Inside MS-DOS 6.2
Second Edition

Mark Minasi
Bill Camarda
David J. Stang, Ph.D.
Kris Ashton
J. D. "Doc" Watson

New Riders Publishing, Indianapolis, Indiana

Inside MS-DOS 6.2
Second Edition

by Mark Minasi, Bill Camarda, David J. Stang, Kris Ashton, and J. D. "Doc" Watson

Published by:

New Riders Publishing
201 West 103rd Street
Indianapolis, IN 46290 USA

All rights reserved. No part of this book may be reproduced or transmitted in any form or by any means, electronic or mechanical, including photocopying, recording, or by any information storage and retrieval system, without written permission from the publisher, except for the inclusion of brief quotations in a review.

Copyright © 1993 by New Riders Publishing

Printed in the United States of America   3 4 5 6 7 8 9 0

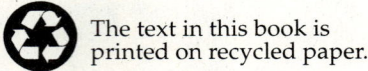 The text in this book is printed on recycled paper.

Publisher
Lloyd J. Short

Associate Publisher
Tim Huddleston

Managing Editor
Matthew Morrill

Acquisitions Manager
Cheri Robinson

Acquisitions Editor
Alicia Krakovitz

Product Directors
Michael Groh
Rob Tidrow

Editors
Rob Lawson
Nancy Sixsmith
Phil Worthington

Acquisitions Coordinator
Stacey Beheler

Publishing Assistant
Melissa Lynch

Editorial Assistant
Karen Opal

Imprint Manager
Kelli Widdifield

Production Analyst
Mary Beth Wakefield

Book Design
Roger Morgan

Production Team
Lisa Daugherty
Rich Evers
Dennis Clay Hager
Juli Pavey
Angela M. Pozdol
Michelle M. Self
Alyssa Yesh

Proofreaders
Danielle Bird
George Bloom
Ayrika Bryant
Karen Dodson
Terri Edwards
Mitzi Foster Gianakos
Wendy Ott
Linda Quigley
Ryan Rader
Tonya Simpson
Suzanne Tully
Dennis Wesner
Lillian Yates

Indexers
Jennifer Eberhardt
Michael Hughes
Joy Dean Lee
Suzanne Snyder

About the Authors

Mark Minasi, owner of Mark Minasi and Company, is a respected consultant and educator in the fields of advanced PC operating platforms and PC technology. He is a contributing editor for *Compute, BYTE,* and *AI Expert,* and author of the number-one, best-selling *Inside OS/2 2.0* (New Riders Publishing). Mr. Minasi has written several books on PC troubleshooting and maintenance. He routinely speaks to large and small groups as a consultant and seminar instructor and has served as Vice President of the Washington, D.C. Capital PC User's Group.

Bill Camarda specializes in writing about computer and telecommunications topics for large corporate clients. Formerly an editor at *Family Computing Magazine,* he is the author of *Bringing the Computer Home.* He coauthored the number-one, best selling *Inside OS/2 2.0* and authored *OS/2 in the Fast Lane* (New Riders Publishing).

David J. Stang is the founder of the National Computer Security Association (NCSA) and is the founder and Chairman of the International Computer Security Association. He is also the editor of *Virus News and Reviews.* Dr. Stang is the author of the International Computer Security Association's *Computer Virus Handbook* and *A Guide to Data Recovery.* He directs the Virus Research Center of the International Computer Security Association and teaches seminars worldwide. He holds a Ph.D. from Syracuse University, an M.S. from the University of Toronto, and a B.S. from Cornell University.

Kris Ashton has worked as a technical support professional for the last ten years. As senior analyst, consultant, and trainer at a major Colorado corporation, she provided extensive support and training to the company's many PC users. Ms. Ashton was instrumental in developing and implementing corporate-wide standards for hardware and software products, including local area networks. She now resides in Virginia, where she provides consulting and training to clients worldwide.

Dr. J.D. "Doc" Watson is an independent consultant, documentation specialist, database developer, and college instructor. He teaches DOS, databases, and Windows at Colorado Mountain College and Colorado Northwestern Community College, located in the Colorado Rockies.

He has written books on DOS and LotusWorks 3.0, and has provided technical support on other titles. Doc is also the technical editor of *Christian Computing Magazine*, for which he writes a monthly technical column and Windows column, and is the full-time pastor of a church in Meeker, Colorado.

Acknowledgments

From Mark Minasi:

Many thanks to my clients, my friends, and my coworkers, who lived through the *Bad Two Months* when this book was being written. (If I haven't returned some phone calls, I'm sorry; I'll get to it soon, I promise...)

Thanks to Kris Ashton, my sweetie and coauthor, who patiently waited for the odd moments when I wasn't writing. She also looked over most of the stuff that I wrote and turned out some pretty good chapters of her own.

Particular thanks go to Christa Anderson, without whom this couldn't have gotten finished. Her running around made much of this possible.

Also many, many thanks to the folks at Microsoft who answered my numerous questions. Until DOS 7...

From Bill Camarda:

Thanks to Mark for the opportunity. And thanks to all the people behind the scenes at New Riders Publishing—you know how to put it all together.

From David J. Stang:

Thanks to Mark Minasi for letting me contribute chapters on my favorite topics. My appreciation also goes to the terrific staff at New Riders for their skill and grace under pressure, in particular, Mike Groh and Rob Lawson. I'd also like to thank users and readers everywhere for their steadfast need to know more and for their willingness to learn. I may be their biggest fan.

From Kris Ashton:

Extra kudos are awarded to Tom Bradley for doing the dirty work of typing in my text. Thanks to Donna, Scott, Jon, and Christa for all their support. And thanks to Mark for giving me the opportunity to explore my writing abilities.

From Doc Watson:

Thanks to Cheri Robinson for thinking of me and for letting me be a part of the best DOS book ever written. And thanks to Mike Groh for his guidance.

The authors wish to thank the following individuals at New Riders for their contributions to this book:

Tim Huddleston, for his insightful direction on setting the right tone for this book.

Cheri Robinson, for keeping everyone on schedule.

Michael Groh and Rob Tidrow for help in reviewing and developing this edition.

Rob Lawson, Nancy Sixsmith, and Phil Worthington, for editing the new material.

Stacey Beheler and Phil Worthington, for formatting the new inserts—a painstaking and important job.

Karen Opal, Stacey Beheler, and Melissa Lynch, for assistance whenever needed.

Trademark Acknowledgments

New Riders Publishing has made every attempt to supply trademark information about company names, products, and services mentioned in this book. The trademarks that follow were derived from various sources. New Riders Publishing cannot attest to the accuracy of this information.

1-2-3, Symphony, and Magellan are registered trademarks of Lotus Development Corporation.

386Max is a registered trademark of Qualitas, Incorporated.

3Com is a registered trademark of 3Com Corporation.

Adaptec is a registered trademark of Adaptec, Inc.

Ami Pro is a trademark of Samma Corporation, a wholly owned subsidiary of Lotus Development Corporation.

ARCnet is a registered trademark of Datapoint Corporation.

AutoCAD is a registered trademark of Autodesk, Inc.

CheckIt is a registered trademark of TouchStone Software Corporation.

COMPAQ is a registered trademark of Compaq Computer Corporation.

CompuServe is a registered trademark of CompuServe, Inc.

dBASE is a registered trademark of Ashton-Tate Corporation.

DELL is a trademark of Dell Computer Corporation.

DesqView and Manifest are trademarks of Quarterdeck Office Systems.

Fastback is a registered trademark of Fifth Generation Systems, Inc.

FoxPro is a trademark of Fox Software, Inc.

IBM, OS/2, Proprinter, PS/2, Quietwriter, and Token Ring are registered trademarks of International Business Machines Corporation and LAN Manager is a trademark of International Business Machines Corporation.

Informix is a trademark of Informix Software, Inc.

Intel is a registered trademark of Intel Corporation.

IPX is a trademark of Sun Microsystems, Inc.

LANTastic is a registered trademark of Artisoft.

LapLink is a registered trademark of Traveling Software, Inc.

LaserJet is a registered trademark of Hewlett-Packard Company.

Macintosh is a registered trademark of Apple Computer, Inc.

Microsoft Excel, Microsoft Paint, Microsoft Publisher, Microsoft Windows, Microsoft Word, MS-DOS, are registered trademarks of Microsoft Corporation, and Windows is a trademark of Microsoft Corporation.

NetWare 386 is a trademark of Novell, Inc.

Norton Utilities is a registered trademark of Symantec Corporation.

Oracle is a registered trademark of Oracle Corporation.

Paradox and Quattro are registered trademarks of Borland International, Inc.

PC Paintbrush is a registered trademark of Z-Soft Corporation.

PC Tools is a trademark of Central Point Software.

Q-DOS is a registered trademark of Gazelle Systems.

Quicken is a registered trademark of Intuit.

RAMPage is a registered trademark of AST Research, Inc.

SpinRite and SpinRite II are trademarks of Gibson Research Corporation.

The Creators of CP/M is a service mark of Digital Research, Inc.

UNIX is a registered trademark of Unix System Laboratories.

Ventura Publisher is a registered trademark of Ventura Software Inc., a Xerox Company.

VINES is a registered trademark of Banyan Systems Inc.

VOPT is a trademark of Golden Bow Systems.

WordPerfect is a registered trademark of WordPerfect Corporation.

XTree is a trademark of Executive Systems, Inc.

Trademarks of other products mentioned in this book are held by the companies producing them.

Warning and Disclaimer

This book is designed to provide information about the MS-DOS 6.2 computer program. Every effort has been made to make this book as complete and as accurate as possible, but no warranty or fitness is implied.

The information is provided on an "as is" basis. The authors and New Riders Publishing shall have neither liability nor responsibility to any person or entity with respect to any loss or damages arising from the information contained in this book or from the use of the disks or programs that may accompany it.

Contents at a Glance

Introduction 3

Part One: Introduction to DOS 6.2 19
   1 MS-DOS 6.2: Almost a Perfect 10 21
   2 An Inside Look: How DOS Works 69

Part Two: Setup and Installation 119
   3 Installing DOS 6.2 121
   4 Taking a Tour of Your Hard Drive 175
   5 Preparing and Setting Up Your Hard Drive 219

Part Three: Optimizing Your Disk with DOS 6.2 273
   6 Creating and Using Directories 275
   7 Managing Disks and Files 315
   8 Tuning Your Disk with DOS 6.2 Tools 383

Part Four: Optimizing Your Memory 435
   9 Understanding PC Memory Types 437
  10 Using the DOS 6.2 Memory Manager 485
  11 Memory Organization and Upgrade Strategies 557
  12 Memory-Management Tips, Tricks, and Troubleshooting 595
  13 Running Third-Party Memory Managers 661

Part Five: Making It Better 715
  14 Using DOS Utilities 717
  15 Writing Batch Files 791
  16 Using DOS 6.2 MultiConfig 861

Part Six: Protecting Your Data 897
  17 A Second Look at Hard Drives 899
  18 Backing Up Your Data 965
  19 Protecting and Recovering Data 1015
  20 Battling Viruses with DOS 6.2 1065
  21 Securing Your PC 1153

12 Inside MS-DOS 6.2

Part Seven: Making Connections under DOS 6.2 .... **1195**
  22 *Interlnk and Other Connectivity Solutions* *1197*
  23 *Using DOS 6.2 with Local Area Networks* *1239*

Part Eight: Command Reference **1269**
    Command Reference *1271*

Part Nine: Appendix **1481**
About the Inside MS-DOS 6.2 Disk *1483*

Index 1507

Contents

Introduction 3

Part One: *19*

1 MS-DOS 6.2: Almost a Perfect 10 .... **21**
    Disk Compression 23
        Compressing Disks On-the-Fly 23
    Protecting Data from Viruses 29
    Keeping in Touch with Communications Support 32
        InterLinking PCs 32
        Connecting Workgroups 34
    Talking with the DOS Manual 35
    Simplifying Customization with Configuration Control 38
    Talking Back to Your Batch Files 44
    Simplifying Memory Management with MemMaker 46
    Arranging Disks with DEFRAG 49
    Repairing Disks with ScanDisk 50
    Checking the System with MSD 2.0a 51
    Improving on Older DOS Versions 52
        Backing Up with Norton Backup 52
        Understanding Memory-Manager Improvements 56
        Undeleting to Bulletproof Files 61
    Looking at Changes in DOS 6.0 and DOS 6.2 63
    Summary 66

2 An Inside Look: How DOS Works **69**
    Why Does Your PC Use DOS? 70
    Understanding the DOS File-Organization System 72
        Looking at Simple Directory Organization 74
        Using DOS Commands To Create and
        Manage Directory Trees 81
    Using DOS Disk-Management Tools 86
    Understanding the DOS User Interface 88
        DOS Says "Hello" with PROMPT 89
        DOS Listens and Obeys with COMMAND.COM 89
        How To Phrase a DOS Command 91

Understanding the DOS Software Foundation 103
  Controlling Hardware 104
  Understanding How Programs Call on DOS
  To Access Hardware 106
  Understanding How DOS Fulfills Requests 110
  Understanding Why Some Programs Bypass
  DOS and BIOS 111
  Understanding TSRs and Device Drivers 113
Summary 116

Part Two: 119

3 Installing DOS 6.2 121
Getting Ready To Install 121
  Step 1: Back Up Your MS-DOS 6.2 Disks 122
  Step 2: Back Up Your Data 123
  Step 3: Inventory Your Computer System 123
  Step 4: Locate Your Current DOS 125
  Step 5: Disable TSRs and Other Problem Programs 126
  Step 6: Read README.TXT 126
  Step 7: Check for Available Space 128
  Step 8: Get a Blank Floppy 129
  Choose Your Own Kind of SETUP 129
  A Few Words about OS/2 131
Running SETUP 132
  Old Programs, New Versions 138
  What Kinds of Things Can Go Wrong? 139
  Installing DOS 6.2 Manually 147
Using EXPAND To Decompress Individual
DOS 6.2 Files 149
  Running UNINSTALL 158
  What If UNINSTALL Fails? 160
  Preparing a Bootable Floppy 162
  What's Different Now? 165
What Setup Does to Windows 166
  Changes to PROGMAN.INI 167
  Changes to SYSTEM.INI 167
  Changes to WINFILE.INI 168
  Other Changes 168
  Documenting Your Installation 169

Summary 171

4 Taking a Tour of Your Hard Drive 175
The Physical Hard Disk Drive 176
How Information Is Stored 179
The Structure of Your Hard Disk 180
    Tracks and Sectors *180*
    Cylinders *182*
    Calculating Disk Storage Capacity *183*
Understanding Drive Performance 183
    Access Time *184*
    Data Transfer Rates and Interleave Settings *184*
Understanding Drive Interfaces 186
    ST-506 Interface *187*
    Integrated Drive Electronics (IDE) *187*
    Enhanced Small Device Interface (ESDI) *188*
    Small Computer Systems Interface (SCSI) *189*
Controller Types XT and AT 190
Disk Structures Imposed by MS-DOS 6.2 191
    Absolute Sectors and DOS Sectors *191*
    DOS Clusters *192*
    The DOS Boot Record *193*
    The Master Boot Record *194*
    DOS (and Other) Partitions *195*
    The File Allocation Table *200*
    DOS Directories *202*
    Lost Clusters and the CHKDSK Command *204*
Floppy Disks 208
    Formatting a Floppy Disk *209*
Summary 216

5 Preparing and Setting Up Your Hard Drive 219
Installing Hard Drives: An Overview 220
    Getting All the Parts *220*
    Installing an IDE Drive *222*
    Installing the First IDE Drive *222*
    Installing the Second IDE Drive *224*
    Installing SCSI Drives *225*
    A Few Words about Low-Level Formatting *227*

16   Inside MS-DOS 6.2

  Configuring Your Drive 228
  Partitioning Your Drive 230
 Formatting Your Drive 233
 Introducing DoubleSpace 234
  An Overview of Data Compression 234
  Reasons NOT To Use DoubleSpace 237
  Warnings before Using DoubleSpace 238
  Basic DoubleSpace Concepts and Components 239
  Understanding DoubleGuard 240
  Working with DoubleSpace 241
  Compressing a Drive with Express Setup 242
  The Compression Process 243
  Using Custom Setup To Compress or Create a Drive 247
  Compressing or Creating Drives from the Command Line ... 251
  Mounting and Unmounting DoubleSpaced Drives 252
  DoubleSpace and Your Floppy Disk 253
  DoubleSpacing Stacker Drives 255
  DBLSPACE/CHKDSK 255
  Defragmenting DoubleSpaced Drives 258
  Deleting Your DoubleSpaced Drive 258
  Changing the Size of a Compressed Drive 261
  Formatting a DoubleSpaced Drive 262
  Getting Information about DoubleSpaced Drives 262
  About DBLSPACE.INI 263
 Understanding the `Error: R6003 - Integer Divide by Zero` Error Message 265
 Understanding Windows Error Messages 266
  The `Corrupt Swap File` Error Message 266
  The `Unsupported DOS Version` Error Message in Windows 3.0 267
 Using a Data-Compression Alternative 268
 Summary 269

Part Three: 273

 6 Creating and Using Directories 275
  Understanding the Root Directory 276
   Root Directory Structure 277
  Understanding Subdirectories 278

Creating Subdirectories 279
    Naming Subdirectories 280
    Subdirectory Size 281
    Nested Subdirectories 282
Introducing Paths 283
Moving from One Directory to Another (CD) 284
    Changing Current Subdirectories on Another Drive 284
PROMPT: Knowing Where You Are 286
    Customizing the Prompt 287
    Listing All Directories 291
    Introducing DELTREE 293
Trailblazing Your Own PATH 294
    Adding a Directory to Your Path 296
    Shortening Long Path Names 296
    Using the SUBST Command 297
    Relative Path Names 298
    More PATH Editing 299
Using TREE To View the Directory Structure 301
    Saving Your Tree to Disk 301
    More Ways To View Your Directory Structure 302
Using the APPEND Command To Find
Nonexecutable Files 303
Using MOVE To Rename Directories 305
Getting Yourself Organized 306
    Inventory Your Current Files 307
    Build a Directory Structure That Makes Sense 308
    Make Space Wherever You Can 310
    Clear Out the Root Directory 310
Summary 313

7 Managing Disks and Files 315
Finding Out What's in Your Directories with DIR 316
    Searching Far and Wide with DIR 317
    Rearranging the Way DIR Presents Information 318
    Using DIR To Locate Files Meeting Specific Criteria 319
    Understanding Attributes 320
    Using DIR with Attributes 321
    Using DIR To Change Sort Order 322

> Using Other DIR Options 323
> Customizing DIR with DIRCMD 324

Finding Out What's in a File 325
Naming Files 325
Using Extensions in File Names 327
> Looking Inside a File 331

Editing with EDIT 333
> Loading EDIT 334
> Getting Around in EDIT 334
> Editing a Document 335

Copying Files 337
> Copying Tricks and Traps 337
> Copying with Overwrite Protection 338
> Using the COPYCMD Environment Variable 340
> Concatenating Files Intentionally and by Accident 341
> Copying between Devices 342
> COPYing ASCII and Binary Files 342
> Verifying the COPY Process 344

Copying Entire Disks with DISKCOPY 346
Copying Smart with XCOPY 347
> Capturing Subdirectories with XCOPY 349
> Backing Up Files with XCOPY 349
> Verifying While Using XCOPY 352
> Using XCOPY /W on a Floppy-Based System 352

Updating with REPLACE 352
> Adding Files with REPLACE 353

Moving Files with MOVE 354
> Understanding the Limitations of MOVE 355
> Verifying MOVEs with the VERIFY Command 355

Comparing Files with FC Is Better than with COMP 356
Erasing Files 359
Renaming Files 360
Naming Volumes and Labels 361
Backing Up Files with DOS 6.2 MSBACKUP and
MWBACKUP 362
> What about the Old Backups? 363
> When Should You Back Up? 364
> Taking a Walk through MSBACKUP and MWBACKUP ... 365

        Starting the Backup *367*
        Performing the Backup *373*
        Understanding Backup Sets and Catalogs *373*
        Saving Setup Files *374*
        Comparing Backups to Originals *376*
        Restoring Files *378*
    Summary 381
8 Tuning Your Disk with DOS 6.2 Tools **383**
    Understanding How a Disk Cache Works 384
        Read Caching *384*
        Write Caching *386*
        Double Buffering and Bus Mastering *388*
    Understanding SMARTDrive 390
        Installing SMARTDrive *391*
        Deciding Where To Load SMARTDrive *392*
        Specifying the Drives To Cache...and How *393*
        Setting Cache Size *394*
        Fine-Tuning SMARTDrive *395*
        Using Double Buffering *396*
        Flushing the Cache *397*
        Reporting the Status of SMARTDrive *397*
        Monitoring Performance with SMARTDrive Monitor *398*
        Looking at Third-Party Disk Caches as Alternatives to
           SMARTDrive *400*
    Reading Directories Faster with FASTOPEN 401
        Using FASTOPEN with UMBs and Expanded Memory *403*
        Deciding How Many Files FASTOPEN Should Track *403*
    Understanding Disk Problems 404
    Understanding Microsoft ScanDisk 405
        Knowing When To Use ScanDisk *406*
        Quitting Everything Else before Starting *406*
        Running Microsoft ScanDisk *407*
        Fixing Problems with ScanDisk *409*
        Creating and Using an Undo Disk *411*
        Understanding ScanDisk's Syntax *412*
        Customizing ScanDisk Using the SCANDISK.INI file *414*
        Using ScanDisk's Errorlevels *415*

20　Inside MS-DOS 6.2

    Understanding Disk Fragmentation 416
        Viewing a List of Fragmented Files 419
        Understanding What Defragmenters Do 420
        Defragmenting a Compressed Drive 421
        Understanding the Risks of Defragmentation 422
    Understanding Microsoft DEFRAG for DOS 422
        Quitting Everything Else before Starting 423
        Running CHKDSK before Defragmenting 423
        Loading Microsoft DEFRAG 424
        Defragmenting Large Disks 431
        Running the DoubleSpace Defragmenter 432
    Summary 433

Part Four: *435*

9 Understanding PC Memory Types 437
    Main Memory versus Secondary Memory
    (RAM versus Disk) 438
        Understanding Main Memory (RAM) 439
        Understanding Secondary Memory (Disk) 440
    Staking Out the First Megabyte 441
        1980: IBM Picks the 8088 441
        Dividing Up the Addresses 442
        A Closer Look at Addresses 442
        Meet the PC's Three Memory Areas 443
    Conventional Memory Stores DOS, Your Programs,
    and Data 444
        Interrupt Vectors and DOS 445
        TSRs and Device Drivers 446
        The Command Shell COMMAND.COM and Your
        DOS Environment 447
        User Programs 450
    Understanding Video RAM 451
        Video RAM Addresses and Video Boards 453
        Details of Video Memory: Text Mode versus
        Graphics Mode 454
        Understanding the Three Video RAM Areas 455
    Understanding the System Reserved Area 458
        Read-Only Memory (ROM) 459

The BIOS ROM	*459*
ROM Addresses	*461*
Buffers and Frames	*461*
Understanding Extended Memory	**463**
Protected Mode	*463*
Protected Mode and Backward Compatibility	*464*
Using Extended Memory under DOS:DOS Extenders	*466*
Understanding Addressing	*472*
Memory: Expanded, LIM, EMS, and Paged	**476**
Summary	**482**

10 Using the DOS 6.2 Memory Manager **485**

What Can Memory Managers Do for You?	**486**
Taking a Few Preparatory Steps	**487**
Setting Up a Basic Configuration	**489**
Preparing a Starter AUTOEXEC.BAT and CONFIG.SYS	*490*
Monitoring Memory with MEM	*491*
Reducing DOS Memory Requirements before the Memory Manager	*495*
Understanding the High Memory Area (HMA)	**496**
What Is the HMA?	*496*
Activating the HMA	*498*
Loading FILES and BUFFERS into the HMA	*499*
Using HIMEM.SYS as an XMS Manager	*501*
Creating and Using Upper Memory Blocks (UMBs)	**504**
What Do UMBs Do?	*504*
How Memory Managers Provide UMBs	*506*
How To Set Up UMBs	*509*
Hexadecimal for Humans: Help for Hex Haters	*510*
Segments and Offsets	*519*
Special Considerations for Integrated Motherboard Machines	*520*
What Goes in UMBs?	*521*
Step 1: Map Upper Memory	**522**
Why Map?	*522*
Other Potential Sources of Memory Conflict	*523*
Using MSD, the DOS 6.2 Memory Scanner	*526*

>   *Using the Documentation for Add-In Boards* 532
>   *Giving the Map to the Memory Manager* 533
>   Step 2: Create UMBs 537
>   *Telling CONFIG.SYS To Create UMBs* 537
>   *Understanding Fragmented UMBs* 537
>   Step 3: Load Programs into UMBs 539
>   *Loading Programs High* 539
>   *Looking at Programs that Load Themselves High* 542
>   *Disabling VCPI Support* 543
>   Using a Memory Manager with Limulation 543
>   *Limulating with EMM386.EXE* 544
>   *Using a Memory Manager for UMBs and Limulation* 548
>   Understanding Shadow RAM 548
>   Sorting Memory and Backfilling 551
>   *Speed Sorting* 551
>   *Memory Backfilling* 552
>   Summary 553
>
> **11 Memory Organization and Upgrade Strategies** 557
>   Buying the Right Memory 558
>   *Looking at RAM Package Types* 558
>   *Buying the Right Speed and Size RAMs* 564
>   *Understanding Why One's Not Enough: Memories Come
>   in Groups* 568
>   Installing the Memory 576
>   *Working Safely inside the PC* 576
>   *Figuring Out Where RAMs Are Installed* 579
>   *Understanding Memory-Installation Methods* 581
>   *Telling the Computer You've Added Memory* 583
>   Testing Memory 584
>   *Why You Must Test RAM* 584
>   *How To Use a Memory Tester* 587
>   Using Cache Memory 588
>   *Memory Speeds in Detail* 589
>   *A Processor Cache Is One Answer to Memory-Speed
>   Problems* 591
>   *How Much Cache Do You Need?* 593
>   Summary 593

Contents **23**

12 Memory-Management Tips, Tricks, and Troubleshooting ..595
   Arranging Programs in UMBs for Maximum
   Space Usage 596
      Placing TSRs into Particular UMBs *597*
      Understanding and Loading Yo-Yo TSRs *601*
      Making Things Easier with MemMaker *608*
      Possible Problems with MemMaker *611*
   Looking at Common Memory-Management Problems 624
      Solving Keyboard Problems Caused by Memory
      Managers *625*
      Solving Other Keyboard Problems *641*
      Solving the Beeps-at-Warm-Boot Problem *641*
      Solving the Problem of Why Some Programs
      Won't Load High *642*
   Using More Tricks To Get More Memory 650
      Stealing Back that ROM *650*
      Restricting Video To Gain 96K *652*
   Making Windows Work with Your Memory Manager 655
      Understanding Why Some Video Drivers Need
      the Monochrome Region *655*
      Mapping Memory under Windows *657*
      Realizing That the DOS Memory Manager
      Must Limulate for Windows To Limulate *657*
      Leaving Space for the Application Program
      Interface Translation Buffers *658*
   Summary 659

13 Running Third-Party Memory Managers **661**
   Setting Up a Testbed Configuration 663
   Looking at MemMaker's Solution to the Test
   Configuration 668
   Looking at Quarterdeck's Solution to the
   Test Configuration 670
      Setting Up QEMM Like DOS 6.2. ....*674*
      Understanding and Using Quarterdeck's Advanced
      Features *678*
      Living on the Edge with Stealth *685*
      Using Optimize, Quarterdeck's Optimizer *686*
      Using Manifest, Quarterdeck's Memory Analyzer *696*

24 Inside MS-DOS 6.2

Looking at Qualitas's Solution to the Test Configuration 702
    Looking at 386Max Features 702
    Understanding Max Syntax 706
    Running Maximize 707
Summary 713

Part Five: 715

14 Using DOS Utilities 717
Editing Files with the DOS Editors 718
    The Full-Screen Editor: EDIT 719
    Changing EDIT's Default File Extension 725
Using SETVER To Set a Program's DOS Version 726
Utilities To Control Floppy Drives 728
    Redirecting Disk Commands with ASSIGN 728
    Making a Copy of a Disk with DISKCOPY 729
    Waking Up DISKCOPY 731
    Comparing Disks with DISKCOMP 732
    Adding External Drives with DRIVER.SYS 733
    Changing a Drive's Format with DRIVPARM 736
Working with Your Keyboard 737
    Using an International Keyboard 738
    Using DOSKEY To Remember Your Commands
    and Create Macros 742
    Make Your Keyboard Faster 750
Understanding and Controlling Video 751
    Video Component I—The Adapter Board 752
    Video Component II—The Monitor 760
    Erasing the Screen with CLS 763
    Getting Fancy with ANSI 763
    An Alternative to DOSKEY Macros 769
    Using MODE CO80,50 To Display 50 Lines 771
Printing 773
    Using Serial Printers 774
    Redirecting Ports with MODE 776
    Identifying and Resolving Timeout Problems 777
    Controlling Screen Prints with GRAPHICS 778
    Background Printing with PRINT 781
Exploring Shell Programs and Program Launchers 783
    A Brief Look at the Norton Desktop for DOS 784

Contents   25

Looking at QBASIC	785
Screen Savers	785
A Screen-Message Program	786
Summary	788

15 Writing Batch Files 791

Batch Files: An Extension of the Command Line	792
Your First Batch File	793
Cleaning Up the Batch File: The ECHO Command	794
Using ECHO To Put Messages on the Screen	796
Understanding DOS Virtual Devices	798
Understanding and Using Input/Output Redirection under DOS	801
Using Redirected Output	802
Using Input Redirection	804
Redirecting Existing Files with Append	805
Using Pipes	806
Sounds and Blank Lines with ECHO	809
Making Choices in Batch Files	811
Receiving User Choices in Batch Files with CHOICE.COM	812
Making Decisions in Batch Files	813
CHOICE, IF ERRORLEVEL, and GOTO Summarized	817
Using CHOICE To Delay a Batch File	820
Specifying Default CHOICEs	820
Waiting for Choices That Never Occur: Preprogrammed Delays	822
Limitations of Using CHOICE To Build Delays	823
Waiting for a Particular Time	823
Refining WAITFOR.BAT	825
Using Replaceable Parameters in Command Files	829
A Batch File To Make and Use a Subdirectory	829
What Does the Command Parser Do with the Parameters?	831
Checking for Replaceable Parameters	832
Understanding and Using Environment Variables in Command Files	835
Adding Comments to Batch Files	838
Connecting Batch Files	839
Building Batch Files That Other Batch Files Can Use	839

26 Inside MS-DOS 6.2

    Putting DELAY in a Batch File 841
    Don't Forget To CALL 842
    Using CTTY NUL 843
    Interactive Batch-File Execution 844
  Understanding a Batch File Toolbox 845
    Day of the Week Utility 849
    File Locator (DW) 849
    Exclude Certain Files from Commands (DW) 850
    Copying Different Disk Formats 851
    Changing the Drive and Directory at Once 853
    Floppy Disk Organizer 853
    A Handy Little Notepad 854
    Log All Computer Activity 856
    The PC Typewriter 857
    Recursive Delete 858
  Summary 859

16 Using DOS 6.2 MultiConfig 861
  What Does MultiConfig Do? 862
  Using Clean Boot and Interactive Boot 863
    Using Clean Boot 864
    Using Interactive Boot 865
    Interactive Boot as a Problem-Solving Tool 867
    Making a Boot Command Always Interactive 868
    Disabling Clean Boot and Interactive Boot 868
  Getting Started with MultiConfig 868
    MultiConfig Step 1: Merge All CONFIG.SYS Files 870
    MultiConfig Step 2: Name the Configurations 871
    MultiConfig Step 3: Set Up the Menu 872
    MultiConfig Step 4: Add Defaults and Timeouts 873
    Coloring Your Menu 874
    MultiConfig Step 5: Put Multiple Configurations in AUTOEXEC.BAT 878
  Using INCLUDE To Simplify a MultiConfig Configuration 885
    Supporting Shared Groups of Statements in MultiConfig ... 885
    The [common] Block 887
  Building More Complex Configurations with Submenus 887
    What Is a Submenu? 887

Contents

Using Submenus	*888*
Suggestions for Using Submenus with Multiple People	*890*
Controlling the NumLock Light with MultiConfig	891
MultiConfig Tips	892
Summary	893

Part Six: 897

17 A Second Look at Hard Drives 899
How Drives Work 899
  Drive Anatomy *901*
  Magnetic Recording *904*
  Tracks and Cylinders *907*
  Sectors *910*
  Encoding Schemes *910*
Understanding the Boot Process 921
  Creating a Master Boot Record *922*
  The Boot Record *924*
  The FATs *932*
  The Root Directory *937*
  Subdirectories *938*
  Hidden System Files and COMMAND.COM *938*
Using FDISK and FORMAT 940
  FDISK: Preparing the Master Boot Record *941*
  FORMAT: Creating the Boot Record, FATS, and Root *945*
  FORMAT Beefs *952*
  UNFORMAT: Secrets of the Recoverable Format *953*
For the Curious 953
  The Size of Things *953*
  Clusters and Slack Space *954*
  Clusters on a Hard Disk *955*
  Cluster Size in a Nutshell *955*
  What Makes a Disk Bootable? *956*
  Where MS-DOS Places Files *958*
Summary 959

18 Backing Up Your Data 965
Getting Motivated 967
Why You Don't Back Up 971
Backup Tips and Tricks 972

Tricks for Improving Backup Frequency	972
Dealing with Dupes	977
Tracking Backups and Archives	979
Storing Backups and Archives	979
Backing Up a Hard Disk to a Hard Disk	981
Understanding MSBACKUP	983
MSBACKUP/MWBACKUP Features	986
Configuring MSBACKUP/MWBACKUP	990
Backing Up Everything with MSBACKUP	993
Backing Up Everything with MWBACKUP	995
Backing Up Selected Files with MSBACKUP/MWBACKUP	996
Restoring from a Backup Set with MSBACKUP/MWBACKUP	997
Comparing Your Source and Your Backups	1001
Trouble in River City	1002
The Price of Integrity	1003
Using XCOPY for Quick Backup	1004
Getting More Out of MSBACKUP/MWBACKUP	1005
Backup Cycles and Retention Periods	1006
Using the Server for Archiving	1007
Backing up MSBACKUP	1007
Making Backups More Efficient with Setup Files	1009
Repairing Catalogs	1010
Looking at a Model BackupPolicy	1011
Summary	1012

19 Protecting and Recovering Data 1015

Preventing Disasters	1016
General Tips for Disaster Prevention	1016
Preventing Media Damage	1018
Using MIRROR To Help Prevent Disaster	1019
Before You Begin	1023
Missing Files	1024
Exploring UNDELETE for DOS	1025
MWUNDEL: Undelete for Windows	1031
UNDELETE's Sentry	1033
Recovering an Erased File Manually	1035
An Alternative to SENTRY	1036
Understanding Which Is the Most Current Version	1038

Directory Disasters 1039
   Differences between the Root Directory
   and Subdirectories 1040
   Recovering a Directory Erased with RD 1042
   Recovering an Overwritten Root Directory 1044
Understanding COMMAND.COM 1045
The Hidden System Files 1047
   Checking for Changes with UNFORMAT 1048
Damaged FATs 1049
   FATs and the Root Directory during File Copy .. 1050
   Using CHKDSK 1051
Understanding the Boot Record 1053
Working with the Master Boot Record 1055
Repairing the Master Boot Record (Partition Table) 1056
Recovering from an Accidental Hard Disk Format 1058
Recovering Files from Damaged Media 1059
   COPY Clues 1060
   Recovery 1061
Summary 1062

20 Battling Viruses with DOS 6.2 1065
Defining a Virus 1066
   Classifying Viruses 1067
   Understanding Where Viruses Come From 1069
   Who Writes Viruses? 1070
   Missile Command (or, Virus Fallout) 1072
Understanding the Virus Threat 1075
   Emergence of New Viruses 1076
   Prevalence 1076
   Infectiousness 1077
   How Much Damage Do Common Viruses Cause? 1077
   What Kind of Damage Can Viruses Cause? 1080
   How Serious Is the Virus Threat? 1081
Preventing Viruses 1082
   Data Disks and Boot Sector Viruses 1084
   Backup 1085
   Access to Bulletin Boards 1086
   Virus Response Teams 1087

Detecting Viruses	1088
Checksumming	*1089*
Scanning	*1091*
TSRs and Device Drivers	*1093*
Virus Scanning with MSAV.EXE	1094
Command Line Options	*1094*
Menu-Driven Operation	*1096*
Speed Consequences of Various Options	*1100*
How Good Is MSAV as a Scanner?	*1100*
A Thorny Boot-Sector Problem	*1102*
The DOS 6.2 Anti-Virus TSR VSAFE.COM	1103
Testing VSAFE.COM	*1106*
Confirming Your Anti-Virus Software's Hunches	1110
False Alarms	*1110*
Suspicious Behavior	*1111*
Real Symptoms	*1114*
Recovering from Viruses	1115
Using an Anti-Virus Product	*1116*
Virus Removal with MSAV	*1116*
How To Remove a Virus	*1118*
Testing Virus Removal with MSAV	*1119*
Home-Grown Virus Removal	1120
Provided Utilities	*1121*
Removal Strategies	1125
Don't Panic	*1125*
Devise an Action Plan	*1125*
Descriptions of Common Viruses	1128
Cascade Family	*1128*
Dark Avenger 1800	*1131*
Dark Avenger 1.31	*1133*
Frodo	*1136*
Green Caterpillar Family	*1139*
Jerusalem.Standard	*1140*
Stoned.Standard	*1146*
Learning More about Viruses	1150
Summary	1151

21 Securing Your PC 1153
Controlling Access to Your PC 1155
Adding a Password System to Your PC 1156
Ensuring That Deleted Files Are Deleted 1161
Replacing Internal Commands 1162
Changing the Name of AUTOEXEC.BAT 1165
Changing the Extension of BAT Files 1168
Logging Bootups 1171
Blanking the Screen 1171
Reprogramming the Keyboard 1172
Permanently Erasing Files 1175
Controlling Access with Menus and Batch Files 1176
Controlling Access with Encryption 1178
Looking at the Problem of Theft 1179
Deterring Theft 1179
Recovering from Theft 1179
Redesigning To Prevent Boot Viruses 1181
Redesigning To Remove Boot Viruses 1182
Redesigning To Prevent File Viruses 1183
MARK and RELEASE 1183
Using Secret Names for COMMAND.COM 1184
Redesigning To Detect Memory-Resident Viruses 1186
Redesigning To Remove (Some) Memory-Resident Viruses 1187
Redesigning To Detect File Viruses Early 1188
File Size Checks 1188
Redesigning To Recover Efficiently 1189
Redesigning To Slow Hackers 1190
Shareware Referenced in This Chapter 1192
Summary 1193

Part Seven: *1195*

22 InterLnk and Other Connectivity Solutions 1197
What Is InterLnk? 1198
What You Need To Run InterLnk 1199
Connecting InterLnk through Parallel Ports 1203
Understanding InterLnk Concepts 1204
Uploading InterLnk to Another MS-DOS System 1205

Including InterLnk in Your CONFIG.SYS File 1208
    What Happens When INTERLNK.EXE Runs? *1211*
    Telling InterLnk When To Install *1213*
    Telling InterLnk When To Search *1213*
    Slowing InterLnk Down *1213*
    Placing the DEVICE=INTERLNK.EXE Statement *1216*
Connecting the Server with INTERSVR.EXE 1216
Using InterLnk Switches at the Command Line 1218
    Running INTERSVR in Black and White *1220*
Using InterLnk To Exchange a File 1220
Running the Client from the DOS Shell 1221
Troubleshooting InterLnk 1222
More InterLnk Applications 1223
Comparing InterLnk with Third-Party Solutions 1224
Linking Your PC to a Macintosh 1224
    Interplatform Sneakernet Using SuperDrive Floppies *1225*
    Running PC Software on the Macintosh *1227*
    Serial Connections between the Mac and PC *1228*
    Networking Macs and PCs Together *1231*
    File Translation *1231*
    Sibling Applications *1232*
    Font Substitution *1233*
    Graphics Formats *1233*
    Compatible File Names *1234*
    Translation and File Transfer Programs *1234*
Summary 1235

23 Using DOS 6.2 with Local Area Networks 1239

Understanding Basic Network Terminology 1240
How DOS Fits In 1242
Planning a LAN 1244
Networking at the Board Level 1246
    ARCnet *1246*
    Ethernet-Style Networks *1247*
    Token Ring Networks (802.5) *1248*
    Fiber Distributed Data Interface (FDDI) *1249*
A Few Words about Wiring 1249
Server-Based or Peer-to-Peer? 1251

Peer-to-Peer Options	1252
LANtastic	*1253*
NetWare Lite	*1254*
Windows for Workgroups	*1256*
Server-Based Options	1257
Novell NetWare	*1258*
Microsoft LAN Manager/IBM LAN Server	*1259*
Banyan VINES	*1260*
Buying a Server	1260
Running Your Network with MS-DOS 6.2	1261
Do You Need a Network Upgrade?	*1262*
Running Networked Applications with MS-DOS 6.2	1265
Summary	1266

Part Eight: Command Reference *1269*

Command Reference **1271**

Part Nine: Appendix *1481*

About the Inside MS-DOS 6.2 Disk **1483**

Index **1506**

Introduction

In the fall of 1993, Microsoft introduced version 6.2 of DOS, the most popular operating system available for personal computers. With version 6.2, DOS provides enhanced features that change the way people use computers. The new features of DOS 6.2 make computing safer and more reliable than ever. Through these enhancements, DOS provides the user with capabilities previously available only as expensive third-party applications.

DOS promises to continue as the premier operating system for personal computing for years to come. Every DOS 6.2 user will benefit from the truly powerful memory-management features, built-in antivirus protection, greatly enhanced backup and undelete commands, and disk optimizer. These advanced capabilities enable you to become productive with *all* the applications you run under DOS.

Inside MS-DOS 6.2, Second Edition prepares the PC-literate individual to take full advantage of DOS 6.2's powerful features. Whether you are an advanced user of MS-DOS or a first-time DOS user, *Inside MS-DOS 6.2, Second Edition* can help you shorten the learning curve and quickly realize the benefits of this powerful operating system.

How This Book Is Different from Most DOS Books

Inside MS-DOS 6.2, Second Edition is designed and written to accommodate the way you work. The authors and editors at New Riders Publishing know that you probably do not have a great deal of time to learn DOS and the new features of DOS 6.2, and that you are anxious to begin using DOS to help you become more productive in your daily work.

This book, therefore, does not lead you through endless exercises for every DOS function and does not waste your time by repeating clearly obvious information. Each chapter introduces you to an important group of related DOS concepts and functions, and quickly shows you how these aspects of DOS relate to your computer system. The chapters also lead you through the basic steps you must follow to incorporate each new concept and function into your own computing work. This book's instructions, however, are fast-paced; they help you become productive in the shortest time possible once you understand the concepts and functions involved.

Inside MS-DOS 6.2, Second Edition is unique in that it contains a wealth of information you need to know to fully understand and control your computer. Very few DOS books take the time to explain how computer viruses attack your computer and how to avoid "infections" from these highly damaging programs. *Inside MS-DOS 6.2, Second Edition* has chapters that go far beyond understanding and using DOS 6.2. This book includes rigorous discussions of the technological hardware—as well as software—underlying DOS 6.2. No matter what level of interest you have regarding DOS, *Inside MS-DOS 6.2, Second Edition* will provide adequate background for all of your questions.

Who Should Read This Book?

Inside MS-DOS 6.2, Second Edition is written for two types of readers: experienced computer users who are new to the DOS environment, and experienced DOS users who want to upgrade to DOS 6.2.

Experienced PC Users Who Are New to DOS

If you are in the first group of readers, you are comfortable using personal computers, whether Intel-based (IBM-PC compatible), Apple Macintosh, or another type of desktop computer. You may be a Microsoft Windows user or have only used DOS through the DOS Shell. This book assumes that you have had some experience using command-line applications and text-based user interfaces. This book also assumes that you are anxious to become productive with DOS 6.2. As an experienced user of personal computers, this book makes the following assumptions about you:

- ✔ You are an experienced PC user who knows the difference between a hard disk and a floppy disk.

- ✔ You know that a file is the computer's basic information container and that files are hierarchically arranged in directories.

- ✔ You know that computers use different kinds of files: text, data (which may be text), executable, and so on. (Executable files normally have an EXE file name extension and text files usually have TXT or DOC extensions.)

- ✔ You can type, and you know the location of the keys on the keyboard.

- ✔ You do not have time to read long passages about computer and software basics; rather, you want to start working with DOS 6.2 as soon as possible.

If you are an experienced PC user who has not yet made the transition to DOS, read the following section.

The Benefits of This Book to New DOS Users

Many different types of DOS books are available, ranging from very basic books to advanced, specialized books for experienced users. Only a few DOS books make a genuine effort to present information with comprehensive explanations, practical examples, and a minimum of hand-holding.

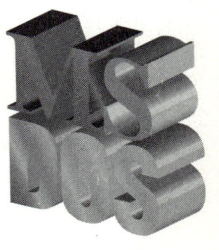

Because of the depth of the topic discussions and the breadth of coverage in *Inside MS-DOS 6.2, Second Edition*, you can use it as a reference long after you have mastered the DOS essentials.

If you have never used DOS, you should start with Chapter 1 and work through Chapter 5. These chapters introduce you to DOS basics, installation, and provide a basis for many of the concepts presented later in the book. Skip over any sections that appear obvious or do not interest you. You can always return to these sections later.

The later chapters of this book deal with more advanced topics that you will encounter as you gain experience with DOS. Whenever possible, practical examples and illustrations are drawn from popular DOS applications.

In these later chapters, you will discover the many new features and power of DOS 6.2. These features combine to provide the user with a highly reliable system suitable for any personal computing task.

DOS Users Who Want To Upgrade to DOS 6.2

If you fall into the second group of readers for whom *Inside MS-DOS 6.2, Second Edition* is written, you are an experienced user of an earlier version of DOS. You either have upgraded to DOS 6.2, or you are considering making the upgrade. This book introduces you to the capabilities that are new to DOS 6.2. You can learn how to apply DOS's latest enhancements to your own computing work without relearning the DOS concepts and functions you already know through your own experience.

Specifically, this book makes the following assumptions about you:

- ✔ You are familiar with the DOS file and directory structure.
- ✔ You know how to create new directories, remove directories, and navigate through the DOS file structure.
- ✔ You are familiar with at least one DOS text editor (either EDLIN, EDIT, or another editor).

✔ You are familiar with the DOS command structure, including switches and parameters.

✔ You know how to start and run applications under DOS.

If you already are a DOS user who is upgrading to DOS 6.2, read the following section.

The Benefits of DOS 6.2 to Experienced DOS Users

If you are upgrading from an earlier version of DOS, you will find that version 6.2 offers even more power and value than the earlier MS-DOS versions.

The advanced memory-management provided by MEMMAKER yields even more usable memory than DOS 5. The new memory management features of DOS 6.2 include an enhanced MEM command and optional parameters for LOADHIGH and DEVICEHIGH.

For the first time, DOS 6.2 enables you to *selectively* load device drivers and other system-management applications from within CONFIG.SYS. With a little practice, the DOS 6.2 *multiple configuration* facility (discussed in Chapter 16) will provide you with greater flexibility than you thought possible.

DOS 6.2 also protects your investment in software and data with MSAV and VSAFE (described in Chapter 20), the all new computer virus fighters. These highly intelligent applications can scan and monitor your system for indications that your system has been infected with any of several thousand different viruses.

The new DEFRAG command (discussed in Chapter 8) provides a built-in DOS disk optimizer. Based on proven technology, DEFRAG can defragment your disk files and neatly organize your directories as a contiguous portion of your hard disk.

Perhaps the most useful new DOS 6 and 6.2 feature is DoubleSpace, the disk expansion utility (also explained in Chapter 8). DoubleSpace effectively doubles your hard disk's capacity with no loss of efficiency or reliability. You'll be happy to know that DoubleSpace is 100 percent transparent in use and is highly configurable.

The Benefits of This Book to Experienced DOS Users

In contrast to many books on DOS 6.2, *Inside MS-DOS 6.2, Second Edition* does not overstate the obvious. The book emphasizes practical examples that demonstrate the subject material without belaboring the point. You should work through as many examples as you like and feel free to experiment.

If you already are an experienced DOS user, you may want to skip over the first two chapters. Starting with Chapter 3, you'll find information on installing DOS 6.2 with special emphasis on hard disk preparation and organization.

The later chapters take a look at making the most of your applications running under DOS. A large part of this book is devoted to advanced topics like disk drive technology, memory management, and practical tips and instructions on creating batch files.

DOS 5 Users

DOS 6.2 is, more or less, just DOS 5 with some window dressing. You'll find, in fact, that at least sixty percent (and that's being conservative) of *Inside MS-DOS 6.2, Second Edition* applies to DOS 5. Virtually every chapter contains a wealth of information for the DOS 5 user—tips, tricks, techniques, and just plain knowledge that the DOS 5 user will not want to live without.

For example, most of the information in the following chapters directly relates to DOS 5: Chapter 2 ("An Inside Look: How DOS Works"), Chapter 4 ("Taking a Tour of Your Hard Drive"), Chapter 5 ("Preparing and Setting Up Your Hard Drive"), Chapter 6 ("Creating and Using Directories"), Chapter 7 ("Managing Disks and Files"), Chapter 9 ("Understanding PC Memory Types"), Chapter 11 ("Memory Organization and Upgrade Strategies"), and Chapter 14 ("Using DOS Utilities").

The following chapters, which at first glance appear to be dedicated totally to DOS 6.2, contain a tremendous amount of information and techniques for the DOS 5 user: Chapter 8 ("Tuning Your Disk with

DOS 6.2 Tools"), Chapter 10 ("Using the DOS 6.2 Memory Manager"), and Chapter 20 ("Battling Viruses with DOS 6.2"). Additionally, Chapter 15 ("Writing Batch Files") is crammed full with procedures and sample batch files that apply to DOS 5, and Chapter 21 ("Securing Your PC") contains a wealth of tricks on PC security that work great with DOS 5.

How This Book Is Organized

Inside MS-DOS 6.2, Second Edition is designed both as a tutorial to help new users learn to master DOS 6.2, and as a reference guide that you can use over and over, long after you have mastered the basics of DOS. The book is divided into parts, each of which covers a specific group of DOS concepts and functions. The parts progress from simple to complex.

Part One: Introduction to DOS 6.2

Part 1 introduces the new DOS user to the DOS environment. In this part of *Inside MS-DOS 6.2, Second Edition*, you'll be exposed to an overview of DOS 6.2 features and utilities. The perspective provided by this part of the book serves as a basis for many of the discussions that follow.

Chapter 1, "MS-DOS 6.2: Almost a Perfect 10," is an enthusiastic overview of DOS 6.2 features.

Chapter 2, "An Inside Look: How DOS Works," explains the DOS file structure, file naming conventions, and command-line basics. It also describes the PATH variable and many details of the internal mechanisms of DOS.

Part Two: Setup and Installation

Part 2 describes the process of installing and optimizing DOS 6.2 for your computer system.

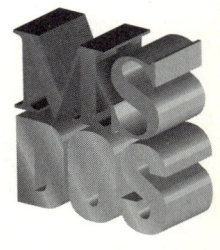

Chapter 3, "Installing DOS 6.2," describes the process of installing DOS 6.2 on your computer. Version 6.2 introduced several new installation options; you will want to consult this chapter before installing DOS 6.2.

In Chapter 4, "Taking a Tour of Your Hard Drive," explains the fascinating technology involved with your hard disk. This chapter presents this information in detail and will become a valuable resource whenever you encounter a problem or have a question about your hard disk.

Chapter 5, "Preparing and Setting Up Your Hard Drive," provides a firm basis for optimizing the space available on your hard disk.

Part Three: Optimizing Your Disk with DOS 6.2

Chapter 6, "Creating and Using Directories," presents strategies and techniques for building the directory and file system on your computer's hard disk.

Chapter 7, "Managing Disks and Files," explains the many, many DOS commands required for successful file management.

Chapter 8, "Tuning Your Disk with DOS 6.2 Tools," describes the new disk optimization and management utilities built into DOS 6.2. Since these utilities are brand new with this release of DOS, even the most experienced DOS user will want to read this chapter.

Part Four: Optimizing Your Memory

DOS 6.2 contains a number of advanced memory management tools and utilities. A thorough understanding of these tools will enable you to maximize your computer's memory.

Chapter 9, "Understanding PC Memory Types," provides the background information necessary for understanding the detailed information that follows.

Chapter 10, "Using the DOS 6.2 Memory Manager," explains how DOS 6.2 effectively uses the memory installed in your computer. Through this detailed discussion you understand the benefits and advances in the DOS 6.2 memory manager.

Chapter 11, "Memory Organization and Upgrade Strategies," explains how to upgrade memory in your computer. The information in this chapter helps you avoid the problems commonly associated with this significant upgrade.

Chapter 12, "Memory-Management Tips, Tricks, and Troubleshooting," offers useful information for those most trying times when nothing seems to go right. Let's face it: you may encounter difficulty after even the most carefully planned and executed upgrade to DOS 6.2. Our author has anticipated the most common and many less likely problems and provides workable solutions to each.

Chapter 13, "Running Third-Party Memory Managers," describes what to look for in a third-party "DOS extender." These applications provide nearly unlimited memory to your DOS applications, making them faster and more reliable. This chapter helps you understand and use the most popular third-party DOS memory products.

Part Five: Making It Better

Many DOS 6.2 users are able to produce their own batch files for automating the most common tasks associated with using their systems. DOS 6.2 also provides a powerful "Multiple Configuration" capability that enables you to start your machine with any one of several configurations that avoid hardware or software conflicts among the peripherals installed on your machine.

Chapter 14, "Using DOS Utilities," describes how to use EDIT, EDLIN, DISKCOPY, and the other DOS utilities. Mastering these applications enhances your productivity with DOS and DOS applications.

Chapter 15, "Writing Batch Files," describes the principles of writing DOS batch files and includes many hints and suggestions to help you write your own batch files that automate many common DOS tasks.

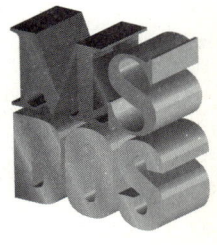

Chapter 16, "Using DOS 6.2 MultiConfig," explains this powerful new feature of DOS. By using MultiConfig, you can avoid many frustrating conflicts between your computer's hardware peripherals and maximize the use of your computer's memory. With MultiConfig, you can selectively load or not load the drivers your hardware (like scanners or sound boards) requires, conserving this valuable memory when it is not needed by your peripheral.

Part Six: Protecting Your Data

Perhaps the most significant features of DOS 6.2 are those which provide a high level of protection for your computer and files. These new features include protection from computer viruses, a number of powerful "undelete" utilities, and a sophisticated backup program.

Chapter 17, "A Second Look at Hard Drives," builds on Chapter 4, discussing hard disks and disk architecture in detail. This chapter also examines the boot sector from the perspective of data protection. How do viruses attack hard disks? What are the different kinds of disk failures that can occur? Turn to this chapter for an in-depth discussion of disk drives.

Chapter 18, "Backing Up Your Data," describes MSBACKUP, the advanced backup program included in DOS 6.2. A disciplined backup schedule will protect your computer's data from all but the most catastrophic failures.

Chapter 19, "Protecting and Recovering Data," discusses the technology behind data recovery. Whether your files were lost by mistake or accident, this chapter explains the process required to ensure adequate recovery.

Chapter 20, "Battling Viruses with DOS 6.2" arms you with practical know-how. Surely one of the most bizarre and dangerous trends in computing is the rise of computer viruses, which can attack your system at any moment. Chapter 20 explains these damaging programs and how DOS 6.2 provides a strong defense against damage or data loss.

Chapter 21, "Securing Your PC," presents a rational approach to ensuring the integrity of the data on your computer. Through thoughtful application of the DOS 6.2 utilities and some plain common sense, you can go a long way toward preventing data loss or damage from either computer viruses or accidents.

Part Seven: Making Connections under DOS 6.2

DOS 6.2 includes several connectivity solutions that permit you to exchange data with other DOS computers and computers connected to PC networks.

Chapter 22, "InterLnk and Other Connectivity Solutions," describes the new DOS 6.2 INTERLNK command. This powerful utility enables you to reliably exchange files with other DOS computers. This chapter also discusses alternative data exchange solutions available to the DOS 6.2 user.

Chapter 23, "Using DOS 6.2 with Local Area Networks," provides background information of interest to anyone considering a PC network system.

Part Eight: Command Reference

The standard DOS 6.2 package does not contain a comprehensive command reference. Although the on-line help available in DOS 6.2 is very good, many users prefer a printed medium. The command reference in *Inside MS-DOS 6.2, Second Edition* substitutes for the on-line help available in DOS 6.2.

Part Nine: Appendix

The Appendix, "About the *Inside MS-DOS 6.2 Disk*," describes each of the applications contained on this book's companion disk.

Conventions Used in This Book

Throughout this book, certain conventions are used to help you distinguish the various elements of DOS, its system files, and sample data. Before you look ahead, you should spend a moment examining these conventions:

- *Shortcut keys* are normally found in the text where appropriate. In most applications, for example, Shift+Ins is the shortcut key for the Paste command.

- *Key combinations* appear in the following formats:

    Key1+Key2: When you see a plus (+) between key names, you should hold down the first key while pressing the second key. Then release both keys.

    Key1,Key2: When a comma (,) appears between key names, you should press and release the first key and then press and release the second key.

- *Hot keys* are used in some menu choices. These on-screen, underlined letters of menu names, file names, and option names enable you to access the item by pressing the indicated letter. For example, the File menu may be displayed on-screen as F̲ile. The underlined letter is the letter you can type to choose that option. (In this book, such letters are displayed in bold, underlined type: **F̲**ile.)

- *Information* you type is in a special **boldface.** This applies to individual letters and numbers, as well as text strings. This convention, however, does not apply to special keys, such as Enter, Esc, or Ctrl.

- *New terms* appear in *italics*.

- *Text that is displayed on-screen,* but which is not part of DOS or a DOS application—such as DOS prompts and messages—appears in a `special typeface`.

Special Text Used in This Book

Throughout this book you will find examples of special text. These passages have been given special treatment so that you can instantly recognize their significance and so that you can easily find them for future reference.

Notes, Tips, Warnings, and Author's Notes

Inside MS-DOS 6.2, Second Edition features many special "sidebars," which are set apart from the normal text. Three distinct types of sidebars are set aside by icons: *Notes*, *Tips*, and *Warnings*.

A ***note*** *includes "extra" information that you should find useful, but which complements the discussion at hand instead of being a direct part of it. A note may describe special situations that can arise when you use DOS under certain circumstances, and tells you what steps to take when such situations arise. Notes also may tell you how to avoid problems with your software and hardware.*

A ***tip*** *provides you with quick instructions for getting the most from your DOS system as you follow the steps outlined in the general discussion. A tip might show you how to conserve memory in some setups, how to speed up a procedure, or how to perform one of many time-saving and system-enhancing techniques.*

A ***warning*** *tells you when a procedure may be dangerous—that is, when you run the risk of losing data, locking your system, or even damaging your hardware. Warnings generally tell you how to avoid such losses, or describe the steps you can take to remedy them.*

An **AUTHOR'S NOTE** has added information you will find informative and, at times, perhaps even entertaining.

New Riders Publishing

The staff of New Riders Publishing is committed to bringing you the very best in computer reference material. Each New Riders book is the result of months of work by authors and staff, who research and refine the information contained within its covers.

As part of this commitment to you, the NRP reader, New Riders invites your input. Please let us know if you enjoy this book, if you have trouble with the information and examples presented, or if you have a suggestion for the next edition.

Please note, however, that the New Riders staff cannot serve as a technical resource for DOS or DOS application-related questions, including hardware- or software-related problems. Refer to the documentation that accompanies your DOS or DOS application package for help with specific problems.

If you have a question or comment about any New Riders book, please write to NRP at the following address. We will respond to as many readers as we can. Your name, address, or phone number will never become part of a mailing list or be used for any other purpose than to help us continue to bring you the best books possible.

> New Riders Publishing
> Prentice Hall Computer Publishing
> Attn: Associate Publisher
> 201 W. 103rd Street
> Indianapolis, IN 46290

If you prefer, you can FAX New Riders Publishing at the following number:

> (317) 581-4670

We welcome your electronic mail to our CompuServe ID:

70031,2231

Thank you for selecting *Inside MS-DOS 6.2, Second Edition*!

MS
DOS

Introduction to DOS 6.2

MS-DOS 6.2: Almost a Perfect 10 21
An Inside Look: How DOS Works 69

Part One:

MS
DOS

CHAPTER 1

MS-DOS 6.2: Almost a Perfect 10

by Mark Minasi

DOS 6.2 is the latest in a long line of versions of what is the most widespread operating system in the world. That long line hasn't been an unbroken string of successes for the DOS architects, however, so it's logical for a PC user to ask, "Should I upgrade? Is DOS 6.2 worth it?" The answer is yes; this chapter explains why.

In some ways, DOS 6.2 might better be named DOS 5.2. That's not a negative comment, just a recognition that DOS 6.2, although different from DOS 5, is nowhere near as different from its forebearer as 5 was from 4.01. In any case, DOS 5 and DOS 6.2 break the mold of the earlier versions of DOS.

DOS 5 was a real success in the PC world and deservedly so; it contained many of the basic DOS utilities that you previously had to buy separately from third-party software vendors. That was a departure for Microsoft; previous DOS releases were a response to new hardware.

DOS 1.1, for example, was introduced to support 360K floppy drives, DOS 2 was introduced for hard disks, 2.1 for the PC Jr and PC Portable floppy drives, DOS 3 to support larger hard disks and 1.2M floppy drives, and so on up to DOS 4, which supported hard disks larger than 32M.

DOS 5, on the other hand, didn't arrive at the behest of some new kind of disk drive; DOS 6.2 continues in the same vein as DOS 5 by venturing forth in areas where DOS has previously feared to tread: virus protection, hard-disk data compression, communications, configuration control, and disk optimization. DOS 6.2 improves DOS's existing support for memory management, data recovery and integrity, and batch files, among other things.

In this book, you learn in detail how to harness the power of DOS. This chapter provides a quick look at all the new features under DOS 6.2 and includes pointers to the other chapters.

AUTHOR'S NOTE

This chapter is a sort of fast-forwarded version of the rest of the book. That means you'll see references to things that aren't defined in this chapter. (For example, although you don't read about XMS managers in this chapter, you do read that the DOS HIMEM.SYS device driver is an XMS manager. For a more complete discussion of XMS managers and other techie specifics, you are referred to the appropriate chapter, in this case, Chapter 11.)

Think of this chapter as something of a travel guide for the rest of the book. If you read no other chapter, read this one. This overview may tell you all you need to know about some parts of DOS, but certain DOS items explained here will whet your appetite for more information. When that happens, just turn to the appropriate chapter and dig in. If you come across sections of this chapter that seem too technical for your taste, don't worry—just skip to the next section. These are the hors d'oeuvres, so no one's watching to make sure that you clean your plate.

> *Whether you are trying to make the decision to buy DOS 6.2; or, having DOS 6.2, you are trying to grasp all its power, this chapter is the place to start.*

Disk Compression

The first few sections in this chapter look at the new DOS features not found in earlier DOSs. First stop in this quick tour is DoubleSpace, the disk compression (the hard disk type, not the spinal type) routine that can actually increase the size of your disk by a factor of two.

Compressing Disks On-the-Fly

DOS 6.2 is fairly large—about 8M, if you install it all—but, because of the new DoubleSpace feature, after installing DOS 6.2, you may have more free disk space than you did before!

DoubleSpace is similar to a product called SpeedStor from AddStor. SpeedStor was sold in the mid-1980s as a device driver (a *device driver* is a program that extends the capabilities of DOS) that got around a limitation that existed in DOS at the time. DOS before DOS 3.3 could not use any part of a hard disk beyond the first 32M.

> *OnTrack Disk Manager from OnTrack Data Systems in Eden Prairie, Minnesota, solved the problem of getting beyond the 32M limit with an inexpensive third-party device driver called DMDRVR.BIN. They soon had competition in the form of similar programs, and SpeedStor was one of the better selling of those programs.*

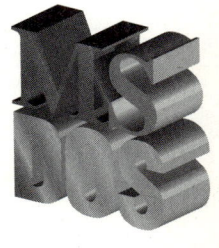

With the advent of DOS 3.3 came one solution to the large-disk problem: DOS 3.3 enabled you to partition a large hard disk, essentially chopping up a disk larger than 32M into several logical disks. Thus, an 80M hard disk could be partitioned into a 32M C drive, a 32M D drive, and a 16M E drive. DOS 4.01 solved the problem even more completely by enabling you to format a disk up to gigabytes (billions of bytes) in size.

Because DOS 3.3 made products like OnTrack and SpeedStor less valuable, those products added features in an attempt to maintain market share. One of the more popular of those features is disk compression.

The leader in the disk compression business is—or was, until DOS 6.2's introduction—Stacker, from Stac Electronics. Another compression product, Double Disk, was licensed by Microsoft as the starting point for what eventually became their DoubleSpace technology.

Disk-Compression Fundamentals

Disk compression involves reformatting the data on the disk so that you can get more data into a smaller space. Although a complete discussion of how data compression works is found in Chapter 5, following is a short description of two methods: run-length encoding and Huffman encoding.

Run-length encoding works well if the data to be compressed shows much duplication. Many graphics files, for example, consist of only 1s and 0s. A 1 appears where ink should appear; a 0 appears where no ink goes (in a monochromatic graphics file). If you consider what most monochromatic images look like, you realize that there are usually large patches, or *runs*, of black in some areas, and large runs of white in other areas. In the data file, those large patches of white are a long string of 0s, and the patches of black are a long string of 1s (see fig. 1.1).

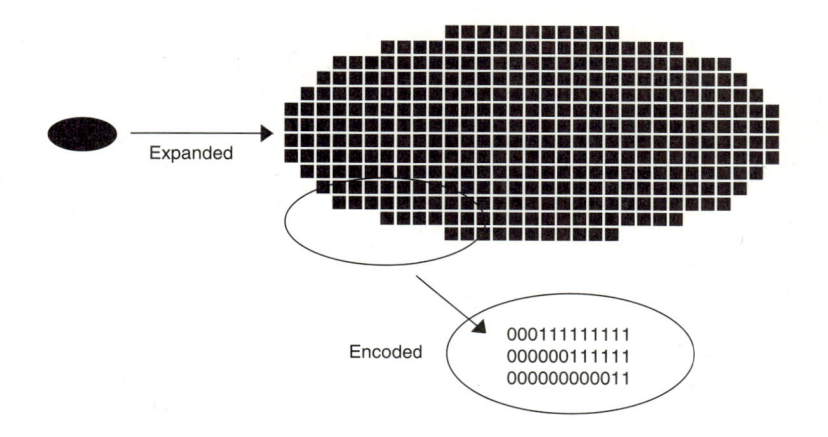

Figure 1.1

A monochrome graphic image, expanded and encoded as 0s and 1s.

In figure 1.1, you see on the left a simple filled-in oval. On the right, you see an expanded version of that oval showing the black and the white parts in detail. The lower right shows how part of the image is encoded as 1s and 0s. It's that part that you need to understand to see how encoding works. The black parts are represented by 1s, the white parts by 0s. In this simple example, a portion of the image looks like the following:

000111111111

000000111111

000000000011

The computer processes this information in a long series of 1s and 0s, more like the following:

000111111111/000000111111/000000000011

The slashes indicate where the line breaks are.

Look at the data again, and you will see that it is a small group of 0s, then a larger group of 1s, then more 0s, 1s, a long group of 0s, and finally two 1s. Each group is a *run*. In a run-length encoding scheme, this might be recast as the following:

0[3]1[9]/0[6]1[6]/0[10]1[2]

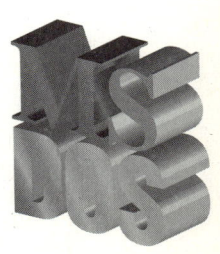

The values in the square brackets indicate a repeat value—the length of a run of 0s or 1s—hence the term *run length*. Some compression schemes go beyond looking for runs of single characters by searching for common pairs or triplets of characters. An analysis of any English text, for example, would show many three-letter triplets consisting of *t*, followed by *h*, followed by *e*.

In the Huffman encoding method, variable-length encoding schemes represent data. Most computers use a standard-length, data-encoding method called *ASCII*, the American Standard Code for Information Interchange. ASCII uses eight bits (bits are 0s or 1s) to describe each letter. Thus, an *A* is represented by eight bits, an *x* by eight bits, a *5* by eight bits, and so on. A Huffman code is different from an ASCII code in that it is a variable-length code. Some characters occur more frequently in English text than others; for instance, the space character appears most commonly, and the letter *Q* appears least commonly. Common characters, such as space or *E* use a short code, perhaps three bits long. Less-common characters use a longer code. The longest codes can be 16 bits long, longer than their ASCII versions. But, because the most commonly occurring characters appear more often than the less common ones, the text ends up shorter with a Huffman code than it would with ASCII.

The DoubleSpace Filter Scheme

Run-length encoding and Huffman codes are good ideas, but virtually all PC programs are designed to work with plain ASCII. If you began storing your data on the hard disk in something other than ASCII, the PC applications you own would no longer work. The DoubleSpace feature in DOS 6.2 gets around that problem by acting as a filter between the disk (which is encoded with some kind of compression scheme once you install DoubleSpace) and the application programs (which expect to see ASCII). Figure 1.2 shows how this works.

Most applications don't directly access the hard disk; they ask DOS to do the disk reading and writing for them. That gives DOS's DoubleSpace device driver the chance it needs to compress data on its way to a disk (when an application program asks DOS to save data to disk) and decompress that data on its way off the disk (when an application program asks DOS to read data from a disk). DOS relies on a set of very important programs called the Basic Input/Output System, or BIOS. *For more information about BIOS, see Chapter 2.*

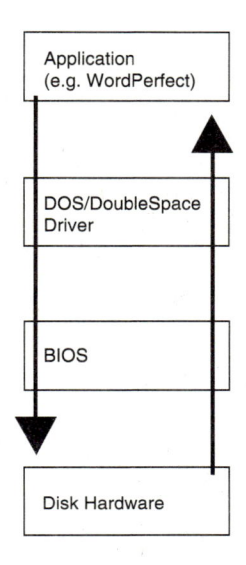

Figure 1.2

The normal flow of information between disks and applications.

The DOS installation program offers you an option to use DoubleSpace on your hard disk. DoubleSpace compresses the files already on the disk and, at the same time, installs the new DOS 6.2 files. That's why you may end up with more free space on your hard disk after you install DOS 6.2. But how important *is* DoubleSpace to DOS 6.2?

> *It's not certain that DoubleSpace is the most important feature of DOS 6.2, but it's reasonable to assert that it will be the most talked-about feature because of its compatibility.*

You now know that DoubleSpace compresses and decompresses data as it's being written to or read from the disk; figure 1.2 shows how that works. Unfortunately, some DOS programs don't use this method of accessing the disk (see fig. 1.3).

Figure 1.3

Flow paths of information between an application and a hard disk.

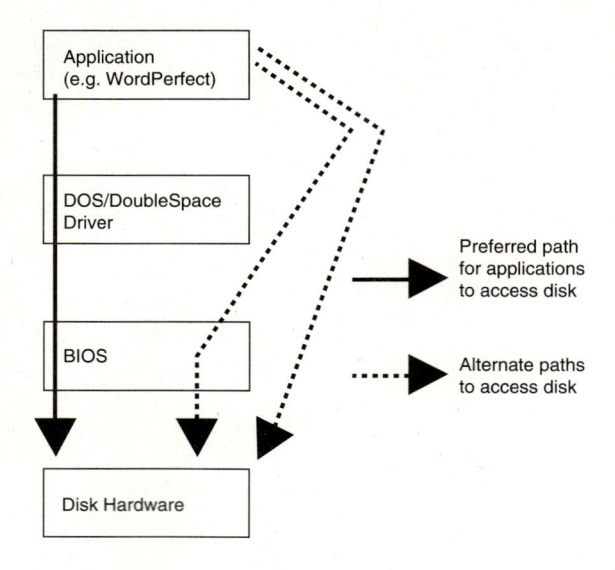

```
┌─────────────────┐
│ Application     │────┐ ┐ ┐
│ (e.g. WordPerfect)│   │ │ │
└────────┬────────┘   │ │ │
         │             │ │ │
         │             │ │ │      ───▶  Preferred path
         ▼             │ │ │             for applications
┌─────────────────┐   │ │ │             to access disk
│ DOS/DoubleSpace │   │ │ │
│ Driver          │   │ │ │      ┄┄▶  Alternate paths
└────────┬────────┘   │ │ │             to access disk
         │             │ │ │
         ▼             │ │ │
┌─────────────────┐   │ │ │
│ BIOS            │───┘ │ │
└────────┬────────┘     │ │
         │               │ │
         ▼      ▼        ▼
┌─────────────────┐
│ Disk Hardware   │
└─────────────────┘
```

As shown in figure 1.3, most DOS applications take the solid-line path when accessing data on the disk. But some programs bypass DOS altogether, accessing a disk through the BIOS, or addressing the hard-disk hardware directly. Either of these latter two methods creates havoc when used with a DoubleSpaced disk.

> **STOP** *Fortunately, most DOS programs use DOS to access disks, but some disk-maintenance programs, such as Gibson Research's SpinRite II or Prime Solutions' Disk Technician, do not use DOS to examine your disk. Because it's essential to use DOS to read and write DoubleSpaced disks, use caution in applying disk-tuning and maintenance programs on a DoubleSpaced disk drive.*

> **NOTE** *Do not use any disk maintenance, tuning, or "speedup" programs on a DoubleSpaced disk until you have checked with the software's manufacturer to ensure that their program will work with the DoubleSpace feature. If you*

don't use DoubleSpace, then any disk-maintenance program that works under DOS 5 should work without trouble under DOS 6.2.

DoubleSpace enables you to either compress an entire existing disk, or use just a portion of the free space remaining on an existing disk, creating a new logical disk drive. *For more information about the pros and cons of each approach, as well as a more in-depth look at DoubleSpacing your disk, see Chapter 5.*

Protecting Data from Viruses

Sometime in the mid-1980s, the PC world got something new to worry about (as if hard disk crashes, accidental formats, power surges, and buggy software weren't enough). Word got around that a kind of program called a *virus* was starting to appear on some PCs. The first virus program that caught national attention was known as the Lehigh virus, named after the college where it was discovered.

DOS 6.2 offers two kinds of virus protection: a virus scanner and a virus shield. Both programs are based on Microsoft Anti-Virus (MSAV), a popular antivirus package marketed by Central Point Software. MSAV is a virus-scanner program that searches through a disk, looking inside every program for a possible virus. MSAV works very quickly; quite a feat when you consider that the list of viruses it checks for contains thousands of programs, such as Bad Boy, Darth Vader, Ogre, Disk Killer, and AIDS, to name just a few.

MSAV can zip through a 30M hard disk in under three minutes. The MSAV program has two versions: MSAV.EXE runs under DOS, and MWAV.EXE runs under Windows.

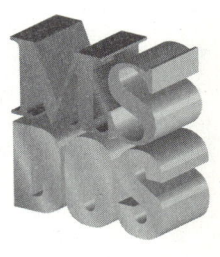

AUTHOR'S NOTE

Lehigh was a virus program that attached itself to an important DOS program called COMMAND.COM (more about this important file in Chapter 2). There were two parts to Lehigh: the worm, which spread the virus to other PCs through floppy disks, and the bomb, which damaged data on the hard disk of the infected system. The worm operated quietly in the computer's memory, scanning any floppy disks inserted into the disk drives. If a copy of COMMAND.COM was on a floppy inserted in the drive, Lehigh's worm quickly inserted a copy of itself into COMMAND.COM, "infecting" that floppy disk. Lehigh kept track of the number of copies of COMMAND.COM it had infected, waiting until it had infected COMMAND.COM on four floppies.

Once Lehigh infected the fourth floppy, the bomb portion of the virus activated. The bomb program was a simple one: it erased the directory of the infected computer's hard disk, effectively destroying all data on that hard disk. Most disks containing Lehigh were ferreted out and erased, but the incident remains something of a watershed in PC history; it was the first really nasty widespread virus.

You have probably heard about viruses for years, and perhaps you have even encountered one. Viruses used to be a curiosity, an unusual event. In 1992, however, as far as I was concerned, viruses came into their own.

In early 1992, I taught a class about DOS memory management at a large government facility. When I arrived for my first class, I was shown to a PC learning lab, a classroom with PCs on the students' desks. I was told that I was the first instructor to use this classroom's brand-new PCs, which had been purchased from a large, well-known PC vendor. In the course of leading the exercises, two students asked me why the amount of free memory reported by the DOS MEM command differed from the values that other students were finding. (You learn about MEM in Chapter 11.) After looking at the students' machines, I could find no differences between them and the other machines. But when I ran a virus checker program on the student's machines, I found that both of the machines in question were infected with the Stoned virus.

Stoned is not a particularly scary virus as viruses go; its effects are typically unimportant, and the virus could almost be ignored. But the very idea that a large PC vendor could ship infected machines to the U.S. government indicates that the virus issue needs attention. (By the way, the PC vendor in this story is not the same vendor that got so much negative press in March 1992 over shipping machines infected with the Michaelangelo virus.)

> **TIP** *You could run MSAV every time you boot DOS, but it is more practical to scan your disk every week or so (or perhaps after you install some software that you suspect could be infected).*

A virus scanner such as MSAV or MWAV reports any damage after it's been done; however, it's of no help in keeping viruses from getting to your disk in the first place. DOS 6.2 offers full-time virus protection in the form of a virus shield, VSAFE.COM. When you run VSAFE, you activate a program that runs continuously in your system, looking over DOS's shoulder and trying to keep DOS from getting in trouble. The following examples demonstrate how VSAFE tries to keep your data safe:

- ✔ Whenever you put a floppy disk in your disk drive, VSAFE checks it almost instantly for common viruses.

- ✔ Some viruses must become "resident" in memory, taking up memory space so that they can monitor disk accesses in the hopes that they can infect new files and disks. VSAFE notices when a program is trying to become resident and warns you. This gives you the option to shut the program down before it can become resident.

- ✔ Viruses do their dirty work by formatting disks or erasing files. The DOS and BIOS commands to do those things are fairly limited in number, and virus shields, such as VSAFE, watch for programs that attempt to activate these DOS or BIOS commands.

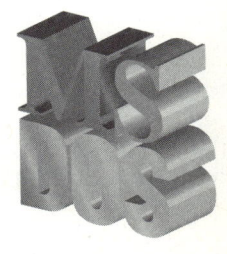

Before the command can be executed, the shield alerts you to the fact that one of your programs has attempted to perform what looks like a destructive act. Of course, this may be a destructive act that you want to perform; in that case, you tell VSAFE to enable the program to do whatever it's doing. But if you did not expect this kind of behavior, then you can go back and run MSAV on the program to determine if it's infected.

PCs need virus protection, and the fact that DOS 6.2 includes antivirus protection shows that DOS is coming to terms with the realities of modern computing.

Keeping in Touch with Communications Support

DOS 6.2 allows two new approaches to hooking up PCs: InterLnk and Workgroup Connection. (Workgroup Connection is available as a separate program that does *not* come with MS-DOS 6.2.)

InterLinking PCs

If you need to transfer an entire subdirectory from a computer on your desk to a laptop—or vice versa—it can be a real pain. And, when you get a computer for a new employee, somebody's got to load the necessary software onto the new computer—which can also be a pain. For a long time, just a few ways existed to transfer large blocks of data from one computer to another:

- ✔ **With a local area network (LAN).** You transfer the subdirectory from the source machine to the server, and then transfer the subdirectory from the server to the target machine.

- ✔ **With a tape drive.** You back up the subdirectory to a tape, take the tape to the computer that you want to transfer the data to, and restore the data on the target computer.

✔ **With floppies.** As with the tape, you back up the data from the source machine onto floppy disks and then restore the information on the target machine from the floppies.

Of these three options, the LAN option is perhaps the most attractive and the simplest. But LANs aren't always available, particularly when laptops are concerned. So a class of programs arose with names like Brooklyn Bridge, LapLink, and FastWire. The first generation of these programs enabled you to connect the serial port of one computer to the serial port of another and then run a program on both computers that enabled you to choose files to transfer. You could tell the program to start transferring, and the program would accomplish the rest. The transfers weren't fast—typically 9,600 bits per second, or about 1,000 characters per second—but it was hands-free. You didn't have to swap floppy disks.

The second generation of these serial-transfer programs introduced two new features. First, maximum transfer rates over serial ports rose to over 100,000 bits per second. Second, programmers figured out how to use the parallel port (previously used only to communicate in a one-way fashion to printers) as a bidirectional, high-speed transfer port supporting up to 500,000 bits per second. Many companies started configuring new systems by setting up one PC and leaving it in their information center, and then linking this special-purpose PC's entire hard disk to each new PC before delivering it to an employee. This assumes, of course, that the company had the legal license and rights to copy the software.

These programs were terrific, but they lacked in one area: to use them, you had to learn a new user interface. And no matter how easy the interface was to learn, it was still a new interface. A third generation of transfer programs changed the interface problem by throwing out the user interface altogether; they used virtual drives. The virtual-drive approach transfers files from computer X to computer Y by running a server program on computer Y and then running a workstation program on computer X. This type of program assumes that computers X and Y both have only one hard disk, drive C. Once connected with the server and workstation programs, computer X sees computer

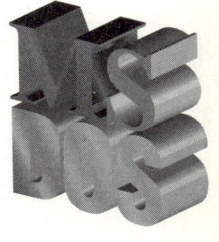

Y's drive C as if it were computer X's own drive D. Transferring files takes place by simply using the familiar DOS COPY and XCOPY commands to transfer data.

DOS 6.2 addresses this area of file transfer. Now you never have to venture far to find one of these serial and parallel transfer programs. Called InterLnk, this new DOS facility makes blasting data from a desktop PC to a laptop PC, or for that matter, from any PC to any other PC, a breeze. *For more information about InterLnk, see Chapter 22.*

Connecting Workgroups

In the fall of 1992, Microsoft released a new version of Windows: Windows for Workgroups. This version of Windows is designed to enable people to build peer-to-peer networks. A *peer-to-peer network* is one in which anyone on the network can share data on his or her hard disk with anyone else on the network. Contrast that type of network with a server-workstation network (the kind more familiar to most LAN users) in which a PC or PCs are dedicated to the task of acting as a shared "file cabinet" of data. Windows for Workgroups comes with a set of network programs called the Workgroup Connection.

DOS 6.2, as the first version of DOS released since Windows for Workgroups, has available as a separate product—this feature does *not* come with the DOS 6.2 package—an updated version of the Workgroup Connection. It is very important for you to understand, however, that Workgroup Connection under DOS is not a stand-alone product (this isn't made abundantly clear in the DOS documentation). In other words, you cannot build a network with just this product; this product enables you only to share printers and files and to send messages by means of a PC running Windows for Workgroups.

If you are using Windows for Workgroups, however, you can do some nifty things, including the following:

- ✔ Send electronic mail between workstations
- ✔ Share disks, files, and printers

Keeping in Touch with Communications Support

- ✔ Schedule activities jointly within a workgroup
- ✔ Play games within a workgroup, such as the Network Hearts game that comes with Windows for Workgroups

Windows for Workgroups has a MAIL program that enables you to compose, send, and receive mail messages; it also has a MICRO program that constantly monitors your mailbox in the background, interrupting your work to tell you when you have received new mail.

Talking with the DOS Manual

Microsoft says that DOS 6.2 is the easiest-to-use DOS yet. In some ways, Microsoft is right. Its MemMaker program makes setting up the Memory Manager easier; the Configuration Manager enables you to tame multiple CONFIG.SYS files; and a new batch command makes it easier for DOS experts to build powerful batch files that can, in turn, make life easier for the users that they help and support. But, at heart, DOS 6.2 is still DOS. Getting anything to work under DOS involves, as magician Penn Jillette says, "knowing what incomprehensible word fragments you have to type in order to back up the greatest script you have ever written." In short, DOS needs documentation.

Microsoft decided to put the bulk of the DOS 6.2 manual right on the PC's hard disk to keep the documentation on-line. Although it's not as easy to read a text from a video screen as it is to read it from a book, it's tremendously convenient to have the manual text just a few keystrokes away.

You may recall that DOS 5 had a fair amount of on-line help as well: you could type **HELP COPY**, or **COPY /?** to see a summary of the syntactic elements of the COPY command. That type of help is still available, although you don't type **HELP COPY** to get the syntactic summary anymore; now you type **DOSHELP COPY** to see that information.

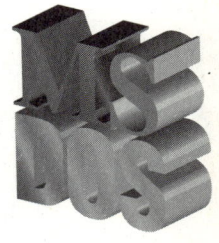

Chapter 1: *MS-DOS 6.2: Almost a Perfect 10*

AUTHOR'S NOTE

Traditionally, the way most DOS documentation is handled is simple: You buy a computer that comes with MS-DOS. The computer arrives in several boxes and you, understandably excited by your new purchase, start opening boxes. (You had better be excited about something you spent thousands of dollars on, right?) The boxes contain a bunch of shrink-wrapped booklets with names such as Read Me First, Getting To Know Your New Computer, MS-DOS Manual, and Other Things You Can Buy from Us Now that You Own a Computer. You probably look over the Read Me First document (maybe you don't—after all, you researched this computer before buying it and you already know what it can do). But the rest is documentation, and who reads that anyway?

Once you set up the computer somewhere, you realize that you have a bunch of books and boxes you have to do something with. You cannot throw the boxes out, because there's a great big notice that came with the computer that states that the computer's manufacturer will not repair any problems with the computer unless the computer is shipped back to the manufacturer in its original box. You put the books in the boxes so that you know where to find them if you ever need them and put the boxes in the garage or the attic.

Sure, you know where the DOS manual is, but when you need to know the syntax of the COPY command, it's too much trouble to paw through a bunch of boxes in the garage just to find the DOS manual. So you do without, which is why most of us are essentially without DOS documentation, until now.

In DOS 6.2, if you type **HELP COPY**, you see an on-line manual that's more than just a summary of the COPY syntax. You see several screens of specific information about how to use the COPY command. You also see references to similar commands, such as XCOPY. Those references are marked in such a way that you can click the mouse on them to have the help system move you to the help screens for the reference word you clicked. This new help system is, therefore, hypertext-like in nature.

Talking with the DOS Manual **37**

> **NOTE**
>
> *With the DOS 6.2 help system, two jump points (Notes and Examples) occur in each help screen. The Notes jump point provides in-depth insight into how to use the command. The Examples jump point, however, is really the key to valuable documentation for many people: concrete examples really nail down the point.*

DOS 6.2's built-in help is more extensive than DOS 5's help. DOS 5 offers on-line help only for DOS command programs invoked from the command line. That means that the DOS 5 on-line help is of no value in finding the syntax of a device driver or a CONFIG.SYS command. DOS 6.2 redresses that problem and gives many examples so that you can get enough information to keep DOS running even if you're stuck somewhere with nothing for documentation but the on-line help.

> **NOTE**
>
> *The file containing the on-line help, HELP.HLP, is a quarter megabyte in size. That one file is larger than all the DOS files for DOS Versions 1.0 through 3.2! That fact points out a striking feature of DOS 6.2: its size. If you install everything that comes with DOS 6.2, you end up using about 8M of disk space. Perhaps that was a significant factor in the decision to include a disk-compression routine with the new DOS.*

The DOS 6.2 help facility also has a Find capability you can use to search for a particular word. You can, for example, search for the word *virus*; Help shows you the first page containing that word. Pressing F3 shows the next page with *virus* on it, and so on.

You can also print help entries with the Help program, but, unfortunately, you cannot use this feature to create a printed manual; the printing capability applies only to specific pages or selected text.

Simplifying Customization with Configuration Control

Disk compression is nice, on-line help is convenient, and InterLnk is good for transferring data from PC to PC. Everyone can probably find something to like in these new features. But the one feature that intermediate-to-advanced users could end up liking best is multiple-configuration control: the Configuration Manager.

If you run more than one complex program, you probably have more than one CONFIG.SYS and AUTOEXEC.BAT file—one for running with the LAN active, another for Windows, another for 1-2-3 Version 3.1, and so on. If your computer has limited memory, you may need multiple configurations because you must sometimes convert some of your memory from extended to expanded; you may also have some configuration files that devote more or less memory to the SMARTDRV disk-cache program. *For more information on types of PC memory, see Chapter 9.*

Even if you don't bother with your CONFIG.SYS and AUTOEXEC.BAT files, you may sometimes rename them or move them so that you can boot your system in a stripped-down configuration to troubleshoot some hardware or software.

More specifically, suppose that you have installed a new local area network (LAN) card in your system and it doesn't seem to work. It fails its diagnostics, but you suspect that the board may be just fine. It's possible that one of the programs you load every day at startup (a screen blanker, memory manager, or the CD-ROM driver) is conflicting with the LAN card. So you want to try booting without any of those programs to test the LAN card again before giving up on it. Such a "clean boot" usually requires that you do something like the following:

1. Copy the old CONFIG.SYS to another file name. Do not use CONFIG.BAK, because it may be overwritten by some installation programs.

2. Copy the old AUTOEXEC.BAT to another file name, in the same fashion as you did for CONFIG.SYS.

Simplifying Customization with Configuration Control 39

3. Erase the old AUTOEXEC.BAT and CONFIG.SYS files.
4. Reboot your system without the CONFIG.SYS and AUTOEXEC.BAT files.
5. Do whatever test you intended to do.
6. Copy the old CONFIG.SYS and AUTOEXEC.BAT files back to where they were and reboot your computer to restore the system.

> **AUTHOR'S NOTE**
>
> *If you have ever actually performed steps 1 through 6, you know that several things can go wrong when you boot without your normal boot files. Here are some of the things that have happened to me:*
>
> ✔ *If you put COMMAND.COM in a directory other than the root of drive C, your system will need a SHELL= statement. If you boot without a CONFIG.SYS file, your system does not contain a SHELL= statement, and the system stops, displays the message* `Bad or missing command interpreter`, *and locks up.*
>
> ✔ *If you need a device driver (one of the programs loaded with the DEVICE= command in the CONFIG.SYS file) to access your hard disk, booting without the CONFIG.SYS file means that your system cannot communicate with its hard disk. Examples of such drivers include OnTrack Disk Manager, Stacker, or many PC-based security systems.*
>
> ✔ *If your CONFIG.SYS or AUTOEXEC.BAT file is complex, you may not want to boot without all their commands; you may want to boot without just a few. That means creating different versions of CONFIG.SYS and AUTOEXEC.BAT, and then managing the versions.*

All these potential problems, as mentioned in the preceding note, are addressed in DOS 6.2. The Configuration Manager's major features include the following:

- ✔ The capability to develop multiple CONFIG.SYS and AUTOEXEC.BAT files, which you select from a menu at boot time with a single keystroke.
- ✔ The option to bypass the CONFIG.SYS and AUTOEXEC.BAT files by pressing F5 at boot time.
- ✔ The option of "single-stepping" through CONFIG.SYS. You hold F8 at boot time, and the system pauses at each line and displays the prompt [Y,N]?. You press Y or N to indicate whether or not that line is to be executed.

> **AUTHOR'S NOTE**
>
> *You get all the details you could want about the Configuration Manager in Chapter 16. But because this is a chapter for the impatient, here's a simple—albeit long—example of how it can make your life easier.*
>
> *Suppose that you have a simple CONFIG.SYS file that looks like this:*
>
> ```
> FILES=60
> BUFFERS=30
> STACKS=9,256
> ```
>
> *(You read more about STACKS in Chapter 2. Information about FILES and BUFFERS is found in Chapter 5. Discussions about HIMEM.SYS and loading DOS high are found in Chapter 11.)*
>
> *Now suppose that you want to add the HIMEM.SYS device driver to your CONFIG.SYS file so that you can run Windows (which requires HIMEM.SYS) and so that you can load DOS high to get more free memory. You need to add two lines to your CONFIG.SYS file so that it looks like this:*
>
> ```
> FILES=60
> BUFFERS=30
> STACKS=9,256
> DEVICE=C:\DOS\HIMEM.SYS
> DOS=HIGH
> ```

Simplifying Customization with Configuration Control

But you don't want to invoke the last two lines every time. You want to be able to choose to load HIMEM.SYS and DOS high when you boot. Under DOS 6.2, your CONFIG.SYS file could look like this in order to achieve the results you want:

```
[MENU]
MENUITEM VANILLA,Boot without memory manager
MENUITEM MEMMGMT,Load DOS high with HIMEM.SYS
MENUDEFAULT=MEMMGMT,5
NUMLOCK=OFF

[VANILLA]
FILES=60
BUFFERS=30
STACKS=9,256

[MEMMGMT]
FILES=60
BUFFERS=30
STACKS=9,256
DEVICE=C:\DOS\HIMEM.SYS
DOS=HIGH
```

When you boot your system, you see the message...

```
loading MS-DOS...
```

...followed by a menu showing you these options:

```
1. Boot without memory manager
2. Load DOS high with HIMEM.SYS
```

You also see a message across the bottom of the screen that says..

```
F5=Bypass startup files F8=Confirm each CONFIG.SYS
file line [NO]
```

On the right is a countdown timer that shows...

```
Time remaining: 05
```

This timer counts down to 04, 03, 02, 01, and finally 00, at which time it automatically loads the files in the MEMMGMT section of the CONFIG.SYS file.

continues

Here's how the magic works: The lines enclosed in square brackets ([]) indicate the beginning of a separate section of the CONFIG.SYS file. This sample CONFIG.SYS file has three sections: [MENU], [MEMMGMT], and [VANILLA]. The [MENU] section is mandatory; the other sections apply only to this particular PC. The presence of the [MENU] section alerts DOS that there are multiple possible CONFIG.SYS file configurations in this file. The MENUITEM commands each announce a configuration. The parameters VANILLA and MEMMGMT give an official system name to each of the two configurations. Because there are only two MENUITEM commands, DOS knows that there are only two configurations to worry about. The phrases "Boot without memory manager" and "Load DOS high with HIMEM.SYS" provide English labels that appear on the menu at boot time. The "MENUDEFAULT=MEMMGMT,5" line tells the computer to wait five seconds for the user to make a selection; if no selection is made, load the MEMMGMT configuration. The "NUMLOCK=OFF" command tells the system to toggle NumLock off on bootup.

After the initial [MENU] section, there are only the [VANILLA] and [MEMMGMT] sections; these are the desired CONFIG.SYS file statements for the two configurations.

You might say that this method seems inefficient: you have to copy the FILES, BUFFERS, and STACKS statements twice. If you rewrite your CONFIG.SYS file using a [COMMON] area, it might look like the following:

```
[MENU]
MENUITEM VANILLA,Boot without memory manager
MENUITEM MEMMGMT,Load DOS high with HIMEM.SYS
MENUDEFAULT=MEMMGMT,5
NUMLOCK=OFF

[VANILLA]

[MEMMGMT]
DEVICE=C:\DOS\HIMEM.SYS
DOS=HIGH

[COMMON]
FILES=60
```

Simplifying Customization with Configuraton Control

```
    BUFFERS=30
    STACKS=9,256
```

In this example, [COMMON] is a predefined "magic" function that gets executed by all configurations. The [VANILLA] section is empty (there's nothing between the [VANILLA] header and the following [MEMMGMT] section). But both the [VANILLA] and [MEMMGMT] sections activate the [COMMON] set of statements. But what if you want some statements common to just some of your configurations and not all of them? You can create a section (a group of commands) and include them in a configuration by adding the line...

```
    INCLUDE xxxx
```

...in which *xxxx* is the name of the section to include. This is easy to see if you rewrite the example CONFIG.SYS file without a [COMMON] area, as follows:

```
[MENU]
MENUITEM VANILLA,Boot without memory manager
MENUITEM MEMMGMT,Load DOS high with HIMEM.SYS
MENUDEFAULT=MEMMGMT,5
NUMLOCK=OFF

[VANILLA]
INCLUDE COMSTUFF

[MEMMGMT]
DEVICE=C:\DOS\HIMEM.SYS
DOS=HIGH
INCLUDE COMSTUFF

[COMSTUFF]
FILES=60
BUFFERS=30
STACKS=9,256
```

This is only the beginning. You never again have to see the...

```
    Bad or missing command interpreter
```

continues

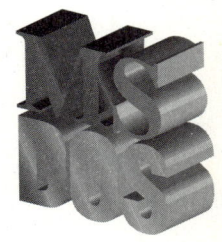

> *...message followed by a system halt. Instead, if you leave out the SHELL= statement or specify a directory where COMMAND.COM cannot be found, you see the following message:*
>
> ```
> Bad or missing Command Interpreter
> Enter correct name of Command Interpreter (eg,
> C:\COMMAND.COM file)
> C>
> ```
>
> *You just enter the fully specified name of COMMAND.COM to get the system up and running. Perhaps the best accolade I can give to DOS 6.2 is that, in the entire time I worked with DOS 6.2 from Beta to final product, I have never had to boot my computer from the floppy drive. Kudos indeed.*

Talking Back to Your Batch Files

The DOS batch language (DBL) is, as anyone who's tried to write programs with it knows, limited. But its greatest limitation is its lack of interactivity. DBL programs can invoke DOS programs, they can make decisions, and they can display information on the screen. What they cannot do is accept a response from a user. With DOS 6.2, however, there's a new external command called CHOICE.COM. *For information about internal and external commands, refer to Chapter 2.*

CHOICE isn't a general-purpose input routine. CHOICE can accept only a single character of input and send that character back to the PC in the form of an ERRORLEVEL datum. *For more information about batch files, including CHOICE and ERRORLEVEL, refer to Chapter 15.*

You can include the CHOICE command in a batch file to accept input from the user of the batch file. You give CHOICE a list of acceptable responses and a prompt. If the user presses something other than one of the acceptable keystrokes, CHOICE beeps and waits for an acceptable keystroke. Once the user presses an acceptable key, CHOICE reports with a numeric code. If, for example, the acceptable keystrokes are E, M, and R, and the user presses E, CHOICE reports code 1 because E is the first in the list of acceptable keystrokes. If the user presses R, CHOICE reports code 3 because R is the third acceptable keystroke. Once CHOICE has a legal keystroke code to report, it terminates with an error code equal to the ASCII code of the key. From there, the remainder of the batch program detects which key the user pressed by testing for various error conditions.

> **AUTHOR'S NOTE**
>
> *Here's a sample batch file, called TEST.BAT, that uses the CHOICE command. If you want to try it, use the EDIT program to create a file that contains the following statements:*
>
> ```
> @ECHO OFF
> CHOICE /C:FL /N What is heavier, a pound of feathers
> or a pound of lead?
> IF ERRORLEVEL 2 GOTO LEAD
> IF ERRORLEVEL 1 GOTO FEATHERS
> :LEAD
> ECHO What LEAD you to that conclusion?
> GOTO END
> :FEATHERS
> ECHO I would say you WINGed that answer!
> :END
> ```
>
> *A sample output would look like the following:*
>
> ```
> C:\>TEST
> What is heavier, a pound of feathers or a pound of
> lead?L
> What LEAD you to that decision?
> C:\>TEST
> What is heavier, a pound of feathers or a pound of
> lead?F
> I would say you WINGed that answer!
> ```
>
> *The batch file starts off with an @ECHO OFF statement, as do most batch files. Then the CHOICE command is invoked with the*
>
> *continues*

> information that the acceptable characters are F and L (`/C:FL`); the CHOICE command also has a prompt to put on the screen (`What is heavier, a pound of feathers or a pound of lead?`). The `/N` option keeps CHOICE from adding `[F/L]?` to the end of the prompt (which it does unless you tell it otherwise).
>
> The two IF ERRORLEVEL statements check for code 2 (L) and code 1 (F). Veteran batch programmers know that you must check ERRORLEVEL values in descending order, hence the L check before the F check. The GOTO statements lead to ECHO statements that display a response on the screen.

NOTE

Although CHOICE isn't the best possible DOS batch language, it's an improvement. DOS's batch language still needs functions, arithmetic capabilities, iteration capabilities, and much more. To see what a batch language should look like, compare DOS's impoverished language to a language such as OS/2's REXX language.

On the other hand, there are enhancements to the DOS batch language. Batch Enhancer, for example, which is included in the Norton Utilities, is a collection of commands that add a lot of power to your batch files. The shareware programs Power Batch and TurboBat provide additional commands and enable you to compile your batch files into EXE and COM files.

Simplifying Memory Management with MemMaker

One of DOS 5's most compelling features was its pair of memory manager programs: HIMEM.SYS and EMM386.EXE. Memory managers do many things, including resolving the "RAM cram" problem

Simplifying Memory Management with MemMaker

brought on by today's typical PC environment. Consider the following excerpt from a CONFIG.SYS file, showing the kinds of programs found in today's typical business PCs:

```
DEVICE=C:\UTILS\SCSI\ASPI4DOS.SYS /P330
DEVICE=C:\DOS\ANSI.SYS
DEVICE=C:\WWG\PROTMAN.DOS /I:C:\WWG
DEVICE=C:\WWG\WORKGRP.SYS
DEVICE=C:\WWG\ELNKII.DOS
DEVICE=C:\UTILS\CORELDRW\CUNI_ASP.SYS /ID:6 /N:1 /
D:MSCD001
DEVICE=C:\DOS\SETVER.EXE
```

Together, these programs take up 90K of the precious bottom 640K that most PC applications must live within, no matter how much memory is actually on the PC. You could have 16M of RAM on your PC, but if you don't have at least 384K free in that bottom 640K, you can't load and run WordPerfect 5.1 (as an example). The programs in the example CONFIG.SYS file are necessary for the PC to communicate with the peripherals inside it. ASPI4DOS.SYS and CUNI_ASP.SYS, for example, enable access to a CD-ROM device. ANSI.SYS enables DOS to display 50 lines on a VGA screen, among other things. PROTMAN.DOS, WORKGRP.SYS, and ELNKII.DOS support the LAN card in the system. SETVER enables DOS 6.2 to support some programs sensitive to the version of DOS under which they run.

Add to this example these programs loaded by the computer's AUTOEXEC.BAT file:

```
DOSKEY
SMARTDRV 1024 512
MSCDEX /V /M:10 /D:MSCD001
MOUSE
```

DOSKEY keeps a command history, enabling you to reuse commands you have already typed. SMARTDRV is a disk cache program that speeds up disk access. MSCDEX supports the CD-ROM drive, and MOUSE is the mouse driver. On a computer with a CD-ROM, this is a stripped down CONFIG.SYS. But, together, these programs take up a lot of space that robs this computer of free RAM in the bottom 640K once it's booted. 250K of RAM is taken up just loading programs that support hardware on the system, before any applications programs are loaded at all! A memory manager's main benefit is that it can solve that problem by moving the programs out of the precious bottom 640K. QEMM, 386Max, and DOS 5's EMM386.EXE all sought to perform that function and solve the RAM shortage problem.

But the DOS 5 Memory Manager required real commitment and understanding to make it work. Merely loading the Memory Manager with your CONFIG.SYS file isn't enough. For DOS 5's Memory Manager to free as much memory as possible, you have to map your PC's memory, examine the size of each program you plan to load in memory, and then fit each program into memory (much as you arrange different sizes of boxes on shelves in a basement). It's not a difficult job, but an exacting one.

In contrast, successful third-party memory managers, such as Quarterdeck's QEMM and Qualitas's 386Max, are shipped with programs that perform this memory arrangement automatically. QEMM has a program called Optimize that probes your computer's memory for every free byte, analyzes every program you load when booting your system, and plans how best to free memory for your DOS applications. Similarly, 386Max comes with a program called Maximize that does essentially the same thing. Programs like Optimize and Maximize have been something of a thorn in Microsoft's side. The automatic nature of the QEMM and 386Max products made them formidable competitors to EMM386.EXE—even though QEMM and 386Max are separate products that cost under $100 and EMM386.EXE is free (at least once you purchase DOS 5).

Because DOS 6.2 is "the easiest DOS ever," it has a memory arranger like Optimize and Maximize; it's called MemMaker. Unfortunately, it's much like Optimize and Maximize. Running Optimize and Maximize on a variety of machines shows that although they're useful sometimes, they're useless at other times. Optimize and Maximize don't run on many PCs, particularly PCs with lots of device drivers and TSR programs—the very machines that would benefit most from a program such as Optimize, Maximize, or MemMaker.

> *The fact that automatic memory arrangers often don't work reflects the fact that having a program try to load other programs at the same time that it monitors DOS's reaction to the programs is an iffy process at best. It's no surprise that MemMaker works like the other memory-management programs: well on some machines, poorly on others.*

You need to try MemMaker for yourself. If it works, fine. If not, you'll have to arrange your memory manager by hand, which is actually the better way to do it. Memory management is discussed in greater detail later in this chapter.

Arranging Disks with DEFRAG

A disk drive is much like a basement. If you have ever lived in a house with a basement, you know what I mean. You move into a new house, and there seems to be an endless supply of space. A whole basement for storing boxes and similar junk! This is how most people feel when they get a larger hard disk.

"200 megabytes!" they exclaim. "I will never run out of space again." But you know the end of this story: The hard disk does indeed fill up (as does the basement). But think about the process of arranging that space in the basement. When you first move in, the boxes are stacked neatly against a wall. Not only do you fill the space, you fill it efficiently. But soon you need something from one of the boxes, and you unstack a few boxes in the process of finding the one that you need. The boxes then go back against the wall, but you're not quite as careful about stacking them. Before you know it, you have a mess in the basement. The boxes aren't stacked right, making it hard to find a box when it's needed. You finally break down and reorganize the basement, neatly restacking the boxes.

A similar process happens on PC hard disks. *Disk fragmentation*, as this process is called, slows down the process of accessing files. If a file is created and destroyed over and over again, DOS eventually fragments it. *Fragmenting* means that part of the file ends up in one location on the hard disk, and another part ends up somewhere else.

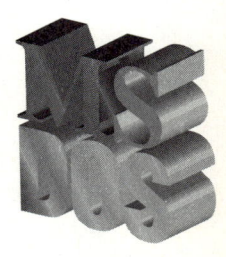

For years, third-party vendors have offered disk defragmenters, which are utilities that pick up fragmented files and replace them on the disk in a single piece. Defragmenting your disks speeds them up and makes them more reliable. One of the better known utilities is Norton SpeedDisk, a utility shipped with the Norton Utilities since Version 4. DOS 6.2 now includes SpeedDisk, although a few features have been removed from it. In DOS, SpeedDisk has been renamed DEFRAG.EXE.

Repairing Disks with ScanDisk

Going back to the house analogy, every homeowner knows that a house demands maintenance and upkeep. There always seems to be something to do around the house: painting the walls, patching the roof, fixing a window, unstopping a drain, replacing a light bulb, mowing the lawn, and on it goes.

The same thing applies to disks—they require maintenance. Quite frankly, when you totally understand how disks work, you may find yourself wondering how in the world they work at all.

A number of things can go wrong with your disks. For one thing, *lost clusters* can develop, which means that DOS thinks that a tiny area of the disk (called a *cluster*) is in use by a particular file, when it isn't in use by any file at all. *Cross-linked files* can also develop, which means that part of two different files are occupying a single cluster. Worst of all, however, areas of a disk can actually become physically damaged, which means that if data was placed in such an area before it was damaged, you will not be able to access your data.

Fortunately, disk upkeep and repair is a lot easier (and cheaper) than home maintenance. Again, powerful third-party products, such as Norton Disk Doctor (included with the Norton Utilities), have been cleaning up the mess for years. DOS has finally joined the club by including ScanDisk with DOS 6.2. ScanDisk is a full-featured disk analysis and repair tool that far surpasses the meager capablities of the CHKDSK command.

Checking the System with MSD 2.0a

Once upon a time, a PC could be described with just a few characteristics: what processor it used, who made its BIOS, how large a hard disk it had, how many floppy drives it had, how much memory, and what kind of video board. Now, however, PC hardware has many, many different types of memory, LAN boards, SCSI peripheral interfaces, mice, and so forth. It would take a long time to describe every PC characteristic; that makes it tough for a PC-support person to walk up to a strange machine and figure out what ails it. Microsoft telephone-support people also have this problem.

> **AUTHOR'S NOTE**
>
> *Asking people to describe their computers over the phone isn't a job most of us would relish: "What kind of processor is in your PC, sir?" "Well, it's got a black case. Does that help?"*
>
> *I recently had a conversation with someone having trouble installing Trident super VGA drivers on a Windows machine. (Trident makes a popular chip set that many super VGA video boards are built around; you need special Trident-specific drivers to get maximum Windows performance from a Trident VGA.) I suggested a number of possible fixes but couldn't quite guess what the problem was. Finally, the fellow with the problem said, "I think I'll just get rid of it. I hate Orchid video boards."*
>
> *The blinders fell from my eyes and I smacked myself for making dumb assumptions. Orchid video boards do not use the Trident chip set; they use the Tseng Laboratories chip set. There's no way to make a Trident driver work on an Orchid board.*
>
> *The point of this story (yes, there is a point) is that if I had had some sort of program to help me quickly inventory that PC, I would have immediately seen that the man didn't have a Trident chip set VGA. And to think that the Microsoft telephone-support people grapple with this sort of thing every day.*

To help telephone-bound service people, Microsoft began shipping a program called MSD (Microsoft System Diagnostics) with Word 5 for DOS. It installed automatically with Word. If you called Microsoft with a tech-support question, the tech-support operator told you to type **MSD**; useful information then appeared on your screen—information that helped the Microsoft person get your problem solved more quickly. MSD also appeared in Windows 3.1, and it is included with DOS 6.2.

> *MSD isn't really a diagnostic tool; it does not test memory or the hard disk. It's more of an inventory program. But it's convenient. You see references to MSD information throughout this book.*

Improving on Older DOS Versions

As you already have seen, DOS 6.2 covers some new ground with disk compression, virus protection, network and communications support, and electronic-mail, to name just a few items. But it also takes pains to repair some problems that have existed in DOS for over ten years. DOS 6.2 makes backups easier and improves on some DOS 5 features, such as the Memory Manager and the UNDELETE command. This section discusses how Microsoft has made the premier PC operating system even better.

Backing Up with Norton Backup

For years, one of the weak points of DOS was its backup software. The DOS BACKUP and RESTORE programs for DOS versions through 4.01 were almost unusable. BACKUP saved a file in a peculiar format, one that only RESTORE could read. But RESTORE was notoriously sensitive, refusing to restore files for the most minor of reasons, leaving users with useless backups.

> **AUTHOR'S NOTE**
>
> *A good reason to do a complete backup is when you upgrade to a newer version of DOS. (Do I have your attention yet?) When they moved from DOS 3.3 to DOS 4.01, many users wanted to repartition their drives so that they could take advantage of DOS 4.01's ability to address drives larger than 32M (the old DOS 3.3 limit). So they used BACKUP to back up their hard drives to a mountain of floppy disks, repartitioned their hard drives (destroying any data left on the disk), installed DOS 4.01, and then tried to restore the data on the floppies.*
>
> *As it turned out, RESTORE for DOS 4.01 only read data generated by BACKUP for DOS 4.01. All those backups made with DOS 3.3 were useless.*
>
> *Although DOS 5's BACKUP and RESTORE commands were a bit better, they still fell tremendously short in terms of ease-of-use and effectiveness.*

Meanwhile, utility vendors Symantec/Norton and Central Point either bundled backup programs with their general utility packages or sold them as separate products. Both products had their adherents and both were indisputably better than the DOS backup and restore utilities. Commercial backup utilities typically offered a few features that the DOS BACKUP and RESTORE programs lacked:

- ✔ **Compression.** Many commercial backup programs could compress files as they saved them, enabling a 1.44M floppy disk to store perhaps 3M of data. Even better, compression could enable a 100M tape drive to store up to 250M of data. But compression has several potentially troublesome aspects: If something goes wrong with a regular backup, such as partial damage to the backup medium, uncompressed data can often be recovered. If something goes wrong in a compressed backup, there's typically no hope of recovery. In addition, compression and decompression take time, slowing down the backup and restore processes.

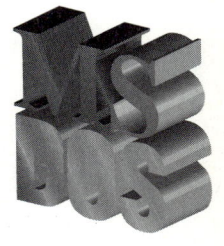

✔ **Fault tolerance.** Some backup programs deliberately write redundant data to the backup disks. The purpose of redundant data is to resolve errors discovered while restoring data. Suppose that you back up some important data onto a series of floppies in 1993. In 1995, you find that you need to restore that data but the floppies holding the data have been partially damaged. Ordinarily, that means you are out of luck. But, if you told your backup program to write the data with fault tolerance, the restoration program tries to reconstruct the data that has been damaged with the redundant information. Some of these systems are quite good. You can, for example, use an ice pick to punch a hole in a floppy-disk backup made with Fastback, a backup product made by Fifth Generation Systems, and Fastback can still restore your data. One drawback is that redundant information takes up space on the disk, reducing the amount of space available for the data to be backed up. Another drawback is that generating and checking the error-correction information takes time, slowing down the backup and restore processes.

If your goal is to perform backups quickly and with the least amount of floppies, tapes, or cartridges, don't use fault tolerance. If, on the other hand, data integrity is your top priority when backing up data, by all means activate the fault-tolerance feature.

✔ **Time activation.** Time activation enables a backup program to activate itself automatically on a daily, weekly, monthly, or annual basis. Some backup programs include a tickler or reminder program that the backup program installs in your AUTOEXEC.BAT file. Every time you boot your system, the tickler program runs. The program quickly looks at your hard disk to determine which files haven't been backed up in a while. Then it presents you with a short message informing you that there are files awaiting backup.

✔ **On-the-fly disk formats.** This kind of format resolves a problem that the DOS BACKUP program had from the beginning: Until DOS 3.3, you needed to know before beginning a backup exactly how many floppies the process would require. Then you had to format that many floppies before beginning the backup process. Once you began backing up, there was no turning back; if your backup required 31 floppy disks, but you had just 30, all would go well for the first 30 floppies. When DOS BACKUP asked for the 31st disk, the entire backup operation would abort if you didn't have another floppy disk ready and formatted, rendering all your work useless. Most commercial programs fix this problem by including the capability to format floppies on the fly. Norton Backup, for example, senses unformatted floppies. If you put an unformatted disk into the floppy drive, Norton Backup automatically formats the disk. If you put a disk already containing data into the floppy drive, Norton Backup asks whether it should erase the data already on the floppy or add the backup data to the existing data.

It's always best to use preformatted disks for backup, whether you format them yourself or buy them preformatted. This enables you to weed out any disks that contain bad sectors, and you require fewer disks for the backup.

If you buy preformatted disks, run CHKDSK on them to ensure that they do not have any bad sectors.

After trying to make PC users happy by modifying BACKUP and RESTORE in DOS 2.0 through DOS 5, Microsoft has removed BACKUP altogether. The new backup program, MSBACKUP, is a new name for the Norton Backup program.

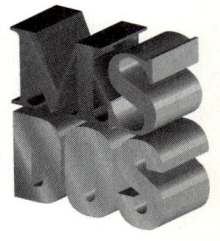

There's much to like in MSBACKUP. It compresses files as it backs them up and offers different levels of fault tolerance. You can set an automatic backup to occur at any time (daily to annually), and the backup is fairly fast and flexible. You can personalize MSBACKUP with a configuration file or, if you like, you can maintain several configuration files so that you can run MSBACKUP with one configuration file for complete disk backups and another for daily incremental backups. MSBACKUP is a great step forward for PC data integrity.

> *MSBACKUP is not perfect (what is?). Although it is a fine program, its lack of DMA support and tape-drive support are serious deficiencies. Yes, backup is faster and more convenient than it used to be, but it is still slow, and users may continue to be lax about this chore.*

Understanding Memory-Manager Improvements

DOS 5's Memory Manager could do about 95 percent of what QEMM or 386Max could do. But DOS 5's EMM386.EXE lacked a few items:

- ✔ You couldn't tell DOS 5 where to load a program when you wanted to load the program above 640K.

- ✔ You couldn't tell DOS 5 that a particular program had a load size too large to fit in upper memory, but that its run size fits within the upper memory space.

- ✔ DOS 5 didn't provide shadow RAM.

Chapters 9-13 offer a more complete discussion of memory managers and memory manager problems and solutions. This section, however, offers a quick look at the strengths of DOS 6.2's Memory Manager.

Understanding Memory Management

Figure 1.4 shows an example of using a memory manager. Look first on the left side of the figure. Most DOS programs are constrained to the bottom 640K of PC memory. Therefore, you must find space not just for your favorite word processor, spreadsheet, or database, you also must use some of that precious 640K for your network drivers,

mouse drivers, and whatever other programs you need to operate your PC (programs known as *device drivers* and *terminate-and-stay-resident programs* or TSRs). At the left of the figure, you see that the two sample TSRs are gobbling up a fair amount of the below-640K space; it is difficult to run many popular DOS applications with the remaining memory.

Figure 1.4 also shows that there is some unused space above 640K. The original PC designers had 1,024K of memory space to work with. (Later PCs have more memory than that but, in general, DOS is unable to use any memory spaces above 1,024K.) So the designers decided to give the bottom 640K to DOS itself, DOS applications, device drivers, and TSRs. The space between 640K and 1,024K was, strictly speaking, still accessible to DOS, but was set aside for the use of PC hardware. Many PCs, however, don't use all that reserved system area. In the figure, you can see that two large areas are unused.

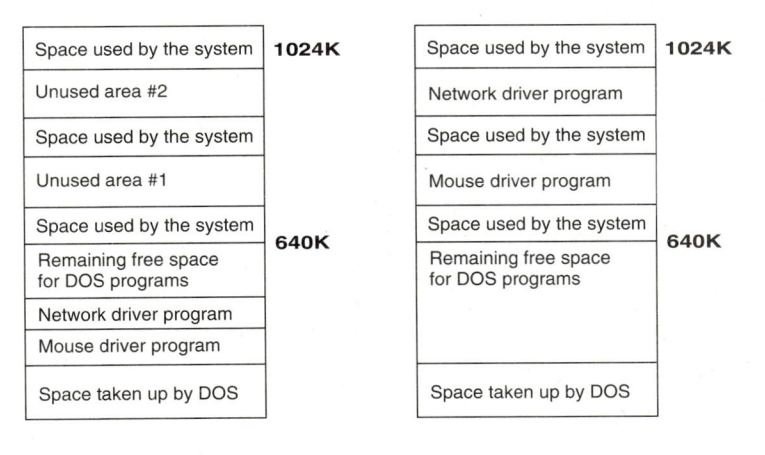

Figure 1.4
Using a memory manager.

Before a Memory Manager	After a Memory Manager
Space used by the system — 1024K	Space used by the system — 1024K
Unused area #2	Network driver program
Space used by the system	Space used by the system
Unused area #1	Mouse driver program
Space used by the system — 640K	Space used by the system — 640K
Remaining free space for DOS programs	Remaining free space for DOS programs
Network driver program	
Mouse driver program	
Space taken up by DOS	Space taken up by DOS

A memory manager fills unused "high" memory areas; it knows how to load TSRs and device drivers into the space between the 640K and 1,024K. Such empty areas are called Upper Memory Blocks or UMBs. On the right side of figure 1.4, you see that the network driver and the mouse driver have been moved to the unused UMBs. Now there is considerably more free space available for the major DOS application—the word processor, spreadsheet, or whatever—in the lower memory area.

Shuffling Programs with Memory Managers

What you have seen so far is what can be done with DOS 5. But DOS 5's Memory Manager is lacking in a few ways. One is the way it places programs in UMBs. For example, you saw in figure 1.4 that the PC had two UMBs. Suppose that the lower UMB was 60K in size, and the upper UMB was 30K. Suppose that the network driver was 59K in size, and that the mouse driver was 25K in size. Remember that no matter where you load a program, it must load completely. You cannot load a program partly in one UMB and partly in another UMB—that does not work. Because the lower UMB is 60K in size, and the network driver is 59K in size, it seems logical to put the network driver in the lower UMB. Because the upper UMB is 30K and the mouse driver is 25K in size, the mouse driver will fit just fine into the upper UMB.

Ah, but what happens when you load the mouse driver—the 25K program—*before* the network driver? DOS 5 has an extremely short-sighted method for placing programs in UMBs. When you tell DOS 5 to load the mouse driver in a UMB, it looks at the available UMBs and sees that one has 30K free and another has 60K free. DOS 5 then loads the mouse driver into the UMB with the most free space—the 60K UMB. Now there's no UMB that can completely hold the 59K network driver.

One answer to this problem has probably suggested itself to you. If you load the larger program—the network driver-first, it gets its pick of the UMBs and the problem is solved. This solution works only sometimes. Some programs are interdependent, meaning that program X must be loaded before program Y. If Y is larger than X, you're back to the same problem. The answer? DOS 6.2's Memory Manager statements. When you use DOS 6.2 to load a program into a UMB, you can specify exactly which UMB you want the program loaded into.

Still No Help for Yo-Yos

For some programs, there's an even more troublesome problem than loading it in a UMB: how DOS sees the total size of the program.

Suppose that you have a driver you want to load in a UMB, such as the Microsoft Mouse Driver 8.2. Using the MEM command, you find that the Microsoft MOUSE.COM driver takes up 17K of RAM. Suppose that you have a UMB with 25K of free space. You logically assume that you can tell DOS to load MOUSE into the 25K UMB. But if you try to do that, DOS refuses to load MOUSE into the UMB.

Programs such as device drivers and TSRs have two parts: the loader portion and the resident portion. In the case of MOUSE, the loader is about 39K and the resident portion is 17K. That means MOUSE appears to DOS to be about 56K in size (39K plus 17K). The loader runs for only a very brief time, but DOS doesn't care about that—it just sees a 56K program trying to fit into a 25K space, and refuses.

What you'd really like to do is to say to DOS, "Look, I know this program looks a little overweight, but I've got it on a strict diet and it's running on the track; it'll be down to fighting weight in no time. So be patient, okay?" But DOS is hearing none of that and refuses to load the "yo-yo" program unless there's enough room for the whole thing, loader and all. For details about MEM, see Chapters 10 and 12.

The major third-party memory managers, QEMM and 386Max, both solve this problem with features called Squeeze for QEMM and FlexFrame for 386Max. Unfortunately, however, DOS 6.2 offers no relief in this area.

Making Your PC Faster

Every PC contains an essential piece of software called the BIOS, the Basic Input Output System. The BIOS contains software the PC must use every time it accesses the hard disk, the floppy drives, the keyboard—all the major peripherals. That important software is stored in a chip called Read-Only Memory (ROM). All you need to know about ROM right now is that it is a kind of memory used for long-term software storage. *You can read more about ROM in Chapter 9. Read more about shadow RAM in Chapter 11.*

ROM has one drawback: it's slow. Some 486-based PCs have ROMs that are so slow that when those PCs execute the programs in ROM, the PCs slow down to the speed of an XT. Memory managers have a trick called *shadow RAM* that speeds things up. Memory managers can copy the contents of the relatively slow ROM into a much faster kind of memory: RAM (Random-Access Memory). The borrowed RAM then acts like ROM, but much faster.

For those systems that cannot offer shadow RAM capabilities, or for those systems that can shadow some RAM and not others, DOS 6.2's Memory Manager now has a shadow RAM feature. As you discover in Chapter 11, shadow RAM can be, at times, a quite undesirable thing, because it sometimes brings Windows to its knees.

For those of you memory-manager experts, there are also a few minor technical changes to EMM386.EXE, the DOS 6.2 Memory Manager (*as covered in greater detail in Chapters 10 and 12*):

- ✔ If you are not running any programs that require *Virtual Control Program Interface* (VCPI) support, the new keyword NOVCPI frees 24K of extended memory.

- ✔ EMM386.EXE is more aggressive in finding empty space in upper memory, meaning that you have more places to stash your favorite device drivers and TSRs.

- ✔ The new NOHIGHSCAN option enables EMM386.EXE to run on systems in which some upper memory cannot be disturbed. Earlier EMM386s could cause some hardware to malfunction simply by probing upper memory.

- ✔ You can set aside upper memory areas for the use of Windows, enabling Windows to create larger DOS sessions.

DOS 6.2's Memory Manager still has a few heights to scale in order to be the best in the business, but it's much closer to those heights than was DOS 5's Memory Manager.

Undeleting to Bulletproof Files

DOS 5 included two levels of undelete protection: simple undeletion and deletion tracking. When you tell the operating system to erase a file, the system doesn't go to the trouble to actually erase it. Instead, DOS just goes to the disk's "table of contents" (two areas called the *directory* and the *file allocation table* or FAT) and marks the file as deleted. It does that by changing the first character of the file's name to a special character that means "deleted" to DOS and by marking the part of the disk that the file resides in as available. DOS doesn't overwrite the data on the hard disk—it just marks it as available for overwriting. It's like evicting people from an apartment but not making them move out until you have found new tenants.

Undeletion programs have relied on this "stay of execution" to do their magic. So long as the data hasn't been overwritten, an undeletion program can guess where the file was previously. It then re-creates the directory and FAT information, making the data into a full-fledged file once again.

AUTHOR'S NOTE

It's hard not to like DOS 5's UNDELETE command. It's of potential use to almost anyone. Actually, it was the first command I used in DOS 5. I'd just installed DOS 5 on my PC's hard disk and intended to clean off a floppy to store a few files on. I meant to type...

```
ERASE A:*.*
```

...but I accidentally typed...

```
ERASE *.*
```

...(note the subtle difference?) and got the message...

```
are you sure?
```

So I pressed Y and watched as my newly installed DOS files were erased in a twinkling. I had also installed DOS 5 to a laptop, so I copied the UNDELETE.EXE program from the laptop to a floppy,

continues

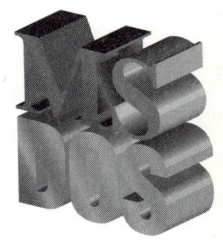

> put the floppy in the PC's floppy drive, and ran UNDELETE.EXE from the floppy drive. In a few minutes, all the files were back, safe and sound. Sigh.
>
> However, as nice as the DOS 5 UNDELETE program is, DOS 6.2 outdoes it with three levels of error protection.

> **TIP**
>
> *It's been said that it takes 21 days to develop a habit, whether good or bad. Well, here's a good one to decrease the "Oops factor."*
>
> *Log on to the drive and directory in which you want to execute a command. Instead of entering* **ERASE A:*.***, *for example, log on to A first, and then enter* **ERASE *.*** *(or the shorthand* **ERASE .***).*

"Taking a guess" is the first level of DOS undeletion protection. Its guesses are usually right, but sometimes they're wrong, which leads to the next level of protection: the undeletion tracker. The tracker is a TSR program that keeps track of what files have been erased recently and what part of the disk they resided on. That makes life easier for the undeletion program; it doesn't need to guess where the file was; it only has to look in the deletion-tracking file to find that information. If the file hasn't been overwritten, it's a snap to reassemble it.

DOS 6.2 includes these two undeletion methods and adds a new level of protection called the *deletion sentry*. Once you activate the deletion sentry, file-erase operations don't actually erase files. Instead, they move the files to a hidden directory. The files in this directory are not counted as taking up disk space, and, in general, you do not see them at all. If you need disk space that these "deleted" files occupy for a new file or files, DOS erases the old files for good. But that doesn't happen often, and the net effect of the deletion sentry is to extend the life of an erased file for a few extra days—time enough for you to realize that you erased a file you didn't mean to erase.

Looking at Changes in DOS 6.0 and DOS 6.2

A few very minor changes were made to old DOS commands in DOS 6.0:

✔ DOS now includes two long-awaited utilities to move files from one subdirectory to another (MOVE) and to eliminate a subdirectory and all of its subdirectories (DELTREE).

✔ A POWER.EXE device driver supports the Microsoft Advanced Power Management (APM) protocol. This is of value only if you have a laptop that supports APM; if you do, the laptop manufacturer will modify the DOS 6.2 SETUP program to install POWER.EXE automatically.

If your laptop supports APM, POWER.EXE boosts a battery charge by 25 percent; if not, it boosts a charge by only about 5 percent. If you don't know whether or not your laptop supports APM, download APMCHK.ZIP from CompuServe. This file contains APM.COM, which is a tiny utility that checks the BIOS and reports whether or not it supports APM.

✔ EDIT and QBASIC now support a /h option that displays the maximum number of lines possible on a screen. Unlike DOS 5, you don't need to preload the ANSI.SYS device driver to use this option in DOS 6.2.

✔ The former HELP command has been renamed DOSHELP.

✔ The COMP (file compare) command has disappeared; its functions are included in the FC command.

✔ FDISK now has a /STATUS option that shows the current status of a disk partition. You accessed this information in previous versions of DOS by typing **FDISK** and then choosing option 4 (Display Partition Information) from the main FDISK menu.

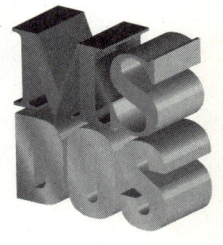

- With DOS 6.2, you don't have to enter the FDISK menu—it reports partition status and returns you to the command line. FDISK also has the undocumented virus killer /MBR option. (*See Chapters 20 and 21 for more information.*)

✔ The GRAPHICS command, which enables you to perform a PrntScrn (print screen) of graphic and text screens, supports a slightly larger group of printers than GRAPHICS did under DOS 5.

✔ The APPEND command enables you to extend the normal DOS PATH limitation of 128 characters. APPEND /X doubles the size of the DOS PATH. (*See Chapter 2 for more details.*)

✔ Like many modern programs, DOS is shipped on disks in a compressed format and requires programs to uncompress it. DOS 5 used a program called EXPAND to uncompress files from its distribution disks. DOS 6.2 uses a more efficient compression approach than DOS 5 and uses a new program called DECOMP. DECOMP has one feature that EXPAND did not have: if you invoke DECOMP with the -Q option, it doesn't uncompress the file; instead, it reports how much disk space the file will require when it *is* uncompressed.

✔ The CONFIG.SYS file FCBS= command used to have two parameters. Now it allows one parameter: the maximum number of file-control blocks open at any one time. This is what was once the first parameter, so any existing CONFIG.SYS files still work. If you include the old second parameter, it is ignored.

✔ The BACKUP command no longer exists. It is replaced by the MSBACKUP program (formerly Norton Backup).

✔ The DIR command has a new option, /C, that reports the compression ratio on compressed DoubleSpace drives. You can use that feature to find out how well DoubleSpace performs when packing your large data files into small spaces.

✔ The MEM command, which enables you to monitor memory usage, almost always produces output longer than a single screen. Either you miss most of the MEM output as it scrolls off the screen, or you have to pipe your output to the MORE filter, or you have to be remarkably quick on the draw with the PAUSE key. Now MEM has a /P option that tells it to pause with each screen of information.

In addition to all the new and powerful features of DOS 6.0, DOS 6.2 adds the following new features and enhancements:

- ✔ DoubleSpace now incorporates DoubleGuard, which prevents other programs from damaging one or more of DoubleSpace's own memory buffers. DoubleSpace also adds automounting of floppy disks, better error messages, smaller memory requirements, and the /UNCOMPRESS switch, which enables you to uninstall DoubleSpace easily.

- ✔ SmartDrive now caches reads on CD-ROM drives. Additionally, write-caching is disabled by default, and SmartDrive flushes its cache to disk after each command executes if write-caching is enabled.

- ✔ DEFRAG can now defragment disks of about twice the size as DOS 6.0.

- ✔ In addition to DOS 6.2's interactive execution of CONFIG.SYS, DOS 6.2 now enables you to interactively execute AUTOEXEC.BAT, as well as all other batch files.

- ✔ The F5 clean-boot feature has been extended with Ctrl-F5, which enables you to do a clean boot without loading DoubleSpace.

- ✔ DIR, MEM, CHKDSK, and FORMAT now separate numbers greater than 1,000 with commas.

- ✔ DISKCOPY no longer requires multiple disk swaps to copy disks—it now makes multiple, one-pass copies.

- ✔ COPY, XCOPY, and MOVE now, by default, ask for confirmation before overwriting a file of the same name.

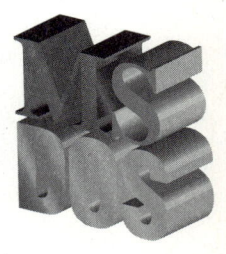

Summary

Is DOS 6.2 worth the cost and trouble of upgrading? For most of us, yes. The continual improvements in data-recovery tools are priceless because the most valuable thing on your computer is your data. Disk compression enables you to put more data on the hard disk, a real blessing if you're using modern disk-hungry software. The improved memory manager enables you to load more programs onto your computer, and the virus protection makes it easier to keep malicious programs from loading into your computer. The e-mail and network support is a convenient add-on if you're already using Windows for Workgroups or LAN Manager, and the InterLnk software will keep the folks who make LapLink, FastWire, and the like burning the midnight oil trying to turn out something better.

Perhaps "something better" is the best way to characterize DOS 6.2. It's not everything that could be desired in an operating system, but it's fine. Whether you have an XT or a Pentium, there's something in the latest DOS for you.

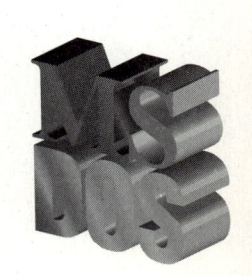

MS-DOS

MS
DOS

An Inside Look: How DOS Works

by Mark Minasi

To many people, understanding DOS means understanding what makes up DOS; that is, learning the syntax of DOS commands and the keystrokes necessary to perform basic functions under DOS. But getting inside DOS means understanding what DOS does and how it does it. Before moving to the sections of the book in which you examine each of the "trees" in DOS, first take a look at the forest. Whether you are a DOS expert or a PC newcomer, this chapter is an unusual overview of the world's most popular operating system.

It is not the purpose of this chapter to teach you DOS commands; this chapter helps you understand what DOS is all about. You learn a few commands in this chapter, but *you learn the details on these commands in Chapters 6 and 7 and in the Command Reference.*

Why Does Your PC Use DOS?

It's easy to view DOS as just another set of incomprehensible commands rather than as your system's dashboard and chassis. DOS acts as the dashboard because you use it to interact with the programs in your computer: to load, control, and terminate them. DOS acts as the chassis because the programs in your computer need DOS to provide a unifying framework on which they can be constructed by program designers. Okay, it may seem like an incomprehensible dashboard and chassis at this point, but it gets easier when you've got the big picture—and that's the purpose of this chapter.

In general, operating systems perform several functions:

- ✔ They provide a file-organization system—a means to keep track of the files on a disk.

- ✔ They provide a set of disk-management tools—programs that enable you to move, copy, erase, create, and view files and directories.

- ✔ They provide a way for you to load and execute programs—in particular, they provide a way for you to issue commands to the operating system to load and execute those programs.

Every operating system has these responsibilities, but each system carries out these responsibilities in different ways. To load and execute a program, for example, you might double-click on an icon (a small picture that represents a program), like you do in the Macintosh, OS/2 Workplace Shell, or Windows environment; or you might type the name of the program you want to execute, like you do in DOS.

The first operating system job, organizing files, is the most important.

AUTHOR'S NOTE

The 10 Commandments of DOS:

*I. **Never be intimidated by DOS**. Remember, DOS is stupid, you are smart.*

*II. **Save and back up your work**. Okay, this is really two commandments, but they go hand-in-hand. Even if you doubt that you'll need that short memo you just wrote, save and keep it for awhile. Back up, back up, back up!*

*III. **Remember correct DOS command phrasing**. What (command name), Where (parameter(s)), and How (switch(es)). (You learn about phrasing later in this chapter.)*

*IV. **Remember the DOS dozen**. The twelve most important command-line DOS commands (in my opinion) are CD, CHKDSK, COPY, CTRL+BREAK, DEL, DIR, DISKCOPY, FORMAT, REN, UNDELETE, UNFORMAT, and XCOPY.*

*V. **Hesitate before pressing Enter**. Capability sometimes breeds cockiness, and cockiness causes calamity. Or, as the Bible puts it, Pride goeth before destruction (Proverbs 16:18).*

*VI. **Undelete a deleted file immediately (if not sooner)**. The longer you wait, the less likely you are to get your data back.*

*VII. **Practice good disk management and maintenance**. Okay, two for one again, but improper management and maintenance cause data loss and general inefficiency.*

*VIII. **Protect yourself against viruses**. The threat is growing, and most users today are in danger.*

*IX. **Write batch files**. There is nothing that makes your work more efficient than batch files. There are numerous examples in this book to get you started.*

*X. **Enjoy your computer!** The first nine commandments help make your work enjoyable, but take a few minutes once in awhile to play a game.*

Understanding the DOS File-Organization System

To understand the whys and wherefores of operating systems, consider any storage medium, electronic or otherwise. How do you, for example, keep track of your paper files—current bills, the deed to your house or the lease to your apartment, tax records, old check stubs, love letters, diplomas, and the like? Ask several people, and you're likely to get several answers:

- ✔ "I have a pile of papers in a drawer. When I need something, I look in there."

- ✔ "I have a file cabinet. I keep file folders for subjects, such as taxes, bills, house payments, and so on."

- ✔ "I have a file cabinet, too, but I organize my file folders alphabetically—bills comes first, and then house payments, and so on."

All three approaches are perfectly valid methods of organizing data. Now think of each piece of paper—each bill, deed, letter—as a file. How do these organizational methods transfer to the computer?

- ✔ **Put it all in a single pile.** Not very efficient, you say? Actually, this method works fine if you have only a few papers. That's how DOS Version 1, 1.1, and 1.25 organized files. These DOS versions supported only floppy disks, not hard disks. Because no floppy disk was larger than 360K, there couldn't be many files to keep track of. Most people organized data further by using filing cabinets to file their floppy disks, labeling the disks with the contents, such as accounting files, games, and so forth. This approach may seem disorganized, but it is the basic approach to file organization.

- ✔ **Keep file folders to organize similar files.** Keeping file folders—one folder for bills, another for awards, and so on—is a good method in small doses. This method works well with a moderate number of file folders, but it's limited in usefulness. As long as you have less than about 20 file folders, the system remains manageable. But can you imagine a file drawer with 200 folders? It would be a nightmare keeping track of that many folders. And even if you alphabetize the folders (as the next person suggested), that would be more work.

> *Before we go on to the alphabetical file-folder approach, you should realize that the disorganized file-folder method is basically the approach taken by the disk structure of DOS 2 through DOS 6. A disk is divided into subdirectories (which function very much like the file folders); you fill the subdirectories with files. The subdirectories are not organized in any way, and neither are the files within the subdirectories.*
>
> *Subdirectories can have subdirectories inside them. A Financial subdirectory can, in turn, have subdirectories such as Taxes, Retirement Planning, Investments, and so on. You learn more about the DOS file organization approach very soon.*

✔ **Use file folders, but alphabetize them.** This approach makes sense when you have many files. OS/2 and Windows NT use file systems like this. Although OS/2 and NT use subdirectories, as does DOS, the first two systems alphabetize their subdirectories automatically. The files inside any subdirectory also are alphabetized.

Placing files in order makes sense, but does it necessarily make sense to order them by name? Many of us have a seemingly disorganized file of personal papers, but the file probably has a hidden organizational method: it's probably ordered by frequency of use. The most often used things end up floating to the front. This may sound flippant, but it's not; some mainframe file systems are arranged like this, and they work just fine. Collections of facts in expert systems (computer programs that mimic the behavior of a human subject-matter expert) use this approach to organize a *knowledge base*, with the most used facts accessed first.

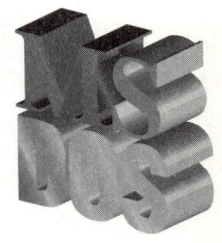

NOTE: *If the idea of ordered directories sounds attractive to you, you may want to look into several DOS utilities that can sort your directories. The new DEFRAG command sorts directories and files, but the sorting is static. After you sort a directory, it remains sorted only until you add files to it.*

Looking at Simple Directory Organization

To see how files are organized in the DOS world, the next sections present a few simple examples. First is a simple floppy-only situation that uses files and no subdirectories. Next, the extra storage concerns that come with having a hard disk are added. Finally, you consider the problems of very large hard disks.

Understanding Floppy Disk File Organization

Suppose that you have a floppy disk containing a drawing program and a few drawings. The files on this disk might be these:

   MYDRAW.EXE

   PC.DRW

   DISK.DRW

   PRINTER.DRW

This disk contains just four files, so it really doesn't require any organizational structure. It's like having an office with only four pieces of paper; there's no point in getting a file cabinet and setting up a large organizational structure. MYDRAW.EXE is the drawing program; the files called PC.DRW, DISK.DRW, and PRINTER.DRW are the drawings you've done so far. On the disk, then, you probably would not set up any subdirectories. One directory already exists, however: the root directory. The *root directory* is indicated by a backslash (\). Microsoft adopted the backslash because they took the idea of sub-directories from UNIX, which uses the forward slash (/) to separate directories. If diagrammed, this simple structure would look like figure 2.1.

Understanding the DOS File-Organization System

> **NOTE**
>
> *In case you're wondering, the terms* directory *and* subdirectory *mean essentially the same thing. Everything is a subdirectory to the main root directory, but sometimes it's easier to call one of the divisions you've made a directory rather than a subdirectory.*

```
\        MYDRAW.EXE
         PC.DRW
         DISK.DRW
         PRINTER.DRW
```

Figure 2.1
One-level disk directory structure.

AUTHOR'S NOTE

Look at the names of the files in figure 2.1. Like names of people, files have different names for different times. If you are Sarah Knight of Columbus, Ohio, then your friends and family probably just call you Sarah. But to the CEO of the company you work for, you may be Sarah Knight, because your CEO has many employees, more than one of whom is named Sarah. To the IRS, you might be Sarah Knight of Columbus, Ohio, 381-44-9023, because the IRS's records include hundreds of millions of people.

You have a complete description of yourself you never use in familiar conversation. You would never, for example, say to your best friend, "Hello. This is Larry James Shoenfeld of 381 Greenway Drive, Altoona, Pennsylvania, USA, Planet Earth, Sol System, Perseid Arm, Milky Way Galaxy." At some level, you use shortened names. And so it is with files. When programs—whether it's the DOS program itself, your word processor, drawing program, or whatever—look for files, they look first in whatever directory has been designated the local or default directory. You can designate which directory is the local or default directory in several different ways, as you will soon see.

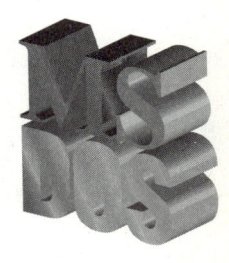

In figure 2.1, you could ask your drawing program to load the file DISK.DRW either by asking for DISK.DRW (as long as the root directory is the default directory, which it must be because there are no other directories on this disk), or by including the name of the directory in the name of the file you request. In this case, you would ask the drawing program to load a file called \DISK.DRW.

Including Drive Names in File Names

Aside from designating directory names, you also must consider the fact that your computer has multiple disk drives. Nearly every computer has at least a drive A (the floppy disk drive) and a drive C (the hard disk). All drives have, at the least, a root directory. Therefore, it is possible that the root directory on drive A contains a file called DISK.DRW, and the root directory of drive C also contains a file called DISK.DRW. Even if you include their directory names, these files are *both* still called \DISK.DRW, so how do you distinguish between the file on drive A and the file on drive C? In the DOS world, you prefix any file name with a drive letter and a colon. The fully specified file name of the DISK.DRW in the root directory of drive C, then, is C:\DISK.DRW.

You usually don't have to fully specify the name of a file. You have probably noticed when using programs that they use a default for directory; they also have default drives. In general, if you start a program on drive C, the program looks for data files on drive C. But that's only "in general." Many people keep their programs on drive C, but put their data files on floppy disks (which use drive A). In that case, they must tell their programs to expect the data on drive A. They do that with the setup options available in most major programs.

File names are divided into two parts, separated by a period. The part to the right of the period is the *extension* and it can't be more than *three* characters long; the part to the left of the period is the *name* and its length can't exceed *eight* characters. If a directory is included in the name, the directory is called the *path* (this path is different from the DOS PATH command, which you learn about soon). If a drive name is included, it is called the *drive* or *drive designator*. If, for example, you ask for the file C:\DISK.DRW, C: is the drive designator, \ is the path, DISK is the file name, and DRW is the file extension.

Understanding the DOS File-Organization System

> *You often hear people use the term* file name *to refer to C:\DISK.DRW, \DISK.DRW, or DISK.DRW. The entire name C:\DISK.DRW—which includes the drive, path, name, and extension—is called the* file specification, *usually abbreviated as* filespec.

File extensions give some indication of the purpose of a file. Table 2.1 lists some file extensions and their common meanings. *See Chapter 7 for a more complete list of file extensions.*

Table 2.1
Common File Extensions and Their Meanings

Extension	Meaning
EXE	Machine language program
COM	Machine language program
BAT	Batch program
SYS	Device driver or configuration file
BIN	Device driver or machine language file
OVL	Overlay file (part of a program loaded later as needed)
DOC	Document data file
TXT	Document or ASCII-text data file
BAS	BASIC language program
ASM	Assembly language program
DRW	Drawing program
PCX	PC Paintbrush format picture
WMF	Windows Metafile format picture
BMP	Windows Bitmap file format picture
Extension	Meaning

continues

Table 2.1, Continued
Common File Extensions and Their Meanings

Extension	Meaning
INI	Files containing setup information for Windows programs
GRP	Files containing information about Windows Program Manager groups
DLL	Dynamic linking library files

Don't worry if you don't know what all those files refer to. You learn about EXE, COM, BAT, BIN, SYS, OVL, and DLL files later in this chapter. The others you'll either run across as you use your computer, or you won't ever have to know what they mean.

Adding Complexity to the Disk Example

Suppose that you add a second program to the floppy disk we're using as an example. The new program is a word processing program called WPROC.EXE. In addition to the word processing program, you have two document files. Together, you have three related files:

WPROC.EXE

TTD.DOC

LETTER.DOC

At this point, it makes some sense to try to organize these files, putting the files relevant to the drawing program in one area and the files relevant to the word processing program in another area. That's where subdirectories come in handy. You can create two directories, one named DRAWNGS and another named WPFILES. Directory names must always start with a backslash: \DRAWNGS and \WPFILES, for example. These directories are subdirectories of the root directory. You could diagram these directories as shown in figure 2.2.

Understanding the DOS File-Organization System

When you create these two directories, there are no files in the root directory, just "pointers" to the \DRAWNGS and \WPFILES directories. On an actual hard disk, however, there are always at least a few files in the root directory at all times; in particular, most of the files you need to boot the computer are in the root directory.

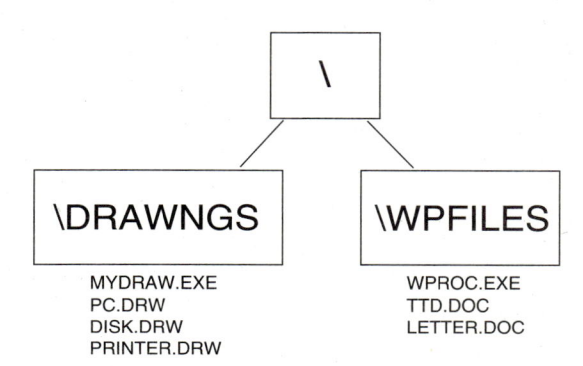

```
              \
             / \
       \DRAWNGS   \WPFILES
      MYDRAW.EXE  WPROC.EXE
      PC.DRW      TTD.DOC
      DISK.DRW    LETTER.DOC
      PRINTER.DRW
```

Figure 2.2

A two-level tree structured directory.

Remember how to write complete file specifications? You can write the complete filespecs for all the files in the \WPFILES directory as A:\WPFILES\WPROC.EXE, A:\WPFILES\TTD.DOC, and A:\WPFILES\LETTER.DOC.

Now you can understand why programs use a default disk drive and a default subdirectory. Wouldn't you rather tell the word processor to load TTD.DOC than A:\WPFILES\TTD.DOC? Even better, because most programs recognize their own file extension, you may not have to type both the file name and extension. WPROC probably requires only that you tell it to load TTD; it assumes the DOC unless you tell it otherwise.

Using Directories beyond Two Levels

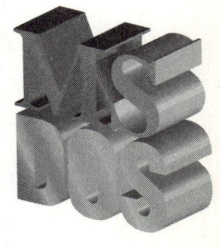

With a moderate number of files, you can end up with a two-level directory like the one in the preceding example: the root and several subdirectories off the root. You probably have one subdirectory for your spreadsheet, one for your word processor, one for DOS, and so on. As you create more and more subdirectories directly on the root directory, you end up back where you started—with too many files in the root directory. (Actually, they're not files; now they're directories that contain files. But at some point, having too many directories can be as unwieldy a prospect as too many files.)

Suppose, for example, that you have too many word processing documents in your \WPFILES directory. You might decide to divide the documents into two subdirectories under the \WPFILES directory, one for personal files and one for business files. Your directory might then look like the one in figure 2.3.

Figure 2.3
A three-level directory.

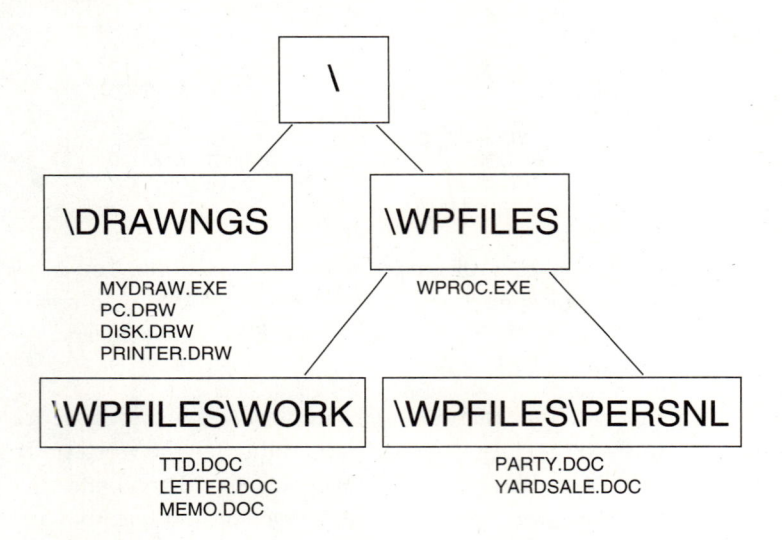

```
                    \
         ┌──────────┴──────────┐
    \DRAWNGS              \WPFILES
   MYDRAW.EXE             WPROC.EXE
   PC.DRW
   DISK.DRW
   PRINTER.DRW
                    ┌──────────┴──────────┐
              \WPFILES\WORK         \WPFILES\PERSNL
              TTD.DOC               PARTY.DOC
              LETTER.DOC            YARDSALE.DOC
              MEMO.DOC
```

The new subdirectories (you could even call them sub-subdirectories) are called WORK and PERSNL. Note that the new subdirectories inherit the names of the directory directly above them, what is sometimes called their *parent* directory. The complete filespecs for the five word processing files are A:\WPFILES\WORK\TTD.DOC, A:\WPFILES\WORK\LETTER.DOC, A:\WPFILES\WORK\MEMO.DOC, A:\WPFILES\PERSNL\PARTY.DOC, and A:\WPFILES\PERSNL\YARDSALE.DOC.

You can make a DOS directory tree go down as many levels as you like.

Using DOS Commands To Create and Manage Directory Trees

You can create, destroy, view, and navigate a DOS directory tree with a few basic commands:

- ✔ The MD (make directory) command creates new subdirectories.
- ✔ The RD (remove directory) command deletes directories.
- ✔ The CD (change directory) command tells DOS which directory you want to use as the current default directory.
- ✔ You change default drives simply by typing the letter of the drive you want to change to.
- ✔ The TREE and DIR /AD commands enable you to view a directory structure.

The following sections discuss each of these commands.

Creating Directories with MD

A blank disk already has one directory on it—the root directory. If you want to create a floppy disk with the same directories as the example presented in the previous sections, place a blank, formatted floppy disk into drive A. Although you could use a preformatted floppy (when you buy the disk, it's already formatted), you will probably have to format your own floppy disks. *Explanations of how to format disks appear in Chapter 7.*

Follow these steps to put two directories on the floppy disk in drive A:

1. Designate the default drive you want to work from. More than likely, your current DOS prompt looks something like this:

    ```
    C:\>
    ```

    This prompt indicates that you're currently using drive C as your default drive, with the root directory of C as your default directory. You want to make drive A the default drive.

Type **A,** and press Enter. The prompt changes to this:

```
A:\>
```

> **NOTE**
> *If DOS displays an error message that says* drive not ready *or* general failure reading drive A, *the floppy disk probably isn't formatted, or perhaps you forgot to close the drive door.*

2. Type the following command and press Enter to create the DRAWNGS directory:

   ```
   MD \DRAWNGS
   ```

   Notice that there's a space between the MD command and the name of the directory you want to create.

   When the directory is successfully created, DOS displays the `A:\>` prompt. Like many DOS commands, MD is the strong, silent type: if it doesn't say anything, the command was successful. You don't see any message like `DRAWNGS directory successfully created`.

   The MD command does not enable you to create a directory that already exists. Try typing the following command again:

   ```
   MD \DRAWNGS
   ```

   DOS displays:

   ```
   Directory already exists
   ```

   > **TIP**
   > *DOS accepts commands in either uppercase or lowercase. You can type* **MD \DRAWNGS** *or* **md \drawngs** *with the same effect.*

3. Create the WPFILES directory by typing the following and pressing Enter:

   MD \WPFILES

When the directory is successfully created, DOS again displays the A:\> prompt.

4. Create the two subdirectories under the WPFILES directory. You use the MD command to create subdirectories as well as directories. Type the following two commands, pressing Enter after each:

    MD \WPFILES\WORK
    MD \WPFILES\PERSNL

NOTE: *In general, DOS commands require that you press Enter after typing them, so you should assume that from now on in this book.*

Viewing Directory Structures with TREE

As you have seen, DOS isn't very talkative. You created a bunch of directories, but all DOS did was grunt A:\> after each command. If you want to see what you've done, you can view your handiwork by typing **TREE**. Your screen will look something like figure 2.4.

```
A:\>tree
Directory PATH listing for Volume INSIDE DOS
A:.
├──DRAWNGS
└──WPFILES
    ├──WORK
    └──PERSNL

A:\>
```

Figure 2.4

Sample output of the TREE command.

The TREE command shows that you have two second-level directories: DRAWNGS and WPFILES. You also have two third-level directories within WPFILES: WORK and PERSNL.

> *If you use TREE on your hard disk, you may find that the tree is so large that it scrolls off the screen. You can make the TREE command pause every time the screen fills up by typing* **TREE | MORE** *instead of just* **TREE**.
>
> *See Chapter 6 for other uses of the TREE command.*

Changing the Current Directory with CD

Inside DOS's memory is an invisible "pointer" that tells DOS where it should look for files. This pointer marks the *current* or *default* subdirectory or directory. The DOS prompt used by most people—PROMPT PG—shows the current directory and default drive. For example, the prompt D:\TOOLS> means that the current drive is D: and the default directory is \TOOLS. You can tell DOS to use a different directory as the current directory with the CD (change directory) command.

On your test floppy disk, you can make \WPFILES\WORK your default directory by typing...

    CD \WPFILES\WORK

The prompt should reflect the new default directory. Move back to the root directory on the floppy disk by typing...

    CD \

Using Relative Directory Addressing

If you followed the example in the preceding section, you should be back at the root directory of the floppy disk. Move to the WPFILES directory by typing...

    CD \WPFILES

Understanding the DOS File-Organization System

Suppose that you want to move from this directory to
\WPFILES\WORK. You could do that by typing...

    `CD \WPFILES\WORK`

...but there is an easier way. Simply type...

    `CD WORK`

The prompt shows `A:\WPFILES\WORK`. This example demonstrates a useful shorthand way of moving from directory to directory. If the CD command does not start with a backslash, DOS assumes that you want it to do a relative directory movement rather than an absolute movement.

> *If you don't type the \ when you give the directory name, DOS moves you to the directory below the current directory. Look at figure 2.3 to see exactly what this means. Two subdirectories are located under \WPFILES: WORK and PERSNL. From \WPFILES, you can type* **CD WORK** *or* **CD PERSNL** *to move to one of those subdirectories. If, however, you want to move to DRAWNGS from \WPFILES, you must tell DOS to make an absolute movement by typing* **CD \DRAWNGS**; *you can't type* **CD DRAWINGS** *without the \ because there is no directory directly below \WPFILES called DRAWNGS.*

You also can reference directories relatively using the .. (dot dot) reference. From the \WPFILES\WORK directory, type the following and press Enter:

    `CD..`

You move up one level, back to \WPFILES. The symbols .. mean the *parent directory* of the current directory. If you keep typing **CD..**, you eventually rise to the root of the directory tree. (By the way, if you think it's odd that the *top* of the directory tree is the *root*, you're not alone. Just file that bit of information away with all the other nonintuitive stuff you learn in the computer business.)

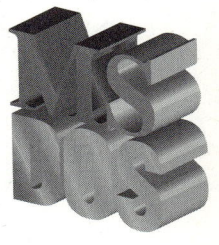

The .. is useful in any DOS context. Suppose that you're in a Windows program like Excel. You click on File Open and then see the File Choose dialog box. The box displays \WPFILES\WORK, but you want to go to \WPFILES. You can type .. and press Enter quicker than you can click on a tree structure. You will also find .. useful in writing batch files, *as you learn in Chapter 16.*

Another directory-reference symbol is a single period (.), which refers to the current directory. Typing **CD.** doesn't do anything of value—you're already in the directory—but it can be used in some cases. If, for example, you want to erase everything in the directory that you're currently in, you can type **ERASE.** instead of **ERASE *.*** *You learn more about the ERASE command in Chapter 7, along with other disk-management commands.*

Using DOS Disk-Management Tools

An operating system must provide its users with some way to manipulate the disk. Table 2.2 summarizes the things that an operating system must be able to accomplish and the commands DOS offers to accomplish those tasks.

Table 2.2
DOS Functions

Function	DOS Command(s)	Comments
See what's on disk	DIR, TREE, CHKDSK/V, DOSSHELL	
Copy files	COPY, XCOPY, REPLACE, DOSBACK, RESTORE, DISKCOPY	

Function	DOS Command(s)	Comments
Move files	None	Requires combination of COPY/ERASE
Erase files	ERASE, DEL	Nothing erases entire trees
Unerase files	UNDELETE	
Rename files	REN, RENAME	
Compare files	FC, DISKCOMP	Old command COMP is gone
Prepare new disks	FORMAT, FDISK, SELECT	
Search for files	DIR /S, PATH, APPEND	
Defragment disks	DEFRAG	
Configure hardware	MODE, POWER	
Support non-English languages	KEYB, CODEPAGE, NLSFUNC, COUNTRY, CHCP	
Control directory structures	MD, RD	
View/modify text files	EDIT, EDLIN, TYPE	

Table 2.2 doesn't present an exhaustive list of DOS commands by any means, just the core commands. You learn more about these commands in later chapters.

Often, more than one command is available to get a particular job done. This means that there's always another reason to read and reread the DOS manual (or any other software you use regularly): you probably will learn alternative methods to get a job done—methods you didn't notice the first time you read the manual.

Chapter 2: *An Inside Look: How DOS Works*

> **AUTHOR'S NOTE**
>
> *You have to copy files for many reasons, but usually, you copy files to back them up, or to move them somewhere because a program needs them. The earliest DOS versions included a simple COPY command; that command exists in DOS 6 today. But the basic COPY command is very inefficient in that it only copies 64K of data at a time and cannot spread a large file over several floppy disks. When COPY first arrived in 1981, those problems were largely irrelevant. But with the arrival of DOS 2 in 1984 came support for hard disks, and hard disks can contain single files considerably larger than the entire capacity of any floppy disk. Because floppy disks were the main backup medium in the early and mid 1980s and the COPY command could not split a large file across several floppy disks, something else was needed.*
>
> *That's when a pair of programs, BACKUP and RESTORE, were introduced. They made their first appearance in DOS 2. BACKUP was seriously flawed in many ways, and that's why it has been replaced with DOSBACK in DOS 6. The 64K-at-a-time problem was addressed with XCOPY (extended COPY) in DOS 3.2.*
>
> *The moral of this story is that if something doesn't look like it makes sense in the DOS world, it may not make sense in the context of today's world, but it does make sense in some years-old context.*

Understanding the DOS User Interface

The third part of an operating system is how it interacts with you, the user. DOS takes care of the data on your hard disk. DOS must provide some way for you to tell it to load and execute program files. The way it does that is called the *user interface* or *UI*. There are several components to how DOS accepts, interprets, and executes your commands.

DOS Says "Hello" with PROMPT

If you have exited from all your application programs, shells, menus, and the like, nothing remains on your computer screen but the DOS user interface, which looks something like C:\> or C:\WP51>. DOS is now in a state that could be described as *expectant*. It's waiting for you to tell it to do something.

If DOS is waiting for a command, why does it print the names of the default drive and directory on the screen? Because you told it to. Well, maybe not you, but somebody put the command PROMPT PG into the AUTOEXEC.BAT file. The PROMPT command tells DOS what to put on the screen while waiting for you to enter a command—it enables you to customize the DOS user interface a bit. You could, for example, tell your computer to "speak" more nicely to you. At the DOS prompt on your screen, type…

    PROMPT Yes, Master?

Now the DOS prompt does not show you the drive or directory, just the message:

    Yes,Master?

PROMPT even has a small programming language built into it. If, for example, you tell PROMPT to display $P, DOS shows the current directory in the prompt. Similarly, $G places the greater-than sign (>) on the screen. Put them together, and you have the prompt that most people use: C:>. Type **PROMPT PG** now, so that your prompt is back to normal. Other PROMPT programming commands include $t (time) and $d (date). *You learn more details about PROMPT and its programming language in Chapter 7.*

DOS Listens and Obeys with COMMAND.COM

Now you know what causes the prompt to appear on the screen. Before going on, however, you should know something about the DOS program that actually puts the prompt on the screen and accepts your typed commands. You've probably seen a file called

COMMAND.COM on some of your disks. COMMAND.COM is the DOS program that supervises interaction with the user. When you type characters on the command line, it is COMMAND.COM that attempts to understand what you are asking for.

> **NOTE** *Any command you issue to DOS activates a program. In the DOS world,* command *and* program *mean the same thing.*

How COMMAND.COM Reads a Command Line

Of course, COMMAND.COM doesn't really "understand" what you type. A better word would be parse. *Parse* means to break a bunch of characters, such as an input line, into pieces before trying to understand the pieces. When someone speaks a sentence to you, you parse the sounds into words. Similarly, when you type **DIR B:** in DOS, COMMAND.COM parses that command into the parts DIR and B:. COMMAND.COM separates pieces of a command using spaces.

The command **DISKCOPY A: B: /V,** for example, tells DOS to activate a program called DISKCOPY, and then tells DISKCOPY that it should copy the disk in drive A: to the disk in drive B:. The /V tells DISKCOPY that it should verify the copy. Figure 2.5 shows how the command is parsed by COMMAND.COM.

Figure 2.5
How COMMAND.COM parses a command.

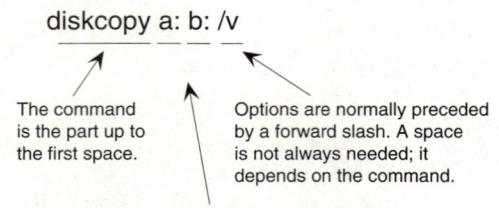

diskcopy a: b: /v

The command is the part up to the first space.

Options are normally preceded by a forward slash. A space is not always needed; it depends on the command.

The arguments or parameters are the items that follow the command, separated by spaces.

As the figure shows, COMMAND.COM assumes that the string of characters up to the first blank is the user's input command. You learn more about parameters, arguments, and options later; for now, just consider the command and what COMMAND.COM does with it.

COMMAND.COM then gives names to each of the separate pieces of the command line. It may be easier to think that COMMAND.COM keeps little containment areas with odd names. The first of these areas is called %0. COMMAND.COM calls the user's input command %0. The second area is called %1, and that's where the first parameter or argument goes. In the example, A: goes into the %1 area. Other internal areas exist that COMMAND.COM calls %2, %3, %4, %5, %6, %7, %8, and %9. (Those are all the areas it has; there is no %10.)

Parameters and arguments mean nothing by themselves; COMMAND.COM has no idea what A:, B:, or /V mean to DISKCOPY. COMMAND.COM's job is to get the DISKCOPY program loaded and hand over to it the tools that DISKCOPY needs to get its job done. In this case, the tools are the arguments A:, B:, and /V.

As another example, suppose that you typed **banana** at the command line. DOS—or, more properly, COMMAND.COM—displays the message bad command or file name. Why? When you type **banana**, COMMAND.COM parses it into %0. (There are no arguments, so there's nothing in %1, %2, and so on.) Because this is not a DOS command, the error message is displayed.

How To Phrase a DOS Command

As an experienced DOS user, you already know that a DOS command consists of three parts: command name, parameter(s), and switch(es). The *command name* refers to the command you want to execute (FORMAT, for example). *Parameters* refer to additional information about the command (adding **A:** to FORMAT tells DOS where you want to execute the command). *Switches* give even more information about how you want a command carried out (adding **/S** to FORMAT A: instructs DOS to put the system files on the formatted disk).

Sometimes even experienced users get parameters and switches mixed up, however. If you keep in mind the following simple phrasing technique, however, this won't happen:

Command name	Parameters	Switches
what	where	how
format	A:	/S

This example shows the three main parts of a command: what we want to do (format a floppy disk), where we want to do it (in drive A:), and how we want to do it (place the system files on the disk).

A simple analogy is that of a delivery man. What he wants to do is deliver a package (command), where he wants to deliver it is to your address (parameter), and how he wants to deliver it is by driving his truck to your address (switch #1), and then walking to your door (switch #2).

How COMMAND.COM Finds the Requested Program

After parsing the input line, COMMAND.COM's next job is to figure out what program you want it to load and to find that program somewhere on disk. COMMAND.COM does that with the following steps (any unclear items in the list are cleared up in the discussion following):

1. COMMAND.COM checks to see whether the command is an internal command. If so, it executes the internal command.

2. If the command is not internal, COMMAND.COM looks for a file with the command's name and the extension COM. If such a file exists, COMMAND.COM loads and executes that file.

3. If no COM file exists, COMMAND.COM looks for a file with the command's name and the extension EXE. If such a file exists, COMMAND.COM loads and executes it.

4. If no EXE file exists, COMMAND.COM looks for a file with the command's name and the extension BAT. If such a file exists, COMMAND.COM loads and executes it.

5. If none of these methods works, COMMAND.COM searches the path, looking in other subdirectories for the COM, EXE, or BAT files.

When you type **DIR**, for example, you activate the **DIR** command, which is a program located inside COMMAND.COM (an internal command). When you type **WIN** to start Windows, you tell COMMAND.COM to find a file called WIN.COM, load it, and execute it.

That's the overview of how COMMAND.COM works; let's move on to a discussion of the details of the steps that COMMAND.COM works through to try to do what you tell it to do.

Commands Internal to COMMAND.COM

COMMAND.COM is to interpret and execute the commands of the user. But it also has a number of side jobs: some commands called *internal* commands. Commercial programs and larger DOS utility programs are contained in COM and EXE files, as you learn in the next section. But basic commands are not housed in external files; they are incorporated in COMMAND.COM. When you type the DIR command (the command that provides a listing of a disk's directory), COMMAND.COM compares the DIR request to an internal table of commands that it knows how to respond to. Because DIR is there, COMMAND.COM knows how to respond to the request. Table 2.3 summarizes the DOS 6 internal commands. For more details, see the discussions elsewhere in this book and in the Command Reference.

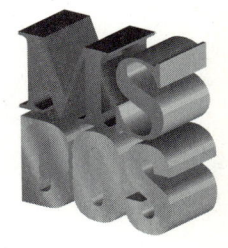

Table 2.3
COMMAND.COM Internal Commands

Command	Function
DIR	Shows information on a file directory
COPY	Copies and merges files
CD	Changes the current subdirectory
MD	Creates subdirectories

continues

Table 2.3, Continued
COMMAND.COM Internal Commands

Command	Function
RD	Deletes subdirectories
DEL	Erases files
ERASE	Erases files
IF	Batch command for decision-making
FOR	Looping command
REM	Enables remarks in batch files
ECHO	Controls how much information DOS shows on screen
BREAK	Tells DOS how often to check for Ctrl-C
CALL	Calls one batch program from another
CHCP	Changes code pages or reports current code page
CLS	Clears the screen
DATE	Displays the date or enables user to change date
XIT	Closes the COMMAND.COM session
GOTO	Batch command
LOADHIGH	Loads a program above 640K into an upper memory block
PATH	Changes the program search path
PAUSE	Displays the message press any key to continue
PROMPT	Changes the command prompt
REN	Renames a file or group of files
SET	Creates or displays environmental variables
SHIFT	Moves the relative position of the parameters in a user command

Command	Function
TIME	Displays or changes system time
TRUENAME	Constructs a complete filespec for a file
TYPE	Copies a file to the screen
VER	Displays DOS version number
VOL	Displays disk volume ID

You can see one of the reasons for COMMAND.COM's 53K size: there are quite a few internal commands, and each of those commands is a program that COMMAND.COM must contain. Internal commands are desirable, however, for several reasons:

- ✔ Many of the commands are essential, like DIR and COPY. Placing them inside COMMAND.COM ensures that they are always close at hand.

- ✔ If not manifested as an internal command, many of these commands would require very small programs. Creating an entire file just to support the VOL command, for example, would mean creating a file of just 40 bytes. But file space is organized into units of a minimum of 2,048 bytes (these units are called *clusters*); a 40-byte file would take up the full 2,048 bytes and waste a good deal of precious space. *For more information about clusters and disks, see Chapter 17.*

- ✔ An internal command already is loaded in memory and, therefore, executes more quickly than an external command.

Internal commands can be smaller, faster, and more efficient than external commands. Of course, not all programs can be internal commands; if they were, COMMAND.COM would become monstrous.

External Commands

If COMMAND.COM does not find an internal command to satisfy your request, it next begins looking for a file with the extension COM or EXE that can perhaps satisfy the request. If you type **banana**, COMMAND.COM looks for a file called BANANA.COM. If COMMAND.COM finds a file by that name in the current directory, it loads the file into memory and instructs DOS to execute the instructions now in memory. If, on the other hand, COMMAND.COM doesn't find a file by that name, it moves on, looking for a file called BANANA.EXE. If the EXE file is present, COMMAND.COM loads it into memory and executes it. A DOS command that is satisfied by a COM, EXE, or BAT file is an *external* command.

Batch Files

If no internal command, EXE, or COM file matches the user's request, COMMAND.COM then looks for a batch file with the extension BAT in the current directory. If such a file exists in the current directory, COMMAND.COM executes the file, line by line. Note that COMMAND.COM executes the file rather than loading the file into memory and passing control to DOS. That's because a batch file is not a true program; it's a sort of super command line with presorted commands that COMMAND.COM executes one at a time, just as if you typed them on the command line yourself. Batch commands enable you to do some simple programming without a compiler or linker. *You learn about batch commands in Chapter 15.*

Continuing with the BANANA example, assuming that no programs named BANANA.COM or BANANA.EXE exist, COMMAND.COM looks for a file called BANANA.BAT; if it finds the file, COMMAND.COM loads and executes it.

AUTHOR'S NOTE

Professional software developers use tools called **compilers** *and* **link editors** *to create computer programs. The programmer first writes the program in a computer language, such as C, COBOL, BASIC, Pascal, or FORTRAN, and then feeds the program into a proper compiler program. (By proper compiler, I mean that you can't feed a file containing Pascal code into a BASIC compiler and expect to get something meaningful.) The compiler feeds its output to a link*

editor, which oversees the linkage of the programmer's program to other programs in the system. The output of the link editor is an EXE file or a COM file. Either type of file is a machine-language file: a set of commands built with the processor's native language. The machine-language file is a set of opcodes (operation codes) that mean nothing to a human without the help of a program called a debugger. To see the contents of a machine-language file, type:

    TYPE COMMAND.COM

You see what looks like gibberish, but it's not gibberish to the PC, thankfully.

COM and EXE files are files containing the basic machine language required to make the PC do anything. Whenever you buy a commercial software package, that package includes at least one COM or EXE file that contains the program itself.

With earlier versions of DOS, there was a difference between the definition of a COM file and an EXE file, but since DOS 3.1, it hasn't mattered whether the file is EXE or COM. DOS can detect which program format the file is in. You can even give an EXE-type program file the extension COM, and it works fine. You also can call a COM-type file an EXE file without trouble.

Although it doesn't matter whether a file is an EXE or COM file, COMMAND.COM does search for files in a particular order. This can lead to a few quirks in DOS behavior. One example happened under DOS with the database program dBASE III.

Once dBASE is installed on a system, you activate dBASE BY entering **DBASE**. Because it's obviously not an internal command, the main dBASE program must either be DBASE.COM or DBASE.EXE. The first version of dBASE III 1.0 was shipped as a COM file. As with so many pieces of software whose version numbers end with .0, however, dBASE III 1.0 had many problems. Ashton-Tate soon released an update, dBASE III+ 1.1. It was installed over the old version of dBASE, but oddly, the new version refused to work, citing a violation of copy protection. An investigation into the problem showed that the new version's main program file was DBASE.EXE. The installation program didn't know

continues

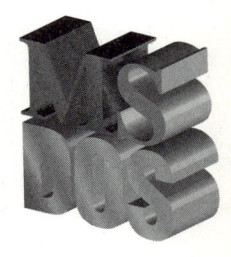

enough to erase the old DBASE.COM file, so the dBASE subdirectory contained all of Version 1.1—including DBASE.EXE—and one remnant of Version 1.0: DBASE.COM. When a user typed **DBASE**, DOS first found and loaded DBASE.COM, which was unable to run because all its support files were gone. To fix this problem, all the user had to do was erase DBASE.COM.

The EXE and COM relationship was exploited by a computer virus known as AIDS II or Companion. Any EXE file could be infected— but so cleverly that the EXE file was unchanged. The method was simple: The virus created a hidden COM file with the same file name. If, for example, a particular subdirectory contained a program called XYZ.EXE, AIDS II created a file called XYZ.COM, and then hid the file. Because hidden program files still run, when COMMAND.COM attempted to execute XYZ, it found XYZ.COM (the virus program) first and executed it. The virus program displayed a message (the usual Look at me kind of message) and then loaded and executed XYZ.EXE (the real program). Because the XYZ.EXE program was started by the XYZ.COM program, control passed back to the XYZ.COM program once the user exited XYZ.EXE. The XYZ.COM program then displayed a farewell message and exited. AIDS II was a virus that only worked because of DOS's idiosyncrasy about running a COM file over an EXE file when it finds both.

The Path

If the current directory yields no files that match the user's request, the problem may be that COMMAND.COM is looking in the wrong place.

Suppose that your current default directory is \DRAWNGS. You want to start your word processor, contained in the file WPROC.EXE. If you type **WPROC**, however, you receive a `bad command or file name` error message from COMMAND.COM. When

COMMAND.COM searched the current directory (\DRAWNGS), the only COM, EXE, or BAT file it found was DRAW.EXE. If, however, you typed **CD \WPFILES** to make the current directory \WPFILES, typing **WPROC** would work because you would be in the directory that contained WPROC.EXE. It is, however, inconvenient to change to the WPFILES directory every time you want to use the word processor. Perhaps you don't keep all your documents in the C:\WPFILES subdirectory; you might want to retrieve files in either \WPFILES\WORK or \WPFILES\PERSNL, for example. It might be more convenient to invoke WPROC from a subdirectory other than \WPFILES. There are two ways to accomplish this.

The first way is to fully specify the command, including the subdirectory. Rather than typing **WPROC**, you type **\WPFILES\WPROC** or **A:\WPFILES\WPROC** to load the program from any directory. The second way involves an important part of DOS called the *path,* which is a list of subdirectory names, separated by semicolons. (For this discussion, let's move the subdirectory examples to drive C because that's the drive you probably use most frequently. Also, let's assume that you added a general-purpose directory called C:\UTILS in which you put your favorite handy utilities.)

A path statement could look like the following:

```
PATH C:\DOS;C:\WPFILES;C:\DRAWNGS;C:\UTILS
```

This statement tells DOS, "When you cannot find COM, EXE, or BAT in the current directory, look for COM, then EXE, then BAT in the C:\DOS subdirectory. If it's not there, look in C:\WPFILES. If there's still no luck, look in C:\DRAWNGS, and, finally, if you haven't found any matching files yet, look in C:\UTILS. If it's not there, give up, and display an error message."

You can see that a long path can slow DOS down; there's a lot of searching to be done. But paths can't get too long; there's a limit of 128 characters to a path. DOS has done a lot of searching before it displays the bad command or file name message.

Chapter 2: *An Inside Look: How DOS Works*

> **AUTHOR'S NOTE**
>
> *You can see how mistyping a command results in the* bad command or file name *message: DOS is looking for a command or file that doesn't exist. And the message itself makes better sense too. Before you see the message, DOS has done the following:*
>
> 1. Looked for an internal command named BANANA.
> 2. Looked in the current subdirectory for a file named BANANA.COM.
> 3. Looked in the current subdirectory for a file named BANANA.EXE.
> 4. Looked in the current subdirectory for a file named BANANA.BAT. (Doesn't it know that they're only in South America?)
> 5. Looked in C:\DOS for a file named BANANA.COM, then BANANA.EXE, then BANANA.BAT.
> 6. Looked in C:\WPFILES for a file named BANANA.COM, then BANANA.EXE, then BANANA.BAT.
> 7. Looked in C:\DRAWNGS for a file named…but you get the picture.
>
> *This may help you understand why a command seems to work sometimes and not others. It may simply be that the program that DOS needs to execute the command isn't on the path. The command works only when you're in the particular directory that contains the files that the command needs to execute.*

If you want to experiment with the PATH command, the syntax is as follows:

    PATH dirname1;dirname2;dirname3;...

The variables *dirname1*, *dirname2*, *dirname3*, and so on are the names of the directories you want DOS to search for in the COM, EXE, and BAT files.

Understanding the DOS User Interface **101**

The following short example using the TREE command (its real name is TREE.COM) assumes that you have put your DOS files into a subdirectory on drive C called \DOS:

1. Starting from the DOS prompt, ensure that you are working from drive C by typing **C:**. If you start DOS with the MS-DOS Shell, you can display a DOS prompt by choosing the Command Prompt option from the main menu.

2. Change to the root directory by typing **CD **.

3. Type **PATH,** and press Enter. You see a report on your current path. \DOS no doubt is in that path. (If it isn't, this exercise won't work.)

4. Type **TREE** to see the tree structure of your C drive displayed on-screen.

> **NOTE**
>
> *In the next steps, you tell DOS to forget the path and then give the TREE command again to prove that DOS can't find TREE.COM unless the \DOS directory is on the path. Once this little exercise is over, however, you don't want to have to retype the original path.*
>
> *Step 5 is a little DOS trick that prevents you from having to retype the path: you load a second copy of COMMAND.COM. Because each copy of COMMAND.COM has its own copy of the path, you can delete the path from the second copy, try the TREE command, and then unload the second copy of COMMAND.COM.*

5. Type **COMMAND** to load a second copy of COMMAND.COM on top of the original COMMAND.COM. You see a prompt and a message:

   ```
   Microsoft (R) MS-DOS (R) Version 6.00/Copyright
   Microsoft...
   ```

If you type **PATH**, you see that the new COMMAND.COM does, indeed, have the old path.

6. Delete the path by typing...

    ```
    PATH ;
    ```

    This command tells DOS to forget your path.

7. Type **PATH**. DOS displays the message:

    ```
    no path
    ```

8. Type **TREE**. DOS displays the error message:

    ```
    bad command or file name
    ```

    DOS cannot find TREE.COM without the path in place.

9. Type **EXIT** to unload the second COMMAND.COM file and restore the path.

Extending the Path with APPEND /X

If you're just getting started with DOS, the 128-character limit on the path may not sound like much of a constraint. But if you install many programs, you soon find that 128 characters isn't nearly as long as you might think. You can, however, extend the DOS path by using the APPEND /X command. This command acts as a kind of supplementary PATH command. Its syntax is as follows:

```
APPEND dirname1;dirname2;dirname3;... /X
```

Once you tell DOS to execute this APPEND command, DOS will look not only in the PATH directories for COM, EXE, and BAT files; it will also look in the subdirectories listed in the APPEND statement.

Be sure to put the **/X** at the end of the command line or this does not work. You can try this command with a modification of the previous exercise:

1. Make sure that you're at the DOS prompt on drive C and the root directory.

2. Load a second copy of COMMAND.COM (for convenience's sake) by typing **COMMAND**.

3. Type this to load APPEND and tell it to include C:\DOS in its directory list:

    ```
    APPEND C:\DOS /X
    ```

4. Type this to tell COMMAND.COM to forget the current path:

    ```
    PATH ;
    ```

    So far, this is much like the previous exercise. In that exercise, however, when you issued the TREE command, you got the bad command or file name message because the path was erased.

5. Type **TREE**. Although this didn't work in the last exercise, it works now because the APPEND command created an auxiliary path that can direct DOS to the TREE.COM command.

6. Type **EXIT** to remove the second copy of COMMAND.COM and restore your original path.

Can you get more on the path than 256 characters? No, not with the current DOS architecture. But perhaps DOS 7?

Understanding the DOS Software Foundation

Now you understand how DOS knows which program to load. But once the program has been loaded, is that the end of DOS's involvement? Not entirely. Once a program has been loaded into memory and is running, it requires some help from the operating system. In fact, you should think of the operating system as the support foundation, the underlying structure that makes it possible for the application to run.

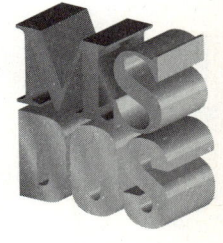

In the DOS world, however, application software may choose to ignore DOS altogether and rely instead on a layer of software under DOS called the *BIOS* (Basic Input Output System). Alternatively, the software may ignore both DOS and BIOS and provide its own structure. Different software uses DOS and BIOS differently, but most software uses a combination of DOS, BIOS, and its own commands.

You have learned what an operating system does for you. It provides a disk-management structure, disk tools, and a means to load programs. But the operating system has another job as well: to support programs.

Operating systems are supposed to simplify the task of writing application programs. But some application programs don't want any help and refuse the services of the operating system; this can create compatibility problems. In the following sections, you learn why these problems arise, and (sometimes) what to do about them.

Controlling Hardware

Consider how many times per session an application program (such as a word processor, spreadsheet, or database, for example) must communicate with your PC's hardware. An application controls hardware when it…

- ✔ Puts information on your PC's screen
- ✔ Prints things
- ✔ Saves things to disk
- ✔ Retrieves things from disk
- ✔ Reads the keyboard

That's not an exhaustive list, but these are probably the most common uses of hardware by application programs. Addressing hardware isn't a simple matter. The program that reads a keystroke from the keyboard goes on for pages and pages of computer code, and it's a relatively difficult program to write; the same can be said of any hardware-addressing code (*code* is a synonym for *program*, as programmers use the word).

NOTE: *A program that addresses and controls computer hardware is often called a* driver. *The part of your word processor that controls your particular printer, for example, is called the* printer driver *for the word processor.*

Now consider the problem of writing application programs. At some point, all application programs must communicate with hardware, whether to read a keystroke, access a file, or whatever. Who writes that program? Should the author of WordPerfect, for example, have to include in the program the job of writing device-control code? No, and there are several main reasons why not:

✔ Good application programmers aren't necessarily good writers of device drivers. Writing these two kinds of programs requires two different specialized skills. You want your device drivers to be as fast as possible. You're probably familiar with the notion that Microsoft Windows requires printer drivers. But did you know that the first version of the Hewlett-Packard LaserJet Windows printer drivers were almost 40 percent slower than the most recent versions? Driver writing should be a specialized business, rather than something that every applications programmer must do.

✔ There's no point in duplicating effort. Everyone writing an application program needs drivers, so why make everyone write them?

✔ The driver programmer must write programs very specific to a particular piece of hardware. Suppose that a new kind of floppy-disk drive appears, one that stores 100M of data on a single 3 1/2-inch disk. In one sense, it's just another kind of disk drive. But in another sense, it's a magneto-optical storage device that uses tricks to stuff great amounts of data into a tiny place, tricks that the WordPerfect programmer must learn in order to read the disks.

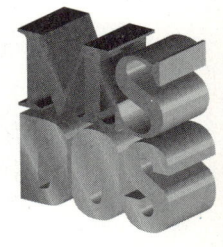

If the WordPerfect programmer insisted on directly controlling the floppy disk hardware, then WordPerfect would have to offer a new version of their word processing software every time some new piece of hardware appeared on the market. (And, to some extent, they actually must do that because WordPerfect refuses DOS's help on some hardware access, but you learn more about that later in this chapter.)

The realization that *application programming* is different from *systems programming* (controlling devices and accessing mass storage) occurred early in the days of the mainframe. The computer industry recognized that tremendous efficiency gains could be made by having a kind of central "library" of driver programs packaged with every computer. That library would be available to any application program. Rather than having to create a file-reading utility program to access the disk, for example, the WordPerfect programmer need only use the driver program built into the PC. A programmer would say that "the application program calls the driver in the library."

Your PC has such a library. That library is called DOS. From a programming standpoint, DOS is just a collection of several hundred small driver and utility programs; a programming library, in other words.

Understanding How Programs Call on DOS To Access Hardware

It's worthwhile taking the time to understand a bit of "programmer talk." This kind of verbiage is bandied about in the more technical trade journals; knowing some techie talk will make explaining the rest of this chapter easier.

Conceptually, an application program communicates with DOS, as shown in figure 2.6.

The application program needs DOS services, such as write a file, read a file, read the keyboard, and so on. DOS offers these services, but the application and DOS need some kind of agreement on how to communicate needs and information. The convention since the first days of DOS has been that an application uses something called INT 21 to call on DOS.

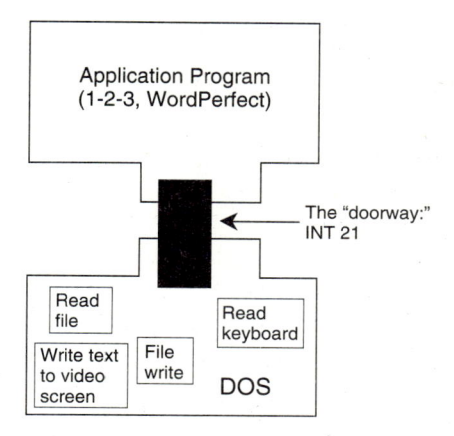

Figure 2.6
How DOS programs use DOS services.

INT 21 is a *software interrupt*. Software interrupts seek to solve a particular problem that any public library software must face: how do the application programs know where to find the library programs?

Once the operating system has been loaded into your PC's memory, the drivers and utility programs are ready for any application program to use (call). But for one program (the application) to call another program (the DOS routine), the caller (the application) must know the address in memory of the callee (the DOS routine). This would be quite difficult without INT 21.

How would WordPerfect, Lotus, Borland, and the other application writers know, for instance, exactly where in memory the routine that sends text to the printer is kept? Without that information, those applications could not print. Interrupts solve these types of problems.

The problem and its solution are best explained with an analogy. Suppose that you go to a building to apply for a job. You should first go to the personnel office, but how do you know where that is? Companies could have a convention that says that personnel offices always go in room 201, but they don't. Instead, you go to the first floor of the building, where you find a listing of job functions and rooms. You look up the personnel office and find that it is in room 405. Now you know where to go.

Think of interrupt vectors as the function listing in the first floor of the building. The first 1,024 bytes of your PC's memory are devoted to holding 256 entries of four bytes. Each four-byte entry (called an *interrupt vector* or *interrupt pointer*) is an address pointing to some location in memory. The 33rd interrupt vector points to DOS.

> **NOTE** *The 21 in INT 21 is not a decimal number; it's a* hexadecimal *number; 21 in hexadecimal is equal to 33 in decimal—hence the INT 21. Don't sweat the hex; it's just something that programmers find convenient. By the way, not all 256 interrupt vectors are used; of those that are, you'll meet some of them later in this chapter.*

A program finds DOS by executing an INT 21 instruction, which tells the CPU to go to a location in the PC's memory—the 33rd four-byte entry—and there find the interrupt vector that points to DOS. Once the program has successfully called DOS, DOS takes over, figuring out whether the program needs a disk read, some screen I/O, or whatever.

> **NOTE** *Think of INT 21 as the "doorway into DOS." INT 21 is known to programmers as the Application Program Interface, or API, for DOS. You see the term* API *in PC magazines now and then. In the DOS context, API refers to a program performing an INT 21 to request a DOS service. DOS fulfills the request and then returns control of the computer to the application. Because DOS is a single-tasking operating system, the application program gets no attention from the computer's CPU while DOS is fulfilling the application request.*

AUTHOR'S NOTE

Before explaining how DOS programs are executed, this is a good place to briefly explain how Windows programs get the services they need.

Windows is a more complex system than DOS, and it offers thousands of API functions. The 256 interrupt vectors on a PC's CPU are not enough interrupt vectors to support all the things that Windows does. Instead, Windows keeps its own internal tables of its utility routines. Instead of executing INT 21, Windows programs ask Windows to find routines with names such as DrawEllipse. These routines are called, as you might imagine, the **Windows API.**

In the DOS world, the total amount of programs that make up DOS add up to only about 70K of memory. For that reason, all of DOS loads into your PC's RAM during the boot process. In Windows, however, that's not possible for two reasons. The first reason is that total Windows functional support is just too big to fit into many PC memories. The second is that third-party application programs want to be able to offer their own extensions to the Windows API. Loading every program with an extension to the API would get pretty messy.

Instead, Windows uses **dynamic linking.** *In dynamic linking, you load just the parts of the operating system you need into memory, when you need them. Windows and Windows programs support this idea. DOS programs, as you can imagine, do not, although some particular DOS applications have been designed to use dynamic linking.*

The files containing the libraries that the Windows programs link to are called **Dynamic Link Libraries,** *or DLLs. You see them on your disk if you have Windows or any Windows programs; their file extension is usually DLL.*

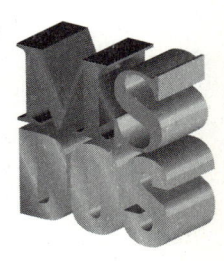

Understanding How DOS Fulfills Requests

You have learned how applications ask DOS to perform system services for them. If you were to look into DOS, however, you would see that DOS doesn't directly control hardware. Instead, DOS acts as a middleman, reformulating the application-program requests to make them palatable to a lower level of software, the *Basic Input Output System* (BIOS).

As you probably know, DOS loads from your PC's hard disk into memory (random access memory or RAM) every time you boot your computer. But BIOS is preloaded into your computer's memory in a special kind of memory chip called *ROM* (read only memory). BIOS is composed of programs that control your PC's hardware. These programs are grouped together by the kind of hardware they support. Just as all the programs that make up DOS share INT 21, so do all BIOS programs connected with the disk share INT 13. The video-control routines all share INT 10, and the keyboard routines share INT 9. *For more information on ROM and RAM, see Chapter 9.*

The following example is a step-by-step analysis of what happens when you type **DIR** and press Enter:

1. COMMAND.COM executes an INT 21, requesting that DOS pass it the next line of typed commands. DOS does not respond until there is a line to offer. In this way, COMMAND.COM waits patiently for your input. (You have not yet typed DIR. COMMAND.COM issued the INT 21 request for the next line of keyboard input immediately after finishing your last command.)

2. Every time you press a key, an INT 9 is generated in the BIOS. The keystroke is passed to DOS, which collects the keystrokes until Enter is pressed.

3. COMMAND.COM sees the command you typed. Because DIR is an internal command, the part of COMMAND.COM that is the DIR program starts executing.

4. The DIR program must read the part of the disk that contains the disk's directory, so it executes an INT 21, asking DOS to read the directory of the disk.

5. DOS knows the specific address on the disk where the directory is kept, and so it executes an INT 13, asking BIOS to read the part of the disk (the "sectors") containing the directory.

6. Once BIOS has finished its job, it passes the directory data to DOS. DOS passes this information to COMMAND.COM.

7. The directory data is in a raw format that means very little to a human user, so COMMAND.COM reformats it to a more meaningful format.

8. COMMAND.COM sends the nicely formatted data to DOS, asking DOS to put the data on the PC screen.

9. DOS uses BIOS's INT 10 to display the data on-screen. INT 10 isn't too smart, however, and can accept only one character of data for each INT 10. DOS, therefore, takes the extensive directory report generated by COMMAND.COM and spoon-feeds it to BIOS, one character at a time.

10. Finally, the data is completely displayed, and COMMAND.COM goes back to waiting for the next command.

Understanding Why Some Programs Bypass DOS and BIOS

You have learned how DOS supports DOS application programs. It's a nice, logical system, but it's not a logical system that is respected all the time. Back in the early 1980s, most people were buying real IBM computers. The BIOS for those IBM PCs was written by IBM programmers. Those computers were running DOS 1.*x* or 2.*x*, written by Microsoft.

It is probably kindest to say that neither the IBM programmers (the BIOS writers) nor the Microsoft programmers (the DOS programmers) made performance their top priority. That made life difficult for writers of applications programs, the brave builders of the early DOS programs. Early DOS programs that "followed the rules" and passed their screens full of information to DOS were very slow, because the

Chapter 2: *An Inside Look: How DOS Works*

early DOS and BIOS routines weren't fast. As a result, many software vendors decided to do things the hard way and write their own driver and system-level programs, essentially reinventing the "wheel" provided by BIOS and DOS—but reinventing it to be a lot faster than BIOS and DOS were. Although writing your own drivers is contrary to the reasons for using common DOS drivers (you read those reasons a few pages back), the gross inefficiency of DOS and BIOS gave application programmers a difficult choice: write their own hardware-accessing code or die out.

> **AUTHOR'S NOTE**
>
> *Not every software house understood the reasoning of "write application-specific drivers or die"—that's why not every early software house exists today. Why do 1-2-3 and WordPerfect have the market shares they do today? Speed: they were faster than the competitors. That logic is less important today because most new computers these days are 25 MHz or faster, but the speed of many popular applications was what got them their initial market share.*
>
> *Even Microsoft, the company setting the software standards, violated the standards with their own products. Multiplan, GW-BASIC, and other early Microsoft products all bypassed DOS and BIOS and directly controlled PC hardware. It's sad that it worked out that way, actually. If DOS's INT 21 interface had been of a quality that third-party vendors could support, it would be much easier for newer operating systems like OS/2 and Windows NT to support older DOS programs.*
>
> *What has occurred is that many DOS applications either bypass DOS and directly call BIOS routines, or bypass both DOS and BIOS and directly control hardware. That's why programs like 1-2-3 require you to specify keyboard and video drivers. 1-2-3 bypasses BIOS and loads its own BIOS. But it must know what kind of hardware to load the BIOS for, and that's what you're helping it to do when you install and configure 1-2-3. Don't think that 1-2-3 is the only example; WordPerfect, Harvard Graphics, Quicken, and thousands of other DOS programs bypass DOS. A smaller number bypass BIOS.*

If so many application programs bypass DOS, why should you understand how DOS fits together? Is it even relevant? Yes. There is one very important function that nearly every program lets DOS handle: file input and output. The vast majority of programs do not use INT 13 to access the disk drives—they leave it up to DOS.

Now you know quite a bit about how DOS programs fit together, and what causes those annoying incompatibilities you sometimes see among DOS programs. But there's one more group of DOS programs you need to understand to get the whole DOS picture: memory-resident and device-driver programs.

Understanding TSRs and Device Drivers

The original DOS 1 manual explained all the INT 21 functions, how to call DOS from inside assembly language programs, and so forth. The manual explained that most DOS functions are handled by INT 21, but that there were a few extra functions that had their own interrupts.

One in particular was INT 27, which was called *terminate-and-stay resident*. Most programs are *terminate-and-exit* programs: when you load a program, the program finds whatever free memory you have and claims it, using the memory for its data. But when you exit that program (when that program terminates), it leaves, freeing whatever memory it was using for the next program. A terminate-and-stay-resident program yields control back to DOS (meaning that the DOS prompt returns to the screen) but retains part of itself in memory, a part of itself that will perform some function in the near future.

In general, terminate-and-exit programs are preferable, both from the user standpoint (it's nice to get your memory back) and the programmer standpoint (it's difficult to write programs that successfully use INT 27; not all programs can). But these *INT 27* programs, as they were originally called, or *TSR* programs as they're called these days (*memory resident* is another term) soon found many uses.

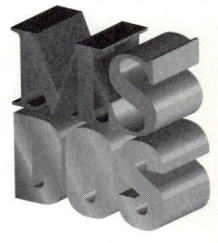

AUTHOR'S NOTE

*Perhaps the first use for a TSR was for keyboard macro programs. Suppose that you work at a firm called Acme Tool & Die, and you type **Acme Tool & Die** many times each day. Every time you press a key, BIOS's INT 9 sends the keystroke to DOS so that DOS can respond to the INT 21 that is requesting the key.*

*But you're tired of typing that sequence all the time. So a programmer friend writes a keyboard macro TSR for you. Now, if you press Ctrl-A, the PC types **Acme Tool & Die** for you, saving you many keystrokes. The TSR that accomplishes this is a little program that "watches" the keyboard. As keystrokes come in, it watches for a Ctrl-A. If the Ctrl-A appears, the keyboard macro TSR jumps in before the BIOS can see the keystroke. The keyboard macro TSR essentially "impersonates" the keyboard at that point, telling BIOS's INT 9 that the keystrokes A, c, m, e, (space), T, o, o, l, (space), &, (space), D, i, and e are coming from the keyboard. BIOS thinks keystrokes are coming from the keyboard, and so passes them to DOS, which passes them to the word processor, spreadsheet, or whatever. Even if you're using a program that bypasses DOS or BIOS, the TSR can step in to impersonate the keyboard hardware.*

How can the TSR do this? It steals the BIOS keyboard interrupt. A keystroke causes the CPU to execute an INT 9, so the CPU looks in the ninth four-byte interrupt vector to see where to go to find the keyboard-handling program. That interrupt vector is supposed to be pointing to the BIOS's INT 9 program. But the TSR changed the interrupt vector to point to the TSR. This technique is called stealing an interrupt or hooking a vector. The technique has the effect of forcing the PC to "wake up" the TSR whenever a keystroke comes in. The TSR then examines each keystroke as it comes in. Most keystrokes are of no interest to this TSR; for these keystrokes, the TSR calls the original INT 9 (the BIOS) to handle the keystroke. Only when Ctrl-A appears does the TSR impersonate the keyboard.

TSRs can be very useful. You use TSR programs to run your memory manager, your network, or perhaps your CD-ROM. If you have an alarm program that reminds you when appointments are drawing near, you are using a TSR. But some TSRs can be harmful for one of two reasons.

First, any TSR that hooks a basic system vector (such as the keyboard, disk, video, printer, and so forth) has assumed a great amount of responsibility. One mistake in the TSR program spells doom for the system, making perfectly good hardware and software look faulty. That's why an important first step in troubleshooting any problem is to reboot DOS without any TSRs, to minimize the possible sources of trouble.

Second, some TSRs are viruses—specifically designed to cause trouble. As an example, you may have heard of the Joshi virus.

One of a virus' programmed goals in life is to reproduce. In a computer context, "reproduce" means that the virus program wants to copy itself onto as many disks as it possibly can. Joshi seeks to spread itself on floppy disks. The way it does this is by hooking INT 13, the disk interrupt. (INT 13 handles both floppy disk and hard disk drives.) Whenever you perform a disk operation, Joshi sees the INT 13 request before the BIOS does because Joshi has changed the INT 13 vector to point to itself. Therefore, whenever DOS issues an INT 13, it thinks it is calling the BIOS, but it actually is calling the virus program. Before doing whatever DOS wants done, Joshi takes a quick look at the disk that the INT 13 operation is supposed to be done on. If Joshi sees that there is already a copy of itself on that drive, it passes the INT 13 request on to the BIOS. But if Joshi sees an uninfected disk, it quickly deposits a copy of itself onto the disk before turning the INT 13 request over to the BIOS.

Some virus-shield programs monitor the interrupt vectors to see whether a program tries to modify them. If a program tries to hook a vector, as virus programs often do while "infecting" your machine—the virus shield informs the user. Furthermore, the shield will, if requested by the user, prevent the virus program from hooking the vector. Viruses are covered in more detail in Chapter 20. Related to TSRs is a kind of program called a device driver. *You read about them in Chapter 9.*

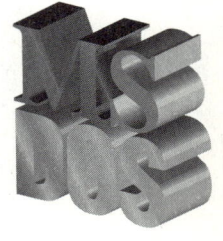

Summary

In this chapter, you learned about what DOS is and what it does. You saw how the pieces of the DOS software world fit together, and how they sometimes don't fit together. Now you have the big picture and can get down to the nitty-gritty of using DOS 6.2.

Although some of this chapter may have, at times, seemed to be a lot of history, understanding this background helps to make clear why the PC world is where it is today. More importantly, it explains why we face some of the constraints that we face today, and helps you understand how software utilities (like the ones shipped with DOS 6.2) attempt to exceed those constraints. The following chapters start you off by getting down to brass tacks about installing and using DOS 6.2.

MS-DOS

Setup and Installation

Installing DOS 6.2 .... *121*

Taking a Tour of Your Hard Drive *175*

Preparing and Setting Up Your Hard Drive *219*

Part Two:

MS-DOS

CHAPTER 3

Installing DOS 6.2

by Bill Camarda

The first step toward using MS-DOS 6.2 is installing it. You can just place Disk 1 in drive A and type **SETUP**, and most of the time everything will be just fine.

But occasionally it won't be.

Then you'll be glad you spent a few minutes beforehand to understand the installation process and plan how you want to use DOS 6.2. This chapter will help you make those plans.

Getting Ready To Install

Getting ready to install DOS 6.2 should be an eight-step process:

1. Back up your MS-DOS 6.2 disks.
2. Back up your data.
3. Inventory your system.

4. Locate your current DOS directory.
5. Disable TSRs and other programs that might interfere with installation.
6. Read README.TXT.
7. Check to see if you have enough space available.
8. Get a blank floppy (two, if you use low-density disks).

Step 1: Back Up Your MS-DOS 6.2 Disks

You've heard this before, but really: *make backup copies of all your MS-DOS 6.2 disks*. Assuming you have only one drive of the same type as your DOS disks, use the following command:

DISKCOPY A: A:

You'll be asked to swap disks until the first disk is completely copied; then insert another one and run the same command again.

Press F3 to display the command again; then press Enter. (We're telling you the shortcut so you'll really back up the DOS 6.2 disks.)

This is the stage when you'll discover if you bought the right size disks. MS-DOS 6.2 is being marketed primarily on high-density 3 1/2-inch and 5 1/4-inch disks; if you need low-density 360K disks, you might have to special-order them.

While you're waiting for delivery, if you happen to have a computer with a compatible high-density disk handy, you may be able to install DOS 6.2 remotely, using its new InterLink feature. See Chapter 22 for the details.

Similarly, if you receive 5 1/4-inch disks when you actually need
3 1/2-inch disks, you can easily copy the 5 1/4-inch disks to 3 1/2-inch
disks by using COPY or XCOPY. Be sure, however, to use the LABEL
command to create the same volume label on the copy that exists on
the original. Naturally, this does not work for copying 3 1/2-inch disks
to 5 1/4-inch disks.

Step 2: Back Up Your Data

Installing a new release of DOS is a rare and important enough
occasion that it makes sense to do a full backup now.

If you use the BACKUP command included with DOS 3 through
DOS 5, remember that you can only restore your data using
RESTORE.EXE—*not* one of the new Microsoft Backup programs that
comes with DOS 6.2.

Step 3: Inventory Your Computer System

In case you have problems, you'll want to know:

- ✔ What kind of computer do you have? What processor are you running? What's the BIOS?
- ✔ How much memory does it have? What kinds?
- ✔ What kind of video are you running?
- ✔ If you are on a network, what kind and version?
- ✔ What version of DOS (and/or other operating systems) are you using now?
- ✔ If you're using a mouse, what kind?
- ✔ What other boards are installed?
- ✔ What disk drives do you have?
- ✔ Which parallel (LPT) and serial ports are active?
- ✔ Which memory-resident programs are running?

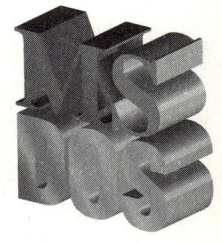

Chapter 3: Installing DOS 6.2

- ✔ Which device drivers are in use?
- ✔ What's in your CONFIG.SYS and AUTOEXEC.BAT files (and in your DOSSHELL.INI and WIN.INI files, if you have them)?

Sounds like a lot of work, and in all honesty, you may not need all that information. But fortunately, MS-DOS 6.2 does it for you—courtesy of Microsoft System Diagnostics (MSD), located on Disk 1 of your (high-density) package.

Before running MSD, exit Windows or the DOS Shell. Then insert Disk 1 of your backup DOS 6.2 disks, and type...

    A:\MSD

You'll see a screen similar to that shown in figure 3.1.

Underneath each item is more detailed information. For example, press M for memory, and you'll see a display like that shown in figure 3.2.

To print a 20+ page detailed report on the innards of your PC, choose Print Report from the File menu (keyboard shortcut Alt,Enter,P). Check Report All in the Report Information box. In the Print to: field, mark where you want to print the file—parallel or serial printer, or disk file. Click on OK, and you're in business.

Figure 3.1

Microsoft System Diagnostics.

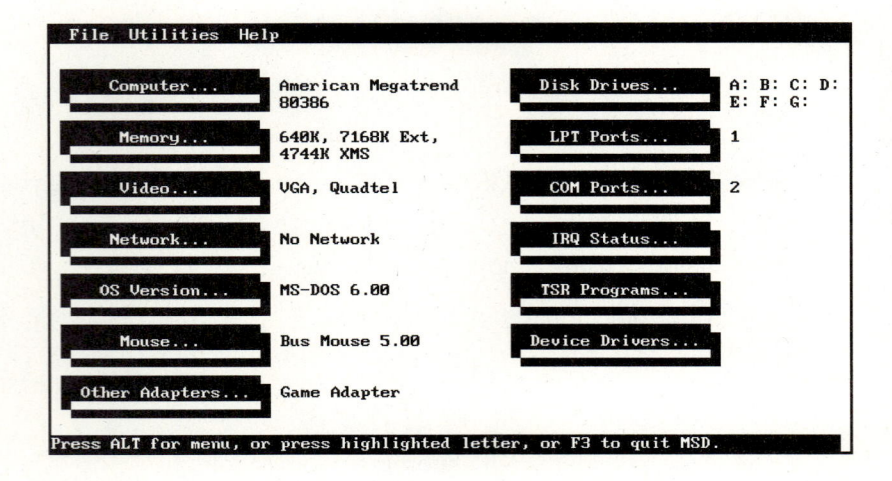

```
 File  Utilities  Help

   Computer...    American Megatrend    Disk Drives...   A: B: C: D:
                  80386                                  E: F: G:
   Memory...      640K, 7168K Ext,      LPT Ports...     1
                  4744K XMS
   Video...       VGA, Quadtel          COM Ports...     2

   Network...     No Network            IRQ Status...

   OS Version...  MS-DOS 6.00           TSR Programs...

   Mouse...       Bus Mouse 5.00        Device Drivers...

   Other Adapters...  Game Adapter

 Press ALT for menu, or press highlighted letter, or F3 to quit MSD.
```

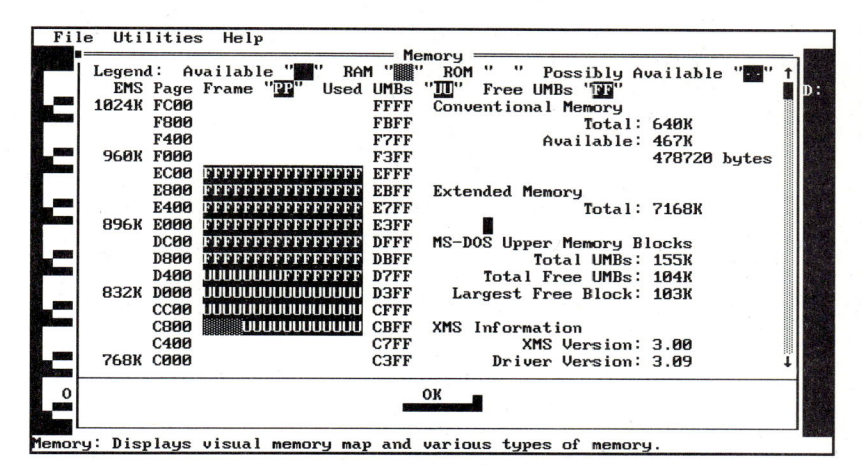

Figure 3.2
MSD Memory Map.

> *On rare occasions, MSD will choke on strange hardware configurations and lock up your system. Just reboot and compile your information manually.*

Step 4: Locate Your Current DOS

SETUP expects to find your current DOS in the subdirectory C:\DOS. If it doesn't, it will create such a subdirectory for the new version of DOS, and leave the old version alone. Usually, this isn't a big problem. One exception, though: DOS 6.2 won't update your SETVER list unless it is in C:\DOS, or in another C drive subdirectory that you specify.

SETVER is a list of programs that DOS knows won't run properly unless it tells them you are running an earlier version of DOS. You may have updated SETVER yourself to include other programs that didn't recognize DOS 5. If DOS 6.2 can't find your SETVER utility in C:\DOS, it simply inserts its new default list, and you have to add all your programs again manually, at the command line.

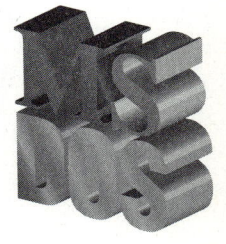

Step 5: Disable TSRs and Other Problem Programs

The SETUP program may have problems with memory-resident programs. It almost definitely will have problems with:

- ✔ Third-party disk caching programs (you can leave SMARTDrive loaded)
- ✔ Active anti-virus programs
- ✔ Programs that protect against inadvertent file deletions (you can leave the DOS Undelete utility alone)
- ✔ Password protection programs

Temporarily disable these before you run SETUP—they can all be reenabled after you finish. If they load from AUTOEXEC.BAT, place the word *REM* in front of each line in AUTOEXEC.BAT, save the file (without adding formatting), and reboot.

You should probably disable your third-party memory manager. It won't interfere with SETUP, but SETUP also won't install the new DOS 6.2 version of HIMEM.SYS if you leave the third-party memory manager running.

Why do you care? You've chosen not to run HIMEM.SYS anyway. Well, someday you might have a problem, and as part of troubleshooting you might want to run the most plain vanilla system possible —your own HIMEM.SYS instead of a third-party memory manager. Little do you (and your technical support person) know: you'll be running an obsolete HIMEM.SYS that wasn't designed to work with MS-DOS 6.2.

Step 6: Read README.TXT

If you're on a network, *check out Chapter 23 for a brief list of network upgrades* that might be necessary to successfully run MS-DOS 6.2.

Then read the README.TXT file that accompanies DOS 6.2 for more detailed information about networks, devices, and applications that might require upgrades or other special treatment.

Getting Ready To Install **127**

The following list covers the installation topics covered in section 1 of README.TXT:

1.1 SpeedStor

1.2 Incompatible hard disk or device driver

1.3 AT&T 6300 computer

1.4 Toshiba with a hard RAM disk

1.5 Tandy with ROM DOS

1.6 Setup displays the `Your computer uses a disk-compression program that is incompatible with Setup` message

1.7 You deleted files from the directory that Setup needs to install the optional Windows programs

1.8 Running Setup if your computer uses Windows NT

1.9 Setup detects that your computer has a non-MS-DOS partition or non-MS-DOS files, and your computer uses Windows NT

1.10 Setup detects that your computer uses DR DOS

1.11 Installing MS-DOS on a drive other than C

1.12 Bypassing the Uninstall disk and using default setup options

1.13 Setup displays the `Your computer uses password protection` message

1.14 Setup displays the `Your computer is using an incompatible delete-protection program` message

1.15 Installing MS-DOS 6.2 on a system with a CorelSCSI UNI_ASP.SYS Driver

1.16 Installing MS-DOS 6.2 on a computer with Micro House DrivePro

1.17 How to set up the Icelandic keyboard

NOTE

The README.TXT file is on disk 1 of 1.2 and 1.44M packages. On lower-density disks, it will be placed elsewhere; the README.1ST file will tell you where.

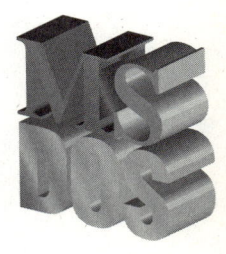

Step 7: Check for Available Space

The MS-DOS 6.2 SETUP program will move all your existing files to a new directory, OLD_DOS.1, and place all its new files in the directory C:\DOS. A few files, such as RESTORE.EXE, are left in place so as not to disrupt your current working environment.

The space requirements for MS-DOS 6.2 are greater than ever. 4.2M for the base operating system and utilities, plus 3.9M for the optional Anti-Virus, Backup, and Undelete utilities if you install both the DOS and Windows versions.

Do you have 8M available on C drive for DOS 6.2? If not, you have several alternatives...

By the way, when SETUP looks for a home for OLD_DOS.1 on your Stacker-compressed disk, it's looking for uncompressed space. So you may think you have enough space; DOS might not.

- ✔ Archive some existing data on floppy disks.

- ✔ Delete some files on your computer. If you are using DOS 5, *it may have placed its predecessor DOS files* in a directory called OLD_DOS.1. If they're still there, this might be a good time to trash them. Type the following:..

    DELOLDOS

- ✔ Install less of DOS 6.2. For example, choose the Windows or DOS versions of the Backup, Anti-Virus, and Undelete utilities. The Windows versions are a little more powerful and, as you can see in table 3.1, a lot bigger.

- ✔ Repartition your drive to make more room on C drive.

Table 3.1
MS-DOS 6.2 Optional Utilities

Utility	Windows	MS-DOS	Both
Anti-Virus	1,056K	848K	1,904K
Backup	1,360K	368K	1,738K
Undelete	256K	32K	288K
All Programs	2,672K (2.61M)	1,248K (1.22M)	3,920K (3.83M)

Remember, repartitioning your drive destroys all the data on it—back up first!

You might want to carefully review your partitioning before upgrading to DOS 6.2, especially if you are running more than one operating system on your computer. See Chapter 5 for a discussion of partitioning.

Step 8: Get a Blank Floppy

The MS-DOS 6.2 SETUP program will create an Uninstall disk that you can use to restore your previous version of MS-DOS if necessary. You'll need one high-density disk (or two low-density disks) to do this. Mark the disk and keep it at hand; you probably won't need it, but if you do, it'll be a lifesaver.

Choose Your Own Kind of SETUP

Several switches are available to define the type of setup you want:

✔ **SETUP/B** runs the setup program in monochrome. (Ideal for black-and-white laptops.)

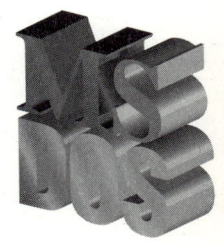

- ✔ **SETUP/E** only installs the optional Windows and DOS anti-virus, backup, and undelete utilities. (Ideal for use after you've run SETUP and decide you want to add one of these programs; for example, if you later migrate to Windows and want to run the Windows versions.)

- ✔ **SETUP/F** performs a minimal setup on a 720K, 1.2M, or 1.44M floppy disk. (Ideal for creating an emergency boot disk, as described later.)

- ✔ **SETUP/I** disables video detection only during the setup process. SETUP may also display indecipherable characters with some monitors. If this happens, run SETUP/I and tell SETUP about your hardware "manually." To disable video detection and hardware detection, use both /I and /U.

> **NOTE** *The SETUP/I option corrects an error in the Microsoft documentation shipped with DOS 6.2.*

- ✔ **SETUP/Q** copies files to hard disk. This is a manual setup that should be used only if the automated setup fails. It won't update your CONFIG.SYS and AUTOEXEC.BAT files; you'll have to do that yourself.

- ✔ **SETUP/U** skips hard-disk detection and installs DOS even if your disk contains incompatible partitions, that is, partitions created by a third-party partitioner DOS doesn't recognize, or partitions created by another operating system.

> **NOTE** *If you need to use both the /Q and /U switch, and if SETUP /U /Q does not work, enter the following:*
>
> **SETUP /Q /U**

A Few Words about OS/2

If you are running OS/2 2 with a previous version of DOS, the two can continue to coexist famously. That's entirely up to you—notwithstanding Microsoft's courteous offer during installation to remove OS/2 2 and save you many megabytes of space.

If you are running OS/2 2 and DOS in "Dual Boot" mode, all your DOS files are already in the C:\DOS directory, including a copy of COMMAND.COM. And your AUTOEXEC.BAT and CONFIG.SYS files already know where to look for them. That's half the battle won right there.

Next, make sure the partition containing both OS/2 and DOS is large enough to contain the DOS upgrade. If so, enter DOS by typing...

     BOOT /DOS

...at an OS/2 command prompt. (You get an OS/2 command prompt from the OS/2 Workplace Shell by double-clicking on OS/2 System, double-clicking on Command Prompts, and then double-clicking on OS/2 Full Screen.)

Now install MS-DOS 6.2 (use the directions that follow), ignoring any reference to `OS/2 Partitions Detected`.

If you are running OS/2 and DOS side-by-side in "Boot Manager" mode, the OS/2 Boot Manager is a 1M partition—probably at the start of your disk—which loads first and asks you which operating system you want to work from.

In this case, DOS and OS/2 are in entirely separate partitions, and Boot Manager will activate whichever operating system you choose. Choose to make the DOS partition active, and install from there.

Unfortunately, when the MS-DOS 6.2 installation program finishes, it doesn't return control to Boot Manager. DOS 6.2, once active, remains active, even after you reboot. The solution is to use FDISK to set the Boot Manager partition as active. (*See Chapter 5 on using FDISK.*) You will recognize it as a 1M "Non-DOS" partition.

In rare instances, you may have to use OS/2's version of FDISK instead. This will require booting OS/2 from its Installation Disk, and then switching to OS/2 Disk 1 and running FDISK from there.

Running SETUP

Assuming that you wish to run a fairly standard setup, insert your backup MS-DOS 6.2 Disk 1 in drive A, and type...

    A:\SETUP

Now press Enter.

The SETUP program's opening screen appears, as shown in figure 3.3:

Figure 3.3
MS-DOS 6.2 SETUP opening screen.

```
Microsoft MS-DOS 6 Setup

    Welcome to Setup.

    The Setup program prepares MS-DOS 6 to run on your
    computer.

    • To set up MS-DOS now, press ENTER.

    • To learn more about Setup before continuing, press F1.

    • To quit Setup without installing MS-DOS, press F3.




ENTER=Continue    F1=Help    F3=Exit    F5=Remove Color
```

Until SETUP starts copying files, you can exit at any time by pressing F3 twice. (F1 gets you help... but not too much.)

Press Enter to continue. You'll be asked to prepare one or two Uninstall disks, as shown in figure 3.4.

DOS now tells you where it plans to install itself and what kind of display it believes you have. Assuming that it finds the previous version of DOS in C:\DOS, that's where it'll want to place the new version, as shown in figure 3.5.

To change any of these items, you can use the up/down arrow keys, press Enter to choose the item you wish to change, and select from the list that is presented.

```
Microsoft MS-DOS 6 Setup

    During Setup, you will need to provide and label one
    or two floppy disks. Each disk can be unformatted
    or newly formatted and must work in drive A. (If you
    use 360K disks, you may need two disks; otherwise,
    you need only one disk.)

    Label the disk(s) as follows:

        UNINSTALL #1
        UNINSTALL #2 (if needed)

    Setup saves some of your original DOS files on the
    UNINSTALL disk(s), and others on your hard disk in a
    directory named OLD_DOS.x. With these files, you can
    restore your original DOS if necessary.

        • When you finish labeling your UNINSTALL disk(s),
          press ENTER to continue Setup.

ENTER=Continue   F1=Help   F3=Exit
```

Figure 3.4
Uninstall screen.

```
Microsoft MS-DOS 6 Setup

    Setup will use the following system settings:

    ┌─────────────────────────────────────┐
    │ DOS Type:        MS-DOS             │
    │ MS-DOS Path:     C:\DOS             │
    │ Display Type:    VGA                │
    │ The settings are correct.           │
    └─────────────────────────────────────┘

    If all the settings are correct, press ENTER.

    To change a setting, press the UP ARROW or DOWN ARROW key until
    the setting is selected. Then press ENTER to see alternatives.

ENTER=Continue   F1=Help   F3=Exit
```

Figure 3.5
Default System Settings.

> **NOTE**
>
> *If you use SETUP /I, SETUP won't check your system and gives the following default settings:*
>
>   DOS Type: MS-DOS (not an OEM version
>   of MS-DOS such as IBM DOS
>   or Compaq DOS)
>
>   MS-DOS Path: C:\DOS
>
>   Display Type: CGA

You can force SETUP to install in another subdirectory, in which case it would edit all your AUTOEXEC.BAT and CONFIG.SYS files accordingly—and leave everything in your C:\DOS directory exactly the way it is.

> *You might want to have DOS' essential files in C:\DOS, and keep other DOS utilities elsewhere. Here's how to do it:*
>
> 1. *Use SETUP /M to create a bootable minimal MS-DOS 6.2 system with hidden system files and COMMAND.COM in the root directory and other essential files in C:\DOS.*
>
> 2. *SETUP will create new CONFIG.SYS and AUTOEXEC.BAT files that reflect this configuration. Edit them to reflect the configuration you ultimately want. For example, make sure all your device drivers are present. And if you want to place your DOS utilities in D:\DOSUTILS, make sure to place that drive and path name in your path statement.*
>
> 3. *Run SETUP /Q (manual installation) to install the basic DOS utilities anywhere you want.*
>
> 4. *If you wish to install Anti-Virus, Backup, or Undelete, run SETUP /E, which places them in any directory you like.*

Next, in figure 3.6, you choose which optional utilities you want to install.

It's easy to blow right past this screen and not do exactly what you intended to do. Any of the three items in the box may be changed by moving the cursor to the item and pressing Enter. Assuming you have Windows, you can install both Windows and DOS versions; only Windows or DOS versions; or neither.

As figure 3.7 shows, DOS won't install Windows utilities unless it detects Windows.

```
Microsoft MS-DOS 6 Setup

      The following programs can be installed on your computer.

                  Program for              Bytes used

      Backup:         Windows only          1,081,344
      Undelete:       Windows only            262,144
      Anti-Virus:     Windows only          1,392,640
      Install the listed programs.

      Space required for MS-DOS and programs:   6,936,128
      Space available on drive C:              21,975,625


      To install the listed programs, press ENTER.  To see a list
      of available options, press the UP or DOWN ARROW key to
      highlight a program, and then press ENTER.

ENTER=Continue   F1=Help   F3=Exit
```

Figure 3.6
Installing optional utilities.

```
Microsoft MS-DOS 6 Setup

      Setup has found Microsoft Windows in the following directory:

      C:\WINDOWS

      To confirm that this is your Windows directory, press ENTER.
      To specify a different directory, type its path, and
      then press ENTER.

      If your computer does not have Windows, neither Backup,
      Undelete, nor Anti-Virus for Windows can be installed.
      Press ESC to return to the previous screen and change
      your selections.



ENTER=Continue   F1=Help   F3=Exit   ESC=Previous Screen
```

Figure 3.7
Locating Windows.

If you still have both Windows 3.0 and 3.1 on your disk in separate directories, make sure SETUP installs these programs in the correct directory, presumably the one containing Windows 3.1.

The next screen, figure 3.8, is your last step before DOS starts copying files:

Press Y and SETUP starts doing its thing. Almost immediately, you'll be asked for your Uninstall disk (figure 3.9):

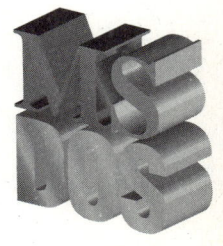

Chapter 3: *Installing DOS 6.2*

Figure 3.8
Last chance to quit.

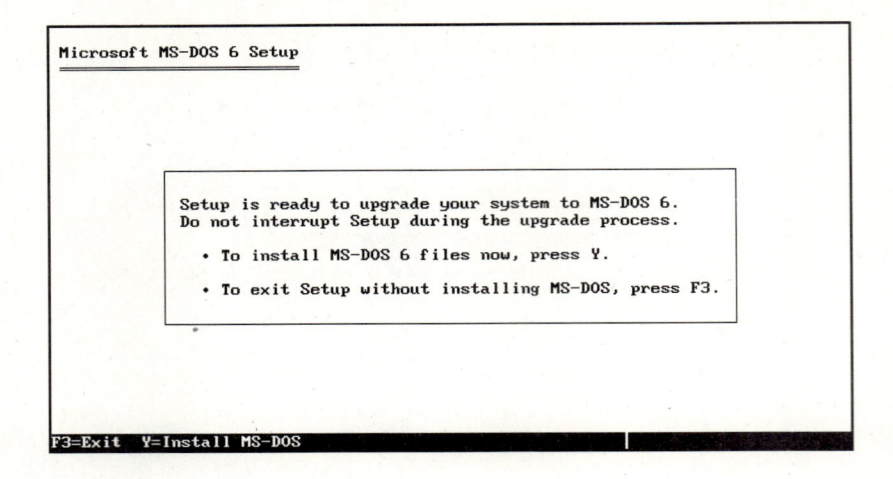

```
Microsoft MS-DOS 6 Setup



     ┌─────────────────────────────────────────────────────────┐
     │ Setup is ready to upgrade your system to MS-DOS 6.      │
     │ Do not interrupt Setup during the upgrade process.      │
     │                                                         │
     │   • To install MS-DOS 6 files now, press Y.             │
     │                                                         │
     │   • To exit Setup without installing MS-DOS, press F3.  │
     │                                                         │
     └─────────────────────────────────────────────────────────┘





F3=Exit   Y=Install MS-DOS
```

Figure 3.9
Inserting the Uninstall disk.

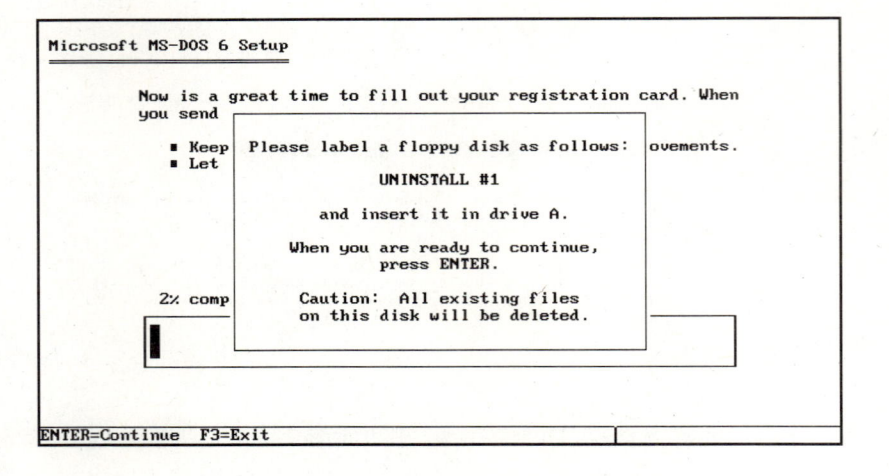

```
Microsoft MS-DOS 6 Setup

    Now is a great time to fill out your registration card. When
    you send
         ┌──────────────────────────────────────────────┐
       • Keep│ Please label a floppy disk as follows:   │ovements.
       • Let │                                          │
             │              UNINSTALL #1                │
             │                                          │
             │        and insert it in drive A.         │
             │                                          │
             │      When you are ready to continue,     │
             │              press ENTER.                │
        2% comp                                         │
             │      Caution:  All existing files        │
    ┌────────│       on this disk will be deleted.      │─────┐
    │        └──────────────────────────────────────────┘     │
    └─────────────────────────────────────────────────────────┘

ENTER=Continue   F3=Exit
```

After you insert it and press Enter, DOS copies UNINSTALL onto the disk (UNINSTAL.EXE). Next, DOS creates a variety of files that tell it the exact state of your system before you began installation, including your old CONFIG.SYS, AUTOEXEC.BAT, boot records, file allocation table, and DoubleSpaced drives.

Your Uninstall disk also contains the files required for an emergency boot in case DOS 6.2 really messes up your system, which is highly unlikely.

Finally, DOS moves your existing DOS files into a new directory, OLD_DOS.1.

> **NOTE** *Uninstall disks won't work if your boot drive has been compressed by a third-party disk compression program. They will, however, work with DoubleSpace.*

Once complete, SETUP proceeds to copy files, prompting you to change disks along the way. SETUP also revises your CONFIG.SYS and AUTOEXEC.BAT files if it finds this necessary—for example, if you have changed your DOS directory and need a new PATH statement.

You can see the progress report at the bottom of figure 3.10:

```
Microsoft MS-DOS 6 Setup

        Now is a great time to fill out your registration card. When
        you send it in, Microsoft will:

            ■ Keep you up to date on the latest product improvements.
            ■ Let you know about related Microsoft products.




    2% complete
   ┌──────────────────────────────────────────────────────────────┐
   │|                                                             │
   └──────────────────────────────────────────────────────────────┘
```

Figure 3.10
Installation progress.

> **NOTE** *If you really hate to swap disks, you can first copy all the disks into a single hard disk subdirectory—we'll call it TEMP6—and install from there. Remember that Disk 1 contains the hidden system files IO.SYS and MSDOS.SYS, which must be unhidden using the ATTRIB command before you copy them, as follows:*
>
>   ATTRIB -S -H A:\IO.SYS
>
>   ATTRIB -S -H A:\MSDOS.SYS
>
> *Then...*
>
>   COPY A:*.* C:\TEMP6

continues

Repeat for each disk; then run Setup from the new directory...

    `C:\TEMP6\SETUP`

After DOS 6.2 installation is complete, you should delete the TEMP6 directory.

After SETUP is complete, you are prompted with the messages in figures 3.11 and 3.12. When you remove the disks and press Enter, the system automatically reboots and attempts to load the new version of DOS.

Figure 3.11
Remove disks.

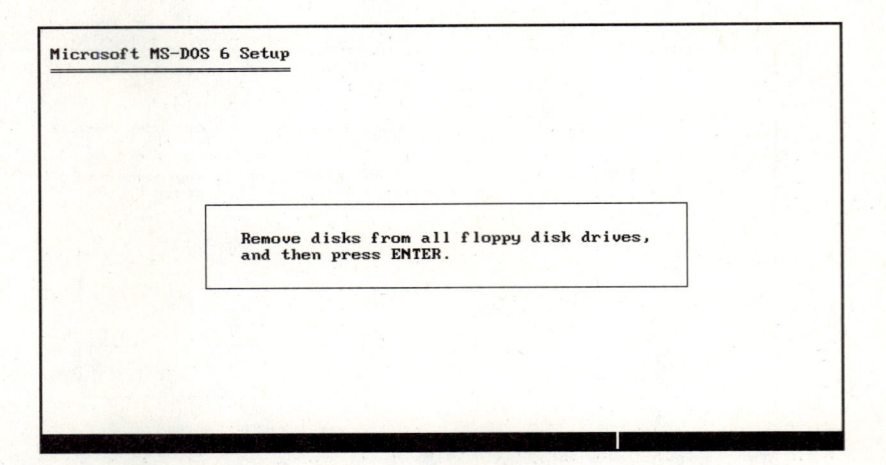

```
Microsoft MS-DOS 6 Setup


              ┌─────────────────────────────────────────┐
              │ Remove disks from all floppy disk drives,│
              │ and then press ENTER.                    │
              └─────────────────────────────────────────┘
```

Old Programs, New Versions

In general, newer is better. MS-DOS 6.2 comes with a variety of programs, including MOUSE.COM and SMARTDRV.EXE, which replace previous versions accompanying DOS and/or Windows. Use the newer versions.

Figure 3.12
Setup complete.

```
Microsoft MS-DOS 6 Setup

         ┌──────── MS-DOS Setup Complete ────────┐
         │ MS-DOS 6 is now installed on your computer. │
         │                                              │
         │ Your original AUTOEXEC.BAT and CONFIG.SYS files, │
         │ if any, were saved on the UNINSTALL disk(s) as   │
         │ AUTOEXEC.DAT and CONFIG.DAT.                     │
         │                                              │
         │  • To restart your computer with MS-DOS 6,   │
         │    press ENTER.                              │
         └──────────────────────────────────────────────┘

ENTER=Continue
```

What Kinds of Things Can Go Wrong?

Well, more than a few. Here are some of them.

- ✔ **SETUP stops running.** You might have a conflict with a memory-resident program. If you can unload it, do so. If not, edit your AUTOEXEC.BAT program to prevent it from loading; then reboot.

    You might have to use UNINSTALL to restore your system to its original condition, and then try again. Running UNINSTALL is described shortly.

    > **NOTE** *SETUP is also incompatible with password-protection programs.*

    If SETUP still won't work, try SETUP /I to disable hardware detection, and provide the correct hardware information yourself.

- ✔ **You can't read the SETUP screens.** Try to run SETUP in monochrome (SETUP /M). If that fails, use SETUP /I and change the default monitor to the type of monitor you're using.

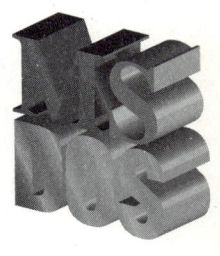

✔ **SETUP complains about DOS files in the root directory.** Before running SETUP, copy these files into a subdirectory on C drive, preferably C:\DOS; then delete the copies in your root directory. Do not move CONFIG.SYS, AUTOEXEC.BAT, or COMMAND.COM.

✔ **SETUP keeps asking for the Uninstall disk.** Use an unformatted disk. If that doesn't work, you'll need to override the parameters DOS expects to find on this particular floppy disk:

1. Quit SETUP and format the disk as a system disk (FORMAT A:/S).

2. Next, create a one-line CONFIG.SYS file on this floppy.

   If you are upgrading from DOS 5, you can do this by loading the DOS Editor by typing...

   `EDIT A:\CONFIG.SYS`

   Using any version of DOS, you can type the line from the command line by first typing...

   `COPY CON A :\CONFIG.SYS`

   Then type...

   `DRIVPARM /D:0 /F:X`

3. Replace X with one of the following numbers, depending on your floppy disk's density:

360K or less:	0
720K:	2
1.2M	1
1.44M	7
2.88M	9

4. If you are using COPY CON, press F6 to end the line and return to your command prompt. If you are using EDIT, choose Save from the File menu to save the file on A drive.

5. Now run SETUP again.

✔ **SETUP refuses to install to a third-party compressed drive.** DOS needs space on the uncompressed host drive in order to install properly. You might try a minimal install on the host drive, or reduce the size of your compressed drive.

✔ **SETUP won't install to some compressed drives at all.** In that case, you must back up your data, delete your compressed drive, restore data (or as much as will fit) to the uncompressed drive, and then run SETUP.

✔ **You suspect that one of the SETUP disks is defective.** Perhaps you are receiving error messages such as `Unrecoverable read error`, `Data error reading...`, or `General failure reading....` A quick test to verify whether or not the disk is defective is to enter **COPY *.* NUL**.

This command reads all the files on the disk and copies them to the NUL device (that is, to nowhere). If you receive another error message, the disk is probably defective. You may be able to repair the damage with a utility such as Norton Disk Doctor (NDD.EXE). If not, call Microsoft Consumer Sales at (800) 426-9400 for a replacement.

✔ **SETUP displays the `UNRECOVERABLE ERROR - ERROR READING FILE SETUP.INI` error message.** This message occurs if you are using an Original Equipment Manufacturer (OEM) version of DOS that does not match your computer (IBM PC-DOS on a ZENITH computer, for example). To cure the problem, reinstall the OEM DOS that came with the computer, and then run Setup again.

✔ **SETUP displays the `Boot sector write error!` message.** The culprit here is the 1993 AMI BIOS chip set, which automatically checks the boot sector for viruses and displays the following message when any program attempts to write to the boot sector:

```
Boot sector write error!
Possible virus!
Do you want to continue  Y/N?
```

To deal with this problem, go to the advanced CMOS setup, and turn off the virus-detection feature. After installing DOS 6.2, you can then re-enable the virus-detection feature.

- ✔ **You receive a critical disk error at the end of SETUP.** This error occurs when the SETUP program has trouble writing to the drive's Master Boot Record (MBR). This problem can be caused if the drive uses a driver that needs to be updated, if your system is using a virus-protection program that does not allow modification of the master boot record, or if there is a problem with the drive's MBR.

    At the very end of the process, SETUP copies the system files (including CONFIG.SYS and AUTOEXEC.BAT), and also rewrites the MBR. If there is any incompatibility, or if anything is out of sync when it attempts to write the MBR, a critical disk error occurs. It does a hardware-compatibility check at the beginning of setup, but it doesn't "write" any code or do anything as intensive as writing the MBR.

    To solve this problem, back up your data (please!), issue the DOS 5 command **FDISK /MBR** to rewrite the MBR, and then run SETUP again. If this does not work, you can try installing DOS 6.2 manually. See Chapter 19 for details about the MBR.

- ✔ **You see the following message:**

    ```
    Hard disk is not readable or Critical disk error.
    ```

    This message most commonly occurs when the ASPI4DOS.SYS device driver is in CONFIG.SYS. Remark out this line (as well as any expanded memory manager that may be present, such as EMM386.EXE or Qemm, install DOS 6.2, and then restore the line(s) in CONFIG.SYS.

- ✔ **SETUP cannot find AUTOEXEC.BAT if you are using 4DOS as your command interpreter and your AUTOEXEC.BAT file is not in the root directory.** Move your AUTOEXEC.BAT file to the root directory before running SETUP. If you have DOS 6.2, edit the AUTOEXEC.BAT file created by SETUP in the root directory, and add the information from your old AUTOEXEC.BAT file.

- ✔ **You receive A `CVF is damaged` message when you boot.** As section 7.17 of the README.TXT file indicates, the most common cause of this message is cross-linked files on the compressed drive. DoubleSpace detects a cross-linked file if two files or directories are recorded in the DoubleSpace file-allocation table as using the same disk space. After you finish the outlined procedure, do the following:

1. Run SETUP with the /F option on a floppy disk in the A drive from the original MS-DOS 6.2 disks so that you have an MS-DOS startup disk with MS-DOS 6.2 files on it (such as CHKDSK, DBLSPACE, and so on).

2. Boot from the new floppy disk, run CHKDSK on the drive from the floppy disk, and correct any errors that it finds.

3. Reboot the machine, and try to change the size of the compressed drive from within DblSpace. Resizing the drive even the slightest amount rewrites the file structure on that compressed drive, and it should solve the problem.

4. After changing the size of the double-space drive, run the DOS DEFRAG utility on the drive.

✔ **SETUP creates a second Tools menu in Norton Desktop for Windows.** If you are a Norton Desktop for Windows user, you soon discover that DOS 6.2 SETUP adds a menu item called Tools, which contains three options: Backup, Anti-virus, and DoubleSpace Info. NDW, however, already provides a Tools menu item for other options. How can you get rid of the DOS 6.2 Tools menu, in case you do not need these DOS 6.2 utilities?

One way to remove the offending Tools menu is by changing a line in DOS 6's WINFILE.INI file. Place a semicolon (;) to the left of the MS-DOS Tools line, as follows:

```
MS-DOS Tools Extensions=C:\DOS\MSTOOLS.DLL
```

It now reads as follows:

```
;MS-DOS Tools Extentions=C:\DOS\MSTOOLS.DLL
```

To replace the menu, remove the semicolon at the front of the line.

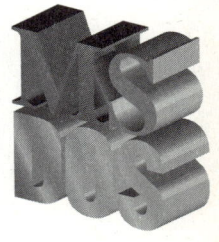

The other way to remove the extra Tools menu is to set MaxWinFileExtensions equal to zero (`MaxWinFileExtensions=0`) in your NDW.INI file, which disables all of the add-ins inherited from File Manager.

✔ **SETUP displays the message `Current drive must be set to A`.** This message appears if you attempt to install the DOS 6.2 Upgrade from a drive other than A. This message occurs when one or more of the following things are true:

1. Your CMOS settings are incorrectly set and do not include your floppy disk drive.

2. You are using a high-capacity optical drive with removable disks (called a *floptical drive*), and the device driver for it is incompatible with SETUP.

3. You are using an external floppy disk drive, and the device driver for it is incompatible with SETUP.

4. You are using a 2.88M floppy disk-controller, which uses an extended BIOS chip set that is incompatible with SETUP.

To complete the MS-DOS 6.2 upgrade , do the following: reboot, create a temporary directory on your hard drive, copy all the files from the distribution diskettes to this directory, and run SETUP from there.

The advantages of this procedure are that no disk changes are required, and an Uninstall disk is also created. The disadvantage is that it requires about 9M of free disk space.

✔ **Halfway through SETUP, the computer stops recognizing the floppy drive and keeps prompting you for the same disk.** The problem may be a TSR program. Remark out (REM) TSRs from AUTOEXEC.BAT and CONFIG.SYS, and try SETUP again.

You can also complete SETUP by following the same procedure as in the situation in which your floppy disk controller is incompatible with the Setup program.

The capability to detect that a disk is changed is called *change line support*. If the problem continues, you may need to set a jumper on the floppy controller or upgrade the system's BIOS. Before working with the hardware, however, try patching the BIOS with a DRIVPARM statement in the CONFIG.SYS. For example, use the following for a 1.2M drive (/f:1) that can detect the change line (/c) that is set up as drive A:

    DRIVPARM=/d:0 /f:1 /c

✔ **If you are running Stacker or SuperStore, SETUP may delete your AUTOEXEC.BAT and CONFIG.SYS from the host and compressed drives if you use the /S switch with Setup.** This is a wierd one. If this situation arises, the disk-compression software does not load when you reboot, and your compressed data is, therefore, not available. Also as a result, the `Error reading file` message is displayed twice during the SETUP procedure, and you are left with only AUTOEXEC.NEW and CONFIG.NEW in the root directory of the boot drive.

What is the cure? You can either rename your AUTOEXEC.NEW and CONFIG.NEW files to their correct names, or do the following:

1. Reboot Setup Disk 1 in drive A. When the `Starting MS-DOS...` message appears, press F5.

2. Replace Setup Disk 1 with Setup Disk 3, and enter **UNDELETE C:** at the prompt.

3. Press **Y** to undelete your CONFIG.SYS and AUTOEXEC.BAT files, and then reboot again.

4. Press **Y** when Stacker displays the following message:
   `Would you like Stacker to update the file(s)?`

✔ **During SETUP, you receive the** `Error updating version table in MSDOS.SYS` **error message.** This happens because SETUP cannot read the SETVER.EXE file in your DOS directory. Correct the error by renaming the current SETVER.EXE file by entering **REN C:\DOS\SETVER.EXE C:\DOS\SETVER.OLD**, and then running SETUP again.

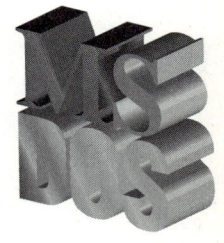

✔ **SETUP does not update your SHELL= line in CONFIG.SYS.** If you are using a third-party command interpreter (such as Norton's NDOS, for example), SETUP does not update the SHELL= command. This may cause problems with MemMaker, the multiple-configuration menus, and the startup function keys (F5 and F8). For best results, either use COMMAND.COM or contact the third-party shell manufacturer for an updated version that supports DOS 6.2.

> *SETUP adds the following SHELL= statement to CONFIG.SYS, if it doesn't already exist:*
>
> ```
> SHELL=C:\DOS\COMMAND.COM C:\DOS /P
> ```
>
> *Also, if your SHELL statement includes the /E switch, SETUP leaves it there.*

✔ **If you are using the PC-KWIK disk cache, SETUP may not detect and disable it.** PC-KWIK's 4.21 installation program adds this line to your AUTOEXEC.BAT file:

```
@CALL C:\PCKWIK\SUPERON
```

The @ symbol is the problem. Because SETUP stumbles over this symbol, it doesn't see the rest of the line and remark it out before it adds DOS 6.2's disk-cache command (SMARTDRV.EXE). You should never run two disk-cache programs simultaneously—either remark out (with REM), or delete one of them.

✔ **After upgrading to DOS 6.2, you discover that your CD-ROM drive no longer operates.** If SETUP finds Microsoft's CD-ROM extension MSCDEX in your AUTOEXEC.BAT file, MSCDEX is updated with version 2.22, which may be incompatible with your CD-ROM drive's device driver.

To solve the problem, replace the new version of MSCDEX with the old one, and be sure that the CONFIG.SYS file has the DEVICE=C:\DOS\SETVER.EXE command. This problem can also occur if you load MSCDEX into an upper memory block (UMB); if this occurs, try loading it into conventional memory.

> **NOTE:** Be sure to check README.TXT for other SETUP subjects.

Installing DOS 6.2 Manually

If you want to place your DOS system files on another hard disk (not C drive), or if SETUP does not run on your computer, as just discussed, you may have to install DOS manually.

Let's walk you through this in detail. First, here's an overview:

Install the basic MS-DOS 6.2 files onto floppy disks. Then copy the new DOS 6.2 system files onto your hard disk. Next, move all your current DOS files from their current subdirectory to a new subdirectory called OLD_DOS.1. Then copy all the DOS 6.2 files into the empty sub-directory where you want to place them. Next, edit CONFIG.SYS and AUTOEXEC.BAT to make sure they can still find your device drivers, programs, and DOS utilities. Finally, reboot into DOS 6.2.

Now, in detail, this is how it's done:

1. Place the first MS-DOS 6.2 disk into drive A.
2. Type the following:

    A:SETUP/F

3. Press Enter to proceed with SETUP.
4. Confirm or change the drive and video options presented by SETUP. (You won't be given an opportunity to install Backup, Undelete, or Anti-Virus, or to create an Uninstall disk.)
5. Press Enter to confirm the installation.
6. When requested, place a new disk in the drive.

You now have a bootable floppy disk containing only the most important MS-DOS files—how many depends on the capacity of the disk.

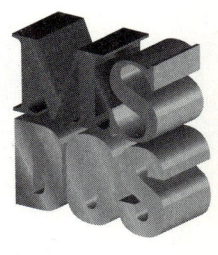

Chapter 3: Installing DOS 6.2

7. Next, copy the new DOS 6.2 system files from this disk to the root directory of the hard drive you want to boot from, using the SYS command. For example, to place system files on drive D, enter...

   `A:\SYS A:\D:`

> **NOTE**: *In DOS 6.2 this command copies not only COMMAND.COM, MSDOS.SYS, and IO.SYS, but also DBLSPACE.BIN, the file that recognizes DoubleSpace compressed drives.*

8. Now create a new directory to which you will copy your old DOS files. If you were using SETUP, it would be named OLD_DOS.1, so for consistency, you might as well do the same.

9. Copy all your current DOS files into that subdirectory. Assuming they are currently in C:\DOS, type...

   `COPY C:\DOS\*.* C:\OLD_DOS.1`

10. Now delete all the old DOS files by entering...

    `DEL C:\DOS\*.*`

11. Now copy all the files from your new DOS boot floppy into the empty C:\DOS subdirectory. Assuming your boot floppy is in drive A, type...

    `COPY A:\*.* C:\DOS`

You now have a bootable C drive which contains only the most important DOS files. The rest are still compressed and contained on your other MS-DOS 6.2 installation disks.

12. Reinsert MS-DOS Disk 1, SETUP.

13. Type **SETUP /Q**. This loads the SETUP program variant which decompresses the basic DOS utilities and places them where you choose.

14. When asked where to install the files, place them in the same subdirectory where you have placed the other DOS files, that is, C:\DOS.

15. Press Y to proceed with SETUP, and then change disks as requested.

You now have MS-DOS 6.2 almost completely installed. Still absent, however, are any of the new DOS utilities: Backup, Undelete, and Anti-Virus.

16. If you wish to install any of these, run SETUP/E.

    SETUP/E corresponds to figures 3.5 and 3.6; you select DOS, Windows, or both versions of each utility, then locate the DOS or Windows subdirectories you want to use, and press Y to confirm installation.

17. Edit your AUTOEXEC.BAT and CONFIG.SYS files to make sure that your DOS files and device drivers are where DOS expects them to be. For example, if you have moved a device driver from C:\DOS to C:\DRIVERS, make the accompanying change in CONFIG.SYS.

18. Empty all floppy disk drives and reboot.

Using EXPAND To Decompress Individual DOS 6.2 Files

Long after installation, the time may come when you need to retrieve a file from one of your MS-DOS 6.2 disks. Perhaps one day you'll receive a friendly DOS message along the lines of...

```
KUMQUAT.EXE is corrupt or missing
```

You didn't know you had a KUMQUAT file. Where is it? How do you get it? The table that follows this discussion tells you. It lists every file that comes with MS-DOS.

In a few cases the files you need will be uncompressed. No problem; you can simply copy them to your DOS directory, by typing...

```
COPY A:\KUMQUAT.EXE C:\DOS
```

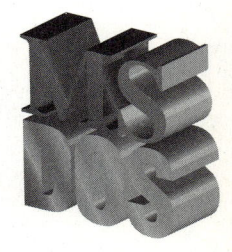

Chapter 3: *Installing DOS 6.2*

More likely, however, the file you need will have been compressed by Microsoft to reduce the number of disks required by DOS. These compressed files replace the last letter of their extension with an underline, as in:

```
MOVE.EX_
```

You'll need to decompress files like these with the EXPAND.EXE utility, as previously described. EXPAND.EXE is installed in your DOS subdirectory and also appears on MS-DOS 6.2 Disk 1—uncompressed, of course—of the 720K, 1.2M, and 1.49M sets; and on Disk 3 of the 360K set.

> **NOTE** *The compression formats used in DOS installation are not the same as those in DoubleSpace or other disk compression programs. EXPAND is the only tool that can uncompress these files.*

EXPAND's syntax is as follows:

```
EXPAND path\sourcefile path\destinationfile
```

In other words, if you want to expand the FILE MEM.EX_, located on drive B, and place it in the subdirectory C:\DOS, type...

EXPAND A:\MEM.EX_ C:\DOS\MEM.EXE

Notice that you must use the full file name of the file as it should appear in the destination directory.

You can also simply type **EXPAND** and have DOS prompt you for the information it needs, as in the following dialog:

```
EXPAND

Type the location and name of the
compressed file you want to expand.
(Example: A:\EGA.SY_)

Compressed file: A:\SMARTDRV.EX_

Type the location and/or name you
want to give the expanded file.
```

Using EXPAND To Decompress Individual DOS 6.2 Files 151

```
(Example: C:\DOS\EGA.SYS)

Expanded file: C:\DOS\SMARTDRV.EXE

a:\smartdrv.ex_ -> c:\dos\smartdrv.exe
1 file expanded
```

Unfortunately, EXPAND doesn't permit wild cards.

Rather than having to rummage through several DOS disks to find the file you're looking for, use our handy table. It lists all files shipped with DOS 6.2. It also lists Supplemental Files that do not ship with MS-DOS 6.2 but are available from Microsoft. These are marked with an S.

Most of these files were part of MS-DOS 5 but have now been dropped from the product. In some cases, SETUP may leave them in your C:\DOS directory so you can keep using them. Otherwise you can copy them in yourself, from your OLD_DOS.1 directory—or expand them from your original DOS 5 disks, using the DOS 5 version of EXPAND.EXE.

A number and letter following S indicate the disk in which the files appeared in the MS-DOS 5.0 720K upgrade package, and whether or not it was compressed there.

NOTE: The EXPAND utility, which is included with Microsoft Windows 3.1 or Windows for Workgroups 3.1, does not correctly expand DOS 6.2 files. It does correctly expand compressed Windows 3.1 and Windows for Workgroups 3.1 files, however.

File Name	Disk	Compressed/Uncompressed?
_SETUP.EXE	1	Uncompressed
4201.CPI	S(3C)	Uncompressed
4208.CPI	S(3C)	Uncompressed
5202.CPI	S(3C)	Uncompressed
8514.VID	1	Compressed
ANSI.SYS	1	Compressed

Chapter 3: *Installing DOS 6.2*

File Name	Disk	Compressed/Uncompressed?
APPEND.EXE	2	Compressed
ASSIGN.COM	S(3C)	Uncompressed
ATTRIB.EXE	1	Uncompressed
AUTOEXEC.BAT	1	Uncompressed
AV.GRP	3	Compressed
BACKUP.EXE	S(3C)	Uncompressed
BK.GRP	3	Compressed
BKAV.GRP	3	Compressed
BKUD.GRP	3	Compressed
BKUPAV.GRP	3	Compressed
BUSETUP.EXE	1	Uncompressed
CGA.GRB	1	Compressed
CGA.INI	1	Compressed
CGA.VID	1	Compressed
CHKDSK.EXE	1	Uncompressed
CHKSTATE.SYS	3	Compressed
CHOICE.COM	1	Uncompressed
COMMAND.COM	1	Uncompressed
COMP.EXE	S(3C)	Uncompressed
CONFIG.SYS	1	Uncompressed
COUNTRY.SYS	1	Uncompressed
CV.COM	S(3U)	Uncompressed
DBLSPACE.BIN	1	Uncompressed
DBLSPACE.EXE	4	Compressed
DBLSPACE.HLP	4	Compressed
DBLSPACE.INF	4	Compressed

Using EXPAND To Decompress Individual DOS 6.2 Files

File Name	Disk	Compressed/Uncompressed?
DBLSPACE.SYS	4	Uncompressed
DEBUG.EXE	1	Uncompressed
DEFRAG.EXE	2	Compressed
DEFRAG.HLP	2	Compressed
DELOLDOS.EXE	2	Compressed
DELTREE.EXE	4	Compressed
DISKCOMP.COM	2	Compressed
DISKCOPY.COM	2	Compressed
DISPLAY.SYS	2	Compressed
DMDRVR.BIN	2	Compressed
DOSHELP.EXE	2	Compressed
DOSHELP.HLP	2	Compressed
DOSKEY.COM	2	Compressed
DOSSETUP.INI	1	Uncompressed
DOSSHELL.COM	1	Compressed
DOSSHELL.HLP	4	Compressed
DOSSWAP.EXE	1	Compressed
DRIVER.SYS	2	Compressed
EDIT.COM	1	Uncompressed
EDIT.HLP	2	Compressed
EDLIN.EXE	S	Uncompressed
EGA.CPI	1(1C)	Compressed
EGA.GRB	1	Compressed
EGA.INI	1	Compressed
EGA.SYS	1	Compressed
EGA.VID	1	Compressed

File Name	Disk	Compressed/Uncompressed?
EGAMONO.GRB	1	Compressed
EMM386.EXE	4	Compressed
EXE2BIN.EXE	S(3C)	Uncompressed
EXPAND.EXE	1	Uncompressed
FASTOPEN.EXE	2	Compressed
FC.EXE	2	Compressed
FDISK.EXE	1	Uncompressed
FIND.EXE	2	Compressed
FORMAT.COM	1	Uncompressed
GORILLA.BAS	S(3C)	Uncompressed
GRAFTABL.COM	S(3C)	Uncompressed
GRAPHICS.COM	2	Compressed
GRAPHICS.PRO	2	Compressed
HELP.COM	2	Uncompressed
HELP.HLP	2	Compressed
HERC.GRB	1	Compressed
HERC.VID	1	Compressed
HIMEM.SYS	1	Compressed
INTERLNK.EXE	4	Compressed
INTERSVR.EXE	4	Compressed
IO.SYS	1	Uncompressed
JOIN.EXE	S(3C)	Uncompressed
KEYB.COM	1	Uncompressed
KEYBOARD.SYS	1	Uncompressed
LABEL.EXE	2	Compressed
LCD.CPI	S(SU)	Uncompressed

Using EXPAND To Decompress Individual DOS 6.2 Files

File Name	Disk	Compressed/Uncompressed?
LOADFIX.COM	2	Compressed
MEM.EXE	1	Compressed
MEMMAKER.EXE	4	Uncompressed
MEMMAKER.HLP	3	Compressed
MEMMAKER.INF	3	Compressed
MIRROR.COM	S(1C)	Uncompressed
MODE.COM	2	Compressed
MONEY.BAS	S(3C)	Uncompressed
MONO.GRB	1	Compressed
MONO.INI	1	Compressed
MORE.COM	1	Uncompressed
MOUSE.COM	2	Compressed
MOVE.EXE	4	Compressed
MSAV.EXE	4	Uncompressed
MSAV.HLP	4	Compressed
MSAVHELP.OVL	4	Compressed
MSAVIRUS.LST	4	Compressed
MSBACKDB.OVL	3	Uncompressed
MSBACKDR.OVL	3	Uncompressed
MSBACKFB.OVL	3	Uncompressed
MSBACKFR.OVL	3	Uncompressed
MSBACKUP.EXE	3	Compressed
MSBACKUP.HLP	3	Compressed
MSBACKUP.OVL	3	Uncompressed
MSBCONFG.HLP	3	Compressed
MSBCONFG.OVL	3	Uncompressed

File Name	Disk	Compressed/Uncompressed?
MSCDEX.EXE	4	Uncompressed
MSD.EXE	1	Uncompressed
MSDOS.SYS	1	Uncompressed
MSHERC.COM	S(2C)	Uncompressed
MSTOOLS.DLL	4	Compressed
MWAV.EXE	4	Compressed
MWAV.HLP	4	Compressed
MWAVABSI.DLL	4	Compressed
MWAVDLG.DLL	4	Compressed
MWAVDOSL.DLL	4	Compressed
MWAVDRVL.DLL	4	Compressed
MWAVMGR.DLL	4	Compressed
MWAVSCAN.DLL	4	Compressed
MWAVSOS.DLL	4	Compressed
MWAVTSR.EXE	4	Compressed
MWBACKF.DLL	3	Compressed
MWBACKR.DLL	3	Compressed
MWBACKUP.EXE	3	Compressed
MWBACKUP.HLP	3	Compressed
MWGRAFIC.DLL	3	Compressed
MWUNDEL.EXE	3	Compressed
MWUNDEL.HLP	3	Compressed
NIBBLES.BAS	S(3C)	Uncompressed
NLSFUNC.EXE	1	Uncompressed
PACKING.LST	1	Uncompressed
POWER.EXE	2	Compressed

Using EXPAND To Decompress Individual DOS 6.2 Files

File Name	Disk	Compressed/Uncompressed?
PRINT.EXE	2	Compressed
PRINTER.SYS	S(3C)	Uncompressed
PRINTFIX.COM	S	Uncompressed
QBASIC.EXE	1	Uncompressed
QBASIC.HLP	2	Compressed
RAMDRIVE.SYS	4	Compressed
README.TXT	2	Uncompressed
REMLINE.BAS	S(3C)	Uncompressed
REPLACE.EXE	2	Compressed
RESTORE.EXE	1	Compressed
SETUP.BAT	1	Uncompressed
SETUP.MSG	1	Uncompressed
SETVER.EXE	2	Compressed
SHARE.EXE	2	Compressed
SIZER.EXE	4	Compressed
SMARTDRV.EXE	4	Compressed
SMARTMON.EXE	2	Compressed
SMARTMON.HLP	2	Compressed
SORT.EXE	2	Compressed
SSTOR.SYS	2	Compressed
SUBST.EXE	2	Compressed
SYS.COM	1	Uncompressed
TREE.COM	2	Compressed
UD.GRP	3	Compressed
UDAV.GRP	3	Compressed
UNDELETE.EXE	3	Uncompressed

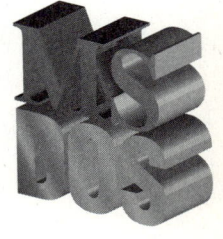

File Name	Disk	Compressed/Uncompressed?
UNFORMAT.COM	1	Uncompressed
UNINSTAL.EXE	1	Uncompressed
VFINTD.386	3	Compressed
VGA.GRB	1	Compressed
VGA.VID	1	Compressed
VGAMONO.GRB	1	Compressed
VSAFE.COM	4	Compressed
WINA20.386	2	Compressed
WNTOOLS.GRP	3	Compressed
XBIOS.OVL	2	Compressed
XCOPY.EXE	1	Uncompressed

BUSETUP.EXE (Bootable Upgrade Setup) is the executable file on Setup Disk 1 that runs only when your machine already has an operating system. If you boot the computer from drive A, which you can do with the upgrade, an AUTOEXEC.BAT file on Setup Disk 1 executes BUSETUP.EXE.

Running UNINSTALL

In the event that DOS does not install properly, you may be prompted to run UNINSTALL. You might also run UNINSTALL in the unlikely event that a program you depend on cannot be made to run under DOS 6.2, even after you tell SETVER to lie to the program about which DOS you're using.

> *Problems are especially unlikely if the program ran smoothly under DOS 5, since there have been few major changes at the core of DOS 6.2 that would create incompatibilities.*

UNINSTALL won't work if you've:

- ✔ Installed onto a disk compressed by a third-party compression program.
- ✔ Deleted files from the subdirectory OLD_DOS.1. (You might be tempted to do this to save space. Fine, but first test your new version of DOS thoroughly.)
- ✔ Moved or renamed OLD_DOS.1 files.
- ✔ Deleted files from the UNINSTALL disk.

Other than that, though...piece of cake.

1. Place the UNINSTALL disk in your floppy drive (we'll assume drive A), and type...

    A:UNINSTAL

2. A screen appears, similar to the Setup screen. Assuming your old DOS files are present, it will say something like:

    ```
    YOUR HARD DISK INSTALLATION WAS SUCCESSFULLY COM-
    PLETED. Continuing with the UNINSTALL program
    removes MS-DOS version 6 system files from the hard
    disk and replaces them with the original DOS. To
    restore the original DOS, press R. To exit, remove
    the UNINSTALL disk from drive A and press E.
    ```

> *If your old DOS isn't present, you'll be told:*
>
>   Nothing to Install
>   Please Remove the Uninstall disk and
>   then press ENTER to restart your system.
>
> *If you don't want to reboot, you can just press F3 twice to escape the Uninstall program, and go back to what you were doing (or trying to do).*

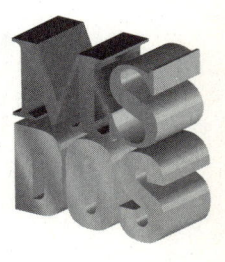

3. Press **R** to continue.

   If you used low-density 360K disks, you are asked to swap disks partway through. Otherwise, Uninstall proceeds to completion.

4. Remove all disks and press any key; the system reboots using your old version of DOS.

> *Although UNINSTALL removes all the files it installed, it does not remove the DEFAULT.* and DOSBACK.* files or the INI files created by optional utilities.*

What If UNINSTALL Fails?

First, whether you want to return to DOS 5 or a version of DOS prior to DOS 5, you need to remove DoubleSpace by carrying out the procedure discussed in the "Deleting Your DoubleSpaced Driver" section of Chapter 5.

Second, if you've already removed DoubleSpace but still can't use UNINSTALL, there may still be some hidden DoubleSpace files in the root directory of drive C. Remove these files by entering the following line at the prompt:

    DELTREE /Y C:DBLSPACE.*

Then remove the following from CONFIG.SYS:

    DEVICEHIGH=C:\DOS\DBLSPACE.SYS /MOVE

Now reboot with the Uninstall disk in drive A.

Third, if you are still unable to remove DoubleSpace, and you want to return to DOS 5 (not a previous version of DOS), follow these steps:

1. To tell the Setup program that your computer uses DOS 5, and enter the following line at the prompt:

       SETVER SETUP.EXE 5.00

2. To remove the read-only attribute from the COMMAND.COM file, enter the following at the prompt:.

    ```
    ATTRIB C:\COMMAND.COM -R
    ```

    Reboot and run the DOS 5 Setup program.

Alternately, if you want to return to a version of DOS prior to DOS 5, follow these steps:

1. If you repartitioned your hard disk drive, you may be unable to see your partitions when you start your computer with a previous version of DOS (versions prior to 4, for example, can only recognize partitions that are 32M or less).

    If you use a pre-DOS 5 partition, back up your data, repartition your drive(s), reformat the drives (use the /S switch on drive C), and then restore your data.

2. If you did not repartition your drive(s) under DOS 6.2, reboot with a system disk from your previous version of DOS in drive A.

3. If you can see all your partitions, enter **SYS C:** at the prompt to transfer the DOS system files to drive C. If SYS fails because it cannot find room on drive C, you can either use the Norton Utilities to make drive C bootable, or you can use FORMAT /S on drive C. Of course, the latter erases all the data on drive C, so be sure to back up first.

4. Copy all the DOS program files from the original DOS disks to the directory that contains your DOS files (usually C:\DOS).

The preceding procedure usually places a copy of COMMAND.COM not only in the root directory, but in the DOS directory as well. Delete the copy in the DOS directory to save a little disk space.

Preparing a Bootable Floppy

Assuming your installation was successful, the next step is to create a bootable floppy that you can use in the event you have problems later.

In the past, formatting a blank floppy with the switch /S (that is, FORMAT A: /S) was all you needed to do in order to make one.

Sometimes it's still that simple. But not always.

If your computer boots from a SCSI drive or a compressed drive, your system must run a specific driver before your hard disk will even be recognized. That driver won't run if you don't run CONFIG.SYS when you boot.

Yet you've got to have an emergency boot floppy, so here goes...

1. Insert Disk 1 of MS-DOS 6.2 into your floppy drive, and type...

    `SETUP /F`

    This tells DOS you want to perform a minimal installation of DOS on a floppy disk.

2. Follow the Setup instructions that begin on the screen shown in figure 3.5. You will have to swap disks several times before you're done.

3. When complete, remove the floppy and reboot. (If you leave the floppy in, DOS will boot from it, and you might not have access to your SCSI or compressed drives.)

    On a 1.44 or 1.2M disk, you now have these basic DOS files. (A 720K disk will not contain the files marked in boldface.)

    IO.SYS (System, Hidden, Read-Only)

    MSDOS.SYS (System, Hidden, Read-Only)

    DBLSPACE.BIN (System, Hidden, Read-Only)

    COMMAND.COM (Read-Only)

    ATTRIB.EXE

    DEBUG.EXE

    EXPAND.EXE

Using EXPAND To Decompress Individual DOS 6.2 Files

FDISK.EXE

FORMAT.COM

RESTORE.EXE

SYS.COM

CHKDSK.EXE

EDIT.COM

QBASIC.EXE

XCOPY.EXE

MSD.EXE

MSAV.EXE

DBLSPACE.EXE

On a 1.44M disk, you'll still have roughly 300K free.

4. Copy the drivers you need, that is, ASPI4DOS.SYS (SCSI drives) or DBLSPACE.SYS (DblSpace-d compressed drives), to the floppy disk.

5. Copy your AUTOEXEC.BAT and CONFIG.SYS files to the floppy by typing...

    ```
    COPY C:\CONFIG.SYS A:
    COPY C:\AUTOEXEC.BAT A:
    ```

6. Edit CONFIG.SYS to make it search the boot floppy for these drivers. For example, the statement...

    ```
    DEVICE=C:\DOS\DBLSPACE.SYS
    ```

    would become...

    ```
    DEVICE=A:\DBLSPACE.SYS
    ```

> **NOTE**
>
> *The SETUP program won't perform a minimal installation of DOS 6.2 to a 360K floppy disk. Here's the workaround:*
>
> *continues*

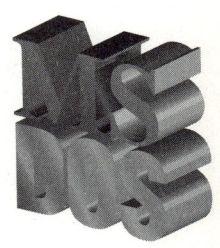

After installing DOS 6.2, insert a formatted disk in drive A and type...

SYS A:

This copies the DOS command interpreter, COMMAND.COM, to the floppy. It also copies the hidden/system files, IO.SYS and MSDOS.SYS, and DBLSPACE.BIN, which enables the floppy to recognize drives using MS-DOS 6.2 DoubleSpace disk compression.

Together, these four files take up about 182K, leaving you 178K for other files. Go to Step 4, and continue.

NOTE

You're probably not using DoubleSpace yet—you just got it. But you might be using Stacker. Here, the files you'll need to copy are STACKER.COM and (generally) SSWAP.COM, and the lines in your CONFIG.SYS file that you'll need to edit will look something like these:

```
device=c:\stacker\stacker.com c:\stacvol.dsk
device=c:\stacker\sswap.com c:\stacvol.dsk /sync
```

Your statements might be a little different.

7. If you still have room, you can add a few more DOS commands to your boot disk. Some suggestions are:

    DELTREE.EXE (31K)

    FC.EXE (18K)

    FIND.EXE (7K)

    MEM.EXE (32K)

    MOVE.EXE (50K)

    RESTORE.EXE (38K)

    UNDELETE.EXE (26K)

    UNFORMAT.COM (12K)

> *If you ignore this advice, you can boot DOS (with no access to special devices) from Disk 1 of the DOS 6.2 disks—or from the UNINSTALL disk that DOS creates when you install DOS 6.2. To use UNINSTALL, boot with the UNINSTALL disk and exit to DOS from within the UNINSTALL program.*

What's Different Now?

Now that you've finished installing DOS 6.2, what's changed?

Well, you may be missing some commands you're used to. Several long-time DOS commands have been consigned to the Supplemental Disk:

- ✔ **ASSIGN.** You are encouraged to use SUBST instead.
- ✔ **BACKUP.** Though, at the last minute, Microsoft returned RESTORE to the DOS 6.2 package—mercifully for people with megabytes of files backed up with the old version of BACKUP.
- ✔ **COMP.** FC is the successor command.
- ✔ **EDLIN.** Would you believe this primitive line editor is finally gone? (Replaced by the EDIT command first included in DOS 5.)
- ✔ **EXE2BIN.** Converted executable files to binary.
- ✔ **GRAFTABL.** Allowed CGA monitors to display extended ASCII characters.
- ✔ **JOIN.** Connected the directory structures of two different drives; often caused more trouble than it prevented.
- ✔ **MIRROR.** Worked with the DOS 5 UNDELETE command to track file deletes; both have been replaced by a new Undelete. You may want to keep the old MIRROR around, though: the MIRROR /PARTN command saves a copy of your partition table to disk, where UNFORMAT can use it to re-create a damaged disk partition. The new Undelete programs can't do that.

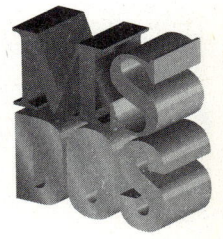

✔ **PRINTER.SYS.** Enabled you to change code pages on a few models of IBM ProPrinters.

If you are upgrading from a previous version of DOS, Setup will leave many of these preceding commands (such as EDLIN and MIRROR) behind in your DOS directory, even as it moves your other old DOS files into OLD_DOS.1.

As mentioned in earlier chapters, however, you have some very significant new features that more than make up for the loss: Defrag, Anti-Virus, DoubleSpace disk compression, a relatively sophisticated backup program, client networking capabilities, memory management, multiple configurations through CONFIG.SYS, DELTREE to eliminate subdirectories and their contents, MOVE to move files in one step, and the list goes on.

If you're running Windows, you have a new Program Group, Microsoft Tools, which contains your new Windows Backup, Anti-Virus, and Undelete programs.

> *And if you happen to be running Norton Desktop for Windows, two menus have been added to its Toolbar: Tools and Information.*

You also have SMARTDrive Monitor, which enables you to track and control the behavior of SMARTDrive—which itself has been updated to recognize compressed drives.

What Setup Does to Windows

DOS 6's optional Windows programs (Microsoft Backup for Windows, Microsoft Anti-Virus for Windows, and Microsoft Undelete for Windows) make a few subtle changes of their own to PROGMAN.INI, SYSTEM.INI, and WINFILE.INI. Windows INI (initialization) files are special startup files that contain crucial information that Windows needs to run. Without INI files, nothing would work.

> *There are times when you want to manually edit certain INI files. Although you can use any ASCII text editor to edit WIN.INI and SYSTEM.INI, the easiest way to edit is to use SYSEDIT, which is a handy editor that resides in the WINDOWS\SYSTEM directory.*
>
> *This utility is not installed in a Windows program group, but you can easily do it yourself. SYSEDIT also enables you to easily edit two other important files: AUTOEXEC.BAT and CONFIG.SYS.*

Changes to PROGMAN.INI

Windows Program Manager uses PROGMAN.INI to store settings, information about groups, and any restrictions you want to place on Program Manager to restrict its use by users. In the [Groups] section, the following line is added if you install the optional Windows-based programs:

    Group<n>=C:\WIN31\WNTOOLS.GRP

WINTOOLS.GRP is the name of the new program group mentioned earlier that contains the Anti-Virus, Backup, and Undelete utilities. The <n> represents the group's number (10, for example).

Changes to SYSTEM.INI

Windows Setup stores hardware information and settings that were specified during Windows installation. If you install the optional Windows utilities, the following line is added to the [386Enh] section of SYSTEM.INI:

    DEVICE=C:\DOS\VFINTD.386

Windows Backup needs this device driver for floppy drive control.

If you are running Windows 3, (you might want to consider upgrading to 3.1), the following list includes all possible changes to the Windows 3.0 SYSTEM.INI file:

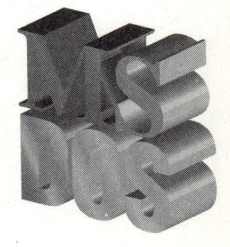

```
SYSTEMROMBREAKPOINT=FALSE

EMMEXCLUDE=A000-FFFF

EMMINCLUDE=<any w= regions>

DUALDISPLAY=TRUE if b000-b7ff is included

NOEMMDRIVER=TRUE if NOEMS is specified
```

Finally, if you use a permanent swap file, DoubleSpace changes the PermSwapDOSDrive setting in the SYSTEM.INI file if you compress a drive that contains your Windows installation.

Changes to WINFILE.INI

Windows File Manager stores its settings in WINFILE.INI. If you install the optional Windows utilities, the following line is added to the [Settings] section of WINFILE.INI:

```
UNDELETE.DLL=C:\DOS\MSTOOLS.DLL
```

Additionally, the following line is added to the [AddOns] section:

```
MS-DOS Tools Extensions=C:\DOS\MSTOOLS.DLL
```

These additions reflect the addition of an add-on utitlity that provides a new command or function, which can be installed onto its menus through a Dynamic Link Library (DLL).

Other Changes

Setup also creates two other files as a result of installing the Windows utilities. Microsoft Backup for Windows creates the WMBACKUP.INI file in the Windows directory. This file stores settings (such as Setup File Name and Path), which Windows Backup uses each time you load it.

Similarly, Microsoft Anti-Virus for Windows creates the MWAV.INI file in the DOS 6.2 directory. This file stores settings default settings such as detection, alarm, and verification options, among others.

What Setup Does to Windows 169

> *Setup may be unable to correctly modify the SYSTEM.INI and PROGMAN.INI files because of TSR programs that are incompatible with Setup. To solve this problem, restore your unmodified backup INI files, disable your TSRs, and then run Setup with the /E parameter.*

Another concern is that you may have trouble reinstalling Windows from your Windows and DOS 5 Upgrade disks after you upgrade to DOS 6.2. In this case, Windows Setup looks for DOS 5 (or earlier versions), and may attempt to reinstall it if it doesn't find it.

To get around this annoyance, install only Windows from either the Windows and MS-DOS 5 for IBM PS/2 package or the Windows and MS-DOS 5.0 Upgrade package by placing Disk 3 in drive A or drive B, logging on to that drive, and entering either **WINSETUP** (normal setup) or **WINSETUP /A** (administrative setup).

Finally, after installing DOS 6.2, you may receive the following error message when you start Microsoft Windows 3.0 or 3.1 in 386-enhanced mode:

```
EMM386: Unable to start enhanced mode Windows due to
   invalid path specification for EMM386
```

The probable cause of this error is an incompatibility between Windows, EMM386.EXE version 4.45, and Central Points VSafe (which comes with DOS 6.2, of course). To solve the problem, change the filespec for VSafe in your AUTOEXEC.BAT file to point to the DOS directory (C:\DOS\VSAFE.COM, for example), and then reboot.

Another cause of this problem is the absence of VSafe (if you do not choose to use it) and the presence of CHKLIST.CPS only. Delete the CHKLIST.CPS file, and add the /Y switch and the path to EMM386.EXE to the EMM386.EXE command in your CONFIG.SYS file.

Documenting Your Installation

Now that your installation has been successfully completed, you may want to write down the current state of your system. Or more precisely, you may want Microsoft System Diagnostics to do it for you...

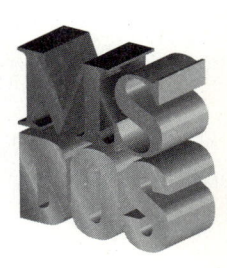

Load MSD. Then print the following sections which may have changed since you ran MSD before installation:

OS Version	Should obviously be DOS 6.2, but you will also get some useful information about your DOS environment
AUTOEXEC.BAT	
CONFIG.SYS	
SYSTEM.INI	If you're running Windows
WIN.INI	If you're running Windows
MSMAIL.INI	If you're running WorkGroup Connection
PROTOCOL.INI	If you're on a network
DBLSPACE.INI	If you're running DoubleSpace
MEMMAKER.STS	If you have extended memory and have run MemMaker

You may want to keep these materials with one set of original MS-DOS disks and UNINSTALL disks. (Keep the originals and backups separate.)

AUTHOR'S NOTE

If all else fails (you've read the Users Manual, the README.TXT file, and especially this book), give the Microsoft Support Services staff a call at one of the following numbers:

1. *For the first 90 days after you acquire the upgrade, call (206) 646-5104, Monday through Friday, 6 a.m. to 6 p.m. Pacific time, excluding holidays. Before you call, note the number on the inside back cover of the Microsoft MS-DOS 6.2 User's Guide. A Product Support Services staff member will ask you for this number before answering your questions.*

2. *If you acquired the MS-DOS 6.2 Upgrade more than 90 days ago, you can call Microsoft OnCall for MS-DOS, at (900) 896-9000, Monday through Friday, 6 a.m. to 6 p.m. Pacific*

time, excluding holidays. The rate for Microsoft OnCall for MS-DOS is $2 per minute. If your line is blocked from accessing 900 numbers, you can reach OnCall for MS-DOS by calling (206) 646-5108. The rate for this number is $25 per call. Please have your VISA, MasterCard, or American Express card ready when you call.

Be sure to have your DOS manuals and disks handy, and you should be at your computer when you call. If you have an OEM release of MS-DOS and cannot obtain support through your OEM or authorized dealer, you can purchase support from Microsoft by calling OnCall for MS-DOS.

Support can also be obtained on CompuServe or by purchasing an annual fee-based program. For additional information about Microsoft support options, call Microsoft Inside Sales at (800) 227-4679, Monday through Friday, 6:30 a.m. to 5:50 p.m., Pacific time, excluding holidays.

And by the way, feel free to register complaints (nicely) and make suggestions concerning DOS and its documentation.

Summary

For most users, installing MS-DOS 6.2 is relatively straightforward. But there can be some surprises in store, and even if your personality tends towards the anarchic, this is an important enough task that you should try to be systematic and organized about it, so that safeguards like UNINSTALL can work for you if you ever need them.

The payoff at the other end is sizable: a DOS that does more than any MS-DOS ever has—maybe more than you ever thought an operating system called MS-DOS ever could, including:

- ✔ Shoehorning more data into the same hard drive (DoubleSpace)
- ✔ Shoehorning more programs into the same 640K, though the 640K limit itself ain't going anywhere (MemMaker)
- ✔ Backing up your data in a reasonably civilized and comprehensible way

✔ Providing a modicum of anti-viral protection (Microsoft Anti-Virus)

✔ Offering workable defragmentation (Microsoft Defrag)

✔ Multiple configurations in CONFIG.SYS—and the ability to walk through a CONFIG.SYS file, one line at a time

✔ Friendlier and more sophisticated UNDELETE utilities

Sure, it's window dressing, not an overhaul of DOS' aging heart and soul. But it works. And you gotta admit the price is right.

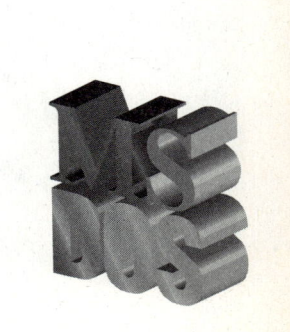

MS-DOS

CHAPTER 4

Taking a Tour of Your Hard Drive

by Bill Camarda

*I*t's easy to forget that DOS stands for *disk operating system*; managing disks has always been one of DOS's core functions. But in order to use MS-DOS 6 to make the most efficient use of your hard drive, you have to understand how the hard drive works—and how it interacts with DOS.

This chapter covers the following topics:

- ✔ The hard drive's physical components
- ✔ Its logical structure
- ✔ Features that affect performance
- ✔ Today's options for purchasing a new drive
- ✔ How DOS superimposes its own structure on the hard drive

You'll learn about the similarities and differences between hard disks and floppies—and how to avoid some common floppy pitfalls.

When you've finished this chapter, you'll have the information you need not only to get the most out of using your current drives with MS-DOS 6, but also to understand your alternatives when you buy a new drive. *See Chapter 17 for a more in-depth discussion of drives.*

> **NOTE** *You'll sometimes hear the term fixed disks, a phrase that dates back to IBM's decision to permanently seal the disks themselves inside air-filtered compartments, along with the rest of the drive system. IBM has more recently taken to calling its PS/2 hard disks "hard files," although its files are no harder than anyone else's. Occasionally, you may also hear the term "Winchester" disk, possibly because an early IBM model was named the 30-30, like the famous Winchester rifle.*

The Physical Hard Disk Drive

If you could look inside your hard disk drive (don't!), the first thing you'd see would be one or more *platters*—flat, coated plates, generally made of aluminum but occasionally of glass (see fig. 4.1). Until recently, nearly all platters were finely coated with iron oxide—rust!—though two new processes, *thin film* and *plated media*, are used in many of today's high-capacity drives.

Early XT hard drives contained two platters. Some of today's high-capacity drives contain as many as 11; a few half-height drives contain only one. In drives with more than one platter, each platter is mounted several millimeters above the next. While the drive is working, all platters spin in parallel, usually at 60 rotations per second—at least *3,600 per minute.* Many newer drives run even faster; some now exceed 5,000 rotations per minute.

Next to the platters, you'd see the *actuator arm*—slightly resembling the arm on an old phonograph turntable. At the end of the arm, hovering one one-thousandth of an inch above each platter, are disk *read/write heads*. Where the arm reaches *between* platters, one read/write head reads the bottom of the platter above it, and another reads the top of the platter below it.

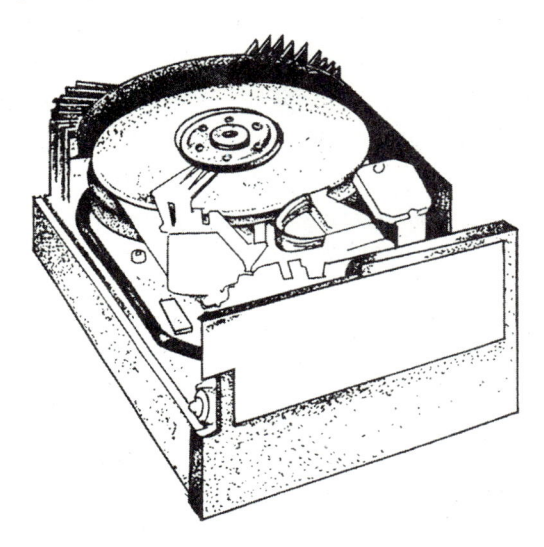

Figure 4.1
Inside a hard disk drive.

This is a good place to define the term *head crash*, that gut-wrenching moment in which one or more of these heads actually makes contact with a platter while the disk is spinning at full speed—potentially tearing off the magnetic surface and scattering it across the disk. In the past, a head crash almost invariably killed the hard drive and destroyed its contents. Newer hard drives are sometimes a bit more resilient, but head crashes are still to be greatly feared.

You see the incredibly fine tolerances involved here—pretty remarkable for a couple-hundred bucks of motors and rusty plates. If you take care of your hard drive, it's somewhat more likely to take care of you.

✔ Don't jostle your computer. And if you have a floor-standing tower system, don't place it where it'll be kicked, or smacked by someone's vacuum cleaner.

- ✔ If possible, don't smoke nearby. Sorry, but smoke particles are many times larger than the space between the head and platter. And they can get inside, despite your hard drive's high-quality, air-filtration system.

- ✔ Do park your heads. Not only when you move the computer, but whenever you shut down the system. Parking the heads allows them to come gently to rest on an area of the disk specifically designed for this purpose—a landing zone. Most drives now park their heads automatically.

- ✔ Do back up your hard drive. You're always one-ten-thousandth of an inch away from potential disaster.

Drive heads are moved by a mechanism called the *head actuator*. Two kinds of head actuators are common: *band stepper* and *voice coil*. Band stepper actuators, the cheaper solution, tend to be found on older, smaller drives. They use stepper motors to move the heads one "step" at a time across the disk.

Unfortunately, they're susceptible to all kinds of problems. They wear out. They lose their alignment, requiring a reformat of the drive about once a year to ensure proper alignment of the heads to the platters. They expand and contract as the temperature changes.

Voice coils, found on newer and larger drives, are *much* more reliable. Voice coil drives also park themselves.

NOTE

Voice coil actuators use magnets similar to those used in audio speakers. The read/write heads are mounted on one end of the actuator arm. At the other end of the arm is a spring that holds the arm toward the center of the disk and an electromagnet. As power to the magnet increases, the magnet pulls the arm, thereby moving the heads toward the outside edge of the disk; decreasing power enables the spring to pull the arm back toward the center.

Depending on how much power is sent to the magnet, the heads move across the disk surface. Because this method is

far less mechanical than a stepper motor, it is extremely fast and reliable, and does not require constant realignment.

How Information Is Stored

Information is stored on hard (and floppy) disks electromagnetically—the same principle used by video and audio cassettes (but with two major differences).

First, video and audio cassettes (except DAT) store *analog* information, whereas the computer disk stores *digital* information. In a digital system, information on the computer disk is divided into bits that are read as either a *one* or a *zero*, depending on their magnetic charge, with no alternatives in between. In other words, there's no such thing as .025 or .06—you're either 1 or 0, on or off.

If a zero is read as a one, a program may not run successfully—or it may deliver someone a million dollars instead of a penny. This is why hard drive controllers contain sophisticated built-in, error-correction mechanisms that check mathematically to make sure all data is correct before it's forwarded to the microprocessor.

The analog videocassette, by contrast, records magnetism in a continuum of intensities that correspond to different types and levels of sound and color. Slight errors are pretty harmless—*human* computers automatically compensate for them.

> **NOTE** *At one time, many tape drives used traditional VHS tapes. But when users found that tapes that did a tolerable job of storing video often fell short when it came to digital information, they quickly learned to use top-of-the-line tapes.*

Second, in audio and videotape, the information moves sequentially past a stationary read/write head. On the hard (or floppy) disk, the disks spin in place—the heads move, and they all move in tandem. Moreover, they can move directly to the next piece of data that you need, wherever it is located.

When drive manufacturers and users look for ways to make hard disks work faster, they often start by improving the efficiency of these drive head movements.

The Structure of Your Hard Disk

A working hard disk contains a complex magnetic map that tells MS-DOS and the disk controller where and how information should be written, and where it can be found after it has been written. This map begins with *tracks* and *sectors*.

Tracks and Sectors

To understand tracks and sectors, start by looking at the top of one hard disk platter—one *surface*. The surface is first divided into several hundred (or more) concentric rings of magnetized particles, called *tracks*, as shown in figure 4.2. The outermost track is numbered Track 0; you then work your way into the innermost track. The number of tracks is dependent on the disk's size and on how densely it can pack data.

Figure 4.2

One hard disk surface divided into tracks.

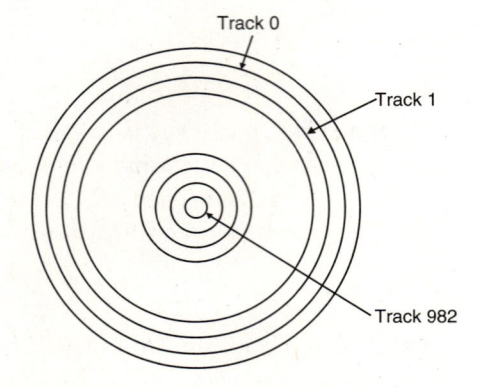

Each track normally contains more than 8K. But because allocating storage space in smaller amounts is more efficient, tracks are sliced into *sectors*.

Each sector contains 512 bytes of storage space, plus a 59-byte sector ID header that includes an address mark to indicate where the sector begins; head, cylinder, and sector numbers; and Cyclical Redundancy Check information designed to detect errors in the sector ID header. (These extra bytes help to explain why a formatted disk contains less storage space than an unformatted disk.) Sectors are shown in figure 4.3.

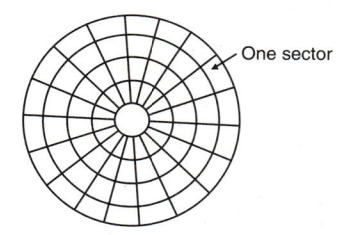

Figure 4.3

Sectors on a hard disk surface.

RLL: Squeezing in More Sectors

At one time, every hard drive track contained 17 sectors. Now, however, you can buy drives with 26, 35, 52 or more sectors per track. The difference is in the encoding technique used. To understand the alternatives, let's look briefly at encoding and what it means.

As you already know, each digital bit of data—each zero or one—corresponds to a positive or negative magnetic charge on a tiny location on the hard drive. When a drive head reads the digital bit "one," it sends a pulse; when it reads "zero," no pulse is sent. Unfortunately, the drive requires regular pulses to maintain its precise internal timing. Reading too many zeros in a row can make the drive's timing start to slip.

How do you provide enough extra pulses to maintain the drive's timing, without wasting too much storage space on bits that don't correspond to useful data?

For years, the standard answer was an encoding technique called *modified frequency modulation (MFM)*. Here's what happens in MFM:

- ✔ 1 is sent as no pulse, followed by a pulse.
- ✔ 0 is sent as a pulse, followed by no pulse.
- ✔ Exception: when a 1 precedes the 0, "no pulse" is sent twice.

With MFM, you can never run more than three zeroes in a row before sending a "one" pulse to the drive controller. This scheme is only moderately efficient, but very safe—a level of safety appropriate for the imprecise band-stepper drives with which MFM most commonly is used.

In the last few years, another encoding scheme, *run length limited (RLL)*, has become dominant, especially in higher-capacity drives. With RLL, up to seven "no pulse" zeroes may pass before a pulse appears. Moreover, the pulses are irregularly placed. The result is that a drive using RLL encoding can store 50 percent more data than the same drive using MFM.

To run RLL, you need a drive precise enough to hold the timing, even if it receives seven consecutive zeroes. Often, these drives also contain safer error correction algorithms. Although connecting an RLL controller to an old MFM band-stepper drive such as the Seagate ST238R is theoretically possible, you're asking for trouble. RLL is much more appropriate for today's newer voice coil, thin-film media drives.

Cylinders

Next, remember that the typical hard disk contains several platters, each of which has a top and bottom surface. And remember that the disk's drive heads move in tandem—able to read simultaneously information at the same track on each surface.

Let's say that your hard drive contains four platters, or eight surfaces. If you move the drive heads to Track 184, you can read all the data contained in every sector in Track 184 *on all eight surfaces*. This top-to-bottom set of bits, shown in figure 4.4, is called a *cylinder*. Note that cylinder numbering, like track numbering, begins with zero.

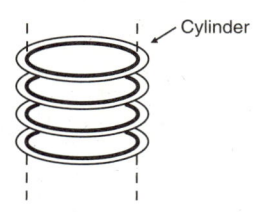

Figure 4.4
Hard disk cylinder.

Most of the time spent searching for information is spent moving the drive heads to the correct location. By making sure that related information is stored on the same cylinder, you make your drive faster and more efficient. This is what disk *defragmentation* accomplishes. *For more information about MS-DOS 6 disk defragmentation, see Chapter 5.*

Calculating Disk Storage Capacity

Now you can understand how a disk's capacity can be calculated. Let's use a recent RLL drive sold by IBM as an example. It has 580 cylinders, 6 surfaces, and 26 sectors per track. Here are the calculations:

26 sectors times 512 bytes per sector = 13,312 bytes

13,312 bytes times 580 cylinders = 7,720,960 bytes

7,720,960 bytes times 6 surfaces = 46,325,760 bytes

46,325,760 bytes divided by 1,048,576 bytes (the number of bytes in a megabyte) = 44.18M

Understanding Drive Performance

There's a lot more to drive performance than the number of milliseconds an advertisement claims it takes to access an average piece of data. In fact, two main factors—access time and data transfer rate—affect the raw speed of a hard drive when it leaves the factory.

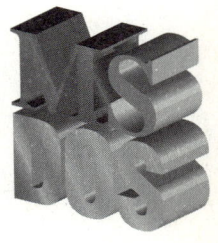

Access Time

Access time describes how long it takes the drive and controller to move the head to the correct cylinder (*seek time*), wait for the correct sector to spin underneath where it can be read (*rotational latency*), and then settle down so that the head can begin to read (*settling time*). Typically, seek time is measured based on a seek 1/3 the distance across the disk, and an average latency of 1/2 revolution.

Note that latency (but not seek time) is reduced when the disk spins faster.

Data Transfer Rates and Interleave Settings

The data transfer rate is highly dependent on how well the disk controller and drive can work together. In the ideal situation, the disk reads a sector of data, the controller checks it, sends it along to the microprocessor, and everyone's all set for the next sector by the time the disk spins to it—in 1/60th of a second or less.

A disk that is capable of working this way (and is formatted to do so) is said to have a *1:1 interleave*. Most of today's high-capacity drives offer 1:1 interleaving.

But it hasn't always been this way. And for many slower drive controllers and PCs, it still isn't.

Consider the problem faced by the engineers of these systems. By the time their controllers would process one sector, the disk would have spun past the next sector, and the controller would have to wait for the disk to spin around again. Nearly 1/60th of a second would be lost for every sector processed.

Instead of placing the disk sectors one after the other, the engineers decided to place the next sector exactly where the spinning disk would arrive at the time the controller was ready for it.

Although this solution was elegant, and certainly necessary, it reduced data transfer rates dramatically. In fact, the 6:1 interleaving in IBM XT hard disks lowered data transfer rates by 83 percent, because only one of every six sectors spinning past was actually being read. Figure 4.5 shows 3:1 interleaving.

Figure 4.5

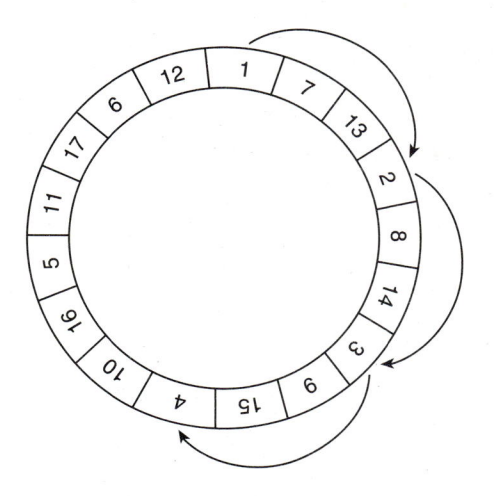

3:1 interleaving.

Changing Interleaving To Improve Efficiency

Users of early ATs, XTs and PCs with slower drives can reset interleaving themselves, often substantially improving efficiency—as long as they don't set interleaving so tight that the controller begins to miss sectors again. This is normally done in connection with a low-level format. You can use the programs shown in table 4.1.

Table 4.1
Programs for Changing Interleaving

Program	Publisher
Calibrate/ Disk Explorer, Norton Utilities	Symantec
Disk Technician Gold DOSUTILS	Prime Solutions OnTrack Computerb Systems
HTEST/HFORMAT Optune SpinRite II	Kolod Research Gazelle Gibson Research

An alternative is to purchase a faster controller, one designed specifically for 1:1 interleaving, as shown in figure 4.6. (You will still need to perform a low-level format to change 3:1 to 1:1.) These controllers, now widely available, work with most drives on 286, 386, and 486 systems.

Interleaving is gradually becoming less of an issue, for two reasons. First, 1:1 interleave drives and controllers are becoming much more common. Second, IDE drives (discussed shortly) are given optimal interleaving at the factory; users can't reset these factory settings.

Figure 4.6
1:1 interleaving.

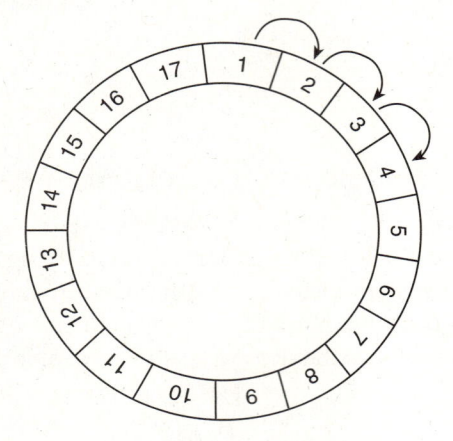

Understanding Drive Interfaces

In the computer industry, it seems as though practically every time technologies grow more powerful, you have to make more complicated choices to take advantage of that power.

Take, for instance, *hard disk interfaces*—the connections between the controller and the drive. You may encounter four different interfaces: ST-506, IDE, ESDI, and SCSI. There are also distinctions between controller interfaces for old XT computers and more recent AT and above computers.

ST-506 Interface

For years, nearly all hard drives followed the *ST-506* standard, first created by Seagate Technologies for its early 5M drives.

ST-506 (sometimes called ST-506/412) was relatively simple. It could handle five to seven million bits of information per second, which was more than enough for smaller drives and slow computers, but represented a bottleneck for larger drives. Usually associated with MFM drives, now ST-506 is commonly used with RLL drives as well.

Under ST-506, two cables connect the drive to the controller: a 20-pin cable for data and a 34-pin cable for control information. Data bits and timing information are intermixed in the data stream received by the controller, however. The controller has to separate them; if either element has an error, it must be sent again. To reduce the number of errors, engineers have kept the cables as short as possible.

Integrated Drive Electronics (IDE)

Recently, the low-end and mid-range drive marketplace has moved to integrated drive electronics (IDE). With IDE drives, the controller circuitry—the intelligence—is mounted directly on the drive. The drive is then either plugged directly into the motherboard, or into a simple "pass-through" board that sends the information into the motherboard.

> **NOTE** *Some refer to IDE as imbedded drive electronics because the drive controller is imbedded right in the drive. Others prefer IDE to stand for intelligent drive electronics because having the controller imbedded in the drive makes the drive an intelligent, self-contained device. Still others prefer integrated development environment because the controller and drive are integrated into one environment.*

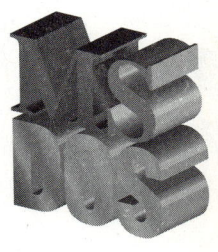

Hardcards, drives mounted directly on a PC expansion board, were the first to use IDE. Laptop hard drives were next, benefiting from IDE's highly integrated "controller-on-a-chip" technology. Nowadays, even desktop drives are likely to be IDE-based; most reasonably priced mid-range desktop drives—say 200M—are IDE drives.

Write-Ahead Caches

Some IDE drives improve performance through the use of a write-ahead cache. The drive anticipates that you will probably need the sectors that immediately follow those you have asked for and reads them into its own cache memory—originally 8K, but nowadays more likely to be 64K or 128K. Then, if and when you do ask for it, it's already there.

> **NOTE**
> *A write-ahead cache is a "hardware cache," into which the drive reads extra sectors, storing them there until you need them.*
>
> *See Chapter 6 for a discussion of SMARTDRV, DOS's built-in software cache—a cache designed to keep frequently used information in RAM so that you don't need to search your drive for it at all.*

Write-ahead caches sometimes confuse programs that test disks and do low-level formatting, but you can't low-level format an IDE drive anyway. They're low-level formatted at the factory, and that's it.

Although IDE manufacturers say the drives will never need a low-level format, this idea may take some getting used to if you're in the habit of performing an occasional low-level format to strengthen your track and sector markings.

Enhanced Small Device Interface (ESDI)

Not as common as they once were, you may still occasionally encounter ESDI drives. ESDI was a standard developed by Maxtor and other drive makers that responded to many of the concerns raised about ST-506.

ESDI drives supported data-transfer rates of 10 or 15 million bits per second (24 million in theory, but rarely in reality). With ESDI drives, you could have many more sectors per track—often 54 or 55. Like IDE, ESDI drives moved some of the intelligence from the controller to the hard drive itself, where the controller can work with more reliable raw data.

Still, ESDI drives are based closely on the old ST-506 standard, and rely on the computer's CPU for drive management. That's a limitation as you call upon your CPU to manage an increasingly heavy load—especially in network environments.

Small Computer Systems Interface (SCSI)

ESDI drives have lost popularity, partly because of the growing popularity of SCSI, the *small computer systems interface*. SCSI (pronounced "scuzzy") has been around for years, but DOS users shied away from it because of its complexity and lack of standardization. It's still complex, but the standards are converging, and if you're careful about purchasing compatible equipment, the advantages of SCSI may well outweigh the disadvantages.

The most enormous advantage is *expandability*. The Macintosh has long used SCSI as a way to hook up not just hard disks but other peripherals as well. Mac users are familiar with creating a SCSI chain in which a hard drive, scanner, CD-ROM, and other peripherals can all work from the same interface. SCSI on the PC offers a similar benefit.

A SCSI drive typically contains three components: the drive, the controller, and a host SCSI adapter. Normally, the drive and controller are *embedded*—they're hardwired together—so that, theoretically, you don't care whether they're communicating through ST-506, ESDI, or smoke signals.

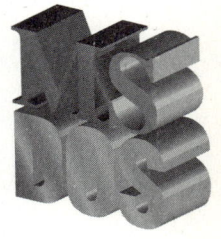

Nor does the specific architecture of your drive (sectors, clusters, drive heads, cylinders, and the like) matter to SCSI. SCSI sends data in blocks; it can send enormous amounts of data at once—up to 30Mbps, six times the rate of the old ST-506 interface.

All information moves from the controller to the system through the host SCSI adapter, which can establish its own bus structure to work alongside your PC's AT, EISA, or Micro Channel bus—offloading much of the work. This host SCSI adapter, in turn, can support seven additional devices, each of which, in turn, can be connected with eight other devices. If that's not enough, you can install four separate SCSI host adapters to the same PC.

Seven times eight times four equals 224. If you add to that your SCSI hard disk, you theoretically can use SCSI to connect 225 devices to your system. Will that hold you for a while?

SCSI Issues To Consider

In the long-term, SCSI may well dominate the market. However, nothing this powerful is ever easy at first, and so it is with SCSI.

First of all, there are *two* SCSI standards; of the two, SCSI-II is more well-defined.

Second, because some incompatibilities still exist between the two standards, be sure that all the SCSI hardware you buy has been tested and optimized together.

Third, you'll usually need a special software driver to connect a device to your SCSI host adapter. These software drivers are generally available for MS-DOS (but may not exist for OS/2, Windows NT, or UNIX).

Fourth, non-SCSI drives need a special *bridge controller* to connect with SCSI.

Controller Types XT and AT

Another way to identify hard disk controllers is by the methods they use to deliver data into the computer's memory. One method, called *direct memory access*, is most commonly used with IBM XT-class computers and drives—hence, drives that use this technology are sometimes called XT-type controllers.

AT-type controllers work differently: here, information is stored on a one-half kilobyte buffer. When the buffer fills, the controller signals the microprocessor that data is available to be read. This *interrupt-driven* method works faster than direct memory access, partly because 80286 (and higher) microprocessors are specifically designed to take advantage of it.

Disk Structures Imposed by MS-DOS 6.2

A hard disk is born unformatted, with no markings in place to tell the controller where to write information or to tell DOS where to find the information after it is written. The organization described earlier—tracks, sectors, and cylinders—is established during *low-level formatting*.

Low-level formatting prepares a hard disk for use by *any* operating system, including MS-DOS, OS/2, Windows NT, or UNIX, to name a few. This distinguishes it from the high-level formatting performed by MS-DOS. *For a detailed discussion of both high-level and low-level formatting, see Chapter 5.*

In this chapter, the focus is on the structure DOS formatting imposes upon a hard disk that has already been low-level formatted.

Absolute Sectors and DOS Sectors

If you've read the description of disk geometry, you know that you can precisely locate any sector if you know its cylinder, sector number, and drive head (surface). The *cylinder* tells you on which circular track the sector appears. If you know the *sector number*, you know which of the track's 17 (or 26, or 35...) sectors you're looking for. And if you know the *drive head*, you know which surface is being read.

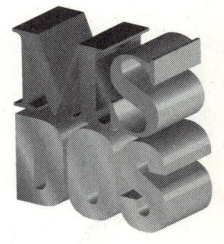

This three-dimensional positioning information is called the disk's absolute sector. DOS assigns a DOS sector number (sometimes called relative sector number) to each absolute sector. DOS sector #0, the first sector assigned to DOS, is set aside as the DOS boot record (described later).

If your disk is formatted entirely for DOS, DOS sector #1 corresponds to cylinder 0, head 1, sector 2. If your disk contains sectors assigned to other operating systems, DOS sector numbering starts with the first cylinder that contains DOS sectors.

In other words, if you have an RLL disk with 26 sectors per track, the first cylinder on head 1 starts with one sector that's "off-limits," and the remaining sectors are numbered 1 through 25. Counting continues on the next head, which contains 26 sectors, numbered 26–51. After all the sectors on every surface in the first cylinder have been counted, the process continues on the next cylinder, and so on, working inward toward the center of the disk.

> **NOTE:** *Cylinder 1, head 0 is set aside for the master boot record, which is described in detail later in this chapter.*

DOS Clusters

Each time you create a file, DOS allocates it a minimum number of adjacent 512-byte sectors. Most people call this grouping of sectors a *cluster*. But DOS—starting with MS-DOS 4—calls it an *allocation unit*. To see what size your allocation units are, just type **CHKDSK** at the command prompt, and then press Enter.

Generally, the larger the hard disk, the larger the cluster size. A 32M hard disk normally uses four-sector clusters, for example, whereas a one-gigabyte drive (1,024M) might use 32- or 64-sector clusters.

> **NOTE**
>
> *When DOS assigns a cluster to a file, that entire cluster becomes unavailable to other files, no matter how small the file may be. If you create a one-byte file on an 80M disk, using 4K clusters, for example, that file is assigned 4K of disk space.*
>
> *Yes, this wastes space; you can even figure out how much space it wastes. Figure that each file wastes 50 percent of its last cluster. Multiply:*
>
> *(0.50) x (the number of files) x (the cluster size)*
>
> *If you have 4,000 files (8K clusters) on a 130M drive, you could lose nearly 16M of storage to wasted clusters.*

Why so wasteful? The larger the cluster, the fewer clusters DOS has to manage—and the fewer clusters DOS must manage, the faster it can run. If you use 8K clusters, for example, DOS can read and write 16 sectors at a time, with one command.

Not only that, clusters help reduce file fragmentation. With 8K clusters, a 40K file can be split into only five locations, max. If every sector stood alone, DOS might have to look in 80 different places! Finally, DOS can use the extra cluster space to accommodate a file as it expands, without having to assign it another cluster.

> **NOTE**
>
> *Different OEM versions of MS-DOS haven't always made the same decisions about cluster size. One well-known example, COMPAQ DOS 3.31, created clusters twice the size of those created by MS-DOS 3.3—making for a noticeably faster system that wasted more disk space. MS-DOS 4 and later versions have adopted COMPAQ's scheme.*

The DOS Boot Record

DOS, like many *people*, isn't good for much when it first wakes up. How does it know where to start and what to do? It looks in the *DOS boot record (DBR)*.

The DBR contains these two elements:

- **The BIOS parameter block**, a detailed description of the contents of your hard disk, including size, cluster size, number of sectors, number of file allocation tables, and more.

- **The bootstrap program**, which reads the BIOS parameter block (BPB) to make sure it's accurate and then, if it is, begins reading the disk. First, it looks for the DOS root directory. Then it looks for the two hidden system files, MSDOS.SYS and IO.SYS. If they are present—if the disk is "bootable"—the bootstrap program loads them. After that, COMMAND.COM loads, and MS-DOS begins to look presentable.

Because someone's got to look for MSDOS.SYS and IO.SYS, there's a DBR on every disk, even unbootable ones. DBRs on floppies serve double duty; they also help DOS determine when you've switched disks, particularly when the new disk is a different density than the disk it replaced.

The Master Boot Record

Now DOS knows how to wake up in the morning, but who kicked DOS in the chops to start the process? And why *DOS*, rather than some other operating system you might have on your disk? You may think *you* put these events in motion, but from DOS's standpoint, the master boot record did.

The master boot record appears in the very *first* sector on the *first* head of the *first* cylinder of your disk, before the DOS boot record or anything else. (And if you're wondering who wakes *it* up, the answer is *firmware*—a brief BIOS routine burned into read-only memory.)

The master boot record contains the disk's *partitioning* information: where each partition begins and ends, which operating system controls each partition, and which one is to be awakened when you flip the switch in the morning.

So what's a partition?

DOS (and Other) Partitions

Partitions are independent data storage areas established on the same hard disk. You use the MS-DOS utility program FDISK to create them. *For more information about partitioning the hard disk, see Chapter 5.*

The simplest partitioning scheme is to define an entire disk as one volume, usually C, which contains DOS and is entirely accessible to DOS. An example of such a master boot record follows:

```
Drive # 80h has 1000 cylinders, 15 heads, 17 sectors (from BIOS).

The following table is from drive 80h, cylinder 0, head 0, sector 1:

            Total_size       Start_partition    End_partition
  Type      Bytes Sectors    Cyl Head Sector    Cyl Head Sector    Rel#
  --------  -------------    ---------------    ---------------    ----
  HUGE Boot 125M  254983      0    1    1       999   14    17      17
```

You can display your master boot record by going to the command prompt and typing this line:

UNFORMAT /PARTN /L

If you want a hard copy of your MBR, add the /P *switch to the end of the line.*

Until MS-DOS 4.0, you couldn't create partitions larger than 32M. This was entirely traceable to *two bytes* in the master boot record. Two bytes are equivalent to 16 bits of information, which was all that DOS set aside to define partition size. That meant that you could have any size partition from 1 to 65,536 sectors (216=64K). Because each sector is half a kilobyte, *voilà*: 32,768 kilobytes (32M).

MS-DOS 4, 5, and 6 dole out two more bytes for this information. Those extra two bytes make *some difference*: now partitions can be as large as two gigabytes.

> **NOTE** *Unfortunately, although your partitions can be two gigabytes, the PC's BIOS still limits your drive to 1,024 cylinders (512M). You can avoid this limitation by using a third-party program such as Disk Manager (OnTrack), Vfeature Deluxe (Golden Bow), or Speedstor (Storage Dimensions), but the nonstandard partitions they create can cause compatibility problems later.*

Just because you can create giant economy-size partitions, that doesn't necessarily mean you want to. Just for convenience, for example, you might want to split a 130M hard drive into two partitions, C and D.

You might keep all DOS programs on one partition and all Windows programs on a second (probably larger) partition, or place DOS and all your programs on one partition, and all your data on another. Or you might make a *functional* distinction: all word processing programs and files on one partition, all database programs and files on another.

> **NOTE** *Be aware that DOS limits you to 512 files in a single root directory. (Actually 509 new files—you've already used two hidden system files and one file for the volume label.) If you manage your disks properly, placing most files in subdirectories, you probably won't reach this limit. But on large disks, this limit could be yet another reason to partition.*

Primary and Extended Partitions

With any version of MS-DOS, you must create one partition that contains the DOS system files and is therefore bootable. This is called the *primary* partition. On typical systems with one or two floppies and a hard drive, it is almost always Drive C, especially now, because MS-DOS 6's setup program won't place DOS anywhere else.

You can also create an *extended partition*, which typically does not contain system files. The extended partition can be divided into as many as 23 *logical drives*, drive D through drive Z. (The limit is simply the letters of the alphabet; A and B are assigned to floppies.)

Don't get crazy, though. You can make your drive just as unwieldy by creating too many logical drives as you can by keeping everything in one drive. Also, be sure to leave enough drive names (letters) for RAM drives and the industry's growing list of Christmas toys: additional hard drives, CD-ROMs, WORM drives, external EHD (extra high density) floppies, et cetera, et cetera, and so forth.

Carefully think through your partitioning ahead of time. After you've created a partition, changing it destroys all the data contained on the partition.

Each partition behaves largely as though it were an entirely separate drive. You can format drive E, for example, without touching drive D or drive F on the same extended partition. (In fact, you *must* format each partition separately.)

Similarly, you can use MS-DOS 6's new DBLSPACE compression program to compress one drive without touching others on the same partition. That makes particular sense if you're running Windows, which uses a swap file that (for performance reasons) should be kept on an uncompressed drive.

At times, however, you will remember that they *are* all the same physical drive. If your drive's master boot record is corrupted, for example, *all* the partitions on your drive are obliterated equally.

Non-DOS Partitions

These days, with OS/2, UNIX, and Windows NT all competing for your desktop, you may want to partition so that you can run two or more different operating systems from the same disk.

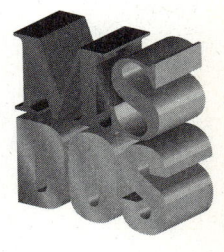

Chapter 4: *Taking a Tour of Your Hard Drive*

When you create multiple partitions that all run under DOS, all partitions are accessible to DOS, which runs on the primary partition and is set to active—is "bootable." It's different if you create multiple partitions for different operating systems, however.

You have to use FDISK in advance to select one partition as *active*. This is the partition the master boot record chooses to run when you turn on the computer (rendering inactive the partition containing your DOS system files). You can see how the master boot record "calls" individual partitions in figure 4.7.

Figure 4.7
Master boot record's relationship to individual partitions.

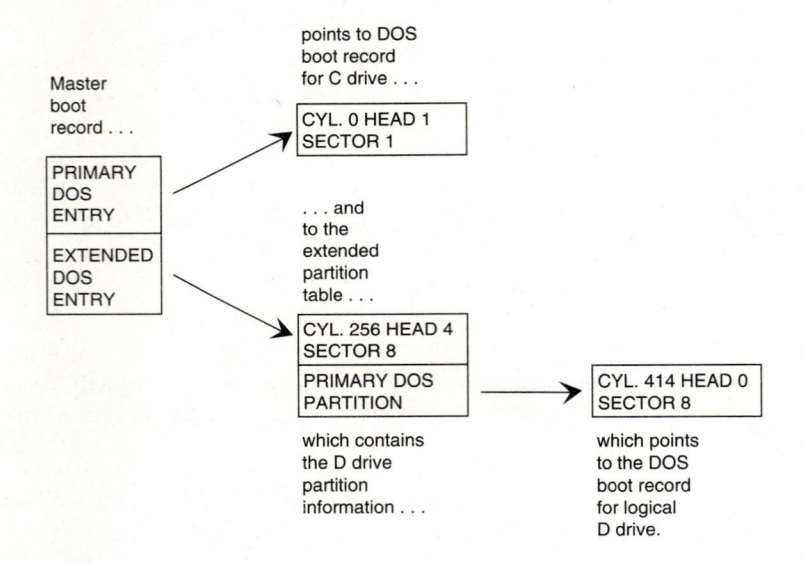

Master boot record . . .

PRIMARY DOS ENTRY → points to DOS boot record for C drive . . . CYL. 0 HEAD 1 SECTOR 1

EXTENDED DOS ENTRY → . . . and to the extended partition table . . . CYL. 256 HEAD 4 SECTOR 8 PRIMARY DOS PARTITION

which contains the D drive partition information . . . → CYL. 414 HEAD 0 SECTOR 8 which points to the DOS boot record for logical D drive.

This not only means that you can't run DOS during that session, but *also* that you can't access any data on the partition containing your DOS system files.

Incidentally, the way disk utility programs create oversized disk partitions is to establish them as non-DOS partitions. Those partitions seem to vanish if their associated device drivers aren't present. Some people may have seen non-DOS partitions on drives they think are running DOS. Worse, they may have been unable to

install older versions of DOS on these partitions. That's because certain third-party products evaded the old 32M limit by creating non-DOS partitions.

Figure 4.8 shows a disk partitioned to run two operating systems.

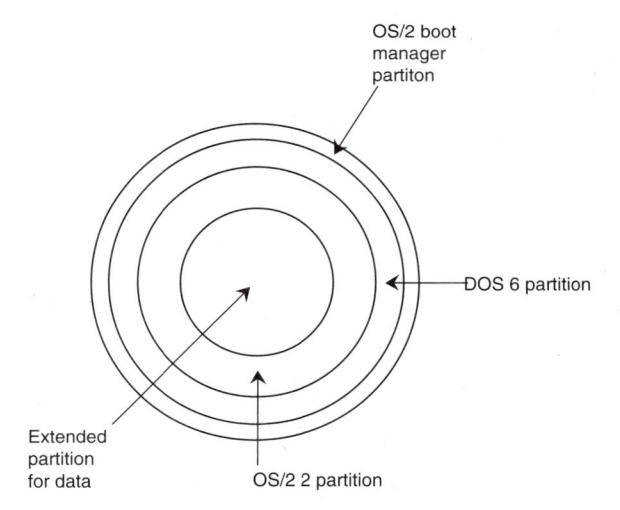

Figure 4.8
Disk partitioned to run two operating systems.

Different operating systems respond differently to this problem. Under OS/2 2.0, for example, you can use OS/2's version of FDISK to create a primary partition for each of two operating systems, and to create an extended partition containing programs and data that (theoretically) are accessible to both. A third primary partition, called Boot Manager, lets you choose which you want to run, as shown in figure 4.9.

I said *theoretically*, because simply giving both operating systems access to the data in a partition doesn't necessarily mean they can do anything useful with it. This partitioning only makes sense if both operating systems can run the same programs and recognize the file system. This isn't much of a problem with OS/2 2.0, which can run most DOS and Windows programs and, optionally, can use the same file system as DOS. But when you start talking about UNIX or other operating systems, that's another story.

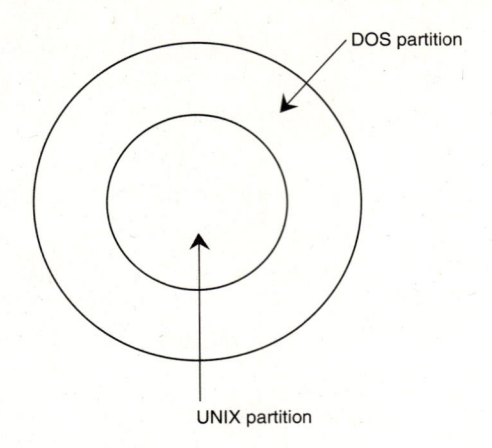

Figure 4.9

Disk partitioned by OS/2 2 to run the same programs and data under either OS/2 or MS-DOS 6.

The File Allocation Table

The following is a quick review of what happens when you load DOS:

1. When you turn on the computer, a routine in ROM searches for the master boot record at the beginning of the disk.

2. The master boot record checks to see which partition is bootable. If it's a DOS primary partition, it hands off to the DOS boot record.

3. The DOS boot record checks out the condition of your DOS partition and kick-starts MS-DOS by loading MSDOS.SYS and IO.SYS, then COMMAND.COM.

Now DOS is loaded. How does it know where to find anything? It searches the FAT.

The *file allocation table (FAT)* is a map that shows exactly what is associated with each cluster contained in your DOS partition. Remember that a given file may be scattered throughout your disk, wherever space was available when you stored it. The FAT is DOS's way to put that file back together seamlessly (albeit slowly) whenever you ask for it.

> **NOTE:** *DOS doesn't go out of its way to fragment your files. It simply places the beginning of a file in the first free cluster, the next chunk in the next free cluster, and so on. As files are deleted and rewritten, scattered free clusters appear throughout the disk—and are then filled with new files.*

If you think that DOS would be in trouble if its FAT were damaged... you're right! The FAT is so important that DOS provides two identical copies. Regrettably, DOS is a little absent-minded about this: it stores the backup right next to the original. Whatever disaster befalls the original is likely to kill the backup, too.

> **NOTE:** *Where have you been keeping your backups lately? (Just wondering.)*

MS-DOS 6 provides a 16-bit FAT for all disks larger than 15M. This means that your FAT can contain information about 65,636 clusters. (Floppy disks and very small hard drive partitions contain 12-bit partitions that are limited to 4,096 clusters.)

FAT Cluster Entries

Every cluster on your disk contains one of the following FAT entries:

Entry	Meaning
0	Empty, available space
BAD	Off-limits; cluster contains bad sector
Reserved	Cluster DOS has set aside for its own purposes
EOF	Last cluster in current file
###	Any *cluster number* (except zero); represents *next* cluster in current file

Here's a typical FAT list:

Cluster #	FAT Entry
288	BAD
289	290
290	291
291	292
292	293
293	EOF
294	308

Here's a typical cross-section of the preceding FAT list.

Cluster 288 is marked as bad. Cluster 289 is a file that's continued from somewhere. You can't tell from this list; it's a *one-way linked list*, which means that you can only follow it forward.

Cluster 289 directs you to 290; 290 directs you to 291, and so on, until 293 presents an end-of-file marker. (The trail of clusters that starts at the beginning of a file and continues to its end is called a *chain*.)

Finally, Cluster 294 appears (you don't know if it's the beginning of a file or the middle) and jumps you forward to 308.

As you can see, you can't tell from looking at the FAT whether 289 and 294 are the beginning of new files or the middle of files that have jumped from somewhere else. If these files did start somewhere else, they could become lost clusters in the event the chain is broken and the FAT no longer properly points to them. More on this a bit later.

DOS Directories

Common sense tells you that DOS somehow needs to know not just where a file *ends*, but where it begins. This information can be found in DOS *directories*. Here, we'll look at the way directories interact with the file allocation table to help DOS locate files. *For information about using directories and subdirectories to manage files, see Chapter 6.*

The Root Directory Table

You've probably walked up to a strange PC and typed **DIR** at the `C:>` prompt, to see what was there. DOS then proceeded to list files, file extensions, date and time the files were created, and file size.

This information comes from the *root directory table,* a set of 32-byte directory entries that DOS creates for each file. Each of these directory entries also includes two bytes that identify the file's *starting cluster*.

DOS generally sets aside up to 16K for a hard disk root directory table (fewer for floppies). Remember the limit of 512 entries in a root directory, mentioned earlier? This is where it comes from.

DOS names the root directory "\," which explains why you use the backslash to identify the root in all your directory commands.

How DOS Finds Subdirectories

You quite likely have more than 512 files on your hard disk. Why don't you get error messages? Because many of your files probably are in subdirectories, and each *subdirectory* represents *one* entry in the root directory table.

A subdirectory entry resembles other DOS file entries, with two exceptions: It states that the subdirectory's size is 0, and it contains a *directory bit* that identifies it as a subdirectory. The most important point is that, like other file entries, the subdirectory entry includes the *starting cluster* of the actual subdirectory list—a pointer that leads DOS to find the list.

When DOS views the subdirectory list (which usually fits into one cluster), it finds the starting clusters that point toward each subdirectory file. It also finds pointers to lower-level subdirectory lists, if they exist. Because the subdirectory lists are themselves files, not a special DOS table, they have no size limitations other than available disk space (and your own convenience).

> **NOTE:** By the way, herein lies the answer to one of those nagging little DOS mysteries: What are those first two lists in your subdirectories (the single and double dots)?
>
> The single dot (.) is the file entry for the subdirectory you're in.
>
> The double dot (..) is the file entry for the parent directory of the current subdirectory.

Following the Chain from Root to File

If you tell DOS to locate the file NOTES.TXT, located in the subdirectory C:\FILES, this is what happens:

1. DOS searches the root directory table for an entry called *files*, which contains a directory bit.
2. DOS looks up the *files* subdirectory entry.
3. DOS searches the subdirectory list for NOTES.TXT and determines its starting cluster.
4. Armed with the starting cluster, DOS searches the FAT to follow the entire chain of clusters that comprises NOTES.TXT.

> **NOTE:** By the way, this process is reversed when you write to a disk. First DOS chooses the clusters it will use, then it writes the data, and only then (after it has accurate starting-cluster and file-size data) does it create the directory list.

Lost Clusters and the CHKDSK Command

Now that you know how DOS locates a file, you can easily understand how things can go wrong. The most common problem is *lost clusters*. If you close your programs and type **CHKDSK** at the command prompt, you may see the following:

Disk Structures Imposed by MS-DOS 6.2

```
Volume Serial Number is CF83-02F7
 186777600 bytes total disk space
     81920 bytes in 2 hidden files
    614400 bytes in 73 directories
 122929152 bytes in 2875 user files
  63152128 bytes available on disk
      8192 bytes in each allocation unit
     22800 total allocation units on disk
      7709 available allocation units on disk
    655360 total bytes memory
    538160 bytes free

Errors found, F parameter not specified
Corrections will not be written to disk
20 lost allocation units found in 8 chains
163840 bytes disk space would be freed
```

Close all your files before running CHKDSK. Open files generate changes in directories and FAT allocations, and not all the updating takes place at the same time. CHKDSK may find lost clusters that are not really lost. If you convert them to files, you'll damage or lose the data they contain. For the same reason, don't run CHKDSK from inside Windows or while the MS-DOS Shell Task Swapper is running.

So how did those clusters (allocation units) get lost? And how worried should you be? To answer the second question first: relax. Lost clusters almost never imply damage to your disk.

Lost clusters *do* mean that the DOS file allocation table includes information about clusters that aren't accounted for in any DOS directory. In other words, DOS has found clusters that *seem* to be files—they've been allocated in the FAT as if they were files. But they're orphaned—cut off from their file names and starting cluster data.

How did it happen? What's in there? What can you do?

How it happened, most likely, is that your program was interrupted while it was writing to disk—but before it could create a complete directory entry. (This sometimes happens when someone turns off a computer without saving files and exiting properly—especially under Windows.)

What's in there probably isn't much. Either it's a temporary file created by one of your programs and never deleted, or it's a file that didn't write to disk properly and therefore was never saved.

But—keeping your expectations low—take a look. At the command line, type...

CHKDSK /F

The /F switch tells CHKDSK to *fix* the problems, not just report them. DOS creates a new directory entry for each chain, *not* for each cluster. DOS follows the FAT directory to the end of each lost chain, placing the entire chain in a single file and then creating a new file for the next lost chain or cluster.

All of these files are placed in the root directory, as files FILE0000.CHK, FILE0001.CHK, FILE0002.CHK, and so on. (If you exceed the 512-file root directory limit, you *could* run out of files.)

To view a file, open it in the DOS editor. (At the command prompt, type **edit file0000.chk**.) If you find a CHK file that seems useful, you can rename it and try to load it in your application program.

More often than not, however, having gone to the trouble of creating all these FILExxx.CHK files, the best thing you can do is to delete them. Well, that's not all bad—you've just recovered a whole bunch of disk space you didn't know you had.

The DOS 6.2 CHKDSK command has a new look—it now uses a comma to separate numbers greater than 1,000. In the previous CHKDSK listing, for example, DOS 6.2 displays the first five lines of the summary as follows:

```
    186,777,600 bytes total disk space
         81,920 bytes in 2 hidden files
        614,400 bytes in 73 directories
```

```
122,929,152 bytes in 2,875 user files
 63,152,128 bytes available on disk
```

CHKDSKs new display also reminds you that DOS 6.2's new ScanDisk utility, a full-featured disk analysis and repair tool, detects and fixes a much wider range of problems and encourages you to use it. See Chapter 8 for more about using ScanDisk.

What CHKDSK Does and Doesn't Do

Mostly, what doesn't it do? It doesn't fix physical problems on your disk. It doesn't identify newly damaged sectors. (The bad clusters it reports were marked that way during low-level formatting.) It doesn't even check the entire disk.

It simply checks to make sure that the FAT and the directories match.

Other FAT Problems

In addition to lost clusters, CHKDSK can report a few other kinds of problems, such as the following:

- ✔ **Invalid clusters.** Clusters that point to a nonexistent Cluster #0, or to a bad sector

- ✔ **Invalid subdirectories.** Subdirectories that don't contain "." and ".." entries

- ✔ **Allocation errors.** Mismatches between the directory's cluster assignments and the number actually allocated by the FAT

- ✔ **Cross-linked clusters.** Clusters that are part of more than one file. This sometimes happens when two open Windows programs use the same file. (CHKDSK can't fix this problem. The only option is to copy each file to a new location and then trash the originals. Even so, you might lose data.)

Chapter 4: *Taking a Tour of Your Hard Drive*

New to DOS 6.2 is ScanDisk, a full-featured disk analysis and repair tool, which you should use instead of CHKDSK /F. See Chapter 8 for more about using ScanDisk.

Floppy Disks

Most of this chapter has focused on hard disks. Floppies generally follow the same principles (stripped down to reflect their smaller sizes).

Like hard disks, floppy disks also contain tracks, sectors, and clusters, for example (but fewer of them). Floppies also permit fewer root directory entries. Table 4.2 shows the different floppy disk formats.

One anomaly is that high-density disks use smaller cluster sizes than low-density disks.

Table 4.2
Floppy Disk Formats

Disk Density	Size	Tracks	Sectors	Cluster Size (Sectors)	Clusters	Root Directory Entries
360K	5 1/4-inch	40	720	2	360	112
720K	3 1/2-inch	40	1,440	2	720	112
1.2M	5 1/4-inch	80	2,400	1	2,400	224
1.44M	3 1/2-inch	80	2,880	1	2,880	224
2.88M	3 1/2-inch	80	5,760	2	2,880	240

Because a double-sided floppy contains two surfaces, each cylinder contains two bits of data. All current floppy disks use MFM encoding.

Because floppy disks take more abuse and are less precise than hard ones, data on floppy disks is packed much less densely, and floppy disks spin much more slowly—about 1/10 as fast as hard drives. Nevertheless, you need to take care of them.

The obvious applies: don't fold, spindle, mutilate, paper clip, staple, or bend floppy disks. Don't leave them in the backseat of a car on a sunny day. Don't reach in and touch the magnetic surface. Don't stick 'em on the fridge with a refrigerator magnet.

But how about the not-so-obvious like storing them next to a telephone, which contains a magnetic field—or taking precautions not to run them through an airport X-ray machine—and instead wiping them clean in the *metal detector*?

Be safe, not sorry.

Formatting a Floppy Disk

MS-DOS 6 maintains the greatly improved DOS FORMAT command that was introduced with MS-DOS 5. FORMAT (as overhauled in MS-DOS 5) not only makes it more difficult to completely destroy your data, but also gives you the option of a quicker format. These improvements join the /F switch (introduced in MS-DOS 4) that makes it easier to specify your formatted disk's density.

> *The procedures for formatting a floppy disk and a hard disk are relatively similar, except that now—thank goodness—DOS provides more safeguards and warnings to make sure that you really want to format your hard disk. For more information about formatting the hard disk, see Chapter 5.*

The simplest format command hasn't changed. If you want to format a floppy disk in drive A, you place it in the drive (after making sure that it doesn't contain files you need), and at the command prompt, type...

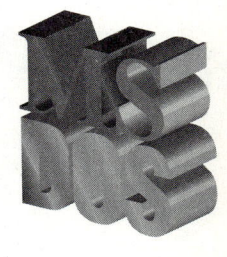

FORMAT A:

On a brand new floppy disk, this command performs the equivalent of both a low-level and high-level format. In contrast to the way FORMAT works on a hard disk, FORMAT *does* identify and mark off bad floppy disk sectors.

Because you haven't said otherwise, the FORMAT A: command formats the disk at the highest density available to drive A. You can set a lower density by adding the switch /F:*n*, in which *n* equals an acceptable disk size. DOS is getting flexible in its old age, and accepts a wide variety of syntax for the following disk sizes:

    160, 160K, 160K

    180, 180K, 180K

    320, 320K, 320K

    360, 360K, 360K

    720, 720K, 720K

    1200, 1200K, 1200K, 1.2, 1.2M, 1.2M

    1440, 1440K, 1440K, 1.44, 1.44M, 1.44M

    2880, 2880K, 2880K, 2.88, 2.88M, 2.88M

Of course, not every drive supports every value.

Next, FORMAT creates a DOS boot record, two clean copies of the file allocation table, a root directory, a unique serial number, and a volume label. If you add the /S switch, it adds the two hidden system files (MSDOS.SYS and IO.SYS) so that you can boot the system from your disk. Together, these two files use approximately 77K.

The DOS 6.2 FORMAT command has a new look— it now uses a comma to separate numbers greater than 1,000. The space summary for a 1.44M disk, for example, is as follows:

```
1,457,664 bytes total disk space
1,457,664 bytes available on disk
      512 bytes in each allocation
          unit
    2,847 allocation units available
          on disk
```

Safe Format versus Unconditional Format

Time was, a DOS format *always* destroyed every single bit of data on your disk, replacing it with an endless string of hexadecimal F6's to ensure that the disk would still read and write properly. Nowadays, this is called an *unconditional format*.

Starting with MS-DOS 5, however, DOS handles things quite differently if it finds data on your floppy disk. Instead of destroying everything, FORMAT merely empties the file allocation table and deletes the first character from all root directory file entries. (It does recheck the disk for bad sectors, though.) This information is placed in a safe location where UNFORMAT can find it later.

DOS calls this a *safe format*.

If you prefer to format a disk the old-fashioned way—to obliterate everything in sight, that is—you can add the U/switch to your format command, as follows:

```
FORMAT A: /U
```

Quick Format

DOS offers another FORMAT option: *quick formatting*. This works like safe formatting, but doesn't recheck the disk surfaces for defective sectors. It really is faster—often 90 percent faster. But you can't quick format a new disk, and you shouldn't quick format a disk if you know it has defective sectors.

The /AUTOTEST and /BACKUP Switches

The DOS 6 (and 5) FORMAT command has two very useful undocumented switches. The first one is the /AUTOTEST switch. If you enter **FORMAT A: /AUTOTEST**, FORMAT doesn't prompt you for a disk, a volume label, or ask if you want to format another disk. It doesn't even display the usual disk-space listing. It just goes! So a fast way to format a stack of new floppy disks is to write FFORMAT.BAT, as follows:

```
@echo off
echo ***** FAST FORMAT *****
:start
```

```
format b: /autotest
echo ^G
echo To exit, press Ctrl-C and Y now, or
echo change disks and press any other
echo key to format another disk. . .
pause > nul
goto start
```

This trick also works with the /F: switch (for example, FORMAT A: /F:720 /AUTOTEST). You also can use this switch with the /U and /S switches but not with the /Q switch. Enter the BELL character (which produces a speaker beep) by holding down Ctrl and pressing **G**.

The other undocumented /AUTOTEST switch is /BACKUP. This one works just like /AUTOTEST, except that it prompts you for a volume label and displays the usual disk-space listing.

> **TIP**
>
> *If you know someone who is still using DOS 3.3, show that person the undocumented /H switch, which will do the same thing as /AUTOTEST. To get the most from it, write the following version of FFORMAT.BAT:*
>
> ```
> @echo off
> echo   ***** FAST FORMAT *****
> :start
> echo N ¦ format a: /h > nul
> echo ^G
> echo Press Ctrl-C or switch disks and
> pause
> goto start
> ```

A FORMAT Menu

Here's a batch file (FO.BAT) that builds on the preceding one. This one creates a menu listing whatever number of formatting options you choose:

```
@echo off
cls
if %1!==! goto list
```

```
if %1==1 goto 1
if %1==2 goto 2
if %1==3 goto 3
if %1==4 goto 4
if %1==5 goto 5
if %1==6 goto 6
:list
echo ===================================
echo    *** DISK FORMATTING OPTIONS ***
echo ===================================
echo    1 - Fast format A:.
echo    2 - Quick format A:.
echo    3 - Format A: with a label.
echo    4 - Format A: with DOS & label.
echo    5 - Format A: at 360K.
echo    6 - Format B: at 720K.
echo ===================================
echo         Type FO <entry number>
goto end
:1
format b: /autotest
echo ^G
echo To exit, press Ctrl-C and Y now, or
echo change disks and press any other
echo key to format another disk. . .
pause > nul
goto 1
:2
format a: /q
goto end
:3
format a:
goto end
:4
format a: /s
goto end
:5
format a: /f:360
goto end
:6
format b: /f:720
goto end
:end
```

To use FO.BAT, type **FO**, followed by a space and an option number. If you type **FO** by itself, your menu appears. The first option is the fast formatting technique discussed earlier. The next three are self-explanatory. The fifth formats a 360K (5 1/4-inch) disk in a 1.2M drive; the sixth formats a 720K (3 1/2-inch) disk in a 1.44M drive. Obviously, you can add or subtract any options you choose, such as adding more options for a B drive. If you are using DOS 3.3, the options are easy to change to match that version. *(See Chapter 15 for more about writing batch files.)*

Waking Up FORMAT

Unless you buy preformatted disks (which is a good idea anyway), you have probably gotten very bored staring at FORMAT's `percent completed` message. There is an easy way to patch FORMAT so that it beeps when the format procedure is complete, enabling you to putter around the office and let FORMAT tell you when it needs attention. Using DSEDIT (a program on the disk accompanying this book), do the following steps:

1. Put DSEDIT.EXE in a directory included in the PATH.

2. Go to your DOS directory and copy FORMAT.COM to a floppy disk so you have a backup copy (just in case). Never patch the original copy of a file.

3. Enter **DSEDIT**. When it starts, press F7 to load a file, and enter **FORMAT.COM**.

4. Press F8 to enter an offset number, and enter **8**.

5. Press the down arrow until you highlight the 1A0 line, and then press the right arrow to highlight byte 3F, which is a question mark.

6. Enter **07**, press Shift+F2 to save the file, and press F10 to exit DSEDIT.

Run FORMAT on a floppy disk, and notice the beep when you are prompted for a volume label. You can easily do similar patches to other DOS commands (see Chapter 14 for ways to patch DISKCOPY) and even to COMMAND.COM (see Chapter 21).

Multitasking FORMAT in Windows

Suppose you're in Windows, and you need to format a stack of floppy disks, but you don't want to stop working to do it. Windows multitasking capability makes this a snap.

First, create a PIF called FORMAT-M.PIF. Enter **32** in KB **R**equired and **64** in KB **D**esired for Memory Requirements, click on the **Wi**ndowed button in Display **U**sage option, and then click on the **B**ackground check box in the Execution option.

Second, run your new PIF, either from the **R**un command, from File Manager, or by creating a new icon. Third, arrange the windows on your screen so that the FORMAT-M box is visible, start formatting a disk, and go back to work. You hear the beep (if you did the patch job) when you need to change disks. Remember, when you multitask a DOS program, system performance drops noticeably, but this trick is worth it.

A Few Tricky Floppy Disk Format Issues

As table 4.2 shows, there are now five major floppy disk formats (not counting the old, single-sided, 5 1/4-inch, 160K/180K MS-DOS 1 disks, or the 2-inch 720K disks briefly sold with the Zenith MinisPort, one of the first notebook PCs).

This plethora of disk formats can cause problems for the unwary user—especially when you interchange 360K and 1.2M floppy disks in a 5 1/4-inch drive, or 720K and 1.44M floppy disks in a 3 1/2-inch drive.

And don't cause your own troubles by trying to format a 360K disk at 1.2M, or a 720K disk at 1.44M.

Swapping 1.2M and 360K 5 1/4-inch Disks

High-density 5 1/4-inch (1.2M) drives *look* as though they ought to work fine with 360K disks. But try borrowing a disk from someone with a 360K drive—listen to him (or her) howl when you return it! You've written to the disk and he (or she) can no longer read it. What's going on here?

Not surprisingly, because it contains 80 tracks instead of 40, a 1.2M drive writes much narrower tracks than a 360K drive. It tries to compensate by doubling its track width when writing to a 360K disk. But because this writing still doesn't quite match the tracks the 360K drive expects, disk errors abound. As mentioned earlier, you won't have this problem if you format new 360K disks first on the high-density drive, using the /F:360 switch.

Swapping 720K and 1.44M 3 1/2-inch Disks

Both 1.44M and 720K 3 1/2-inch drives write the same track widths. So you can format anything anywhere, right? Sorry—not necessarily. To keep the tightly packed data bits from interfering with their neighbors, 1.44M disks store weaker magnetic charges than 720K disks, which means that you need a stronger magnetic field to lay down data on the 1.44M disk.

But not all disk drive subsystems can tell the difference—especially those without a media sensor to read the extra hole that's now built into high-density drives. A high-density disk might not notice that your 720K drive is trying to write to it—even if it's formatted at 720K. Conversely, after a 1.44M drive blasts its powerful magnetic charges at a 720K disk, you might have trouble revising or reformatting it.

Summary

On a day-to-day basis, MS-DOS protects you from the complexities of the drive hardware. You organize your files into subdirectories and directories, and DOS takes care of everything going on underneath—that's what it's there for.

But sometimes—in the following situations—you'll need to know more:

✔ When you need to recover lost data

✔ When you want your drive to work faster

✔ When you need to restructure the way your drive holds data

✔ When you're working with more than one kind of floppy disk

With the information in this chapter under your belt, you can move on to installing and formatting your hard drive (Chapter 5), setting up your file systems for maximal efficiency (Chapters 6 and 7), and restoring data, in the event you *do* lose it (Chapters 18 and 19). *Remember that Chapter 17 goes into even more detail about the physical properties of drives and about how DOS is stored on drives.*

Later, when you're considering buying a new hard drive, you can return to this chapter—and Chapter 17—for help in evaluating your options.

MS DOS

CHAPTER 5

Preparing and Setting Up Your Hard Drive

by Bill Camarda

In Chapter 4, you learned the basics of how your disks operate and how DOS superimposes its own structure on them. Now, roll up your sleeves, and you can start to use this information.

You'll get a quick guide to physically installing the two kinds of hard drives that are currently most popular: IDE and SCSI drives. Then, you'll walk through the partitioning process, deciding how to divide your disk for maximum efficiency.

Buying a new drive is one way to get more disk storage. But there's another. The bulk of this chapter introduces you to *DoubleSpace*, the disk compression feature built into DOS for the first time.

Should you use DoubleSpace? How does it work? And can it really double the space on your hard drive for a fraction of the cost of buying a new one?

Installing Hard Drives: An Overview

A multibillion-dollar industry has conspired to get you to purchase a new disk drive. It's the computer hardware and software industry. In the last decade, drive manufacturers have cut the per-megabyte cost of disk storage by nearly 95 percent, which is like trading in your old Plymouth Duster for a new model that gets 500 miles per gallon.

Meanwhile, software developers led by Microsoft, are making software that is getting fatter and fatter. Graphics eat up storage space like there's no tomorrow. And *then* there's video.

So maybe you're installing a new drive. This overview focuses primarily on the two most common kinds of drives sold today, IDE and SCSI.

Getting All the Parts

Make sure you get all the parts you need to get the job done. Drives are often sold *bare*, meaning you only get the drive mechanism and some basic mounting hardware. Chances are, you'll also need:

- ✔ **Adapter cards**. These cards range from extremely simple and cheap IDE adapters to fairly complex and expensive SCSI adapters. Since the IDE adapter is so simple, some recent PCs include them directly on the motherboard.

NOTE: You may hear these cards referred to as controller cards because earlier ST-506 and ESDI drives required separate controller cards. IDE and SCSI, otherwise as different as day and night, both move the controller function onto the drive itself.

Installing Hard Drives: An Overview

✔ **Mounting hardware.** This hardware, which includes rails, enables the drive to sit neatly where it belongs—instead of falling onto your motherboard like a rock.

✔ **Cables.** Cables connect your drive to the adapter or motherboard; usually either a 40-wire cable for IDE drives, or a 50-wire cable for SCSI drives. (Today's hard drive cables are straight-through. They don't do the twist like floppy cables do.)

✔ **Faceplate.** A *faceplate,* or *bezel,* covers the front of the drive and often contains the drive-in-use light.

✔ **Power connector.** Attaches the drive to your power supply.

✔ **Documentation.** Some of the best hard drive documentation is provided by third-party mail order vendors, not the manufacturers themselves, some of whom are notorious for incomprehensible technical materials that say little or nothing about actually installing the drives.

You may especially need information on configuring the system and any jumpers that will need to be set or disabled.

It's common for all these items to be packaged together in a "kit."

If you're installing your drive into an older PC or XT with a 5 1/4-inch drive enclosure, you may also need a drive bay adapter to fit today's smaller (3 1/2-inch) drives into the space left for it.

One thing that doesn't come in a kit is *space in your computer.* Now you know why those ads tout three, five, six, or even eight expansion bays.

Depending on your situation, you may have to install a larger power supply (such as a 200-watt supply). A rule of thumb is that if your existing power supply is less than 100 watts (the rating appears on a label on top of the power supply), you should replace it. If you don't, you may end up with slow performance, overheating, or even drive failure.

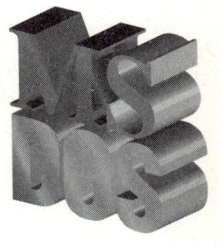

Installing an IDE Drive

As you've read in Chapter 4, the IDE interface is relatively simple. Electronically, it behaves almost exactly like a standard AT-bus expansion slot, with a few specialized functions added. In fact, sometimes it's called an *AT attachment*.

Before IDE, older drive standards transferred data much more slowly than your PC's bus, creating a bottleneck. Since IDE can work at the same speed as the bus, the bottleneck is eliminated (though others, like the disk's own data transfer rate, remain).

In general, installing an IDE drive is extremely straightforward—and even easier if you already have one IDE drive. As always, there's an exception: older IDE drives are not universally interchangeable; to match one, you might have to pick a model from the same manufacturer.

Most current IDE drives share the 3 1/2-inch form-factor. 3 1/2-inch refers to the disk platter, not the drive's external measurements, which are usually 5.75 inches × 4 inches, and either 1 inch or 1.6 inches high. Nearly all 3 1/2-inch drive bays will support either height.

Installing the First IDE Drive

Start by turning the computer off (!). Then prepare your drive's new home.

1. Install the mounting rails.
2. If you need to adapt a 5 1/4-inch drive bay, install the bay adapter.

If this is your first IDE drive, install the IDE adapter card—or locate the IDE connectors on your motherboard.

Installing Hard Drives: An Overview

To install the card:

1. Carefully press the board's edge connectors into an empty motherboard slot, making sure that the board is lined up facing the same direction as each other board.

2. Tighten the screw that connects the board to the rear of the computer's case.

3. Connect the IDE cable between the drive and the adapter card.

By now, this has been pretty thoroughly foolproofed. The cable contains three identical 40-pin connectors, as shown in figure 5.1:

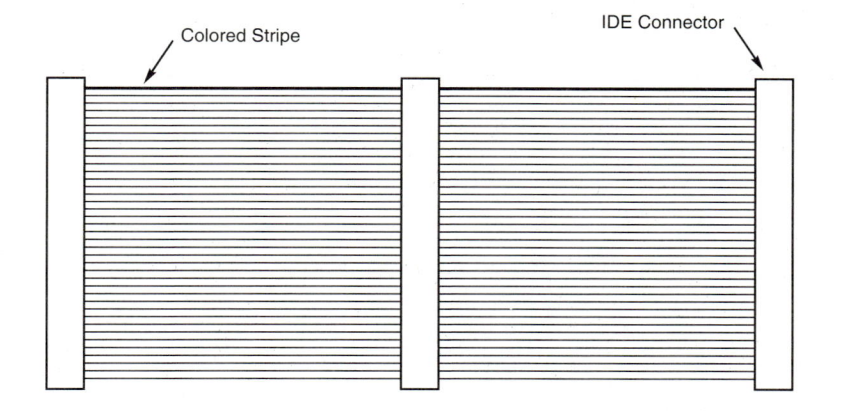

Figure 5.1
IDE cable.

One connector plugs into your IDE adapter card or motherboard. The others connect one or two IDE drives. One edge of each cable contains a colored stripe (usually red or blue), corresponding to the cable's Pin 1. Pin 1 on one end connects to Pin 1 on the other—there's no switching or funky cable twists to worry about.

Where's Pin 1 on the adapter and drive? Usually, the dead giveaway is the number *1* printed above it.

In some cases, you're physically prevented from installing an IDE cable wrong, because they only fit together the right way. Do, however, make sure that both rows of pins are connected.

TIP: Depending on the layout of your computer, you might want to connect the cables after step 4.

4. Slide the drive onto the drive mounting rails you've installed (or are already there).

5. Connect the four-wire cable extending from the power supply. Again, note that it can be properly connected in only one way; don't force it.

6. Once everything is correctly connected, tighten the screws that hold the drive in place.

NOTE: Many old hard disk controllers also contained a floppy disk controller. If you are removing an old drive and controller, make sure your floppy disk still has something to connect to. Most IDE cards do contain a floppy connection.

If your system still supports floppies even after you disconnect your old controller, but doesn't support 1.2M or 1.44M floppies, you may want to use the IDE card's floppy support instead.

Normally, you can enable or disable floppy support on both the motherboard and IDE card by disconnecting the appropriate jumpers.

7. Finally, configure your drive using your computer's SETUP program (*not* MS-DOS 6 SETUP). This is discussed later in this chapter.

Installing the Second IDE Drive

If you already have an IDE drive, you already have an IDE adapter card. This *should* mean you don't need one. But again, early implementations of the IDE standard weren't always as interoperable as they should have been.

NOTE: *If you have problems making your two IDE drives work together, replace the old card (you can do it for $15-$30) with a new one, and configure the new drive as master.*

If you're relatively sure that both IDEs will work together, simply daisy-chain them: plug the first drive into the second, and the second into the IDE adapter. Next, you'll have to set jumpers on each drive to make one the "master" and the other the "slave." Start out by making the new drive the slave; if that doesn't work, switch them.

Then proceed with the rest of the installation as previously described.

Installing SCSI Drives

SCSI's another ball of wax. As you read in Chapter 4, SCSI is more than a drive interface. It's an entirely separate bus that can theoretically move data among many devices, without even bothering with your computer's AT, EISA, or Micro Channel bus. (*If only* it was standardized enough to really do so.)

Some aspects of installing an SCSI drive are the same as IDE: you'll still need to mount the drive on rails, and you'll still need to make sure it fits in the expansion bay you've assigned to it. Like IDE drives, most SCSI drives are 3 1/2-inch, though a few 1+ gigabyte SCSI drives still use the old 5 1/4-inch form factor.

And like IDE, SCSI uses an adapter rather than a controller—traditional disk controller functions are located on the drive itself. But that's where the similarities come to a crashing halt. The SCSI adapter is much more complicated than the IDE adapter.

The first complexity *you* have to face is setting the device number for your hard drive. (If you've been sensible enough to purchase your adapter and drive together, this may have been done.) The number can be anything from 0 to 6; the adapter itself is usually number 7. No two devices can have the same number.

The higher the number, the higher the priority it gets from the SCSI adapter. Therefore, hard disks are commonly given the number 6.

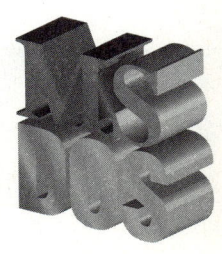

Some devices, however, require a specific SCSI number. You'll have to work around those requirements.

The next complexity you have to worry about is *termination*. SCSI devices are daisy-chained; one connects to the next, then it connects to the next, all the way through to the adapter.

At each end of the chain, you need to damp down the electrical signals so they stop right there, and don't bounce back from whence they came. This is done with a *terminator*—essentially, a set of electrical resistors. Chances are, your host adapter already contains a terminator.

If your drive is the only other SCSI device you're installing, it needs to be terminated as well. Check—your drive may already be terminated, too.

> **NOTE** *In rare cases, your adapter will be in the middle of a SCSI chain, in which case, you'll need to remove its terminator.*

When they're properly numbered and terminated, install the SCSI adapter card; it installs just like any other PC card. Connect the cables. Internal SCSI devices use a 50-pin cable; external drives either use a 25-pin cable or an oversized 50-pin Amphenol connector.

Most SCSI cables are marked to indicate proper connections, as with IDE cables. However, some aren't—so be a little more careful to check the documentation and get it right.

You don't have to run your hardware's SETUP program when you install an SCSI drive, but you will probably have to install a special device driver, such as the increasingly popular ASPI drivers developed by Adaptec.

ASPI drivers manage the two treacherous zones of nonstandardization in an SCSI subsystem: the connection between your drive and your SCSI adapter, and the connection between your SCSI adapter and your PC.

The disadvantage of ASPI—or any hard disk driver—is that if it's corrupted, or can't be found, your drive becomes inaccessible.

A Few Words about Low-Level Formatting

Neither IDE nor SCSI drives need to be low-level formatted; that was done at the factory. Other drives do, however. For example, old ST-506 drives benefit from occasional low-level reformatting.

Don't low-level format an IDE drive. Doing so may result in wiping out the factory-marked defect list and may even destroy the drive.

Remember, low-level formatting utterly wipes out all data on your drive. UNFORMAT does nothing against a low-level format.

You're generally best off doing low-level formatting with a utility designed specifically for the purpose, such as OnTrack Disk Manager, which is often shipped with drives. However, most ST-506 drives can be formatted directly, using a low-level format program built directly into the drive controller.

You can access it with the DEBUG command. Type...

DEBUG

...and press Enter.

Your command prompt disappears. You now type the memory location where the ROM low-level formatting program resides. On Western Digital controllers, that's usually:

G=C800:5

On other controllers, it's **G=C800:6** or, for Adaptec RLL controllers, **G=C800:CCC**.

> **NOTE:** *SCSI drives usually are low-level formatted. Controllers that support low-level formatting, however, can be accessed through DEBUGs G=C800:5. Disk Manager and SpeedStor do not work with most SCSI drives.*

Now, you'll have to answer some questions. Be prepared. Three are especially important:

- ✔ Number one is your choice of interleave. (See the discussion in Chapter 4.)

- ✔ Number two is "Are you dynamically configuring the drive?" **Yes** means you want to perform a custom installation; **No** means just do the default stuff and follow any hardware jumper settings you see.

- ✔ Number three is a request for a list of bad tracks. These should appear on a sticker on your drive. If you don't enter these, you may find yourself storing data on bad sectors later.

Configuring Your Drive

Your computer either comes with a built-in SETUP program or one on an accompanying disk. If you have an IDE drive, you need to use SETUP to match your disk drive against a preset table of drives (commonly 47 different kinds) stored in your computer's BIOS.

If you have an SCSI drive, you don't have to bother with this. In fact, you don't even want SETUP to know you've installed a drive—you want your hardware to always go through appropriate channels (that is, your SCSI bus).

Back to IDE: In the old days, matching your drive against the computer's list was relatively easy. There was one list of drives, the one built into the BIOS of IBM PCs. But drives have proliferated, and so have BIOSs.

If you're lucky, you have a ROM BIOS, like AMI's, that allows you to add your exact drive to its list. If not, see what's on *your* computer's list, and come as close as possible.

Most new IDE drives give you some flexibility, through a feature called *automatic sector translation*. With it, you can multiply...

cylinders * heads * sectors/track

...to get a total number of available sectors.

Then you can choose any drive table entry containing the same number of sectors, or more.

> *No matter what kind of drive you have, never tell Setup you have more sectors than you really do.*

If your drive doesn't have automatic sector translation, you have to be more careful. Narrow down your list like this:

1. If your drive uses write precompensation, eliminate those that don't—or use substantially different amounts of it.

2. Don't pick a drive with more heads or cylinders than you really have.

3. Among those that remain, play *The Price Is Right*: Choose the drive closest to your actual capacity, without going over.

If you don't have a customizable BIOS, and you can't find a drive on your list that *remotely* resembles the one you've just installed, you have three choices:

✔ Purchase an add-on ROM that enables you to add new drives to your drive table. Manufacturers of these so-called ROM dubbing kits include OnTrack Systems, Golden Bow, and Washburn & Co.

✔ Purchase an entirely new set of ROMs, such as AMI or Phoenix ROMs.

✔ Use software like DiskManager or SpeedStor to make DOS think you're running a standard drive.

The last choice is the least appealing, because it won't work if you ever change operating systems. Even within DOS, if the software doesn't run, neither will your drive.

Partitioning Your Drive

Chapter 4 discussed primary and extended partitions, logical drives, and non-DOS partitions. These may all be created using DOS' FDISK program. FDISK writes into your disk's partition table the information DOS needs to find the physical space it has been allocated on a hard disk.

To run it, type **FDISK** at the command prompt.

Changing your partitions destroys all data on the partitions you change.

The opening screen offers the following options:

```
1.   Create DOS Partition or Logical DOS Drive
2.   Set active partition
3.   Delete partition or Logical DOS Drive
4.   Display partition information
Enter choice: [1]
Press Esc to exit FDISK
```

If you have multiple hard disks, you'll have a fifth option:

```
5.   Change current fixed disk drive
```

Make your choice by selecting the number and pressing Enter. You can always leave FDISK by pressing Esc repeatedly until you arrive at the opening screen, and then pressing Esc once more.

If you have just installed your first drive, you must create at least one primary partition and set at least one partition to active. Start by choosing **1**. On the next screen, choose **1** again, Create Primary DOS Partition. You see the following message:

Installing Hard Drives: An Overview   231

```
Current fixed disk drive: 1
Do you wish to use the maximum available size for a
Primary DOS Partition and make the partition active?
(Y/N)
```

If you already have a primary DOS partition, you'll be given details about it, for example:

```
Current fixed disk drive: 1
Partition    Status   Type     Volume Label   Mbytes   System   Usage
  C: 1         A      PRI DOS    Mydisk         20     FAT 12    93%
Primary DOS Partition already exists.
Press Esc to continue.
```

Pressing Esc returns you to the main menu; if you want to create a new Primary DOS partition, you will have to wipe out the one you already have.

If you have no primary DOS partition and you want to create a single partition containing all the space on your drive, press **Y**. Note that MS-DOS 6.2 has long since shed the limitation of 32M partitions that plagued DOS for years.

Assuming you have only one drive, FDISK will now restart. Since there is no data on the drive, you'll need to insert a floppy boot disk in order to boot DOS. The next step will be to use FORMAT to format the partition.

If you want to create a smaller partition, enter N instead. You'll see a message like this:

```
Total disk space is 150 Mbytes (1 Mbyte = 1048576 bytes)
Maximum space available for partition is 130 Mbytes
Enter partition size in Mbytes or percent of disk space
(%) to create a Primary DOS Partition.
```

To create a 30M DOS Partition, therefore, you could either type **30%** or **20%**.

Chapter 5: *Preparing and Setting Up Your Hard Drive*

> **NOTE**
> *Even if you use a percentage, the partition, once created, will not change even if the available space on the disk changes.*

If you want, you can assign the remaining space to an Extended DOS Partition by choosing 2 (Create Extended DOS Partition) at the next screen. Once again, you will have the option of specifying the extended partition's size in megabytes or as a percentage of the remaining space.

Unless you're splitting your disk between operating systems, that is, making room for OS/2, assign all the remaining space to the extended partition. If you are leaving room for another operating system, *make sure you leave enough room*—a complete OS/2 installation, for example, requires 30M at minimum.

Finally, you must set one partition as active, or else DOS won't be able to boot from the disk. Return to the main FDISK menu and choose item 2, Set Active Partition. You will be shown a list of all available partitions; highlight the one you want to make active.

If you determine that you must restructure your disk, you can delete some or all of its partitions. Once again, remember this will destroy all data on those partitions—back them up first.

At the main FDISK menu, choose item 3, Delete Partition or Logical DOS Drive. You'll then be given a choice of what you want to delete:

Choose one of the following:

```
    1.    Delete Primary DOS Partition
    2.    Delete Extended DOS Partition
    3.    Delete Logical DOS Drive(s) in the Extended DOS
    Partition
    4.    Delete Non-DOS Partition
    Enter choice: [ ]
    Press Esc to return to FDISK Options
```

To delete the Primary DOS Partition, choose 1. You will be shown details about your Primary partition(s), and given the following message:

```
WARNING! Data in the deleted Primary DOS Partition will
be lost. What primary partition do you want to delete?[1]

Press Esc to return to FDISK Options
```

If you want to delete the partition, confirm the number of the partition and press Enter. As an extra precaution, FDISK will ask you to provide the partition's volume name. If you provide the correct name, you'll be warned one last time:

```
Do you wish to continue (Y/N)
```

Pressing **Y** will delete the partition and your data.

> *Third-party utilities exist to handle partitioning. However, they usually create non-DOS partitions, which must be accessed by means of specific drivers.*
>
> *DOS 6 FDISK can remove non-DOS partitions created with Disk Manager, SpeedStor, and HARDRIVE.SYS (from Priam, now UNITEX). You need to back up the data you want to keep and find out how many cylinders the drive has. FDISK only sees 1024 cylinders; you cannot use the cylinders greater than 1024 if you partition the drive with FDISK.*
>
> *So, except for the 1024-cylinder limitation, the other limitations that once accompanied DOS partitioning are gone. Moral: Use FDISK whenever possible.*

Formatting Your Drive

Once you've partitioned your drive and set one partition as active, you have a drive that DOS can recognize—but still not access. Now you need to perform a high-level format, using the DOS FORMAT command.

FORMAT creates the disk partition's DOS Boot Record, File Allocation Table and root directory. Next, it demarcates the boundaries of every sector on the disk, writing dummy data to every available space on the disk. As it proceeds, it rereads this data to ensure that it has been written accurately.

To perform a high-level format on a new disk partition, from an MS-DOS 6.2 boot floppy or other drive, enter...

```
FORMAT C: /S
```

The /S switch tells FORMAT to place all DOS system files on the hard drive, so you can henceforth boot directly from the hard drive. The next step is to install DOS itself, as described in Chapter 3.

Introducing DoubleSpace

Now, the *pi'ece de résistance*, DoubleSpace—the most tangible reason why many people are upgrading to MS-DOS 6.

At this writing, a 120M hard drive, with installation kit, runs around $300 through mail order. But if you've already got a 120M hard drive, MS-DOS 6's DoubleSpace promises to give you the equivalent of another one for $99 or less—along with all its other features. Call it *better living through data compression*.

This section explains the magic and tells you how to take advantage of it—all the while helping you sidestep some of the potential pitfalls introduced by DoubleSpace or any other compression program.

An Overview of Data Compression

The primary data compression technique used in DoubleSpace, Stacker, and most other modern data compression programs was first invented in 1977 by Abraham Lempel and Jacob Ziv. It's therefore called the Lempel-Ziv (LZ) method, or occasionally the LZ77 method, after the year in which they introduced it.

The basic idea behind LZ is that strings of bytes constantly reappear throughout your files. This is especially apparent in text files, but is also true in graphics and most other files.

Whenever LZ sees a new string of bytes, it assigns them a short code. Then if it sees that string of bytes again, it simply substitutes the code for them.

Suppose you put a simplified version of LZ to work on the opening lines of Yeats' *The Second Coming*:

> Turning and turning in the widening gyre
> the falcon cannot hear the falconer;

Whenever the compression algorithm sees the letters turn, it substitutes a code, in this case an exclamation point. And so on, as it sees additional combinations. Then, when it sees a duplicate, it swaps in a code from this table:

Text	*Code*
turn	= !
in	= @
fal	= #
con	= $
the	= %
an	= ^
g(spacebar)	= &

The result is...

!@&^d !@& % widen$&gyre

% #$ c^not hear % #$er;

...roughly 60 percent compression, right there.

That, in a more sophisticated, much more bulletproof version, is what DoubleSpace does.

In theory, the larger a "dictionary" of combinations a compression program has available to it, the more it can compress a file. However, larger dictionaries can significantly slow compression.

Data compression programs also monkey with the way DOS allocates chunks of data. Typically, DOS allocates data in groups of 512-byte sectors, called *clusters* or *allocation units*, as described in Chapter 4. A cluster might consist of 4, 8, or even 16 sectors. Once a cluster is assigned, all the leftover space in the cluster is unavailable to any other file.

That's prime turf for finding more space. DoubleSpace presents itself to DOS as using normal 8K clusters, but internally, it allocates space in single sectors.

The trade-off for all of this hocus-pocus is time. You will probably notice that compressed drives run a little bit slower than regular drives. Not drastically slower—but enough that you wouldn't want to DoubleSpace a network drive or a Windows swap file.

Notwithstanding the name *DoubleSpace*, data compression has a widely different effect on varying types of files.

Database and graphics files tend to be very compressible. Spreadsheet compressibility varies widely. Programs tend to be only moderately compressible. Encrypted files and files that have already been compressed, such as ZIP and ARC files, generally can't be compressed at all.

> *Trying to compress already-compressed files can actually expand them, so DoubleSpace doesn't even try—it simply marks them as uncompressable.*

On the whole, consider yourself fortunate to actually double your space. However, 1.6-to-1 to 1.8-to-1 compression ratios are reasonable to expect.

> **NOTE**
>
> *By the way, you may occasionally hear reference to two kinds of file compression algorithms: lossless and lossy. Lossy file compression algorithms are willing to lose slight amounts of information in exchange for remarkable compression ratios—often at least 100 to 1.*
>
> *That's cool (or usually cool) for large graphics and video files, which require enormous amounts of bandwidth to transmit. After all, you can appreciate your TV even though the image isn't absolutely perfect.*
>
> *The search for better and better lossy compression is at the heart of attempts to bring full-motion video to the desktop. JPEG (Joint Photographics Expert Group) is one example of a recent lossy compression standard.*
>
> *However, back here on Earth, a few bits missing from your company's accounting system would not be welcome. Hence, DoubleSpace, Stacker, PKZIP, and others of their ilk stick to lossless compression.*

Reasons NOT To Use DoubleSpace

If you need absolute rock-solid safety, if you can't sacrifice an iota of disk speed, or if you simply refuse to back up your data, you might think twice about using a compression program.

Also, if you are thinking about switching to OS/2 or Windows NT, be wary: DoubleSpace currently supports neither. Microsoft may one day choose to support Windows NT.

Microsoft has promised that NT will support a version of the *Microsoft Real-Time Compression Interface* (MRCI), the software interface to compression/decompression services used by DoubleSpace. But that is not the same as saying that files will automatically be interchangeable.

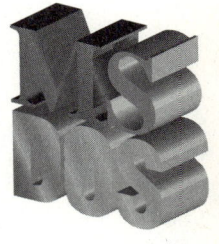

Warnings before Using DoubleSpace

As mentioned earlier in this chapter, you may want to create a separate uncompressed boot partition for DOS and your most critical device drivers, so if you ever have a problem at startup accessing drives that have DoubleSpace, you can still boot and then work on the problem from an uncompressed drive.

Also, be aware that you can't decompress an entire compressed drive. You *can*, however, copy all the contents of a compressed drive to another compressed drive (or drives), and then delete the compressed drive, assuming you have the space available.

DOS 6.2 now provides the /UNCOMPRESS switch. Assuming you have enough disk space, use the DBLSPACE /UNCOMPRESS [drive:] command to uncompress the drive. This also removes DBLSPACE.BIN from memory.

Some "older" users (those who are resistant to change, which is not always bad) like to quote the old expression, "The more you complicate the plumbing, the easier it is to stop up the drain." Although AddStor and Stac Electronics have been doing safe disk compression for years, users who have lost data and volumes take issue with the word "safe."

You don't get anything without paying for it; that is, there are trade-offs with disk compression. For one thing, the DoubleSpace driver consumes 43K of RAM (although you can load it high). Perhaps more serious is the hindrance to disk performance. Disk reads suffer by two percent, and writes suffer by 25-40 percent when you are writing large files.

If you choose to write compressed data to floppy disks and then use them on another PC, that PC must also have

DoubleSpace installed; neither SuperStore nor Stacker have this problem.

Removing DoubleSpace from your disk (in case you don't like it) is not an easy task.

See the "Using a Data-Compression Alternative" section at the end of this chapter for a way to compress data without using DoubleSpace.

That's the rub, of course: for most people, the whole point of using data compression is to use more space than they would otherwise have available.

Finally, Microsoft reports that DoubleSpace may occasionally make communications applications less reliable if your computer uses first-generation 8250 UARTs to manage serial communications. Microsoft speculates that this may be due to DoubleSpace's heavy use of some interrupts that were less frequently used before.

A better UART, such as the 16550AFN, can solve this problem and is usually relatively inexpensive to add. *(See Chapter 22 for a more detailed discussion of UARTs.)*

> **NOTE** *Short of replacing your UART, you might try disabling SMARTDrive write-caching on your DoubleSpace host drive. (See Chapter 8 for a discussion of SMARTDrive write caching.)*

Basic DoubleSpace Concepts and Components

When you DoubleSpace a drive, DOS creates a *Compressed Volume File* (CVF) that contains all the files that were previously on your drive.

This file still exists on your *uncompressed* host drive. You don't see it because it's a system-hidden, read-only file. But type **ATTRIB** on the host drive, and it will be listed—under the name DBLSPACE.000 or a similar name.

Under normal circumstances DOS wouldn't recognize DBLSPACE.000 as anything more than a gigantic invisible file. But DBLSPACE also includes these two files:

- ✔ DBLSPACE.BIN, an extension to DOS that recognizes and controls compressed drives, ensuring that they present themselves to you almost exactly like regular disks.
- ✔ DBLSPACE.SYS, a device driver that determines whether DBLSPACE.BIN will load in conventional or upper memory.

You'll notice that if you format a system disk under DOS 6, DBLSPACE.BIN will be one of the hidden files that appears on your disk. DBLSPACE.BIN loads even before CONFIG.SYS or AUTOEXEC.BAT—an example of what Microsoft means when it talks about integrating DoubleSpace more tightly into DOS than third-party compression vendors can.

However, if for some reason, DBLSPACE.BIN doesn't run, your compressed drives won't be recognized.

When you want access to a compressed drive, you have to mount it. DBLSPACE does this automatically for hard drives, but not for floppies.

Because each DoubleSpaced drive consists of a hidden CVF that behaves like a drive, but is contained on a host drive, you need two drive letters to account for both the CVF and the host. DoubleSpace swaps letters so that your current drive retains its letter after compression, and a new, higher letter is assigned to the host drive.

Understanding DoubleGuard

DOS 6.2 adds a feature to DoubleSpace that will make users less apprehensive about using DoubleSpace. DoubleSpace uses certain memory buffers to hold its critical data structures, and it is possible for a stand-alone or TSR program to damage one of those buffers. To prevent this, Mircrosoft added DoubleGuard, which calculates a checksum every time it modifies its buffers, and then verifies that checksum before actually writing the buffers to disk.

If DoubleGuard detects that another program has violated its memory buffers, it pops up an error message and shuts down the system before any damage is done. Additionally, DoubleGuard also makes a periodic check to ensure that its own code has not been corrupted.

If you receive a DoubleGuard error, restart the computer and enter **SCANDISK /ALL** at the prompt. This runs DOS 6.2's new full-featured disk analysis and repair utility, which detects and repairs any problems that might have been caused by the program that violated DoubleSpace's memory. Also make a note of any programs that were running when the error occurred. By a process of elimination, try to ascertain which one caused the problem and exactly what you were doing when the problem occurred. *See Chapter 8 for how to use ScanDisk.*

You can expect about a two percent performance penalty when using DoubleGuard. You can turn off DoubleGuard, which you may decide to do if DoubleSpace doesn't cause you any problems. To turn off DoubleGuard, enter **DBLSPACE /DOUBLEGUARD=0** at the prompt. To turn DoubleGuard back on, enter **DBLSPACE /DOUBLEGUARD=1** at the prompt. You will have to reboot before the change will take affect.

Working with DoubleSpace

You can work with DoubleSpace in two ways:

- ✔ From the command line, using parameters and switches much like any other DOS command

    or

- ✔ From the DoubleSpace menu-driven program, which loads when you type **DBLSPACE** at the command prompt.

There are also two ways to get help about DoubleSpace:

- ✔ From the command line, type **DBLSPACE /?** to get a one-line listing of the appropriate syntax for each DoubleSpace command.

✔ Or type **HELP DBLSPACE** or **HELP DBLSPACE / SWITCHNAME** to get DOS' somewhat more detailed on-line help about each element of DoubleSpace.

Do you know where your emergency boot disk is? You might think of keeping it within sight for the next few pages.

Compressing a Drive with Express Setup

The easiest way to create a DoubleSpace drive is to use the DoubleSpace program. Type **DBLSPACE** at the command prompt, and you will see the following screen:

```
Microsoft DoubleSpace Setup
===========================

Welcome to DoubleSpace Setup.

The Setup program for DoubleSpace frees space on your hard
disk by compressing the existing files on the disk. Setup
also loads DBLSPACE.BIN, the portion of MS-DOS that pro-
vides access to DoubleSpace compressed drives. DBLSPACE.BIN
requires about 40K of memory.
    o To set up DoubleSpace now, press ENTER.

    o To learn more about DoubleSpace Setup, press F1.

    o To quit Setup without installing DoubleSpace, press
F3.

    ENTER=Continue      F1=Help        F3=Exit
```

Press Enter to continue.

> **6.2** *Under DOS 6.2, DBLSPACE.BIN now consumes only 32K with automounting off; it consumes 36K with automounting on. See the Note in the "DoubleSpace and Your Floppy Disk" section, later in this chapter, for more information about automounting.*

> **NOTE** *F1 gives you a modicum of help from anywhere inside the DBLSPACE program.*

You now have a choice: Express Setup and Custom Setup.

Express Setup compresses your entire C drive. It also swaps drive names, so that the compressed drive appears to be C drive, and the host drive appears to be drive H (if you have only one hard disk partition; if you have two, it will start with drive I and work backward).

To proceed with Express Setup, make sure Express Setup is highlighted and press Enter. If you have a floppy disk in A drive, remove it—DoubleSpace will need to reboot during the compression process. Then, to start compressing, press **C**.

> **NOTE** *You can't compress a drive that's already packed to the gills. DoubleSpace needs at least 1M free space to compress a hard disk, 200K free to compress a floppy disk.*

The Compression Process

DoubleSpace begins the compression process by running CHKDSK to mark off any bad clusters. It then searches for any existing compressed drives; if they exist, they must be taken into account when DoubleSpace assigns drive names. (DoubleSpace can't coexist with Stacker compressed drives.)

> **NOTE:** *DoubleSpace will only work with the version of SMARTDRV.EXE that ships with MS-DOS 6. This installs automatically with DOS 6. If for some reason you're using an older version of SMARTDrive, you'll be warned to update it before you begin.*

> **6.2:** *To ensure that it does not write any of its data structures onto unmarked bad disk sectors, DoubleSpace does a surface scan of the entire disk before compressing it. If it finds an unreliable sector, it moves the data to a reliable sector, and it marks the unreliable one as unusable. See Chapter 8 for how to use ScanDisk, DOS 6.2s full-featured disk analysis and repair utility.*

Next, DoubleSpace creates a preliminary DBLSPACE.INI file, which will later be edited to include information DoubleSpace needs to mount your compressed drives properly.

Then, DoubleSpace reboots, continuing the compression process with a screen like this:

```
Microsoft DoubleSpace Setup
============================

DoubleSpace is now compressing drive C.

Start time:  12:00:45 pm

Current time:           12:00:47 pm

Estimated finish time:      12:28 am

Time left:   About 28 minutes

Currently Compressing:      C:\IO.SYS

            0% complete
Compressing files...
```

The actual compression process will take awhile—figure roughly a minute per megabyte, perhaps less if you have a very fast system.

Note that DoubleSpace's estimate of the time it will take to compress a drive may vary substantially from the actual time it takes, because different types of files behave differently.

When DoubleSpace finishes compressing the drive, it runs some tests, and then runs Microsoft Defrag, which defragments the entire drive, making sure that all clusters of the new Compressed Volume File are next to each other—reducing the amount of time your drive will need to read files within the CVF. This will also take a few minutes.

You then receive a report similar to this:

```
Microsoft DoubleSpace Setup
============================

DoubleSpace has finished compressing Drive C.

Free space before compression:      26.0 MB

Free space after compression:       44.5 MB
Compression ratio:          1.7 to 1

Total time to compress:             20 minutes

DoubleSpace has created a new drive I that contains
2.0 MB of uncompressed space. This space has been set
aside for files that must remain uncompressed.
To exit from DoubleSpace and restart your computer, press
ENTER.
```

2.0M of uncompressed space is the default setting.

If you then press Enter, you get this message:

```
DoubleSpace is making final modifications to your
AUTOEXEC.BAT and CONFIG.SYS files, and will then restart
your computer to enable the compressed drive.
Preparing final DBLSPACE.INI file...
```

In CONFIG.SYS, DoubleSpace adds a line similar to this:

```
DEVICEHIGH=C:\DOS\DBLSPACE.SYS /MOVE
```

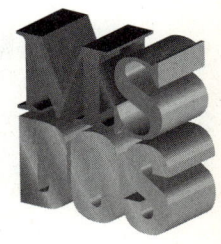

Chapter 5: *Preparing and Setting Up Your Hard Drive*

> **NOTE** *You may have even seen a line like this if you have an XT or original PC (which don't even have upper memory). Because all DBLSPACE.SYS does is determine whether DBLSPACE.BIN will load in conventional or upper memory, you can safely delete it (or, better, disable it by adding the word* **REM** *in front of it) if you don't have upper memory.*

DoubleSpace may also change drive assignments in AUTOEXEC.BAT if necessary. DBLSPACE.INI is described in more detail later in this chapter.

Even after compression, the host drive will still contain a copy of COMMAND.COM and your system-hidden, read-only files in addition to your DBLSPACE.000 compressed drive.

It also leaves room on your uncompressed drive for your Windows swap file, if it detects that you have Windows. This is because Windows' speed is highly dependent on the speed of its swap file, and DoubleSpace inevitably slows down reads and writes. *See the Windows error messages, later in this chapter, for more information.*

> **NOTE** *The uncompressed drive left by Express Setup may not contain other device drivers that could be essential to your system, such as SCSI hard disk drivers.*
>
> *If you have these drivers, or other information you want to boot even if something happens to your DoubleSpace drive, plan for a larger uncompressed boot partition, and choose Custom Setup.*

> **NOTE** *DoubleSpace creates a drive identified by the letter H if you have drives A, B, and C only. Here's the reason: to avoid conflicts with existing drives, DoubleSpace examines the existing drive assignments during installation to find the highest drive letter currently in use. It then skips the next four letters and assigns the fifth letter to the new DoubleSpace drive.*

Using Custom Setup To Compress or Create a Drive

Custom Setup gives you more control; it permits you to compress a different drive, or compress just part of a drive. You may especially want to use Custom Setup when you need more control over how DoubleSpace assigns drive names.

To use Custom Setup, select it when you are given the choice of Express or Custom Setup. You will then be given the choice to `Compress an existing drive` or `Create a new empty compressed drive`.

Compressing an existing drive will squish the existing files on whichever drive you choose. (Express Setup compressed your existing C drive.)

Creating a new empty compressed drive will transform some or all of the empty space you already have available on a drive into a larger, empty compressed drive.

If you want to compress a current drive, press Enter. Custom Setup will display the screen shown in the following screen:

```
Microsoft DoubleSpace Setup
===========================

DoubleSpace will compress drive C to create free space on it.
Certain files, such as the Windows permanent swap file, must
remain uncompressed. When DoubleSpace compresses  drive C, it
also creates a new uncompressed drive to contain files from
drive C that must remain uncompressed. DoubleSpace creates
the new uncompressed drive using the following settings:

Free space on new uncompressed drive:          2.00 MB
Drive letter of new uncompressed drive:        H:
                                               Continue

To accept the current settings, press ENTER. To change a
setting, press the UP or DOWN ARROW key to select it.
Then, press ENTER to see alternatives.

ENTER=Continue        F1=Help F3=Exit ESC=Previous screen
```

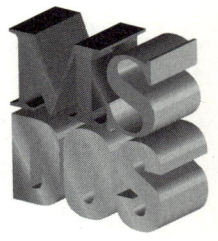

To change either of these default values, use the up-arrow key to highlight it, and press Enter. A new screen will appear, as follows:

```
Microsoft DoubleSpace Setup
============================

You can specify the amount of free space the new
uncompressed drive will contain. (The more space the new
drive contains, the less there will be on drive C.)

The new drive will be used to store files that must
remain uncompressed.
If you are not sure how much space is  required, use the
recommended size, which DoubleSpace calculates based on
your system's needs. For more information, press F1.

   Free space on new uncompressed drive:    [8.00  ] MB

To accept the current value, press ENTER.

To enter a different value, type the number you want, and
then press ENTER.

   ENTER=Continue       F1=Help F3=Exit ESC=Previous screen
```

Type your replacement value or letter, and press Enter. When you have both the drive letter and free space the way you want them, press the down-arrow to continue and press Enter. Then press C to begin compression. DoubleSpace will follow the procedure just described.

If, instead, you want to create a new compressed empty drive, choose that option. You will be given a choice of all existing hard drive partitions, as follows:

```
Microsoft DoubleSpace Setup
============================

Select the drive you want to use. DoubleSpace will
convert that drive's free space into a new compressed
drive.
                 Current              Project Size
   Drive         Free Space           of New Drive
   C             14.4 MB              27.7 MB
```

Introducing DoubleSpace **249**

```
To accept the current selection, press ENTER.

To select a different drive, press the UP ARROW or DOWN
ARROW key until the drive you want is selected, and then
press ENTER. If there are more drives than fit in the
window, you can scroll the list by pressing the UP ARROW
DOWN ARROW, PAGE UP, or PAGE DOWN key.

ENTER=Continue       F1=Help F3=Exit ESC=Previous screen
```

Highlight the drive you want, and press Enter. You will be given a chance to change the drive size on the next screen:

```
Microsoft DoubleSpace Setup
============================

DoubleSpace will use the free space on drive C to create
a new compressed drive. DoubleSpace creates the new
compressed drive using the following settings:

  Free space to leave on drive C:      | 8.00 MB   |
  Compression ratio of new drive:      | 2.00 to 1 |
  Drive letter of new drive:           | H:        |
                                       | --->      |
                                       | Continue  |

To accept the current settings, press ENTER.

To change a setting, press the UP or DOWN ARROW key to
select it. Then, press ENTER to see alternatives.

ENTER=Continue       F1=Help F3=Exit ESC=Previous screen
```

Again, you can change each of these settings by highlighting it, pressing Enter, and changing the setting. Compression ratio of new drive sets DoubleSpace's estimate of how much empty space you will have on the new drive.

NOTE *As previously mentioned, if you have a wide variety of files, you may find 2-to-1 to be optimistic. On the other hand, database and graphics files may compress even more than 2-to-1.*

Drive letter of new drive represents the first available drive letter DoubleSpace sees. For Drive letter of new drive, note that you are choosing the drive letter of the new compressed drive, not the host drive, which won't change.

Watch out for overlapping drive letters. Be careful to make sure that DoubleSpace doesn't map the new drive onto a letter that you're not using now, but do use occasionally. For example, you may sometimes load a RAM drive or a network drive—make sure you don't use the same drive letter for a compressed drive.

If you make this mistake, and later load a network (or InterLnk), you may get the following error message:

```
A network drive has been connected using
drive letter E. To use drive C, you must
first remove the network drive or assign
it a different drive letter.
```

Remove the network connection, and edit DBLSPACE.INI to change the host drive name. (Editing DBLSPACE.INI is discussed later in this chapter.)

Press Enter when you have the settings correct; remove any floppy disks from A drive; then press C to begin creating the new drive. Note that this is a much quicker process than compressing an existing drive, and also does not require a defragmentation.

When complete, DoubleSpace mounts the new drive and then displays a message similar to this:

```
Microsoft DoubleSpace Setup
============================

DoubleSpace has created drive H by converting free space
from drive C.

Space used from drive C:         10.0 MB
Free space on new drive:         18.0 MB
Compression ratio:               1.8 to 1
```

```
Total time to create:               2 minutes
Drive C still contains 15.2M of free uncompressed space.
To quit DoubleSpace and restart your computer, press
Enter.

ENTER=Continue   F1=Help
```

> *You can't tell DoubleSpace to compress only a specific directory. But you can create a compressed drive from empty space, then use the MOVE command to move a subdirectory, or another set of files, into it.*

Compressing or Creating Drives from the Command Line

If you prefer, you can compress an existing drive from the command line, using the DBLSPACE/COMPRESS command. First, you specify the drive you wish to compress; then use the /NEWDRIVE= switch to specify the name you want to reassign to its host-drive incarnation; then use the /RESERVE= switch to specify how much space you want to keep uncompressed on the host drive.

For example, to compress D drive, specify drive K as the host drive, and reserve 10M to the uncompressed drive K, enter...

DBLSPACE/COMPRESS D: /NEWDRIVE=K /RESERVE=10

You can also use this abbreviated syntax...

DBLSPACE/COM D:/NEW=K /RES=10

Similarly, you can create a compressed drive using empty space on an existing drive, by means of the DBLSPACE/CREATE command.

The syntax is similar, but not identical. First, specify the host drive. Then use /NEWDRIVE= to specify the letter of the new compressed drive. Then, you can use /RESERVE= to specify the amount of space to leave uncompressed on your host drive.

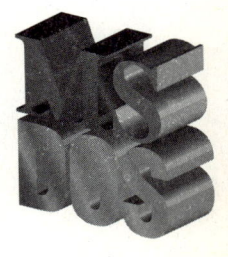

For example, to create a compressed drive K on the host C drive, and leave 5MB uncompressed on C drive, enter...

    `DBLSPACE/CREATE C: /NEWDRIVE=K /RESERVE=5`

The acceptable abbreviation for /CREATE is /CR.

Note that here—but not in /COMPRESS—you can choose to specify how much space the compressed drive should *take* from the uncompressed host, rather than how much space it should leave alone. This can be a bit more intuitive. Use the /SIZE (or /SI) switch.

For example, if you wanted your new drive to use 20M of empty space on the host drive, you would type...

    `DBLSPACE/CREATE C: /NEWDRIVE=K /SIZE=20`

You can use /RESERVE or /SIZE but not both.

Mounting and Unmounting DoubleSpaced Drives

When you boot a computer with a hard disk that used DoubleSpace, DOS automatically makes the connection between the compressed drive and its drive letter. This is called *mounting* the drive. (For years, UNIX users have used a *mount* command to gain access to remote file systems—this is a variant on that idea.)

Normally, you would only unmount a compressed drive when you want to perform an operation on it, that is, defragmenting or resizing a drive. In these cases, DoubleSpace unmounts and remounts the drive automatically.

Occasionally, however, you might need to unmount and remount a drive manually, perhaps to change a drive assignment.

To unmount compressed Drive G, enter...

    `DBLSPACE /UNMOUNT G:`

To remount the drive, enter...

    `DBLSPACE /MOUNT G:`

DoubleSpace and Your Floppy Disk

Now that you can DoubleSpace those 1.44M disks, who needs a 2.88M drive?

Well... *maybe*.

You would think that DOS would recognize its own DoubleSpace drives and run them transparently. You'd be wrong: DoubleSpace floppies don't automount. DOS normally treats the disk like any other 100 percent-full disk; the only visible file is a 178-byte file called READTHIS.TXT. When you do, you're told:

```
This disk has been compressed by MS-DOS 6 DoubleSpace.

To make this disk's contents accessible, change to this
drive and then type
    DBLSPACE/MOUNT
at the command prompt.
```

All the other space, of course, is taken up by the system-hidden, read-only file DBLSPACE.000, your compressed volume.

Even worse, you can't even manually mount a DoubleSpace floppy from within Windows—or even a DOS session generated by Windows. You have to exit Windows altogether, or else suffer the message:

```
You are running Windows. To run DblSpace, you must first
quit Windows.
```

This is a royal pain in the you-know-what. A woefully inadequate workaround is to include the statement...

DBLSPACE /MOUNT A:

...in your AUTOEXEC.BAT file. Then, after DOS boots from the hard disk, insert your compressed floppy in A drive, and it will automatically be mounted. If the next statement is...

WIN

...then Windows will load after the disk is mounted.

However, if you remove that floppy and insert a new one, you'll have to exit Windows and manually mount the new one all over again.

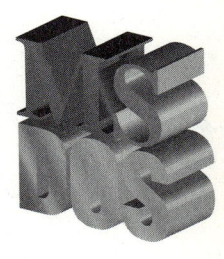

> **NOTE:** Of course this means you can't boot from a DoubleSpace floppy, because the system already must be running in order to mount it.
>
> By the way, DoubleSpace also supports Bernoulli drives.

> **6.2:** All the preceding is academic if you are using DOS 6.2. Compressed floppy disks and other compressed removable media now mount automatically under both DOS and Windows. This increases DoubleSpace's resident size by 4K, but the increase will probably be well spent.
>
> Still, you can turn off automounting, if you wish, by entering **DBLSPACE /AUTOMOUNT=0** at the prompt. You will, of course, have to reboot before the change takes effect.

Using DoubleSpace and RAM Drives

With the advent of Windows, which eats all the memory it can get its hands on, RAM drives have been going out of style. Still, if you use them, DoubleSpace can (roughly) double their size, too, with only a minor reduction in RAM drive speed.

Let's say you now have a RAM D drive: and you want to create a compressed RAM drive G: on the host RAM drive. In AUTOEXEC.BAT, enter...

    DBLSPACE /CREATE D: /NEWDRIVE=G: /RESERVE=0.0015

We've chosen /RESERVE=0.0015 to minimize the wasted RAM used by the host RAM drive.

There's only one issue: your RAM drive now has a different drive name. If you have batch files that used D drive, you'll have to change them to reflect the new drive name.

DoubleSpacing Stacker Drives

Well, first of all, should you? Not necessarily. You won't necessarily get better performance. In fact, DoubleSpace roughly matches the performance of Stacker 3.0, and often falls short.

And Stacker 3.0 does have several features that aren't available on DoubleSpace, including:

- ✔ *Stacker Anywhere*, which lets you compress a disk that can be uncompressed on a system that doesn't have Stacker.

- ✔ *Previewing*, which tells you how much a disk will compress before you actually compress it.

If you're happy with Stacker, therefore, there's no universally compelling reason to switch. Also, if you have the Stacker co-processor card, DoubleSpace won't work with it.

On the other hand, DoubleSpace is exceptionally well-integrated into DOS, and the outlook is for it to be increasingly well-integrated in future versions. Now that disk compression is part of DOS, using DoubleSpace could simplify your configuration and make it a little bit easier to troubleshoot problems. If nothing else, you have one less vendor support line to call.

Both Stacker and DoubleSpace are relatively reliable; early Stacker 3.0 upgraders have reported some problems, but then DoubleSpace isn't perfect either.

One way or another, you will have to decide; you can't run Stacker on one drive and DoubleSpace on another.

DBLSPACE/CHKDSK

DoubleSpace CVFs contain internal structures that DOS never sees. Table 5.1 shows the layout of a CVF:

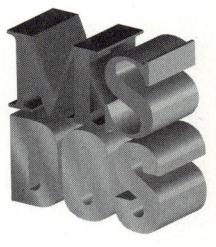

Table 5.1
Internal View of Compressed Volume File

Name	Size	Description
MDBPB	1 sector	Contains MS-DOS 4 BPB and DoubleSpace information, especially the maximum capacity of the compressed drive.
BitFAT	Varying	Contains one bit for each sector of available file space in the CVF (sector heap). Sectors in use are marked "1," unused sectors "0."
Reserved1	1 sector	Reserved.
MDFAT	Up to 256K	4-byte entries that map FAT clusters to clusters in the CVF sector heap, and mark whether each cluster's data is compressed.
Reserved2	31 sectors	Reserved.
Boot Sector	1 sector	DoubleSpace drive boot sector.
Reserved3	Varying	Reserved.
FAT	Varying	Standard MS-DOS FAT for DoubleSpace drive.
Root Directory	32 sectors	DoubleSpace drive root directory.

Name	Size	Description
Reserved4	2 sectors	Reserved.
Sector Heap	60 sectors	Sectors available to store new data as needed.
2nd Stamp	1+ sector	Last sector(s) of CVF; contains 2nd DoubleSpace signature.

All this means you can have a perfectly clean host drive, and still have cross-linked or lost clusters on your compressed drive. "Classic" CHKDSK won't catch this. DBLSPACE/CHKDSK will.

If you have a compressed drive, and you run CHKDSK on the host drive, DOS will automatically load and run DBLSPACE/CHKDSK when "Classic" CHKDSK finishes. You can also run DBLSPACE/CHKDSK separately at any time.

DBLSPACE/CHKDSK works like regular CHKDSK in one respect: entering it without a switch only displays lost clusters. Using the /F switch chains those lost clusters that can be fixed, and turns them into files.

In particular, DBLSPACE/CHKDSK checks the MDFAT, which translates the FAT clusters that DOS sees into the locations where DoubleSpace has actually placed the compressed data.

Beginning with DOS 6.2, DoubleSpace no longer includes the /CHKDSK switch. Replacing it is the ScanDisk utility, which is a full-featured, disk-repair tool. See Chapter 8 for more about using ScanDisk.

Defragmenting DoubleSpaced Drives

Regular defragmentation programs don't work on compressed drives, because all they do is defragment the files that are visible to DOS—not the internal structure of the Compressed Volume File. In fact, they can even increase the fragmentation of a compressed drive.

That's why there's a DBLSPACE/DEFRAGMENT program. DBLSPACE/DEFRAGMENT (or, in compressed lingo, DBLSPACE/DEF), consolidates all the *used* sectors within the CVF. It's most often used before you shrink a compressed drive; it's not really designed to make a compressed drive run faster.

To defragment compressed D drive, enter...

`DBLSPACE/DEF D:`

To defragment your current (compressed) drive, enter...

`DBLSPACE/DEF`

When you run Microsoft Defrag on a host drive, it automatically runs DBLSPACE/DEF when it finishes. Since DBLSPACE/DEF has been known to take much longer than the host defragmentation, you may want to cancel it. You can press Esc at any time to safely stop defragmenting.

Occasionally, you may defragment a compressed drive and still be told that it's too fragmented to shrink. In that case, you may have clusters which DBLSPACE/DEF could not move. Try using Microsoft Defrag with the /H switch that permits it to move hidden files...

`DEFRAG /H`

Deleting Your DoubleSpaced Drive

You can't uncompress a compressed drive, but you *can* move its information elsewhere and then delete it.

6.2 *In response to DOS 6 user requests, DOS 6.2 now provides the /UNCOMPRESS switch. Assuming you have enough disk space, use the DBLSPACE /UNCOMPRESS [drive:] command to uncompress the drive. This also removes DBLSPACE.BIN from memory.*

First, defragment the drive using DBLSPACE/DEFRAG. Next, shrink the drive as much as possible—creating as much space as possible on the host drive in the process. To do this, type DBLSPACE/SIZE.

Next, back up the compressed drive's contents. If you have a tape backup system, use that. If the amount of space on your uncompressed host drive now exceeds the space used on the compressed drive, you can XCOPY your compressed files to your uncompressed host drive. For example, if DoubleSpace displays your compressed drive as C, and your host drive as K, enter...

    XCOPY C:*.* K: /E /S

If you have *most* of the space you need on your uncompressed drive, you can finish XCOPYing to floppies after XCOPY reports running out of space on the host drive.

Then type **DBLSPACE/DEL**, followed by the compressed drive you want to delete, for example:

    DBLSPACE/DEL H:

You are then asked the following:

    Deleting drive H will permanently erase it and all the
    files it contains.
    Are you sure you want to delete drive H?

Press **Y**. DoubleSpace will respond:

    DoubleSpace is deleting drive H.
    DoubleSpace has deleted drive H.

This works, unless you want to delete a compressed C drive, your boot drive. DoubleSpace will tell you:

    Drive C is your startup disk drive and should not be
    deleted.

Now things get a bit more convoluted, but stay with it.

After you've followed the preceding instructions to back up your files, change to the host drive. Next, clear the system-hidden and read-only attributes on the files DoubleSpace in the root directory by typing...

ATTRIB -S -H -R DBLSPACE.*

> *Your compressed volume file is usually named DBLSPACE.000, but might have a different number in its extension if you have more than one compressed drive, or if you formerly had another one and deleted it.*
>
> *To make absolutely sure you are deleting the correct drive, run DBLSPACE /LIST first.*

Then delete them. If you have only one compressed drive in your root directory, this will work:

DEL DBLSPACE.*

> *Make sure not to delete the DBLSPACE files in your DOS directory (DBLSPACE.EXE, DBLSPACE.HLP, DBLSPACE.BIN, DBLSPACE.INF and DBLSPACE.SYS), or else you won't be able to run DBLSPACE in the future.*

Now edit your CONFIG.SYS and AUTOEXEC.BAT files. If you now have no DBLSPACE files, delete the device driver line. (It begins DEVICE=C:\DOS\DBLSPACE.SYS or DEVICEHIGH=C:\DOS\DBLSPACE.SYS.) If you instructed a program to load from a compressed drive name, edit it to load from its original uncompressed drive.

Finally, reboot; your system should appear as it originally did, sans compressed drive.

Introducing DoubleSpace

> After you delete a DBLSPACE drive, DOS might still recognize that drive name until you reboot. In fact, you can actually run a directory on the no-longer existing compressed volume.
>
> Eventually, though, you'll crash your system if you keep it up. Better to just reboot and put the whole compressed drive behind you.

Changing the Size of a Compressed Drive

You can shrink or expand a compressed drive—assuming there's enough available space to do it. Use the DBLSPACE/SIZE command.

As you just saw, entering DBLSPACE/SIZE without any parameters shrinks the current compressed volume as far as possible: zero bytes free. You can, of course, take a more measured approach. The following command assigns compressed drive H exactly 40M of the space on its host drive:

```
DBLSPACE /SIZE=40 H:
```

Conversely, you can define how much space should be left on the host drive by adding the /RESERVE switch. In this example, 10M will remain. Note that the drive name in the command is still the compressed drive:

```
DBLSPACE /SIZE /RESERVE=10 H:
```

You can "grow" the compressed drive to fill all the space available, with the following command:

```
DBLSPACE /SIZE /RESERVE=0 H:
```

Before changing the size of a drive, DoubleSpace first unmounts it, and then remounts it when finished with the task.

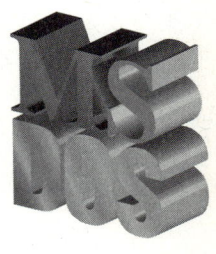

Formatting a DoubleSpaced Drive

DoubleSpace provides a special utility, DBLSPACE /FORMAT, for formatting compressed drives. When you use DBLSPACE /FORMAT, the result is an empty compressed volume *that can't be unformatted.*

To format the compressed D drive, enter...

DBLSPACE /FORMAT D:

If you format a host drive, eliminating its data, you also eliminate any compressed drive contained within it.

Getting Information about DoubleSpaced Drives

You can always get information about the status of your DoubleSpaced drives from the command prompt by typing...

DBLSPACE/INFO (or DBLSPACE/I).

You'll get a report like this:

```
DoubleSpace is examining Drive C.

Compressed drive C (HOST_FOR_C) was created on 01-31-93
at 12:01 pm. Drive C is stored on uncompressed drive H in
the file DBLSPACE.000.

                 Compressed      Uncompressed
                 Drive C         Drive H
Total space:     32.60 MB        20.32 MB
Space used:      8.13 MB         17.86 MB
Space free:      24.48 MB**      2.46 MB

The actual compression ratio is 1.6 to 1.

** based on estimated compression ratio of 2.0 to 1.
```

> **NOTE:** *DoubleSpace sometimes reports estimates of remaining space that are substantially off-base. DoubleSpace might estimate that it can compress additional files more than it actually will be able to.*
>
> *Here's an extreme example. Suppose you have 10M of uncompressed space left over. DoubleSpace thinks that when you fill that space, it will be able to compress the new files at 1.7 to 1. Therefore, it reports you have 17M remaining.*
>
> *Then you come along with 12M of ZIP files that can't be compressed at all. Lo and behold, DoubleSpace reports that you're out of space even before you finish.*
>
> *Take DoubleSpace's estimates with a grain of salt.*

DBLSPACE/LIST (or DBLSPACE/L) will give you a detailed list of exactly which drives are which. This sample listing reports that C drive is compressed and appears as DBLSPACE.000 on the host D drive.

```
Drive  Type                      Total Free  Total Size  CVF File name
-----  ----                      ----------  ----------  -------------
  A    Floppy drive                0.00 MB     1.39 MB
  B    Removable-media drive     No disk in drive
  C    Compressed hard drive      22.58 MB   189.26 MB   D:\DBLSPACE.000
  D    Local hard drive            4.99 MB   124.24 MB
  E    Available for DoubleSpace
  F    Available for DoubleSpace
  G    Available for DoubleSpace
  H    Available for DoubleSpace
  I    Removable-media drive     No disk in drive
```

About DBLSPACE.INI

One of the hidden files on your host drive is DBLSPACE.INI, which controls many aspects of how DoubleSpace works. If you clear the system, hidden and read-only bits on DBLSPACE.INI, you can see its contents, something like this:

```
MaxRemovableDrives=1
FirstDrive=G
LastDrive=K
MaxFileFragments=128
ActivateDrive=K,C0
```

MaxRemovableDrives counts the number of floppies, Bernoulli drives, and other removable media that DoubleSpace will need to keep track of. *FirstDrive* represents the first letter that can be assigned to a DoubleSpace drive; in almost all cases, leave it alone. *LastDrive* represents the last letter that may be assigned.

MaxRemovableDrives and LastDrive can be controlled through the Options item in the Tools menu of the DoubleSpace program. You can't set LastDrive to a letter lower than a drive letter already assigned to a DoubleSpace drive, but you may want to set it higher, in the event you plan to create more DoubleSpace compressed volumes on your hard drive.

ActivateDrive instructs DBLSPACE to activate both the host drive and its compressed drive. *MaxFileFragments* displays the number of fragments that a compressed volume file may contain. Note that this doesn't have anything to do with the fragmentation of the host drive and isn't affected by defragging the host drive.

You may occasionally get an error message, indicating that you have too many fragments, and that your compressed drive cannot be mounted. In rare instances even running the DBLSPACE/DEFRAG utility, which is specially designed to defragment a compressed volume, won't solve the problem. Try increasing MaxFileFragments in DBLSPACE.INI.

If you are using DoubleSpace under DOS 6.2, you'll find two other entries in DBLSPACE.INI: the `AutoMount=` *line and the* `Doubleguard=` *line.*

Automount indicates whether or not compressed floppy drives and other compressed removable media are automatically mounted when accessed. `0` *indicates that automounting is off;* `1` *indicates that automounting is on.*

Doubleguard indicates whether or not the DoubleGuard feature is enabled. 1 *indicates that DoubleGuard will constantly check its memory for damage by other programs;* 0 *turns this feature off.*

Editing DBLSPACE.INI is even more dangerous than editing CONFIG.SYS. It's a bomb waiting to go off. Save and print your current DBLSPACE.INI. Remember to use a text editor that won't add formatting. If DBLSPACE.INI is damaged, not only will DoubleSpace not be able to find your compressed drives...your system may not boot at all.

Even worse, since a DOS 6 boot floppy will quickly look to the contents of DBLSPACE.INI, that won't work either! You'll have to boot from a DOS 5 or older boot floppy and then immediately edit DBLSPACE.INI back the way it was when you started.

Understanding the Error: `R6003 - Integer Divide by Zero` Error Message

This error message can occur because of corrupted DoubleSpace files or incompatible TSR programs. To solve this sticky problem, do the following:

1. From Disk 1 of the original DOS 6 Upgrade disk, copy DBLSPACE.BIN to the root directory of your host drive.

2. From Disk 3 of the 3 1/2-inch set or Disk 4 of the 5 1/4-inch set, expand the DBLSPACE.EX_ file to DBLSPACE.EXE, and then cold boot the computer.

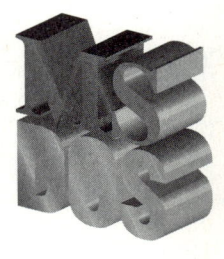

3. If the problem persists, the solution is a matter of trial and error. Reboot again, and then press F5 or F8 to eliminate device drives and TSRs.

Understanding Windows Error Messages

When using DoubleSpace on a system with Windows, there are a number of unique error messages you may encounter. You may see one of these messages after installing DoubleSpace or after attempting to create a *permanent swap file* (PSF) on a compressed drive.

The `Corrupt Swap File` Error Message

As the DOS 6 README.TXT file says, if you use a Windows permanent swap file, it must be located on an uncompressed drive. If your permanent swap file is on a compressed drive, Windows displays the following message when it starts:

```
The permanent swap file is corrupt
```

The reason you cannot create a PSF on a compressed drive is because Windows accesses a PSF directly through the disk controller if the 32-Bit Disk Access (FastDisk) option is selected, and through the BIOS if this option is not selected. Because both of these methods access your hard disk at a level that is below compressed drives, Windows reads invalid data, which causes the error message. So, because Windows performs direct disk read/write operations to a PSF, the swap file must be located on a physical hard disk, not a CVF.

To work around this problem, delete the PSF, and create a PSF on your host drive (the drive that actually contains the DoubleSpace CVF). Also, when you create a new PSF on the host drive, you may receive the following warning:

```
Windows will not use more than the virtual memory speci-
fied by the Recommended Size. Are you sure you want to
create a larger swap file?
```

As long as the PSF is not larger than four times your physical memory, Windows can use a swap file that is larger than the recommended size.

If there is not enough disk space on an uncompressed drive for a swap file, you must either delete files from the host drive or reduce the size of the compressed drive. If your compressed drive is C and your host drive is H, for example, you can use the following command to decrease the size of the compressed drive, creating 12M of free space on the host drive (H):

```
DBLSPACE   /SIZE   /RESERVE=12 C:
```

If you receive the error message `Drive is too fragmented to resize`, enter **DEFRAG /H** at the DOS prompt.

The Unsupported DOS Version Error Message in Windows 3.0

If you are running Windows 3.0 in Real mode (in order to run SWAPFILE.EXE), you may receive the following message:

```
Unsupported DOS version; upgrade to DOS version 3.1 or
higher
```

Obviously, this message is wrong. If you have Windows 3.0a, you can work around this problem by running SPATCH.BAT, which is located on your original MS-DOS 6.0 disks.

If you have Windows 3.0, you must use the version of SPATCH.BAT that is available on the MS-DOS 6 Supplemental Disks. As an alternative, you can modify the SPATCH.BAT file provided with the MS-DOS 6 Upgrade by using an ASCII text editor, such as MS-DOS Editor, to change the SET ADDR= line in SPATCH.BAT from SET ADDR=2df2 to SET ADDR=2dc0. The version of SPATCH.BAT on the MS-DOS 6 Supplemental Disks works on both the Windows 3.0 and Windows 3.0a SWAPFILE.EXE files.

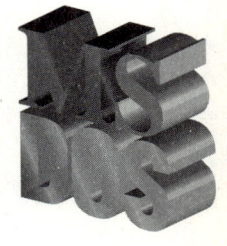

If you have Windows 3.0 (not 3.0a), and you run the version of SPATCH.BAT provided with MS-DOS 6 Upgrade, your SWAPFILE.EXE file will be corrupted. You can restore this file by copying the SWAPFILE.SAV file as SWAPFILE.EXE to your Windows directory. The SWAPFILE.SAV file is not always easy to find because it is placed in the directory from which you ran SPATCH.BAT. If you run SPATCH.BAT from the root directory of your C drive, for example, use the following command to restore your PSF:

```
COPY C:\SWAPFILE.SAV C:\WINDOWS\SWAPFILE.EXE
```

You can order the MS-DOS 6 Supplemental Disks with the form in the back of the MS-DOS 6 User's Guide (and $5.00, of course).

Using a Data-Compression Alternative

If you do not want to use DoubleSpace, but you still want the advantages of data compression, there is an easy-to-use alternative: a data-compression program such as PKZIP or LHA. One of these utilities enables you to compress an entire directory to one file, expand it for use, and then update the archive and clear the directory when you're done. You can download the PKZIP or LHA utilities from any bulletin board or CompuServe.

The PKZIP utilities are shareware and require a registration fee, but LHA is freeware (no fee). The downside is that LHA compresses and uncompresses a little slower than PKZIP.

Using either PKZIP or LHA, here's how you can do data compression and decompression on whole directories. First, make sure that PKZIP and PKUNZIP (or LHA) are in a directory that is included in your PATH statement in AUTOEXEC.BAT.

Suppose you use WordPerfect 5.1, which takes up about 5M of space. Create your ZIP file by changing to the WP51 directory and entering this command (if you are using LHA, omit the hyphen):

```
PKZIP  -M  WP  *.*
```

This command shrinks the directory to about half the size. Now create the following WP.BAT batch file:

```
@echo off
cd\wp51
pkunzip wp.zip
wp
pkzip -u -m wp *.*
```

When you enter your usual WP command, the batch file expands the directory. Run WordPerfect—when you're done, the batch file continues by updating the ZIP file and deleting all the individual files in the directory. Granted, this technique is slow, but again, it consumes only about half the space and frees you from some of the negative aspects of DoubleSpace; the best thing to do is type **WP**, and then go get a cup of coffee.

Many of the DoubleSpace error mesages are a wee bit cryptic, (for example, the infamous `The CVF is damaged`) *message. DOS 6.2 addresses this shortcoming by replacing these messages with clearer messages that tell what corrective measures you need to take.*

Summary

You've now walked through the procedure of installing a disk, from screwdriver to data compression. You've learned about installing the two most popular types of drives, IDE and SCSI, both from a hardware and software standpoint. You've walked through setting up partitions and formatting your new disk. And you've nearly doubled its available space.

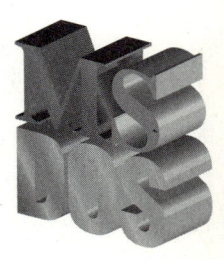

Almost every one of these topics represents an area of transition. SCSI drives may finally be coming of age, as the SCSI-2 standard and drivers like ASPI increasingly become popular. If so, the interface might actually meet its potential of connecting literally hundreds of devices without adding overhead to your PC's main bus.

Increasingly, users will be using partitioning to make room for more than one operating system—non-DOS partitions, as DOS parochially calls them.

Finally, Microsoft is positioning DoubleSpace and the associated Microsoft Real-Time Compression Interface as a way for third parties to build data compression into all kinds of products. (Who knows; maybe they'll even decide to support DoubleSpace on Windows NT?)

MS-DOS

Part Three:

Optimizing Your Disk with DOS 6.2

Creating and Using Directories 275
Managing Disks and Files 315
Tuning Your Disk with DOS 6.2 Tools 383

MS
DOS

CHAPTER 6

Creating and Using Directories

by Bill Camarda

So you've just formatted your hard disk. This vast storage area is available to you, with all the infrastructure in place for you to do just about anything you want with it.

Now you have a decision to make. In six months, which do you want: an orderly, comprehensible file system that makes you more productive, and the envy of your friends and colleagues—or an awful mess that confuses the daylights out of you and anyone else who must use your computer?

For many DOS users, the file system "just happens" as they slowly learn—a little bit at a time—about the way MS-DOS handles directories, subdirectories, and files. But this is one area in which the payoff for understanding what you're doing now, instead of later, is tremendous.

The commands described here and in the next chapter are the ones you'll probably use most often, on a daily basis. We'll walk through the commands first: there's more to them than you may have picked up on your own.

Then I'll describe a strategy for keeping things in order. And if you've inherited (or evolved) a chaotic file system, you'll learn some techniques for clearing the underbrush and turning over a new leaf.

Understanding the Root Directory

Whenever you format a disk—hard or floppy—DOS creates a root directory, named "\". (Every DOS partition on the hard drive gets its own root directory, too.) To distinguish between root directories on different disks, just pay attention to the drive name: A:\, B:\, C:\, D:\, and so on.

This root directory is physically located in the control area of your disk, after the DOS boot record and the file allocation table (FAT).

Every file or subdirectory you place on the hard drive "grows from" the root directory. To make the point even more visual, DOS uses the term *directory tree* to mean any directory list that shows the relationship of files and directories to the root (see fig. 6.1).

Figure 6.1

A sample directory tree.

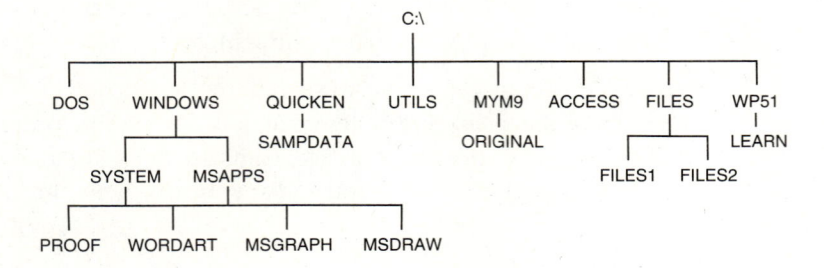

```
                              C:\
  ┌──────┬────────┬────────┬───┴──┬────────┬────────┬────────┐
 DOS  WINDOWS  QUICKEN  UTILS   MYM9   ACCESS    FILES     WP51
         │        │              │              ┌─┴──┐      │
         │     SAMPDATA        ORIGINAL       FILES1 FILES2 LEARN
      ┌──┴──┐
   SYSTEM  MSAPPS
      ┌─────┼──────┬──────┐
    PROOF WORDART MSGRAPH MSDRAW
```

Root Directory Structure

If you read Chapter 4, you know that the root directory has a specific structure. It consists of one 32-byte entry for each file. Of those 32 bytes, 22 take care of the following items:

- ✔ File name (8 bytes)
- ✔ File extension (3 bytes)
- ✔ File attributes (1 byte, which contains 6 bits that set aspects of the file's behavior, plus 2 more that aren't used)
- ✔ Time the file was last changed
- ✔ Date the file was last changed
- ✔ Starting cluster
- ✔ File size

The other 10 bytes are reserved by DOS "for future use."

When DOS establishes a specific location for the root directory, it also establishes a specific size: 512 entries (16K) on a hard disk, fewer on floppies. Table 6.1 shows how DOS assigns root directory sizes.

Table 6.1
Root Directory Size

Disk Capacity	Entries	Root Directory Size
360K	112	3.5K
720K	112	3.5K
1.2M	224	7K
1.44M	224	7K
2.88M	448	14K

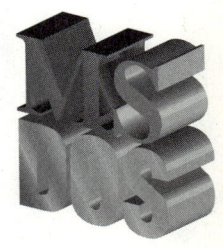

> **NOTE:** *You may have noticed that when you format a disk, you get slightly less usable space than DOS says you will. A disk formatted at 720K, for example, gives you 730,112 bytes, which equals only 713K. The root directory, along with the FAT and DOS boot record, account for this "missing" space.*

Understanding Subdirectories

If this were MS-DOS 1, you would now know all you needed to know about the DOS file system. A root directory was all you got. You could squeeze 64 file names onto a single 160K disk, and that's it.

It quickly became obvious that this wasn't good enough. In developing DOS 2, Microsoft and IBM had two models to choose from. They could follow the lead of CP/M, DOS's predecessor, and simply allow users to divide their disks into smaller chunks, along the lines of today's disk partitions.

Or they could follow the example of UNIX, creating a hierarchical file system that allows for many levels of subdirectories, each of which may contain not only files, but also other subdirectories.

They chose the UNIX path…which quickly led to the DOS file-system structure we use today.

> **NOTE:** *The root directory name "\," like many aspects of the DOS file system, traces its roots to UNIX. In UNIX, however, it's called "/" (forward slash). DOS did things backwards because it was already using the forward slash for switches, as in the command DIR A: /P. (UNIX uses hyphens for this purpose, as in: LS -L.) Early on, the backslash bewildered not only UNIX users, but also DOS users overseas, whose keyboards often didn't contain a backslash.*
>
> *The use of a dot (.) to name the current directory and a double dot (..) for the parent directory are lifted directly from UNIX.*

Creating Subdirectories

If you have just used the DOS setup program to install DOS on the hard disk of a new computer, you already have one subdirectory, DOS, located on drive C—hence, C:\DOS.

To view this subdirectory from the command prompt in the root directory of drive C, just type **DIR**. The file list includes…

```
AUTOEXEC.BAT
CONFIG.SYS
COMMAND.COM
DOS     <DIR>
```

The word <DIR> appears next to the subdirectory's name, indicating that it is a subdirectory under the C:> root directory. The first two files—AUTOEXEC.BAT and CONFIG.SYS—are the only files that must appear in your root directory, no matter what else is in the root directory.

COMMAND.COM, the command interpreter that displays the DOS prompt and processes your commands, typically is placed in both the root directory and C:\DOS. These file names are shown without a <DIR> notation, indicating that they are part of the current directory.

If you are in the root directory of drive C, you can make a new subdirectory, DATAFILS, by using the MD (make directory) command…

MD DATAFILS

…and, of course, press Enter.

If, on the other hand, you were in another subdirectory on drive C, you could still create a new subdirectory directly underneath the root directory by using the backslash (\) to indicate that you wish to begin at the root, as follows:

MD \DATAFILS

When you create a subdirectory, DOS creates an entry for it in the root directory. This entry is almost identical to the entry DOS would create for a regular file, except that it contains a length of zero, and it includes a directory bit which indicates that DOS should read the entry as the pointer to a subdirectory, not as a file.

If you ask to list the contents of that subdirectory, DOS goes to the starting cluster of the subdirectory, as listed in the root directory.

Naming Subdirectories

Because a subdirectory closely resembles a file, the rules for naming them are the same:

- ✔ Directory names can be up to eight characters long. Although adding a three-character extension to subdirectory names is legal, it's not recommended (because of the possibility of confusing files with subdirectories—already a potential problem, as you'll see).

- ✔ Acceptable characters include the entire alphabet, all numbers, and the following special characters:

    ^ $ ~ ! # % & - { } ( )

- ✔ Extended characters—foreign language, line-drawing, and scientific characters that are built into your system but don't correspond to keys on your keyboard—are acceptable.

- ✔ DOS control characters are not acceptable. They are the first 32 characters in the IBM character set, 0–31, below the 128 ASCII characters that include the alphabet, all numerals, and basic punctuation. (Perhaps the most familiar is character 003, Ctrl-C, which halts a command in progress.)

- ✔ The following characters, most of which have other DOS functions, are not acceptable:

    , \ < > | * ? +

- ✔ You can use a period only to designate an extension (one, two, or three acceptable characters must follow it).

- ✔ You can't give a directory a name that DOS has already reserved (AUX, CON, or PRN, for example).

NOTE

In the past, some users added extended characters to directory names to provide a modicum of security for the files contained in those directories. The theory was that not every casual snooper knows how to generate the extended characters.

In particular, some people used the DOS blank character generated by pressing Alt and then typing 255 on the numeric keypad. This looks like the entry created with a spacebar, as in:

```
FILE NAM.DOC
```

But when a casual user enters a space after `FILE`*, DOS will assume the directory name has ended and report an error message due to the incorrect syntax.*

Nowadays, however, anyone who knows the MS-DOS Shell or the Windows File Manager can get around this. You can do a little better (but not much) by using the ATTRIB +H file attribute command to hide each confidential file. (Be careful to keep track of these hidden files somewhere. You could lose them yourself.)

This gimmick can still be defeated with the View All Files command in the MS-DOS Shell, or the DIR /A command, but you have to know that the files exist, and how to display them.

Well, heck, it's something.

Two other restrictions on directory naming are pretty obvious. First, you can't place a subdirectory in a parent directory that doesn't exist; and second, you can't give a subdirectory the same name as a file contained in its parent directory.

Subdirectory Size

Because a subdirectory resembles a file, it doesn't share the same size restraints as your root directory does. So, when you have a choice, how large should you make your subdirectories?

There are two answers. First, how long a list of files do you find convenient to manage? 20, 30, 50 files?

And, second, how many files can DOS conveniently manage? If you can keep your subdirectories to a single cluster, DOS will find them faster. On large drives, it's rarely an issue: a 130M hard drive, with 8K clusters, can store 256 subdirectory lists in a cluster. On smaller, slower drives, it might be a different story. *For more information about clusters, refer to Chapter 4.*

By the way, to the extent that occasional defragmenting improves your drive's performance on data files, it also improves performance on multiple-cluster subdirectory lists.

> *The DOS command MKDIR performs exactly the same function as MD. Through MS-DOS 5, the manual's official Command Reference referred to only MKDIR, not the shortcut. In MS-DOS 6, the manual contains no Command Reference, but the on-line reference HELP MD gets you the same information as HELP MKDIR.*

Nested Subdirectories

Unless you tell it otherwise, DOS creates the subdirectory in the directory you are working in. If you're working in the root directory on drive C, therefore, your new subdirectory appears in a directory list, like this:

```
AUTOEXEC.BAT
COMMAND.COM
CONFIG.SYS
DATAFILS <DIR>
DOS <DIR>
```

Suppose, however, that you create a subdirectory from the DOS subdirectory. The new subdirectory, called a *nested* subdirectory, is placed in the subdirectory you're working in (and is described as C:\DOS\DATAFILS).

> **NOTE:** *Backslashes are used to separate each directory level. Note also that the DOS subdirectory isn't a particularly good place for your data files—but more on that later in this chapter.*

Technically, every disk only has one directory—the root directory. All the others are subdirectories. Sometimes, different levels are distinguished by calling the higher-level subdirectory the *parent* and the lower-level subdirectory inside it the *child*.

> **TIP:** *As a general rule, don't go deeper in your directory structure than two or three levels under the root (C:\WORD\DOCS, for example). It doesn't take long to grow weary of typing long path names.*

Introducing Paths

The line...

    C:\DOS\DATAFILS

...is an example of a *path*. Paths are well-named; they describe the path DOS must take to get to a specific location, starting with the root directory and moving through each subdirectory level.

You can create many subdirectory levels—subdirectories within subdirectories. But DOS does set limits. You have to be able to reach all your subdirectories with a path no more then 66 characters long—including the root directory and all punctuation.

> **NOTE:** *The paths we're discussing here are related to, but not the same as, the PATH statement which, when included in your AUTOEXEC.BAT file, provides DOS with a default group of paths to follow. More on the PATH statement later.*

Moving from One Directory to Another (CD)

The Change Directory command enables you to move from one subdirectory to any other subdirectory on the current drive. When you issue this command, the subdirectory you move to becomes the current directory.

To move from a parent to a child directory, type **CD**, followed by the name of the child directory, such as the following syntax:

`CD directoryname`

To move down two levels, you'd use both the name of the subdirectory and *its* child subdirectory, as in...

`CD CHILD\GRNDCHLD`

Because you're starting from the current directory, you don't have to begin with a backslash.

To move from a child directory to a parent directory, remember that DOS understands two dots (..) to mean the parent of any current directory...

`CD..`

To move somewhere else on the drive, type **CD** followed by a path statement that leads from where you are to wherever you want to be. Start with a backslash (\) to tell DOS you want to begin at the root directory of your current drive...

`CD \FRIEND\FRNDSKID`

(That first backslash was missing from the previous example, because you wanted that path to begin with the *current subdirectory*.)

Changing Current Subdirectories on Another Drive

What if you want to move to a subdirectory on another drive? You'll have to change to that drive first.

Moving from One Directory to Another (CD)

Which brings up a perhaps subtle point (as illustrated by fig. 6.2): *every drive has its own working directory.* CD, an internal DOS command, can change that directory from wherever you invoke it. By definition, changing the working subdirectory on the current drive takes you to the new working subdirectory.

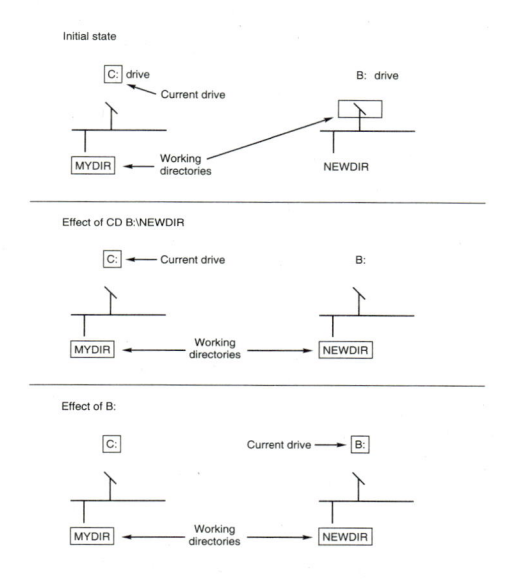

Figure 6.2

An illustration of change in working subdirectories.

At point (A) in this figure, drive C is the current drive whereas the directory named \MYDIR is the working directory on drive C. The root directory (\) on drive B is the working directory on that drive, even though drive B is not the current drive.

Point (B) shows the effect of issuing the CD B:\NEWDIR command. The working directory on drive B changes to \NEWDIR, even though C: remains the current drive.

At point (C) the user changes the current drive to drive B by logging onto it by entering **B:** at the keyboard. The working directory on drive C remains \MYDIR, whereas the working directory on drive B remains \NEWDIR.

Changing the working directory on another drive does not affect where you are working now. When you change to that drive, however, you are placed in the working directory you have just specified—not in the root directory of that drive.

To report the current directory on drive B, type…

    `CD B:`

To change the current directory on drive B, type…

    `CD B:\NEWDIR`

Then, to move to B:\NEWDIR, type…

    `B:`

> **TIP**
>
> Create one or more *temporary* or *working directories*, which serve as temporary work areas, and name them T1, T2, or W1, W2, and so on. You can, for example, use these directories as a place to uncompress files you've downloaded from a BBS.
>
> After examining the files, you can then decide where to move them. You can also throw miscellaneous files into such directories until you have time to do something permanent with them; some users create a JUNK directory for this purpose.

PROMPT: Knowing Where You Are

The default DOS setting displays a prompt that tells you your current path. If you're working in WPDOCS, a subdirectory of the root directory on drive D, for example, you normally see this prompt…

    `D:\WPDOCS>`

Your system might only be displaying the drive name, however:

    `D:>`

…in which case, you might think you were in the root directory when you really were in a subdirectory—and you could accidentally cause some real damage.

As you've learned, you can always find out what the current directory is by typing CD at the command prompt. But wouldn't it be nice to not have to ask?

To make sure that the prompt automatically displays the drive and current directory, list your AUTOEXEC.BAT file by typing **TYPE \AUTOEXEC.BAT**. If you find the line…

    PROMPT PG

…you know that the DOS prompt is displaying the entire path. (Including a PROMPT command forces DOS to take a moment to reread your drive and update the prompt after each command.)

Customizing the Prompt

Actually, $P tells DOS to display the path; $G tells DOS to display the greater-than (>) symbol. You can customize your prompt in any way you'd like by using the following metastring characters:

A metastring is a combination of one or more text characters with a metacharacter. Now do you understand? A metacharacter, incidentally, is a character that DOS does not interpret literally, but instead sees as a command to behave in a certain way. For example, the * and ? file name wild cards are metacharacters. In the case of PROMPT, the $ metacharacter indicates that DOS should substitute a specific item for the text characters that follow it.

$_ adds a linefeed; use it to create multiline prompts.

$B lets you include a pipe (|).

$D adds the current date.

$E lets you add an ANSI escape sequence.

$G adds the greater-than symbol (>).

$H lets you backspace to delete a character.

$L adds the less than symbol (<).

$N adds the current drive.

$P adds the path.

$Q adds an equal sign (=).

$T adds the current time.

$V adds the MS-DOS version number.

You can also follow the PROMPT command with any string of text you want to include in your PROMPT:

`PROMPT IT'S$T$!$_GET DOWN TO WORK!`

…to see that there's more than one way to get rid of the dreaded C:> prompt!

> ### AUTHOR'S NOTE
>
> *PROMPT is one of the most harmless DOS commands there is. You can "play" with it all day and not hurt a thing. But PROMPT is also very versatile, and it enables you to do some very practical (and fun) things. Here are a few examples of what you can do with PROMPT.*
>
> *If you need to be serious and business-like, try this prompt:*
>
> ```
> PROMPT $v$_$d  $t$h$h$h$_Current Directory $q
> $p$_Your Command:
> ```
>
> *This command produces an impressive result that is similar to this:*
>
> ```
> MS-DOS Version 5.0
> Thu  07-25-1991  16:40:10
> Current Directory = C:\DOS
> Your Command:
> ```
>
> *Note the three $h characters. They erase the hundredths of a second that the $t prints; put in three more to erase the seconds altogether. Also notice the two spaces between $d and $t.*
>
> *If you install ANSI.SYS (and invest a little time), you can design even more elaborate prompts. For example, the following prompt puts the date and time in the upper right corner of your screen, jumps to the next line, and gives the current drive and directory:*

PROMPT: Knowing Where You Are

```
PROMPT $e[s$e[1;67H$d$e[2;67H$t$h$h$h$e[u$_$p$g
```

The following variation of the command adds some reverse video:

```
PROMPT
$e[s$e[1;67H$d$e[2;67H$t$h$h$h$e[u$_$e[7m$p$g$e[m<space>
```

If you have a color monitor, the following command, followed by the CLS command, displays the familiar current drive and directory prompt, but also changes your display to white letters (foreground) on a blue background:

```
PROMPT $P$G$E[44;37m
```

*Make sure you separate the color codes (**44** and **37**) with a semicolon, and that the letter **m** is in lowercase. If you want the foreground in high-intensity white, use the following syntax:*

```
PROMPT $P$G$E[44;37;1m
```

By placing the preceding command in your AUTOEXEC.BAT file, your screen takes on the new configuration on bootup. Other combinations are possible by using the ANSI color codes and attribute codes (refer to ANSI.SYS in the Command Reference for more information).

Here's one more prompt that will really impress your friends. As you type this long command, allow the cursor to wrap to the second line by itself (the & character is used to show where you should type a space):

```
PROMPT $e[44;37;1m$e[6C/
$b$_&&&\'o.o'$_&&&$q(___)$q$_&&&&&&U$_MEOW!&$P$G
```

*Notice that the **44;37;1m** portion of the command defines the color and intensity of the characters. This can be easily changed to suit your own taste. If all goes well, your prompt should now look like the following (if you are in the DOS subdirectory):*

```
       /¦
    \'o.o'
   =(___)=
       U
 MEOW!  C:\DOS>_
```

continues

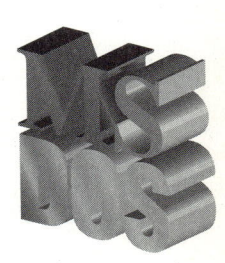

> *When you design elaborate prompts, put them in a batch file (MEOW.BAT, for the above example) so that you have to input the PROMPT line each time you want to change prompts. Also, use the batch command CALL in AUTOEXEC.BAT to call your PROMPT command (CALL C:\BATCH\MEOW.BAT, for example).*
>
> *Enjoy! See Chapter 14 for more information about PROMPT and ANSI.SYS.*

Prompts are stored in DOS' environment—a small area in memory where DOS keeps a variety of important system settings, known as environment variables. In MS-DOS 5 and 6, the default environment space set aside by DOS is 256 bytes; before that, it was 160 bytes. In addition to PROMPT, the environment space stores the following environment variables:

- ✔ Any PATH and APPEND commands you're using (as described later in this chapter)

- ✔ The COMSPEC statement, which tells DOS where to find COMMAND.COM

- ✔ Any SET statements, which establish custom environment variables your batch files and programs can use

- ✔ DIRCMD, which enables you to define exactly how your DIR lists are displayed (see Chapter 7)

- ✔ TEMP, which locates your temporary file directory and is used by Microsoft Windows as well as some other programs

- ✔ WINDIR=, which locates your Windows subdirectory if you are running Microsoft Windows

- ✔ MSDOSDATA=, which tells DOS where to look for files such as the Microsoft Anti-Virus initialization file and Microsoft Backup files

If you add a long prompt, and you already have long PATH or APPEND statements, DOS tries to increase the environment space. If it can't—because memory-resident programs are in the way, for example—you'll see a message telling you that you are...

```
Out of environment space
```

You don't want to increase environment space indiscriminately, because it comes straight out of your 640K conventional memory for program execution. But increasing it a little won't hurt much.

In MS-DOS 5 and 6, you can place the following line in your CONFIG.SYS file to increase environment space from the current 256 bytes to 320 bytes:

```
SHELL=COMMAND.COM /E:320 /P
```

You can increase or decrease environment space in 16-byte chunks. If you ask for another value, MS-DOS rounds up to the next higher multiple of 16.

The preceding SHELL=COMMAND.COM statement assumes that COMMAND.COM is in your root directory. If it's elsewhere, you must specify the exact path. If, for example, it's in your C:\DOS directory, then instead use...

```
SHELL=C:\DOS\COMMAND.COM /E:320 /P
```

Be careful when you edit the shell line in your CONFIG.SYS file. If DOS can't find the path to COMMAND.COM (or another command processor you may be using, such as the third-party 4DOS), your system will not run.

Listing All Directories

Now that you know where you *are*, you might want to know where you could be. The DIR command, which is covered in detail in the next chapter, generally is used to list files. You can list all directories on the current drive, however, by using the following syntax:

```
DIR /AD
```

or

```
DIR *.
```

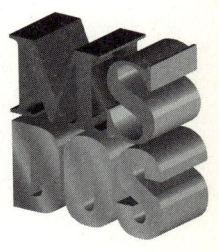

Of course, to list all directories on another drive and path, include the drive and path, such as the following:

    DIR D:\MAINDIR /AD

or

    DIR D:\MAINDIR*.

To list all subdirectories in the root of the current drive—and to display them five-across so that you can see all of them at once—use the following syntax:

    DIR \ /AD /W

or

    DIR *. /W

Want a printout? Add >PRN to the end of the line to redirect the output to your first parallel printer.

> ### AUTHOR'S NOTE
>
> *From MS-DOS 1 through MS-DOS 5, one gripe remained constant: There was no easy way to delete a subdirectory together with all its contents. To delete a subdirectory, you had to…*
>
> *First delete all the contents of every subdirectory it contained…*
>
> *Then delete those "child" subdirectories themselves…*
>
> *Then make extra sure you had eliminated every possible file in every nested subdirectory. (If any of these subdirectories included hidden, read-only, or system files, you had to use the ATTRIB or DIR /A: command to find them; then you had to change their attributes; then you could delete them….)*
>
> *Then, at long last, you would change directories (CD) to the root directory and use the remove directory command (RD or RMDIR) to delete the subdirectory itself (by typing **RD**, followed by the name of the subdirectory).*
>
> *The frustration this caused led to shareware DOS utilities with names like NUKE and KILLDIR, which did the job in one fell swoop.*

Introducing DELTREE

In MS-DOS 6.2, the polite, ineffectual RD command is still around. But Microsoft has introduced its own subdirectory serial killer, DELTREE.

To delete a subdirectory, type **DELTREE**, followed by the drive and path, including the subdirectory name, as follows:

`DELTREE C:\FILES`

To delete more than one subdirectory at a time, when both subdirectories are in your current path, type the following:

`DELTREE FILES1 FILES2`

You get one warning per subdirectory; use the following syntax:

```
Delete directory "c:\files" and all its subdirectories?
[yn]
```

To proceed, press **Y**, and press Enter.

Note that DELTREE is every bit as vicious as any third-party utility that came before it. DELTREE cares not a whit about the read-only, hidden, or system file attributes that the commands DEL and ERASE carefully respect.

DELTREE's options can make it even more indiscriminate. The /Y switch, for instance, used before the drive and path name, as in the following:

`DELTREE /Y C:\FILENAME`

...even eliminates DELTREE's request that you confirm each subdirectory deletion.

Moreover, because DELTREE accepts wild cards, you can delete several subdirectories from a drive simultaneously. In fact, DELTREE *.* executed at the root directory has the same effect as a DOS quick format (FORMAT /Q). *It eliminates not only all subdirectories but also all files in the root directory.*

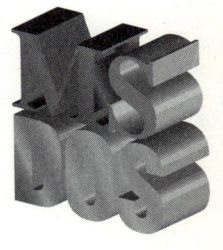

> **TIP**
>
> Before using DELTREE with wild cards to delete multiple subdirectories, use the following directory command to list, one page at a time, exactly what you're preparing to delete:
>
> `DIR [DRIVENAME]:[PATH] /A /S /P`

If you were terribly distracted, and you've just this instant confirmed a global DELTREE deletion by mistake, press Ctrl-C (or Ctrl-Break) right now and stop the wanton destruction before it goes any further.

In the unlikely event that you very recently created the directory structure on the disk, you may be able to restore most of your files by using the UNFORMAT command.

> **TIP**
>
> Some utilities and installation programs enable you to create directory names with illegal characters (such as spaces). Because a directory name with a space or other illegal character is not expected, DEL was not designed to work with them.
>
> DELTREE, however, can delete illegal directories. To delete the illegal directory MY WORK, for example, enter **DELTREE "MY WORK"** at the prompt. Be sure to include the quotation marks.

Trailblazing Your Own PATH

If you ask DOS to find a program, it looks only in its current directory unless you tell it otherwise. What happens if you have a directory tree like the one shown in figure 6.3, in which you're working in the 92FILES subdirectory, and you want to load WordPerfect (wp) in the WP51 subdirectory, somewhere else on the disk?

Well, you could type **C:\WP51\WP** every single time you want to access WordPerfect. But doing that every single day is not only a hassle, but also is bound to produce the following message:

```
    Bad command or file name
```
or...
```
    Path not found
```
...any time you make a typographical error.

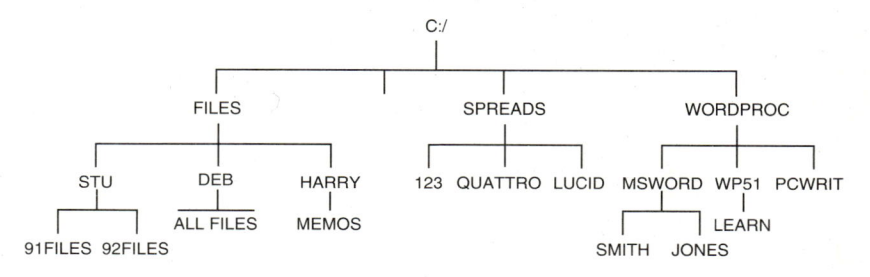

Figure 6.3
Complex directory tree.

Alternatively, you can instruct DOS once to clear a path to each directory you might want to use during a session. This is where the PATH command shines.

PATH tells DOS where to look for a program or batch file in the event that the file can't be found in the current directory. You can use PATH from the command line. More typically, however, you'll place it in your AUTOEXEC.BAT file so that DOS runs it automatically whenever you start up.

> *PATH tells DOS only where to find executable files, which it recognizes by their extensions—BAT, COM, or EXE. You can use the APPEND command, described later in this chapter, to specify search routes for data files.*
>
> *In addition, many applications will look through the directories in the PATH variable to find their data files.*

When you install MS-DOS 6.2, SETUP normally places the PATH statement...

```
    PATH C:\DOS
```

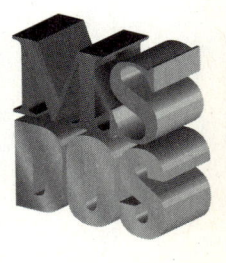

...in the AUTOEXEC.BAT. If this line is present, you can access all DOS commands from anywhere in your system—even from drives other than C. If this line isn't present, you'll only be able to run commands that are built into COMMAND.COM (so-called *internal commands*) unless you're in the directory that contains the DOS commands, that is, C:\DOS.

To check your current path, type **PATH** at the command prompt. (Because PATH is an internal DOS command, this works—no matter where you start from.)

Adding a Directory to Your Path

You can add a new directory to your path by adding a semicolon followed by the complete path and directory...

    PATH C:\DOS;C:\TEXTPROC\WP

This path tells DOS that after it looks for the program in the current directory, it should look first in the DOS subdirectory and then in the WP subdirectory contained within the TEXTPROC subdirectory. In other words, this PATH statement *does not create a path* to all subdirectories in TEXTPROC—only to the one you have specifically included.

Because a path statement executes in order, you should always place the programs you use most often early in the path statement.

> *When DOS processes a path statement, it must read each entire subdirectory to ensure that a program isn't present, before going on to the next one. All else being equal, you may want to place smaller directories ahead of longer ones and more frequently used paths (such as \DOS) ahead of those used less often (such as \MYGAMES).*

Shortening Long Path Names

As you already know, you can use no more than 66 characters to describe a subdirectory. DOS also sets a 127-character limit on the length of PATH statements (the same limit as the one placed on other DOS commands).

If you're running short of space, a good first step is to shorten the names of directories and subdirectories wherever possible. You can shorten directory and subdirectory names by using the new MOVE command, described later in this chapter, or the MS-DOS Shell RENAME command.

Make sure that no two subdirectories share the same name. In the case of MS-DOS Shell program items, also edit the Command Line in the program's Properties to ensure that double-clicking the associated icon still invokes a command line that executes correctly.

Also, be aware that some programs may still expect to find their components in the same subdirectories where you originally placed them at installation—that is, in subdirectories with their original names.

After you've installed Microsoft Excel for Windows in its default EXCEL subdirectory, for example, the program looks for library files in C:\EXCEL\LIBRARY, even though they're now located in C:\EX\LIBRARY. This problem can be avoided if you choose shorter directory names during each program's installation or setup process.

Using the SUBST Command

Another less-than-perfect approach to squeezing more into a 127-character path is to use the SUBST command. SUBST identifies a specific drive and path, and tells DOS to view it as if it were a new logical drive. Instead of including (for example)...

    `C:\MAINDIR\SUBDIR\CHILDDIR`

...in your path statement, you first tell DOS to...

    `SUBST E: C:\MAINDIR\SUBDIR\CHILDDIR`

...and from then on, you include `E:\;` in your path statement instead of `C:\MAINDIR\SUBDIR\CHILDDIR`.

Well, you've saved 22 characters in your path statement, but you may have lost more than you've gained, because you can't use SUBST with a long and growing list of important DOS commands, including the following: ASSIGN, CHKDSK, DISKCOMP, DISKCOPY, FASTOPEN,

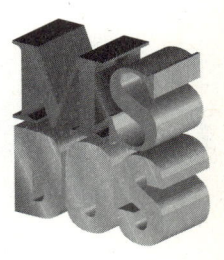

FDISK, FORMAT, INTERLNK, JOIN, LABEL, MIRROR, MSBACKUP, PRINT, RECOVER, RESTORE, and SYS.

A few more notes on SUBST:

- ✔ Don't SUBST to a drive name you're using for something else—you'll make the drive inaccessible.

- ✔ If you are creating a SUBST drive above drive E, you will have to insert a new LASTDRIVE= statement in your CONFIG.SYS file. Say, for example, that you already have logical drives C and D, and a CD-ROM drive E. Now you want to set aside drives F and G to be substituted. Include the statement...

    `LASTDRIVE=G`

    ...in CONFIG.SYS, and reboot. (Note that there's no colon after the G.)

Why not just include LASTDRIVE=Z and grab all 26 available drive names? Because you'll waste nearly 2.5K of valuable conventional memory if you do.

Using TRUENAME

Once you start mucking about with SUBST (or for that matter, with ASSIGN or JOIN), you can easily lose track of what your substituted drives really are. ("Where did that drive Q come from, anyway?") TRUENAME, one of DOS' biggest (and still undocumented) open secrets, can tell you. Type...

`TRUENAME Q:`

...and DOS returns the true file and subdirectory (unlike CD, which returns the substitute drive name).

Relative Path Names

Up to this point, your PATH statements have told DOS exactly which root directory to begin with, and where to proceed from there. These are called *explicit* paths. PATH statements also can include *relative* paths that tell DOS to proceed from wherever you currently happen to be. To include a relative path, omit the drive name and first backslash from the path you want to create...

    PATH SUBDIR1\SUBDIR2

In this example, if you were working in the root directory, this sample path would make DOS look first in C:\SUBDIR1 and then in C:\SUBDIR2. On the other hand, if you were working in the subdirectory D:\WINDOWS\MSAPPS, the path would make DOS look first for D:\WINDOWS\MSAPPS\SUBDIR1 and then for D:\WINDOWS\MSAPPS\SUBDIR2.

If you commonly search for a parent directory from its child or grandchild subdirectory, you can use the two-dot (..) aliases in relative PATH statements, like this...

    PATH ..;..\..;C:\;C:\DOS;C:\WP51;C:\WINDOWS;C:\EXCEL

This example tells DOS to look up one subdirectory level from wherever it is, and then another. Only then will DOS move to the C: root directory and to the specified subdirectories growing out of it.

More PATH Editing

Sometimes, when you install a program, the program's installation utility automatically edits your PATH statement. You might not like the results. Some programs, for example, place themselves at the beginning of the path—ahead of programs you might use much more often. Good for the software publisher (the program loads faster). Bad for you (all your other programs load slower).

Don't hesitate to reedit the path yourself. Remember these tips:

- ✔ Each list (except the last one) should end with a semicolon.
- ✔ Include the drive name in each path. (The PATH command can bring in information from different drives, including floppies—but if you search for files on an empty floppy drive, you'll get an `Abort, Retry, Fail?` message. DOS won't skip to the next subdirectory.)

✔ If you have two programs with the same name (batch files, perhaps) in different directories, DOS executes the one it finds first.

✔ Within a single directory, DOS executes COM files first, then EXEs, and then BATs. (Remember, FILENAME.COM, FILENAME.EXE, and FILENAME.BAT are all different files, even though the first eight characters are the same.)

✔ Don't add a space before a semicolon.

If you've already started a session, and you now expect to work for awhile in one or two directories that aren't in your path, you can create a new path from the command prompt. This path replaces the one established by your AUTOEXEC.BAT file (until you reboot or change it again).

And you can eliminate paths altogether, by including the following line in your AUTOEXEC.BAT file, or by typing it at the command prompt:

```
PATH ;
```

To check that you really did eliminate the path, type **PATH** at the command prompt. The result is...

```
No path
```

With no path defined, DOS will only search the current directory for programs.

> **NOTE** It's hard to imagine a good reason for eliminating the path altogether. Conceivably, a path could result in the message `Out of environment space`, if it were used with an extremely long PROMPT message or APPEND list. But even in this case, you'd be more likely to make up the difference by slightly increasing the size of your environment, as described earlier.

Using TREE To View the Directory Structure

As mentioned at the beginning of this chapter, the best way to think about a disk's directory structure is to picture it as a tree, growing out of your root directory. (Think of a banyan tree—very flat and wide.)

The quickest way to see your directory tree from the command line is to use the TREE command...

TREE

...or, if you want to display the directory tree on another drive...

TREE B:

A typical drive C tree appears on-screen in the next section.

TREE is context-sensitive; *that is, if you invoke it from a subdirectory, TREE displays only those directories immediately beneath it. If you often want to see the structure of your entire disk (drive C, for example), write a batch file that contains the line* TREE C:\. *See Chapter 15 for more information on writing batch files.*

Saving Your Tree to Disk

You may want to save your tree to disk by redirecting it to a file name. Type...

TREE >DOSTREE.TXT

The list displays beautifully in MS-DOS 6.2's text editor, EDIT, which uses all 256 IBM character-set characters precisely as IBM originally intended. But it'll accumulate some unwanted characters if you try to load it in a word processor such as Word for Windows...

```
Directory PATH list
Volume Serial Number is CF83-02F7
C:.
```

```
_---DOS
_---WINDOWS
   |   _---SYSTEM
   |   ¿---MSAPPS
   |       _---PROOF
   |       _---WORDART
   |       _---MSGRAPH
   |       _---MSDRAW
   |       _---EQUATION
   |       _---GRPHFLT
   |       _---TEXTCONV
   |       ¿---NOTE-IT
```

The solution is the TREE command's switch /A, which converts IBM's graphics characters into standard ASCII characters. It ain't pretty, but it works, as you can see from the following sample output:

```
Directory PATH list
Volume Serial Number is CF83-02F7
C:.
+-DOS
+-WINDOWS
|    +-SYSTEM
|    \-MSAPPS
|        +-PROOF
|        +-WORDART
|        +-MSGRAPH
|        +-MSDRAW
|        +-EQUATION
|        +-GRPHFLT
|        +-TEXTCONV
|        \-NOTE-IT
```

More Ways To View Your Directory Structure

TREE, as described in the preceding section, displays only subdirectories. But used with the switch /F (for *files*), TREE also displays the contents of those subdirectories (except hidden files).

If you need a list of all files, each with its full path name, try the command...

    CHKDSK /V

...in which /V stands, appropriately enough, for *verbose*.

Also, TREE/F and CHKDSK/V can be redirected to your disk or printer.

Using the APPEND Command To Find Nonexecutable Files

You've already learned that PATH tells DOS where to look for BAT, COM, and EXE executable files. But what do you do when the PATH statement directs you to a program, you try to load the program, and it fails because it can't find its support files?

The APPEND command is DOS' attempt to solve this problem. You can think of it as a PATH statement for nonexecutable files: it tells DOS where to look for them if they can't be found in your current directory. Ordinarily, APPEND (like PATH) is placed in the AUTOEXEC.BAT file, but you can run it from the command line as well.

When you issue the APPEND command, the files in your appended directories seem to MS-DOS (and your applications) to be in the current directory.

But be cautious: APPEND is trickier than it looks. *You can easily trick yourself while you're tricking DOS.*

To tell DOS to search the C:\FILES and C:\FILES2 subdirectories after it searches the current directory, type...

    APPEND C:\FILES;C:\FILES2

Normally, APPEND is an external command, but you can place an APPEND statement in your environment space so that SET commands can affect how APPEND behaves. First, type...

    APPEND /E

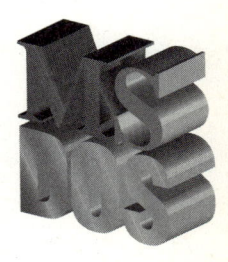

Press Enter. Then, immediately type the APPEND statement you normally would use...

```
APPEND C:\FILES;C:\FILES2
```

(These two statements may be inserted together in AUTOEXEC.BAT.)

Again like PATH, you can see which directories are currently appended by typing **APPEND** at the command prompt and pressing Enter. You can specify different appended directories at any time by typing a new APPEND statement. And you can "unappend" all appended directories by typing...

```
APPEND;
```

You can direct APPEND to search for program files as well as data files by adding the /X:ON switch when you first run APPEND...

```
APPEND C:\FILES;C:\FILES2 /X:ON
```

Using /X:OFF limits the search to data files.

Don't use APPEND with Windows or Windows Setup. Don't use APPEND with ASSIGN, JOIN, or SUBST. Don't use APPEND to tell DOS where it can find additional data files outside the current directory.

Be very cautious. Remember that, to a program, the appended files look as if they're part of the current directory. So, in most cases (databases tend to be the exception) the current directory is where the data files are saved. Now you have two copies of the data file—a new one in the current directory, and an old one in the directory in which you originally placed it. Is that what you really want?

Similarly, don't use APPEND to find auxiliary program files that will be updated by writing entirely new versions to disk. The same problem will occur.

Using MOVE To Rename Directories

Until MS-DOS 6, there was no easy way to rename directories from the command line (although the MS-DOS 5 Shell introduced a RENAME option that worked for both directories and file names).

MS-DOS 6 introduced the new command MOVE, which is used primarily for moving files between directories, but can be used also to rename directories. *For more information about moving files between directories, see Chapter 7.*

MOVE moves files, which you'd expect, given its name. But it doesn't move directories—it only renames them. You specify the path name of the directory you want to rename, and then the path name of the new directory, for example...

```
MOVE C:\DIR1 C:\DIR2
```

You can dispense with the drive and path if the directory or directories are in your current path...

```
MOVE DIR1 DIR2
```

In either case, DOS responds with the full path names as it lets you know that the renaming was successful...

```
C:\DIR1 => C:\DIR2 [OK]
```

If you ask to relocate the directory at the same time you rename it, DOS refuses...

```
C:\DIR1 => C:\DOS6\DIR2 [PERMISSION DENIED]
```

If you accidentally switch the syntax and place the new name before the old one, DOS again refuses...

```
C:\DIR2 => C:\DIR1 [NO SUCH FILE OR DIRECTORY]
```

Chapter 6: *Creating and Using Directories*

> **NOTE**
> You can use MOVE to build batch files that take different actions or display different messages depending on whether the MOVE has been successful. Like many other DOS commands, MOVE returns an ERRORLEVEL of 0 to batch files dependent on it. See chapter 15 for a more detailed discussion of batch files.

> **TIP**
> Again, some utilities and installation programs enable you to create directory names with illegal characters (such as spaces). Like DELTREE, MOVE can deal with these illegal directories; that is, you can use it to rename illegal directories. To rename the illegal directory MY WORK, for example, enter **MOVE "MY WORK" MY_WORK** at the prompt. Be sure to include the quotation marks.

Getting Yourself Organized

With these tools, you can begin to sort through a disorderly directory structure and bring order out of chaos.

Your ultimate goal is to keep your root directory as uncluttered as possible, and to organize all the files in your other directories in as coherent a way as possible.

Some people maintain a root directory with as few as two file entries, CONFIG.SYS and AUTOEXEC.BAT, plus subdirectories. That might be a bit compulsive for some tastes, but you should be able to keep it down to a half-dozen file entries without too much trouble.

> **STOP**
> In some cases, if you move files from the root directory, you'll immediately have to tell DOS (or Windows) where they went (otherwise, your system won't run). Don't trash files until you know where they are.

Inventory Your Current Files

Haul out the old pencil and paper, and inventory where you are now. You'll want to answer the following questions:

1. **What does your root directory look like?** Realistically, it shouldn't have more than a half-dozen files—not including subdirectory entries. Again, you can recognize subdirectory entries by the <DIR> tag next to them. If you think you have too many files in your root directory, you may want to see a five-wide list of your files. Here, subdirectories are bracketed. To print a five-wide copy of your root directory, enter...

    DIR C:/W >PRN

    To print a directory list that shows everything in each directory and subdirectory, with file size as well as the date and time of creation, enter...

    DIR C:\ /S/O >PRN

    The list could be surprisingly long.

2. **How full is your hard drive?** The answer to this question will help you determine how many programs and files you'll want to move off the hard drive and onto floppy disks.

    (MS-DOS 6.2's DBLSPACE compresses roughly twice as much junk onto the same size disk. But ignore that for the time being. If you're planning to use DBLSPACE, it'll work faster and leave more space if you clear off the flotsam and jetsam ahead of time.)

3. **What programs do you have?** Is each major program installed in its own subdirectory? Are minor programs (such as TSR memory-resident programs) organized into a single subdirectory?

4. **What data-file names are associated with each of your programs?** Lotus 1-2-3, for example, generates WK1 files. Microsoft Word normally generates DOC document files and BAK backup files.

5. **Where does each of your programs currently store its files?** At minimum, you want to make sure that each program is using a default storage directory which makes sense—not simply dumping all your new files on the root directory.

6. **Does your disk contain old versions of software that you no longer use?** Often, during a transition period, maintaining old and new software side-by-side—making sure to install them in entirely separate directories—makes sense. (Many users maintained both Windows 3 and 3.1 on the same disk for months after upgrading to 3.1. Do you still need them both?)

   If you've fully converted to the new software, you can archive the old version on floppy disk (or haul out your existing backup disks when you need them—you do have them, right?).

7. **Do you have multiple copies of the same files? Which are the most recent?** Use View All Files in the DOS Shell to quickly see and analyze duplicates.

8. **What's in your PATH and APPEND statements?** Have you restricted APPEND to associating program files and databases, or eliminated it entirely? Does your PATH statement reflect the directories you really use most often? Have you been slowing down your computer by including directories that no longer exist or are rarely used?

Build a Directory Structure That Makes Sense

Now think about designing the structure for data directories—the one that would work best for you. Outline the functional areas in which specific subdirectories would make sense.

Do you primarily use word processing programs? Then perhaps you should maintain a different subdirectory for each type of document you work on, as shown in figure 6.4.

```
                       TEXT PROC
         ┌────────────────┼────────────────┐
      ARTICLES      MEMOS        PROPOSLS       BIZPLANS
```

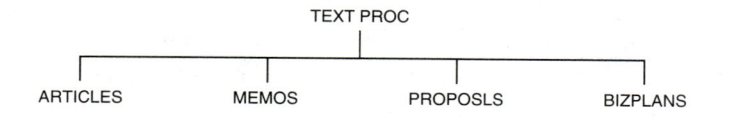

Figure 6.4

Sample structure for word processing files.

Do you work on projects on which you need to use several applications, moving information between files that were generated in different application programs?

In that case, you might want to build a directory structure in which all related project files are placed together, even if they are created by different applications (see fig. 6.5).

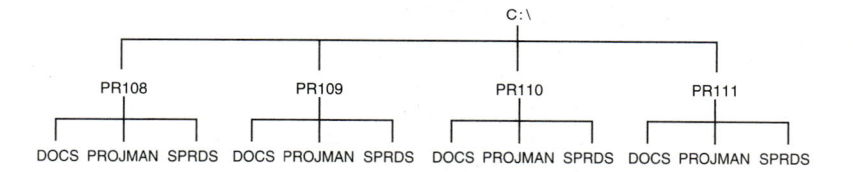

```
                                C:\
         ┌────────────────┬─────────────────┬────────────────┐
       PR108            PR109             PR110            PR111
    ┌────┼────┐     ┌────┼────┐      ┌────┼────┐      ┌────┼────┐
  DOCS PROJMAN SPRDS DOCS PROJMAN SPRDS DOCS PROJMAN SPRDS DOCS PROJMAN SPRDS
```

Figure 6.5

Sample structure for project-related files.

Notice that in both options, you are building a directory structure that is wide and shallow. Nothing is harder to access, slower, or more annoying than multiple levels of deeply nested subdirectories...

```
C:\LIBRARY\SCIENCE\PHYSICS\RELATIVE\EINSTEIN\BOMBLTRS
```

> *For optimal speed, try to keep subdirectories to within one cluster. Each directory list requires 32 bytes.*
>
> *Also, don't use extensions in directory names—you're likely to start confusing them with files.*
>
> *For more information about how many bytes fit into one cluster on your hard disk, see Chapter 4.*

After you have created the appropriate directories, move your files into them.

Make Space Wherever You Can

It's always easier to fill up a hard drive than to clear one out, but here's an orderly way to approach the problem:

- ✔ Delete any empty subdirectories. (Use RD—it won't work if your subdirectories aren't empty, and that'll be your cue to look inside.)
- ✔ Back up current copies of all files on floppies, and delete duplicates and older copies as appropriate.
- ✔ After you've backed up your files to floppies, delete any redundant BAK (backup) files created by your software.
- ✔ Determine which recent files can be maintained on floppies; make sure they're backed up, and then delete them from the hard drive.
- ✔ After you move their data files into new directories, or onto floppies, back up outdated copies of programs and then delete them from the hard disk.
- ✔ Exit Windows and any other program that creates TMP files. If you still see TMP files on the root directory, delete them.
- ✔ Consider deleting program functions you know you will never use. If you never include clip art in your documents, for example, you might want to delete the large clip art libraries that come with most Windows word processors. You can always reinstall the libraries later, if you change your mind.

Clear Out the Root Directory

If your root directory is really cluttered, you may not know what some of the files are. Start by moving the ones you do know.

If your word processing files all have the TXT extension, create a temporary C:\TEXTFILE subdirectory and move them all there...

```
MOVE C:\*.TXT C:\TEXTFILE
```

...until you have the time to check them more closely. Do the same for other program extensions you recognize.

If you've scattered shareware utilities all across your root directory, you may want to collect them in C:\UTILS (and add C:\UTILS to your path if you want them accessible from anywhere). If you have many batch files (BAT), move all of them (except AUTOEXEC.BAT) into a subdirectory called C:\BATCH, and add that to your path as well.

Make sure that all your DOS files (except AUTOEXEC.BAT, CONFIG.SYS, and COMMAND.COM) are located in the C:\DOS directory. For now, also leave files with the following extensions in your root directory: INI, BIN, SYS, or 386. Also leave the files CHKLIST.MS and CHKLIST.CPS, which Microsoft Anti-Virus needs to make sure that your directory hasn't been infected.

AUTHOR'S NOTE

In some cases, in which programs have scattered incomprehensible file names across your root directory, you may be better off reinstalling them and then deleting the extra files in your root directory. You'll get to choose the program's directory name. Whenever you can, choose shorter names. They make for shorter PATH statements, and less room for typos.

Copy the old data files you need into their new directories—or onto floppy disks. (If they're in an older format that will eventually have to be converted, you may want to place them temporarily in a subdirectory of their own.) When you're sure that no useful data remains in the old program hulk, nuke it with DELTREE.

Moving WINA20.386

If you are running Windows, perhaps you now want to move WINA20.386 into your Windows directory. To do so, you'll need to change two things.

First, in your CONFIG.SYS file, add the statement...

    SWITCHES=/W

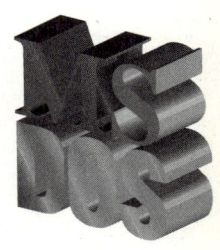

Chapter 6: *Creating and Using Directories*

> **NOTE:** SWITCHES is a command that performs two obscure, unrelated functions which need doing but don't fit into any other DOS command. SWITCHES=/W is one function. The other function is SWITCHES=/K, which makes DOS treat a 101-key keyboard like an 84-key AT-style keyboard.

Then, in your Windows SYSTEM.INI file, add the statement…

```
DEVICE=C:\WINDOWS\WINA20.386
```

Next time you reboot and load Windows, it searches for WINA20.386 in this new location. By the way, you can delete WINA20.386 altogether if you never plan to use Windows.

Moving COMMAND.COM

Finally, if you want to save 55K more disk space, you can move COMMAND.COM into your C:\DOS directory (or, more precisely, remove it from your root directory because you currently have two copies of it). But you must change your CONFIG.SYS statement immediately, before rebooting, or else DOS won't be able to find COMMAND.COM.

To tell DOS that it can find COMMAND.COM in C:\DOS, include the following statement in your CONFIG.SYS file…

```
SHELL=C:\DOS\COMMAND.COM C:\DOS /E:256 /P
```

`/E:256` tells DOS to use the default environment size of 256 bytes.

`/P` tells COMMAND.COM to ignore requests to exit and to remain in memory, no matter what.

Finally, once you've done all this, replace your AUTOEXEC.BAT PATH statement with an updated one reflecting your new preferences.

Everyone does this: log on to drive A, having forgotten to put a disk in it, only to see the following annoying message:

```
Not ready reading drive B
Abort, Retry, Fail?
```

*Upon pressing **F**, you then see:*

```
Current drive is no longer valid>
```

Then you enter another drive letter and start over. The undocumented /F switch, however, makes the oversight more bearable by displaying a combined prompt:

```
Not ready reading drive B
Abort, Retry, Fail? Current drive is no
longer valid>
```

Summary

MS-DOS' tree-shaped, hierarchical directory system gives you the power to set up your files any way you want—if you understand it. You can use the TREE command to more easily visualize the directory structure. DOS shortcuts like "." and ".." simplify getting where you want to go. And, with DELTREE and MOVE, MS-DOS 6.2 makes changing your directory structure easier, too.

It's worth the effort, because a poorly organized hard disk means you have to spend a lot more time finding and re-creating files—and you'll be doing it on a system that might even run slower than it has to.

One day, MS-DOS may sport a 21st-century file system that's smart enough to help you organize your work. In the short term, perhaps a 32-bit file system will be made available that permits English-language file names. But for now, you're on your own—just use the tools DOS gives you, and you'll be in business.

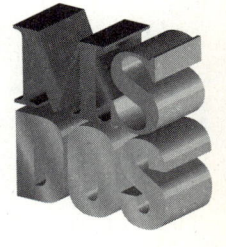

MS-DOS

CHAPTER 7

Managing Disks and Files

by Bill Camarda

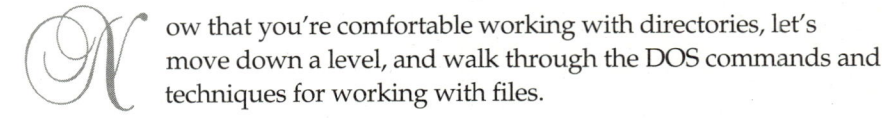

Now that you're comfortable working with directories, let's move down a level, and walk through the DOS commands and techniques for working with files.

In this chapter, you learn how to list, copy, delete, move, and rename files. You learn how to change the attributes of a file. And you learn how file attributes can be part of a backup strategy that includes DOS 6.2's all-new backup and restore programs—a major improvement over anything DOS provided before.

Finding Out What's in Your Directories with DIR

What could be simpler? If you want to know what's in your root directory, type…

DIR

…and there it is…

```
Directory of C:\

COMMAND   COM         53405   12-06-92    6:00a
DOS           <DIR>           11-15-92    1:41p
DSVXD     386          5741   12-06-92    6:00a
WINDOWS       <DIR>           11-15-92    1:42p
AUTOEXEC  BAT           150   12-18-92    9:40a
CONFIG    SYS           238   12-27-92    7:24a
EXCEL         <DIR>           11-15-92    1:59p
WINWORD       <DIR>           11-15-92    2:13p
MSPUB         <DIR>           11-15-92    2:29p
UTILS         <DIR>           11-15-92    3:29p
CSERVE        <DIR>           11-15-92    3:46p
MOUSE         <DIR>           11-15-92    3:55p
WP51          <DIR>           11-15-92    4:20p
NORTON        <DIR>           11-15-92    4:49p
       14 file(s)          59534    bytes
                        51904512    bytes free
```

This directory list contains 14 entries, including 10 subdirectories. The subdirectories each have a file size of zero—remember, that's how DOS counts subdirectories. (That means you can't use a simple DIR list to determine how much disk space you've used.)

> *The DOS 6.2 DIR command has a new look—it now uses a comma to separate numbers greater than 1,000. In the preceding DIR listing, for example, DOS 6.2 displays COMMAND.COM's size as 53,405, and displays the totals as follows:*
>
> ```
>        14 file(s)          59,534
>                        51,904,512
> ```

Finding Out What's in Your Directories with DIR **317**

The *bytes free* list reflects DOS's assessment of space remaining available for use on the current drive. Until MS-DOS 6.2, this number could be relied on with certainty. But now, if you're using DBLSPACE, the *bytes free* number is just an estimate.

> **NOTE**
>
> *Whenever you or DBLSPACE change the file-compression ratio used to determine your remaining space, the number of bytes free reported by DIR changes as well.*
>
> *You may discover that DIR and CHKDSK report different amounts of free disk space. The culprit here is Delete Sentry, which increases the amount of free space that MS-DOS reports (through interrupt 21h function 36h) to programs by the size of all deleted files stored in the hidden SENTRY directory.*
>
> *This affects the amount of free space reported by the DIR command, Windows File Manager, and many other programs. CHKDSK, on the other hand, reports the true amount of free disk space because it bypasses Delete Sentry and examines the FAT directly.*

Searching Far and Wide with DIR

As you've seen, typing **DIR** by itself gives you a list of only the files in the current directory. You can use a path name to specify any other directory, as with these examples:

DIR C:\WORD5	lists the subdirectory C:\WORD5.
DIR WP51	lists the subdirectory WP51 located in the current directory.
DIR \MYM9	lists the subdirectory MYM9 one level below the current root directory.
DIR B:\FILELIST	lists the subdirectory FILELIST in the root directory on drive B.

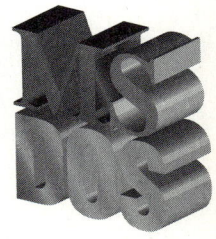

DIR ..	lists the parent directory of the current subdirectory.
DIR ..\..	lists the grandparent directory of the current subdirectory.

Rearranging the Way DIR Presents Information

If, like many users, you have hundreds or thousands of files on your disk, simply typing **DIR** and letting the file names fly past you on the screen may not be an ideal way to get the information you want. Fortunately, DIR enables you to control the floodgates with a few switches:

DIR /P	displays the file list information one screen at a time.
DIR /W	displays the file names five wide without showing other information, as in this example:

```
Volume in drive C has no label
Volume Serial Number is CF83-02F7
Directory of C:\

COMMAND.COM    BEFSETUP.MSD   [DOS]        DSVXD.386 [WINDOWS]
AUTOEXEC.BAT   CONFIG.SYS     [QUICKENW]   [EXCEL]   [CHAOS]
[WINWORD]      [MSPUB]        [TRUETYPE]   [UTILS]   [CSERVE]
[MOUSE]        [PARTABLE]     [FTM]        [MTEZ]    [WP51]
[WORD5]        [SMARTCOM]     [NORTON]     [MYM8]    [APPRENTC]
    20 file(s)       125189   bytes
                              63520768 bytes free
```

You can also redirect the "rushing water" that DIR may result in:

DIR >FILE NAME.EXT	pours the directory list into a file called FILE NAME.EXT.
DIR >PRN	sends the list to your parallel-interface printer.

Using DIR To Locate Files Meeting Specific Criteria

DIR enables you to list only the files that meet your specific needs. You can do this by using wild cards or attributes.

Using DIR with Wild Cards

DIR is an ideal command to use with DOS's two wild card characters, * and ?. For example:

DIR *.TXT	lists all files in the current directory with the extension TXT.
DIR 92*.*	lists all files whose file names begin with 92, regardless of the length of the file name or extension.
DIR ?LIST.DBF	lists all files where one character exists in place of the question mark.

When you use an asterisk, you tell DOS to include any file that contains a letter or letters in the position where you have placed the asterisk. FILE.DOC, for example, would include both FILE1.DOC and FILE NAME.DOC.*

Conversely, using a question mark limits DOS to including files that substitute one character for the wild card. FILE?.DOC, for example, would include FILE1.DOC, but not FILE NAME.DOC.

Using DIR To Search for One File

You can narrow DIR's search through the directory so that it searches for one file. By combining the DIR command with the file name you are looking for, you determine if the file exists in the current directory, as in...

    DIR FIRST.COM

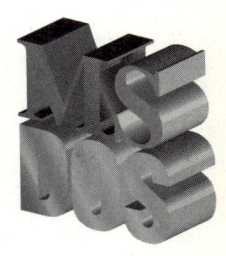

You can add the /S switch...

`DIR FIRST.COM /S`

...which tells DIR to search all subdirectories within the current directory.

If you specify a root directory as the starting point, as in...

`DIR \FIRST.COM /S`

...you are telling DIR to search the entire disk for the specified file.

If more than one file with the specified file name exists, DOS lists them all, one directory at a time.

> *NOTE: If you use the same syntax, but choose the name of a directory, DOS lists all files in that directory and stops there without searching the rest of the disk.*

Understanding Attributes

To understand how DIR works with attributes, you have to first understand what attributes are, what they do, and how you can control them with the ATTRIB command.

ATTRIB enables you to set or clear any of four attributes for each file:

- **A**   Archive (You haven't backed up the file since you last changed it.)
- **R**   Read-only (The file can't be changed.)
- **H**   Hidden (The file shouldn't appear in an ordinary file list unless you say otherwise.)
- **S**   System (The file is a critical system file.)

> *NOTE: DOS automatically gives the IO.SYS and MSDOS.SYS files the system, hidden, and read-only file attributes.*

When you set an attribute for a file, that attribute is included in the file's directory entry. You can then use the attributes to choose which files to list, copy, or back up.

To view the attributes on all files in the current directory, type…

> `ATTRIB`

To view the attributes of a specific file, type…

> `ATTRIB`

followed by the file name…

> `ATTRIB 4Q92.XLS`

To set an attribute, type **ATTRIB**, a plus sign (+), the initial of the attribute you want to set, and the file's entire path name. For example, to make C:\FILES\FILE NAME.EXT a read-only file, type…

> `ATTRIB +R C:\FILES\FILE NAME.EXT`

The ATTRIB command follows the same path rules as other DOS commands: if a file is in the current directory, you don't have to specify the entire drive and path name.

To clear an attribute, use the same syntax but replace the plus (+) sign with a minus (-) sign…

> `ATTRIB -R C:\FILES\FILE NAME.EXT`

Like DIR, ATTRIB works with the wild cards * and ?. To clear the archive bit on every file in the subdirectory C:\JONES, type…

> `ATTRIB -A C:\JONES\*.*`

By clearing the archive bit, you tell backup programs that this file has not changed since it was last backed up and, therefore, does not need to be backed up again.

Using DIR with Attributes

You can use the DIR /A (attribute) switch, along with the attribute initial or initials of your choice, to control which files to list.

To show all the read-only files on the current directory, type...

    DIR /AR

To show all files that contain the archive and hidden attributes, type...

    DIR /AHA

When you specify more than one attribute, the search is narrowed to files that contain every attribute you specify.

> ***Hidden and system files with /A...*** *You can use the /A switch all by itself, even without the H or S attribute initials, to get a list that includes hidden and system files, such as IO.SYS and MSDOS.SYS.*

DIR can work with one attribute you can't reset with the ATTRIB command: the directory bit. That's why, as mentioned in the last chapter, you can get a list of just subdirectories by typing...

    DIR /AD

Using DIR To Change Sort Order

Starting with DOS 5, DIR provides powerful sorting options with the /O (order) switch. DOS's default setting is /ON, which sorts alphabetically by file name. (You can type...

    /O:N

...if that's less confusing.) But now you can sort in reverse alphabetic order by file name with the switch /O-N. Table 7.1 lists all the options you can use with the /O switch.

> *In this case, /O is the switch; the character or characters that follow it tell the switch how to behave. The /A switch works similarly; other DIR switches are not modifiable this way.*

Table 7.1
Sorting Options for Use with the /O Switch

Option	Sort Results
N	Alphabetically by file name
-N	Reverse alphabetically by file name
E	Alphabetically by extension
-E	Reverse alphabetically by extension
D	Oldest file to newest file (DOS dates files by when they were last changed)
-D	Newest file to oldest file
S	Smallest file to largest file
-S	Largest file to smallest file
G	All subdirectories first, then all files, one subdirectory at a time
-G	All files first, one subdirectory at a time, then all subdirectories

Using Other DIR Options

You can use the DIR command with the /B (bare) switch to strip off all information except file names. The result is a list like this, which can be used directly in batch files:

```
AUTOEXEC.BAT
COMMAND.COM
DOS
DSVXD.386
EXCEL
WINA20.386
WINDOWS
WP51
```

You can also use the /L switch to display file names in lowercase (the switch doesn't affect extended characters).

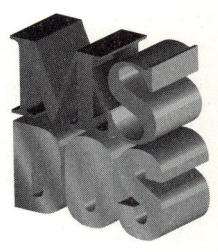

> *For a sample batch file using DIR, see the Batch File Toolbox in Chapter 15.*

Customizing DIR with DIRCMD

With all the customization options available for the DIR command, you may have one very specific preference for listing your files. For example, you may like to list files by extension, one directory at a time, in lowercase. You might also prefer to include hidden files. If this is true, your DIR command looks like this:

DIR /OE /A /S /L

Although you can type this command every time you want a directory list, with DOS 5 and 6.2, you can make this command your default. The SET DIRCMD= statement, placed in the AUTOEXEC.BAT file, puts your DIR preference in DOS's environment space. DOS then uses these preferences in place of its own. For this example, the statement...

SET DIRCMD=/OE /A /S /L

...should be included in your AUTOEXEC.BAT. (Note that the word *DIR* is not included in the SET DIRCMD= statement.)

> *As always, any changes you make to AUTOEXEC.BAT don't take effect until you reboot. But if you also enter the SET DIRCMD= statement at the command prompt, the change takes effect immediately.*
>
> *You can always override the SET DIRCMD= statement by specifying different parameters when you give the DIR command. DIR's behavior reverts to the default preferences after you give the single command—until you change SET DIRCMD=.*

Finding Out What's in a File

You've been looking at lists of files, but let's get back to first principles: What is a file? Think of a file as any grouping of bytes that, taken together, have a common purpose: usually to perform a function or present information.

In Chapter 4, you saw that each file in the root directory has a 32-byte list. This is also true of subdirectory files. These lists contain the file's name, extension, attributes, starting cluster, and other information. You also saw that DOS maintains a File Allocation Table to keep track of the clusters assigned to each file, so that it can follow the chain from a file's starting cluster to the end of the file.

Each file also contains an end-of-file marker, equivalent to Ctrl+Z, or character 26 in the IBM character set. You'll see later how some DOS commands stumble over this end-of-file marker.

Naming Files

DOS gives you a great deal of latitude in naming a file. You can use…

- ✔ One to eight characters
- ✔ An optional extension of one to three characters
- ✔ Any alphanumeric character (A-Z, 0-9)
- ✔ These symbols:

    ! @ # $ % ^ & ( ) ' ' { } ~ - _

- ✔ Any high-bit ASCII character (those characters above 127 in the IBM Extended ASCII Character Set)

NOTE: Stay away from the special high-bit ASCII characters if you expect to change character sets frequently—as you would if you work in different languages.

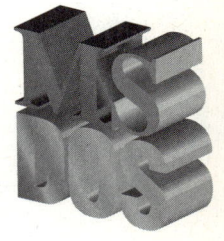

Chapter 7: *Managing Disks and Files*

AUTHOR'S NOTE

DOS recognizes two types of files: executable and nonexecutable. There are three primary types of executable files: COM, EXE, and BAT files.

COM and EXE files contain your programs. The COM extension, a holdover from DOS's predecessor CP/M, dates back to the days when assembly-language programs had to squeeze into 64K of very expensive RAM. COM programs load byte-for-byte into memory and are therefore sometimes called memory-image files.

DOS 6.2 contains 19 COM files—including the mother of all COM files, COMMAND.COM. Some of these files, like HELP.COM and EDIT.COM, load other programs not subject to the constraints of a COM file. Others, like FORMAT.COM, behave internally in essentially the same way their CP/M ancestors did.

Most application programs you use nowadays are EXE files. So are most of the 46 external commands that accompany DOS 6.2— including DOS's new backup and antivirus programs.

Unlike COM files, EXE files can take advantage of all the conventional memory DOS throws their way. This is because EXE files are segmented to handle data, code, and the stacks that hold the current state of a program while the computer is busy handling I/O interrupts.

Batch (BAT) files are the third type of executable file. AUTOEXEC.BAT is the most well-known of these files. BAT files represent combinations of DOS commands in ASCII format.

Because people can name their files any way they like, DOS generally doesn't rely on the file extension to determine how a file behaves. For example, you can't make DOS run a graphics file as if it were a program by simply renaming it with an EXE extension.

Nonexecutable files cover the waterfront from word processing text files to graphics files to overlay files that a program requires in order to run successfully.

Besides the space character, you can't use the following in naming a file:

- Characters DOS reserves for its own use:

    * ? + = / \ ; : " , < > [ ]

- Names DOS reserves for its own devices:

    AUX, CLOCK$, COM1, COM2, COM3, COM4, CON, LPT1, LPT2, LPT3, NUL, PRN

You probably don't want to use file names already taken by DOS for internal or external programs.

You can try to give one of your files the same name as an internal command name, but when DOS looks for a program, it usually begins with a long, searching look deep inside itself. (You didn't know DOS was so introspective, did you?) Needless to say, it'll find its own program before yours every time—unless you instruct DOS otherwise by including a specific path in your command.

Using Extensions in File Names

Use some discretion in naming files—at least in your choice of extensions. First of all, *do use* extensions so that you won't confuse your files with subdirectories. DOS doesn't limit your choice of extensions—at least not beyond the restrictions already presented. Many programs, however, use a specific file extension and attempt to filter out data files with other extensions unless you specifically tell them otherwise.

Moreover, a wide variety of extensions have become common. Knowing what they are can help you the next time someone shows up with a mystery disk and asks what all the files are.

Table 7.2 presents a list of the most commonly used file extensions and what's most likely to be contained in the files that use them.

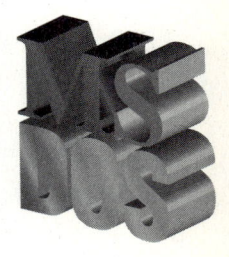

Table 7.2
Common File Extensions

Extension	Likely Contents
$$$	Temporary or incorrectly stored file
000	DBLSPACE file
ARC	File compressed using ARC utility
ASC	ASCII (text) file
ASM	Assembler code file
BAK	Backup file created by Microsoft Word or other program
BAS	BASIC program file
BAT	Batch file
BIN	Device driver or machine language file
BMP	Graphics file in Windows bitmap format
C	C source code file
CBL	COBOL source code file
CFG	Program configuration/setup information file
CGM	Graphics file in Computer Graphics Metafile format
CHP	Ventura Publisher chapter file
CLP	Windows clipboard file
CNF	Program configuration/setup information file
CNV	Data conversion file
COM	Command (executable) file
CPI	Code-page information file specifying international keyboard
CPP	C++ source code file
CPS	Microsoft Anti-Virus checksum file
DAT	Data file

Using Extensions in File Names

Extension	Likely Contents
DBF	dBASE II, III, III+, and IV database file
DIF	Data Interchange Format file
DLL	Windows Dynamic Link Library file
DOC	Word processing document file
DRV	Device driver file, especially printer driver
DRW	Drawing program
EXE	Executable file
FNT	Font file
FON	Font file
FOR	FORTRAN source code file
FOT	TrueType font file
GIF	Graphics file in Graphics Interchange Format
GRP	Windows Program Group file
HLP	Help file
ICO	Windows icon file
IDX	Q&A index file
IMG	Graphics file in GEM format
INF	Information file generated by DOS utility
INI	Initialization file (for example, WIN.INI, DOSSHELL.INI)
LET	Letter or other document file
LGO	Windows video graphics mode file
LIB	Program library file
LST	Program listing file
MDX	dBASE IV index file
ME	READ.ME file (last-minute program information)

continues

Table 7.2, Continued
Common File Extensions

Extension	Likely Contents
MSG	Program message file
MSP	Microsoft Paint file
NDX	dBASE III index file
OVL	Program overlay file
OVR	Program overlay file
PAS	Pascal source code file
PCX	Graphics file in PC Paintbrush format
PIF	Windows program information file
PUB	Microsoft Publisher file
QNX	Quicken data file
REC	Windows Recorder macro file
RES	Windows Resource file
RFT	DCA-RFT document interchange file
RLE	Windows opening screen image file
SAM	Ami Pro
SYS	System file/device driver file
STY	Microsoft Word or Ventura Publisher style sheet
TIF	Graphics file in Tagged Image File Format (TIFF)
TMP	Temporary file
TTF	TrueType font file
TXT	Word processing file, usually ASCII
WAV	Windows sound file
WK1	Lotus 1-2-3 Version 2 worksheet
WK3	Lotus 1-2-3 Version 3 worksheet

Extension	Likely Contents
WKQ	Quattro Pro worksheet
WKS	Lotus 1-2-3 Version 1 worksheet
WMF	Graphics file in Windows Metafile format
WRI	Windows Write file
WRK	Symphony spreadsheet
XLC	Microsoft Excel chart
XLS	Microsoft Excel worksheet
YAL	Arts & Letters graphics file
ZIP	Compressed file in ZIP format

Looking Inside a File

DOS provides a variety of ways to look at the contents of a file. The oldest and simplest one is the TYPE command. You type **TYPE** plus the file name and extension of the file you want to look at, as in...

    TYPE FILE NAME.EXT

DOS then scrolls the contents of the file across the screen. If the file is all or mostly text, you can get a very good idea of what's inside the file. If not... well, figure 7.1 shows what's inside Microsoft's recently released Access 1.0 database program (MSACCESS.EXE).

In figure 7.1, TYPE is attempting to display the IBM Character Set equivalents to the program code and other data actually included in the file. (The figure shows a rare glimpse of the actual text of the error message ACCESS would display if you tried to load it without Windows.)

You have better luck if you display this file using a language more akin to the program's. View File Contents (in the DOS Shell) shows binary on the left, hexadecimal in the center, and ASCII equivalents on the right, as shown in figure 7.2. In this figure, the file at least *looks* organized.

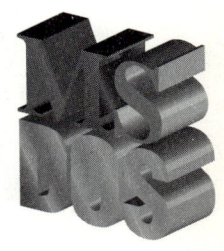

Chapter 7: *Managing Disks and Files*

Figure 7.1
The contents of Microsoft Access 1.0, as displayed by the TYPE command.

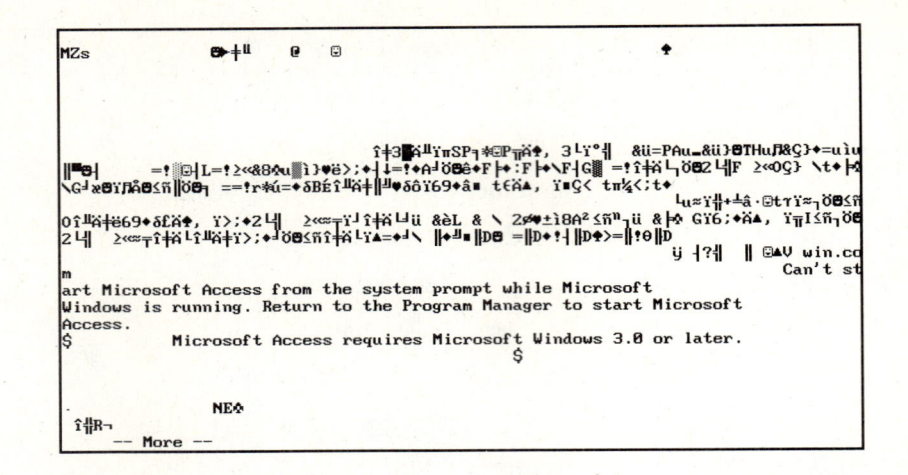

Figure 7.2
The contents of Microsoft Access 1.0, as displayed in the DOS Shell's View File Contents window.

> **NOTE**
>
> You may know that MSACCESS.EXE contains 1,324,672 bytes. So why does TYPE only show one or two screens and then return to the DOS prompt?
>
> MS-DOS's own programs, such as TYPE and EDIT, end their processing when they arrive at an end-of-file marker.

Other applications may use the Ctrl+Z (end-of-file) character for other purposes. If you use TYPE or EDIT to display such a file, the file may end unexpectedly without displaying all its contents.

The DOS Shell's View File Contents window solves this problem, too: it knows all and shows all.

Editing with EDIT

DOS 5 and 6.2 include a real text editor to replace EDLIN, the line editor only a very forgiving programmer could love. EDIT and EDLIN both shipped with DOS 5; with DOS 6.2, EDLIN has landed in the dustbin of history.

EDIT (its opening window is shown in fig. 7.3) looks like a word processor and can be run with either the keyboard or a mouse. Use EDIT instead of your word processor when you want to take a quick look at a text file. Or use it when you want to create or edit a text file with no extraneous formatting—for example, your AUTOEXEC.BAT or CONFIG.SYS file.

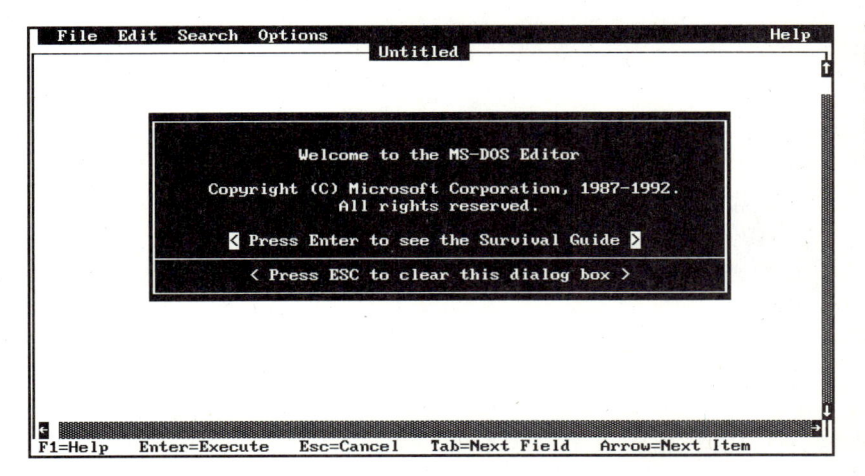

Figure 7.3

The opening windows for DOS EDIT.

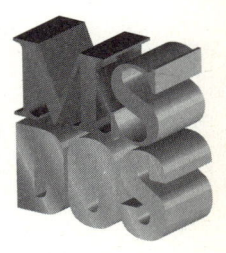

> **NOTE**
>
> *Because EDIT is actually a stripped-down version of DOS 6.2's QBASIC programming interface, both EDIT and QBASIC must be in your path for EDIT to run properly.*

Loading EDIT

To load EDIT from the command prompt, just type **EDIT**. Or you can directly load a file (or create a new file) by typing **EDIT** and the path and file name, as in…

EDIT FILE NAME.EXT

or…

EDIT D:\BATCHFLS\NEWBATCH.BAT

If you load EDIT without a file name, press Esc to clear the Welcome dialog box that appears. To create a new file, choose New from the File menu. With the mouse: click on File and then click on New. With the keyboard: press Alt to activate the menus, press Enter to open the File menu, move the cursor to New, and press Enter.

To open an existing file, select File Open instead. EDIT displays all the files with the TXT extension in the current directory (see fig. 7.4). In the File Name box, you can type a complete new path and file name. Or you can tab (or move the mouse) to the file name in the Files box. Or you can change the drive in Dirs/Drives.

> **NOTE**
>
> *To learn how to change EDIT's default, see Chapter 14.*

Getting Around in EDIT

You can press F1 (or right-click the mouse) anywhere within EDIT to get help.

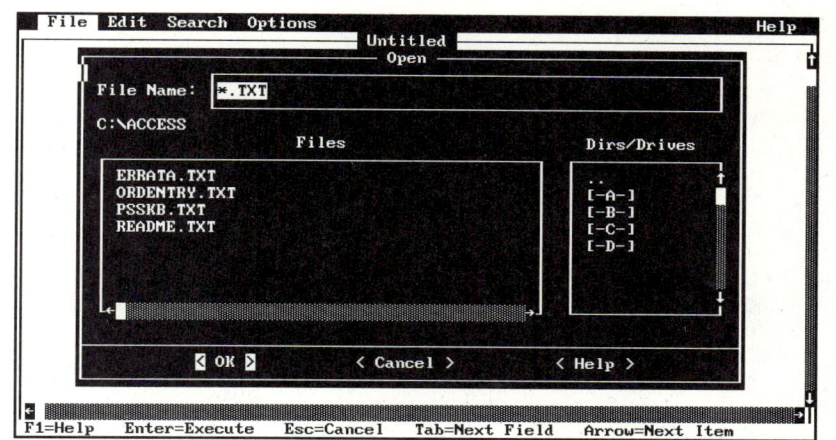

Figure 7.4

Opening an existing file in DOS EDIT.

EDIT provides cut, copy, and paste capabilities in the **E**dit menu; find and change capabilities are in the **S**earch menu. If EDIT had word-wrap and formatting features, you might think you were using a real low-end word processor. (But those features would detract from its prime function: to provide a smooth way of working with pure text files that must be executed by DOS.)

Use the **P**rint command in the **F**ile menu to print the entire file; alternatively, you can print only text you have selected with the mouse or keyboard. To select text from the keyboard, press and hold down Shift as you use the arrow keys to select the text you want. To select text by using the mouse, press and hold down the left mouse button as you move the mouse to highlight the text you want. Then release the mouse button.

Editing a Document

Once you have the text display window (without the Welcome box), you can start typing or editing. Move the cursor to the location where you want to work (either with the mouse or with the keyboard arrow keys).

EDIT provides several shortcuts for moving in a document; you can see these shortcuts in the HELP: Shortcut Keys screen (see fig. 7.5). To do so, follow these steps:

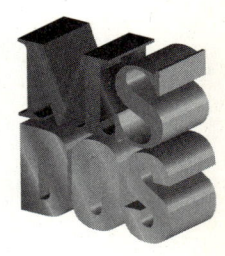

Chapter 7: *Managing Disks and Files*

1. In Edit, press F1 for Help.
2. Move to the word *Keyboard* that appears between triangles near the top of the screen.
3. Select Keyboard by pressing Enter or double-clicking.
4. Move to the Shortcut Keys option, and select it by pressing Enter or double-clicking.

Figure 7.5

The DOS EDIT Help: Shortcut Keys screen.

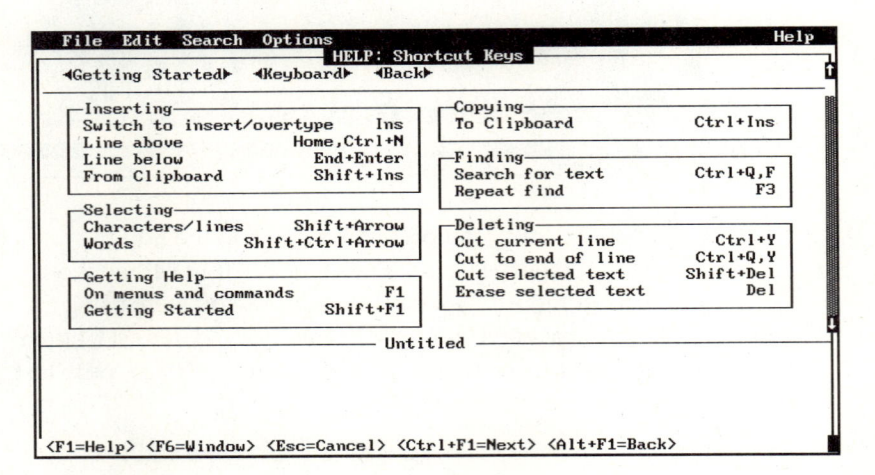

```
 File  Edit  Search  Options                                    Help
                     ┌─── HELP: Shortcut Keys ───┐
 ◄Getting Started►  ◄Keyboard►  ◄Back►
 ┌─Inserting────────────────────┐  ┌─Copying─────────────────────┐
 │ Switch to insert/overtype Ins│  │ To Clipboard      Ctrl+Ins  │
 │ Line above         Home,Ctrl+N│  └─────────────────────────────┘
 │ Line below          End+Enter│  ┌─Finding─────────────────────┐
 │ From Clipboard      Shift+Ins│  │ Search for text    Ctrl+Q,F │
 └──────────────────────────────┘  │ Repeat find             F3  │
 ┌─Selecting───────────────────┐   └─────────────────────────────┘
 │ Characters/lines  Shift+Arrow│  ┌─Deleting────────────────────┐
 │ Words        Shift+Ctrl+Arrow│  │ Cut current line    Ctrl+Y  │
 └──────────────────────────────┘  │ Cut to end of line Ctrl+Q,Y │
 ┌─Getting Help────────────────┐   │ Cut selected text  Shift+Del│
 │ On menus and commands     F1│   │ Erase selected text    Del  │
 │ Getting Started     Shift+F1│   └─────────────────────────────┘
 └──────────────────────────────┘
                     ──── Untitled ────

 <F1=Help> <F6=Window> <Esc=Cancel> <Ctrl+F1=Next> <Alt+F1=Back>
```

Adjusting EDIT Colors and Finding Help Files

The **O**ptions menu enables you to adjust your display colors. (If you load a file and can't see it, double-check the **O**ptions **D**isplay command to make sure that the background and foreground colors aren't identical.) The **H**elp **P**ath command permits you to locate DOS EDIT Help if it isn't in the current path.

If you're a DOS old-timer, you may be wondering what happened to EDLIN, the primitive line editor that DOS has traditionally provided. It's no longer shipped with DOS; EDIT is now the DOS editor.

If you're inexplicably attached to EDLIN, however, you can get it with the MS-DOS 6.2 Supplemental Disk, or simply copy EDLIN from an older version of DOS—it works fine.

See Chapter 14 for more information about EDLIN.

Copying Files

By now you've looked at and listed files to your heart's content. This section starts you off actually acting on the files—copying, moving, renaming, and deleting them. We start with COPY, the basic DOS command for copying files.

In its simplest permutation, COPY is used to copy a file from the current directory to a floppy disk, as in…

    COPY 2Q93REPT.XLS A:

That's all some people use it for. But you can combine COPY with wild cards to copy large groups of files by typing…

    COPY *.XLS A:

If you use path names, you can copy files to or from other locations by entering…

    COPY C:\DIR1*.* A:\FILES

In all these examples, the COPY command is followed first by the source file (or files) to be copied and then by the destination.

Copying Tricks and Traps

COPY can be trickier than it looks, for a few reasons:

✔ Unlike many DOS commands, COPY makes assumptions. For example, if you type…

    COPY B:\JONESFILE.DOC

…COPY assumes that you want to copy JONESFILE.DOC into the current directory.

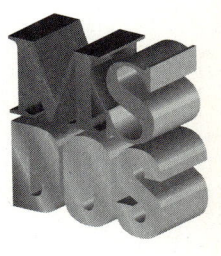

- COPY assumes that you don't want to change the file name when you copy it. Although that's usually appropriate, COPY doesn't hesitate to copy a file over another file by the same name.

  If you do want to change the file name on the destination drive, type the new file name after the destination path—if any—and before any switches...

  `COPY B:\NOTEBOOK.DOC C:\OLDFILES\OLDNOTES.DOC`

  To copy the file with another name to the same disk, type...

  `COPY B:\EXERCISE.DOC EXERCISE.BAK`

  *It's too easy to type **COPY *.* A;** instead of **COPY *.* A:**. If you type a semicolon instead of a colon, COPY will copy all the files to a new file called A in the current directory instead of to drive A.*

  Be sure to reread your command syntax after you type it and press Enter.

- COPY overwrites existing files of the same name in the destination directory without questioning you. To avoid unintentional overwriting, run a directory list on the destination directory before you copy files to it.

  After twelve years of DOS, COPY finally warns you if you are about to overwrite an existing file of the same name. See the next section for details.

Copying with Overwrite Protection

For years, DOS users have screamed for overwrite protection when copying files with COPY. Well, its finally here. Who says persistence doesn't pay off?

> ## AUTHOR'S NOTE
>
> *Because COPY can create copies of files with new file names, a slight typing error can cause you considerable confusion, placing files where you didn't expect them with names you didn't expect.*
>
> *Suppose that you're working in drive C and you want to place GRAPH.WK3 into the WRKSHEET subdirectory on drive D. To do this, you intend to type COPY GRAPH.WK3 D:\WRKSHEET. But for a moment, you forget that the destination directory is on a different drive—and instead you type...*
>
> ```
> COPY GRAPH.WK3 WRKSHEET
> ```
>
> *This produces another copy of GRAPH.WK3 in the current directory with the new name WRKSHEET.*
>
> *Next month, when you look for the file on D:\WRKSHEET, it isn't there. There is, however, a file called WRKSHEET in the drive C root directory, which (because it doesn't have an extension) looks an awful lot like a subdirectory.*
>
> *The following week, you notice WRKSHEET on C drive, assume that it's the subdirectory that you are looking for, and try to copy another file into it by entering...*
>
> ```
> COPY GRAPH2.WK3 C:\WRKSHEET
> ```
>
> *But you've now accidentally copied the file C:\WRKSHEET over the file GRAPH2.WK3. It was bad enough that your original file GRAPH.WK3 was renamed and misplaced—but now it no longer exists.*
>
> *Combining this copying mistake with a wild card is one way people fill their root directories with so much crud that it requires surgery to extract it all.*

By default, COPY (as well as XCOPY and MOVE) now warns you if you are about to overwrite a file of the same name, and prompts you for confirmation. For example, if MYFILE.DOC already exists on drive A and you attempt to copy a file of the same name to drive A, you will see the following prompt:

```
Overwrite A:MYFILE.DOC (Yes/No/All)?
```

To carry out the copy process, you must first type **Y**, and (for added safety) press Enter. A nice touch is the All choice, which will replace all other duplicate file names without further confirmation.

> *To prevent the COPY command from bogging down your batch files with continual confirmation messages, COPY will behave exactly like it always has when you use it in a batch file. It will simply overwrite any existing file of the same name with no confirmation.*

There are also two new switches with the DOS 6.2 COPY command, both of which relate to overwrite confirmation. The /Y switch instructs COPY to go ahead and replace any existing files without prompting you for confirmation. The /-Y switch instructs COPY to prompt you for confirmation when replacing an exising file. The reason for this switch is explained in the next section.

Using the COPYCMD Environment Variable

Like the DIR command, COPY now has its own environment variable. The COPYCMD environment variable enables you to specify your preference for the way COPY behaves—whether or not it prompts for overwrite confirmation. The following command, for example, instructs COPY to skip overwrite confirmation, and causes COPY to act like it always has:

    SET COPYCMD=/V

With this variable set, you can then use the /-Y switch from the command line if you want to override the COPYCMD setting and instruct COPY to once again prompt you for overwrite confirmation. With the preceding variable set, for example, entering this command…

    COPY MYFILE.DOC A: /-Y

will override the environment setting and prompt you for overwrite confirmation if a file of the same name already exists on drive A.

Be aware that COPYCMD supports only the /Y switch. Using the /V switch with COPYCMD, for example, accomplishes nothing (see the Verifying the COPY Process section later in this chapter).

Concatenating Files Intentionally and by Accident

Concatenation is something else COPY can do that's really powerful when you do it for a good reason... but really disastrous when you do it by mistake. *Concatenation* means combining several files into one. This can be useful if you have multiple ASCII files you want to combine.

I emphasize *ASCII files* because if you combine several files formatted by a specific application, that application may be confused by the concatenated file and either load only the first section, or nothing at all. Worse, if you concatenate binary program files, you almost always wind up with a useless lump of bytes.

> *Concatenation is also occasionally useful when you use COPY to copy data from one device to another, as described in the following section.*

The normal way to concatenate files is to separate the source files with plus (+) signs and then give the name of the new file you want to create, as in typing...

    COPY FILE1.ASC + FILE2.ASC TWOFILES.ASC

You can also use wild cards to concatenate by entering...

    COPY *.ASC ALLFILES.ASC

This command merges all the ASC files in the current directory into one concatenated file called ALLFILES.ASC.

To borrow from Lord Acton, "If power corrupts, this much power can corrupt your files into an absolute mess." Suppose that you want to copy all your files into the directory ALLFILES. Unfortunately, you forgot you don't have a directory by that name. Or, more likely, it's not on the path you specified.

So instead of copying all the files into a subdirectory in usable form, you shuffle them all together in a new file that's worthless to you.

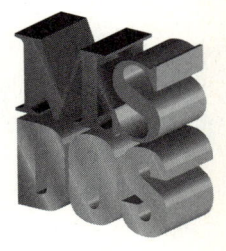

The giveaway here is the statement:

```
1 file copied
```

This message tells you that one new destination file was created when you expect more.

> **NOTE:** *You can get around problems like these by using XCOPY, which has the sense to ask whether you're trying to copy to a directory or a file.*

Copying between Devices

Most people think of COPY as strictly a mechanism for working with files, but you can use it to copy data to and from devices as well.

As you may know, DOS has built-in support for several devices: COM1 (AUX), COM2, COM3, and COM4 serial ports; LPT1 (PRN), LPT2, and LPT3 parallel ports; the keyboard (CON); the system clock (CLOCK$); and NUL (a phony device used to accept discarded output). Some of these devices, like PRN, only accept information; others, like CON, only send it. With serial ports, information can go both ways.

> **STOP:** *Be aware of what you're sending to and from devices: in some cases, copying to a device that doesn't exist can lock up the system (while it looks obsessively for the nonexistent output device).*

COPYing ASCII and Binary Files

There are two ways to copy a file:

- ✔ Make a binary copy by copying everything in the file, end-to-end, exactly as it existed in the original.

✔ Create a text (ASCII) file by adding a Ctrl+Z (IBM character 26) end-of-file marker to the end of whatever you're copying.

> **AUTHOR'S NOTE**
>
> *You can use COPY to turn your hot new Pentium workstation into a typewriter. (Hey, sometimes a typewriter is what you need.) The command...*
>
> ```
> COPY CON LPT1
> ```
>
> *...tells the computer to accept input from your keyboard and copy it to the printer connected to the first parallel port (LPT1).*
>
> *Sometimes you can combine COPY's capability to concatenate, combined with its capability to copy to a file, to send multiple statements to a device at once. For example, you might want to instruct your printer directly (not through any application software) to print in boldface and compressed type.*
>
> *Let's say you have one short file, BOLD.PRN, that contains the commands your printer needs to print boldface type. Another file, COMPRESS.PRN, contains the commands for compressed type. To do both at once, you enter...*
>
> ```
> COPY BOLD.PRN /B +COMPRESS.PRN LPT1
> ```
>
> *Note that the /B switch indicates that both files should be read as binary files, and that it should appear after the first file.*

COPY nearly always guesses right about which approach to take. If you want a conventional copy, COPY makes a binary copy. If you concatenate files, COPY assumes that the files are probably ASCII files that need an end-of-file marker.

However, you can override these default settings by using the /A (ASCII) or /B (binary) switch with COPY. Note that this switch can be used with the source portion of the COPY statement, the destination portion, or both.

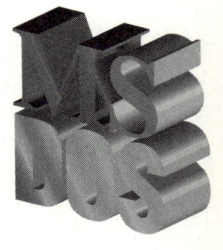

Chapter 7: *Managing Disks and Files*

The following command reads the source file C:\CURRENT\SOURCE.DOC as a binary file and copies it to text file A:\FILE.ASC:

```
COPY C:\CURRENT\SOURCE.DOC /B A:\FILE.ASC /A
```

Unfortunately, the /A switch can cause you trouble if you use it with a binary file. When you use the /A switch, the first time COPY sees character 26 in the file—regardless of why it's there—COPY ends the file right there, leaving you with an incomplete, useless file.

Verifying the COPY Process

COPY can give you a partial assist in verifying that your copying has been done properly. If you add the /V (verify) switch to the COPY command, COPY compares what it has actually written against the contents of its memory buffer. In other words, COPY /V doesn't check the copy against the original—it only checks to make sure that it copied what it tried to copy. That's almost always good enough.

Not surprisingly, /V slows down the COPY process significantly, because it rereads each destination file from disk. You may want to use it only for your most critical copies.

AUTHOR'S NOTE

You might assume that when you use COPY to copy a file, DOS simply reads the file into memory and plunks it down at the destination. But there's more going on, and understanding the process that COPY follows may help you understand how to keep things from going wrong.

When you use COPY, it performs the following tasks, one step at a time:

1. *COPY asks, "Is the source a file or a DOS device?"*

2. *If the source is a DOS device, DOS displays the device name and waits for ASCII input from that device (unless you used the /B switch to tell it to expect binary input).*

3. If the source is a file, COPY prepares to copy the file in binary format (unless you used the /A switch to tell it to expect ASCII input). COPY then starts searching for the file's directory.

4. COPY reads the directory to find the first file that matches your request. (There may be many if you used a wild card.)

5. COPY displays the file name and copies the first 64K of the file into memory (or the entire file, if the file is less than 64K).

6. COPY then asks, "Is the destination a file or a DOS device?"

7. If the destination is a DOS device, COPY searches for the device. When COPY finds it, it writes the first 64K to the device, copies another 64K from the source and writes it to the device, and so on until it finishes. COPY follows any instructions you give it about writing in ASCII or binary format.

8. If the destination is a file, COPY searches for the destination directory.

9. If COPY finds that the destination file name matches a file name in the path you specified, it looks to see whether you're copying one file or several to that name.

10. If you're copying several files to a single name, COPY assumes that you are concatenating (merging) them and starts the process. Otherwise, COPY assumes that you are simply copying the source file to the destination directory and giving the file the destination name you specified. Again, COPY follows any instructions you give it about writing in binary or ASCII format.

11. COPY writes the first 64K into the destination file and goes back to the source for more, alternately reading and writing 64K chunks until it's finished.

Copying Entire Disks with DISKCOPY

DOS provides a command specifically designed to copy the contents of an entire disk to another disk with an identical format: DISKCOPY copies everything, including subdirectory structure, hidden files, and system files. The only difference between a DISKCOPY copy and the original disk is the serial numbers on the disks. DISKCOPY is ideal for backing up the programs you buy.

New to DOS 6.2 (finally!) is the no-swap DISKCOPY. DISKCOPY now stores all the copied data on the hard disk and then copies all of it to the destination in one shot. Even better, after the copy process completes, you see this prompt:

```
Do you wish to write another duplicate of
this disk (Y/N)?
```

This prompt enables you to make multiple copies of the same disk without having to repeat the original copy step. If you prefer the old multi-pass method, you can force this by adding the /M switch to the command.

The normal syntax for DISKCOPY is simply:

```
DISKCOPY sourcedrive destinationdrive
```

For example:

```
DISKCOPY B: A:
```

However, most people do not have two identical drives. You may have one 1.44M drive and one 1.2M drive, or one 360K drive and one 720K drive. Because DISKCOPY won't work across different size drives, you can use XCOPY (described in the following section), or you can use DISKCOPY to copy files on the same drive, as in:

```
DISKCOPY A: A:
```

DISKCOPY copies into memory as much data as it can and then prompts you to place a destination disk in the same drive. DOS 6.2 copies all data from the source disk onto your hard drive, and then copies it to the destination disk all at once.

It writes the data to the second disk and prompts you to place the source disk back in. This swap process continues until DISKCOPY finishes: usually three swaps at most.

You can add the /V switch to tell DISKCOPY to verify the accuracy of writes. Because you use DISKCOPY primarily to duplicate original program disks, it may be worth the (significant) added time to use /V switch.

DISKCOPY destroys any data that may be present on the destination disk.

Copying Smart with XCOPY

XCOPY is COPY's younger, smarter brother. Introduced in DOS 3.2, it's ideal for these situations:

- ✔ Copying multiple files
- ✔ Copying files larger than 64K (but smaller than the available space on the destination disk)
- ✔ Copying subdirectory structures
- ✔ Selecting files to copy based on whether they've already been copied

Although XCOPY won't concatenate files, for many users that's another advantage: one less thing to go wrong. (XCOPY also won't copy to or from a device.)

Unlike COPY (which reads files in chunks of 64K at most), XCOPY can read as much data as you have available conventional memory—and then write it all to the destination in one pass. Typically, that means XCOPY can handle six to nine times as much data at once.

However, unlike COPY, XCOPY is an external program: that means that it loads a bit more slowly and has to be in the current path. That's why people usually stick with COPY for very small file-copy operations.

XCOPY assumes that you are copying entire subdirectories, unless you tell it otherwise. Therefore, these two commands do the same job…

```
XCOPY A:\ B\
COPY A:\*.* B:\*.*
```

…except that XCOPY usually does it much faster.

In fact, if you're copying files into the current directory, you can make the process even simpler. XCOPY assumes that you want to place files in the current directory unless you tell it differently. To place all the files on drive A in your current directory, simply enter…

XCOPY A:*.*

You can also copy all the files in one directory or path to or from any other directory or path by typing…

XCOPY D:\WORDPROC C:\OLDFILES

You can also specify file names in an XCOPY command—most often with wild cards by entering…

XCOPY A:\93*.XLS B:

Alternatively, you can use the /p (pause) switch to specify multiple files and ask XCOPY to stop and confirm if you want to copy each one by typing…

XCOPY A:\ B:\ /P

Like COPY, XCOPY now warns you if you are about to overwrite a file of the same name and prompts you for confirmation.

Capturing Subdirectories with XCOPY

By default, XCOPY doesn't capture files located in subdirectories within the directory you specify. However, you can use the /s switch to copy the contents of all subdirectories. In fact, XCOPY will create the subdirectories on the destination if they don't already exist. For instance, you can enter…

    XCOPY A:\ B:\ /S

…and, by itself, the /s switch doesn't copy empty subdirectories. But if you use the /e switch too, it will. You have to use both /s and /e by entering…

    XCOPY A:\ B:\ /S /E

Backing Up Files with XCOPY

Whenever DOS changes a file, it sets the file's archive bit. That's DOS's way of telling you that you have a file that needs to be backed up. (Disk crashes are DOS's other way to tell you this.)

You can use XCOPY and the archive-bit information to copy all the files that have changed since you last backed up your disk. You'll be copying all files that have their archive bits set—in other words, all files that have been changed since you last backed them up.

Let's say that you want to copy onto drive A all the files in the subdirectory C:\FILES, which have changed since your last backup. Let's say you also want to clear their archive attributes so that they will not automatically be backed up the next time, unless they change again. Then enter…

    XCOPY C:\FILES A: /M

If your backup needs are simple—small files, for example—this may be the only file-backup strategy you need.

Two switches are involved to make backups with XCOPY:

/A   copies all files with archive bits set—but does not clear the archive bits.

/M   copies all files with archive bits set—and clears the archive bits.

Chapter 7: *Managing Disks and Files*

If you only use XCOPY to create backups—and the only way you make backups is with XCOPY—using /M makes sense. The /M switch clears the archive bits so that the next time you make a backup with XCOPY, you won't have to waste time and disk space making duplicate copies of files you've already archived.

Using /M also makes sense if you are copying more files than one destination disk can hold. Normally, XCOPY halts when it runs out of space. Giving the command again simply recopies the same files—and you run out of space again.

Here's how you can use /M to solve the problem:

1. Set the archive attributes of all the files you want to copy by using the ATTRIB command. Type...

    `ATTRIB +A C:\FILES\*.*`

2. Run XCOPY for these files, using the /M switch to clear archive attributes on each file successfully copied by entering...

    `XCOPY C:\FILES /M`

    As expected, XCOPY terminates when the first destination disk is full—before it has copied every file.

3. Insert a new, formatted disk and give the same XCOPY command again. (Press F3 to display the last command without retyping it.)

    XCOPY only copies the files that still have an archive attribute set—but none of the ones whose archive bits have already been cleared.

> **NOTE** *See Chapter 18 for more about backup and how to use DOS's excellent XCOPY command as an alternative for daily backups.*

There are disadvantages to clearing the archive attributes with the XCOPY /M switch, however. Unless you reset the bits manually (or write a batch file to do it), the archive bits are no longer set when you want to use them for a formal backup (using a dedicated backup program). As another example, you might use XCOPY to make a set of copies to give to a colleague.

> *Don't forget that you can reset a file's archive bit yourself by using the ATTRIB +A command.*

You can also use the /D: switch to copy all files created or changed on or after a certain date by typing...

```
XCOPY E:\ B:\ /D:04/06/93
```

Make sure that you use the /D: switch with a date syntax DOS recognizes. In the U.S., these are acceptable formats:

```
month:day:year
month/day/year
month-day-year
```

AUTHOR'S NOTE

XCOPY's biggest advantage in making backups is its relative simplicity. It's right there at the command line. You can just type a few letters and you're off...

```
XCOPY C:\ A:\ /S /M
```

XCOPY also has the advantage of creating files that are immediately usable. Contrast that with the backup files MSBACKUP and MWBACKUP create: these files are in a special format that must be specifically restored.

XCOPY has some disadvantages, however. It won't split a file across more than one disk. In the best case, you leave lots of unused space on the destination disk. In the worst case, you can't use XCOPY to back up a file that's bigger than the destination disk. You can't use XCOPY if you have a 3M multimedia file and only 1.44M floppies to back it up on.

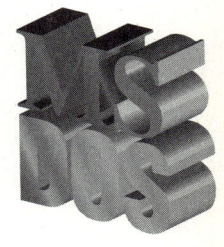

Verifying While Using XCOPY

Like COPY and DISKCOPY, XCOPY accepts the /V switch that checks to ensure that the copy written to disk matches the copy held in memory. (Again, /V does not actually compare the source file with the copied version.)

Using XCOPY /W on a Floppy-Based System

Because XCOPY is an external command, it has to be loaded and run when you call it. If you have to run XCOPY from a floppy disk, and you want to XCOPY files to or from the same drive, you can use the /W switch to load XCOPY into memory and then have the system pause while you switch disks.

> *XCOPY won't copy hidden or system files such as MSDOS.SYS and IO.SYS.*

Updating with REPLACE

The DOS REPLACE command gives you an easy way to update a directory's files or to add files to that directory.

Suppose that you have several copies of a file with the same name, but of various vintages. Now suppose that the only purpose served by the older files is to confuse people.

To update all the files with REPLACE, specify the path and name of the newest version of the file followed by the path containing the file or files you want to replace.

In rare cases, you can use REPLACE to update software—but be careful: new versions of software often contain different files than the old versions. Even if you replace the main EXE file, other old files may remain to confuse the new version. If the program or its update included an Install or Setup program, use that instead.

Device drivers are one possible candidate for replacement—as long as you have backups of your previous versions.

The following command updates all copies of DATABASE.DOC on drive C's root directory, making them identical to A:\DATABASE.DOC:

    REPLACE A:\DATABASE.DOC C:\

Because REPLACE doesn't change file names, you don't have to include a file name after the destination path. As with XCOPY, if you don't include a destination path, REPLACE replaces files in the current directory.

To change every version of DATABASE.DOC in all subdirectories in drive C, use the same /S switch that works with XCOPY by entering...

    REPLACE A:\DATABASE.DOC C:\ /S

When you use REPLACE, you run the risk of accidentally replacing a current file with an older version. The /U (update) switch can help prevent this accident. For example...

    REPLACE A:\DATABASE.DOC C:\ /S /U

...tells REPLACE only to replace a specified file if the replacement version is newer. REPLACE won't replace hidden or system files (although you can always clear the hidden or system attributes and *then* replace those files). REPLACE won't swap read-only files either—unless you use the /R switch:

    REPLACE A:\DATABASE.DOC C:\ /S /R

Adding Files with REPLACE

The default REPLACE command doesn't place a file in any subdirectory that doesn't already contain a file by that name. But you can use REPLACE to place new files into a subdirectory—or to replace them in a directory from which you may have deleted them. Just use the /A (add) switch by typing...

Chapter 7: *Managing Disks and Files*

> **REPLACE A:*.DOC C:\WORDPROC /a**

REPLACE replaces any files that already exist in the destination subdirectory—and adds the files that don't exist.

> **NOTE**
>
> *As with XCOPY, you can use the /W switch to tell REPLACE to pause so that you can swap floppies. You can also use the /P switch to have REPLACE prompt you to confirm each file replacement.*

Moving Files with MOVE

Before DOS 6.2, moving files was a two-part process: copy the files into the new location and then delete the files from the original location. You could get the move function from shareware programs, but not from DOS. With DOS 6.2, however, there's a real-life MOVE command.

MOVE works both within a drive and across drives. The syntax is as follows: type **MOVE**, then specify the file or files you want to move, and then specify the destination. For example, type…

> **MOVE C:\WORD5\DATA.DOC C:\NEWWORD**

If you are moving files from the current directory, you don't have to include the current directory in the path. Here's an example of moving a file from the current directory:

> **MOVE FILE NAME.EXT B:\DISKFILE**

But if you're moving files *to* the current directory, you do need to indicate it. Use the DOS . (dot) shortcut by entering…

> **MOVE C:\DISKFILE\FILE NAME.EXT .**

If you are moving a single file, you can use MOVE to change the file name on the destination drive by typing…

> **MOVE C:\WORD5\DATA.DOC A:\NEWDATA.DOC**

You can also use wild cards with MOVE by entering…

> **MOVE A:*.* B:**

> *Like COPY, MOVE doesn't question you if you tell it to overwrite an existing file on the destination directory. It just goes ahead and does it. List the directory on the destination directory first—to make sure that you aren't about to destroy a file you need.*

> **6.2** *Like COPY and XCOPY, MOVE now warns you if you are about to overwrite a file of the same name and prompts you for confirmation.*

Understanding the Limitations of MOVE

There are some things MOVE won't do that you might expect it to do:

- ✔ It won't rename more than one file at a time. An errant command such as…

    ```
    MOVE C:\NEWFILES\*.DOC C:\OLDFILES\*.BAK
    ```

    …evokes this message…

    ```
    Cannot move multiple files to a single file
    ```

- ✔ As the preceding message implies, MOVE won't concatenate.
- ✔ MOVE doesn't have a /V switch to verify the move (see the following section).

Verifying MOVEs with the VERIFY Command

MOVE does not have a /V switch to verify that the files it moves have been accurately written. Microsoft says that when the file is being moved within a disk, the file is not actually rewritten: its subdirectory address is changed.

However, MOVE also works across drives. If you want to verify the accuracy of those writes, use the VERIFY command, which works the same way as the COPY /V switch. At the command prompt, type…

`VERIFY ON`

DOS rechecks all writes against the contents of its buffer until you disable the VERIFY command by typing…

`VERIFY OFF`

Like /V, VERIFY can slow down moves across drives by 60 percent or more, so you may want to use it sparingly. To check whether VERIFY is currently turned on or off, type…

`VERIFY`

> **NOTE** *You can see how the MOVE command is used to rename subdirectories in Chapter 6.*

Comparing Files with FC Is Better than with COMP

DOS 5 included two commands for comparing the contents of files: COMP and FC. In DOS 5, COMP worked only if you had two files that were exactly the same size. As soon as it found ten differences, it halted the comparison.

COMP was useful in comparing short batch files or in determining whether two longer data files were identical. Beyond that, it wasn't especially helpful. FC was a lot more flexible: in true Darwinian manner, FC is the file-comparison command that survives in DOS 6.2.

The syntax for FC is as follows: type **FC**, then any relevant switches, then the first file to be compared, and then the second file. (Unlike many DOS commands, FC places switches *before* file names.) If both files are not in the current directory, specify complete paths.

FC can compare only two files, and you cannot use wild cards to specify file names. FC behaves differently, depending on whether you are comparing ASCII (text) files or binary files. FC compares ASCII files line-by-line; it compares binary files byte-by-byte.

For ASCII comparisons, FC offers a wide variety of switches to refine and streamline your search:

- **/A** tells FC if it finds several lines in a row that are different to display only the first and last lines of that chunk.
- **/C** tells FC to treat uppercase and lowercase letters as identical and not display them as differences.
- **/T** tells FC not to include 8 spaces in place of each tab it comes across.
- **/W** tells FC to compress white space (tabs and spaces) and not compare white space at the beginning and end of each file.
- **/LB#** tells FC to increase or reduce the number of lines it can fit in its buffer. The default is 100 lines; you can increase this if you are comparing a long file with many small changes.

Normally, FC assumes that a file is an ASCII file unless it has an extension normally used by binary files (EXE, COM, SYS, OBJ, LIB, BIN). You can force a binary comparison with the /B switch. If you use /B, however, none of the other switches are available. Conversely, you can force an ASCII comparison of files that FC believes are binary files by using the /L switch.

Following is a simple example of an ASCII comparison that uses no switches. Suppose that you want to compare two price lists: PRILISTR.DOC and PRILISTS.DOC. You want to know when you introduced the new product called *Quotches*. Type the following command...

    FC PRILISTR.DOC PRILISTS.DOC

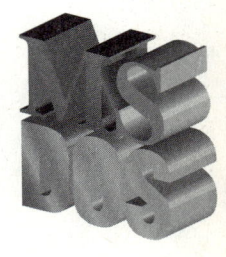

Chapter 7: *Managing Disks and Files*

FC displays each line in which a difference between two files exists, along with adjacent lines for context:

```
Comparing files PRILISTR.DOC and PRILISTS.DOC
***** PRILISTR.DOC
As of 12/30/92, our new price list is as follows:

***** PRILISTS.DOC
As of 3/30/93, our new price list is as follows:

*****

***** PRILISTR.DOC
Pludges        $2.79
Wizzums        $3.39
***** PRILISTS.DOC
Pludges        $2.79
Quotches       $6.59
Wizzums        $3.39
*****
```

As you can see, Quotches was introduced with the 3/30/93 price list.

A note about this example: both files used were pure text files. If you use a word processor or other program that includes special characters for text formatting, differences in these characters may also show up when FC compares files.

If you use the /N switch, you can add line numbers so that you can more easily find the differences when you go back into the files later. For instance, typing…

FC /N PRILISTR.DOC PRILISTS.DOC

…produces this output:

```
Comparing files PRILISTR.DOC and PRILISTS.DOC
***** PRILISTR.DOC
    1:  As of 12/30/92, our new price list is as follows:
    2:
***** PRILISTS.DOC
    1:  As of 3/30/93, our new price list is as follows:
    2:
*****
```

```
***** PRILISTR.DOC
    7:     Pludges      $2.79
    8:     Wizzums      $3.39
***** PRILISTS.DOC
    7:     Pludges      $2.79
    8:     Quotches     $6.59
    9:     Wizzums      $3.39
*****
```

Erasing Files

Take your pick: DOS recognizes both the DEL and ERASE commands to delete files. Both commands work the same. To delete a file in the current directory, you can type either of these commands:

```
DEL FILENAME.EXT
ERASE FILENAME.EXT
```

NOTE *Although DEL and ERASE do the same thing, I prefer to use DEL because it's shorter and because it's consistent with the new DELTREE command you can use to delete a subdirectory and all its contents (see Chapter 6).*

You can delete file names other than those in the current directory by including their complete path names:

DEL C:\EXCEL\92RESULT.XLS

You can also use wild cards with DEL:

DEL C:\OBSOLETE*.*

Any time you try to delete all the contents of a subdirectory, you get the following message:

```
All files in directory will be deleted! Are you sure (Y/N)?
```

If you press **Y**, DEL deletes all the files. There are two ways to slow this process down and lower the risk that you'll delete something you want. The first is to give the DIR command with the same path you plan to DEL. That shows you what you're about to delete.

Chapter 7: *Managing Disks and Files*

> *If you are confident that you don't need an* `Are you sure (Y/N)?` *prompt after entering DEL *.*, then write the following DELALL.BAT batch file:*
>
> ```
> @echo off
> echo Y ¦ del *.* > nul
> ```
>
> *If you want to delete all the files in a directory without DEL prompting you for confirmation, change to the proper directory and enter* **DELALL**. *The piping symbol (¦) passes the ouput from the ECHO statement (Y followed by a carriage return) to the DEL command. DEL thinks the user answered* **yes** *to its confirmation message and deletes all the files in the current directory. Be careful!*

Alternatively, you can use the /P switch with DEL. DOS prompts you with each file name before you delete it:

```
filename.ext, Delete (Y/N)?
```

AUTHOR'S NOTE

The day will come when you use DEL or ERASE with a file that you wish you hadn't. That's the day you should drop your mouse and hurry to Chapter 19 to read about retrieving deleted files.

I recently had a client trash the root directory of her hard drive by entering **DEL..** *from a subdirectory off the root, thinking this would delete all the files in the current directory. The result was a mess. But .. refers to the parent directory, so DEL.. deletes the directory immediately above the current directory.*

Renaming Files

The REN command can rename single files or groups of files. First you specify the file's current name, and then the file's new name:

REN FILE1.DOC FILE1.BAK

Wild cards work with REN, too:

```
REN *.DOC *.BAK
```

One good use for REN is to rename groups of files restored by the UNDELETE command. When UNDELETE can't find a complete file name, the files it restores begin with #.

Although you can rename files on a different path, REN does not move them. (That's what MOVE's for.) So this works...

```
REN D:\BACKUPS\89FILE.DOC 89ARCHIV.DOC
```

But this doesn't...

```
REN D:\BACKUPS\89FILE.DOC A:\89ARCHIV.DOC
```

Unlike COPY, MOVE, and many other DOS file commands, REN stops before renaming a file if it finds an existing file by that name. You see this message:

```
Duplicate file name or file not found
```

You can use MOVE to rename a directory (see Chapter 6), or you can do so from the DOS Shell or Windows File Manager. You can use LABEL to rename a disk, as described in the following section.

Naming Volumes and Labels

Whenever you format a hard disk or floppy disk, DOS assigns the disk a random serial number: two 4-digit combinations of letters and numbers, connected with a hyphen. For example: 4166-0BD8.

When you format a disk, DOS asks if you want to name (label) the disk:

```
Volume label (11 characters, ENTER for none)?
```

Chapter 7: *Managing Disks and Files*

Although you can't change the serial number (unless you reformat the disk), you can see the serial number and label by using the VOL command. Typing **VOL** at the command prompt gets you a response like this:

```
Volume in drive C is NEWLABEL
Volume Serial Number is 4166-0BD8
```

You can also use VOL to see other drives by typing...

VOL B:

You can change the disk's label (without glue remover). Type **LABEL**, followed by the drive name, followed by the new label you want to use, as in...

LABEL B: WPERFECTFLS

You can use up to 11 characters to name the disk. Sounds like file names, right? But it's a little different: you *can* use spaces in a volume name, but you *can't* use periods or any of the following punctuation marks:

* ? / \ | . , ; : + = [ ] ( ) $ ^ < > "

> **NOTE**
> *DOS displays all label names in uppercase, no matter how you type them.*

Backing Up Files with DOS 6.2 MSBACKUP and MWBACKUP

COPY and XCOPY might be all you need to back up your files. But people who create a lot of files, or change them frequently, usually find these two commands lacking. For example, COPY and XCOPY stop dead in their tracks when a destination disk runs out of room. Although you can use archive attributes with XCOPY to get around this problem, you still have no way to split large files over disks.

DOS 2 introduced a BACKUP command so weak that it spawned a multimillion-dollar market for third-party backup programs that work better and faster and give the user more control. BACKUP was upgraded somewhat in DOS 3.3, but it still had plenty of limitations.

With DOS 6.2, Microsoft scraps BACKUP altogether and includes two complete backup programs based on Symantec's Norton Backup for DOS and Windows. When you install DOS 6.2, you are given the opportunity to install Microsoft Backup for DOS (MSBACKUP). If you have Windows, you are also offered Microsoft Backup for Windows (MWBACKUP)—or the opportunity to install both.

MSBACKUP for DOS may not run successfully from within Windows, although it runs fine if you first end the Windows session. Although the two packages are similar, the Windows package has some advantages, and you should run it instead of the DOS version if you have Windows.

Both programs are a major step forward, but they still share two major limitations: they don't support tape-backup units, nor do they have DMA support. So if you use one, you'll have to keep using the software you're already using. The new DOS backup programs do, however, support network drives and Bernoulli boxes.

What about the Old Backups?

Microsoft Backup for DOS and Windows cannot read backups made with the earlier DOS BACKUP utility. You can still use the BACKUP command, but first you have to get it. As of this writing, BACKUP is not on the DOS disks, though it is on the Supplemental Disk that can be ordered from Microsoft. RESTORE, however, has made it back into the regular package.

> **NOTE:** BACKUP may already be on your disk, in the OLD_DOS.1 directory where DOS placed the old DOS files when you upgraded. If the file isn't there, you can get it from your old DOS distribution disks.

Here's a sample procedure for retrieving and expanding compressed versions of BACKUP.EXE and RESTORE.EXE that came with DOS 5. (This example assumes that your copy of DOS 5 came on 3 1/2-inch 720K disks.)

1. Place DOS 5 disk #3 in your drive.

2. Copy the file EXPAND.EXE to the directory where DOS is installed (usually C:\DOS).

3. Assuming that C:\DOS is in your current path, type the following commands:

   ```
   EXPAND A:\BACKUP.EX_ C:\DOS\BACKUP.EXE
   EXPAND A:\RESTORE.EX_ C:\DOS\RESTORE.EXE
   ```

When Should You Back Up?

In answering the age-old question "How often should I back up?" the standard response may sound flippant: "How much work can you afford to lose?"

You should do your own cost-benefit analysis. It's the same as buying an insurance policy. Ask yourself:

- ✔ How much time are you willing to invest in regular incremental backups against the possibility (really, the likelihood) that you will one day lose data?

- ✔ How much data can you afford to lose?

- ✔ If you lose data, how much will you realistically be able to reconstruct?

- ✔ How long will it take to reconstruct the data, compared with the time it would take to back up your files?

- ✔ How important is the data you might not be able to reconstruct?

Backing Up Files with DOS 6.2 MSBACKUP and MWBACKUP

After you ask these questions, you might decide that a complete daily backup is essential. (If your computer contains the company's entire accounting system, this is a reasonable conclusion.) On the other hand, if you're a light PC user, weekly or biweekly incremental backups might be sufficient.

With DOS 6.2, two new elements may shift the balance towards increased backups:

- ✔ The new graphical interface-based backup programs make backups a little easier. If you resisted using DOS's BACKUP program, you may find that the DOS command-line elements you didn't like are gone; they're replaced with a program you can understand and might even like.

- ✔ Microsoft's new disk-compression program, DBLSPACE, presents many new opportunities to lose data. The extensive DBLSPACE beta test shook out quite a few problems, but some may remain. Although the underlying technology for DBLSPACE is borrowed from Speedstor, some of the formats have changed, and the way it has been integrated into DOS is new.

    Moreover, DBLSPACE, like Windows, utterly depends on the presence of certain files, such as DBLSPACE.INI and DSVXD.386. If one of these files is deleted or damaged, you may not have access to any of the information on your compressed drive.

Although you may never have problems with DBLSPACE, the disk-compression program introduces a significant new risk factor. Err on the side of more backups.

Taking a Walk through MSBACKUP and MWBACKUP

MSBACKUP and MWBACKUP work similarly and create backup files that are compatible with each other. You can load MSBACKUP

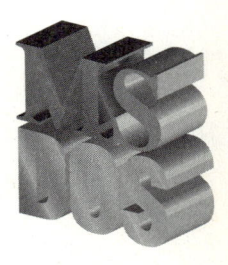

Chapter 7: *Managing Disks and Files*

from the command prompt by typing **MSBACKUP**. The Windows version is called Backup and can be found in a new Windows Program Group: Microsoft Tools (installed during the DOS 6.2 Setup process).

Figures 7.6 and 7.7 show you the opening screens of these programs.

Figure 7.6

The opening screen of Microsoft Backup for DOS (MSBACKUP).

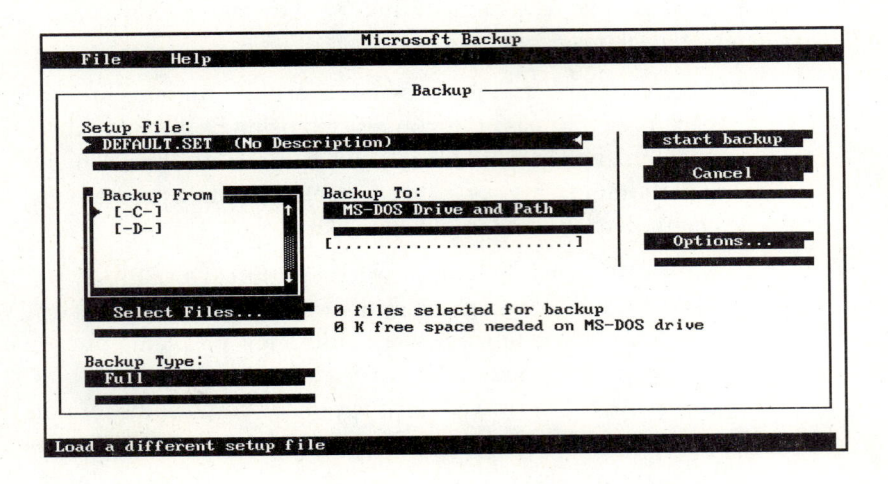

Figure 7.7

The opening screen of Microsoft Backup for Windows (MWBACKUP).

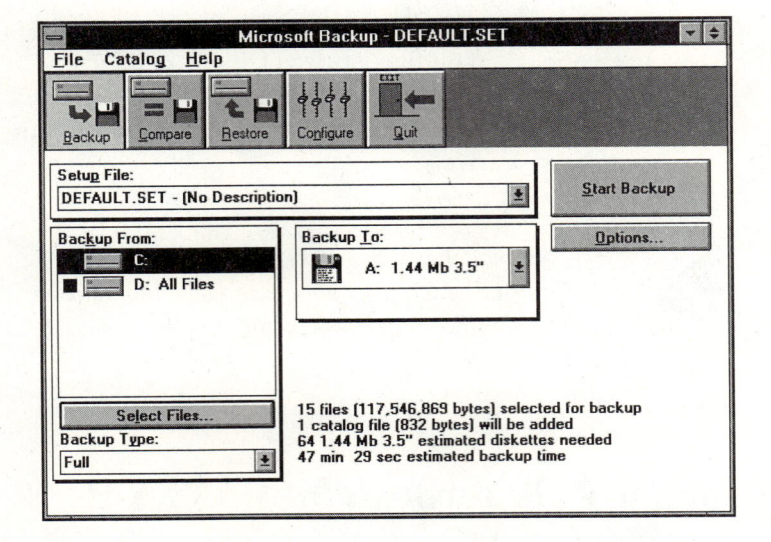

At the top of both screens are two menus: **F**ile and **H**elp. If you don't have a mouse, you can use the keyboard commands Alt+F and Alt+H to open the menus. This is the same convention used by the DOS Shell.

> **NOTE**
>
> *Because backup programs must often know the correct time and date to perform backups correctly, MSBACKUP and MWBACKUP require a working system clock. If your system does not have one, use the TIME command to set the current time, and the backup programs will function properly.*

> **AUTHOR'S NOTE**
>
> *When you load MSBACKUP or MWBACKUP for the first time, you will be asked to run a compatibility test. This test selects some small files from your system, copies them to the drive, and then checks to make sure that they were written accurately and can be restored.*
>
> *Because backup programs really aren't perfect at identifying the peculiarities of every system, you really should run this test. In fact, you should run it for each of your current drives—and any time you add a new drive to your system. You need two identical disks for each test; they don't have to be formatted. To run the Compatibility Test, choose Co**n**figure from the main menu, and then choose Com**p**atibility Test. Choose the drive you want to test, and then click on **S**tart Backup.*

Starting the Backup

To prepare a backup, choose **B**ackup. The Backup screen that appears enables you to set specific preferences for your backup. The following sections describe each of these options.

Chapter 7: *Managing Disks and Files*

> **NOTE:** *If you want to use DOS BACKUP's other major areas—*Compare, Restore, Configure, *or* Quit*—press Escape to get back to the main menu. In the Windows version, the other areas appear as large icons on the current screen.*

Specifying Where To Put the Backup Files

The Backup To option enables you to set the destination drive where the backup files are to be placed.

Doing Full, Incremental, and Differential Backups

The Backup Type option gives you three backup options: full, incremental, and differential.

- ✔ A *full backup* archives every file you specify. You might want your first backup to be a full backup (excluding programs you already have original copies of). This process clears the archive bit of every file it backs up. When you change files after the backup, the archive attributes for those files are reset.

- ✔ An *incremental backup* archives only files that have changed since your last full or incremental backup (the program recognizes that files have changed by looking at their archive attributes). Incremental backups clear the archive attributes.

- ✔ A *differential backup* archives files only if they have been created or changed since your last full backup. Moreover, a differential backup *does not clear* the archive attribute, so that the next time you perform a full or incremental backup, these files are backed up again.

Understanding Disk-Backup Options

The Options enable you to specify several disk-backup options. Underlined items in the following list indicate options included in the default settings:

Verify Backup Data compares the data on the backup disks with the data in the source files. This option slows down the backup process considerably, but may be worth it for the most critical backups.

Compress Backup Data compresses backup data so that you use fewer disks. (The backup programs do not use the same compression formats as DBLSPACE.)

Password Protect Backup Sets prohibits users from restoring a set of backup files without a password you specify.

Prompt Before Overwriting Used Diskettes helps you make sure that you aren't destroying old files or backup sets.

Always Format Diskettes forces the backup program to format each new disk, even if it is already formatted.

Use Error Correction on Diskettes instructs the backup program to add Error Correction Codes (ECCs) to disks. ECCs include redundant information that helps the program decipher missing data if it is lost. If you don't use the Verify option, you should at least use ECC.

Keep Old Backup Catalogs tells the backup program not to overwrite an existing catalog, even if it was created on the same day. If this option is disabled, the program creates up to two new catalogs on the same day and overwrites the older one if you ask for a third. When this option is enabled, the program provides new names for up to 26 catalogs in a single day.

Audible Prompts beeps in the event of an error.

Quit after Backup automatically leaves the program after the current backup is finished.

370 Chapter 7: *Managing Disks and Files*

> **NOTE**
>
> *A* backup catalog *is a file that appears on the last backup disk and contains the information required to accurately restore all your data:*
>
> ✔ *Names of the files contained in the backup set*
>
> ✔ *How many files the backup set contains*
>
> ✔ *The name of the setup file you used to back up these files*
>
> ✔ *The source disk's directory structure*

Selecting Specific Files To Back Up

The Select Files option enables you to choose the drive that contains the files you want to back up.

When you choose the drive, a display similar to the one in the DOS Shell or File Manager appears. Figure 7.8 shows the display that appears for the DOS version; figure 7.9 shows the Windows version. You can use this screen to mark the subdirectories and files you want to back up. To select or deselect a file or directory with the mouse, double-click on it (single-click on it with the right mouse button). With the keyboard, use the tab, arrow, and Enter keys.

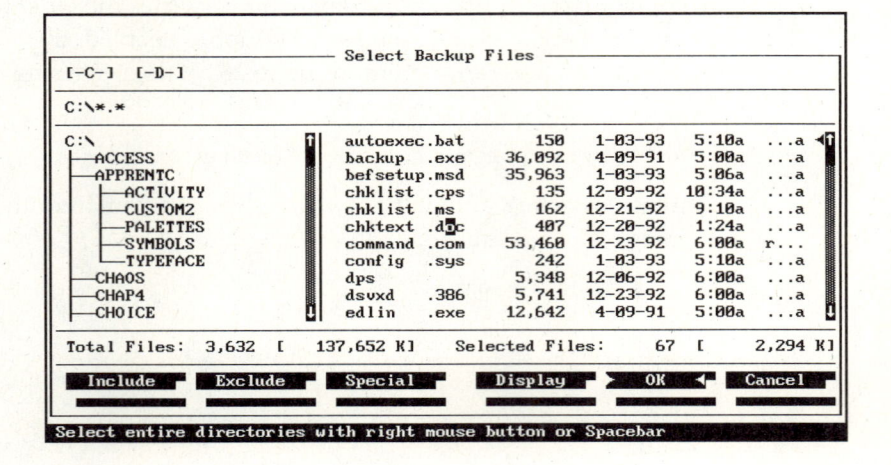

Figure 7.8

The Select Backup Files screen for Microsoft Backup for DOS.

```
┌─────────────────────── Select Backup Files ───────────────────────┐
│ [-C-]   [-D-]                                                      │
│ C:\*.*                                                             │
│ C:\              ▲    autoexec.bat      150   1-03-93   5:10a  ...a│
│ ├─ACCESS         │    backup   .exe  36,092   4-09-91   5:00a  ...a│
│ ├─APPRENTC       │    befsetup.msd  35,963   1-03-93   5:06a  ...a│
│ │  ├─ACTIVITY    │    chklist .cps     135  12-09-92  10:34a  ...a│
│ │  ├─CUSTOMZ     │    chklist .ms      162  12-21-92   9:10a  ...a│
│ │  ├─PALETTES    │    chktext .doc     407  12-20-92   1:24a  ...a│
│ │  ├─SYMBOLS     │    command .com  53,460  12-23-92   6:00a  r...│
│ │  └─TYPEFACE    │    config  .sys     242   1-03-93   5:10a  ...a│
│ ├─CHAOS          │    dps             5,348  12-06-92   6:00a  ...a│
│ ├─CHAP4          │    dsvxd   .386   5,741  12-23-92   6:00a  ...a│
│ ├─CHOICE         ▼    edlin   .exe  12,642   4-09-91   5:00a  ...a│
│ Total Files:   3,632 [   137,652 K]  Selected Files:  67 [  2,294 K]│
│  ┌─Include─┐ ┌─Exclude─┐ ┌─Special─┐   ┌─Display─┐ ► ┌─OK─┐ ◄ ┌─Cancel─┐│
│ Select entire directories with right mouse button or Spacebar      │
└────────────────────────────────────────────────────────────────────┘
```

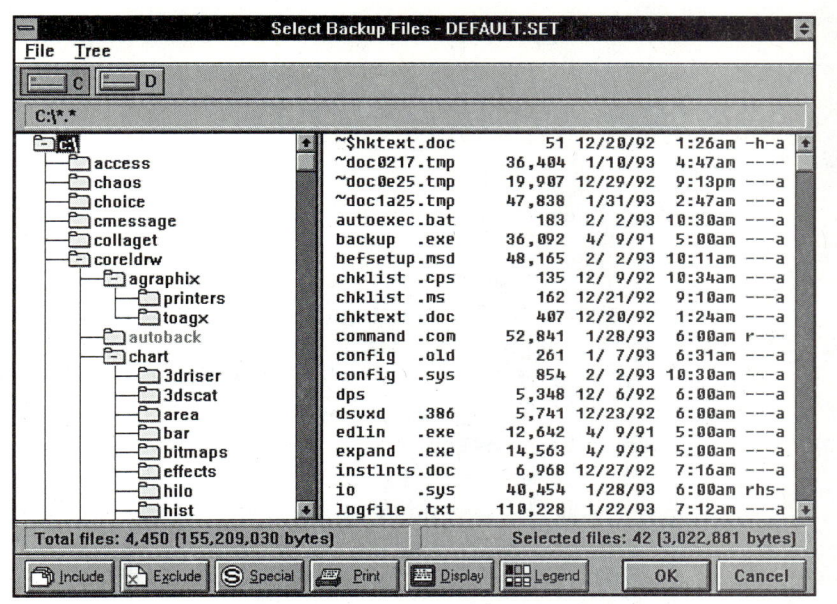

Figure 7.9

The Select Backup Files screen for Microsoft Backup for Windows.

You can use Include and Exclude to specify files or groups of files that are always (or are never) backed up. You might, for example, never want to back up *.BAK files because they're already duplicate files. Add the appropriate statement within the Include/Exclude box (in the DOS version of the Backup program, there are separate Include and Exclude boxes). Click on OK when you're finished selecting files.

To make it easier to choose files, the Display option helps you sort files by name, extension, size, date, or attributes. You can also use the Display filter with wild cards to eliminate certain files from each list.

Backing Up Files by Date

Special Selections enable you to back up files created on a specific date or dates. To back up by date, click on Apply Range in the Backup Files by Date Range box. Then specify the beginning and ending dates of the files you want to back up. To back up files created on a specific date or dates, click on the Special box at the bottom of the screen. This opens a new screen, Special Selections. To back up by date, check the Apply Range checkbox in the Backup Files in Date Range box. Then specify the beginning and ending dates of the files you want to back up.

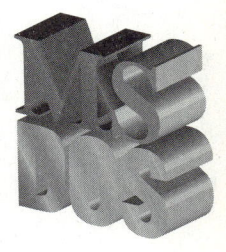

Chapter 7: *Managing Disks and Files*

You can also use **S**pecial Selections to exclude the following kinds of files:

- ✔ Copy-protected files
- ✔ Read-only files
- ✔ System files
- ✔ Hidden files

For most aspects of the backup program, the DOS and Windows versions are very similar. Here is one area where the Windows version is significantly better: In the Windows version, when you select drives, directories, or files, Backup tells you what you can expect Backup to do, based on the options and specifications you have already set. Backup uses the selection icons shown in figure 7.10. You can view these icons by clicking **L**egend in the Select Backup Files window.

Figure 7.10

Selection icons for Microsoft Backup for Windows.

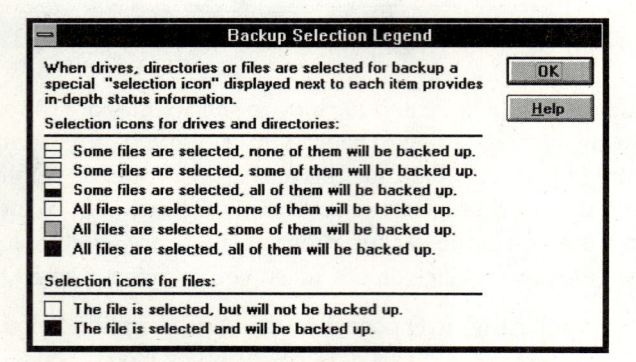

The Windows version of the backup program also offers the **P**rint function, which prints the names of all files on the current disk or of all files on all the disks currently in your system. (However, **P**rint won't print only the file names you specified to be backed up.)

The date that Microsoft Backup for Windows displays when you print a directory listing is actually a month ahead. If the date is 09/22/93, for example, the date will appear as 10/22/93 in the footer of each page when you print the directory listing. This is a bug for which there is as yet no cure.

The Windows version also includes a File menu on the Select Backup Files screen that enables you to quickly select or deselect all files in a directory or drive; the Tree menu enables you to view your files and subdirectories at any level.

Performing the Backup

Once you choose the files you want to back up in the Select Backup Files screen, click on OK. From the Backup screen, select Start Backup. A screen appears to show the progress of the backup (see fig. 7.11).

Figure 7.11

The Backup Progress screen for Microsoft Backup for Windows.

You are asked to insert new disks as required. Backup will format them for you if necessary, though this will slow down the process somewhat. You can halt Backup at any time by clicking on Cancel.

Understanding Backup Sets and Catalogs

When the backup is complete, you have a *backup set*, which includes all the files you have backed up, and a *backup catalog*, which describes the contents of the backup set. The backup catalog is stored on your hard drive, in the directory containing the backup program (usually C:\DOS or C:\WINDOWS).

The backup catalog uses one of the following extensions:

    FUL   Full backup

    INC   Incremental backup

    DIF   Differential backup

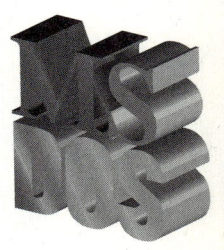

The backup set has the extension 001. Unlike the old DOS BACKUP command that created backup sets simply named BACKUP, the new version creates file names that actually offer useful information.

- ✔ The *first character* in the name of the backup set created by the backup program corresponds to the first drive containing source files included in this set.

- ✔ The *second character* corresponds to the last drive containing source files included in this set.

- ✔ The *third character* corresponds to the last digit of the year you created the backup (for example, *3* for *1993*).

- ✔ The *fourth and fifth characters* represent the month in which you created the backup (January=01, December=12).

- ✔ The *sixth and seventh characters* correspond to the day of the month on which you created the backup.

- ✔ The *last character* is a letter that indicates where this backup stands in the sequence of backups created on the same day. *A* indicates that it is the first backup you created; *Z* refers to the 26th backup.

Each backup set has a corresponding backup catalog. Now you can decipher the name of one: The backup catalog CD30406A.FUL indicates that you made a full backup containing files from drive C and drive D, on April 6, 1993—and it was the first backup you made that day.

> *If your backup catalogs are not on your current (working) disk, you can look elsewhere. Click the arrow next to Restore From, and then click on the drive that contains the catalog you're looking for.*

Saving Setup Files

In preparing a backup, you may create a very detailed set of file and option choices.

Suppose that you only want to back up specific types of files on specific drives. You want to do a differential backup—and you only want to capture files changed after a specific date. You use specific Include and Exclude criteria. Because the files are especially important, you want to verify that they're accurately backed up—and you want to use Error Correction Codes. Because you're paranoid, you don't even want to take the chance of compressing these files. Because these files are *so* important, you want to create a password to prevent snoopers from getting at the backup disk.

Why should you have to re-create all these specifications the next time you run this backup? You don't. Both DOS and Windows versions of the backup program enable you to save your backup choices in a setup file.

Make all your backup choices, but before you select Start Backup, first choose Save Setup As from the File menu. The Save Setup File window opens (see figs. 7.12 and 7.13).

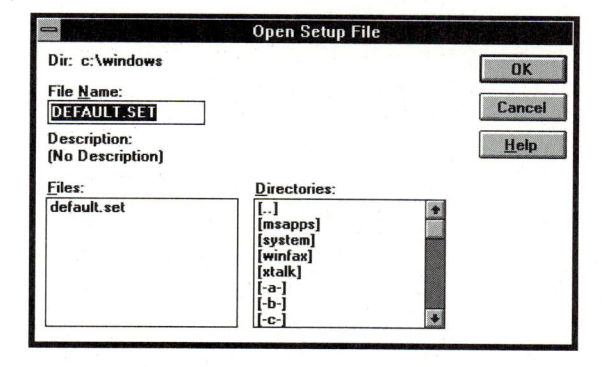

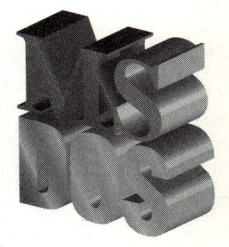

Figure 7.12

The Save Setup As window for Microsoft Backup for Windows.

Type a new file name (using the default extension SET). If you want, you can also type a description of the backup procedure you are saving. Together, the file name and description can take up to 40 characters. Then select OK or Save. The next time you do a backup and want to use a procedure other than DEFAULT.SET, choose the setup file you want from the Setup Files list in the Backup window.

Chapter 7: *Managing Disks and Files*

Figure 7.13

The Save Setup File windows for Microsoft Backup for Windows.

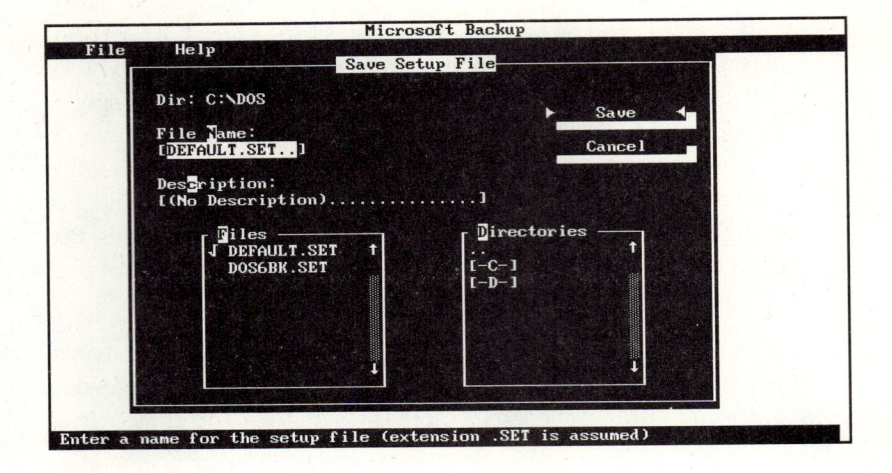

```
                           Microsoft Backup
    File      Help
                          ┌─ Save Setup File ─┐
         Dir: C:\DOS
                                              ▶  Save  ◀
         File Name:
         [DEFAULT.SET..]                         Cancel

         Description:
         [(No Description)...............]

         ┌─ Files ──────┐        ┌─ Directories ─┐
         │ √ DEFAULT.SET│        │ ..            │
         │   DOS6BK.SET │        │ [-C-]         │
         │              │        │ [-D-]         │
         └──────────────┘        └───────────────┘

    Enter a name for the setup file (extension .SET is assumed)
```

> **NOTE** *The SET file is an ASCII document you can look at in the EDIT text editor. But hands off unless you know what you're doing.*

Comparing Backups to Originals

To be really sure of a quality backup, you may want to compare the backup to your original files. Comparing the two sets of files does more than just tell you about any problems: it gives the backup program a chance to correct the problem.

To compare the originals with the backup, follow these steps:

1. Select **C**ompare from the main menu. The Compare opening screen appears (see figs. 7.14 and 7.15).

2. Choose the backup set catalog you want to use from the list that appears under Bac**k**up Set Catalog. (In the DOS version of the Backup program, press Tab to move the cursor to the Bac**k**up Set Catalog box and then press Enter to see the list of available catalogs. In the Windows version of backup, click on the down arrow next to the list.)

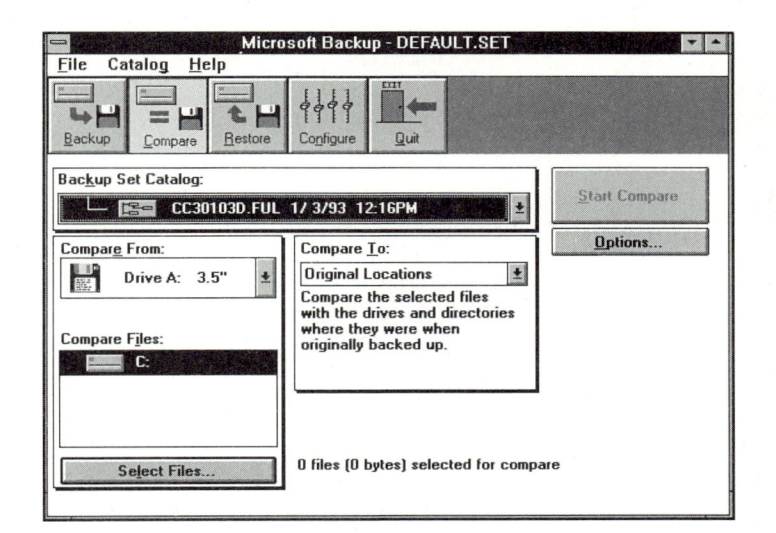

Backing Up Files with DOS 6.2 MSBACKUP and MWBACKUP   **377**

Figure 7.14

The Compare opening screen for Microsoft Backup for Windows.

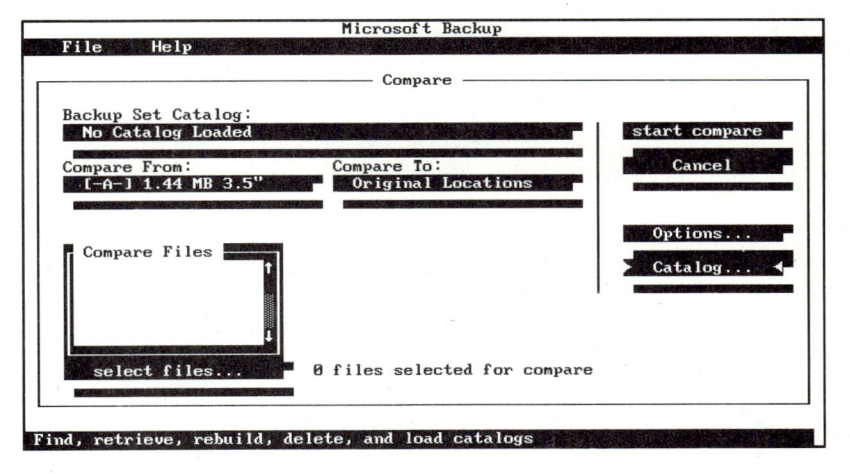

Figure 7.15

The Compare opening screen for Microsoft Backup for DOS.

3. In the Compare From window, choose the drive or path that contains the backup files. If the backups are on your hard drive, select MS-DOS Drive and Path from the Compare From window. Then return to the Compare window and type the drive and path in the box that appears underneath.

4. In the Compare Files window, choose the files to compare based on the drives you originally backed them up from.

For example, to compare all the files in the backup drive that were originally on drive C, select drive C. (Double-click on the drive name to select All Files.)

To compare only some of the files backed up from a given drive, select the drive name and then choose Se**l**ect Files. Then specify the files you want to compare.

5. In the Compare **T**o window (yes, there sure are a lot of *compares* here), tell the backup program whether the source files are still in their original locations or have been moved to alternative drives or directories.

6. Select **S**tart Compare.

A Compare Progress screen appears. Notice the Corrections item; it indicates how many corrections have been made during the course of the comparison.

Restoring Files

Of course, the ultimate purpose of a backup is to be able to restore files from it in the event of an emergency. The new DOS 6.2 backup programs make this process relatively easy. Instead of using a separate RESTORE command, you load the MSBACKUP or MWBACKUP program and click on the **R**estore box on the opening screen. You will see the Restore window (see figs. 7.16 and 7.17).

If you receive the `Incorrect DOS Version` *error message after entering the RESTORE command, it's probably because DOS is trying to launch the RESTORE.COM file, which is from earlier versions of DOS. The DOS 6.2 upgrade does not remove any unrecognized commands in the DOS directory, so the old RESTORE.COM and the new RESTORE.EXE both exist in the DOS directory. DOS, therefore, tries to launch the COM file first. To cure the problem (you guessed it), delete RESTORE.COM.*

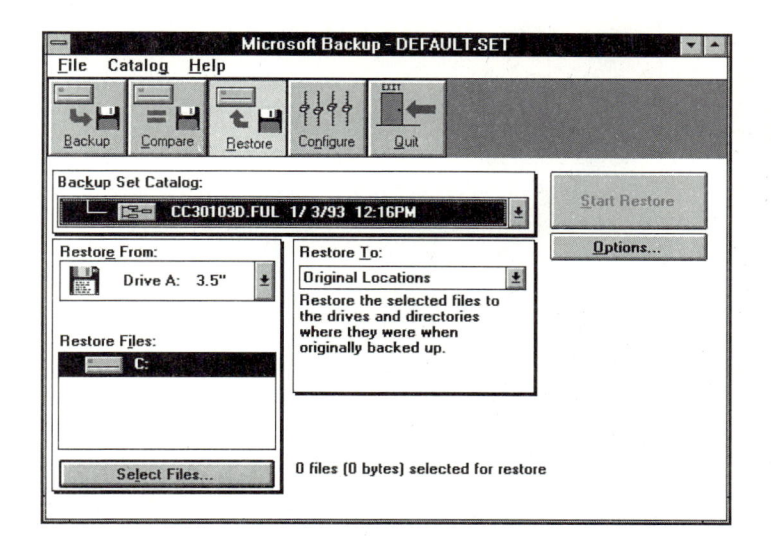

Backing Up Files with DOS 6.2 MSBACKUP and MWBACKUP **379**

Figure 7.16
The Restore screen for Microsoft Backup for Windows.

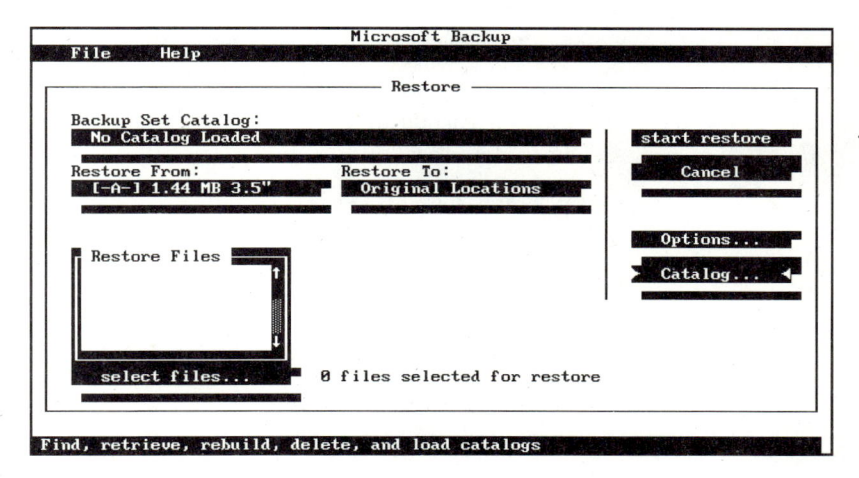

Figure 7.17
The Restore screen for Microsoft Backup for DOS.

From the Restore window, follow these steps:

1. Pick a backup set to restore from the Backup Set Catalog list.
2. In the Restore From window, choose the drive containing the backup files.

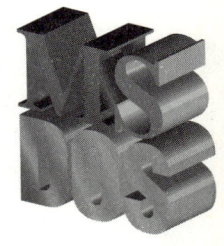

3. In the Restore F<u>i</u>les window, select the drive which originally contained the files you want to restore. Then click on Select Files to mark the files you want to restore. Select the subdirectories that contained the original files you want to restore, and then select the individual files you want. In Microsoft Backup for DOS, to select or deselect all of the files in a subdirectory, press the spacebar or right-click the mouse. In the Windows version, choose **S**elect All or D**e**select All from the File menu. To select or deselect individual files, click on them.

4. In the Restore **T**o window, specify whether you want the files to be restored to their original locations or elsewhere.

5. Select **O**ptions and choose any appropriate options from the following list:

   ✔ Verify Restore Data: Double-checks the restored files against the files contained on the backup disk.

   ✔ Prompt Before Creating Directories: Asks for confirmation before creating a subdirectory on a drive that doesn't already contain that subdirectory.

   ✔ Prompt Before Creating Files: Does the same for each file that doesn't exist.

   ✔ Prompt Before Overwriting Existing Files: Provides a check against accidentally overwriting a perfectly good file with an older version.

   ✔ Restore Empty Directories: Restores all directories, even if you haven't chosen to restore the files contained in them.

   ✔ Audible Prompts: Beeps in the event of an error.

   ✔ Quit After Restore: Leaves the program automatically after the current restoration is completed.

Summary

DOS continues to evolve, sometimes as much by subtraction as addition. With DOS 6.2, EDIT is crowned as the DOS editor, and EDLIN slips into history. FC becomes the DOS file comparison utility (Windows still doesn't have one), and COMP spirals towards oblivion.

Meanwhile, MOVE takes the place of a thousand shareware utilities, providing a reasonably safe way of moving files (though no way to prevent inadvertent file overwrites on your destination disk or subdirectory).

Best of all, Microsoft Backup programs for both DOS and Windows are solid backup packages that do everything but stand on their heads (and, oh yes, back up to tape).

Pretty crafty negotiators, those Microsoft people, who are apparently paying no royalties on these miniature versions of Symantec's Norton Backup for DOS and Windows. It'll be interesting to see what they beg, borrow, or otherwise acquire for MS-DOS 7.

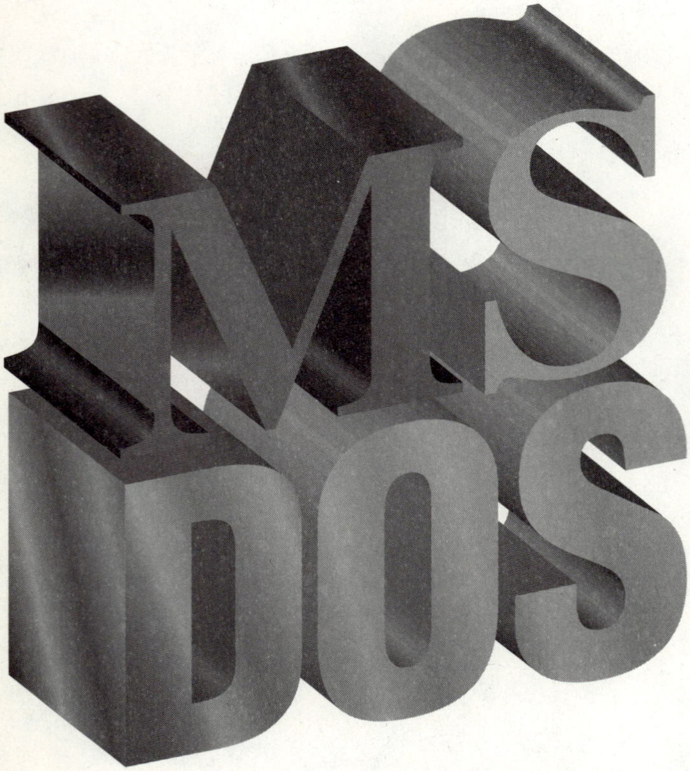
MS
DOS

CHAPTER 8

Tuning Your Disk with DOS 6.2 Tools

by Bill Camarda

---

*I*t's the search for the Holy Grail: how to improve your computer's performance without spending more money. The best place to start looking for a performance boost is your hard-disk drive because disks are the only mechanical devices in your computer—and the slowest.

DOS 6.2 provides three important tools that can help you significantly reduce the number of disk searches and the time they take:

✔ SMARTDrive, which enables you to use fast RAM memory as a disk cache, storing information until your processor needs it

✔ FASTOPEN, which places frequently used files in memory so that DOS doesn't have to perform lengthy directory searches

✔ Microsoft DEFRAG, a DOS utility that allows you to reorganize the disk's files to reduce the amount of time that the disk drive's heads must waste simply moving back and forth

Understanding How a Disk Cache Works

Your computer's memory works in nanoseconds. (That's the way it's measured: 60ns, 80ns, 100ns, and so on. Your hard drive, on the other hand, works in milliseconds (17ms, 28ms, and so on). This means memory works roughly a million times faster than hard drives. Which obviously means that anything stored in memory is retrieved a whole lot faster than if it's stored on disk.

Read Caching

Read caching is the first thing disk-cache programs try to do. Whenever you read a file, the disk cache makes a copy and places it in memory. This is called *read caching*; it works as shown in figure 8.1.

Figure 8.1
Read caching.

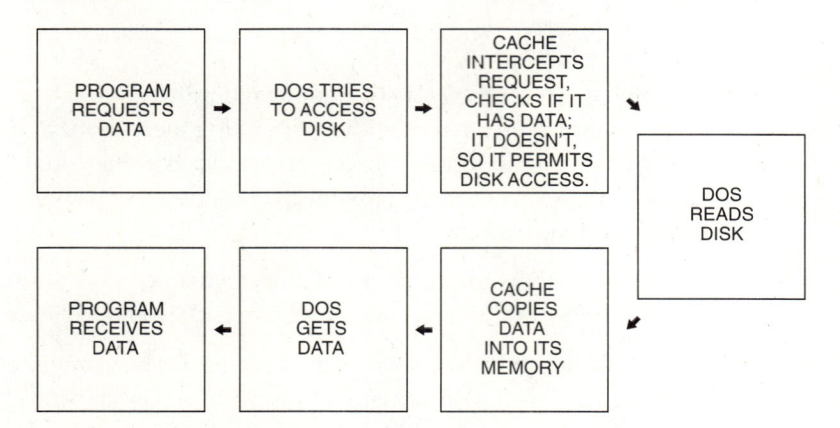

PROGRAM REQUESTS DATA → DOS TRIES TO ACCESS DISK → CACHE INTERCEPTS REQUEST, CHECKS IF IT HAS DATA; IT DOESN'T, SO IT PERMITS DISK ACCESS. → DOS READS DISK

PROGRAM RECEIVES DATA ← DOS GETS DATA ← CACHE COPIES DATA INTO ITS MEMORY

With all this data rushing through it, the cache quickly runs out of space. So it tries to set priorities, anticipating what you're most likely to need and discarding the rest. This is why a very small disk cache (one of about 256K or 512K) doesn't do much good—it is quickly overwhelmed by a few disk reads.

On the other hand, once you get up to 2M, the default SMARTDrive setting for Windows, a cache can usually make enough good guesses that it has most of what you need. Unless, of course, you request data you haven't asked for before. Then it doesn't matter what size disk cache you have: DOS still has to go to disk. This is why increasing cache size past 2M doesn't help as much as you expect.

Two fundamental ideas govern how a read cache decides what to keep in memory:

1. If you read a sector of a disk, you'll probably want to read the same sector again soon.

2. You're also likely to read the next sector, so the cache might as well load that even though you haven't asked for the sector yet.

Some disk caches discard sectors based on an LRU (least recently used) algorithm. Others use an LFU (least frequently used) algorithm. There's little practical difference between the two.

If the cache finds what it's looking for—and it's not unreasonable to expect an 80-percent "hit rate"—DOS skips the trip to disk, as shown in figure 8.2. It's important to note that a read cache is safe even if you lose power, because all the data it contains has been copied from disk and still exists there.

Figure 8.2

How a read cache eliminates disk reads.

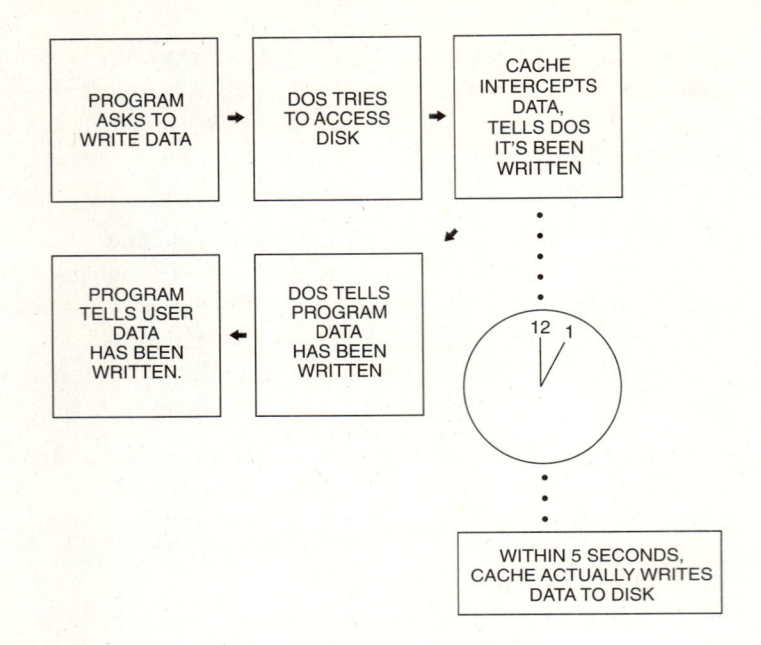

```
PROGRAM          DOS TRIES        CACHE
ASKS TO     →    TO ACCESS   →    INTERCEPTS
WRITE DATA       DISK             DATA,
                                  TELLS DOS
                                  IT'S BEEN
                                  WRITTEN

PROGRAM          DOS TELLS
TELLS USER       PROGRAM
DATA       ←     DATA
HAS BEEN         HAS BEEN
WRITTEN.         WRITTEN

                                  WITHIN 5 SECONDS,
                                  CACHE ACTUALLY WRITES
                                  DATA TO DISK
```

Write Caching

When your program sends data to be written to disk, a write cache holds a copy of it—so it's right there if you need it again. In addition, when you write a file, chances are you've only changed a small part of it; a write cache writes only sectors that have changed.

Many write caches, including SMARTDrive, hold data in cache until the system is less busy and only then writes to disk. From your application program's standpoint, the data has been written to disk, and the program continues to operate just as if it had been. Microsoft calls this write-behind; in OS/2, it's called *lazy writes*.

Write-behind is at work when the computer tells you that data's been written to disk but you haven't seen the hard-drive light go on. Figure 8.3 shows how it works.

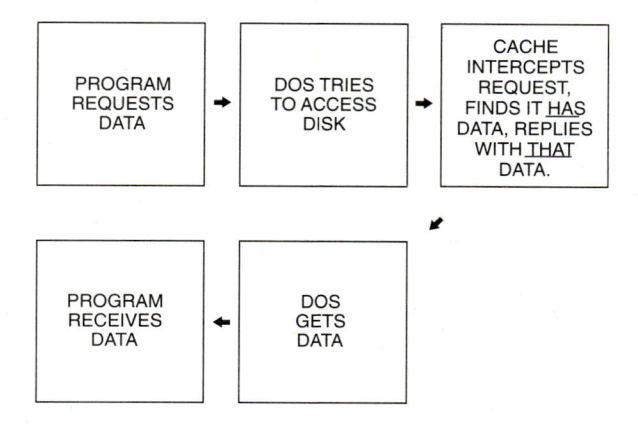

Understanding How a Disk Cache Works

Figure 8.3
Write-behind caching.

```
PROGRAM          DOS TRIES         CACHE
REQUESTS   →     TO ACCESS   →     INTERCEPTS
DATA             DISK              REQUEST,
                                   FINDS IT HAS
                                   DATA, REPLIES
                                   WITH THAT
                                   DATA.
                                       ↓
PROGRAM          DOS
RECEIVES   ←     GETS
DATA             DATA
```

> **AUTHOR'S NOTE**
>
> As previously mentioned, the salient point about write caches is that the cache tells you that data has been written to disk correctly when it really hasn't been. You're not unreasonable to be troubled by this. But SMARTDrive's write-behind caching has many safeguards:
>
> ✔ It writes everything to disk within five seconds, no matter what.
>
> ✔ It recognizes normal reboots like Ctrl+Alt+Del and "flushes the cache" onto disk before rebooting.
>
> ✔ If you're using Windows, SMARTDrive regularly saves temporary files, so a very recent copy of your file is probably in your \TEMP directory somewhere.
>
> But SMARTDrive isn't foolproof. A few things can go wrong that SMARTDrive isn't ready for:
>
> ✔ The power can fail while you're using a DOS program that doesn't save temporary files (another reason to invest in a true, nonswitching, uninterruptible power supply).
>
> *continues*

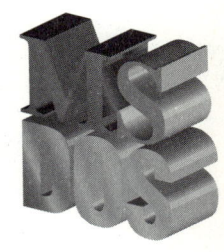

- ✔ You might have a disk-hardware problem. You thought the file was saved, so you quit the program—and now that you found there's a problem, you have no way to save the file: it's trapped in the cache, which has no way to write it to disk.

- ✔ You might be using a program that changes the way DOS reboots. SMARTDrive recognizes normal Ctrl+Alt+Del reboot requests and disk resets that use the standard INT21 interrupt. It doesn't recognize reboots that involve INT19 or jump to FFFF:0000. Program categories that may cause problems include:

  - ✔ Third-party boot managers that enable you to choose which CONFIG.SYS and AUTOEXEC.BAT files you want to use. With DOS 6.2's new MultiConfig feature, you may have less need for these.
  - ✔ Some keyboard-remapping programs.

With SMARTDrive, you can decide for yourself whether to use write caching.

If you are using DOS 6.2 and have write-caching enabled, SmartDrive now uses the default /F switch to instruct SmartDrive to flush its cache to the disk after each command executes. In case you're still concerned about data loss due to lazy writes, DOS 6.2 disables write caching by default by adding the /X switch to SMARTDRV during Setup. Don't fret, however, if you install DOS 6.2 on a system that already has write-caching enabled, Setup will leave it that way.

Double Buffering and Bus Mastering

Some SCSI disk-controller cards and a few ESDI controller cards use a technique called *bus mastering* to get data to and from memory.

Many of these bus-mastered controllers do not work properly with a disk cache without use of a special technique called *double buffering*.

To understand this, you need to understand how a conventional disk controller gets data to and from memory. Typically, the hard-disk controller places 512-byte chunks of data in memory directly, without involving the system's CPU. This is called *Direct Memory Access* (DMA); it means that the CPU must let the disk controller control system memory while the transfer is underway. To make the transfer, the disk controller sends the 512 bytes to the PC's DMA controller and tells it where to place them in memory.

When you introduce a disk cache, it's the cache program—not the disk controller—that holds the 512 bytes and tells the DMA controller where to put them. *Hold that thought.*

Where's the disk cache loaded? If you have upper-memory blocks (UMBs) on a 386 or 486 system, you'll probably want the cache there because the cache can't load in extended memory, and you don't want to waste conventional memory. UMBs are *remapped* memory locations, however, and although they appear to be in the space between 640K and 1024K (and therefore addressable by DOS), in reality, they're part of extended memory—above 1024K.

That's a problem for the DMA controller, which needs an actual physical memory location to read from and write to. Otherwise data gets written into thin air—or overwritten on top of something else.

To solve this thorny problem, Microsoft came up with Virtual DMA Services, which intercepts DMA requests and translates them so that both SMARTDrive and the DMA controller get the memory addresses they need.

All this works for DMA controllers that interact directly with your CPU. When bus mastering comes along, things change a bit. Suddenly, DMA is delegated to the disk controller, which contains its own DMA chip.

Everything should be OK: the translation still goes on, it just goes on somewhere else. But in fact, some bus-mastering controllers don't support the Microsoft standard. Once again, information gets written to the wrong addresses—or the DMA controller looks in the wrong place for the information it must send to the CPU.

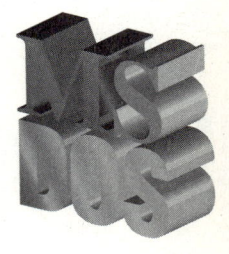

That's where double buffering comes in. Double buffering sets up a new memory buffer—in conventional memory—and squeezes all DMA transfers through it. Double buffering is never necessary on MFM, RLL, or IDE drives; it is only sometimes necessary on SCSI and ESDI drives. (Newer SCSI and ESDI drives, especially those with ASPI drivers, are more likely to support the Microsoft standard.) But if your SCSI or ESDI drive is behaving strangely, try enabling double buffering. IBM PS/2s and compatibles with Micro Channel Architecture may also require double buffering.

> **NOTE**
> *Some Adaptec controller boards require you to disable double buffering.*

> **TIP**
> *The quick way to see if you need double buffering is to first make sure that DEVICE=C:\DOS\SMARTDRV.EXE /DOUBLE_BUFFER is in your CONFIG.SYS file, reboot, and then enter **SMARTDRV** at the prompt. This displays a status report for all your system drives. Look at the buffering column. If any drive lists Yes or a dash (-), keep the double buffering driver installed. Yes means that double buffering is required; a dash means SMARTDrive cannot determine whether double buffering is required. If every entry in the buffering column reads No, you can remove the line from CONFIG.SYS file.*

Understanding SMARTDrive

SMARTDrive has a history. The SMARTDRV.SYS program released with Windows 3 was a finicky beast: it was restless in upper memory, incompatible with third-party hard-disk partitions like those created by On Track's Disk Manager, and unable to work with many drives that were in the least nonstandard.

Understanding SMARTDrive 391

If that wasn't bad enough, it was a *track-buffer cache*, meaning that it stored the contents of an entire disk track, often caching files you were unlikely ever to use. And it cached only reads from disk, never writes to disk.

DOS 5 and Windows 3.1 improved SMARTDrive considerably. With Windows 3.1's SMARTDRV.EXE, the modern SMARTDrive took shape. It's...

- ✔ Comfortable in upper memory (you usually don't even have to ask; it goes there all by itself when the opportunity arises).
- ✔ Capable of read and write caching—so you at least get to choose how dangerously you want to live.
- ✔ Block-oriented—so it stores more of the files you're caching for.
- ✔ Compatible with nearly any hard drive, including SCSI drives and Bernoulli boxes.

All that with no increase in price; it's still free with your choice of DOS or Windows.

If you run Windows, DOS 6.2 offers another major refinement: SMARTDrive Monitor, a Windows-based utility that can help you monitor SMARTDrive's performance.

Installing SMARTDrive

SMARTDrive works only if you have a PC with a hard disk and extended or expanded memory—which means it won't work with an 8088 or 8086-based system.

Normally, DOS 6.2 installs SMARTDrive for you. But if it hasn't—or if you have just upgraded your system and now want to run SMARTDrive—here's how to install it:

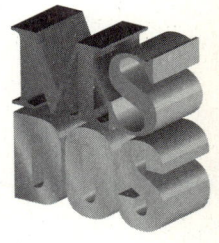

Include the SMARTDrive program (and its path) in your AUTOEXEC.BAT file. The following command sets up SMARTDrive with its default settings:

C:\DOS\SMARTDRV

NOTE: In earlier versions of DOS, SMARTDrive was a SYS file you included in CONFIG.SYS. In DOS 6.2, you include SMARTDrive in CONFIG.SYS only when you need double buffering.

Deciding Where To Load SMARTDrive

By default, the SMARTDrive program loads into upper memory blocks (between 640K and 1024K) if they are available. Note that you don't have to include a LOADHIGH statement; it happens automatically.

In some cases, however, you may need to load SMARTDrive into lower memory. In these cases, you can use the /L switch:

C:\DOS\SMARTDRV /L

Conversely, DOS may sometimes decide to install SMARTDrive low, when in fact it will work in upper memory. This occasionally happens when DOS senses a bus-mastering disk controller that it doesn't believe can coordinate properly with SMARTDrive in upper memory.

Because loading SMARTDrive low eats up 31K of conventional memory, if your disk-controller manual says it supports SMARTDrive loaded high, delete the /L and see what happens.

TIP: This might also be a good time to run MemMaker and see where it thinks SMARTDrive can run most efficiently.

Specifying the Drives To Cache...and How

By default, SMARTDrive caches all hard disks and floppy disks, except for compressed drives. (Normally, SMARTDrive caches the host drive, so it is redundant to also cache the compressed drive contained within it.)

> **NOTE** *A DoubleSpace disk is actually a large, invisible file on a host drive. Therefore, from SMARTDrive's point of view, the data is already coming off the host drive—to cache the compressed drive too, you'd be making another copy of the same data. See Chapter 5 for a more in-depth discussion of DoubleSpace.*

Also by default, SMARTDrive activates both read and write caching on all hard drives; it activates only read caching on floppy drives. The theory is that you can remove a disk from the floppy drive before SMARTDrive writes to it. SMARTDrive normally ignores CD-ROM and network drives.

> **6.2** *CD-ROM drives are notoriously slow, so DOS 6.2 automatically caches reads on CD-ROM drives. You can ignore CD-ROM drives, however, by using the /U switch. Be aware that if you use the /U switch, you can enable CD-ROM drive caching on individual drives from the command line by using the drive parameter. For example, if you load SMARTDrive with the /U switch, which we'll assume disables caching of your CD-ROM drive E, you can enable caching by entering* **SMARTDRV E** *at the prompt.*

You can change these default settings for any drive. These changes can be made either in AUTOEXEC.BAT or from the command line while SMARTDrive is running. Suppose that you want to change C drive; you have the following options:

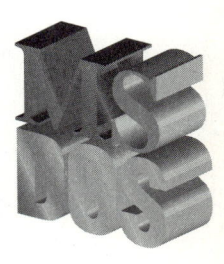

SMARTDRV C-	disables read and write caching on drive C.
SMARTDRV C	enables read caching and disables write caching.
SMARTDRV C+	enables read and write caching on drive C.

The same syntax works on any drive, including floppy drives. You can even cache a drive resident on an Interlink server. For example, if the InterLnk server drive C has been redirected to drive F on the client system, this command enables read and write caching of this drive:

`SMARTDRV F+`

You can also specify different settings for different drives:

`SMARTDRV A- B+ C+`

NOTE: You can only read cache a CD-ROM (Read-Only Memory) drive.

Setting Cache Size

By default, SMARTDrive's minimum cache size is 256K. Depending on the amount of extended memory SMARTDrive senses, it sets cache sizes as shown in table 8.1.

Table 8.1
SMARTDrive's Default Cache Sizes

Extended Memory	Initial Cache Size	Windows Size Cache
1M or less	All available extended memory	No cache
1-2M	1M	256K

Extended Memory	Initial Cache Size	Windows Size Cache
2-4M	1M	512K
4-6M	2M	1M
6M+	2M	2M

In other words, when you first load DOS, SMARTDrive sets aside memory as an initial cache (the amount shown in column 2). Because Windows requires more memory, if you load Windows on a system containing 6M of memory or less, SMARTDrive shrinks itself and gives Windows the extra memory. When you exit Windows, the cache returns to its normal size. This process isn't dynamic during a Windows session: once Windows opens, the cache shrinks; when Windows closes, the cache increases.

If you have substantially more than 6M of memory, you can experiment with larger cache sizes—although they don't always improve the system's performance, especially under Windows.

To set SMARTDrive's cache size, specify the initial cache size and the Windows cache size as follows:

```
SMARTDRV 1024 512
```

If you don't have Windows, don't use the second number:

```
SMARTDRV 1024
```

Fine-Tuning SMARTDrive

Microsoft gives you the tools to spend your life fine-tuning SMARTDrive. In general, the default settings are quite good, but you may improve performance through a little experimentation.

/B:#   sets the size of the read-ahead buffer.

As mentioned in the earlier discussion of read-caching, one way a cache anticipates the data you may want is to read the sectors following the one you asked for. Normally, SMARTDrive reads 16K ahead (/B:16), but you can increase or decrease this amount.

/E:# sets the element size.

The *element size* is the smallest chunk of data SMARTDrive can move at once: 1024, 2048, 4096, or 8192.

Note that /B: must be an exact multiple of /E; increasing either one can increase the amount of conventional memory SMARTDrive requires, even if most of SMARTDrive is loaded into upper-memory blocks.

Using Double Buffering

If you need double buffering (see "Double Buffering and Bus Mastering," earlier in this chapter), install SMARTDrive using a separate DEVICE command in CONFIG.SYS:

```
DEVICE=C:\DOS\SMARTDRV.EXE /DOUBLE_BUFFER
```

This command creates a separate 2.5K buffer in conventional memory and runs all disk transfers through it. If you don't need double buffering, remark the statement out (using REM) and see how the system runs (if nothing else, DOS gives the 2.5K back to you—and it might run a hair faster, too):

```
REM DEVICE=C:\DOS\SMARTDRV.EXE /DOUBLE_BUFFER
```

Even with the `DEVICE=SMARTDRV` *statement included in CONFIG.SYS, you still must run SMARTDrive from the AUTOEXEC.BAT file or the command line if you want disk caching installed.*

Flushing the Cache

When you use a write-behind cache, before shutting down you may want to make sure that the cache writes (or commits) its contents to disk. You can do that by entering this command:

SMARTDRV /C

Similarly, you can clear all the contents of a cache and at the same time write them to disk by entering....

SMARTDRV /R

Reporting the Status of SMARTDrive

You can always find out whether SMARTDrive is loaded and how it is running by typing this at the command prompt:

SMARTDRV /S

A report like the following displays:

```
Microsoft SMARTDrive Disk Cache Version 4.0
Copyright 1991,1992 Microsoft Corp.
Cache size: 2,097,152 bytes
Cache size while running Windows: 2,097,152 bytes
    Disk Caching Status
    drive   read cache      write cache     buffering
    ---------------------------------------------------
        A:      yes             no              no
        B:      yes             no              no
        D:      yes             yes             no
        E:      yes             no              no
        F:      yes             no              no
        G:      yes             no              no
For help, type "Smartdrv /?".
```

Note that this report excludes drive C, a drive compressed using the DoubleSpace program.

Incidentally, if all the entries in the buffering column say *no*, as in the listing shown here, it's a pretty good sign that you can disable double buffering without harm.

Monitoring Performance with SMARTDrive Monitor

SMARTDrive now comes with a Windows-based monitoring program named SMARTDrive Monitor, which enables you to see how SMARTDrive is behaving and to change many of its parameters.

To open SMARTDrive Monitor, double-click on the Windows Smartmon icon. The main SMARTDrive Monitor screen appears, as shown in figure 8.4.

Figure 8.4

The SMARTDrive Monitor opening screen.

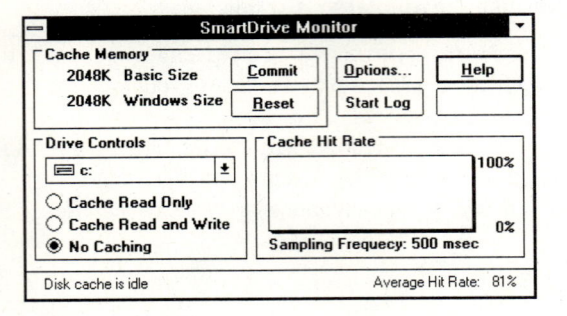

The Cache Memory options (at the top of the opening screen) permit you to **C**ommit all elements in the write cache to disk immediately (corresponding to typing **SMARTDRV /C** at the command line). The **R**eset button allows you to empty the cache and start filling it with new information (comparable to typing **SMARTDRV /R**).

You can't change the size of the cache from Windows; this is set when SMARTDrive first loads.

The Drive Controls options permit you to change the read/write settings of any drive, including Interlink drives.

The Cache Hit Rate monitors how often SMARTDrive contains sectors that would otherwise have required disk access. The Average Hit Rate, shown at the bottom right of the screen, represents the percentage of hits since SMARTDrive started or was last reset.

The **S**tart Log button enables you to maintain a log file of SMARTDrive's success for as long as you want; the default is 120 minutes.

The **O**ptions button opens another window, shown in figure 8.5.

Figure 8.5

The SMARTDrive Monitor Options screen.

The SMARTDrive Monitor Options window enables you to control the following:

- ✔ How often SMARTDrive Monitor measures the hit rate (from 50 to 10,000 ms) and how often it displays the result.

- ✔ Where it keeps the log and how long it records log information before stopping. You can replace the suggested file name with any other name. Include another path if you don't want to store the file in the current directory.

    The log file appears as a long list of system-clock ticks, cache accesses, and the number of times the cache contained what you needed. Following is a sample of a log file:

    ```
    ticks,    total,   hits
    690352,   17052,   14871
    ```

```
692329,    17174,    14979
694087,    17423,    15220
694911,    17647,    15444
696503,    17756,    15553
696613,    17758,    15555
700458,    17761,    15558
708202,    17768,    15563
708752,    17770,    15565
712981,    17878,    15668
```

- ✔ Whether read/write drive settings you change during a Windows session are permanently included in the AUTOEXEC.BAT file (or another DOS batch file).

You can keep the SMARTDrive Monitor on-screen at all times by checking the Always on Top box in the control menu—the menu you see when you click the square in the very top left-hand corner of the screen. When you minimize SMARTDrive Monitor, its icon displays (see fig. 8.6).

Figure 8.6
The SMARTDrive Monitor minimized icon.

Looking at Third-Party Disk Caches as Alternatives to SMARTDrive

You don't have to use SMARTDrive if you don't want to; there is a long list of popular alternatives. One of the most popular is Super PC-Kwik from Multisoft, which—unlike SMARTDrive—dynamically changes its size depending on the memory requirements of the application currently running.

Other popular disk caches include these:

- ✔ MCache, included in The Mace Utilities from Fifth Generation Systems

- ✔ NCache-F and NCache-S, included in the Norton Utilities from Symantec
- ✔ PC Cache, included in PC Tools from Central Point Software

Reading Directories Faster with FASTOPEN

The idea behind FASTOPEN is noble: You use some files over and over again. FASTOPEN sits in memory, tracking the location of those files in its name cache. The next time you need one of those files, DOS doesn't have to start at the root directory and follow a trail of subdirectories to the file's starting cluster. It already knows where the file is.

FASTOPEN can significantly improve your system's performance, especially if you use a subdirectory structure three or four levels deep.

The reality of FASTOPEN is noble, too—if you follow the rules and use FASTOPEN only where it's intended to be used. Keep in mind that FASTOPEN only knows where you left the file when you last worked with it. It's easily bewildered. If you move a file without opening it—or if you leave one file open and open another—you risk serious data loss. Hence...

- ✔ Don't use FASTOPEN with Windows 3 or 3.1.
- ✔ Don't run FASTOPEN from the DOS Shell.
- ✔ Don't run FASTOPEN while DOS Shell task swapping is enabled.
- ✔ Don't defragment a disk while FASTOPEN is active. (If you do, reboot immediately after defragmenting is complete.)
- ✔ FASTOPEN won't work on a floppy drive. This is logical, because FASTOPEN doesn't have any way of tracking floppy swaps.
- ✔ FASTOPEN won't work on a network drive. If you run NetWare, that software maintains its own directory cache.

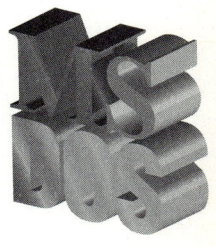

- ✔ Only load FASTOPEN once. (If you place an INSTALL=FASTOPEN.EXE statement in CONFIG.SYS, don't include a FASTOPEN statement in AUTOEXEC.BAT.) DOS displays the following error message if you try to place two copies in memory:

    ```
    FASTOPEN already installed
    ```

- ✔ You can't change FASTOPEN settings during a session; you have to reboot. (If FASTOPEN settings are kept in CONFIG.SYS or AUTOEXEC.BAT, edit these files before rebooting.)

- ✔ Don't load any disk device drivers after FASTOPEN loads. If a disk device driver must run from AUTOEXEC.BAT or the command line, don't run FASTOPEN until after the driver is loaded.

- ✔ Don't use FASTOPEN with SUBST. (If this were DOS 5, you would not want to use it with ASSIGN or JOIN either, but these commands are no longer part of the official DOS 6.2 package.)

Having said all that, FASTOPEN can really help in straightforward single-tasking environments, especially if...

- ✔ You have large, deep directories.
- ✔ You use database programs, compilers, or DOS applications like AutoCAD that often reopen the same files.

So, at long last, here's how to use FASTOPEN: You can install FASTOPEN as part of CONFIG.SYS, run it from AUTOEXEC.BAT, or run FASTOPEN from the command line. In AUTOEXEC.BAT or at the command line, the normal syntax is as follows:

```
FASTOPEN drive:=#files
```

In other words, specify the number of files on each drive that you want to have held in memory. You can specify a number of files for each hard drive. The total number of all files must be between 10 and 999. For example, if you want to make room for 75 files on drive C and 50 files on drive D, the AUTOEXEC.BAT statement looks like this:

```
FASTOPEN C:=75 D:=50
```

You can theoretically specify FASTOPEN settings for up to 24 logical drives (C through Z). If you want to run FASTOPEN with the default setting of 48 files per drive, you still have to specify the drive or drives these files should come from:

```
FASTOPEN C:
```

Using FASTOPEN with UMBs and Expanded Memory

FASTOPEN actually consists of two components: the program that monitors file usage and maintains the name cache, and the name cache itself. By default, these are kept together in conventional memory. But you can place them both in upper-memory blocks. You can also move the name cache to expanded memory compatible with the Lotus-Intel-Microsoft standard.

To load FASTOPEN into UMBs, use the LOADHIGH command; notice that you have to specify the entire path and file name:

```
LOADHIGH C:\DOS\FASTOPEN.EXE C:20 D:20
```

To load the name cache into expanded memory, add the /X switch:

```
LOADHIGH C:\DOS\FASTOPEN.EXE C:20 D:20/X
```

To install FASTOPEN through CONFIG.SYS, use the INSTALL statement:

```
INSTALL=C:\DOS\FASTOPEN.EXE C:20 D:20
```

The /X switch may also be used with FASTOPEN in an INSTALL statement placed in your CONFIG.SYS file.

Deciding How Many Files FASTOPEN Should Track

In DOS 6.2, Microsoft sets FASTOPEN's default to 48 files on the current drive. Beyond this, the typical recommendation has been one file per megabyte on the hard drive.

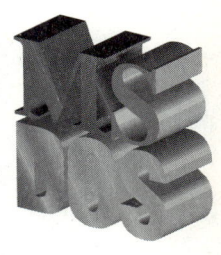

FASTOPEN itself requires 5520 bytes in memory; each file you tell FASTOPEN to make room for consumes another 48 bytes. Telling FASTOPEN to keep track of 100 files instead of the default 48 costs you almost 2.4K of memory ((100-48)*48=2496 bytes).

When the FASTOPEN name cache gets too long, DOS can spend more time looking at FASTOPEN than it would have spent looking for the file the conventional way. Depending on your system, this tends to happen at around 200 files.

Understanding Disk Problems

Back in Chapter 4, we explored some basic principles of disks. In order to fully understand what can go wrong with your disks, well take a little time here to review briefly those principles and add a few others.

As you recall, the *file allocation table* (FAT) keeps track of every cluster on a disk, using one of five entries: 0, BAD, Reserved, EOF, or a cluster number. A *cluster*, of course, is a grouping of a specific number of contiguous 512-byte sectors. Also referred to as an *allocation unit*, a cluster consists of 4, 8, or 16 sectors, depending on the disk. Similarly, a *subdirectory entry* is assigned space as if it were just another file, but instead of containing data, it contains other file names.

One potential problem is the *lost cluster*, which occurs when a cluster in the FAT is marked as being in use when it is, in fact, not a part of any files allocation chain. These lost clusters take up disk space that you could be using for other files.

Another problem, the *cross-linked file*, occurs when two or more FAT entries point to the same cluster; in other words, a cross-linked file means that a single cluster has been allocated to two different files. A variation on this theme is the *circular chain*, which occurs when one FAT entry points back to the same entry that just pointed forward to the present entry. An *invalid cluster* points to a nonexistent Cluster #0 or to a bad sector, and an *invalid subdirectory* is one that does not contain the . or .. entries.

These problems are typically caused when the computer is shut off or rebooted while a program still has files open or when it is still writing data to disk (which in essence is the same thing). Moral? Properly exit Windows, programs, and DOS shells before shutting down.

Another problem that occurs on disks is the *bad cluster*. Unlike these other problems, which are simply *logical* problems, the bad cluster is a *physical* problem, that is, a physical defect that has developed on the disk since its original low-level format.

Another key term is *boot sector* (see Chapters 4 and 17), which occupies the very first sector of a floppy disk and the second sector of a hard disk (since the partition table occupies the first sector of a hard disk). The boot sector contains two things: the bootstrap program, which reads in the operating system, and a list of the key characteristics of that disk, such as: size, cluster size, and number of sectors. Speaking of the *partition table* (which is contained in the *master boot record*), it records what drives are installed on the computer, where each begins and ends, which operating system controls each partition, and which operating system is active. While it is a serious thing for either of these to be damaged, they are fairly easy to fix (see Chapter 19).

Understanding Microsoft ScanDisk

Now that we've reviewed a few key terms, we're ready to discover how DOS 6.2 repairs disk problems. Continuing to fight the war of the disk utilities, Microsoft included ScanDisk, a full-featured disk analysis and repair tool, with DOS 6.2. Similar to Norton Disk Doctor and other such tools, ScanDisk checks a drive for errors and corrects problems in the following areas:

- ✔ **Media descriptor.** Checks to see that the code that identifies the drive as an MS-DOS drive is in place.

- ✔ **Directory structure.** Checks to see if the tree structure and each individual directory in the structure is valid.

- ✔ **File system.** Checks for lost clusters and cross-linked files.

- ✔ **File allocation tables (FATs).** Checks to see if both copies of the FAT match.

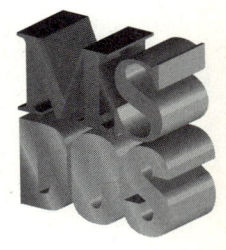

✔ **Surface scan of the drive.** Checks every area of the disks surface for physical errors (bad clusters) and moves any data in such an area to a safe area and marks the damaged area as unusable. It also confirms that data can be reliably written to and read from the drive.

ScanDisk also analyzes DoubleSpace drives, checking the volume header (MDBPB), volume file structure (MDFAT), compression structure, and volume signatures. ScanDisk can regenerate and repair certain damaged portions of a CVF and recover the data in many cases. During a surface scan of a DoubleSpace drive, ScanDisk confirms that data can be decompressed.

Although ScanDisk very comprehensively finds and fixes errors on hard drives, DoubleSpace drives, floppy disk drives, RAM drives, and memory cards; it does not work on CD-ROM drives, Network drives, or drives created by using ASSIGN, SUBST, JOIN, or INTERLNK.

Knowing When To Use ScanDisk

Here are a few suggestions of when you should use ScanDisk:

✔ When files or directories seem to be missing but were not deleted.

✔ When you have trouble accessing a disk.

✔ When your disk starts behaving erratically.

✔ When you experience problems when trying to run applications.

✔ When you want to ensure disk integrity as a part of regular disk maintenance, such as just before you defragment your disk.

Quitting Everything Else before Starting

When a file is in use, DOS updates the FAT and the directory structure to reflect any changes that have occurred. The problem, however, is that such updates are not always recorded immediately. So, if you run ScanDisk when other programs, such as Windows and the DOS Shell task swapper, are running, some files might still be open. To a program like ScanDisk, which is designed to be used on disks where files are unchanging, these files appear to be lost clusters or chains. Needless to say, this can cause you great grief in the form of corrupted or lost data. So, do not use ScanDisk to repair a drive when other programs are running.

With the above warning in mind, you can, however, *check* your disk for errors without actually fixing the errors. As we'll see later, you can do this by adding the /CHECKONLY switch to the SCANDISK command. Even at this, the /CHECKONLY switch will not do a surface scan.

> **NOTE** *If you run SCANDISK /CHECKONLY from within Windows, ScanDisk might detect errors that do not exist when Windows is not running. If ScanDisk detects any problems, you should exit Windows and run ScanDisk again to be sure the problems are real. For best results, you should run ScanDisk only from the DOS command line.*

Running Microsoft ScanDisk

To run ScanDisk on the current drive, enter **SCANDISK** at the prompt. Alternately, if you want to run ScanDisk on another drive, add the drive letter to the command—**SCANDISK D:**, for example.

When ScanDisk starts, it will immediately check the media descriptor, FATs, directory structure, and file system. During this initial phase, you can press **P** at any time to pause the scanning process. When this phase completes, ScanDisk will begin its surface scan (if you give it the go ahead) and will display a graphical representation of your disk, as illustrated by figure 8.6. You can also pause the surface scan at any time by pressing **M** for More Info or Esc. You can also exit ScanDisk at any time by selecting Exit.

Chapter 8: *Tuning Your Disk with DOS 6.2 Tools*

The graphical representation displays the following important pieces of information:

- ✔ The letter of the drive being scanned.
- ✔ The total number of clusters on the disk.
- ✔ The number of clusters so far examined.
- ✔ The number of clusters found to be bad.
- ✔ The number of clusters each rectangle represents.
- ✔ Unused clusters, which are marked with a blue and black rectangle; these clusters are currently free.
- ✔ Some used clusters, which are marked with a faded blue rectangle; these clusters are partially in use, but have portions that are not in use.
- ✔ Used clusters, which are marked with a solid blue rectangle; these clusters are currently in use.
- ✔ Some bad clusters, which are marked with a B; these clusters indicate that some, but not all, of the clusters in this area are bad.

Figure 8.7 shows a ScanDisk surface scan.

Fig. 8.7

ScanDisk surface scan.

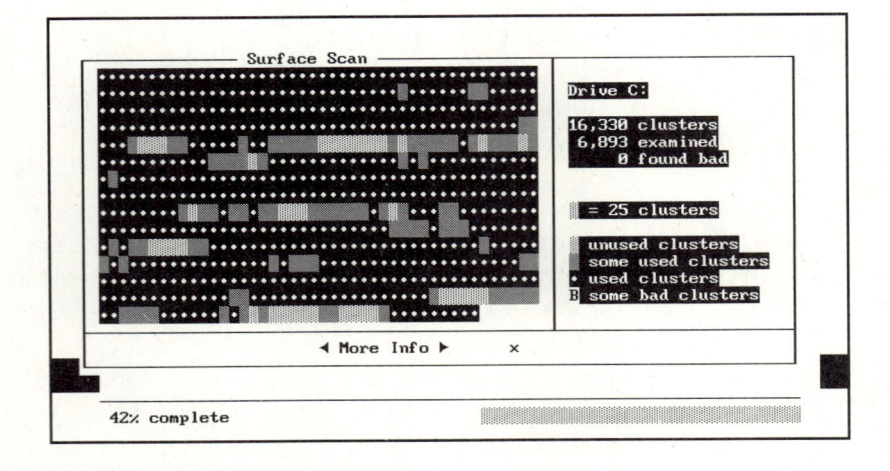

You can also check multiple drives with a single command. Entering **SCANDISK C: D:**, for example, will run ScanDisk on both drives. Similarly, entering **SCANDISK /ALL** will scan all your hard-disk partitions, as well as all mounted DoubleSpace drives, but will not scan any floppy drives.

> **NOTE** *If you run ScanDisk on a mounted or unmounted compressed drive, it offers to check the host (physical) drive first. In general, you should allow it to do this because an error on the host drive could cause problems with the compressed drive.*

You can also run ScanDisk on a DoubleSpace compressed volume file (CVF), in case it won't mount, for example. To repair a CVF named DBLSPACE.000 located in the root directory of drive C, for example, enter **SCANDISK C:\DBLSPACE.000**.

Fixing Problems with ScanDisk

If ScanDisk doesn't find any problems, you can pretty much sit back and relax. If ScanDisk does find a problem, however, it displays the Problem Found dialog box, briefly explains the problem, and describes what will happen if you fix it.

Figure 8.8 illustrates a typical Problem Found dialog box that occurs during the File Structure analysis. In this case, ScanDisk has detected lost clusters. You can also press **M** for more specific information about how many lost clusters were found.

Most Problem Found dialog boxes have a Fix It button and a Don't Fix It button. To have ScanDisk correct the problem, choose the Fix It button. As you can see, fixing this problem does exactly the same thing as the CHKDSK /F command does—it saves the lost clusters as files in the root directory.

Figure 8.9 illustrates another typical Problem Found dialog box. In this case, data is stored in a damaged area of the disk. If you want to see what file is actually stored in the damaged area, press **M** for More Info (see fig. 8.10).

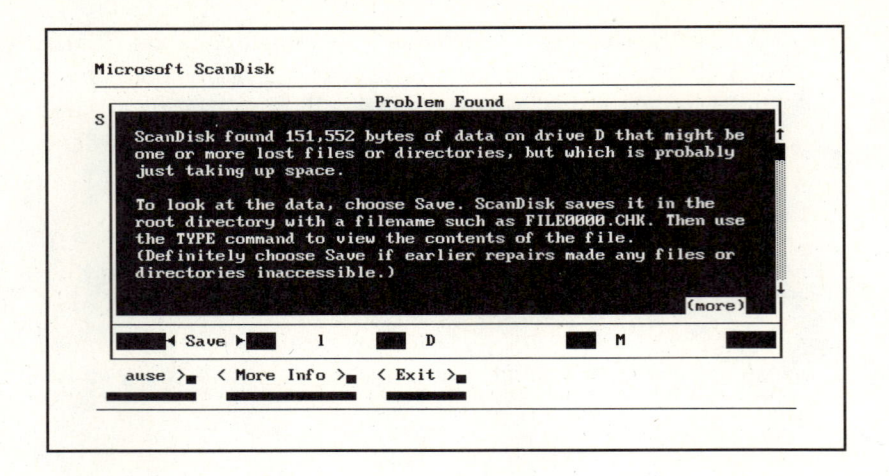

Chapter 8: *Tuning Your Disk with DOS 6.2 Tools*

Figure 8.8
ScanDisk lost cluster Problem Found dialog box.

```
Microsoft ScanDisk
┌─ Problem Found ─┐
ScanDisk found 151,552 bytes of data on drive D that might be
one or more lost files or directories, but which is probably
just taking up space.

To look at the data, choose Save. ScanDisk saves it in the
root directory with a filename such as FILE0000.CHK. Then use
the TYPE command to view the contents of the file.
(Definitely choose Save if earlier repairs made any files or
directories inaccessible.)
                                                        (more)

      ◄ Save ►      1           D            M
   ause >   < More Info >   < Exit >
```

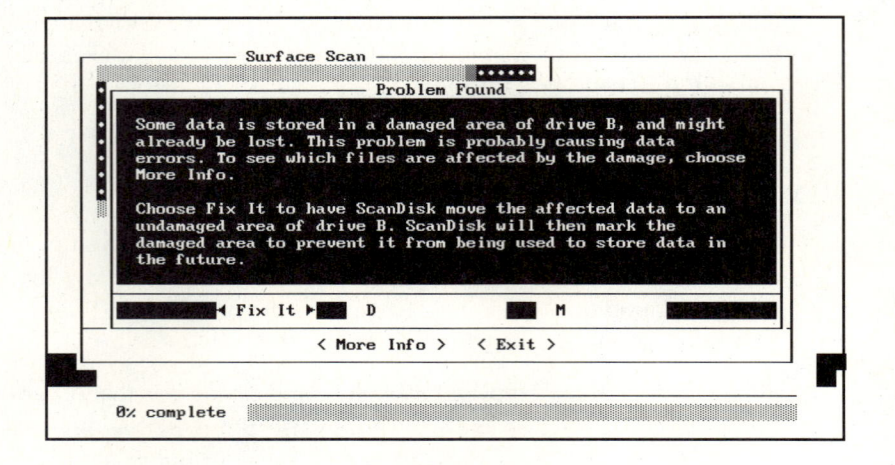

Figure 8.9
ScanDisk damaged disk area Problem Found dialog box.

```
┌─ Surface Scan ─┐
┌─ Problem Found ─┐
Some data is stored in a damaged area of drive B, and might
already be lost. This problem is probably causing data
errors. To see which files are affected by the damage, choose
More Info.

Choose Fix It to have ScanDisk move the affected data to an
undamaged area of drive B. ScanDisk will then mark the
damaged area to prevent it from being used to store data in
the future.

         ◄ Fix It ►    D              M
            < More Info >   < Exit >
0% complete
```

In this example, selecting Fix It will instruct ScanDisk to move the affected data to an undamaged area of the disk and then mark the damaged area as unusable.

One other strength of ScanDisk is that it can fix cross-linked files. In contrast, CHKDSK can only *detect* cross-links but cannnot fix them. DiskScan also detects and fixes cross-linked sectors within a CVF.

Understanding Microsoft ScanDisk **411**

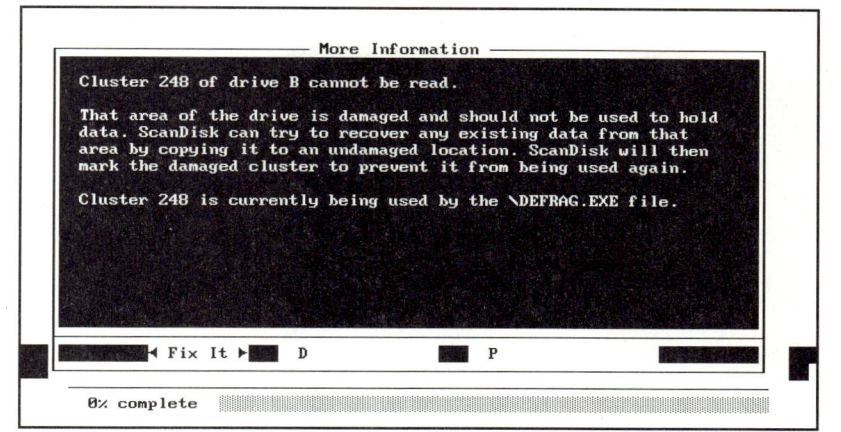

Figure 8.10

ScanDisk More Information dialog box.

Naturally, you can use ScanDisk on floppy disks as well as hard disks. Actually, you might find more errors on floppies. In fact, you might even find errors on a distribution disk that you just purchased. I've seen it happen more than once that a program would not install because of a bad sector on the distribution disk. You may, therefore, want to run ScanDisk on distribution disks before you try to install the program.

Creating and Using an Undo Disk

If you choose to fix a problem that ScanDisk finds, ScanDisk asks you if you want to create an Undo disk (see fig. 8.10), which contains information that specifies which drive it applies to, as well as information on every change that ScanDisk made to that drive. If you want to restore ScanDisks changes, you can use this Undo disk to do so.

Be aware that you can restore your disks previous state only if you haven't changed it in any way since making repairs. In fact, don't even try to undo ScanDisks changes if any files on the drive have changed. If you use the Undo disk after you update a file or directory, or even after you copy or delete a file, you might damage your drive structure and lose data.

Figure 8.11
ScanDisk Create Undo Disk prompt.

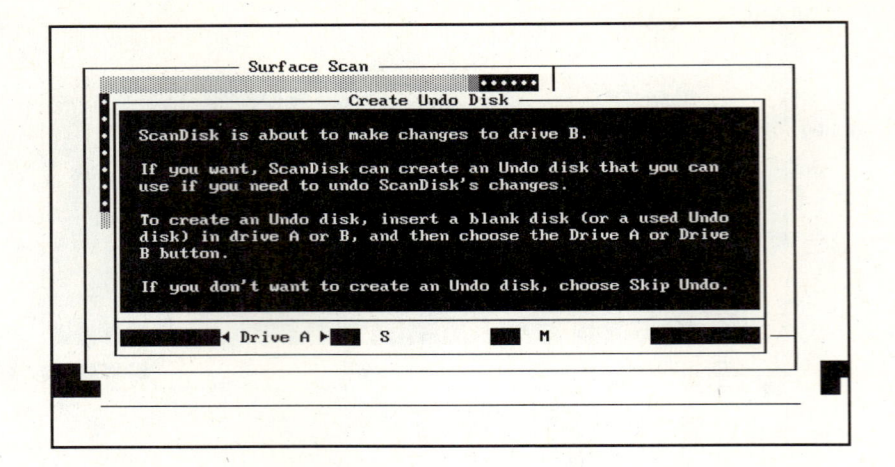

```
┌─ Surface Scan ─────────────────────┐
│        ┌─ Create Undo Disk ─┐       │
│  ScanDisk is about to make changes to drive B.
│
│  If you want, ScanDisk can create an Undo disk that you can
│  use if you need to undo ScanDisk's changes.
│
│  To create an Undo disk, insert a blank disk (or a used Undo
│  disk) in drive A or B, and then choose the Drive A or Drive
│  B button.
│
│  If you don't want to create an Undo disk, choose Skip Undo.
│
│       ◄ Drive A ►    S           M
└─────────────────────────────────────┘
```

To create an Undo disk, simply insert a blank, formatted floppy disk in drive A or B, and then choose the corresponding button in the dialog ScanDisk displays. To use an Undo disk, place it in drive A and enter **SCANDISK /UNDO A:**.

*Be aware that you will be asked only once if you want to create an Undo disk. Once you answer **no** to the Create an Undo Disk prompt, you will not be asked again, even if ScanDisk finds other errors.*

Understanding ScanDisk's Syntax

The basic syntax for running ScanDisk is as follows:

```
SCANDISK drivename: drivename: volume-name path\filename
/option
```

In this syntax, *drivename* refers to the drive you want to scan and can be multiple drives, as in SCANDISK C: D:, for example. Entering **SCANDISK** alone will scan the current drive.

Volume-name refers to the name of the unmounted DoubleSpace volume file you want to scan. To check the DBLSPACE.000 CVF in the root directory of drive H, for example, enter **SCANDISK H:\DBLSPACE.000**.

Path\filename refers to the file or files you want to examine for fragmentation. This does allow wildcards, but, like CHKDSK, it does not check subdirectories. To check the WINWORD\DOCS directory on drive D for fragmentation, for example, enter **SCANDISK /FRAGMENT D:\WINWORD\DOCS*.*** or log on to the directory and enter **SCANDISK /FRAGMENT *.***.

/Option refers to one or more of the following switches:

- **/ALL.** Checks and repairs all fixed drives, but does not scan floppy drives.

- **/AUTOFIX.** Fixes damage without prompting you first. By default, /AUTOFIX saves the lost clusters as files in the drive's root directory. If you want ScanDisk to delete lost clusters rather than save them, add the /NOSAVE switch. You cannot use the /AUTOFIX switch with the /CHECKONLY or /CUSTOM switches.

- **/CHECKONLY.** Scans a drive for errors, but does not repair any damage. You cannot use this switch with the /AUTOFIX or /CUSTOM switches.

- **/CUSTOM**. Runs ScanDisk using the configuration settings in the [Custom] section of the SCANDISK.INI file. This is especially useful for running ScanDisk from a batch file. You cannot use this switch with the /AUTOFIX or /CHECKONLY switches.

- **/MONO.** Runs ScanDisk in monochrome mode for use with a monochrome display.

- **/NOSAVE.** Instructs ScanDisk to delete any lost clusters it finds instead of saving their contents as files in the root directory of the drive. This can be used only with the /AUTOFIX switch.

- **/NOSUMMARY.** Prevents ScanDisk from displaying a full-screen summary after checking each drive.

- **/SURFACE.** Instructs ScanDisk to go ahead and perform a surface scan after its intitial scan of the drives other areas instead of pausing and asking you if you want to do a surface scan. If you use /SURFACE with /CUSTOM, /CUSTOM overrides the Surface setting in the [Custom] section of the SCANDISK.INI file.

- **/UNDO.** Restores the changes ScanDisk made during its scan using the Undo disk created during the scan. To use an Undo disk, place it in drive A, and enter **SCANDISK /UNDO A:**.

You can restore your disks previous state only if you haven't changed it in any way since making repairs. If you use the Undo disk after you update a file or directory, or even after you copy or delete a file, you might damage your drive structure and lose data.

Customizing ScanDisk Using the SCANDISK.INI file

Perhaps the only shortcoming of ScanDisk is that you cannot customize it through menus such as Microsoft BACKUP or DEFRAG. You can, however, customize ScanDisk by directly editing SCANDISK.INI, which contains settings that determine many aspects of ScanDisks behavior. The [ENVIRONMENT] section controls general aspects of ScanDisks behavior. Most of the settings in SCANDISK.INI, however (that is, those in the [CUSTOM] section), determine how ScanDisk will behave if you start it with the /CUSTOM switch.

To view and edit SCANDISK.INI, change to the DOS directory and enter **EDIT SCANDISK.INI**. After loading the file into the editor, read the comments in each section for an adequate explanation of how to customize how ScanDisk operates. Here are a few ideas:

In the [ENVIRONMENT] section, change `Display=Auto` to `Display=Mono`, instead of using the /MONO switch every time you run ScanDisk.

To do a more thorough surface scan of a disk, change `NumPasses=1` to a larger number, such as 3 or 4. Naturally, increasing this number will proportionally increase the time it takes to scan the disk. Using a large number, such as 10, is useful for lengthy overnight scanning, but you will also want to change other settings according to the next point.

In the [CUSTOM] section, you might want to change `Surface=Never` to `Surface=Always` and change `Bad_Clusters=Prompt` to `Bad_Clusters=Fix`. This will allow ScanDisk to run unattended when you want to do something else or when you want to run a very thorough overnight scan.

If you do not want ScanDisk to prompt you for an Undo disk, change `Undo=Prompt` to `Undo=Never`.

Using ScanDisk's Errorlevels

When ScanDisk returns to the command prompt, it sets ERRORLEVEL to one of the following:

- ✔ **0.** ScanDisk did not detect any problems on the drive(s) it checked.

- ✔ **1.** ScanDisk could not run because the command-line syntax was incorrect.

- ✔ **2.** ScanDisk terminated unexpectedly due to an out-of-memory error or an internal error.

- ✔ **3.** The user chose to exit before ScanDisk had finished.

- ✔ **4.** ScanDisk completed all logical checks on all drives, but the user exited from one or more surface scans before the scans were complete.

    Errorlevel 4 is not returned, however, if the user chose to bypass the surface scans completely.

- ✔ **254.** ScanDisk found disk problems and corrected them all.

- ✔ **255.** ScanDisk found disk problems, but not all problems were corrected.

The value of these errorlevels is that you can use them in batch files to better automate your disk-maintenance chores. Let's assume you want to run ScanDisk before you run DEFRAG, but want to ensure that DEFRAG runs only after ScanDisk says all is well. MAINTAIN.BAT will do this for you:

```
@echo off
scandisk
if errorlevel 255 goto quit
if errorlevel 254 goto defrag
if errorlevel 4 goto quit
if errorlevel 3 goto quit
if errorlevel 2 goto quit
if errorlevel 1 goto quit
if errorlevel 0 goto defrag
:defrag
defrag
goto end
:quit
echo Some kind of error occurred!
:end
```

After running ScanDisk, this batch file determines whether or not to run DEFRAG by processing the errorlevel that ScanDisk returns. DEFRAG runs only if it repairs all the problems it found (errorlevel 254) or if it doesn't find any problems at all (errorlevel 0). If you want MAINTAIN.BAT to be more specific about what error occurred, you can easily change each GOTO statement to point to another label instead of quit. For example, you can change the errorlevel 255 line to read:

```
if errorlevel 255 goto notall
```

Then add the following label and routine:

```
:notall
echo AN ERROR OCCURRED! DEFRAG WILL NOT RUN!
echo ScanDisk found disk problems, but not all
echo problems were corrected.
goto end
```

Finally, you can, of course, add any switches you wish to the SCANDISK command. *See Chapter 15 for more on writing batch files.*

Understanding Disk Fragmentation

To understand disk fragmentation, you need to understand what DOS does when it's told to write a file. To simplify only slightly, DOS looks

Understanding Disk Fragmentation   417

for the first available cluster and places the first chunk of the file there. If the adjacent clusters happen to be free, DOS places the next chunks of data there. Figure 8.12 shows a contiguous file. Figure 8.13 shows what happens after you keep this up for a while, placing new files of various sizes, one after the other.

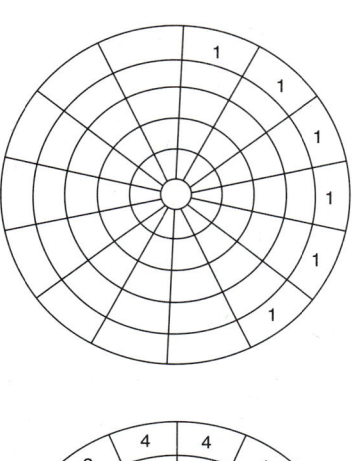

Figure 8.12

Writing clusters to an unfragmented disk.

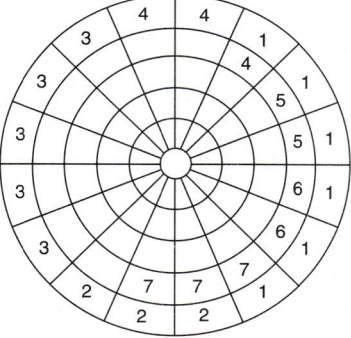

Figure 8.13

An unfragmented disk with many contiguous files.

Suppose that you erase file #3 and file #5. DOS marks those clusters as free in the File Allocation Table (see fig. 8.14).

Now suppose that you write a new file, file #8. DOS places it in the space left by the deleted file #3—but has one cluster of space left over. When you write another new file, file #9, DOS starts at the last free cluster left over after writing #8. DOS then jumps to the free clusters created when you deleted file #5. It fills all those clusters and because it still isn't finished writing the file, hops over the remaining files and writes the rest of the file into the first free clusters at the end of the disk. File #9 is fragmented, as shown in figure 8.15.

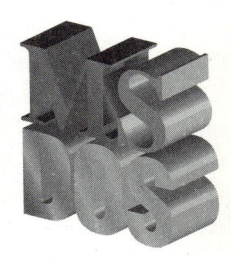

Figure 8.14

The disk after two files are deleted.

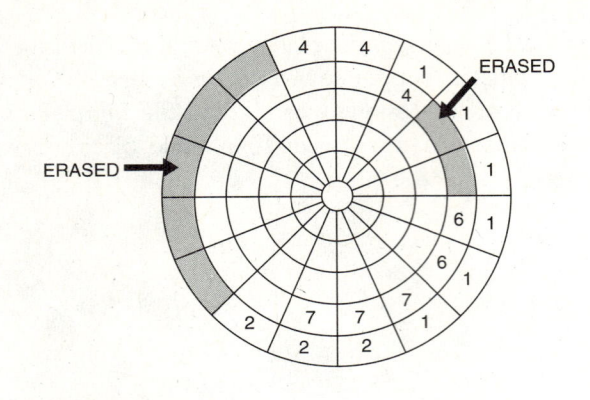

Figure 8.15

The fragmented file #9.

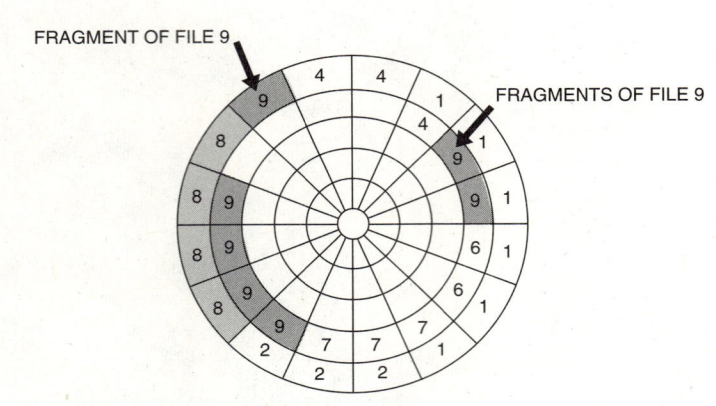

You can see that the longer you work, the more fragmented files become. DOS has changed the way it places files over the years, but for the most part, it still splits new files into the first available clusters.

> **NOTE** *When DOS writes new changes to an existing file, it tries to write the entire file to a new location. This limits fragmentation but also leaves scattered fragments of previous versions of the file throughout the disk.*

If you install a new program on a seriously fragmented disk, the EXE file may be written in one place and its support files—Windows Dynamic Link Libraries or Quattro VROOM modules, for example—may be placed somewhere else entirely.

Viewing a List of Fragmented Files

You can see which files are fragmented on your current directory by typing this:

`CHKDSK *.*`

CHKDSK searches each subdirectory on the drive, listing the files that are fragmented. Following is a sample output of CHKDSK:

```
C:\DOS\MSD.EXE Contains 9 noncontiguous blocks
C:\DOS\QBASIC.EXE Contains 4 noncontiguous blocks
C:\DOS\DEFRAG.EXE Contains 3 noncontiguous blocks
C:\DOS\QBASIC.HLP Contains 10 noncontiguous blocks
C:\DOS\DOSSHELL.EXE Contains 3 noncontiguous blocks
C:\DOS\README.TXT Contains 3 noncontiguous blocks
C:\DOS\MWBACKUP.HLP Contains 8 noncontiguous blocks
C:\DOS\MWBACKR.DLL Contains 2 noncontiguous blocks
C:\DOS\MWUNDEL.EXE Contains 2 noncontiguous blocks
C:\DOS\VSAFE.COM Contains 4 noncontiguous blocks
C:\DOS\DBLSPACE.EXE Contains 6 noncontiguous blocks
```

So who cares? DOS still knows where to find your files—that's all that matters, right?

AUTHOR'S NOTE

There are two reasons file fragmentation matters. The first is speed. Nearly everything going on in your computer happens electronically—except for disk access; that's a mechanical process that moves like molasses in comparison. The slowest part of disk access is usually the seek time — the time it takes for the drive heads to arrive at the cylinder where the data is.

Many seeks are relatively short—typically 5 to 16 milliseconds. If you have write-ahead disk caching enabled, many of these seeks don't happen at all: the information is already in the RAM cache. But sometimes a seek requires the head to move almost the entire radius of the drive. (Drive manufacturers assume that your average seek is one-third of the distance from front to back.) You might have

continues

situations where one 16K chunk of code repeatedly calls another that lives all the way at the other end of the disk. Even if a cache is present, that cache may constantly have large chunks of data running through it— so it may have to return to disk for this data.

All this seeking time adds up. On some systems, fragmented disks can reduce performance substantially. On other systems, there's less of a performance hit. One reason some disks don't benefit as much from defragmentation is that they're not that fragmented. The programs you installed a year ago stayed exactly where they were. It's your data files that are fragmented, and then only the files and subdirectories that won't fit into a single cluster.

There's a second reason to defragment your disk: safety. It's easier to recover a damaged file if all the clusters are contiguous. This is just common sense: Remember that DOS depends on a very tenuous pointer system to find its files. If a file begins in cluster 308, a pointer directs DOS to look next in cluster 462, then 537, then 551, and so on. If one of the pointers disappears, what tells DOS where to go next? Nothing. What tells the clusters that follow which file they belong to? Nothing. They're orphaned. If the pointer disappears from a text file, you may be able to make the connection. If it's an executable file, that's another story. See Chapter 20 for a detailed discussion of data recovery.

Understanding What Defragmenters Do

At the least, this is what a defragmentation program does: assembles all the fragments of each file into contiguous clusters. This solves at least one of the problems mentioned above: slow movement through a file.

Once you defragment a drive, you can't undelete anything you deleted beforehand.

A slightly more sophisticated defragmentation program, of the kind that's become common in the last few years, can also put all the files in a given directory together. That helps respond to the modularity of modern programs that load and unload separate support files repeatedly. After defragmentation with such a sophisticated program, all the support files are on the same cylinder—or on cylinders that are quite close by.

Such a program also places all subdirectories at the front of the disk, adjacent to the main directory, which shortens seeks as you move through the hierarchical file system. Some defragmenters go a step further and rearrange files within a directory following your preferences (for example, in alphabetical or date order).

These programs make it a little more convenient to use your directories, but no more so than including a DIRCMD= command in your environment space would. DIRCMD= enables you to set your preferences for how the DIR command displays directories. See Chapter 7 to learn more about DIRCMD=.

Defragmenting a Compressed Drive

Things get more interesting when you use data compression. As you recall from Chapter 4, DOS normally assigns a full cluster to any file—even a one-byte file. The extra slack space is used when the file expands. One way a data-compression program squeezes more information into fewer bytes is by using this slack space while still presenting the image of a normal cluster arrangement to DOS.

One of the goals of defragmenting a compressed drive is to make sure that each compressed cluster is no larger than it has to be. You want to make sure, for example, that a 6K file uses only 6K of space within the compressed drive—even though it's behaving all the while as if it uses standard-sized clusters.

A conventional defragmentation program won't do this; you need a special defragmentation utility such as DBLSPACE/DEFRAG or Stacker's SDEFRAG.

In the case of DoubleSpace, when you run Microsoft DEFRAG , after it finishes working its magic on your host drive, it automatically "spawns" DBLSPACE/DEFRAG to perform defragmentation on your compressed disk.

DBLSPACE/DEFRAG also moves all data to the front of the compressed disk and leaves blank space at the end. This is especially desirable if you wish to reduce the size of your compressed disk because you now can eliminate all the space at the end of the compressed disk.

Note, however, that the DoubleSpace defragmenter does not make sure all files within the compressed disk are physically contiguous on the disk. So in and of itself, it won't make the drive run faster.

Understanding the Risks of Defragmentation

Most of what a defragmenter does involves physically reading information from a disk and placing it in a new location. This means that information is overwritten and deleted as it is moved. A good defragmentation program doesn't erase old file pointers until it finishes reconstructing the file.

Still, if you have a few extra minutes, you should probably choose a verify option to double-check that all data has been written to disk correctly. And you can certainly lose files if the power fails while you're defragmenting. You might want to wait until the thunderstorm is over before you start.

Understanding Microsoft DEFRAG for DOS

Microsoft DEFRAG for DOS is a stripped-down version of Norton SpeedDisk, one of the best and most popular disk-defragmentation programs. DEFRAG does everything described in the preceding sections.

Quitting Everything Else before Starting

Remember that some programs, notably Windows 3.1 and the DOS Shell task swapper, may leave disk files open in a way that makes them look like lost clusters and chains. This can confuse any program that needs to know which clusters are connected to which file—as a defragmenter does. Before running Microsoft DEFRAG (or CHKDSK), exit Windows and close the DOS Shell. Close any other multitasking programs that are running and remove TSRs from memory.

In particular, make sure that you aren't running FASTOPEN, which stores the locations of files in memory. DEFRAG mentation changes those locations and may cause FASTOPEN to damage files.

If you plan to defragment often, you may want to use DOS's new MultiConfig features to create a separate boot file that doesn't load TSRs or other problem applications. Then, before you defragment, press Ctrl+Alt+Del and choose that option from the boot menu.

You can also boot from a floppy disk.

Running CHKDSK before Defragmenting

Before you defragment a disk, you should first run CHKDSK /F to dispose of any lost clusters and chains, which result in allocation errors that reduce a defragmenter's efficiency. CHKDSK converts lost clusters and chains to files named FILE0000.CHK, FILE0001.CHK, and so on, which you can then delete. You wind up with more disk space, and the defragmentation program takes slightly less time.

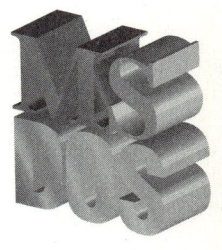

Chapter 8: *Tuning Your Disk with DOS 6.2 Tools*

> **6.2** ScanDisk does a much more thorough and efficient job of disk analysis and repair than CHKDSK. It is, therefore, recommended that you run ScanDisk instead of CHKDSK before running DEFRAG.

Loading Microsoft DEFRAG

There are two ways to work with Microsoft DEFRAG for DOS: load the program and run it from its graphical interface, or give specific parameters at the command prompt and just let it roll. Let's take these options one at a time.

Defragging from DEFRAG's Graphical Interface

To load Microsoft DEFRAG and use its graphical interface, type **DEFRAG** at the command prompt. After Microsoft DEFRAG tests your system memory, it asks you to specify which drive you want to defragment (see fig. 8.16).

Figure 8.16

The Microsoft DEFRAG for DOS opening screen.

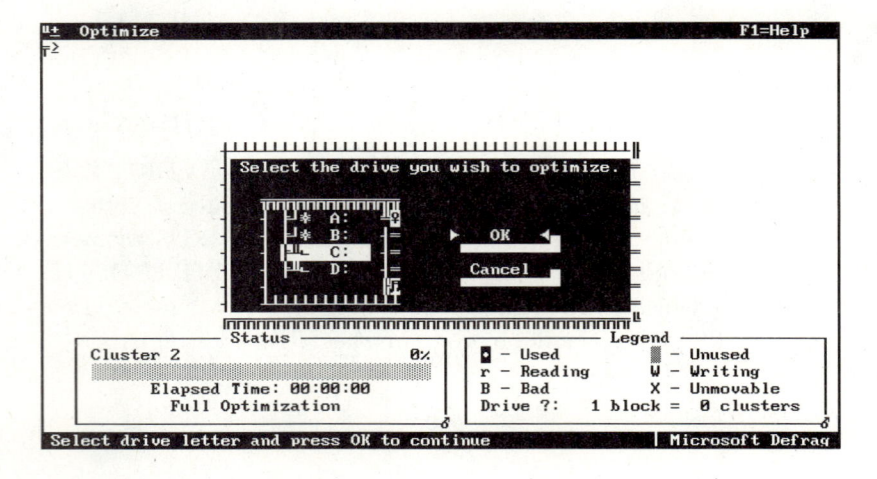

Any disk volume is acceptable: floppy disks, hard disks, or compressed drives. Choose one and click on OK. Microsoft DEFRAG displays a screen showing the contents of the current drive as illustrated by figure 8.17.

Understanding Microsoft DEFRAG for DOS **425**

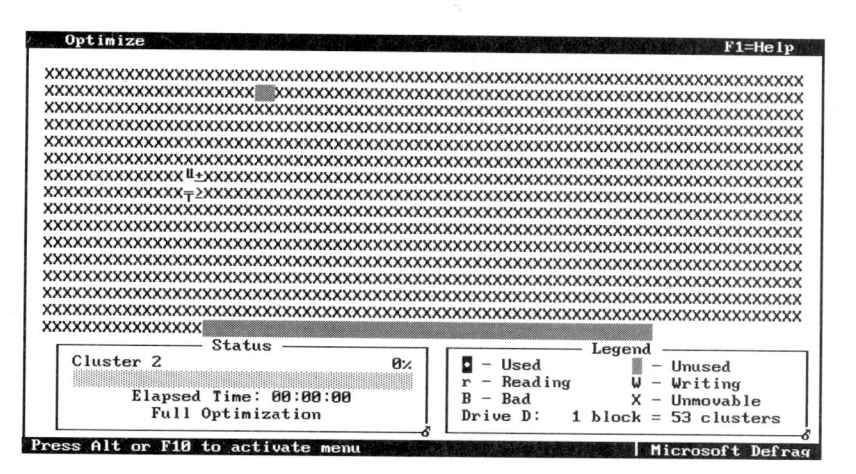

```
┌ Optimize ─────────────────────────────────────────── F1=Help ┐
│ XXXXXXXXXXXXXXXXXXXXXXXXXXXXXXXXXXXXXXXXXXXXXXXXXXXXXXXXXX   │
│ XXXXXXXXXXXXXXXXX■XXXXXXXXXXXXXXXXXXXXXXXXXXXXXXXXXXXXXXXX   │
│ XXXXXXXXXXXXXXXXXXXXXXXXXXXXXXXXXXXXXXXXXXXXXXXXXXXXXXXXXX   │
│ XXXXXXXXXXXXXXXXXXXXXXXXXXXXXXXXXXXXXXXXXXXXXXXXXXXXXXXXXX   │
│ XXXXXXXXXXXXXXXXXXXXXXXXXXXXXXXXXXXXXXXXXXXXXXXXXXXXXXXXXX   │
│ XXXXXXXXXXXXXXXXXXXXXXXXXXXXXXXXXXXXXXXXXXXXXXXXXXXXXXXXXX   │
│ XXXXXXXXXXXXX ⌂± XXXXXXXXXXXXXXXXXXXXXXXXXXXXXXXXXXXXXXXXX   │
│ XXXXXXXXXXXXXX⊤≥ XXXXXXXXXXXXXXXXXXXXXXXXXXXXXXXXXXXXXXXXX   │
│ XXXXXXXXXXXXXXXXXXXXXXXXXXXXXXXXXXXXXXXXXXXXXXXXXXXXXXXXXX   │
│ XXXXXXXXXXXXXXXXXXXXXXXXXXXXXXXXXXXXXXXXXXXXXXXXXXXXXXXXXX   │
│ XXXXXXXXXXXXXXXXXXXXXXXXXXXXXXXXXXXXXXXXXXXXXXXXXXXXXXXXXX   │
│ XXXXXXXXXXXXXXXXXXXXXXXXXXXXXXXXXXXXXXXXXXXXXXXXXXXXXXXXXX   │
│ XXXXXXXXXXXXXXXXXXXXXXXXXXXXXXXXXXXXXXXXXXXXXXXXXXXXXXXXXX   │
│ XXXXXXXXXXXXXXXXXXXXXXXXXXXXXXXXXXXXXXXXXXXXXXXXXXXXXXXXXX   │
│ XXXXXXXXXXXXXX                                               │
│   ┌─── Status ─────────────┐  ┌──── Legend ────────────────┐ │
│   │ Cluster 2         0%   │  │ ◆ - Used      ▓ - Unused   │ │
│   │ ▓▓▓▓▓▓▓▓▓▓▓▓▓▓▓▓▓▓▓▓▓▓ │  │ r - Reading   W - Writing  │ │
│   │ Elapsed Time: 00:00:00 │  │ B - Bad       X - Unmovable│ │
│   │ Full Optimization      │  │ Drive D:  1 block = 53 clusters │
│   └────────────────────────┘  └────────────────────────────┘ │
│ Press Alt or F10 to activate menu           │ Microsoft Defrag│
└──────────────────────────────────────────────────────────────┘
```

Figure 8.17
Microsoft DEFRAG drive map.

- ✔ Used clusters are marked with a solid white rectangle containing a diamond.

- ✔ Bad clusters are marked with a *B*. These clusters are marked when the disk is low-level formatted and are ignored by DEFRAG.

- ✔ Unused clusters are marked with a faded rectangle.

- ✔ Unmovable files are marked with an X. These files include all system or hidden files, and may also include some programs protected by an older copy-protection scheme that requires a program to remain in the sectors where it was originally installed. (Lotus 1-2-3 used a protection scheme like this through Version 2.1.)

> **NOTE**
> *Leaving system files in place dates back to the days before DOS 5, when the DOS boot record required that MSDOS.SYS and IO.SYS start at cluster #2. Even now, it makes sense—for stability reasons—to leave system files alone; Microsoft DEFRAG does not offer a way to move them.*

Chapter 8: *Tuning Your Disk with DOS 6.2 Tools*

Note that each rectangle (or block) on a drive map corresponds to a specific number of clusters, depending on the size of the disk you're mapping. For a 360K floppy disk, each block equals one cluster; for a 130M hard disk, each block equals 53 clusters.

Microsoft DEFRAG also makes a recommendation about how to proceed, based on how fragmented the disk is. In figure 8.18, Microsoft DEFRAG recommends full optimization.

Figure 8.18
DEFRAG recommendations.

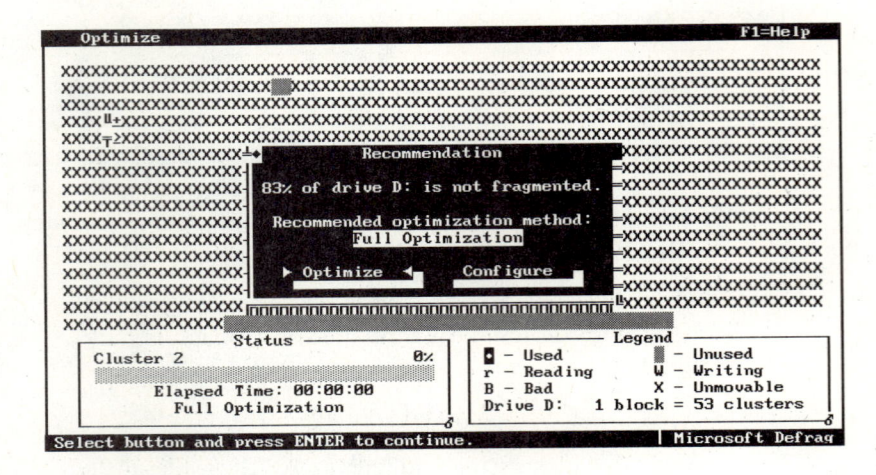

```
Optimize                                                             F1=Help
XXXXXXXXXXXXXXXXXXXXXXXXXXXXXXXXXXXXXXXXXXXXXXXXXXXXXXXXXXXXXXXXXXXX
XXXXXXXXXXXXXXXXXXXXXXX■XXXXXXXXXXXXXXXXXXXXXXXXXXXXXXXXXXXXXXXXXXXX
XXX"XXXXXXXXXXXXXXXXXXXXXXXXXXXXXXXXXXXXXXXXXXXXXXXXXXXXXXXXXXXXXXXX
XXX┬²XXXXXXXXXXXXXXXXXXXXXXXXXXXXXXXXXXXXXXXXXXXXXXXXXXXXXXXXXXXXXXX
XXXXXXXXXXXXXXX┴┌─────────────────────────────┐XXXXXXXXXXXXXXXXXXXXX
XXXXXXXXXXXXXXXX│         Recommendation      │XXXXXXXXXXXXXXXXXXXXX
XXXXXXXXXXXXXXXX│ 83% of drive D: is not fragmented. │XXXXXXXXXXXXXX
XXXXXXXXXXXXXXXX│ Recommended optimization method:  │XXXXXXXXXXXXXXX
XXXXXXXXXXXXXXXX│       Full Optimization           │XXXXXXXXXXXXXXX
XXXXXXXXXXXXXXXX│                                   │XXXXXXXXXXXXXXX
XXXXXXXXXXXXXXXX│  ▶ Optimize        Configure      │XXXXXXXXXXXXXXX
XXXXXXXXXXXXXXXX└───────────────────────────────────┘XXXXXXXXXXXXXXX
XXXXXXXXXXXXXXX┬□□□□□□□□□□□□□□□□□□□□□□□□□□□□□□□□□□□┴XXXXXXXXXXXXXXX
XXXXXXXXXXXXXXXX▒▒▒▒▒▒▒▒                          ┌─── Legend ──────┐
┌──── Status ────┐                                 │ ■ — Used    ▒ — Unused │
│ Cluster 2                        0%              │ r — Reading W — Writing│
│ ▒▒▒▒▒▒▒▒                                         │ B — Bad     X — Unmovable│
│ Elapsed Time: 00:00:00                           │ Drive D:  1 block = 53 clusters│
│ Full Optimization                                └────────────────┘
└────────────────┘
Select button and press ENTER to continue.          │ Microsoft Defrag
```

DEFRAG's options are as follows:

Full Optimization   Moves all directories to the front of disk

                                Defragments all files

                                Moves all empty space to the end of the disk

                                Can take a while

Unfragment files only   Leaves directories alone

                                Defragments all files

                                Leaves empty space in place

                                Runs very quickly

No optimization necessary No action taken

Understanding Microsoft DEFRAG for DOS

If you accept the recommendation, choose **O**ptimize (click on it or press Enter). If you want to change the recommendation, click on **C**onfigure or press C.

> *Clicking on **O**ptimize doesn't open the **O**ptimize menu—it starts the defragmentation process.*

Looking at the DEFRAG Optimize Menu

Choosing Configure opens the Optimize menu, which gives you the following choices:

Begin Optimization	starts the defragmentation.
Drive	gives you another chance to change drives.
Optimization Method	enables you to change DEFRAG's recommendation.
File Sort	enables you to re-sort the order in which each directory displays after the disk is optimized. The File Sort option doesn't actually move files—it only changes the order in which they are listed (see fig. 8.19).
Map Legend	adds just a tiny bit of detail to the descriptions of each symbol on the bottom right of your disk map screen.

When you finish making your choices, choose Begin Optimization; Microsoft DEFRAG begins working. You can watch it move blocks around. An R appears where DEFRAG reads a file; a W appears where it writes; and each optimized block is displayed in yellow.

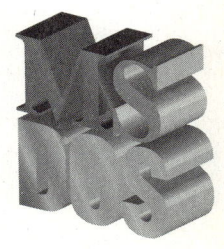

Chapter 8: *Tuning Your Disk with DOS 6.2 Tools*

Figure 8.19
The Microsoft DEFRAG File Sort window.

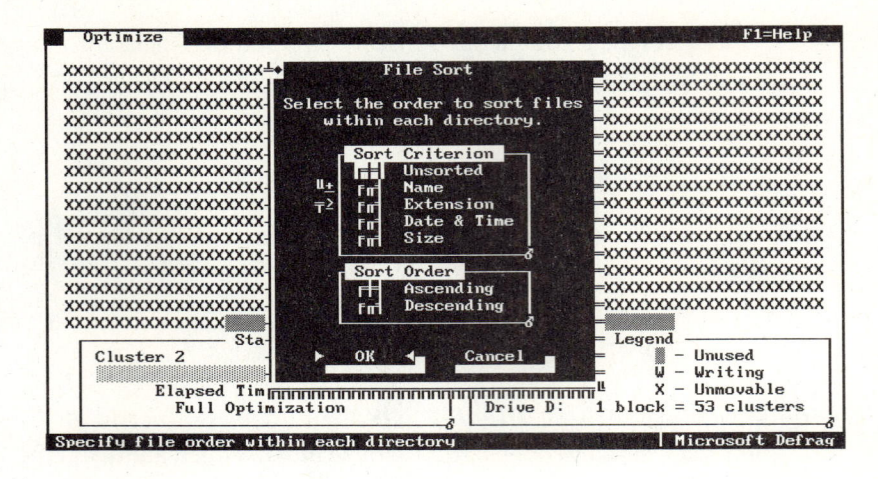

```
Optimize                                                              F1=Help
XXXXXXXXXXXXXXXXXX┌──────────── File Sort ────────────┐XXXXXXXXXXXXXXXXXXX
XXXXXXXXXXXXXXXXXX│  Select the order to sort files  │XXXXXXXXXXXXXXXXXXX
XXXXXXXXXXXXXXXXXX│         within each directory.   │XXXXXXXXXXXXXXXXXXX
XXXXXXXXXXXXXXXXXX│ ┌─ Sort Criterion ──────────────┐ │XXXXXXXXXXXXXXXXXXX
XXXXXXXXXXXXXXXXXX│ │     Unsorted                  │ │XXXXXXXXXXXXXXXXXXX
XXXXXXXXXXXXXXXXXX│ │     Name                      │ │XXXXXXXXXXXXXXXXXXX
XXXXXXXXXXXXXXXXXX│ │     Extension                 │ │XXXXXXXXXXXXXXXXXXX
XXXXXXXXXXXXXXXXXX│ │     Date & Time               │ │XXXXXXXXXXXXXXXXXXX
XXXXXXXXXXXXXXXXXX│ │     Size                      │ │XXXXXXXXXXXXXXXXXXX
XXXXXXXXXXXXXXXXXX│ └───────────────────────────────┘ │XXXXXXXXXXXXXXXXXXX
XXXXXXXXXXXXXXXXXX│ ┌─ Sort Order ──────────────────┐ │XXXXXXXXXXXXXXXXXXX
XXXXXXXXXXXXXXXXXX│ │     Ascending                 │ │XXXXXXXXXXXXXXXXXXX
XXXXXXXXXXXXXXXXXX│ │     Descending                │ │XXXXXXXXXXXXXXXXXXX
─── Sta ──────────│ └───────────────────────────────┘ │── Legend ─────────
 Cluster 2        │      ▶  OK  ◀       Cancel        │       - Unused
                  └───────────────────────────────────┘    W  - Writing
 Elapsed Time                                              X  - Unmovable
        Full Optimization                Drive D:   1 block = 53 clusters
Specify file order within each directory                   Microsoft Defrag
```

> **NOTE**
>
> *If you return to a disk after optimizing it, blocks that were optimized are displayed as "used."*
>
> *During the process of defragmenting a disk, blocks which are being optimized are displayed in yellow. But once you leave Microsoft DEFRAG and then come back to it, DEFRAG makes no distinction between the blocks you previously optimized and those that simply happen to be used, but have never been optimized.*

> **AUTHOR'S NOTE**
>
> *You can press Esc at any time to halt a defragmentation partway through the process. This is safe: Microsoft DEFRAG finishes writing the current cluster and makes sure that the directory and FAT listings are updated to the point when you stopped the defragmentation. Here are some times when you may want to stop defragging before it finishes normally:*
>
> ✓ *When you want to rearrange the listings in directories but not actually defragment the disk. (Microsoft DEFRAG optimizes directories before it defragments files. As soon as you see the message* Optimizing Directories complete, *press Esc.)*

> ✔ When you want to defragment the physical disks but not the compressed volumes. (Microsoft DEFRAG automatically spawns a separate program, called DBLSPACE/DEFRAG, to defragment any compressed volume contained within the drive you specified. If the compressed drive is nearly full, this can take a very long time.)
>
> Although you can run DBLSPACE/DEFRAGMENT separately, it's more effective to run it immediately after you run Microsoft DEFRAG on the host drive.

Defragging from the Command Line

The choices available from within Microsoft DEFRAG for DOS are also available from the command line. The basic syntax for running DEFRAG from the command line is as follows:

    DEFRAG drivename: /opttype

In this syntax, /opttype is the type of optimization you want to do. You may substitute one of the following switches:

| /F | for full optimization. |
| /U | unfragments files only. |

If you want to sort files, follow the /F or /U switch with one of these /S switches:

/SN	sorts alphabetically by name.
/SN-	reverses sort alphabetically by name.
/SE	sorts alphabetically by extension.
/SE-	reverses sort alphabetically by extension.
/SD	sorts from oldest file to newest.
/SD-	sorts from newest file to oldest.
/SS	sorts from smallest file to largest.
/SS-	sorts from largest file to smallest.

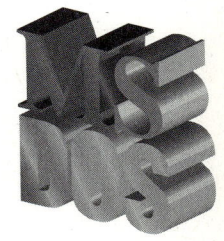

After the /S switch, you can include any of the following switches that are available only from the command line:

/V	verifies that files have been written correctly.
/B	reboots after defragmentation (use this switch if you have been running FASTOPEN or another program that might be confused by your files' new physical locations).
/SKIPHIGH	forces Microsoft DEFRAG to load in conventional memory, even if upper memory is available.
/H	moves hidden files.

You can use these three switches to affect how the DEFRAG utility behaves:

/LCD	displays Microsoft DEFRAG with the LCD color scheme.
/BW	displays Microsoft DEFRAG in black and white.
/G0	disables the graphical mouse and character set.

The following command defragments drive D's files but does not close up any empty space. It also reverse-sorts directory listings by extension, verifies all file writes, moves all hidden files, and reboots when it finishes:

```
DEFRAG D: /U /SE- /V /H /B
```

Microsoft DEFRAG also has one more, undocumented, switch: /MULTITASK. This switch enables you to run DEFRAG from a DOS session within Windows after giving you the warning shown in figure 8.20.

Consider using Microsoft DEFRAG from within Windows only if you're defragmenting a drive you're sure doesn't contain any files left open by Windows.

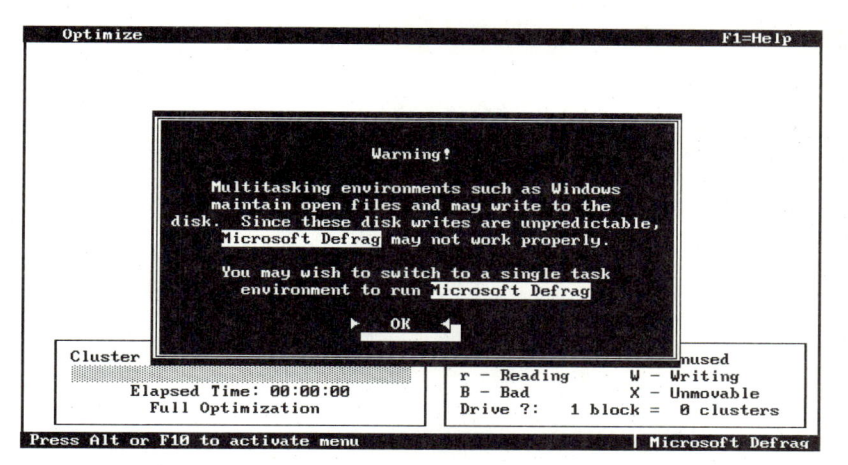

Figure 8.20

The warning that appears when running DEFRAG with the /MULTITASK switch.

Defragmenting Large Disks

Microsoft DEFRAG runs in conventional memory. The more conventional memory you can liberate, the larger a disk you can defragment. Regardless of how much memory you have, however, you're bound to run out of room if you defragment some very large disks.

DEFRAG needs room to load and run; it also needs room for two copies of the File Allocation Table. In addition, DEFRAG needs 16 bytes of free conventional memory per file plus 48 bytes of free conventional memory per subdirectory.

You may run out of memory if you have a very large disk. On 386 and above systems with extended memory, the following procedure may give you enough memory to do the following:

1. Run MEM/CLASSIFY to see how much available memory you already have.

2. Edit CONFIG.SYS as follows:

    ```
    [menu]
    menuitem=normalload
    menuitem=defragload
    [normalload]
    include all your current CONFIG.SYS statements here
    [defragload]
    DOS=HIGH
    ```

```
DOS=UMB
DEVICE=C:\DOS\HIMEM.SYS
DEVICE=C:\DOS\EMM386.EXE NOEMS I=A000-B7FF
```

If you have DoubleSpace installed, also include this statement:

```
DEVICEHIGH=C:\DOS\DBLSPACE.BIN /MOVE
```

3. Reboot.

4. From the boot menu, choose the defragload option.

5. Type **MEM** to see how much memory you now have.

6. If there is more memory available than before, run Microsoft DEFRAG.

7. Either reboot and choose the normalload option or edit CONFIG.SYS back the way it was before this procedure. Don't try to run the system with the defragload configuration. It's just a temporary measure to get you defragmented.

> *Another trick that sometimes works on systems with large disks and limited memory is to first defragment files; only then do a complete defragmentation the second time around.*

Many defragmenters have trouble with very large disks. One that doesn't is Golden Bow's VOPT; it can handle up to 16,378 files, 1,023 directories, and partitions up to 1 gigabyte.

Running the DoubleSpace Defragmenter

As already mentioned, if you defragment a drive containing a DoubleSpace-compressed volume, DBLSPACE/DEFRAG runs automatically after the regular DEFRAG finishes. DBLSPACE/DEFRAG scrunches all the compressed data together at the beginning of the DoubleSpace volume, leaving the end of the volume blank.

Although DBLSPACE/DEFRAG is most effective if you run it immediately after running the regular DEFRAG program on the same drive, you can run it separately by typing...

    DBLSPACE /DEF C:

If you leave off the name of the drive, DBLSPACE/DEFRAG tries to defragment a compressed volume on the current drive.

> **AUTHOR'S NOTE**
>
> *How often should you defragment a disk? Well, that depends on who you talk to. I'd say at least once a week. Your disk probably won't fragment by more than 10 percent in that time, so defragmentation shouldn't take long.*
>
> *If you're putting stuff on a new disk, install the programs first. DOS places them in contiguous clusters that won't ever have to be defragmented. That also leaves less space for the data to become scattered across—which definitely speeds defragmentation and might even slightly improve performance between defrags.*

Summary

This chapter has covered the three main tools DOS 6.2 provides to help improve the performance of your computer's disk drive—without costing you a dime.

SMARTDrive's disk caching enables you to substitute high-speed memory for low-speed disk access—often as much as 80 or 90 percent of the time.

FASTOPEN, used in the right circumstances, can eliminate repetitive searching for the same files.

Microsoft DEFRAG can speed your disk seeks by reorganizing your disks so that entire files are contiguous.

It's all free with DOS 6.2—all you need to spend is some time.

MS-DOS

Optimizing Your Memory

Understanding PC Memory Types 437
Using the DOS 6.2 Memory Manager 485
Memory Organization and Upgrade Strategies 557
Memory-Management Tips, Tricks, and Troubleshooting 595
Running Third-Party Memory Managers 661

Part Four:

MS DOS

CHAPTER 9

Understanding PC Memory Types

by Mark Minasi

Confused by the terms "extended," "expanded," "conventional," and the like? So are most people. In this chapter, you learn about the kinds of memory on your system and how to use that memory as productively as possible. This text relies heavily upon DOS 6.2 for examples, for two reasons. The first and most obvious reason is that this book is about DOS 6.2. Second, if you've already got DOS 6.2, you probably can do anything you need to do to manage memory without having to spend more money for a third-party memory manager. (If you know what you're doing, you don't need a third-party memory manager.) In some cases, QEMM-386, from Quarterdeck, and 386 to the Max, from Qualitas, may solve a problem that DOS 6.2 can't. *For more information about third-party memory managers, see Chapter 13.*

You probably know that there are many kinds of memory these days, although you may not have heard of all of them. The five most common types of memory are the following:

- ✔ Conventional
- ✔ "Reserved," or "adapter segment" areas
- ✔ Video RAM areas
- ✔ Extended
- ✔ Expanded, also called *EMS (Expanded Memory Specification)* or *LIM (Lotus-Intel-Microsoft)* areas

Memory used to be easy to understand. Computers (pre-PC) all had something like 1K, 4K, 16K, 32K, 48K, or 64K. Then the PC came along with bigger numbers—up to 640K of memory! More total memory, but not more confusing; so far, more is better.

Now memory's "extended," "expanded," "LIM," and "conventional," not to mention ROM (and "UMBs" and "the HMA"). Why so many kinds of memory? Before I go on, you need to know that nobody planned this. It just kind of "growed that way."

The plethora of memory types is largely the result of unfortunate planning—nobody ever thought the PC would need more than 640K of memory. Here's a look at how memory works.

Main Memory versus Secondary Memory (RAM versus Disk)

The PC, like all computers, must have both main and secondary memory. Why must it have two kinds of memory? Basically, it's a speed-versus-cost tradeoff, with data longevity thrown in for good measure. *Main memory* is for transient storage of information the computer is working on right this minute; *secondary memory* is for long-term storage of data and programs.

Understanding Main Memory (RAM)

Main memory is a high-speed data-storage medium the CPU can read from or write to. *High speed* here means that reading from or writing to memory takes less than a microsecond (a millionth of a second). The other, more popular, name for such memory is RAM, the acronym for *random access memory*. Now, "random access memory" doesn't tell us much; here's what it means. *Random access* means that you have a certain number of memory locations—millions on most modern computers—and that each location is as easy for the CPU to get to as any other location.

Suppose that you want to play a song on an album. All you have to do is pick up the phonograph's tonearm and put the tonearm down over the appropriate track. Playing the third song is just as easy as playing the ninth song. A phonograph, then, is a random access device, like the RAM in your system. The "random access" part of the term RAM isn't very descriptive because most kinds of storage are random access.

The alternative is *sequential access*, such as you find on a cassette tape. Suppose, in contrast, that you wanted to play the very same song on a cassette tape, but that the song was at the end of the tape. You can't simply tell your cassette deck to play song number 9; you have to fast-forward the tape to song number 9. Once you're at song number 9, it's much easier to get to song number 10 than to, say, song number 3.

In addition to being very fast, RAM is a relatively expensive storage medium. In 1993, the amount of RAM hardware you'd need to store the text of an average size book (about one megabyte) cost around $40. One megabyte of secondary storage costs a tenth of that amount. And RAM is *volatile*, which means that any break in a steady stream of power causes it to lose whatever data it is storing. Some of the chips inside your PC's case are its RAM hardware. *For additional information about those chips, how to identify them, and how to upgrade them, see Chapter 11.*

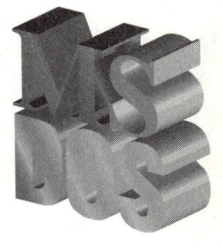

Understanding Secondary Memory (Disk)

In contrast to RAM, secondary memory is the storage space on a hard or floppy disk, a tape drive, optical disk drive, or Bernoulli-type cartridge. Because floppy disks, hard disks, optical drives, and Bernoulli cartridges are all random-access devices, most secondary memory is also random access. How, then, are disks different from RAM? Disks store data, but at rates that are hundreds of thousands of times slower than main memory. Hard disks—the fastest kind of secondary storage in general use—take longer than a millisecond (1/1,000 second) to respond to requests; as you've already read, main memory responds in less than one microsecond, or in nanoseconds (1/1,000,000,000 second).

Because RAM and disk storage capacities usually are described in megabytes, trying to understand the difference between RAM and disk space can be confusing. When I mention that Windows runs best with 8 megabytes of RAM, for example, someone often responds "That's no problem—I've got 60 megabytes on my computer." The reference, almost certainly, is to disk space, not memory space. And disk space is not volatile. If you put a data file on a computer's hard disk, turn off the computer, and walk away from it for a week, the data is still there when you return. With memory, as soon as you've powered down, the data goes to Data Heaven, or wherever data goes.

To illustrate data volatility, suppose that you power up your computer, fire up WordPerfect, and start typing. Where do your keystrokes go—to primary or secondary storage (RAM or disk)? The answer is RAM. Type 100 pages of text without saving it, and then turn off your computer. All your hard work is gone. But if you save the file to disk before turning off the computer, the data is still accessible.

While you're editing a file, WordPerfect keeps it in RAM simply because RAM is so fast. When you save a file, it is saved to disk simply because disk space is nonvolatile.

In short, the big differences between disk space and RAM space are as follows:

1. RAM is volatile (it does not retain data when you turn off the PC), but disk drives retain the data stored on them even if the power is turned off.
2. PCs tend to have much more disk space than RAM space.
3. RAM is much faster than disk.

In the remainder of this chapter—and the next four—you learn more about working with RAM, rather than disk. But much of the rest of the book covers disks in detail.

Staking Out the First Megabyte

Why is DOS limited to 640K? Many of the constraints we face today have their roots in the past, a past 13 years ago....

1980: IBM Picks the 8088

In the summer of 1980, after ignoring the home computer market ("home computer" is what we called a PC in those days) for six years, IBM started to develop a new microcomputer, the one eventually called the IBM Personal Computer. The goal of the small design team was to build a computer that could compete with the Apple II, the market leader at the time. The PC had a good start in that it was based on a much more powerful central processing unit (CPU) chip than the Apple's.

When a computer designer picks a CPU for a PC, he or she simultaneously imposes a number of constraints on that computer system—how fast it can go, what sort of hardware supports it, and how much memory it can address. As you probably know, the CPU chip that IBM selected was the Intel 8088. At that time, one of the powerful features was that the 8088 could address ("talk to") up to 1024K—one megabyte, or 1,048,576 bytes—of RAM.

Dividing Up the Addresses

Planning a new computer is kind of like planning a new community. Before breaking ground on a planned community, a zoning board or planning board determines what use will be made of all the land space. Thus, the planners of a new community start with some unused land, perhaps fallow farmland. After acquiring the land, they must plat it into lots, and then determine which lots will hold residential buildings, which ones commercial buildings, industrial buildings, local government, and so on. We could say that before any buildings are built, a planner must allocate addresses. Before any buildings are built, the planner decides that any buildings built on address "X" must be residential, and any on a given address "Y" must be commercial.

So it is with PC design. Before any memory is placed in the system, the computer planner knows that the CPU can address a certain amount of memory—1024K, in the case of the 8088 CPU—and that groups of addresses must be set aside for particular functions. The memory chips that get hooked up to the computer are basically identical, whether they're conventional, extended, expanded, or any other kind. What's important is the *address* of that memory.

A Closer Look at Addresses

Let's take a moment and refocus on exactly how memory addresses differ from memory. Memory addresses are on the CPU chip—they are some of the little legs that extend off the chip. When a designer plunks a CPU down in the middle of a newly designed memory board, he or she has already put the memory addresses in that computer. *Adding memory* means attaching memory chips to the addresses that already exist on the motherboard—addresses that physically are nothing more than wires extending off a CPU chip. You've already read my land analogy: you start with vacant lots—they're the computer's addresses. Then you put buildings on the land—the buildings correspond to memory chips placed on a particular address. Finally, some buildings are used and some are not used—that corresponds to memory that's filled with programs and data versus free memory space.

If that analogy's not helpful, try this one. Imagine a tall pole extending from the ground to the sky. On that pole are cup hooks—small hooks a cup or a mug could hang from. There are a million of these cup hooks, because it's a tall pole. (Hey, trust me: go with me on this story a bit, okay?) This pole is used for storing small things: to store something, you just hang a cup on a cup hook and then place whatever you want to store in the cup. (For the nitpickers, the handles on the cups are arranged so that the cups hang at an angle so that items don't fall out of them. Imagine also that you have a ladder tall enough to let you get to the millionth cup.)

Each hook is an address. An 8088 has 1024K of addresses. But you can't store anything at an address. First, memory has to be attached to that address—a cup must be hung on that cup hook. In PC terms, a memory chip must be attached to a CPU's memory address before the CPU can store something at that address.

Sorry if the analogies seem like overkill, but believe me, the whole question of memory versus memory addresses is one of the toughest things to understand about memory management.

Meet the PC's Three Memory Areas

In the early days, a PC's entire universe consisted of just 1024K of addresses. Figure 9.1 shows a simple memory map—a rough overview of those addresses. A *memory map* is a common tool for diagramming memory addresses and the uses of memory put in those addresses.

This memory map needs a few words of explanation. Note that it has decimal addresses on the left and hexadecimal addresses on the right—that's what "A0000," "FFFFF," and the like are. You've got to get used to hex addresses early on because you'll have to use hex when you work with memory managers. At each boundary point, you see two hex numbers: the hex value of the last address in the lower area, and the hex value of the first address in the higher area. The last hex address of the area labeled "conventional memory" is 9FFFF, for example, and the first hex address of the video RAM area is A0000. On the decimal side of the map, note that the last address is 1024K-1, not 1024K; because the first memory address is 0 and there are only 1024K of addresses, the last address must be 1024K-1. *If you're "hexaphobic," Chapter 10 offers four hexaphobia.*

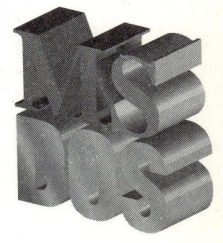

Figure 9.1
The three major PC memory address ranges below 1024K.

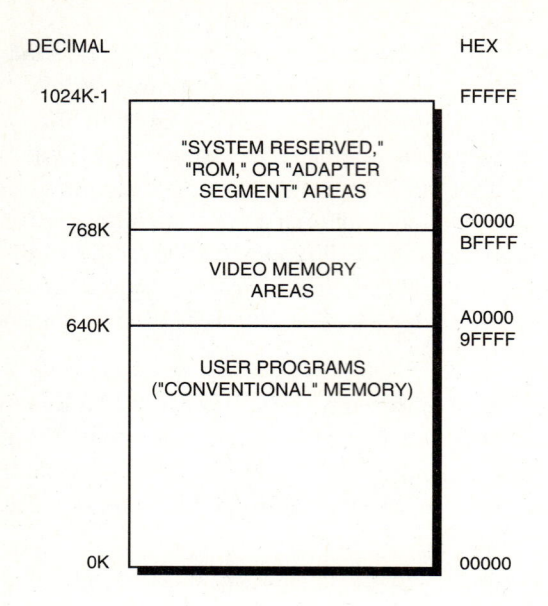

```
DECIMAL                                              HEX
1024K-1  ┌─────────────────────────┐                FFFFF
         │   "SYSTEM RESERVED,"    │
         │   "ROM," OR "ADAPTER    │
         │     SEGMENT" AREAS      │
  768K   ├─────────────────────────┤                C0000
                                                    BFFFF
         │    VIDEO MEMORY         │
         │        AREAS            │
  640K   ├─────────────────────────┤                A0000
                                                    9FFFF
         │    USER PROGRAMS        │
         │ ("CONVENTIONAL" MEMORY) │
         │                         │
         │                         │
   0K    └─────────────────────────┘                00000
```

> **NOTE**
>
> *In computers with only 1024K of addresses, the last memory address must be 1024K-1 (because the first address is 0).*

The three memory areas, conventional, video, and system reserved, are the foundation of the PC's memory structure. For more details about each area, read on....

Conventional Memory Stores DOS, Your Programs, and Data

PCs running DOS and DOS programs can use 640K of main memory. The first 640K of memory addresses are called "conventional" (or sometimes "user") memory addresses. Any memory wired to those addresses serves for storing "user programs" (that phrase is in quotes because other programs also draw from those addresses). DOS loads in that memory, as do some "helper" programs called TSRs and device drivers, which you'll learn about in a minute. The BIOS

Conventional Memory Stores DOS, Your Programs, and Data

programs that form the lowest level of software in much of the PC world also keep a little data in the low 640K. The *K* refers to 1024; 64K, for example, equals 64 x 1024, which equals 65,536 bytes of data. Each byte can hold the equivalent of about one character. Assuming that your PC has memory in at least the first 640K of addresses, let's take a look at how that very important 640K gets filled. Figure 9.2 shows what memory might look like on a PC running WordPerfect 5.1.

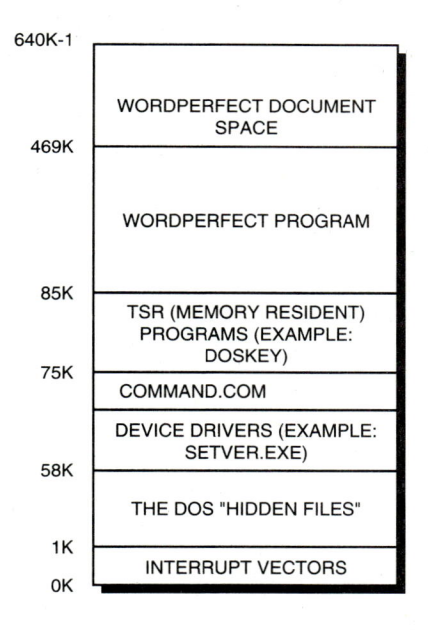

```
640K-1 ┌─────────────────────────┐
       │                         │
       │  WORDPERFECT DOCUMENT   │
       │         SPACE           │
 469K  │                         │
       ├─────────────────────────┤
       │                         │
       │   WORDPERFECT PROGRAM   │
       │                         │
  85K  ├─────────────────────────┤
       │  TSR (MEMORY RESIDENT)  │
       │   PROGRAMS (EXAMPLE:    │
       │        DOSKEY)          │
  75K  ├─────────────────────────┤
       │      COMMAND.COM        │
       ├─────────────────────────┤
       │ DEVICE DRIVERS (EXAMPLE:│
       │       SETVER.EXE)       │
  58K  ├─────────────────────────┤
       │   THE DOS "HIDDEN FILES"│
   1K  ├─────────────────────────┤
       │    INTERRUPT VECTORS    │
   0K  └─────────────────────────┘
```

Figure 9.2

An example of conventional memory use under WordPerfect 5.1.

The map shows decimal memory addresses and hex addresses. Read it from the bottom up—the lower positions in the figure are the lower addresses. The following sections examine in some detail the memory uses shown in figure 9.2.

Interrupt Vectors and DOS

The bottom 1K is an area used by the CPU as a kind of table of contents of hardware support programs called "software interrupts;" the table of contents is composed of pointers to those programs, called "interrupt vectors." The table of interrupt vectors is a fixed size of 1024 bytes (400, in hexadecimal). (Again, trust me for a bit on the hex.

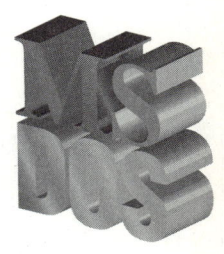

Conversion routines are coming in Chapter 10.) One interrupt points to the program that controls your disk drives, another to the video board, and so on. As you can see from figure 9.2, DOS loads just above the interrupt vectors in this example. Chapter 10 shows you how to load DOS high and also describes DOS loaded entirely in conventional memory. *For a discussion of software interrupts and interrupt vectors, refer to Chapter 2.*

> **NOTE** As you can see, DOS 6 takes up the next 57K. (Your copy of DOS probably takes up a different number of bytes; the number is determined by how you've set your BUFFERS, FILES, STACKS, and LASTDRIVE.)

TSRs and Device Drivers

The next 15K are taken up with device drivers and memory-resident programs, known as *TSRs* (terminate-and-stay-resident programs). You probably use these every day in your work.

Device drivers are programs that either allow DOS to support a new piece of hardware, or add new capabilities to an existing piece of hardware. Device drivers are loaded in the CONFIG.SYS file with the DEVICE= statement. Some examples of device drivers include the following:

- ✔ The ANSI.SYS device driver that extends your system's capability to respond to a new set of video commands, the ones specified in the ANSI X3.64 standard.

- ✔ A mouse driver, like MOUSE.SYS, that enables your system to recognize and control your mouse.

- ✔ The memory manager drivers HIMEM.SYS and EMM386.EXE that we will meet later, which make your previously useless memory above 1024K into a useful resource for your software. *For a more detailed discussion of the HIMEM.SYS and EMM386.EXE memory manager drivers, see Chapter 10.*

Conventional Memory Stores DOS, Your Programs, and Data

TSR programs do much the same thing, but because they are loaded from AUTOEXEC.BAT, they load after any device drivers. The following are a few examples of TSR programs:

- ✔ MOUSE.COM is an alternative way to load software support for your mouse.

- ✔ The program to use your IRMA board, if you've got an IRMA board—you know, the one that connects you to the mainframe when you press both Shift keys—is one example.

- ✔ DOS comes with a small utility, DOSKEY, that remembers the last twenty-or-so commands I've typed, so that if I make a mistake, I can call up a previous command, edit it, and resubmit it to the PC. If you don't use DOSKEY yet, use it.

- ✔ Many virus and antivirus programs are TSRs.

- ✔ Network shells and protocol stacks usually are TSRs. Novell NetWare users may find the commands NET and IPX in their AUTOEXEC.BAT files, for example.

TSRs and device drivers are useful, but they've got a price: they take up space in your precious 640K of conventional memory. As you'll see in Chapter 10, one of the capabilities of a memory manager product is to load those programs out of the 640K area. *If you need more background on TSRs and device drivers, see Chapter 2.*

Device drivers and TSRs tend to slow down performance. To see this, clean boot your system and time how long it takes for the DIR C:*.* /S command to complete. Then load all your drivers, run the command again, and notice the difference. Moral: run as few drivers as possible.

The Command Shell COMMAND.COM and Your DOS Environment

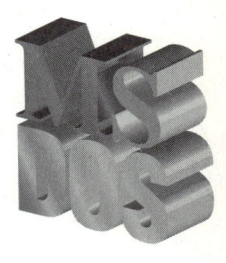

Between the device drivers and TSRs is the command interpreter, COMMAND.COM. It accepts command-line commands and passes them to DOS for execution. COMMAND.COM takes about 5K of memory, depending on whether you've increased the size of your environment.

The *environment* is an area maintained by COMMAND.COM to hold items called "environment variables." To see your environment variables, type **SET** from the DOS command line. When I do that on my computer, this is what I see:

```
CONFIG=VAN
COMSPEC=C:\DOS\COMMAND.COM
BLASTER=A220 I10 D3 T4
PROMPT=$P$G
PATH=C:\DOS;C:\UTILS\CORELDRW;C:\WWG
TEMP=C:\TEMP
TMP=C:\TEMP
```

What exactly do these environment variables do? An *environment variable* is a piece of information stored in memory for the convenience of some program. Some environment variables are used by DOS, others may be used by applications programs. CONFIG=VAN, the first environment variable on my system, for example, tells my system that I'm using MultiConfig, the DOS configuration manager, and that I've chosen to boot with the "VAN" configuration. VAN doesn't mean anything to anyone but me—it's just what I choose to call one of my configurations, the "vanilla" configuration in which I boot with no TSRs or device drivers. *For more information about MultiConfig, see Chapter 16.*

COMSPEC is a variable DOS uses to remind itself where COMMAND.COM is located on the disk. BLASTER is a variable used by the software that comes with the Sound Blaster Pro board I have in my system. When I run one of the utilities that came with the Sound Blaster Pro, that utility must know the I/O address of the board (220), the interrupt number (10), the DMA channel (3), and the version (4) of the digital signal processing (DSP) chip on the board.

The BLASTER line means absolutely nothing to DOS or DOS programs, except a few Sound Blaster Pro-aware applications—programs that use a Sound Blaster board if one exists in your PC. Understand that something does not have to be part of DOS to use an environment variable—any program can add variables to the environment, provided that there is space to do so. Furthermore, the variables need not mean anything to any program but the one that put the value in there in the first place.

You use the SET command to set environment variables. To insert an environment variable called GREETING that contains the value HELLO, for example, you just type...

```
SET GREETING=HELLO
```

...from the DOS command prompt. No program uses the variable, but that's no trouble; all it does is take up a little space. The command set all by itself lists the current environment variables.

The PROMPT and PATH environment variables are the way COMMAND.COM remembers what command prompt to put onscreen and where to search for files when executing programs, respectively. (For more background on how COMMAND.COM displays command prompts and locates executable files, refer to Chapter 2.) TEMP and TMP are conventions that many programs in the DOS world—including DOS itself—use to know where to place "temporary" files.

While we're on the subject of the environment, it's worth noting that the environment is a preallocated area in memory, one that can fill up. By default, COMMAND.COM sets aside 256 bytes for the environment, which may not be enough. If you have a long path, it can chew up a substantial amount of that space. By including a SHELL statement in your CONFIG.SYS file, you can tell COMMAND.COM to allocate additional space. Stripped down, that statement looks like this:

```
SHELL=pathCOMMAND.COM path /E:nnnn /P
```

with *path* the subdirectory containing COMMAND.COM, and *nnnn* the number of bytes to allocate to the environment. The path variable must appear twice, by the way, so that COMMAND.COM knows where COMMAND.COM itself is. Otherwise, you may get an error message that looks like...

```
unable to reload command interpreter
```

Suppose, for example, that you store COMMAND.COM in the C:\DOS subdirectory of your PC, and you wanted to allocate 1024 bytes for your environment. The SHELL statement in your CONFIG.SYS file would look like…

```
SHELL=C:\DOS\COMMAND.COM C:\DOS\ /E:1024 /P
```

If you ever get an…

```
out of environment space
```

…error message, just up the environment size through the SHELL statement and reboot. Problem's solved. One other side item: environment variables can be no more than 256 bytes long. Generally, however, they are much shorter than that because they're typically set through SET statements. COMMAND.COM restricts SET statements (as it does all command-line commands) to no more than 128 characters.

User Programs

The WordPerfect program (WP.EXE) takes up the next 384K of conventional memory, with the remainder available for WordPerfect documents. Again, the top address is 640K minus one, rather than 640K, because we started counting at zero, not one.

> **AUTHOR'S NOTE**
>
> *The vast majority of DOS programs claim that they can run only in the low 640K of your PC's memory, and that's largely true. That's why the 640K conventional memory area is so important. If your program can live only in conventional memory and the conventional memory is full, getting more memory won't help.*
>
> *One of my users said recently of her 4M computer, "We need to buy more memory for my PC—I'm running out of memory." She was indeed running out of memory, but with an old application that couldn't use any more memory than 640K. As far as that application was concerned, the memory beyond 640K didn't even exist. It's*

> definitely not true that all memory is created—or addressed—equal.
> But why is there a 640K barrier in the first place, and can anything
> be done about it? Part of the answer lies with the next group of
> memory addresses, the addresses set aside for video RAM.

Understanding Video RAM

People often speak of DOS and DOS programs as having a "640K barrier" or "640K limitation," but that's not actually true. Almost all DOS programs are written to run on the 8088 chip (and, of course, its successors, the 286 and later). Any 8088 program can address up to 1024K of memory—in theory. Nothing about DOS or the 8088 requires that the story end at 640K. Nevertheless, 640K is a very real barrier for most systems. Why?

Don't blame Microsoft. Don't blame IBM. Blame everybody.

Well, okay, the initial blame for the 640K limitation can be laid at IBM's door. They (remember the 1980 PC designers—they're the guys) decided that the PC would use memory-mapped video, and that the video would be located at 640K. But there's more.

The video board—the circuit board that acts as an interface between the CPU and the monitor—in an IBM machine must contain some memory. That memory is shared between the circuitry on the video board and the CPU. The CPU "puts data on the screen" by putting data into this video RAM. The video circuitry sees the data in the memory and interprets it as graphical or textual information.

Video memory is memory used by video boards to keep track of what's to be displayed on-screen. When a program puts a character on the screen, or draws a circle on the screen, it actually makes changes to this video memory. IBM set aside 128K for video memory, but most video boards don't actually need or use that much memory space. The answer to the original question ("Where does the 640K limit come from?"), however, is that the video RAM must go somewhere, and the original PC designers placed it from 640K through 768K. Even if more memory for user programs existed above 768K, most programs could not use that memory because most programs insist on contiguous blocks of memory. As you'll see later, a small workaround for this problem is to load TSRs and device drivers above 768K—a major reason to use memory managers.

> **AUTHOR'S NOTE**
>
> *You may be saying, "Why doesn't someone just build a PC with the video addresses higher up? Or put some memory above 768K? Then there'd be more space for conventional memory." Well, the answer to the first question is, "It wouldn't work." Remember the analogy I used, comparing a planning commission and PC hardware design? In the PC world, it's kind of like the world has changed, but the planning commission's rule hasn't. Perhaps some old curmudgeon who's been on the commission for years is saying, "I don't see why we should change the plan...it's been a good plan for the last 50 years; it'll be a good plan for 50 more."*
>
> *Who's the curmudgeon in this story?*
>
> *Every major software vendor.*
>
> *You see, virtually all major software products don't use DOS to address the video hardware; rather, they directly manipulate the video hardware (you read about this in Chapter 2). All those major software programs were written assuming that the video memory is where it's supposed to be—between 640K and 768K. If you move the video memory, all the programs—1-2-3, WordPerfect, you name it—stop working. So the installed base of software compels the hardware to remain static in some ways.*

The answer to the second question ("Why not put some extra memory above 768K?") is that DOS programs generally are capable only of addressing memory that's all in one piece—memory that is contiguous. If you had a 640K block of memory below the video section (which is what you usually have) and, say, a 128K block of memory above 768K, then each DOS program would have to fit entirely into either the 640K block or the 128K block. A program can't be divided between the memory blocks, so a sort of fetish on DOS's part—that each program fit entirely within some memory space—was a contributing factor to the 640K limitation. Memory started at address 0 and moved up until it found an obstruction—the video RAM.

Video RAM Addresses and Video Boards

Video boards use the addresses from 640K through 768K. But how did they use the addresses? Table 9.1 shows the major types of video boards through PC history and how they used the addresses.

Table 9.1
Video Memory Use

Video Board	Addresses Used	Total Memory on Video Board
Color Graphics Adapter (CGA)	736K-768K (B8000-BFFFF)	16K-32K (depending on vendor)
Monochrome Display Adapter (MDA)	704K-736K (B0000-B7FFF)	16K-32K (depending on vendor)
Enhanced Graphics Adapter (EGA)		
(in text mode)	736-768K (B8000-BFFFF)	256K
(in graphics mode)	640-704K (A0000-AFFFF)	256K
Video Graphics Array (VGA) and super VGAs		
(in text mode)	736-768K (B8000-BFFFF)	256K
(in graphics mode)	640-704K (A0000-AFFFF)	256-1024K

The memory address space used differs from total memory on the video board for the EGA and VGA because they use a technique called "paging" that enables them to put a great deal of memory on the video board—more memory means better video—without taking up a lot of the CPU's total 1024K memory address space. (The previous section on video memory and paging explains paging.)

The EGA and VGA do not use the memory addresses between B0000 and B7FFF (the addresses the MDA uses). That's so that your system can run two monitors. Why run two video boards and monitors? Some debugging systems let you test-run your program with program output going to the CGA, EGA, or VGA monitor while debugging information is displayed on the MDA.

Details of Video Memory: Text Mode versus Graphics Mode

You probably have noticed that the EGA, VGA, and super VGA adapters have two modes—text and graphics—and that these two modes use different amounts of memory. Text mode is an older, simpler way to manage video. When a video adapter is in text mode, it can accept only commands from the CPU to put characters on the screen. In text mode, a video board cannot draw pictures, display shapes, or show bit maps like the familiar Windows wall-paper pictures.

But text mode has two very positive features. First, it's fast. In text mode, a video board has a very simple job: just display one of 256 characters. Because the design of each character is prestored in a chip on the video board, the board can blast the text out onto the screen. Second, text mode does not require much memory. The typical PC text screen is 80 characters wide by 25 lines deep. Each character on the screen can be represented by two bytes of data: the first byte is the character itself, and the second describes the color in which to display the character and whether it should be inverse video, blinking, or highlighted. Because there are 2,000 positions (80 × 25) to keep track of on a screen, at two bytes apiece, a video board can store an entire screen in just 4,000 bytes.

In graphics mode, on the other hand, the CPU can control, through the video board, every single pixel on the screen. The video board enables the CPU to draw pictures, display bit maps—you name it. That's the good part. The bad part of graphics mode is that the CPU not only *can*

control every dot on the screen, it *must* control every dot on the screen. The simple operation of putting some text on the screen becomes much more complex in graphics mode. On a VGA graphics screen, for example, the CPU must manipulate about a quarter of a million pixels. To put text on the PC's screen, the CPU must actually draw each character onto the screen. The process requires a great deal of memory, as well as 150K of RAM for a single VGA screen.

How do I get 150K of RAM? The screen has 640 pixels across and 480 pixels down; half a byte is needed to represent the 16 VGA colors. Multiply 640 times 480 times 1/2 (.5) divided by 1024 (1024=1K) equals 150K exactly. Resolution higher than VGA requires even more memory, which is why super VGA boards may have one or more megabytes of memory. But now that you know that video boards use 256K or more of RAM, consider the question: how does 256K—or, for that matter, a megabyte or more—fit into just 128K of addresses?

Understanding the Three Video RAM Areas

The key to understanding video memory is to recognize that 128K of memory *addresses* are set aside for video, and 256K or more of *memory*. Viewed in that light, the whole thing seems a bit less impossible.

The 128K set aside for video memory isn't just laid out as one big 128K block; rather, there are three separate and distinct video memory areas, as shown in figure 9.3.

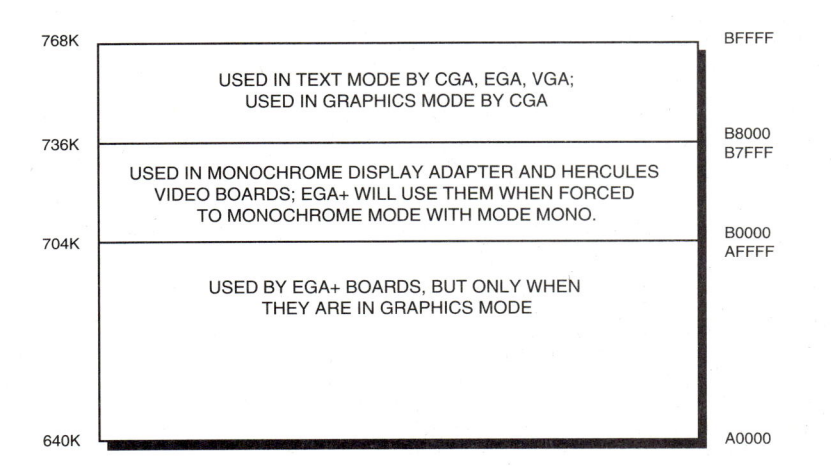

```
768K ┌────────────────────────────────────────────────┐ BFFFF
     │         USED IN TEXT MODE BY CGA, EGA, VGA;    │
     │         USED IN GRAPHICS MODE BY CGA           │
736K ├────────────────────────────────────────────────┤ B8000
     │                                                │ B7FFF
     │   USED IN MONOCHROME DISPLAY ADAPTER AND HERCULES │
     │   VIDEO BOARDS; EGA+ WILL USE THEM WHEN FORCED │
     │   TO MONOCHROME MODE WITH MODE MONO.           │
704K ├────────────────────────────────────────────────┤ B0000
     │                                                │ AFFFF
     │         USED BY EGA+ BOARDS, BUT ONLY WHEN     │
     │         THEY ARE IN GRAPHICS MODE              │
     │                                                │
     │                                                │
640K └────────────────────────────────────────────────┘ A0000
```

Figure 9.3

How the video addresses on a PC are divided up.

On EGA and higher graphics boards, graphics activity takes place in the bottom 64K of the video area. This area is accessed only in graphics mode; the addresses between 640K and 704K (A0000-AFFFF in hex) on your PC are essentially "vacant lots"—addresses without memory attached to them—when the video board is not in graphics mode. The 32K of addresses from 704 through 736K (B0000-B7FFF in hex) was designated for the Monochrome Display Adapter (MDA), although IBM MDAs only used memory from 704 through 708K (B0000-B0FFF hex), a 4K area. Later MDA improvements like the Hercules Graphics Controller and clones used the entire 32K region. Your PC will use this monochrome region only if one of the following is true:

- Your PC has a monochrome display adapter installed.

- You have shifted your VGA into monochrome-compatible mode by using the MODE MONO command.

- You are using one of the super VGA boards and video accelerators that use this memory area when they are in a graphics mode with resolution beyond 640×480×16 colors.

Do not confuse "monochrome monitor." *Monochrome adapter* refers to a video board that puts out a particular kind of signal designed for a particular kind of monitor. Of the four kinds of video adapters referred to in table 9.1, three of them—CGA, EGA, and VGA—support color output. But color monitors are expensive. In all three cases, the marketplace has seen the introduction of monitors that, although electrically compatible with the color signal, displayed colors only as shades of gray, green, or amber. Those monitors also were called monochrome monitors, causing confusion with the monochrome display adapter. The upshot is that having a monochrome VGA monitor does not mean that you have a monochrome display adapter on your system.

The top 32K, the range of addresses between 736K and 768K (B8000-BFFFF hex), originally was used by the Color Graphics Adapter (CGA) in either text or graphics mode. Even EGAs and VGAs use this area whenever a CGA graphics program is running. That's a pretty rare occurrence these days; however, it's hard to think of too many popular programs that use CGA graphics. The most common use for B8000 through BFFFF is to support text mode in the EGA and later video boards. Text mode is essential. The system can't boot up without it.

But let's get back to that "where does all the memory go?" question. Anyone who's bought a super VGA board has heard of VGA boards with 256K, 512K, or 1024K of memory. Where does this memory go, given that only 64K of addresses are set aside for VGA graphics? The answer is in a technique called "paging."

> **NOTE** *Paging is a process commonly used in the computer world to shoehorn a great deal of memory into just a few addresses.*

To help you understand paging, let's return to the zoning and planning board story. Suppose that the story's mythical planned community has 1,024 building lots and that lots 640 through 703 are set aside for an industrial park. All 64 lots are quickly populated with small one-story buildings. But, soon thereafter, there's a demand for more floor space in that industrial park. The planning commission is approached for more lots, but they won't relent. How can the town get more floor space in the industrial park without using more building lots—addresses? Simple: build up or add more floors. Memory paging is like that. It sort of adds extra floors—and an elevator—to memory addresses.

As you may recall, the video RAM is not on the motherboard; rather, it's on the video board. (Even on computers that don't have a separate video board, the video RAM is implemented on separate memory chips that are physically separate from the main system RAM. The rest of this discussion still applies to those computers.) Paging hardware on the VGA board allows the video board to present only 64K of its 256K (the amount of memory on a normal VGA) to the CPU at a time. A standard VGA, then, has four 64K pages and, as it turns out, each page has a job. One page governs the blue part of the screen, another the red, another the green, and the final one the intensity of an image.

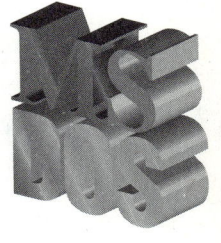

The process of generating a complete VGA graphics screen goes something like this:

1. Issue the command to bring in ("page in") the blue 64K.
2. Draw the blue part of the screen in the blue memory page.
3. Issue the command to page in the green page.
4. Draw the green part of the image.
5. Issue the command to page in the red 64K page.
6. Draw the red part of the screen.
7. Issue the command to page in the intensity page.
8. Designate the areas that need high intensity and low intensity.

You'll see this notion of paging in many places in the computer world. As you'll see later, the video RAM area is the place in which the real memory management "wizards" squeeze out those extra vital few bytes of space.

Understanding the System Reserved Area

Above 768K sits an area called the *reserved*, the *system*, or sometimes the *adapter segment* area of memory. It's the area in which the original PC designers planned to put things called ROMs—read-only memories. We'll get to ROMs in a minute. But first, why put this system stuff so high in memory?

When you turn on your PC, the CPU gets power, like the other components in the system. But where does the CPU go for its marching orders? After all, it doesn't just wander around the PC's memory looking for programs to run. So where does it look?

By design, the 8088 and later CPUs go to address FFFF0 in hexadecimal, or 16 bytes below 1024K, when they are powered up. (Again, don't sweat the hex; this is covered in the next chapter.) The CPU goes to just about the very top of memory looking for startup instructions.

If this PC is going to work, it had better be ready with some startup programs for the CPU, and those programs must start at FFFF0. But there's a problem with that idea. *For information on hex and decimal conversion, see Chapter 10.*

You see, programs must reside in memory, and the memory I've talked about so far is RAM. Earlier in this chapter I mentioned that RAM is volatile—remove power from it, and it forgets its contents. But the memory around the top of 1024K can't be allowed to forget its commands; those commands have to be sitting there, ready for the computer whenever it powers up. What to do? Simple. Use ROM—read-only memory.

Read-Only Memory (ROM)

So far, I've talked about memory and RAM as if they were identical. Another kind of memory exists, however, that is not used as much as RAM but is important nonetheless. Unlike RAM, which the CPU can write data to or read data from, this other kind of memory cannot be altered. It can only be read, which is why it's called "read-only memory." This is memory that someone (usually the computer manufacturer) loads just once with a special device called a PROM blaster or an EPROM programmer. You can read information from ROMs, but you can't write new information to them. (Well, you can write the information, but the ROM ignores you. Think of ROM as a chip that can give advice, but can't take it.)

Why have a memory chip in which you can only store information once? Well, it has the virtue of being nonvolatile. Unlike normal RAM, the ROM doesn't lose its memory when you turn off the machine. The first, most obvious need for ROM is to store the startup program the PC needs. (If you're a coffee drinker, think of ROM as being like coffee for your PC—to get it going in the morning.)

The BIOS ROM

The ROM that contains that startup software is called the BIOS ROM (the Basic Input/Output System ROM). It contains not only the startup code, but also some vital programs the system uses on a second-by-second basis to control your video system, floppies, hard disk, keyboard, and other basic hardware. Those programs, as you may recall from Chapter 2, are accessed through interrupt vectors. INT 9 points to the program in the BIOS that handles the keyboard, INT 13 points to the code supporting the drives, and INT 10 points to the video code. Thus, when DOS reads your floppy, it does so by calling on the BIOS routine that reads your floppy drive. That's why the BIOS is so important: the BIOS determines in large measure how compatible with the IBM standard your PC is.

As you'd expect, IBM's BIOS is the standard of compatibility. Back in the early 80s, the first cloners developed BIOSs that conformed in varying degrees to the IBM standard; the question "Does it run Lotus 1-2-3 and Microsoft Flight Simulator?" was the acid test of compatibility. Nowadays, I suppose the question is "Does it run OS/2 and Windows?" Three companies—Phoenix Software, Award Software, and American Megatrends, Incorporated (AMI) derive large incomes from their main business of writing very compatible BIOSs for clone makers. The availability of compatible BIOSs has simplified the business of cloning considerably.

Because it is memory, ROM needs an address. And, again, the system BIOS ROM needs an address range that includes FFFF0. Thus, most system BIOSs take up the addresses between 960K and 1024K (F0000-FFFFF hex). A few systems, however, (such as PS/2s) have an "extended" BIOS that ranges all the way from 896K through 1024K (E0000-FFFFF hex).

Now, most software on your system won't be stored in ROM. Because changing ROM involves replacing a chip in your system—never a fun task—hardware designers use ROM to store software that won't change very often.

ROMs are also found on expansion boards like LAN, video, or scanner interface cards, to name a few examples. On those ROMs are pieces of software that allow the system to control those boards. Or the ROM may contain code that, like the system BIOS, initializes the board when the system powers up. In essence, we can say that ROM on a circuit board contains the software that tells the system how to use a circuit board.

As you know, software changes from time to time. And I've said that ROM contains software. Occasionally, you can fix a problem by *upgrading the ROM*—getting the latest version of the ROM-based software from the manufacturer.

ROMs usually can be identified fairly easily. They generally are larger chips than the basic RAM chips. They're usually 24- or 28-pin chips; they are socketed (which makes them easy to change); and they often bear a paper label with a version number or some such printed on it.

ROM Addresses

Because ROMs are memories, albeit inflexible ones, they require a place in the memory addresses in the reserved area between 640K and 1024K. Suppose that you have in your system a board that contains a ROM. That ROM must be attached to some memory addresses somewhere in the 0 through 1024K range. As you now know, the ROMs really should be addressed somewhere in the 768 through 960K range, because the addresses below 768K are for video RAM and the addresses above 960K are for the main system BIOS ROM.

VGA boards, for example, have a BIOS on a ROM between 24K and 32K in size. That ROM usually sits at either 768K or 896K, depending on the kind of computer. Assuming that the VGA BIOS was at 768K and that it was 32K long—the usual size these days—then the VGA BIOS ROM would extend from 768K to 800K (C0000-C7FFF hex).

Buffers and Frames

Some boards need a little memory space reserved for them. A LAN board, for example, may need some storage space. A few examples of these boards follow:

- ✔ LAN boards have 16K of ROM that contains a sort of network-level BIOS. They also have a RAM buffer that can be adjusted so that it is as small as 8K or as large as 64K.

- ✔ Many Ethernet boards these days have a 32K RAM buffer; that RAM buffer must have an address within the CPU's address range.

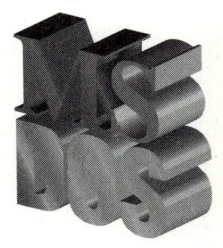

Chapter 9: Understanding PC Memory Types

- ✔ Some old ARCnet cards have up to 64K of ROM.
- ✔ Basic VGA boards have 24K of ROM, but Super VGA boards usually have 32K of ROM.
- ✔ Many hard disk controllers have ROM, particularly hard disk controllers that offer some kind of high performance, like bus mastering, ESDI, SCSI, or caching controllers.
- ✔ Scanner interface cards like the one supplied with the Hewlett-Packard ScanJet include some ROM.
- ✔ A kind of memory board called an "expanded" or LIM memory board needs 16K to 64K of "page frame" memory space to buffer transfers into and out of LIM memory. This type of memory board is described later in this chapter.

All of those memory pieces must fit somewhere in the reserved area from 640K to 1024K in the PC's memory address space.

Before leaving this section, take a look at figure 9.4, which shows the memory map with reserved areas added.

Figure 9.4
PC memory map showing all areas, from 0 to 1024K.

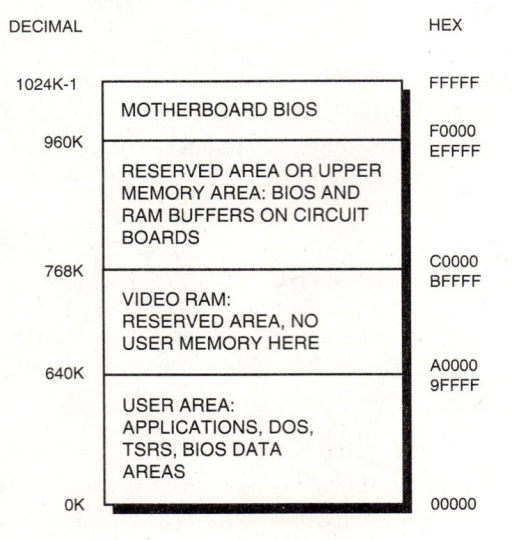

DECIMAL		HEX
1024K-1	MOTHERBOARD BIOS	FFFFF
960K		F0000 / EFFFF
	RESERVED AREA OR UPPER MEMORY AREA: BIOS AND RAM BUFFERS ON CIRCUIT BOARDS	
768K		C0000 / BFFFF
	VIDEO RAM: RESERVED AREA, NO USER MEMORY HERE	
640K		A0000 / 9FFFF
	USER AREA: APPLICATIONS, DOS, TSRS, BIOS DATA AREAS	
0K		00000

This memory map (fig. 9.4) is how the original PC designers laid out the first PC. The layout of that first 1024K became a standard that no software or hardware designer dared violate, at the cost of 100 percent compatibility with IBM PCs. But with more complex PCs, came more memory—and a chance to get to more space.

Understanding Extended Memory

As part of the march of electronic progress, Intel didn't stop with the 8088 but continued making faster, more powerful chips. The 8088 was in some ways little more than a glorified calculator chip; it could address quite a bit of memory for a microprocessor, but little else. In the years since the 8088 appeared, however, Intel has designed and built microprocessors for which the prefix "micro-" seems more and more silly. The power of such modern microprocessors as the 486 and the Pentium rivals that of mainframes.

What does a chip need to rival the power of mainframes? Well, for one thing, an even larger address space than a mainframe. Starting with the 80286's introduction in 1981, Intel chips have been able to address megabytes and megabytes. An 80286 can talk to ("address") 16 megabytes; an 80386 or 80486 can talk to 4 gigabytes (one gigabyte is 1024M) of RAM. Over time, normal RAM above the 1M level has come to be known as "extended memory." Why does memory above 1024K get a completely new name? Largely because the 286 and later chips have "split personalities." And that has to do with another mainframe-like feature found on many chips: memory protection.

Protected Mode

You're probably aware that large mainframe computers run multiple programs simultaneously. Basically, the memory space of the computer gets parceled out to the applications: perhaps an E-mail program needing about 350K runs in the background, a word processor in the foreground requires 800K, and perhaps a spreadsheet that takes up around 1200K is in the background. (The programs I'm talking about here are not DOS programs, as you can tell from the size of the spreadsheet.)

Each of these programs has its own separate memory areas, and each one's expected to stay in its place. But what about the odd program that accidentally strays from its area? Perhaps you bring the spreadsheet up into the foreground and try to place a graphic inside the spreadsheet, making the spreadsheet grow considerably. As the spreadsheet grows, what happens if it accidentally grows into the word processor's area? Or, worse yet, suppose that your computer were acting as a server on a local area network, and one program (a virus, or the like) tried to peek into the memory of the LAN server program itself—the program that contains the system passwords?

Do you see why memory protection is a good idea, and why mainframes have memory protection? Hardware built into the mainframe CPU keeps track of which application gets to use what memory. If an application tries to reach out of its space, the protection hardware senses what's happening and stops the application, probably by ending the program and informing the user. Until 1981, none of the Intel CPUs had this built-in memory protection, but the 286 and later chips all have the feature. These chips can also address memory beyond 1024K, but only while in protected mode.

> *The 8088, 8086, and earlier chips cannot under any circumstances address memory beyond 1024K; thus, they can never have extended memory.*

Protected Mode and Backward Compatibility

If protected mode sounds like a neat idea, it is. An operating system can just plunk a program down into an area in memory, and kind of put a "force field" around the program. Provided that the application behaves itself and stays only in its assigned area, all is well. But if the application attempts to access some part of memory for which it isn't authorized, the memory protection circuitry in the CPU detects the access attempt and generates a sort of "red alert," forcing the CPU to set aside what it's doing and deal with the delinquent program. (That "red alert" is called a general protection fault, or "GP fault.") Dealing with the delinquent program typically means shutting down the program before it can do any damage. Basically, programs that run while in protected mode don't try to do anything with memory without first requesting memory blocks from the operating system. Then, after the OS has granted them an area in memory, the programs load their data into their spaces and stay there.

That's the good part about protected mode; but it's also the problem with running DOS programs under protected mode. You see, the whole notion of first asking the operating system—DOS—for permission before using memory is totally unknown in the DOS world. A program written for DOS pretty much assumes that no other program is in the system, and just takes whatever memory it wants without asking for it. Adding memory protection and the ability to address 16M to the 286 made it more powerful, but also made it incompatible with the 8088.

Now, because designing and releasing a new chip that was totally incompatible with any previous Intel offerings would be suicidal, Intel gave the 286 and subsequent chips split personalities: when they boot up, they act just like an 8088, except faster. In this initial boot-up mode, the chips can address up to 1024K of memory, no more. This 8088 emulation mode is called "real mode." When speaking of Windows or OS/2, people sometimes refer to DOS programs as "real mode programs." With a few instructions, any chip from the 286 on can shift over to protected mode, and from there to lots of memory beyond 1024K. But, again, when the 286 (or later) chip is in protected mode, it can't run programs designed for real mode—DOS and DOS programs, that is.

> **NOTE**
>
> *At this point, you may be saying to yourself, "Well, if this wonderful protected mode gives access to tons more memory, and makes it easy to run multiple programs without having them crash each other, why don't we have a version of DOS that uses the silly thing!" The answer is, we do. It's called OS/2. OS/2 hasn't caught on for a number of reasons, however. Rumor has it that DOS 7.0*
>
> *continues*

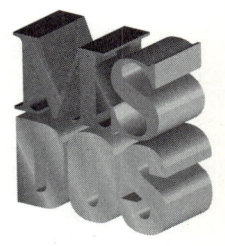

will offer not only the capability to run both existing DOS real-mode programs, but also a way for developers to access protected memory. But those are only rumors at this moment.

Anyway, much of this protected mode discussion is all about why the memory above 1024K on a 286 or later computer gets the special "extended memory" name. The reason is that because the CPU must be in protected mode to access memory above 1024K, and DOS programs don't run in protected mode, memory above 1024K exists in a 286 or later computer but is essentially useless under DOS. That memory gets another name to set it apart from the accessible conventional memory.

Using Extended Memory under DOS: DOS Extenders

Am I saying that DOS programs absolutely cannot use extended memory? By no means. One class of DOS programs uses a DOS extender so that it can use extended memory. Basically, a DOS extender is a tiny protected-mode operating system that unlocks the door to extended memory and provides tools with which programmers can use that memory. Examples of programs built with DOS extenders include Paradox 4.0, 1-2-3 Version 3.*x*, AutoCAD, and Harvard Graphics Version 3.*x*. This need for extended memory explains why 8088-based machines cannot run 1-2-3 Version 3.0.

DOS memory managers, which also work with extended memory, clearly contain a DOS extender. If you need to make the DOS extenders contained in memory managers work with the DOS extenders in application programs, Windows, or OS/2, you'll find that some do… but some don't. Is there some kind of overall rule?

Early DOS Extenders

Back in the days when OS/2 was still under development, and Windows was just a curiosity that no one used for anything serious—before the days of programming environments that make it easy for programmers to use extended memory—a number of companies started writing DOS programs that could access extended memory on 286 and later computers. Accessing extended memory requires installing a "supervisor" program, a program to make sure that no program treads upon another program's territory. OS/2, Windows, and Windows NT are all examples of supervisor programs. Given that all these DOS programs wanted was to support themselves—and no other programs—in extended memory, they didn't need a very big "supervisor" program.

The Intel chip world has more than just one "supervisor." Programs can have one of four levels of privilege, called "rings." To understand the privilege rings, think of four rings nested one inside the other, with ring 0 in the middle and ring 3 on the outside. Ring 0 has the highest priority; the program with ring 0 privilege sits in the "command center" of the CPU, and ring 0 is intended for use by the operating system. Ring 1 programs have less privilege than ring 0 programs; ring 1 typically is used for device drivers. Ring 2 is of lower privilege and is typically unused. Ring 3, at the lowest level of privilege, is intended for user programs.

The notion of the rings is useful because the idea is that the device drivers can control memory in an application program's memory areas—ring 1 is of a higher privilege level than ring 3—but a deranged device driver cannot damage an operating system area. Similarly, buggy applications can damage only their own memory areas; they can't touch other applications, the device drivers, or the operating system.

Early programs that used extended memory lived entirely in ring 0, because it was just easier for an applications programmer to put the whole program in ring 0. The programmer didn't really have to learn anything about the rings or privilege levels. That worked fine, provided that only one of those programs was running in the computer at any time. Oracle and Informix are examples of early programs that used extended memory; other examples are VDISK.SYS (the "RAM disk" program that came with DOS 3.0 and later versions of DOS up to DOS 5.0) and the IBMCACHE.SYS disk cache program that IBM shipped with the PS/2s. None of those programs would coexist with other programs running in extended memory.

> **NOTE**
>
> *Most old programs that used extended memory didn't even have a formal DOS extender product attached to them. Rather, they used a feature (INT 15, function calls 87 and 88) that is built into most PC BIOSs. Of the hundreds of built-in utility programs in a BIOS, these two will find out how much extended memory is on your PC (that's INT 15, function call 88), and then transfer data into or out of some area in extended memory (that's INT 15, function call 87). All a simple extended-memory-using program would do is stuff data up in extended memory, saving and retrieving it as needed with INT 15 function calls. That's why the earliest crop of extended-memory-using programs are sometimes called "INT 15 programs."*
>
> *All went well until someone tried to run a program that used extended memory (an INT 15 program or something built upon an early DOS extender) in a computer at the same time another supervisor was running—running a DOS extender program while a memory manager was active, for example. That lead to a fight between the memory manager and the DOS extender over who got to be the supervisor, because only one supervisor program at a time is supposed to be active in a PC. The two supervisors slugged it out, and the PC lost. The simple act of running the 1988 vintage of Oracle (a database) on a system that uses 386 to the Max (a memory manager) would result in a lockup, for example. Clearly, some kind of rapprochement between ring 0 programs was necessary.*

The Virtual Control Program Interface (VCPI)

As a result of incompatibility problems, the makers of DOS extender products got together and developed a method by which DOS extenders could peacefully coexist. The *virtual control program interface* (VCPI, to us acronym-lovers) provides an agreement through which two or more DOS extenders can coexist. The VCPI defines an organized, agreed-upon method in which one DOS extender makes a note about how it has memory organized, saves that note somewhere, and then hands control over to the second DOS extender, which then reorganizes memory to suit itself. When the time comes for the second DOS extender to hand control back to the first one, it does so by restoring things to the way it found them and then passing the baton back to DOS extender number one. Each program that uses a DOS extender is a ring 0 program. The big thing the VCPI does is to provide for the orderly transfer of power from one ring 0 program to another.

Much of what a DOS extender must do is keep track of which section of memory is being used by each part of the program it is extending. This information is kept with some data structure in memory called "page tables." The technical names for these tables are the local descriptor table (LDT) and the global descriptor table (GDT). Almost all DOS extenders use page tables (they must, for reasons related to how the 286 and later chips dole out extended memory) but all organize the tables differently. And that's the big problem: two programs keeping GDTs that are organized differently are bound to step on one another at some point. But that doesn't happen if you run only one program at a time and switch the entire memory image when you move from one VCPI-compliant program to another. Which is pretty much what happens with VCPI-compliant programs. They can't multitask with each other because each sees the GDT in different ways. But they can share the GDT, in the sense that each can unload its own GDT and reload another VCPI program's GDT before passing control to that program.

> **NOTE** *There are two standards for making DOS extenders coexist. The virtual control program interface (VCPI) won't work with OS/2, NT, or Windows in 386 mode. The DOS protected mode interface (DPMI), implemented correctly, will enable an extended program to work under Windows, OS/2, or NT.*

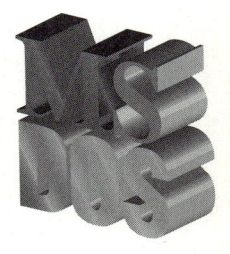

For that reason, VCPI applications cannot work reliably in the multitasking framework of Windows 386-enhanced mode. They probably will work in standard mode, however, for the simple reason that standard mode switches context instead of multitasking. When you activate a DOS program under standard mode, the memory image of standard mode gets swapped out to disk, "clearing the desk" for the next VCPI program. Examples of programs that follow the VCPI standard are 1-2-3 Version 3.0, Paradox 3.5, AutoCAD, FoxPro, and Interleaf Publisher.

> **AUTHOR'S NOTE**
>
> *If all this talk of GDTs and LDTs isn't clear, consider the following analogy. An assembly plant runs 24 hours a day in three shifts. The plant has a day manager, an evening manager, and a night manager. The way each manager does his or her job is totally different, but all of them must use the desk that sits in a good observation point above the assembly line floor. The managers have made an agreement: no matter what happens on any manager's shift, that manager has to leave a clean desktop—the way he or she found it—at the end of the shift. There's no way that two of these managers could work at the desk at the same time, but they can share it in an eight-hours-at-a-time way. So it is with VCPI-compliant programs: they can context-switch among themselves, but they cannot multitask among themselves.*

One problem you may find with VCPI programs is that VCPI programs can access extended memory in two ways. A few are built around INT 15; this form of VCPI was an early attempt to tame the old bear, before the VCPI folks gave up and developed another approach, one built upon a system of memory allocation called the eXtended Memory Specification, or XMS. Most VCPI programs use this newer XMS method. XMS programs will not run unless a device driver whose job is to serve as an XMS manager is active in memory. (The HIMEM.SYS program you'll meet in Chapter 10 is one example of such a program.) INT 15-type VCPI programs require that you preallocate memory for them with a parameter on your HIMEM.SYS invocation, using the /INT15=*nnnn* switch. If you were planning to run an INT 15-type VCPI application that needed a megabyte of extended memory, for example, your HIMEM.SYS invocation in CONFIG.SYS would look like...

    device=c:\windows\himem.sys /int15=1024

For more information about HIMEM.SYS, see Chapter 10.

The DOS Protected Mode Interface (DPMI)

The next turn in the road for the DOS extender saga appeared with the advent of Windows 3.1. Windows uses a DOS extender, but—because it supports a multitasking operating system—can't just yield the command chair (ring 0). If a VCPI program asks the Windows multitasking engine to step aside for a while, the Windows multitasking engine essentially replies, "Are you crazy? I've got to manage these sessions, keep track of four programs printing at the same time...unless you can manage all these Windows programs, Mr. DOS program, I'm afraid I can't let you get to ring 0." Windows can't clear out memory in anticipation of the DOS program's load; if it did, Windows couldn't multitask.

So (getting back to the analogy of the industrial plant and its three managers) the next step was to teach all these managers how to share a desk—that is, to get all DOS extender programs to agree on how to address the GDT and LDT page tables, so that they could all have page tables in memory at the same time, allowing smooth multitasking of DOS extender applications and Windows. The resulting standard is called the DOS protected mode interface, or DPMI. The basic difference between Versions 3.0 and 3.4 of Lotus 1-2-3 is that 3.4 is DPMI compliant but 3.0 is VCPI compliant.

DPMI programs have two components: a DPMI server and a DPMI client. The *DPMI client* is the application program itself, which is written to operate in ring 3. The *DPMI server* is the ring 0 part, the part that actually allocates and deallocates memory. The client requests that the server allocate and deallocate memory; the server responds to those client requests. The way DPMI applications coexist is that each DPMI server must be willing to obey some well-defined client commands such as, again, "allocate memory" and "deallocate memory."

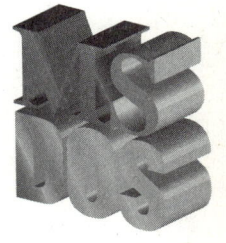

All DPMI servers should be indistinguishable, so that when a DPMI application loads, it first checks whether a DPMI server is already installed. If a DPMI server is already loaded, the DPMI server built with the application that's currently loading just doesn't bother loading. If a DPMI server is not currently in memory, the application's DPMI server takes up residence in ring 0, ready to serve the memory commands of any DPMI-aware application.

DPMI applications should run without trouble in a DOS box under Windows, provided that (1) you give them XMS memory in the PIF for the DPMI-compliant application, and (2) the vendor has implemented DPMI correctly. Not all software vendors implement DPMI completely correctly. Lotus is one example. Even though 1-2-3 version 3.1 is a DPMI-compliant application, and as such uses extended memory, it won't run properly unless you create an expanded memory page frame. Look for DOS extender applications to be DPMI-compliant. Borland's Paradox 4.0 is the DPMI-compliant version of Paradox, and the three big memory managers—EMM386, which ships with DOS 5.0 and Windows 3.1, QEMM-386 (from Quarterdeck), and 386 to the Max (from Qualitas)—are all working on DPMI compliance.

As time progresses, more and more DOS programs that use memory managers will switch to DPMI compliance, and so will run much more easily under Windows.

Understanding Addressing

Because XT-type machines are based on 8088/8086 chips, they cannot have extended memory. ATs and 386-based machines can. When you see your computer count up to 1024K, 2048K, 4096K, 8192K, or 16384K (the most common memory sizes) during the power-on self test, you know that it has some extended memory.

Let's take a simple example—an old 286 with 1024K of memory. The 1024K is RAM, all of which must be given addresses. You may recall from the earlier part of this chapter that the addresses from 0 to 640K are meant to be filled so that conventional memory space exists. Addresses 640K through 1024K must be left alone because they're intended for memory from other sources—the video board and add-

Understanding Extended Memory 473

in cards. Putting 640K of the 1024K in the 0-640K range leaves 1024K minus 640K, or 384K. Where does that memory get placed? In the extended memory addresses, making it extended memory.

You can see how it looks on our memory map, shown in figure 9.5.

I want to emphasize why the memory gets allocated this way—not to belabor the point, but because the subject causes a lot of confusion for users. This breaking up of memory perplexes some people. Here's further explanation.

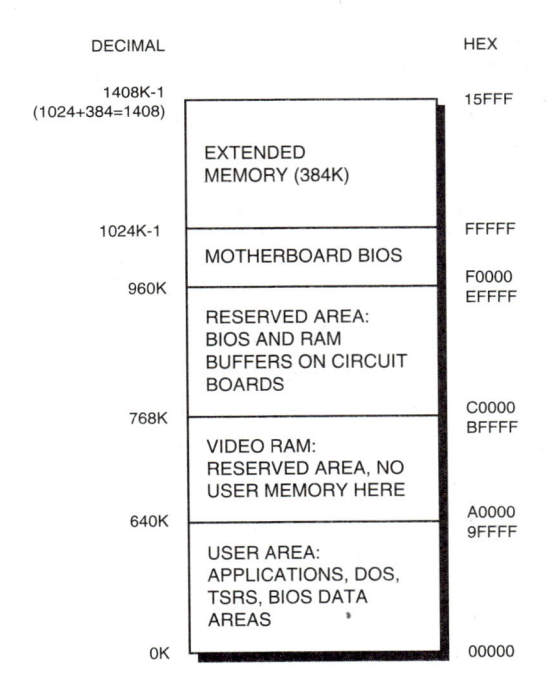

```
         DECIMAL                                    HEX
         1408K-1                                    15FFF
       (1024+384=1408)
                         ┌─────────────────────┐
                         │                     │
                         │   EXTENDED          │
                         │   MEMORY (384K)     │
                         │                     │
         1024K-1         │                     │   FFFFF
                         ├─────────────────────┤
                         │   MOTHERBOARD BIOS  │   F0000
         960K            │                     │   EFFFF
                         ├─────────────────────┤
                         │   RESERVED AREA:    │
                         │   BIOS AND RAM      │
                         │   BUFFERS ON CIRCUIT│
                         │   BOARDS            │
         768K            │                     │   C0000
                         ├─────────────────────┤   BFFFF
                         │   VIDEO RAM:        │
                         │   RESERVED AREA, NO │
                         │   USER MEMORY HERE  │
         640K            │                     │   A0000
                         ├─────────────────────┤   9FFFF
                         │   USER AREA:        │
                         │   APPLICATIONS, DOS,│
                         │   TSRS, BIOS DATA   │
                         │   AREAS             │
         0K              └─────────────────────┘   00000
```

Figure 9.5

Memory map of a PC with 1024K total memory: 640K conventional, 384K extended.

The key is to understand that there's a difference between memory and memory addresses. Remember my analogy, early in this chapter, between designing a computer and designing a town? Well, let's suppose that we're designing a town built (conveniently enough) on 1,024 one-acre lots. Suppose that we zone the first 640 lots for residential use, the next 128 for industrial, and the remaining 256 for commercial buildings. We now have addresses, purposes for those addresses, but nothing in those addresses. Sure, there's now a lot called "200 First Avenue," but it's only a muddy rectangle of ground. If you send mail there (that is, if you try to store data there), it just sits outside and rots.

After the town has been zoned, we start putting houses in the residential addresses—filling our PC with memory. But suppose that someone selling prefabricated houses shows up with 1024 houses? That's the situation a computer designer is faced with when building a computer with 1024K of RAM. First, she plunks down houses in the first 640 lots, filling the "conventional" addresses.

The zoning board (that is, the requirements of PC hardware compatibility) precludes one putting any of the houses in the top 384 addresses. (Here, the computer designer plays the roles of both the planning board and the prefabricated house vendor.) The top 384 lots do not have normal system RAM (houses) in them; rather, they have special RAM. On a PC, that area is filled in with some RAM physically located on the video board, and perhaps some ROM located on the motherboard or add-in boards. That, too, is worth stressing: the memory in the video area isn't taken from the system's main memory. When you buy a PC with 1024K of memory, none of that memory is ROMs or video RAM. A PC with 1024K of RAM actually has a fair amount more than 1024K of RAM, if you count the RAM on the video board and the ROMs and RAM buffers on the expansion boards. And that memory is not counted when your system does its power-up memory count. There is simply nowhere to put the extra 384 houses, which is why XTs and PCs (8088-based computers) don't have more than 640K of system RAM.

Now let's move along to the 286 and later chips. Because these chips have memory limitations of 16M or more, now we have to zone the addresses above 1024K. Continuing the town planning analogy, suppose that after our town has been operating for 30 years, a community springs up outside our original 1024 lots. We'd call that a suburb of the town; it might have a different tax rate, be governed differently, and have different levels of access to the privileges accorded town residents. Suburbanites might have to pay a fee to use the town parks, for example, whereas the town residents might be able to use the parks for free. So it is also with extended memory—the addresses above 1024K are not accessible to the vast majority of DOS programs, as you learned earlier in this discussion.

To return to the case of the vendor of prefab houses who shows up in our new town with 1,024 houses—again, she puts houses on the first

640 spaces, and is then told that she cannot put houses on the top 384 addresses. "What will I do with these extra 384 houses?" she wails. "Take them out to the suburbs," she's told. She puts the remaining 384 houses in the extended addresses, because the 384 addresses she skipped (from 640 to 1024) will be filled with buildings from another source.

Now, to get back to the original question: what's happening with a 286 computer that counts up to 1024K on power-up? First, understand that 1024K is a count only of program memory. More memory is in the computer—video RAM on the video board, system BIOS ROM on the motherboard, and ROMs and perhaps small RAM buffers on add-in cards in the system—but is not counted. The 1024K fills the first 640K. It cannot fill any of the addresses between 640K and 1024K, or the PC will have program memory in the same addresses as video memory or ROM. Just as you can't put two houses on the same lot, so also two separate memories wired to the same address would both malfunction. The extra 384K of RAM gets addressed starting at 1024K and going up to 1408K.

If you're still stuck, the next two figures may be of additional help. First, consider figure 9.6—the case of putting 1M of RAM into a 286-based system. On the left is the memory itself. On the right are the addresses on which we'll hang the memory. Figure 9.7 shows how you have to place the memory.

One more point hangs some people up: I've said that the reserved area from 640K to 1024K contains memory, but it's not completely full. Usually, plenty of unused addresses are between 768K and 1024K— a fact that created the memory manager market in the first place. Many people seem to feel that all of the addresses from 0 through 1024K must be filled by something before any addresses above 1024K can be filled. But that's not true. You could build a computer with 128K of conventional memory, video RAM between 640K and 768K, a few ROMs between 768K and 1024K, and 6M of extended memory above 1024K. (You'd have trouble finding software that would run on it, but you could do it.)

Extended memory is simple for programmers to use, provided that those programmers have a DOS extender or an operating environment that supports extended memory. The tremendous memory demands of today's programs make using extended memory a necessity for many programs built in the 90s. But extended memory wasn't always easy to work with (which leads to the following discussion of expanded memory).

Figure 9.6
The 286 memory allocation (before).

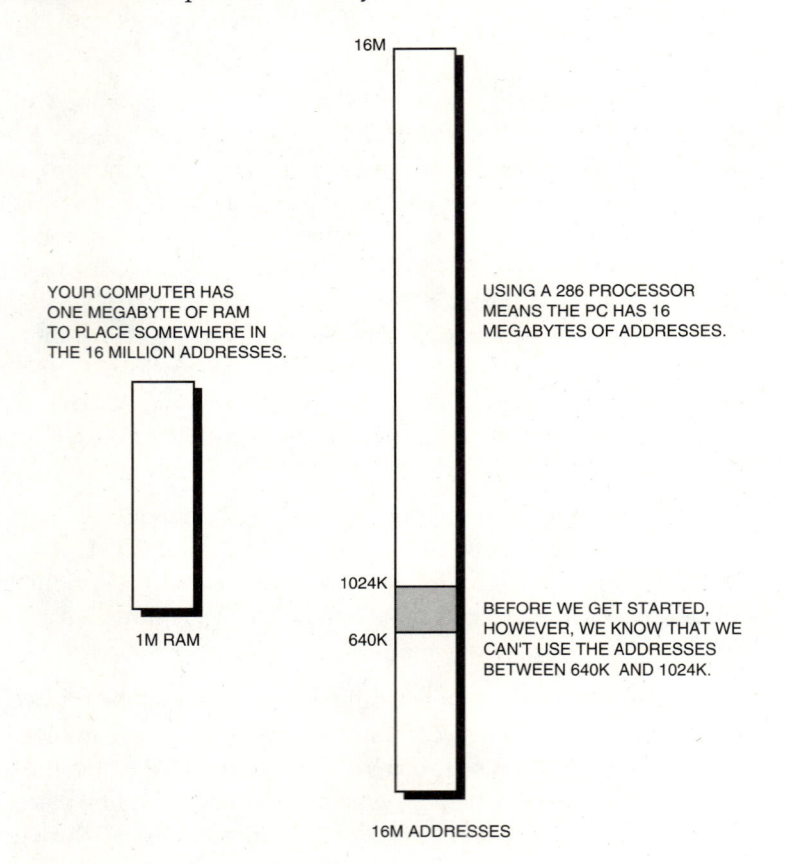

16M

YOUR COMPUTER HAS ONE MEGABYTE OF RAM TO PLACE SOMEWHERE IN THE 16 MILLION ADDRESSES.

USING A 286 PROCESSOR MEANS THE PC HAS 16 MEGABYTES OF ADDRESSES.

1M RAM

1024K
640K

BEFORE WE GET STARTED, HOWEVER, WE KNOW THAT WE CAN'T USE THE ADDRESSES BETWEEN 640K AND 1024K.

16M ADDRESSES

Memory: Expanded, LIM, EMS, and Paged

Expanded memory, intended to be a short-term solution to the RAM cram problem, turned out to be a long-term hassle. The story begins in 1985. At that time, the bestselling program of any kind on the planet was 1-2-3 Version 1A, a program that became popular because it was

Memory: Expanded, LIM, EMS, and Paged

fast and because it could use all 640K of the PC's memory. Because previous spreadsheets had been confined to 64K, 1-2-3 quickly became quite popular.

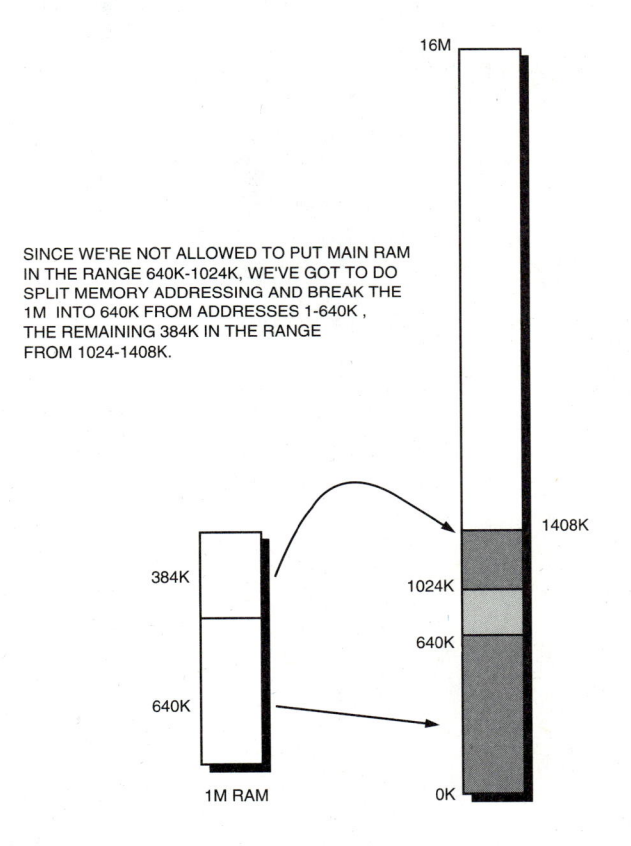

Figure 9.7

The 286 memory allocation (after).

SINCE WE'RE NOT ALLOWED TO PUT MAIN RAM IN THE RANGE 640K-1024K, WE'VE GOT TO DO SPLIT MEMORY ADDRESSING AND BREAK THE 1M INTO 640K FROM ADDRESSES 1-640K, THE REMAINING 384K IN THE RANGE FROM 1024-1408K.

In accordance with one of those Murphy's Laws that seems to dictate that there never is "enough" in the memory department, however, even 640K wasn't enough. People soon had spreadsheets that packed a 640K PC to the rafters. But memory constraint or not, 1-2-3 Version 1A was a hit.

The first Lotus product to use expanded memory was Symphony, but the first important product to use it was 1-2-3 Version 2.1. Since 2.1, all Lotus 2.x upgrades—2.2, 2.3, and 2.4—use expanded memory.

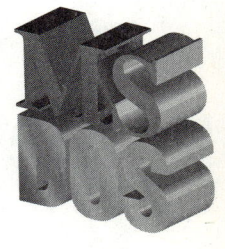

Chapter 9: Understanding PC Memory Types

> **AUTHOR'S NOTE**
>
> *When Lotus announced Version 2.0 of 1-2-3, there was a mad dash to get a copy. People who bought 1-2-3 Version 2.0 were disappointed, however, to find that this version took up more memory space than version 1A. Thus, any spreadsheets that packed the memory up to the 640K rafters—and there were plenty—would not run under 2.0 for love nor money. Lotus took a lot of flack over this, and so sought a short-term solution. (The long-term solution, in Lotus's eyes, was OS/2 1.0 and 1-2-3 Version 3.0, which was under development; they saw 1-2-3 Version 2.0 as just a way station.)*
>
> *In search of a short-term solution, Lotus called up Intel, the chip designers, and asked what could be done. Lotus and Intel developed a paged memory system (remember paging, in the video discussion?) they called "expanded memory." The solution involved buying a new kind of memory board, called an AboveBoard, that Intel built. (I'll explain, in a bit, the details of how it works.) Now, that board was of no value until you did two things, both having to do with software: first, you had to load a device driver (called EMM.SYS) that served as the manager of those pages of expanded memory—sort of a "reservations agent" for the expanded pages; and second, you had to find an application that knew how to use expanded memory.*
>
> *In the final days of the design of the expanded memory board, Microsoft got involved; the system became known as the "LIM" specification, referring to Lotus, Intel, and Microsoft. The original version, called LIM Version 3.2, was soon followed by LIM 4.0, which incorporated some improvements designed by AST into their clones of the AboveBoard, clones called the RAMPage board. (Get it? RAM ... page? Paging?) Because it is known also as the Expanded Memory Specification, or EMS, you'll hear expanded memory referred to in three ways: as "expanded" memory, "LIM" memory, or "EMS" memory.*

To summarize: Lotus, Intel, and Microsoft collaborated on a new kind of memory board, a hardware standard that allowed DOS programs access to more memory—8 megabytes under LIM 3.2, 32 megabytes under LIM 4.0. A reasonable question at this point is, "Why did they go to so much trouble? Why didn't they just use a DOS extender to give 1-2-3 access to extended memory?"

> *For most users, LIM memory is useful with Lotus 1-2-3 Version 2.x and WordPerfect Version 5.1. Both applications automatically use LIM if it is present, which gives them considerably more available memory. LIM usually is not required by those applications unless you're working with large data files.*

If you think about the time frame, you'll have the answer. Extended memory exists only on 286 and later computers. But 286 computers were scarce and expensive in 1985, and 386s didn't exist as commercial products until 1986. If Lotus had used a DOS extender, they would have solved the problem for upscale clients only, rather like a vendor today saying, "We've got the software you need, but it'll only run on a Pentium with 64 megabytes of RAM."

How does LIM work? Basically, the system doesn't view LIM memory as memory. All the PC knows is that "pages" of storage are available—16K-sized pages. LIM can support up to 2,000 of these pages, hence the 32M maximum size. Because LIM boards allocate 64K of memory—enough space for four pages—somewhere in the reserved area between 640K and 1024K, a program can manipulate up to four pages at a time. LIM is manipulated, then, by pulling in a page from LIM memory to the memory in the reserved area (this memory is called a "page frame," and moving data to and from LIM and page frames is called "paging"), reading and modifying the page frame, and possibly writing the page frame back to the LIM memory.

When a LIM-aware program like 1-2-3 wants to use some expanded memory, it does something like this:

1. The application asks whether an expanded memory manager is present. (It does this with a software interrupt, INT 67.)

2. If the expanded memory manager is present, 1-2-3 asks it how many pages of LIM are free.

3. The expanded memory manager tells 1-2-3 how many pages are unallocated.

4. 1-2-3 then asks the expanded memory manager to allocate all free pages to 1-2-3. That is not, by the way, the standard behavior of LIM-aware programs; 1-2-3 just happens to be a memory hog, and so grabs any available memory.

When 1-2-3 wants to use some of the LIM, it just tells the expanded memory manager to grab four pages from the LIM area and put them in the page frame. Then 1-2-3 can modify the page frame directly, because the address of the page frame is within the 1024K address space of the 8088. When those areas are full, 1-2-3 can tell the LIM board to whisk them back to the LIM area, get some more, and so on. As you may recall, this movement back and forth is called "paging."

In case you're wondering—yes, paging does take time. Expanded memory can be a trifle slow to use, but it's still much faster than reading and writing disk drives. And you'd probably agree that having some slower paged memory is better than having no memory at all. Even if you're willing to accept the speed cost, this is not a panacea: remember that only software written specially for the paged memory can use expanded memory. Many DOS applications can use LIM, but most cannot. As time goes by, fewer and fewer new applications will use LIM. Now, however, it's useful for your PC to support LIM.

On 8088 and most 80286 computers, you need a specific memory board (such as Intel's AboveBoard or the AST RAMPage cards) to support LIM. But as you'll discover in the next section, you can achieve LIM compatibility with just software on 386-type (and later) machines. A 386 can make extended memory behave from an application software's point of view; the extended memory looks like expanded memory. (Some 286s can do that also, but not many.)

Now that you've looked at conventional, video, reserved, extended, and expanded memory, here are the highlights of what you've learned so far:

✔ **Conventional Memory**

   Available to all PCs

   Limited to 640K by virtue of the video memory's location

   Virtually every program can use this memory

   By default, DOS, device drivers, and TSRs load in conventional memory

Memory: Expanded, LIM, EMS, and Paged

✔ **Video RAM**

  Physically located on the video board

  Uses paging to cram a lot of video memory into a small number of addresses

  Ranges from 640K through 768K

✔ **Reserved Area**

  Addresses used for ROMs, and in particular for BIOS ROM

  On some boards, a small amount of RAM buffer fits in this space

✔ **Extended Memory**

  Only possible with machines based on 286 and later chips; not possible with XTs

  Only a subset of DOS programs (such as 1-2-3 Version 3.4 and Harvard Graphics 3.0) can use it; these programs must use DOS extenders

  Used by Windows 3.1, OS/2, UNIX

✔ **Expanded Memory**

  Also called LIM (Lotus-Intel-Microsoft) memory or EMS (Expanded Memory Specification) memory

  Can be used with any PC machine: PCs, XTs, and ATs

  Useful under DOS with programs that can use it, such as Lotus Version 2.x and WordPerfect 5.1

  All 386+ computers (and a few 286-based machines) can make their extended memory act like expanded memory

> *If you're having trouble remembering which memory is extended and which is expanded, try this trick: I always remember extended versus expanded by pronouncing the latter "exPanded" to remind me that it is "Paged."*

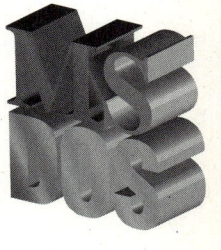

Summary

This chapter explained the different kinds of memory on your PC. The knowledge gained here will stand you in good stead in the following chapter, where you'll learn how to use your DOS 6.2 memory manager to put your memory to work.

MS-DOS

MS
DOS

CHAPTER 10

Using the DOS 6.2 Memory Manager

by Mark Minasi

The last chapter may have contained technical detail that seemed a bit daunting, but in this chapter, you see why you needed last chapter's information. In this chapter, you use your knowledge about memory as a foundation as you learn how to use a memory manager—in particular, the DOS 6.2 memory manager. The DOS 6.2 memory manager is a very good memory manager and can do 95 percent of what you need a manager for; additionally, if you own DOS 6.2 , the memory manager is free. Some third-party memory managers are more powerful than DOS's memory manager, and you'll look at them in Chapter 13. Just because some memory managers have some features that DOS 6.2 lacks, however, don't feel shortchanged if you use DOS 6.2 's memory manager; you'll find that if you want to maintain maximum compatibility with major PC software, you usually can't use the really high-tech features of the third-party memory managers anyway.

What Can Memory Managers Do for You?

The Intel 80386 programming manual is over 300 pages long. In that manual is a 12-page section that describes with little fanfare all the things that the 386 can do to manage memory.

Just 12 pages. But those 12 pages have changed the world. Without the capabilities described in those 12 pages, it would be impossible to do any of the things you read about in this chapter; those 12 pages are the acorn from which has sprung the oak of the memory-management business today. Just 12 pages have been parleyed into six major features, available to a lesser or greater degree in memory managers today. Memory managers can do the following things:

- ✔ Create and utilize the High Memory Area (HMA), just above the 1024K address range.

- ✔ Create and utilize Upper Memory Blocks (UMBs), which lie between 640K and 1024K—spaces the memory manager uses for TSR and device-driver programs, moving them out of the precious 640K of conventional memory to free more space for applications programs.

- ✔ Convert extended memory to expanded memory, making it possible for applications that rely on expanded memory to run on systems that only have extended memory.

- ✔ Maintain both extended (XMS) and expanded (EMS) memory managers so that more than one program can utilize these memory types without conflict.

- ✔ Create *shadow RAM* whereby ROMs are copied to RAM to improve the speed of your computer.

✔ Rearrange the address order of memory in your PC so that faster memory appears in lower addresses, effectively "sorting" memory.

✔ Fill in any empty addresses below 640K with memory taken from extended memory to "backfill" the low 640K.

Just because all these features exist doesn't mean I recommend you use them; in fact, I suggest that you restrict yourself to using only the first four. In this chapter, you learn more about each of these features and how to use them with the DOS 6.2 memory manager, where possible.

Taking a Few Preparatory Steps

Before you start managing memory, we have to lay some groundwork, and I have to warn you about a few things. Most of the actual "work" of memory management involves modifying the AUTOEXEC.BAT and CONFIG.SYS files; because those files are extremely important to your system, it is imperative that you take a few steps to protect them.

If you're already comfortable with how to make a bootable floppy and use the F5 and F8 keys to control how your system boots, then skip this section. But otherwise, you should be prepared to do three things:

1. Back up the existing AUTOEXEC.BAT and CONFIG.SYS files. If you're not sure how to do that, the following two commands do the job:

    ```
    COPY C:\AUTOEXEC.BAT C:\AUTOEXEC.BEF
    COPY C:\CONFIG.SYS C:\CONFIG.BEF
    ```

    Then, any time you want to restore AUTOEXEC.BAT and CONFIG.SYS to their original state, just reverse the process, copying the BEF files (BEF for *before*) like this:

    ```
    COPY C:\AUTOEXEC.BEF C:\AUTOEXEC.BAT
    COPY C:\CONFIG.BEF C:\CONFIG.SYS
    ```

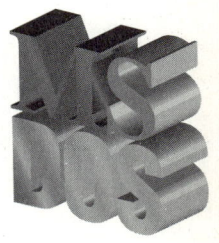

2. Understand how to use the Shift, F5, and F8 keys to control how your system boots.

   If you want your system to boot and bypass CONFIG.SYS altogether, press Shift or F5 when the Loading MS-DOS... message appears. You don't have to hold it, just press and release one of those keys when the Loading... message appears. Your system skips all the CONFIG.SYS commands, going right to the AUTOEXEC.BAT commands.

   If you want DOS to pause at each line in CONFIG.SYS, displaying the line and asking if you want to execute that line, press F8 when the Loading MS-DOS... message appears. In this way you can check for mistyped commands in CONFIG.SYS. Press Y if you want the line executed, or N if you want DOS to skip that line. *For more information about using the Clean Boot feature from DOS 6.2, see Chapter 17.*

3. Make a boot floppy in case you change AUTOEXEC.BAT or CONFIG.SYS so that your system becomes nonbootable.

> *To make a bootable floppy disk, get a blank disk (or one that doesn't contain any data you care about) and put it in drive A. It has to go in drive A because that's the boot floppy drive. Some PCs can boot from drive B, but they're rare. Then type...*
>
> **FORMAT A: /S**
>
> *The /S switch makes the disk bootable. After the disk is formatted, type...*
>
> **COPY C:\CONFIG.SYS A:**
>
> *...and press Enter to copy the CONFIG.SYS file to the floppy. Do the same with the AUTOEXEC.BAT file:*
>
> **COPY C:\AUTOEXEC.BAT A:**
>
> *Then test the boot disk by rebooting with the floppy in drive A. If the system boots without trouble, you have a good boot disk. Write-protect it and put it aside just in case you need it.*

You may think that these three steps are overly risk-averse, and you may feel you can move on in this text without going to the trouble of backing up AUTOEXEC.BAT and CONFIG.SYS; you may also think that formatting a floppy and getting a boot disk ready is an unnecessary step you can easily skip. But don't skip those steps! Believe me, at some point you'll render your system nonbootable when you mess around with a memory manager. And then you'll be glad you have a bootable floppy.

Setting Up a Basic Configuration

Let's start examining memory management with a simple DOS configuration. This configuration provides a starting point, an initial DOS configuration we can improve with memory management. If you want to follow along with the examples in this chapter, it's best for you and me to work from roughly the same CONFIG.SYS and AUTOEXEC.BAT; that way, your screens look basically the same as mine. That's basically the same—your computer is almost certainly different than mine, so the output differs somewhat, but don't worry; you can't duplicate my results exactly, nor do you need to.

You'll meet two important programs that comprise the bulk of the DOS memory manager, files named HIMEM.SYS and EMM386.EXE. I assume you've installed your DOS files to the C:\DOS drive and directory; if your files are in a different location, make the adjustments to my references as you go. If you use Windows, you'll find that Windows also contains files named HIMEM.SYS and EMM386.EXE. Should you use the HIMEM.SYS and EMM386.EXE that ship with Windows or DOS? Use the newest files. At the time of DOS 6.2's release, the HIMEM.SYS and EMM386.EXE that came with DOS were newer (and therefore more desirable for use), so use them. However, by the time you read this, an even newer set of memory-manager files may be shipping with a new version of Windows. Check the dates on HIMEM.SYS and EMM386.EXE and use the most recent ones.

> **NOTE:** If you use Compaq DOS, note that Compaq renames HIMEM.SYS to HIMEM.EXE; EMM386.EXE is named CEMM.EXE. Treat the two files exactly as described in this book, but just remember to call them by their Compaq names or DOS won't find them. If you end up using the Windows version of HIMEM.SYS instead of the DOS HIMEM program, you can use Windows HIMEM.SYS on the Compaq without experiencing any trouble.

The starter CONFIG.SYS and AUTOEXEC.BAT we'll work from have a few memory-resident programs. A few of these programs will be helpful in explaining what a memory manager does because they take up RAM that the memory manager seeks to free up.

Preparing a Starter AUTOEXEC.BAT and CONFIG.SYS

We start with a fairly minimal CONFIG.SYS and AUTOEXEC.BAT. Later, we add a few memory-resident programs to see how to load them high. The starter files include the video-screen driver ANSI.SYS. ANSI.SYS was pretty useless before DOS 5 but has picked up a few uses in later versions of DOS. One value of ANSI.SYS is that you can shift the video screen to 50-line mode. SETVER is included as well, even though it's not of much value. Because the DOS installation program automatically includes it in CONFIG.SYS, however, we'll assume the device driver is in CONFIG.SYS and use it in the examples. Your CONFIG.SYS should look like this:

```
BUFFERS=30
FILES=60
DEVICE=C:\DOS\SETVER.EXE
DEVICE=C:\DOS\ANSI.SYS
SHELL=C:\DOS\COMMAND.COM C:\DOS\ /P /E:2048
```

The SHELL= statement tells DOS that COMMAND.COM is in the C:\DOS subdirectory. The /e:2048 sets the size of a memory area called the environment. *You learned about the environment in Chapter 2;* you learn more about it in the chapters on batch files and MultiConfig. FILES is set to 60 for Windows; and BUFFERS is set to 30 (you get fewer Windows "GP Fault" error messages with higher FILES numbers). AUTOEXEC.BAT also is simple, but includes a few TSRs so that we can load them high later. AUTOEXEC.BAT looks like this:

```
PROMPT $p$g
PATH C:\DOS;C:\UTILS
DOSKEY /BUFSIZE=30000
MOUSE
VSAFE
```

PROMPT and PATH are familiar commands to you by now. DOSKEY is a command-history program that recalls all keyboard commands from the time you booted up to now. BUFSIZE=30000 is an option that makes DOSKEY take up more memory space than it usually does. I'm doing that because I want to construct a "before" picture that's memory constrained so that we can use the DOS 6.2 memory manager to recover a large amount of memory space. I'm restricting the examples to programs that are fairly common so that you can follow along. In real life, you'll probably have some fairly hefty network drivers that chew up tons of memory; think of the large buffer size on DOSKEY as being a simulation of that. MOUSE loads the mouse driver; in my case, it's Version 8.20 of the Microsoft Mouse driver, the driver that ships with DOS 6.2. VSAFE is the DOS 6.2 virus-shield program.

Monitoring Memory with MEM

Your goal in managing memory is to move as many programs as possible out of the low 640K of memory and into some other area of memory. To do that, you need a tool that enables you to examine memory, to find out what programs are loaded in memory and taking up space, how much space they take up, and exactly where in memory they are loaded. The tool to do that is a DOS utility called MEM.

From the command prompt, just type **MEM** to see a screen like the one in figure 10.1. What you see in this simple MEM output (you learn about other MEM options later) is that total conventional memory is 639K.

Chapter 10: *Using the DOS 6.2 Memory Manager*

Figure 10.1

MEM output before memory management.

```
C:\>mem

Memory Type         Total  =   Used   +   Free
----------------   -------    -------    -------
Conventional         639K       172K       467K
Upper                  0K         0K         0K
Adapter RAM/ROM      385K       385K         0K
Extended (XMS)     19456K     19456K         0K
Expanded (EMS)         0K         0K         0K
                   -------    -------    -------
Total memory       20480K     20013K       467K

Total under 1 MB     639K       172K       467K

Largest executable program size      467K   (478256 bytes)
Largest free upper memory block        0K        (0 bytes)
The high memory area is available.
C:\>
```

The DOS 6 MEM command gave us a new look from the DOS 5 MEM command, but DOS 6.2 gives us a newer look still—it now uses a comma to separate numbers greater than one thousand. In the preceding MEM listing, for example, DOS 6.2 displays the Total memory line as:

```
Total memory     20,480K    20,013K    467K
```

Conventional memory isn't a full 640K because this computer, like many others, reserves the top 1K of the conventional area for an extended BIOS data area. It's a pain, but a lot of computers nowadays do it. There's usually nothing that you can do about it.

The conventional memory line in the MEM output says that 467K of conventional memory is free. It reports 385K of adapter RAM/ROM, which isn't necessarily adapter ROM and RAM; what it really means is "memory the memory manager isn't using right now." Until you load a memory manager and tell it how to go forth and conquer the nooks and crannies in memory, DOS only sees the 639K of conventional memory; the rest is essentially invisible to DOS and gets the generic name *adapter RAM/ROM*.

> **NOTE:** *Adapter RAM/ROM is the sum of excluded UMB space, memory used by BIOS and adapter cards, and expanded memory services (EMS) page frame(s). You should take the Adapter RAM/ROM line with a grain (or even a bucket) of salt. In the original design (early betas), this line was supposed to reflect the amount of memory between 640K and 1M that had been converted to UMBs. If MEM reported 256K of upper memory, for example, it therefore reported 128K of Adapter RAM/ROM.*
>
> *The final release of DOS 6 doesn't do this, however. MEM now looks at the amount of RAM you have, rounds up the answer to the nearest megabyte, if it isn't an exact multiple of one megabyte, and places the difference on the Adapter RAM/ROM line. So, what's the point? Good question!*

MEM also reports about 19M of XMS memory. That's not really true, strictly speaking. Although there is certainly 19M of extended memory on the example computer, remember that extended memory is different than XMS memory. XMS memory is extended memory being managed by an XMS memory manager. Because we haven't loaded an XMS memory manager yet, there is no XMS memory. I think what the MEM output means to say is that there are 19-plus megabytes of RAM that could be managed by an XMS manager. Notice also that MEM not only reports more than 19M of XMS memory, it also claims that all that memory is used. Both pieces of information are inaccurate, but don't let that worry you. MEM is confused because we haven't loaded a memory manager yet, I suppose. Finally, there is no expanded memory because we haven't loaded a memory manager that provides LIM memory yet.

MEM reports 172K of memory used. Used by what? You can find more in-depth information about what's using memory with MEM's /C parameter. MEM/C produces a lot of output, so I'll utilize a very handy new parameter that cropped up with DOS 6.2 : /P; /P is short for *pause* because it makes DOS pause after displaying each screen of

Chapter 10: *Using the DOS 6.2 Memory Manager*

information. You see the first screen's output in figure 10.2. We don't need the second screen, because it doesn't contain information relevant to the low 640K of memory.

Figure 10.2
The first part of the MEM/C output before activating a memory manager.

```
Modules using memory below 1 MB:

Name           Total        =    Conventional   +    Upper Memory
────────────────────────────────────────────────────────────────────
MSDOS          68445  (67K)       68445  (67K)         0     (0K)
SETVER           672   (1K)         672   (1K)         0     (0K)
ANSI            4208   (4K)        4208   (4K)         0     (0K)
COMMAND         6784   (7K)        6784   (7K)         0     (0K)
VSAFE          44960  (44K)       44960  (44K)         0     (0K)
DOSKEY         33632  (33K)       33632  (33K)         0     (0K)
MOUSE          17296  (17K)       17296  (17K)         0     (0K)
Free          478368 (467K)      478368 (467K)         0     (0K)

Memory Summary:

Type of Memory      Total         =      Used        +      Free
────────────────────────────────────────────────────────────────────
Conventional       654336  (639K)      175968 (172K)      478368 (467K)
Upper                   0    (0K)           0   (0K)           0   (0K)
Adapter RAM/ROM    394240  (385K)      394240 (385K)           0   (0K)
Extended (XMS)   19922944 (19456K)   19922944 (19456K)         0   (0K)
Expanded (EMS)          0    (0K)           0   (0K)           0   (0K)

Press any key to continue . . .
```

MEM/C gives the same information you saw with MEM but with some detail. The top part of the output lists the programs loaded in memory-MSDOS, SETVER, ANSI, COMMAND, VSAFE, DOSKEY, and MOUSE. Notice that the TSRs are not reported in exactly the same order in which you loaded them. Next to each program is the total memory they take up, a report of how much conventional memory they take up, and finally how much upper memory they take up. The upper-memory numbers are all zero at the moment, so don't worry about them for a while.

Look at the Conventional column; you see that conventional memory is being taken up by first DOS itself (67K), then by SETVER (1K) and ANSI (4K), and then by COMMAND.COM (7K). Notice that device drivers load before COMMAND.COM, which in turn loads before TSRs. VSAFE comes after COMMAND, weighing in at 44K, followed by DOSKEY (33K) and the mouse driver (17K). The extended memory numbers are bogus, as before.

That's the lay of the land in memory before memory management. Now let's start installing the memory manager.

Reducing DOS Memory Requirements before the Memory Manager

You can increase the amount of free space under DOS by a bit even before you load a memory manager by reducing these four numbers:

- The size of the environment in the SHELL statement
- The number of BUFFERS=
- The number of FILES=
- The number of STACKS=

> **NOTE:** *Many people (including me) use values for all four that are probably larger than necessary, forcing DOS to waste some memory space in the bottom 640K. The reason we do it is simple: it makes Windows more stable. That sounds a bit nebulous—"it makes Windows more stable"—but it's advice you hear from many knowledgeable people, some of them at Microsoft. Windows can be flaky and we crank up these values to put a cushion between DOS and Windows. That way, when Windows ventures into parts of memory into which it should not tread, it treads on expendable parts of memory. I know that this sounds shaky, but from an empirical point of view, it works.*

If you don't run Windows, or if you're willing to live dangerously, you can adjust these values downward. The environment value is set with the /e: parameter in the SHELL statement in CONFIG.SYS; a value of 2048 is much too big for normal use; 512 is fine and saves 1.5K of memory. Each time you reduce the number of buffers by 1, you reclaim 524 bytes of RAM. Each file handle takes up 48 bytes of memory. And the size taken up by the STACKS command can be computed by multiplying the number of stacks (the first number) by the size of each stack (the second number). For example, Windows automatically puts the line STACKS=9,256 into your CONFIG.SYS; that uses 9 times 256 bytes, or 2305 bytes.

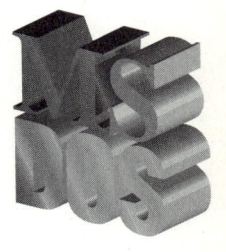

Even better, if you keep the FILES and BUFFERS values low enough, the DOS memory manager can move them out of the low 640K altogether; read on.

Understanding the High Memory Area (HMA)

Chapter 9 explained that the 286 and later chips have the tremendous capability to access memory beyond 1024K, but that this extended memory requires special programming to use the CPU's protected mode. Because the vast majority of DOS programs are not written to use protected mode (those that are, recall, are built with programming tools called DOS extenders), it may seem there's nothing more to do if you need more memory. It's not quite the end of the story, however; a few tricks let you claw a few K back from the clutches of protected mode. The first trick involves an area called the High Memory Area.

What Is the HMA?

The first trick comes from a bug in the design of the 286 and later chips. You may recall that in *real mode*—the mode the 286 uses when running DOS—the 286 can only address 1024K of memory. That's not the whole story, actually; a 286 can access not only 1024K of memory in real mode, it can access almost another 64K, raising the roof to 1088K. That extra 64K is taken from extended memory. That means that the example cited in Chapter 9 of a 286-based computer with 1M of RAM (which had 640K of conventional memory and 384K of extended memory) would have a new memory map like the one shown in figure 10.3.

The discovery of 64K of "new" memory isn't as wonderful as it might sound; that 64K lives fairly far from the rest of the DOS applications. DOS applications generally need conventional memory to be contiguous; dangle the 64K in the HMA under Word's nose, for example, and it can't use it. You can't offer most DOS programs a bunch of scattered and fragmented memory. In general, all DOS programs, both applications and utilities, prefer to load all in one place. As with the case of extended and expanded memory, we see that merely having a kind of memory available isn't much use without programs that can utilize that kind of memory. To use the HMA, you need programs written specifically to use the HMA; you can't just load anything into it. Additionally, you can load only one program into the HMA, so you're wise to find a program whose size is around 64K; otherwise, much of the HMA is wasted space. Before the release of DOS 5 in June 1991, only a handful of programs could load into the HMA.

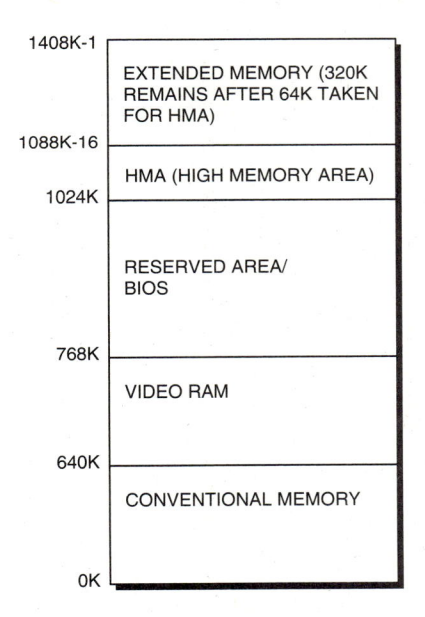

```
1408K-1  ┌─────────────────────────┐
         │ EXTENDED MEMORY (320K   │
         │ REMAINS AFTER 64K TAKEN │
         │ FOR HMA)                │
1088K-16 ├─────────────────────────┤
         │ HMA (HIGH MEMORY AREA)  │
1024K    ├─────────────────────────┤
         │                         │
         │ RESERVED AREA/          │
         │ BIOS                    │
         │                         │
768K     ├─────────────────────────┤
         │                         │
         │ VIDEO RAM               │
640K     ├─────────────────────────┤
         │                         │
         │ CONVENTIONAL MEMORY     │
         │                         │
         │                         │
0K       └─────────────────────────┘
```

Figure 10.3

A memory map of computer with 1M of RAM, showing the location of the HMA.

If you run DOS 6.2 (or DOS 5 for that matter), you can put most of DOS into the HMA to leave more conventional memory for normal DOS applications. To get the benefits of an HMA, of course, you need a computer with at least 64K of extended memory—meaning that it has to be a 286 or better to use this feature of DOS 6.2.

After you load DOS into the HMA—you see how to do that in just a moment—you see quite a change in free memory. Figure 10.4, for example, shows what memory might look like on a 1M PC before loading DOS high. DOS takes up about 70K of RAM. Create the HMA and load most of DOS into it (not all of DOS can load into the HMA), and you have a situation like the one in figure 10.5.

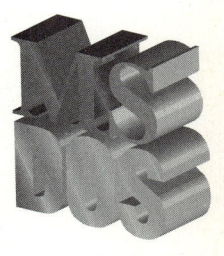

Chapter 10: *Using the DOS 6.2 Memory Manager*

About 52K of DOS moves from conventional memory to the HMA. This is a simple step; the really nice part about loading DOS high is that you can do it on a 286-based computer; most of the remaining memory-manager features are impossible on 286 computers.

Figure 10.4
Free DOS conventional memory before loading DOS into the HMA.

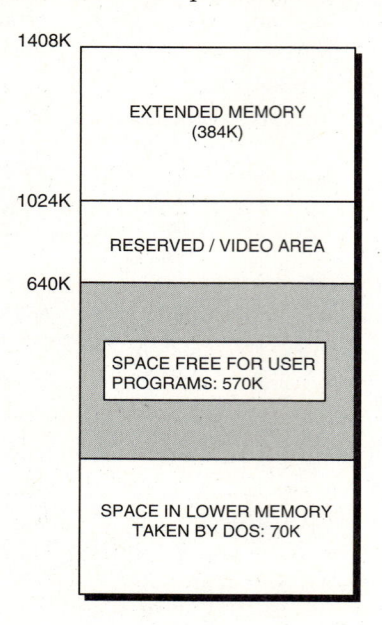

```
1408K ┌─────────────────────────┐
      │                         │
      │   EXTENDED MEMORY       │
      │        (384K)           │
      │                         │
1024K ├─────────────────────────┤
      │   RESERVED / VIDEO AREA │
 640K ├─────────────────────────┤
      │  ┌───────────────────┐  │
      │  │ SPACE FREE FOR USER│ │
      │  │ PROGRAMS: 570K    │  │
      │  └───────────────────┘  │
      │                         │
      │                         │
      │  SPACE IN LOWER MEMORY  │
      │  TAKEN BY DOS: 70K      │
      └─────────────────────────┘
```

Activating the HMA

Assuming that you have a 286 CPU or better and at least 64K of extended memory, loading DOS 6.2 high is simple. Just add these two lines to CONFIG.SYS:

```
DEVICE=C:\DOS\HIMEM.SYS
DOS=HIGH
```

By the way, if you've got Compaq DOS, recall that the file's name is HIMEM.EXE, not HIMEM.SYS.

Put the HIMEM statement at the beginning of CONFIG.SYS; any subsequent memory-management statements must follow this statement.

The `DOS=HIGH` statement can go anywhere in CONFIG.SYS, but I usually put it a line or two after the HIMEM.SYS invocation. Later in this chapter, you see that another memory-management program follows, one called EMM386.EXE; I keep all three of those statements close together in CONFIG.SYS, but HIMEM goes first.

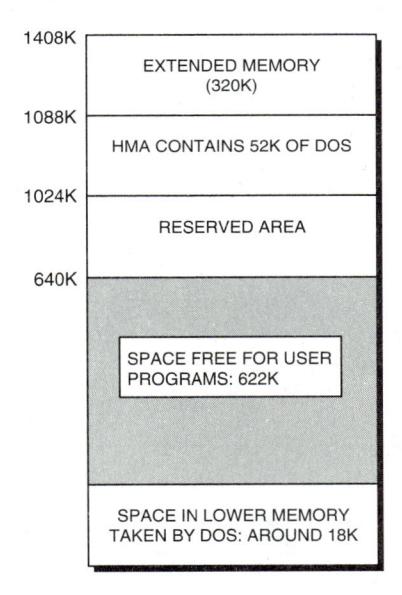

Figure 10.5

Free DOS conventional memory after loading DOS into the HMA.

```
1408K ┌─────────────────────────┐
      │   EXTENDED MEMORY       │
      │       (320K)            │
1088K ├─────────────────────────┤
      │ HMA CONTAINS 52K OF DOS │
1024K ├─────────────────────────┤
      │    RESERVED AREA        │
 640K ├─────────────────────────┤
      │                         │
      │  SPACE FREE FOR USER    │
      │   PROGRAMS: 622K        │
      │                         │
      ├─────────────────────────┤
      │  SPACE IN LOWER MEMORY  │
      │ TAKEN BY DOS: AROUND 18K│
      └─────────────────────────┘
```

Loading FILES and BUFFERS into the HMA

Recall that the value of the FILES and BUFFERS statements affects the size of DOS. Both the file handles and the buffers can load in the HMA, provided there's enough space for them—and that makes things a bit complex. DOS insists on loading all the BUFFERS high or none of them; it insists on loading all the file handles high or none of them. You can discover this for yourself with a little experimentation.

Chapter 10: *Using the DOS 6.2 Memory Manager*

The starter CONFIG.SYS, when modified to load DOS high, looks like the following:

```
DEVICE=C:\DOS\HIMEM.SYS
DOS=HIGH
BUFFERS=30
FILES=60
DEVICE=C:\DOS\SETVER.EXE
DEVICE=C:\DOS\ANSI.SYS
SHELL=C:\DOS\COMMAND.COM C:\DOS\ /P /E:2048
```

The resulting output from MEM/C looks like figures 10.6 and 10.7.

Figure 10.6

The output from MEM/C after loading DOS high (part 1).

```
Modules using memory below 1 MB:

Name           Total        =   Conventional   +   Upper Memory

MSDOS         16077  (16K)       16077  (16K)       0    (0K)
HIMEM          1104   (1K)        1104   (1K)       0    (0K)
SETVER          672   (1K)         672   (1K)       0    (0K)
ANSI           4208   (4K)        4208   (4K)       0    (0K)
COMMAND        4704   (5K)        4704   (5K)       0    (0K)
VSAFE         22848  (22K)       22848  (22K)       0    (0K)
DOSKEY        33632  (33K)       33632  (33K)       0    (0K)
MOUSE         17296  (17K)       17296  (17K)       0    (0K)
Free         553840 (541K)      553840 (541K)       0    (0K)

Memory Summary:

Type of Memory       Total       =      Used      +      Free

Conventional        654336  (639K)     100496  (98K)     553840 (541K)
Upper                    0    (0K)          0   (0K)          0   (0K)
Adapter RAM/ROM          0    (0K)          0   (0K)          0   (0K)
Extended (XMS)    20317184 (19841K)    221184 (216K)   20096000 (19625K)
Expanded (EMS)           0    (0K)          0   (0K)          0   (0K)
Press any key to continue . . .
```

Figure 10.7

The output from MEM/C after loading DOS high (part 2).

```
VSAFE         22848  (22K)       22848  (22K)       0    (0K)
DOSKEY        33632  (33K)       33632  (33K)       0    (0K)
MOUSE         17296  (17K)       17296  (17K)       0    (0K)
Free         553840 (541K)      553840 (541K)       0    (0K)

Memory Summary:

Type of Memory       Total       =      Used      +      Free

Conventional        654336  (639K)     100496  (98K)     553840 (541K)
Upper                    0    (0K)          0   (0K)          0   (0K)
Adapter RAM/ROM          0    (0K)          0   (0K)          0   (0K)
Extended (XMS)    20317184 (19841K)    221184 (216K)   20096000 (19625K)
Expanded (EMS)           0    (0K)          0   (0K)          0   (0K)
Press any key to continue . . .

Total memory      20971520 (20480K)    321680 (314K)   20649840 (20166K)

Total under 1 MB    654336  (639K)     100496  (98K)     553840  (541K)

Largest executable program size           553728 (541K)
Largest free upper memory block                0   (0K)
MS-DOS is resident in the high memory area.
C:\>
```

Understanding the High Memory Area (HMA)

You can see that DOS's use of conventional memory has dropped to 16K, a 51K improvement. There's a new program loaded—HIMEM.SYS—that takes up 1K. COMMAND.COM also has dropped in size from 7K to 5K, a bonus from the memory manager. Notice the last line of the second part of the MEM output: `MS-DOS is resident in high memory area`. That's a confirmation that what you wanted DOS to do, it did.

Did DOS load all the buffers high or low? MEM does not report directly where the buffers ended up, but a little experimentation shows where they are. I tried some different values for `BUFFERS=` in CONFIG.SYS and got quite different results. Up to and including `BUFFERS=45`, DOS took 16253 bytes. But at `BUFFERS=46`, DOS jumped from 16K in size to over 40K in size. Obviously, the 46th buffer didn't take up over 24K of space; it was the buffer that made all the buffers together too large to fit in the HMA, causing them all to move down to conventional memory.

> *TIP: If you use the SMARTDRV.EXE disk-cache program that comes with DOS, you can drop the number of buffers to 10 and see no performance decrease.*

Don't misread me: I didn't tell you to keep `BUFFERS=` below 46; there's nothing magic about the 46th buffer—the magic number happened to be 46 on my system because of my FILES and other values. It's worth taking a minute or two and experimenting with your system to find out how high you can set the BUFFERS value before all the buffers tumble into conventional memory. You find the same behavior for the FILES value.

Using HIMEM.SYS as an XMS Manager

Recall from Chapter 9 that programs share extended memory using the XMS standard, a standard whereby a device driver (the XMS manager) serves as a "clearinghouse" for requests from programs that can use extended memory, a clearinghouse that must never give out the same section of memory to two different programs lest they crash each other. HIMEM.SYS is an XMS manager. Look back at figure 10.7 to see that MEM reports about 20M of RAM available in the form of XMS memory.

Recall also that a few older programs do not use XMS to access extended memory; they instead use BIOS interrupt vector INT15 to transfer data to and from extended memory. *Refer to Chapters 2 and 9 for more about interrupt vectors.* Programs that use INT15 in general can't coexist with XMS programs; because they are unaware of XMS, they run roughshod over memory that XMS tries to manage. You can get XMS programs to live with INT15 programs with an option on the HIMEM.SYS driver. Suppose that you have an INT15 program that needs 1024K of extended memory. You make both the INT15 program and the XMS programs happy by setting aside 1024K for the INT15 program; the rest goes to the XMS programs. You set aside the 1024K with the /INT15= parameter on HIMEM.SYS, making the HIMEM.SYS invocation look like this:

```
DEVICE=C:\DOS\HIMEM.SYS /INT15=1024
```

Don't use the /INT15 parameter unless you're sure you need it; in this example, the 1024K of memory is now denied to Windows or other XMS programs.

AUTHOR'S NOTE

There is a side effect from using the old INT15 programs. Dozens of old programs were written to be PC "status checkers"—programs that report how many floppy drives you have, how large a hard disk, how much memory, and so on. Most of them also report the amount of expanded and extended memory on your system. Where do they get this information? The expanded-memory number is easy to come by: the programs test to see whether there's an expanded memory manager present in memory; if there is, the status program interrogates the manager about how much expanded memory there is.

To find out how much extended memory is on a system, some status programs do the same thing for extended memory as they do for expanded memory: look around for an XMS manager and query it if

it is present. Because XMS hasn't been around for that many years, older status checkers don't use XMS to find out how much extended memory is on a system; instead, they use INT15.

One of the things that HIMEM.SYS tries to protect the system from is old INT15 programs because they can wreak havoc on an XMS system. As a result, HIMEM.SYS intercepts all incoming INT15 calls in an effort to nip INT15 programs in the bud. When an INT15 program queries the system to find out how much extended memory is in the system, HIMEM.SYS intercepts the call, returning the message "there's no extended memory on this system." (There's an exception to this if you've used the /INT15 option.) This arrangement means that an older PC status checker may report that there is no extended memory if HIMEM.SYS is loaded. Don't worry about it if you see something like that—it just means that progress has left your status checker behind.

For those interested in some more details about how INT15 worked, here are the specifics: The earliest programs that used extended memory did it with two programs built right into the BIOS on a 286 or advanced computer: Move_Block and Determine_Memory_Size, known to programmers as INT15 functions 87 and 88, respectively. The Determine_Memory_Size function counts the amount of extended memory in the system by looking at the "total extended memory found" area created by the BIOS when the computer does the Power On Self Test (POST). A program then used extended memory by preparing the data it wanted to move to extended memory in a block of conventional memory, and then moved the data to some arbitrary extended-memory location with INT15/87. INT15/87 can also move data from extended memory back to conventional, as you probably expected. These two commands—"How much extended memory do I have?" and "Please move this data to or from extended memory."—are the basis of older programs like VDISK.SYS, the first group of programs that addressed extended memory in any way.

Programs don't still use INT15 because there was no provision in INT15 for one program using extended memory to warn another extended-memory- using program about its memory usage. Consequently, the only reliable way to use INT15 programming is to use no more than one INT15 program at any point in time.

Creating and Using Upper Memory Blocks (UMBs)

The HMA isn't the only place where extra DOS memory can be stashed. The discussions of memory in Chapter 9 mentioned the video-RAM area between the addresses of 640K and 768K, and the system-reserved area between 768K and 1024K. You may recall, from the discussion of the ROM-buffer portion of the reserved area, that add-in circuit boards may contain ROM and that the ROM, like all memory, must have an address; the ROM reserved area is where ROM addresses are found. Together, those regions from 640K through 1024K are called the Upper Memory Area (UMA).

In this section, you see how to fill previously unused spaces in the UMA to create Upper Memory Blocks (UMBs) and how to fill those handy little areas with TSRs and device drivers.

What Do UMBs Do?

Let's review what we know so far about the UMA:

- ✔ **The UMA includes the addresses from 640K through 1024K.** The video addresses between 640K and 704K, and 736K through 768K are taken up with basic video functions. Addresses 960K through 1024K are usually taken up with the system BIOS, although you see later that some of the 960K-through-1024K area is usable by memory managers. Some computers have a BIOS that goes from 896K through 1024K; these are typically computers with highly integrated motherboards, with the video and disk circuitry located right on the motherboard rather than on a separate circuit card. And some add-in cards incorporate ROMs that contain important software to enable the PC to control those cards.

- ✔ **Not only ROMs are found in the UMA.** Although the original intent for the part of the UMA that ranges from 768K to 1024K was for ROMs, some boards need a little RAM "window" that

Creating and Using Upper Memory Blocks (UMBs)

they can control. The most common example is a LIM or EMS (expanded) memory board that requires a 64K "page frame"—a 64K window of RAM somewhere between 768K and 960K. In the video-RAM area are the video-RAM buffers that hold display images at any instant in time. Many LAN boards incorporate a shared memory section—a small part of memory shared by both the electronics on the LAN board and the CPU.

✔ **Not all of the reserved area is used.** The reserved area from 768K to 960K adds up to 192K, a fair amount of space. Of that space, a typical PC may have only a 32K ROM for video support and a 64K EMS page frame, leaving 96K of addresses unused. The monochrome video region is usually unused. The fact that some space in the UMA is unused is the key to moving TSRs and device drivers out of conventional memory. Recall that the 640K limitation is not the true limitation of real mode (the original 8088 processor mode that DOS is written in): the actual limitation is 1024K; for a 286 or better machine the limitation is 1088K. Theoretically, DOS could use memory located in the 768K to 960K area, if there were a way to put memory there.

There *is* a way to put memory there—if you have a 386-class computer (386SX, 386SXL, 386SL, 386DX, 486SX, 486DX, 486DX2, 486SLC, 486DLC, or a Pentium). The 386 has a wonderful ability to rearrange memory with software—you don't fumble with jumpers and DIP switches to stuff memory into the open holes between 768K and 960K. After you stuff memory into those empty spaces, you can then put programs into those spaces. If it's not immediately obvious why that's a terrific thing, take a look at figures 10.8 and 10.9.

In figure 10.8, you see that the space below the 640K address range has been severely reduced by three programs: ANSI, DOSKEY, and SMARTDRV. There are unused memory addresses between 768K and 960K, addresses with no memory attached to them. In figure 10.9, you see the situation after an ideal job of memory management: memory has placed in the heretofore unused addresses, and the three TSR and device-driver programs have been loaded into the newly created memory spaces, called Upper Memory Blocks (UMBs).

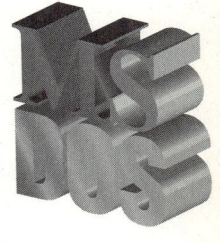

Figure 10.8

A PC with little free conventional memory before memory management.

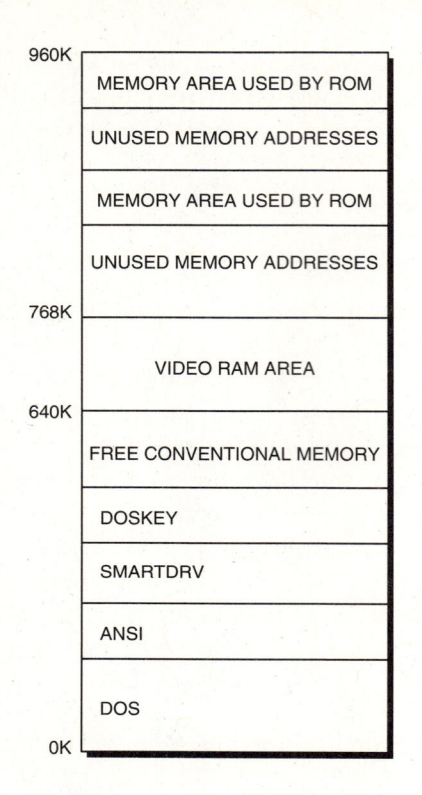

```
960K ┌─────────────────────────────┐
     │  MEMORY AREA USED BY ROM    │
     ├─────────────────────────────┤
     │  UNUSED MEMORY ADDRESSES    │
     ├─────────────────────────────┤
     │  MEMORY AREA USED BY ROM    │
     ├─────────────────────────────┤
     │  UNUSED MEMORY ADDRESSES    │
768K ├─────────────────────────────┤
     │                             │
     │      VIDEO RAM AREA         │
640K ├─────────────────────────────┤
     │   FREE CONVENTIONAL MEMORY  │
     ├─────────────────────────────┤
     │          DOSKEY             │
     ├─────────────────────────────┤
     │         SMARTDRV            │
     ├─────────────────────────────┤
     │           ANSI              │
     ├─────────────────────────────┤
     │           DOS               │
  0K └─────────────────────────────┘
```

How Memory Managers Provide UMBs

It's worth underscoring exactly what's going on with these unused spaces. In figure 10.10, you see that this PC has memory filling all the addresses under 1024K except for a range in the reserved memory area. (If you're waiting for me to explicitly name the unused memory ranges, I won't; the actual spans of unused areas vary from PC to PC, as you learn later in this chapter.) There's plenty of extended memory, but extended memory has addresses above 1024K, making it largely inaccessible to DOS programs.

In figure 10.11, you see how the 386 can make memory management possible. The 386 and later chips actually can take a slice of extended memory and change its apparent address, "moving" it to the range of addresses in the reserved area and making this block of extended memory seem to possess addresses below 1024K—which makes it accessible to DOS programs.

Creating and Using Upper Memory Blocks (UMBs) 507

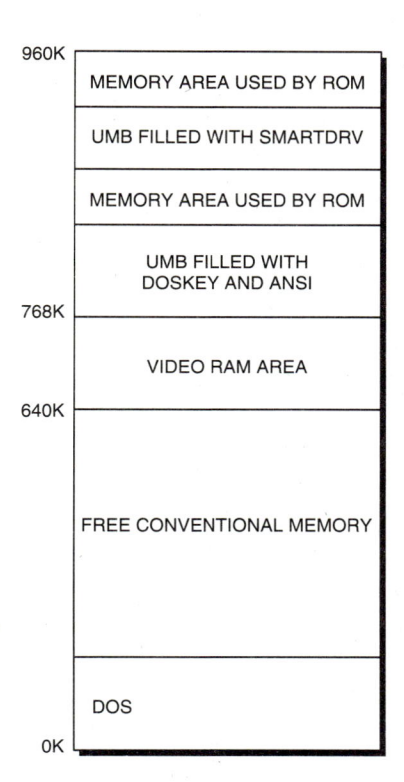

```
960K ┌─────────────────────────┐
     │ MEMORY AREA USED BY ROM │
     ├─────────────────────────┤
     │ UMB FILLED WITH SMARTDRV│
     ├─────────────────────────┤
     │ MEMORY AREA USED BY ROM │
     ├─────────────────────────┤
     │      UMB FILLED WITH    │
     │     DOSKEY AND ANSI     │
768K ├─────────────────────────┤
     │                         │
     │     VIDEO RAM AREA      │
640K ├─────────────────────────┤
     │                         │
     │                         │
     │  FREE CONVENTIONAL MEMORY│
     │                         │
     │                         │
     │                         │
     ├─────────────────────────┤
     │          DOS            │
 0K  └─────────────────────────┘
```

Figure 10.9

A PC with more free conventional memory after memory management.

This movement of memory is impossible with the 286 or earlier computers. But the 386 sees two kinds of memory addresses: *physical addresses*, which are the only kind that existed in the Intel world before the 386, and *logical addresses*, which are the things changed in the example in figure 10.11. DOS software can run in memory whose logical address is below 1024K, even if its physical address is above 1024K. That is the key, and the heart, of memory management; without it, UMBs could not be created nor programs loaded into them.

Chapter 10: *Using the DOS 6.2 Memory Manager*

Figure 10.10
Memory and addresses for a typical PC before using a memory manager.

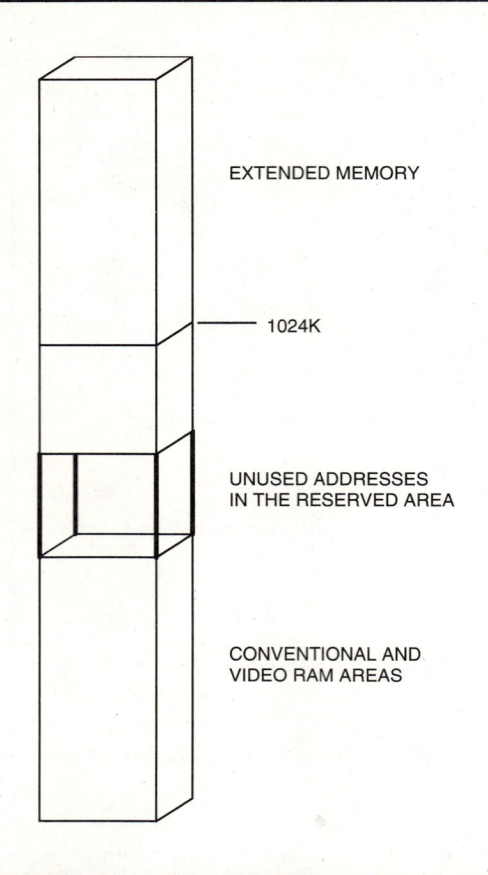

EXTENDED MEMORY

1024K

UNUSED ADDRESSES IN THE RESERVED AREA

CONVENTIONAL AND VIDEO RAM AREAS

AUTHOR'S NOTE

If the notion of logical and physical addresses is difficult to grapple with (for most folks, it is difficult—I have an instructor who taught memory-management classes for months before he really got it), consider this analogy: I currently live at 5400 Wilson Blvd, and have lived there for 10 years. Soon, I hope to move to 5409 Tenth Street. All my friends, family, and business associates know that my address is 5400 Wilson, and I don't want to go to the trouble of informing several hundred people of my new address. So I ask the Post Office to forward my mail in perpetuity. (Yes, yes, I hear your objections about whether or not the mail actually would be

forwarded—but it's just a story; pretend that this would work.) If I did that, then everyone would think that my address was 5400 Wilson, but it would actually be 5409 Tenth. In that case, you might say that my logical address was 5400 Wilson, but my physical address was 5409 Tenth.

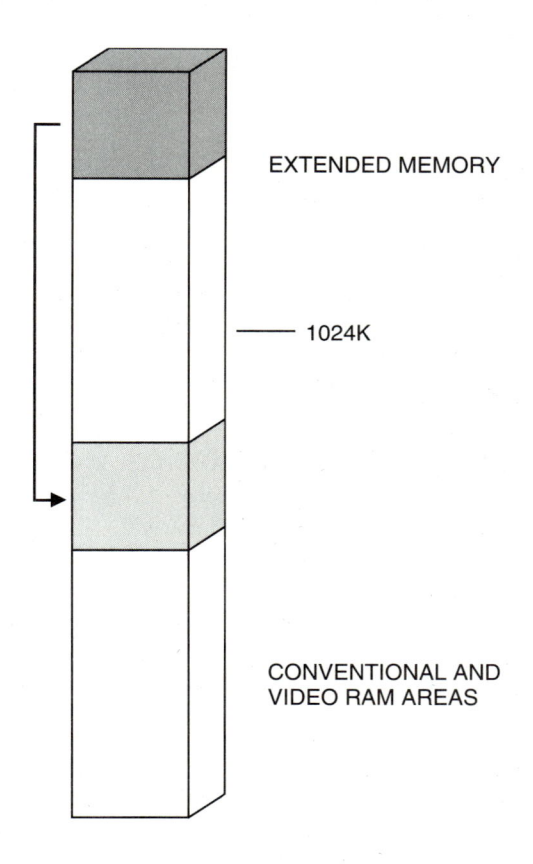

Figure 10.11
Extended memory moved to the unused reserved area.

EXTENDED MEMORY

1024K

CONVENTIONAL AND VIDEO RAM AREAS

How To Set Up UMBs

How do you do UMB memory magic? Well, you need a memory manager that can provide and use UMBs. There are three steps to using upper memory areas:

1. Identify the areas between 640K and 1024K that are unavailable—that is, the areas used by a ROM or RAM buffer—so that you can locate the areas that are available in that area.

2. Fill the available areas with memory using a memory manager to create UMBs.

3. Load TSRs and device drivers into the UMBs.

Remember those steps; many people skip the first one, to their peril.

Hexadecimal for Humans: Help for Hex Haters

Before you can do anything with memory management, you've got to be able to sling hexadecimal around with some facility. The first step of memory management is to map memory so that you can tell the memory manager which areas it should use and which it should avoid. Unfortunately, that's got to be done in hexadecimal. Memory managers also typically report data back to you in hex, expecting that you understand numbers in that format. Therefore, if you've been avoiding getting to know hex, avoid no more. (If you're comfy with hex, just skip this section.)

Hex is just an alternative way to express numerical values. Hex is used instead of decimal because many software notions closely tied to hardware notions—memory addresses, for example—translate more easily on a really low level into hex, much more easily than they do into decimal.

Looking at a Specific Example of How Memory Addressing Works

This example is of value to anyone trying to understand what's really happening in memory management.

On the hardware level—the wires and the chips—memory addresses are neither in hex nor decimal; they are in *binary*, a number system composed entirely of 1s and 0s. The reason for that is because there are a number of wires that run between the CPU chip itself and the

Creating and Using Upper Memory Blocks (UMBs)

memory. The CPU controls a large number of those wires, called *address lines*, to enable the CPU to direct the memory to fetch or store a piece of information. For example, when the CPU says, "store the value *41* in location 1511 in memory," it must pass at least two pieces of information to the memory: the data to be saved, and where to put the data. Remember that the CPU and the memory are separate chips on a circuit board called the *motherboard*. How can a CPU communicate a number like *1511* over a wire? Here's an Important Fact: a PC—or any computer—can transmit only one of two signals over a wire: a 0 or a 1.

Having said that, let's look more closely at how many wires have to run between the CPU and the memory. Imagine the simplest CPU-to-memory connection possible: one with only one wire between the CPU and the memory (see fig. 10.12).

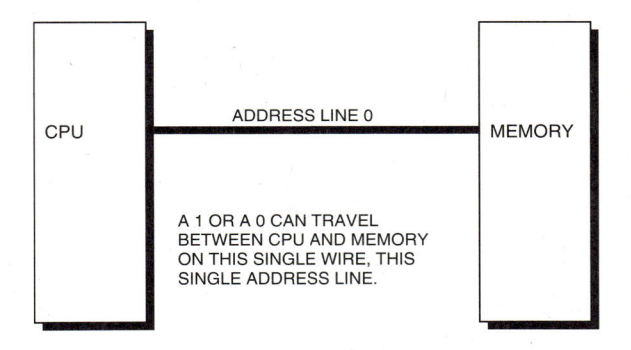

```
┌─────┐                           ┌──────┐
│     │      ADDRESS LINE 0       │      │
│ CPU │───────────────────────────│MEMORY│
│     │                           │      │
└─────┘                           └──────┘
         A 1 OR A 0 CAN TRAVEL
         BETWEEN CPU AND MEMORY
         ON THIS SINGLE WIRE, THIS
         SINGLE ADDRESS LINE.
```

Figure 10.12

A simple one-wire CPU-to-memory interface (supports only two memory locations).

Because there's only one wire between the CPU and the memory, the CPU has only two options when requesting memory in this overly simple example: the CPU can put a 0 on the request line, or the CPU can put a 1 on the request line. That wire between the CPU and the memory, by the way, is called an *address line*; it is address line number 0, because in the computer business, as you've seen, we number address lines from 0 up. In a computer like this, you could only have two memory addresses: a far cry from the roughly one million addresses that an 8088 can address, or the billions that the 386/486/Pentium family can address. But now consider a computer with two address lines (see fig. 10.13).

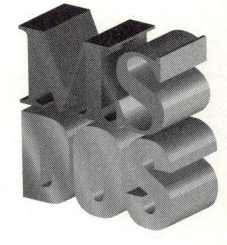

Chapter 10: *Using the DOS 6.2 Memory Manager*

Two wires support four memory addresses; here's why. The CPU can transmit a 1 or a 0 on the first wire, and the CPU can transmit a 1 or a 0 on the second wire. That means that there are four possible combinations of signals on the two address lines, like so:

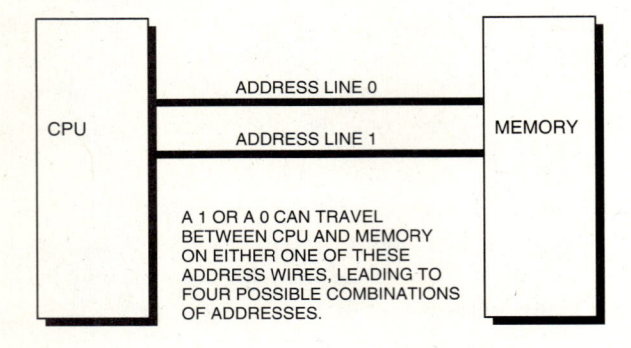

Figure 10.13
A two-wire CPU-to-memory interface (supports four memory locations).

```
                ADDRESS LINE 0
    CPU      ─────────────────────      MEMORY
                ADDRESS LINE 1
             ─────────────────────

         A 1 OR A 0 CAN TRAVEL
         BETWEEN CPU AND MEMORY
         ON EITHER ONE OF THESE
         ADDRESS WIRES, LEADING TO
         FOUR POSSIBLE COMBINATIONS
         OF ADDRESSES.
```

Value on Address Line 0	Value on Address Line 1
0	0
0	1
1	0
1	1

These are the only possible combinations. A computer like this can support only four memory locations; still pretty lame, but getting better. Add a third address line; look at how many combinations are possible with three address lines:

Value on Address Line 0	Value on Address Address Line 1	Value on Address Line 2
0	0	
0	0	1
0	1	0
0	1	1

Creating and Using Upper Memory Blocks (UMBs)

Value on Address Line 0	Value on Address Address Line 1	Value on Address Line 2
1	0	0
1	0	1
1	1	0
1	1	1

Eight combinations in all. Notice how the numbers rise rapidly—two, four, and then eight addresses. In general, if a system has x address lines, the system can support a number of memory locations equal to 2 raised to the power of x—2 multiplied by itself x times.

Now consider a real-life CPU, the 8088. It has 20 address lines, meaning that it can support 2-to-the-20th power addresses; multiply 2 by itself 20 times, and you get the value 1,048,576—which you know by its more common name, 1 megabyte. A 286 adds 4 address lines, for a total of 24 address lines, but the impact is significant: 24 address lines lets the 286 address 2-to-the-24th-power addresses: 16,777,216 memory locations—or 16 megabytes.

But back to why hex is useful here. Suppose that your PC needs to address a ROM whose address *in decimal* is 786,432 (I picked that because that's where the BIOS ROM for most VGA boards is located). Referring to the address as 786,432 is a convenience for us humans; the CPU has no idea what decimal is. Instead, it places on the 20 address wires the combination 11000000000000000000, a 20-bit address. Remember that 1s and 0s are all the CPU understands.

Well, 1s and 0s are all well and good for electronic devices, but they're hell on us humans. So a hardware engineer developed a fast shorthand way of writing out long strings of binary ones and zeroes called hexadecimal. Here's how it works.

1. Take the binary string of numbers and divide it into 4-bit groups, like so: 1100 0000 0000 0000 0000. If it doesn't divide evenly into 4-bit groups, pad to the left with zeroes.

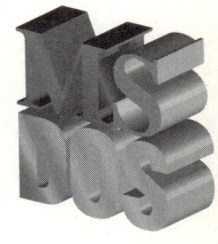

2. Notice that any 4-bit group can have only 16 possible values (2 raised to the 4th power is 16). You can write all the possibilities to prove that this is right: 0000, 0001, 0010, 0011, 0100, 0101, 0110, 0111, 1000, 1001, 1010, 1011, 1100, 1101, 1110, and 1111.

3. To make the string shorter to write, assign a one-character shorthand for each possible 4-bit combination. Use table 10.1.

   Why are there numbers from some combinations and letters for others? Mainly because we ran out of digits; there are sixteen 4-bit combinations but only ten digits.

4. Substitute the hex digit for the 4-bit combination to get the hex value of the memory address. In the example we've been working with, 1100 corresponds to C, 0000 corresponds to 0, and the four 0000 combinations correspond to 0, so the hex value for the binary 1100 0000 0000 0000 0000 is C0000.

Table 10.1
Hex Digits and Corresponding Binary Values

Binary Value	Hex Digit
0000	0
0001	1
0010	2
0011	3
0100	4
0101	5
0110	6
0111	7
1000	8
1001	9
1010	A

Binary Value	Hex Digit
1011	B
1100	C
1101	D
1110	E
1111	F

Do you see now why hexadecimal has become the common method for describing memory addresses? It's a simple translation of the actual underlying memory addressing system, a shorter way to write strings of 1s and 0s.

Converting between Hex and Decimal

I'm certain that some of you skipped the preceding example because you're saying, "Forget the theory, Mark—how the heck do I *do* this?" There are three easy ways to convert between hex and decimal:

✔ Use the built-in hex-to-decimal conversion capability in the Windows Calculator

✔ Use QBASIC, which ships with DOS, to convert numbers

✔ Use my Hex Cheat Sheet, coming up in a few pages

All are effective, nearly pain-free methods to convert between one number and the other.

Converting Hex with the Windows Calculator

Most Windows users don't know it, but the Windows Calculator can convert hex, decimal, binary, and another number system called *octal*. If you're wondering why you never noticed this capability of the Calculator, it's because the Calculator hides its lamp under a bushel. When you first fire up the Calculator, it appears in a basic, standard mode, kind of a Clark-Kent interface. If you click on **V**iew and **S**cientific, the Calculator steps into a phone booth and emerges as a full-featured scientific calculator.

Press F5 or click on the Hex radio button (the Dec radio button is deselected). You can then type a hexadecimal number, press F6 or click on Dec, and the display shows the decimal equivalent. You can convert decimal to hex the same way: select Dec, enter the decimal number, and then select Hex.

Converting Hex with DOS 6.2

If you don't have Windows handy, maybe you have DOS 6.2 around. (I hope so, or why are you reading this book?) The QBASIC programming language that comes with DOS 6.2 is a powerful tool. Of special interest are the two programs in QBASIC that you can use to convert between hex and decimal.

Create a file with the DOS editor, the Windows Notepad, Edlin, or whatever program you use to produce ASCII files—don't use a word processor unless it has an option for ASCII files. Type this simple program into the file...

```
INPUT "Number to convert from hex to decimal:"; a$
inval& = VAL("&h" + LTRIM$(a$) + "&")
PRINT "Decimal equivalent="; inval&;" or ";inval&/1024;"K"
system
```

Call the program CONVHEX.BAS. To run it, all you need to do is type...

```
QBASIC /RUN CONVHEX
```

...making sure that CONVHEX.BAS is in the current subdirectory; if it isn't, include its full name in the command: **QBASIC /RUN C:\DOS\CONVHEX**. (The **QBASIC /RUN CONVHEX** command assumes that CONVHEX.BAS is in the C:\DOS subdirectory and that C:\DOS is in the PATH). You must use QBASIC, the BASIC that ships with DOS 6.2 : GWBASIC or BASICA do not do the job. Quick BASIC 4.5, if you have it, works just fine.

To go the other way—to convert from decimal to hex—use the following program. Call it CONVDEC.BAS, and handle it as you handled CONVHEX.BAS:

Creating and Using Upper Memory Blocks (UMBs) 517

```
INPUT "Number to convert from decimal to hex:"; a&
hval$=hex$(a&)
PRINT "Hex equivalent=";hval$
system
```

Save this program to an ASCII file called CONVDEC.BAS; invoke it by typing...

QBASIC /RUN C:\DOS\CONVDEC

Using a Memory Map

All that clicking and typing is okay, but when it comes down to it, I think there are only about 512 people in the whole world who understand hex, and 300 of them live in Taiwan. The third answer to the hex problem is the best: an upper memory map, a hex cheat sheet. You can see one in figure 10.14.

What the cheat sheet shows you is the following:

- ✔ The hex values for the memory addresses from 640K to 1024K in 8K increments
- ✔ The corresponding decimal values
- ✔ Examples of common boards that include ROM and the addresses that those ROMs use

When you hear someone refer to a range of addresses, like 768K through 800K, what they really mean is, the addresses that start at and include 768K through the addresses that end at but do not include 800K.

> **TIP**
> *Address ranges include the starting addresses but exclude their ending addresses. Consider the statement "the addresses from 768K through 800K are taken by a ROM but addresses 800K through 832K are unused." Two ranges were mentioned, and both included 800K. That's impossible: 800K can't be taken by a ROM and be unused. Therefore we have the convention that a range includes the starting address but excludes the ending*

Chapter 10: *Using the DOS 6.2 Memory Manager*

address. That's what I mean when I express a range as, for example, 640-647.9. I don't really mean that the ending address is 647.9; what I really mean is "up to but not including 648K."

Figure 10.14
A hexadecimal cheat sheet.

HEX ADDRESS	DECIMAL ADDRESS (K)	COMMON USAGES OF THESE AREAS
FE000-FFFFF	1016-1023.9	SYSTEM BIOS AREA
FC000-FDFFF	1008-1015.9	
FA000-FBFFF	1000-1007.9	
F8000-F9FFF	992-999.1	
F6000-F7FFF	984-991.9	
F4000-F5FFF	976-983.9	
F2000-F3FFF	968-975.9	
F0000-F1FFF	960-967.9	
EE000-EFFFF	952-959.9	EXTENDED BIOS FOR PS/2 AND PCS WITH INTEGRATED MOTHERBOARDS, AS WELL AS COMMON LOCATION FOR BUILT-IN SETUP PROGRAM / ROM LOCATIONS FOR INTEGRATED VGA: VGA ROM / SUPER VGA ROM
EC000-EDFFF	944-951.9	
EA000-EBFFF	936-943.9	
E8000-E9FFF	928-935.9	
E6000-E7FFF	920-927.9	
E4000-E5FFF	912-919.9	
E2000-E3FFF	904-911.9	
E0000-E1FFF	896-903.9	
DE000-DFFFF	888-895.9	TYPICAL DEFAULT EMS PAGE FRAME
DC000-DDFFF	880-887.9	
DA000-DBFFF	872-879.9	
D8000-D9FFF	864-871.9	
D6000-D7FFF	856-863.9	
D4000-D5FFF	848-855.9	
D2000-D3FFF	840-847.9	
D0000-D1FFF	832-839.9	
CE000-CFFFF	824-831.9	SOME AT HARD DISK CONTROLLER ROMS
CC000-CDFFF	816-823.9	
CA000-CBFFF	808-815.9	
C8000-C9FFF	800-807.9	
C6000-C7FFF	792-799.9	8514 ROM / VGA ROM / SUPER VGA ROM
C4000-C5FFF	784-791.9	
C2000-C3FFF	776-783.9	
C0000-C1FFF	768-775.9	
BE000-BFFFF	760-767.9	EGA+ TEXT, CGA TEXT, CGA GRAPHICS
BC000-BDFFF	752-759.9	
BA000-BBFFF	744-751.9	
B8000-B9FFF	736-743.9	
B6000-B7FFF	728-735.9	MONOCHROME REGION; ALSO USED BY SOME VIDEO ACCELERATOR BOARDS
B4000-B5FFF	720-727.9	
B2000-B3FFF	712-719.9	
B0000-B1FFF	704-711.9	
AE000-AFFFF	696-703.9	EGA+ GRAPHICS AREA
AC000-ADFFF	688-695.9	
AA000-ABFFF	680-687.9	
A8000-A9FFF	672-679.9	
A6000-A7FFF	664-671.9	
A4000-A5FFF	656-663.9	
A2000-A3FFF	648-655.9	
A0000-A1FFF	640-647.9	

Here are a few examples so that you can get the hang of reading the chart in figure 10.14. A typical super-VGA ROM ranges from 768K through 800K; what's that in hex? The range 768-775.9 (which means the range from 768K up to but not including 776K) is C0000-C1FFF; its starting address is C0000 hex. What hex address replaces the "through 800K" part? Remember that the range extends to just before 800K, which this chart refers to as 799.9. The range that ends in 799.9 is 792-799.9, which in hex is C6000-C7FFF. The hex value for "just before 800K" is C7FFF. The range 768K to 800K in hex is, then, C0000-C7FFF.

Now consider the most common location for the system BIOS: from 960K through 1024K. 960K is in the 960-967.9 range, and is F0000 in hex. Just before 1024K is the end of the last interval, or FFFFF. The range in hex for 960K through 1024K is F0000-FFFFF.

The cheat sheet shows that the job of a PC configuration and installation person is not an easy one: it's fairly easy to put two boards that have conflicting ROM addresses in the same machine; when you do that, you often find that neither board works. Some AT-type hard-disk controllers, for example, use the addresses from CC000-CFFFF; although they're not on the chart, some Token-Ring local area network adapters also use that area. Put both boards in a system and neither works. Both boards may be perfectly fine, but the conflict makes them not function. For the sake of this book, I assume that you have all your hardware installed correctly; consult a book on PC upgrade and maintenance to find out more about installing new circuit boards.

Segments and Offsets

While I'm here, I may as well explain something that'll cause no end of confusion otherwise: segments and offsets.

PC memory management takes place in the area between 0 and 1024K or, to be exact, from location 0 through location 1024K-1 (with the exception of the HMA, of course, but it's not relevant here). The hex value for 0 is, of course, 00000; the hex value for 1024K-1 is FFFFF. FFFFF is as high as you can go with five hex digits; add 1 to FFFFF, and you get 100000—a six-digit number. In hex, Fs work the same way 9s do in decimal.

CPUs designed before the 80386, however, have registers (places to put data) that can handle only four hex digits, so the largest address that those machines can handle is FFFF—65,535. Not very impressive, and far short of the 1,048,576 memory locations that the 8088 can address. (They didn't build larger registers into these chips because Intel was concerned about backward compatibility with chips even older than the 8088: the 8080 and 8085 chips.) So the 8088—and any chip mimicking the 8088, as all chips must do when they run DOS—must address all parts of memory in two parts: a segment and an offset.

Segments and offsets are both represented by registers that hold four hex digits. How, then, does an 8088 employ full 20-bit (5-hex digit) addresses? Simple: the segment address is assumed to have a hex 0 tacked onto the end of it. For example, if an 8088 segment register holds 1000, and the offset register holds 5, what's the address? Well, the segment's value gets an extra 0 tacked onto the end, so it counts for 10000 rather than 1000; then the offset is added, yielding a 5-digit address of 10005.

DOS programs could never refer directly to address C0000; they get the address information in two pieces—a segment address of C000 and an offset of 0000. The segment and offset are often written with a colon between them: C000:0000. The leading zeros on the offset are not, strictly speaking, required.

Special Considerations for Integrated Motherboard Machines

Although different computers may or may not have different ROMs, one ROM you can be relatively certain your computer has is a VGA ROM. Because you have to find the ROMs in your system before you can get your PC ready for bulletproof memory management, here's a heads-up on where to look for VGA ROMs.

About half of PCs have the VGA circuitry on a separate board plugged into the PC's expansion slots; about half have integrated video, meaning that the video circuitry is incorporated right onto the PC's motherboard. The VGA ROM's address tends to be 768K to 800K (C0000-C8000) if the VGA is on a separate board, or 896K to 928K (E0000-E8000) if you have a computer with integrated video on the motherboard.

Some computers give you the option to relocate the VGA BIOS from E0000 down to C0000; Dell computers are one example of that. Others like those in the Compaq line put two copies of the VGA BIOS on the system: one at C0000 and one at E0000.

The PS/2 line of computers are perhaps a worst-case scenario for upper memory because they have an extended BIOS that ranges all the way from 896K through 1024K (E0000-FFFFF); that's 128K of addresses you can't put UMBs into, unfortunately.

What Goes in UMBs?

So we have two UMBs, one 16K in size and another 136K in size. As with the HMA, you have the problem that DOS programs can't generally use noncontiguous memory. If you want to load a program into a UMB, it's got to be a UMB that the entire program fits in. The kinds of programs that fit in spaces from 16K to 128K in size are TSRs and device drivers.

Recall the AUTOEXEC.BAT and CONFIG.SYS files we've been working with. ANSI.SYS is a device driver—one that modifies the way your video behaves. The DOSKEY TSR is a program that remembers previous keystrokes, simplifying the repetition of commands. ANSI.SYS ordinarily robs your system of 4K; DOSKEY also takes 4K—and that memory comes out of your precious conventional memory space. Although that 8K isn't much, this is just an example.

If we put ANSI.SYS and DOSKEY into UMBs, we end up with more conventional memory. (If you're wondering "How?," hang on: it's coming up.)

Step 1: Map Upper Memory

The most vital step necessary to make a memory manager work is the step of mapping upper memory to lay out exactly what's being done with the addresses between 640K and 1024K. The reason why this is so important is simple: memory managers aren't too bright when it comes to finding available and unavailable memory spaces. Before popping TSR and device driver programs into the empty memory space above 640K, the question of what's empty and what's not empty *must* be determined.

Why Map?

If you don't explicitly tell the memory manager (I'll show you how in a bit) where it can and can't go, you leave those decisions up to the memory manager itself. Although memory managers are fairly capable in the area of memory mapping, they're not perfect, and that leads to subtle instabilities in the system. Note that I said *subtle*: that's the mean part about it. If the system blew up, you'd know there was something wrong and that it was time to do something drastic. But that's often not what happens; instead, Windows gets `general protection` errors, DOS programs lock up at odd times, or your network doesn't work. So consider this first step the bulletproofing step of memory management.

The vast majority of reference materials do not stress the importance of mapping your own memory; instead, they suggest that you trust the memory manager to handle most of the memory mapping but to step in and override it now and then. I say absolutely not: I've solved countless memory-management problems with explicit memory mapping.

AUTHOR'S NOTE

Here's an example of why you must map memory. IBM Token-Ring LAN boards have a bit of RAM and a bit of ROM on them. That RAM and ROM are addressed somewhere in the address range 768K through 960K; the addresses the RAM and ROM use should be avoided by a memory manager seeking to fill empty spaces with UMBs.

But here's the rub: the Token-Ring board's memory actually hides until the network is active. There's nothing to read there; if you write data, it disappears. For all intents and purposes, the RAM and ROM are not there at all until you load the Token-Ring device drivers. If you load your memory manager before the Token-Ring device drivers, the memory manager sees what look like wide-open spaces just begging to be filled with UMBs. So it moves memory into those addresses, essentially "blacktopping" over the Token Ring memory, and eventually loading programs into that area. All is well until the network is activated. The Token-Ring memory then awakens, shoves aside any UMBs in its area, and crashes any programs loaded in the same space as the Token-Ring RAM. Had the Token-Ring RAM areas been excluded with a map, then no conflict would have occurred.

In general, memory managers have problems coping with boards that contain RAM rather than ROM. ROMs are, in general, fairly easy to find, but RAMs can be a bit of trouble. There's just no well-established way to identify RAMs in a system; a memory manager can easily overwrite an existing RAM on an add-in board with a UMB.

Other Potential Sources of Memory Conflict

You can find other common sources of memory conflicts. One is to actually run two memory managers at the same time, or a DOS extender that hasn't been built to be compliant with a standard that makes it compatible with memory managers.

Chapter 10: *Using the DOS 6.2 Memory Manager*

In general, ROM chips are simple to locate; most memory managers don't stumble over them. That's because there is a standard "signature" that ROMs are supposed to contain: the first three bytes of the ROM should contain a hex 55 in its first address, an AA value in the second address, and a value in its third address that indicates how long it is (a value computed by dividing the total length of the ROM by 512—don't ask me why).

Here's a simple example using DEBUG. I'll start DEBUG from a command prompt and then ask DEBUG to display the first few bytes starting at C0000. Look back at the hex cheat sheet in figure 10.14 to see that C0000 is a common location for the ROM on a video board. Start DEBUG by typing its name at a DOS prompt; you see a minus sign (–). That's DEBUG's prompt. Then type...

```
D C000:0 L 3
```

...and press Enter. That command says *dump* (that's what the *d* means) the data appearing in the memory whose addresses start at C000:0 and continue for a *length* (that's what the *l* means) of 3 bytes (that's what the *3* is). Exit DEBUG by pressing Q (for *quit*). If you have a PC with a separate video board rather than one with the video built right onto the motherboard, you'll see something like this:

```
UC:\DOS>DEBUG
-D C000:0 L 3
C000:0000 55 AA 40                              U.@
-Q
C:\DOS>
```

Notice that the dump command was written in segment:offset format; if I had tried to get DEBUG to dump at address C0000—a 5-digit address—DEBUG would have returned an error message. The L 3 says "dump a sequence of 3 bytes." You see that the response was 55 AA 40. The 55 AA means that it's a ROM. The 40 means "multiply 40 hex by 512 decimal to find out how long I am." 40 hex is 64 decimal, and 512 is one half of 1K, so this ROM extends for 64 times 1/2K, or 32K.

All this makes life easier for memory managers, but it's not always reliable. For example, at least one video board (based on older ET-4000 chip sets) misleads the system about how much memory it has. The

Step 1: Map Upper Memory

old ET-4000s told the system they were 24K ROMs rather than 32K ROMs, with the result that the memory manager inadvertently truncated the last 8K of the video ROM, to no good end.

In addition to prevaricating ROMs, memory managers stumble over RAM buffers because they do not have a signature.

> **AUTHOR'S NOTE**
>
> *You may be asking, "Isn't there an easier way—some program that does the dirty work for me?" If you've been messing with memory managers for a while, you may not be wondering: you may be getting a bit steamed up. Whenever I do a memory-management class, there's always somebody who looks ready to burst if I don't let him comment on what I'm saying. If I call on him, I usually get a comment like this:*
>
> *This is all very good, Mark, but you're working too hard; there are many programs that find high memory for you. I use Quarterdeck Manifest all the time, and it works great for me.*
>
> *A very common statement. Unfortunately, it's wrong. Manifest and programs like it do a very good job of sniffing out areas of upper memory that are already used, but they don't do the whole job; they can't always find RAM buffers or prevaricating ROMs. There's just no substitute for having the actual documentation on the system you're working on.*
>
> *I know, however, that many of you don't always have the time to find the documentation and need to take an educated guess about what the upper memory area of a PC looks like. If you must map a computer without the documentation, try one of the following programs:*
>
> - ✔ *Checkit, from Touchstone*
> - ✔ *System Sleuth, from Dariana*
> - ✔ *MSD.EXE, a program that comes with DOS 6.2 and Windows 3.1*
> - ✔ *Manifest, a Quarterdeck product*
>
> *continues*

Chapter 10: *Using the DOS 6.2 Memory Manager*

> ✔ *At Last! from RYBS*
>
> ✔ *ASQ from Qualitas*
>
> *All good programs, conscientiously built. But again, none of them can detect (for example) the Token-Ring board if its drivers aren't loaded. 3Com 3C503 boards use shared memory in the range of CC000-CFFFF, but those RAM buffers seem invisible to most memory-mapper programs.*
>
> *If you must use a memory-scanner program, be sure to first load the device drivers for all the boards in your system; that makes it easier for the memory scanner to find everything in the system.*

Using MSD, the DOS 6.2 Memory Scanner

DOS 6.2 (and Windows 3.1) ships with a fairly decent memory scanner called MSD. It can be fooled by peek-a-boo memory like the others, but it's no worse than any of the memory scanners you pay money to procure. Here's a short walk-through of MSD.

> **NOTE** *If you are using DOS 5, you can still use MSD. If you are running Windows 3.1, you can find MSD in your Windows directory.*

You start MSD by typing **MSD**. Run MSD without any active memory managers to get the most accurate picture of your upper memory area. You then see an opening screen like the one in figure 10.15. After a few seconds, you see a menu screen as in figure 10.16.

Step 1: Map Upper Memory **527**

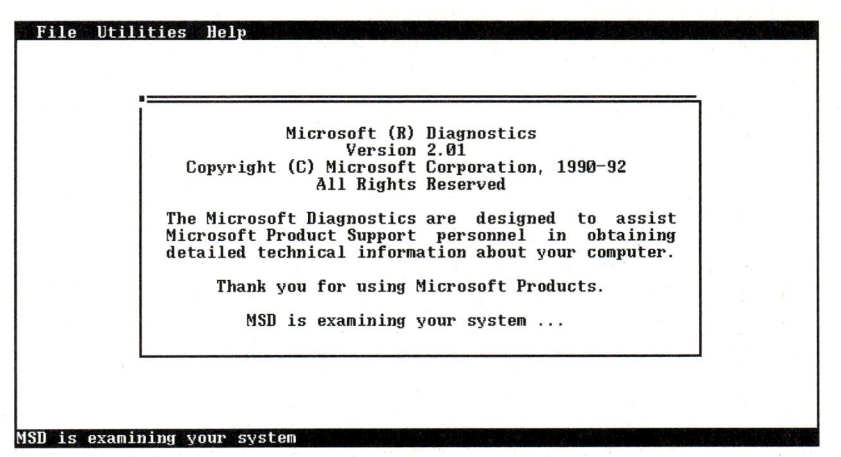

Figure 10.15
The opening MSD screen.

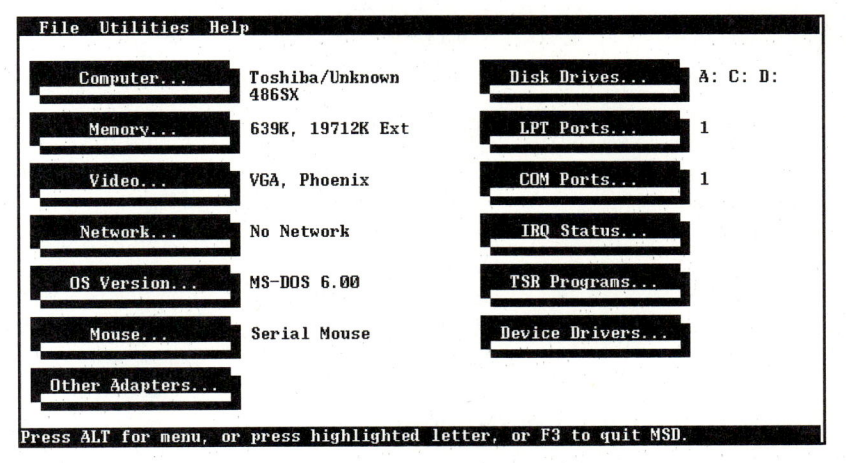

Figure 10.16
The MSD menu for a simple PC.

This opening screen indicates that this computer has 640K of conventional memory and 19712K of extended memory. MSD sees no network. Unfortunately, this points out the problem I've been discussing: this computer *does* have a network board installed and most of the network drivers are already resident in memory. The final network command hasn't been issued, however, so MSD doesn't see the network. To look further into this computer's memory with MSD, press M. A more detailed memory screen appears (see fig. 10.17).

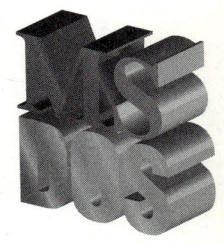

Figure 10.17

A memory view with MSD.

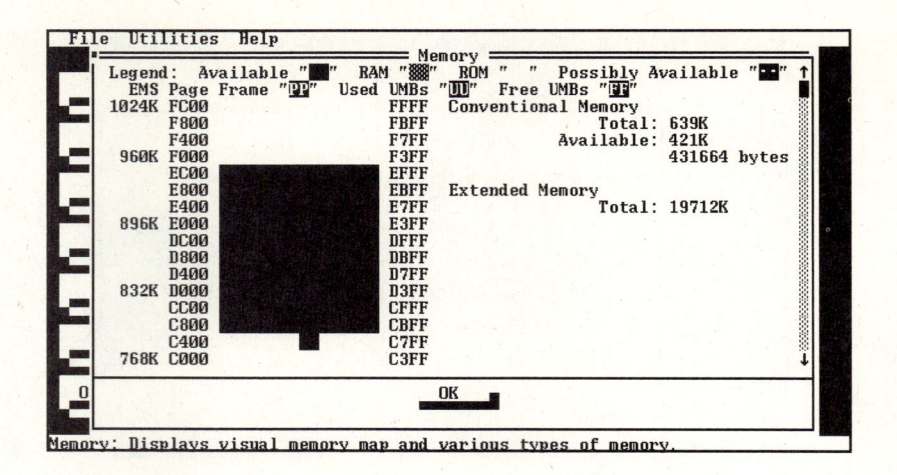

```
 File  Utilities  Help
                            ┌──────── Memory ─────────┐
      Legend:   Available " "   RAM "▓"    ROM  " "  Possibly Available "▪" ↑
        EMS  Page Frame "PP"   Used UMBs "UU"  Free UMBs "FF"
      1024K  FC00                      FFFF   Conventional Memory
             F800                      FBFF              Total: 639K
             F400                      F7FF          Available: 421K
       960K  F000                      F3FF                431664 bytes
             EC00                      EFFF
             E800                      EBFF   Extended Memory
             E400                      E7FF              Total: 19712K
       896K  E000                      E3FF
             DC00                      DFFF
             D800                      DBFF
             D400                      D7FF
       832K  D000                      D3FF
             CC00                      CFFF
             C800                      CBFF
             C400                      C7FF
       768K  C000                      C3FF                             ↓
                                 ┌────────┐
         0                       │   OK   │
                                 └────────┘
 Memory: Displays visual memory map and various types of memory.
```

The MSD output starts at 768K and goes to 1024K. If you're following along on your PC, that's not the end of the story. You can press PgDn to start the view at 640K and show the video regions. This map shows ROM as black areas, unused addresses as white areas, and any RAMs that MSD can detect as dithered areas. (There aren't any RAM areas visible on this map.) Notice that the hex memory addresses are only four digits long; that's because, as you soon see, memory managers want to see memory addresses with the rightmost digit lopped off.

MSD indicates that there's a ROM in the C0000-C7FFF range, a ROM you can guess is the video ROM. But notice that MSD indicates that there's a small unused area in that C0000-C7FFF range, something worth exploring in detail a little later. MSD then declares the entire C8000-EFFFF region fair game.

It's dead wrong. It's dead wrong for a few reasons. First, there's a LAN board in this computer that uses a RAM buffer from C8000 through CFFFF—800K through 832K. Second, this particular computer is a laptop with an auto-resume feature that does not work unless I leave the range from E8000 through EFFFF unused. I'm not aware of a memory manager anywhere that knows about auto-resume features. But how can I stack the cards in MSD's favor so that it can take a better stab at the network RAM buffer?

Step 1: Map Upper Memory   529

It's easier for a memory-scanner program to find RAMs on a network card if the network is active; so exit MSD (press Enter and then F3 if you're following along) and load the network drivers. Then reenter MSD and press M to see the memory details again; the memory view screen looks a bit different, as you see in figure 10.18.

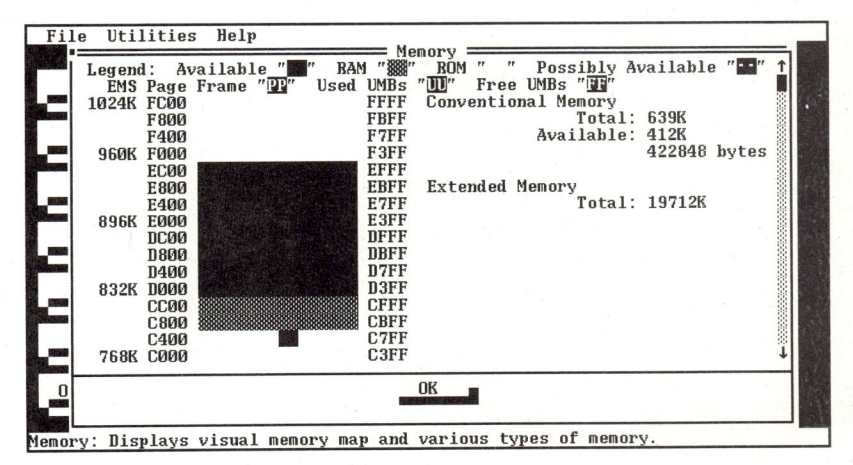

```
File  Utilities  Help
                            ═══ Memory ═══
         Legend:   Available "■"  RAM "▓"  ROM " "  Possibly Available "▒"
           EMS Page Frame "PP"  Used UMBs "UU"  Free UMBs "FF"
    1024K  FC00                  FFFF   Conventional Memory
           F800                  FBFF                Total: 639K
           F400                  F7FF            Available: 412K
     960K  F000                  F3FF                   422848 bytes
           EC00                  EFFF
           E800                  EBFF   Extended Memory
           E400                  E7FF                Total: 19712K
     896K  E000                  E3FF
           DC00                  DFFF
           D800                  DBFF
           D400                  D7FF
     832K  D000                  D3FF
           CC00                  CFFF
           C800                  CBFF
           C400                  C7FF
     768K  C000                  C3FF
                              OK
Memory: Displays visual memory map and various types of memory.
```

Figure 10.18

The memory view with the network drivers loaded and the network RAM buffer active.

Now you see a dithered region from C8000 through CFFFF, which is where the RAM buffer for the LAN board is. After the driver was loaded, MSD's guess about which areas were usable and which were not usable got better.

Before leaving MSD, let's look more closely into that open area in the VGA ROM. It's visible in figure 10.18 as the small white space between C4000 and C7FFF—almost exactly between, starting somewhere around C6000. You can check it out in greater detail with DEBUG. Exploring the ROM area takes only a few DEBUG commands, as shown in figure 10.19.

Don't be scared by the DEBUG stuff; after all, some DOS program has to have the worst user interface, right? Remember that DEBUG insists on referring to memory addresses in segment:offset format; that means that address C6000 is referred to as C600:0 if you want DEBUG to do anything with that address.

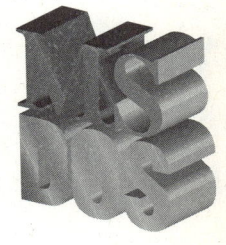

Figure 10.19

A DEBUG session that examines empty spaces in ROM.

```
C:\>debug
-d c500:0 1 10
C500:0000  CC 88 00 00 00 00 00 22-22 88 88 22 22 88 88 22   .......""..""..".
-d c600:0 1 10
C600:0000  FF FF FF FF FF FF FF FF-FF FF FF FF FF FF FF FF   ................
-d c6ff:0 1 10
C6FF:0000  80 6E 09 10 2B FB 73 04-80 6E 08 10 FE CC 75 AE   .n..+.s..n....u.
-q

C:\>
```

1. In the first line of the screen, I load DEBUG. It responds with the hyphen prompt.

2. In the second line, I ask DEBUG to dump 16 bytes starting at C5000. I do that by typing...

    D C500:0 L 10

    C5000 (C500:0) is the starting address. The length of my request is 16 bytes; 16 in decimal is 10 in hex—hence the L 10.

3. In the third line, DEBUG responds with the hex values it found in memory in the 16 bytes starting at C5000. What I am looking for are the values FF in all locations; that means they are unused memory addresses. Because there are many different values in this range, I know that this range of addresses is taken.

4. In the fourth line, I skip to C6000 and make the same request. I didn't try C5800 or some other point in between C5000 and C6000 because of a simple fact of life about memory managers: they only work in addresses in increments of 1000 hex, or 4096 decimal—a 4K interval. There is no point in checking whether there's a small free area in the C5000-C5FFF range because you can't say to the memory manager, "Use part of the C5000-C5FFF range, but avoid the other part of it."

Step 1: Map Upper Memory   531

Memory managers can't do that. If a single byte in a 4K interval has information in it, you must tell the memory manager to avoid the entire 4K that the byte is in.

> **NOTE** *Memory managers can only manipulate memory in 4K chunks. All addresses in memory-manager commands must lie exactly on 4K boundaries.*

5. In line 5, DEBUG responds with a dump of the values I asked for. They're all FFs, indicating an unused area. Hmmm...looks promising. But I can only tell my memory manager to exploit a range starting at C6000 if the entire region from C6000-C6FFF (the entire 4K area) is unused.

6. In line 6, I ask DEBUG to show me the last 16 bytes of the C6000-C6FFF region by requesting a dump of the 16 bytes starting at C6FF:0.

7. In line 7, DEBUG shows me the bytes in the second half of that area; unfortunately, their values are not FF; that means I don't have a complete 4K unused area starting at C6000, so I can't exploit that space. Too bad.

8. I press Q to quit DEBUG.

DEBUG looks scary if you haven't used it much, but I find that just the D or dump command can be quite powerful and isn't really difficult after you get past the segment:offset stuff. Remember these few things, and DEBUG can be your oyster (as in "The world is your oyster."):

- ✔ Start dumping at XX00:0, where XX can be anything. You ensure that you start your search on a 4K boundary with the 00:0. Because you don't need to see a lot of data, add the l 10 to get only 16 bytes. For example, examine CC000 by typing **D CC00:0 L 10** and pressing Enter.

- ✔ All values must be FF, or you should avoid that area of memory. There are the occasional exceptions, but stick with the FF rule and you'll find free areas—as long as they aren't some kind of peek-a-boo memory.

✔ After you find a candidate area, dump the end to check that it's free. If d XX00:0 l 10 showed FFs (XX is some pair of hexadecimal digits), next type **D XXFF:0 L 10** and look for all FF values. For example, if I find FF values after I type the **D CC00:0 L 10** command, I check the end of that 4K area with **D L 10**. If you really want to be sure that a 4K area is unused, dump the whole thing by typing **D XX00:0 L 1000** and stand back. Data zips by on the screen, but all you're looking for is a pattern: if there's nothing but FF values, the data looks consistent as it scrolls up the screen. But even 1 byte that's not FF sticks out like a sore thumb as it scrolls by.

As you can probably see by now, memory mapping can be some real work if not done properly.

Using the Documentation for Add-In Boards

There's no way around it. The most dependable way to find out what's usable memory and what's not is with your documentation. Documentation falls into several categories:

✔ Straightforward, clear documentation. Hey, don't scoff; there's more and more of this all the time. Many board manufacturers understand that we have to do memory-management stuff and that we're in trouble without good documentation. Documentation like this typically says something like...

> The XYZ board has a 16K BIOS chip located at CC000

This means that there's a ROM of 16K extending from CC000 to CFFFF. (If you're unclear about how I got that, go back to the cheat sheet or add 16K-1 to CC000 using the Windows Calculator.)

✔ Documentation written without the last digit in the ROM address. Although you often see something like the preceding example, you may see a line like...

Step 1: Map Upper Memory

> The XYZ board has a 16K BIOS chip located at CC00

Thus far, you've seen memory addresses expressed with 5 hex digits; where's the fifth digit on this one? As you may have guessed, the documentation in this case is employing the segment address; it lops off the rightmost zero: instant segment!

- ✔ Micro Channel and EISA configuration utilities. The big difference between PCs built around the old ISA (Industry Standard Architecture) bus and those built around the newer MCA (Micro Channel Architecture) or EISA (Extended Industry Standard Architecture) bus is that ISA boards are usually configured with hardware but MCA or EISA boards are usually configured with software. What that means is that you may be able to get a complete top-to-bottom map of ROMs and RAM buffers just by running the Reference Disk on your PS/2.

If there's no way to get documentation or information from your hardware vendor, by all means use one of the memory-scanning programs mentioned earlier, but be aware that you're not doing complete justice to your system. And you might want to read the section later in this chapter that discusses how to look for upper memory areas by hand. Too many people complain to me, "The person who had this job before me took the documentation when he left." Most vendors can be quite helpful; just phone them and explain the problem; you'll probably have a new manual in no time.

Giving the Map to the Memory Manager

Assume that you've gotten the information on your computer's upper memory map. You know what addresses your memory manager should avoid and which it should dive into and exploit. Now, how do you communicate that information to your memory manager?

Under DOS 6.2, the job of memory manager is divided up between two device drivers: HIMEM.SYS and EMM386.EXE.

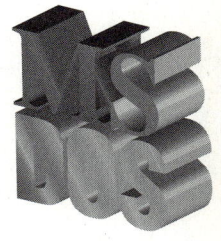

> *If you're working with Compaq DOS, the files are named HIMEM.EXE and CEMM.EXE, respectively.*

HIMEM.SYS must load before EMM386.EXE. In its simplest form, EMM386.EXE creates UMBs for you if you just include it in CONFIG.SYS as a device driver. Modified, the CONFIG.SYS we used as a starting point earlier now looks like this:

```
FILES=60
BUFFERS=30
DEVICE=C:\WINDOWS\HIMEM.SYS
DEVICE=C:\WINDOWS\EMM386.EXE NOEMS
DOS=HIGH
DEVICE=C:\DOS\SETVER.EXE
DEVICE=C:\DOS\ANSI.SYS
```

The NOEMS parameter on EMM386 is explained in the discussion about using LIM memory with a memory manager, but basically it tells the memory manager to provide no EMS—that is, don't convert any extended memory to expanded memory. What the modified CONFIG.SYS does is load EMM386.EXE and allow it to sniff out the occupied and unoccupied areas in upper memory. Recall that there's a RAM buffer on the local area network card in the range 800K to 832K (C8000-CFFFF). Summarized, the memory situation on the sample computer looks like this:

Address Range	Contents
A0000-AFFFF	VGA graphics area
B0000-B7FFF	Monochrome text area, free on this computer
B8000-BFFFF	VGA text area
C0000-C7FFF	VGA BIOS ROM
C8000-CFFFF	Ethernet RAM buffer
D0000-EFFFF	Free
F0000-FFFFF	System BIOS

Step 1: Map Upper Memory

This map isn't totally accurate: the area between E8000-EFFFF should be left unused so that the laptop's auto-resume feature works, but I'm willing to give up the auto-resume feature in return for some extra upper memory.

The map information is transmitted to the memory manager by adding parameters to the DEVICE= line for EMM386.EXE. Any area that can be used (or *included*, in memory manager parlance) is indicated with an I= range; any area that should be avoided (or *excluded*) should be indicated with an X=. With the I= and X= parameters, only use segment addresses: trim off the rightmost digit. Here's what it would look like for the sample computer:

```
DEVICE=C:\DOS\EMM386.EXE NOEMS X=A000-AFFF I=B000-B7FF
X=B800-CFFF I=D000-EFFF X=F000-FEFF
```

> **NOTE** *Even though that last line broke across two printed lines, it should be typed as a single line in CONFIG.SYS. Please pay attention to that last caveat: it's probably the single most common error that people make when reading text like this.*

Notice that I explicitly excluded all the way into the Fs for this computer. In general, you need not explicitly exclude the F region (from F0000 through FFFFF) because the DOS memory manager won't attempt to use it unless you tell DOS to use it. If you wonder why the last exclude goes only to FEFF rather than FFFF, it's because of a bug in DOS 6.2's memory manager: it won't let you exclude up to FFFF without issuing an annoying message at boot time. I've seen a few notebooks—the ones made by Tandon and DataWorld—lose the capability to do warm boots (Ctrl+Alt+Del) if you run EMM386.EXE. They can do warm boots if you exclude all the way up to FFFF, but you get an annoying message from EMM386 every time you boot if you exclude up that far. For some reason, such an exclude statement leads to the message...

```
specified memory ranges overlap
```

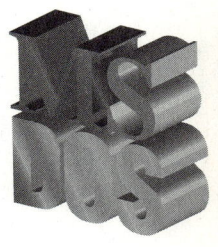

Chapter 10: *Using the DOS 6.2 Memory Manager*

If this happens to you—the warm boot problem—then add the ALT+boot parameter to your EMM386 invocation; that'll usually fix the loss of warm boot capabilities.

After adding parameters to the DEVICE= line for EMM386.EXE and rebooting to run CONFIG.SYS, type `MEM/C/P` to see output something like that in figures 10.20 and 10.21. There's not much difference in this output because we're not finished creating and using UMBs. But notice that the new program, EMM386.EXE, takes up 4.1K of conventional space.

Figure 10.20

The output from MEM/C/P after loading EMM386.EXE and mapping memory (part 1).

```
Modules using memory below 1 MB:

Name           Total        =   Conventional   +   Upper Memory
--------       -----            ------------       ------------
MSDOS          16093  (16K)     16093   (16K)      0      (0K)
HIMEM           1104   (1K)      1104    (1K)      0      (0K)
EMM386          4144   (4K)      4144    (4K)      0      (0K)
SETVER           672   (1K)       672    (1K)      0      (0K)
ANSI            4208   (4K)      4208    (4K)      0      (0K)
COMMAND         4704   (5K)      4704    (5K)      0      (0K)
VSAFE          22848  (22K)     22848   (22K)      0      (0K)
DOSKEY         33632  (33K)     33632   (33K)      0      (0K)
MOUSE          17088  (17K)     17088   (17K)      0      (0K)
Free          550928 (538K)    550928  (538K)      0      (0K)

Memory Summary:

Type of Memory        Total        =       Used       +        Free
--------------      --------              ------             --------
Conventional          655360  (640K)     104432  (102K)     550928  (538K)
Upper                      0    (0K)          0    (0K)          0    (0K)
Adapter RAM/ROM       393216  (384K)     393216  (384K)          0    (0K)
Extended (XMS)      19922944 (19456K)    171008  (167K)   19751936 (19289K)
Press any key to continue . . .
```

Figure 10.21

The output from MEM/C/P after loading EMM386.EXE and mapping memory (part 2).

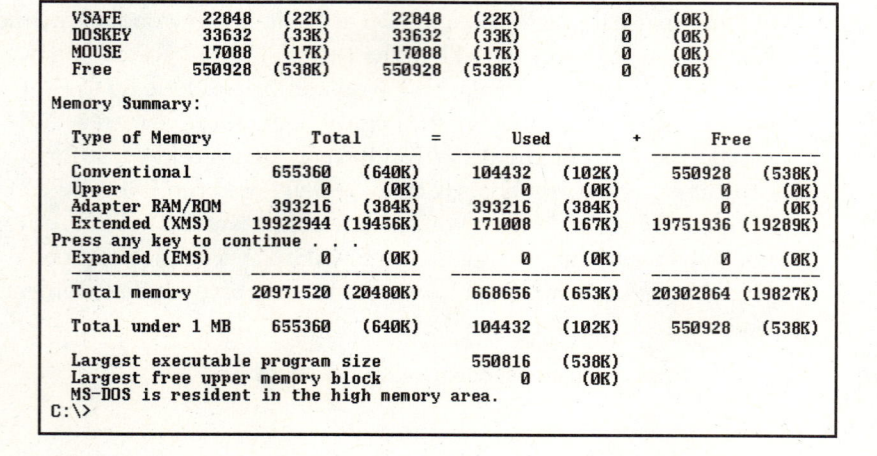

```
VSAFE          22848  (22K)     22848   (22K)      0      (0K)
DOSKEY         33632  (33K)     33632   (33K)      0      (0K)
MOUSE          17088  (17K)     17088   (17K)      0      (0K)
Free          550928 (538K)    550928  (538K)      0      (0K)

Memory Summary:

Type of Memory        Total        =       Used       +        Free
--------------      --------              ------             --------
Conventional          655360  (640K)     104432  (102K)     550928  (538K)
Upper                      0    (0K)          0    (0K)          0    (0K)
Adapter RAM/ROM       393216  (384K)     393216  (384K)          0    (0K)
Extended (XMS)      19922944 (19456K)    171008  (167K)   19751936 (19289K)
Press any key to continue . . .
Expanded (EMS)             0    (0K)          0    (0K)          0    (0K)

Total memory        20971520 (20480K)    668656  (653K)   20302864 (19827K)

Total under 1 MB      655360  (640K)     104432  (102K)     550928  (538K)

Largest executable program size           550816  (538K)
Largest free upper memory block                0    (0K)
MS-DOS is resident in the high memory area.
C:\>
```

Step 2: Create UMBs

Now that the UMA is mapped out, let's exploit its unused areas.

Telling CONFIG.SYS To Create UMBs

This part is easy. Just change the DOS=HIGH line in CONFIG.SYS to DOS=HIGH,UMB. The notebook CONFIG.SYS (which may not be right for your computer; adjust the I= and X= parameters if necessary) looks like this:

```
FILES=60
BUFFERS=30
DEVICE=C:\WINDOWS\HIMEM.SYS
DEVICE=C:\DOS\EMM386.EXE NOEMS X=A000-AFFF I=B000-B7ff
X=B800-CFFF I=D000-EFFF X=F000-FEFF
DOS=HIGH,UMB
DEVICE=C:\DOS\SETVER.EXE
DEVICE=C:\DOS\ANSI.SYS
```

There are no changes to make to AUTOEXEC.BAT at this stage. Reboot and run MEM/C; you'll see that MEM/C has more to say (see figs. 10.22 and 10.23).

Look closely for the one very important difference between figures 10.22 and 10.23 and the earlier figures 10.20 and 10.21. Look in the Upper Memory column. Figure 10.20 showed all the values in the Upper Memory column to be 0; figure 10.22 shows a free memory value of 155K for upper memory. Now that the upper memory is there, let's use it.

Understanding Fragmented UMBs

Before we do anything with the UMBs, however, look at the summary of the memory situation a few pages back that listed the free and busy areas in the PC's memory. There were two unused memory address ranges: the 32K monochrome area and 128K of unused addresses between 832K and 960K (D0000-EFFFF). It would be useful to check out which UMBs ended up there. MEM/F (the F option is for *free*)

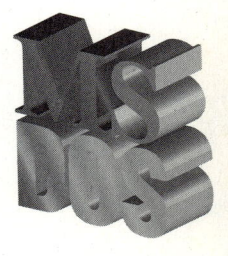

Chapter 10: *Using the DOS 6.2 Memory Manager*

gives that information. You can see the output from MEM/F in figure 10.24. The lower part is the Free Upper Memory section. It details two regions of size 27K and 128K; these correspond to the two upper memory blocks. By the way, notice that you haven't got 155K free in one big contiguous block, but rather in two separate blocks—the UMBs are fragmented. *You'll see in Chapter 12 that fragmented UMBs can lead to problems.* The reason the first one is not 32K in size, but rather 27K, is that some of EMM386.EXE loads into the UMB.

Figure 10.22

The output from MEM/C/P after DOS=HIGH,UMB (part 1).

```
Modules using memory below 1 MB:

Name           Total           =   Conventional   +   Upper Memory
----           -----               ------------       ------------
MSDOS          16093   (16K)       16093   (16K)      0       (0K)
HIMEM           1104    (1K)        1104    (1K)      0       (0K)
EMM386          4144    (4K)        4144    (4K)      0       (0K)
SETVER           672    (1K)         672    (1K)      0       (0K)
ANSI            4208    (4K)        4208    (4K)      0       (0K)
COMMAND         4704    (5K)        4704    (5K)      0       (0K)
VSAFE          22848   (22K)       22848   (22K)      0       (0K)
DOSKEY         33632   (33K)       33632   (33K)      0       (0K)
MOUSE          17088   (17K)       17088   (17K)      0       (0K)
Free          709680  (693K)      550912  (538K)    158768  (155K)

Memory Summary:

Type of Memory       Total              Used           +    Free
--------------       -----              ----                ----
Conventional        655360  (640K)    104448  (102K)     550912  (538K)
Upper               158768  (155K)         0    (0K)     158768  (155K)
Adapter RAM/ROM     234448  (229K)    234448  (229K)          0    (0K)
Extended (XMS)    19922944 (19456K)   171008  (167K)   19751936 (19289K)
Press any key to continue . . .
```

Figure 10.23

The output from MEM/C/P after DOS=HIGH,UMB (part 2).

```
VSAFE          22848   (22K)       22848   (22K)      0       (0K)
DOSKEY         33632   (33K)       33632   (33K)      0       (0K)
MOUSE          17088   (17K)       17088   (17K)      0       (0K)
Free          709680  (693K)      550912  (538K)    158768  (155K)

Memory Summary:

Type of Memory       Total              Used           +    Free
--------------       -----              ----                ----
Conventional        655360  (640K)    104448  (102K)     550912  (538K)
Upper               158768  (155K)         0    (0K)     158768  (155K)
Adapter RAM/ROM     234448  (229K)    234448  (229K)          0    (0K)
Extended (XMS)    19922944 (19456K)   171008  (167K)   19751936 (19289K)
Press any key to continue . . .
Expanded (EMS)           0    (0K)         0    (0K)          0    (0K)

Total memory      20971520 (20480K)   509904  (498K)   20461616 (19982K)

Total under 1 MB    814128  (795K)    104448  (102K)     709680  (693K)

Largest executable program size    550800  (538K)
Largest free upper memory block    131056  (128K)
MS-DOS is resident in the high memory area.
C:\>
```

Step 2: Create UMBs **539**

```
C:\>MEM/F
Free Conventional Memory:

  Segment        Total
  -------   -------------
   00708          80    (0K)
   00794          16    (0K)
   01985          96    (0K)
   0198B       87664   (86K)
   02EF2      463056  (452K)

  Total Free: 550912  (538K)

Free Upper Memory:

  Region   Largest Free    Total Free     Total Size
  ------   ------------   ------------   ------------
     1      27712  (27K)   27712  (27K)   27712  (27K)
     2     131056 (128K)  131056 (128K)  131056 (128K)
C:\>
```

Figure 10.24
The output from MEM/F showing two separate UMBs.

> **TIP**
> *If you want EMM386.EXE to not load part of itself into UMBs, specify the NOHI option in the EMM386.EXE invocation; I've never had a use for it myself, but it's one of those things you should try when the system locks up mysteriously.*

Step 3: Load Programs into UMBs

After the upper memory blocks are created, you're ready to use them.

Loading Programs High

Two DOS commands are used to load programs into UMBs:

- ✔ DEVICEHIGH replaces the DEVICE statement in CONFIG.SYS to load device drivers into UMBs.

- ✔ LOADHIGH, when used as a prefix for a TSR invocation, loads TSRs into UMBs.

DEVICEHIGH just takes the place of the DEVICE statement that's been in DOS since Version 2. It attempts to load a device driver into a UMB. If it's not successful, however, it just loads the driver into conventional memory without any complaint. For example, instead of the ANSI.SYS invocation we've been using...

    DEVICE=C:\DOS\ANSI.SYS

We can load ANSI.SYS high with...

    DEVICEHIGH=C:\DOS\ANSI.SYS

The LOADHIGH command, which can be abbreviated to LH, prefixes the command you normally use to load a program. The program then loads into a UMB, if there's one big enough to hold the program. For example, instead of invoking the DOSKEY program with the single line...

    DOSKEY

You can invoke it so that it loads high with...

    LH DOSKEY

If the device drivers and TSRs are loaded high, the sample CONFIG.SYS looks like this:

```
FILES=60
BUFFERS=30
DEVICE=C:\WINDOWS\HIMEM.SYS
DEVICE=C:\DOS\EMM386.EXE NOEMS X=A000-AFFF I=B000-B7FF
X=B800-CFFF I=D000-EFFF X=F000-FEFF
DOS=HIGH,UMB
DEVICEHIGH=C:\DOS\SETVER.EXE
DEVICEHIGH=C:\DOS\ANSI.SYS
```

AUTOEXEC.BAT looks like this:

```
PROMPT $p$g
PATH C\DOS;C:\UTILS
LH DOSKEY /BUFSIZE=30000
LH MOUSE
LH VSAFE
```

Boot the computer to try out these configurations; the output of MEM/C looks like figures 10.25 and 10.26.

Step 3: Load Programs into UMBs 541

```
Modules using memory below 1 MB:

Name            Total      =  Conventional  +  Upper Memory
----            -----         ------------     ------------
MSDOS           16061  (16K)   16061  (16K)       0    (0K)
HIMEM            1104   (1K)    1104   (1K)       0    (0K)
EMM386           4144   (4K)    4144   (4K)       0    (0K)
COMMAND          4704   (5K)    4704   (5K)       0    (0K)
VSAFE           22848  (22K)       0   (0K)   22848   (22K)
SETVER            672   (1K)       0   (0K)     672    (1K)
ANSI             4256   (4K)       0   (0K)    4256    (4K)
DOSKEY          33632  (33K)       0   (0K)   33632   (33K)
MOUSE           17088  (17K)       0   (0K)   17088   (17K)
Free           709664 (693K)  629360 (615K)   80304   (78K)

Memory Summary:

Type of Memory          Total      =       Used      +       Free
--------------          -----              ----              ----
Conventional           655360  (640K)    26000   (25K)   629360   (615K)
Upper                  158800  (155K)    78496   (77K)    80304    (78K)
Adapter RAM/ROM        234416  (229K)   234416  (229K)        0     (0K)
Extended (XMS)       19922944 (19456K)  171008  (167K) 19751936 (19289K)
Press any key to continue . . .
```

Figure 10.25

The output of MEM/C/P after loading programs high (part 1).

```
ANSI             4256   (4K)       0   (0K)    4256    (4K)
DOSKEY          33632  (33K)       0   (0K)   33632   (33K)
MOUSE           17088  (17K)       0   (0K)   17088   (17K)
Free           709664 (693K)  629360 (615K)   80304   (78K)

Memory Summary:

Type of Memory          Total      =       Used      +       Free
--------------          -----              ----              ----
Conventional           655360  (640K)    26000   (25K)   629360   (615K)
Upper                  158800  (155K)    78496   (77K)    80304    (78K)
Adapter RAM/ROM        234416  (229K)   234416  (229K)        0     (0K)
Extended (XMS)       19922944 (19456K)  171008  (167K) 19751936 (19289K)
Press any key to continue . . .
Expanded (EMS)              0    (0K)        0    (0K)        0     (0K)

Total memory         20971520 (20480K)   509920  (498K) 20461600 (19982K)

Total under 1 MB       814160  (795K)   104496  (102K)   709664   (693K)

Largest executable program size       629264  (615K)
Largest free upper memory block        52688   (51K)
MS-DOS is resident in the high memory area.
C:\>
```

Figure 10.26

The output of MEM/C/P after loading programs high (part 2).

You can see that all the memory numbers for the device drivers and TSRs moved from the Conventional column to the Upper Memory column, leaving 615K of conventional memory free. That's not bad: look back to figure 10.1 to remind yourself that before any memory management, the PC only had 467K of free conventional memory. (I hope that's reward enough for all the details I've put you through.)

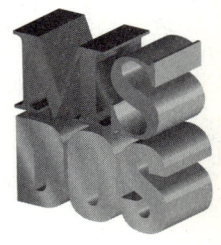

Looking at Programs that Load Themselves High

Before moving on, I should mention that there are some TSR programs that should not be loaded high simply because they load themselves high. One close-to-hand example is SMARTDrive Version 4.1, the version of SMARTDrive that ships with DOS 6.2, and version 4.0 that shipped with Windows 3.1.

SMARTDrive used to be a device driver under DOS 5 and earlier, but now it's primarily a TSR—I say primarily because you load it as a device driver in a few circumstances.

Try adding SMARTDrive to the notebook computer example: just add the line SMARTDRV to AUTOEXEC.BAT, resulting in an AUTOEXEC.BAT that looks like this:

```
PROMPT $p$g
PATH C\DOS;C:\UTILS
LH DOSKEY /BUFSIZE=30000
LH MOUSE
LH VSAFE
SMARTDRV
```

I won't show you the MEM/C output, but MEM reports that SMARTDRV.EXE loaded itself into a UMB. The important thing to see here is that I didn't have to prefix the program name with LH or the like: it loads high automatically.

> *If you want SMARTDRV to load itself low, you can force it to load low with the /L option. You may find that if you want maximum performance from SMARTDRV, you have to load it low. SMARTDRV is a bit slower when run from a UMB.*

The Workgroup Connection network programs also load themselves high automatically, provided that there are UMBs present into which they can fit. As time goes on, you'll see more and more programs that load themselves high automatically.

Disabling VCPI Support

Recall from Chapter 9 that some members of the class of programs called *DOS extenders* use a compatibility standard called VCPI, the Virtual Control Program Interface. Examples of VCPI-compliant programs are AutoCAD and Harvard Graphics 3.

Part of what EMM386.EXE offers is built-in support for the memory-switching required of any VCPI-compliant application. (The memory manager also must be VCPI compliant to work with a VCPI application.) The programming to support VCPI requires about 20K of RAM, however, and Microsoft knew that not everyone needs VCPI support.

Consequently, you can tell EMM386.EXE not to load VCPI support by including the NOVCPI parameter on the EMM386.EXE invocation. If you do that, you save about 20K of extended memory. No, it's not much extended memory, but it's better than nothing.

Using a Memory Manager with Limulation

Expanded memory is of less importance than it used to be, but there's still a wealth of programs out there that rely on or are enhanced by the presence of some expanded memory. If, like most 386/486/Pentium users, you don't have any expanded (also called LIM or EMS) memory, but rather have extended memory, it would be nice to be able "to emulate LIM," or to say it more specifically, *to limulate*. Limulation, the conversion of extended memory to expanded memory, is the third major feature of a memory manager.

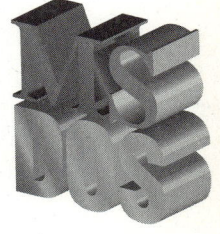

> **AUTHOR'S NOTE**
>
> *It's possible to do limulation with a 286 machine, but only with a small subset of 286 machines. This creates a difficult buying decision for 286 owners: when buying a memory board for your 286, should you buy extended or expanded memory? Many 286 memory boards are reversible for extended or expanded memory. These are good buys because you may need expanded today and want to use extended later.*
>
> *In general, limulators for 286s are not a good idea because full LIM 4.0 powers can't be emulated, and the 286 isn't built to limulate. If you must do this, I strongly recommend either replacing your 286-based motherboard with a 386-based motherboard; if you don't have a computer that allows for easy motherboard replacement, another approach is to purchase one of the many 386SX "daughtercards" that replace the existing 286 CPU. These small circuit boards are pin-for-pin compatible with the 286. It's not a great answer, but it's better than nothing. I've experimented with a few of these and have found them a bit troublesome to get to work with Windows or other non-DOS operating environments. They are, however, inexpensive (around $200 for the cheaper ones) and may be the only solution possible for you poor suckers stuck with a pile of PS/2 Model 50Zs and 60s.*

Limulating with EMM386.EXE

In its earliest incarnation, EMM386.SYS, as it was named in the DOS 4 days, was only a limulator. As it is even now if you invoke EMM386.EXE in CONFIG.SYS with no parameters:

```
DEVICE=C:\DOS\EMM386.EXE
```

This statement does not create any UMBs, but it gives you the ability to use LIM memory. The amount of LIM is, by default, equal to the amount of extended memory: EMM386.EXE changes memory from extended to expanded as needed. If you want to restrict the amount of LIM memory available, however, you can do that by specifying an amount of LIM in the EMM386.EXE invocation. For example, to restrict the amount of available LIM to 512K, change the EMM386 invocation like so:

```
DEVICE=C:\DOS\EMM386.EXE 512
```

So far, so easy. Of some concern is the effect expanded memory has on the upper memory area between 640K and 1024K. You may recall that expanded memory requires a 64K page frame that it shuttles data in and out of so that LIM-aware DOS programs can use data stored in LIM. That can be a big problem.

Consider that a LIM page frame needs 64K of UMB space, which could easily be more than half of the total UMB space we have. Furthermore, 64K must be a contiguous 64K—you can't give it 16K here, 32K here, and round off with 16K from somewhere else. The LIM page frame must start on a 16K boundary, so you can't use just *any* 64K for the page frame. The page frame must start at address X0000, X4000, X8000, or XC000, where *X* is some hexadecimal digit: C0000, C4000, C8000, or CC000 are acceptable but C7000 is not. All that is a bit restrictive—and memory-gobbling besides-so the moral of the story is if you can avoid limulation, do so because limulation chews up UMBs pretty quickly.

EMM386.EXE ought to be smart enough to find a contiguous 64K all by itself, but it cannot place the frame in either an included or excluded area; so it mutters a *nolle prosequi*...

```
WARNING: Unable to set base page frame address-EMS
unavailable
```

...and denies you any LIM memory.

The first order of business, then, is to help EMM386.EXE place a page frame. There are several methods that do that:

✔ Leave an unused area of exactly 64K in the UMA, neither included nor excluded, so that the page frame goes into that unused space.

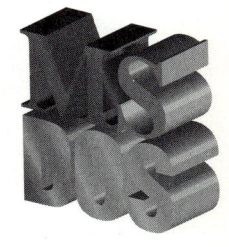

✔ Use the FRAME= parameter. Include a FRAME=*nnnn* parameter, where *nnnn* is a hex address, and EMM386.EXE places the 64K page frame starting at that address. EMM386.EXE trusts that the 64K area starting at *nnnn* is free, so make sure that the whole 64K area is free. The FRAME= parameter allows EMM386.EXE to put a frame inside included space. There is also a slightly shorter version of the FRAME= parameter: the /p parameter. For example, instead of including FRAME=C000 in the EMM386.EXE invocation, include /pC000 to have the same effect. If you wonder why there are two basically identical parameters for EMM386.EXE, so do I. My guess is that EMM386.EXE has been around a long time and has accumulated several generations' worth of parameters, some of which are a bit redundant.

✔ Instead of typing out the entire FRAME= parameter, use two or three predefined letter codes to direct EMM386.EXE to place the frame at particular locations. For example, instead of using FRAME=C000, you can just include the M1 parameter. There are M*n* parameters for *n*=1 through 14. The Mn parameters place the frame at the following locations:

M1	C0000
M2	C4000
M3	C8000
M4	CC000
M5	D0000
M6	D4000
M7	D8000
M8	DC000
M9	E0000
M10	80000
M11	84000
M12	88000
M13	8C000
M14	90000

Using a Memory Manager with Limulation

It's reasonable for you to ask why Microsoft offers these extra redundant parameters. All I can say is, "Danged if *I* know." One value to the "Mn" parameters is that they take up less space on the CONFIG.SYS line.

Suppose you want to do limulation on the sample PC. Currently, the EMM386.EXE statement looks like this:

```
DEVICE=C:\DOS\EMM386.EXE NOEMS X=A000-AFFF I=B000-B7FF
X=B800-CFFF I=D000-EFFF X=F000-FEFF
```

To get expanded memory, you must first remove the NOEMS parameter and then place the frame. This computer has 64K of contiguous space starting at D000 at which you can place the frame. Just add a FRAME=D000 parameter to make the invocation look like this:

```
DEVICE=C:\DOS\EMM386.EXE X=A000-AFFF I=B000-B7FF X=B800-
CFFF I=D000-EFFF X=F000-FEFF FRAME=D000
```

Recall that although this line may have broken on the page, you should not break it in CONFIG.SYS.

The effect of removing NOEMS and adding FRAME= is that you get LIM services but not UMBs. (To get LIM and UMBs, stay tuned for a couple of paragraphs.)

> *You can't always get LIM to work on a computer. If you have lots of adapters with lots of RAM buffers or ROMs, you may not be able to find 64K of contiguous space. This is a particular problem with a PS/2 computer with the BIOS that extends from 896K through 1024K (E0000-FFFFF); I've seen computers where it was just plain impossible to find 64K of contiguous unused address space starting on a 16K boundary. So draw your memory map carefully when limulating.*

Using a Memory Manager for UMBs and Limulation

You've already done the hard work, so the rest is simple. You've seen that the NOEMS parameter provides UMBs but no expanded (LIM or EMS) memory. Using no parameter provides only LIM memory. To get both expanded memory and UMBs, you need the RAM parameter. Make sure that the FRAME= statement is in place, and put a LIM size number in if you want to restrict the amount of LIM memory provided by the system.

To add UMBs, for example, to the last invocation, use this EMM386.EXE statement:

```
DEVICE=C:\DOS\EMM386.EXE RAM X=A000-AFFF I=B000-B7FF
X=B800-CFFF I=D000-EFFF X=F000-FEFF FRAME=D000
```

Understanding Shadow RAM

Many memory managers offer a feature called shadow RAM. It's a popular feature, but one that I recommend you use with care.

As you learned in previous chapters, your computer has some essential system software called the BIOS—the Basic Input/Output System. It's not really a *system* (whatever that means); it's just a collection of small programs your computer depends on to communicate with its hardware. For example, one part of BIOS is the program known as INT10; it performs video functions. Every time DOS needs to display some data on the screen, it does so by calling the INT10 program many times: once for each character DOS wants to display.

BIOS is part of the chain that extends from application to hardware: in theory, an application makes requests of DOS, which makes requests of BIOS, which in turn controls the hardware. By the way, I say *in theory* because, *as you saw in Chapter 2, some DOS programs bypass DOS and the BIOS altogether*. INT10 is a particularly apt example because the video routines in DOS and the BIOS are fairly slow and inefficient; that's why most applications bypass the BIOS in the first place.

BIOS is different from other software in that it isn't loaded from disk into memory. Instead, it's preloaded into a special kind of memory called ROM, or Read-Only Memory. *Chapter 9 discusses ROM in more detail.* There's one small bad feature, however: even though ROMs are memory and memory is fast—much faster than disk—ROMs are a good deal slower than RAM. Up to four or five times slower, in fact, which means that every time your computer executes a BIOS program, it's forced to slow down.

What ROM shadowing or shadow RAM does is to copy the ROMs to RAM, providing RAMs that mimic the ROM function but have the speed of RAM. Sounds good, eh? It can be...but it can pose problems as well.

The good part is the greater speed, which is no small potatoes. On a cheap, no-name 486 that I work with, shadow RAM sped up a program that wrote data to the video screen only through the BIOS by a factor of 10 over the same test when I didn't shadow.

But it's got problems. The first problem is that it may just plain crash the floppy drives. The BIOS program that affects your floppy drive—INT13—is very sensitive to timing and is often designed with the relatively slow speed of ROM in mind. I've seen computers whose floppies behave erratically when ROM is shadowed. The second problem is that the programs that provide shadow RAM don't always implement shadow RAM properly. ROMs are supposed to have a checksum value in them that DOS can use to ensure that they haven't been damaged. That checksum isn't always properly implemented when the ROM is copied to RAM. Because of that, Windows or OS/2 often doesn't like shadow RAM. If some software becomes unstable after you install shadow RAM on your system, get rid of shadow RAM. The shadow RAM feature is either a built-in feature offered by your system's SETUP program or as part of the memory-manager program.

Don't be too sad about having to put aside shadow RAM: it looks good on benchmark programs but it's not that relevant to the real world. Think about where it's useful: when the BIOS is called. The fact is that most DOS applications bypass the BIOS altogether and manipulate the hardware directly to gain speed. If you try Lotus 1-2-3 or

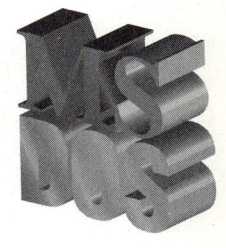

WordPerfect with and without shadow RAM, you'll see no speed difference whatsoever because the BIOS isn't used by either of those programs. In fact, the biggest user of BIOS is probably DOS, which means that the most visible effect of shadow RAM is that it can make the DIR command blazingly fast...which doesn't really seem like that much of a feature.

Anyway, assuming that you want to try shadow RAM on your system, there are a few ways to implement it:

- ✔ Many PCs have a shadow-RAM feature built right into their BIOSes. You activate or deactivate shadow RAM on these systems by running that PC's setup program. Unfortunately, some PCs do not offer the option of disabling shadow RAM: many PS/2 computers shadow the video and main system BIOS whether you want them to or not.
- ✔ Third-party, memory-manager products like QEMM and 386Max offer shadow-RAM features, but they can only shadow RAM if you use that third-party memory manager.
- ✔ EMM386.EXE offers a shadow-RAM capability, albeit not a very good one.

In DOS 6.2, EMM386.EXE gained the capability to shadow a ROM. To shadow a ROM, specify its address with the ROM=nnnn parameter. So, for example, you could take the EMM386.EXE statement that we saw before and shadow the video BIOS. The invocation looked like this:

```
DEVICE=C:\DOS\EMM386.EXE NOEMS X=A000-AFFF I=B000-B7FF
X=B800-CFFF I=D000-EFFF X=F000-FEFF
```

To shadow the video ROM, just change this statement like so:

```
DEVICE=C:\DOS\EMM386.EXE NOEMS X=A000-AFFF I=B000-B7FF
ROM=B800-C7FF X=B800-CFFF I=D000-EFFF X=F000-FEFF
```

NOTE *Don't expect too much in terms of performance improvement because so many programs bypass the BIOS anyway, making shadowing irrelevant. Additionally, EMM386.EXE unfortunately doesn't do a very good job of shadowing.*

Sorting Memory and Backfilling

Two memory-management features that first appeared in the early days of memory management you should know about. Although they're both pretty much irrelevant in today's hardware world, activating either feature can give many modern software programs (Windows, DOS extender products, and the like) heartburn. The two features are called *speed sorting* and *backfilling*.

Speed Sorting

In early 386 computers, it wasn't uncommon to see the first 256K of RAM implemented as fairly slow 64K chips (in case you're wondering, cost was the reason); empty sockets offered RAM expansion from that point on. Most 386 owners opted for mildly more expensive and faster memory for expansion memory with the result that they had 256K of slow memory in the bottom addresses, and a megabyte or two of fast memory from address 256K up.

The problem is that the memory that gets the most use is the bottom 640K. It seemed a shame that nearly half of it—256K—was slow, while much of the nearly useless extended memory was so fast. The wonderful capability of the 386 chip to reshuffle memory was employed by early memory-manager products; it was fairly common in the late 80s for a memory manager to time each section of the PC's memory and move the fastest memory down into the 0-to-640K range. That's called *memory sorting*.

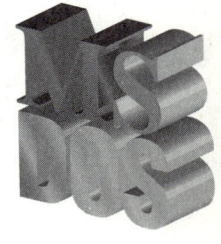

Memory sorting makes no sense in today's PCs because they generally have blocks of equal-speed memory at least 4M in size, if not 16M in size; I don't think there's been a computer sold in years that adds memory in 256K modules. You should disable the speed-sorting feature anyway, because there's the chance that the algorithm that tries to implement it can cause memory-manager havoc. If your memory manager offers memory sorting, disable it. EMM386.EXE does not do speed sorting.

Memory Backfilling

One of the first popular 386-based motherboards had 1024K of RAM on its motherboard. The designers of this motherboard which was based on an early Chips and Technologies chipset, got a bit lazy; that's where the story—and the feature—come from. On this motherboard, the 1024K of RAM wasn't divided as it normally is (640K conventional, 384K extended). Instead, it was divided into 512K of conventional memory and 512K of extended memory. Using the memory-shuffling capabilities of the 386, the earliest memory managers included a neat feature that moved 128K from extended memory to conventional memory, "backfilling" conventional memory from extended memory.

A good and useful feature, but, like shadow RAM, not an advisable one. Windows and other DOS-extender programs don't coexist well with backfilling. For most of us, it's a moot point and not worth worrying about. But you never know when you'll run into a memory manager that thinks it must backfill, and as a result creates a mess with Windows or similar programs. EMM386.EXE doesn't backfill—at least, I *think* it doesn't backfill (there aren't too many of those old motherboards to try it out on). If you use another memory manager, it's a good idea to check whether it has a backfill feature; if it does, disable it.

> **AUTHOR'S NOTE**
>
> In this chapter, you learned how to use the major features of memory managers—in particular how to implement them with EMM386.EXE and HIMEM.SYS, the DOS 6.2 memory manager programs.
>
> If it seems I've thrown a lot of commands at you, you may be a bit fuzzy on where they go. Here's a summary of how to use memory managers in CONFIG.SYS:
>
> 1. HIMEM.SYS should appear before EMM386.EXE and any device drivers to be loaded high or that employ extended memory.
>
> 2. If there are any device drivers that will not be loaded high but that use XMS memory, they can appear anywhere after HIMEM.
>
> 3. EMM386.EXE should follow HIMEM.SYS and be before any device drivers to be loaded high.
>
> 4. The DOS=HIGH,UMB statement can go anywhere in CONFIG.SYS, but I usually place it after EMM86.EXE just to keep track of it.
>
> After the DOS=HIGH,UMB statement, you can load any device drivers you want to load high.

Summary

In this chapter, you learned about the three major uses of memory managers:

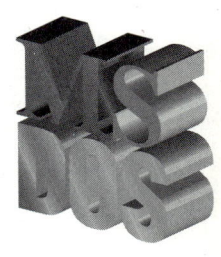

- ✔ To create and use the High Memory Area (HMA)
- ✔ To create and use Upper Memory Blocks (UMBs)
- ✔ To convert extended memory to expanded memory

You can load DOS into the HMA, freeing up over 50K of space in the conventional area. With some careful mapping, parts of the address range between 640K and 1024K can be opened up, making room to load TSRs high. The mapping is a pain, but it must be done. It's accomplished by "including" and "excluding" areas in the upper memory area. Finally, a memory manager can create LIM memory, but at the cost of 64K in the UMB space for a page frame.

In the next chapter, you learn how to choose and install more memory in your system...now that you know what to do with it.

MS-DOS

MS DOS

CHAPTER 11

Memory Organization and Upgrade Strategies

by Mark Minasi

Now that you know what you can do with memory beyond the familiar 640K level, you're probably thinking about getting more memory so that you have something to manage with DOS 6.2's memory manager. Before you try to choose and install more RAM, read this chapter; it gives you the information you need to keep from making mistakes.

Adding memory involves a few basic steps:

1. You must buy the right type and number of memory devices.
2. You must install the memory correctly.
3. You must test the memory before relying on it.

Chapter 11: *Memory Organization and Upgrade Strategies*

Once you learn about upgrading memory, the chapter finishes with a brief discussion about a special kind of memory called *cache memory*.

Buying the Right Memory

Remember how confusing it was to buy your PC? New terminology, different brands that seemed to offer the same kind of hardware for very different prices? Well, it's the same for memory. As when you buy a PC, the time you spend learning how to buy memory wisely is time well spent.

When buying memory, you've got to be sure that you...

- ✔ Buy memory packaged in a format compatible with your computer: DIP chips, SIMMs, or proprietary modules.
- ✔ Buy memory of the right speed and capacity (nanoseconds and megabytes).
- ✔ Buy memory in the right increments.

Looking at RAM Package Types

When the PC first appeared, there was only one kind of memory upgrade hardware available. It was a small chip that stored 16,384 bits of data and was called a 16K RAM. You could buy nine of these chips and plug them into empty sockets on the PC's motherboard. As the industry has grown, however, alternatives have appeared: memory has gotten denser, cheaper, faster, and easier to install. The developers, though, followed several paths, which have led to a real profusion of memory packages. Following is an overview of the different memory-package types.

To find out which of these memory types you should buy, you can pop the top on your PC and take a look inside to see what you've currently got. Alternatively, you can consult the documentation that accompanied your computer. (Don't say that the documentation doesn't tell you anything; although it's true that PC documentation

Buying the Right Memory **559**

can often be terrible, one thing that all PC system documentation covers is RAM requirements.)

AUTHOR'S NOTE

Before examining chip packages in detail, you should first understand the term data path. Any piece of hardware that uses data must be able to read and write that data; in order to read and write data, the hardware has to have a place built into it that does the reading and writing. Think of it this way: memory is something like a warehouse for your data. Every warehouse has a loading dock. The loading dock on any memory package is the set of wires used to transfer data into or out of the memory. The wider a memory device's loading dock, the more data can be transferred to or from that memory device at any instant in time.

For example, consider two different kinds of memory devices. The first is called a one-megabit chip (it has the capacity to hold 1,024K bits of data). The second is called a 256K nybble chip (it has the capacity to hold 256K of 4-bit groups of data called nybbles). (You know that 4 bits is a nybble, and you almost certainly know that 8 bits is a byte.) The capacity of the 256K nybble chip is 256K times 4 bits, or 1,024K bits. That means that both chips have the same capacity; so why give them different names? Although the capacity of both warehouses is the same, they've got different-sized loading docks. You can load or unload only a single bit at a time with the 1-megabit chip, but you can load or unload 4 bits simultaneously with the 256K nybble chip.

That turns out to be important later: not only do memory devices have data paths, CPUs have them as well. You have to be sure that your memory devices collectively provide a data path of a width that supports the CPU's data path. For example, if you wanted to buy memory for a CPU with a 16-bit data path, and you were looking at memory devices like the 1-megabit chip, recall that each memory chip has a data path of just 1 bit. The CPU's 16-bit data path, then, requires you to add memory in increments of 16 chips so that the memory circuitry can transfer enough data to satisfy the CPU's needs. If that's not totally clear, don't worry about it: there's a lot more detail and examples coming up in the section called "Understanding Why One's Not Enough: Memories Come in Groups."

Bit DIP-type RAM

The oldest kind of memory device is a memory chip with a single-bit data path. These chips, also called DRAMs (Dynamic Random Access Memories), are packaged in a Dual Inline Pin (DIP) container, the most common chip package. Figure 11.1 shows a DIP package.

Figure 11.1
A nybble-type chip package.

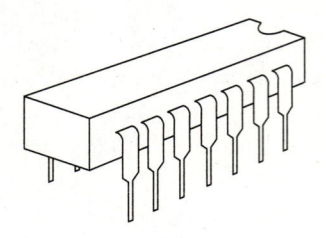

DIP chips with a single-bit data path are typically added to PCs in multiples of eight or nine. They are inserted into sockets soldered directly onto the PC's motherboard or onto a special memory expansion board.

Nybble DIP-Type RAM

Around 1985, some motherboards started appearing with sockets for DIP-type chips that were a bit longer than normal; they held chips with a couple of extra pairs of legs. Those chips organized their internal data a bit differently, allowing an outside device (like a CPU) to request not 1 bit at a time, but 4 bits (a nybble). Nybble DIP memory chips look like bit-type DIP memory chips, but longer (see fig. 11.2).

Figure 11.2
A nybble-type DIP package.

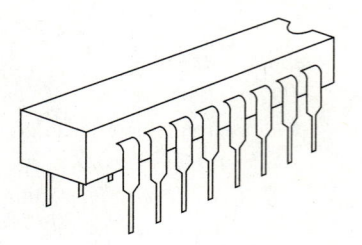

Nybble chips are inserted into nybble-sized sockets. Nybble memories are more convenient to install than bit-type memories, and must generally be installed in pairs or in pairs with a single bit-type chip added. Nybble DIPs are also a type of dynamic RAM.

In general, inserting bit-type memory into sockets intended for nybble-type memory, or vice versa, does not work and can permanently damage the memory.

RAM in SIMM Packages

You've read that bit-type DIP memory is generally installed in multiples of eight or nine. Those are a lot of chips to insert when it's memory-upgrade time, but bit-type DIP chips were a real blessing back in the days of expensive RAM chips. You could run diagnostic programs to tell you exactly which chip was at fault, so that all you had to do was replace a single bad chip, not all eight or nine.

As time went on, however, memory chips became inexpensive (under five dollars), and the annoyance of installing nine or more chips began to outweigh the benefits of being able to troubleshoot down to the chip level. In 1987, PCs that used Single Inline Memory Modules (SIMMs) were introduced. SIMMs are basically small circuit boards with eight or nine bit-type DIP chips soldered onto them (see fig. 11.3).

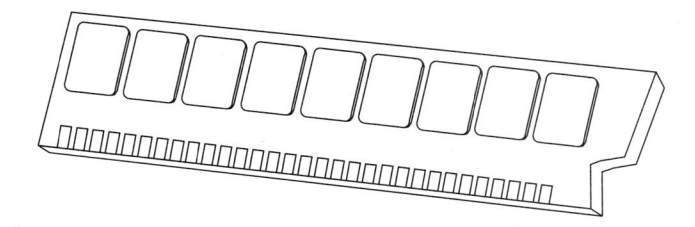

Figure 11.3

A Single Inline Memory Module (SIMM).

SIMMs offered the convenience of snapping in a small circuit board in less time than it takes to insert a single chip—and in lots less time than it takes to insert eight or nine bit-type DIP chips!

AUTHOR'S NOTE

By the way, when you read advertisements for memories, you'll see reference to SIMMs that are 1M×9 versus 1M×8, or 256K×9 versus 256K×8, and so on. Don't worry about the sizes (1M, 256K, and the like) but understand that ×8 and ×9 refer to the number of bit-type DIP chips on the SIMM itself. You read earlier that most PCs use bit-type DIP chips in multiples of nine, but a few use multiples of eight. As far as I know, all PCs use SIMMs with an equivalent of 9 bit-type chips on them. Macintoshes, on the other hand, use SIMMs with an equivalent of eight bit-type chips. So don't buy ×8 SIMMs for your PC unless you're absolutely sure that you've got an oddball PC that doesn't use the normal ×9 SIMMs.

RAM in SIPP Packages

SIMMs are small circuit boards with edge connectors: little gold fingers that, when snug against corresponding gold fingers in a SIMM socket, provide the electrical connections needed for the PC to use the SIMM. Chips, on the other hand, do not use edge connectors; they use small metal pins that are pushed into holes in a socket. A few computers use a variation of a SIMM that looks like a SIMM but has pins like a chip. It's called a Single Inline Pin Package, or SIPP. It works just like a SIMM, but is more difficult to install and remove because it's easy to break off the little pins. You can see a SIPP in figure 11.4.

Figure 11.4

A Single Inline Pin Package (SIPP).

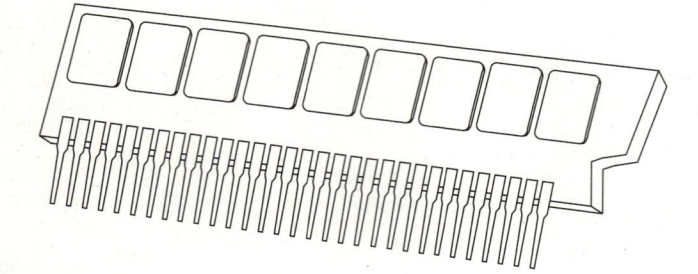

The question of whether you need SIMMs or SIPPs is determined by the kind of sockets that are on your motherboard. SIMMs are far more common than SIPPs.

Proprietary SIMM

When you read advertisements for SIMMs, notice that they refer to different kinds of SIMMs. Some SIMMs are just called SIMMs and others are called IBM SIMMs, Toshiba SIMMs, or the like. Most PCs use an industry-standard SIMM with nine chips on a board; IBM and a number of other vendors use a nonstandard SIMM of their own making. Unfortunately, these proprietary SIMMs are usually more expensive than the generic SIMMs, suggesting that it's perhaps a good idea to avoid buying PCs that use proprietary SIMM types.

Proprietary Memory Modules

SIMMs don't make sense for all PCs. Because they stand up on the motherboard of a PC, it's hard to find room for them on a low-profile laptop. As a result, some PC manufacturers build their own memory devices. For example, the IBM PS/2 Model 80 employs a strange proprietary memory device that looks like a futuristic high-rise condominium. The Toshiba 4400SXC computer uses memory that looks like a thick credit card. There is an emerging laptop standard called the PCMCIA (Personal Computer Memory Card Industry Association) that will probably become the next standard in memory. Like the Toshiba memory device, PCMCIA slots enable PC manufacturers to offer add-in devices like memory, modems, and the like in a small form. PCMCIA was originally intended for laptops, but don't be surprised to see PCMCIA slots on desktop PCs soon. Assuming, of course, that desktop PCs will even exist in a few years. If notebook PCs keep catching up to desktops in price and features, the familiar beige box on the desktop will probably go the way of the card reader and the light pen: interesting side trips on the way to truly useful computing.

Buying the Right Speed and Size RAMs

Merely knowing that you need SIMMs for your PC is not enough. A quick glance at a recent memory ad shows references to things like *SIMM/256KX9 80ns*, *SIMM/16MBX9 70ns*, *SIPP 1X9/70*, *DRAM 1MBX1 60ns*, and *DRAM 1MBX4 80ns* memories. Perhaps you can understand some—if not all—of what these ads refer to. *SIMM/256KX9* is a SIMM with the equivalent circuitry of nine chips, rather than eight chips. *SIPP 1X9* refers to another 9-bit equivalent device. *DRAM 1MBX1* refers to a bit-type DIP memory chip; the *X1* means that there's a data path of 1 bit. The *X4* in the last reference means that the chip is a nybble-type chip, with a data path of 4 bits.

But what about the rest of it? The two items you must be able to decipher from the ads are the size and the speed of the memory device.

Understanding RAM Sizes

RAM is not available in random sizes; it tends to appear in sizes that are powers of two or powers of four. Over time, memories have appeared whose sizes were 256 bytes, then 1,024 bytes (1K), then 4K, and then 16K (at about the time the PC arrived on the market). PC memories continued to grow, quadrupling in size with each jump: the 16K memories commonplace in 1981 gave way to 64K memories, which yielded to 256K, then 1024K (1M), 4M, until now we're seeing 16M modules advertised.

I often joke about the imminent appearance of 1G memories, but consider: if 16M memories are available today, three generations from now (in terms of chip generations, not human generations) we'll see memories whose sizes are 16 x 4 x 4 x 4 megabytes in size; that's 1,024M or 1 gigabyte. The time between when 16K RAMs were common and when 1024K RAMs became widespread was about 8 years; perhaps by the turn of the century, we'll all have at least a gigabyte of RAM on our PCs.

In today's market, most memory is in the 1M and 4M size (low-end PCs use 256K SIMMs or DRAMs). You find exceptions to all rules in the proprietary market. For example, although you can't find 2M memory modules among standard SIMMs, you can find them in PS/2

memories, Compaq memory modules, and proprietary laptop memories, to name a few.

Understanding RAM Speed

Last on the list of memory characteristics is the speed of the memory. You've probably heard the term *megahertz* (sounds like "a lot of pain," doesn't it?) and are no doubt aware that bigger megahertz means a faster PC. For example, a 50 MHz 486 is (all other things equal) faster than a 25 MHz 486. Faster computers generally need faster memory. Memory speed, however, isn't measured in megahertz. It's usually expressed in another way: access time.

The megahertz (MHz) unit refers to a circuit that drives the entire computer, a circuit called the clock circuit. Each time the clock goes *tick*, some work gets done. (Think of it as being like a coxswain on a rowing team. The coxswain sits up front, saying *stroke, stroke, stroke...* while the oarsmen row in time to his voice.) The more *tick*s per second, the more work the CPU does. One megahertz means one million ticks per second; 50 megahertz means 50 million ticks per second.

Any device keeping up with such a rapid pace must be fast, and the faster the device, the more expensive. That's one reason why a 50 MHz 486DX computer is more expensive than a 25 MHz 486DX computer: the parts that go into a 50 MHz 486DX are basically the same parts that go into the 25 MHz 486DX, but they're more expensive because they're harder to make.

So faster computers need faster memory. But memory speed is measured in nanoseconds (ns) of access time. A nanosecond is one billionth of a second; *access time* is roughly the amount of time required for a memory device to retrieve a piece of data. The stated access time is the longest the CPU will ever have to wait for the memory to respond to the CPU's request.

Technically speaking, between the time the CPU requests data from the memory and the time the memory delivers it, two operations actually take place. First, the memory must be precharged so that the act of reading a bit in the memory does not also erase that bit from the memory cell.

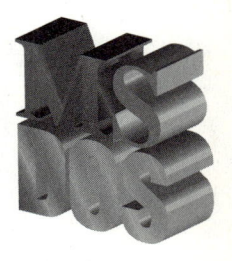

That takes some time, after which the actual memory access occurs. The amount of time required for the memory access is the access time. The access time added to the precharge time is the total amount of time a CPU must wait for data from a memory device. On some memories, the precharge time can be quite significant—almost equal to the access time.

Unfortunately, the only source of information on a RAM's precharge times is the manufacturer's data sheet on that RAM. Those sheets are available on request from chip manufacturers, but most of us never think to request them.

Larger numbers mean faster when talking about megahertz, but smaller means faster when discussing access times on memories. You see memory ads these days that offer access times of 100ns, 80ns, 70ns, 60ns, 53ns, and even 40ns.

In general, if a computer needs memories of a particular access time, that computer can use faster memories as well. For example, if your PC's documentation says it needs 80ns memories, 70ns memories usually work too (subject to some restrictions, as explained in the next section).

Before moving on to a more involved discussion of whether or not to buy faster memories, here's one more thing about proprietary memories. Now you have the background information you need to read memory ads, but be aware that if you're buying a specialized proprietary memory device (like the nonstandard SIMMs that IBM uses on its PS/2 computers), you usually don't have to worry about memory speeds. In fact, you probably won't see memory speeds advertised for proprietary modules. Because these memories are intended for one particular computer model, there's no need for the vendors to advertise speed; they need only advertise size and price.

Buying Memory of Uniform Speed

What speed memory should you buy? There are several pieces in the answer to that puzzle.

✔ **Speed is good.** Because there is a certain amount of engineering "slack" between one memory and another—and between one PC system and another—there's some comfort in buying the fastest memories possible. That way, if you end up with memory that's a hair slower than advertised, or if you have a PC that's a hair faster than advertised, you don't end up with memory errors. (Once, the most common source of memory errors was faulty memory modules; nowadays, it's most likely that "bad memory" is just "slow memory.")

> *Buying fast memory does not make your PC run faster. Your PC runs at a particular speed (whatever its clock rate is), and it assumes that everything can keep up with it; if something doesn't keep up, the PC considers that component a failed component.*

✔ **Speed is expensive.** Although speed is good, buying lightning-fast chips is costly. For example, a memory ad in a recent magazine offers 1-megabyte SIMMs (*1M X 9* in memory lingo) in speeds from 100ns to 40ns. The 100ns SIMMs cost $32; the 40ns SIMMs cost $69. From the point of view of saving money, the best answer may be to consult your PC documentation, find what speed memories the PC needs, and then buy those memories. In essence, this philosophy says to buy the slowest memories you can get away with.

✔ **Speed should match across your PC's memory.** Although you can buy faster memories than your system needs and experience no trouble on most PCs, some PCs are quirky. A few clones I've run into require memories of a single speed. A 386DX-20 motherboard I populated with 16M of RAM with the intention of running OS/2 could not run OS/2, even though it could run Windows. Stringent memory tests showed that putting memories of different speeds in different memory banks caused occasional nonrepeating memory errors. OS/2 is more careful in examining the memory it uses than Windows is; hence OS/2 became the "canary in the coal mine" that alerted me to the problem.

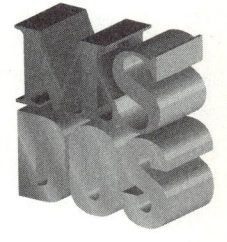

✔ **Speed must match within a memory bank.** You learn in the next section that you add memory to your PC in specific minimum increments called *memory banks*. Within a bank, the speeds *must* be constant.

Having expressed all these mildly contradictory points of fact and advice, what's the happy medium? Consider that memories are a lot cheaper than they were just a few years ago (even expensive memory is cheap). Consider further that as you upgrade the memory on your computer with denser memory (for example, if you replace some 1M SIMMs with 4M SIMMs so that you can put more RAM in a fixed number of sockets), you can recycle the 1M SIMMs into some other PC. If you bought fast SIMMs in the first place, you should have a wide variety of computers you can put the 1M SIMMs into. I usually put the fastest memories I can afford into a computer and make sure that any subsequent RAM additions are of the same speed as the initial batch of memory.

Understanding Why One's Not Enough: Memories Come in Groups

As you've read, memory chips come in varying sizes and speeds. But they also have a final characteristic: you must install them in groups. In general, you can't simply add one SIMM to a computer and end up with upgraded memory. Typically, you add two or four chips, or you don't bother at all. (Proprietary memory systems are an exception. Most proprietary systems feature memory devices that can be upgraded one at a time.) As you learned earlier in this chapter, memory chips have a capacity and a data path (the size of the "front door" of the chip). PC processors also have "front doors" of various sizes. Table 11.1 lists the data paths for the most common CPU chips.

Table 11.1
Common PC CPUs and Data Paths

CPU	Data Path
8088	8
80188	8

CPU	Data Path
8086	16
80186	16
80286	16
80386SX	16
80386SL	16
80386DX	32
80486SX	32
80486DX	32
80486SLC	16
80486DLC	32
80486DX2	32

As CPU technology improved, data paths widened. The 8088, a chip designed in 1978, has an 8-bit data path and can read or write 8 bits at a time. The 80286 and 80386SX have a 16-bit data path, enabling them to transfer twice as much data in one operation. Most of the 386 family, released by Intel at least 10 years after the 8088's inception, have 32-bit data paths. The data path determines how a PC's memory banks are arranged, which then determines how many chips you must install at a minimum when upgrading memory.

Looking at an 8088 Memory Bank

Consider the 8088 memory chip. (I know, I know: you don't have an 8088 any more. Except for the original PC I'm keeping around on the off chance that the Smithsonian will want it one day, I don't have an 8088 either. But it's a lot easier to diagram—and visualize—an 8-bit data path than a 32-bit data path.)

Figure 11.5 shows a partial diagram of an 8088 chip. The 8 chip legs you see on it are the eight data pins on the CPU.

Figure 11.5

An 8088 CPU with eight data pins.

CPU DATA PATH

Suppose that you want to add bit-type DIP memories to the computer for this CPU. Each bit-type DIP memory has a data path of 1 bit. Figure 11.6 shows a bit-type DIP memory chip next to the CPU, with the memory's single-bit data path connected to one of the data bits on the 8088 CPU.

Figure 11.6

An 8088 CPU with a single RAM chip added.

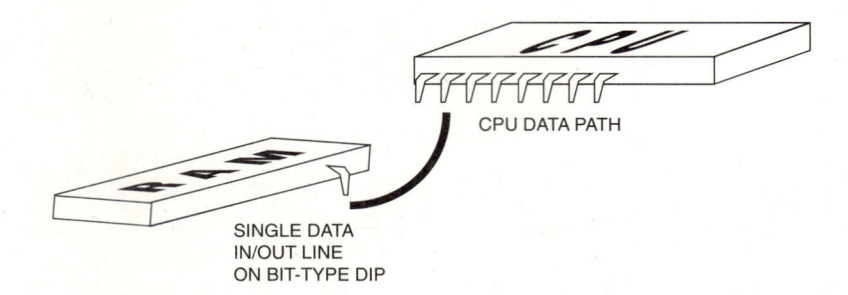

CPU DATA PATH

SINGLE DATA IN/OUT LINE ON BIT-TYPE DIP

You can see that this single chip won't meet the needs of this CPU, which must be able to read or write 8 bits simultaneously. This memory chip can only serve on one line of the CPU's 8-bit data path. Figure 11.7 suggests what you'd have to do to add memory to this PC in an effective manner.

Figure 11.7

An 8088 CPU with a memory bank added (not all chips displayed).

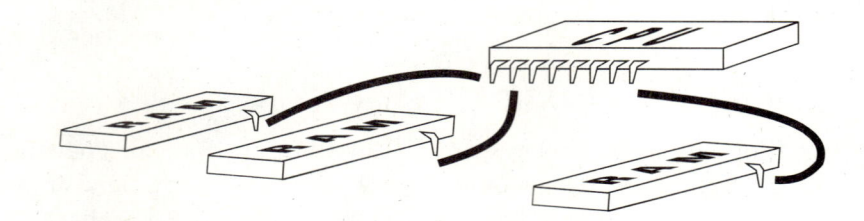

There wasn't really room in the diagram for eight chips, but you can see how eight chips would work together to form a memory bank.

But that's not the whole story; earlier in this chapter I said that most PC memory banks use multiples of 9 chips, not 8. Most PCs add a ninth chip called a *parity chip*. In the simplified arrangement shown in figure 11.8, the ninth chip is labeled with a *P*. The ninth memory chip and another chip, called a *comparator*, are used to check the integrity of the data in memory.

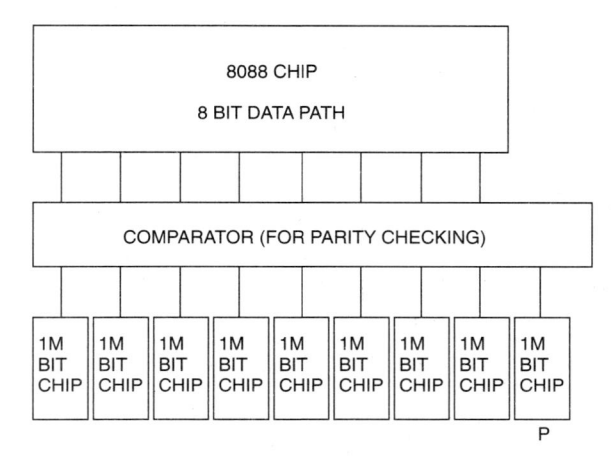

```
┌─────────────────────────────────────────┐
│              8088 CHIP                  │
│           8 BIT DATA PATH               │
└─────────────────────────────────────────┘
      │  │  │  │  │  │  │  │
┌─────────────────────────────────────────┐
│      COMPARATOR (FOR PARITY CHECKING)   │
└─────────────────────────────────────────┘
      │  │  │  │  │  │  │  │  │
   ┌──┐┌──┐┌──┐┌──┐┌──┐┌──┐┌──┐┌──┐┌──┐
   │1M││1M││1M││1M││1M││1M││1M││1M││1M│
   │BIT││BIT││BIT││BIT││BIT││BIT││BIT││BIT││BIT│
   │CHIP││CHIP││CHIP││CHIP││CHIP││CHIP││CHIP││CHIP││CHIP│
   └──┘└──┘└──┘└──┘└──┘└──┘└──┘└──┘└──┘
                                        P
```

Figure 11.8

An 8088 CPU with a memory bank that includes a parity chip.

When 8 bits of data are written to RAM, the comparator generates the ninth parity bit based on the contents of the other 8. When the data is read back, the comparator uses the parity chip to check whether the 8 bits of data have been damaged by a hardware error in the memory, a power surge, or the like. If the comparator detects an error, it generates a software interrupt (*software interrupts were described in Chapter 2*) called a *nonmaskable interrupt* (NMI) because the error can't be ignored. What the CPU does with the information that corrupted data was found in a memory location depends on the kind of computer you've got; IBM computers respond by putting the words `Parity Check` on the screen and then locking up the computer. You must turn the PC off and on again to get it to respond.

The value of the comparator in checking for corrupt data is the reason why so many memory banks consist of 9 chips. Most XT memory banks require 9 chips: there is no value in adding 2 or 3 bit-oriented memory chips when the CPU needs all 9 to work.

Now suppose that you want to build a memory bank from nybble chips. Recall that each nybble provides 4 bits; 2 nybbles provide 8 bits. Because your computer probably uses a ninth parity bit, you have to match 2 nybble chips with a single-bit chip, as shown in figure 11.9.

Figure 11.9

An 8088 memory bank built from nybble chips.

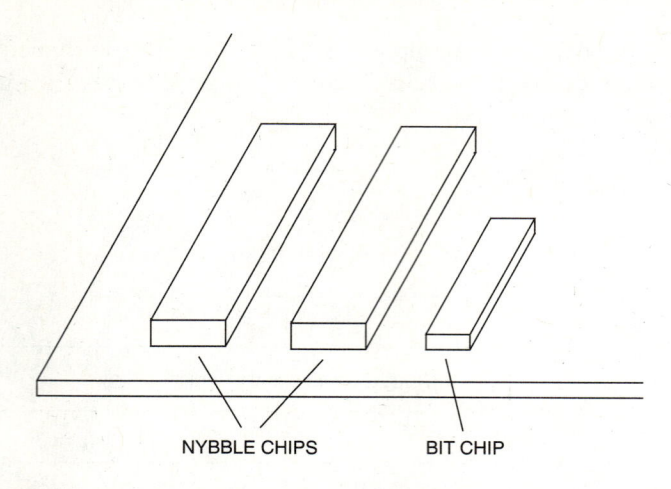

NYBBLE CHIPS   BIT CHIP

If this 8088 used a 1M SIMM, how many SIMMs constitute a memory bank for an 8088? A generic SIMM is the equivalent of nine 1-bit chips; just one SIMM provides everything the 8088 needs.

Building Memory Banks for 16-bit Computers

What you've learned so far explains how 8088 memory banks work. But you probably don't have an 8088-based computer; you probably have a PC based on a 286 CPU, or perhaps a 386SX or 386SL. Recall that 286 and 386SX computers don't have an 8-bit data path—they've got a 16-bit data path. Therefore, 8 or 9 memory chips can't do the job for them. Because the 286's front door or data path is 16 bits wide, you need sixteen 256K-bit chips to create a memory bank for the 286—if the 286 computer was designed to work without parity. With parity, you need a parity bit for each 8-bit group (that's 2 extra bits in the bank), for a total of 18 chips. The minimum number of memory bit chips you add to a 286 system is 18. If you use nybble chips, you need 4 nybbles and 2 bits (hmmm, this is starting to sound like a dog-food commercial). With ordinary SIMMs that provide 9 bits, you need 2 SIMMs to provide a full bank for 286, 386SX, or 386SL systems.

Buying the Right Memory

NOTE: *Some vendors, like IBM and Toshiba, have designed their own special proprietary 16-bit SIMMs. That's why the IBM PS/2 model 55SX, which uses a 386SX, only requires 1 SIMM to make a bank: it's a special 16-bit SIMM.*

On a typical 386SX computer, you see room for 4 SIMMs. Since a 386SX requires 2 normal SIMMs for a single bank, that means that a 386SX computer with 4 SIMM sockets has room for *two* banks of RAM.

The rules for configuring that memory are as follows:

1. For computers that use banks of multiple SIMMs (such as 286 and later CPUs), all SIMMs in a bank must be the same size and speed.

2. It may be possible to put any size SIMM you like in a bank, but not always. Lots of SX machines can't take 4M SIMMs. Other motherboards restrict you from putting in a second bank that is smaller than the first bank; for example, if you use 1M SIMMs in bank 0 (the first bank), you can't use 256K SIMMs in bank 1 (the second bank).

Assuming that the hypothetical 386SX computer can take 4 SIMMs, how many possible memory configurations are there? Table 11.2 summarizes all the possibilities.

Table 11.2
Memory Configurations Possible with a 16-bit Data Path

Bank 0	Bank 1	Total (M)
256	0	0.5
1,024	0	2
4,096	0	8
256	256	1

continues

Table 11.2, Continued
Memory Configurations Possible with a 16-bit Data Path

Bank 0	Bank 1	Total (M)
256	1,024	2.5
256	4,096	8.5
1,024	256	2.5
1,024	1,024	4
1,024	4,096	10
4,096	256	8.5
4,096	1,024	10
4,096	4,096	16

Don't take the four-SIMM-motherboard comment as gospel—there are also 386SX computers whose motherboards can only hold two SIMMs, and some that will use *eight* SIMMs. Four just seems to be the most common arrangement. Notice that there are some particularly inefficient layouts. Some 386SX computers—notebooks in particular—ship with 1M of RAM, but it's arranged by filling all the SIMM sockets with 256K SIMMs. As an exercise, you might want to map out all the possibilities for an SX motherboard that supports eight SIMM sockets (as some 386SX-based motherboards do).

Building Memory Banks for 32-bit Computers

The 386DX and all the 486 CPUs have a 32-bit data path. A 32-bit data path plus 4 bits for parity means that a 386 that used bit chips would require 36 chips per memory bank—a lot of chip stuffing! Although I've never seen such a computer, a 386 that uses nybble memory requires only 9 nybble chips to create a 32-bit memory bank; it needs 4 normal 9-bit SIMMs. If the computer used 16-bit SIMMs, you would need only 2 SIMMs to make a complete 386 memory bank. Commonly, 386DX and 486 motherboards have room for 8 SIMMs, so let's take a look at the possibilities there: if there's room for 8 SIMMs, that means that there are just 2 banks because the 32-bit data path of these CPUs demands 4 SIMMs per bank. The combinations look like the ones in table 11.3.

Table 11.3
Possible Memory Bank Combinations with a 32-bit Motherboard

Bank 0	Bank 1	Total (M)
256	0	1
1,024	0	4
4,096	0	16
256	256	2
256	1,024	5
256	4,096	17
1,024	256	5
1,024	1,024	8
1,024	4,096	20
4,096	256	17
4,096	1,024	20
4,096	4,096	32

As with 16-bit configurations, you can have some really undesirable combinations for 32-bit configurations. Perhaps the worst is the 2M arrangement in which all the SIMM sockets are filled with 256K chips. Notice that there's a tough choice if you want 8M of RAM. You really need 8M to make Windows or OS/2 work well, and you will probably want 32M eventually, but to get 8M you have to fill the motherboard with 1M SIMMs. And you'll have to throw away those SIMMs when you upgrade to 16M—an upgrade that requires four 4M SIMMs.

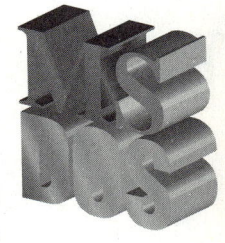

Most modern PC CPUs can accommodate quite a lot of memory. Unfortunately, many motherboards aren't designed well and cannot accept very much memory. When you buy a PC, look closely at how much memory you can put on the motherboard. You should get a motherboard that will accept at least 16 megabytes, even if you're not going to use it immediately: believe me, you'll get there eventually.

Installing the Memory

Once you purchase the memory chips, or SIMMs, how do you put them in? There are two parts to this process: First, follow some basic good "technician sense" as you work inside your PC. Second, know where to put the memories.

Working Safely inside the PC

Inserting chips or SIMMs isn't hard, but there are a few things you should take care of before doing in-PC spelunking.

Preparing the Work Area

Before you start disassembling the PC, prepare your work area. Make sure that you have enough space to put the monitor on the table next to the PC. Set out a pad or notebook and pen, and a clean empty cup. It is a good idea if you don't stand on carpeting, especially a shag carpet, when you handle chips (see the following section).

Reducing the Possibility of Static Damage

Static electricity is a possible evil that all PC hardware faces. Simply shuffling your feet across the rug as you walk toward a PC can generate over 50,000 volts of static charge. When you touch the PC's case, the spark you feel has the capacity to scramble data in your PC's memory, leading to spurious memory-failure messages. But the memory already in your system is moderately well-protected: any static charge is dissipated through many chips, rather than targeted at just one.

TIP

Even though a static charge is dissipated through the computer and may not damage a single chip, that's not to say you shouldn't do something about reducing static in your normal daily PC usage: static electricity can permanently damage chips. But the amount of damage from a static zap on a chip inside a PC is nothing next to the amount of damage you can inflict by touching a chip or a SIMM that's not yet installed. There's no point in plunking down your hard-earned cash for memory devices and then destroying them the first time you touch them.

You can minimize static damage to PC components by doing two things:

- ✔ Leave the memory devices in their antistatic shipping containers until you are ready to install them.

- ✔ Get an antistatic wrist strap. A wrist strap is usually attached to a coiled cord like a telephone cord and has a grounding clip of some kind on the other end. Some grounding clips are plugged into a wall outlet and use the ground connection built into every three-prong outlet; others have an alligator clip you can clip to some grounded object, like the case of your PC's power supply. (By the way, if you intend to ground yourself to your PC's power-supply case, leave the power supply plugged in—but turned off!—as you disassemble your PC.)

Writing Everything Down

Whenever you install things, keep notes. Whenever you buy a PC, get a spiral-bound notebook; whenever you learn something about the PC, write it in the notebook. *Writing* doesn't just refer to text; you should diagram things as you disassemble a machine so that you know where everything goes when you reassemble that machine.

> **AUTHOR'S NOTE**
>
> *You'll find that you'll have to make some battlefield command decisions when you're under the hood of your PC, such as "Is the memory board filled left-to-right or right-to-left?" The documentation doesn't say. So you try it both ways and then find something that works. That knowledge is golden, a real enhancement to the documentation for your PC, so take the all-important step of writing it down.*
>
> *Sometimes an installation doesn't work when all indications tell you it should. Keeping notes enables you to walk away from a problem for a while and come back to it later, perhaps with better insight. Your notebook is invaluable: there's nothing more frustrating than saying, "Let's see…I solved this problem before…and I wish I could remember how I did it."*

Having a Bootable Floppy Ready

In the process of disassembling the PC, you may end up doing something that makes your machine temporarily unable to boot from the hard disk. Have a bootable floppy on hand in case this happens; it might not be a bad idea to have a diagnostic program like CheckIt from TouchStone Software or QAPlus from DiagSoft on a floppy as well.

Parking the Hard Disk

Most hard disks park themselves automatically when you power down a PC, but it can't hurt to run a disk-head parking program before you shut down your computer. Most diagnostics programs, like CheckIt and QAPlus, include a head-parking option.

Keeping the Screws Organized

As you pull screws and small brackets out of a PC, you'll find that reassembling the PC is much easier if you keep track of…

✔ Where the screws came from

✔ Where you put them down when you removed the screws

Too many people lay the screws down on the top of the table they're working at and accidentally sweep them off the table onto the floor. It's awfully embarrassing if you don't know where a screw came from when you reassemble the PC (true technicians never end up with "extra parts").

> *To keep from having extra parts, put the screw back in its screw hole whenever you remove a screw to disassemble something—even if the item is disassembled. That way, when you put the PC back together, you know where all the screws are.*

Removing the Board to Which You Are Adding Memory

Many people just reach inside the PC and shove new chips into the PC's motherboard. Although that's the easy way, it stresses the motherboard. It's better policy to remove the motherboard from the PC and then install the memory directly onto it.

Figuring Out Where RAMs Are Installed

Memory devices aren't always installed on the motherboard. Memories can be installed in one of three locations:

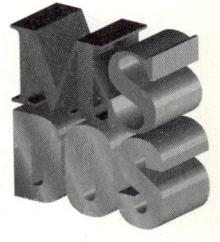

✔ **On the PC motherboard.** This is the most common location for memory. Modern PCs tend to either use SIMMs or some kind of proprietary memory device, although some older motherboard designs may have sockets for DIP-type bit or nybble chips. When you buy a PC, make sure that the motherboard has enough room for lots of memory: it should have lots of SIMM sockets and be able to use high-capacity SIMMs. Most 486-type motherboards have room for 8 SIMMs, but you can find motherboards that accommodate 16 SIMMs. Make sure that you can put either 1M or 4M SIMMs into the sockets; if possible, get a motherboard that supports 16M SIMMs. Although you probably won't buy them now—they're expensive—getting a motherboard with room for 16 SIMMs, each with a maximum size of 16M, means you have expansion possibilities for up to 256M of RAM. That's about as obsolescence-proof as you can get.

- ✔ **On a normal plug-in expansion card.** Never, never, never, *never* get an AT-bus or EISA-bus memory expansion card for your PC. Because bus slots in the ISA and EISA world run at only 8 MHz, any expansion memory in those slots can only serve the PC at 8 MHz, a totally unacceptable speed. However, you should be aware that there indeed *are* AT-bus and EISA-bus memory expansion cards.

- ✔ **On a local bus memory-upgrade card.** Some PCs have special 32-bit, high-speed "local bus" slots with matching high-speed memory-expansion boards. For example, you add memory to Compaq PCs by purchasing, populating, and installing a board that only works on a Compaq PC, but that can accommodate up to 16, 32, or 64 megabytes of RAM, depending on the Compaq model. When you buy a PC or plan memory upgrades, follow the same advice here as for working with memory expansion on the motherboard: buy the memory-expansion option that gives you the greatest ultimate memory capacity.

The third is my favorite option for memory expansion, largely because it's the easiest. You really should remove a board from the PC before adding memory to it: doing so keeps the board from flexing and breaking the small printed-circuit traces that are the highways the electrons run on (the electrons make the PC work). The downside to this practice is that on a PC that accepts memory expansion directly on the motherboard, you have to take the motherboard out to upgrade the memory. Getting the motherboard out is a pain in the neck; getting a local-bus memory upgrade card out is a three-minute job. Just another thing to keep in mind when buying PCs....

Understanding Memory-Installation Methods

Once you figure out where the memory devices go, you have to insert them.

Inserting Chips

Before taking the chips out of their antistatic packages, lay out some aluminum foil or conductive foam. Spill the chips out on the foil or foam and put all five fingers on the foil. Any minor static differences between your fingers are evened out. Now you can pick up the chips with impunity.

Make sure that you align the chip properly. Take a look at a chip and notice that there's a notch at one end of the chip (sometimes it's not a notch, it's just a dimple). The socket you're about to put the chip into usually has a notch at one end too. Make sure that the chip notch is on the same side as the socket notch.

Notice that the legs of the chip are splayed rather than straight up and down. Don't bend the legs before inserting the chip: that angle on the legs helps hold the chip in the socket. Just align the legs on one side and then use your fingers to guide the legs on the other side into their socket holes. Because the chip wants to spring out at this point, push it firmly into the socket. If you lined everything up correctly, a simple push fits it right in.

Inspect the chip to make sure that you didn't bend any chip legs when you inserted the chip.

Inserting SIMMs

SIMMs are the memory modules of choice on most PCs these days. Figure 11.10 shows how to remove a SIMM (inserting a SIMM is the reverse process).

Figure 11.10
Removing a SIMM.

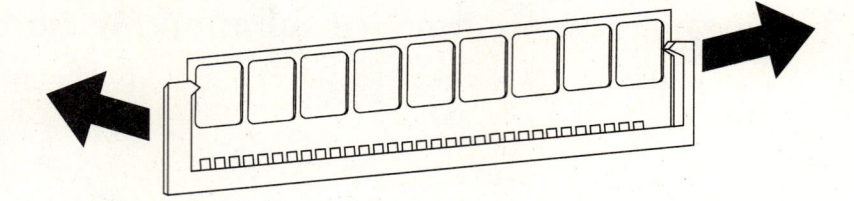

FIRST, GENTLY PULL ASIDE THE PLASTIC TABS THAT HOLD THE SIMM IN PLACE. BE GENTLE, AS THE TABS ARE EASILY BROKEN.

ONCE THE TABS HAVE BEEN PUSHED OUTWARD, ROTATE THE SIMM FORWARD. IT THEN COMES RIGHT OUT OF ITS SOCKET.

Notice that the SIMM leans backward in its socket. Figure 11.10 shows that each SIMM is held in place by a tab on either side of the device. You remove a SIMM by pulling the tabs out very gently with your fingernails, rotating the SIMM forward, and pulling it out of its socket. Replace it in reverse. Because SIMMs lie on top of one another, you'll probably have to remove all the SIMMs to get to the last SIMM.

> **NOTE**
> *The toughest thing about installing SIMMs is not breaking the little tabs. You can always tell when a SIMM was installed by a first-timer: there's a rubber band holding the SIMM into the socket because the tabs are broken.*

SIPPs are much like SIMMs, except that they have a single row of holes on the motherboard for their pins. Line up the pins carefully, press down firmly, and as you press, watch to make sure that none of the pins buckle. Then hope that you never have to take the SIPP out. If you do have to take out a SIPP, use a needlenose pliers and work the SIPP out a little at a time from the right and left.

Telling the Computer You've Added Memory

Once the memory is installed on your PC, you've got to inform the PC that the memory is there. How you do that varies from PC to PC. Some PCs automatically sense the presence of new memory the first time you power them up with that memory in place. Others require you to run the SETUP program that came with the PC; you just have to run it. The SETUP program senses the new memory and adjusts the PC's configuration memory, telling the PC to expect to see a certain amount of memory every time it powers up. A few PCs require that you change the position or setting of DIP switches or jumpers on the PC's memory board; thankfully, that method is going out of style. Check your PC's documentation to find out what you have to do to reconfigure your PC to accept the new memory.

You're more than likely to see an error message of some kind when you first start up the computer with new memory. That's because the PC is configured to expect a certain amount of memory—no more, no less. When it finds a different amount (a bigger amount, but a different amount in any case), the PC's powerup routines emit some kind of error message. Don't worry about it; just run the SETUP program or whatever is necessary to reconfigure the PC to accept the new memory, and then reboot. If the PC still doesn't like the memory, then be concerned. Make sure that you've installed the memory devices properly and configured the PC correctly for that memory.

Testing Memory

Once you install new memory in your system, don't immediately fire up Windows and gloat about the amount of free space the Program Manager displays. Before you even *think* of entrusting data to new memory, you must test the memory. There's a decent chance that your new memories are faulty, either because they have a subtle manufacturing error that slipped past the manufacturer's quality control, or because you may have damaged the memory when installing it or because you may have not installed it correctly.

Don't think that the PC's Power On Self Test (POST)—the set of simple checks the PC does on powerup—is of any value in diagnosing memory errors. The POST is totally ineffective in detecting any but the most egregious memory hardware errors. Spend a little money and get a high-quality memory-test program now and save heartache and mysterious program crashes later.

Why You Must Test RAM

It's particularly important to test new devices because if something's going to fail, it's likely to do so in the first few weeks of operation. Testing most devices is fairly easy: you run the self-test on a new printer, run a graphics program on a new video board, or format a disk in a new floppy drive. But when it comes to memory (and hard disks), the story is quite different.

Most memory failures aren't nice, well-behaved situations in which a memory chip dies altogether. Many memory problems are interactive in nature. Think of memory as a giant group of single-information cells. Each cell contains a bit. Most simple memory tests, like the one that occurs on system power-up, fill memory with 1s and then read the 1s to make sure that they're still there; then it does the same with 0s. This isn't a very good way to test memory; in fact, it's probably the least strenuous test. Figure 11.11 shows a representation of a better test, as well as the problem that the test is designed to detect.

The test works like this: It fills an area of memory with zeros and places a single 1 in the middle of them. You may be able to imagine the potential problem this method detects: the sheer number of 0 charges surrounding the 1 "drain power" from the 1, undesirably changing its value. This is called the mountain/valley test because the 1 is a mountain (large charge) surrounded by a valley (the 0 small charge).

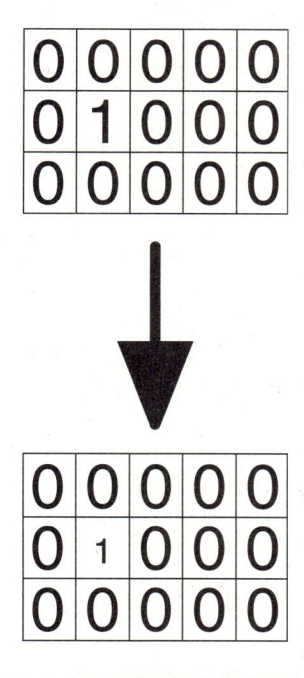

Figure 11.11
The mountain/valley memory test.

AUTHOR'S NOTE

A memory test related to the mountain/valley test is the checkerboard test. Another is the walking-bit test. I learned about a walking-bit error with the first 386 PC I owned.

Errors were creeping into my data files, text with values changed randomly. An A became a 0 now and then and other subtle changes like that. I originally blamed my storage devices and started keeping documents on floppy disks. Then I noticed that it only seemed to affect larger documents; it started to look like I had poltergeists in my PC.

continues

Then I realized that if the problem only occurred in large documents, that was a clue. Only when I loaded a large document did the memory up near 640K get any exercise; what if I had some kind of memory error there? I ran the normal diagnostic tests (back in 1986, there really weren't any good memory-testing programs on the market) but couldn't pin down a problem. Then I got some extremely useful advice from a friend.

"You might have a walking-bit error," Chris suggested. And then he explained how it worked. "Sometimes you have a situation where a memory location in one part of memory affects a memory location way off in another part of memory. Call the first part X and the second Y. Suppose that you test location X all by itself. It checks out fine; so does location Y when you test it by itself. But now put all 0s into location Y; because the memory location is one byte in size, that's 00000000 in binary. Now put a particular pattern into location X—say 1111111. When you look back at location Y, you find that at least one of the bits has flipped from 0 to 1."

Chris's advice sounded strange, but I sat down and wrote a program to test it. It started out at the bottom of memory and put 0s in all locations up to 640K. Then it put all 1s into the lowest location in memory and checked all locations above it to see whether they still equaled 0. If that check turned out all right, the test went to the next location in memory, filled it with 1s and checked for 0s again. I moved in this way up to the top of memory—that's why they call it the walking-bit test: the 1s march up to the top of memory.

And you know, Chris was right. When I put a 1 into location 536,133, a 1 appeared in location 617,551. I replaced the memory, and we lived happily ever after.

Now I don't have to write walking-bit test programs; they are built into my 2 favorite memory-test programs: Checkit and QAPlus. But I'm amazed at how useful memory testing is. Of the hundred or so PCs I tested in 1992 in the process of installing them, I found faulty memory in 10 of them. Again, all the errors were subtle errors, errors that the POST didn't catch.

> *The silver lining to finding a machine with faulty memory is that it gave me a chance to cross-check other diagnostic programs. I found that Checkit and QAPlus pretty much agreed with each other about errors. Some very expensive diagnostics, however, sailed right past this kind of memory error. Don't think that Checkit and QAPlus can be outpaced by another package just because the other package is more expensive: I found $700 packages that crashed when they found a real live memory error.*

How To Use a Memory Tester

Once you purchase a memory-test program, you should be aware of a few tips on using the program effectively.

✔ Make sure that your memory manager is disabled before you test memory. Although this step is not always necessary, most memory tests cannot reliably test memory when a memory manager is present.

✔ Make sure that the error is a RAM error. Recently I ran memory diagnostics on a 486 system with 8M of RAM. After a few hours' operation, memory errors started appearing *in every part of memory*. The 8M of RAM was implemented as 8 separate 1M SIMMs, so the fact that memory errors were appearing throughout the memory address space meant that all 8 SIMMs were defective.

Or did it? The simultaneous failure of 8 SIMMs seemed a remote possibility. It seemed more likely that something in common to the SIMMs was the source of the trouble. That "something in common" had to be something on the motherboard. Sure enough, a replacement motherboard worked fine with the original 8 SIMMs.

✔ Be sure to run the memory diagnostic in slow-test mode. Both CheckIt and QAPlus offer a normal-test and a slow-test mode.

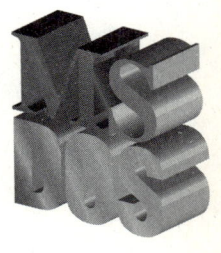

Run the slow test; the slow test does a walking-bit, checkerboard, and other extensive tests. Don't be surprised if the test takes hours: I've waited overnight for a test of 16M of RAM on a slow computer. Remember that the time spent waiting is time well spent.

✔ Run the memory test in continuous mode and log errors to a disk file. Some diagnostic programs stop at the first error and prompt you to acknowledge the error before the program moves on to test the next memory location. You want to be able to start the diagnostic program and walk away for a day or two; you don't want to have to baby-sit the program. Both CheckIt and QAPlus have logging capabilities that store error information in a disk file and continue to run unattended after an error is detected. Be sure to activate those features before you leave the PC to do unattended diagnostics.

After you test (*burn in*, as techies say) your memory, you're ready to make the most of it with the DOS 6.2 memory manager (as described in the preceding chapter). Before you leave this chapter on memory hardware, however, you may wonder how "processor caches" that you may have heard about fit into the memory picture. The last section in this chapter is about memory caches.

Using Cache Memory

Nobody makes cheap memories fast enough to keep up with a computer faster than about 20 MHz. Memory faster than that costs more than 10 times more than regular memory. But making a fast computer involves getting fast memories, so how can a PC designer make a reasonably priced machine?

There are two kinds of memory: dynamic and static. Dynamic is slower than static but a lot cheaper. Unfortunately, dynamic memory isn't fast enough to keep up with today's CPUs. Dynamic memory is slower partly because it must be refreshed. When you store data in a static RAM, it remembers the data until you turn off the power or change the memory. Not so with dynamic RAMs: they forget what you tell them within 4 milliseconds. The PC must have hardware to refresh the contents of the dynamic memory every few milliseconds.

As you learned earlier in this chapter, RAM speed is described by its access time. Access time is only part of the total amount of time required for a chip to respond to a request; the total time is called the *cycle time*. Access time, like cycle time, is measured in nanoseconds (ns), or billionths of a second. Typical access times range from 250ns (very slow) to 40ns for dynamic RAMs, but as fast as 15ns for static RAMs.

Memory Speeds in Detail

On 286/386 machines, memory must be able to respond to a CPU request in two clock ticks. *Clock ticks* are the reciprocal of the clock rate: 8 MHz means 8 million clock ticks per second, so each clock tick is 1/8,000,000 second. If you divide 1 by 8 million (use a calculator), you get 0.000000125. That's 0.125 microseconds or 125 nanoseconds. Do this computation, and you'll get a table like table 11.4.

Table 11.4
Relation of Clock Rates to Time Intervals in PC Clocks

Clock Rate (MHz)	Clock Duration (ns)
10	100
12	83.33
16	62.5
20	50
25	40
33	30.3
50	20

Memory must be able to respond to a memory request in two clock ticks. For example, the memory for a 10 MHz computer must respond in 2 x 100ns or 200ns. Most people think that the access time is the only time the memory requires when fetching data—but there's another part: the charging time. Memory chips have a charging time that may equal or exceed the access time. Typical charging times are shown in table 11.5.

Table 11.5
Charging Times for Common Access Times

Access Time	Plus Charging Time	Equals Cycle Time
200	170	370
150	120	270
120	90	210
100	75	175
80	65	145

The simple formula for determining how long memory requires to respond to a request is this:

Memory Cycle Time = Memory Access Time + Memory Charging Time

Suppose that you want to design a computer using a 10 MHz clock and 256K, 120ns chips. You have to keep an entire memory cycle below 2 x 100 = 200ns. Remember that the cycle time equals the access time plus the charge time; you know that the access time is 120ns. If the charge time for the 120ns 256K chips is 90ns, the total cycle time for the chips is 120 + 90 = 210ns. The memory chips are 10ns too slow.

You could install faster memories (for more money) or slow down the processor to make the machine work. But there's a third alternative: add wait states. A *wait state* is an extra clock tick added to each memory access. Instead of requiring that each memory cycle be done in just two clock ticks (200ns in this case), you relax the constraint, requiring that a cycle be finished in three clock ticks (300ns—plenty of time for the memory to complete its 210ns cycle).

Although this may sound like a good alternative, consider: a 10 MHz computer is supposed to get a memory access done in two cycles.

With one wait state, it takes three cycles, or 300ns. What speed computer would you need to do a memory access in two clock ticks with no wait states? One with a 300/2 or 150ns clock tick. That's a 6.7 MHz computer—considerably slower than a 10 MHz computer. Adding a wait state really means slowing the computer down by 50 percent whenever memory accesses occur.

Put together memory-cycle times and clock durations, and you end up with some bad news: even with 53ns chips, you can't build a computer faster than 20 MHz and have the memory keep up with the CPU.

A Processor Cache Is One Answer to Memory-Speed Problems

Another answer to the memory/CPU speed mismatch is a processor cache.

As you know, memories come in different speeds. From 1981 to 1986, memory chips got faster at about the same rate as processors: an 8 MHz computer could generally be outfitted with memory of like speed without emptying your wallet.

Then 16 MHz came around. At 16 MHz, the usual dynamic memory chips couldn't keep up. Because nobody makes a dynamic memory chip with a 126ns total cycle time, PC manufacturers would be forced to either insert wait states (a sleazy way, as you've seen, of making a slow machine sound fast), or they'd have to look elsewhere for faster memories.

Faster memory does exist: it's static RAM, and it's expensive: ten times or more the cost of dynamic RAMs of comparable size. One company did indeed use all-static memory, but they soon discontinued the product (cost no doubt had something to do with it).

As has happened before, a leaf was taken from the mainframe's book, and cache memory was included in most 16 MHz and faster computers. *Cache memory* is a small amount (generally no more than 64K) of expensive static RAM, RAM fast enough for the CPU to address at no-wait-state speed. The computer also has a larger amount, perhaps megabytes, of the relatively slower 80-or-so ns dynamic memory. The last piece of hardware the PC needs is a cache controller to manage the various kinds of memory.

> *Do not confuse processor cache with disk cache. Processor cache is a high-speed memory chip with support hardware. A disk cache is a PC program designed to use the normal PC DRAM to help the operating system respond to requests from a program or the user for data from the hard disk. You read more about disk caches in Chapter 8.*

A cache controller tries to use the relatively small cache to speed up the much larger RAM by using an assumption about computer use. The idea is that computer programs tend to stay within one area of code for a while, move to another area and stay there for a while, and so on. The same phenomenon occurs with data. The cache controller gets an idea of what part of memory to work with and guesses that the CPU will soon need the data that follows in that part of memory. Then it goes to that area in the slow dynamic memory and grabs a piece of it—not the whole 64K; it's usually only about 4K—and transfers it into the cache. If the cache guessed right, the next data the CPU needs won't be in the slow memory: it's in the cache. The cache is fast enough to accept reads and writes at zero-wait-state speed.

If the cache didn't guess right, the CPU must go to the slow dynamic memory and endure two or more wasted CPU clock cycles—two or more wait states. This means that your cache better be a good guesser, or you have a two-wait-state machine. In practice, caches are right 80 to 99 percent of the time, so you end up with a zero-wait-state machine 80 to 99 percent of the time and a two-wait-state machine the other 20 to 1 percent of the time.

Most 386 machines use the Intel 80385 cache controller to handle cache management. The 486 actually includes the 80385 controller right in the 486 CPU and comes with 8K of static RAM for the cache.

How Much Cache Do You Need?

Some machines come with the basic 8K of cache that the 486 has built into it; others have an external processor cache with typical sizes of 64K or 256K. A logical question is "How much cache do I need?"

Certainly, bigger is better with cache, but if you do singletasking DOS-kinds of operations, you won't see much performance difference with a cache larger than 64K. But if you have Windows, OS/2, UNIX, or some other kind of multitasking environment, 256K pays for itself with the time it saves you.

Summary

In this chapter, you learned how to choose and install more memory for your PC, giving your PC more memory for Windows, OS/2, or DOS memory management. Although you may know a lot about memory and memory management, the next chapter explains some of the problems that can occur as you try to do memory management—as well as some solutions to the problems and some "expert tricks" to squeeze more out of your PC's memory manager.

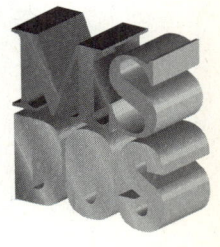

MS
DOS

CHAPTER 12

Memory-Management Tips, Tricks, and Troubleshooting

by Mark Minasi

Chapter 10 showed you how to use DOS 6.2 to do the basic things that memory managers do. But that was really just the start; you find that memory managers can pose some real challenges if you want to get the most out of them.

> **NOTE:** *If you haven't read Chapter 10 yet, please read it before tackling this chapter. Reading Chapter 11 before this chapter isn't necessary, but Chapter 10 is essential.*

In this chapter, you learn how to arrange upper-memory blocks (UMBs) in such a way that you get as many programs as possible into the UMBs and as few programs as possible eating up space in conventional memory. Unfortunately, there's more to it than just loading everything high: not all programs can load high and some do not load high for seemingly mysterious reasons. Worse yet, some programs stop working if you load them high. This chapter shows you how to attack those particular problems so that you can stuff as much as possible in the memory areas above 640K. But if you're successful in convincing more and more programs to load high, you'll probably run up against another problem: running out of UMB space. In this chapter, I also show you a few tricks to maximize the amount of free space you can get out of the UMA.

Arranging Programs in UMBs for Maximum Space Usage

Most folks who have just learned about memory management dive right in and change all their `DEVICE=` statements to `DEVICEHIGH=` statements, put an `LH` in front of all TSR invocations (as a matter of fact, I've seen people blindly put `LH` in front of every command in AUTOEXEC.BAT), then dust their hands off, smile contentedly, and figure that they've pretty much completed the dirty work of memory management.

Sometimes it is that easy, but not always. Doing memory management in this way is like clearing out space in your house by opening the attic door and tossing things into the attic. If you have a really big attic, everything probably goes in without a hitch. But if you try to put a great many things in a smallish-sized attic, you get the most stuff in the attic by comparing each box you want to store in relation to the other boxes you want to store, and then arranging them in some kind of neat, organized manner. In this section, you learn how to do that with a memory manager by placing TSRs into particular locations in memory and by learning how to deal with the dreaded yo-yo TSR.

Placing TSRs into Particular UMBs

Suppose that you have two UMBs in your system. The first is 64K in size, the second is 32K in size. Your upper-memory-block situation might look like the one in figure 12.1.

Before going any further, let's review a constraint faced when putting programs into upper memory blocks. In figure 12.1, the total amount of UMB space available is 64 plus 32: 96K of UMB space. Can you load a single 96K program into upper memory? Absolutely not: the vast majority of DOS programs can load only into a *contiguous* area of memory. Whatever program you plan to put in the 64K UMB must fit entirely in that UMB; whatever program you plan to put in the 32K UMB must fit entirely in that UMB.

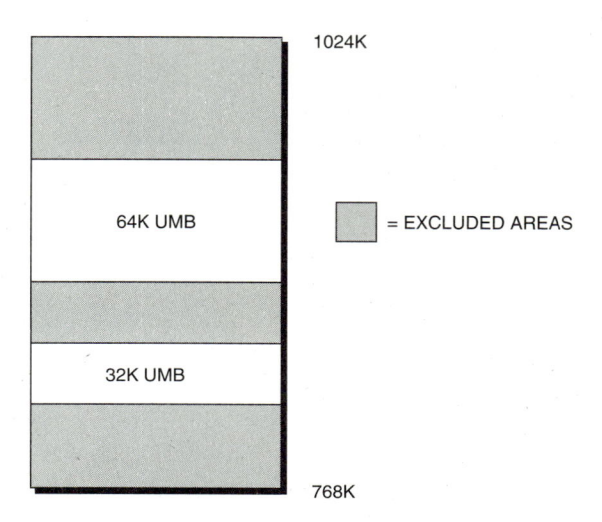

Figure 12.1

An upper-memory arrangement with two UMBs.

But what about loading two programs into these UMBs: one 32K in size and another 64K in size? You should have no trouble doing that: put the 64K program in the 64K UMB and the 32K program in the 32K UMB. But it's not always that easy.

Chapter 12: *Memory-Management Tips, Tricks, and Troubleshooting*

If you load the 32K program (call it P1) first, it ought to be smart enough to see that it fits in the 32K UMB, but it isn't. Instead, when DOS loads a program in a UMB, it chooses the UMB into which it loads a program in this way:

When asked to load a program into upper memory, DOS selects the upper-memory block with the most free space.

That means that DOS puts the 32K program in the 64K UMB (see fig. 12.2).

Figure 12.2

UMB free space after loading a program into the large UMB.

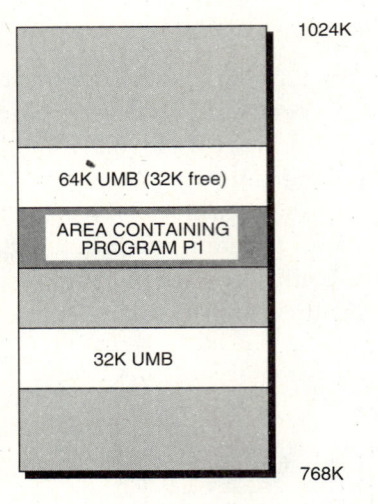

```
                                              1024K
    ┌─────────────────────┐
    │                     │
    │                     │
    │  64K UMB (32K free) │
    │                     │
    │  AREA CONTAINING    │
    │     PROGRAM P1      │
    │                     │
    │                     │
    │     32K UMB         │
    │                     │
    └─────────────────────┘
                                              768K
```

Although there's 64K of free space, it's not 64K of contiguous free space. If you try to load the 64K program (call it P2) into upper memory, it can't load high.

The obvious answer to this problem is "load the big one(s) first." If you load the 64K program first, it would go into the larger UMB because no other program had taken it up yet. The smaller program would end up in the smaller UMB, and all would be well. Naturally, however, you can't simply say "load the big ones first" and let it go at that, for two reasons:

- ✔ **Some programs must be loaded in a particular order (you can't load programs in just any order).** For example, if you use an IBM Token-Ring LAN board, you have to load three device drivers in memory in a particular order. The drivers are 1K, 9K, and 29K in size, in the order in which they must be loaded (sort of a worst-case scenario)—three drivers that must be loaded in ascending order of size!

✔ **All device drivers must load before all TSRs.** Recall that two kinds of programs can be loaded into upper memory: device drivers and TSRs. Even if you could always specify the order in which you load programs in CONFIG.SYS and AUTOEXEC.BAT, you can't get around the fact that all CONFIG.SYS statements load before AUTOEXEC.BAT statements, meaning that TSRs load after device drivers.

The answer is to tell DOS to somehow load the small program into the small UMB, and the large program into the large UMB. DOS 6.2 enables you to do this by first assigning a unique identification number to each UMB and then specifying a numbered UMB in the DEVICEHIGH or LOADHIGH statement.

> *For some reason, Microsoft shifts terminology after you number UMBs. If you refer to UMBs by number, they're not called UMBs in the Microsoft documentation any more; they're now called regions. Don't be confused: just remember that UMBs and regions are the same thing. (My guess as to what led to the differing terms is that Microsoft basically copied the terminology used by Quarterdeck's QEMM-386 product; Quarterdeck uses the term regions.)*

EMM386.EXE *numbers UMBs—oops, regions—*sequentially from low addresses up. Figure 12.3 shows how this works for the example we've been working with.

The smaller UMB, the 32K one, is *region 1*. The larger UMB, the 64K one, is *region 2*. By the way, there is also a *region 0*. It's the conventional memory area. You can use those region numbers to force DOS to use one UMB in preference to others when loading a program high. The way that you do this (a feature new to DOS 6.2, for those of you who have some familiarity with DOS 5) is with the /L:n parameter, found on both the DEVICEHIGH and LOADHIGH commands.

Figure 12.3

Numbered regions (UMBs) in DOS 6.2.

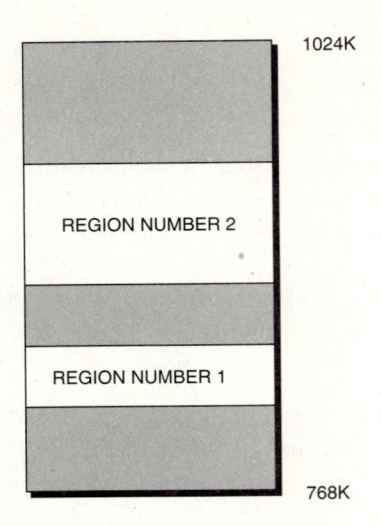

```
                    1024K
   ┌──────────────┐
   │▓▓▓▓▓▓▓▓▓▓▓▓▓▓│
   │▓▓▓▓▓▓▓▓▓▓▓▓▓▓│
   ├──────────────┤
   │              │
   │REGION NUMBER 2│
   │              │
   ├──────────────┤
   │▓▓▓▓▓▓▓▓▓▓▓▓▓▓│
   ├──────────────┤
   │              │
   │REGION NUMBER 1│
   │              │
   ├──────────────┤
   │▓▓▓▓▓▓▓▓▓▓▓▓▓▓│
   └──────────────┘
                    768K
```

You already know that you can tell DOS to load a device driver high by including a DEVICEHIGH= statement in your CONFIG.SYS file. If you had a device driver called P1.SYS, for example, you can tell CONFIG.SYS to load it into an upper-memory block by including…

    DEVICEHIGH=P1.SYS

…in CONFIG.SYS. You can add the region parameter /L:1 to force DOS to load P1.SYS into the lower 32K UMB; the appropriate command would look like this:

    DEVICEHIGH /L:1 =P1.SYS

Assuming that you want to place program P2.SYS into the second region, you end up with the following two statements in CONFIG.SYS:

    DEVICEHIGH /L:1 =P1.SYS
    DEVICEHIGH /L:2 =P2.SYS

You can use the /L: parameter on LOADHIGH statements as well. The syntax for loading a TSR high into a particular region with the LH command is very much like it is for the DEVICEHIGH command: just include an /L: parameter. If P1 and P2 were TSRs instead of device drivers, the section of AUTOEXEC.BAT that loads them might look like this:

    LH /L:1 P1
    LH /L:2 P2

> **NOTE**
>
> *If you specify a particular region, but the region can't accommodate the program (the region is too small), DOS just loads the program low, even if some other region could accommodate the program.*

You can, if you like, specify that DOS load a program into one of several UMBs. Suppose that you had five UMBs and you wanted P1 to go into either region 1 or region 4. The LH command for P1 would look like this:

```
LH /L:1;4 P1
```

After the /L: parameter, you can specify a list of region numbers.

> **AUTHOR'S NOTE**
>
> *The power of the /L: parameter cannot be understated. Merely trying to load a pile of programs into upper memory in a scattershot way may sometimes work, but more often than not you find that simply putting DEVICEHIGH where DEVICE used to be and sticking LH in front of each TSR invocation usually leads to a bunch of programs that don't load high, even though there's a fair amount of free space in upper memory. When you use the /L: parameter, on the other hand, you can fit programs into upper memory just like you probably store things in your closet: nice and organized, with a minimum of wasted space.*
>
> *If all this sounds like a lot of work, it's really not that bad. Stay tuned and you soon learn about MemMaker. MemMaker is a DOS 6.2 program that does some of the upper-memory arrangement work for you.*

Understanding and Loading Yo-Yo TSRs

Sometimes you have an open space in a UMB and you have a program that would fit in there nicely, perhaps with a little space left over. So you tell DOS to load it high, and you reboot. But the program doesn't load high. What's going on?

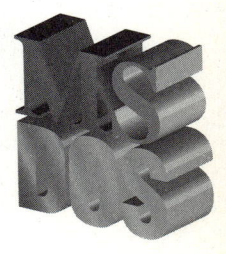

A Sample Yo-Yo: The Mouse Driver

When DOS 6.2 was first introduced, I tried loading the Microsoft Mouse 8.20 driver into a UMB, but found that it was seemingly impossible. This was the situation: I had a computer with very little space for UMBs (it had one of those 128K extended BIOSs and a number of add-in cards that included some RAM or ROM, leaving it only 64K of UMB space, all in one region). Its memory situation looked like figure 12.4.

Figure 12.4

Memory map for a PC before loading the mouse driver high.

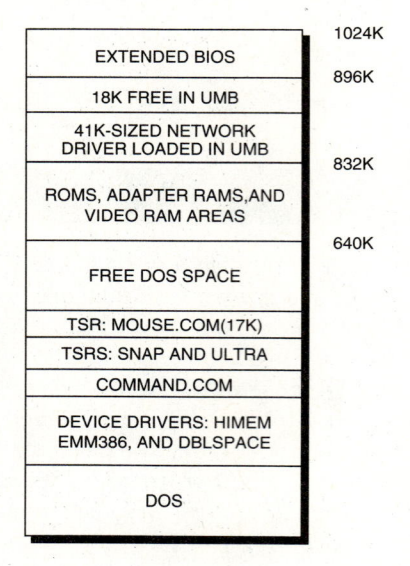

EXTENDED BIOS	1024K
	896K
18K FREE IN UMB	
41K-SIZED NETWORK DRIVER LOADED IN UMB	
	832K
ROMS, ADAPTER RAMS, AND VIDEO RAM AREAS	
	640K
FREE DOS SPACE	
TSR: MOUSE.COM(17K)	
TSRS: SNAP AND ULTRA	
COMMAND.COM	
DEVICE DRIVERS: HIMEM EMM386, AND DBLSPACE	
DOS	

Don't worry about all the details of the diagram; I just wanted you to have an overview of what was going on in memory before I tried loading MOUSE.COM high. A MEM/C on this computer looked like figure 12.5.

As you can see, NET loaded high without any trouble, leaving a free space of 18,880 bytes. MOUSE (which hasn't tried to load high yet) only takes 17,296 bytes and should fit without trouble into the UMB.

I changed the MOUSE line in AUTOEXEC.BAT to LH MOUSE, rebooted, and did another MEM/C. Things looked exactly the same. Everything took up the same amount of space, and the mouse driver still loaded in low memory. I checked to make sure that I hadn't mistyped something. What was happening?

Arranging Programs in UMBs for Maximum Space Usage

```
Modules using memory below 1 MB:

Name         Total         =   Conventional     +   Upper Memory
----         -----             ------------         ------------
MSDOS        17517   (17K)     17517   (17K)        0       (0K)
HIMEM         1152    (1K)      1152    (1K)        0       (0K)
EMM386        4144    (4K)      4144    (4K)        0       (0K)
DBLSPACE     43984   (43K)     43984   (43K)        0       (0K)
COMMAND       4992    (5K)      4992    (5K)        0       (0K)
SNAP        105872  (103K)    105872  (103K)        0       (0K)
ULTRA         6144    (6K)      6144    (6K)        0       (0K)
MOUSE        17296   (17K)     17296   (17K)        0       (0K)
NET          41632   (41K)         0    (0K)    41632      (41K)
Free        473040  (462K)    454160  (444K)    18880      (18K)

Memory Summary:

Type of Memory       Total        =      Used        +      Free
--------------       -----               ----               ----
Conventional        655360  (640K)     201200  (196K)     454160  (444K)
Upper                60512   (59K)      41632   (41K)      18880   (18K)
Adapter RAM/ROM     332704  (325K)     332704  (325K)          0    (0K)
Extended (XMS)    19922944 (19456K)     49152   (48K)   19873792 (19408K)
Press any key to continue . . .
```

Figure 12.5

The results of MEM/C for a PC before loading the mouse driver high.

To get some insight into why the mouse driver didn't load, let's look at what happens when you type **MOUSE**, or when MOUSE appears in AUTOEXEC.BAT. Figure 12.6 shows how a TSR like MOUSE loads.

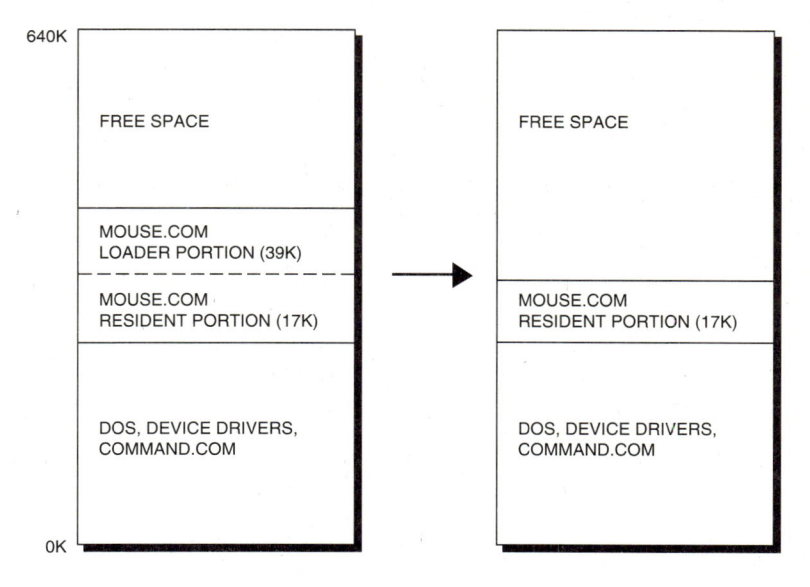

Figure 12.6

How a TSR loads into memory.

Before a Terminate-and-Stay-Resident program can fix itself in memory, that is, before it can "stay resident," it first must load into memory and adjust some internal data structures. Then it must inform DOS that it will remain resident; DOS doesn't know that a program will remain resident until after DOS has loaded the program. When loading, the mouse driver must "get its bearings" by figuring out whether it is a bus mouse, an InPort mouse, a serial mouse, and so on. The code to get the mouse ready to be resident is, believe it or not, considerably larger than the actual resident portion of the code. The part of the mouse driver that loads the mouse driver is 39K in size; the driver itself is 17K in size. The MOUSE.COM file for mouse driver Version 8.20 says that it's 56K in size. That means that when DOS loads the program MOUSE.COM, DOS thinks that it's 56K in size. There's really no way for DOS to know that even though MOUSE seems pretty rotund at the moment, it will soon slim down to a svelte 17K. Such a rotund-to-slim TSR is called a *yo-yo TSR*.

And that's why DOS refused to load MOUSE.COM high: the UMB had only 18K free and thought I asked it to load a 56K program into that 18K space!

Loading the Mouse Yo-Yo High

DOS 6.2 can't load MOUSE high unless you have a UMB with 56K of contiguous space. In this example, the computer has a 64K UMB before loading NET, so why not load mouse before NET? If I do that, I get a MEM/C listing like the one in figure 12.7.

Both the NET and MOUSE programs load high without any trouble. I suppose that you could conclude from this example that you should load the yo-yos first.

That's not very good advice, however, if you think about it. What if both NET and MOUSE are yo-yos? There'd be no way to get them both to load high. *Furthermore, as explained in Chapter 10, it's not always possible to choose the load order of programs.*

Unfortunately, with DOS 6.2, there aren't any alternatives. With Quarterdeck or Qualitas, there are options ("squeeze" and "flexframe," respectively) that solve the problem of yo-yo TSRs.

Arranging Programs in UMBs for Maximum Space Usage **605**

```
Modules using memory below 1 MB:

Name             Total            =  Conventional    +   Upper Memory
--------       -----------          ---------------      ---------------
MSDOS           17517   (17K)        17517   (17K)           0    (0K)
HIMEM            1152    (1K)         1152    (1K)           0    (0K)
EMM386           4144    (4K)         4144    (4K)           0    (0K)
DBLSPACE        43984   (43K)        43984   (43K)           0    (0K)
COMMAND          4992    (5K)         4992    (5K)           0    (0K)
SNAP           105872  (103K)       105872  (103K)           0    (0K)
ULTRA            6144    (6K)         6144    (6K)           0    (0K)
MOUSE           17296   (17K)            0    (0K)       17296   (17K)
NET             41632   (41K)            0    (0K)       41632   (41K)
Free           473040  (462K)       471456  (460K)        1584    (2K)

Memory Summary:

Type of Memory       Total           =     Used         +      Free
----------------   --------------       --------------      ---------------
Conventional         655360  (640K)       183904  (180K)      471456  (460K)
Upper                 60512   (59K)        58928   (58K)        1584    (2K)
Adapter RAM/ROM      332704  (325K)       332704  (325K)           0    (0K)
Extended (XMS)     19922944 (19456K)       49152   (48K)    19873792 (19408K)
Press any key to continue . . .
```

Figure 12.7
The MEM/C listing after rearranging TSRs.

How Memory Managers Handle Yo-Yo Programs

Both Qualitas (maker of 386Max) and Quarterdeck (maker of QEMM-386) allow yo-yo programs to grow and then shrink into a UMB. Basically, the commands to make that happen require that the memory manager's LOADHIGH command know the ultimate size of the TSR. That way, it knows whether or not it's acceptable to try to fit a TSR into a particular part of memory. A memory manager with a yo-yo option loads a yo-yo TSR by first loading the entire TSR (loader and resident portion) into upper memory. Figure 12.8 shows how a memory manager with yo-yo capabilities loads MOUSE.COM into the 64K UMB after NET has loaded.

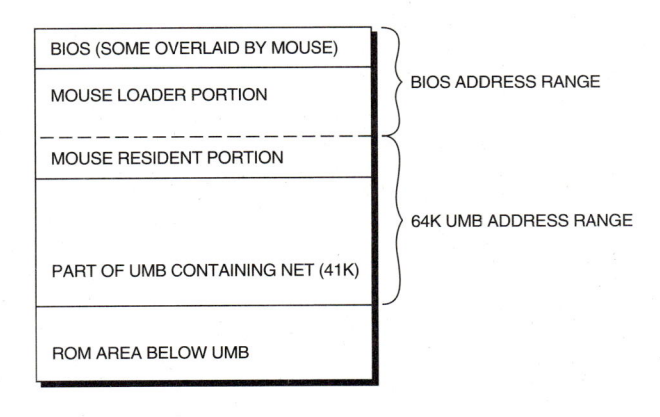

```
┌─────────────────────────────────────┐  ┐
│ BIOS (SOME OVERLAID BY MOUSE)       │  │
│                                     │  ├ BIOS ADDRESS RANGE
│ MOUSE LOADER PORTION                │  │
├─────────────────────────────────────┤  ┘
│ MOUSE RESIDENT PORTION              │  ┐
│                                     │  │
│                                     │  │
│                                     │  ├ 64K UMB ADDRESS RANGE
│ PART OF UMB CONTAINING NET (41K)    │  │
│                                     │  │
├─────────────────────────────────────┤  ┘
│ ROM AREA BELOW UMB                  │
└─────────────────────────────────────┘
```

Figure 12.8
MOUSE.COM loading into a UMB too small for the loader portion of the program.

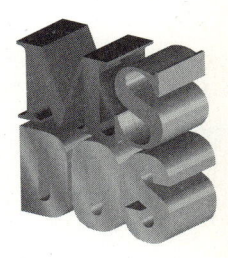

Notice that some of the MOUSE.COM program overlays the BIOS. This isn't an acceptable situation if it were going to go on forever (it means that that part of the BIOS is overwritten, and the programs in that part of the BIOS don't work, crashing the system). But the whole idea behind handling yo-yos is that the loader part of a TSR only runs for a brief time and probably does not require any BIOS services. The loader portion then disappears, leaving the BIOS (or whatever else was immediately following it in memory) intact.

> *It's a real shame that Microsoft omitted some kind of yo-yo handling from DOS 6.2; it's the sole general-purpose feature of the Quarterdeck and Qualitas products that DOS 6.2 lacks. When I urged Microsoft to include it in the DOS 6.2 beta test program, the Microsoft folks claimed that it would make DOS 6.2 "too unstable." True, there is a possibility that the loader portion of a TSR could, in its brief life, call on some service it had overlaid. But anyone who uses Quarterdeck or Qualitas on a regular basis can vouch for the fact that in the real world, yo-yo support is both necessary and fairly reliable. Yes, loading a program with yo-yo support in QEMM or 386Max does cause a system crash now and then, but it's rare. On the other hand, there's nothing rare about needing yo-yo support. Probably one third of the popular TSR programs have significantly different load sizes and resident sizes.*

Determining the Load Size of a Program

In order to handle a yo-yo TSR, you should know how large it is when it loads. To get that information, usually figure that it's equal to the size of the TSR program itself. If you need actual values, try Quarterdeck's Optimize or Qualitas's Maximize program (these programs ship with the vendors' memory managers). In the process of analyzing your setup, they also find load sizes.

Understanding Reverse Yo-Yo Programs

Now you know about TSR and device drivers that shrink in size after loading, causing DOS to mistakenly think that they can't load into some UMBs that they actually could fit into. But what about the reverse? Do programs exist that *grow* after DOS loads them, potentially overgrowing other programs, crashing themselves and the other programs?

Yes, such programs exist, but they're rare. But Microsoft thought that they were important enough to include support for them in the LOADHIGH and DEVICEHIGH commands.

Recall that you can tell DOS to put a program (for example, PROG) into a particular UMB (for example, the second region) with the /L: option. If PROG is a TSR, the command looks like this:

```
LH /L:2 PROG
```

You may have decided to load PROG into region 2 because PROG.EXE was 2,672 bytes in length and the second UMB was about 2,700 bytes in length, and you figured that they'd be a good match. Suppose that every time you loaded PROG high, it crashed the system, but when you loaded PROG low, it didn't crash. There are a lot of potential causes for that, but let's examine just one.

In figuring out the reason for the crash, you wondered whether PROG was a yo-yo of some kind. You find that PROG.EXE, the file containing the PROG program itself, is 2,672 bytes long. After you load PROG into low memory, you type…

```
MEM/C
```

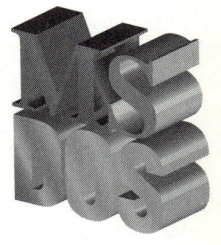

MEM/C reports that the file uses 8,726 bytes of memory. Now you know that PROG is a reverse yo-yo—a program that grows after loading. When you load it into low memory, it doesn't crash because there's plenty of space for it to grow (it finishes growing before giving control of the PC back to DOS). When you load it into a UMB with only about 2,700 bytes of free space, however, PROG grows and overwrites something else—a RAM buffer on an add-in card, a ROM, or perhaps a program in an adjacent UMB. Because you know that PROG loads at 2,672 bytes and then quickly grows to 8,726 bytes, you can keep PROG from causing trouble by warning LOADHIGH to set aside 8,726 bytes when loading PROG. You do that by adding a comma and the final load size to the /L: parameter of the LOADHIGH statement, like so…

```
LH /L:2,8726 PROG
```

> **NOTE**
> *Actually, when you give this command, LOADHIGH does not load PROG into region 2 because region 2 only has about 2,700 bytes free. LOADHIGH recognizes that there's not enough space to put PROG in that region. In that case, you may want to specify a number of potential load regions, as you learned earlier that you can do with the LH command.*

Making Things Easier with MemMaker

By now, you are thinking it is easier to color-coordinate, choose, and arrange the furniture in your house than it is to hand-place each TSR and device driver into a particular UMB. That's why Microsoft has included with DOS 6.2 a program called MemMaker.

MemMaker examines your device drivers, TSRs, and upper memory to try to maximize the amount of programs it can move from conventional memory to UMBs. In the process, it asks you a few questions about how you want your system arranged, and then does its best to tweak your memory manager.

> **STOP**
> *MemMaker is not very smart at all. It certainly does the best job a program can do, but its powers are massively inferior to what you can do with a drawing of upper memory, a list of the programs and program sizes you want to load into upper memory, and a little time. But MemMaker never makes things worse because it has an undo feature (it usually can't cause any massive damage that it can't fix). It can't hurt to run it on a system, particularly when it's a system you may not have time to optimize.*

Running MemMaker

To start MemMaker working for you, just type **MEMMAKER** at a DOS prompt. (Make sure that you're out of Windows before you do this—never try to run MemMaker from inside Windows.) Figure 12.9 shows the opening screen when the program is run on the PC with the 64K UMB and the network and mouse programs you read about in the preceding sections. The opening screen is an introductory screen. Press Enter to move to the next screen (see fig. 12.10).

```
Microsoft MemMaker

    Welcome to MemMaker.

    MemMaker optimizes your system's memory by moving memory-resident
    programs and device drivers into the upper memory area. This
    frees conventional memory for use by applications.

    After you run MemMaker, your computer's memory will remain
    optimized until you add or remove memory-resident programs or
    device drivers. For an optimum memory configuration, run MemMaker
    again after making any such changes.

    MemMaker displays options as highlighted text. (For example, you
    can change the "Continue" option below.) To cycle through the
    available options, press SPACEBAR. When MemMaker displays the
    option you want, press ENTER.

    For help while you are running MemMaker, press F1.

                Continue or Exit? Continue

  ENTER=Accept Selection   SPACEBAR=Change Selection   F1=Help   F3=Exit
```

Figure 12.9

The opening MemMaker screen.

```
Microsoft MemMaker

    There are two ways to run MemMaker:

    Express Setup optimizes your computer's memory automatically.

    Custom Setup gives you more control over the changes that
    MemMaker makes to your system files. Choose Custom Setup
    if you are an experienced user.

              Use Express or Custom Setup? Express Setup




  ENTER=Accept Selection   SPACEBAR=Change Selection   F1=Help   F3=Exit
```

Figure 12.10

The introductory MemMaker screen.

The following note corrects an error in the Microsoft documentation.

> *If you receive the* `Not enough conventional memory` *error message, you can work around the problem by doing the following:*

1. Reboot, and then bypass all the commands in CONFIG.SYS by pressing **N** for all commands except HIMEM.SYS, EMM386.EXE, SHELL, and CHKSTATE.SYS.

2. Press **N** to skip processing the AUTOEXEC.BAT file.

3. At the DOS prompt, enter:

    `FIND /I "MEMMAKER" AUTOEXEC.BAT,`

    It should display a line similar to this:

    `C:\DOS\MEMMAKER.EXE /SESSION:13396`

4. Enter this line at the prompt. MemMaker should now work normally.

MemMaker gives you the option of running it in Custom mode or Express mode. In Custom mode, you have a little more control over what MemMaker does when it fools around with CONFIG.SYS and AUTOEXEC.BAT. Because I already told you that I'm not totally confident of MemMaker's capabilities, I changed the option to Custom by pressing the spacebar. On the other hand, there's nothing wrong with selecting the Express option—MemMaker can undo anything it does. After you make your selection, you see another explanatory screen like the one in figure 12.11.

As you've learned, the big effect that *limulation* (converting extended memory to expanded memory) has on UMBs is that limulator programs must steal 64K of contiguous UMB space for the LIM page frame. MemMaker knows this and prefers to avoid a page frame; not limulating means more UMB space and more programs that can be loaded out of conventional memory. I don't use expanded memory and so answer No to the question about expanded memory, but that's

Arranging Programs in UMBs for Maximum Space Usage **611**

not necessarily the right answer for you. Take stock of the applications you use before answering this question.

After you respond to the question about expanded memory, a new screen appears, looking something like the one in figure 12.12.

```
Microsoft MemMaker

   If you use any programs that require expanded memory (EMS), answer
   Yes to the following question.  Answering Yes makes expanded memory
   available, but might not free as much conventional memory.

   If none of your programs need expanded memory, answer No to the
   following question.  Answering No makes expanded memory unavailable,
   but can free more conventional memory.

   If you are not sure whether your programs require expanded memory,
   answer No.  If you later discover that a program needs expanded
   memory, run MemMaker again and answer Yes to this question.

   Do you use any programs that need expanded memory (EMS)? No




ENTER=Accept Selection   SPACEBAR=Change Selection   F1=Help   F3=Exit
```

Figure 12.11
MemMaker asks whether you need expanded memory.

```
Microsoft MemMaker

                        Advanced Options

   Specify which drivers and TSRs to include in optimization?    No
   Scan the upper memory area aggressively?                      Yes
   Optimize upper memory for use with Windows?                   No
   Use monochrome region (B000-B7FF) for running programs?       No
   Keep current EMM386 memory exclusions and inclusions?         Yes
   Move Extended BIOS Data Area from conventional to upper memory? Yes


   To select a different option, press the UP ARROW or DOWN ARROW key.
   To accept all the settings and continue, press ENTER.



ENTER=Accept All   SPACEBAR=Change Selection   F1=Help   F3=Exit
```

Figure 12.12
MemMaker presents its advanced options.

Possible Problems with MemMaker

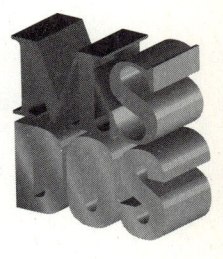

There are two potential problems with MemMaker that may or may not apply to you: how MemMaker reacts to some SCSI drives and how it reacts to hard disk drivers. These problems are discussed in the following sections.

MemMaker and SCSI Drives

If you are using a SCSI hard drive, MemMaker may hang if a device driver loads into upper memory before the SMARTDrive double_buffer driver. To solve this problem, reboot, choose Cancel And Undo when MemMaker prompts you, make sure the `DEVICE=C:\DOS\SMARTDRV.EXE /DOUBLE_BUFFER` line appears first in CONFIG.SYS, and then run MemMaker again.

MemMaker and Hard Disk Drivers

MemMaker cannot function properly if your boot drive cannot be written to until a device driver is loaded. To make MemMaker work, do the following:

1. Use the SYS command to create an MS-DOS 6.2 bootable floppy disk; and then copy MEMMAKER.EXE, CHKSTATE.SYS, HIMEM.SYS, EMM386.EXE, and SIZER.EXE to it.

2. Copy your AUTOEXEC.BAT and CONFIG.SYS files to your bootable floppy disk, and then modify them so they properly start your system. If you have a device statement such as `DEVICE=DRV.SYS`, for example, edit the statement so it looks specifically at drive C for the hard disk driver (`DEVICE=C:\DRV.SYS`).

3. Reboot with your bootable floppy disk, and then enter **MEMMAKER** at the A prompt.

4. When MemMaker finishes, copy the modified AUTOEXEC.BAT and CONFIG.SYS files to drive C, and then edit them to ensure that the path statements for HIMEM.SYS and EMM386.EXE point to the hard drive.

Using MemMaker's Advanced Options

After you pass the expanded-memory question, MemMaker offers some advanced options (see fig. 12.12). Let's look at them one at a time.

- ✔ **Specify which drivers and TSRs to include in optimization?** If you already have a program where you like it, or if you know for a fact that a particular program should not load into a UMB, this is your chance to tell MemMaker. If you say Yes to this question, MemMaker shows you screens like the one in figure 12.13, prompting you about every TSR and device driver to find out whether you want to "include this program in the optimization process," which just means "should I try to move it around in memory?"

    The SNAP program mentioned in figure 12.13, in case you're wondering, is a screen-capture program. Tell MemMaker to avoid working with a program if you know that the program must stay where it currently is. In the vast majority of cases, you can let MemMaker include all drivers and programs in its optimization process. One situation in which you might want to specify drivers and programs to include is if you use a SCSI-type hard disk. The common SCSI driver, ASPI4DOS.SYS, not only frequently malfunctions if MemMaker moves it around, it sometimes requires loading before EMM386.EXE to work reliably.

```
Microsoft MemMaker


\collage\snap

Include this driver or program in the optimization process? Yes










ENTER=Accept Selection    SPACEBAR=Change Selection    F1=Help    F3=Exit
```

Figure 12.13

MemMaker prompts whether to optimize the SNAP program.

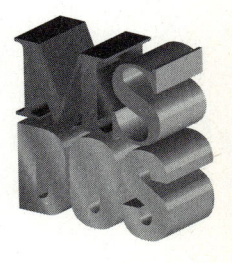

✔ **Scan the upper memory area aggressively?** Under DOS 5, EMM386.EXE never even attempted to place UMBs in the addresses above 896K (E0000-FFFFF). If you answer *Yes* to this question, MemMaker adds the include statements required to make EMM386.EXE use those areas.

On the other hand, if you correctly and completely map your upper memory area, this question is irrelevant and can be answered **No** with no loss of software capabilities. You can select a later MemMaker option telling MemMaker to respect existing includes and excludes. You are strongly recommended to explicitly map your upper memory area by hand; doing so significantly reduces the probability of a conflict between your memory manager and an add-in card.

> **NOTE**
>
> *I recommend answering **No** to this question because I've seen MemMaker erase the information on a PC's setup CMOS chip while aggressively searching memory.*

✔ **Optimize upper memory for use with Windows?** Windows requires up to 24K of memory somewhere in the 0 to 1024K address range for something called Application Program Interface Translation Buffers (APITBs). If 24K is free in the upper memory area, Windows puts the buffers in that free area. If not, Windows puts the buffers in the 0 to 640K range, reducing the amount of free memory available to DOS sessions under Windows. Because that requires some clarification, let's stop talking about MemMaker for a minute and consider APITBs.

> **AUTHOR'S NOTE**
>
> *Windows sets aside the 24K of APTIBs so that it has a drop-off point where it can leave data for DOS, and where DOS can leave data for Windows. For example, most people don't know that Windows cannot do file input and output operations; it relies on DOS to read and write files. But Windows, as you probably know, does most of*

its work in extended memory; DOS cannot access extended memory. If a Windows program like Excel wants Windows to write a spreadsheet to disk, the data is probably located entirely in extended memory, so Windows can't simply say to DOS, "write the data from extended memory to disk." DOS can't see the data in extended memory. Instead, Windows grabs some of the data that Excel wants written to disk, places it somewhere that DOS can see (any area below the 1024K address line) and then asks DOS to write that data to disk. As you've guessed, "somewhere that DOS can see" is the 24K of APITBs. By the way, the 24K of APITBs is actually six separate 4K buffers; each buffer can be placed anywhere, and they don't have to be contiguous.

If Windows must place the APITBs in the 0 to 640K range, it cannot release that area to any DOS sessions it creates. This means that any DOS program running under Windows has its free memory restricted a bit. Although it's not the end of the world, it is an undesirable situation. Instead, Windows tries to place the APITBs into unused space in the upper memory area. Unused space either means an unused address you haven't filled with an upper memory block or free space in an existing UMB—either option works just fine for Windows. (In case you're confused, recall that the upper memory area—UMA—is the name for the addresses between 640K and 1024K; an upper-memory block—UMB—is an address range in the UMA that did not contain any memory before a memory manager filled it with RAM by borrowing that memory from extended memory.) The 24K of APITB space, by the way, is not a fixed amount. Depending on the kinds of hardware you have, Windows may need no more than 8K of APITB space.

Assuming that you want Windows to put the APITBs somewhere other than the 0-to-640K range, you have to make sure that either you leave 24K of potential UMB space untapped, or you leave 24K of UMB free. With DOS 6.2's EMM386.EXE program, there is an option to do just that: the WIN= option. It works in a similar fashion to the I= (include) and X= (exclude) options you met in Chapter 10. You just put WIN=XXXX-YYYY on the EMM386.EXE invocation line, where XXXX-YYYY is a range of hexadecimal addresses; EMM386.EXE then knows not to put

continues

UMBs in that range of addresses. The WIN= option differs from excluding that range of addresses because any addresses excluded by the DOS memory manager are avoided by the Windows memory manager (yes, there is one) as well. Any areas excluded by the DOS memory manager aren't available to the Windows memory manager for use as APITBs. The WIN= parameter basically says, "Exclude this from the DOS memory manager, but don't exclude it from the Windows memory manager."

Anyway, the bottom line is whether you should answer Yes or No to MemMaker's question about optimizing upper memory for use with Windows. Actually, it doesn't matter a whole lot, because most of us have at least a few K of unused UMB space—probably enough to accommodate 8 to 24K of Windows APITBs. You might as well answer Yes if you use Windows; the worst thing that can happen is that you end up with 24K less UMB space. Even that's not such a bad thing, because if you didn't set aside the space for Windows in upper memory, Windows takes it out of the conventional memory of your DOS sessions under Windows, rendering the whole matter a wash anyway.

If that's not clear, let's do a little arithmetic. Imagine that you're running Windows on a DOS machine with exactly 24K of UMB space; you don't have any TSRs. Before running Windows, DOS shows 610K of free space. You fire up Windows and start a DOS session. When you run MEM, it probably lists about 600K of free space (there's a bit of unavoidable overhead between running DOS by itself and running DOS sessions under Windows). Expect to lose about 10K when you run a DOS session under Windows—completely independent of the need for APITBs. Meanwhile, Windows has taken the 24K of unused UMB space for its APITBs.

Now imagine that you're running a DOS machine with exactly 24K of UMB space, but you also have exactly 24K of TSRs. If you do not load the TSRs into the UMBs, DOS by itself shows the same 610K of free space it showed before, minus the 24K for TSRs, or 586K. When you run Windows and start a DOS session under Windows, you see about 576K free (586K minus the 10K of overhead).

If you take that same PC and load the 24K of TSRs into the 24K of UMBs, you leave no upper memory space free: there are no unused addresses to accommodate UMBs, and there is no free space left in *any UMB. DOS by itself shows 610K free. How much memory do you have for a DOS session under Windows? If you remove 10K for the usual Windows overhead, you have 600K—except that Windows, hasn't yet found a place to put the APITBs. Windows has to find space for the APITBs in the conventional memory area. That means that the free space for a DOS session on this computer under Windows is 600K minus 24K, or 576K.*

The moral of the story is that if your UMBs are packed to the rafters, it's irrelevant whether or not you set space aside for Windows (assuming that you do most of your work under Windows). If memory isn't packed to the top, the WIN= parameter isn't terribly important, but it does serve as a kind of reminder for MemMaker to leave some space unused in upper memory.

✔ **Use monochrome region (B000-B7FF) for running programs?**
As you learned in Chapter 10, a 32K region of upper memory is set aside for the monochrome display adapter (MDA). If the video board you use is not compatible with the MDA—as most are not (you're probably working with something that is VGA or super-VGA compatible)—the monochrome region from 704K to 736K (B0000-B7FFF) should be filled with a UMB.

You may not want to fill the monochrome region with a UMB, however, if you have certain super-VGA or video accelerator/coprocessor boards and are running Windows. Some, but not all, drivers for Windows video accelerators and super-VGA boards require access to that region. If you include the monochrome region on a plain-Jane VGA board, Windows runs without a problem. If Windows (actually, the Windows video driver) doesn't like the fact that you're using the monochrome region, you get an error message that looks like this when you start Windows:

```
Windows cannot set up an upper memory block at segment
B000.
Exclude this address space by using the syntax of your
memory manager.
For more information see the README.WRI file. Type WIN/S
to start
Windows in standard mode and choose the Read Me icon.
```

Chapter 12: *Memory-Management Tips, Tricks, and Troubleshooting*

In English, what Windows is telling you to do is to exclude the monochrome region by adding X=B000-B7FF to the EMM386.EXE statement. So should you tell MemMaker to avoid the monochrome region? Initially, let MemMaker use the monochrome region; after MemMaker is done, try to run Windows. If you shouldn't be using the monochrome region under Windows, you'll know immediately—the error message, as you've seen, isn't subtle.

- ✔ **Keep current EMM386 memory exclusions and inclusions?** This is an easy question. The answer is *yes, Yes, YES!* (Assuming, of course, that you followed my advice and mapped your upper memory from stem to stern. If you haven't followed my advice about mapping yet, do so now.)

- ✔ **Move Extended BIOS Data Area from conventional to upper memory?** Some computers, like PS/2s and Compaqs, set aside an area at the top of the 640K space for the use of their BIOSs (it's called the *Extended BIOS Data Area*). It typically takes up about 1K of RAM. MemMaker can tell EMM386.EXE to move that area up to a UMB on some systems. This won't work on every PC, and the majority of PCs don't have an Extended BIOS Data Area to begin with. It can't hurt to give MemMaker the option to move the area, so go ahead and let it. By default, EMM386.EXE tries to do this anyway. If you want EMM386.EXE not to try to put the Extended BIOS Data Area into upper memory, specify the NOMOVEEXBDA parameter on the EMM386.EXE invocation line.

After you answer the Advanced Options questions on the screen shown in figure 12.12 and press Enter, MemMaker looks for your copy of Windows on disk, if you've got one on disk. It then confirms that it has indeed found the correct copy of Windows, as you see in figure 12.14. MemMaker then causes some disk activity and displays a screen like the one in figure 12.15.

In order to analyze your memory-resident programs, MemMaker must boot the system so that it can examine load sizes and discover yo-yos. Press Enter from the first warning screen; MemMaker reboots your system for the first time. Then you see another MemMaker

Arranging Programs in UMBs for Maximum Space Usage

screen warning you of a second reboot. As the second reboot occurs, keep an eye on the screen, watch for any messages like...

```
driver load failed
```

...that indicate that MemMaker has done something bad in its arrangement of files. After the second boot, you see a MemMaker screen like the one in figure 12.16.

```
Microsoft MemMaker

  MemMaker found a copy of Windows in the following directory:

    C:\W31

    * If this is the copy of Windows you are currently using,
      press ENTER to continue.

    * If your current copy of Windows is in a different directory,
      type the path of that directory, and then press ENTER.







ENTER=Continue   F1=Help   F3=Exit
```

Figure 12.14
MemMaker confirms the location of Windows files.

```
Microsoft MemMaker

  ┌──────────────────────────────────────────────────────────┐
  │ MemMaker will now restart your computer.                 │
  │                                                          │
  │ If your computer doesn't start properly, just turn it off│
  │ and on again, and MemMaker will recover automatically.   │
  │                                                          │
  │ If a program other than MemMaker starts after your computer│
  │ restarts, exit the program so that MemMaker can continue.│
  │                                                          │
  │     * Remove any disks from your floppy-disk drives and  │
  │       then press ENTER. Your computer will restart.      │
  │                                                          │
  └──────────────────────────────────────────────────────────┘

ENTER=Continue
```

Figure 12.15
MemMaker warns you before first system reboot.

Chapter 12: *Memory-Management Tips, Tricks, and Troubleshooting*

Figure 12.16
MemMaker makes a final confirmation.

```
Microsoft MemMaker

Your computer has just restarted with its new memory configuration.
Some or all of your device drivers and memory-resident programs
are now running in upper memory.

If your system appears to be working properly, choose "Yes."
If you noticed any unusual messages when your computer started,
or if your system is not working properly, choose "No."

Does your system appear to be working properly? Yes




            ENTER=Accept Selection   SPACEBAR=Change Selection   F1=Help   F3=Exit
```

In this screen, MemMaker says, "If everything looks good to you, I'll make my suggested changes permanent." Press Enter to display a final "scorecard" of how MemMaker did (see fig. 12.17).

Figure 12.17
The final MemMaker report of memory saved.

```
Microsoft MemMaker

MemMaker has finished optimizing your system's memory. The following
table summarizes the memory use (in bytes) on your system:

                                Before          After
    Memory Type                 MemMaker        MemMaker        Change

    Free conventional memory:   434,304         523,424         89,120

    Upper memory:
       Used by programs          28,800         117,920         89,120
       Reserved for Windows           0               0              0
       Reserved for EMS               0               0              0
       Free                      97,248           8,064

    Expanded memory:            Disabled        Disabled

Your original CONFIG.SYS and AUTOEXEC.BAT files have been saved
as CONFIG.UMB and AUTOEXEC.UMB.  If MemMaker changed your Windows
SYSTEM.INI file, the original file was saved as SYSTEM.UMB.

ENTER=Exit   ESC=Undo changes
```

Checking MemMaker's Work

In figure 12.17, you saw that I gave MemMaker a pretty large bunch of programs to load high and not too much UMB space to load them into—and it did a pretty good job, at first look. But when I rebooted my system, I found that the EDIT command no longer worked; it locked the system, requiring me to power off and on.

Arranging Programs in UMBs for Maximum Space Usage

The reason for the crash is quite unexpected: MemMaker insists on adding /L: options to all `LOADHIGH` and `DEVICEHIGH` statements, including the region number to load the program to and the maximum load size—whether it's needed or not. Figure 12.18 shows my CONFIG.SYS file with all the /L: options added. Notice all the commands inserted before the menu options—they're MemMaker's handiwork.

```
DEVICE=C:\DOS\HIMEM.SYS
DEVICE=C:\DOS\EMM386.EXE NOEMS HIGHSCAN novcpi x=a000-c7ff i=c800-efff
BUFFERS=44,0
FILES=61
DOS=UMB
LASTDRIVE=H
FCBS=4,0
switches=/k
[menu]
menuitem van,Vanilla
menuitem normal,Normal
menuitem interlink,Add interlink support
menuitem withnet,Add network support
menudefault=normal,2
numlock=off

[standard]
DEVICEHIGH /L:1,12048 =C:\DOS\SETVER.EXE
DOS=HIGH
DEVICEHIGH /L:1,9072 =C:\DOS\ANSI.SYS
DEVICEHIGH /L:1,44064 =C:\DOS\DBLSPACE.SYS
rem devicehigh=c:\dos\power.exe adv:max

[van]
-- More --
```

Figure 12.18
A sample CONFIG.SYS file after MemMaker finishes.

The particular computer I ran MemMaker on had only one large UMB, and plenty of space to load programs, so there was absolutely no value to including all the /L: options. For whatever reason, merely taking the /L: parameters out of the CONFIG.SYS file made the system boot and operate just fine.

Is this an unusual result from running MemMaker? It appears not. Another computer uses fairly run-of-the-mill hardware and is totally unable to use MemMaker. When MemMaker tries to reboot the system, it puts the PC in an endless loop of reboots. Another generic 486DX system with very plain hardware (standard VGA, IDE hard disk, two serial ports, and a parallel port) crashes when MemMaker tries to reboot the system but works after I turn the PC off and then on again. I don't mind telling you that all this odd behavior as a result of using MemMaker doesn't exactly raise my confidence level about the product. So take MemMaker's advice with a grain or two of salt.

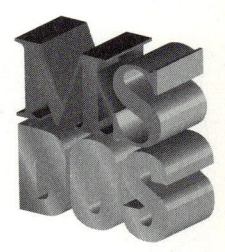

Using MEMMAKER.STS

As it runs on your system, MemMaker creates a fact-filled file called MEMMAKER.STS in the DOS subdirectory. Here's an excerpt from a MEMMAKER.STS file:

```
[MemmakerData]
State= DONE 12809
AvailConvMemoryBefore=599760
AvailUpperMemoryBefore=77488
UsedUpperMemoryBefore=64928
WindowsUpperMemoryBefore=0
EMSUpperMemoryBefore=0
AltSysFiles=False
WindowsXlat=False
CustomMode=True
AutoexecBatCheckSum=21729
ConfigSysCheckSum=55210
SystemIniCheckSum=0
WindowsLocation=C:\W31

[SizeData]

Command=C:\DOS\SETVER.EXE
Line=8
FinalSize=768
MaxSize=12048
FinalUpperSizes=0
MaxUpperSizes=0
ProgramType=DEVICE

Command=C:\W31\WORKGRP.SYS
Line=25
FinalSize=4416
MaxSize=7280
FinalUpperSizes=0
MaxUpperSizes=0
ProgramType=DEVICE

… more entries are in here…

Command=C:\W31\mouse.COM /Y
Line=10
FinalSize=17088
```

```
MaxSize=56928
FinalUpperSizes=0
MaxUpperSizes=0
ProgramType=PROGRAM
```

This file is divided into sections by headings whose names are surrounded by square brackets, similar to the INI files you've probably seen in Windows. The two section names here are `[MemMakerData]` and `[SizeData]`. The `[MemMaker Data]` section isn't very interesting: it parrots back the settings you selected when you ran MemMaker. But the [SizeData] section tells a number of things that MemMaker discovered about a program when it analyzed it. Each entry contains a number of items of information about programs in your CONFIG.SYS or AUTOEXEC.BAT file. The first item of information is the command itself—SETVER.EXE in the case of the first program—and the line on which it appears in CONFIG.SYS or AUTOEXEC.BAT.

The `FinalSize` line tells how much space a program takes up after it's loaded and settled down; MaxSize tells the maximum amount of space that the program requires in either loading or running. Notice, for example, the entry for MOUSE.COM: it reports a FinalSize of 17088 bytes—the run size we saw before—and a MaxSize of 56928 bytes—the loading size for this driver.

I'm not sure what the `FinalUpperSizes` and `MaxUpperSizes` lines are: they always equal zero. The final item, `ProgramType`, reports whether the program is a device driver (DEVICE) or a TSR program (PROGRAM). All in all, a useful set of information.

> **AUTHOR'S NOTE**
>
> *One of DOS 6.2's neatest new features is called MultiConfig. It enables you to combine a number of different CONFIG.SYS/ AUTOEXEC.BAT pairs into a single large CONFIG.SYS and AUTOEXEC.BAT that enables you to load with any one of those configurations. You can read about how to use MultiConfig in Chapter 16.*
>
> *If you use MultiConfig—and you will, believe me, once you see how flexible it can make controlling your system's configuration—you*
>
> *continues*

have to be careful about it when running MemMaker. MemMaker is largely unaware of MultiConfig; in the process of moving lines around in CONFIG.SYS, MemMaker usually trashes your nicely divided-up configurations. Commands supposed to be executed only in one configuration may now show up in all configurations.

Microsoft's advice is that you separate the various configurations back into separate AUTOEXEC.BAT/CONFIG.SYS pairs before running MemMaker. Run MemMaker on each one of them, then paste your MultiConfig CONFIG.SYS and AUTOEXEC.BAT back together by hand.

Yuck, eh? Microsoft claims that it "would be a lot harder than you think" to make MemMaker more aware of multiple configurations. In any case, be aware of this problem.

When all is said and done, is running MemMaker a good idea? I say "yes," but I also say again that there's no program around that can do all your memory arranging for you. The best way is the old-fashioned way: tune the memory manager by hand and you end up with a system that's got more free memory and runs more stably. That does not mean that you shouldn't run MemMaker—MemMaker can do a quick-and-dirty job of memory scanning and program arranging that can save you time when you begin the process of arranging your PC's memory. Just understand that MemMaker is the first or second step in memory management…not the only one.

Looking at Common Memory-Management Problems

Memory managers are terrific things: they've given a new lease on life to poor old DOS. But they can cause their own troubles. Whether it's an incapability to warm boot a computer, phantom keystrokes, or programs that don't work when loaded high, there are a number of common problems understood by memory-management experts.

Because you're reading this chapter to become a memory-management expert, it seems that now is the right time to meet some of these memory-management puzzlers and their corresponding solutions.

Solving Keyboard Problems Caused by Memory Managers

Back when DOS 5 appeared—the first DOS that featured EMM386.EXE and the capability to load programs high—I got copies for all my employees, and we installed them on the couple of dozen machines in the office. Soon, however, a few odd problems began to crop up.

The most puzzling thing happened to my marketing director Donna Cook. Donna complained that her keyboard was malfunctioning, particularly while she was in WordPerfect for DOS. Looking over her shoulder as she worked, I saw that as she typed a line of text in lowercase, random uppercase characters appeared, almost as if some ghostly finger periodically pressed Shift. You can see a typical screen (with Edit, rather than WordPerfect—the problem occurred in several programs) in figure 12.19. That seemingly minor problem led to a lot of investigation, and two possible answers.

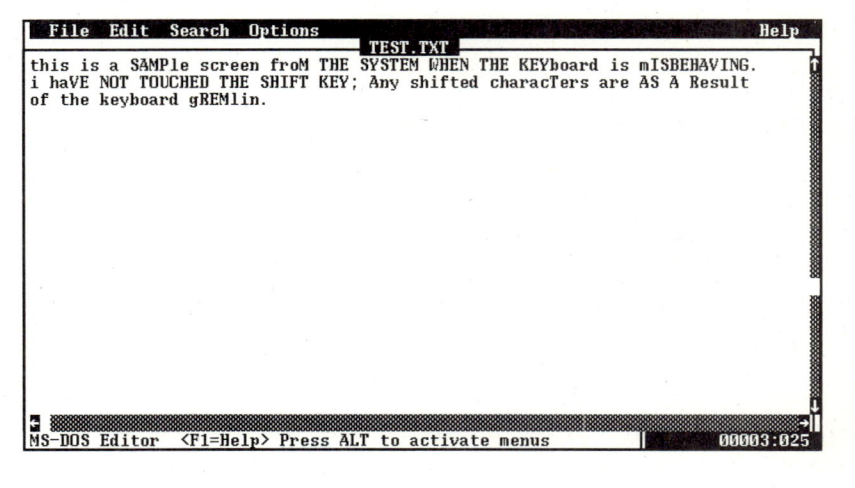

Figure 12.19

A ghostly finger pressed Shift.

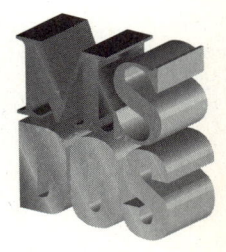

Solution: Using and Understanding Alternative A20 Handlers

Ever notice the message as HIMEM.SYS loads that refers to `A20 handler number X loaded`? Recall that early PCs were based on the 8088 CPU; the address space of the 8088 was only 1024K in size. The 8088 could not access more than 1024K in RAM (*see Chapter 9*).

Now consider this: what happens when the 8088 CPU's instruction pointer is poised at top of memory—location 1024K-1—and then it receives an instruction that says, "Go to the next location?" (I know that this seems like a kind of Zen question—"Where do we go when we go nowhere?"—but it's important, as you'll see.)

In this case, the 8088 *wraps around* the address value. Looking at it in hex for a minute, the 8088 has address registers only five hex-digits wide; any numbers bigger than five hex digits lose all but the rightmost five digits (*truncated* is the technical term). In hex, the top 8088 address is FFFFF. Add 1 to FFFFF, and you get 100000, a six hex-digit number. But, as I just said, any digit past the fifth is lopped off, making the result 00000. If this wraparound is difficult to understand, think of a car's odometer. Older cars had only five digits on the odometer. After your car exceeded 99,999 miles, the odometer wrapped around to 00000 once again.

In contrast, however, the address register of the 286 isn't five hex-digits wide; it's six hex-digits wide. Add 1 to FFFFF on a 286, and you get 100000 with no wraparound. Continuing the odometer analogy, this is like newer cars that have six digits on the odometer: they have to pass 999,999 miles before they wrap around.

Okay, you say, big deal. The 8088 wraps around beyond FFFFF. An interesting curiosity—but how is it relevant to today?

Believe it or not, some DOS programs depend on this wraparound. The reason is mainly a program-development tool popular in the PC business in the late 80s, a "program linker" that offered the option to create large programs that wouldn't take up much space on disk. The linker used a programming trick, however, that only worked if run on an 8088 that wrapped addresses around above FFFFF.

All the programs developed with that linker, however, worked fine on 99.9 percent of the PCs on the market, even if they were built around a 286 or later CPU. Those CPUs could mimic the 8088's wraparound, thanks to IBM. When IBM engineers designed the AT back in 1983, they faced a problem. The AT was designed around the 286 chip, which can address more than 1024K, as you know. As you also know, the 286 doesn't wrap around addresses, so it provides the trick that makes it possible for the High Memory Area (HMA) to exist. (Recall that the HMA allows real-mode programs to exploit 64K more of space, raising the roof to 1088K rather than 1024K.) The issue of compatibility with the earlier PC and XT concerned the AT engineers. As useful as the HMA might be, it could also pose a problem: what about those DOS programs that relied on address wraparound at 1024K? They wouldn't work because the address after 1024K-1 would no longer be 0; it would be 1024K. The IBM AT development team wanted the AT to be as 100-percent compatible with the PC as possible.

The original PC's designers had included on the PC bus the capability to address any location in the PC's 1024K address space. That address space can be completely expressed with 20 wires (as is said in technospeak, *20 address lines*). The address lines on the PC bus are labeled A0 through A19. Because the 286 chip addressed up to 16M of RAM, the AT's expanded version of the PC bus (later known as the ISA, or Industry Standard Architecture bus) needed more address lines—24 in fact. Any access of memory above 1024K-1 energized these extra address lines. At exactly 1024K, address line A20 is activated.

The IBM engineers decided to make the AT more compatible with the PC by putting an electronic "gate" on A20 (see fig. 12.20). (The 286's address lines A21, A22, and A23 aren't shown in figure 12.20 to keep the diagram simple.) The gate acts like a microscopic drawbridge, letting data pass from the CPU to the RAM, or blocking those signals. When the gate is closed (remember, *closed* means *connected* in electronic talk), A20 signals can pass and the HMA can be accessed. When the gate is open, A20 signals cannot pass, and the AT behaves like the 8088: the address wraps around above 1024K-1. The procedure is sort of like putting a piece of tape over the sixth digit on a new car's odometer to make it 100-percent, old-car compatible if you follow my analogy.

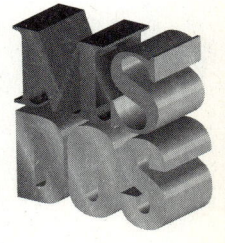

Figure 12.20
A 286 PC and an A20 gate.

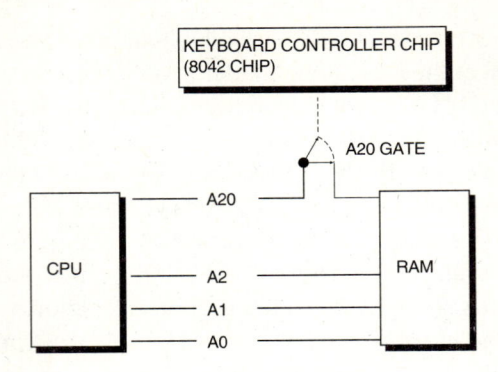

```
                    ┌──────────────────────────┐
                    │ KEYBOARD CONTROLLER CHIP │
                    │      (8042 CHIP)         │
                    └────────────┬─────────────┘
                                 ╎
                                 ╎    A20 GATE
                                 •──╱
                          A20 ──┘  
           ┌─────┐                        ┌─────┐
           │     │────── A20 ─────────────│     │
           │ CPU │────── A2  ─────────────│ RAM │
           │     │────── A1  ─────────────│     │
           │     │────── A0  ─────────────│     │
           └─────┘                        └─────┘
```

The keyboard controller chip acts as the gatekeeper. Believe it or not, HIMEM has to close A20 by sending a command to the keyboard controller. The AT's designers probably did it that way because the keyboard controller, the 8042 chip, is a completely separate and distinct microcomputer. That's *microcomputer*, not *microprocessor*.

The difference is that a microprocessor is just a CPU. A microcomputer has RAM and ROM, like the 8042 keyboard controller chip does. That single chip is actually as powerful as the original stand-alone microcomputers of the mid-70s. Furthermore, because the keyboard controller is its own computer-inside-a-computer, it has a program running inside it that controls the keyboard. But that microcomputer can lose its way, just as the main processor sometimes loses its way. When the keyboard controller experiences software confusion (a buggy keyboard driver mis-programs it) or a hardware trouble (perhaps a static charge partially scrambles the keyboard controller's memory), the keyboard typically locks up.

> *Have you ever had your PC's keyboard lock up, and the PC ignores the Ctrl+Alt+Del sequence? What's really mysterious is when that happens on a computer with a hardware reset key. Push the reset key, and the computer reboots but complains of a keyboard failure. What happens is that the hardware reset switch resets the main processor, not the keyboard processor. Whatever's bothering the keyboard processor wasn't affected by your pressing the reset key.*

IBM probably used the keyboard controller to control the A20 line so that the keyboard controller could be programmed to do things like alter the state of the A20 gate while the PC's main processor was busy booting the system. It's not a bad idea, but what went wrong was one of two things. First, not every PC hardware designer uses the keyboard controller to manipulate the A20 line. Second, the keyboard controller normally services the keyboard; ask it to do too many things at once (service the keyboard and police the A20 gate) and some things can fall through the cracks.

Not all 286 or later PCs use the keyboard controller to control the A20 gate. For example, when IBM designed the PS/2, it did away altogether with the keyboard controller's involvement with A20 and built a separate circuit to do the A20 gate-swinging. When IBM broke the AT mold, the floodgates opened on innovation among other PC vendors: other vendors decided to showcase their creativity also. As a result, Microsoft built into HIMEM.SYS support for 17 different approaches to altering the state of the A20 gate. These methods are chosen with the /MACHINE: option (it can be abbreviated "/M:") on HIMEM.SYS. HIMEM must, then, contain the A20 handler, the program that opens and closes the A20 gate.

Forcing HIMEM To Use an Alternative A20 Handler

Before HIMEM can function properly in your system, it must determine which of the A20-handler methods works on your particular PC. In most cases, HIMEM chooses the correct handler approach. But sometimes it doesn't, leading to odd side effects and ghostly keystrokes.

An incorrect A20 handler is one reason for unusual keyboard behavior; so one thing to try when trying to solve a keyboard problem is to force HIMEM to use different A20 handlers. Try it yourself on a troublesome machine. For example, to invoke HIMEM.SYS with A20 handler number 5, include this line in CONFIG.SYS:

```
DEVICE=C:\DOS\HIMEM.SYS /M:5
```

> *Before you do this, make sure that you have a bootable floppy handy. Typically, only one or two A20 handlers work on a given system; forcing HIMEM to use any other A20 handler locks up the system. (I know; you can also press F5 when you boot to bypass CONFIG.SYS and the HIMEM statement, so you may not need a bootable floppy. But I'm a belt-and-suspenders kind of guy; when you set up memory managers on a few hundred machines, you'll be a belt-and-suspenders kind of person, too.) That way, you can recover from the system lockup that usually results from trying to boot with an incorrect machine type.*

Installing a New Keyboard Controller

You may find, however, that none of the alternative A20 handlers solves your keyboard problems. You may boot your system 17 times using the /M:1 through /M:17 parameters on HIMEM.SYS, and still not exorcise the ghostly keystrokes. Some older keyboard controllers have sloppy programs in them, sloppy programs that were never really noticed until you made some demands of them. Some clones and compatibles need a new keyboard controller chip to resolve their memory problems; consult your PC's manufacturer (not the keyboard's manufacturer) if your keyboard malfunctions under Windows and no machine type fixes the problem. Before you do that, however, try the other remedies in this section.

Getting Applications To Lay Off the Keyboard Controller

Donna was mainly troubled by the keyboard-Shift ghost when she was in WordPerfect 5.1 for DOS. The ghost seemed to only haunt that application—was there some reason, I wondered?

I thought back a few years, and realized the answer. How did WordPerfect get to be Numero Uno in the word processing business in the first place? Well, it wasn't its easy-to-use, friendly user interface; and it wasn't its usage of industry-standard keystrokes like Esc and F1.

Looking at Common Memory-Management Problems

WordPerfect got to be number one in the word processing business because it was fast—blindingly fast. No other word processor on the market could keep up with the fleet fingers of most fast secretaries. The features came later...the speed came first.

If you look back at Chapter 2, you realize where WordPerfect gets its blinding speed: WordPerfect bypasses DOS and BIOS to directly address the keyboard hardware, cutting out the middleman and speeding itself up in the process. At any instant in time, WordPerfect is figuratively standing over the keyboard controller, saying, "Do you have any new keystrokes for me? How about now? How about now? How about now?..." over and over again. The keyboard controller is constantly saying to WordPerfect, "Not yet not yet not yet not yet..." and DOS is trying to tell the keyboard controller, "Hey, stop paying attention to the keyboard for a second so that I can get you to move the A20 gate..." It's understandable that the keyboard controller might end up giving some false information to WordPerfect now and then.

The answer is to tell WordPerfect to chill out and access the keyboard controller through DOS, like many other applications.

"But wait, Mark," you say. "I thought that WordPerfect needed to go directly to the keyboard controller to achieve acceptable keystroke-response time." Although that was once true, it was true in the days of WordPerfect 4.2, which mainly ran on 4.77 Mhz 8088-based PCs. You probably run WordPerfect on a 25Mhz 80386DX PC, so you'll almost certainly feel no difference if you tell WordPerfect to lay off the keyboard controller and wait in line for keystrokes from DOS like everybody else.

You tell WordPerfect to get its keystrokes from DOS and BIOS by invoking WordPerfect with the /nk option. Instead of starting up WordPerfect by typing **WP**, you type **WP /nk**.

> *I have solved a number of ghostly keyboard problems by telling applications to access the keyboard through DOS. The only problem with the method is that for it to be totally effective, I'd have to tell you how to tell all programs to go through DOS and BIOS to get their*

continues

> keystrokes. I don't know how to do that for more than a few applications and besides, most applications that directly address the keyboard don't give you the option to force the application to work through DOS or BIOS.

Loading an Alternative Keyboard Driver

The fourth thing you can try when exorcising an A20 poltergeist is to load an alternative keyboard controller program. Folks who work with non-American keyboards have been doing this for years with the KEYB command. Americans have never had the need to understand keyboard drivers and code pages, and so there was never an international keyboard map for the U.S. keyboard. That changed with DOS 5, and it continues with DOS 6.2. You may find that loading the U.S. keyboard driver solves your keyboard problems. You load it with the following statement:

```
KEYB US,437,C:\DOS\KEYBOARD.SYS
```

For those who are wondering, 437 refers to a character-set mapping method called a *code page*.

Solution: 386 Max Fixes TSRs Hooking Keyboard Controller

Although I've laid much of the blame for keyboard and memory manager problems at the door of HIMEM.SYS, its partner EMM386.EXE must assume its share of the blame as well.

The first troubleshooting step when keyboard gremlins pop up is to load DOS low and continue to load device drivers and TSRs high. If the problem goes away, you have a HIMEM.SYS-related problem; one of the previously explained remedies should solve your problem. If the problem persists, EMM386.EXE is the likely culprit.

How DOS Reads a Keyboard without TSRs

To understand why EMM386.EXE is likely to be the cause of keyboard gremlins, consider how TSR programs interact with the keyboard hardware. In figure 12.21, the user has pressed the r key, and the

Looking at Common Memory-Management Problems   633

keystroke has been transmitted to the keyboard controller. The keyboard controller must get DOS to read the keystroke quickly because the keyboard controller has no storage space; if another keystroke comes in before DOS comes to collect the current r keystroke, the keyboard controller loses the older keystroke so that it can hold onto the most current keystroke from the keyboard.

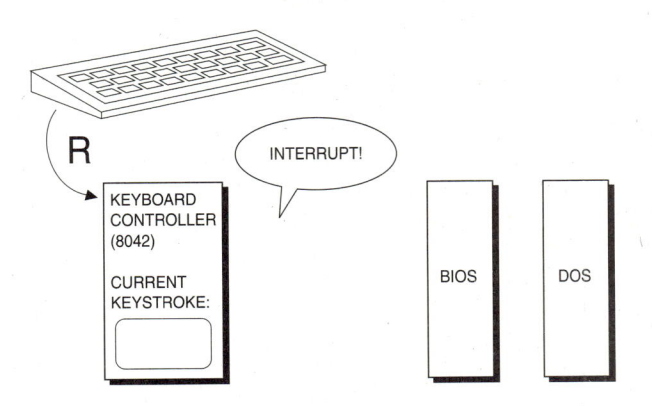

Figure 12.21

How DOS reads a keystroke (part 1).

The keyboard controller forces DOS to pay attention to it by generating a hardware interrupt (IRQ1, for you techies). A hardware interrupt is kind of like a bell that goes off near the CPU, forcing the CPU to drop everything and respond. That causes the CPU to execute software interrupt 9 (INT9, as described in Chapter 2, if you've forgotten software interrupts). INT9 points to the BIOS's keyboard routines in this simple example.

The BIOS INT9 routine instructs the keyboard controller to display the current keystroke (see fig. 12.22). The keyboard controller then displays the r, and the BIOS INT9 program acknowledges that it got the keystroke. Figure 12.23 shows the display of the keystroke in a rounded rectangle, kind of like a TV screen, but in actuality it's presented on I/O address 60 hex. (You do not have to follow the details about which interrupt is which and what I/O port is used, or even what an I/O port is—the detail is here for the curious.)

Because BIOS accepted the character, the keyboard controller no longer retains the r in its keystroke display (that is, the code for r no longer sits at I/O address 60). BIOS transfers the keystroke to DOS, which maintains a keyboard buffer that enables you to type ahead of the program you're using (see fig. 12.24).

Figure 12.22

How DOS reads a keystroke (part 2).

Figure 12.23

How DOS reads a keystroke (part 3).

Figure 12.24

How DOS reads a keystroke (part 4).

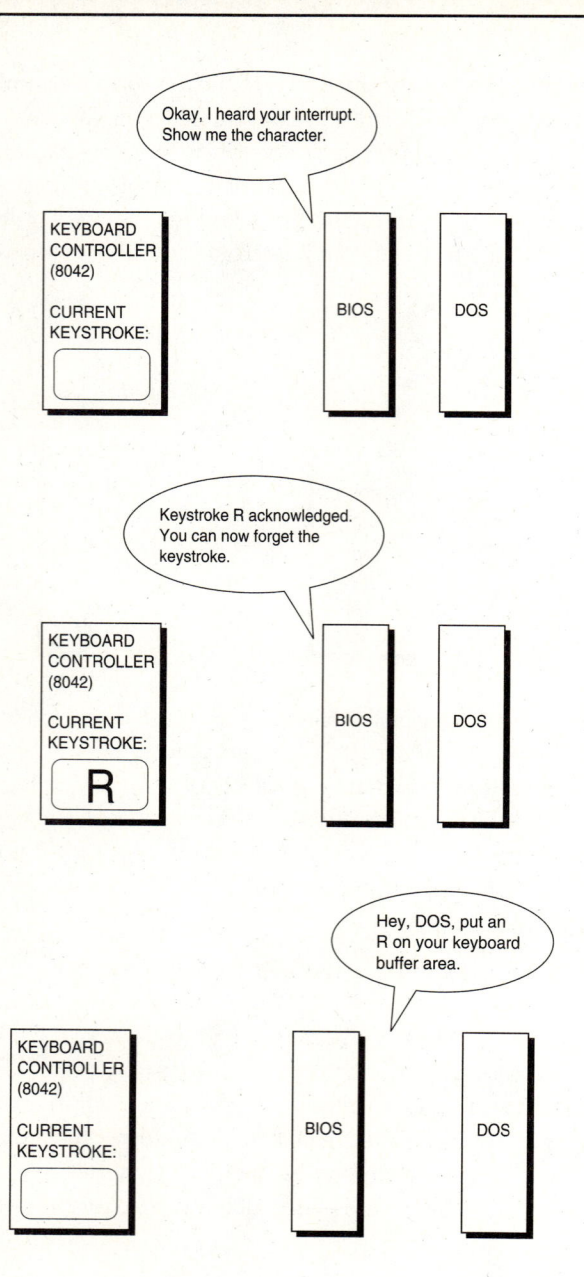

How DOS Reads a Keyboard with TSRs

To the preceding example, suppose that you add a TSR program that enables you to run a terminal-emulation program in the background (like many 3270-emulation programs that large corporations use). The idea behind a terminal-emulation program is that you load it at boot time and then work in your usual DOS application until you need to access the mainframe computer that the PC is hooked up to. The terminal-emulation software essentially "sleeps" until awakened by a particular keystroke; typical keystrokes are Ctrl+Alt or Left Shift+Right Shift. The terminal-emulation program then "wakes up," takes over the screen, and performs its terminal-emulation duties.

This example examines how an emulation program knows to wake up when you press Left Shift+Right Shift. In figure 12.25, the incoming keystroke causes the keyboard controller to issue an interrupt. Notice that when the emulator loaded, it placed itself first in line for any incoming keystrokes; from its position at the front of the line, it looks for the Shift+Shift combination that causes it to spring into action.

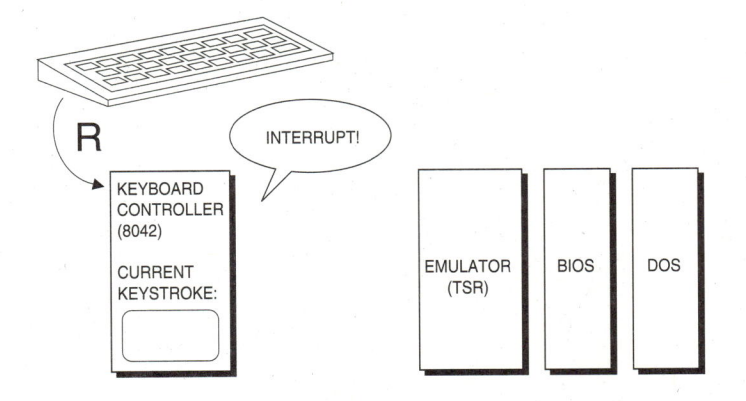

Figure 12.25

How TSRs intercept keystrokes (part 1).

Figure 12.26 shows how the emulator responds to the keyboard controller as the BIOS does normally, requesting that it display its keystroke.

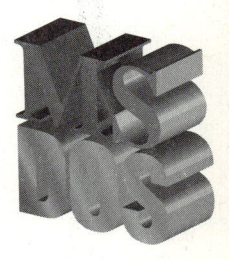

Figure 12.27 shows where things get a bit different. The emulator looks at the keystroke (which turns out to be a lowercase r) but does not acknowledge it, forcing the keyboard controller to retain the

keystroke. The emulator then fakes an interrupt to the BIOS, "waking up" the BIOS and directing it to request the next keystroke from the keyboard controller.

Figure 12.26

How TSRs intercept keystrokes (part 2).

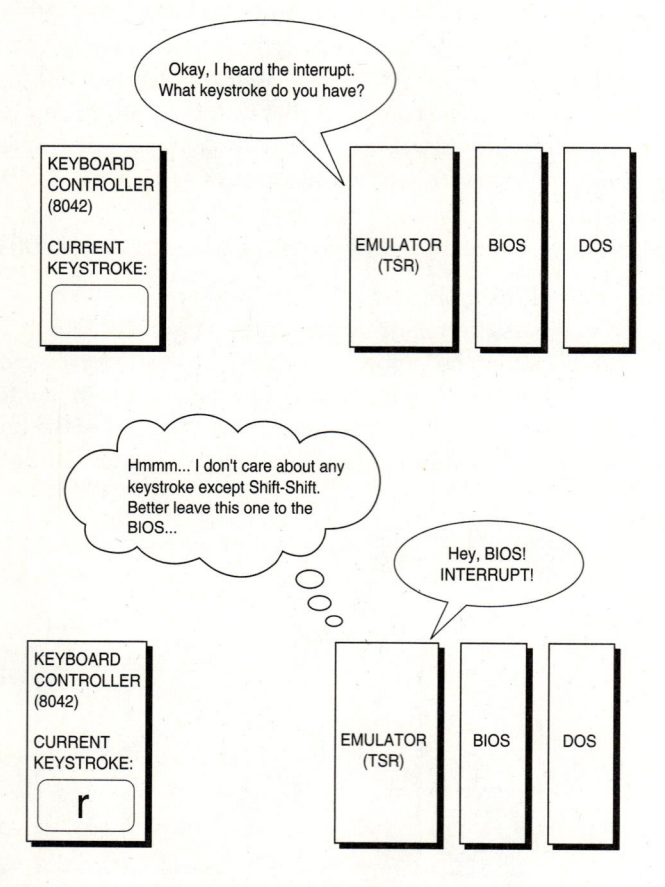

Figure 12.27

How TSRs intercept keystrokes (part 3).

Two things are worth mentioning here. First, the BIOS doesn't realize that it isn't the first program to query the keyboard controller, and it behaves as though the keyboard controller hadn't already been asked to display the character. Second—and here's the part very few people know—keyboard controllers have a maximum amount of time that they display a keystroke on I/O address 60 (the current-keystroke display). The time between when the first program says, "Display the current keystroke on I/O address 60" and the time that a program says, "Okay, I acknowledge receipt of the keystroke—you can forget it now," cannot exceed a few milliseconds. (How many milliseconds varies from keyboard controller to keyboard controller.)

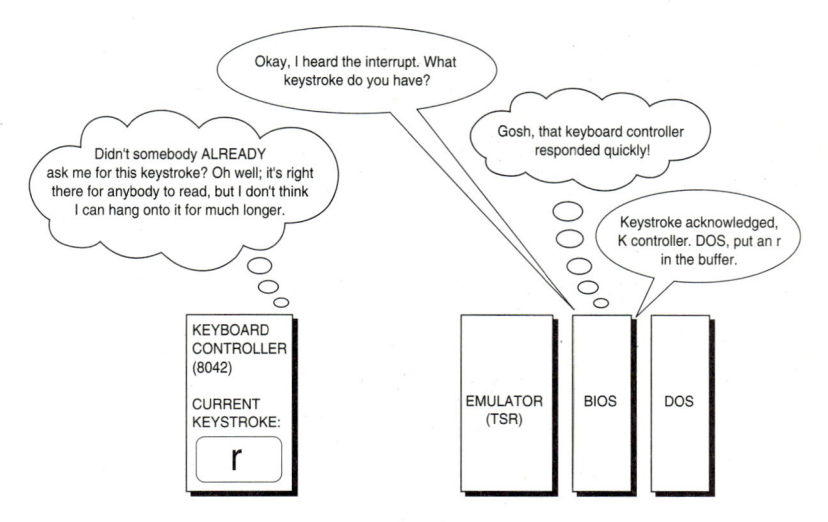

Figure 12.28

How TSRs intercept keystrokes (part 4).

> **NOTE**
>
> *Once a program has said, "Show me the current keystroke," it or some other program had better grab that keystroke fast or the keyboard controller ends up losing or garbling the character.*

Figure 12.28 shows the rest of what happens to get the keystroke from the keyboard controller to DOS: BIOS asks the keyboard controller for the keystroke. The keyboard controller is already displaying the keystroke, but no matter; it responds to BIOS by saying, "Here it is." BIOS reads the keystroke and passes it to DOS; end of story.

How TSRs Can Cause Keyboard Read Failures

In the preceding example, a single TSR was inserted into the chain from keystroke to BIOS to DOS. That single TSR made the keyboard controller wait a bit longer than usual. Let's lengthen the chain by loading EMM386.EXE. EMM386.EXE inserts itself at the head of the chain and monitors the keyboard as a matter of course (it monitors *all*

Chapter 12: *Memory-Management Tips, Tricks, and Troubleshooting*

system activity). Although it doesn't have to monitor everything, that's the way EMM386—and most other memory managers—are designed.

Figure 12.29 dramatizes in one picture what goes on when you have two programs—EMM386 and an emulator—in line for keystrokes before BIOS. (I say *dramatizes* because in actuality, two programs wouldn't cause any trouble. Trouble is more likely to happen to someone with six or seven programs in the chain, but it's easier to draw just two programs in the chain.) Following is a step-by-step account of what happens in figure 12.29.

Figure 12.29
How a memory manager can cause garbled keystrokes.

8042: INTERRUPT!
EMM386: What keystroke do you have?
8042: r
EMM386: Hmmm... not interesting. INTERRUPT!
Emulator: What keystroke do you have?
8042: Didn't I do this already?...r
Emulator: Hmmm...Not interesting. INTERRUPT!
BIOS: What keystroke do you have?
8042: [The keystroke display has timed out.] Actually, I'm not sure. I think it was a shifted R.
BIOS: Shifted R acknowledged. DOS, put a shifted R in the buffer.

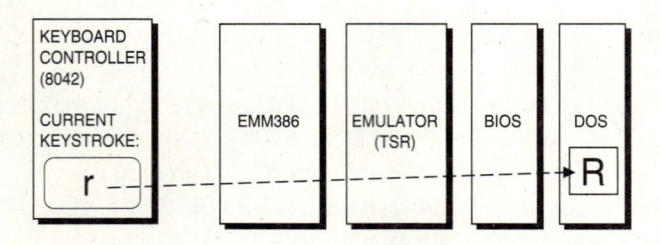

```
KEYBOARD
CONTROLLER
(8042)              EMM386    EMULATOR    BIOS    DOS
                              (TSR)
CURRENT
KEYSTROKE:
    r  ------------------------------------------>  R
```

1. The 8042 keyboard controller receives a keystroke from the keyboard.

2. The 8042 issues an interrupt, requesting that some piece of software take the keystroke so that the 8042 has room for a subsequent keystroke. First in line is EMM386.EXE, which doesn't actually look for keystrokes but does monitor the activity of the 8042.

3. EMM386 says to the 8042, "Show me the keystroke you're holding."

4. The 8042 shows EMM386 the keystroke. EMM386 didn't want the keystroke—it just wanted to *see* the keystroke. Now that the keyboard controller has displayed the keystroke, the timeout countdown has begun. When the countdown is over, the character in the 8042 is no longer reliable. EMM386, meanwhile, fakes an interrupt, activating the next program in the chain.

   The next program in the chain is Emulator. But Emulator is a real-mode program, and EMM386 runs in protected mode. Before EMM386 can hand control over to Emulator, EMM386 must shift the PC from protected mode to real mode. That takes a few milliseconds, which may not sound like much, but remember the clock is ticking on the 8042's retention of the keystroke.

5. After the PC has shifted to real mode, Emulator says to the 8042 keyboard controller, "Show me your keystroke." The 8042 obliges—in fact, it was showing the keystroke already.

6. Emulator sees that the keystroke (an r) is not the keystroke it's looking for (it's waiting for a Shift+Shift) and fakes an interrupt so that the next program in the chain takes over. The next program in the chain is the BIOS.

7. The BIOS is unaware that any other program has already talked to the keyboard controller about this keystroke and so says, "Show me the keystroke." The 8042 attempts to comply, but it has timed out and no longer has a reliable keystroke. It ends up reporting not only the r, but also a spurious CapsLock keystroke.

8. The BIOS acknowledges receipt of the keystroke so that the keyboard controller can forget about the keystroke.

The net effect is random groups of shifted characters.

How To Fix Keyboard and Memory-Manager Problems

There are two things you can do about keyboard problems caused by too many TSRs: either lengthen the timeout period on the keyboard controller or shorten the chain of programs accessing the 8042.

The only way to extend the keyboard controller's timeout period is to replace it (a drastic move). Replacing the controller chip may, however, be the only way to solve the problem.

An easier way to fix the ghost-key problem is to look closely at the number of TSR programs you run. Believe it or not, nearly every TSR hooks the keyboard in some way. One way to reduce or eliminate the keyboard problem is to trim the list of TSRs.

> *Even SMARTDRV.EXE monitors the keyboard to determine when the system is inactive. (Recall from the discussion in Chapter 8 on SMARTDrive that the DOS disk-cache software waits for inactivity before writing data to disk.) Other common TSRs that monitor the keyboard include DOSKEY (the command history program), GRAPHICS (a printscreen-enhancement program), BREAK and other DOS programs, as well as most third-party TSRs.*

Recall that the memory manager itself is one of the programs that stands in line for keystrokes. The memory manager makes things worse than most TSRs because the memory manager not only adds delays, as do all TSRs, it also forces a shift between protected and real mode. The addition of precious milliseconds to accomplish this shift makes the memory manager a particularly troublesome member of the keyboard chain.

The only thing you can do about that is to not use EMM386.EXE. For that matter, don't use Quarterdeck's QEMM; it does the same things as EMM386.EXE. But Qualitas's 386Max leaves the keyboard alone, making it the memory manager of choice when you've got a troublesome keyboard.

Solving Other Keyboard Problems

If you experience keyboard problems after installing DOS 5 or 6.2, there are several procedures you can follow to troubleshoot these problems.

Although there are actually two ways to read from enhanced keyboards, some older TSRs that hook into the keyboard interrupt don't know both of these, and therefore fail to operate properly. Add the following line to CONFIG.SYS to force the system to use conventional keyboard functions rather than extended keyboard functions:

```
SWITCHES=/K
```

> **TIP** *If you are using ANSI.SYS, add the /K switch, which has the same effect. (You must, in fact, use both these procedures if you are using ANSI.SYS.)*

Keyboard problems also occur because of BIOS problems. If you are using an AMI BIOS, check the last two digits of the serial number. (You see the serial number displayed when you reboot the computer.) If they are K7, the BIOS can cause keyboard problems in Windows and on networks. Upgrading to K8 may correct the problem.

Solving the Beeps-at-Warm-Boot Problem

The first time I worked with one of the 386SX notebooks in my office, I noticed an odd problem whenever I rebooted the system. If I used the DOS 5 memory manager to load programs high, and I pressed the warm-boot key sequence Ctrl+Alt+Del, the laptop emitted a *beep-beep-beeeeep* sound and then locked up. (Appropriately, the final *beeeeep* was in a minor key.) The only thing that fixed the problem was to exclude the region F0000-FFFFF, making it possible to warm boot but causing EMM386.EXE to produce the following annoying message...

```
User specified ranges overlap. Press any key to
continue....
```

After pressing a key, all was well—but it was annoying to have to press that key.

Shortly after discovering this problem, I worked on an NEC 486DX PowerMate; it had the same problem. I noticed that both the laptop and the PowerMate used basically the same BIOS—PhoenixVIEW video BIOS Version 1.00 and PhoenixBIOS A386 Version 1.01.

A call to Phoenix got the advice to "use Quarterdeck; it seems not to have the problem." (Hey, *thanks*, Phoenix.) A call to Microsoft, on the other hand, got the problem fixed in DOS 6.2. If you hear *beep-beep-beeeeep* when you try to warm boot, and you're using EMM386.EXE, add the parameter ALTBOOT to your EMM386.EXE invocation. When I added ALTBOOT to the line in my CONFIG.SYS that loads EMM386.EXE, the beeps went away forever.

Solving the Problem of Why Some Programs Won't Load High

As you try to squeeze more and more free space out of conventional memory, you will find that a number of programs just don't want to load high. It's as if these device drivers and TSRs had a fear of heights: they start misbehaving when loaded above 640K.

You can't make all problem programs load high, no matter what you do. Some programs have to be upgraded before they work anywhere but in conventional memory.

The majority of programs that won't load high do so for one of two reasons:

- ✔ Some programs don't work when DOS is loaded high, even if the programs themselves are loaded in conventional memory.

- ✔ Some programs perform Direct Memory Access (DMA) operations, not all of which work if performed in upper memory.

The following sections look at both categories of problem programs.

Some Programs Don't Like DOS Loaded High

As mentioned elsewhere, I use Iomega's Bernoulli Box cartridge storage device to do backups. Using it is pretty simple: you disconnect the printer from your PC, plug the drive into your parallel port, include a device driver named RCD.SYS in CONFIG.SYS, and reboot. Instantly, you've got a new drive G, H, or whatever the next unused drive letter is.

When I first tried that back with DOS 5, however, the driver wouldn't work (DOS 6.2 has the same result). After playing around with some device settings in the hope that I'd hit on one that would make the Bernoulli Box work, I tried loading DOS low. The Bernoulli Box worked.

Since then, I've occasionally run across programs that just plain don't work if DOS is loaded into the HMA. I don't know why the Bernoulli driver didn't work, but there are a number of late-80s DOS programs that use a program-linking utility called CVTPACK to create smaller EXE files. EXE files run through CVTPACK are compressed in a manner similar to the way that DoubleSpace compresses files on your hard disk. The benefit of CVTPACK was that software vendors could ship programs on a smaller number of floppy disks that would take up less space on your hard disk.

Before it can execute, any CVTPACK program must decompress itself; it does this each time you execute it. And that's where the trouble occurs. The decompressing algorithm assumes that any addresses above 1024K wrap around to zero (as described in "Using and Understanding Alternative A20 Handlers," earlier in this chapter).

HIMEM.SYS tries to detect these programs and provide the address wraparound for them, but it can't always detect when a program uses CVTPACK. When that happens, you get the following error message:

```
packed file is corrupt
```

You may be able to run the program anyway with the LOADFIX program. If you want to run a program called PROG, for example, you run it under LOADFIX by typing...

LOADFIX PROG

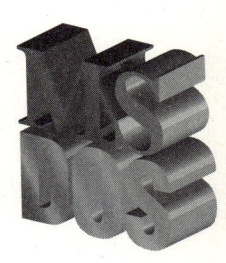

At that point, PROG either works or it doesn't. If it doesn't, your choices are either to not use HIMEM.SYS when you want to run PROG or contact PROG's vendor to find out when a HIMEM.SYS-aware version of the program will be available.

Another subclass of programs exists that won't run when DOS is loaded high. The problem that these programs face is that they were written assuming that they would be loaded above DOS in memory. That was a good assumption until DOS 5 introduced a version of DOS that could load above 1024K; because DOS 5 appeared in 1991, hopefully new versions of these products have arrived that are compatible with DOS when it's in the HMA.

If You DMA into a TSR in a UMB, You're SOL

Sorry—couldn't resist that title. In Chapter 10, you learned exactly what happens to supply the memory for an Upper Memory Block (UMB). Memory-address regions that have no memory attached to them but that are within the low 1024K address range can be filled with memory from addresses above 1024K. Recall the analogy of moving from 5400 Wilson Boulevard to 5409 Tenth Street and having mail forwarded from 5400 Wilson to 5409 Tenth Street in perpetuity so that you don't have to tell anyone you've moved.

In this analogy of the move, your actual physical address is 5409 Tenth Street. Your logical address—the one you seem to inhabit because your mail gets to you even if it's addressed to you there—is 5400 Wilson Boulevard.

So it is with programs in UMBs. Although they are physically located in extended memory, they behave as if they were operating out of memory in the 768 to 1024K range.

Disk Transfers and DMA

One function that some TSRs must perform is Direct Memory Access (DMA). The purpose of DMA is, simply stated, speed. Take, for example, the way a disk controller transfers data to and from the PC.

Looking at Common Memory-Management Problems

Every time a disk-read operation happens, the controller board holds 512 bytes of data from the disk drive. Those 512 bytes of data have to be transferred from the disk controller to the PC's memory because, like the keyboard controller in the example a few pages back, the 512-byte storage area is all the hard disk controller has. The data must be moved out of the controller and into the PC's RAM as soon as possible, both to make room for more data and to allow the CPU to use the data quickly.

There are two ways to accomplish the controller-to-RAM transfer: programmed Input/Output (PIO) and Direct Memory Access (DMA).

With PIO, each byte is transferred first from the controller to the CPU and then from the CPU to RAM. It's simple to do and doesn't involve any special hardware—just a short program that runs on the CPU and loops 512 times to grab a byte from the controller, transfer it to RAM, and go back for more. It's simple, but it has one major problem: it's not very fast.

A quicker approach involves designing a PC with a few extra chips on the motherboard to support Direct Memory Access. With DMA, the program that wants to read data from the hard disk just points to the 512-byte region of RAM into which the hard-disk data is to be transferred, and says, in effect, "hard-disk controller, put the data here." The data can then be transferred directly from the hard-disk controller to the desired location in RAM.

Although that sounds like the CPU's not involved at all in a DMA transfer, that's not true. What actually happens is that the program that wants to do the DMA gets permission from the CPU to do the DMA and then instructs a chip called the DMA controller to get ready to do the DMA. When the 512-byte chunk of data makes it into the controller, the DMA chip knows to grab it and put it in the proper place in RAM.

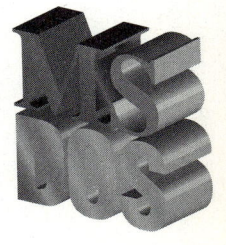

SMARTDrive is one TSR that directs DMA operations. Because SMARTDrive takes over the nitty-gritty disk operations for the PC, it is the program that issues the DMA instructions, telling the DMA controller, "Place the incoming data here into a data area I've created inside myself." SMARTDrive, like all disk-cache programs, is a program that should be loaded high because it can burn up 20 to 40K of RAM space. If SMARTDrive is loaded high, that means that *all* of SMARTDrive is loaded high, including the data area inside SMARTDrive that's been set aside as a buffer for incoming (and outgoing) data.

DMA Needs Physical Addresses, Not Logical Ones

Here's the problem. When SMARTDrive is in a UMB, it has a physical address over 1024K and a logical address below 1024K. Because SMARTDrive is totally unaware that it's sitting in extended memory that's masquerading as below-1024K memory, it just says to the DMA controller, "Transfer the disk data to me here at (for example) 815K."

The trouble is, the DMA controller needs *physical* addresses, not logical ones. There is no memory at 815K; it's just an unused address. If you try to do a DMA to that address, you send data to addresses without memory, and the data essentially walks off a cliff.

Return to the forwarding-address analogy. Suppose that you order a product from a mail-order company and give your (logical) address of 5400 Wilson Boulevard. You know that the product will find its way to 5409 Tenth Street because all your mail is forwarded. But suppose that the mail-order company uses Federal Express? Then the package goes to the actual physical address of 5400 Wilson Boulevard, and you'll never see it.

One Answer: A Virtual DMA Controller

For most TSRs that do DMA operations, sending data to an address whose logical value is different from its physical value isn't a problem. That's because EMM386.EXE includes a virtual DMA controller: a software traffic cop that constantly monitors the system for DMA operations. Any time a program tries to communicate with the DMA controller to initiate a DMA transfer, the virtual DMA controller senses the attempt and looks over the shoulder of the operation. If the DMA operation is intended to go into low memory—where logical and physical addresses are equal—the virtual DMA controller does not interfere. But if a DMA operation requests a DMA to an address whose logical value is different from its physical value, the virtual DMA controller steps in and invisibly alters the target address of the

DMA operation to its actual physical value, rather than the logical value that SMARTDrive (or any other TSR that does DMA) mistakenly requested.

Bus Master Boards Don't Work with the Virtual DMA Controller

Most DMA operations are protected from being misdirected by EMM386.EXE's virtual DMA controller. But there is a class of high-performance peripherals that communicate with the PC using their own kind of homegrown DMA called *bus mastering*. Bus mastering is a type of DMA designed to offer high-performance data-transfer rates—but it doesn't go through the standard DMA controller. A bus-master board includes its own on-board DMA hardware that the standard DMA controller is totally unaware of.

If the standard DMA controller is unaware of the bus-mastering activities, so too is the virtual DMA controller. Therefore, any TSR that attempts input/output operations with a bus-master device while that TSR is in a UMB will fail.

> *How you solve the problem depends on the particular TSR you're working with. Microsoft wrote SMARTDrive, however, to successfully cache both run-of-the-mill controllers and bus-master controllers. You may have to tell SMARTDrive to double buffer, however—see what follows.*

You can tell SMARTDrive to load a small portion of itself down in conventional memory—where logical address equals physical address—so that SMARTDrive directs all its DMA operations through that area. The rest of SMARTDrive can, then, live up in a UMB without you having to fear data loss. Putting an extra "transshipment point" in conventional memory for SMARTDrive is called *double buffering*. You enable the double buffer for SMARTDrive by putting a SMARTDrive invocation not only in AUTOEXEC.BAT (the place from which SMARTDrive is usually started) but also by adding…

```
DEVICE=C:\DOS\SMARTDRV.EXE /double_buffer
```

…to CONFIG.SYS.

Although this is how to fix a DMA-into-a-UMB problem when you use SMARTDrive, there may not be a way to do it for other device drivers and TSRs. If a new device fails, or starts failing after you set up all the memory-management commands in AUTOEXEC.BAT and CONFIG.SYS, try loading the device driver or TSR into low (conventional) memory. If that solves the problem, call the vendor and get an updated driver. For example, in the case of the Bernoulli Box drivers that wouldn't work when DOS was loaded high, Iomega quickly offered upgraded drivers compatible with DOS 5.

> **AUTHOR'S NOTE**
>
> *Before moving on, let me finish this section with two more things to try if you experience some kind of crash while using EMM386.EXE.*
>
> *First, did you map all your UMA? I may sound like a broken record here, but let me tell you a story to back up how important this is.*
>
> *A large company (a very large company) bought a bunch of big-name software and hardware: IBM PS/2s, IBM Token-Ring boards, Novell NetWare, Microsoft Windows, MS-DOS, and Lotus Ami Pro. They gave it to thousands of users after doing some testing.*
>
> *All went well for a while, but soon complaints started coming in. It seemed that if you performed a specific sequence of events—turn the PC on, log on to the Novell server, start Windows, and double-click on the Ami Pro icon—Windows crashed. Add any intermediate steps to the process and the crash usually didn't occur, which is why the support folks hadn't noticed the problem.*
>
> *Anyway, the company brought Microsoft in and paid them a ton of money (I'm being vague here because they're clients of mine, they're generally very smart people, and they're my friends) to look things over. Microsoft agreed that there was definitely a problem. "It's not our software that's at fault, however," they decided, and left.*
>
> *Then the company brought in IBM to look at the IBM stuff. The IBM folks looked over the setup and agreed that there was definitely a problem. "It's not our hardware that's at fault, however," they decided, and left.*

Next was Novell. Novell charged its usual enormous per-second-elapsed fee to look over the network, attached sniffers and protocol analyzers, and agreed that there was definitely a problem. "It's not our network software that's at fault, however," they decided, and left.

The firm went so far as to call in Lotus, who looked over Ami Pro, and...well, you know what they said. The support people at this large company were desperate. That's when they called me.

I flew out to see them and heard the saga of the "Mysterious Windows Crash." I looked things over a bit and asked for the documentation on the boards installed in the PCs. Then I constructed a map of the UMA, put it on EMM386.EXE, rebooted the system, logged on to the server, fired up Windows, and double-clicked on Ami Pro's icon. Need I tell you the result?

All that was left to do was for me to adjust my hat, get back on old Paint, proclaim, "Well, I guess my work here is done," and ride off into the sunset. Since then, I've solved dozens of memory-management problems merely by mapping memory stem to stern—including or excluding the addresses from A0000 through FFFFF.

The second (and last) thing to try if your system crashes when you load EMM386.EXE is to use the NoHiScan parameter on the EMM386.EXE invocation. For instance, instead of...

```
DEVICE=C:\DOS\EMM386.EXE NOEMS X=A000-CFFF I=D000-EFFF
X=F000-FEFF
```

...use this...

```
DEVICE=C:\DOS\EMM386.EXE NOEMS X=A000-CFFF I=D000-EFFF
X=F000-FEFF NoHiScan
```

The idea behind NoHiScan (you can capitalize it any way you like, by the way) is that EMM386.EXE searches through memory looking for places where it's safe to place UMBs and places where it's unsafe to place UMBs. That process is irrelevant if you've mapped memory completely between 640K and 1024K, but the process of scanning can sometimes cause a board with a RAM buffer in the UMA to malfunction, locking up the system. NoHiScan just

continues

> says, "don't go poking around memory looking for available locations." EMM386.EXE isn't very bright about finding available memory locations anyway; that's why you're mapping memory in the first place.

Using More Tricks To Get More Memory

If you're still reading after a hundred-odd pages of memory-management information, you've probably explored every nook and cranny of your PC between the addresses of 704K and 960K. There is, of course, no point looking for potential UMB space between 640K and 704K; that space is used by the video board. Similarly, 960K through 1024K is always taken up with the system's BIOS ROM, so those addresses are unavailable.

Or are they? In the following sections, we look at when, where, and how to recapture upper memory and conventional memory space from places you ordinarily wouldn't look.

Stealing Back that ROM

Wouldn't it be nice if you could stuff programs into the whole area from 768K through 1024K, rather than having to yield the space to ROM? Although that's not totally feasible, it's not impossible to reclaim *some* ROM space.

Remember what we've said about ROMs so far: they contain important programs that communicate with your computer's hardware to both start up the hardware and to use it on an ongoing basis during the day.

Take a look at that previous sentence: "...to start up the hardware..." refers to the fact that the BIOS contains PC startup programs used when the computer is first powered up—and never again during the day. A typical PC's BIOS takes up 64K from F0000 through FFFFF (960K to 1024K). Suppose that the first 32K of that 64K were startup programs; you could tell the memory manager to fill in the first 32K of ROM space with UMBs and claim another 32K of space for UMBs.

That's not a fanciful statement. For example, one of the computers I use has an EMM386.EXE statement that looks like this:

```
DEVICE=C:\WINDOWS\EMM386.EXE NOEMS X=A000-C7FF I=C800-F7FF
```

What this statement says is that the first 32K of my BIOS ROM is essentially erasable. (Look back to the hex cheat sheet in Chapter 10 if that's not clear.) It also means that I've got one big UMB from addresses C7FFF (800K) through F7FF (992K)—192K! You can stuff a lot of TSRs in there!

The logical question is, "How did you know how far you could venture into your ROM space?" The answer is: I didn't know. I do know, however, that ROM designers tend to put the discardable stuff—the startup stuff—in the beginning of the ROM, so I always start including from the bottom. I also know that memory managers cannot work with increments of memory smaller than 4K. So I search from bottom to top. Here's how:

> *Make sure that you've got a bootable floppy disk before you go any further. Although the F5 alternative will probably work, it never hurts to be sure.*

1. Install a UMB over the first 4K of your BIOS ROM by adding the parameter I=F000-F0FF to your EMM386.EXE invocation. Be sure that you don't also have a parameter that says X=F000-FEFF; then you'd have both an include and an exclude statement that referred to the same location. When EMM386.EXE sees both an include and an exclude statement that refer to the same location, the exclude takes precedence. In this case, it means you won't get your UMB.

2. Reboot and then test to be sure that you haven't overwritten any essential part of the system's ROM. Do that by reading and writing data on the floppy and hard disks. If the system

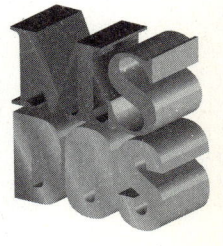

booted without hanging, the video and hard-disk read operations work. To test other areas, put a floppy disk into a floppy drive and copy a file from the hard disk to the floppy, and from the floppy back to the hard disk. Do a printscreen as well. If the system doesn't lock up while doing that, it's probably all right to go on the next step.

3. Include the next 4K of your BIOS ROM by adding an include statement like I=F100-F1FF to your EMM386.EXE statement. Repeat step 2.

4. Do the same thing for the ranges F200-F2FF, F300-F3FF, F400-F4FF, F500-F5FF, F600-F6FF, F700-F7FF, F800-F8FF, F900-F9FF, FA00-FAFF, FB00-FBFF, FC00-FCFF, FD00-FDFF, and FE00-FEFF. Don't bother trying FF00-FFFF: that's *always* controlled by the memory manager.

You can do all this in 15 reboots. The process doesn't take very long, and it's worth spending some time to look for those "upper memory nuggets"—they're pure gold. Don't be surprised if you find that the free areas are scattered, rather than all in one place. After you have this information, write it down so that you'll be able to use it for any other computers that have the same system BIOS.

Restricting Video To Gain 96K

The first area above 640K is a large area used by the video board. As you learned in Chapter 9, PC video boards all use a set of memory addresses from 640K through 768K to place memory that holds the current video image. That 128K of addresses is not always fully used, but because it's still allocated, normal DOS programs are shut out of the entire area. A closer look at the 128K shows how you can grab 96K more RAM for DOS programs. Figure 12.30 shows how that memory area is used by the most popular video boards. (*You saw this diagram in Chapter 9; it's repeated here for convenience.*)

The bottom 64K of the area (addresses 640K through 704K) is used only by DOS when displaying graphics on a video board of type EGA or more advanced (called *EGA+* for this discussion). When an EGA+

board operates in text mode, it doesn't touch that area; it works only in the range 736K through 768K. (An EGA+ board never uses the range from 704K through 736K, by the way.) That means that if you know you're not going to use the graphics mode with some program, you can safely move the top of DOS's conventional memory from 640K to 736K, resulting in a memory map like the one in figure 12.31.

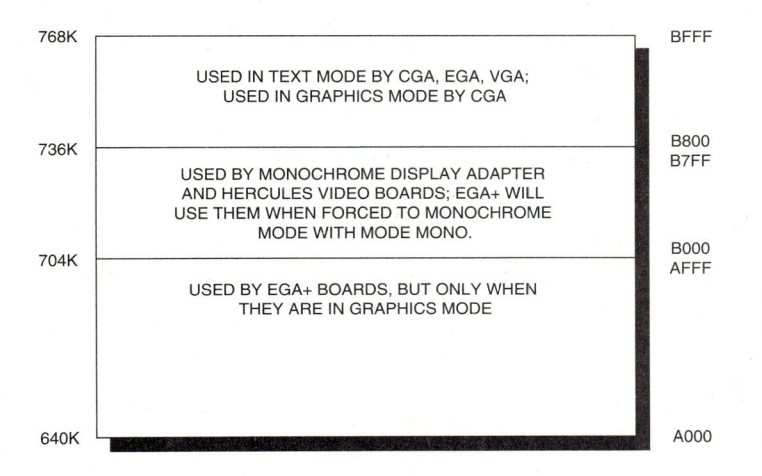

```
768K ┌─────────────────────────────────────────┐ BFFF
     │   USED IN TEXT MODE BY CGA, EGA, VGA;   │
     │      USED IN GRAPHICS MODE BY CGA       │
736K ├─────────────────────────────────────────┤ B800
     │                                         │ B7FF
     │   USED BY MONOCHROME DISPLAY ADAPTER    │
     │   AND HERCULES VIDEO BOARDS; EGA+ WILL  │
     │  USE THEM WHEN FORCED TO MONOCHROME     │
     │         MODE WITH MODE MONO.            │
704K ├─────────────────────────────────────────┤ B000
     │                                         │ AFFF
     │   USED BY EGA+ BOARDS, BUT ONLY WHEN    │
     │         THEY ARE IN GRAPHICS MODE       │
     │                                         │
640K └─────────────────────────────────────────┘ A000
```

Figure 12.30

PC video-memory regions.

To do this small feat of magic, just add I=A000-B7FF to your EMM386.EXE invocation, and you'll see a MEM output like the one in figure 12.32.

Of course, there is a catch. Because this trick treads all over the VGA graphics area, you cannot run any programs that use VGA graphics—no print previews, no Windows, and so on. But, before you rule out this trick as infeasible, consider: you can still use CGA graphics. You can always run Windows in CGA mode (well, okay, only in extremis). Similarly, the WordPerfect Print Preview feature doesn't look completely terrible in CGA mode. I submit to you that it's a hard choice if you have one of those stodgy old programs that won't use either XMS or EMS memory and insists on tons of conventional memory. This little trick may save the day for you sometime.

Chapter 12: *Memory-Management Tips, Tricks, and Troubleshooting*

Figure 12.31

A memory map after including video regions and loading DOS high.

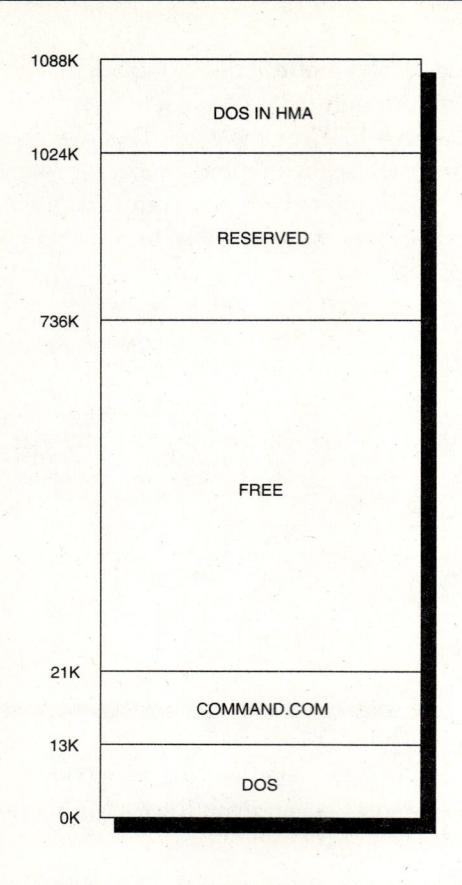

```
1088K ┌─────────────────┐
      │  DOS IN HMA     │
1024K ├─────────────────┤
      │                 │
      │  RESERVED       │
      │                 │
 736K ├─────────────────┤
      │                 │
      │                 │
      │                 │
      │  FREE           │
      │                 │
      │                 │
      │                 │
  21K ├─────────────────┤
      │  COMMAND.COM    │
  13K ├─────────────────┤
      │  DOS            │
   0K └─────────────────┘
```

Figure 12.32

The output from MEM after including video regions and loading DOS high.

```
C:\>MEM

Memory Type          Total  =   Used  +   Free
-----------------   ------    ------    ------
Conventional          736K       21K      715K
Upper                 155K        0K      155K
Adapter RAM/ROM       133K      133K        0K
Extended (XMS)      15360K      612K    14748K
-----------------   ------    ------    ------
Total memory        16384K      765K    15619K

Total under 1 MB      891K       21K      871K

Largest executable program size       715K  (732560 bytes)
Largest free upper memory block       155K  (158816 bytes)
MS-DOS is resident in the high memory area.

C:\>
```

Making Windows Work with Your Memory Manager

Despite the fact that the box claims it is an operating system, Windows requires DOS to run. DOS is the foundation on which the house of Windows is built; as you know, the best house in the world won't last long if built on a shaky foundation. That's why DOS memory management is essential for the stability of Windows. In my experience, at least 70 percent of the "mysterious" Windows problems I've seen have been caused by a memory manager that was incorrectly set up.

You have read about a few aspects of Windows memory management in this and other chapters, so I can cover the effects of memory managers on Windows fairly briefly. The four things you should know about Windows and memory managers are these:

- ✔ You may not be able to include the monochrome region as a UMB if you use a super-VGA driver with Windows.

- ✔ Windows 3 required you to echo every include and exclude statement with an EMMINCLUDE and EMMEXCLUDE statement; that's not necessary under 3.1, but it's another reason to be sure to completely map your memory.

- ✔ Windows cannot provide expanded memory to your DOS applications unless your DOS memory manager provides limulation.

- ✔ Windows requires between 8K and 24K of memory for Application Program Interface Translation Buffers (APITBs). The memory either comes from unused UMA space or conventional memory.

Understanding Why Some Video Drivers Need the Monochrome Region

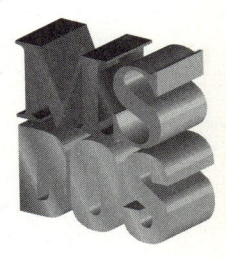

The 32K monochrome region between B0000 and B7FFF can be a useful place to stash a few programs if you tell your memory manager to include it as a UMB. As you read earlier in this chapter, however, Windows doesn't always let you use that region because some super-VGA drivers require that area.

To find out whether your super-VGA driver requires the area, just include B000-B7FF in your memory manager, reboot, and try to run Windows. If you see the following error message, the video driver requires the monochrome area:

```
Windows cannot set up an upper memory block at segment B000.
Exclude this address space by using the syntax of your memory
manager.
For more information see the README.WRI file. Type WIN/S to start
Windows in standard mode and choose the Read Me icon.
```

If you see this message, don't give up yet. You can get from Microsoft two Windows drivers that may enable you to use the monochrome region. The drivers are files named MONOUMB.386 and MONOUMB2.386. You use MONOUMB.386 with EMM386.EXE; use MONOUMB2.386 with Quarterdeck's QEMM or Qualitas's 386Max. Copy whichever file you use to your Windows directory and then edit a file in the Windows directory called SYSTEM.INI (you can use the DOS 6.2 EDIT program to edit SYSTEM.INI). Look in SYSTEM.INI for [386enh] on a line by itself. Add a line below the [386enh] line that says this if you're using MONOUMB.386 with EMM386.EXE:

DEVICE=MONOUMB.386

If you're using MONOUMB2.386 with Quarterdeck's QEMM or Qualitas's 386Max, add a line that says this:

DEVICE=MONOUMB2.386

Save SYSTEM.INI and try running Windows. There's a good chance that Windows will lock up when you try to start it. If that happens, remove the line from SYSTEM.INI and tell your memory manager to exclude B000-B7FF. But if Windows doesn't crash, you can use the monochrome region for a UMB.

Mapping Memory under Windows

Windows must perform memory-management functions both for itself and for DOS sessions that run under it. That means that it's just as essential to map memory for the Windows memory manager as it is to map memory for the DOS memory manager. With Windows 3, you mapped memory with commands in the SYSTEM.INI file by repeating the I= and X= parameters from EMM386.EXE. Each I= statement in EMM386.EXE became an EMMINCLUDE= in SYSTEM.INI; each X= statement in EMM386.EXE became an EMMEXCLUDE= in SYSTEM.INI.

The Windows 3.1 memory manager, however, works more closely with the DOS memory manager. If Windows detects the presence of a DOS memory manager, it follows the lead of the DOS memory manager, keeping it around to perform some functions and replacing it for some others. In any case, the map you give to the DOS memory manager is transferred to the Windows memory manager, so you don't have to worry about EMMINCLUDEs and EMMEXCLUDEs with Windows 3.1. In fact, any EMMEXCLUDEs and EMMINCLUDEs in SYSTEM.INI are overridden by any I= and X= parameters in the EMM386.EXE statement. If you mapped your memory from A0000 through FFFFF, any EMMEXCLUDE or EMMINCLUDE statements are moot.

Realizing That the DOS Memory Manager Must Limulate for Windows To Limulate

If you intend for any DOS programs that run under Windows to have expanded memory available to them, you must first set up your DOS memory manager to provide expanded memory.

With Windows 3, the Windows memory manager could provide expanded memory even if the DOS memory manager did not. But Windows 3.1's closer integration with the DOS memory manager—an improvement over Windows 3 in general—causes this negative side effect.

The amount of expanded memory that the DOS memory manager provides is, however, irrelevant to the amount of expanded memory that Windows can provide. Even if you restrict the amount of memory that EMM386.EXE converts from extended to expanded to 256K, a DOS program running under Windows can be given access to megabytes and megabytes of expanded memory by Windows. It seems that Windows relies on the DOS memory manager for some of the job of managing expanded memory, but not all of it.

Leaving Space for the Application Program Interface Translation Buffers

Earlier in this chapter, you learned that Windows requires up to 24K of memory space somewhere for the Application Program Interface Translation Buffers (APITBs). The APITBs aren't very large, so even if they are in your lower 640K, it's not a terribly big memory hit. The larger concern is that the buffers not overlay ROMs and RAM buffers. Here are the sizes of the APITBs:

- ✔ 4K for file I/O
- ✔ 4K for paging (virtual memory) support in 386 mode
- ✔ 16K for networking

That's 24K in total—8K if you're not attached to a network. I already covered what you need to know about APITBs in the discussion about MemMaker, so let me just review the two major concerns about APITBs:

- ✔ Make sure that you've mapped upper memory so that Windows doesn't mistakenly put an APITB over an existing RAM or ROM in the reserved area. This is the same memory-management defensive tactic I've mentioned before.

- ✔ Avoid making Windows put the APITBs in conventional memory. Windows puts the buffers in conventional memory only if it cannot find 24K of space in the UMA that is either available but not mapped, or in an unused UMB. Recall that you can use the WIN= parameter to set aside space for Windows' APITB use.

Summary

Although memory management is a powerful tool, it can bring new problems to your system—problems you'd rather avoid...but can't. If you want to get the most free conventional space possible for your DOS programs (if you didn't, you probably wouldn't be reading this chapter), there's no substitute for rolling up your sleeves and hand-tweaking your configuration.

You saw in this chapter that there's a peculiar connection between memory management and your keyboard hardware. If you see odd behavior from your keyboard after you start using a memory manager, you now have the tools you need to attack and eliminate the problem.

You can also get more memory for your DOS programs by including the video area: raising the roof from 640K to 736K. Your system ROMs are a good place to start looking for places to put extra UMBs, and it's worth spending a little time to make sure that your programs are all tucked into upper memory in the most efficient arrangement possible. If they're not, you can use the /L: parameter to make them use the space better. Master these tricks, and you'll be a memory-management maven. Good luck!

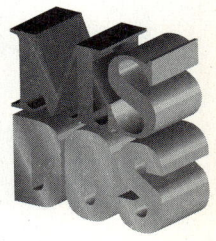

MS
DOS

Chapter 13

Running Third-Party Memory Managers

by Mark Minasi

emory management as a software category was created in 1987 by Qualitas with their 386Max product; Quarterdeck's QEMM product quickly outstripped it in market share. Qualitas and Quarterdeck have been slugging it out for years, with each product coming up with some feature that the other lacks, only to have the other add that feature in its next release—as well as some other feature that the first one doesn't have, which starts the whole process all over again.

This is a terrific thing for those of us who use memory managers: this never-ending horse race means more and better features. In other software markets like word processing and spreadsheets, it seems that the major vendors are content to add marginal features and that they have no real pressure to improve performance. But memory managers were a niche market; a lot of people didn't use a memory manager because they were hard to set up right. (They *still* are, in fact, as you've seen in the last few chapters.) In addition to QEMM and 386Max, there were a half-dozen other memory managers of varying quality. They all had audiences, even the bad ones, mainly because there wasn't much general awareness in the PC business about memory managers.

The appearance of DOS 5 in 1991 changed the picture in that DOS 5 included EMM386.EXE, a memory manager that—if you were to grade it—would probably receive a B+ at best. But the fact that DOS came with a memory manager raised the ante; no third-party memory manager that simply matched EMM386.EXE's capabilities found any takers in the user community. Although it's not widely remembered these days, DOS 5 EMM386.EXE was the first DOS memory manager that fit cozily with Windows at a time when running a DOS memory manager with Windows was to invite data loss.

The basic memory-management capabilities of EMM386.EXE, as well as its smooth fit to Windows, created a new "floor" in memory-management features. Some memory managers couldn't seem to get out of the basement, however, and they passed away to the Great Software Graveyard.

The two top third-party memory managers (ironic, isn't it, that Qualitas and Quarterdeck created the memory-manager market, but when Microsoft entered it with a DOS freebie memory manager, the two Qs became *third-party software vendors*?) saw opportunity, however, where others saw imminent ruin. They went back to the drawing board and returned with a bunch of new features, as well as improvements to programs that attempt to automatically handle the ugly details of setting up a memory manager. Those features, in turn, spurred Microsoft to improve the DOS memory manager further by adding shadow RAM, the capability to place particular programs into particular UMBs, and the MemMaker program.

Of course, the story isn't over yet. If you think Terry Myers at Quarterdeck or Bob Smith at Qualitas is going to roll over and yield the memory-management field to Microsoft, you're sorely mistaken.

This chapter looks at QEMM and 386Max, focusing particularly on answering three questions:

✔ How can you use these products to match the memory-management capabilities of EMM386.EXE?

✔ What can these products do that EMM386.EXE cannot? Is it safe to use the extra features?

✔ How do the programs that parallel MemMaker—programs that automatically set up memory arrangements—compare to and exceed MemMaker in power?

Setting Up a Testbed Configuration

Just for comparison purposes, I cooked up an ugly—but not unreasonable—configuration to which I subjected the DOS, Quarterdeck, and Qualitas memory managers. Just in case you want to duplicate these results or want to know how similar or different the test configuration was to a system you own, here are the details on the hardware and the software.

The computer on which the tests were done is a 50Mhz 486DX clone using an Opti chipset, an AMI BIOS dated June 1991, and an H-level keyboard controller. It has a local bus VGA with an S3-based chipset (meaning that we have to exclude the monochrome region so that the Windows drivers work for this video board). The hard disk is a 535M IDE drive with no hardware cache on the controller. It has one serial port and one parallel port, with a Logitech Microsoft-compatible mouse attached to the serial port.

The workstation is connected to an Ethernet network with a 3Com 3C503 16-bit board that supports a thin Ethernet connection. Shared memory is disabled on this card. An NEC CDR83 internal CD-ROM is attached to the system through an Adaptec 1542B SCSI controller. Because no hard disks are attached to this SCSI controller, its BIOS has been disabled. The PC also contains a Sound Blaster Pro FM/MIDI sound card.

Chapter 13: *Running Third-Party Memory Managers*

The initial CONFIG.SYS file for this computer looks like the following:

```
DEVICE=C:\DOS\HIMEM.SYS
DEVICE=C:\DOS\EMM386.EXE X=A000-C7FF I=C800-EFFF
BUFFERS=10,0
FILES=60
DOS=UMB
LASTDRIVE=N
FCBS=4,0
DOS=HIGH
DEVICE=C:\UTILS\SCSI\ASPI4DOS.SYS /P330
DEVICE=C:\UTILS\CORELDRW\CUNI_ASP.SYS /ID:6 /N:1 /D:MSCD001
DEVICE=C:\DOS\ANSI.SYS
DEVICE=C:\WWG\PROTMAN.DOS /I:C:\WWG
DEVICE=C:\WWG\WORKGRP.SYS
DEVICE=C:\WWG\ELNKII.DOS
DEVICE=C:\DOS\SETVER.EXE
STACKS=9,256
SHELL=C:\DOS\COMMAND.COM C:\DOS\ /E:2048 /P
DEVICE=C:\DOS\DBLSPACE.SYS /MOVE
```

Notice that EMM386.EXE does not provide UMBs initially: neither the RAM nor NOEMS parameters are on the invocation. Notice that the upper memory map is pretty simple: one big exclude and one big (160K) include.

Moving down to the device drivers, the ASPI4DOS.SYS driver supports the Adaptec SCSI adapter. The CUNI_ASP.SYS is a SCSI driver for the CD-ROM. PROTMAN.DOC, WORKGRP.SYS, and ELNKII.DOS are device drivers for the Workgroup Connection. Finally, the DBLSPACE.SYS device driver moves DBLSPACE.BIN, the driver that allows DOS to do on-the-fly disk compression, from the top of conventional memory to a UMB.

The AUTOEXEC.BAT file on the PC looks like the following:

```
SET BLASTER=A220 I10 D3 T4
@ECHO OFF
PROMPT $p$g
PATH C:\DOS;C:\QEMM;C:\UTILS\CORELDRW;C:\WWG;C:\WGS;C:\WINDOWS;C:\UTILS
SET TEMP=C:\TEMP
```

```
DOSKEY
C:\MOUSE\MOUSE
C:\DOS\MSCDEX.EXE /S /V /M:10 /D:MSCD001
C:\DOS\SMARTDRV.EXE /Q
C:\WWG\NET START
SET SOUND=C:\SBPRO
C:\SBPRO\SBP-SET /M:12 /VOC:12 /CD:12 /FM:12
NET USE * \\ACMA\F /YES
SNAP F:\SCREENS
```

In AUTOEXEC.BAT, you see the usual stuff: DOSKEY and MOUSE you've met before. SET BLASTER, SET SOUND, and SBP-SET are statements that initialize Sound Blaster Pro; none are memory resident. NET START and NET USE set up the Workgroup Connection, and SNAP is the screen-capture program I'm using to write this book. When you boot the PC with these AUTOEXEC.BAT and CONFIG.SYS files, you get MEM/C output like figures 13.1 and 13.2.

```
Modules using memory below 1 MB:

Name         Total        =   Conventional   +   Upper Memory
--------     ---------        ------------       ------------
MSDOS        18333  (18K)     18333  (18K)       0      (0K)
HIMEM         1152   (1K)      1152   (1K)       0      (0K)
EMM386        8112   (8K)      8112   (8K)       0      (0K)
ASPI4DOS      5184   (5K)      5184   (5K)       0      (0K)
CUNI_ASP     18768  (18K)     18768  (18K)       0      (0K)
ANSI          4208   (4K)      4208   (4K)       0      (0K)
PROTMAN        128   (0K)       128   (0K)       0      (0K)
WORKGRP       4368   (4K)      4368   (4K)       0      (0K)
ELNKII       10400  (10K)     10400  (10K)       0      (0K)
SETVER         736   (1K)       736   (1K)       0      (0K)
DBLSPACE     44112  (43K)     44112  (43K)       0      (0K)
COMMAND       4704   (5K)      4704   (5K)       0      (0K)
MOUSE        15840  (15K)     15840  (15K)       0      (0K)
DOSKEY        4144   (4K)      4144   (4K)       0      (0K)
MSCDEX       36576  (36K)     36576  (36K)       0      (0K)
SMARTDRV     28800  (28K)     28800  (28K)       0      (0K)
SNAP        105952 (103K)    105952 (103K)       0      (0K)
NETBEUI      36208  (35K)     36208  (35K)       0      (0K)
REDIR        86064  (84K)     86064  (84K)       0      (0K)
Press any key to continue . . .
```

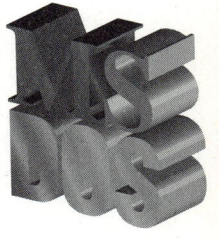

Figure 13.1
MEM/C output for the basic configuration (part 1).

NOTE *The NET commands used in this chapter are available from Microsoft as a separate utility that is not packaged with MS-DOS 6.2.*

Chapter 13: *Running Third-Party Memory Managers*

Figure 13.2
MEM/C output for the basic configuration (part 2).

```
Free          221520   (216K)      221520   (216K)           0     (0K)
Memory Summary:

Type of Memory          Total       =        Used       +        Free
----------------    ----------------    ----------------    ----------------
Conventional            655360   (640K)      433840   (424K)      221520   (216K)
Upper                        0     (0K)           0     (0K)           0     (0K)
Adapter RAM/ROM         393216   (384K)      393216   (384K)           0     (0K)
Extended (XMS)*       15728640 (15360K)     2605056  (2544K)    13123584 (12816K)
----------------    ----------------    ----------------    ----------------
Total memory          16777216 (16384K)     3432112  (3352K)    13345104 (13032K)

Total under 1 MB        655360   (640K)      433840   (424K)      221520   (216K)

*  15296K of XMS memory is configured for XMS/EMS sharing.
    2624K of this amount is in use as EMS.
   12672K is available for either XMS or EMS.

Total Expanded (EMS)                        16056320 (15680K)
Free Expanded (EMS)                         13369344 (13056K)
Largest executable program size               221232   (216K)
Largest free upper memory block                    0     (0K)
MS-DOS is resident in the high memory area.
Press any key to continue . . .
```

After everything has been loaded, this PC has a mere 216K of RAM available. I'd say this is a believable configuration (except for the screen-capture program). Notice how much space is taken up by the Workgroup Connection programs: PROTMAN, WORKGRP, ELNKII, NETBEUI, and REDIR add up to 137,168 (137K)!

NOTE

The truth is that this configuration crashed all three of the programs that are supposed to automatically arrange programs into upper memory and free conventional memory. MemMaker (the DOS program), Optimize (the Quarterdeck program), and Maximize (the Qualitas program) all either refused to load because of insufficient memory or crashed on general principles and could not recover.

Each of the three programs had to be nursed through any kind of optimization procedure. *I made that sentence bold because I want to stress that when it comes to memory management, for stability and functionality there's no substitute for hand-arranging memory. (Now that I've gotten that old soapbox out, let me move along....)*

Setting Up a Testbed Configuration

Something interesting happens when you change the CONFIG.SYS line `DOS=HIGH` to `DOS=HIGH,UMB`: three DOS 6.2 programs—SMARTDRV, NET, and REDIR—automatically load themselves into UMBs! After making the single change, `DOS=HIGH` to `DOS=HIGH,UMB`, you can see the resulting MEM/C output in figures 13.3 and 13.4.

```
Modules using memory below 1 MB:

  Name           Total        =    Conventional   +   Upper Memory
  --------    ---------------      ----------------    ----------------
  MSDOS         18333   (18K)        18333   (18K)         0    (0K)
  HIMEM          1152    (1K)         1152    (1K)         0    (0K)
  EMM386         3120    (3K)         3120    (3K)         0    (0K)
  ASPI4DOS       5184    (5K)         5184    (5K)         0    (0K)
  CUNI_ASP      18768   (18K)        18768   (18K)         0    (0K)
  ANSI           4208    (4K)         4208    (4K)         0    (0K)
  PROTMAN         128    (0K)          128    (0K)         0    (0K)
  WORKGRP        4368    (4K)         4368    (4K)         0    (0K)
  ELNKII        10400   (10K)        10400   (10K)         0    (0K)
  SETVER          736    (1K)          736    (1K)         0    (0K)
  DBLSPACE      44112   (43K)        44112   (43K)         0    (0K)
  COMMAND        4704    (5K)         4704    (5K)         0    (0K)
  MOUSE         15840   (15K)        15840   (15K)         0    (0K)
  DOSKEY         4144    (4K)         4144    (4K)         0    (0K)
  MSCDEX        36576   (36K)        36576   (36K)         0    (0K)
  SNAP         105952  (103K)       105952  (103K)         0    (0K)
  NETBEUI       36208   (35K)            0    (0K)     36208   (35K)
  REDIR         86064   (84K)            0    (0K)     86064   (84K)
  SMARTDRV      28800   (28K)            0    (0K)     28800   (28K)
Press any key to continue . . .
```

Figure 13.3

MEM/C output for the basic configuration with UMBs (part 1).

```
  SNAP         105952  (103K)       105952  (103K)         0    (0K)
  NETBEUI       36208   (35K)            0    (0K)     36208   (35K)
  REDIR         86064   (84K)            0    (0K)     86064   (84K)
  SMARTDRV      28800   (28K)            0    (0K)     28800   (28K)
Press any key to continue . . .
  Free         409696  (400K)       377568  (369K)     32128   (31K)

Memory Summary:

  Type of Memory          Total      =        Used         +        Free
  ------------------   -----------------    -----------------    -----------------
  Conventional           655360   (640K)      277792  (271K)      377568  (369K)
  Upper                  183200   (179K)      151072  (148K)       32128   (31K)
  Adapter RAM/ROM        210016   (205K)      210016  (205K)           0    (0K)
  Extended (XMS)       15728640 (15360K)     2519040 (2460K)    13209600 (12900K)
  ------------------   -----------------    -----------------    -----------------
  Total memory         16777216 (16384K)     3157920 (3084K)    13619296 (13300K)

  Total under 1 MB       838560   (819K)      428864  (419K)      409696  (400K)

  Largest executable program size            377280  (368K)
  Largest free upper memory block             12240   (12K)
  MS-DOS is resident in the high memory area.

C:\>
```

Figure 13.4

MEM/C output for the basic configuration with UMBs (part 2).

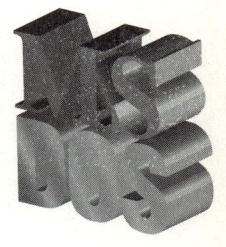

Free memory now soars to 369K. Ironically, that is about the best free-memory value you see in this chapter. The fact that some DOS programs load themselves high confuses at least one memory-optimizer program, which is part of the trouble.

Looking at MemMaker's Solution to the Test Configuration

Before jumping into discussions of the third-party memory managers, let's give MemMaker a chance to rearrange things.

MemMaker first booted the system with the intention of determining the sizes of all the programs, so MemMaker could get the data it needed to find the best arrangement of programs in upper memory. That attempt failed, however, because some line in CONFIG.SYS caused EMM386 to emit an `unsupported DMA mode` message, forcing a crash and reboot.

MemMaker offered to analyze memory again with more conservative settings, but I wanted to find out what it had choked on. I restored CONFIG.SYS and AUTOEXEC.BAT to their pre-MemMaker settings and ran MemMaker again. But this time, I pressed F8 as the `Starting MS-DOS...` message appeared to make DOS pause at each line of CONFIG.SYS. In this way, I saw that the analysis boot crashed at the CUNI_ASP.SYS driver, one of the programs that supports the CD-ROM. I decided to place the SCSI driver (ASPI4DOS.SYS) and the CD-ROM driver before HIMEM.SYS and EMM386.EXE. Additionally, I put them on the "don't touch these drivers" list that MemMaker keeps in the file MEMMAKER.INF (it's in the C:\DOS directory, in case you ever want to add something to it). When I reran MemMaker, I got another crash.

> **NOTE** *Even after shuffling drivers, the system crashed, partially because MemMaker insists on loading HIMEM and EMM386 first—it even rearranges all the device drivers to make sure of it.*

Looking at MemMaker's Solution to the Test Configuration

Then I tried removing the ASPI4DOS.SYS and CUNI_ASP.SYS drivers altogether before running MemMaker (that's another option for files you put in MEMMAKER.INF, by the way) to no avail. The device driver that MemMaker choked on after I removed the CD-ROM stuff was ANSI.SYS, certainly a driver above reproach. That meant that what was crashing MemMaker was the way it scans high memory looking for open spaces.

Once I'd exonerated the CD-ROM drivers, I gave MemMaker the chance to try loading programs high again, but, in its words, "with conservative settings." No crash this time. The resulting CONFIG.SYS file looked like this:

```
CONFIG.SYS:
DEVICE=C:\DOS\HIMEM.SYS
DEVICE=C:\DOS\EMM386.EXE NOEMS X=A000-C7FF I=C800-EFFF
BUFFERS=10,0
FILES=60
DOS=UMB
LASTDRIVE=N
FCBS=4,0
DOS=HIGH
DEVICE=C:\UTILS\SCSI\ASPI4DOS.SYS /P330
DEVICEHIGH /L:1,22688 =C:\UTILS\CORELDRW\CUNI_ASP.SYS /ID:6 /N:1 /
D:MSCD001
DEVICEHIGH /L:1,9072 =C:\DOS\ANSI.SYS
DEVICE=C:\WWG\PROTMAN.DOS /I:C:\WWG
DEVICEHIGH /L:1,7280 =C:\WWG\WORKGRP.SYS
DEVICEHIGH /L:1,11328 =C:\WWG\ELNKII.DOS
DEVICE=C:\DOS\SETVER.EXE
STACKS=9,256
SHELL=C:\DOS\COMMAND.COM C:\DOS\ /E:2048 /P
DEVICE=C:\DOS\DBLSPACE.SYS /MOVE
```

The resulting AUTOEXEC.BAT file looked like this:

```
SET BLASTER=A220 I10 D3 T4
@ECHO OFF
PROMPT $p$g
PATH C:\DOS;C:\QEMM;C:\UTILS\CORELDRW;C:\WWG;C:\WGS;C:\WINDOWS;C:\UTILS
SET TEMP=C:\TEMP
```

```
LH  /L:1,6400 DOSKEY
LH  /L:1,34816 C:\MOUSE\MOUSE
LH  /L:1,36576 C:\DOS\MSCDEX.EXE /S /V /M:10 /D:MSCD001
LH  /L:0;1,42496 /S C:\DOS\SMARTDRV.EXE /Q
C:\WWG\NET START
SET SOUND=C:\SBPRO
C:\SBPRO\SBP-SET /M:12 /VOC:12 /CD:12 /FM:12
LH  /L:0;1,35488 /S NET USE * \\ACMA\F /YES
SNAP F:\SCREENS
```

I'll spare you the entire output from MEM/C, but the simple MEM output is in figure 13.5.

Figure 13.5
MEM output after MemMaker optimization.

```
C:\>mem

Memory Type         Total  =    Used  +    Free
----------------    -----       -----      -----
Conventional         640K        299K       341K
Upper                155K        120K        35K
Adapter RAM/ROM      229K        229K         0K
Extended (XMS)     15360K       2436K     12924K
----------------    -----       -----      -----
Total memory       16384K       3084K     13300K

Total under 1 MB     795K        419K       376K

Largest executable program size         341K  (349424 bytes)
Largest free upper memory block          35K   (35408 bytes)
MS-DOS is resident in the high memory area.

C:\>
```

MemMaker ends up with 376K of free space—not much more memory for a lot of effort. Now let's see what the competition can do.

Looking at Quarterdeck's Solution to the Test Configuration

After DOS itself, the best-selling memory-management product is QEMM-386 from Quarterdeck Office Systems. It does everything that DOS's EMM386.EXE does—and more. The fact that QEMM does things that EMM386.EXE doesn't do isn't necessarily a reason to buy

Looking at Quarterdeck's Solution to the Test Configuration   671

QEMM, because you may not need QEMM's extra features or you may not be able to use those extra features.

QEMM does all these things that DOS 6.2 does:

- ✔ It provides an HMA, so if you include the DOS=HIGH statement in CONFIG.SYS, most of DOS loads high.

- ✔ It creates and exploits UMBs with its LOADHI.COM TSR and LOADHI.SYS device driver.

- ✔ It converts extended memory to expanded memory.

- ✔ It enables you to choose a UMB to move a program into when loading programs high.

- ✔ It shadows RAM.

- ✔ It does not force you to preassign some memory to be expanded or extended; QEMM maintains a pool of memory that can be either extended or expanded as needed.

- ✔ It comes with a memory-analysis program that does a pretty good job of figuring out what ROMs can be overwritten, how to best load your TSRs and device drivers high, and the like. For many machines, the Optimize utility eliminates much of the grunt work you heard about in preceding chapters. The utility is also better than most programs at detecting RAMs, ROMs, and the like in the UMA—but it's not going to solve all memory-management problems.

- ✔ It supports the VCPI (Virtual Control Program Interface) standard, and so functions properly with AutoCAD, Paradox 3.5, 1-2-3 release 3.1, and any other VCPI-compliant program. Like EMM386.EXE, QEMM does not support DPMI. In general, if you plan to run a VCPI-compliant program, you should be sure that QEMM (or any other memory manager) provides expanded memory. In the case of QEMM, you do that by not using the NOEMS parameter—see the later section on setting up QEMM.

- ✔ Quarterdeck's not exactly wild about broadcasting this information, but QEMM creates upper memory blocks completely compatible with the upper memory blocks EMM386.EXE uses. That means that you can use the built-in DOS 6.2 LOADHIGH and DEVICEHIGH statements with the QEMM386.SYS device driver.

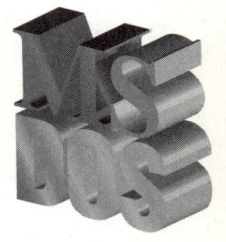

Additionally, QEMM does some extra things: some old and obsolete, some logical and useful, and some a bit daring and not recommended. In the "old and obsolete" category, QEMM can...

- ✔ Backfill conventional memory (not very useful unless you've got a very old 386-type system). *Backfilling memory is discussed in Chapter 10.*

- ✔ Sort memory by speed (again, not of relevance in today's world). You want to avoid this feature for two reasons: first, it's largely irrelevant to today's computers. It's not unusual to see a PC with a single bank of four 4M SIMMs—a total of 16M in just one bank. Remember that you cannot have varying memory speed in a single bank. Second, just about any product built on a DOS extender, such as Windows, fails if you sort memory while running it. So avoid this feature.

Machines saw varying memory only when they had a large number of banks of memory, each composed of 36 64K-bit DRAM chips (see Chapter 11 if you've forgotten these). In those days, each bank of memory was 256K in size; a 2M system was composed of eight banks (that's eight times 36 chips, or 288 chips!). Each bank could run at different speeds. The idea was that if you had a bunch of fast extended memory but slow conventional memory, the memory manager would put the fast stuff in the 0 to 640K range where it would see a lot of use, and move the slower memory to the extended range, where it presumably would be infrequently used.

In the category of "nifty features," QEMM boasts a number of goodies:

- ✔ First and most useful is a "squeeze" feature that handles yo-yo TSRs by letting you temporarily steal space from a UMB, a ROM, or an EMS page frame while the yo-yo is loading. It gives back the space once the yo-yo has settled down to its final size.

- ✔ As I remind you for the thousandth time to be sure to hand-map your memory, it's worthwhile to mention that much of the

Looking at Quarterdeck's Solution to the Test Configuration **673**

information you need to put together a map of upper memory is in a machine-readable format on Micro Channel-based PCs. Quarterdeck has cleverly designed QEMM to seek out and utilize that information.

✔ Recall that DOS loads the DOS buffers into the HMA, if they all fit. QEMM ships with a program called BUFFERS.COM that enables you to fit almost all your buffers into UMBs, no matter how many you have.

✔ Quarterdeck ships a nifty memory analyzer called Manifest, a system status/information report program that's kind of a combination of MEM and MSD, although it can't do everything that MSD does.

✔ I'm not sure whether to put this in the "nifty" category or the upcoming "impressive-sounding but dangerous" category: QEMM and Manifest can examine your BIOS ROMs to find the parts that can probably be overwritten. It's not 100-percent reliable, but it gives you some ideas when you're looking for a little more upper memory space.

✔ You learned in the last chapter how to set up the DOS memory manager so it would grab 96K of addresses ordinarily assigned to video RAM. The trick was a little cumbersome, however, because it required modifying CONFIG.SYS and rebooting. In contrast, QEMM offers a program called VIDRAM that enables you to steal that 96K of addresses and give them back on-the-fly, so that you needn't modify CONFIG.SYS (or set up a MultiConfig system) and reboot every time you want to steal or give back the video system.

Finally, in the "Buck Rogers Memory Management" category, Quarterdeck has a feature called Stealth that lets QEMM actually put UMBs in the same addresses as active ROMs. I'm not quite sure where to put this next item, but since Version 5 (the current version is 6.2) of QEMM, Quarterdeck has increasingly taken the posture that memory-manager options need not be documented or explained in any detail. Their opinion, as stated in the READ.ME file for Version 6.2, is...

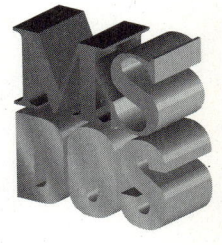

```
Our experience has shown that many people who have
trouble with QEMM386 have added parameters which they do
not fully understand. We recommend that you do NOT add
any other parameters unless the default ones are not
working well.
```

Earlier, the file states...

```
In general, INSTALL and OPTIMIZE will automatically place
the parameters you need and most users will not need any
additional parameters.
```

> **NOTE** *There's something disturbingly self-fulfilling about Quarterdeck's comments. Important options, like the /SQF and /SQT parameters, are not documented except to say that they are "internal Squeeze parameter[s] generated by the Optimize program." Well, heck, the Squeeze function is the coolest thing about QEMM—are we supposed to just trust that Optimize knows what's best for us? Of course, any memory-management expert's going to play around with the parameter to try to figure out what it does, and of course the system's going to end up crashing—what else can be expected when the silly parameter's not documented?*

Let's examine QEMM first as a substitute for DOS 6.2's EMM386.EXE, then as an improvement on it, and finally in combination with Optimize, its automatic memory-arranger program.

Setting Up QEMM Like DOS 6.2.

Before looking at any of QEMM's extra nifty features, the following sections explain how to convert AUTOEXEC.BAT and CONFIG.SYS to QEMM format so that you can use QEMM as a straightforward replacement for DOS 6.2.

Loading the QEMM Device Driver

QEMM uses only one device driver, QEMM386.SYS, that performs the duties previously assigned to HIMEM.SYS and EMM386.EXE. You do not want backfilling, speed sorting, or LIM memory; the testbed PC is pretty memory-crunched, so you can't afford 64K of UMB space for the LIM page frame. You *do* want UMBs. As with DOS 6.2's EMM386.EXE, it's best to map memory explicitly. Assuming that the QEMM files are in a subdirectory called C:\QEMM, the driver invocation looks like this:

```
DEVICE=C:\QEMM\QEMM386.SYS NOEMS RAM X=A000-C7FF I=C800-EFFF
```

The parameters look familiar (I think Microsoft hired some ex-Quarterdeck people when they built their memory manager) but there's one difference. Recall from the discussion of how to set up EMM386.EXE in Chapter 10 that the NOEMS and RAM parameters are mutually exclusive. For EMM386.EXE, RAM means *supply LIM memory and UMBs*. NOEMS, in contrast, means *supply UMBs, but do not supply LIM memory*.

For QEMM386.SYS, however, the parameters refer to separate options. NOEMS means *don't provide LIM memory*. If you don't specify it, you get LIM memory by default. RAM means *provide UMBs*. If you don't specify it, you don't get UMBs. The effects of these two parameters are summarized in table 13.1.

Table 13.1
QEMM Parameters To Control LIM and UMBs

RAM	NOEMS	Result
No	No	LIM memory, no UMBs
No	Yes	Neither; shadow RAM and other features can still exist
Yes	No	Both LIM memory and UMBs lose 64K of UMB to page frame
Yes	Yes	UMBs only, no LIM memory

The Quarterdeck manual recommends changing the
DOS=HIGH,UMB statement to `DOS=HIGH`, but I don't agree. If you
don't specify the UMB, the DOS memory utilities—MEM,
LOADHIGH, and DEVICEHIGH—don't recognize the upper
memory blocks and so cannot report on their status (in the case of
MEM) or use them (in the case of LOADHIGH and DEVICEHIGH).
Furthermore, programs that load themselves high (like SMARTDrive
and Workgroup Connection) cannot see the UMBs and so cannot load
themselves high if you leave the UMB off the DOS= statement.

On the off-chance that QEMM thinks it detects memory of varying
speeds, you should add the NOSORT parameter to the
QEMM386.SYS invocation line. That disables memory-speed sorting.
A NOFILL parameter tells QEMM not to backfill, but it's unlikely that
will be an issue anyway.

QEMM provides XMS services and creates a High Memory Area. Its
support of the HMA is fully XMS-compliant, so DOS 6.2 has no
trouble loading in the HMA if you include the DOS=HIGH statement
in CONFIG.SYS when you use QEMM.

Loading Device Drivers and TSRs High with QEMM

The `DEVICEHIGH=` statements you used with DOS 6.2 are replaced by
QEMM with a device driver called LOADHI.SYS whose job it is to
load a device driver into a UMB or, as Quarterdeck's documentation
calls it, a *region of high RAM*. Its basic syntax looks like this:

```
DEVICE=C:\QEMM\LOADHI.SYS [/R:n] programname
```

In this syntax, *n* is the number of the memory region to put the
program into (just like the /L: parameter on DOS 6.2's `LOADHIGH` and
`DEVICEHIGH` statements) and *programname* is the program (a device
driver, in this case) to load into a UMB. (I'll stick with the DOS terminology in this chapter instead of using Quarterdeck's term *region*.) Just
blindly loading everything high results in a CONFIG.SYS that looks
like the following:

Looking at Quarterdeck's Solution to the Test Configuration

```
DEVICE=C:\QEMM\QEMM386.SYS NOEMS RAM X=A000-C7FF I=C800-EFFF
BUFFERS=10,0
FILES=60
DOS=UMB
LASTDRIVE=N
FCBS=4,0
DOS=HIGH
DEVICE=C:\QEMM\LOADHI.SYS C:\UTILS\SCSI\ASPI4DOS.SYS /P330
DEVICE=C:\QEMM\LOADHI.SYS C:\UTILS\CORELDRW\CUNI_ASP.SYS /ID:6 /N:1 /
D:MSCD001
DEVICE=C:\QEMM\LOADHI.SYS C:\DOS\ANSI.SYS
DEVICE=C:\QEMM\LOADHI.SYS C:\WWG\PROTMAN.DOS /I:C:\WWG
DEVICE=C:\QEMM\LOADHI.SYS C:\WWG\WORKGRP.SYS
DEVICE=C:\QEMM\LOADHI.SYS C:\WWG\ELNKII.DOS
DEVICE=C:\QEMM\LOADHI.SYS C:\DOS\SETVER.EXE
STACKS=9,256
SHELL=C:\DOS\COMMAND.COM C:\DOS\ /e:2048 /p
DEVICE=C:\QEMM\LOADHI.SYS C:\DOS\DBLSPACE.SYS /MOVE
```

The LOADHIGH or LH statements are replaced with a program called LOADHI.COM. Its simplified syntax looks like this:

```
C:\QEMM\LOADHI [/R:n] programname
```

In this syntax, *n* again refers to a UMB's number, and *programname* refers to the program you're trying to load into a UMB. Just loading everything from AUTOEXEC.BAT with LOADHI, you get an AUTOEXEC.BAT file that looks like this:

```
SET BLASTER=A220 I10 D3 T4
@ECHO OFF
PROMPT $p$g
PATH C:\DOS;C:\QEMM;C:\UTILS\CORELDRW;C:\WWG;C:\WGS;C:\WINDOWS;C:\UTILS
REM notice that now that QEMM is on the path, I can just say LOADHI
SET TEMP=C:\TEMP
LOADHI DOSKEY
LOADHI C:\MOUSE\MOUSE
LOADHI C:\DOS\MSCDEX.EXE /S /V /M:10 /D:MSCD001
LOADHI C:\DOS\SMARTDRV.EXE /Q
LOADHI C:\WWG\NET START
SET SOUND=C:\SBPRO
```

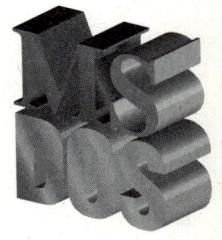

```
C:\SBPRO\SBP-SET /M:12 /VOC:12 /CD:12 /FM:12
LOADHI NET USE * \\ACMA\F /YES
LOADHI SNAP F:\SCREENS
```

When I reboot, I get a lot of error messages announcing that it's not possible to load programs up high because there isn't room. But some things do get up there, and free space goes to 378K—9K better than before, with EMM386 and MemMaker.

Shadowing RAM with QEMM

You don't have to tell QEMM anything to get it to shadow a ROM; if it detects a ROM, it shadows it by default. To get QEMM to not shadow a ROM, either exclude the ROM with the X= parameter or use the NOSHADOWROM or its shortened version, NOSH on the QEMM386.SYS invocation line.

Understanding and Using Quarterdeck's Advanced Features

If what you've seen so far is all that Quarterdeck's good for, there is no point in buying it. But QEMM offers more features, as described in the following sections.

Loading Yo-Yo Programs with QEMM's Squeeze Feature

Despite its many improvements over DOS 5, DOS 6.2 still can't handle TSRs that load large and then become small—so-called *yo-yo TSRs*. Take the Microsoft version of MOUSE.COM, for example. Although it's not present on the testbed computer used in this chapter, I use it on a number of other systems. I tend to load MOUSE early in my AUTOEXEC.BAT files because it's a yo-yo program. It loads at 56K and shrinks down to a 17K resident size. Because all that the DOS memory manager cares about is the load size of a program, not its final size, MOUSE appears to DOS's memory manager to be 56K in size. If I don't load it early in the boot process, DOS 6.2 can't load it high at all.

Looking at Quarterdeck's Solution to the Test Configuration

The problem is that DOS 6.2 just plain doesn't understand yo-yo programs. You can't make DOS 6.2 understand that you need some memory just for an instant so that the mouse driver can load, and that you will give the memory back to DOS 6.2 immediately.

Although DOS can't understand it, QEMM can. As it turns out, LOADHI has two options that do it: /SQF and /SQT. Both options are "squeeze" options that direct QEMM to borrow memory either from the page frame (SQF) or somewhere else in high memory (SQT), load the program, and then give the memory back when finished. For this to work, however, you have to tell LOADHI how large the program will eventually be with the /RES parameter, which communicates the *resident size* that the program eventually takes up.

QEMM ships with a program somewhat like a combination of MSD and MEM called *Manifest*. (You'll read more about Manifest later in this chapter.) A look at Manifest when MOUSE is loaded low shows that the driver ends up to be 16K in size, so I can change the line that loads the mouse driver to look like this:

```
C:\QEMM\LOADHI /RES:16134 /SQT C:\DOS\MOUSE
```

The result of this change is that the mouse driver loads high without having to place the invocation in a particular location in AUTOEXEC.BAT.

NOTE: You cannot use the /SQF parameter in this case because the system is configured without EMS memory and so does not have a page frame. If you limulate on your system, however, you can use either /SQF or /SQT.

Squeeze often needs to know exactly from where to borrow RAM. You can specify a range of RAM to borrow by including a range after the /SQT parameter, like so:

```
C:\QEMM\LOADHI /RES:16134 /SQT=D000-D5FF C:\DOS\MOUSE
```

This works only if the space immediately following the space where the mouse driver loads is D0000-D5FFF, meaning that you pretty much have to specify a region number when squeezing. Let's look at a specific example, like MOUSE, because it's such a convenient yo-yo. You have a copy you can try this out on; it comes with DOS 6.2.

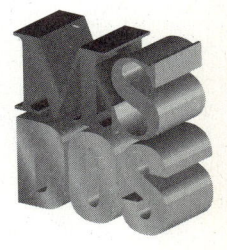

The testbed PC has a UMB from C8000-EFFFF. That's too easy, however: MOUSE fits in there without any work at all, so we'll restrict the mouse driver's space a bit by excluding everything but a 32K space at D0000 and a 32K space at E0000. The QEMM386.SYS invocation then looks like this:

```
DEVICE=C:\QEMM\QEMM386.SYS NOEMS RAM X=A000-CFFF I=D000-
D7FF X=D800-DFFF I=E000-E7FF X=E800-FFFF
```

> **NOTE** *The QEMM386 invocation line wrapped around to a new line because it wouldn't fit on a single printed line, but you shouldn't break the line if you are following along and want to type it into CONFIG.SYS. Type it all on one line.*

Now you have two upper memory regions of 32K each. If you try to load MOUSE into either one, you get the message from LOADHI...

```
not enough room to load MOUSE high
```

MOUSE has a load size of 57,120 bytes. If I want it to load at address D0000, at the start of region 1, I need enough space to load 57,120 bytes starting at D0000. Add 57,120 decimal to D0000 hex (cheat and do it the way I do it, with the Windows calculator) and you find that the entire mouse program can load from D0000 to DDF20.

Now we have to tell Squeeze to temporarily use the range D0000-DDF20 as a UMB. But remember that memory managers only work in blocks of 4K; we have to round the range D0000-DDF20 up to the next 4K, making the desired range D0000-DDFFF. Because D0000-D7FFF is already a legal UMB, we only need to borrow the range from D8000-DDFFF. Do that with this /SQT parameter:

```
LOADHI /R:1 RES=17280 /SQT=D800-DDFF MOUSE
```

The region number is a necessity because /SQT=D800-DDFF is meaningless if LOADHI tries to load the mouse to the E000-EFFF region. The /RES=17280 parameter tells LOADHI how large the program will eventually become.

In review, here are the steps to squeeze a program:

1. **Determine the program's load size and its run size.**
   MemMaker's MEMMAKER.INF gives exact load sizes, but the size of the COM file is a good indication. Add 1K to the COM file's size to get a safe, conservative estimate of the load size of a file. You can get the run size by just loading the program low and then running the MEM/C program. In the MOUSE example, the load size and run size were 57,120 and 17,280 bytes.

   Be aware, however, that some programs load to larger or smaller sizes according to how much free space they perceive or what hardware they sense. For example, I've seen the MOUSE.COM version 8.20 driver load in sizes between 16,100 and 17,400 bytes. It's probably not a bad idea to add 1K to the run size you see in the MEM/C output just to be on the safe side.

2. **Decide on the region you'll load it into.** Make sure, of course, that no other program can use that region. If you're going to do this squeeze stuff, you've got to specify exactly which region *each* program occupies. In the mouse example, you want to put the mouse driver into the UMB starting at D0000; that's region number 1.

3. **Add the starting location of the UMB to the load length of the program.** That tells you the top piece of memory you need to load this program. You want the result in hex. In the mouse example, D0000 (hex) + 57120 (decimal) equals DDF20.

4. **Round the result up to the nearest FFF.** In the mouse example, DDF20 rounds up to DDFFF.

5. **Exactly delineate the range of memory for /SQT to borrow.** The range you're borrowing from starts right after the UMB you're trying to load your program into. In the mouse example, you're trying to put the driver into a UMB that ends at D7FFF; the area that follows it immediately is D8000.

The end of the space to "borrow" with /SQT is the result from step 4. In the mouse example, that means that the borrowed area is the range D8000-DDFFF. Specify that range with your /SQT= parameter. Be sure to lop off the rightmost digit as always with memory-manager parameters.

Whew! If that looks like some work, it is. Most of the time, you can let Optimize—which you will meet soon—do the hard work for you. But sometimes Optimize develops blind spots, and the only fix is to wade in and set up the loading instructions by hand.

Loading BUFFERS, FILES, LASTDRIVE, and FCBs into UMBs

Earlier, you learned that DOS 6.2 can load file buffers or file handles into the HMA, provided that *all* of them fit in the HMA. If all the buffers can fit in the HMA, but not all the file handles can fit in the HMA, then the buffers go high and the file handles go low. FCBs (File Control Blocks) and the drive-letter table, two other types of internal DOS storage areas, load low in any case.

Each of these internal DOS file areas requires some conventional memory. As you learned in Chapter 10, each buffer requires 528 bytes; each file handle requires 112 bytes. Adding a drive letter by incrementing LASTDRIVE costs 80 bytes per drive letter. Each FCB takes 53 bytes of memory.

Quarterdeck ships QEMM with four programs: FILES.COM, BUFFERS.COM, LASTDRIV.COM, and FCBS.COM. The job of each of these programs is to create file handles, file buffers, drive-letter entries, or FCBs in an upper memory block. Assuming that you have unused UMB space, any one of these programs can create extra conventional memory by moving one or more of these internal file areas to a UMB.

These programs do not move the initial BUFFERS, FILES, LASTDRIVE, or FCBS values to UMBs. Instead, they create additional internal DOS file areas. The way you use them is to allocate only the minimum BUFFERS, FILES, LASTDRIVE, and FCBS in CONFIG.SYS and then use the corresponding Quarterdeck programs to create more internal file areas.

Looking at Quarterdeck's Solution to the Test Configuration

> **AUTHOR'S NOTE**
>
> *People often ask, "What determines how many BUFFERS, FILES, LASTDRIVEs, and FCBs I must have?" The answer is that it depends on the programs you run. The documentation for any program on your system should include recommendations for these four DOS parameters if the program requires unusual values for the parameters. Most people boot up with at least FILES=20 and BUFFERS=20, so most programs don't mention how many FILES and BUFFERS they need if they don't need more than 20. Similarly, LASTDRIVE is fairly irrelevant for the vast majority of DOS programs, although a few (Windows SETUP is an example) do not recognize a drive letter above E (the default value for LASTDRIVE) unless there is a LASTDRIVE statement in CONFIG.SYS that specifies the last drive letter it can expect to see. FCBs are fairly irrelevant nowadays, so you'll probably never need to worry about them.*

Suppose that you need a large value for BUFFERS=, say 50, because of a database program you use. You need a few BUFFERS (one or two is sufficient) to get the system started, but 50 buffers is a big hit on conventional memory; if the BUFFERS can't all fit in the HMA—and that many almost certainly will not—all 25K or more of them live in the low 640K. With Quarterdeck, you can have a BUFFERS=2 statement in CONFIG.SYS and then create 48 more buffers in a UMB (assuming that you have a UMB with 25K of space) by adding...

LOADHI BUFFERS +48

...to CONFIG.SYS. You can do the same thing for file handles with the FILES.COM program, for LASTDRIVE with the LASTDRV.COM program, and FCBs with the FCBS.COM program. The general syntax looks like:

LOADHI *program* **+n**

In this syntax, *program* is BUFFERS, FILES, LASTDRV, or FCBS; *n* is the number of those internal areas to create. The plus sign (+) is essential; without it, the program—BUFFERS, FILES, LASTDRV, or FCBS—just reports the number of internal areas you currently have.

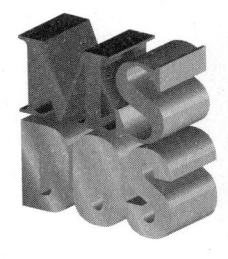

> **NOTE:** *Small items like this may seem unimportant, but sometimes a few K here or there make the difference between getting a large program to load high or not. Even if you choose not to use the QEMM386.SYS device driver as your memory manager, the BUFFERS.COM, FILES.COM, LASTDRV.COM, and FCBS.COM programs still work fine with DOS 6.2's EMM386.EXE.*

Using VIDRAM To Capture 96K of Video RAM for DOS

In Chapter 12, you learned how to include the range A000-B7FF in an EMM386.EXE invocation to add 96K of contiguous memory to the top of DOS's 640K. The price you pay for doing this is that you cannot run EGA, VGA, super-VGA, or 8514-type graphics programs.

When 386 PCs first appeared, it wasn't completely silly to buy a computer with a CGA video board or a monochrome video board. As a result, a fair number of people had computers that never used the range of addresses from 640K to 704K (A0000-AFFFF), or perhaps from 640K to 736K (A0000-B7FFF).

For those people, Quarterdeck wrote VIDRAM. VIDRAM adjusts DOS's internal memory tables to use either the range from 640 to 704K (if you have a monochrome display adapter) or from 640K to 736K (if you have a color graphics adapter). The result is more conventional memory.

Of course, as time has gone on, VGA hardware is now practically given away. More and more people have VGAs. If you have a VGA, VIDRAM can still be of use to you. You may want to be able to switch to a CGA-emulation mode (with conventional memory available up to 768K) so that you can do some text-mode or CGA-graphics work, and then switch back to 640K-conventional mode for doing Windows or other graphics work.

You install VIDRAM by just typing **VIDRAM ON**. You either see a short message and return to the DOS prompt or you see the system lock up. (It should be obvious, but please don't experiment with VIDRAM when you can't afford to crash the system.) If the latter event occurs, you're either running some program that uses the VGA graphics or the monochrome area, causing the system to crash, or you have a system that for some reason won't let you add the extra 96K to DOS. Not all PCs let this work. It just takes a minute to find out, and it's useful information.

To restore the system to a default 640K conventional-memory arrangement, type **VIDRAM OFF**.

Living on the Edge with Stealth

It's likely that more ink has been spilled about Quarterdeck's Stealth feature for QEMM than about any other feature of Quarterdeck's flagship software product. Stealth can be explained in just a sentence or two. The whole idea of memory management is to use the unused portions of the memory addresses below 1024K or, if you're using an XMS provider that can create an HMA, the addresses below 1088K. When the CPU is in real mode, it is trapped below 1088K, imposing a real, solid, final lid on memory expansion for basic DOS programs. The idea behind Stealth is to use just about all that 1088K—even the part with the ROMs in it.

When activated, Stealth relocates your ROMs outside the 0 to 1088K memory-address range, opening up all the ROM area to UMBs. This results in up to 256K of UMBs, and *contiguous* UMBs at that! Because those ROMs are needed by the system, however, QEMM constantly monitors any attempts to use the ROMs. When it senses a program trying to use the services of a ROM, it whisks the UMB that has stolen the ROM's addresses off to a far-distant memory location and restores the ROM. It keeps the ROM where it's supposed to be just long enough for the program that needs it to use it, and then rewhisks (I know it's not a word, but it gets the point across, right?) the ROM off to the far-distant memory location and restores the UMB.

There is, of course, a catch. Because all this memory-whisking takes some time, you notice that some DOS programs slow down tremendously when you activate Stealth. Also, not all computers can have their ROMs Stealthed without problems. One of the functions of Optimize (covered in the next section) is to test whether or not a PC can support Stealth.

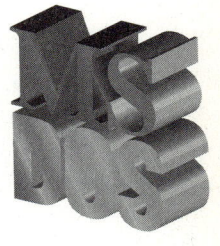

Chapter 13: *Running Third-Party Memory Managers*

> *My advice to you about Stealth is don't do it. Stealth is a neat idea, a fascinating demonstration of what amazingly clever coders can do, but it doesn't have the kind of industrial-strength solidity you and I need to get our day's work done.*

Using Optimize, Quarterdeck's Optimizer

In an earlier attempt at gaining some memory, we loaded everything high, rebooted, and waited to see the results. But the scattershot "load everything high" approach is not the best answer. After all, as the management books say, "a failure to plan is a plan sure to fail" or something like that. As you've seen, you can hand-fit programs to UMBs to maximize the amount of free conventional memory available. But that's a lot of work, or so it seems. That's why Quarterdeck was the first in the marketplace with an automatic memory optimizer called Optimize. Let's follow it through an optimization.

When you start up Optimize from the DOS prompt—and that should be a DOS prompt outside of Windows—you see an opening screen like the one in figure 13.6. Press Enter to continue, and Optimize advises you that it's about to start changing your startup files, as you see in figure 13.7.

Figure 13.6
The opening Optimize screen.

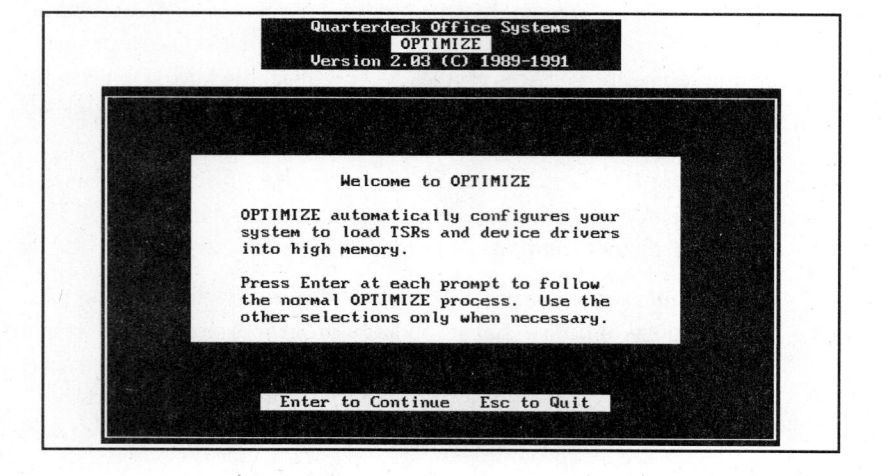

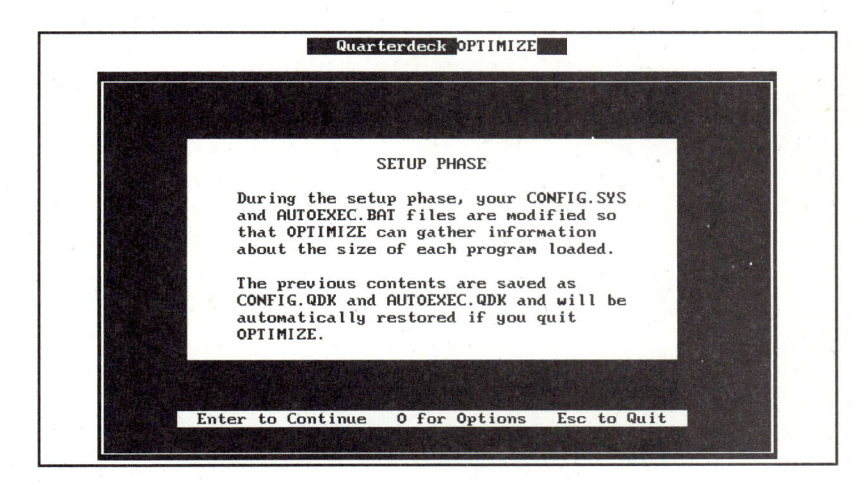

Looking at Quarterdeck's Solution to the Test Configuration

Figure 13.7
The Optimize Setup Phase screen.

```
                    SETUP PHASE
    During the setup phase, your CONFIG.SYS
    and AUTOEXEC.BAT files are modified so
    that OPTIMIZE can gather information
    about the size of each program loaded.

    The previous contents are saved as
    CONFIG.QDK and AUTOEXEC.QDK and will be
    automatically restored if you quit
    OPTIMIZE.

    Enter to Continue    O for Options    Esc to Quit
```

In the Setup Phase, Optimize changes AUTOEXEC.BAT and CONFIG.SYS to add small loader programs to the device drivers and TSRs. The job of these loader programs is to monitor a program's loading behavior—load size and final size—to help Optimize figure out how best to fit programs into UMBs and then to alert Optimize about any yo-yos so that it can handle them. Once that's done, Optimize is ready to reboot your system so that the loaders can gather their information. Optimize alerts you that it's about to enter the Detection Phase with a screen like the one in figure 13.8.

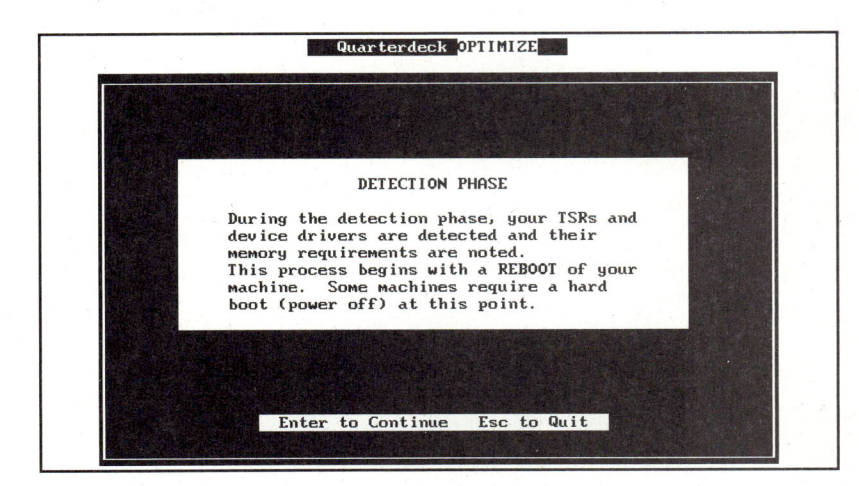

Figure 13.8
The Optimize program, about to enter the Detection Phase.

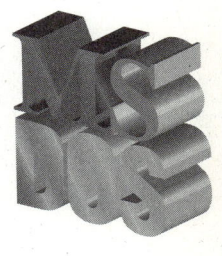

```
                   DETECTION PHASE
    During the detection phase, your TSRs and
    device drivers are detected and their
    memory requirements are noted.
    This process begins with a REBOOT of your
    machine.  Some machines require a hard
    boot (power off) at this point.

          Enter to Continue    Esc to Quit
```

Chapter 13: *Running Third-Party Memory Managers*

Then Optimize reboots your system; a pile of messages flash by as the loaders put programs into memory. Optimize then examines all possible ways to put the programs into UMBs to maximize the amount of free conventional memory once all is said and done. It reports its findings with a screen like the one in figure 13.9.

Figure 13.9

The Optimize Analysis report.

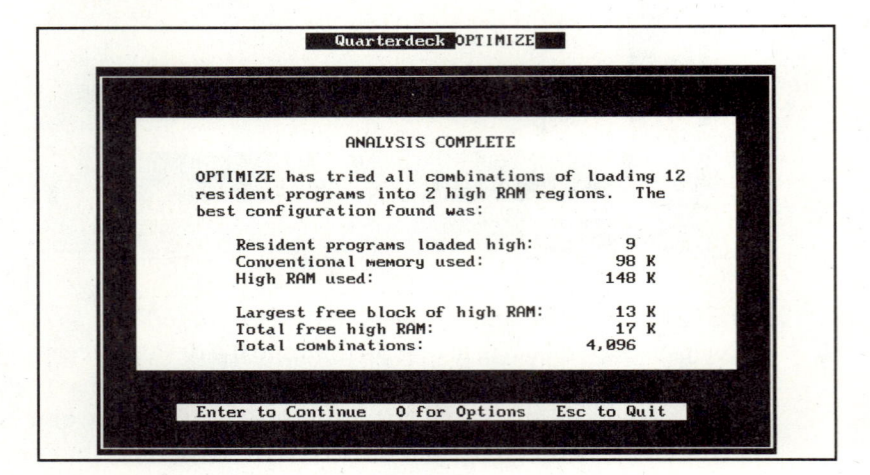

```
┌─────────────────── Quarterdeck OPTIMIZE ───────────────────┐
│                                                            │
│                                                            │
│                      ANALYSIS COMPLETE                     │
│                                                            │
│      OPTIMIZE has tried all combinations of loading 12     │
│      resident programs into 2 high RAM regions.  The       │
│      best configuration found was:                         │
│                                                            │
│           Resident programs loaded high:         9         │
│           Conventional memory used:             98 K       │
│           High RAM used:                       148 K       │
│                                                            │
│           Largest free block of high RAM:       13 K       │
│           Total free high RAM:                  17 K       │
│           Total combinations:                4,096         │
│                                                            │
│                                                            │
├────────────────────────────────────────────────────────────┤
│       Enter to Continue    O for Options    Esc to Quit    │
└────────────────────────────────────────────────────────────┘
```

Note that it says it tried 4,096 combinations. Some people seem to think that Optimize is suggesting it must do 4,096 reboots to test memory. That's not happening at all. In fact, that number has nothing to do with rebooting.

AUTHOR'S NOTE

Imagine that you have three programs to load high (call them P1, P2, and P3) and two UMBs to load them into (call them UMB1 and UMB2). Suppose that none are yo-yos and have load sizes equal to their run sizes for the sake of simplicity. P1, P2, and P3 are 25K, 12K, and 19K in size, respectively. UMB1 and UMB2 are 20K and 40K in size, respectively. Your job (assuming you wanted to be an Optimize-type program) is to figure out how to minimize the amount of unused UMB space by finding the combination of programs and UMBs that results in the least unused UMB space. The possibilities are outlined in table 13.2; draw a picture for yourself if that makes it clearer.

Looking at Quarterdeck's Solution to the Test Configuration

Table 13.2
UMB/Program Combinations

Program P1	P2	P3	Feasible?	UMB Space Remaining
1	1	1	No	
1	1	2	No	
1	2	1	No	
1	2	2	No	
2	1	1	No	
2	1	2	No	
2	2	1	Yes	4K
2	2	2	No	

The first line of the table looks at the possibility of putting all three programs into the 20K-sized UMB1. The sum of space needed is 25+12+19, or 56K—they'll never fit in UMB1. The combination is not feasible.

The second line looks at putting programs P1 and P2 (25K+12K) into UMB1 (20K), and P3 (19K) into UMB2 (40K). P3 goes in okay, but P1 and P2 can't fit in UMB1. It's not feasible.

The third line tries putting P1 and P3 (25K+19K) into UMB1 (20K)—there's no point finishing this line because it's also not feasible.

The fourth possibility puts P1 (25K) into UMB1 (20K)—no good. The fifth possibility has P1 (25K) in UMB2 (40K) and P2 and P3 (12K+19K) in UMB1 (20K)—again, no good. The sixth possibility has P1 and P3 (25K+19K) in UMB2 (40K)—closer, but no cigar.

The seventh possibility has P1 and P2 (25K+12K) in UMB2 (40K)—so far, so good—and P3 (19K) in UMB1 (20K). Hurrah—it's feasible! Leftover UMB space is 3K in UMB2 and 1K in UMB1. The last possibility (putting all three programs into UMB2) is impossible.

continues

Of the eight combinations considered, only one was even feasible. That's the one suggested. There are eight combinations because there were two UMBs and three programs. Two to the third power is eight. In general...

> *The number of memory combinations = (the number of UMBs) raised to the power of (the number of programs).*

I recently came across a PC with a single large UMB and three small 4K UMBs that it was able to reclaim from the BIOS ROM in the Fxxxx region. With the monochrome region (this PC could safely use the monochrome region with Windows and its video adapter), it had five UMBs. I asked it to optimize 12 programs. Grab your calculator and you'll see why it claimed to have examined 244,140,625 possibilities (and some people say there's no good reason to have the speed of a 486). That number is five raised to the twelfth power. (By the way, it got the analysis done in 23 seconds.)

After Optimize shows you its analysis report, you can press Enter to move on to the next step; but Optimize will, if you want, show you the information it's gathered, along with specifics about what it thinks is the best arrangement of programs in upper memory. Press **O** to see the options screen (see fig. 13.10).

Figure 13.10
The Optimize Analysis Options screen.

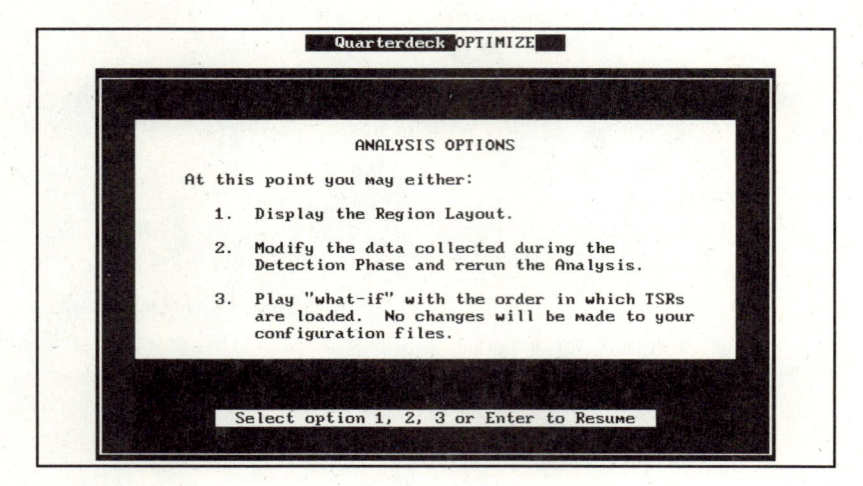

```
┌──────────────── Quarterdeck OPTIMIZE ────────────────┐
│                                                      │
│                    ANALYSIS OPTIONS                  │
│         At this point you may either:                │
│                                                      │
│           1.  Display the Region Layout.             │
│                                                      │
│           2.  Modify the data collected during the   │
│               Detection Phase and rerun the Analysis.│
│                                                      │
│           3.  Play "what-if" with the order in which │
│               TSRs are loaded.  No changes will be   │
│               made to your configuration files.      │
│                                                      │
│                                                      │
│       Select option 1, 2, 3 or Enter to Resume       │
└──────────────────────────────────────────────────────┘
```

Looking at Quarterdeck's Solution to the Test Configuration

The first option shows you where Optimize plans to place your programs in conventional and upper memory. Press 1 to see it (see fig. 13.11).

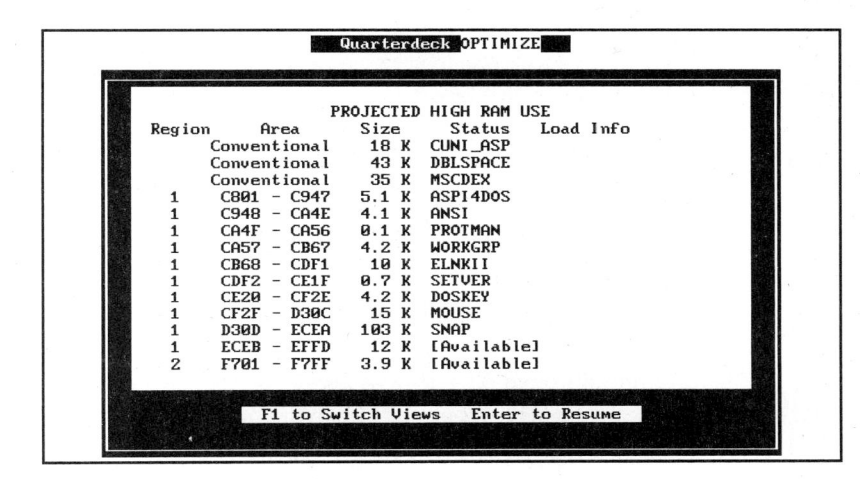

```
                    Quarterdeck OPTIMIZE

                    PROJECTED HIGH RAM USE
    Region     Area        Size    Status      Load Info
               Conventional  18 K  CUNI_ASP
               Conventional  43 K  DBLSPACE
               Conventional  35 K  MSCDEX
       1    C801 - C947     5.1 K  ASPI4DOS
       1    C948 - CA4E     4.1 K  ANSI
       1    CA4F - CA56     0.1 K  PROTMAN
       1    CA57 - CB67     4.2 K  WORKGRP
       1    CB68 - CDF1      10 K  ELNKII
       1    CDF2 - CE1F     0.7 K  SETVER
       1    CE20 - CF2E     4.2 K  DOSKEY
       1    CF2F - D30C      15 K  MOUSE
       1    D30D - ECEA     103 K  SNAP
       1    ECEB - EFFD      12 K  [Available]
       2    F701 - F7FF     3.9 K  [Available]

            F1 to Switch Views    Enter to Resume
```

Figure 13.11

The Optimize report of projected high RAM use.

Optimize thinks that this is how upper memory will end up. This is how it intends to set up the programs in UMBs and in conventional memory. You can't change this display, you can only examine it. Press Enter to return to the Analysis Options screen and then press 2 to see the next options screen (see fig. 13.12).

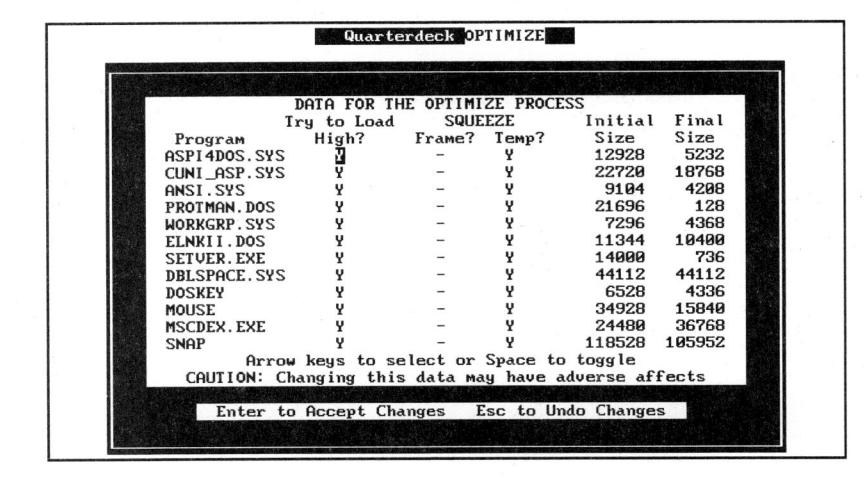

```
                Quarterdeck OPTIMIZE

               DATA FOR THE OPTIMIZE PROCESS
              Try to Load    SQUEEZE       Initial    Final
   Program      High?    Frame?  Temp?      Size      Size
   ASPI4DOS.SYS   Y        -       Y        12928     5232
   CUNI_ASP.SYS   Y        -       Y        22720    18768
   ANSI.SYS       Y        -       Y         9104     4208
   PROTMAN.DOS    Y        -       Y        21696      128
   WORKGRP.SYS    Y        -       Y         7296     4368
   ELNKII.DOS     Y        -       Y        11344    10400
   SETVER.EXE     Y        -       Y        14000      736
   DBLSPACE.SYS   Y        -       Y        44112    44112
   DOSKEY         Y        -       Y         6528     4336
   MOUSE          Y        -       Y        34928    15840
   MSCDEX.EXE     Y        -       Y        24480    36768
   SNAP           Y        -       Y       118528   105952
          Arrow keys to select or Space to toggle
      CAUTION: Changing this data may have adverse affects
         Enter to Accept Changes    Esc to Undo Changes
```

Figure 13.12

The Optimize screen that lets you control which programs load high and which to squeeze.

Optimize assumes at the outset that you want to load all programs high and so puts a Y next to each program in the column *Try to Load High?*

> **NOTE:** *The programs NETBEUI and REDIR do not appear on Optimize's data screen. That's because, for some reason, the Workgroup Connection programs do not announce themselves as TSRs in a fashion that Optimize can recognize. Remember that—it'll get Optimize in trouble later.*

The next two columns refer to the Squeeze option. The *Frame?* column has a dash (-) next to every program name. That's because the testbed PC is running without a page frame; /SqueezeF can't operate without a page frame. The only Squeeze option available to the Optimize program, then, is the /SQT, or *temporary*, option.

This screen also lists *Initial Size* and *Final Size* for the various programs. There are some massive disparities between the two numbers, as you see if you look at PROTMAN.DOS, SETVER.EXE, or MOUSE. (By the way, if you wonder why the mouse driver's load and run sizes aren't the 56K and 17K mentioned earlier, it's because this particular machine didn't use the Microsoft Mouse driver.) The MSCDEX.EXE program is a reverse yo-yo; it goes from a 24K load space to a 36K run space.

If you press Escape, you return to the Analysis Options screen. Skip the third option—there's nothing of value there. Press Enter to see a screen like figure 13.13.

From the Final Phase screen, press Enter. Optimize enters the final phase, where it actually puts the plan it just developed into place. After the boot, Optimize summarizes how effective its analysis was. You see the result of Optimize's analysis in figure 13.14.

No, you're not reading that wrong. Optimize actually ended up offering less memory after analysis than before; 24K less, in fact.

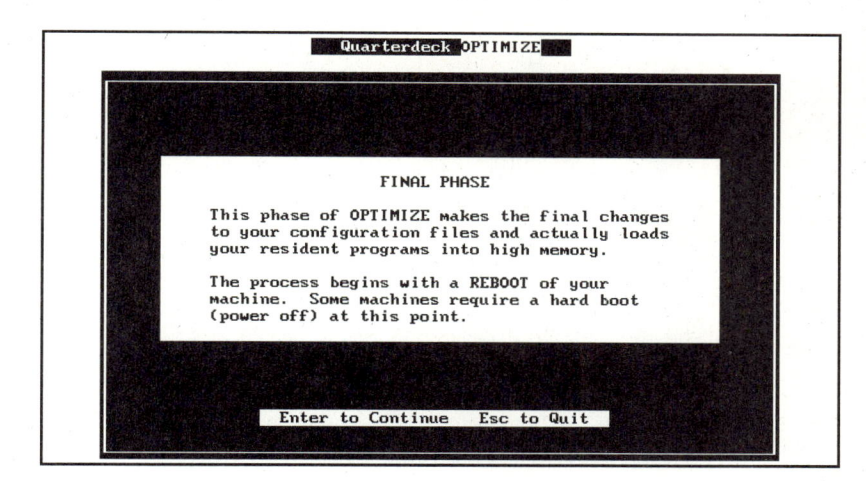

Looking at Quarterdeck's Solution to the Test Configuration 693

Figure 13.13
The final phase of Optimize.

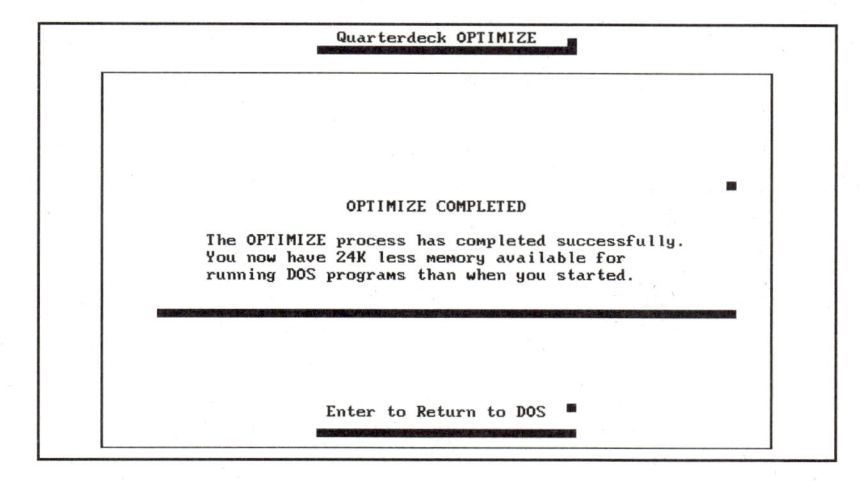

Figure 13.14
Optimize's performance summary.

To see what happened, take a look at the resultant CONFIG.SYS and AUTOEXEC.BAT files. CONFIG.SYS looks like this:

```
DEVICE=C:\QEMM\QEMM386.SYS NOEMS RAM X=A000-C7ff I=C800-EFFF
BUFFERS=10,0
FILES=60
DOS=UMB
LASTDRIVE=N
FCBS=4,0
DOS=HIGH
```

Chapter 13: *Running Third-Party Memory Managers*

```
DEVICE=C:\QEMM\LOADHI.SYS /R:1 C:\UTILS\SCSI\ASPI4DOS.SYS /P330
DEVICE=C:\UTILS\CORELDRW\CUNI_ASP.SYS /ID:6 /N:1 /D:MSCD001
DEVICE=C:\QEMM\LOADHI.SYS /R:1 C:\DOS\ANSI.SYS
DEVICE=C:\WWG\PROTMAN.DOS /I:C:\WWG
DEVICE=C:\QEMM\LOADHI.SYS /R:1 C:\WWG\WORKGRP.SYS
DEVICE=C:\QEMM\LOADHI.SYS /R:1 C:\WWG\ELNKII.DOS
DEVICE=C:\QEMM\LOADHI.SYS /R:1 C:\DOS\SETVER.EXE
STACKS=9,256
SHELL=C:\DOS\COMMAND.COM C:\DOS\ /E:2048 /P
DEVICE=C:\DOS\DBLSPACE.SYS /MOVE
```

AUTOEXEC.BAT looks like this:

```
SET BLASTER=A220 I10 D3 T4
@ECHO OFF
PROMPT $p$g
PATH
C:\DOS;C:\QEMM;C:\UTILS\CORELDRW;C:\WWG;C:\WGS;C:\WINDOWS;C:\UTILS
REM notice that now that QEMM is on the path, I can just say LOADHI
SET TEMP=C:\TEMP
C:\QEMM\LOADHI /R:1 DOSKEY
C:\QEMM\LOADHI /R:1 C:\MOUSE\MOUSE
C:\DOS\MSCDEX.EXE /S /V /M:10 /D:MSCD001
C:\DOS\SMARTDRV.EXE /Q
C:\WWG\NET START
SET SOUND=C:\SBPRO
C:\SBPRO\SBP-SET /M:12 /VOC:12 /CD:12 /FM:12
NET USE * \\ACMA\F /YES
C:\QEMM\LOADHI /R:1 SNAP F:\SCREENS
```

QEMM intends to load everything high except DBLSPACE.SYS, CUNI_ASP.SYS, PROTMAN.DOS, MSCDEX, SMARTDRV, and the network redirector (loaded by the NET USE * \\ACMA\F /YES command). But what actually was loaded high? Figures 13.15 and 13.16 show the output from MEM/C.

Looking at Quarterdeck's Solution to the Test Configuration

```
Modules using memory below 1 MB:

  Name          Total     =  Conventional  +  Upper Memory
  ----          -----        ------------     ------------
  MSDOS         18333  (18K)  18333  (18K)       0   (0K)
  RSTRCFG          96   (0K)     96   (0K)       0   (0K)
  QEMM386        3104   (3K)   3104   (3K)       0   (0K)
  LOADHI         1360   (1K)   1360   (1K)       0   (0K)
  CUNI_ASP      18768  (18K)  18768  (18K)       0   (0K)
  PROTMAN         128   (0K)    128   (0K)       0   (0K)
  DBLSPACE      44112  (43K)  44112  (43K)       0   (0K)
  COMMAND        4704   (5K)   4704   (5K)       0   (0K)
  MSCDEX        36576  (36K)  36576  (36K)       0   (0K)
  SNAP         105952 (103K) 105952 (103K)       0   (0K)
  REDIR         86064  (84K)  59280  (58K)   26784  (26K)
  ASPI4DOS       5232   (5K)      0   (0K)    5232   (5K)
  ANSI           4208   (4K)      0   (0K)    4208   (4K)
  WORKGRP        4368   (4K)      0   (0K)    4368   (4K)
  ELNKII        10400  (10K)      0   (0K)   10400  (10K)
  SETVER          768   (1K)      0   (0K)     768   (1K)
  MOUSE         15840  (15K)      0   (0K)   15840  (15K)
  DOSKEY         4144   (4K)      0   (0K)    4144   (4K)
  SMARTDRV      28800  (28K)      0   (0K)   28800  (28K)
Press any key to continue . . .
```

Figure 13.15

The output from MEM/C after Optimize (part 1).

```
  MOUSE         15840  (15K)      0   (0K)   15840  (15K)
  DOSKEY         4144   (4K)      0   (0K)    4144   (4K)
  SMARTDRV      28800  (28K)      0   (0K)   28800  (28K)
Press any key to continue . . .
  NETBEUI       36208  (35K)      0   (0K)   36208  (35K)
  Free         394000 (385K) 362880 (354K)   31120  (30K)

Memory Summary:

  Type of Memory        Total      =      Used       +      Free
  --------------        -----             ----              ----
  Conventional        655360  (640K)   292480  (286K)   362880  (354K)
  Upper               167872  (164K)   136752  (134K)    31120   (30K)
  Adapter RAM/ROM     225344  (220K)   225344  (220K)        0    (0K)
  Extended (XMS)    15728640 (15360K) 5242880 (5120K) 10485760 (10240K)
  -------------     -------- -------- ------- ------- -------- --------
  Total memory      16777216 (16384K) 5897456 (5759K) 10879760 (10625K)

  Total under 1 MB    823232  (804K)   429232  (419K)   394000  (385K)

  Largest executable program size         361648  (353K)
  Largest free upper memory block          21904   (21K)
  MS-DOS is resident in the high memory area.

C:\>
```

Figure 13.16

The output from MEM/C after Optimize (part 2).

These two figures show that SNAP is in low memory instead of high memory; something must have crowded it out of a UMB. Among the programs we expect to find low but that appear high, however, are parts of REDIR and SMARTDRV! That explains what happened. In the discussion about squeezing, earlier in this chapter, recall the comment that you've got to know what regions all programs go into if you try to arrange even one program? Well, SMARTDRV and REDIR messed things up because, unbeknownst to Optimize, those two

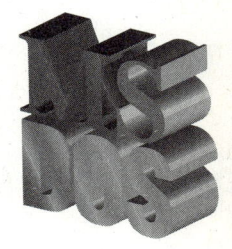

programs load themselves high when they see UMBs. Once
SMARTDRV and REDIR grabbed some upper memory space, there
was no space for SNAP, so that huge TSR dropped into conventional
memory and caused the `24K less memory after Optimize` message.
And the message was right: MEM/C shows 354K of available
memory, 24K less than the 378K we got just trying to load everything
high.

Using Manifest, Quarterdeck's Memory Analyzer

If you run QEMM with `DOS=HIGH` rather than `DOS=HIGH,UMB`, you find
that MEM/C can no longer see any programs loaded with
LOADHI.SYS or LOADHI.COM. They simply don't appear on the
MEM/C output. Nor do the UMBs—MEM/C reports no UMBs at all.
To find out what's happening in upper memory in this situation, use
Quarterdeck's Manifest utility, shipped with QEMM. There's a lot that
QEMM can do—not all of it is useful and much of it is flashy—so I'll
restrict this discussion to showing you how Manifest replaces and
improves on MEM/C.

You start Manifest from the DOS command line by typing **MFT**. You
see an opening banner, followed by the initial System/Overview
screen (see fig. 13.17).

The opening screen doesn't show a lot of essential information, but it
can be used to explain the Manifest menu system. Along the left side
of the screen is a column of categories: System, First Meg, and so on.
You select a category by pressing the up or down arrow. Along the
top of the screen is a row of topics; these topics change with the
category. Once you select a category, you choose a topic by moving
the cursor right and left. I'll refer to Manifest options using the convention *category/topic*; for example, the screen in figure 13.17 is the
System/Overview screen.

If you move to First Meg/Overview, you see a screen like figure 13.18.
To see the rest of the report, press PgDn (see fig. 13.19).

Looking at Quarterdeck's Solution to the Test Configuration

AUTHOR'S NOTE

Perhaps now you can see why Quarterdeck advises changing your `DOS=HIGH,UMB` statement to `DOS=HIGH`. If you don't tell the DOS programs that load themselves high that there's a high place to load to, they stay put. If you specify `DOS=HIGH` rather than `DOS=HIGH,UMB`, SMARTDrive won't detect the UMBs and won't preempt SNAP. It would seem, then, that the smart thing to do would be to change `DOS=HIGH,UMB` to `DOS=HIGH` and then reboot. Or so I thought.

When I started experimenting with EMM386, QEMM, and 386Max, I fully expected to show you that Optimize gives you a decent amount of free conventional memory. But that's when I found out that the Workgroup Connection redirector under DOS 6.2 can not only detect UMBs built by DOS, it can also detect UMBs built by Quarterdeck—even if you specify `DOS=HIGH`.

Although it sounds like we're up against a wall, we can sneak in a DOS 6.2 command to solve the problem. Remember that LH under DOS also has region control. To force a program that self-loads into a UMB so that it doesn't self-load into a UMB, fix its appearance in AUTOEXEC.BAT to use this syntax:

```
LH /L:0 programname
```

To fix the NET USE * \\ACMA\F /YES command, change it to `LH /L:0 NET USE * \\ACMA\F /YES`. (Don't worry about all that bizarre network syntax; Chapter 23 explains all you need to know about the Workgroup Connection.) Once you force NET into low memory, the amount of free memory goes from 354K to 368K. Still not as good as the 378K initially, but better. As I've said before, don't trust "automatic" programs; you can always do better by hand-fitting programs into UMBs. Sometimes the blunderbuss approach (load them all high) works better than Optimize as well.

Why doesn't Optimize know about this problem? Simple: this version of Optimize was released before DOS 6.2 was even in beta. All I can say is that I'm sure that the Quarterdeck folks will have another version of QEMM available soon, complete with a version of Optimize that's DOS 6.2 savvy.

Chapter 13: *Running Third-Party Memory Managers*

Figure 13.17

The Manifest System/Overview screen.

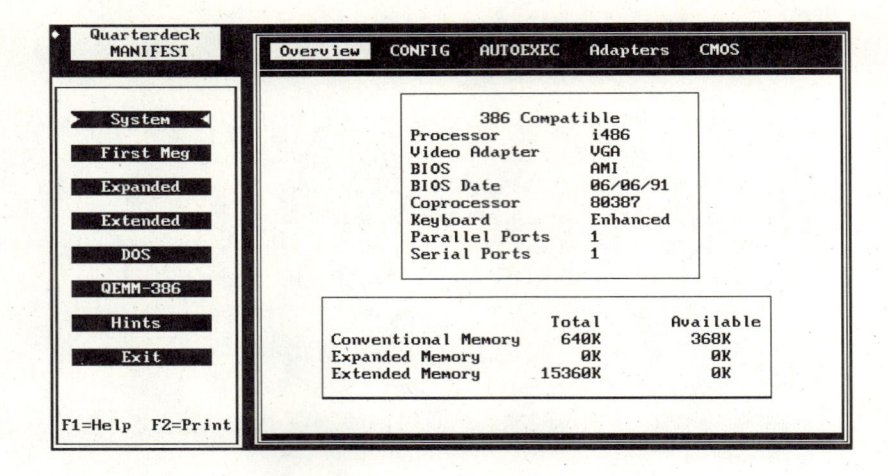

```
┌─────────────────┐ ┌──────────────────────────────────────────────┐
│  Quarterdeck    │ │ Overview  CONFIG  AUTOEXEC  Adapters  CMOS   │
│   MANIFEST      │ │                                              │
│                 │ │         ┌──────────────────────────────┐     │
│  ┌───────────┐  │ │         │       386 Compatible         │     │
│  │▶ System  ◀│  │ │         │ Processor          i486      │     │
│  └───────────┘  │ │         │ Video Adapter      VGA       │     │
│  ┌───────────┐  │ │         │ BIOS               AMI       │     │
│  │ First Meg │  │ │         │ BIOS Date          06/06/91  │     │
│  └───────────┘  │ │         │ Coprocessor        80387     │     │
│  ┌───────────┐  │ │         │ Keyboard           Enhanced  │     │
│  │ Expanded  │  │ │         │ Parallel Ports     1         │     │
│  └───────────┘  │ │         │ Serial Ports       1         │     │
│  ┌───────────┐  │ │         └──────────────────────────────┘     │
│  │ Extended  │  │ │                                              │
│  └───────────┘  │ │         ┌──────────────────────────────┐     │
│  ┌───────────┐  │ │         │             Total   Available│     │
│  │   DOS     │  │ │         │Conventional Memory   640K  368K│   │
│  └───────────┘  │ │         │Expanded Memory         0K    0K│   │
│  ┌───────────┐  │ │         │Extended Memory     15360K    0K│   │
│  │ QEMM-386  │  │ │         └──────────────────────────────┘     │
│  └───────────┘  │ │                                              │
│  ┌───────────┐  │ │                                              │
│  │   Hints   │  │ │                                              │
│  └───────────┘  │ │                                              │
│  ┌───────────┐  │ │                                              │
│  │   Exit    │  │ │                                              │
│  └───────────┘  │ │                                              │
│                 │ │                                              │
│ F1=Help F2=Print│ │                                              │
└─────────────────┘ └──────────────────────────────────────────────┘
```

Figure 13.18

The Manifest First Meg/Overview screen (part 1).

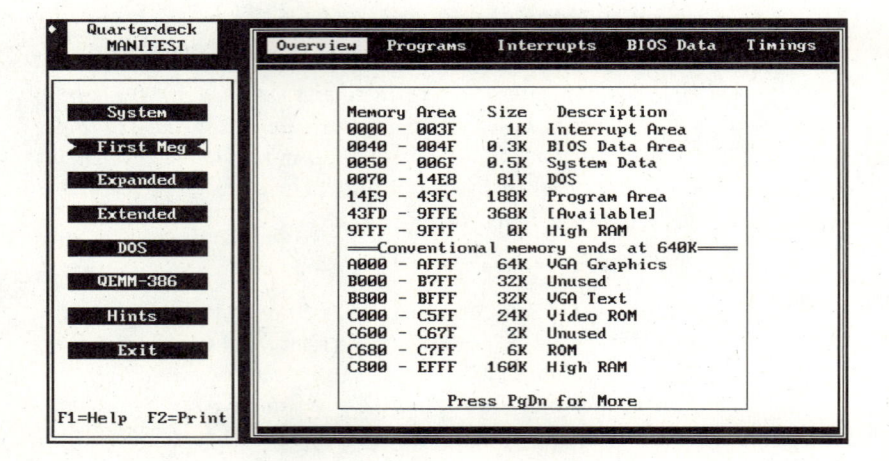

```
┌─────────────────┐ ┌──────────────────────────────────────────────┐
│  Quarterdeck    │ │ Overview  Programs  Interrupts  BIOS Data  Timings │
│   MANIFEST      │ │                                              │
│                 │ │  Memory Area    Size   Description           │
│  ┌───────────┐  │ │  0000 - 003F     1K    Interrupt Area        │
│  │  System   │  │ │  0040 - 004F    0.3K   BIOS Data Area        │
│  └───────────┘  │ │  0050 - 006F    0.5K   System Data           │
│  ┌───────────┐  │ │  0070 - 14E8    81K    DOS                   │
│  │▶First Meg◀│  │ │  14E9 - 43FC   188K    Program Area          │
│  └───────────┘  │ │  43FD - 9FFE   368K    [Available]           │
│  ┌───────────┐  │ │  9FFF - 9FFF     0K    High RAM              │
│  │ Expanded  │  │ │  ═══Conventional memory ends at 640K═══      │
│  └───────────┘  │ │  A000 - AFFF    64K    VGA Graphics          │
│  ┌───────────┐  │ │  B000 - B7FF    32K    Unused                │
│  │ Extended  │  │ │  B800 - BFFF    32K    VGA Text              │
│  └───────────┘  │ │  C000 - C5FF    24K    Video ROM             │
│  ┌───────────┐  │ │  C600 - C67F     2K    Unused                │
│  │   DOS     │  │ │  C680 - C7FF     6K    ROM                   │
│  └───────────┘  │ │  C800 - EFFF   160K    High RAM              │
│  ┌───────────┐  │ │                                              │
│  │ QEMM-386  │  │ │            Press PgDn for More               │
│  └───────────┘  │ │                                              │
│  ┌───────────┐  │ │                                              │
│  │   Hints   │  │ │                                              │
│  └───────────┘  │ │                                              │
│  ┌───────────┐  │ │                                              │
│  │   Exit    │  │ │                                              │
│  └───────────┘  │ │                                              │
│                 │ │                                              │
│ F1=Help F2=Print│ │                                              │
└─────────────────┘ └──────────────────────────────────────────────┘
```

There's nothing new in this report up to 640K. But Manifest is smart enough to know about the VGA graphics area and the VGA text area. It shares the ignorance that all Quarterdeck products seem to have about Windows and super-VGAs, however: it claims that the B000-B7FF monochrome region, which I explicitly excluded because my super-VGA card needs it to run Windows, is unused. Just for chuckles, I once ran a DOS session under Windows and ran Manifest in that session. Manifest still claimed that the area was unused! Don't believe everything you read on a screen.

Looking at Quarterdeck's Solution to the Test Configuration 699

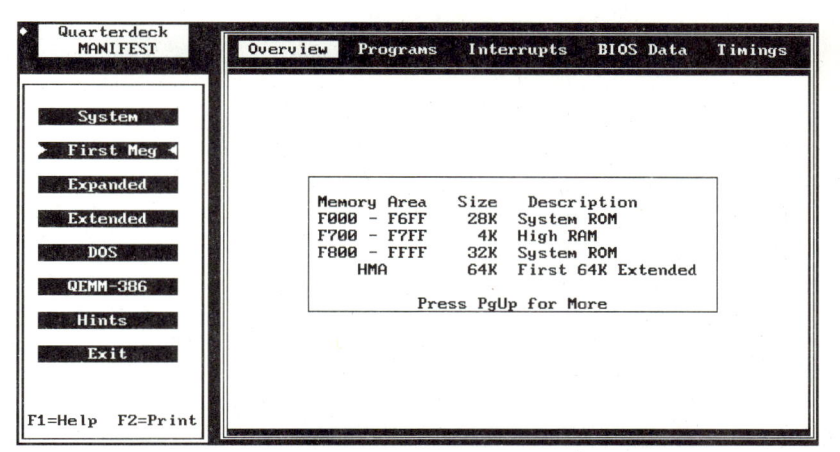

```
  Quarterdeck
    MANIFEST        Overview   Programs   Interrupts   BIOS Data   Timings

    System
  ► First Meg ◄
    Expanded
                         Memory Area    Size    Description
    Extended             F000 - F6FF    28K     System ROM
      DOS                F700 - F7FF     4K     High RAM
                         F800 - FFFF    32K     System ROM
    QEMM-386             HMA            64K     First 64K Extended
    Hints                        Press PgUp for More
     Exit


F1=Help  F2=Print
```

Figure 13.19

The Manifest First Meg/Overview screen (part 2).

Manifest then correctly detects that my video ROM is divided up into two parts, with 2K of unused space between them. Why it tells me that is a wonder because memory managers can only allocate areas in chunks of 4K. A 2K UMB could not exist—it's impossible. (Well, not impossible. But to use that 2K area, a memory manager would have to create a 4K area that partially contained the ROM it would otherwise overlap. A lot of work for a tiny space in memory.) Manifest sees the High RAM—its name for UMB—and the system ROM. Manifest claims that the 4K range of memory from F7000-F7FFF is High RAM, which means that QEMM386.SYS must have detected a section of ROM it guessed was overwritable. Let's hope for the sake of the system's stability that it was right. (You can always explicitly exclude an area you want QEMM to stay out of.)

If you want the kind of detail you see with the DOS 6.2 MEM/C command—which doesn't work with QEMM if you specify DOS=HIGH with no corresponding DOS=UMB—choose First Meg/Programs. The screen looks like figure 13.20; press PgDn twice to see the rest of it (see figs. 13.21 and 13.22).

The Manifest memory listing may be easier to comprehend than the MEM/C listing. Manifest gives a nice, bottom-to-top display of what's in memory relative to the other things in memory. You can see not only what loaded high and low, but also details of how some programs break up into data areas and program areas. And the simple hex ranges to the left of each entry assist you should you want to try to move programs to other regions.

Chapter 13: *Running Third-Party Memory Managers*

Figure 13.20

The Manifest First Meg/Programs screen (part 1).

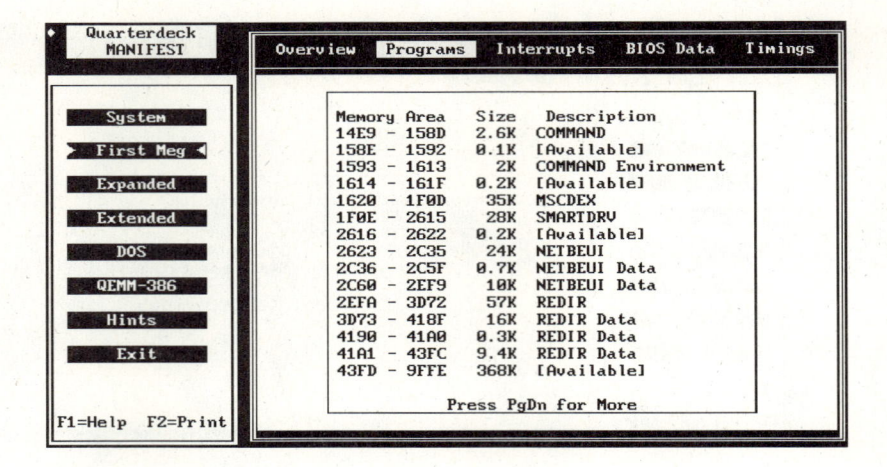

```
┌─────────────────────────────────────────────────────────────────────┐
│ ♦ Quarterdeck                                                       │
│   MANIFEST     Overview  Programs  Interrupts  BIOS Data  Timings   │
│  ┌─────────┐  ┌──────────────────────────────────────────────────┐  │
│  │ System  │  │ Memory Area    Size   Description                │  │
│  │►First Meg◄│ │ 14E9 - 158D    2.6K   COMMAND                    │  │
│  │ Expanded│  │ 158E - 1592    0.1K   [Available]                │  │
│  │ Extended│  │ 1593 - 1613     2K    COMMAND Environment        │  │
│  │   DOS   │  │ 1614 - 161F    0.2K   [Available]                │  │
│  │ QEMM-386│  │ 1620 - 1F0D    35K    MSCDEX                     │  │
│  │  Hints  │  │ 1F0E - 2615    28K    SMARTDRV                   │  │
│  │  Exit   │  │ 2616 - 2622    0.2K   [Available]                │  │
│  └─────────┘  │ 2623 - 2C35    24K    NETBEUI                    │  │
│               │ 2C36 - 2C5F    0.7K   NETBEUI Data               │  │
│               │ 2C60 - 2EF9    10K    NETBEUI Data               │  │
│               │ 2EFA - 3D72    57K    REDIR                      │  │
│               │ 3D73 - 418F    16K    REDIR Data                 │  │
│               │ 4190 - 41A0    0.3K   REDIR Data                 │  │
│               │ 41A1 - 43FC    9.4K   REDIR Data                 │  │
│               │ 43FD - 9FFE    368K   [Available]                │  │
│ F1=Help F2=Print │        Press PgDn for More                    │  │
│               └──────────────────────────────────────────────────┘  │
└─────────────────────────────────────────────────────────────────────┘
```

Figure 13.21

The Manifest First Meg/Programs screen (part 2).

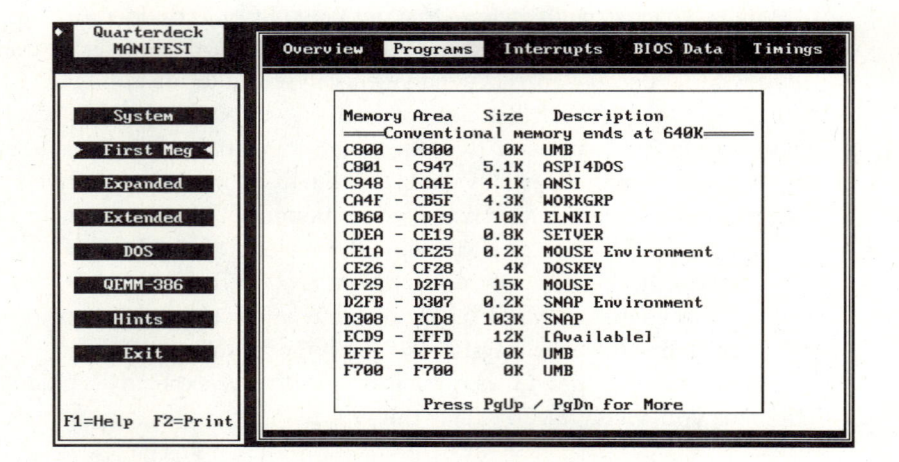

```
┌─────────────────────────────────────────────────────────────────────┐
│ ♦ Quarterdeck                                                       │
│   MANIFEST     Overview  Programs  Interrupts  BIOS Data  Timings   │
│  ┌─────────┐  ┌──────────────────────────────────────────────────┐  │
│  │ System  │  │ Memory Area    Size   Description                │  │
│  │►First Meg◄│ │═══Conventional memory ends at 640K═══           │  │
│  │ Expanded│  │ C800 - C800     0K    UMB                        │  │
│  │ Extended│  │ C801 - C947    5.1K   ASPI4DOS                   │  │
│  │   DOS   │  │ C948 - CA4E    4.1K   ANSI                       │  │
│  │ QEMM-386│  │ CA4F - CB5F    4.3K   WORKGRP                    │  │
│  │  Hints  │  │ CB60 - CDE9    10K    ELNKII                     │  │
│  │  Exit   │  │ CDEA - CE19    0.8K   SETVER                     │  │
│  └─────────┘  │ CE1A - CE25    0.2K   MOUSE Environment          │  │
│               │ CE26 - CF28     4K    DOSKEY                     │  │
│               │ CF29 - D2FA    15K    MOUSE                      │  │
│               │ D2FB - D307    0.2K   SNAP Environment           │  │
│               │ D308 - ECD8    103K   SNAP                       │  │
│               │ ECD9 - EFFD    12K    [Available]                │  │
│               │ EFFE - EFFE     0K    UMB                        │  │
│               │ F700 - F700     0K    UMB                        │  │
│ F1=Help F2=Print │     Press PgUp / PgDn for More                │  │
│               └──────────────────────────────────────────────────┘  │
└─────────────────────────────────────────────────────────────────────┘
```

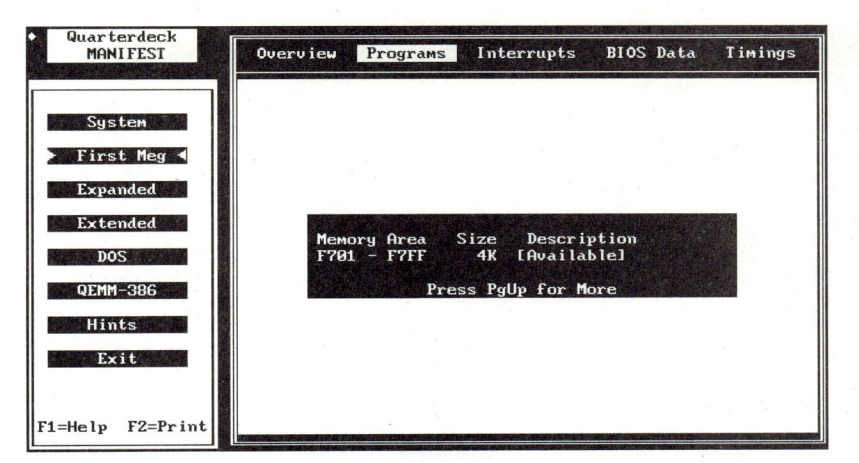

Looking at Quarterdeck's Solution to the Test Configuration

Figure 13.22

The Manifest First Meg/Programs screen (part 3).

> **AUTHOR'S NOTE**
>
> Although earlier versions of QEMM were difficult to work with, the competition from DOS 5 inspired Quarterdeck to produce a fine-quality memory manager that can match DOS 5 and DOS 6.2 feature for feature. It can even present the kind of information that DOS does in a more palatable form. No doubt Quarterdeck's answer to DOS 6.2 will be even better.
>
> On the negative side, Quarterdeck's documentation is downright scanty. It devotes less than a dozen pages to the central QEMM386.SYS program, and even less to LOADHI.COM and LOADHI.SYS. Vital parameters like /SQT=xxxx-yyyy (the parameter that Squeeze revolves around) are described as an "internal Squeeze parameter generated by the Optimize program." In other words, "Don't worry yore pretty lil' head 'bout those details—ol' Uncle Optimize will handle all the difficult stuff." That might be an acceptable answer if ole Uncle Optimize didn't get into the corn squeezin's now and then and leave things worse than he found them.
>
> All in all, QEMM is a good package, but better documentation would make it a great package.

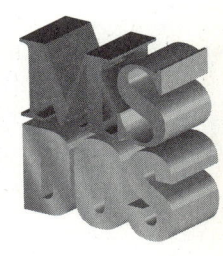

Looking at Qualitas's Solution to the Test Configuration

The company longest in the memory management business is Qualitas, a software company based just outside Washington, DC, in neighboring Bethesda, MD. In 1987, Qualitas began shipping a product called 386 To The Max (usually shortened to 386Max or Max), a program that sorted memory, backfilled, and limulated—the usual stuff for memory managers in those days. Over time, it's added features to keep up with its Q competitor on the west coast, Quarterdeck. Qualitas also offers a special version of Max specially tuned for IBM PS/2 machines called *Blue Max*. Everything that applies to Max also applies to Blue Max, so I don't have much to say about Blue Max here.

386Max shares many features with QEMM and EMM386.EXE (but not all of them), and it has a trick or two of its own up its sleeve. For example, Quarterdeck introduced the world to automatic optimizers like Optimize, but Qualitas introduced us to the idea of creating new UMBs by wholesale overwriting of unnecessary ROMs.

Looking at 386Max Features

Rather than take a lot of space describing Max's features, most of which parallel ones already described for QEMM or EMM386, the following sections briefly describe the features in three groups: the old stuff, the modern stuff, and the unusual stuff.

Obsolete Max Features

Like the other memory managers, Max has some ancient, useless features:

- ✔ Memory sorting is still on Max's list of features. Don't use it.
- ✔ Max can backfill memory if necessary.

✔ Disk-cache and RAM-disk programs are shipped with 386Max. Truthfully, better programs from other third-party software vendors are available, so there's no real reason to use QCache or 386Disk, the two Qualitas utilities.

Mainstream Max Features

Max also has all the modern, mainstream features:

✔ Since its first release, Max has automatically added as much conventional memory as possible, given your video board. In 1987 I worked for a while on a 386DX machine that had a monochrome display board; Max booted that PC up every day with 704K of conventional memory. It almost made me regret moving to a VGA.

✔ Max loads device drivers high by using its 386LOAD.SYS device driver.

✔ TSRs load high with either 386LOAD.COM or the basic 386Max command 386MAX LOADHIGH.

✔ You can specify the upper memory region in which to place a program with the PRGREG= (*program region*) parameter. It works exactly like the /L: parameter on DOS 6.2, including the notion that region 0 is conventional memory.

✔ You don't have to prerestrict memory. Like the others, you need not decide in CONFIG.SYS how much memory to set aside for expanded memory. Instead, 386Max's SmartMemory feature converts from extended to expanded memory as needed.

✔ Max was the first memory manager to understand and solve the problem of yo-yo TSRs. Max calls its feature the flexframe feature. It corresponds to the /SQF feature of QEMM. There is no equivalent to QEMM's /SQT currently in 386Max. That means that you cannot accommodate yo-yo programs unless you're limulating—which means that you have to give up 64K of contiguous UMB space. (Damned if you do, damned if you don't....) Just as with QEMM, Max needs to know the size of a yo-yo before it can flexframe it. But Max needs to know the load size, not the run size, to get the job done.

Max to the Max: Special Max Features

Max has some special features that separate it from the pack:

- ✔ **A separate profile file.** By now, you've noticed that memory-manager invocation lines can run on and on and on, making CONFIG.SYS files hard to print and read. Max gives you the option of putting all your parameters into an ASCII file so that each parameter gets its own line in a file that's easily viewed, edited, and printed.

- ✔ **VGAswap.** In VGAswap, a feature that moves your video ROM into the monochrome region, Max has a sort of Stealth Jr. I don't use it because it gives Windows fits and won't work on systems with super-VGA. But if you run a basic suite of DOS applications that aren't graphical, VGAswap can be useful because it essentially takes the monochrome region (normally a separate 32K UMB) and makes it contiguous with the UMB that often appears starting at 800K.

  More specifically, many computers have a section of UMA from 704K up that looks like this:

  704K-736K: monochrome region (unused, a UMB goes in there)

  736K-768K: VGA text region (used, no UMB in there)

  768K-800K: VGA ROM

  800K-something: unused address (unused, a UMB goes in there)

  This results in a fragmented set of UMBs: one in address range 704K to 736K and one in the range 800 to whatever. By moving the VGA ROM down to the monochrome region, Max opens up the 768K to 800K range for a UMB, defragmenting the UMBs. Although it won't work in all situations, it's convenient when it can.

- ✔ **ROMSearch.** All the big-three memory managers aggressively seek out areas of ROM that can be overwritten safely, but 386Max consistently finds the most areas that can be overwritten. Max comes with a program called ROMSearch that looks for

Looking at Qualitas's Solution to the Test Configuration

these open spaces. You needn't run ROMSearch, however: it's run automatically as part of Maximize, the 386Max automatic optimizer like MemMaker and Optimize.

By the way, the Max documentation doesn't call putting UMBs on top of inactive ROMs *overwriting* or *stealing* ROMs: it calls it *compressing* ROMs.

> *Qualitas goes beyond mere ROM scanning with their product Blue Max. Realizing that a lot of people have IBM PS/2 computers, Qualitas did extensive research into what could be overwritten in the BIOSs of PS/2 computers. The capability to overwrite ROM was a particularly important feature to add to a memory manager for PS/2 computers because PS/2s have a system BIOS that stretches from 896K through 1024K (E0000-FFFFF). One PS/2 I saw running Blue Max had recovered a 56K contiguous space from inside the BIOS. If you use PS/2s and you're running out of upper memory space, do not miss Blue Max.*

✔ **DPMI support.** All memory managers support VCPI, but 386Max can serve as a full-fledged DPMI server. Recently, Microsoft wanted to start shipping a DPMI server with their professional C language development tool. Microsoft developed one but then decided that Max did a better job at providing DPMI services. Microsoft C 7 ships with a copy of 386Max.

✔ **Documentation.** Just when I was starting to suspect that it was illegal to fully document a memory-manager product, Qualitas delivers a manual at least five times thicker than Quarterdeck's, chock full of troubleshooting advice and—believe it or not—examples!

✔ **ASQ.** Max comes with a program called ASQ that is a kind of combination memory-management tutorial and memory-viewer/analyzer along the same lines as Manifest. Qualitas will even give it to anyone who requests it (at least they did the last time I checked). Think of it as being very much like MSD with a lot of explanatory tutorial information added.

Understanding Max Syntax

Max shares many features with QEMM, so I don't want to repeat myself. Instead, let me compare the actual commands used to make the programs work.

The first is the memory manager itself, 386MAX.SYS. Its invocation line is a bit shorter than the others:

```
DEVICE=C:\386MAX\386MAX.SYS PRO=C:\386MAX\386MAX.PRO
```

All the options are organized into an ASCII text file called 386MAX.PRO. Set up for the initial testbed arrangement, it looks like this:

```
EMS=0                   ; no expanded memory
RAM=A000-C800           ; exclude this region
USE=C800-F000           ; include this region
```

This is a feature of Max I really like: each option gets its own line and you can even add a *comment* to each line.

> **NOTE** *The terminology Max uses is a bit different than what we're used to. What we're used to calling an* exclude *is referred to by Max as* RAM=; *an include is* USE=. *Notice also that the ranges are written differently than we're used to. The range we've been calling A000-C7FF, Max calls A000-C800. Not totally accurate, but probably easier to teach to a memory-management tyro.*

Max needs no options to create UMBs; in fact, there is no option to create them. Instead, it has a NOHIGH option that you can use on the chance that you'll want to *not* create UMBs some day.

You load device drivers high with the 386LOAD.SYS device driver. In its simplest form, it looks like this:

```
DEVICE=C:\386MAX\386LOAD.SYS PROG=devicedrivername
```

In this syntax, *devicedrivername* is the fully specified path and filename of the device driver. If you want to load a yo-yo (assuming that you are limulating) with a load size of *s* bytes, and want to load the program into region *n*, the load statement looks like this:

```
DEVICE=C:\386MAX\386LOAD.SYS FLEXFRAME SIZE=s PRGREG=n
PROG=devicedrivername
```

Similarly, you can load a TSR with a program called *386LOAD.COM*. All the options apply in the same way as for 386LOAD.SYS.

Running Maximize

Enough preliminaries; let's let the memory optimizer, Maximize, loose. The first time I ran Maximize, it crashed rather severely with a run-time error from the C compiler it was created with; the only message was...

```
run-time error R6009/ -not enough space for environment
```

This doesn't mean that Maximize is less stable than Optimize or MemMaker. Remember that the other two programs had considerably more free memory to start with. Their underlying memory managers created UMBs that NET recognized, and NET loaded itself high, giving the managers about 80K more free space to work with.

My workaround for 386Max was to remove the large SNAP and NET programs from AUTOEXEC.BAT, freeing up enough space to get Maximize going. Then I ran Maximize to create a starting point. That "optimized" system gave me enough room to put back NET and SNAP and rerun Maximize. The opening screen looks like figure 13.23.

Maximize asks a few basic questions and then displays a screen warning you that the first reboot is about to occur (see fig. 13.24). Maximize then gives you the option to control which programs to load high (see fig. 13.25).

In this screen, Maximize shows you what is already being loaded high (these programs have the HIGH designation) and which programs are currently being analyzed (these programs have the MAXIMIZE designation). At this point, you can tell Maximize not to try to load a program high.

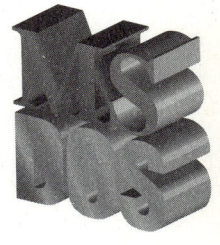

Chapter 13: *Running Third-Party Memory Managers*

Figure 13.23
The opening Maximize screen.

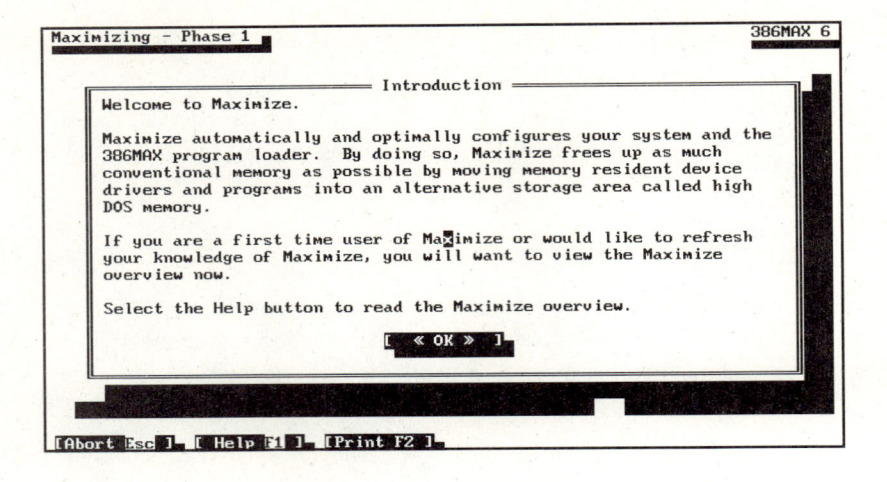

```
Maximizing - Phase 1                                          386MAX 6
┌──────────────────── Introduction ────────────────────┐
│ Welcome to Maximize.                                 │
│                                                      │
│ Maximize automatically and optimally configures your system and the │
│ 386MAX program loader.  By doing so, Maximize frees up as much      │
│ conventional memory as possible by moving memory resident device    │
│ drivers and programs into an alternative storage area called high   │
│ DOS memory.                                          │
│                                                      │
│ If you are a first time user of Maximize or would like to refresh   │
│ your knowledge of Maximize, you will want to view the Maximize      │
│ overview now.                                        │
│                                                      │
│ Select the Help button to read the Maximize overview.│
│                                                      │
│                      [ « OK » ]                      │
└──────────────────────────────────────────────────────┘
[Abort Esc ]  [ Help F1 ]  [Print F2 ]
```

Figure 13.24
The Maximize screen before the first reboot.

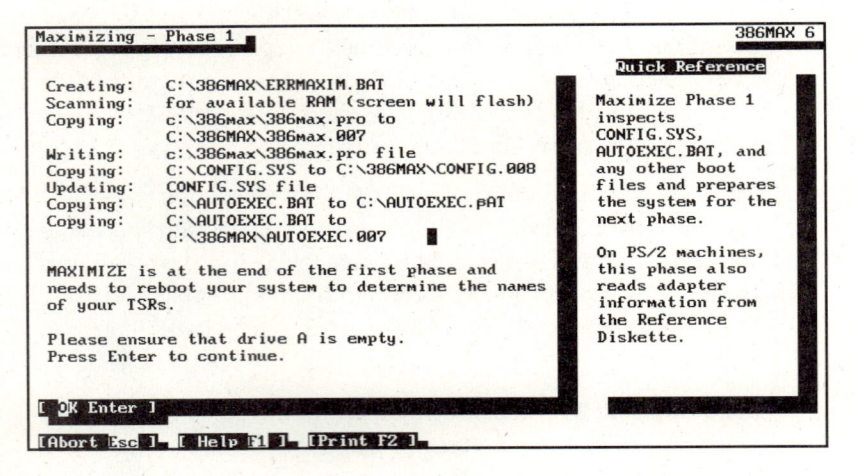

```
Maximizing - Phase 1                                          386MAX 6
                                                      ┌─Quick Reference─┐
 Creating:   C:\386MAX\ERRMAXIM.BAT                   │ Maximize Phase 1│
 Scanning:   for available RAM (screen will flash)    │ inspects        │
 Copying:    c:\386max\386max.pro to                  │ CONFIG.SYS,     │
             C:\386max\386max.007                     │ AUTOEXEC.BAT, and│
 Writing:    c:\386max\386max.pro file                │ any other boot  │
 Copying:    C:\CONFIG.SYS to C:\386MAX\CONFIG.008    │ files and prepares│
 Updating:   CONFIG.SYS file                          │ the system for the│
 Copying:    C:\AUTOEXEC.BAT to C:\AUTOEXEC.pAT       │ next phase.     │
 Copying:    C:\AUTOEXEC.BAT to                       │                 │
             C:\386MAX\AUTOEXEC.007                   │ On PS/2 machines,│
                                                      │ this phase also │
 MAXIMIZE is at the end of the first phase and        │ reads adapter   │
 needs to reboot your system to determine the names   │ information from│
 of your TSRs.                                        │ the Reference   │
                                                      │ Diskette.       │
 Please ensure that drive A is empty.                 │                 │
 Press Enter to continue.                             │                 │
                                                      │                 │
 [ OK Enter ]                                         │                 │
[Abort Esc ]  [ Help F1 ]  [Print F2 ]
```

Unfortunately, Maximize's user interface isn't always what you're looking for. In figure 13.26, I tried to direct Maximize to load the NET command high, but Maximize doesn't recognize that NET is a TSR, mainly because NET itself doesn't remain resident; a few pieces of NET called REDIR and NETBEUI stay resident. You can see this by noting that neither "maximize" nor "LOADHIGH" is written next to NET. I was unable to convince 386Max to load the network drivers high.

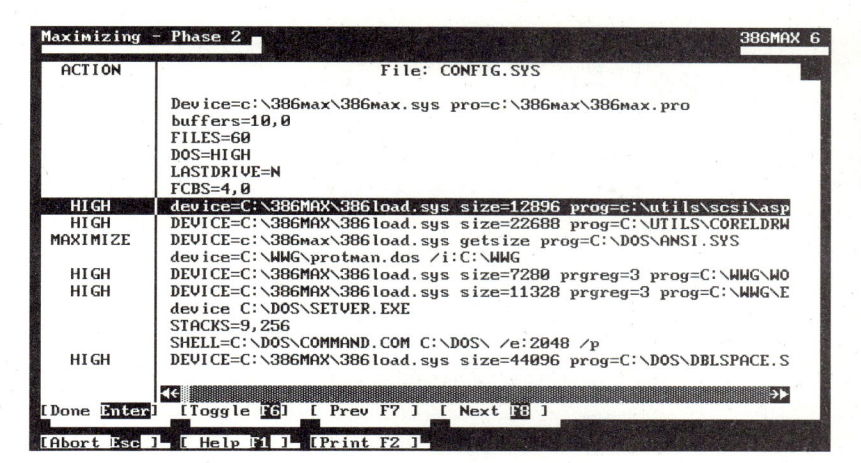

Looking at Qualitas's Solution to the Test Configuration

Figure 13.25
Maximize allows you to choose programs to load high or analyze.

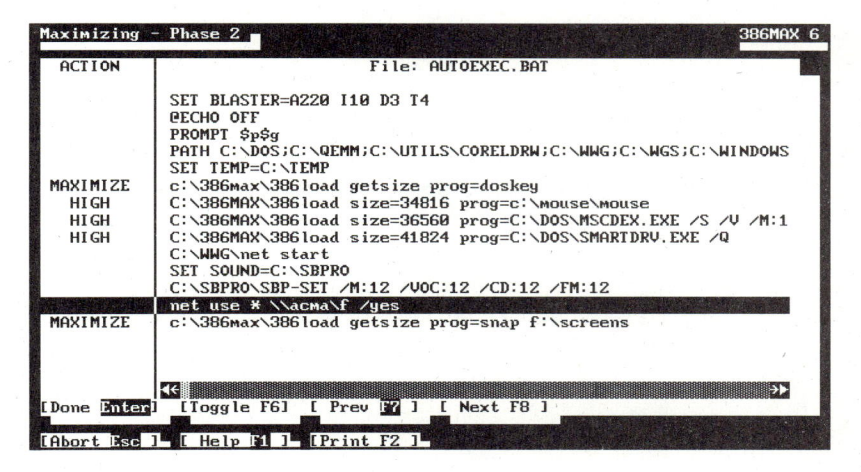

Figure 13.26
A TSR that Maximize doesn't recognize as such.

Maximize then offers its VGAswap feature. Like other memory managers, Maximize can't sense the fact that it will crash the system if it does the VGAswap. Figure 13.27 shows the screen that asks whether I want to use the VGAswap feature. After I choose No, Maximize reboots a second time. After that reboot, an analysis screen appears (see fig. 13.28).

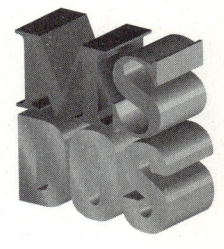

Chapter 13: *Running Third-Party Memory Managers*

Figure 13.27
Maximize offers the VGAswap option.

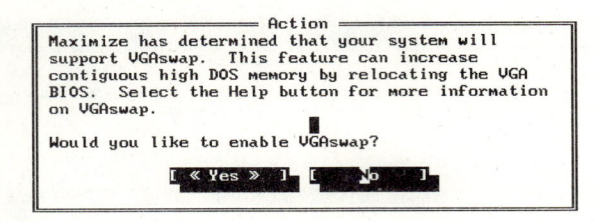

```
================= Action =================
Maximize has determined that your system will
support VGAswap.  This feature can increase
contiguous high DOS memory by relocating the VGA
BIOS.  Select the Help button for more information
on VGAswap.

Would you like to enable VGAswap?

           [ « Yes » ]    [    No    ]
```

Figure 13.28
Maximize analyzes upper memory combinations.

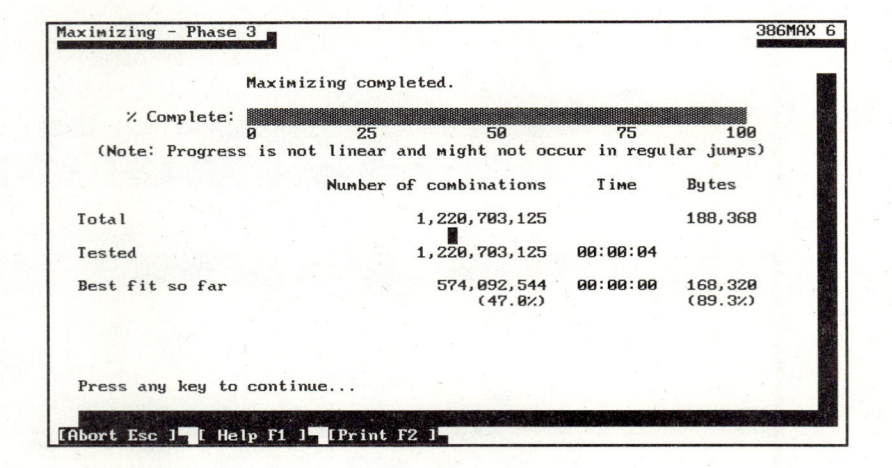

```
Maximizing - Phase 3                                     386MAX 6

                    Maximizing completed.
      % Complete:
                   0        25       50       75      100
               (Note: Progress is not linear and might not occur in regular jumps)

                         Number of combinations     Time      Bytes
       Total                  1,220,703,125                  188,368

       Tested                 1,220,703,125       00:00:04

       Best fit so far          574,092,544       00:00:00   168,320
                                    (47.0%)                  (89.3%)


       Press any key to continue...


[Abort Esc ]  [ Help F1 ]  [Print F2 ]
```

As with Optimize, Maximize brags about the millions of combinations it had to consider to find the one it thinks will net the most conventional memory. So far, Maximize looks much like the other programs you've seen. But it separates itself from the pack in the next few screens. Figure 13.29 is the first screen of a series showing how Maximize allows you to group TSRs.

When you group programs, you tell Maximize that a group of programs must load in a particular order. If you don't group, Maximize rearranges the load order of your programs to give itself more flexibility in maximizing conventional memory.

Figure 13.30 shows the third network driver in CONFIG.SYS marked. Like the other two network drivers, this one is being included in Group A. All you need do to create a group is to move the cursor over a program and press F6. Maximize then asks whether it should create a new group for this program or add it to an existing group. It then reorders the programs and reboots a final time.

Looking at Qualitas's Solution to the Test Configuration 711

Figure 13.29
The introductory message about program grouping.

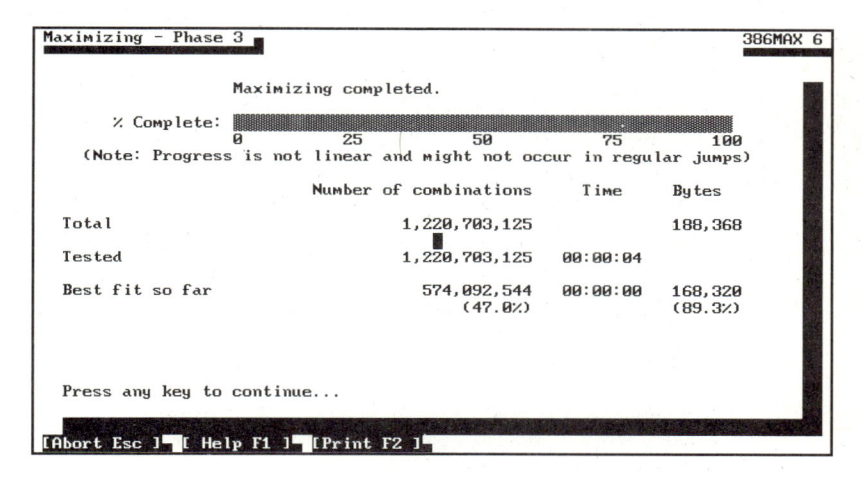

Figure 13.30
Grouping programs in Maximize.

Once 386Max was done, CONFIG.SYS looked like this:

```
DEVICE=C:\386MAX\386MAX.SYS PRO=C:\386MAX\386MAX.PRO
BUFFERS=10,0
FILES=60
DOS=HIGH
LASTDRIVE=N
FCBS=4,0
DEVICE=C:\DOS\SETVER.EXE
STACKS=9,256
SHELL=C:\DOS\COMMAND.COM C:\DOS\ /E:2048 /P
DEVICE=C:\DOS\DBLSPACE.SYS /MOVE
DEVICE=C:\386MAX\386LOAD.SYS SIZE=12896
PROG=C:\UTILS\SCSI\ASPI4DOS.SYS /P330
DEVICE=C:\386MAX\386LOAD.SYS SIZE=9072 PRGREG=3
PROG=C:\DOS\ANSI.SYS
DEVICE=C:\386MAX\386LOAD.SYS SIZE=22688
PROG=C:\UTILS\CORELDRW\CUNI_ASP.SYS /ID:6 /N:1 /D:MSCD001
```

```
DEVICE=C:\WWG\PROTMAN.DOS /I:C:\WWG
DEVICE=C:\386MAX\386LOAD.SYS SIZE=7280 GROUP=1
PROG=C:\WWG\WORKGRP.SYS
DEVICE=C:\386MAX\386LOAD.SYS SIZE=11328 PRGREG=3 GROUP=1
PROG=C:\WWG\ELNKII.DOS
```

The AUTOEXEC.BAT FILE looked like this:

```
SET BLASTER=A220 I10 D3 T4
@ECHO OFF
PROMPT $p$g
PATH
C:\DOS;C:\QEMM;C:\UTILS\CORELDRW;C:\WWG;C:\WGS;C:\WINDOWS;C:\UTILS;C:\386MAX
SET TEMP=C:\TEMP
C:\DOS\SMARTDRV.EXE /Q
C:\WWG\NET START
SET SOUND=C:\SBPRO
C:\SBPRO\SBP-SET /M:12 /VOC:12 /CD:12 /FM:12
C:\MOUSE\MOUSE
C:\DOS\MSCDEX.EXE /S /V /M:10 /D:MSCD001
C:\386MAX\386LOAD SIZE=118304 PROG=SNAP F:\SCREENS
C:\386MAX\386LOAD SIZE=6400 PROG=DOSKEY
NET USE * \\ACMA\F /YES
```

386Max netted 397K of free conventional space—the winner. Why did 386Max turn in the best performance? Well, first of all, all three memory managers performed relatively closely; no memory manager left the others in the dust. Remember that Maximize needed more hand-holding than the others; perhaps that gave it some kind of hint about an optimal memory arrangement that the others lacked. One thing that certainly affected Maximize's performance was that it was much more aggressive and successful in finding areas in the system's BIOS ROM that could be successfully overwritten. At least, they seem to be successfully overwritten. I may yet find that some basic and important function of my computer doesn't work because an area of ROM was overwritten. In any case, congratulations to Max.

> **AUTHOR'S NOTE**
>
> 386Max is clearly a world-class memory manager, good competition for DOS and QEMM. But Max suffers from instability in some of its programs, and some of its status reports are horribly laid out. Further, it offers less free memory for DOS sessions under Windows than if you use either QEMM or EMM386.EXE.
>
> Experience has shown that once Max is on your computer and set up properly, it's quite reliable. My advice for the prospective Max user is that you not allow VGAswap and, as always, that you hand-exclude the sensitive spots in your memory. And don't forget Blue Max if you're using PS/2 computers—Blue Max and PS/2s are a hand-tooled fit.

Summary

All three of the memory managers here are top quality products.

DOS 6.2's EMM 386/HIMEM combination is a powerful evolutionary step up from the DOS 5 memory manager, which was quite good all by itself. It lacks a few features that the two Qs have—squeeze being the most prominent—but it doesn't cost anything if you already own DOS 6.2.

Quarterdeck's QEMM is the better selling of the two major third-party memory managers. Its Optimize program is probably the easiest of the three to use. Additionally, QEMM creates UMB structures that are compatible with DOS 6.2's UMB structures, making it possible to mix the two memory managers a bit.

Of the three, 386Max is the most unused. It uses notation that's different from the other two, and is the most aggressive of the three in finding memory and using it. Its unusual UMB structure enabled it to control memory in my test configuration more exactly than could QEMM or EMM 386. And it is the memory manager of choice when you're having "ghost keyboard" problems.

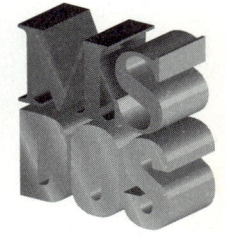

MS
DOS

Part Five:

Making It Better

Using DOS Utilities 717
Writing Batch Files 791
Using DOS 6.2 MultiConfig 861

MS
DOS

Chapter 14

Using DOS Utilities

by Kris Ashton

You've already learned about many of the MS-DOS utility programs available. Earlier chapters introduced you to utilities used to manage memory, as well as those used to work with disk directories and files. Future chapters explore additional disk utilities used for data backup and recovery, virus utilities, and more.

In this chapter you learn how to use MS-DOS commands and device drivers to customize your MS-DOS environment, add new devices to your system, or optimize devices you already have, making them work more efficiently.

The chapter begins with a discussion of the MS-DOS commands EDIT and EDLIN—programs used to create and edit your system's startup files. As you work to customize your MS-DOS environment, you will find many opportunities to work with these startup files. This section introduces the editors you might use and compares their features.

The section on floppy disk utilities helps you control your new or existing floppy drives. In this section, you learn how to use the DRIVER.SYS device driver and the DRIVPARM command to add external drives to your system or to set or change the logical format for a floppy disk drive. You explore the DISKCOPY and DISKCOMP commands used to copy and compare floppy disks, and the ASSIGN command for redirecting drive input and output.

The section on keyboard utilities introduces you to the DOSKEY command, useful for managing a history of keyboard commands and creating keyboard macros. The KEYB command is handy when you want to configure your keyboard for international use. You also learn how to speed up your computer's keyboard.

The section on displays begins with a discussion of how the computer's video system works. Then you learn how to use device drivers to control output to the screen, as well as how to use the MODE and PROMPT commands to set some of the characteristics of the display. The section on printers shows you how to use the GRAPHICS command to control printing of graphics, the MODE command to configure serial printers and redirect print output, and the PRINT command to print text files while you work on other tasks.

In the final section of the chapter, you learn about alternate shells and program launchers you can use to more easily accomplish many of the commands discussed in this chapter.

Editing Files with the DOS Editors

DOS 6.2 ships with two text-editing programs you can use to create and edit MS-DOS batch files, simple documents, and program source code. You cannot use the MS-DOS editors, which were designed to work with ASCII text files, to create text or documents that contain any type of formatting, such as underline, boldface, fonts, or graphics.

The Full-Screen Editor: EDIT

The MS-DOS full-screen text editor, EDIT, is very easy to learn and use and provides more capabilities than the EDLIN command. With EDIT, you don't have to learn cumbersome commands or work with line numbers. With your entire text file displayed on-screen, you can move the cursor anywhere on the screen, to the point at which you want to begin editing. This and other EDIT features work in much the same way as many word processors.

When you work with EDIT you can use your mouse or keyboard to scroll through a file. All cursor-control keys—including PgUp, PgDn, Home, and End—are supported. The editor also has pull-down menus and dialog boxes to help you perform common editing tasks such as search-and-replace, cut-and-paste, and file opening and saving. To perform these tasks in EDLIN, you have to memorize constantly changing line numbers and single-letter commands.

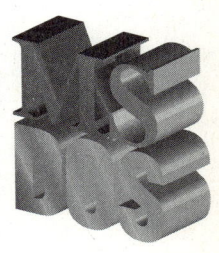

Using the Editor

The MS-DOS editor's executable file, EDIT.COM, is located in the directory that contains the MS-DOS utility files (typically C:\DOS). If the DOS directory is on your system path, or you are working in the C:\DOS directory, just enter the following command to start the editor...

    EDIT

...and press Esc to clear the opening screen. You'll see a blank editing screen with a menu bar along the top (see fig. 14.1). Now you are ready to create a new file or edit an existing file.

If you know the name of the file you want to edit, just type...

    EDIT *file name*

The Editor will open with your file displayed and ready to edit.

Figure 14.1

The MS-DOS Editor's editing screen.

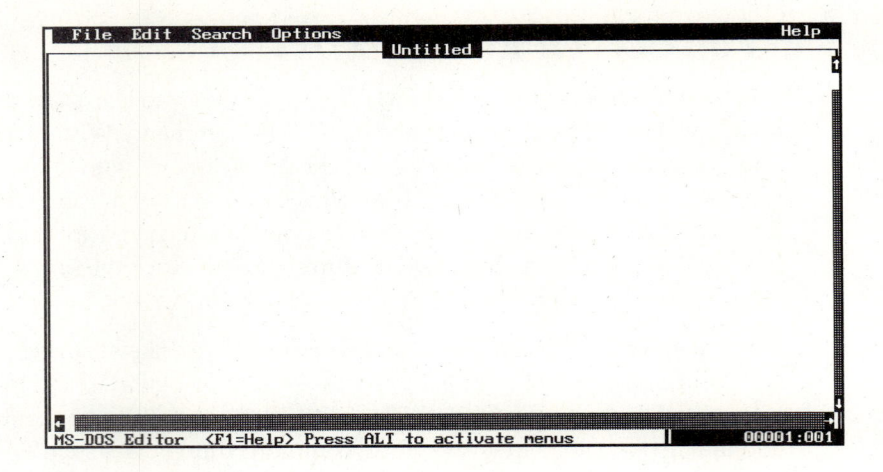

```
  File  Edit  Search  Options                                         Help
┌──────────────────────────── Untitled ──────────────────────────────────┐
│                                                                       ↑│
│                                                                        │
│                                                                        │
│                                                                        │
│                                                                        │
│                                                                        │
│                                                                        │
│                                                                        │
│                                                                        │
│                                                                        │
│                                                                        │
│                                                                        │
│                                                                        │
│                                                                       ↓│
│←                                                                      →│
└────────────────────────────────────────────────────────────────────────┘
 MS-DOS Editor  <F1=Help> Press ALT to activate menus          00001:001
```

> **NOTE**
>
> *EDIT.COM is really another MS-DOS program (QBASIC.EXE) in disguise. (EDIT does not contain the programming support found in QBASIC.) For the Editor to run, QBASIC.EXE must be on the system path. If it is not, or if the file has been erased, you see the message* `Cannot find file QBASIC.EXE`. *In general, having the DOS directory as part of your path is a good idea.*

Working with the Menus

The MS-DOS Editor uses a standard menu similar to those found in many other applications. Typically these applications have many of the same menu commands. Many applications contain File, Edit, and Help menus, for example. There are often other menus as well, depending on the application program. All the menus work the same; they are called *pull-down or drop-down* menus.

To access any menu on the screen, simply point to it with the mouse and *select* it (press the left mouse button). When the corresponding menu drops down, point to the option you want and click the mouse.

If your system doesn't have a mouse, or if you prefer using the keyboard, just press Alt to activate the menu bar. The Editor's menu bar contains five selections—File, Edit, Search, Options, and Help. When you press Alt, the first letter of each selection is highlighted (or underlined, on some systems). To select an option, simply press the highlighted letter. The menu that drops down displays the commands available from that menu. To select one of these options, just press the highlighted letter. If you prefer, you can use the cursor keys to move to a particular selection and then press Enter.

The File Menu

The File menu contains commands for opening, saving, and printing files, and for exiting the Editor. The File menu contains the following commands:

New creates a new file. If a file is already displayed on-screen when you select this option, you are prompted to save that file.

Open opens an existing file. Again, you can first save a file that's already displayed.

Save saves the file, using the current file name. If the file displayed hasn't been named, the program senses that and uses the Save As option instead.

Save As saves a file that hasn't been named, or lets you change the name of the file (thus saving another copy of the file with a different name).

Print prints the file.

Exit is used to exit the Editor. If the current file hasn't been saved, you are prompted to save or to exit without saving.

Many programs require that you "select" something, such as text, before other options can become available. To select some text, place the mouse pointer at the upper left corner of the text. Hold down the mouse button, drag the mouse pointer to the lower right corner of the text, and then release the button. The text should be highlighted. Now you can do things with the selected text, such as cut or copy it.

The Edit Menu

The commands on the Edit menu enable you to copy, move, and delete text in a file. Editing your files by using these commands—including duplicating lines of text without retyping them—is easy. All the commands available from the Edit menu have keyboard equivalents, which are discussed later in this chapter. The Edit menu contains the following commands:

Cut deletes selected text from the file and places it in a temporary storage buffer called the *clipboard*. You use this command when you want to remove text from one part of a file and insert it at another point.

Copy copies selected text from the file into the clipboard. As with Cut, you can paste the text into another part of the file, or into another file.

Paste inserts previously cut or copied text from the clipboard into the file. The text is inserted at the cursor's current location.

Clear cuts text from the file without saving it in the clipboard.

The Search Menu

The Search menu includes commands that let you find text in the file, repeat the last Find command, and change text by using a search-and-replace method. These commands are useful for editing large text files and for making changes to items that appear more than once in the file. The Search menu contains the following commands:

Find locates an occurrence of a text string.

Repeat last find repeats the previous Find command. Alternatively, you can activate this command by pressing F3 instead of using the menu.

Change finds a text string, then changes it to something else.

The Options Menu

The Options menu contains commands that enable you to work with the appearance of your display or change tab settings. These commands are useful for customizing your editing environment. The Options menu contains the following commands:

Display changes the color of the text and of the background. Simply choose the colors you want from a scrolling list. Display is also used for setting the tabs (normally set every eight spaces). Tabs are useful for entering complex batch files or program listings; by indenting sections of text, you make it easier to read and follow. Finally, you can toggle the display of scroll bars on or off while editing.

Help path indicates the location of the file QBASIC.HLP, the on-line help system for the Editor. QBASIC.HLP normally is located in the C:\DOS directory, which should be on your system path; if so, you do not need to specify the file's location.

The Help Menu

With the Help menu commands you can access the on-line help system associated with the Editor (not the general on-line help). The Help menu contains the following commands:

Getting Started is used for general help in the Editor.

Keyboard gets help about keyboard equivalents used in the Editor. See table 14.1 for a list of these keyboard commands.

About displays the version number of the EDIT program.

Work Faster by Using Your Keyboard

The more you work with the MS-DOS Editor, the less you'll use the menus. Rather, you probably will use the program's built-in keyboard equivalents. The advantage of working this way is that you can work faster when you use keys instead of menus. Table 14.1 lists the keyboard commands used in the Editor.

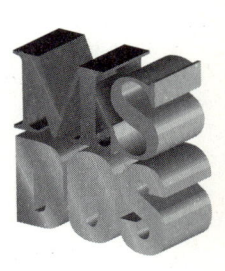

Chapter 14: *Using DOS Utilities*

Table 14.1
Keyboard Equivalents for EDIT Commands

Command	Key
Select character or line	Shift+arrow key
Select word	Shift+Ctrl+arrow key
Select line	Shift+End
Toggle insert/overwrite	Ins
Insert line above	Home, Ctrl+N
Insert line below	End, Enter
Insert from clipboard	Shift+Ins
Delete current line	Ctrl+Y
Delete to end of line	Ctrl+Q,Y
Cut selected text to clipboard	Shift+Del
Delete selected text	Del
Copy selected text to Clipboard	Ctrl+Ins
Search for text	Ctrl+Q,F
Repeat find	F3
Help on menus and commands	F1
Help—Getting Started	Shift+F1

Understanding Dialog Boxes

After you make selections from the Editor's menus, a screen often appears so that you can enter information or make additional selections. With these screens, called *dialog boxes*, you tell the program what you want it to do or which file you want to work with. The File Save As dialog box, shown in figure 14.2, is typical of these screens. It appears when you select Save **A**s from the Editor's **F**ile menu.

Editing Files with the DOS Editors **725**

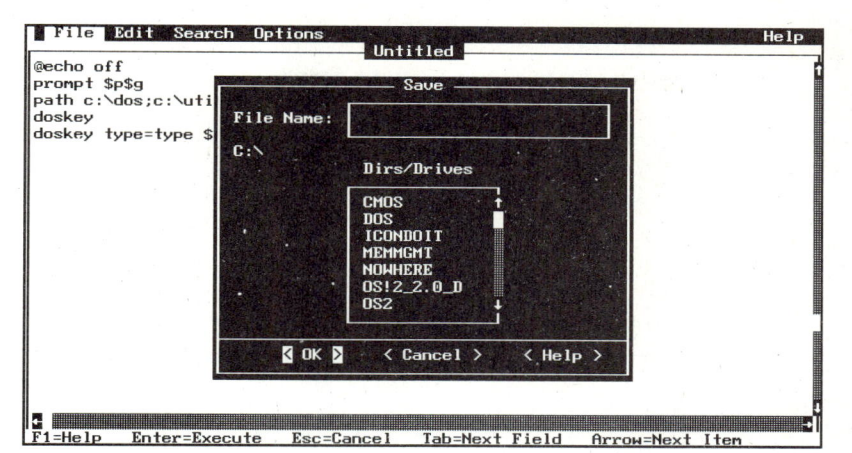

Figure 14.2

The MS-DOS Editor's File Save As dialog box.

> Use Tab to move from one field to another in a dialog box. Some fields, such as the Dirs/Drives field, contain scroll bars that enable you to use your mouse pointer or cursor keys to search for and select something. If text in a field is highlighted, simply start typing new text. You do not need to delete the existing text first.

Changing EDIT's Default File Extension

It is annoying to have to change the default *.TXT list of files to *.* so that other files will be listed. Well, using DSEDIT (a program on the disk accompanying this book; see also Chapter 21 for more information), makes it easy to patch QBASIC.EXE so that the default listing is all files (*.*) by following these steps:

1. Put DSEDIT.EXE in a directory included in the PATH.

2. Go to your DOS directory, and copy QBASIC.EXE to a floppy disk so you have a backup copy (just in case). *Never patch the original copy of a file.*

3. Enter **DSEDIT**. When it starts, press F7 to load a file, and then enter **QBASIC.EXE**.

4. Press F8 to enter an offset number, and enter **366**.

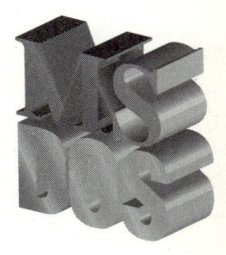

5. Press the down arrow until you highlight the 70 line, press the right arrow to highlight byte 54 (the letter T), and then enter **2A** (an asterisk).

6. Press the right arrow once to highlight byte 58 (an X), change it to **00,** and repeat it for the next byte (another T).

7. Press Shift+F2 to save the file; press F10 to exit DSEDIT.

Run EDIT, select File, Open, and notice that the default listing of files in the current directory is now *.*. You can easily do similar patches to DOS commands (refer to Chapter 4 for how to patch FORMAT and later in this chapter for how to patch DISKCOPY) and even COMMAND.COM (see Chapter 21).

Using SETVER To Set a Program's DOS Version

Some of the applications or device drivers loaded on your system might have trouble operating under DOS 6.2. Programs designed to work with a specific version of MS-DOS might report errors, or simply not work at all. Perhaps you can upgrade the application to a version that works with DOS 6.2. Or you can use the SETVER command to trick these programs into believing that they're operating with a different version of MS-DOS (other than 6).

Suppose, for example, that the application "banana.exe" is installed on your system. Suppose also that "banana" fails to work with DOS 6.2. After consulting the documentation (you do have the documentation, right?), you learn that banana is designed to work with MS-DOS 3.3 or later versions. Your system seems to fit the qualifications, but a call to the software vendor reveals that MS-DOS 3.3, 4.01, and 5 are supported, but not DOS 6.2—and a banana upgrade is not yet available. You are able to work around the situation by entering the following command...

```
SETVER banana.exe 5.0
```

You see a warning message on the screen, followed by the message...

```
Version table successfully updated
The version change will take effect the next time you
restart your system
```

When you restart your system, the change takes effect and "banana" should operate properly.

> *To update the system version table, the device driver SETVER.EXE must be included in your CONFIG.SYS file. Include the following in CONFIG.SYS:*
>
> **DEVICE=C:\DOS\SETVER.EXE**
>
> *or*
>
> **DEVICEHIGH=C:\DOS\SETVER.EXE**

You can use the SETVER command to specify not only the MS-DOS version needed for applications, but also the one for device drivers. Just remember to put the SETVER device statement in CONFIG.SYS before the statement that loads the particular device driver.

Entering **SETVER** at the prompt after it is installed displays the complete list of applications in the version table. The DOS 5 Upgrade and DOS 6 Upgrade Setup add several programs and device drivers to SETVER's version table, so even if you haven't added any programs to the version table, you still see a list.

If you install an updated version of the application, you may need to remove its entry from the version table. Do this by using /D. To remove the PROGRAM.EXE from the version table, for example, enter **SETVER PROGRAM.EXE /D**, and then reboot.

> *You many want to contact your software manufacturer to see if your program works with MS-DOS 5 or 6.2. Some programs depend on obsolete DOS functions that may not be present in DOS 5 or 6.2. Adding an incompatible program to the version table may result in lost or corrupt data or system instabilities.*

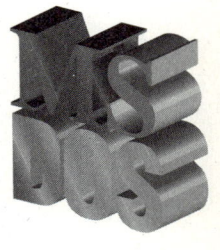

Utilities To Control Floppy Drives

Earlier chapters introduced you to the DOS 6.2 commands used for working with files and directories. Most people are comfortable moving around in the DOS file system, and can easily copy and delete files and work with directories. Some DOS commands and drivers that affect disk drives might be less familiar.

These commands and device drivers enable you to connect external disk drives to your system, provide a way to reassign drive IDs, copy and compare the contents of disks, and create and modify logical drives. This section explores some of these useful but esoteric commands.

Redirecting Disk Commands with ASSIGN

The ASSIGN command redirects disk commands from one logical drive ID to another. When you use the ASSIGN command to redirect a drive, all drive input and output goes to the redirected drive, instead of to the actual physical drive.

One use for the ASSIGN command is to switch the drive IDs to allow software to be installed. Let's assume, for example, that you have on your system a 5 1/4-inch drive that is designated drive A, and a 3 1/2-inch drive that is designated drive B.

Suppose that you recently purchased a program you want to install on your system's hard drive (the program was shipped on 3 1/2-inch floppy disks). The instructions call for the software to be installed from drive A. You try to install it from drive B, but the program refuses to install, insisting on drive A. ASSIGN to the rescue! In this case, enter the following command...

```
ASSIGN a=b b=a
```

...to reverse the drive IDs, enabling you to install the software as if the disks were in drive A. When you finish installing the software, enter the following command to return the drive IDs to their original settings...

```
ASSIGN
```

NOTE: *Sometimes reassigning the drive IDs with ASSIGN does not work when you're installing software from a specific drive. In that case, your options are to get the software on a disk of the correct size, or to open your computer and swap the ends of the floppy drive cable that connect to the drives. Before moving drive cables, consult a book on PC troubleshooting and maintenance.*

STOP: *Use caution with the ASSIGN command. You shouldn't use this command with other commands that modify the boot sectors or file allocation table of a disk—programs like ERASE, DOSBACK, FDISK, or FORMAT. It is easy to forget that the drives have been redirected, and important information can be destroyed. Fortunately, not many situations require the use of the ASSIGN command.*

Making a Copy of a Disk with DISKCOPY

The DISKCOPY command copies the contents of a floppy disk to another floppy disk. The original disk is called the *source* disk, and the second (or copy) disk is called the *target* disk. The general form of the DISKCOPY command is as follows:

```
DISKCOPY drive1 drive2
```

In this general form, *drive1* indicates the source disk drive and *drive2* indicates the target disk drive. Both the source disk and the target disk must be capable of being formatted identically. That is, you cannot use DISKCOPY to copy from a 3 1/2-inch disk to a 5 1/4-inch disk. You can use DISKCOPY to copy between two drives of the same size, even if they are of different capacities. To do this, simply put the disk of lower capacity in the source drive. The target disk assumes the same formatting as the source disk.

The DISKCOPY program reads as much information from the source disk as it can fit into the computer's memory in one pass. If more than one pass is required to copy the entire disk, the program prompts you to swap the disks.

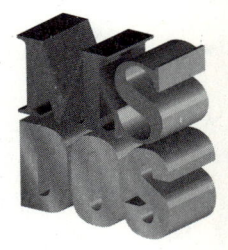

NOTE *A shareware program, DCOPY.EXE, that copies a high-density disk in one pass is included on the disk included with this book.*

The target disk doesn't have to be formatted—DISKCOPY formats as it copies. If the target disk is unformatted, DISKCOPY displays the message `Formatting while copying`. The copying process is just somewhat slower than copying onto a formatted disk.

It might go without saying, but any information on the target disk is destroyed during the DISKCOPY process.

STOP *DISKCOPY does not check to see whether or not any information is on the source disk—it just copies the disk. If the source and target disks get switched, you could end up with two copies of a blank disk! It's best to write-protect the source disk when using this command.*

DISKCOPY works only with removable drives, such as floppy disks. If you specify a hard disk as the source or destination disk, you see the following message:

```
Invalid drive specification
Specified drive does not exist or is non-removable.
```

Typically, DISKCOPY is used to make exact copies of floppy disks. Suppose that you want to make a copy of a high-density disk in drive A—a 3 1/2-inch drive—and that you don't have a second 3 1/2-inch drive. Follow these steps to make the copy:

1. Insert the source disk in drive A and close the drive door. *Be sure to write-protect the disk first.*

2. Enter the command...

    DISKCOPY A: A:

    (In this case, the source and target are the same). You see the following prompt...

    ```
    Insert SOURCE diskette in drive A:
    ```

DISKCOPY reads information from the disk and stores as much as it can in the computer's memory. Then you see the prompt...

```
Insert TARGET diskette in drive A:
```

3. Remove the source disk and replace it with the target disk.

4. Repeat steps 1-3 until you see the message...

```
Copy another diskette?
```

Because DISKCOPY makes an exact copy of the source disk on the target disk, any fragmentation on the source disk is transferred to the target disk. To avoid copying fragmented disks, use the MS-DOS COPY or XCOPY commands rather than DISKCOPY. *For more information on fragmentation, refer to Chapter 6.*

You can use DISKCOPY to make a copy of a startup disk (often called a "boot disk"). Because DISKCOPY makes an exact copy of a disk, it copies the MS-DOS hidden files that a startup disk needs.

Waking Up DISKCOPY

You have probably gotten bored waiting for DISKCOPY to prompt you for the next disk. There is an easy way to patch DISKCOPY so that it beeps when you need to insert a disk, enabling you to putter around the office. Using DSEDIT (a program on the disk accompanying this book; see also Chapter 21 for more information), do the following steps:

1. Put DSEDIT.EXE in a directory included in the PATH.

2. Go to your DOS directory and copy DISKCOPY.COM to a floppy disk so you have a backup copy (just in case). Never patch the original copy of a file.

3. Enter **DSEDIT**. When it starts, press F7 to load a file and enter **DISKCOPY.COM**.

4. Press F8 to enter an offset number, and enter **11**.

5. Press the down arrow until you highlight the 1C0 line, press the right arrow to highlight byte 3A, which is a colon, and enter **07**.

6. Press the down arrow three times to line 1F0, press the left arrow to highlight the colon in that line, and enter **07** again.

7. Press Shift+F2 to save the file, and press **F10** to exit DSEDIT.

Run DISKCOPY, and notice the beep when you are prompted for either the source disk or the target disk.

> *You can easily do similar patches to other DOS commands (see Chapter 4 for how to patch FORMAT) and even COMMAND.COM (see Chapter 21).*
>
> *See Chapter 15 for two alternatives to DISKCOPY.*

Comparing Disks with DISKCOMP

You use the DISKCOPY command, introduced in the preceding section, to make an exact copy of a disk. After copying a disk, you can use another command to verify that it copied correctly. The DISKCOMP command is used to compare two floppy disks to make sure that no differences exist between them. Because the DISKCOPY and DISKCOMP commands are related, the restrictions concerning disk size and capacity apply to both.

To compare disks, using one disk drive, follow these steps:

1. Place the first disk in drive A and enter the command...

    DISKCOMP a: a:

    DISKCOMP responds with...

    ```
    Insert FIRST diskette in drive A:
    ```

2. Press Enter to begin the verification process. DISKCOMP reads the disk's format and reports the message...

```
Comparing 80 tracks
18 sectors per track, 2 side(s)
```

After DISKCOMP reads as much disk information as will fit in the computer's memory, you see...

```
Insert SECOND disk in drive A:
```

3. Insert the second disk in drive A and press Enter.

4. Repeat steps 1-3 until you see the message...

```
Compare OK
```

If the two disks are not the same, DISKCOMP displays a message similar to...

```
Compare error on side 2, track 64
Compare process ended
```

Finally, (shades of DISKCOPY) a prompt asks whether you want to compare additional disks.

You can save time by using DISKCOPY to verify the target as it is making the copy. To do this, use the following command...

DISKCOPY drive1 drive2 /V

The shareware program DCOPY.EXE also has a verify option.

Adding External Drives with DRIVER.SYS

DRIVER.SYS is a device driver that enables you to create logical drives you can use to refer to your system's physical floppy drives. A *logical drive* is, in essence, a pointer to a physical drive. Most systems do not need this device driver; their physical floppy drives carry the appropriate drive IDs for normal use. Systems with an external disk drive, however, might need DRIVER.SYS to make the drive work properly. You can use DRIVER.SYS also to assign a new ID to an existing drive.

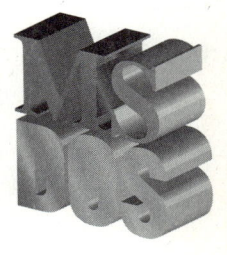

Installing DRIVER.SYS

Before you can do any of these tasks, you have to install DRIVER.SYS in your CONFIG.SYS file, using a DEVICE= statement. Before installing the device driver, take time to study the following section that describes the switches and parameters used to control drives.

The general form of the DRIVER.SYS statement is as follows:

```
DEVICE=D:PATH\DRIVER.SYS [/D:]NUMBER [/F:]FACTOR
[/T:]TRACKS [/S:]SECTORS [/H:]HEADS [/C]
```

The `D:PATH\` parameter specifies the location of the DRIVER.SYS file (usually the C:\DOS directory).

The /D switch specifies the drive number, and is required. The first physical floppy drive in the system is designated as drive 0; the second physical drive (if present) as drive 1. External drives, if installed, are given the next available drive number. When you assign a new drive ID to an existing drive, you indicate its current drive number.

The /F switch specifies the form factor or type of drive. Generally, the /F switch is all that is necessary to specify a drive's type. If you use the /F switch, you can omit the switches mentioned later in this list that also control type. Be sure to check with your drive's manufacturer for the correct form-factor value. The following are valid form-factor values:

Value	Form Factor
0	160K/180K or 320K/360K
1	1.2M
2	720K (3 1/2-inch) or other
7	1.44M (3 1/2-inch)
9	2.88M (3 1/2-inch)

The default form-factor setting is 2.

You should be able to assign most drive IDs by using the /F switch only. If you need to specify the number of tracks and sectors on the drive, however, you can use these additional switches:

/H:HEADS specifies the number of heads in the disk drive. Valid values are from 1 to 99; the default value is 2.

/S:SECTORS specifies the number of sectors per track. Valid values are from 1 to 99; the default value depends on the value of the /F factor, as shown in the following list:

Form Factor	Number of Sectors
/F:0	/S:9
/F:1	/S:15
/F:2	/S:9
/F:7	/S:18
/F:9	/S:36

/T:TRACKS specifies the number of tracks per side. Valid values are 1 to 99; the default value is 80, unless /F is 0, in which case the default value is 40.

Be sure to check the documentation for your particular drive before using any of these switches.

Finally, the /C switch specifies *change-line support*, which simply means that the disk drive can detect when the drive door is opened and closed. MS-DOS operations with disk drives are faster with change-line support than without it. With change-line support, you don't have to make DOS verify a new disk—it is "told" that when you open and close a drive door, it's usually because you are swapping disks. To determine whether your disk drive has change-line support, refer to the documentation for your floppy drive.

Adding an External Drive

Suppose that you just purchased an external 5 1/4-inch 1.2M drive for your computer system. The first step in adding this drive to your system is to determine its drive type. When you know this, you can construct the proper DRIVER.SYS statement.

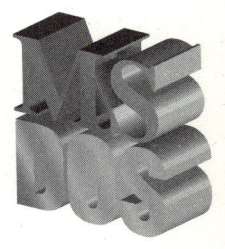

According to the form-factor value table, a 1.2M drive is type 1. To install the drive onto your system, add...

```
DEVICE=C:\DOS\DRIVER.SYS /D:1 /F:1 /C
```

...to your CONFIG.SYS file. This statement assumes that your system has one existing physical drive; hence, the designation "1" indicating that this is the second drive. The drive is given the next available drive letter after all previous drives have been defined.

> **NOTE**
> *Some external drives may come with their own device drivers. Use the one that the manufacturer ships with the drive. If DRIVER.SYS is also needed, the documentation will say so.*

Changing a Drive's Format with DRIVPARM

The DRIVPARM command is used in CONFIG.SYS to modify the format MS-DOS uses when communicating with an existing logical disk drive. You use the command whenever you install an external disk drive, or when you want to configure a drive to a format other than its default. The DRIVPARM command can be used also to change the format you previously set with DRIVER.SYS.

The general form of the command is:

```
DRIVPARM=/D:DRIVE /C /F:TYPE /H:NUMBER /I /N /S:SECTORS /T:TRACKS
```

/D:*DRIVE* identifies the drive number. Drives are numbered sequentially; the first drive (A) is number 0, the second drive (B) is number one, and so on.

/F:*TYPE* specifies the type of drive. The following drive types are supported:

Value	Form Factor
0	160K/180K or 320K/360K
1	1.2M
2	720K (3 1/2-inch drive)

Value	Form Factor
5	Hard disk
6	Tape
7	1.44M (3 1/2-inch drive)
8	Read-write optical disk
9	2.88M (3 1/2-inch drive)

/C indicates whether the drive supports change-line support (the ability to detect when the drive door has been opened and closed).

/H:*NUMBER* indicates the number of drive heads.

/T:*TRACKS* specifies the number of tracks.

/I is used if the computer's ROM BIOS does not support the 3 1/2-inch drive.

/N is used if the drive is a nonremovable type.

To reconfigure your B drive to a 1.2M format, enter the following command in your CONFIG.SYS file...

```
DRIVPARM=/D:1 /F:1 /C
```

This command causes the second drive in the system, drive B, to be configured as 1.2M (type 1) and activates change-line support.

Use the DRIVER.SYS device driver to define the relationship between logical and physical drives. Refer to the previous section to learn about DRIVER.SYS.

Working with Your Keyboard

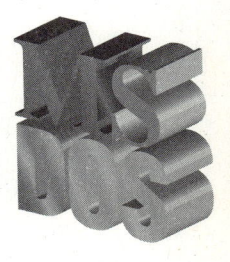

DOS 6.2 contains several utilities that enable you to control and customize your computer's keyboard. You can use the KEYB command to configure your keyboard for a language other than United States English. Use the DOSKEY command to create keyboard macros

and maintain a keyboard command history. Using MODE CON, you can control the rate at which keys on your keyboard repeat, and how long MS-DOS waits before it begins to repeat the key. This is the command to use when you want to speed up your keyboard.

Using an International Keyboard

To configure your keyboard for a specific language other than United States English, use the KEYB command. KEYB changes the layout of the keyboard and its characters to one of five foreign languages: Multilingual (Latin I), Portuguese, Nordic, Canadian-French, and Slavic (Latin II). MS-DOS uses a facility called code page switching to accomplish this.

What Is a Code Page?

You may recall that computers use ASCII codes to represent characters, numbers, and symbols. These characters are contained in a *code page*, which is simply a table with 256 entries, each of which represents a different ASCII letter, number, or symbol.

By default, MS-DOS uses the code page, called the *hardware code page*, that is built into your computer system. There is a code page for your keyboard and for your screen. MS-DOS uses the character set contained in your system's hardware code page unless you specify otherwise.

Most of the characters in the hardware code page are oriented toward United States English. If you want to use a foreign-language keyboard, you can change the character set available to MS-DOS by specifying an alternate code page (sometimes called a *prepared code page*). MS-DOS then translates the characters you type on your keyboard into the appropriate other-language characters in your data files.

MS-DOS cannot interpret keyboard commands or display its messages, dialog boxes, or help screens in another language unless you have purchased and installed a foreign-language version.

> *Prepared code pages are available for your display using the device driver DISPLAY.SYS and for your printer using the device driver PRINTER.SYS. Refer to the Command Reference for information about these device drivers.*

Using the KEYB Command

You can start the KEYB program in three different ways:

✔ Enter...

KEYB

...at the command prompt. The general form of the command is:

```
KEYB [COUNTRY-CODE] [CODE-PAGE FILENAME] [/E] [/ID:NUMBER]
```

COUNTRY-CODE, a two-letter abbreviated name of a particular country, specifies the keyboard code to use. The following values are supported for the country code:

Code	Language
be	Belgium
br	Brazil
cf	Canadian-French
cz	Czech
sl	Slavic
dk	Denmark
su	Finland
fr	France
gr	Germany
hu	Hungary
it	Italy

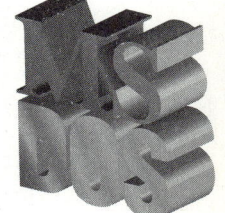

continues

Code	Language
la	Latin America
nl	Norway
pl	Poland
sp	Spain
sv	Switzerland (French)
sg	Switzerland (German)
uk	United Kingdom
us	United States
yu	Yugoslavia

CODE PAGE refers to one of six code pages, or translation tables, MS-DOS uses to translate the keys you type into their foreign-language counterparts. The possible code page values follow:

Code Page	Language	Description
437	United States	Contains characters for English and most other European languages
850	Multilingual	Contains characters for most of the (Latin I) languages that use the Latin alphabet
852	Slavic (Latin II)	Contains characters for Slavic languages that use the Latin alphabet
860	Portuguese	Contains characters for English and Portuguese
863	Canadian-French	Contains characters for English and Canadian-French

Code Page	Language	Description
865	Nordic	Contains characters for English, Norwegian, and Danish

FILE NAME includes the drive, directory, and name of the keyboard definition file. KEYBOARD.SYS, the default name, is included as part of MS-DOS and is located in your \DOS directory.

/E indicates that you want to use an extended keyboard with an 8086 computer.

/ID:NUMBER specifies which of two keyboard layouts you want to use. This value works only for countries that have more than one keyboard layout for the same language—France, Italy, and the United Kingdom. The ID codes for those countries are as follows:

Country	ID code
France	120,189
Italy	141,142
United Kingdom	166,168

As an example of how to use the command, suppose that you wanted to use a Spanish (Latin American) keyboard. Enter...

    KEYB LA

✔ Include an INSTALL command for KEYB.COM in your CONFIG.SYS file. This is useful if you wish to enable a specific keyboard layout each time you use your system. To use this option, enter the following general command in your CONFIG.SYS file...

    INSTALL=KEYB country-code

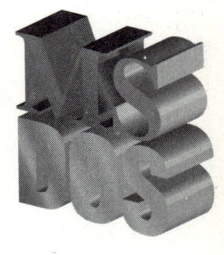

Another way to start KEYB is useful if you want to enable a specific keyboard layout each time you use your system. You include an INSTALL command for KEYB.COM in your CONFIG.SYS file. If you want to use the Latin American keyboard each time you use your computer, for example, you add the following command to CONFIG.SYS...

```
INSTALL=KEYB LA
```

✔ The third way to start KEYB is to include an appropriate KEYB command in your AUTOEXEC.BAT file. This method is essentially the same as enabling KEYB with an INSTALL command. The difference is that by using INSTALL, the command loads from your CONFIG.SYS file. This may be important to you if you are trying to load device drivers and TSRs into upper memory blocks—sometimes the order in which these programs are executed determines whether they are loaded high or into conventional memory. For more information about loading device drivers and TSRs high, see the previous chapters on memory management.

Using DOSKEY To Remember Your Commands and Create Macros

DOSKEY is a memory-resident program that maintains a history of commands you enter at the command prompt. DOSKEY also provides a means for recalling, editing, and resubmitting these commands. The commands are stored in the *command buffer*, a memory area created when you execute the DOSKEY program. By default, the command buffer is 512 bytes in size; you can, if need be, increase or decrease the command buffer size.

DOSKEY can also be used to create keyboard macros. A *macro* is a command or string of commands to which you assign a name. You execute a macro by entering its name at the command prompt; MS-DOS then executes the command(s) contained in the macro.

Macros are very similar to *batch files*—lists of commands you normally would enter at the command prompt but that are contained in a file. When you want to execute all the commands in the file, you simply enter the name of the batch file. *For more information about batch files, see Chapter 15.*

You should be aware of a few differences between macros and batch files. First, macros are stored in memory, whereas batch files are stored on disk. Because macros reside in memory, they execute faster than batch files, whose individual commands must be loaded from disk and executed in sequence. There is a price to pay for speed, though—memory. Both the DOSKEY program and the command buffer take up space in memory—approximately 4K if the command buffer is the default size of 512 bytes.

The second difference involves the size of a macro versus the size of a batch file. It is possible to create a batch file of nearly unlimited length, in which each command exists on a line by itself. The size of a macro, on the other hand, is limited to no more than 128 characters; all must be entered on one line.

Installing DOSKEY

To load the program, enter the following command...

    DOSKEY

This installs the program with the default command buffer size of 512 bytes. After the program is loaded, it stores your most recently used commands in the command buffer. The number of commands it stores depends on the size of the buffer and the complexity of the commands you enter.

The DOSKEY program and its command buffer can be loaded into an upper-memory block with this command:

    LOADHIGH DOSKEY

With DOSKEY installed, you can enter complex commands. That is, you can combine more than one command on the command line, provided that you type no more than 128 characters on the command line. If you enter multiple commands on the same line, you must separate them with a special separator character by pressing Ctrl+T.

Suppose that you want to back up your Excel worksheet files to a floppy disk, but first need to format one. To format a floppy disk and back up the files in one step, enter the following command...

```
FORMAT A: <CTRL-T> COPY C:\EXCEL\*.XLS A:
```

When you press the Ctrl+T combination, the carriage return symbol (↵) appears on the command line. Remember—you can string together as many commands as you want, as long as the total number of characters does not exceed 128.

Using Command Recall

DOSKEY keeps track of the commands you enter at the command prompt so that you can recall and resubmit them without retyping. You also can edit the command before resubmitting. To select the last command you entered, for example, simply press the up-arrow key. As you continue pressing the up-arrow key, DOSKEY cycles through all the commands in memory until you find the one you want. To resubmit the command, press Enter.

The other keys DOSKEY uses to make recalling and editing commands easy are listed and described in table 14.2.

Table 14.2
DOSKEY Editing Keys

Key	Function
Up-arrow	Displays previous command in command list
Down-arrow	Displays next command in command list
F7	Displays entire list of commands (which are numbered)
F8	Cycles through commands that begin with a letter you first specify
F9	Prompts for the number of a command in the list; to recall a command, enter its number
PgUp	Displays oldest command in the list

Key	Function
PgDn	Displays most recent command in the list
Esc	Clears command from command line

After you have selected a command from the command list, you can either press Enter to resubmit the command as is, or you can edit it. To edit a command, use the right- and left-arrow keys to move the cursor to the point at which you want to begin editing. Because DOSKEY is in replace mode by default, whatever you type replaces what is already there. If you want to insert characters, you must first press Ins to switch to insert mode. (Press Ins again to toggle back to replace mode.)

Adjusting the Command-Buffer Size

After working with DOSKEY, perhaps you'll want to change the default command buffer size of 512 bytes to something larger. You change the size of the buffer by adding the /BUFSIZE switch to the command, as in the following example:

```
DOSKEY /BUFSIZE=1024
```

In this example, the size of the command buffer is set to 1,024 bytes when the command is executed.

Creating and Executing Macros

One of DOSKEY's most powerful features is its ability to create and execute command macros. To use the macro function, you first must load the DOSKEY program by itself or with a buffer size. Then you issue the command a second time, followed by the macro definition. The general form of the command to create a macro is as follows:

```
DOSKEY MACRONAME=COMMAND MACRO
```

After the macro has been defined, simply enter the macro name—MS-DOS executes the macro command(s).

Suppose, for example, that you want to create a macro to make a backup of your Excel worksheets. To create this macro, enter...

```
DOSKEY EBACK=COPY C:\EXCEL\*.XLS A:
```

In this example, the name of the macro is EBACK. When you enter the macro name EBACK, MS-DOS executes the command COPY C:\EXCEL*.XLS as if you had entered it on the command line.

You learned earlier that you can use DOSKEY to enter complex commands from the command line, by including a special character (Ctrl+T) to separate the individual parts of the command. You can do the same thing with macros—that is, you can create a macro that consists of a series of commands. In this case, the separator character you use is $T.

Let's say that you want to create a macro to copy a group of Excel worksheets from your hard disk to a backup disk, as in the preceding example, and then—after the files are copied—you want to erase them from the hard disk. Enter the following complex command to create the macro...

```
DOSKEY MOVEM=COPY C:\EXCEL\*.XLS A: $T ERASE C:\EXCEL\*.XLS
```

Saving Macros

Remember that because macros are stored in memory, they are lost if your PC is reset or turned off. Although you could reenter them at the beginning of each PC session, that involves a lot of unnecessary typing. There are a couple of ways around the problem...

- ✔ Add the commands to create the macros to your AUTOEXEC.BAT file.
- ✔ Redirect the command that creates a macro to a batch file, then execute the batch file. To do this with the EBACK macro from the preceding example, enter...

```
DOSKEY EBACK=COPY C:\EXCEL\*.XLS A: > EB.BAT
```

This command puts the DOSKEY macro command into a file called EB.BAT. You execute the macro by entering the name of the batch file (EB) at the command prompt. (With just a single command macro, redirecting it to a batch file and then executing the batch file doesn't make much sense. Entering EBACK is probably just as easy as entering EB.)

This technique is more useful if you have many macros to define. In this case, you might create a *macro batch file*, a file that contains all the macros you need for your session. Just add the name of the macro batch file to AUTOEXEC.BAT; the macros you need will be created when you start up your computer.

Remember that DOSKEY does not save macros to files, but retains them in memory during your session. The first step to creating a macro batch file is to use the DOSKEY command's /MACROS option to display the macros that are stored in memory. Then you simply redirect the contents of the command buffer to a file, which you include in AUTOEXEC.BAT. Follow these steps:

1. To create the command macros you want to save to a file, enter each one from the command prompt, using the preceding example as a guideline.

2. To list the macros you have created, enter...

    DOSKEY /MACROS

3. To save the macros to a file, enter...

    DOSKEY /MACROS>FILENAME.BAT

4. Edit FILE NAME.BAT so that the word DOSKEY appears at the beginning of each line.

5. Include FILE NAME.BAT in your AUTOEXEC.BAT file. When you start up your PC, the batch file will create the macros you specified.

If you include in AUTOEXEC.BAT a command that's the name of a batch file, MS-DOS won't be able to return to AUTOEXEC after the included batch file has executed. If you include a batch file name in AUTOEXEC.BAT, it should be the last command in the file.

Using Replaceable Parameters in Macros

Many of the command macros you create will function on their own, without any additional input or direction. At times, however, you might need to pass into a DOSKEY macro additional information that's used by the macro during processing.

Suppose that you want to create a macro to copy files from one directory to another, or perhaps to a floppy disk, and then erase them. You learned earlier how to create a static macro to do this, and it works well if the names of the drives, directories, and files are always the same. Creating a more generic macro might be more useful. You need to use replaceable parameters to do this.

With MS-DOS, you can use up to nine parameters in a DOSKEY macro. DOSKEY parameters use the $ character and a number to define a position in a command at which a replacement will be made. Valid parameters are $1 through $9.

To create a generic DOSKEY macro that copies files, then erases them from their original location, follow these steps:

1. Enter the following command, including parameters for the source and destination of the file(s) to copy and then erase...

    DOSKEY GCOPY=COPY $1 $2 $T ERASE $1

    In this example, GCOPY is simply the name of the macro. $1 represents the source file that is to be copied and then erased, and $2 represents the destination file. MS-DOS interprets the $T parameter as a carriage return.

2. To execute the macro, enter the command **GCOPY** followed by the source name and destination of the files to be processed. You do not have to specify the location of the files to be erased—DOSKEY uses the location determined by the first replaceable parameter.

In addition to the replaceable parameters just discussed, DOSKEY supports several other parameters. Table 14.3 lists the parameters used with the DOSKEY command.

Table 14.3
DOSKEY Parameters

Parameter	Function
$G or $g	Use either of these characters to redirect output to a device, such as a printer or a file. $G is the equivalent of using the redirection (>) symbol for output.
GG or gg	Use these double characters to append output to an existing file rather than replace the contents of the file. GG is the equivalent of using the double redirection (>>) symbol.
$L or $l	Use these characters to read input from a device or file rather than from the keyboard. $L is the equivalent of using the redirection (<) symbol for input.
$B or $b	Use these characters when you normally would use the pipe (	) character in a command.
$T or $t	Use these characters to separate commands in a macro command line.
$$	Use these characters wherever you would normally place a single dollar sign ($).
$1 through $9	Use these characters to represent replaceable parameters in a macro.
$*	Use these characters to save the text that follows a macro name as a single replaceable parameter.

Examples of Useful Macros

Many simple MS-DOS commands lend themselves well to becoming macros. Descriptions of some particularly useful ones follow:

- ✔ **DOSKEY DIR=DIR $1 /P** displays a specified directory with the "pause" option. Simply enter the DIR command with the name of the drive or directory; DOSKEY uses this macro to display the directory one screen (or page) at a time. To display the directory of drive D and cause it to pause, for example, enter...

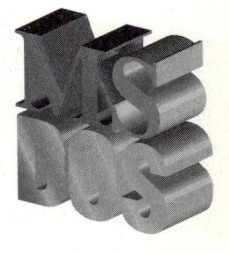

    DIR D:

Using this macro may help you avoid having to enter the command twice; the "pause" option often seems forgotten.

✔ **DOSKEY TYPE=TYPE $1 $BMORE** types on-screen the contents of an ASCII file, using the "more" option. The more option causes the file being typed on-screen to pause scrolling at each fill page. You see the message -more- at the bottom of the screen, indicating there is more text. To display a file called README.DOC, for example, enter...

    TYPE README.DOC

The " | more" option is added automatically to the TYPE command.

✔ **DOSKEY QF=FORMAT $1 /Q /U** performs a quick unconditional format of a floppy disk you specify. To perform a quick unconditional format of a floppy disk in drive A, for example, type...

    QF A:

Make Your Keyboard Faster

Did you know that you can make your keyboard faster? You can configure your system to speed up your keyboard's response time by using a version of the MODE command, MODE CON.

The MODE CON command makes your keyboard faster by controlling its *typematic rate*—the rate at which a key repeats itself when held down. Two components of the MODE CON command control different aspects of the keyboard rate.

The first typematic component controls the rate (the number of times a second) at which a key repeats. The second component controls the *delay time*—how long you have to hold down the key before it begins to repeat. Both components must be specified, as in the following general command:

    MODE CON RATE=X DELAY=Y

The value used for RATE can range from 1 to 32. A rate of 1 causes the key to repeat twice a second; a rate of 32 causes the key to repeat 30 times a second. The default value for rate is 20 for AT-type keyboards, 21 for IBM PS/2 keyboards.

The delay number can be 1, 2, 3, or 4. These numbers represent the number of quarter-seconds of delay you want. The number 1 causes a delay of 1/4 second before repeating a key, for example. The number 4 causes a delay of a full second. The default value for delay is 2.

To create the fastest keyboard repeat rate, add the following command to your AUTOEXEC.BAT file:

```
MODE CON RATE=32 DELAY=1
```

These values cause a key to repeat 30 times per second; MS-DOS waits 1/4 of a second before beginning to repeat the key.

Before using the MODE CON command, be sure that the ANSI.SYS device driver is installed in your CONFIG.SYS file.

Understanding and Controlling Video

Your computer's video system is in many ways its most important component; consider the time you spend in front of it each day. Several MS-DOS utilities can help you get the most from your video system. Before discussing these utilities, however, let's consider how your video system works.

Your computer's video system consists of two separate components: the video adapter board and the monitor. Both components must be present, and must be matched, for the video system to function properly.

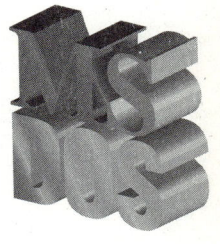

Video Component I—The Adapter Board

Your computer's video adapter board has the task of translating your computer's instructions into something the monitor can display. The video adapter board controls many aspects of displaying an image on-screen, such as resolution and color. The first thing you need to know about your display system, though, is what mode it's operating in.

Text and Graphics Modes

The first computer monitors used text mode to display information on-screen. In *text mode*, the screen is divided into a matrix of individual character positions. Many screens display 80 columns by 25 lines—2,000 individual character positions—for example. Any character position can display one of 256 different characters contained in a character set; the character set is defined by the display's code page (discussed earlier in this chapter). Although there can be many character sets, only one can be in use at any given time.

Most character sets contain some graphics characters, which a programmer or a user can combine to create graphic images on the screen. These images can never be very sophisticated, however, because they are created from individual characters of a predetermined size. What is needed to create better graphics, then, is a way to work with smaller areas of the screen.

In *graphics mode*, an image sent to the screen can be divided into thousands of individual dots, called *pixels* (or picture elements). Each dot on the screen can be adjusted independently, using color or intensity. Most computers sold today include a video system that displays in graphics mode.

Video Resolution—How Sharp Is That Picture?

One of the first things you hear about a particular video adapter is its *resolution*—the number of pixels across and down the screen. You probably have heard numbers like 640 by 480, which simply means the adapter can generate 640 pixels across the screen and 480 pixels down the screen. In most cases, the higher the numbers, the better the resolution. Some adapters can even generate more than one resolution. Table 14.4 lists some of the common video resolution standards.

Table 14.4
Video Resolution Standards

Standard	Mode	Resolution
Monochrome Display Adaptor (MDA)	Monochrome text only	720x350
Color Graphics Adapter (CGA)	Color graphics	320x200, 4 colors 640x200, 2 colors
Hercules Monochrome Graphics	Monochrome graphics	720x348
Enhanced Graphics Adapter (EGA)	Color graphics	640x350, 64 colors
Multicolor Graphics Array (MCGA)	Color graphics	320x200, 256 colors 640x480, 2 colors
Video Graphics Array (VGA)	Color graphics	640x480, 16 colors 320x200, 256 colors
Extended Graphics Array (XGA)	Color graphics	640x480, 65,536 colors 1024x768, 256 colors
8514/A	Color graphics	1024x768, 256 colors
Super VGA (SVGA)	Color graphics	Up to 1024x768, 256 colors

The effect of resolution varies according to the size of the screen. Because resolutions are defined by the number of dots across and down a screen, the size of the screen determines the size of the dots. Consider a 13-inch monitor, for example. An adapter that can display 640 by 480 has to create 307,200 individual pixels to cover the screen (640x480). An adapter that displays at a resolution of 1024 by 768 must create 786,432 pixels on the same screen area. Clearly, when more pixels are placed in the same amount of screen, the pixels are much smaller when you use the higher-resolution adapter. In fact, any text generated by this monitor-adapter combination may be too small to read comfortably.

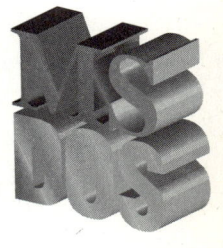

Increasing resolution does improve a computer's display, however, and in some cases enables applications to show more text without the need to scroll the display. The important thing to keep in mind is that a smaller display works well with resolutions up to and including VGA, whereas XGA, 8514/A, and SVGA adapters lend themselves well to larger displays.

Adding Color

Another important aspect of your display adapter is its ability to display color. Color video adapters can generate anywhere from 4 to more than 16 million colors, depending on the capabilities of the particular adapter and the mode you select. Although the capability to create and display all these colors might seem to be a good thing, the reality frequently is not so good.

> **NOTE**
>
> *You probably have heard the terms "8-bit video" and "24-bit video," which describe the number of bits the video board uses to generate colors.*
>
> *Standard VGA uses 4-bit video, of which you may not have heard. With 4-bit video, 4 bits are used to describe 16 different colors (2^4=16). (16 combinations of 4 bits—each combination describing a different color—are possible.)*
>
> *8-bit video uses 8 bits to describe 256 different colors (2^8=256). 24-bit video, sometimes referred to as "true color," uses 24 bits to describe 16,777,216 different colors (2^{24}=16,777,216). Because true color is fairly expensive, few applications take advantage of it.*

Creating and displaying all those colors takes time. Systems that generate more than the basic 16 colors of VGA are slower than those that don't. (Generally, these systems are estimated to be from three to ten times slower!) If you have the type of video adapter that can display these colors, you probably should consider using a video coprocessor (discussed in the next section). You must also consider the application software you are using.

You see, most software available today cannot display all the colors your adapter might be able to create. Imagine your word processor or spreadsheet for a moment. You normally type documents or enter data in one color. Sometimes, during editing, you might add color to indicate important aspects of your work. But in the end, most documents are printed in black and white.

A growing number of applications—desktop publishing and graphics programs—can take advantage of these colors. These programs are built with color production in mind. When you use them, however, consider again one of the biggest requirements of this hardware combination—time. (Specifically, SVGA without a coprocessor will take a lot of time to draw graphic images when using 256 or 16x106 colors.)

The Performance Hit

Creating high-resolution graphic images of many colors might seem like a good thing, but the reality is that doing so puts a strain on your system. Creating those images takes CPU power, and storing them takes memory. Your computer's CPU and memory have to work overtime to manage all the individual pixels and colors on your screen. What can you do to improve this situation? First, enhance the graphics creation process by adding an accelerator or coprocessor to your system. Second, think about using local bus video. And finally, add additional memory to the video system, in the form of VRAM (*video RAM*).

Speed Up Video with an Accelerator or Coprocessor

Most video boards are not very intelligent. They rely on the processing power of the computer's CPU to generate and color the pixels on-screen. By adding an accelerator or coprocessor to your system, the lion's share of video computing power is moved directly onto the video board.

A *video accelerator* moves information between the CPU and the video board in much the same fashion as a standard video board. The biggest difference, however, is its ability to move less information in a single operation. Also, video accelerators often have image drawing tools built into their circuitry. Consider how this works when you draw a simple circle.

With a standard video board, the CPU must tell the video board how to draw the circle—that is, the CPU must generate instructions to calculate the location and color of every pixel in the circle. With an accelerator, the CPU sends one instruction to the video board: "Draw a circle, so large, using a medium-thick line, and color it red." Because the video accelerator contains tools to draw and color circles, no additional instructions are needed from the CPU.

Video accelerators usually are specific in the roles they support—they do not speed up *all* video functions. Probably the most popular type of video accelerator is one that supports *bit blitting*—moving large numbers of pixels from one area of the screen to another. Programs that are extremely graphical in nature, such as Microsoft Windows, benefit greatly from a bit-blitting accelerator.

The alternative to the accelerator is the *graphics coprocessor*, a special-purpose CPU, similar to a math coprocessor. In the same way that a math coprocessor can speed up numerical calculations, a video coprocessor speeds up the entire process of creating and displaying graphic images.

A coprocessor varies from an accelerator in that it speeds up all video operations—not just certain tasks. Also, because a coprocessor is programmable, it can be upgraded as software improves and graphics functions are added. The most popular coprocessor boards are based on the Texas Instruments TI34010 and TI34020 CPU chips, although other proprietary coprocessors are available.

Just because your system has a coprocessor doesn't mean it always uses it. The adapter may use the coprocessor for its highest resolutions, but not for standard VGA. This situation, unfortunately, is very common. If you buy a video coprocessor, make sure that it supports all the video modes you want to use.

Local Bus Video: The Express Bus

You have already seen how the use of a video accelerator or coprocessor can speed up your video system. In both cases, a reduced number of instructions are sent to the video board for processing. It seems a natural next step to reduce the amount of time these instructions take to travel from the CPU to the video board. The two possible ways to do this are by speeding up the transfer or widening the transfer pathway.

When you work with expansion boards in your system, you face a limitation of the computer's basic architecture. You see, no matter how fast your CPU is, or how good your video coprocessor is, all data is transferred around inside the computer at a speed of 8 MHz—the speed of the computer's bus. You can think of a bus as a method of collecting and distributing electronic signals and information from one part of a computer to another. The parts of the bus you see (call it the "interface," if you like) are the expansion slots in which boards are placed.

Another characteristic of a bus is its data path. On the original IBM PCs, the data path of the bus was 8 bits wide. On IBM ATs and later machines, the width of the bus was widened to 16 bits. With a 16-bit-wide bus, twice as much information could be transferred in a single operation.

The combination of 8 MHz speed and an 8- or 16-bit data path are the most noticeable features of a bus type called ISA (Industry Standard Architecture). The two other types of buses are MCA and EISA. IBM uses MCA (Micro Channel Architecture) in many of their PS/2 computers. EISA (Enhanced Industry Standard Architecture) is a new bus type intended to offer the advanced features of MCA (at a lower price). One such feature, found on both MCA and EISA buses, is a 32-bit data path.

Local bus video combines the best of the two ways to speed things up. First, a local bus video board is placed in a special 32-bit-wide slot on the computer's motherboard. These special slots are not something you can just add to your system—you must buy a specific motherboard that incorporates them. The slots also communicate directly with the CPU, using a private bus that runs at the same speed as the CPU.

Can local bus video really make a difference? Consider a standard VGA board, which transfers data along a 16-bit-wide pathway at a speed of 8 MHz. A local bus slot on a 386DX or 486, 33MHz machine transfers data along a 32-bit-wide pathway at 33MHz. At twice the width and four times the speed, you can see what an improvement local bus video can make.

> *Some computer dealers are using a new term, "VL-bus" (VESA Local bus), to indicate local bus video. VL-bus boards meet the standards determined by VESA, the Video Electronics Standard Association. When buying a system with local bus video, make sure that it follows VESA standards.*

CRAM on Some Video Memory

Another aspect of the video system that you must consider is the amount of video memory needed to store high-resolution images in many colors. The higher the resolution you work with and the more colors you want, the more memory your video board requires. A standard VGA, for example, comes with 256K of RAM on the board, and can display 256 colors with 320x200 resolution. If you want to use the higher resolution mode, 640x480, you either have to work with 16 colors or add more memory to the board. A super VGA board displaying 256 colors at 1024x768 resolution requires 1M of RAM. The following table gives you an idea of the amount of memory these and several other video modes require:

Resolution	Number of Colors	Usual Memory Configuration
320x200	256	256K
640x480	16	256K
800x600	16	256K
1024x768	16	512K
640x480	256	512K

Resolution	Number of Colors	Usual Memory Configuration
800x600	256	512K
1024x768	256	1M

When you're adding memory to your video adapter board, remember this: You can't put any old memory chips on these boards. Video memory (often called "VRAM" or "Video RAM") is "dual-ported" RAM, which means that the computer can simultaneously write to and read from the memory. This is unlike normal RAM, which can either be written to or read from, but not both at once. Dual-ported RAM is very fast (read "expensive").

Get the Drivers

Drivers are special programs that other applications require to display an image on a screen. Most applications provide basic drivers for VGA systems. After VGA, however, there is no standard on how adapters create and display images, which means that each adapter board you buy needs its own drivers. If you use more than one MS-DOS application, you may need drivers for each one. Be sure that the board you buy has drivers for each mode the board supports. (An SVGA board that can display 640x480 and 1024x768 needs drivers for both modes, for example.)

Checking frequently with the manufacturer of your adapter to get the most recent drivers is important. Many companies provide the drivers for little or no cost, provided they are still in business. Often the manufacturer makes the drivers available on bulletin board services. Buying your adapters from a big-name company with a consistent track record is probably best—you may well avoid the problem of outdated drivers. And be sure to ask for the drivers for Microsoft Windows or OS/2 if you work with these systems.

> *Having trouble finding SVGA drivers? Many SVGA boards are based on the Tseng Laboratories ET4000 chip set. Drivers for one ET4000-based board may work on another.*

Video Component II—The Monitor

Your computer's monitor displays images on a screen by shooting a beam of electrons from an electron gun onto a phosphor-coated screen. When the beam strikes the screen, the phosphors glow for a very short time and then fade away. To keep a picture on the screen, the beam must continually sweep across the screen to keep the phosphors glowing. The beam scans the screen from side to side on one line, then drops down and scans another line, and so on until it reaches the bottom of the screen. Then the beam returns to the top of the screen to begin scanning again.

Two terms are used to describe the rates at which the electron beam scans. The *vertical scanning frequency*, or *vertical refresh rate* as it is sometimes called, describes the number of times per second the electron beam scans and repaints the entire screen. The *horizontal scanning frequency* describes the number of times per second the beam scans each line on the screen. These scanning frequencies work together and must also be supported by your video adapter board.

Cause To Flicker—Vertical Refresh Rate

If a monitor's electron beam repaints the screen too slowly, you may notice that the monitor flickers. A flickering monitor translates into eyestrain for the user using it. The point at which flicker is perceived varies from person to person, but for most people, a monitor that repaints the screen 60 times per second (60 Hz) is not perceived as flickering. In general, faster refresh rates translate into less visible flicker on-screen and reduced eyestrain.

Refresh rate is determined to a certain extent by the video mode you use. VGA screens generally are scanned at between 60 and 70 Hz. The scan rate for super VGA has been set by VESA at 72 Hz. At 50 Hz, almost everyone perceives flicker; at 60 Hz, you may not notice it, but it may tire your eyes; and at 72 Hz, the screen is essentially flicker-free.

> *The term "ergonomic" is sometimes used to refer to monitors that support a 72 Hz refresh rate.*

Horizontal Scanning Frequency

As an electron beam sweeps across the screen, it paints lines of dots. The number of lines and dots painted depends on the resolution of the screen. A VGA display, for example, may display 640 dots across the screen and 480 lines down. When considering the horizontal scanning frequency, we usually are concerned with the number of lines that must be scanned, and how fast they are scanned.

Consider a basic VGA display that refreshes the screen 60 times per second and has 480 lines on-screen. If the electron beam scans all 480 lines 60 times per second, the monitor has a scanning frequency of 28,800 lines per second, or 28.8 KHz. Super VGA using 1024x768 mode, refreshing at 72 Hz, has a scanning frequency of about 55.3 KHz.

> *Some monitors have extra lines that are scanned but which you can't see. When you examine the technical specifications for a monitor, the scanning frequency might appear higher because of this. Standard VGA, for example, usually specifies a scanning frequency of 31.5 KHz.*

Multisync Monitors

When a graphics adapter sends a signal to a monitor, the monitor must be able to handle both the refresh rate and the scanning frequency. These frequencies vary according to the mode you work with.

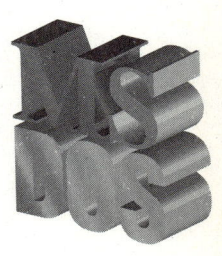

If you buy a *fixed frequency* monitor (one that locks the frequency for VGA), you might not be able to use it with a super VGA adapter board.

Multifrequency monitors (also called *multisync* or *multiscan*) can adjust themselves to a range of scanning frequencies. The higher the range, the more flexibility you have in using your monitor with different adapter boards, now or in the future. Some monitors automatically adjust themselves to any frequency within their range. Others work only with a small number of predefined frequencies (you might have to set or change them manually or through software).

> *When a multisync monitor switches modes (when you switch from a high-resolution graphical program like Microsoft Windows to a text-based DOS program, for example), it may make a clicking or popping sound and the picture may jump around for a few seconds or even momentarily disappear. This is perfectly normal.*

More Cause To Flicker—Interlaced versus Noninterlaced

Ideally a monitor should repaint the screen in one pass, scanning every line as it goes. Some monitors, instead of scanning every line, scan every other line (this is called *interlacing*). Scanning in this manner causes the electron beam to scan the screen *twice*—once for the even-numbered lines and once for the odd-numbered lines. If your eyes are sensitive to this type of scanning, you might see the screen flicker. Even if you do not see flicker, it is still there and can cause eye fatigue.

Noninterlaced monitors, which scan every line on the screen, from top to bottom, in a single pass, do not create flicker. These monitors cost more than interlaced monitors but are well worth the extra price. Before buying one, though, be sure that your video adapter board can produce a noninterlaced image.

Dot Pitch

Another important aspect of your monitor is its *dot pitch*—the distance between the dots on the screen. Dot pitch is measured in millimeters (mm); the larger the number, the farther apart are the dots on the screen and the grainier the image. A monitor with a .28mm dot pitch creates sharper images than one with a .31mm dot pitch. On a small screen, a smaller dot pitch such as .28mm is better to have. On a larger screen, a dot pitch of .31mm or even .34mm produces good results.

Erasing the Screen with CLS

The CLS command is used to erase the entire display. Anything displayed on-screen is cleared and the cursor returns to the home position (the screen's upper left corner). If you have enabled enhanced screen colors or attributes, they remain in effect when the screen is cleared. The CLS command affects only what is on the screen, not what is in memory.

Getting Fancy with ANSI

ANSI.SYS, a device driver supplied with MS-DOS, controls certain display functions, such as screen color, text attributes, cursor position, and display modes. The ability to control the screen is most useful when you are working at the DOS command prompt, or using simple programs that don't control the screen directly.

Many of the application programs you work with control the screen colors and other attributes for you. Lotus 1-2-3, for example, is responsible for creating the blue borders around a worksheet and the color of text in a protected cell, among other attributes. Programs such as Word Perfect have a comprehensive setup program that enables you to control not only the color of the screen, but also the text attributes. When you use application programs like these, you don't need to use ANSI.SYS.

Before you can work with the screen-control functions, you must install ANSI.SYS in your CONFIG.SYS file. To install the device driver, enter either...

    DEVICE=C:\DOS\ANSI.SYS

or...

    DEVICEHIGH=C:\DOS\ANSI.SYS

...in CONFIG.SYS. This statement assumes that the MS-DOS utility files are stored in your C:\DOS directory. You might be able to load the device driver into an upper-memory block on your computer. To do so, just change the word "device" to "devicehigh." ANSI.SYS occupies about 4.1K of memory space.

ANSI and the PROMPT Command

Many of the functions ANSI controls can be activated by using the MS-DOS PROMPT command. You are probably already familiar with using this command to display the name of the current directory and the greater-than (>) sign. (If not, the command is PROMPT PG.) You can use PROMPT to display several other system parameters, such as time and date or MS-DOS version number. Table 14.5 lists the parameters available for use with PROMPT.

Table 14.5
PROMPT Parameters

Parameter	Displays
$Q	= (equal sign)
$$	$ (dollar sign)
$T	System time
$D	System date
$P	Current drive and directory
$V	MS-DOS version number
$N	Current drive

Parameter	Displays
$G	> (greater than sign)
$L	< (less than sign)
$B	| (vertical bar sign)
$_	Carriage return-linefeed
$H	Backspace
$E	ASCII code 27 (the Escape character)

ANSI.SYS doesn't normally have to be active on your system for you to use these PROMPT parameters. In one instance, however, you do need to use the device driver—when you're using the $E (escape) parameter. Use the escape parameter with other control codes in the PROMPT command to set or change characteristics of the screen, such as screen color, text color, text attributes, and cursor location.

Using PROMPT To Set Screen Attributes

To control the visual characteristics of text on a display—including attributes such as bold, underline, blinking, and reverse video—use the ANSI.SYS device driver in combination with the PROMPT command. You can use these commands also to change the color of the text and of the screen.

To set the color of the screen as well as the color and attributes of the text, issue an ANSI control code sequence following this general format:

    Esc[N;N;N...M

In this statement, `Esc[` is typed as **$E[**. In the remainder of the statement, substitute the text attribute, foreground (text) color, and background color values separated by semicolons. Don't forget to add the M, to indicate to MS-DOS that you want to work with the settings for display colors. See table 14.6 for a list of these settings.

Table 14.6
Display Settings for ANSI.SYS

Text Code	Attributes Effect
0	All attributes default
1	Bold text
4	Underline text
5	Blinking text
7	Reverse video
8	Hidden text

Foreground Code	Color Effect	Background Code	Color Effect
30	Black	40	Black
31	Red	41	Red
32	Green	42	Green
33	Yellow	43	Yellow
34	Blue	44	Blue
35	Magenta	45	Magenta
36	Cyan	46	Cyan
37	White	47	White

Suppose that you want to change the color of your display from the default black to blue. At the same time, you want to enable the bold attribute for the text, to make it easier to read on the blue background. To set the display with these characteristics, enter the following PROMPT command...

    PROMPT $E[1;37;44M

This command tells MS-DOS to display bold, white text on a blue background. And you probably should add the path and greater-than sign to this prompt statement; otherwise, you'll get a blank screen. Just add **PG** at the end of the preceding statement without spaces or punctuation.

You can use the PROMPT statement to create some interesting effects. Suppose, for example, that you want to create a prompt that displays the date and time and then, on the next line, the path in one color and the greater-than sign in another color. To create this prompt, enter...

```
PROMPT $D$_$T$_$E[1;31M$P$E[1;36M$G
```

In the preceding command, $D displays the date, $_ creates a carriage return-line feed, and $T displays the time. Then, carriage return-line feed and set the colors—bold, red path and bold cyan greater-than sign. Everything you type at the command line will be in cyan, because that is the last color command encountered by MS-DOS.

Using ANSI To Move the Cursor

In addition to using ANSI and PROMPT to change the display colors and text attributes, you can use them to control the cursor's location on the screen. That is, you can specify the exact row and column coordinates at which you want the cursor to appear. To do this, you type the escape character, followed by a particular cursor-movement command. Take care when you use these codes—they are case-sensitive. Table 14.7 lists the codes available for controlling the cursor's position.

These codes are case-sensitive (small f, not capital F).

Table 14.7
Cursor-Movement Commands

Command	Effect
Esc[*row,col*H	Moves cursor to specified row and column; if no row and column are specified, cursor returns to row 0, column 0.
Esc[*row,col*f	Same as Esc[*row,col*H.
Esc[*lines*A	Moves cursor up by specified number of lines.

continues

Table 14.7, Continued
Cursor-Movement Commands

Command	Effect
Esc[*lines*B	Moves cursor down by specified number of lines.
Esc[*columns*C	Moves cursor right a specified number of columns; if number is not specified, cursor moves one column to right. If cursor is at right edge of screen, it won't wrap to next line.
Esc[*columns*D	Moves cursor left a specified number of columns; if number is not specified, cursor moves one column to left. If cursor is at left edge of screen, it won't wrap to preceding line.
Esc[s	Saves cursor's current position.
Esc[u	Restores cursor to position saved with Esc[s.
Esc[2J	Clears screen and returns cursor to row 0, column 0.
Esc[K	Erases any characters from cursor position to end of line.

Let's look at an example. Suppose that you want to display the system date and time in the upper left corner of the screen and that you want the cursor to return to the beginning of the next line. To set up your screen for this example, enter...

```
PROMPT $E[0;50H$D $T$_$P$G
```

In this example, the $E[0;50H indicates that the cursor is to be moved to row 0, column 50. Then the date is displayed ($D), followed by two spaces, followed by the time ($T). The cursor is returned to the next line with the carriage return-line feed control code, $_. Although you can move the cursor to the beginning of the next line in other ways, the easiest way probably is to use the carriage return-line feed code.

Practice combining different attributes with a complex PROMPT statement. Create a prompt that displays the date and time in the upper left corner of the display in cyan and then returns the cursor to the beginning of the next line. Then set the prompt to display the path in red, with two greater-than signs in green.

To create such a prompt, enter...

```
PROMPT $E[1;36M$E[0;50;H$D $T$E[K$_$E[1;31M$P$E[1;32M$G$G
```

An Alternative to DOSKEY Macros

DOSKEY provides you not only command recall, but keyboard-macro capability as well. The price you pay for macros is memory, however. There is an alternative to using DOSKEY if you can't spare the memory—you can reprogram your keyboard using ANSI.SYS and batch file. This sounds technical, but it's really quite easy.

First, make sure ANSI.SYS is installed. Suppose, for example, that you want to reprogram F1 to change to the A drive each time you press it. To do this, execute this command:

```
PROMPT $e[0;59;"A:";13p
```

As you know, the $e characters is PROMPT's way of inserting the escape character. The scan code for F1 is 0;59. The drive designation "A:" is put in quotes to show what F1 is being programmed to do. Finally, 13p is the scan code for the Enter key.

Each time you press F1, an A: automatically prints on the screen, and the Enter character is sent to the printer, changing to drive A. Using this technique, you can also launch any DOS command, any executable program, or batch file.

Instead of manually entering this ANSI sequence every time you boot up, the most effective way is to put all these commands in your AUTOEXEC.BAT file, or (better still) put them in a batch file called NEWKEYS.BAT, which can be called from within AUTOEXEC.BAT with the CALL command.

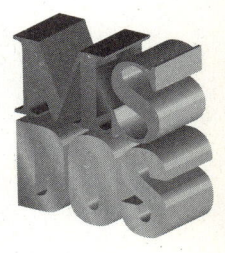

Although you can use PROMPT statements to set these ANSI sequences, they must be inserted before an ECHO OFF statement in the batch file because the sequences display on-screen. Thus, it is better to use another technique using ECHO.

Many word processors (WordPerfect and Word, for example) and text editors enable you to directly insert the escape character, which is displayed as a left arrow. This insertion is done by holding down the Alt key, entering **27** on the numeric pad, and releasing Alt. The DOS 6.2 Editor is an excellent choice for building NEWKEYS.BAT. To insert the escape character, press Ctrl+P, and then press Esc. Here's a sample NEWKEYS.BAT file that includes all 12 F keys:

```
echo {ESC}[0;59;"A:";13p
echo {ESC}[0;60;"B:";13p
echo {ESC}[0;61;"C:";13p
echo {ESC}[0;62;"dir /p";13p
echo {ESC}[0;63;"xcopy a:*.* c: /w";13p
echo {ESC}[0;64;0;64p
echo {ESC}[0;65;"xcopy b:*.* c: /w";13p
echo {ESC}[0;66;"xcopy c:*.* a: /w";13p
echo {ESC}[0;67"del *.*";13p
echo {ESC}[0;68;"cls";13p
echo {ESC}[0;133;"edit";13p
echo {ESC}[0;134;"my.bat";13p
```

TIP: If you use CTTY NUL to prevent the screen echo, make sure the preceding commands execute before the CTTY NUL command. See Chapter 15 for details on using CTTY NUL.

Notice the /W switch with XCOPY, which causes XCOPY to wait for you to insert the proper disk before it begins copying. You can use it as a safeguard to see that everything is okay before you begin.

Note also that there is no programming statement for F6 (scan code 0;64) because its the end of file marker (^Z). If you don't use COPY CON much, go ahead and reprogram F6.

> *Reprogramming the function keys in this manner does not affect the function keys in your application programs, such as word processing programs. Such programs take over the keyboard directly.*

If you need to change the keys back to their default values, OLDFKEYS.BAT does it quickly, as follows:

```
@echo off
echo {ESC}[0;59;0;59p
echo {ESC}[0;60;0;60p
echo {ESC}[0;61;0;61p
echo {ESC}[0;62;0;62p
echo {ESC}[0;63;0;63p
echo {ESC}[0;64;0;64p
echo {ESC}[0;65;0;65p
echo {ESC}[0;66;0;66p
echo {ESC}[0;67;0;67p
echo {ESC}[0;68;0;68p
echo {ESC}[0;133;0;133p
echo {ESC}[0;134;0;134p
```

Using MODE CO80,50 To Display 50 Lines

In the preceding section, you worked with PROMPT commands that set attributes for the screen. Although ANSI and PROMPT work well together to control these functions, there is no function or combination of functions that changes the number of lines on the screen. To do that, you use the MODE command. The general form of the command is as follows:

    MODE DISPLAY,LINES

Table 14.8 lists the options available for the *display*. The number of *lines* can be 25, 43, or 50 for most displays (except monochrome and CGA). Changing the number of lines on these displays is not possible. Figure 14.3, shown in three examples, shows the differences in the number of lines displayed on a VGA display.

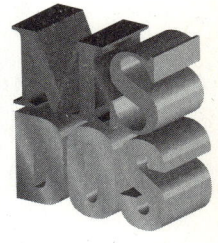

Chapter 14: *Using DOS Utilities*

Table 14.8
Display Settings for MODE Command

Setting	Effect
40 or 80	Indicates the number of columns of the display
bw40 or bw80	Indicates a monochrome display and the number of columns
co40 or co80	Indicates a color display and the number of columns

Figure 14.3

Directory displays showing 25-line, 43-line, and 50-line displays.

```
Volume in drive C is MS-DOS_5
Volume Serial Number is 199A-65C2
Directory of C:\DOS

.            <DIR>        06-04-92   10:45a
..           <DIR>        06-04-92   10:45a
EGA      SYS      4885   12-23-92    6:00a
FORMAT   COM     22591   12-23-92    6:00a
NLSFUNC  EXE      7036   12-23-92    6:00a
COUNTRY  SYS     17066   12-23-92    6:00a
EGA      CPI     58870   12-23-92    6:00a
ASSIGN   COM      6399   05-08-91   12:00p
HIMEM    SYS     14144   12-23-92    6:00a
KEYB     COM     14983   12-23-92    6:00a
COMP     EXE     14282   05-08-91   12:00p
KEYBOARD SYS     34694   12-23-92    6:00a
ANSI     SYS      9065   12-23-92    6:00a
ATTRIB   EXE     11165   12-23-92    6:00a
CHOICE   COM      1754   12-23-92    6:00a
CHKDSK   EXE     12267   12-23-92    6:00a
EDIT     COM       413   12-23-92    6:00a
DBLSPACE BIN     50848   12-23-92    6:00a
DOSHELP  TXT      1540   05-08-91   12:00p
Press any key to continue . . .
```

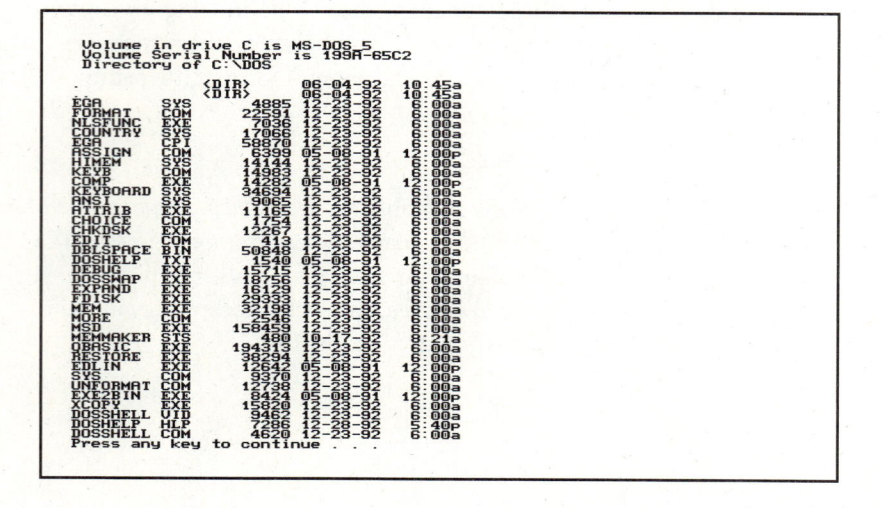

```
Volume in drive C is MS-DOS_5
Volume Serial Number is 199A-65C2
Directory of C:\DOS

.            <DIR>        06-04-92   10:45a
..           <DIR>        06-04-92   10:45a
EGA      SYS      4885   12-23-92    6:00a
FORMAT   COM     22591   12-23-92    6:00a
NLSFUNC  EXE      7036   12-23-92    6:00a
COUNTRY  SYS     17066   12-23-92    6:00a
EGA      CPI     58870   12-23-92    6:00a
ASSIGN   COM      6399   05-08-91   12:00p
HIMEM    SYS     14144   12-23-92    6:00a
KEYB     COM     14983   12-23-92    6:00a
COMP     EXE     14282   05-08-91   12:00p
KEYBOARD SYS     34694   12-23-92    6:00a
ANSI     SYS      9065   12-23-92    6:00a
ATTRIB   EXE     11165   12-23-92    6:00a
CHOICE   COM      1754   12-23-92    6:00a
CHKDSK   EXE     12267   12-23-92    6:00a
EDIT     COM       413   12-23-92    6:00a
DBLSPACE BIN     50848   12-23-92    6:00a
DOSHELP  TXT      1540   05-08-91   12:00p
DEBUG    EXE     15715   12-23-92    6:00a
DOSSWAP  EXE     18757   12-23-92    6:00a
EXPAND   EXE     16129   12-23-92    6:00a
FDISK    EXE     29333   12-23-92    6:00a
MEM      EXE     32198   12-23-92    6:00a
MORE     COM      2545   12-23-92    6:00a
MSD      EXE    158459   12-23-92    6:00a
MEMMAKER STS       480   10-17-92    8:21a
QBASIC   EXE    194313   12-23-92    6:00a
RESTORE  EXE     38294   12-23-92    6:00a
EDLIN    EXE     12642   05-08-91   12:00p
SYS      COM      9370   12-23-92    6:00a
UNFORMAT COM     17738   12-23-92    6:00a
EXE2BIN  EXE      8424   05-08-91   12:00p
XCOPY    EXE     15820   12-23-92    6:00a
DOSSHELL VID      9462   12-23-92    6:00a
DOSHELP  HLP      7286   12-28-92    5:40p
DOSSHELL COM      4620   12-23-92    6:00a
Press any key to continue . . .
```

```
Volume in drive C is MS-DOS_5
Volume Serial Number is 199A-65C2
Directory of C:\DOS
.            <DIR>       06-04-92  10:45a
..           <DIR>       06-04-92  10:45a
EGA      SYS      4885  12-23-92   6:00a
FORMAT   COM     22591  12-23-92   6:00a
NLSFUNC  EXE      7036  12-23-92   6:00a
COUNTRY  SYS     17066  12-23-92   6:00a
EGA      CPI     58870  12-23-92   6:00a
ASSIGN   COM      6399  05-08-91  12:00p
HIMEM    SYS     14144  12-23-92   6:00a
KEYB     COM     14983  12-23-92   6:00a
COMP     EXE     14282  05-08-91  12:00p
KEYBOARD SYS     34694  12-23-92   6:00a
ANSI     SYS      9065  12-23-92   6:00a
ATTRIB   EXE     11165  12-23-92   6:00a
CHOICE   COM      1754  12-23-92   6:00a
CHKDSK   EXE     12267  12-23-92   6:00a
EDIT     COM       413  12-23-92   6:00a
DBLSPACE BIN     50848  12-23-92   6:00a
DOSHELP  TXT      1540  05-08-91  12:00p
DEBUG    EXE     15715  12-23-92   6:00a
DOSSWAP  EXE     18756  12-23-92   6:00a
EXPAND   EXE     16129  12-23-92   6:00a
FDISK    EXE     29333  12-23-92   6:00a
MEM      EXE     32198  12-23-92   6:00a
MORE     COM      2546  12-23-92   6:00a
MSD      EXE    158459  12-23-92   8:21a
MEMMAKER STS       480  10-17-92   6:00a
QBASIC   EXE    194313  12-23-92   6:00a
RESTORE  EXE     38294  12-23-92   6:00a
EDLIN    EXE     12642  05-08-91  12:00p
SYS      COM      9370  12-23-92   6:00a
UNFORMAT COM     12738  12-23-92   6:00a
EXE2BIN  EXE      8424  05-08-91  12:00p
XCOPY    EXE     15820  12-23-92   6:00a
DOSSHELL VID      9462  12-23-92   6:00a
DOSHELP  HLP      7286  12-28-92   5:40p
DOSSHELL COM      4620  12-23-92   6:00a
DOSSHELL GRB      4421  12-23-92   6:00a
DEFRAG   EXE     74657  12-23-92   6:00a
GORILLA  BAS     29998  10-23-92   8:29a
GRAFTABL COM     11205  05-08-91  12:00p
DEFRAG   HLP      9227  12-23-92   6:00a
MOUSE    COM     56408  12-23-92   6:00a
QBASIC   HLP    130810  12-23-92   6:00a
Press any key to continue . . .
```

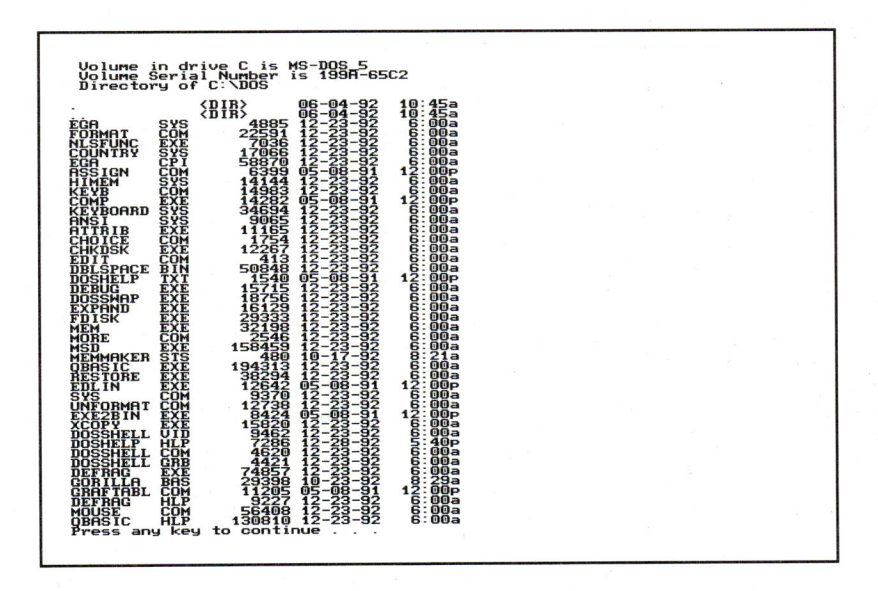

Suppose that you have a standard VGA display, which defaults to 80 columns by 25 lines, and that you want to fit more of the DIR display on your screen. To display 50 lines, for example, rather than the usual 25, type...

MODE CO80,50

To return to the default of 25 lines, type...

MODE CO80

Remember that for this command to work, the device driver ANSI.SYS must be installed in your CONFIG.SYS file. And be aware that all display systems might not support the command.

Printing

You can use a variety of utilities to control your printer when you're working with MS-DOS. When you work with application programs you don't need to use any of these commands, because the application program controls the printer for you. But you might have to install a specific printer driver for the applications. This printer driver—not MS-DOS—tells the computer what kind of printer you have.

MS-DOS knows your printer, not by the name "HP LaserJet III" or "Epson LQ1050," but rather by the physical port the printer's connected to. MS-DOS supports three *parallel* printer ports (LPT1, LPT2, and LPT3) as well as four *serial* ports, to which you can connect printers (among other things). Connecting a parallel printer to a serial port is possible. If you do this, you must tell MS-DOS to redirect the output from the parallel port (as the application software sees it) to the serial port (as MS-DOS and the hardware see it).

This section begins with a discussion of the MODE command, which is used to control a serial printer, redirect output, and resolve timeout problems. The PRINT command, used to print ASCII text files, and the GRAPHICS command, used to print graphics screens, are discussed also.

Using Serial Printers

When you connect a serial printer to one of your computer's serial ports, you have to tell MS-DOS how to communicate with that printer. (You don't have to do this when you work with parallel printers.) With serial printers, more communications settings are involved than with parallel printers.

The MODE command sets the system's serial port parameters. The parameters defined in the MODE command must match the communication parameters of the printer connected to the port. Refer to your printer's user manual to determine the communication parameters for your printer.

The general form of the command is as follows:

```
MODE COMn B,P,D,S,R
```

COM*n* refers to the name of the communications (serial) port the printer is connected to. It can be COM1, COM2, COM3, or COM4.

B is the *baud rate*—the speed at which data is sent to the printer. Valid baud rates are 110, 150, 300, 600, 1200, 2400, 4800, 9600, and 19200.

P is the *parity*—used on some systems for error checking. Values for parity are none, even, odd, mark, space. The default value when working with printers is even.

D is the number of *data bits*—the number of bits used to make up each character. With PCs, each character (or byte) consists of 8 bits. With some systems, however, only 7 bits are used to define each character. The possible values are 5 through 8. With serial printers, the default is 7.

S is the number of *stop bits*—used to mark the end of each character. The possible values for stop bits are 1 or 2. If your printer's baud rate is 110, the number of stop bits is 2. For all other baud rates, 1 stop bit is used.

R is the *retry value*—used by MS-DOS to determine what action to take in the event the printer is not responding or is not available. The possible actions are as follows:

> **E** checks status of a busy port and returns an error.
>
> **B** checks status of a busy port and returns a busy message.
>
> **P** continues retrying until the port accepts the output.
>
> **R** checks status of a busy port and returns a ready message.
>
> **N** takes no retry action (this is the default).

See the next section for a more complete discussion of the retry value.

> *Note: Generally, the name of your serial port(s) is determined by jumpers or DIP switches on the serial board or by configuring the serial port with software. On ISA motherboards, only two serial ports can be active at one time—COM1/COM2, COM3/COM4, COM2/COM3, or COM1/COM4—because COM1 and COM3 use the same interrupt, and COM2 and COM4 use another interrupt. ISA does not support interrupt sharing.*

Suppose, after checking your printer manual, that you wanted to configure your COM1 port for 2400 baud, no parity checking, 8 data bits, 1 stop bit, and continuous retry. To set up the port for these parameters, enter...

```
MODE COM1 2400,N,8,1,P
```

The N stands for no parity checking.

Redirecting Ports with MODE

You might, on occasion, need to connect a parallel printer to a serial port, but your software expects to communicate with the printer through a parallel port. The most common example of this type of situation is when you use a printer-sharing device. With a *printer-sharing* device, you can connect more than one PC to a printer. A typical printer-sharing device supports both parallel and serial ports. You use the parallel ports to connect PCs that are 6 feet or less from the device; the serial ports are used to connect PCs that can be as much as 50 feet away.

Suppose that you have a serial connection to a printer-sharing device. Because the printer you are ultimately connecting to is parallel, and that's what your software expects (some software doesn't recognize serial ports), you need to *redirect* the output from one port to another. That is, you must make your software (and ultimately MS-DOS) think that it is communicating with the parallel port, when in fact it is communicating with the serial port.

Before redirecting the output, you must define the communications parameters for the serial port. Then you can redirect the output. Use these commands to redirect LPT1 to COM1...

```
MODE COM1 9600,N,8,1,R
MODE LPT1:=COM1:
```

To specify any other port, simply substitute the appropriate port names. Any parallel port can be redirected to any serial port.

NOTE: *Sometimes you see the name of a port followed by a colon, as in LPT1:, and sometimes the colon is not part of the name, as in LPT1. Both forms are equivalent.*

Identifying and Resolving Timeout Problems

When MS-DOS attempts to access a printer port on your computer, the port might not be available. The printer might be off-line or already in use, or there might be some other problem with communications. When any of these problems occur, the system *times out*—it stops trying to send information through the port and instead generates an error.

If you are working at the DOS command prompt and get a printer timeout error, you can usually select "Retry" in response to the error. The printer might then be able to print. Application programs have different ways of handling the timeout problem; the program you are using determines what your response should be. In some situations, your system might just freeze.

To avoid these problems, you can use the retry value of "P" with the MODE command to tell MS-DOS to try to send information to the printer forever. Enter...

```
MODE LPT1: ,,P
```

...to enable infinite retry. The two commas are required; they act as placeholders for the values the MODE command normally expects.

Before using this command, be sure that a printer is connected to your system. Otherwise, your system will lock up the first time you try to print.

TIP: *If you are using the MODE command to control a network printer, do not use any of the retry values.*

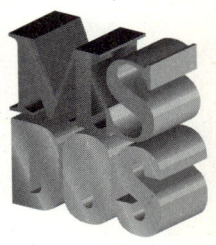

Controlling Screen Prints with GRAPHICS

As you learned earlier, your monitor uses two display modes: text mode and graphics mode. MS-DOS and most DOS applications display in text mode. When you press PrtScr on your keyboard, the text displayed on your monitor prints on your printer. When you have graphics displayed, however, the screen does not print properly when you press PrtScr. To print the graphic image, you need to use the MS-DOS command GRAPHICS.

The GRAPHICS command enables you to print graphics on a printer. GRAPHICS, a memory-resident program, interprets the display that you see as graphics to something your printer can understand and print properly. If the display contains text, the GRAPHICS command has no effect and passes the text directly to the printer. And GRAPHICS has no effect if the printer you are using does not have a graphics mode.

Using the GRAPHICS Command

The GRAPHICS command supports CGA, EGA, and VGA graphics modes. Before using PrtScr to print any graphics, enter...

```
GRAPHICS [PRINTER] [D:PATH\FILENAME] [/R] [/B] [/LCD]
```

The *PRINTER* parameter indicates the type of printer you are printing to. The GRAPHICS command uses the printer type to determine how to convert what is on the screen to what should be printed on the printer. The printer types supported by the GRAPHICS command are in table 14.9.

Table 14.9
Printer Types Supported by GRAPHICS

Type	Description of Printer
COLOR1	IBM PC Color Printer (black ribbon)
COLOR4	IBM PC Color Printer (red, green, blue, and black ribbon)
COLOR8	IBM PC Color Printer (cyan, magenta, yellow, and black ribbon)

Type	Description of Printer
HPDEFAULT	Any Hewlett-Packard PCL printer
DESKJET	Hewlett-Packard DeskJet printer
GRAPHICS	IBM Personal Graphics printer, IBM Proprinter, or IBM Quietwriter printer
GRAPHICSWIDE	IBM Personal Graphics printer (11-inch-wide carriage)
LASERJET	Hewlett-Packard LaserJet printer
LASERJETII	Hewlett-Packard LaserJet II printer
PAINTJET	Hewlett-Packard PaintJet printer
QUIETJET	Hewlett-Packard QuietJet printer
QUIETJETPLUS	Hewlett-Packard QuietJet Plus printer
RUGGEDWRITER	Hewlett-Packard RuggedWriter printer
RUGGEDWRITERWIDE	Hewlett-Packard RuggedWriterWide printer
THERMAL	IBM PC-compatible Thermal printer
THINKJET	Hewlett-Packard ThinkJet printer

D:*PATH\FILE NAME* specifies the location and name of the printer profile.

/R causes the graphics to be printed as they appear on-screen—in reverse. (That is, graphics are printed with white characters on a black background instead of the usual black characters on a white background.)

/B is used with color printers to enable or disable printing of the background. You must use the /B switch if you want the color background of your graphics display to print on the printer; otherwise, the background is the color of the paper. Use this switch only if you have specified color4 or color8 as the printer type.

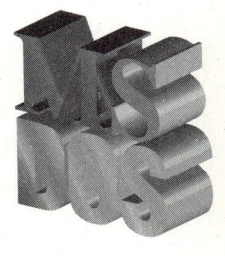

/LCD is used to print, with the proper aspect ratio, images displayed on LCD (liquid crystal display) monitors. If the /LCD switch is not specified, the graphics are printed with the default CGA aspect ratio.

Modifying the Printer Profile

Normally, you use GRAPHICS.PRO, the printer profile included with MS-DOS. Because this is the default file, normally located in the DOS directory, specifying it in the command is not necessary. If you need to access special capabilities of your printer, however, you'll have to modify GRAPHICS.PRO to suit your needs. To modify the profile used by GRAPHICS, first make a backup copy of the file GRAPHICS.PRO, which is located in the DOS directory. Then edit the file, using your printer manual to obtain the proper codes to activate the functions you want.

> **NOTE** *Neither the structure nor the syntax of GRAPHICS.PRO is documented. You'll have to study the file to see how it's structured. Then, if you are familiar with your printer's control codes and capabilities, you should be able to modify GRAPHICS.PRO to suit your needs.*

After you edit the profile, you might want to save it with a different name. If you do so, remember to use the new file's name when you invoke the GRAPHICS command.

Printing a Graphics Screen

To print the contents of a graphics screen, press the Shift+PrtScr combination. If your computer uses 320x480 color graphics mode and the printer type you specify is graphics or color1, the GRAPHICS command prints the display in as many as four shades of gray. If the computer is in 640x480 color graphics mode, the screen is printed sideways on the paper.

You can't use the Shift+PrtScr combination to print the contents of a screen to a PostScript printer. PostScript is a "printer definition language," which means that anything sent to the printer must be accompanied by the proper programming commands for the printer. If you press PrtScr or Shift+PrtScr, your printer starts printing page after page of PostScript programming commands rather than the screen print you expected.

Background Printing with PRINT

The MS-DOS PRINT command is a memory-resident utility that enables background processing of print jobs. Background printing lets you continue working with your PC while MS-DOS prints files to your printer. Because printing in the background is a multitasking activity, the PRINT command has parameters that control the amount of CPU time allocated to the PRINT function.

In a *multitasking* environment on a PC, a single CPU is shared among all the currently running applications. If you choose to PRINT in the background, you might want to increase or decrease the amount of time the CPU allocates to this process. Multitasking options are just some of the options you can specify with the PRINT command.

The general form of the PRINT command is as follows:

```
PRINT [/D:DEVICE] [/B:BUFSIZE] [/U:BUSYTICK] ]/M:MAXTICK]
[/S:TIMESLICE] [/Q:MAXFILES] [/T] [D:PATH\FILENAME(S)/C]
[/P]
```

/D:*DEVICE* specifies which device you want to print to. For a parallel printer, you can specify PRN, LPT1, LPT2, or LPT3. For a serial printer, the value can be COM1, COM2, COM3, or COM4. If you do not specify a device, you are prompted for one. The default is PRN (this is the same as LPT1). PRN and LPT1 are interchangeable. Although PRN is used as LPT1, it cannot be used as LPT2 or LPT3.

/B:*BUFSIZE* sets the size of the internal print buffer. The default is 512 bytes (about 1/4 page) and the maximum is 16,384 bytes (about 8 pages). Increasing the buffer size usually makes printing faster.

/U:*BUSYTICK* specifies the number of clock ticks (each 1/18 of a second) the PRINT program waits for a printer to become available. The default is 1, but you can specify up to 255.

/M:*MAXTICK* indicates the maximum number of clock ticks the printer can use to print any individual character. If the time is exceeded, an error is generated. The default is 2; 255 is the maximum.

/S:*TIMESLICE* sets the number of clock ticks allocated for background printing. The default is 8; 1-255 are allowed. If you increase the timeslice value, background printing gets a greater share of the CPU's time, causing any other applications you may be using to run slower.

/Q:*MAXFILES* specifies the maximum number of files that can be placed in the *print queue* (a list of files waiting to be printed). The default is 10, but you can specify from 4 to 32 files.

/T clears the print queue.

D:*PATH\FILE NAME(S)* indicates the file(s) to be printed.

/C cancels printing of a specified file.

/P places a file in the print queue and puts PRINT in print mode.

To load the PRINT command with all its default settings, type...

```
PRINT
```

MS-DOS responds with a message that the program has been installed...

```
Name of list device [PRN]:
Resident part of PRINT installed
PRINT queue is empty
```

Alternatively, you can specify a file name to be printed. This form of the command can be used whenever you want to print something to your printer. If you use the options that control clock ticks, you must specify them only the first time you issue the PRINT command.

> **NOTE** *The PRINT command cannot be used on a network printer. Most network operating systems have their own commands to queue and print in the background.*

Exploring Shell Programs and Program Launchers

When you work with MS-DOS commands at the command prompt, you are interacting with a program called COMMAND.COM, the MS-DOS *command interpreter*. The command interpreter enables you to control your disks, files, and any devices that are attached to your system. For some people, interfaces like COMMAND.COM are not very easy to work with. Many users find the syntax of the commands somewhat cryptic and become frustrated trying to master them.

Alternatives to the DOS command prompt exist, in the form of a program called a *shell*, which is an application program that works with MS-DOS but presents a somewhat prettier face. DOS shell programs tend to be graphical, with menus and dialog boxes from which to select commands. This section introduces you to The Norton Desktop for DOS. The Norton Desktop is just one example of many fine programs that provide a shell and a package of useful utilities. Here are some others you might consider:

- ✔ XTree and XTree Gold
- ✔ Lotus Magellan
- ✔ PC Tools
- ✔ Geoworks Desktop
- ✔ Mace Utilities

- ✔ DirectAccess DOS
- ✔ Norton Commander
- ✔ DESQview
- ✔ Windows

A Brief Look at the Norton Desktop for DOS

The Norton Desktop for DOS is one example of the type of program you can buy that provides you with a simple graphical interface for DOS. It has many of the same features as the DOS Shell, with a few exceptions.

Unfortunately, the Norton Desktop doesn't have a Task Swapper (or any other method that enables you to work with several programs simultaneously). Rather, Norton Desktop concentrates on file utilities. The program contains all the usual menu options for moving, copying, renaming, and deleting files, as well as options for working with directories. It adds other options to the list—options for data recovery, file compression, and file protection. Figure 14.4 displays some of the options with Norton Desktop.

Figure 14.4

Some of the options in the Norton Desktop for DOS.

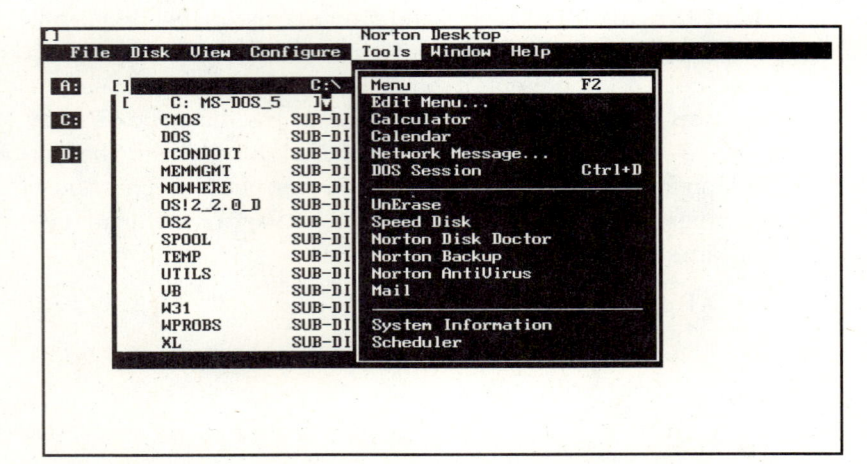

When you click on the Tools menu in Norton Desktop, you see several options that represent the basic set of Norton Utilities. You see options for programs such as...

UnErase gets back deleted files.

Speed Disk unfragments your hard disk. (Don't use this program with a DoubleSpace disk!)

Norton Disk Doctor tries to fix damaged files.

AntiVirus detects and eradicates viruses.

System Information provides information about the configuration of your system.

Scheduler, **Mail**, **\Calendar**, **Calculator** is a set of personal productivity tools.

With the Norton Desktop, as with the MS-DOS Shell, you can launch programs by double-clicking on their names in the directory list. But you can't create program groups in which to store icons.

Looking at QBASIC

Unlike IBM's BASICA and Microsoft's GWBASIC, QBASIC (a scaled-down version of QuickBasic, that first shipped with DOS 5) is a real programming language that enables you to do some pretty sophisticated stuff. Admit it, you like GORILLA.BAS!

Even an introduction to QBASIC programming is beyond the scope of this book, but this chapter includes a few sample programs for you to play with.

Screen Savers

Today's high-tech VGA screens don't really need screen-saving, but users like them anyway. Three lines of code create the simplest screen saver around, SSS.BAS (SimpleScreenSaver):

```
CLS
WHILE INKEY$ = "": WEND
SYSTEM
```

> *In case you forgot, you can run a QBASIC program from the command line by entering* **QBASIC /RUN <program name>**. *Also, you might want to write batch files to launch QBASIC programs.*

This blanks your screen until you press any key, at which time (because of the SYSTEM command) you return to DOS. You may want a prettier screen than this, however, so with a few more lines of code you can create STARS.BAS, as follows:

```
DEFINT A-Z
RANDOMIZE TIMER
VidMode = 9
VHeight = 350
VWidth = 640
SCREEN VidMode
WHILE INKEY$ = ""
VColor = RND * 15
y = VHeight * RND
x = VWidth * RND
PSET (x, y), VColor
WEND
SCREEN 0
SYSTEM
```

A Screen-Message Program

QBASIC and Quick BASIC are capable of creating powerful programs. If you are interested in easy Windows programming, Microsoft Visual BASIC is astounding.

Here's a simple, practical, little program that serves two purposes: it is a while-you-were-out messaging program and a screen saver (when no security is required). Run the program, and then type in a short message that you want to appear on the screen while you are away from the computer. The message (in random colors) and the current time change positions on the screen to prevent burn-in. If you don't want to display a message, press Enter. The program is as follows:

```
CLS : W = 40: WIDTH W
INPUT "Message to display: "; R$
S = LEN(R$)
RANDOMIZE TIMER
Back1:
ROWNUM = INT(RND * 20) + 1
COLNUM = INT(RND * (W - 5)) + 1
CLS
IF INKEY$ <> "" THEN SYSTEM
COLOR (ROWNUM MOD 8) + 8
LOCATE ROWNUM, COLNUM
PRINT R$
L = 1
ROWNUM = INT(RND * 20) + 1
COLNUM = INT(RND * (W - 8)) + 1
COLOR (ROWNUM MOD 8) + 8
Back2:
LOCATE ROWNUM, COLNUM
IF L >= 1000 THEN GOTO Back1
PRINT TIME$;
L = L + 1
GOTO Back2
SYSTEM
```

This program is also useful for telling those you trust how to use the utility so they can leave you a message. Be warned, however, that messages are not saved; once you exit, the current message is gone.

If you do not have a color monitor, delete the two COLOR (ROWNUM MOD 8) + 8 lines. You can also decrease the type size by changing W=40 to **W=80**. You can also decrease or increase the interval at which the screen changes by editing the IF L >= 1000 THEN GOTO Back1 line (the smaller the number, the faster the screen changes).

> **AUTHOR'S NOTE**
>
> *Here's one more. For a long time, I wanted an ASCII chart to which I could quickly refer. Sure, there are a lot of them in books, but, hey, I use a computer! So I wrote the following little utility (ASC.BAS), which automatically creates an ASCII table in an ASCII text file called ASCII.ASC in the current directory:*
>
> ```
> OPEN "ASCII.ASC" FOR OUTPUT AS #1
> FOR i = 32 TO 255 STEP 12
> FOR y = 0 TO 11
> IF i + y < 99 THEN PRINT #1, " ";
> IF i + y < 256 THEN PRINT #1, i + y; CHR$(i + y);
> NEXT y: PRINT #1,
> NEXT i
> CLOSE #1
> END
> ```
>
> *To complete this addition to your DOS toolkit, write the following batch file (ASC.BAT) to display the file on your screen (be sure to include the full path to the file):*
>
> ```
> @echo off
> cls
> echo.
> echo ASCII Table
> type <path>ascii.asc
> echo.
> ```

Summary

In this chapter, you learned about the programs and commands you can use to get more out of your floppy drives, keyboard, printer, and display. You also learned how the video system on your computer works, and some things to consider as your video requirements grow. You were introduced to the two MS-DOS editing programs used to create and edit your system's startup files, where many of the commands you learned about are entered.

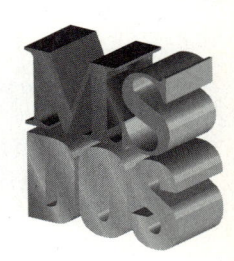

MS-DOS

MS
DOS

CHAPTER 15

Writing Batch Files

by Mark Minasi

Microsoft and IBM have been working on DOS for more than 11 years. During that time, DOS not only has evolved in response to new hardware, it has been improved to meet the needs of its users. In instances where a need has gone unfulfilled, a third-party vendor often has filled the gap.

You might think that DOS would be perfect by now, but it isn't. Specialized needs always arise, or a tool might be required to fix a single, one-time problem. That's why DOS includes batch language capability, DOSKEY macros, and the QBasic language interpreter.

DOSKEY macros are discussed in Chapter 14, and entire books have been written about QBasic. In this chapter, I'll introduce you to batch files.

Batch files are a method of combining several DOS commands to solve a specific problem. I hesitate to call it a "programming language" for two reasons: it tends to scare people away unnecessarily, and it's not much of a programming language anyway. QBasic is a bona fide programming language, with hundreds of language elements, dozens of functions, and odd syntactic conventions, all of which add up to a lot of power, but that can take months to master. Batch files are rather simple, and can be mastered in a day or two.

DOS 6.2 brings us yet another reason to learn batch files: MultiConfig. As you'll learn in the next chapter, you cannot use the power of DOS 6.2's configuration manager without knowledge of batch files.

This chapter introduces commands and then provides examples for their use. Some commands bring up other questions, which give me an opportunity to introduce other commands. I hope to introduce you to some new batch commands, and give you the confidence to write your own.

Batch Files: An Extension of the Command Line

Throughout much of this book, you've learned how to use the power of DOS 6.2's command line to control DOS and your PC. You learned in Chapter 2 that you don't issue commands such as DIR or COPY directly to DOS, but to an intermediate program called a *user shell* or *command interpreter* called COMMAND.COM. That's necessary because DOS has no idea what a DIR, COPY, or ERASE command is. (And here you thought you were the only one having trouble understanding those DOS commands.) COMMAND.COM then interprets, or translates, your commands into a sequence of operations that DOS understands.

If COMMAND.COM's job is to take a command from the keyboard and translate it to something DOS understands, why not enable COMMAND.COM to read commands from a file and translate them into something that DOS understands? That's what a batch file is all about.

Your First Batch File

I'll start by showing you an example of a simple batch file. It won't be very useful, but it will at least demonstrate a point. We'll save the spectacular stuff for later.

DOS files have an internal "flag" called the archive attribute. It is either on or off. If it's on, the file has not been backed up. This archive attribute is used by incremental backup programs to know which files have changed since the previous backup.

If you could see the files for which archive bits are set, you would know which files have not been backed up. If you're a master of the DIR command, you already know how to do this: type **DIR /AA**, which is short for "Give me a directory listing, but only show me the files whose archive bits are set." To see the files for which the archive bits are *not* set, type **DIR /A-A**.

I don't know about you, but I'm forever fumbling around with the slash keys; I type a backslash when I mean a forward slash, and vice versa. So any time I can slash the need for slashes, I do it. Instead of typing DIR /AA, I type **DNB**, short for "Directory of files that need backup." You can build DNB in one simple step: using the DOS editor or equivalent, create a file called DNB.BAT. The file should contain one line: DIR /AA.

The following step-by-step procedure shows you how to do this:

1. Rather than cluttering your hard disk with batch files, you might want to create your own subdirectory to keep your batch file experiments. I call mine BATCHTST; you can create a subdirectory with that name by typing **MD \BATCHTST**.

2. Change to that directory by typing **CD \BATCHTST**.

3. Now open the Editor to create DNB.BAT by typing **EDIT DNB.BAT**.

4. A blank edit screen should now appear. Type **DIR /AA**. It is not necessary to press Enter.

5. Save the file by pressing and releasing Alt, then pressing **F** for the File menu. Then press **X** for the eXit option. The editor

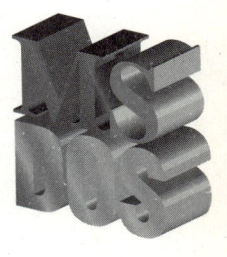

prompts you that you're about to exit the editor, and asks if you want to save the unsaved data in the editor. The yes option already is highlighted, so just press Enter.

You now can start the batch file by simply typing **DNB** and pressing Enter. You'll see a screen similar to figure 15.1.

Figure 15.1

Sample output of DNB batch program.

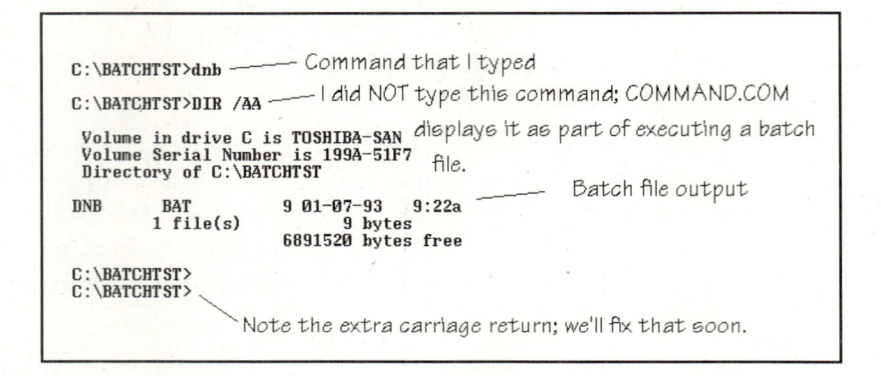

```
C:\BATCHTST>dnb          ── Command that I typed
C:\BATCHTST>DIR /AA      ── I did NOT type this command; COMMAND.COM
Volume in drive C is TOSHIBA-SAN   displays it as part of executing a batch
Volume Serial Number is 199A-51F7  file.
Directory of C:\BATCHTST
DNB     BAT       9 01-07-93  9:22a    ── Batch file output
     1 file(s)           9 bytes
                   6891520 bytes free

C:\BATCHTST>
C:\BATCHTST>
          ── Note the extra carriage return; we'll fix that soon.
```

I've annotated the output of the batch program to make it easier to understand. First, I typed **DNB** to start the batch file. As you read in Chapter 2, typing commands at the DOS prompt tells COMMAND.COM to search for files with the same names as the commands. Presumably, no files are called DNB.COM or DNB.EXE, and no internal commands are named DNB, therefore COMMAND looks for (and finds) a file called DNB.BAT.

After COMMAND.COM finds DNB.BAT, it examines each line (in this case, only one) and executes it as if it you had just typed it in.

Cleaning Up the Batch File: The ECHO Command

Before leaving this batch file, let's make it more presentable. Refer to figure 15.1 and the other notes that I put on the figure.

First, you see C:\BATCHTST>DIR /AA on the screen. You don't want a batch file to show the commands that are in your batch file, you just

Cleaning Up the Batch File: The ECHO Command

want the batch file to run. (It looks sleeker that way.) Basically, COMMAND.COM executes a batch file using the following simple approach:

1. Display the next command to be executed on the command line.
2. Execute the command.
3. If there's another command, go to step 1; otherwise, stop.

We need a way to get COMMAND.COM to skip step 1 every time it sees a new command. We want to tell COMMAND.COM, "Don't tell me what you're going to do, make like a Nike ad and just do it!"

Such a command does exist—the ECHO OFF command. Add ECHO OFF to a batch program and DOS no longer displays the commands (echoing them, in DOS terminology) before executing them. Let's add the command to DNB.BAT, creating a new batch file we'll call DNB2.BAT. It will appear as follows:

```
ECHO OFF
DIR /AA
```

If you're still not comfortable with the editor, review Chapter 14. In DOS's EDIT program, just position the cursor on the first character of the first line and press Enter. You want ECHO OFF to be the first line of the batch file because DOS executes the commands in the order in which they appear, and you want to issue the order to DOS to stop echoing commands as soon as possible. Run DNB2, and your screen should resemble figure 15.2.

```
C:\BATCHTST>dnb2

C:\BATCHTST>ECHO OFF
 Volume in drive C is TOSHIBA-SAN
 Volume Serial Number is 199A-51F7
 Directory of C:\BATCHTST

DNB2     BAT        19 01-07-93   5:02p
DNB      BAT         9 01-07-93   5:02p
        2 file(s)          28 bytes
                      6889472 bytes free
C:\BATCHTST>
```

Figure 15.2

Sample output of DNB2.

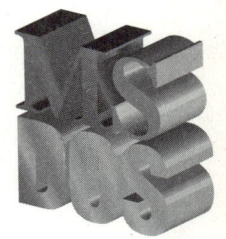

Hmmm... that's not exactly what we were looking for. The DIR /AA line no longer appears, but ECHO OFF does. Why is this? Didn't we tell COMMAND.COM not to echo commands?

We did, but think about how commands get executed: first show them, then do them. By the time COMMAND.COM executes the ECHO OFF command, it already has shown it. This presents something of a chicken-and-egg dilemma. How do you issue a command to the batch processor (that is, COMMAND.COM) to tell it to stop echoing commands, but tell it not to echo that very command?

You couldn't, until DOS 3.3 introduced the @ prefix. By typing @ in front of any command, you tell COMMAND.COM not to display that single command. It's sort of an ECHO OFF command for just one command. Doing so makes the command appear as smooth as was originally intended. The third variation of this example batch file—call it DNB3.BAT—then appears as follows:

```
@ECHO OFF
DIR /AA
```

Run it, and you'll see a screen similar to figure 15.3.

Figure 15.3

Output of the version of DNB3.BAT, with extraneous DOS messages removed.

```
C:\BATCHTST>dnb3

 Volume in drive C is TOSHIBA-SAN
 Volume Serial Number is 199A-51F7
 Directory of C:\BATCHTST

DNB2         BAT        19 01-07-93    5:02p
DNB          BAT         9 01-07-93    5:02p
DNB3         BAT        20 01-07-93    5:23p
        3 file(s)          48 bytes
                      6887424 bytes free
C:\BATCHTST>
```

That's not a bad-looking utility! But it needs a title, or something.

Using ECHO To Put Messages on the Screen

The ECHO command can help us with that too, because ECHO is three commands in one. When invoked with ECHO ON, ECHO keeps COMMAND.COM from echoing commands to the screen. (ECHO OFF reverses the process.) Simply typing ECHO at the DOS prompt causes the batch processor (COMMAND.COM) to report on the status of ECHO. But typing ECHO followed by any message other than ON or OFF causes ECHO to put that message on the screen. Figure 15.4 illustrates these three modes.

```
C:\BATCHTST>echo hello           ─── Using ECHO to display "hello"
hello            Using ECHO to turn on command echo (it was
C:\BATCHTST>echo on              already on)
C:\BATCHTST>echo ─── Using ECHO to report status of command
ECHO is on                       echoing
C:\BATCHTST>echo off   ─── Using ECHO to turn command echo off
echo on ─── Using ECHO to turn command echo back on (note no
C:\BATCHTST>echo How are you?    command prompt when ECHO OFF)
How are you?
C:\BATCHTST>            ─── Using ECHO to display "How are you?"
```

Figure 15.4

Different uses of ECHO.

The first line shows ECHO with a message (`hello`) on the screen. The second line shows ECHO as it is used to turn command echoing on or off. Here, it turns it on, which is the state that it was in anyway. In the third line, ECHO by itself reports on the state of command echoing; ECHO reports that command echoing is ON. After that, I used ECHO to turn command echoing off, which has the side effect of telling COMMAND.COM not to show a command prompt. That's why the next line appears without C:\BATCHTST> in front of it. On that next line, I turned command echoing back on, and finally I used ECHO to again display a message, `How are you?`

Now let's use the message display feature of ECHO to put some introductory information in our small batch file. Rather than merely displaying files, let's put a title at the top of the report announcing that these files have not been backed up. I can do that with a few ECHO statements, so that the latest version of DNB—DNB4.BAT—appears as follows:

```
@ECHO OFF
ECHO ***************** NOTE! *****************
ECHO The following files have not been backed up!
ECHO Back them up soon!
DIR /AA
```

Figure 15.5 displays a sample output.

Figure 15.5

Sample output of DNB4 with introductory title.

```
C:\BATCHTST>dnb4
******************** NOTE! ********************
The following files have not been backed up!
Back them up soon!

 Volume in drive C is TOSHIBA-SAN
 Volume Serial Number is 199A-51F7
 Directory of C:\BATCHTST

DNB2         BAT        19 01-07-93   5:02p
DNB          BAT         9 01-07-93   5:02p
DNB3         BAT        20 01-07-93   5:23p
DNB4         BAT       147 01-07-93   7:10p
        4 file(s)         195 bytes
                      6885376 bytes free

C:\BATCHTST>
```

This is an improvement, but can we get rid of the introductory words from DIR—the `Volume in drive C...` and `Volume Serial`, and `Directory of...` lines? Yes, but first we'll have to take a look at something that we had to get to sooner or later—virtual devices and redirection.

Understanding DOS Virtual Devices

Most of the DOS commands that you've learned so far—such as DIR, COPY, and ERASE—have related primarily to files and paths on the PC's disks. This is to be expected, as most of an operating system's job lies with storage devices. A PC has other types of input/output devices, however, and those also are managed by the operating system. DOS must control the following in particular:

✔ Screen

✔ Keyboard

✔ Serial ports

✔ Parallel ports

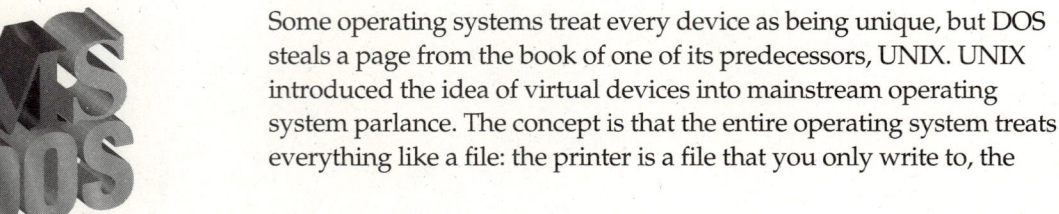

Some operating systems treat every device as being unique, but DOS steals a page from the book of one of its predecessors, UNIX. UNIX introduced the idea of virtual devices into mainstream operating system parlance. The concept is that the entire operating system treats everything like a file: the printer is a file that you only write to, the serial ports are files that may be read or written, the screen can only be written, the keyboard only read, and so on. This simplifies the command structure because it means that everything gets couched in file terms.

In DOS, for example, you don't need a special command to print an ASCII file; you only need to copy the file to the printer. To print your CONFIG.SYS—never a bad idea, as it's an important file, and you can refer to it more easily as you read this book—you would type...

    COPY C:\CONFIG.SYS PRN

PRN is the name of the generic printer device. By the way, if you've got a laser printer, nothing will happen until you take the printer offline and then press the form feed button. The names of the other devices are listed in table 15.1.

Table 15.1
Names and Functions of DOS Virtual Devices

Device Name	Description
LPT1	First parallel port
LPT2	Second parallel port
LPT3	Third parallel port
COM1	First serial port, if present
AUX	First serial port, if present
COM2	Second serial port, if present
COM3	Third serial port, if present
COM4	Fourth serial port, if present
PRN	First parallel port
CLOCK$	System clock device
NUL	The null device
CON	The screen (for output)
CON	The keyboard (for input)
MOUSE$	The pointing device

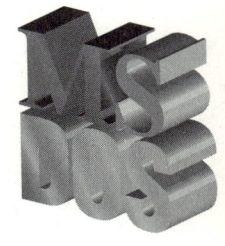

Many of these devices are inaccessible except to programmers, but the COM*n*, LPT*n*, NUL, and CON devices are useful in many situations. First, there's the previous print-the-file example, a handy way to print a file. As another example, consider modems. Modems are controlled with a programming language first created by Hayes Microcomputer Products for their original Smartmodem product. Smartmodem commands are all in uppercase, and all start with AT.

One example is the command ATT, which instructs the modem to dial by touch tone. The alternative would be ATP, to dial pulse. Suppose your modem was connected to the COM2 serial port, and that this modem worked best with a string of commands, such as ATTM0E0 (dial with tone, turn off the modem's speaker, and don't echo commands). It would be a simple matter to store the ATTM0E0 string in a file (call it MODEM), and then type...

    COPY MODEM COM2

...before using the modem.

Another common usage of virtual devices is the COPY CON command, as shown in the following example:

1. Type **COPY CON TEST.TXT**, and press Enter.

2. Type **I am now creating an ASCII file.** and press Enter.

3. Press Ctrl+Z, and press Enter.

You'll see a message such as `1 file(s) copied`. You've just created a file called TEST.TXT. Your disk's directory will confirm this. Type...

    TYPE TEST.TXT

...and you'll see the line that you typed.

What happened here? You copied from the console device—that is, the keyboard—to a file called TEST.TXT. As long as you typed, the contents of the "file" was dumped into TEST.TXT. Anything that you type will go into this file. How do you stop the process? Well, as you saw, the Ctrl+Z sequence stops it, as Ctrl+Z has been the "end of file" marker for operating systems from CP/M in the late 1970s to MS-DOS today. Each time you create a text file with a text editor, that text editor appends a Ctrl+Z to the end of that text file when the file is saved to disk.

Again, CON is a dual-purpose device. When used as input, it represents the keyboard. When used as output, it represents the screen. Try typing **COPY TEXT.TXT CON**; the result will be that you'll see the file shown on the screen; in effect, copying something to the console device displays it on the screen.

The NUL device is the "do nothing" device. Sending output to NUL essentially eliminates it. If a program insists on creating some kind of report that you do not want, tell the program to write the report to the NUL device—you can put in NUL anywhere that you would put a file.

Copying a file to NUL does not produce any copies, but it does have a side effect—it forces DOS to read the file before realizing that the file's not going anywhere. Thus, you can use NUL as a cheap "floppy tester." Just put the disk that you'd like to test in drive A, and type **COPY A:*.* NUL**. While the process doesn't create files, it causes the system to read every sector that has a file in it. (This does not read any sectors that don't contain files.)

By the way, you also can get some odd results with virtual devices. Use the TYPE, DIR, or COPY commands just for fun, as follows:

```
TYPE CLOCK$
TYPE CON:
```

Understanding and Using Input/Output Redirection under DOS

DOS not only learned of virtual devices from UNIX, it also picked up on a related idea, *redirection*. Consider the following question: When you type **DIR**, where does COMMAND.COM put the output? Most people would answer, "On the screen, of course." But that's only partly true. When the Microsoft programmers wrote the DIR command, they didn't write the program to put its output on the screen, they wrote the program to put its output on the standard output device, or, as programmers refer to it, STDOUT. The program lets the operating system decide what is the standard output device. By default, that's the screen, of course, and so the output from the DIR command usually shows up on the screen. But try typing...

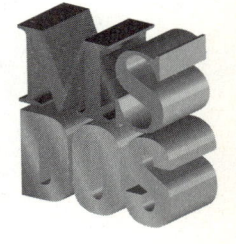

```
DIR >DIROUT.TXT
```

Chapter 15: *Writing Batch Files*

You will not see any output on the screen. That's because by typing **>DIROUT.TXT**, you told DOS to change the definition of STDOUT, just for the duration of this command, to a file named DIROUT.TXT. Type…

    TYPE DIROUT.TXT

…and you'll see what looks like normal directory output captured in an ASCII text file.

From the operating system's point of view, applications have one input, called STDIN (standard input), and two outputs, called STDOUT (standard output) and STDERR (standard error). Think of it as pictured in figure 15.6.

Figure 15.6
Standard inputs and outputs in a DOS program.

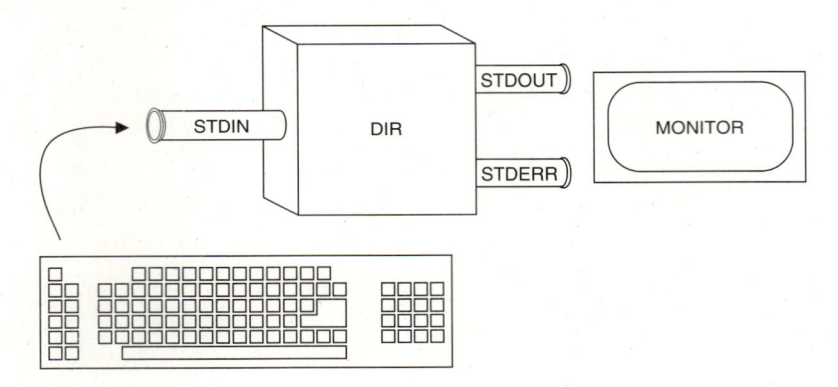

The program, DIR, has a standard input device that is, by default, the keyboard. It has the standard output device that is, by default, the monitor screen, and a standard output stream for error messages that is also the monitor screen. By redirecting DIR's output, you create a situation such as that depicted in figure 15.7.

Using Redirected Output

Output redirection has many uses. After it has been captured to a file, the output of the DIR command can be included in documentation, such as `once you install Word Blaster, you will have a directory with the following files included in it...` Or you

Understanding and Using Input/Output Redirection under DOS

could use the virtual devices with redirection, as in the following examples:

```
DIR >PRN

COPY X Y >NUL

ECHO ATTM0E0 >COM2
```

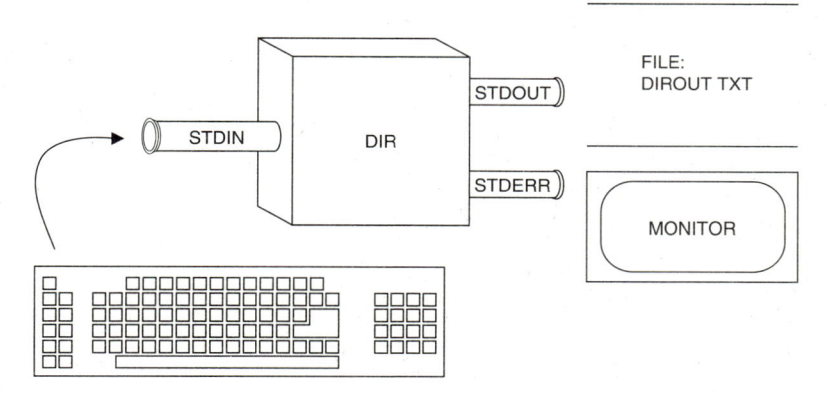

Figure 15.7
DIR's ouput redirected to a file.

In the first example, you redirect the output of the DIR command to the printer, and get a printout of the current directory. Be sure you have a printer attached before trying this, or DOS will respond that your printer is out of paper.

In the second example, you execute a normal COPY command, copying from X to Y. But perhaps this command is part of a batch file that you have written for your users, assuming that you are a DOS support person. Each time your users run the batch file, however, they see the computer emit an output message such as `one file(s) copied`, and they wonder what that means. Rather than having to explain it hundreds of times, you'd like to just get rid of the message. You do that by sending the standard output of the COPY command off to the NUL device, DOS's "black hole."

Recall in the early section the discussion about using virtual devices to program a "smart" modem. In that discussion, you saw that a hypothetical smart modem might require the setup string ATTM0E0, a sequence that tells it to dial touchtone, shut off the speaker, and suppress command echoing. Rather than creating a file and copying the file to COM2, a simpler method is to just use ECHO.

Consider what ECHO does. When you type **ECHO Hello**, what is happening? You might think that ECHO puts the word "hello" on the screen. But that's not the entire story. ECHO puts "hello" on the standard output device—which is, by default, the screen. But ECHO can be redirected to any virtual device as well. If you type...

```
ECHO Hello, there > PRN
```

...the words `Hello, there` will be printed. In fact, you'll find that ECHO, when redirected, is quite a powerful tool.

Try this time-saving use of ECHO: You may know that laser printers require a full page of data before they'll print; they are full-page printers, printing an entire page at a time. Until they get a full page, they hold the partial page in their memory. If you've got a partial page in your printer, however, you can force it to print the page by taking the printer off line, pressing the form feed key, and putting the printer back on line. That can be a nuisance, however. With the following command, you can force your printer to perform the same function:

```
ECHO ^L>PRN
```

Don't type ^L by pressing Shift+6, then L; type it by pressing Ctrl+L. This forces your printer to execute a form feed. If you find that sequence useful, why not make it a batch file? Such a batch file might be called EJECT.BAT, and might appear as follows:

```
@ECHO OFF
ECHO ^L>PRN
```

Using Input Redirection

Less useful, but still valuable, is input redirection. Just as the output of a program can be diverted to a file, a program can search a file for the input that it normally gets from the keyboard. Take, for instance, the ERASE command. If you try to erase an entire directory called \X by typing **ERASE *.***, you get the response `\X\*.*, are you sure (y/n)?` You must then press y and Enter to execute the command. You can do the same thing in one step with input redirection. Try it, but first create a directory that you don't mind erasing, as follows:

Understanding and Using Input/Output Redirection under DOS 805

1. Type **MD \JUNK**
2. Type **XCOPY C:\DOS \JUNK**
3. Type **CD \JUNK**

You'll need a file containing the letter y to act as the response to the question "Are you sure?". Create it with the COPY CON command that you saw in the earlier discussion about virtual devices, as follows:

4. Type **COPY CON RESPONSE**
5. Type **Y**, and press Enter.
6. Press Ctrl+Z, and press Enter. You should now have a file called RESPONSE that contains a Y.
7. Type **ERASE *.* <RESPONSE**. You'll see the are you sure? message, but it will be automatically answered from the RESPONSE file. There will be no files left in the directory, save for RESPONSE itself; DOS will not erase it, as it's being read by the ERASE process.
8. To clean up, erase the RESPONSE file by typing **CD **, and then typing **RD \JUNK**.

> **TIP**
>
> *An easier way to do input redirection is to use DELALL.BAT:*
>
> ```
> @echo off
> echo Y ¦ del *.* > nul
> ```
>
> *This pipes a Y through the DEL command, making DOS think you entered a **Y** at the* Are you sure (Y/N)? *prompt.*

Redirecting Existing Files with Append

What happens if you redirect some output to a file that already exists? Unfortunately, the information in that file is erased. That can be a real problem. Suppose you want to run three programs, called PROG1, PROG2, and PROG3, one after the other, and you want to capture the output of each to a file called OUTPUT.TXT. If you type the commands **PROG1>OUTPUT.TXT**, **PROG2>OUTPUT.TXT**, and **PROG3>OUTPUT.TXT** in sequence, you will only see the output of PROG3 in the file OUTPUT.TXT, because each separate redirection command began by first sweeping away any existing files named OUTPUT.TXT.

The solution to this problem is to append new output. Rather than typing >, type **>>**. It means "redirect output to this file, but do so starting at the end of the file." Recast, the previous example would appear as follows:

```
PROG1>OUTPUT.TXT
PROG2>>OUTPUT.TXT
PROG3>>OUTPUT.TXT
```

Notice that the first line still uses the > symbol. That's because you don't want anything currently in OUTPUT.TXT—assuming that such a file already exists—cluttering up your output.

Using Pipes

You have seen how DOS programs have input and output *sockets* called STDIN, STDOUT, and STDERR; only STDIN and STDOUT are accessible with the redirection symbols > and <. I've discussed STDERR because it is a DOS entity associated with each program. You've also seen that, at least until now, those sockets ordinarily attach to input/output devices such as the keyboard and screen, but can be redirected to files or virtual devices. Pipes take this notion a step further, enabling two programs to attach the output socket of one program to the input socket of another. Called piping, this is drawn schematically in figure 15.8.

To pipe the output of one file to the input of another, use the ¦ character. It's the vertical bar on your keyboard with a hole in the middle of it, and can be typed by pressing Shift+backslash. You would pipe the output of program X into the input of program Y by typing **X¦Y**.

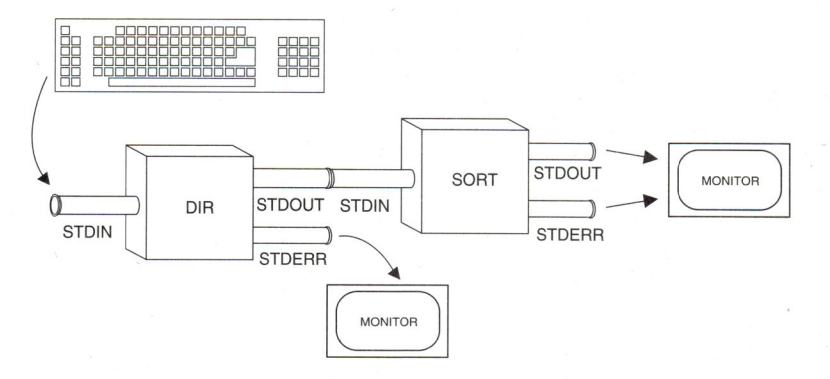

Figure 15.8

Connecting (piping) the output of one program to the input of another program.

Here's an example. Ordinarily, the DIR command produces output that is not ordered in any manner; it just shows the files in whatever order they happen to have fallen. STDOUT goes to the monitor, as we've seen. DOS also has a program called SORT.EXE. To use this program, type **SORT,** and feed it a few lines. It will sort those lines and display them, as follows:

1. At a DOS command prompt, type **SORT**.

2. As was the case with COPY CON, anything that you type goes into the SORT program. Type a line of text, and press Enter.

3. Type several more lines, pressing Enter between each one.

4. When you are finished, press Ctrl+Z, and then press Enter. Remember, Ctrl+Z is the end-of-file marker, signalling to SORT that your input is completed.

You will see all of your lines arranged so that they are in alphabetical order, or *collation sequence*. Collation sequence refers to the fact that every character has an ASCII code, a value somewhere between 32 and 126. For example, capital A has code 65, the lowercase a has code 97, the digit 0 has code 48, and a blank space has a code 32. SORT just orders them according to their codes, so any lines starting with digits would come before lines starting with capital letters, which would precede lines starting with lowercase letters.

If you have completed the previous steps correctly, your screen should resemble figure 15.9.

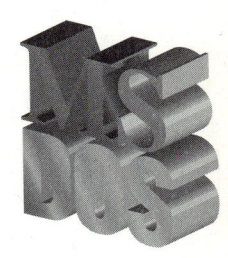

Figure 15.9

A sample run with SORT.

```
C:\BATCHTST>sort
A first line.
a second line, but with a lowercase "a".
Be sure to note that the uppercases are before lowers.
1 sure thing is that numbers are before letters.
^Z
1 sure thing is that numbers are before letters.
A first line.
a second line, but with a lowercase "a".
Be sure to note that the uppercases are before lowers.

C:\BATCHTST>
```

Executed by itself, SORT isn't very interesting. But when the output of a program such as DIR is piped into SORT, you see the value of SORT, or any similar program. Such programs (called filters) are valuable add-ons that give new powers to preexisting programs. DOS comes with three filter programs, as follows:

- ✔ SORT puts lines of data in collation sequence.
- ✔ FIND looks for matches with a particular sequence of characters.
- ✔ MORE stops a program after every screen's worth of output and prompts - More -.

FIND matches a stream of input against particular character strings. Suppose, for example, you wanted to find every BASDEV statement in your CONFIG.SYS. Just pipe it into FIND with the TYPE command, as follows: **TYPE TYPE C:\CONFIG.SYS¦FIND** *device*, and only the lines with "device" in them will be displayed.

Not impressed? Well, FIND is going to be the filter that puts the icing on the cake for DNB.BAT. Recall that earlier in the chapter we wanted to be able to show only lines with file names on them, and filter out the volume label and serial number information. Look back at figure 15.5, and notice that the lines that we're looking for all include the colon (:). Type **FIND** after the DIR command, and we get DNB5.BAT, as follows:

```
@ECHO OFF
ECHO ****************** NOTE! ******************
ECHO The following files have not been backed up!
ECHO Back them up soon!
DIR /AA¦FIND ":"
```

The output becomes a bit prettier, as you see in figure 15.10.

```
C:\BATCHTST>dnb5
******************** NOTE! ********************
The following files have not been backed up!
Back them up soon!
 Directory of C:\BATCHTST
DNB2         BAT         19 01-07-93    5:02p
DNB          BAT          9 01-07-93    5:02p
DNB3         BAT         20 01-07-93    5:23p
DNB4         BAT        147 01-07-93    7:10p
DNB5         BAT        156 01-07-93   10:47p
C:\BATCHTST>
```

Figure 15.10

Results of the FIND command with the DIR header removed.

You could clean it up even more by clearing the screen at the start of the batch file, leading to the final DNB, DNB6.BAT, as follows:

```
@ECHO OFF
CLS
ECHO ****************** NOTE! *****************
ECHO The following files have not been backed up!
ECHO Back them up soon!
DIR /AA¦FIND ":"
```

I'll spare you the sample output.

> *There is an easier way to do this: use DIRs /B (bare) switch, which suppresses DIRs heading information and summary.*

Sounds and Blank Lines with ECHO

It is sometimes useful to have a program that causes the computer to emit a beep. This is easily done after you know that the Ctrl+G character is the "bell" character, named for the fact that on old teletype machines it would ring a bell. Computers don't have bells, of course, but it's too late to rename it the "beep" character. In any case, type the following two-line batch file whenever you need your computer to make a noise:

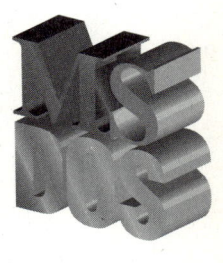

```
@ECHO OFF
ECHO ^G
```

Again, don't type the ^ symbol and then G. Press Ctrl, then press G, then release the G, and then release Ctrl; ^G then appears on the screen. Try it out, but not too often—unless you *want* to irritate the people in the room with you.

Perhaps you're also wondering how to echo a blank line. Most all batch programmers have tried to show a blank line on the screen by typing ECHO on a line by itself in the batch file. For example, consider the following batch file:

```
@ECHO OFF
ECHO This is the first line.
ECHO
ECHO
ECHO
ECHO You should have seen three blank lines.
```

If you run this batch file, your output should appear as follows:

```
This is the first line.
ECHO is OFF
ECHO is OFF
ECHO is OFF You should have seen three blank lines.
```

Each ECHO line was executed as ECHO without arguments by COMMAND.COM, and ECHO without arguments is, you'll recall, a request for a status report about command echoing.

The correct way to ECHO a blank line is to issue the command ECHO with a period immediately following. Recast, the batch file above could be written as follows:

```
@ECHO OFF
ECHO This is the first line.
ECHO.
ECHO.
ECHO.
ECHO You should have seen three blank lines.
```

This batch file will have the desired effect.

By now you've learned a bit about controlling the output of a batch file. But listening is at least as important as talking, so let's take a look at how to solicit information from the user.

Making Choices in Batch Files

Your disk contains a batch file called MENU.BAT. Try it out; when you type **MENU**, you get a menu like the one that you see in figure 15.11.

```
***************** Information Menu *******************
     Choice          Action
       W             Receive a pearl of wisdom
       D             See the directory
       N             Make a little noise
       X             Exit the menu
Please choose W, D, N, or X?
```

Figure 15.11
MENU.BAT opening screen.

It's a silly menu system that dispenses some questionable wisdom, shows a directory, makes a beep, or exits the system. What you'll learn from seeing how to build this, however, is how to accept input from the keyboard with a batch program (DOS 6.2 makes it easier than it's ever been), and how to make decisions in batch files.

Let me introduce you to MENU.BAT. Don't expect to understand all of it at once, but I think you'll be surprised at how much you do understand already. It appears as follows:

```
@echo off
:top
cls
echo *************** Information Menu ******************
echo.
echo   Choice    Action
echo.
echo    W        Receive a pearl of wisdom
echo    D        See the directory
echo    N        Make a little noise
echo    X        Exit the menu
echo.
choice /C:wdnx /n Please choose W, D, N, or X?
If errorlevel 4 goto end
if errorlevel 3 goto beepit
if errorlevel 2 goto dirit
if errorlevel 1 goto wisdom
```

```
:wisdom
echo As you travel down the highway of life,
echo a bird in the hand will make steering difficult
echo and shifting virtually impossible
goto nextone
:dirit
dir
goto nextone
:beepit
echo 
goto nextone
:nextone
pause
goto top
:end
cls
echo Thanks; see you next time!
```

Receiving User Choices in Batch Files with CHOICE.COM

The heart of any interactive batch program is CHOICE.COM. In its simplest form, CHOICE asks the user for a single key, which must be either Y or N; the case of the letter is ignored. You'll probably find CHOICE more useful in an expanded mode, however, where it provides the opportunity to specify a prompt and choices other than Y and N. With those options added, CHOICE appears as follows:

```
CHOICE /C:listofchoices prompttext
```

The *listofchoices* option is a sequence of characters that are the only acceptable answers to the CHOICE command. For example, the option /C:XYZ would tell CHOICE to only accept the keystrokes X, Y, or Z. The *prompttext* option is the text of a prompt to put on the screen, sort of a built-in ECHO. For example, consider a batch file containing the following command:

```
CHOICE /c:vcs Do you prefer vanilla, chocolate, or strawberry?
```

A user of the batch file would see this prompt:

```
Do you prefer vanilla, chocolate, or strawberry?[V,C,S]?
```

The *[V,C,S]?* is tacked onto the prompt by default, and can be suppressed with another option on the CHOICE command, the */N* option. Thus, if the command were typed as follows:

```
CHOICE /c:vcs /n Do you prefer vanilla, chocolate, or strawberry?
```

The output would then appear as follows:

```
Do you prefer vanilla, chocolate, or strawberry?
```

NOTE: If you press any key besides v, c, or s, the PC beeps at you. This is clearly an input command designed by an old-time programmer. I can just hear the head software designer now: "We'll make those turkeys answer the question!"

Making Decisions in Batch Files

Now that the user has chosen from some characters, what is to be done with them? Before I answer that, a warning. In general, I like to introduce a reader to just one command at a time, but in this case I need to introduce three things at once. (None of them are hard, but I wanted you to be ready.)

Using Return Codes and ERRORLEVEL

The user's choice gets transmitted to the subsequent line of the batch file through a built-in batch function called ERRORLEVEL. It's called ERRORLEVEL because it was introduced to DOS 2 to solve this problem: Suppose you want to write a batch program that first executed program X, and then executed program Y, but should only execute Y if X completed successfully? How could the batch program know whether or not X completed successfully?

The answer is that each DOS program has the option of leaving when exiting DOS with a number between 0 and 255 called a *return code*. A value of 0 means everything worked out fine. A value between 1 and

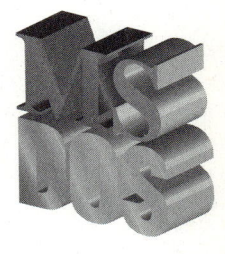

255 means... well, it means just about anything a program wants it to mean. Most DOS programs, both those shipped with DOS by Microsoft and those offered by third-party vendors, do not make use of this potentially valuable feature.

I've got to explain ERRORLEVEL in order to get to the pay dirt in CHOICE, however, so assume that my mythical program X returns 0 if all turned out right, or 1 if X couldn't perform its duty for some reason. The batch file could then be written to say "first do X, and then do Y if X terminated with a return code of 0." How would this be done? With the ERRORLEVEL value. The ERRORLEVEL test is `IF ERRORLEVEL n command` in which *command* is any DOS command. It has a companion version: `IF NOT ERRORLEVEL n command`.

It takes a while to grow accustomed to ERRORLEVEL. It works like this: if the return code from the previous program is equal to *n* or greater, then execute *command*. Otherwise, do nothing. To build the simple batch file discussed above, where X runs and then Y runs if X was successful, you would write the batch file as follows:

```
X
IF NOT ERRORLEVEL 1 Y
```

IF NOT ERRORLEVEL 1 Y means "do Y if the ERRORLEVEL from X was not greater than or equal to 1." "Not greater than or equal to" is the same as "less than," so IF NOT ERRORLEVEL 1 Y means "do Y if the ERRORLEVEL from X is less than 1."

When your batch files use the CHOICE command, the command returns the value of the user's choice by way of ERRORLEVEL. The previous CHOICE example in this chapter appeared as follows:

```
CHOICE /c:vcs /n Do you prefer vanilla, chocolate, or strawberry?
```

Here, you're telling CHOICE to accept only the characters v, c, or s. After the user has pressed one of those three characters, CHOICE sets ERRORLEVEL to 1 if the choice was v, 2 if the choice was c, or 3 if the choice was s. Let's write a simple batch file that uses that CHOICE statement and makes (somewhat) appropriate responses to the user's choice. It might look like the following batch file, which I call ICECREAM.BAT:

Making Choices in Batch Files

```
@echo off
CHOICE /c:vcs /n Do you prefer vanilla, chocolate, or strawberry?
if errorlevel 3 echo Strawberry ... tart and sweet.
if errorlevel 2 echo Well, chocolate's certainly an old standby!
if errorlevel 1 echo Fruit of the vanilla bean. My choice as well.
```

You see an example in figure 15.12.

```
C:\BATCHTST>icecream
Do you prefer vanilla, chocolate, or strawberry?V
Fruit of the vanilla bean.  My choice as well.
C:\BATCHTST>
C:\BATCHTST>
C:\BATCHTST>icecream
Do you prefer vanilla, chocolate, or strawberry?C
Well, chocolate's certainly an old standby!
Fruit of the vanilla bean.  My choice as well.
C:\BATCHTST>
C:\BATCHTST>
C:\BATCHTST>icecream
Do you prefer vanilla, chocolate, or strawberry?S
Strawberry ... tart and sweet.
Well, chocolate's certainly an old standby!
Fruit of the vanilla bean.  My choice as well.
C:\BATCHTST>
```

Figure 15.12

Sample run of ICECREAM.BAT, showing a problem with ERRORLEVEL.

The sample response of v seems to work out all right. But answering **c** not only gets the response for c, it also gets the response for v. Answering **s** gets all three responses.

What caused this problem? The nature of ERRORLEVEL. The statement `IF ERRORLEVEL 3 ECHO Strawberry...` means "if the value of ERRORLEVEL is greater than or equal to 3, echo `Strawberry....`" Therefore, that statement only gets executed if you have an error level of 3 or greater, but the only possible value of ERRORLEVEL in this batch file at that point is three, since there are only three possible responses. But the second statement, `IF ERRORLEVEL 2 ECHO Well...` will get executed if ERRORLEVEL is greater than or equal to 2—which means that message appears if the user presses either s or c. `IF ERRORLEVEL 1...` executes in any case.

It appears as if this batch file is almost correct. What does it need to work properly?

One word: GOTO.

GOTO Keeps You Jumping

So far, you've seen batch files with lines that execute in nice, sequential fashion; the second line executes after the first line but before the third line, and so on. The DOS batch language's GOTO command enables your batch programs to jump around. GOTOs need a place to jump to, however, so the batch language also supports a label—any line starting with a colon (:). The GOTO command appears as follows:

```
GOTO labelname
```

A line with a label appears as follows:

```
:labelname
```

For example, try the following batch file, appropriately named FOREVER.BAT:

```
@ECHO off
:top
ECHO Help! I can't stop!
GOTO TOP
```

This places the message…

```
Help! I can't stop
```

…on the display over and over and over. Instead of putting commands such as ECHO at the end of IF ERRORLEVEL statements, it's usually a good idea to issue the GOTO command somewhere, and perform the actions that you're trying to do out there. That way, you can devote more than one line to an action. If you replace the ECHOs with GOTOs in ICECREAM.BAT, you'll end up with a reworked version I'll call IC2.BAT, which appears as follows:

```
@ECHO off
CHOICE /c:vcs /n Do you prefer vanilla, chocolate, or strawberry?
if errorlevel 3 goto strawberry
if errorlevel 2 goto chocolate
if errorlevel 1 goto vanilla
:strawberry
ECHO Strawberry ... tart and sweet.
goto end
:chocolate
```

```
ECHO Well, chocolate's certainly an old standby!
goto end
:vanilla
ECHO Fruit of the vanilla bean. My choice as well.
GOTO end
:end
```

CHOICE, IF ERRORLEVEL, and GOTO Summarized

Now this simple batch file works as intended. The primary things to learn from this batch file are as follows:

✔ When testing error levels, always test the highest value first and work down. In IC2.BAT, I tested ERRORLEVEL 3 before ERRORLEVEL 2 because ERRORLEVEL 2 isn't satisfied only if the ERRORLEVEL value equals 2—it's satisfied if the ERRORLEVEL value equals 2 or greater. Putting the IF ERRORLEVEL 2 statement before the IF ERRORLEVEL 3 statement would mean that the IF ERRORLEVEL 3 statement would never get executed, because the IF ERRORLEVEL 2 GOTO CHOCOLATE statement would jump down to the :CHOCOLATE line.

✔ Test a number of choices, as follows: CHOICE, then IF ERRORLEVELS, then labels. Use IC2.BAT as a model. Many batch files will end up looking like IC2.BAT. Here's a more general template. Don't type this in exactly; it won't work. It's just intended to guide you in building a batch file based on user inputs and alternatives. The actual batch statements are in uppercase and the general terminology or notes are in lowercase.

```
@ECHO OFF
CHOICE ...whatever the CHOICE statement ends up looking like...
IF ERRORLEVEL n GOTO CHOICEn [where n is the largest choice]
IF ERRORLEVEL n-1 GOTO CHOICEn-1 ...
[other ERRORLEVELs here]
IF ERRORLEVEL 3 GOTO CHOICE3
IF ERRORLEVEL 2 GOTO CHOICE2
```

```
IF ERRORLEVEL 1 GOTO CHOICE1
:CHOICEn
[whatever you want to do if the user picks choice number n.]
GOTO END
:CHOICEn-1
[whatever you want to do if the user picks choice n-1]
GOTO END
[labels for other alternatives...]
:CHOICE3
[actions if user picks choice 3]
GOTO END
:CHOICE2
[actions if user picks choice 2]
GOTO END
:CHOICE1
[actions if user picks choice 1]
GOTO END
:END
```

Note all the GOTO END commands. If you don't include them, the program finishes whatever option you chose and then wanders through all of the options of a lower number—kind of like our earlier problem with ICECREAM.BAT.

Now take another look at MENU.BAT. This time, I've numbered the lines to make them easy to refer to. Don't type the file with the numbers—it won't work that way.

```
(1)@echo off
(2):top
(3)cls
(4)echo *************** Information Menu ******************
(5)echo.
(6)echo   Choice    Action
(7)echo.
(8)echo    W    Receive a pearl of wisdom
(9)echo    D    See the directory
(10)echo   N    Make a little noise
(11)echo   X    Exit the menu
(12)echo.
(13)choice /C:wdnx /n Please choose W, D, N, or X?
(14)If errorlevel 4 goto end
```

Making Choices in Batch Files

```
(15)if errorlevel 3 goto beepit
(16)if errorlevel 2 goto dirit
(17)if errorlevel 1 goto wisdom
(18):wisdom
(19)echo As you travel down the highway of life,
(20)echo a bird in the hand will make steering difficult
(21)echo and shifting virtually impossible
(22)goto nextone
(23):dirit
(24)dir
(25)goto nextone
(26):beepit
(27)echo ^G
(28)goto nextone
(29):nextone
(30)pause
(31)goto top
(32):end
(33)cls
(34)echo Thanks; see you next time!
```

One unique aspect of this program is that it runs over and over; our other programs have all been kind of one-shot batch files. That's why there's a label near the top of the batch file on line 2 called :top. This is used later to restart the menu, as you'll see.

Line 3 clears the screen to get it ready for the menu, and lines 4-12 put the menu on the screen.

> *An even easier way to display a menu is to create a small text file that's arranged the way you want the screen to appear, and then TYPE the line from inside your batch file.*

Line 13 requests the user's choice. The options are *w* (ERRORLEVEL=1), *d* (ERRORLEVEL=2), *n* (ERRORLEVEL=3), or *x* (ERRORLEVEL=4).

Line 14 tests for the highest ERRORLEVEL, which in this case is the EXIT command. Lines 15-17 contain the other IF ERRORLEVEL commands, which, as you can see, are arranged in descending order.

Line 18 starts the section in response to a *w* alternative. It's just a few ECHO statements and then a GOTO command to a label called nextone, which tells the system to get ready for the next option that the user selects.

Line 23 starts the response for the *d* option. Note that while the IF ERRORLEVEL commands must be in descending order, there's no need for the actual labeled areas to appear in any order.

Line 26 contains the label that the system goes to if the user presses *b*, and the following lines contain a Ctrl+G and then move on to nextone.

At line 29 is the label nextone. It tells the system to pause and wait for a key to be pressed, and then goes back to the :top label—effectively restarting the batch file.

> *The PAUSE command instructs the system to wait for a key to be pressed, then enables COMMAND.COM to execute the next batch command. The PAUSE command does not record a keystroke, unlike CHOICE.*

Line 32 begins the exit sequence, and is accessible only if the user enters **x**. It clears the screen and says goodbye.

Using CHOICE To Delay a Batch File

A discussion of CHOICE would not be complete without talking about its timeout feature. Suppose you want to give a user two options, but only a certain number of seconds in which to make the choice?

Specifying Default CHOICEs

Consider, for example, the most important batch file in your system, AUTOEXEC.BAT. This is a batch file like any other, but it has one

Using CHOICE To Delay a Batch File

special property—it runs automatically when you boot your system. Suppose you'd like AUTOEXEC.BAT to offer you the option to log onto your network each time you boot up, rather than automatically logging you on, as the network programs burn up a large amount of RAM. A fragment of your AUTOEXEC.BAT might resemble the following:

```
[...previous lines...]
choice /c:yn Would you like to log onto the network
if errorlevel 2 goto nonet
net logon
:nonet
[...following lines...]
```

That would work well. We're not using the /N *noprompt* option, so the choice message will read Would you like to log onto the network [Y/N]? If you press N, the result is an ERRORLEVEL of 2, causing the batch file to skip to the :nonet label, bypassing the NET LOGON command. Pressing Y causes an ERROR-LEVEL of 1, which will be ignored by the IF ERRORLEVEL 2 statement; therefore, the logon occurs.

That works well, but it means you must be sitting in front of your computer while it boots. I don't know about your PC, but mine seems to take about two minutes to boot because of all the memory managers, network drivers, and other programs it contains. For me, rebooting usually means an opportunity to get a refill on my diet Dr. Pepper. But if my AUTOEXEC.BAT includes any CHOICE statements, then I've got to babysit the PC while it's booting. Now, nine-tenths of the time, I'm going to press Y. AUTOEXEC.BAT would be smarter if it would just give me two seconds to press y or n, and then log me on if I don't do anything.

CHOICE enables "this default" with the /T:, or *time* option. It looks like /T:C,N where C is the character to assume if no key is pressed within the time limit, and N is the number of seconds to wait. If I rewrite the above fragment of AUTOEXEC.BAT to wait two seconds for my response—an adequate amount of time if the user is sitting at the PC waiting to press a key—then it'll look like the following:

```
[...previous lines...]
choice /c:yn /t:y,2 Would you like to log onto the network
if errorlevel 2 goto nonet
net logon
:nonet
[...following lines...]
```

Waiting for Choices That Never Occur: Preprogrammed Delays

That's nifty, but the /t parameter on CHOICE also can be used for something that I'm sure Microsoft didn't intend—as a "snooze" command. Sometimes you'll want to write batch files that tell the PC to just do nothing for a certain amount of time. Here's a trick to do just that. The following batch file, called ONEMIN.BAT, makes your PC pause for one minute between two messages:

```
@echo off
echo See you in a minute!
choice /c:{255} /t:{255},60 /n
echo Told you I'd be back!
```

There's just one trick to typing this in: don't type {255} as "left curly brace, 2, 5, 5, right curly brace"; it's meant to represent you typing the following sequence of keystrokes.

1. Press Alt and hold it down.

2. Using the numeric keypad (not the numbers across the top of the keyboard) type **2**, **5**, and **5**.

3. Release Alt.

You have inserted an ASCII code that is recognized by the computer as a character, but doesn't show on the screen and has no corresponding key on the keyboard. The CHOICE command is basically saying, "Wait 60 seconds for the user to enter a keystroke, but the only choice in keystrokes is this ASCII code that doesn't correspond to any keys on the keyboard except for this one odd-ball Alt-key combination." The net effect is to wait for 60 seconds. To wait more or fewer seconds, just include the CHOICE /c:{255} /t:{255}, 60 statement in your batch files, and change the 60 to a different value.

Limitations of Using CHOICE To Build Delays

Before you start relying on this method to build-in delays to a batch file, be aware of a limitation. The CHOICE command, like most DOS commands, assumes that it works in a single-tasking environment.

That's not a safe assumption these days, particularly with a version of DOS that includes three Windows applications. If you run a batch file that includes a CHOICE delay in a DOS session under Windows and switch away from that session in the middle of the preprogrammed delay, time essentially stops for the DOS session. Let's say you told the batch program to wait for one minute before proceeding, and then immediately switched away from the DOS session to the Windows desktop and did some work with Windows applications for a few hours. When you returned to the DOS session, you'd find that the DOS batch file would still be waiting for that minute to go by, because it is totally unaware of any time spent while you've switched away from it. Keep this in mind if your batch files run under Windows.

If you want to be sure that a DOS program running under Windows waits the correct amount of time even after you switch away from it, check the Background box in the Settings window.

Waiting for a Particular Time

Sometimes you don't want to wait a certain length of time; you want to wait *until* a particular time. The CHOICE command cannot accomplish this, but a DOS command is available that can make a batch file aware of the time.

The TIME Command

You probably already are aware of the TIME command. It appears as follows:

```
C:\BATCHTST>TIME
Current time is 12:42:41.03p
Enter new time:
```

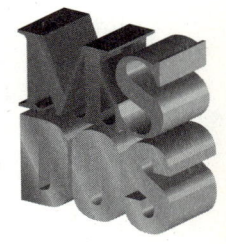

After you press Enter, the DOS prompt returns. How can this be of value in a batch file? Well, we've got two stumbling blocks to overcome.

First, each time the TIME command is issued, it insists that you press Enter (or enter a new time and press Enter) before it returns control of the PC to DOS. You obviously don't want the user of your batch file to have to press Enter each time the TIME command is run. What's the answer?

Perhaps you've figured out by now that a simple input redirection can make TIME happy. I just create a text file called ENTER that contains one blank line. I then redirect that into the TIME command, and TIME responds as if you've pressed Enter. An example follows:

```
C:\BATCHTST>TIME <Enter>
Current time is 12:42:41.03p
Enter new time:
C:\BATCHTST>
```

You don't have to press any keys; the TIME command just returns you to the DOS prompt. One problem down, one to go.

The second problem is to get a batch file to recognize a particular time. The FIND command does the job, but it gets complicated. You issue the TIME command, but you pipe the output of TIME—which includes, among other things, the current time—into FIND, with instructions for FIND to look for some sequence of numbers that corresponds to the time you're waiting for, such as 3:37.

If FIND is successful, it returns an ERRORLEVEL of 0; otherwise, it returns an ERRORLEVEL of 1 or greater. You can use that information to build a batch file that waits for a certain time. A first attempt might appear as follows:

```
@echo off
:top
time<enter ¦ find "3:31:"
if errorlevel 1 goto top
```

Notice that the time 3:31: is specified rather than 3:30. Had you told FIND to look for 3:30, it would have been satisfied with any time whose seconds portion was 30 and whose minutes portion was 3.

Using CHOICE To Delay a Batch File

By adding the colon at the end, you ensure that you are asking for *hours:minutes*. Look back at the sample output of TIME—12:42:41.03p—to see what is meant.

You could use something like WAITFOR in any batch file. You could, for instance, tell your PC to run an unattended tape backup of your hard disk every night at 11 p.m., as follows (assuming your tape backup program is called TBACKUP):

```
@echo off
:top
time<enter | find "11:00:"
if errorlevel 1 goto top
tbackup
```

Refining WAITFOR.BAT

Before you try to automate all of your house's functions on your computer with remote control hardware and a few batch files, understand that limitations exist. First, notice the inability to distinguish between a.m. and p.m. I don't know how to resolve that problem.

If you have used the WAITFOR command and told it to wait for any significant length of time, you probably noticed that the hard disk runs continuously while it's waiting. Let's examine this first.

In the process of piping data from STDOUT of one program to STDIN of another program, DOS temporarily stores the piped data in a temporary file. This means that every time you type **TIME<enter | find...**, the command creates and then destroys a small file. I estimate that the time/find statement could end up looping about five to ten times per second, which means that waiting four hours to back up a tape would require that your hard disk perform about 72,000 unnecessary accesses. Not very conducive to long disk life, is it?

You have two possible solutions: send the temporary file to a disk that won't wear out, or tell the batch file that it need not check the time quite so often.

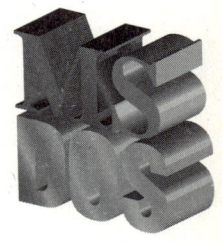

Put Temporary Files on a RAM Drive

My problem with the current version of WAITFOR.BAT is that it beats the heck out of your hard drive; it not only could be used to control a timed backup procedure, it could be used as a burn—in program for a new hard disk.

One way to avoid this would be to put the temporary files on a drive that won't wear out, a drive without moving parts—some kind of "solid state" drive. There is such a thing—it's called an *electronic disk*, *RAM disk*, or *RAM drive*.

The idea with a RAM drive is that you allocate some memory—either conventional, extended, or expanded, although extended is recommended—and run a program that tells DOS that memory isn't memory, it's a disk drive. A RAM drive is good in that it's fast, blindingly so, and won't wear out. A RAM drive, however, has at least one weak point: if you turn the PC off, everything in the RAM drive is lost. This means RAM drives are very good for storing data that needs to be stored quietly and quickly, but temporarily.

What kind of data is important enough to create, but not important enough to want to keep after you turn off the PC? Temporary data, that's what. Many programs create temporary files in the process of doing their work. For example, when you ask a word processor to generate a table of contents for a document, it does so by scanning the entire document, looking for items that must go into the table of contents. Prior to doing that, however, the word processor creates a file that retains any items that need to go into the table of contents; when it's done generating the table of contents, it doesn't need the file any longer, and so it erases it.

When a graphics program converts a large graphical file from one format, such as PC Paintbrush PCX format, to another format, such as Aldus Tagged Image File Format (TIFF), it usually creates some kind of intermediate file that, again, gets erased as soon as the operation is finished. Many Windows programs create temporary files, and you've already seen that DOS itself creates temporary files during pipe operations.

Notice that if a temporary file gets lost due to a power failure, buggy software, or whatever, it doesn't matter. If the operation that needed the temporary file was interrupted, all you need to do is restart the operation and the temporary file is re-created, and after it's re-created, it gets erased after the operation has been completed anyway.

You can tell Windows and DOS programs that create temporary files where to put those temporary files with an environment variable called TEMP. You probably have a line in your AUTOEXEC.BAT as follows:

```
SET TEMP=C:\DOS
```

Now, not every program looks to the TEMP variable; some programs just make a mess wherever they feel like it. But DOS and most Windows programs look to the TEMP variable for guidance about where to put temporary files, which returns us to the subject of RAM drives.

If you have extended memory that you don't need for your programs, you can convert that memory to a RAM drive with the RAMDRIVE.SYS program. The entire syntax for RAMDRIVE.SYS is in the Command Reference, but, simplified, you can include the following line in your CONFIG.SYS:

```
DEVICE=C:\DOS\RAMDRIVE.SYS nnnn /E
```

Here, *nnnn* is the amount of extended memory, in K, that you want to devote to the RAM drive. This statement must appear somewhere after HIMEM.SYS in your CONFIG.SYS file. If you place it before HIMEM.SYS, RAMDRIVE.SYS won't be able to run because it needs an XMS driver to run. *(See Chapter 9 if you've forgotten what an XMS driver is.)* After RAMDRIVE.SYS loads, you'll see a message similar to the following:

```
Microsoft RAMDrive Version 3.07 virtual disk F:
Disk size: 4096K
Sector size: 512 bytes
Allocation unit: 4 sectors
Directory entries: 64
```

The only part of these messages that you need to be concerned with is the drive letter that RAMDRIVE.SYS has been assigned—F:, in the case of my example. Modify the AUTOEXEC.BAT to point to that drive, such as by typing **SET TEMP=F:**, and reboot. Now if you run WAITFOR.BAT, you won't see any disk activity.

Be warned, however, that Windows uses the same temporary area as DOS, and Windows programs may create temporary files that are many megabytes in size. If you only run DOS programs, using a RAM disk for temporary files is probably a good idea. If you also run Windows programs, however, be sure to create a RAM disk that's large enough to accommodate the Windows programs. That's probably tough to do, however, as you would need a great deal of RAM to be able to meet Windows' need of at least 8M of RAM to be useful and create a multi-megabyte RAM drive.

Perhaps we can find an alternative.

Combine CHOICE Delays with WAITFOR

The WAITFOR command checks the time several times per second, almost like anxious children waiting for their parents to awake on Christmas morning. Why not teach WAITFOR to check the time only every minute or so? Recall that you can get a batch file to wait about a minute by adding the line **CHOICE /c:{255} /t:{255},60 /n** to the batch file. Put that in the loop before each time check. Then WAITFOR.BAT would appear as follows (call it WAITFOR3.BAT):

```
@echo off
:top
choice /c:{255} /t:{255},55 /n
time<enter ¦ find "11:00:"
if errorlevel 1 goto top
```

I think you will like this version better. Note that I wrote it so that it checks time once every 55 seconds, rather than once every minute; I just wanted to be sure that a small inaccuracy in CHOICE didn't make WAITFOR3.BAT miss the appointed minute.

Notice that WAITFOR has a time value, such as 11:00:, built into it. It would be much more useful—or at least elegant—if you could call it with a time to wait until. That way, you could type **WAITFOR 5:32:**, rather than having to edit WAITFOR to get it to wait for a different time. You would do that with replaceable parameters.

See the Batch File Toolbox, at the end of this chapter, for two practical examples.

Using Replaceable Parameters in Command Files

You are accustomed to DOS programs that accept parameters and arguments on the command line. For example, when you type **DIR B:**, the B: is an argument to the program DIR. (*See Chapter 2 if you've forgotten how DOS executes a command.*) These are sometimes called run-time arguments because they're not incorporated in the DIR program; you specify them when you run the DIR program. Run-time arguments make programs more flexible, and it's simple to add them to DOS batch programs.

A Batch File To Make and Use a Subdirectory

Here's an example of a batch file in which run-time parameters really make the batch program useful. When users get a floppy full of information, the natural reaction is to create a subdirectory for the disk and then copy the disk to the subdirectory. That involves a sequence such as the following:

```
MD \newsub
CD \newsub
COPY a:*.*
```

That is what's supposed to happen. But it's common to forget to CD after MD-ing. The result is that you have the subdirectory and you have the data on the disk, you just don't have the data in the subdirectory on the disk. It would be nice to have a command that performs the functions of the MD and CD commands in one shot, enabling you to, say, type **MCD \newsub**, and then copy to your heart's content. A batch file to both create and move to \newsub: would require just three lines, as follows:

```
@ECHO OFF
MD \newsub
CD \newsub
```

This batch file, however, would only create a subdirectory called newsub. What if you wanted a subdirectory called sub2? You would type...

```
@ECHO off
MD \sub2
CD \sub2
```

You see the pattern emerging. The batch file appears as...

```
@ECHO OFF
MD [subdirectory name]
CD [same subdirectory name]
```

As mentioned before, it would be nice if you could write MCD.BAT so that you could type **MCD \newsub**, and somehow communicate the \newsub back to the MD and CD commands. You can, with replaceable parameters. It would appear as follows:

```
@ECHO OFF
MD %1
CD %1
```

The %1 is the replaceable parameter. Recall from Chapter 2's discussion of how COMMAND.COM chops up a command line—*parses* it—that COMMAND.COM searches for spaces in the command line. The first item that COMMAND.COM sees is interpreted as the command that COMMAND.COM must execute, either as an internal command, COM, EXE, or BAT file. Subsequent items are put into temporary holding spaces called %1, %2, %3, %4, %5, %6, %7, %8, and %9. There is even a %0—the command itself.

For example, if you type the command **abc dog lincoln house justice** the command parser executes abc, whatever that turns out to be, pass-ing to the parameters %1=dog, %2=lincoln, %3=house, %4=justice, and %5 through %9 =?, or null—empty.

What Does the Command Parser Do with the Parameters?

In the case of MCD.BAT, say you have typed **MCD \NEWSUB**. The command parser goes through the following steps:

1. It puts \NEWSUB into %1 and activates MCD.BAT.

2. The first line of MCD.BAT is the usual @echo off, just as you've seen earlier in this chapter.

3. The second line is md %1. The command parser knows that it has to resolve the % variables before executing the line, so it looks up %1, and comes up with \NEWSUB. It then reassembles the command to MD \NEWSUB, and executes that.

4. The third line again contains a % variable. Convert the %1 to \NEWSUB, and the command to be executed is CD \NEWSUB. And the batch file is done.

To see in more detail how replaceable parameters work, try out the following batch file, called SEEVARS.BAT:

```
@ECHO OFF
ECHO The first replaceable parameter (%%1)=%1
ECHO The second replaceable parameter (%%2)=%2
ECHO The third replaceable parameter (%%3)=%3
ECHO The fourth replaceable parameter (%%4)=%4
```

Now type **seevars log dog bog fog**, and **seevars sherpa doppelganger**. You'll see output similar to that in figure 15.13.

```
C:\BATCHTST>seevars log dog bog fog
The first replaceable parameter (%1)=log
The second replaceable parameter (%2)=dog
The third replaceable parameter (%3)=bog
The fourth replaceable parameter (%4)=fog
C:\BATCHTST>seevars sherpa doppelganger
The first replaceable parameter (%1)=sherpa
The second replaceable parameter (%2)=doppelganger
The third replaceable parameter (%3)=
The fourth replaceable parameter (%4)=
C:\BATCHTST>
```

Figure 15.13

Sample output from SEEVARS.BAT.

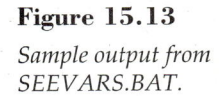

In this example, the ECHO statements are simply putting messages on the screen. The messages only vary from run to run because the replaceable parameters get inserted in place of the %1, %2, and so on by COMMAND.COM before the ECHO statements are actually executed. There's nothing to the right of = on the third and fourth variables in the second example because you typed in only two parameters. This isn't an error, because, as mentioned before, there are always the parameters %1 through %9, regardless of whether or not they are empty.

Checking for Replaceable Parameters

Now that you know how to use replaceable parameters, you might see a potential problem: if you've written a batch file that needs replaceable parameters, it needs replaceable parameters. Consider what happens to MCD if you forget to type in replaceable parameters. The second line, md %1, becomes simply md, as there's nothing in %1. The command MD all by itself causes an error, because the operating system doesn't know what directory to make. The command CD all by itself just requests a report from the operating system on the name of the current subdirectory.

You can check to see if you've received a parameter using the IF command. You used IF ERRORLEVEL to check return codes, but there is another version of IF—the *evaluation* IF. It appears as follows:

```
IF firstitem == seconditem command
```

In this case, *firstitem* and *seconditem* are any string of characters, and *command* is any batch command, such as GOTO END or ECHO HELLO. The == symbols mean "is equal to," and, if you're wondering why DOS doesn't just use a plain old equal sign (=), it's probably because much of DOS was written by programmers using the C language, and the C language uses == to test for equality. (It's kind of a macho techie programmer thing.)

Here's an example of the IF == command. In this batch file, called SECRET.BAT, you must guess a secret password. It appears as follows:

```
@ECHO OFF
IF %1==swordfish goto rightanswer
ECHO You didn't get it this time!
```

```
GOTO end
:rightanswer
ECHO Correct!
:end
```

Try it with *secret opensesame*, *secret password*, and *secret swordfish*. As swordfish is the correct password, the first two tries won't work, and your screen appears something like figure 15.14.

```
C:\BATCHTST>secret opensesame
You didn't get it this time!
C:\BATCHTST>
C:\BATCHTST>secret password
You didn't get it this time!
C:\BATCHTST>
C:\BATCHTST>secret swordfish
Correct!
C:\BATCHTST>
C:\BATCHTST>secret
Syntax error
You didn't get it this time!
C:\BATCHTST>
```

Figure 15.14

Sample output from SECRET.BAT.

Try it without a parameter, and you'll get the error message at the bottom of the figure. The problem stems from the comparison %1==swordfish, which only works if there's something on both sides. If there is no parameter, there's nothing on the right-hand side of this expression. Again, how do you protect your command files against this kind of "user input" problem? The following program, INPUTTST.BAT, shows the way:

```
@ECHO OFF
IF "%1a"=="a" goto nogood
ECHO Good--you entered a parameter!
GOTO end
:nogood
ECHO You didn't enter a parameter. Try again, but this time
ECHO type "INPUTTST parameter," where "parameter" is any
ECHO combination of characters.
:end
```

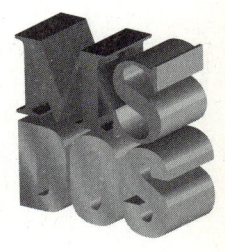

Try that, and you'll see that it "traps user errors," to use programmer lingo. The user might or might not have typed in a parameter. If the user typed a parameter, such as X, the X substitutes for the %1. Then the comparison becomes IF Xa==a ..., which fails, as the character sequence Xa is different from the character sequence a. On the other hand, suppose the user didn't type anything. Then the test would be IF a==a, as the %1 would be empty, and there would be no difference between the two sides of the test. When this test succeeds, it means the user forgot the parameter, and the batch file needs an error message—or, as programmers sometimes call it, a "nastygram."

Apply input checking to MCD.BAT, and it might resemble MCD2.BAT, as follows:

```
@ECHO OFF
IF "%1"=="" goto nogood
MD %1
CD %1
GOTO end
:nogood
ECHO ^GError: please use this program like so:
ECHO MCD subname
ECHO where "subname" is the name of the subdirectory that you
ECHO wish to create.
:end
```

Note the ^G in the error message. That's a Ctrl+G, and it makes the system beep to get the user's attention. Whenever possible, write your batch files to be as "bulletproof" as possible, not only so your users won't be tripped up, but because over time you may forget the batch file's function yourself.

Before leaving MCD.BAT, let's add the *coup de grace* to this batch file—full DOS 6.2 documentation compatibility. To what do I refer? Why, on-line help, of course! All respectable DOS 6.2 programs can be invoked with the /? option, leading them to display a few lines of self-explanation. By reworking the file a bit, you end up with MCD3.BAT, as follows:

```
@ECHO OFF
IF "%1"=="" goto nogood
IF "%1"=="/?" goto explain
MD %1
CD %1
GOTO end
:nogood
ECHO ^GError: this program needs an input argument!
```

```
GOTO explain
:explain
ECHO please use this program like so:
ECHO MCD subname
ECHO where "subname" is the name of the subdirectory that you
ECHO wish to create.
:end
```

Invoke it with **/?**, and you get an output similar to the one in figure 15.15.

```
C:\BATCHTST>mcd3 /?
please use this program like so:
MCD subname
where "subname" is the name of the subdirectory that you
wish to create.
C:\BATCHTST>
```

Figure 15.15

MCD3.BAT output with help displayed.

Kinda makes me feel like a real programmer.

Understanding and Using Environment Variables in Command Files

Replaceable parameters are one kind of a larger class of programming tools called environment variables or batch variables. Variables are places in memory that programmers use to hold transient information, temporary "scratch pad" areas. Just as you saw that MCD would be silly without replaceable parameters, some programs would be impossible without variables.

A variable is named by any string of characters with a percent sign (%) at the front of it. The name must start with a letter: %f, %mydata, or %varname are all perfectly legal names, but %7 is not, nor is %4data, as it would be confused with the replaceable parameters.

Variables are stored in a section of COMMAND.COM called the environment. You've already got a few variables in your environment. Type **set**, and you'll see a display similar to the one in figure 15.16.

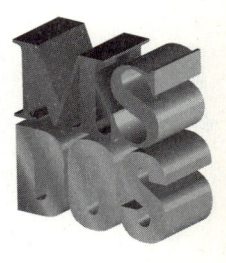

Figure 15.16

Displaying environment variables.

```
C:\BATCHTST>set
CONFIG=withnet
COMSPEC=C:\DOS\COMMAND.COM
PROMPT=$p$g
PATH=C:\DOS;C:\W31;C:\UTILS;D:\UTILS
TEMP=f:\

C:\BATCHTST>
```

The figure shows a number of prestored environment variables. They are used by the operating system for various purposes. For example, the TEMP command, as you've read earlier in this chapter, tells DOS, some DOS programs, and most Windows programs where to put temporary files.

Again, notice that this applies to some DOS programs and most Windows programs. The environment variables are only of use to programs that choose to use them; they're a set of iron rules that applications programs must follow. The environment variables that are on your system will probably vary in names and values from the ones on mine, but the five that you see in figure 15.16 are variables used by DOS and many DOS and Windows programs. A summary of what they do follows:

- ✔ CONFIG is used by the DOS MultiConfig feature to communicate from CONFIG.SYS to AUTOEXEC.BAT which of the multiple possible configurations were selected by the user.

- ✔ COMSPEC identifies the location of the command-line shell. It is required when DOS must reload part of COMMAND.COM from the disk.

- ✔ PATH you already have met. This environment variable holds the current value of the program search path that COMMAND.COM uses.

- ✔ PROMPT controls what user prompt you see: the C:\ prompt is presented by DOS, and controlled by this environment variable. You've learned in previous chapters how to use PROMPT to modify the DOS prompt.

All of these environmental variables (and any new ones that you define) are immediately accessible from inside batch files; just surround the variable's name with percent signs, and COMMAND.COM substitutes the value inside the variable for the variable's name.

For example, suppose you wanted a batch file that would report the status of the location for the temporary files. The batch file would alert the user that no location had been specified for temporary files, or would report that location. Such a batch file might appear as follows:

```
@ECHO off
IF "%TEMP%"=="" goto notemp
ECHO Current location for temporary files=%TEMP%
GOTO end
:notemp
ECHO ^GWarning! You have not specified a TEMP variable.
:end
```

Here's another command file—actually a pair of batch files—that you can use to modify your path as you go. The first, called ADDPATH, enables you to temporarily add a subdirectory to your path without retyping the entire PATH statement. The second batch file deletes the temporarily added element to the PATH.

The ADDPATH command file appears as follows:

```
@ECHO off
IF ""=="%1" goto messup
SET oldpath=%path%
SET path=%1;%path%
GOTO end
:messup
ECHO Please use this batch file with the subdirectory that
ECHO you wish to add to the path, as in "addpath c:\wp"
:end
```

Its twin, DELPATH.BAT, is simpler:

```
@ECHO off
SET path=%oldpath%
```

The ADDPATH command file checks to see if a parameter is included, and issues an error message if not. It also stores the current path to a new environment variable called OLDPATH. The OLDPATH variable is kept around so that it's easy to restore the path to its pre-ADDPATH state.

The DELPATH variable uses that information to return PATH to its former state. The command SET PATH=%OLDPATH% just takes the value in OLDPATH and copies it into PATH.

Some very complex command files can be built with environment variables. Environment variables are the key to building multiple configurations under MultiConfig, as you'll learn in the next chapter.

Adding Comments to Batch Files

You read earlier that you should add error checking and messages to batch files as a safeguard against accidental misuse of a batch file, and to jog your memory about a batch program you've already written. In general, all good programmers document their work. (In general, we should all give to charity. In general, we should all be kind and helpful to people in need. Getting the idea about documentation in the real world?)

Documenting your work means adding statements in regular English within the program to help anyone who is trying to figure out what you did in the program, or to help you figure out what you were trying to do if you forget. Programmers believe they'll never forget how they built such a labor of love, but they often do. The explanatory statements the batch language enables programmers to add (they are not executed) are prefixed with the word REM, short for remark. A typical REM statement might be...

```
REM This next line tests for user input.
```

This line doesn't accomplish anything except make your life easier when you're trying to remember what a batch file is supposed to do. Fully commented, a MCD2.BAT batch file might appear as...

```
@ECHO off
REM Directory maker and changer
REM Written by: Mark Minasi 10 January 1993
REM Combines the functions of "MD" and "CD"
REM
REM The next line checks that the user enters a parameter
if a%1==a got nogood
```

```
REM if you got to this line, the user used a parameter; now make
rem the directory, and change to it.
MD %1
CD %1
REM Now jump over the error message.
GOTO end
:nogood
REM Explain what went wrong, with suggestions for next time.
ECHO ^GError: please use this program like so:
ECHO MCD subname
ECHO where "subname" is the name of the subdirectory that you
ECHO wish to create.
REM Exit point
:end
```

That's overdoing it a bit, but you see the point: bigger and uglier batch files definitely need comments. Get in the habit while you're doing small batch files, and you'll stay in the habit when you do larger ones.

Connecting Batch Files

All programmers eventually end up with a "toolkit" of useful programs they use again and again. Consider, for example, the CHOICE delay command that I've used in a few batch programs. To wait 30 seconds, I add the line `CHOICE /c:{255} /t:{255},30 /n` at an appropriate location in the batch file. To wait 50 seconds, I would add `CHOICE /c:{255} /t:{255},50 /n` where needed, and so on.

But that's awfully cumbersome. Wouldn't it be better if I could just put a command in my batch file such as `DELAY 30` or `DELAY 50`? That would be no problem.

Building Batch Files That Other Batch Files Can Use

First, let's build a batch file called DELAY.BAT that accepts a command-line argument of the number of seconds to wait. By now, this should be easy to build, as follows:

```
@ECHO off
REM DELAY.BAT by Mark Minasi January 1993
REM delays a batch file for "n" seconds.
REM Requires DOS 6.2 or later, and MUST be called with a
REM number of seconds to delay
if "%1"=="" goto error
CHOICE /c:{255} /t:{255},%1 /n
GOTO end
:error
ECHO ERROR in DELAY: no delay time specified
ECHO DELAY should be called with number of seconds
ECHO to delay.
:end
```

Notice the input checking. This is particularly important if we plan to use this batch file within other batch files, because if one batch file activated DELAY without the proper parameters, DELAY wouldn't work correctly, which in turn would make the other batch file work incorrectly, and could make for a major debugging nightmare. This way, I've built in a bit of the "belt-and-suspenders" mentality that is essential for programmers.

Notice also the REM statements. This is positively essential for a tool that is to be used repeatedly. Six months from now, I probably won't remember that DELAY requires a delay time in seconds. As a matter of fact, if I forget what DELAY does, I can just type **DELAY**, and DELAY informs me.

Notice finally that the batch file is 13 lines long, and, of those lines, only one line—the CHOICE command—does any "real" work. That's not unusual; good programs must be well documented, and they should understand that they work in an environment of other programs. All the other "padding" makes life easier for the users of DELAY in the long run—and because the major user of DELAY probably will be me, I should have a vested interest in seeing those goals achieved.

Did you know, for example, that in the Microsoft Windows programs that support FastDisk (the 32-bit disk access), 90 percent of the code simply makes sure the hardware that FastDisk runs on will be compatible with FastDisk, so that it doesn't lose any data? Some folks might call that wasteful use of program space, but I wouldn't—I've lost data at the hands of buggy operating systems in the past.

Putting DELAY in a Batch File

Now let's experiment with DELAY. This first batch file, called TD1.BAT, displays a message, waits five seconds, and displays another message, as follows:

```
@ECHO off
ECHO Hello from TD. Next message in 5 seconds...
DELAY 5
ECHO Goodbye from TD.
Sample output from TD1.BAT looks like this:
C:\BATCHTST>TD1
Hello from TD. Next message in 5 seconds...
C:\BATCHTST>
```

Running this, I experienced a five-second delay before the command prompt returned, so it appeared to work. The second ECHO never appeared, however. Why?

It has to do with the manner in which COMMAND.COM executes batch files. It processes one line at a time, as you've seen. But when one of the lines in a batch file tells COMMAND.COM to run another batch file, COMMAND.COM begins executing the second batch file, forgetting the original batch file. COMMAND.COM basically has no memory when it comes to batch files calling batch files.

> **AUTHOR'S NOTE**
>
> *Think of it this way. You're sitting at your desk, hard at work designing an attractive invitation to the pool party you're having in two weeks. Then your boss has the nerve to come in and ask you to look over a report and add any comments that you may have. So you put aside the invitation, look over the report, make comments on it, and return it to your boss. Then you return to the invitation.*
>
> *What you did would be called, in computer terms, a* push and pop. *You have in your brain a kind of minute-by-minute "things to do" list. Earlier, the first item on the list was "work on the party*
>
> *continues*

invitation," and you were executing that program, so to speak. Then your boss issued a priority interrupt ("Do it now, Olson, or you're fired, and don't call me Chief!"), so you put "comment report" at the top of the "things to do now" list. But you didn't erase "work on the party invitation"—you just pushed it down lower on the list. Once you finished "comment report," then "work on party invitation" just popped up to the top of the list.

What you've demonstrated is that you're smarter than COMMAND.COM. Left to itself, COMMAND.COM has only one item in its "things to do" list. If something new arrives on the list, it knocks other things off the list. That's the problem, you see: it executed some of TD1.BAT, then started on DELAY.BAT. Then, by the time it finished DELAY.BAT, COMMAND.COM had forgotten that it was working on another batch file previously.

Don't Forget To CALL

You can solve this problem by warning COMMAND.COM that the next command in the batch file is another batch file, and so COMMAND.COM should be prepared to pick up where it left off in the first file. A new and improved TD2.BAT incorporates this change, as follows:

```
@ECHO off
ECHO Hello from TD. Next message in 5 seconds...
CALL DELAY 5
ECHO Goodbye from TD.
```

Now a sample output appears, as follows:

```
C:\BATCHTST>TD2
Hello from TD. Next message in 5 seconds...
Goodbye from TD.
C:\BATCHTST>
```

Problem solved. Remember, whenever you call a batch file from a batch file, use the CALL command. I've seen many people build themselves nice, big AUTOEXEC.BAT files in which

AUTOEXEC.BAT tries to execute a batch file, and stops when it's done with the second batch file, never finishing AUTOEXEC.BAT. This happens because the builders of the batch file didn't remember the CALL command.

Using CTTY NUL

The CTTY (Change Console Device) command, an internal command that came with DOS 2, changes the standard input/output device (the keyboard and monitor) to some other device (such as a terminal or teleprinter) and back again. When using CTTY, you must specify a device that can both receive input and send output. For example, entering `CTTY PRN` is silly because your printer is an output-only device; your computer sits there, waiting for input from the printer that never comes.

Although this command has little meaning for PC users, there is a very practical use for CTTY. Even when using ECHO OFF in batch files (as well as the @ symbol), unwanted screen clutter still occurs at times. You can clean up the screen totally by inserting `CTTY NUL` into the batch file before the commands that produce the screen clutter.

Unlike CON, which refers to the console (keyboard), and PRN, which refers to the printer, the NUL device refers to a device that does nothing. (Think of NUL as a "black hole"—you can send things there that you never want to see again.)

NUL is mostly used as a destination to redirect output to when you don't want output from a program run from a batch file to be seen on the screen. For example, this command copies MYFILE.TXT to drive A and prevents the `1 file(s) copied` message from appearing on the screen:

    COPY MYFILE.TXT A: > NUL,

Place the CTTY NUL command before any lines that echo information to the screen, but make sure you insert CTTY CON before the batch file ends to reactivate the keyboard. If you forget, you'll be locked out of the machine and have to reboot. To be on the safe side, always make sure that the batch file runs correctly before inserting the CTTY NUL command.

Chapter 15: *Writing Batch Files*

> *If you use the ANSI.SYS and Esc sequences to reprogram your keyboard, make sure these commands run before the CTTY NUL command or they won't work. Chapters 14 and 21 contain an example of how to reprogram your keyboard.*

Interactive Batch-File Execution

DOS 6.2 enables you to boot interactively by manually selecting the lines of your CONFIG.SYS file that you actually want to execute. DOS 6.2 also enables you to do this with AUTOEXEC.BAT.

As an added bonus, DOS 6.2 also enables you to interactively execute any batch file by using COMMANDs new /Y switch. To do this, enter `COMMAND /Y /C [batname]`. Use the following batch file (INTERACT.BAT), for example:

```
@ECHO OFF
ECHO Line 1
ECHO Line 2
ECHO Line 3
```

Entering `COMMAND /Y /C INTERACT` results in the following, if you press **y** for each line:

```
INTERACT [Y/N]?y
ECHO OFF [Y/N]?y
ECHO Line 1 [Y/N]?y
Line 1
ECHO Line 2 [Y/N]?y
Line 2
ECHO Line 3 [Y/N]?y
Line 3
```

Alternately, pressing **n** for a line prevents that line from being executed. Obviously, this switch is extremely useful for "walking" through a batch file for debugging purposes.

Understanding a Batch File Toolbox

One of the neatest things about the PC is that it enables you to do a lot of things yourself, unlike other platforms (such as the Mac) that lock you into their way of doing things. One way the PC gives you a lot of power is through batch files. Indeed, you can create some astonishingly powerful utilities using batch files alone.

> **TIP**
>
> *There are many other batch files in this book that you may want to reference and include in your toolbox.*

> **AUTHOR'S NOTE**
>
> *Using the technique you learned in the Using CHOICE To Delay a Batch File section, you can create your own alarm utilities. I've been known to sleep in my office (yes, during the work on this book), and of course, I needed an alarm clock to get me up so I could continue to work on my current project. So, instead of going down to Wal-Mart and buying another alarm clock, I just wrote ALARM.BAT.*
>
> *Make sure you also create a file called "CR," which contains a single carriage return. Use EDIT to create ALARM.BAT, as follows:*
>
> ```
> @echo off
> if %1!==! goto oops
> cls
> echo Alarm is set for %1
> time < cr | find "%1"
> if errorlevel 1 goto check
> goto alarm
> :check
> cls
> echo.
> echo Alarm is set for %1
> ```
>
> *continues*

```
time < cr ¦ find "Current"
choice /c:<255> /t:<255>,55 /n
time < cr ¦ find "%1"
if errorlevel 1 goto check
:alarm
echo ^G
echo Press Ctrl+Break to shut off alarm...
goto alarm
:oops
echo.
echo   Syntax = ALARM 11:30:
echo.
:end
echo.
```

To run ALARM.BAT, enter **ALARM**, and then enter a time (**11:30**, for example—remember to include the colon). The batch file then displays the alarm time and the current time until the system time reaches the specified time. The alarm itself is simply a Ctrl+G in an endless loop. Keep in mind that this technique does not recognize AM or PM, so you are stuck with a 12-hour alarm clock (what do you expect from a batch file?).

Using the same technique, you can also create a message-alarm utility that not only beeps, but displays a specified message. After creating ALARM.BAT, edit it as follows, and resave it as ALARM2.BAT:

```
@echo off
if %1!==! goto oops
if %2!==! goto now
echo.
echo                *** Message Alarm ***
echo.
echo To display a message when your alarm goes off,
echo type each line followed by the Enter key. After
echo the last line, press F6, and Enter once again.
copy con alarm.msg > nul
:now
   cls
   echo Alarm is set for %1
```

```
    time < cr ¦ find "%1"
    if errorlevel 1 goto check
    goto alarm
:check
    cls
    echo.
    echo Alarm is set for %1
    time < cr ¦ find "Current"
    choice /c:<255> /t:<255>,55 /n
    time < cr ¦ find "%1"
    if errorlevel 1 goto check
:alarm
    echo ^G
    if %2!==! goto end
    type alarm.msg
    echo.
    pause
    if not exist alarm.msg goto end
    del alarm.msg
    goto end
:oops
echo.
echo Syntax = ALARM 11:30: M (optional if you want a
echo   message displayed)
echo.
:end
echo.
```

To run ALARM2, enter the command, followed by the alarm time, a space, and an **M** if you want to enter a message, which you do by means of the COPY CON command. Unlike ALARMCLK, ALARM beeps only once when it senses the specified time, and then displays and deletes the message you entered.

*If the alarm in Windows Calendar or your favorite PIM doesn't suit you, try ALARM2.BAT instead. Run it in a small DOS window at the bottom of the screen, and set its background processing priority to **25**.*

continues

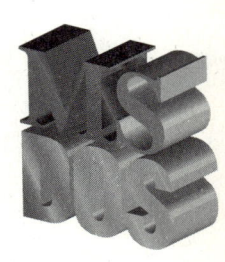

You can also use this technique to run a program at a specified time. For example, you can easily edit ALARM.BAT to create RUNAT.BAT. Edit the :Alarm routine to simply run the program of your choice, such as MSBACKUP, for example.

In case you are using a version of DOS prior to DOS 6.2, there is another way to produce the delay that the two alarm batch files need—create your own program using DEBUG. To do this, create the following ASCII text file and save it as WAITASEC.SCR. Be sure to leave a blank line after the Q:

```
N WAITASEC.COM
E 0100 BF 5B 00 33 C0 33 C9 33
E 0108 D2 BE 82 00 38 4C FE 74
E 0110 2D AC 3C 0D 74 16 2C 30
E 0118 72 F7 3C 09 77 F3 8B DA
E 0120 D1 E2 D1 E2 03 D3 D1 E2
E 0128 03 D0 EB E5 0B D2 74 0E
E 0130 B8 D6 00 F7 E2 33 D2 BB
E 0138 0A 00 F7 F3 8B F8 B8 40
E 0140 00 8E D8 BB 6C 00 8B 77
E 0148 02 03 3F 13 F1 8B 07 8B
E 0150 57 02 38 4F 04 74 03 83
E 0158 C2 18 3B D6 72 06 77 0E
E 0160 3B C7 73 0A B2 FF B4 06
E 0168 CD 21 74 E1 FE C1 8A C1
E 0170 B4 4C CD 21
RCX
0074
W
Q
```

To create the program, enter **DEBUG < WAITASEC.SCR** at the prompt. Now simply replace the CHOICE command in the batch files with **WAITASEC 46**, which will delay the computer for about 55 seconds.

Day of the Week Utility

Ever wonder on which day of the week a certain day will fall, such as Christmas Day 1999? Here's a cute little batch file that uses a little redirection and the DATE command to find out for you:

```
@echo off
cls
echo.
echo            *** WhatDay Utility ***
echo.
echo To see on which day of the week a certain day falls,
echo first type TODAY'S date (e.g. 9-23-93), press Enter,
echo then F6, and Enter once again.
copy con today.now > nul
echo.
echo Now enter the date you want to check.
date
echo.
echo Take note below of the day on which your special
echo date falls, then press Enter TWICE to end...
echo.
date
pause > nul
date < today.now > nul
del today.now
echo.
```

File Locator *(DW)*

Beginning with DOS 5, the DIR command finally gave us some power. A case in point is the /S switch, which lists files in subdirectories. Using the FIND filter, FINDFILE.BAT searches the current drive and directory for a single file or multiple occurrences of a file name, but it does not accept wildcards.

```
@echo off
if %1!==! goto oops
echo.
echo ***** FindFile Utility *****
echo.
echo Searching for %1
```

```
echo Please wait...
dir\ /s /b ¦ find "%1" /i ¦ more
goto end
:oops
echo.
echo Syntax = FINDFILE {filename.ext}
echo.
:end
echo.
```

Exclude Certain Files from Commands *(DW)*

There may be times when you want to carry out a command on all files in a directory except one, or perhaps on all but a certain group of files, such as all DOC files, for example. DELBUT.BAT hides the file(s) you want to keep, deletes all the others, and then unhides your keepers. Naturally, this accepts wildcards, such as *.DOC or D*.*.

```
@echo off
if %1 !==! goto oops
attrib +h %1
echo Y ¦ del *.* > nul
attrib -h %1
goto end
:oops
echo.
echo Syntax = %0 {filename.ext}
echo Wildcards are permitted.
echo.
:end
```

COPYBUT.BAT adds a slight twist to DELBUT.BAT. It copies all the files in a directory to a specific destination but leaves certain files behind. Note that the DEL line will *not* prompt you for confirmation.

```
@echo off
if %1 !==! goto oops
if %2 !==! goto oops
attrib +h %1
copy *.* %2
attrib -h %1
```

```
goto end
:oops
echo.
echo Syntax = %0 {filespec} {filespec}
echo Wildcards are permitted.
echo.
:end
```

One other variation on this theme is SPACE.BAT, a utility that will tell you how much space a group of files consumes.

```
@echo off
if %1 !==! goto oops
attrib +h %1
dir /ah /p
echo Look at the bottom of the directory display
echo to see how much disk space %1 consumes.
echo.
pause
attrib -h %1
goto end
:oops
echo.
echo Syntax = %0 {filespec}
echo Wildcards are permitted.
echo.
:end
```

Copying Different Disk Formats

DISKCOPY can't copy disks of differing formats, so what can you do? Just create COPYAA.BAT, which creates a temporary directory on drive C, copies all the files from the source disk to it, copies all those files back to the target disk, and then deletes the files and the directory on drive C. This does not work if the source disk has any subdirectories (no, not even if you use XCOPY). Naturally, with a couple of minor changes, you can create COPYBB.BAT, as follows:

```
@echo off
echo.
echo ***** A: to A: Copy Utility *****
echo.
```

```
echo Place SOURCE diskette in Drive A: and
pause
md c:\copyaa
copy a:*.* c:\copyaa
echo ^G
echo.
echo Place TARGET diskette in Drive A: and
pause
copy c:\copyaa\*.* a:
echo Y ¦ del c:\copyaa\*.* > nul
rd c:\copyaa
echo ^G
echo ^G
echo Done!
echo.
```

A variation of this is COPYAB.BAT, which *does* utilize XCOPY to copy all the files and directories from A to B. This is handy if you have a laptop with a 3 1/2-inch drive and need to use files from your desktop PC. COPYAB also displays the volume label of A and prompts you to type it in for B.

```
@echo off
echo.
echo ***** A: to B: Copy Utility *****
echo.
echo Place SOURCE diskette in drive A and
echo the TARGET diskette in drive B.
pause
echo Copying files. Please wait...
xcopy a:\ b: /s /e > nul
echo ^G
echo.
vol a:
echo.
echo If A has a volume label, enter it now.
abel b:
echo.
echo Done!
```

Changing the Drive and Directory at Once

Ever get irritated that you have to change first to a drive and then to a directory? Wouldn't it be more efficient to be able to do it in just one step? You can with CDD.BAT. Just type **CDD** followed by as many as three directories:

```
@echo off
if %1 !==! goto syntax
%1:
if %2 !==! goto end
cd \%2
cd %3 > nul
cd %4 > nul
goto end
:syntax
echo.
echo Syntax = %0 Drive Directory Directory Directory
echo.
:end
echo.
```

Floppy Disk Organizer

You can go out and buy a special program that will organize and catalog all your floppies, but FLOPORG.BAT is a cheap, fast, and easy way to do this. After choosing C to catalog a disk, the program shows you the contents of the disk, sorts it in alphabetical order, and then writes it to FLOPDIRA.TXT. You can then use the catalog directly from disk, or you can print it. Naturally, with a couple of changes, you can redo the program for drive B. The listing is as follows:

```
@echo off
:start
echo ================================
echo    *** Floppy Disk Organizer ***
echo --------------------------------
echo    C - Catalog a Floppy Disk
echo    X - Exit the Program
echo ================================
echo.
```

```
choice /C:cx Press
if errorlevel 2 goto no
if errorlevel 1 goto yes
:yes
echo.
echo Please put a floppy in drive A
echo and then press a key to continue.
pause > nul
dir a: /w /p /on
echo.
dir a: /on >> flopdira.txt
goto start
:no
```

A Handy Little Notepad

NOTE.BAT provides a quick way to jot down a note (shopping list, memo, and so on). You can then save and print it, save it only, or print it only. Enter the command with a file name to enter your text by means of COPY CON. The utility not only checks to see whether it a file name is entered, but it also checks to see if that file name already exists.

Notice that the lines for the notepad ruler wrap to the next line on this page. You type each one on one line. Also take note of the Alt+12 lines; entering Alt+12 on the numeric key pad enters a form feed to the printer. The listing follows:

```
@echo off
cls
if %1!==! goto oops
if exist %1 goto error
echo ==================
echo *** Quick Note ***
echo ==================
echo.
echo Type your note with a carriage return at the end of each line.
echo Press F6 and Enter again when done.
echo.
echo         5    10   15   20   25   30   35   40   45   50   55   60
65   70   75   80
```

```
echo +----+----+----+----+----+----+----+----+----+----+----
+----+----+----+----+
copy con %1 > nul
echo.
echo ============================
echo       * File Destination *
echo ----------------------------
echo      A - Save and Print
echo      S - Save Only
echo      P - Print Only
echo ============================
choice /C:asp Press
if errorlevel 3 goto print
if errorlevel 2 goto save
if errorlevel 1 goto both
:Both
echo.
echo Your note has been saved. Please
echo make sure your printer is ready.
echo.
pause
echo.
echo Printing your note...
copy %1 prn > nul
echo <Alt+12> > prn
echo.
goto end
:Save
echo.
echo Your note has been saved.
echo.
goto end
:Print
echo.
echo Please make sure your printer is ready.
echo.
pause
echo.
echo Printing your note...
copy %1 prn > nul
echo <Alt+12> > prn
del %1
```

```
echo.
goto end
:oops
echo.
echo You forgot to enter a file name.
echo    Syntax = NOTE {filename.ext}
echo.
goto end
:error
echo.
echo A file named %1 already exists.
echo Reenter the command with another file name.
echo.
:end
echo Done!
echo.
```

Log All Computer Activity

LOG.BAT is a quick way to log all the activity on your computer. There are two examples given here, but you can use as many as you need. After typing **LOG**, type a parameter, such as **WP** (word processor) or **SS** (spreadsheet). Naturally, you have to plug in the correct directory and program name for each example. The batch file then puts the date and time the program was started and ended in a log file called PROGRAM.LOG, which resides in the root directory. If no parameter is typed, the batch file reminds you of the syntax. Add the proper parameters for your system in a list under :oops. The listing is as follows:

```
@echo off
cd\
if %1!==! goto oops
if %1==wp goto wp
if %1==ss goto ss
:wp
   type start.wp > start.wp
   dir start.wp ¦ find "START" >> program.log
   del start.wp
       cd\<directory>
<program name>
```

```
    cd\
     type end.wp > end.wp
     dir end.wp ¦ find "END" >> program.log
     del end.wp
     goto end
:ss
    type start.ss > start.ss
    dir start.ss ¦ find "START" >> program.log
    del start.ss
        cd\<directory>
    <program name>
    cd\
    type end.ss > end.ss
    dir end.ss ¦ find "END" >> program.log
    del end.ss
    goto end
:oops
echo Type LOG followed by one of the following:
echo                WP     SS
:end
```

The PC Typewriter

As you learned in Chapter 7, you can use the COPY CON LPT1 command to copy directly from the console to the printer. PCTYPE.BAT takes advantage of this by enabling you to type in multiple lines and then print them; or type an individual line, print it, type another, print it, and so on. The latter choice provides an easy way of filling in a check or other form. This utility also illustrates a way of providing instructions for your batch files. The listing follows:

```
@echo off
echo =================
echo * PC Typewriter *
echo =================
echo.
choice /c:yn Do you need instructions?
if errorlevel 2 goto pctype
echo.
echo Instructions: To type multiple lines, type each
echo line,pressing Enter at the end of each one. After
```

```
echo the last line, press F6 and echo Enter once again.
echo.
echo To type individual lines, type a line, press Enter,
echo F6, and Enter again. Then press Y to enter the next
echo line or N to exit.
:pctype
echo.
choice /c:im Enter Individual lines or Multiple lines?
if errorlevel 2 goto start
copy con lpt1
goto end
:start
copy con lpt1
echo.
choice /c:yn Enter another line?
if errorlevel 2 goto end
goto start
:end
echo.
```

Recursive Delete

Here's one more. Utilizing the SHIFT command, RDEL.BAT recursively deletes a list of files without having to type multiple commands:

```
@echo off
echo.
echo   ***** Recursive Delete *****
echo.
:loop
if %1 !==! goto end
del %1
echo Deleting %1
shift
goto loop
:syntax
echo Syntax = %0 <filename>  <filename>   etc.
:end
echo.
echo Nothing to do!
echo.
```

The syntax is: RDEL *<filename> <filename>*, and so on. The utility deletes the first listed file, displays its name, then shifts the processing to the next file while GOTO loops back to the beginning. This process continues until the IF statement fails to find a file name in the list, at which time the batch file ends.

A nice feature about this technique is that if you enter a file that doesn't exist, you see a `File not found` message; the next line says it deleted that file, but, of course, it really didn't delete it.

Summary

You've seen that DOS batch language provides access to one of COMMAND.COM's greatest strengths—its *programmability*, or the power to prestore commands in batch files. Batch files enable you to take a repetitive task and automate it, freeing you to be more productive. (I even got a chance to preach a bit of "that old-time religion" about documenting programs, one of my favorite topics.)

MS DOS

CHAPTER 16

Using DOS 6.2 MultiConfig

by Mark Minasi

What's the best thing about DOS 6.2?

Many people like the disk compression routines built into DOS 6.2. I hate to be a party pooper, but I just don't trust disk compression, and I never will. (That doesn't mean you shouldn't either; I'm just a bit hidebound about a few things.) Other people like the new virus scanner and shield stuff. I say that it's been a long time coming, but it's no fun having to check your system for malicious programs written by antisocial cretins with nothing better to do. As a laptop user, InterLnk is certainly nifty, but after years on the road I've been carrying LapLink as a matter of habit anyway, so that brings no real improvement in quality of life for me.

Those DOS 6.2 features are nice, but I don't think any of them is the best one. As a matter of fact, I think it's no contest.

The best DOS 6.2 feature? MultiConfig.

I have one computer that has 10 sets of CONFIG.SYS/ AUTOEXEC.BAT files—one for normal DOS work, one for remote access, one for playing around with the CD-ROM, one for when I attach the Bernoulli box and do backups . . . you get the drift.

How often do you find yourself having to set up a "vanilla" AUTOEXEC.BAT/CONFIG.SYS combination, to make a program work more smoothly? Or rooting around for a bootable floppy because some CONFIG.SYS experiment went awry, and your system won't boot from the hard disk?

One of the great annoyances of the world, along with flossing your teeth and doing the dishes, is juggling configurations. MultiConfig solves all that. I said earlier that InterLnk is nice, but that LapLink (not to mention FastLynx and Brooklyn Bridge, and FastWire and PC Hooker, for that matter) has already solved that problem. Third-party, multiple-boot configuration utilities have been available for years, but they've never really worked. That's not a slap at the people who've worked hard to design and build those utilities, it's just recognition of the fact that multiple-configuration control works best when built into the operating system.

When you see how easy it is to make it work, I think you'll agree.

What Does MultiConfig Do?

The MultiConfig feature of DOS 6.2 can accomplish the following:

- ✔ It enables you to merge many AUTOEXEC.BAT/CONFIG.SYS combinations into one CONFIG.SYS/AUTOEXEC.BAT.

- ✔ It adds a simple front-end menu system to multiple configurations, enabling you at run-time to decide which configuration is best for your work today.

✔ It enables you to designate a particular configuration as a default configuration that loads after waiting a specified number of seconds for you to choose a configuration.

✔ It enables you with a keystroke (F5) to skip the entire CONFIG.SYS/AUTOEXEC.BAT.

✔ It enables you with another keystroke (F8) to stop DOS at each line in the CONFIG.SYS, prompting you (Y/N?) whether or not to activate that particular line.

✔ It enables you to designate any line in the CONFIG.SYS as one DOS prompts you about before executing.

✔ It enables you to shut off the NumLock light on your enhanced keyboard—a function that is completely irrelevant to the maintenance of multiple configurations, but is quite welcome to us old-timers who think that God intended for the Ctrl key to sit next to our left pinkies, and can't seem to remember not to use the numeric keypad for cursor control keys. (It's an affliction known as "original PC keyboard fixation.")

Before going any further in this chapter, please back up your AUTOEXEC.BAT and CONFIG.SYS files. If you follow along with the discussion of MultiConfig, then you'll end up modifying AUTOEXEC.BAT and CONFIG.SYS. Please back those files up before modifying them. (Our lawyers make us include this line.)

Using Clean Boot and Interactive Boot

Even if you don't mess around much with the CONFIG.SYS and AUTOEXEC.BAT files, you sometimes must rename or move them so that you can boot your system in a "vanilla" configuration, a stripped-down setup required to troubleshoot some faulty hardware or software.

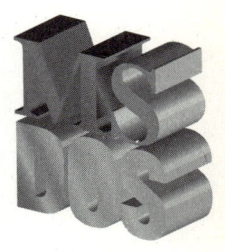

More specifically, suppose that you've installed a new Local Area Network (LAN) card in your system. It doesn't seem to work—it fails its diagnostics—but you suspect that the board is fine. Perhaps one of the programs you load each day upon startup (your screen blanker, your memory manager, or maybe the CD-ROM driver) is conflicting with the LAN card. So you'd like to try booting without any of those programs to test the LAN card again before giving up on it.

Such a *clean boot* usually requires that you save your old CONFIG.SYS/AUTOEXEC.BAT, then type a new basic one and try to reboot (although you would have to have a bootable floppy on hand in case you didn't type the new CONFIG.SYS/AUTOEXEC.BAT file correctly).

If you've ever done that, you know that a number of things can go wrong when you boot without your normal boot files. A few that have happened to me include the following:

- ✔ If you put your COMMAND.COM file in a directory other than the root of the drive C, your system needs a SHELL= statement. If you boot without a CONFIG.SYS file, your system won't contain a SHELL= statement, and the system will stop during the boot with a message that says `Bad or missing command interpreter`, followed by a system lockup.

- ✔ If you need a device driver (one of the programs loaded with the DEVICE= command in CONFIG.SYS) to access your hard disk, then booting without CONFIG.SYS leads to a booted system that can't communicate with its hard disk. Examples of this include OnTrack Disk Manager, Stacker, or many PC-based security systems.

Using Clean Boot

In DOS 6.2, all you've got to do is reboot your system and wait for the message to appear on the screen that says `Starting MS-DOS...`; then just press and release F5, activating the clean boot feature. You'll see a message that says MS-DOS is bypassing your CONFIG.SYS and AUTOEXEC.BAT files.

DOS will have booted, with the DoubleSpace driver loaded, if you use DoubleSpace on any of your volumes. It also gives you a PATH=C:\DOS, a nice touch.

> **NOTE** *If you are using DOS 6.2, you also can skip the loading of DoubleSpace by pressing Ctrl-F5 for a truly clean boot. You might want to do this for troubleshooting purposes or for those times when you need every single byte of memory for a certain program, such as Falcon 3.0 or other game.*

> **NOTE** *If your keyboard does not recognize F5 due to some malfunction, you can instruct DOS to skip your CONFIG.SYS/AUTOEXEC.BAT by pressing and holding down either Shift key. Begin pressing the key once the Starting MS-DOS... message appears, and don't release it until the system has finished booting. You will not see the* `MS-DOS is bypassing your CONFIG.SYS and AUTOEXEC.BAT files` *message if you bypass the startup files with the shift key, unlike when you bypass them with the F5 key.*

Using Interactive Boot

You also might find yourself wanting a selective boot rather than a clean boot—that is, a boot process that enables you to interactively eliminate one or more lines. This is a better alternative than copying the CONFIG.SYS somewhere else so that you can restore it later, using the REM command to delete the suspect lines, then rebooting again.

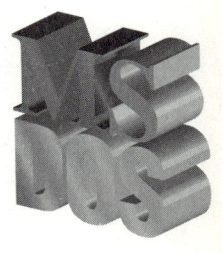

With DOS 6.2's interactive boot feature, it's a piece of cake. All you've got to do is wait for the `Starting MS-DOS...` message, then press F8. As the system boots, you'll see each line of CONFIG.SYS, together with the [Y,N]? prompt. You just press **Y** or **N** as the prompts appear—you need not press Enter—and you can then accept or reject each statement as it appears.

For example, suppose that you have a simple CONFIG.SYS that appears as follows:

```
device=c:\dos\himem.sys
files=60
dos=high
```

If you press F8 as your system boots, you see something like the following:

```
FILES=60 [Y,N]?
DOS=HIGH [Y,N]?
DEVICE=C:\DOS\HIMEM.SYS [Y,N]?
Process AUTOEXEC.BAT [Y,N]?
```

I've left off the responses, but I want you to notice something. The order in which the commands are presented is not necessarily the order in which you put them in the CONFIG.SYS; instead, you're seeing them in the order in which DOS executes them.

> *Notice that the prompts only occur for each CONFIG.SYS line. All that Interactive Boot says about AUTOEXEC.BAT is* Process AUTOEXEC.BAT [Y,N]? *Interactive Boot really only controls CONFIG.SYS on a line-by-line basis, not AUTOEXEC.BAT. In fact, MultiConfig largely only controls the execution of CONFIG.SYS. That does not mean that it's impossible to support multiple configurations in a single AUTOEXEC.BAT—by no means—but what it does mean is that you'll have to do a lot of the work with the batch commands that you learned in Chapter 15 (that's why we put that chapter first).*

In light of the previous note, after asking you if you want to process AUTOEXEC.BAT, DOS 6.2 does an interactive execution just like CONFIG.SYS. This new feature now enables you to easily support multiple configurations with a single AUTOEXEC.BAT. See Chapter 15 for another new feature of DOS 6.2's interactive batch-file execution.

Interactive Boot as a Problem-Solving Tool

Actually, that's a kind of neat side effect of Interactive Boot.

Did you ever have some error message flash by that you couldn't read because the screen cleared, or something else scrolled off the screen? Use Interactive Boot. Because it stops and prompts you between statements, you get a chance not only to see the messages, but also which program issued which message.

I used Interactive Boot when I was writing Chapter 13 and comparing the memory manager optimization performance of MemMaker, Quarterdeck's Optimize, and Qualitas' Maximize. MemMaker froze partway through its analysis, and I suspected that it was the SCSI driver on my PC that was killing it.

Now, back in the old days (before Interactive Boot), you would have had to make up a different CONFIG.SYS, one without the SCSI drivers, and then run MemMaker on that CONFIG.SYS to figure out if it was, indeed, the SCSI drivers that were making MemMaker freeze. As a matter of fact, I almost did that until I realized that I had a better answer. I just waited for MemMaker to do its first reboot as part of its analysis process, and I pressed F8 as it started the boot. By putting CONFIG.SYS in *single-step mode*, I was able to determine that it was not the SCSI driver crashing MemMaker after all, but EMM386.EXE in its *aggressive memory search* mode.

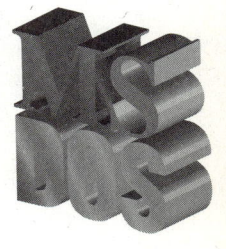

Making a Boot Command Always Interactive

You may find that you want the option to accept or reject activating a particular statement every time you boot. You can do that under DOS 6.2 by placing a question mark before the equal sign (=) in any statement. If you regularly use the ANSI.SYS device driver, for example, but sometimes want to bypass loading it, write its invocation line in CONFIG.SYS as follows:

```
DEVICE?=C:\DOS\ANSI.SYS
```

You then get the [Y,N]? prompt next to it each time you boot the system, whether you pressed F8 or not.

Disabling Clean Boot and Interactive Boot

As valuable as the Clean Boot and Interactive Boot features are, you might want to disable them, perhaps for reasons of security. In that case, just add...

```
SWITCHES=/N
```

...to your CONFIG.SYS. Whenever DOS sees that command in a CONFIG.SYS, it disables Clean Boot (either through F5 or the Shift keys) and Interactive Boot (F8).

It would seem logical that you'd have to put this command on the first line of CONFIG.SYS for this to work, but it'll actually work no matter where you place it in a CONFIG.SYS file.

Getting Started with MultiConfig

As you've read elsewhere in this book, DOS 6.2 includes a serial and parallel port-based file transfer program called InterLnk. Setting up InterLnk involves two parts: a device driver called INTERLNK.EXE, and a TSR called either INTERSVR.EXE or INTERLNK.EXE, depending on whether your PC will be acting as a server (INTERSVR.EXE) or a client (INTERLNK.EXE).

I don't want to explain InterLnk in detail—that's what Chapter 22 is about—but I want to show you how to set up a PC to be able to act as an InterLnk client. Suppose that you have the following basic CONFIG.SYS (I'm sure yours is more complicated, but I want a simple CONFIG.SYS so that the basic principles of using MultiConfig are easy to see):

```
FILES=60
BUFFERS=30
STACKS=9,256
DEVICE=C:\DOS\HIMEM.SYS
DOS=HIGH
```

To make your PC act as an InterLnk client or server, you've got to add the INTERLNK.EXE device driver. So, on the days when you want to work with InterLnk, you'd need a CONFIG.SYS that appears as follows:

```
FILES=60
BUFFERS=30
STACKS=9,256
DEVICE=C:\DOS\HIMEM.SYS
DOS=HIGH
DEVICE=C:\DOS\INTERLNK.EXE
```

Basically, you've got two CONFIG.SYS files—one for *normal* operations and one for *InterLnk* operations. Let's call them that just for convenience's sake—the normal and the InterLnk configurations.

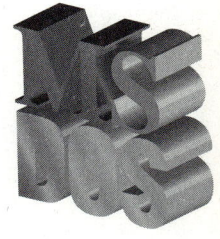

Now, I don't know how you kept track of stuff like this before DOS 6.2, but I had a subdirectory called C:\CONFIGS that had CONFIG.SYS and AUTOEXEC.BAT files for different uses. I might, then, have kept the CONFIG.SYS for normal operations in a file called CONFIG.NRM and the CONFIG.SYS for InterLnk operations in a file called CONFIG.ILK. I'd do the same for the AUTOEXEC.BATs, and would have an AUTOEXEC.NRM and an AUTOEXEC.ILK. Then I would prepare to execute normal operations by typing **COPY C:\CONFIGS\CONFIG.NRM C:\CONFIG.SYS**, and **COPY C:\CONFIGS\AUTOEXEC.NRM C:\AUTOEXEC.BAT** for the AUTOEXEC.BAT.

Using MultiConfig on these files requires several steps; let's take them one step at a time.

MultiConfig Step 1: Merge All CONFIG.SYS Files

With MultiConfig, you put both CONFIG.SYS files into the same ASCII text file. (I say both, but if you had almost a dozen configurations as I do, the better phrase is "all configurations.") Don't name it CONFIG.SYS just yet, as it's still going to need some work. For now, call it CONFIG.ALL.

If you want to merge a number of CONFIG.SYS files into a single file, you'll find that the DOS EDIT program has no "merge file" capability. But here's a simple way to do it right from the DOS command line. If you want to merge CONFIG.NRM and CONFIG.ILK into a file called CONFIG.ALL, just type **COPY CONFIG.NRM+CONFIG.ILK CONFIG.ALL**. *Then you can bring CONFIG.ALL into the EDIT program and add the lines necessary for MultiConfig support.*

The configurations will be separated with MultiConfig commands, so leave a blank space or two in the file between each configuration. My CONFIG.ALL file looks like the following at this point:

```
FILES=60
BUFFERS=30
STACKS=9,256
DEVICE=C:\DOS\HIMEM.SYS
DOS=HIGH
FILES=60
```

```
BUFFERS=30
STACKS=9,256
DEVICE=C:\DOS\HIMEM.SYS
DOS=HIGH
DEVICE=C:\DOS\INTERLNK.EXE
```

MultiConfig Step 2: Name the Configurations

MultiConfig separates the commands to be executed as CONFIG.SYS statements and the commands that are to be MultiConfig commands by requiring that MultiConfig commands be enclosed in square brackets ([and]). The first MultiConfig statements to add are the identifiers for these two configurations.

You can call these two configurations anything you want, so keep calling them "normal" and "InterLnk." Just put those names in square brackets above each configuration. Your CONFIG.ALL file will then look like the following:

```
[normal]
FILES=60
BUFFERS=30
STACKS=9,256
DEVICE=C:\DOS\HIMEM.SYS
DOS=HIGH
[InterLnk]
FILES=60
BUFFERS=30
STACKS=9,256
DEVICE=C:\DOS\HIMEM.SYS
DOS=HIGH
DEVICE=C:\DOS\INTERLNK.EXE
```

Just for convenience's sake, let's call each group of lines headed by a line in square brackets a block, so in this case this CONFIG.SYS contains a block called normal and a block called InterLnk.

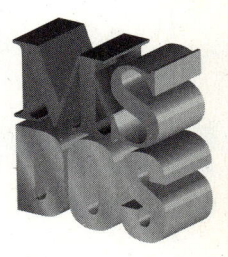

Now, if you were to attempt to boot using this file as your CONFIG.SYS, DOS would treat it as if it were blank. None of the commands would execute. None of these commands would execute because MultiConfig would recognize two configurations called normal and InterLnk, but there would be no MultiConfig statements telling DOS to actually use either of these configurations. That comes in the next step.

MultiConfig Step 3: Set Up the Menu

Most of the directives to MultiConfig go in a block called [menu]. In the [menu] block, you enumerate the alternative configurations, tell MultiConfig what the menu should look like, what options it should take as default, how long to wait for user response, even what color to put on the screen! Just for starters, we'll enumerate the configurations. You do that with the Menuitem command. It appears as follows:

```
MENUITEM configurationname,menutext
```

Here, *configurationname* is the name in brackets of a configuration, such as normal or InterLnk in our example, and *menutext* is just the English text that MultiConfig should display when showing the menu. Add the [menu] block, and CONFIG.ALL appears as follows:

```
[menu]
menuitem normal,Standard setup
menuitem InterLnk,Setup with InterLnk driver
[normal]
FILES=60
BUFFERS=30
STACKS=9,256
DEVICE=C:\DOS\HIMEM.SYS
DOS=HIGH
[InterLnk]
FILES=60
BUFFERS=30
STACKS=9,256
DEVICE=C:\DOS\HIMEM.SYS
DOS=HIGH
DEVICE=C:\DOS\INTERLNK.EXE
```

Now you can copy CONFIG.ALL to C:\CONFIG.SYS, and reboot. You'll see the Starting MS-DOS... message, and a couple of seconds later you'll see a screen containing the following menu:

```
MS-DOS 6.2 Startup Menu
=======================

     1. Standard setup
     2. Setup with InterLnk driver
Enter a choice: 1
```

The bottom line of the screen reminds you that you can access Clean Boot by pressing F5, or Interactive Boot by pressing F8. Press 1 and Enter, and the system boots in the normal setting. Try rebooting again and press 2, and you'll see the InterLnk driver load.

Congratulations—you've built your first MultiConfig menu!

MultiConfig Step 4:
Add Defaults and Timeouts

It would be a nuisance to have to hover over your PC each time it boots, pressing 1 to start the standard setup and 2 now and then when you need InterLnk. It would be much preferable to tell MultiConfig, "If I don't press any keys for two seconds, assume that I want the normal configuration."

You can do that with the MENUDEFAULT command, as follows:

    MENUDEFAULT *configurationname*[,*timeout*]

In this command, *configurationname* means the same thing as it did in the MENUITEM command—the name that is surrounded by square brackets preceding the block of CONFIG.SYS statements defining a configuration. In this example, you could specify either normal or InterLnk. You can add a number to define a timeout, the maximum number of seconds for MultiConfig to wait before taking the default. If you don't specify a timeout, MultiConfig waits forever at the MS-DOS 6.2 Startup Menu, but the bouncebar is already positioned on the default item.

Now, in this example, I'd like to tell MultiConfig to give me two seconds to make a choice, and if I don't make a choice within two seconds, then just load and use the "normal" configuration. I can do that by adding the following line to the [menu] block of CONFIG.SYS:

    MENUDEFAULT normal,2

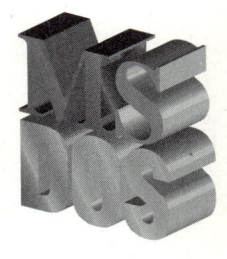

It can go anywhere in the [menu] block. The CONFIG.SYS file now appears as follows:

```
[menu]
menuitem normal,Standard setup
menuitem InterLnk,Setup with InterLnk driver
menudefault normal,2
[normal]
FILES=60
BUFFERS=30
STACKS=9,256
DEVICE=C:\DOS\HIMEM.SYS
DOS=HIGH
[InterLnk]
FILES=60
BUFFERS=30
STACKS=9,256
DEVICE=C:\DOS\HIMEM.SYS
DOS=HIGH
DEVICE=C:\DOS\INTERLNK.EXE
```

Now boot the system with your hands off the keyboard. You'll see MultiConfig count down, and then load the "normal" configuration. Then try booting again, and press 2; you'll see that it overrides the default, loading the InterLnk driver.

Coloring Your Menu

If you have a color monitor, you can customize the colors of your MultiConfig menu with the MENUCOLOR command, as follows:

```
MENUCOLOR foreground,[background]
```

Here, *foreground* and *background* are numbers representing the colors that the PC text screen can display—16 in all. The *foreground* option is a mandatory value, but *background* is optional; if you don't specify a number, you get the normal black background.

I'm really not sure why Microsoft made this part of MultiConfig in the first place. DOS has needed a simple program that enables you to change the color of your DOS screen for a long time—and I thought that this was it when I first read about the MENUCOLOR command.

MultiConfig, however, only retains its colors during the execution of CONFIG.SYS; after AUTOEXEC.BAT begins executing, the screen goes back to white-on-black. It doesn't even do it cleanly; there's usually a messy combination of color and black and white on the screen until you execute the CLS command.

I can think of only one good reason for coloring menus. One use for MultiConfig that I'll suggest later is to enable a single PC to be shared among several people, each of whom has his or her own AUTOEXEC.BAT/CONFIG.SYS file. It's possible to build MultiConfig menus within menus, with different colors for each menu. Giving each of the users who shares a machine a differently colored menu provides quick visual proof that they have their menu, not someone else's.

You can see the colors in table 16.1.

Table 16.1
MENUCOLOR Color Codes

Code	Color
0	Black
1	Blue
2	Green
3	Cyan (aqua)
4	Red
5	Magenta
6	Brown
7	Low-intensity white
8	Gray
9	Bright blue
10	Bright green
11	Bright cyan

continues

Table 16.1, Continued
MENUCOLOR Color Codes

Code	Color
12	Bright red
13	Bright magenta
14	Yellow
15	Bright white

I guess what troubles me about this command is the wasted time that can result. There are 240 foreground/background combinations, and it seems some folks just won't rest until they've seen them all. To save those people time, a QBASIC program called MPREVIEW.BAS that previews all the foreground/background color combinations more quickly than 240 reboots follows:

```
REM Opening declarations
DECLARE SUB REFRESH ()
TRUE = -1
FALSE = NOT TRUE
ESCAPE$ = CHR$(27)
UPA$ = CHR$(0) + CHR$(72)
DOWNA$ = CHR$(0) + CHR$(80)
RIGHTA$ = CHR$(0) + CHR$(77)
LEFTA$ = CHR$(0) + CHR$(75)
REM Start out with black background, white foreground
FG = 7
BG = 0
CALL REFRESH
LOCATE 15, 1
PRINT "Current colors: MENUDEFAULT"; STR$(FG); ",";
PRINT MID$(STR$(BF), 2)
DONE = FALSE
REM Main body of program. Scans for Escape, up, down,
REM left, and right arrows. If it finds one, it either
REM exits (Escape) or alters the foreground/background
and REM re-draws the screen in the new colors.
WHILE NOT DONE
```

```
            A$ = INKEY$
            CHANGED = FALSE
            IF A$ <> "" THEN
             SELECT CASE A$
             CASE ESCAPE$
              DONE = TRUE
             CASE UPA$
              FG = FG + 1
              IF FG > 15 THEN FG = 0
              CHANGED = TRUE
             CASE DOWNA$
              FG = FG - 1
              IF FG = -1 THEN FG = 15
              CHANGED = TRUE
             CASE RIGHTA$
              BG = BG - 1
              IF BG = -1 THEN BG = 15
              CHANGED = TRUE
             CASE LEFTA$
              BG = BG + 1
              IF BG = 16 THEN BG = 0
              CHANGED = TRUE
             CASE ELSE
              BEEP
             END SELECT
             IF CHANGED THEN
              COLOR FG, BG
              CALL REFRESH
              LOCATE 15, 1
              PRINT "Current colors: MENUDEFAULT"; STR$(FG); ",";
        MID$(STR$(BG), 2)
             END IF
            END IF
        WEND
        SUB REFRESH STATIC
        CLS
        PRINT "MS-DOS Startup Menu"
        FOR i = 1 TO 21: PRINT chr$(205); : NEXT: PRINT
        PRINT
        PRINT "  1. Your first menu choice"
        PRINT "  2. Your second menu choice"
```

```
PRINT
PRINT "Enter a choice: 1"
LOCATE 20, 1
PRINT "INSTRUCTIONS:"
PRINT "Move the up and down arrows to change foreground
color,"
PRINT "and the left and right arrows to change background
color."
PRINT "Press ESC to exit."
END SUB
```

Basically, this program uses a subroutine called REFRESH to put a dummy version of the MultiConfig startup menu on the screen. The program starts by setting the colors to white-on-black, then constantly scans the keyboard for a keystroke. When a keystroke appears, it checks to see if it's the Esc key, an arrow key, or something else. If it's the Esc key, it exits the program. If it's an up-arrow key, it selects the next foreground color; if it's a down-arrow key, it selects the previous foreground color. Left and right arrows pick next and previous background colors, and any other key just produces a beep. When you find a combination that you like, copy the MENUCOLOR statement that you see on the screen into your CONFIG.SYS file.

MultiConfig Step 5: Put Multiple Configurations in AUTOEXEC.BAT

Now that you've merged two CONFIG.SYS files into one using MultiConfig, complete with a startup menu, defaults, timeouts, and even colors, it's time to see what MultiConfig does for AUTOEXEC.BAT. The answer is, "not much."

Enough tools are available, however, to enable you to link CONFIG.SYS configurations to AUTOEXEC.BAT configurations.

Let's return to the two-configuration approach that we've been following so far. Suppose that two AUTOEXEC.BATs are available, one for the normal configuration, and another for the InterLnk configuration. The normal AUTOEXEC.BAT might appear as follows:

```
PROMPT $P$G
PATH C:\DOS
DOSKEY
```

The InterLnk AUTOEXEC.BAT might appear as follows:

```
PATH C:\DOS
INTERSVR
```

Let me first show the people who are comfortable with batch language programming how to combine these AUTOEXEC.BATs into one AUTOEXEC.BAT, and then I'll present a simple "formula" for combining batch files that anyone who can use an editor can follow.

Keeping MultiConfig Combined AUTOEXEC.BATs Separate (For Those Who Are Batch-Savvy)

The key to combining two (or more) AUTOEXEC.BAT files into a single batch file, and then extracting them, is an environment variable called CONFIG. CONFIG contains the name of the configuration that you selected—in our example, that means either normal or InterLnk. You then use IF ... == commands and GOTO commands to determine what part of the AUTOEXEC.BAT file gets executed. Our example AUTOEXEC.BAT would appear as follows:

```
@ECHO OFF
IF %config%==normal GOTO normal
IF %config%==InterLnk GOTO InterLnk
:normal
PROMPT $P$G
PATH C:\DOS
DOSKEY
GOTO end
:InterLnk
PATH C:\DOS
INTERSVR
GOTO end
:end
```

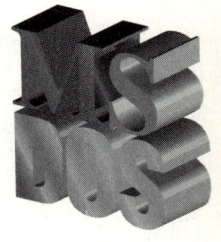

Keeping MultiConfig Combined AUTOEXEC.BATs Separate (For Those Who Are Not Batch-Savvy)

Some batch experts might view the previous example as a trifle inefficient, but it follows a nice, simple formula that anyone can use to quickly combine a number of configurations into a single AUTOEXEC.BAT file. Assuming that you had three configurations named c1, c2, and c3, you would build the AUTOEXEC.BAT file as follows:

```
@ECHO off
IF %config%==c1 GOTO c1
IF %config%==c2 GOTO c2
IF %config%==c3 GOTO c3
:c1
[put the C1 commands here]
GOTO end
:c2
[put the C2 commands here]
GOTO end
:c3
[put the C3 commands here]
GOTO end
:end
```

This "skeleton" of a batch file should help underscore how to build an AUTOEXEC.BAT file that supports three configurations; you can easily see how to extend it to four, five, or any number of configurations.

At the risk of being obvious, remember that the lines in brackets should not be typed literally; they're intended to be English instructions to you.

Perhaps even more generally, you can assemble a combined AUTOEXEC.BAT file by following these steps:

1. The first line of your combined AUTOEXEC.BAT should be @ECHO OFF, as explained in the previous chapter. So, the AUTOEXEC.BAT file appears as follows so far:

    ```
    @ECHO OFF
    ```

2. Examine your CONFIG.SYS's [menu] section that you assembled earlier in the chapter and write down the names of all the configurations. Take the name of the first configuration and incorporate it in an IF statement, as follows:

   ```
   IF %config%==[name of configuration] GOTO [name of configuration]
   ```

You should replace [*name of configuration*] with the actual name of the first configuration. Do that for each configuration name. For example, suppose that you find that your CONFIG.SYS has a menu section that appears as follows:

```
[menu]
menuitem standard,Normal stuff I use
menuitem maxmemory,Setup to give maximum free memory
menuitem wingcomm,Configuration to run Wing Commander II
menudefault ...
```

That means you've got three configurations named standard, maxmemory, and wingcomm. (Notice that I did not include configurations named normal or InterLnk—I didn't want you to think they were mandatory.) You'd prepare the first configuration IF to appear as follows:

```
IF %config%==standard GOTO STANDARD
```

In the previous example, notice that ==standard is in lowercase. The case in the IF statement must match the case of the named configuration, or it won't work.

You'd then assemble the other IF statements, one for each of the two other configurations. Your AUTOEXEC.BAT file would appear as follows:

```
@ECHO OFF
IF %config%==standard GOTO STANDARD
IF %config%==maxmemory GOTO MAXMEMORY
IF %config%==wingcomm GOTO WINGCOMM
```

3. Create a section of the AUTOEXEC.BAT file for each of the configurations. Each section should have two lines. The first line is the name of the configuration preceded by a colon (:), and the second line should say GOTO END. The last line in

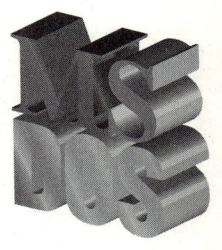

the batch file should say :END. If you do that, the
AUTOEXEC.BAT appears as follows:

```
@ECHO OFF
IF %config%==standard GOTO STANDARD
IF %config%==maxmemory GOTO MAXMEMORY
IF %config%==wingcomm GOTO WINGCOMM
:WINGCOMM
GOTO END
:MAXMEMORY
GOTO END
:STANDARD
GOTO END
:END
```

4. For each section, insert the AUTOEXEC.BAT file for that section between the label with the colon at the beginning of it and the GOTO END command. Save this file; you're done. For example, suppose that the AUTOEXEC.BAT file for the "standard" configuration appears as follows:

```
PROMPT $P$G
PATH C:\DOS
DOSKEY
PRINT /Q
SMARTDRV
```

And suppose that the configuration for the "maxmemory" configuration appears as follows:

```
PROMPT $P$G
PATH C:\DOS
LH DOSKEY
```

Then suppose that the configuration for the "wingcomm" configuration appears as follows:

```
CD\GAMES\WC2
WC2
```

You'd insert these files into the AUTOEXEC.BAT file that you're building to end up with a final AUTOEXEC.BAT file that appears as follows:

```
@ECHO OFF
IF %config%==standard GOTO STANDARD
IF %config%==maxmemory GOTO MAXMEMORY
IF %config%==wingcomm GOTO WINGCOMM
:STANDARD
PROMPT $P$G
PATH C:\DOS
DOSKEY
PRINT /Q
SMARTDRV
GOTO END
:MAXMEMORY
PROMPT $P$G
PATH C:\DOS
LH DOSKEY
GOTO END
:WINGCOMM
CD\GAMES\WC2
WC2
GOTO END
:END
```

There you have it—a quick and painless way to integrate your configurations under DOS 6.2. Note the following three things:

- ✔ The configuration names get passed to AUTOEXEC.BAT in the same case that you wrote them in the CONFIG.SYS. If the configuration name was InterLnk, then don't write the IF statement IF %config%==InterLnk GOTO …, as that'll never match. The case must match.

- ✔ If you read Chapter 15, you know about the CALL statement. That would provide an alternative to inserting the various AUTOEXEC.BATs physically into the master AUTOEXEC.BAT. If you wanted, you could have had batch files called STANDARD.BAT, MAXMEM.BAT, and WINGCOMM.BAT, and then inside the sections you could have simply inserted CALL STANDARD, CALL MAXMEM, or CALL WINGCOMM. That would make the final AUTOEXEC.BAT appear as follows:

```
@ECHO OFF
IF %config%==standard GOTO STANDARD
IF %config%==maxmemory GOTO MAXMEMORY
IF %config%==wingcomm GOTO WINGCOMM
:STANDARD
CALL STANDARD
GOTO END
:MAXMEMORY
CALL MAXMEM
GOTO END
:WINGCOMM
CALL WINGCOMM
GOTO END
:END
```

Now, there is an even more compact way of doing this that involves just doing the CALL statements from inside the IFs; the AUTOEXEC.BAT would appear as follows:

```
@ECHO OFF
IF %config%==standard CALL STANDARD
IF %config%==maxmemory CALL MAXMEM
IF %config%==wingcomm CALL WINGCOMM
```

That's an acceptable alternative, and it certainly makes converting a bunch of configurations to a single AUTOEXEC.BAT file easier, but it won't work if the CONFIG variable gets altered by one of the batch files. The chances of that happening, however, are small, so this may be the simplest method of unifying AUTOEXEC.BATs for most people.

✔ I've been using GOTO statements that jump the batch files to labels that have the same names as the configurations, but you don't have to do that. I do it as a helpful reminder.

Now, if you're a batch expert, you've probably noticed that I could have reorganized some of the statements to make the AUTOEXEC.BAT file smaller. That's certainly true, and if you want to do that for your AUTOEXEC.BAT, then go ahead. I didn't because I like the clearly-defined separate areas for the different configurations. This clear separation makes it possible for me to keep the configurations separate, something that'll no doubt be important because all of the configurations may change over time, and this gives them all "room to breathe."

Using INCLUDE To Simplify a MultiConfig Configuration

Let's get back to the CONFIG.SYS part of MultiConfig. In my example, I ended up with a CONFIG.SYS that appeared as follows:

```
[menu]
menuitem normal,Standard setup
menuitem InterLnk,Setup with InterLnk driver
menudefault normal,2
[normal]
FILES=60
BUFFERS=30
STACKS=9,256
DEVICE=C:\DOS\HIMEM.SYS
DOS=HIGH
[InterLnk]
FILES=60
BUFFERS=30
STACKS=9,256
DEVICE=C:\DOS\HIMEM.SYS
DOS=HIGH
DEVICE=C:\DOS\INTERLNK.EXE
```

Supporting Shared Groups of Statements in MultiConfig

You'll notice that a group of statements was common to both configurations. There are just a few statements that you can expect all configurations to have—perhaps an essential device driver, FILES/BUFFERS/LASTDRIVE/STACKS statements, and the like. In the case of my example configuration, the commands that were common to the two configurations are as follows:

```
FILES=60
BUFFERS=30
STACKS=9,256
DEVICE=C:\DOS\HIMEM.SYS
DOS=HIGH
```

You can save yourself some typing by extracting some common block of statements, making it a block by giving it a block name, and then using the MultiConfig command INCLUDE. Just remove the group of statements from all configurations that use it, and precede it with a name in brackets, just like the configurations that you've been building so far. Then, where the group of statements used to be in each configuration, insert the phrase **INCLUDE [*blockname*],** in which *blockname* is whatever you called the block of statements common to the configurations.

For example, if I create a block called *shared* that contains the statements shared between the configurations, then the CONFIG.SYS appears as follows:

```
[menu]
menuitem normal,Standard setup
menuitem InterLnk,Setup with InterLnk driver
menudefault normal,2
[shared]
FILES=60
BUFFERS=30
STACKS=9,256
DEVICE=C:\DOS\HIMEM.SYS
DOS=HIGH
[normal]
INCLUDE shared
[InterLnk]
INCLUDE shared
DEVICE=C:\DOS\INTERLNK.EXE
```

You can have as many INCLUDE blocks as you like. For example, you might have an INCLUDE block with your memory management commands (EMM386/HIMEM/DOS=HIGH,UMB), another with InterLnk commands, and so on.

The [common] Block

There is a predefined block called [common] which, if included in your CONFIG.SYS, will automatically be executed at the end of every configuration. Just include the line, [common], and then follow it by whatever statements you want to see executed no matter what configuration gets selected.

Building More Complex Configurations with Submenus

We're used to working with menu systems under the DOS Shell, Windows programs, or OS/2 applications; those menu systems are typically two-level menu systems, however—select an option, and more suboptions appear.

What Is a Submenu?

For example, I'm looking right now at the menu on a Windows program, Ami Pro. The Ami Pro menu offers these options: File, Edit, View, Text, Style, Page, Frame, Tools, Window, and Help. That's the "top level" menu. But if I click the mouse on, say, the Window menu item, then I get another menu below that, a kind of submenu that offers the options New window, Tile, and Cascade.

MultiConfig offers you the capability to add a second level of menus to your MS-DOS Startup Menu using the SUBMENU command. For example, recall the normal versus InterLnk example that I've been using throughout this chapter. InterLnk can be used in either server or client mode. You could put together a menu with three options on it: Normal, InterLnk-Server, or InterLnk-Client. Or you could have a top level menu that just offered normal and InterLnk options, and then if you chose InterLnk, you'd get a second-level menu that offered either client or server. Note that just because you put a submenu on InterLnk does not require that you put a submenu on the other options, such as Normal.

Using Submenus

The SUBMENU command appears as follows:

```
SUBMENU menublock,menutext
```

Here, *menublock* is the name of a block—a section of CONFIG.SYS with that name at the top of it enclosed in square brackets. Menutext is the text that you want displayed on the Startup Menu. You then create a block called, again, [*menublock*] that contains menu commands, just like the original block called [*menu*].

When last we looked at the normal/InterLnk example, the CONFIG.SYS appeared as follows:

```
[menu]
menuitem normal,Standard setup
menuitem InterLnk,Setup with InterLnk driver
menudefault normal,2
[shared]
FILES=60
BUFFERS=30
STACKS=9,256
DEVICE=C:\DOS\HIMEM.SYS
DOS=HIGH
[normal]
INCLUDE shared
[InterLnk]
INCLUDE shared
DEVICE=C:\DOS\INTERLNK.EXE
```

Now I want to make the InterLnk option a submenu rather than a configuration. To do that, I'll change the line `menuitem InterLnk,Setup with InterLnk driver` to `submenu InterLnk,Setup with InterLnk driver`.

After I do that, however, MultiConfig expects the [InterLnk] block to contain menu commands, not CONFIG.SYS commands. So the new [InterLnk] block should contain a menu for the InterLnk server and client commands. That menu will have new menuitems, contain menudefaults, include new colors, and even contain more submenus. The new [InterLnk] block will be fairly simple to build, as you can see in the following:

Building More Complex Configurations with Submenus

```
[InterLnk]
menuitem server,Load InterLnk as server
menuitem client,Load InterLnk as client
```

Then I'll have to build two new blocks, the [server] and [client] blocks. They'll actually contain the same text in the CONFIG.SYS, but will look different in the AUTOEXEC.BAT. Those new blocks will appear as follows:

```
[client]
INCLUDE shared
DEVICE=C:\DOS\INTERLNK.EXE
[server]
INCLUDE shared
DEVICE=C:\DOS\INTERLNK.EXE
```

I bothered with two different configurations because the commands in the AUTOEXEC.BAT have to be different in this situation. A piece of the AUTOEXEC.BAT might look like the following:

```
IF %config%==client GOTO CLIENT
IF %config%==server GOTO SERVER
...
:CLIENT
PROMPT $P$G
PATH C:\DOS
INTERLNK
GOTO END
:SERVER
C:\DOS\INTERSVR
GOTO END
:END
```

In the server configuration, there's no need to set PROMPT and PATH, as the server computer just sits there with an InterLnk status report on the screen; you can't get a DOS prompt or execute programs anyway. Put the whole CONFIG.SYS together, and it appears as follows:

```
[menu]
menuitem normal,Standard setup
submenu InterLnk,Setup with InterLnk driver
menudefault normal,2
[shared]
```

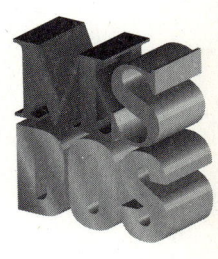

```
FILES=60
BUFFERS=30
STACKS=9,256
DEVICE=C:\DOS\HIMEM.SYS
DOS=HIGH
[normal]
INCLUDE shared
[InterLnk]
menuitem server,Load InterLnk as server
menuitem client,Load InterLnk as client
[client]
INCLUDE shared
DEVICE=C:\DOS\INTERLNK.EXE
[server]
INCLUDE shared
DEVICE=C:\DOS\INTERLNK.EXE
```

In case it's not clear yet, submenus don't change anything about the way you write your AUTOEXEC.BAT file. The only way that submenus, or the main menu for that matter, can affect AUTOEXEC.BAT is through communicating the value of the CONFIG environment variable.

Suggestions for Using Submenus with Multiple People

Now, in general, the idea of putting menus inside menus, with the possibility of menus inside them and so on, seems to be of value only to people who are overly fastidious. There is an application that's tailor-made for submenus, however.

Many PCs are shared by several people. For example, some companies have a pool of laptop computers that people borrow for business trips. One of the biggest gripes the people who use those computers have is that when they get the laptop back after someone else has used it, the configuration has been all messed up.

In many households, all the family members share a computer, and they all want to be able to keep their configurations separate and distinct. Public access computers such as the ones starting to appear in public libraries may need to serve multiple duty as connecting points to databases of very different types, requiring different access methods.

MultiConfig can help these types of problems with its single-level menu. In the household, Mom, Dad, and Junior could each have a menu item. But with submenus, it's possible for Mom to have three of her own configurations, Dad to have a couple, and Junior to keep separate the fourteen different configurations he needs to run all his games.

An arrangement such as this actually provides a use for the MENUCOLOR command, as I mentioned before. One way to be sure that you haven't accidentally activated someone else's menu is to color each menu differently. This is more useful than would seem at first glance. Suppose that Dad sits down to use the PC. He reboots and (out of habit) presses 2, then 1, and Enter, as that combination always gets him to the configuration he typically uses.

Instead of ending up in Quicken, however, he finds himself (or, rather, finds his cursor) being chased by the minions of the ravenous bug-blatter beast of Traal. What's happened to Dad, of course, is that he accidentally got into Junior's menu. But if the screen had turned red when he got to Junior's submenu, he would have noticed it (Dad uses a menu whose background is a sedate gray), and rebooted straight off.

Controlling the NumLock Light with MultiConfig

Before finishing this chapter with some tips, let me mention one final MultiConfig command: NUMLOCK. If you include in a menu or submenu block the command NUMLOCK=OFF or NUMLOCK=ON, the state of the NumLock light on your keyboard is set. I hate to admit it, but this is another one of my favorite DOS 6.2 features. I just can't seem to break myself of the habit of using the numeric keypad for cursor movement, so my attempts to press Page Down and then End just end up sticking a *31* at the beginning of the document that I was just trying to examine.

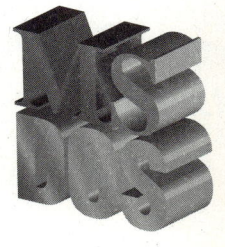

> **NOTE:** The use of NUMLOCK= is not restricted to start-up menus and multiple configurations. You can use this command anywhere in CONFIG.SYS.

> **NOTE:** The preceding note corrects an error in the Microsoft documentation shipped with DOS 6.2.

MultiConfig Tips

MultiConfig was a long time in coming, but I imagine that it'll be an even longer time before the software world adjusts to it. For that reason, let me share with you a few tips—notes from the front, so to speak.

- ✔ Prior to running a memory management optimizer program, break up the CONFIG.SYS into multiple CONFIG.SYS files and then rerun the optimizer on each CONFIG.SYS. Then reassemble the CONFIG.SYS files back into a single CONFIG.SYS.

  No one can blame Quarterdeck or Qualitas for not recognizing MultiConfig statements in CONFIG.SYS; 386Max and QEMM Versions 6.0 and 6.02 were shipped before DOS 6.2 appeared. That's why it's not that big a deal that Quarterdeck's Optimize and Qualitas' Maximize don't understand MultiConfig—they are not aware of, and do not optimize, any CONFIG.SYS statements that don't get executed during their optimization procedures. Unless you hover over Optimize/Maximize while they're running, and continually direct MultiConfig to choose some alternate configuration, then all you'll end up with after running Optimize or Maximize is a configuration optimized solely for your default MultiConfig choice.

MemMaker, on the other hand, was written by Microsoft, and should know better—but doesn't. I'm sure that the MemMaker programmers are different people, and probably even inhabit different offices, than the MultiConfig programmers, but they all get their Jolt cola from the same soda machines in the Microsoft cafeteria, for goodness' sakes! My advice to you prior to using the MemMaker memory manager optimizer is the same, unfortunately: tear apart the configurations, optimize each separately, and then recombine them by hand.

✔ Look closely at your AUTOEXEC.BAT and CONFIG.SYS files after installing a program. Most programs that mess with your CONFIG.SYS and AUTOEXEC.BAT files end up doing things that defeat the purpose of MultiConfig—they put drivers at the top of the CONFIG.SYS, or at the bottom of the CONFIG.SYS, or whatever. Get in the habit of inspecting your CONFIG.SYS and AUTOEXEC.BAT immediately after any installations.

✔ Always end your CONFIG.SYS with a [common] block. That way, any device drivers automatically added to the end of CONFIG.SYS—which is the most common place to insert new drivers—automatically get loaded.

✔ Add SWITCHES=/f to your CONFIG.SYS. There is a built-in two-second delay during the "Starting MS-DOS…" message that's annoying and unnecessary. Adding this line gets rid of the delay.

Summary

MultiConfig is a welcome new member of the family of DOS features. It's one of those things that works much better as a built-in feature than as a third-party add-on, and it's to Microsoft's credit that they added this feature to DOS 6.2.

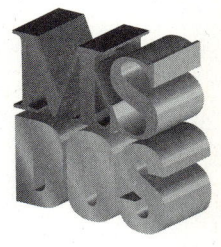

The DOS 6.2 SETUP program does not automatically set up MultiConfig, so you must do the rearranging for MultiConfig yourself, but it's not that hard to do. In this chapter, you've learned the steps needed to bring together the myriad configurations that you've probably had lying around all this time. Remember, however, that automatic installation programs and memory optimizers do not yet understand MultiConfig, so you should keep an eye on their work.

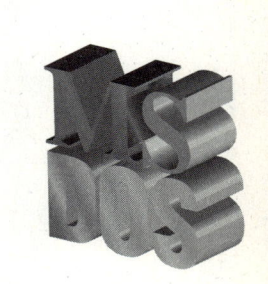

MS
DOS

Part Six:

Protecting Your Data

A Second Look at Hard Drives 899
Backing Up Your Data 965
Protecting and Recovering Data 1015
Battling Viruses with DOS 6.2 1065
Securing Your PC 1153

MS
DOS

CHAPTER 17

A Second Look at Hard Drives

by David Stang

Life is full of mysteries. For computer users, one of the biggest mysteries is how the computer stores information. We know it's a mystery because users do the silliest things as they try to prevent data loss or recover data. If you understand the basics of how drives work and how MS-DOS works with them, you can do all sorts of clever things to protect your information and recover information when it seemingly disappears.

How Drives Work

Computer designers have used many approaches to storing information. To better understand how drives work, you should know a bit about their history... their evolution.

On *punched tape*, a strip of sturdy paper, a hole punched in a certain position meant a 1; no hole in that position meant a 0. Punched tape was cheap and not affected by RFI, EMP, or other electromagnetic problems. But because only about 10 bytes fit an inch of tape, you'd need more than 31 miles of it to hold the contents of today's 20M hard disk.

Punched cards were somewhat more flexible than punched tape. You could enter a line of program instruction (up to 80 characters [bytes]), eject the card, and then type the next instruction. Programmers usually coded programs by hand on a "coding sheet," then typed them with the card punch. The card decks—like the paper tape—were immune to the effects of electromagnetism. And with up to 80 bytes per card, and perhaps 50 cards in a one-inch deck, you would need a card deck only 416 feet thick to store 20M of information—a substantial improvement over the 31 miles of paper tape!

The first random-access storage devices—*disk packs*—were removable sets of "platters" coated with iron oxide. Because they weren't sealed, disk packs were vulnerable to dust and smoke, which could cause the heads—positioned close to the surface—to crash. Unlike paper tape or punched cards, the heads on the drive could move to any location with equal ease to read information. Unlike tape and punched cards, which were *sequential access* devices, a disk pack was a *random access* device and far more useful for speedy storage and retrieval.

Project developers of the first hard disk, developed by IBM, called it a *Winchester*. It amounted to a sealed disk pack—heads and platters placed in one sealed, dust-free box. In a sense a step backward—because every set of platters needed its own set of heads and a mechanism for moving them—it was destined to dramatically outsell the disk pack.

The first floppy drive and disk also were IBM inventions and also a step back toward the disk pack (with the platter removable and the heads staying in the machine). But in this design, the heads touched the surface of the disk and couldn't crash, which made the device ideal for normal human environments.

Storage has come a long way since the early days of computing. Over the last 10 years, we've stabilized on the hard disk and floppy drive technology and have seen only gradual changes. Drive speed, capacity, and reliability have improved, and prices have dropped.

Drive Anatomy

This section looks at the anatomy of the 5 1/4-inch and 3 1/2-inch *floppy disks, the hard disk, and the tape drive. See the last portion of Chapter 4 for a discussion of floppy disk formatting.*

Floppy Disks

Figures 17.1 and 17.2 show the components of a 5 1/4-inch floppy disk and a 3 1/2-inch floppy disk, respectively.

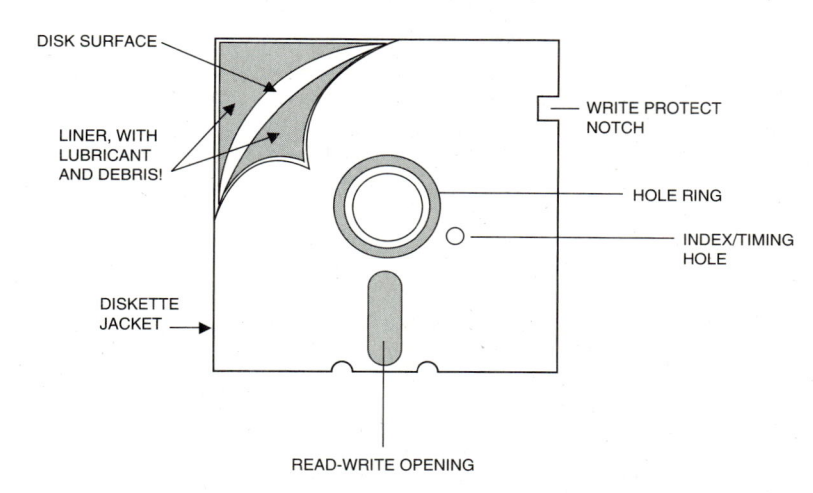

Figure 17.1
A 5 1/4-inch floppy disk.

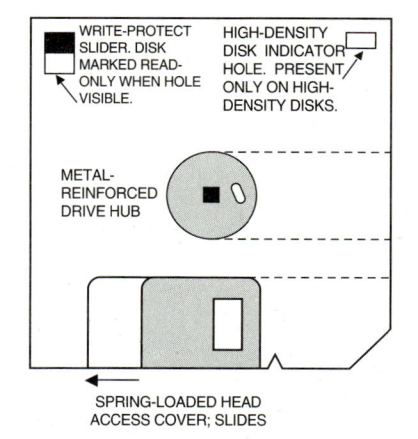

Figure 17.2
A 3 1/2-inch floppy disk.

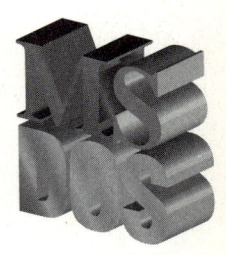

The *disk jacket* is fairly stiff fiberboard in the 5 1/4-inch disks and rigid plastic in the 3 1/2-inch disks. The jacket makes the disk more rigid and protects it from dust, fingerprints, smoke, scratches, and—to some extent—butterscotch pudding. It contains a *liner* that picks up dust that might otherwise abrade the surface.

The *disk hub* is the center of the disk. When the disk drive door is closed, the drive clamps down on this hub, and the pressure enables the disk to spin in its jacket when the drive motor turns the clamp. Normally, 360K floppies have a *hub ring* to help with reliable centering, but 1.2M floppies do not. (The 1.2M drives spin the disk as the door closes, before clamping. Because the spin helps with the centering, the hub ring is not necessary.) In the 3 1/2-inch disk, a metal hub ring ensures precise alignment against the drive spindle.

The *read-write* opening is a window, through which the drive's read-write heads come into contact with the disk for read and write operations.

How does the drive determine whether it is spinning the floppy too fast or too slow? On a 5 1/4-inch disk, an *index* or *timing hole* is used to find the first sector of the selected track. On a 3 1/2-inch disk, a *sector notch* on the floppy next to the disk spindle is used to help find the first sector. Both the hole and the notch give feedback to a servomechanism (*servo* means self-regulating) on the drive to help regulate disk rotation speed.

Unfortunately, there is no consistent way to determine whether or not a disk is write-protected. On a 5 1/4-inch disk, a closed notch means that the disk is write-protected. On 3 1/2-inch disks, the opening is protected with a sliding metal shutter—if it's open, the disk is write-protected.

On an 8-inch disk, an open notch on the side of the jacket means that the disk is write-protected. You can make the 8-inch disk "writable" by placing a small adhesive tab over the opening.

Hard Disks

Hard disks have more parts than floppies have. Following are a few key parts:

✔ **Rigid aluminum disks or platters** are coated with magnetic particles. A few years ago, such a surface stored 5M, whereas today, a 3 1/2-inch drive can store 40M or more per platter.

✔ **A disk spindle motor** is positioned below the disks, spins them at a constant rate—normally 3600 rpm. Today's drives draw a fair amount of power (10 to 30 watts). The smaller and lighter the disks, the less current this motor needs.

The Conner CP-2024 20M drive is just 1/2-inch tall, weighs less than eight ounces, and draws only 1.5 watts of power when it is idle. The Conner CP-4044, a 40M drive, is 3/4-inch tall, 3 1/2-inches wide, weighs 8.8 ounces, and draws 47 milliwatts of power when idle (1.4 watts while reading or writing). The motor that turns the spindle may be a *pancake motor* nestled below the spindle.

✔ **A read-write head** (one per surface) is mounted in an assembly and attached to a motor. The head is a magnet, made from one or more turns of copper wire in a ring or core of ferrite. The ferrite core has a thin gap on the side facing the disk. When current flows through the copper wire, the disk surface under the gap in the ferrite core is magnetized and a bit is written. The direction in which the current flows determines whether the magnetization is from north to south or south to north, a 1 or a 0.

To do its work, the delicate head rides a cushion of air, poised a mere hundred-thousandth of an inch from the surface. The head rests on the surface when your computer is off, but glide on this cushion of air when it is on. The air cushion is a wind of up to 54 miles per hour.

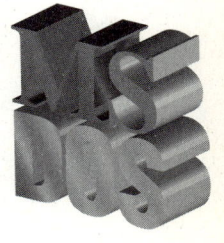

✔ **A stepper motor** or **voice-coil mechanism** moves the head assembly. *Stepper motors* move the heads in a fixed increment, or step, across the surface. Each increment defines a cylinder. *Voice-coil mechanisms*, on the other hand, use information stored on the top of the first platter to help determine where to move the heads. Generally, drives with voice-coil mechanisms are faster and more expensive than those with stepper motors. All floppy drives use stepper motors; almost all drives that offer access times of less than 28 milliseconds use voice-coil technology.

- ✔ An enclosure that separates the motors from the disks and heads, isolates the heat created by the motors. This enclosure is sealed, except for a filter to permit air movement in or out. The filters not only keep dust out, but also equalize the inside and outside air pressure.

NOTE: No air current passes through the special, dense filters which are part of the sealed motor enclosure. However, an airplane ride in baggage can cause enough change in pressure taking off and landing that there is some flow through the filters. Without these filters, drives would either blow up or implode.

Magnetic Tapes

Magnetic tape, a sequential device that can hold 60M or more, is made of mylar coated with iron oxide, with a slick final coating to help the heads glide. The heads in a tape drive, like those in a floppy drive, touch the tape, preventing a crash. Like the disk, hard disk, and disk pack, the surface of the tape is a coating of iron oxide on a mylar tape, with a slick final coating to help the heads glide.

Magnetic Recording

The surface of a hard or floppy disk is covered with very fine oxide particles that are "grown" in a laboratory and applied to the surface (that's why disk packs, tape, hard disk platters, and the insides of floppy disks are a rusty brown). As the disk rotates, the particles can be magnetized by the head (to a plus or minus charge, indicating 1 or 0, respectively). With disks and magnetic tape, the vehicle for this oxide is mylar (a plastic). On a hard disk, the rigid platters are often made of aluminum.

Motion Sensitive

The drive uses two motions to move information under the read/write head. As the disk rotates, the head travels along the radius of that rotation and is able to access every point on the disk's surface. An analogy is the plotter's pen or typewriter's ball or dot-matrix printer's print head, which moves east-west while the paper moves north-south. The logic board coordinates the north-south and east-west motion so that all points on the surface can be addressed.

Heads and Necks: Connected or Just Close?

Because the strength of magnetic fields drops exponentially as you move away from the source of the field, all heads must be close to the media they read so that they can detect weak magnetic fields. And to place magnetic information close together, each 0 or 1 must be represented with a very weak field. The magnetic field on a floppy is so weak that you'll never be able to get one to stick to the refrigerator.

On a floppy disk, the only way to be sure that the head is a constant distance from the surface is to make the head actually touch the surface at all times. And this is truly what happens. When you close the drive door, you force two spring-loaded heads down against the portion of the disk exposed by the read-write window on the jacket. This pressure permits a weak magnetic signal to be used for writing, another weak magnetic signal to work for reading, and ensures that the floppy won't literally flop up and down as it is read or written to (thereby changing signal strength).

Clever, but with a downside. First, the heads touching the floppy create heat that can damage the floppy. (After a read or write, remove your floppy—you'll feel the heat.) To prevent heat buildup, disk drive speeds are kept low: 300 rpm for 3 1/2-inch and 360K floppies, 360 rpm for 1.2M floppies. Floppy disk drives rotate the floppy disk during read or write operations only. The time your drive takes to accelerate from 0 rpm to 300-360 rpm is another reason for the relative slowness of a floppy disk drive. Both this latency and the slow rotation speed—done to keep things cool—also mean slower data transfer than in a hard disk.

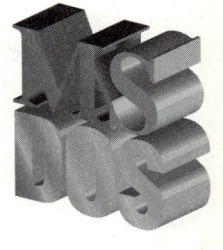

To speed access time, hard disks are designed for faster, constant rotation. The head has to be lifted off the drive a bit to eliminate friction, heat, and wear. When the hard disk is turned on, the heads lift off the surface, raised by the swirling air current inside the drive, until they float like a glider at a height of about 10 millionths of an inch. This slim gap is only a few air molecules thick—not large enough to see and certainly not large enough for a smoke particle, hair, or piece of lint to fit through.

But if a piece of dust somehow got between the head and the platter, it would slam into the head, bouncing it up and then letting it slam down into the surface, digging a circular trench where your cylinder or track of data used to be. To avert this tragedy, a hard disk is manufactured in a clean room (far more dust-free than an operating room in a hospital) and then sealed so that anything entering the drive must pass through a dense filter.

For obvious reasons, opening a hard disk voids the warranty.

AUTHOR'S NOTE

I mentioned that drive rotation speeds are 360 rpm (for 1.2M floppies), 300 rpm (for other floppy capacities), or 3600 rpm (for hard disks). Avid students of wall current might note that these speeds are convenient multiples of 60. The AC power from your wall is 60Hz, which translates to 60 cycles per second, 3600 cycles per minute. Can this be coincidence, or do we let the power company help control our drives?

Early 8-inch drives operated on AC, and may have used the 60Hz frequency to determine their speed, but modern disk drives operate completely on DC. The fact that drives operate at a speed which is some multiple of the AC frequency is a historical artifact.

Tracks and Cylinders

A *track* is the area under the head where the head does not move and the disk completes a full revolution. The number of tracks (or positions) a head can address is a function of the radius and the needed thickness of a track. An 8-inch disk has a larger radius, and thus could theoretically accommodate more tracks than a 5 1/4-inch disk. The required width of a track is defined by recording *sensitivity*; with a lower sensitivity, a greater amount of information can be stored. See Chapter 4 for an introduction to tracks and cylinders.

Tracks: The Denser, the Smarter

The more rigid the surface and the tighter the manufacturing tolerances, the closer tracks can be. *Track density*, in part, defines how much data can be stored. Track density can be measured in TPI (tracks per inch). Table 17.1 shows how different media differ in capacity, TPI, and tracks.

Table 17.1
Capacities, TPI, and Tracks for Different Storage Devices

Device	Capacity	TPI	Tracks per Side
8-inch SD Floppy	300K		
8-inch DD Floppy	600K		
5 1/4-inch SD Floppy	180K	24	40
5 1/4-inch DD Floppy	360K	48	40
5 1/4-inch Quad Density			80
5 1/4-inch High Density	1.2M	96	80
3 1/2-inch	720K		80
3 1/2-inch	1.44M		80
Zenith 2-inch	720K		80

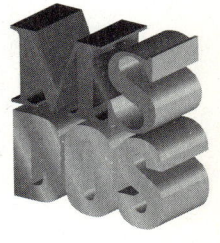

Tracks can be placed closer together on the rigid surface of the hard disk than on the less-rigid floppy. The 3 1/2-inch disk is quite rigid—but less so than the hard disk—and achieves very high TPI compared to the 5 1/4-inch and 8-inch floppy disks. Its metal hub permits more exact centering and, consequently, denser recording.

Side Walls

One way to increase the storage capacity of a surface is to place information closer together—tighten the TPI. Another way is to increase the surface area. A surface with a large radius (5 1/4-inches, for example) can record more than one with a smaller radius (such as two inches) if TPI is held constant. But adding sides is an easier way to double surface area—and storage capacity—without increasing the overall size of the drive by much. Although adding sides might affect height slightly, it won't affect width and depth.

A double-sided drive offers twice the capacity of a single-sided drive but—because only an extra read-write head need be added—doesn't cost much more. In a hard disk, you can add *platters* (plates, both sides of which can be read). Some examples are shown in table 17.2. Note that each platter has two sides and potentially two heads, but might have only one.

Table 17.2
**Representative Hard Disks:
Platters, Heads, and Capacity**

Drive	Platters	Heads	Capacity
Seagate ST-225	2	4	21.4M
Seagate ST-4038	3	5	31.9M
Priam HD 60	4	7	56.7M
Seagate ST-4096	5	9	76.5M
Maxtor XT-1140	8	15	117.5M

When floppy disks are made, both sides are coated with gallium oxide. (If only one side were coated, the disk would warp.) Then both sides are tested. If both sides meet the standards, the disk is put in a jacket, labeled "double-sided," and sold for a double-sided price. If only one side passes, the good side is placed "up" in the jacket and sold as "single-sided." But because *your* disk drive probably doesn't impose such a tough standard, and because MS-DOS marks as "bad" any imperfections on either side during formatting, folks find that single-sided 180K disks formatted as double-sided 360K disks are quite serviceable—and much cheaper than "official" double-sided disks.

> **AUTHOR'S NOTE**
>
> *As you will recall from Chapter 4's discussion, a cylinder is a set of tracks—one track per surface—that can be read from or written to without moving the head. In any drive that has two or more surfaces, the heads are mounted as a unit and all move together. Thus, if one head must move over to track 3 of the first side, all the other heads move also. If your entire file is located in a single cylinder, when the heads reach this cylinder they don't need to move again to read it all. A common way to improve the speed of the drive is to split files across surfaces, with each head reading or writing a portion of the file.*

Numbered and Tagged

As pointed out in Chapter 4, the outside track is called track 0. The top side is called side 0. On a drive with two heads, track 0 on side 0 plus track 0 on side 1 constitute cylinder 0. On a double-sided drive with 40 tracks, there also are 40 cylinders, with cylinder 0 on the outside and cylinder 39 on the inside.

On a hard disk drive with two platters and four heads, there are four sides, named side 0, side 1, side 2, and side 3. Such a drive has four tracks named 0 and one cylinder 0 that contains these four tracks. *For more information on naming and numbering tracks, see Chapter 4.*

Sectors

With today's technology, we should be able to read 10K-100K hunks of information from a drive's surface at once. But the basic rules for drives were developed long ago, when dinosaurs roamed the earth and a 512-byte block was considered plenty. Thus all drives, whether floppy or hard disk, read data 512 bytes at a time. Such a unit in a track is called a sector. The number of sectors you have depends entirely on recording density. Floppies have fewer sectors than hard disks, as you can see from table 17.3. *For more information about floppy disk sectors, see Chapter 4.*

Table 17.3
Calculating Storage Capacity (Floppy and Hard Disks)

Disk Type	Size	Sectors per Track X	Bytes per Sector X	Tracks per Side X	Number of Sides =	Capacity
DSDD	5 1/4-inch	8	5K	40	1	160K
DSDD	5 1/4-inch	9	5K	40	1	180K
DSDD	5 1/4-inch	8	5K	40	2	320K
DSDD	5 1/4-inch	9	5K	40	2	360K
DSDD	5 1/4-inch	15	5K	80	2	1.2M
DSDD	3 1/2-inch	9	5K	80	2	720K
HD	3 1/2-inch	18	5K	80	2	1.44M
ST225 hard disk	5 1/4-inch	17	5K	615	4	20.91M
ST238R hard disk	5 1/4-inch	26	5K	615	4	31.98M

Encoding Schemes

Although all sectors contain only 512 bytes of information, you can see from table 17.3 that some hard disks have more sectors per track than others. Why? It has to do with the techniques used to encode the information on the disk. Basic encoding schemes include modified frequency modulation (MFM) and run length limited (RLL). For now, all you need to know is that these two types exist. *For more information about these encoding schemes, see Chapter 4.*

When IBM began shipping hard disks with XTs, it chose MFM encoding. This encoding approach became so popular that many programs were written that assumed that the drives they would run on would have 17 sectors per track. As people bought the first RLL drives, they discovered such naive programs wouldn't work.

Rather than be blamed for the errors of programmers, some hardware companies developed translating controllers that made the RLL drive look like an MFM drive to the computer. To do this, the controllers reduced the number of sectors per track reported to MS-DOS and increased the number of cylinders reported to MS-DOS. The net result was that all sectors were still present and accounted for, with the controller doing the accounting job.

Sector translation is also useful for large drives that exceed IBM's original idea of a good time. In the XT, the BIOS sets an upper limit of 63 sectors per track, 16 heads, and 1,024 cylinders. None of today's hard disks seem to use this many sectors per track or this many heads, but some exceed 1,024 cylinders. Sector translation can convert more cylinders to more heads or more sectors per track. Through translation, the original XT BIOS actually permits 63 x 16 x 1,024 = 1,032,192 total sectors. At half a kilobyte each, this works out to 528,482,304 bytes (504M) possible per drive.

> **NOTE** *Sector translation is terrific for everyone but the authors of low-level formatters. Such software must directly address sectors, heads, and cylinders, which is not possible with a "deceptive" translating controller.*

As compared with MFM encoding, RLL encoding reduces the amount of data-checking information that must be stored by performing the checks on longer blocks of data. Storage with RLL uses fewer flux reversals for a given amount of data. You can store on the same surface almost twice the amount of data you can store with MFM encoding. Because information is packed together more tightly, data transfer can be higher with RLL than with MFM.

Formatted versus Unformatted Capacity

A drive's theoretical capacity is defined at the factory by the number of cylinders and surfaces it has and the density with which information can be recorded. During the formatting process, some of the drive's storage space is used by sector addresses, system files, FATs, and directories. Sector addresses, system files, FATs, and directories all are defined later in this chapter. For more information about them, see Chapter 4.

Furthermore, the formatting process may discover and set aside "bad sectors" that should not be used for storage. All of this reduces effective storage space. A 110M drive before formatting might offer only 90M of storage space after formatting.

> *Because some vendors advertise unformatted capacity, be sure to ask what a drive's formatted capacity is before you buy it. Or run CHKDSK to see for yourself. Using CHKDSK, which comes with MS-DOS 6, you can check the space allocation on your disk. Note that this works for local hard drives only—not for network drives.*

Figure 17.3 shows CHKDSK syntax and parameters. An example of CHKDSK output is shown in figure 17.4.

Figure 17.3

Syntax and parameters for using CHKDSK.

```
C:\>chkdsk/?
Checks a disk and displays a status report.

CHKDSK [drive:][[path]filename] [/F] [/V]

  [drive:][path]  Specifies the drive and directory to check.
  filename        Specifies the file(s) to check for fragmentation.
  /F              Fixes errors on the disk.
  /V              Displays the full path and name of every file on the disk.

Type CHKDSK without parameters to check the current disk.

C:\>
```

How Drives Work

```
C:\>chkdsk

Volume 200 MB     created 11-07-1992 6:28p
Errors found, F parameter not specified
Corrections will not be written to disk

     10 lost allocation units found in 2 chains.
  81920 bytes disk space would be freed

 392478720 bytes total disk space
     90112 bytes in 3 hidden files
    450560 bytes in 54 directories
  88383488 bytes in 2284 user files
 303472640 bytes available on disk

      8192 bytes in each allocation unit
     47910 total allocation units on disk
     37045 available allocation units on disk

    655360 total bytes memory
    416912 bytes free

C:\>
```

Figure 17.4

What appears onscreen after you type **CHKDSK**.

Because only one file can be placed in a cluster, some unused space is left on the disk in the last cluster for nearly every file we store. Thus, a drive with 90M of storage space available after formatting might be able to store as little as 45K of files, depending on the size of those files.

> **NOTE** *On a drive with a 2K cluster, a one-byte file must use 2K (2 × 1,024 bytes) of storage space. A 90M drive can store 90 × 1,024 × 1,024 bytes. Thus, only 45 × 1,024 files can be stored on this drive. At one byte each, only 45K of data is actually stored on a 90M drive!*

MS-DOS has trouble counting beyond 65,536, which happens to be 64K or 2^{16}. Numbers larger than 64K often cause it trouble. To simplify the counting task, MS-DOS doesn't count sectors directly. Rather, it counts groups of sectors, called clusters, so that it doesn't have to count so high.

MS-DOS follows a few simple rules with clusters:

- ✔ Only one file per cluster, even if there is space for part of another.

- ✔ If a sector in the cluster is bad, the entire cluster should be marked as bad.

Clusters really help MS-DOS keep its total count of locations relatively small. In fact, MS-DOS works hard to find a file you request. To read just the first character of a file, MS-DOS has to do the following:

1. Find the file name in the current or specified directory.

2. Read the starting cluster stored at the end of this entry.

3. Convert this to a sector number by subtracting 2 from the cluster number (because the first cluster number is 2), multiply by the number of sectors per cluster, then add the offset of the first data sector. The offset may be something like 12 (1 boot sector plus 4 FAT sectors plus 7 directory sectors).

4. Tell the controller to read this sector number.

Addressing Sectors

Although sectors usually are described as looking like pie slices, a sector is really an arc in a circle—the track—and looks more like a crescent moon. A stack of such sectors, each a bit shorter, begins to look like a slice of pie.

Each track is a concentric ring. In each track are many 512-byte sectors. Because most of your files are larger than 512 bytes, you need a system for identifying the pieces of a file and their many 512-byte locations.

Early floppy disks were "hard sectored." A small hole denoted the starting position of each sector, and a light passing through this hole alerted the drive that another sector had been reached. Beginning with the IBM PC in 1981, soft-sectored disks became popular. With "soft sectoring," information identifying the sector is written to disk during the formatting process and then read back as the disk spins.

Floppy Disk Sector Addressing

On a floppy, the information identifying sectors includes:

- ✔ The *sector address*, to tell the drive where the sector is; its four bytes include

    A byte for this sector's track (0-39)

    A byte for this sector's side (0 or 1)

    A byte for the sector number (1-9)

    A byte to indicate sector size in bytes (0 = 128 bytes, 1 = 256 bytes, 2 = 512 bytes, 3 = 1024 bytes)

- ✔ *Special synchronization bytes*, to help prepare the drive for a read or write

- ✔ *Gap bytes*, which provide some filler, to make timing less critical in reading a sector

The rules for this formatting are defined in the controller and hard disk so that any version of MS-DOS has the same chances of reading a given drive.

Hard Disk Sector Addressing with Embedded Servos

A *servo* is a mechanism that gives feedback. A sensor in a coffee maker, for instance, can turn the hot plate on when the temperature falls too low, and the sensor can turn off the hot plate when the temperature gets too high. The sensor and switch for the hot plate constitute a servo-mechanism permitting the coffee maker to regulate the temperature of your coffee.

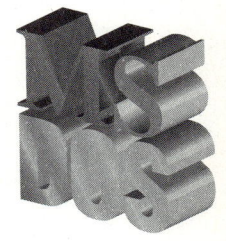

On a hard or floppy disk, a servo tells the heads where they are located. That is, on a disk drive, the heads read position information from the platter and report this info to the logic board on the drive. The logic board decodes this information and determines if the heads are where they should be, or if they are at a lower or higher track. If at a lower track, the logic board directs the heads to a higher track; if higher, to a lower track. The heads report back, and the process continues. This feedback loop can both move the heads and maintain their position.

An *embedded servo* intermixes positioning information on the drive with the data you are storing. Each track contains some such positioning information, as does each sector. If your hardware diagnostic program reports an even number of heads, you know that your hard disk has an embedded servo.

If, on the other hand, your diagnostic program reports an odd number of heads, your hard disk has a *dedicated servo*—the alternative to an embedded servo. The "missing" head is actually there but is used on a platter dedicated to servo information; servo information does not have to be provided on other surfaces. The advantage of a dedicated servo is that it usually is faster than an embedded one.

An embedded servo also has advantages, however. It can be more accurate than a dedicated servo, particularly for drives subjected to changing temperatures.

With an embedded servo, two kinds of information are written: information that occurs only once per track (and which precedes the first sector or follows the last sector) and information that is repeated for each sector.

The information written once per track includes Gap 1 information and Gap 4 padding. *Gap 1 information*, which occurs at the start of each track, before the first sector begins, consists of 16 bytes of 4E hex (01001110 in binary). *Gap 4 padding*, at the end of the track, also is done with 4E hex.

Most of the information on a track occurs once per sector, rather than once per track, however. Here is the format for a given sector in the track:

- ✔ **Synchronization bytes** (all 0s) are placed at the beginning of every track to help prepare the drive for a read.

- ✔ An **ID Field** consists of the following 7 bytes:

    ID field address marks—always an A1 hex (10100001 in binary), then an FE hex (11111110 in binary)—tell the controller that the address of this sector follows.

A byte to identify the cylinder for this sector. Because a single byte can identify only 256 cylinders, drives with more cylinders have a problem here. The solution is to use the least significant bits of the cylinder number. Thus, cylinder 257 is 100000001 in binary (nine digits); the eight least significant bits are 00000001. This would make the cylinder look like cylinder 1—were it not for the next clever byte.

A clever byte whose bits have two meanings. The first three bits are the most significant bits of the cylinder number. (Thus, for cylinder 256, in the preceding example, these bits would be 001.) The next five bits identify this sector's head number—the number of the head that will read this sector.

A byte to identify the sector number on this track (1-17 on most hard disks).

Two bytes for a cyclic redundancy check (CRC) to detect errors in the previous five bytes of this ID field. The CRC bytes also are known as error correction code (ECC). Such code not only is used to verify whether what is now being read matches what was written earlier, but also allows a small amount of correction! For instance, if you write a string of As to your hard disk, and a gremlin changes one to a B, the ECC can find and fix it. ECC can repair strings of up to 11 bits of error per sector.

✔ **Gap 2 information** consists of 16 bytes:

A write splice of three bytes of 00 hex

An ID pad of 13 bytes (again 00 hex) that fill out the length of the ID field and enable the drive's phase lock oscillator to synchronize with the data field, in preparation for a read

✔ The bytes of the **data field** look like this:

A data field address mark, which contains two bytes: A1 hex and F8 hex

512 bytes of data

Two bytes for a cyclic redundancy check, to detect errors in the data field

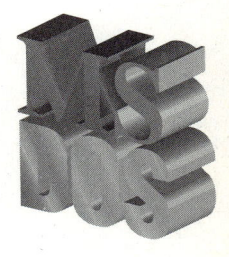

A write splice of three bytes of 00 hex

✔ **Gap 3**—a data pad—consists of 15 bytes of 4E hex, which pad the sector to the proper length. If this is the last sector of the track, the Gap 4 pad (mentioned earlier) begins. Otherwise, the sync information for the next sector begins at the end of Gap 3.

How Information Is Stored

If you've made it this far, you know that the surface of a floppy or hard disk is coated with microscopic magnetic particles, each of which has a north and a south pole. When a read-write head does its work, it creates a magnetic field that orients these particles so that north is up or down. Several magnetic particles are affected when the heads create a magnetic pulse; these particles comprise a *magnetic domain*. The head orients the particles in one direction by sending electricity through its own magnet in one direction, and orients the particles in the other direction by sending the electricity through its magnet in the other direction.

As you learned earlier in this chapter, a character can be represented by eight bits. Thus, an uppercase A is represented, in ASCII, by 10000010. But instead of storing the pattern itself (+ - - - + -), the head stores information on how the pattern changes "flux reversals." When the head writes a 1, it changes polarity (from north to south or vice versa) from whatever it had been doing; when it writes a 0, it doesn't change polarity. Thus, the pattern of the A, of a 10000010, might look like this if the previous bit written were an S: NNNNNNSS. In short, only a binary 1 motivates the head's current to change direction. This change in the magnetic orientation is called a *flux change*.

> *Drives code a change in bits as N, nonchange as S. Thus, a long string of 0s would be stored exactly like a long string of 1s—as a long string of Ss. A sequence of alternating 0s and 1s, on the other hand, would be stored as a string of Ns. Deciphering this coding requires knowledge of only one fact: the nature of the first bit (0 or 1). The checksum info stored for each sector indicates whether the bit in the sector is 0 or 1.*

Before going on, pause to admire the lowly floppy drive:

- ✔ The information stored is awfully small. On the outside track—which has a diameter of about 5 inches, a circumference of about 15.7 inches—you can store 9 sectors of 512 bytes (or 4,608 bytes). At 8 bits per byte, you can store 36,864 bits in this 15.7 inches, or 2,348 bits per inch. And the magnetic field created by each of these is too weak to affect any of the adjacent fields.

- ✔ The information moves pretty fast. The drive can read all 36,864 bits of a track in one revolution. At 300 rpm, it reads 11,059,200 bits per minute, translating them to characters and getting them all into memory where you can use them. Pretty speedy!

How a Drive Reads

When the heads read information from the disk's surface, they are able to sense the passing magnetized sections of the disk, distinguish between the polarity of the field (a 0 or 1), and amplify the weak current these magnetic fields create. The amplified signal is then converted from fuzzy analog signals to precise digital pulses. Drive electronics then sift through the pulses to determine which are *clock pulses* involved with synchronizing the drive and which are other information.

When the drive finds the sector address it reads it, comparing it with what the controller is looking for. If this is not the correct sector, the search continues; if it is the correct sector, the drive then reads the data, calculates a CRC, and compares it with the CRC it has just read. If the two CRCs match, the data is passed on through the controller. If they don't match, the controller tells the drive to try again.

If the controller retries several times and continues to find a mismatch between the CRC it calculates and the CRC it reads, it reports a *hard error*. Such an error may be with the sector read versus its CRC (the message is `Sector not found`) or with the data read versus its CRC (the message is `Data error reading drive`).

> **NOTE**
>
> *Any error that is not repeatable (one caused by a bit of dust or a minor power fluctuation during the read, for example) is called a soft error and might not be reported to the user because DOS makes the drive try again 3-5 times. But if all attempts by DOS fail, you call it a hard error and get an* `Abort Retry Ignore Fail` *message.*

Assuming that a clean data stream of bits is coming from the heads, the controller then *deserializes* them, converting them into bytes of information which then are placed in a buffer on the controller and transmitted out of the controller and through the bus. The number of bytes transmitted at one time (8, 16, or 32) is determined by the computer and how the controller attaches to its bus.

Where does the information go when it leaves the controller? That is determined by which CPU—or *central processing unit*—is in your computer. The CPU interprets the instructions that are in memory and executes them.

In an 8088, the CPU is a bit too slow to keep up with the speed at which your controller can send it information. So the PC and XT use a direct memory access (DMA) chip for the job. This chip sets up a direct pipeline to memory you've set aside to temporarily store the data coming from the controller. In your CONFIG.SYS file, the statement BUFFERS=20 creates 20 storage compartments in RAM, each exactly the size of one sector (512 bytes). The DMA chip fills these compartments; then the CPU copies them to other memory locations, as required by the software you are running. After all buffer locations are filled, the DMA chip cycles through them again, filling the first again, then the second, and so on.

Micros with faster CPUs, such as the 80286 and 80386, don't need DMA for the job. The CPU accepts the information from the controller, pops each sector into a buffer, then moves the information from each buffer to the memory location requested by your application software.

> **NOTE**
>
> *During a disk write, this process is reversed. Information in memory is sent through the CPU in 512-byte blocks to the MS-DOS buffers, then passed through the DMA controller (in the 8088) or CPU (in faster machines) to the hard disk controller. On the controller, the data waits in another buffer until the heads are correctly positioned over the sector where it is to be placed. Finally, the heads write it to the disk's surface.*

Understanding the Boot Process

In the first part of this chapter, you grappled with the physical facts of storage. Now you are going to look at how MS-DOS is stored on your drive, and how—when loaded—it is able to manage other things stored there.

When you *boot* (turn on) your machine, code stored in the ROMs on your motherboard is executed. This code runs the *POST* (the Power on Self-Test) and then loads into memory a very low form of operating system. This program, called the *BIOS* (for Basic Input-Output System), contains instructions to determine whether the floppy drive is ready to read and whether there is a hard disk that is ready to read. (As this question is answered, you see the floppy and then the hard disk drive lights come on.)

If both drives are ready, the BIOS checks whether a floppy disk is in drive A and whether the door is closed. If so, the very first sector of the floppy (side 0, cylinder 0, sector 1) is loaded and executed. If no disk is in drive A, the light goes out and the hard disk light comes back on. The computer tries reading from the very first sector of the hard disk (side 0, cylinder 0, sector 1).

> **NOTE**
>
> *On a hard disk, this first sector is called the* master boot sector. *It contains a program (the* master boot record*) and a database (the* partition table*). The program and database together tell the computer where to position the*

continues

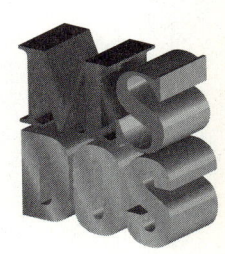

heads for the next read, which will be of the boot record, located in the boot sector. The boot record usually is located on side 1, cylinder 0, sector 1 of the hard disk—on the other side of the first platter, just below the master boot record.

On a floppy disk, the boot sector is the first sector read. Floppies don't have a master boot sector. For more information about the boot record, the master boot record, and partitions, see Chapter 4.

As noted in Chapter 4, after reading the boot record, the process continues—reading two file allocation tables, a root directory, two hidden system files, CONFIG.SYS, COMMAND.COM, and AUTOEXEC.BAT (in that order).

Because the process has many steps, and we'll take them one at a time, reading this part will take a bit longer than the normal boot process takes to complete!

Creating a Master Boot Record

If you see the message...

```
General Failure Error Reading Drive C:
```

...when you turn on the computer, it is surely the result of a failure to read and understand the master boot sector's information. This area might be damaged, a virus might have modified this region beyond recognition, the drive might have been dropped while it was spinning, or perhaps someone has run a low-level format program.

What does all this stuff in the master boot record mean?

The master boot record (MBR) is sometimes referred to as the partition table, but I would rather say that the master boot record *contains* the partition table. This master boot record, a one-sector file, is created when FDISK is run. FDISK, a powerful utility included with MS-DOS 6.2, configures your hard disk so that you can run MS-DOS. A hard disk that has never been partitioned with FDISK does not have a master boot record. Floppies never have one.

If the MBR exists, it contains information on the number of partitions and the location of the boot record in each. It also contains information about which partition is active. From the MBR, the heads move to the active partition and read the boot record (as distinguished from the master boot record) there.

The MBR, a variable-length file, contains information on each partition created with FDISK. For each partition, the following information is defined:

- The *boot indicator*, which asks Can we boot from this partition? For one partition, the answer must be yes (coded as 80 hex). For all other partitions, the answer must be no (coded as 0).

- Where to find the boot record to be used, including information on the *system indicator* (12-bit DOS FAT, 16-bit DOS FAT, or unknown operating system), head, sector, cylinder (for the first partition only), *relative sector* (number of sectors preceding this partition), and number of sectors in this partition. All this location information takes only 12 bytes per partition.

- The MBR ends with a *signature*—a pair of bytes set to 55AA hex to indicate a valid master boot record.

The location of the MBR is *totally inflexible*. It *always* resides on side 0, track 0, sector 0. If this part of the surface is damaged, you can't have a good MBR, and FDISK and FORMAT are likely to fail. Hard disk manufacturers are extra careful in testing track 0 to ensure that it begins life in good shape. Nevertheless, your head probably uses this track fairly often, increasing the chance of injury. Before proceeding, FDISK verifies that track 0 is usable. Unlike some earlier versions of FDISK, running it in MS-DOS 6 does not automatically destroy (by verifying) the locations of the boot record, FAT, root directory, two system files, and COMMAND.COM. *For more information about the boot record, the master boot record, and partitions, see Chapter 4.*

Don't try to repartition a drive that already has good data on it. FDISK will destroy some of your data forever.

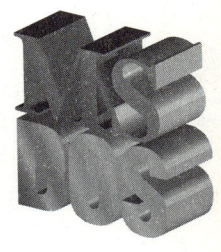

If you'd like to look at your own MBR, copy DSEDIT.EXE (on the *Inside MS-DOS 6.2* disk) to your hard drive, and then type...

DSEDIT

During the boot process, the MBR tells your hard disk controller which partition is active and where it begins. The heads move to this location and read the MS-DOS boot record. If no partition is marked as active, you can't boot from the hard disk. To ensure booting from the hard disk, choose Display partition information before you quit FDISK (see fig. 17.5), and ascertain that one part is marked "active" or "A." Not to worry. FDISK is covered at length later in this chapter.

Figure 17.5
The FDISK main menu.

```
                    MS-DOS Version 6.00
                    Fixed Disk Setup Program
                (C)Copyright Microsoft Corp. 1983 - 1992

                         FDISK Options

    Current fixed disk drive: 1

    Choose one of the following:

    1. Create DOS partition or Logical DOS Drive
    2. Set active partition
    3. Delete partition or Logical DOS Drive
    4. Display partition information


    Enter choice: [1]




    Press Esc to exit FDISK
```

The Boot Record

Like the program in the master boot sector, the only time the program in the boot sector runs is when you are booting your computer. But the boot record also contains a fine variety of useful information about your drive that comes in handy whenever MS-DOS needs to know about the drive. This information, stored at the top of the boot record, is especially handy when you swap floppy disks in a drive, because MS-DOS needs to know whether you've just replaced the last disk with one of the same capacity.

The first three bytes of the boot record (E9 XX XX hex or EB XX 90 hex) instruct the computer to jump past the interesting information that follows these bytes and run the bootstrap program located at the end of that jump. This *bootstrap program* loads the operating system from the drive.

The following crucial drive information is located between those three jump bytes and the bootstrap program bytes:

- ✔ **OEM name and version (eight characters).** The *OEM* is the *original equipment manufacturer*. Disks formatted with MS-DOS 6.2 from Microsoft show "MSDOS 6.2" as seven of these eight characters. If your DOS 6.2 comes from IBM or from COMPAQ, these eight characters of information may include the letters "IBM" or "COMPAQ." Almost every program I've ever seen ignores the OEM name and version. In this location, "HAL" or "HI MOM" would cause no offense.

- ✔ **Number of bytes per sector.** This 2-byte value, which begins the BIOS parameter block, is almost always 512 (ASCII). The *BIOS parameter block*, a database for the BIOS, helps with drive-related, input-output tasks.

- ✔ **Sectors per cluster.** This 1-byte number is always a power of 2 (1, 2, 4, 8, and so on).

- ✔ **Reserved sectors.** Starting at sector 0, one sector (sector 1) is always reserved for the boot record. If some hard disk makers set aside more for their own use, this can be stored in this 2-byte number. Reserved sectors are passed over as the boot process looks for the first copy of the FAT. *File allocation tables (FATs) are discussed in Chapter 4.*

- ✔ **Number of FATs (a 1-byte number).** All versions of MS-DOS, including MS-DOS 6.2, have two file allocation tables (FATs). The first is used more often than the second (which is for emergency recovery of files should the first become damaged).

- ✔ **Number of root directory entries.** The root directory is a fixed-length file, with 32 bytes used by each entry. During the boot process, you need to know how much to read. The answer is stored in this 2-byte number.

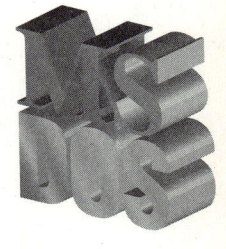

- ✔ **Sectors on the drive.** In this position of the boot record, a 2-byte number is useful only to describe the number of sectors on a drive of 32M or smaller. The 2-byte value can only hold a value of up to 256×256 = 65,536.

  NOTE: If the drive exceeds 32M, this field contains 0 and the information on drive size is stored in the Huge Sectors field (described a little later). On a 32M drive, you want to store 32×1024×1024 = 33,554,432 bytes. At 512 bytes per sector, you need to manage 33,554,432/512 = 65,536 sectors. We could use a three-byte number here, but that wouldn't be backward-compatible with various older programs that read these two bytes. So we use the new Huge Sectors field for large drives.

- ✔ **Media descriptor byte.** This byte tells MS-DOS which type of drive or disk this one is. MS-DOS passes the information to device drivers. Sometimes the information is checked to see whether you've changed disks in your floppy drive. Sometimes the information is repeated as the first byte of the header of the FAT. The following bytes commonly are used:

    F0 (1.44M or 2.88M floppy or other media types)

    F8 (hard disk)

    F9 (1.2M)

    FA (320K)

    FB (640K)

    FC (180K)

    FD (360K or 8 inches)

    FE (160K or 8 inches)

    FF (320K)

- ✔ **Sectors per FAT (a two-byte number).**
- ✔ **Sectors per track (a two-byte number).**

Understanding the Boot Process **927**

- **Number of read-write heads on the drive (two bytes).**
- **Number of hidden sectors (four bytes).**
- **Huge sectors (four bytes).** Number of sectors if the drive is larger than 32M ("Sectors on the drive" field is 0). This field marks the end of the BIOS parameter block.
- **Drive number.** It specifies whether the drive is the first hard disk drive (contains 80h) or not (00h). Used internally by MS-DOS 6.2.
- **Reserved-unused.** (We'll wait for MS-DOS 7 to see what happens here.)
- **Extended boot signature record (29h).**
- **Volume serial number or ID.**
- **Volume label (11 characters).**
- **Type of file system.** An 8-byte ASCII label is used. Either FAT12 or FAT16 (followed by three spaces) identifies which is used. (Floppies are likely to show FAT12; the hard disk, FAT16.)
- **Bootstrap routine.** Program whose main function is reading the information from the fields described here, then loading the remainder of the operating system: FATs, root directory, hidden system files, and COMMAND.COM.
- **Boot sector signature (stored as the last two bytes).** In hex, 55AA. (In ASCII, it looks a bit like my dog on his back waiting to get his tummy rubbed.)

Figure 17.6 shows a boot sector from a 1.44M floppy, formatted by MS-DOS 6.2.

Boot Sectors: Some Varieties

The contents of the boot sector vary according to drive type. Table 17.4 provides some examples of the information contained in a boot sector.

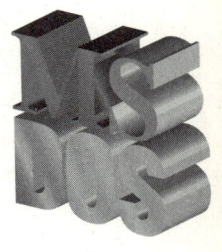

Chapter 17: *A Second Look at Hard Drives*

Figure 17.6

The boot sector of a 1.44 floppy.

```
Side 0, Cylinder 0, Sector 1                              Hex format
                                                      Offset 0, hex 0
EB3C904D 53444F53 362E3000 02010100 02E00040 0BF00900  ë<ÉMSDOS6.0.☻☺☺.♠♣.♠♦≡○.
12000200 00000000 00000000 000029F8 1A522A4E 4F204E41  ‡.☻..........)°►R*NO NA
4D452020 20204641 54313220 2020FA33 C08ED0BC 007C1607  ME    FAT12    ·3└ÄÐ╝.│▬.
BB780036 C5371E56 1653BF3E 7CB90B00 FCF3A406 1FC645FE  ╗x.6┼7▲V.S¿>|╣♂.■ñ♠▼Eã
0FB80E18 7C884DF9 894702C7 073E7CFB CD137279 33C83906  ☼╕♫↑|êM·ëG☻╟.>|√═♥ry3╚9♠
137C7488 8B0E137C 890E207C A0107CF7 26167C03 061C7C13  .|t^ï♫.|ë♫ |á►.|≈&▬|.♠∟|‼
161E7C83 060E7C83 D200A350 7C891652 7CA3497C 89164B7C  ▬▲|âÀ♫|âÐ.úP|ë▬R|úI|ë▬K|
B82000F7 26117C8B 1E0B7C03 C348F7F3 0106497C 83164B7C  ╕ .≈&◄|ï▲♂|♥├H≈≤☺♠I|â▬K|
00BB0005 8B16527C A1507CE8 9200721D B001E8AC 0072168B  .╗.♣ï▬R|íP|Φ.r↔░.Φ¼.r▬ï
FBB90B00 BEE67DF3 A6750A8D 7F20B90B 00F3A674 18BE9E7D  √╣♂.¥µ}≤ªu◙ì⌂ ╣♂.≤ªt↑¥₧}
E85F0033 C0CD165E 1F8F048F 4402CD19 585858EB E88B471A  Φ_.3└═▬^▼Å♦ÅD☻═↓XXXδΦïG→
48488A1E 0D7C32FF 7E30306 497C1316 4B7CBB00 07B90300  HHè▲.♪|2.≈π♥I‼.▬K|╗..♣.
505251E8 3A0072D8 B001E854 00595A58 72BB0501 0083D200  PRQΦ:.r┘░.ΦT.YZXr╗♣☺.â╨.
031E0B7C E2E28A2E 157C8A16 247C8B1E 497CA14B 7CEA0000  ♥.♂|Γrè..|è▬$|ï▲I|íK|Ω..
7000AC0A C07429B4 B08B0700 CD10EBF2 3B16187C 7319F736  p.¼◙└t)┤░ï.═►δ≥;▬↑|s↓≈6
187CFEC2 88164F7C 33D2F736 1A7C8816 257CA34D 7CF8C3F9  ↑|■┬^▬O|3╥≈6→|^▬%|úM|°├∙
C3B4028B 164D7CB1 06D2E60A 364F7C8B CA86E98A 16247C8A  ├┤☻ï▬M|▒♠╥µ◙6O|ïÊå⌐è▬$|è
36257CCD 13C30D0A 4E6F6E2D 53797374 656D2064 69736B20  6%|═‼├♪◙Non-System disk
6F722064 69736B20 65727226 720D0A52 65706C61 63652061  or disk error♪Replace a
6E642070 72657373 20616E79 206B6579 20776865 6E207265  nd press any key when re
6164790D 0A00494F 20202020 20205359 534D5344 4F532020  ady♪◙.IO      SYSMSDOS  
20535953 000055AA           Press Enter to continue  SYS..U¬
1Help  2Hex  3Text  4Dir  5FAT  6Partn  7   8Choose  9Undo  10QuitNU
```

Table 17.4
What's in the Boot Record?

Information	360K	1.2M	720K	1.44M	Hard Disk
Media descriptor (hex)	FD	F9	F9	F0	F8
Bytes per sector	512	512	512	512	512
Sectors per cluster	2	1	2	1	4
Number of FATs	2	2	2	2	2
Root directory entries	112	224	112	224	512
Sectors per FAT	2	7	3	9	64
Number of sectors	720	2,400	1,440	2,880	65,467
Offset to FAT	1	1	1	1	1
Sectors per track	9	15	9	18	17
Sides/heads	2	2	2	2	9
Hidden sectors	0	0	0	0	17

Looking at Your Own Boot Record

MS-DOS 6.2 comes with a program, DEBUG, that enables you to look at your boot record. To use this program, type the following:

```
DEBUG
-L 100 0 0 1
-D
-Q
```

If you run DEBUG on a 1.44M floppy in drive A, you see the display shown in figure 17.7.

```
C:\>debug a:
File not found
-l 100 0 0 1
-d
3FE3:0100  EB 3C 90 4D 53 44 4F 53-36 2E 30 00 02 01 01 00   .<.MSDOS6.0.....
3FE3:0110  02 E0 00 40 0B F0 09 00-12 00 02 00 00 00 00 00   ...@............
3FE3:0120  00 00 00 00 00 00 29 F8-1A 52 2A 4E 4F 20 4E 41   ......)..R*NO NA
3FE3:0130  4D 45 20 20 20 20 46 41-54 31 32 20 20 20 FA 33   ME    FAT12   .3
3FE3:0140  C0 8E D0 BC 00 7C 16 07-BB 78 00 36 C5 37 1E 56   .....|...x.6.7.V
3FE3:0150  16 53 BF 3E 7C B9 0B 00-FC F3 A4 06 1F C6 45 FE   .S.>|.........E.
3FE3:0160  0F 8B 0E 18 7C 88 4D F9-89 47 02 C7 07 3E 7C FB   ....|.M..G...>|.
3FE3:0170  CD 13 72 79 33 C0 39 06-13 7C 74 08 8B 0E 13 7C   ..ry3.9..|t....|
-q

C:\>
```

Figure 17.7

The boot record of a 1.44M floppy, as shown by DEBUG.

What's on the Bottom of Your Boot?

You probably have turned on your computer many times with a data disk in drive A, only to see the message Non-System disk or disk error. Replace and strike any key when ready. on the screen. Did you ever wonder where this message comes from?

It is at the very bottom of every boot record. The boot program contains instructions to load the two hidden system files and is given their names (as the final entries of the boot record). If they can't be located, the boot record displays the error message. Because these two files are not copied to a drive unless you use the /S option with FORMAT, all data disks created without the /S option display the message if you try to boot from them. The next section covers FORMAT and its options in greater detail.

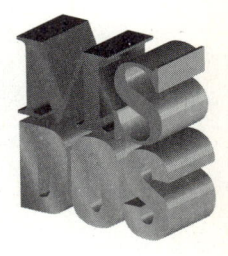

When you see this message, you might have something else to think about other than taking your unbootable disk out of drive A. It is possible that your computer has just been infected with a boot virus. A *boot virus* moves the boot record to some other location and then places itself in the boot sector of a floppy disk.

> **NOTE**
>
> Although not all disks are bootable, FORMAT creates a boot record on all of them.
>
> When you boot with a disk infected with a boot virus, the computer runs whatever program is in the boot sector, thus running the virus. The virus goes into memory and prepares to infect other drives. It then calls the original boot record program, which it has copied to some other location on your disk. When the boot record runs, it instructs the drive to read the FATs and root directory, and try to load and execute the hidden system files. If they are not found, you see the dreaded `Non-System disk or disk error` message. This message, we now know, occurs after you've accidentally booted with an unwanted disk. And it may mean that a boot virus has secretly loaded.
>
> If you want to be careful, you should reboot with a write-protected, uninfected bootable disk. Then run MSAV, the anti-virus utility that comes with MS-DOS 6, from your hard disk to check your hard disk's master boot record and boot record, or to check the floppy you just accidentally tried to boot with.

How does the `Non-System disk or disk error` message get into the boot sector? It is contained in FORMAT.COM. You can find it there by using any sector editor, such as the Norton Utilities (see fig. 17.8).

Understanding the Boot Process

```
format.com═══════════════════════════════════════════Hex format═
  Cluster 144, Sectors 2,576-2,591        File offset 3,584, hex E00
16247C8A 36257CCD 13C30D0A 4E6F6E2D 53797374 656D2064 ▌$!è6%!=!!|♪♂Non-System d
69736B20 6F722064 69736B20 6572726F 720D0A52 65706C61 isk or disk error♪◙Repla
63652061 6E642070 72657373 20616E79 206B6579 20776865 ce and press any key whe
6E207265 6164790D 0A00494F 20202020 20205359 534D5344 n ready♪◙ IO      SYSMSD
4F532020 20535953 000055AA 0002B200 0002B039 02CA0E46 OS   SYS..U¬.▓..⌐9☻◙♀F
41543132 20202046 41543136 20202000 00000000 001A00B2 AT12   FAT16     ....→.▓
201300B0 00FF0000 00000008 000900B2 3F0B00B0 008F00B0  !!. ▒.....▓?♂.▒.Å.▒
413A0000 00000050 4154483D 464F524D 41541200 B2001A00 A:.....PATH=FORMAT‼.▓..
B0020201 00027000 8002FF01 00080002 0F00B200 1000B002 ░☻☺.☻p.Ç☻.☻.☻☺.▓.►.▓
01010002 40004001 FE010008 00010F00 B2001000 B0020201 ☺☺.☻@.@☺■☺.☻.☺☼.▓..►░☻☺
00027000 D002FD02 00090002 0F00B200 1000B002 01010002 .☻p.╨☻²☻.○.☻☼.▓.►.▓☺☺.☻
40006801 FC020009 00010F00 B2001000 B0020101 0002E000 @.h☺ⁿ☻.○.☻☼.▓.►.▓☺☺.☻α.
6009F907 000F0002 0F00B200 1000B002 02010002 7000A005 `○∙•..☼.▓.►.▓☻☺.☻p.á♣
F9030009 00020F00 B2001000 B0020101 0002E000 400BF009 ∙♥.○.☻☼.▓.►.▓☺☺.☻α.@♂≡○
00120002 0F00B200 1000B002 02010002 F0008016 F0090024 ..☻☼.▓.►.▓☻☺.☻≡.Ç▬≡○.$
00020F00 B2000F00 B08001C0 018000C0 00000000 0026170E .☻☼.▓.☼.░Ç☺╚.Ç.╚.....&↨◙
00B20008 00B04517 00006417 0600B200 1202B001 0000FFFF .▓..░E↨..d↨.☻▓.‼☻░☺.. 
0500B200 1A00B058 3A5C434F 4D4D414E 442E434F 4D0E00B2 ♣.▓.→.░X:\COMMAND.COM♫.▓
007200B0 434F4D53 5045433D 0000583A 5C434F4D 4D414E44 .r.░COMSPEC=..X:\COMMAND
2E434F4D 1800B200 0800B02D 53746163 6B212D2D 53746163 .COM↑.▓..░-Stack!--Stac
6B212D2D 53746163 6B212D2D 6B212D2D 53746163 6B212D2D k!--Stack!--Stack!--Stac
6B212D2D 53746163                                     k!--Stac
                              Press Enter to continue
1Help 2Hex 3Text 4Dir 5FAT 6Partn 7     8Choose 9Undo 10QuitNU
```

Figure 17.8

Sector of FORMAT.COM with original message.

> ⬥ **STOP**
>
> *This experiment is designed so that you can remind yourself to check for possible viruses if you have accidentally booted with an unwanted floppy. We recommend that you read the experiment thoroughly, and then if you decide to proceed, do so only with a copy of FORMAT.COM. Be sure to keep your MS-DOS 6.2 master disks in a safe and secure place.*

In this experiment, you modify FORMAT.COM so that a message other than Non-System disk... appears.

1. Copy FORMAT.COM to another name, such as FARMAT.COM. Then use an editor (such as Norton Utilities) to find the message `Non-System disk or disk error. Replace and press any key when ready.`

2. Replace this message (it occurs twice) with `Boot virus warning! Scan now! Check C: or A: after booting clean!` Don't trample the carriage return-line feed (0D0Ah) if you want your message to appear on two lines (see fig. 17.9).

continues

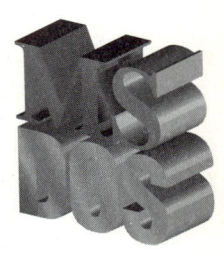

Figure 17.9

Sector of FARMAT.COM with modified message.

```
farmat.com                                           Hex format
 Cluster 10,852, Sectors 173,904-173,9    File offset 3,584, hex E00
16247C8A 36257CCD 13C30D0A 426F6F74 20766972 75732077 ▌$¦è6%!=‼¦♪◙Boot virus w
61726E69 6E672120 5363616E 206E6F77 210D0A43 6865636B arning! Scan now!♪◙Check
20433A20 6F722041 3A206166 74657220 626F6F74 696E6720  C: or A: after booting
636C6561 6E210D0A 0A00494F 20202020 20205359 534D5344  clean!♪◙.IO     SYSMSD
4F532020 20535953 000055AA 0002B200 0002B039 02CA0E46 OS   SYS..U¬.◙▌..◙ ◙♀║F
41543132 20202046 41543136 20202000 00000000 001A00B2 AT12    FAT16     ...→.▓
201300B0 00FF0000 00000008 000900B2 3F0B00B0 008F00B0  !!.▐.....◙.▓?♂.◙.Å.
413A0000 00000050 4154483D 464F524D 41541200 B2001A00 A:.....PATH=FORMAT‡..▓.
B0020201 00027000 8002FF01 00000002 0F00B200 1000B002 ░...○.○.p.C◙.◙.◙*.▓.▶.░
01010002 40004001 FE010008 00010F00 B0020201 ☺☺.◙@.@.■◙.◙.◙*.▓.▶.░░.
00027000 D002FD02 00090002 0F00B200 1000B002 01010002  .○.╨☻²☻.◙.◙*.▓.▶.░░.☺
40006801 FC020009 00010F00 B2001000 B0020101 0002E000 @.h☺ⁿ☻.◙.◙*.▓.▶.░░.8*
6009F907 000F0002 0F00B200 1000B002 02010002 7000A005 `.·•.☼.◙.▓.▶.░░.☻p.á◘
F9030009 00020F00 B2001000 B0020101 0002E000 400BF009 ∙♥.◙*.▓.▶.░░.☻◦.@♂≡◦
00120002 0F00B200 1000B002 02010002 F0008016 F0090024 .‡.◙*.▓.▶.░░.Ξ=≡◦.$
00020F00 B2000F00 B00001C0 018000C0 00000000 0026170E .◙*.▓.*.╝◙└.L...&‡♫
00B20008 00B04517 00006417 0600B200 1202B001 0000FFFF .▓.◙.E‡..d‡♦.▓.t◙░.
0500B200 1A00B058 3A5C434F 4D4D414E 442E434F 4D0E00B2 ♦.▓.→.░X:\COMMAND.COM♫.▓
007200B0 434F4D53 5045433D 0000583A 5C434F4D 4D414E44 .r.░COMSPEC=..X:\COMMAND
2E434F4D 1800B200 0800B02D 53746163 6B212D2D 53746163 .COM↑.▓.◘.░-Stack!--Stac
6B212D2D 53746163 6B212D2D 53746163 6B212D2D 53746163 k!--Stack!--Stack!--Stac
6B212D2D 53746163                Press Enter to continue k!--Stac
1Help  2Hex    3Text   4Dir   5FAT   6Partn   7       8Choose 9Undo  10QuitNU
```

3. After saving your work, try formatting a nonbootable floppy with FARMAT A:/Q/U, then try booting with this disk. The message on the screen is the test. If your screen displays the message you've just entered, you've successfully modified the message of the boot record.

```
Boot virus warning! Scan now!
Check C: or A: after booting clean!
```

Such modifications will be included in every disk you format with your modified version of FORMAT.COM. If users follow your advice—scanning immediately after accidentally booting with an unknown floppy—they have a better chance of stopping a virus early.

The FATs

The *file allocation table* (FAT) is located immediately after the DOS boot sector. The FAT serves as a miniature database; DOS uses it to keep track of all the clusters on a drive. From the FAT alone, you can reconstruct a file—but without a clue as to its name.

The FAT is a *one-way linked list*. Because a given entry points only to the next sequential entry—not also to the previous entry—you must start at the top of the file and read down to determine what goes with what.

The FAT contains one entry for every cluster on your logical drive. The first two bytes (the first entry), are reserved for special information. These two bytes contain the media descriptor, a code that designates what kind of device this FAT is dealing with. Table 17.5 shows the common media descriptors and their meanings.

Table 17.5
Media Descriptor Bytes and Drive Types

Media Decimal	Descriptor Hex	Byte Binary	Disk Drive Type
240	F0	11110000	1.44M 3 1/2-inch disk
248	F8	11111000	Hard disk
249	F9	11111001	1.2M 5 1/4-inch or 720K 3 1/2-inch disk
252	FC	11111100	180K 5 1/4-inch single-sided, double-density disk
253	FD	11111101	360K 5 1/4-inch double-sided, double-density disk
254	FE	11111110	160K 5 1/4-inch single-sided, single-density disk
255	FF	11111111	320K 5 1/4-inch double-sided, single-density disk

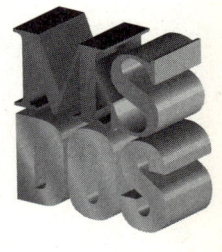

12-Bit FAT versus 16-Bit FAT

The reason the media type is read first in the FAT is that it defines how the FAT is coded. FAT entries are 16 bits on any logical drive that has at least 4,086 clusters (a 20M partition on a hard disk, for example). For any smaller logical drive (a 6M hard disk partition, for instance, or any floppy), a 12-bit FAT is used. A FAT 12 bits wide can store FFF as its maximum value.

In a 16-bit FAT, the first row contains two bytes: the media descriptor byte and a spacer byte of FF hex. This row, in the computer's counting system, is row 0.

The 16-bit FAT's second row (row 1 in the computer's counting system) contains two spacer bytes of FF hex.

The third row of a 16-bit FAT (officially row 2) is where things start to get interesting. This entry tells the story about the second cluster of the drive and is the first "real" entry of the FAT. MS-DOS begins cluster numbering with 2, and this row number describes its cluster number.

Each entry contains one of the five facts shown in table 17.6.

Table 17.6
What's in the FAT, and What It Means

Value (HEX)	Interpretation
Not in use by a file (empty, awaiting some action)	
0000	Cluster is available for use. This hexadecimal value for the two bytes is the same as 0 in decimal, 0000000000000000 in binary.
FFF0-FFF6	Cluster is not used but is reserved. Don't use it for a file. This range of values is 65,520 to 65,526 in decimal, and 1111111111110000 through 111111111110110 in binary.
FFF7	This is a bad cluster. Don't use it! In decimal, this value is 65,527. In binary, it is the pattern 1111111111110111.

Value (HEX)	Interpretation
	In use by a file
0002-FFEF	Cluster is used by a file. Go to the cluster value indicated to find information on the next cluster of the file. These patterns in decimal range from 2 through 65,519. In binary, the pattern is from 0000000000000010 through 1111111111101111.
FFF8-FFFF	This is the last cluster for this file. It can range from 65,528 through 65,535 in decimal, from 1111111111111000 through 1111111111111111 in binary.

What does the FAT look like? The fact is, it is a magnetic pattern and isn't visible at all. The closest representation you have is a string of 0s and 1s. In a typical 16-bit FAT for a hard disk, with 65,636 entries of 16 bits each, you'd see a string of 65,536 5 16 = 1,048,576, 0s and 1s. In all of this mess, there won't be even one carriage return. Try turning in a term paper that looks like that, and see what grade you get!

Because there is no standard, you can represent this mess any way you choose. One clean way is with a list, in English, like that shown in table 17.7.

Table 17.7
Imaginary FAT

Cluster*	FAT Entry
2	3
3	4
4	End of file
5	Available
6	Available
7	Bad
..	

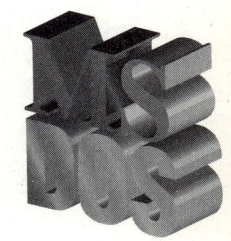

continues

Table 17.7, Continued
Imaginary FAT

Cluster*	FAT Entry
..	
65,536	

*In reality, the information in this column isn't placed in the FAT, but is inferred by MS-DOS. DOS counts down and figures out the cluster number from the FAT entry number, or "row number."

In this imaginary FAT, a file in cluster 2 continues in cluster 3. The file in cluster 3 continues in cluster 4. The file in cluster 4 ends somewhere in that cluster. Clusters 5 and 6 are available and can be used by another file. Cluster 7 contains one or more bad sectors and shouldn't be used.

Although the FAT view shown in table 17.7 is easy to understand, you'd need many sheets of paper (or screens on your monitor) to view 65,636 entries. A more efficient viewing approach is that used by programs like NU, the Norton Utilities. The FAT shown in figure 17.10 is identical to the one shown earlier.

Figure 17.10

Sector 16 in the first copy of the FAT.

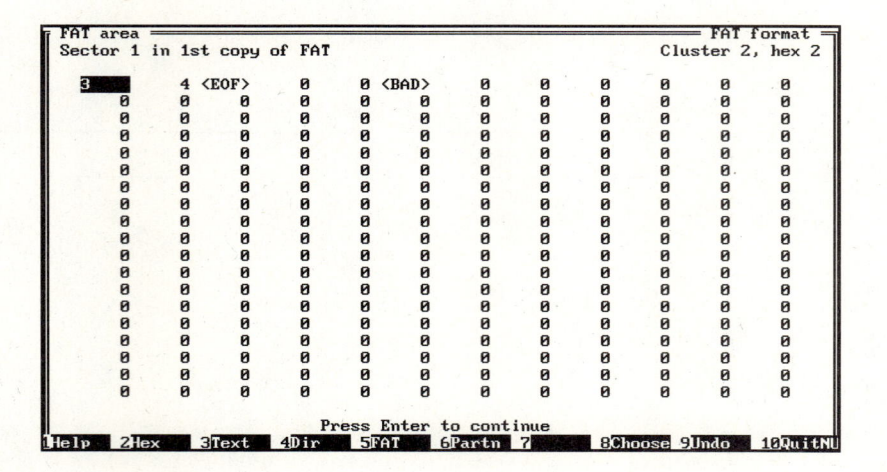

The Root Directory

The root directory is located immediately after the second (backup) copy of the FAT. You can imagine it as a small database in which each record is 32 bytes wide. The fields of this database, and their widths, are shown in table 17.8.

Table 17.8
What's in the Root Directory?

Information	Size in Bytes	Comment
File name	8	
Extension	3	
Attributes	1	One attribute per bit; 8 binary attributes
Reserved	10	Unused (wasted, for now)
Time	2	Coded, to make it fit
Date	2	Coded, to make it fit
Starting FAT entry	2	2 bytes for MS-DOS 3 and later
File Size	4	
Total	32 bytes per entry	

The root directory always has a fixed length, even when empty, but this length depends on the media type (see table 17.9). Large hard disks, which can hold more files, are entitled to more entries.

Table 17.9
Root Directory Size by Drive Type

Drive Type	Sectors for Root	Entries for Root
160K	4	64
180K	4	64

continues

Table 17.9, Continued
Root Directory Size by Drive Type

Drive Type	Sectors for Root	Entries for Root
360K	7	112
1.2M	14	224
720K 3 1/2-inch	7	112
1.44M 3 1/2-inch	14	224
Hard disk	32	512

Subdirectories

Root directories and subdirectories all use 32 bytes to describe a file. However, the size of the root directory is fixed. *Subdirectories*—any directory listed in the root or another directory—are variable in size, from one entry to an unlimited number of entries. This is because a subdirectory is nothing more than a special MS-DOS file. When a file is added to a subdirectory, the subdirectory file grows by 32 bytes. This may or may not increase the number of clusters required by the subdirectory.

Like all files, a subdirectory can become fragmented. On a typical hard disk, a subdirectory fills a cluster at 64 files. The 65th entry is likely to be located far away on the hard disk, causing a slight pause in reading the directory.

Hidden System Files and COMMAND.COM

In the days of DOS 5, the two hidden system files had a variety of names, depending on whose DOS you had (Compaq, IBM, Microsoft, or others). These files were actually "archive, read-only, system, and hidden" in their attributes. The first of these files, IO.SYS, establishes the basic input-output functions DOS requires. The second,

MSDOS.SYS, sets up things for the higher level functions of COMMAND.COM. These basic functions have not changed in MS-DOS 6.2, although the files have grown as tricks have been added. See table 17.10 for the new scale weights. (Like me, DOS has gained weight with age.)

Table 17.10
Differences in System-File Sizes between MS-DOS 5 and 6.2

File Name	Size in MS-DOS 5	Size in MS-DOS 6.2
IO.SYS	33,430 bytes	39,590 bytes
MSDOS.SYS	37,394 bytes	37,416 bytes
COMMAND.COM	About 47,845 bytes (depended on version)	53,022 bytes

When the boot record executes, it reads the FATs and the root and then determines whether the two hidden system files (IO.SYS and MSDOS.SYS) are present. If they are, MS-DOS learns from them what to do next.

One of the things that must be known before leaving any stage of the boot process is where to go next. IO.SYS gives us a hint. At offset 37,855 of IO.SYS, a reference to \CONFIG.SYS defines the file to be read after MSDOS.SYS. You can change its location and name (for security reasons) by *patching* IO.SYS, provided that you work within the space limitations of this file (a total of 11 characters, including the path, are available). Thus, you could change it to \DOS\C.SYS. The file to be read after CONFIG.SYS, defined at offset 37,947 of IO.SYS, is \COMMAND.COM. This reference, like the one \CONFIG.SYS, can be *patched*, that is, replaced with code using a sector editor such as DSEDIT, which is provided on the *Inside MS-DOS 6.2* disk. *See Chapter 21 for some guidance on using this editor.*

DOS doesn't know the name of a file to be processed after COMMAND.COM until booting has loaded COMMAND.COM, where the text \AUTOEXEC.BAT is at offset 8,031. As with the other text references, you can change this one if you want to.

In MS-DOS 5 and earlier versions, reconfiguring your machine was a nuisance. It could be done by saving various copies of CONFIG.SYS and AUTOEXEC.BAT in a directory, under meaningful names, and writing a batch file that copied a selected CONFIG.SYS and AUTOEXEC.BAT from this directory to the root, renaming in the process, then asking you to reboot (or running REBOOT.COM, on the *Inside MS-DOS 6.2* disk).

> *A little bit about REBOOT. Type **REBOOT**, and presto, your computer reboots and restarts. For example, you might have a few batch files to give yourself a "different" computer.*

To reconfigure your machine in MS-DOS 6.2, press F5 during booting when you see the message `Starting MS-DOS...` in the upper left of your screen. F5 bypasses the startup files (CONFIG.SYS and AUTOEXEC.BAT). Then you can confirm each CONFIG.SYS line by pressing F8. Thus, you can add mutually exclusive lines in CONFIG.SYS, and select the ones you want during the boot process.

MS-DOS 6.2 displays the lines of CONFIG.SYS, one at a time, and gives you a `[Y,N]?` option. After moving through CONFIG.SYS, MS-DOS 6.2 asks whether to `Process AUTOEXEC.BAT [Y,N]?`. If you answer no, AUTOEXEC.BAT is ignored. If you answer yes, every line of AUTOEXEC.BAT is processed—DOS doesn't ask you about them.

> *If you are troubleshooting CONFIG.SYS, the F8 key is a handy way to keep an error message on-screen while you record what it says and where it came from.*

Using FDISK and FORMAT

When you have a brand new computer on your hands—one that doesn't have MS-DOS preloaded by the manufacturer—you must prepare yourself for using FDISK and FORMAT.

FDISK: Preparing the Master Boot Record

FDISK.EXE is a utility provided with MS-DOS to partition a hard disk into one or more logical drives. Using it, you can divide your hard disk into just a single drive (C), two drives (C, D), or more. With MS-DOS 6.2, each of these partitions can be as large as 2 gigabytes. (A *gigabyte* is 1,024 megabytes, or 1024×1024×1024 bytes. Two gigabytes is more than two billion bytes.)

If you typed at 60 words per minute, 40 hours a week, 52 weeks a year, and your average word was only about 6 characters long, filling a hard disk partition this big would take you nearly 24 years. By then, you might have more than just wrist strain!

You should know that FDISK is a very dangerous program. If you run it and create a partition in which there was none, you cause no harm. But if you change the size of a partition, you will surely lose information in other partitions. Consider this horror story:

John has a hard disk, previously partitioned into drives C (20M) and D (20M). He wants to change his partition table so that it defines a logical drive C of 40M. To do this, he must delete D and C, then create C. When he is finished, C starts in the same place it once did, and it is readable. But the root directory for his files that were once on D is now sitting out in nowhere land, and MS-DOS cannot find it. Nor can MS-DOS find the FATs he once had for files on D. Every file on D is now effectively lost.

The moral to the story is: if you are running FDISK to change your partitions, back up all your drives first, and when you are done with FDISK, restore from your backups.

continues

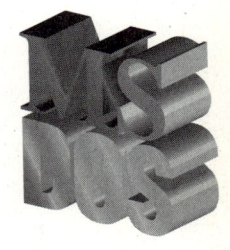

> *Because FDISK is such a potentially dangerous program, we recommend that you do not install it on a user's machine, but rather keep a copy locked away for the use of those whose job it is to set up computers in the organization. Even if a user never accidentally runs the program, your organization has to pay the storage costs for this thing: at 57,224 bytes per FDISK.EXE, a thousand users will require about 57M to store it, a cost of several hundred dollars.*

FDISK is a useful, useless, and dangerous program! Useful because you now can organize any drive you own into a single logical drive, for greater simplicity in accessing files. Useless because once you have used it to partition your hard disk, you may never need it again. You'll probably use it less than five minutes every two years. Dangerous, because if you make a simple error in using the program, you lose much of the information on your disk or can't access the drive at all.

If you want to look at how your hard disk is partitioned, without modifying the information, type...

FDISK /STATUS

...which tells you how many partitions you have, what percent of your total drive surface has been partitioned, and the size of each partition (see fig. 17.11). This feature of FDISK is new with MS-DOS 6.2.

Figure 17.11
Output of FDISK/STATUS.

```
                   Fixed Disk Drive Status
Disk   Drv   Mbytes   Free   Usage
 1            202       0    100%
       C:     202


      (1 MByte = 1048576 bytes)
C:\>
```

If you want to replace the main program in the master boot sector without modifying the data about your logical drives (the partition table), type...

FDISK /MBR

This replaces just the first 224 bytes of the master boot record, overwriting whatever is there with a combination of a program stored in FDISK.EXE and information that FDISK is able to find in memory (in the BIOS) about the drive. FDISK /MBR is a safe combination to use. You can use it effectively to remove any boot virus (such as Stoned) that has infected the master boot record. To remove such a virus, begin by booting from an uninfected, write-protected floppy. This will remove the virus from memory. Now execute the command...

FDISK /MBR

You should not run FDISK/ MBR if any of the following things are true of your disk:

- ✔ *The disk was partitioned using Storage Dimensions' SpeedStor utility with the /BOOTALL option.*
- ✔ *The disk has more than four partitions.*
- ✔ *The disk is using certain dual-boot programs.*

Now run MSAV or your favorite virus scanner to determine whether the virus is gone. It should be, if the virus infected the master boot record. Note that FDISK /MBR is available only in MS-DOS 5 and 6.2.

If you get confused, you can enter the standard...

FDISK /?

...but this won't offer any help. All you'll see on your screen is this:

```
C:\>FDISK /?
Configures a hard disk for use with MS-DOS.

FDISK

C:\>
```

You're most likely to use FDISK when you set up your hard disk, deciding how to partition the disk. You can use FDISK to do the following:

- ✔ Create a primary MS-DOS partition
- ✔ Create an extended MS-DOS partition
- ✔ Set a partition to active
- ✔ Delete a partition
- ✔ Display partition information
- ✔ Choose a different hard disk to partition (if your computer has more than one hard disk)

You can always safely use FDISK to view your partitions. The very first time you run FDISK, or after a major calamity, you will see no partitions defined. Here are some rules to follow:

- ✔ All hard disks must have an MS-DOS partition if you will be running MS-DOS.
- ✔ If you have no partitions on your hard disk, and create one, it is called the "primary partition."
- ✔ Only if you have a primary partition can you create a secondary partition.
- ✔ If you have one physical hard disk, your primary partition is called C. Your first secondary partition will be D; the next one, E, and so on.
- ✔ You may have up to 24 partitions. These drive letters (C, D, E, and so on) refer to "logical drives," to distinguish them from your single physical hard disk.
- ✔ If you have two physical hard disks, the primary partition on the first hard disk is C, and the primary partition on the second hard disk is D. The lettering process then goes back to the first hard disk, where all extra partitions are lettered sequentially (E, F, etc.). The process then continues on the second hard disk (N to Z).

You will absolutely need to run FDISK if, when you run it with FDISK /STATUS, you see the message...

    no partitions defined

...or...

    no partition marked active

Normally, if you need to use FDISK and you have anything of value on your hard disk, start by carefully backing up everything. Then run FDISK and choose menu option 4, Display Partition Information. If you want to increase the number of partitions, you have to make one or more partitions smaller if all the space on your hard disk has been assigned to existing partitions. If you want to make a partition smaller, you need to delete it and then create it again, this time specifying a new size.

FDISK does have limitations: it's limited to 1,024 cylinders, it won't work on any drive created with SUBST, and (fortunately for network managers) it won't work on a network or InterLnk drive. The hard disk you modify with FDISK must be physically connected to your computer. For information about SUBST, see Chapter 6.

FORMAT: Creating the Boot Record, FATS, and Root

On hard disks and on floppies, FORMAT.COM creates a boot record, two new FATs, and a new root directory. Used with the /U parameter, it erases your files beyond the reach of UNFORMAT—so that UNFORMAT can't recover. Unless you use the /Q option, it also scans your drive for unreadable sectors and records these bad sectors in the FATs.

Before you insert your floppy into the drive, take a look at it. Look at the label to be sure that you don't need anything on this boy anymore.

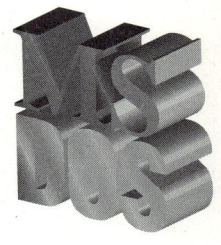

NOTE: Look at the disk. If it is a 5 1/4-inch disk with a hub ring on the top side, it's a 360K disk. You would be better off formatting it in a 360K drive than in a 1.2M drive, because the 1.2M drive writes a narrower track that the 360K drive can have trouble reading.

If it is a 5 1/4-inch disk with no hub ring, don't try formatting it as a 360K disk in any drive. The surface of these 1.2M floppies has a coating that—because it doesn't change its magnetic encoding easily—requires the high current of the 1.2M drive for writing. Sometimes such disks are unreliable in 360K drives.

If it is a 3 1/2-inch disk, check it for one or two holes at the label end. Disks with two holes are intended for 1.44M use; those with one, for 720K use.

The only good exception to the principle of not trying to squeeze more onto a floppy than it was intended to hold is the single-sided 5 1/4-inch disk. Such disks actually are coated on both sides and almost always work perfectly as double-sided disks.

After you've decided what you are going to do with the disk, make sure that what you plan to do is safe. I never format a floppy without first popping it in the drive and issuing the DIR command to see what is on it. General failure error is satisfying—it generally means that nothing ever was on the disk and the boot record does not exist.

NOTE: You can save yourself a megabyte or two of lost data every year if you look before you let FORMAT leap. Even though MS-DOS 6.2 comes with UNFORMAT, you won't be motivated to unformat something until you figure out that you've formatted over it. After it's gone, you aren't likely to figure out where it went.

The syntax of the FORMAT program is as follows:

```
FORMAT d: [/V[:label]][/Q][/U][F:size][/B¦/S]
FORMAT d: [/V[:label]][/Q][/U][T:tracks/N:sectors]/S]
```

Using FDISK and FORMAT

```
FORMAT d: [/V[:label]][/Q][/U][/1][/4][/B¦/S]
FORMAT d: [/Q] [/U] [/1] [/4] [/8] [/B¦/S]
```

The order in which you enter these parameters is unimportant, as is the case: format c: /s works just as well as FORMAT C: /S. FORMAT always requires a drive designator (a drive letter followed by a colon)—if you don't add one, you'll see the message: Required parameter missing. If you don't provide any of the command-line switches (/U, /Q, /V, and so on), MS-DOS 6.2 formats the disk to the default for the drive type. (If your drive can read and write both 720K and 1.44M floppies, for instance, FORMAT assumes that the disk is a 1.44M floppy.) Following are detailed descriptions of FORMAT's switches:

/? is the magic trick for a quick reminder on which FORMAT switches you might want to use. HELP FORMAT gives you plenty of additional detail (about as much as you'd cover in an MS-DOS course).

/B is a truly pointless switch. At one time, we had to save some space for the hidden system files in case a user might later want to make the disk bootable with the SYS command. This is no longer needed, but in the name of backward-compatibility, the amazing trick has been retained.

The parameter /B creates two dummy files. IO.SYS is first entered in the root directory and given a correct size, current date and time, and starting cluster number (2). It is marked as system and hidden, but not read-only. Then MSDOS.SYS is added to the root directory, with a correct size for the program, the current date and time, and starting cluster number (usually 24). It, too, is marked as system-hidden. The FAT also is written with entries for these files.

The files created by /B are dummy files, and cannot boot, even if COMMAND.COM is added to the disk. You will see the message

`Non-System disk or disk error. Replace and press any key when ready.` /B does not copy COMMAND.COM to the floppy. /S does.

The hidden system files created by /B are slightly larger than those created by /S, ensuring that there will be adequate room for the real files should the user later decide to make the disk bootable. With the /B option, the two files completely fill sectors, and are multiples of 512 in size. /B uses the current date and time for IO.SYS and MSDOS.SYS. /S uses the date and time found on these files on the source disk. /B does not mark IO.SYS or MSDOS.SYS read-only or archive. /S does. /B marks all other directory entries as erased. /S marks them as unused.

/F:size — is a handy way to override the default for your floppy disk drive. If you put a 720K disk in a 1.44M drive, and don't indicate something like /F:720, MS-DOS and your drive will attempt to create a 1.44M floppy of it. This won't work, and your friends might laugh at you and your error message. You have the following size options:

Floppy DiskType	Valid Switches
160K 5 1/4-INCH SS, DD	160, 160k, 160kb
180K 5 1/4-INCH SS, DD	180, 180k, 180kb
320K 5 1/4-INCH DS, DD	320, 320k, 320kb
360K 5 1/4-INCH DS, DD	360, 360k, 360kb
720K 3 1/2-INCH DS, DD	720, 720k, 720kb
1.2M 5 1/4-INCH DS, DDDD	1200, 1200k, 1200kb
1.44M 3 1/2-INCH DS, DDDD	1440, 1440k, 1440kb, 1.44, 1.44m, 1.44mb
2.88M 3 1/2-INCH DS, XHD	2880, 2880k, 2880kb, 2.88, 2.88m, 2.88mb

Using FDISK and FORMAT 949

/N:*sectors* will help you impress your Macintosh-using friends. Use this switch in conjunction with the /T switch to indicate the disk format (/T comes later in this list). With /N you specify the number of sectors per track. For instance, /N:9 means 9 sectors per track.

> **NOTE** *You must use /N in conjunction with /T. (But you can forget them both and use /F instead!)*

/1 formats a single side (the top) of a floppy disk.

/4 formats a 360K floppy in a 1.2M drive (but many 360K drives will have trouble reading this).

/1 /4 (used together) create a 180K, 5 1/4-inch, single-sided floppy.

/8 formats a floppy with eight sectors per track, ensuring compatibility with MS-DOS Version 1.*nn*.

/Q does a quick format of a disk, replacing the FATs and root directories with new (empty) ones. You can use /Q when you want to do a hasty cleanup of used floppies, but you shouldn't use it to prepare new disks or if you are trying to use FORMAT to destroy a boot sector virus. This switch doesn't replace the boot sector, nor does it check whether the disk can be read.

/S is my very favorite switch. With it, you can convert a helpless mylar doughnut into a boot thang, and enjoy the awesome power of your PC. With /S, you copy the hidden system files (IO.SYS and MSDOS.SYS) and the MS-DOS shell COMMAND.COM. If FORMAT can't find one or more of these files, it asks you to insert a disk containing them.

/T:*tracks* is incompatible with /F and requires both /N and a good memory. You are recommended to use the /F switch instead.

/U does an *unconditional* format of the drive specified, preventing any data recovery from a floppy and reducing the chances of data recovery from a hard disk. Use this option only if you want to permanently destroy files, perhaps for security purposes. Formatting is faster with /U than without it; for the speediest formatting, try /Q and /U at the same time. See the index entry for UNFORMAT for information on what might befall you if you try this trick.

/V:*label* writes a volume label to the root of the drive, and also places it in the boot sector of the disk. If you don't specify /V, FORMAT asks you for a volume label when it has nearly finished the job. Many users never add volume labels, but sometimes they can be handy. You can, for example, use your name —11 letters or less—to help in recovery from theft. You also can label disks "Disk 1," "Disk 2," and so on for a setup program to use to determine whether or not the correct disk is in the drive. If you are formatting several floppies at once, each is given the same volume label you entered with /V. See index entries for DIR, LABEL, and VOL commands.

/AUTOTEST formats the disk without any prompts (such as insert disk prompt, volume label prompt, and format another disk prompt) or the usual disk-space listing.

/BACKUP is similar to /AUTOTEST. Formats the disk without any prompts except the volume-label prompt. Also, unlike /AUTOTEST, it displays the usual disk-space listing.

When FORMAT finishes running, it puts an error level into the environment. If FORMAT was run from a batch file, then the batch file can continue in various ways based on what happened, according to this error level.

A 0 means that FORMAT completed with no problem. A 3 means that the user pressed Ctrl-C or Ctrl-Break to stop FORMAT, a 4, that some other fatal error occurred. A 5 means that the user answered the question `Proceed with Format (Y/N)?` with N.

If you are a master of MS-DOS 5, you won't see much new in the preceding information—except the support for 2.8M floppies, the increased flexibility of the /F switch, and the error levels on exit. If you look inside FORMAT.COM, you'll find three undocumented, non-working switches (at least, I didn't figure them out). /SELECT seems to do nothing; /BACKUP doesn't like the syntax, nor does /AUTOTEST.

If you direct FORMAT at a hard disk, you get the following message:

```
WARNING, ALL DATA ON NONREMOVABLE DISK
DRIVE x: WILL BE LOST!
Proceed with Format (Y/N)?
```

Don't answer Y without careful thought.

Do not use FORMAT on a drive referenced by SUBST, on remote network disks, or InterLnk drives.

Enter **FORMAT A:** to create the following:

✔ A boot record

✔ Two FATs

✔ A root directory

Entering **FORMAT A:/S** does all this and also copies two hidden system files and COMMAND.COM.

FORMAT Beefs

Although FORMAT.COM has improved over the past decade along with MS-DOS, there are still a number of objections to it. Each version seems to ask us for patience—perhaps we should finally accept our fate. MS-DOS trainers routinely spend significant class time trying to help students understand this potentially dangerous tool, and support people routinely work with users who have inadvertently committed suicide with the program.

Here are some key problems with the program:

- ✔ FORMAT destroys all files on the floppy by overwriting them. Because FORMAT does not check in advance whether files are on a floppy, many users have lost files when they formatted a disk in the wrong drive, or formatted the wrong disk in the right drive. Although UNFORMAT can save you, it won't if you don't notice the disaster right away (something you are unlikely to be able to do after valued files disappear!).

- ✔ FORMAT destroys the root directory and FATs, replacing them with empty root directories and FATs on floppies as well as hard disks. Despite the warning message…

    ```
    WARNING, ALL DATA ON NON-REMOVABLE DISK DRIVE C: WILL BE LOST!
    Proceed with Format (Y/N)?
    ```

    …many megabytes have disappeared through user errors.

- ✔ FORMAT contains no helpful prompts or menu to help users get what they want. Thus—unless they remember the secret command-line switch /F:360—users will find themselves formatting a 360K floppy as a 1.2M floppy in a 1.2M drive.

UNFORMAT: Secrets of the Recoverable Format

In the days before MS-DOS 5, FORMAT always overwrote files on your floppy with F6 hex. In MS-DOS 5 and 6.2, FORMAT won't overwrite any files on the floppy unless you use the /U option. The information from the FAT and root directory is copied to the final cluster(s) of the drive. This location is not given entries in the FAT or root directory, nor is it marked bad in the FAT. Running UNFORMAT.COM can bring your files back if you haven't overwritten their original locations.

> *The good news about UNFORMAT is that you waste no space on your drive with the recovery information—all space is usable. The bad news is that unless you run UNFORMAT immediately after the FORMAT disaster, your chances of unformatting successfully are slim. The syntax is:*

```
UNFORMAT [drive letter]
```

For the Curious

I know some of you out there are just itching for more numbers, and I can give them to you in the form of odds and ends concerning drive preparation.

The Size of Things

A 360K floppy has two sectors (or 1,024 bytes) per cluster. With 354 clusters, the maximum number of files you could have is 354. But there are only 112 root directory entries. If you try to place more than that in the root on a 360K floppy, you'll get a `File creation error` message. You can create a directory, if you want, to hold any extra small files. Or you can use an archive-compression program to pack two or more little files into one little file.

The number of files you can fit on a floppy or hard disk can be limited by the number of entries permitted in the root directory, if you try to place everything in the root. It also can be limited by the number of clusters available, because only one file can be placed in a cluster.

Clusters and Slack Space

How large is a file? The question has two correct answers, which rarely agree. Information on the number of bytes the file uses is kept in the root directory. Thus, when you type DIR, you see that a file of 5 bytes has a size of 5.

On the other hand, the smallest unit of disk storage that MS-DOS can manage is a cluster—a chunk of two or more 512-byte sectors.

On a standard 360K floppy, a cluster includes two sectors, or 1,024 bytes (1K). Thus, on a 360K floppy, a 5-byte file shows a size of 5 when you type DIR. But a before-and-after comparison of space remaining shows a loss of 1K. Try the following experiment to compare real and effective file size on a floppy.

To check the size of files on a floppy:

1. Insert a 360K floppy in your machine and type…

    DIR

2. Record the space remaining (see fig. 17.12).

Figure 17.12

The space remaining on a 360K disk.

```
A:\>dir

 Volume in drive A has no label
 Volume Serial Number is 475D-10FC
 Directory of A:\

DATAPATH COM      2162 02-22-91   6:42p
        1 file(s)          2162 bytes
                         359424 bytes free

A:\>
```

3. Copy a small file to the disk (any size under 1K).

4. Type **DIR** again.

5. Record the space remaining, as well as the size of this file (see the directory listing in fig. 17.13).

6. Subtract this from the space remaining in Step 2.

You should come up with a difference of 1,024 bytes or 1K.

Clusters on a Hard Disk

Because a hard disk usually puts more sectors in a cluster than a 360K floppy does, a small file can occupy even more physical space on the hard disk than on the 360K floppy. You can repeat the preceding experiment to determine the size of a cluster on your hard disk.

```
A:\>dir
 Volume in drive A has no label
 Volume Serial Number is 475D-10FC
 Directory of A:\

DIRCOMP  COM        874 02-22-91   6:42p
DATAPATH COM       2162 02-22-91   6:42p
       2 file(s)       3036 bytes
                     358400 bytes free

A:\>
```

Figure 17.13

The space remaining on a 360K disk after a 874-byte file was copied to it.

Cluster Size in a Nutshell

So how big are clusters? It depends on the device! The information is in table 17.11.

Table 17.11
Cluster Size for Different Drive Types

Device	Sectors/Cluster	No. K/Cluster
360K floppy	2	1
1.2M floppy	1	1/2
ST225 (20M hard disk)	4	2

Now for a magic trick. Show your friends how you can copy more than 360K worth of files to your 360K floppy.

1. On your hard disk, make a directory called TEMP and change to it by typing…

    MD \ TEMP
    CD \ TEMP

2. Run CHKDSK to find how many bytes are free.

3. Run MAKETXT1 (on the accompanying disk) by typing…

    MAKETXT1

4. Create 200 files. On your hard disk, 200 files take 2K each (each takes one cluster of 2K).

5. Run CHKDSK again. Your space available should be reduced by 400K.

6. Now copy all 200 files to a formatted 360K floppy. Because cluster size is only 1K on the floppy, 200 files should fit with no problem.

What Makes a Disk Bootable?

The only surefire way to make a disk bootable is to type…

FORMAT A: /S

A disk is bootable only if certain conditions have been met. Thanks to FORMAT/S, you don't have to worry about any of the following:

✔ The first two directory entries in the root directory are the names of the hidden system files.

✔ The names in the root agree with the names recorded in the MS-DOS boot sector.

✔ The two hidden system files are positioned as the first two files in the data area.

✔ COMMAND.COM is located in the root directory.

> **NOTE**
>
> *To find out whether the two hidden system files have to have any particular attributes, make a bootable floppy, and then use ATTRIB or Norton's FA to make the files nonhidden, nonsystem. Will the floppy still boot? The answer is yes.*

Is COMMAND.COM position-sensitive? Try the following experiment:

Must COMMAND.COM be the third file in the directory (the first nonhidden file)? Try renaming it to X, then copying X to COMMAND.COM. Do a DIR to check your work, and reboot with the floppy. Follow these next steps to see what happens:

1. Format a floppy with the command...

    `FORMAT A:/S`

2. Type...

    `DIR`

    You should see only one file listed—COMMAND.COM—because IO.SYS and MSDOS.SYS are hidden. COMMAND.COM is really the third file in the directory.

3. Check your work, and prove that the disk is bootable by pressing Ctrl-Alt-Del. Can you boot from this floppy? You should be able to. If not, try FORMAT A:/S again.

4. Make COMMAND.COM the fourth file on this disk by renaming COMMAND.COM to something else, as follows...

    `REN A:COMMAND.COM OLDBOY`

5. This step is optional. To prove that this disk is no longer bootable (because COMMAND.COM won't be found), try booting from it now.

6. Now recover COMMAND.COM by name, making it the last file in the root directory...

    `COPY A:OLDBOY A:COMMAND.COM`

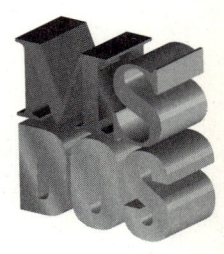

7. Type...

   `DIR`

   ...to see what is on the disk. You should see OLDBOY first and COMMAND.COM second.

8. Now try rebooting. What happens?

You should still be able to boot with the floppy, even though COMMAND.COM is the fourth file in the directory.

Other projects for you to try: can COMMAND.COM be hidden? Read-only? What is the advantage of doing this?

Why not compare FORMAT.COM's /B and /S switches? Find out what a disk formatted with /B or /S looks like. How do the boot sectors differ? (If you've forgotten, you can look up the answers in the "FORMAT: Preparing the Boot Record" section of this chapter.)

Where MS-DOS Places Files

If you start with an empty disk, each file begins in the next available cluster and runs in consecutive clusters.

Erasing a file from a set of files has the following effect:

- ✔ The directory for the file has only one byte changed—the first character of the file name is replaced with a lowercase Sigma.
- ✔ The FAT entries for the file are replaced with 0.
- ✔ The file is not touched.

When a file is copied to a drive that has an erased file, here's what happens:

- ✔ If you are using MS-DOS 3.3, the file is placed in the first available cluster into which the entire file will fit contiguously. Hence, if a large file is erased and a small file is copied, the erased file is partially replaced.

- ✔ If there is no place in the FAT that can hold the entire file as a contiguous unit, the first available cluster is occupied, and the file is scattered across all subsequent available clusters.

- ✔ In MS-DOS versions earlier than 3.3, the preceding procedure was always used, resulting in fragmentation and slower reads.

Summary

Now that you have completed this chapter, you may appreciate tables 17.12-17.14. They summarize the key facts about drives that have been discussed.

Table 17.12
Where Is It?

Item	Location
MBR/Partition record	First sector, first track, first side (sector 1, track 0, side 0) on a hard disk; area is reserved, even if no partitioning is done (does not exist in floppies)
Boot record	First sector of first track of first side (sector 1, track 0, side 0) on floppies; always sector 2, track 0, side 0 on hard disks
FAT #1	Size depends on results of format and information stored in boot record; begins immediately after boot record, on track 0, side 0
FAT #2	Begins immediately after first FAT; same size as FAT #1
Root directory	Begins immediately after FAT #2, on track 0, side 0
Data area	Begins immediately after root directory; fills remainder of disk
Root subdirectories	Maintained as files in data area; can be anywhere

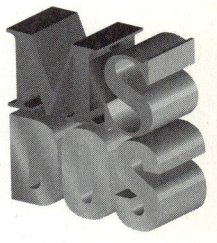

In the decimal numbering system, which begins with 0, there are 10 digits, (9 is the 10th digit). Many of the counting systems in the computer world use 0 to represent the first value, 9 to represent the 10th value. But sometimes 1 means 1. And in one case, at least, 2 means 1. Table 17.13 summarizes the values used to indicate starting points in different components.

Table 17.13
Where Numbering Starts for Various Components

Component	Starting Number
Cylinder	0
Cluster	2
Drive number	0
Head	0
Memory location	0
Parallel port	1
Sector	0 or 1
Serial port	1
Side	0
Track	0

Information about the device is stored in the boot record, the directories, the FATs, the master boot record, and even in CMOS. Often, a given piece of information is stored in two places as a double check.

Table 17.14
Where Does It Come From?
Sources of Information on the Drive

Information	Source
Bytes/sector	Boot record
Disk heads	Boot record

Information	Source
MS-DOS version	Boot record
FATs, number of	Boot record
File, attributes	Directory
File, date of creation/last edit	Directory
File, size in bytes	Directory
File, starting sector for	Directory
File, time of creation/last edit	Directory
Media descriptor byte	1st byte in both FATS; also in boot record
Partition, number of sectors in	MBR/partition table
Partition, relative starting sector	MBR/partition table
Partition, starting cylinder for	MBR/partition table
Partition, starting sector for	MBR/partition table
Partition to boot from	MBR/partition table
Partition, starting head for	MBR/partition table
Reserved sectors	Boot record
Root entries, maximum #	Boot record
Sectors containing parts of a file	FAT
Sectors, hidden	Boot record
Sectors, total	Boot record
Sectors per cluster	Boot record
Sectors per FAT	Boot record
Sectors per track	Boot record
System ID	Boot record

From a shopper's standpoint, computer drives have gotten faster, cheaper per megabyte, physically smaller, and larger in capacity. But

Chapter 17: *A Second Look at Hard Drives*

from the standpoint of DOS, drives haven't changed much. And from the user's standpoint, drives are probably just as mysterious as ever.

Understanding how drives work will help you feel more in charge of your computer and will reduce the frequency with which you do totally stupid or dangerous things to them. If the auto industry improved as fast as computer drives, our cars would cost 10 cents, go a zillion miles an hour, and never run out of gas.

MS DOS

CHAPTER 18

Backing Up Your Data

by David Stang

"There are only two types of computer users: those who have lost valuable data and those who are about to." —Paul Mace.

"There are only two types of computer users: experienced users, who have lost a great deal of information, and inexperienced users, who have not lost much yet. Neither of them back up." —David Stang.

Before computers, life had two certainties: death and taxes. Today, you must add data loss to the list. Let me promise you now that data loss is as certain as taxes, but it can be much more costly. It is as certain as death, and just might seem more painful, depending on which comes first. Backing up won't make disaster less likely, but it can ensure a dramatic recovery from most disasters.

Backups are one of the simplest means of ensuring that you have a copy of your files when they disappear from your computer.

Several things can cause the information in your machine to disappear:

- ✔ You delete a directory by mistake.
- ✔ You save a new version of a spreadsheet, for example, over an old version that you wanted to keep.
- ✔ You copy all your files from one directory to another and delete them from the source directory, only to discover later that the destination directory never existed. Instead, all your files have been copied to a single file bearing the source directory name, and only the last file to be copied still exists.
- ✔ You format a floppy with the /U switch without checking its contents first.
- ✔ A virus infects your computer, and you let those helpful folks from MIS, DP, ADP, or the help desk clean up with FDISK, FORMAT, or who knows what.
- ✔ You've had your el-cheapo hard disk for 366 days, and it came with a one-year warranty.
- ✔ Murphy lives in your town.
- ✔ 107 other reasons.

According to Jon William Toigo, author of *Disaster Recovery Planning: Managing Risk and Catastrophe in Information Systems*, 90 percent of disaster recovery involves restoring backup data. If you do back up often and properly, if your backups are perfect and you can always restore what you've backed up, if your backups are stored in an absolutely safe place, and if you have already done everything to make the backup process more efficient, then skip this chapter, you fibber!

For those of you wanting to continue, this chapter is organized as follows:

- ✔ Getting motivated—some inspirational reading for those who hate to back up.
- ✔ Why we don't back up—some reasons that backups are not done regularly, if at all.
- ✔ Backup tips and tricks—some good tricks that even the lazy can appreciate.
- ✔ Using MSBACKUP—the main point in a chapter on backing up in a book about DOS 6.2.
- ✔ Using MWBACKUP—an equally important topic if you spend your days in Winders (that's how folks in some parts of the country say it).
- ✔ Getting more out of MSBACKUP—a short section on efficiency.
- ✔ Looking at a model backup policy—an even shorter section for those in search of rules.

Never have fewer than two copies of your data. If you save data to your hard disk, back it up to a floppy; if you save your data to a floppy, back it up on another floppy. Remember: the only data you need to back up is the data you care about.

Getting Motivated

In its introduction to MSBACKUP, Microsoft tells us, "Statistics show that most hard disks represent an average of 2,000 hours of work." If you have 10M of treasures on your hard disk, and you created it at a rate of 180 bytes a minute (30 words per minute at 6 bytes a word), you have an investment of 58,254 minutes—970 hours. I don't know about you, but I don't want to relive any of those hours. It was hard enough the first time.

Lori Dietrich, supervisor of planning and business analysis at the Dorsey and Whitney law firm in Minneapolis, lost the hard disk on her machine and "thought it was the end of the world." If the information was so important, why wasn't it backed up? Well, she wasn't sure how, and so had been backing up to the same hard disk. "Now," she says, "I always back up to floppies, no matter how large the spreadsheet is."

When asked for 10 tips on hard disk management and data recovery, 3Com's Greg Heumann remarked, "The first five tips are to back up. In the end, it's the only sure bet there is."

The problem is not merely one of user laziness or overconfidence. Entire organizations often fail to back up. In one investigation, the General Accounting Office reported the following:

- ✔ The IRS National Computer Center has no designated backup processing site.
- ✔ Computer capacity problems may make it impossible for one service center to back up another, as currently proposed.
- ✔ The IRS does not always maintain backup tape files containing data and programs necessary to continue operations.

Choosing to store your information on floppies can be a swell idea if you don't have much data, but if you have 40M of data, you may need as many as 110 floppy disks for the job. If you are going to buy a hard disk big enough to store a lot of information, you also need to figure out how to back it up efficiently and frequently.

Few organizations store backup disks far away from the originals. And few users always perform backups as conscientiously as they should.

Although catastrophic loss of data is not a daily occurrence on your desktop, you might benefit from the following "Grim Fairy Tale" (based on a true story).

> **AUTHOR'S NOTE**
>
> *Once upon a time, there was a secretary who had been drilled on how much her life would be improved when the computers came. When she got a computer, she found herself in a windowless, overheated sweatshop, with three times the typing she used to have. One evening she typed her resignation on the firm's computer and printed out two copies. Then she typed...*
>
> ```
> DEL *.*
> ```
> *...erasing all the files on the hard disk, including the annual report that was about to be delivered to the annual meeting of the board of directors.*
>
> *Moral: back up everything, and keep a copy of the backups in a safe place. Learn how recovery utilities can recover erased files. (And don't promise rose gardens to secretaries who have to sit on the thorns.)*

Backing up is a terrific means of avoiding the consequences of hard disk failure, malicious users, and natural disasters such as fire. It also can help you recover from viruses that prove to be unremovable with your favorite anti-virus program. (If, for example, you find yourself with the Form virus, the anti-virus product provided with DOS 6.2, MSAV, will remove the virus from your hard disk, but may render your 1.44M floppy disks unreadable.) Unless you plan to study the next chapter on data recovery carefully, a backup of such disks would be your only salvation!

And backing up can be handy if you need to go back to a previous version of your work. Suppose that you are working with a group on an important report. You work all day on modifying a section of the report, only to find tomorrow that your boss is furious (she wrote that section) and wants the original back in, your changes out! How can you do this? With a restore from yesterday's backups, of course—if you've made them.

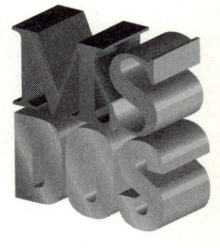

This archiving quality of backing up has helped programmers who have coded, tested, and found that a module or routine worked fine, coded some more, and then tested, only to find that the module that once worked no longer does. Did they change some code? What did the original coding look like? Only backups may help them find their mistake.

A special form of backup, called archiving, also is useful for giving you more free space on your hard disk. *Archiving* is the process of removing information from on-line storage (usually hard disks) and placing it on another off-line medium (such as tape or floppy). Note the difference between archiving and backing up. *Backing up* is the process of copying information from on-line storage to off-line storage. It doesn't remove the information from on-line storage.

Archiving is normally done for one of two reasons:

- To free on-line storage space, because the files archived have been infrequently accessed or won't be needed for some time.
- To secure files by removing them from on-line access.

By backing up to good quality media, labeling carefully, and storing carefully, you can now remove whatever you have backed up from the source drive (turning this backup into an archive), without fear that it has been permanently lost. If you have some large files you won't be accessing in the next few months, you might want to archive them. If you have some programs you don't think you will be using again for some time, you can archive them.

Archiving is facilitated by placing the archives on a random-access medium, such as a removable hard disk, removable Bernoulli cartridge, or floppy, and storing the archives as DOS-readable files. If archiving is done with ordinary tape drives, the files need to be restored to the hard disk before they can be accessed because the tape drive is a sequential-access medium. If you use MSBACKUP to do your archiving rather than COPY or XCOPY, you also must use RESTORE before using an archived file.

By removing the only copy of a file that is on your hard disk, you are entrusting your fate to your backups. With a program such as MSBACKUP, used with all the integrity options, and with trustworthy media that is carefully labeled and stored, you are safe. (Please note, however, that the author is not interested in being held responsible for lost information, if something should go wrong.)

Why You Don't Back Up

Why don't you back up more often? It may be the reliability of computers that is ultimately to blame. If you lost data nearly every day, as we did in the early days of computing, you would certainly back up conscientiously. But most of you have never seen flames burst from your hard disk. Without frequent disaster, who can really believe it will happen to them?

The joylessness and "boredumb" of backing up doesn't help much, either. When backing up is tedious, time-consuming, and confusing, and when it is unrewarded by disaster, you are rarely tempted to do it.

But the main reason that users in organizations don't back up is that it isn't their job! Every organization must decide who is responsible for the information in the computers. Those who are designated as responsible should be rewarded for caring for it and punished for not caring for it.

Your employers have compounded the problem with the equipment they bought you. Your desktop seems to have a complete computer, with its mouse, VGA monitor, and huge hard disk. But how is that hard disk to be backed up? To floppies? That's just silly. In the first few months of backing up to floppies, your labor will cost the organization more than a nice tape drive would have cost. Organizations should not buy computers to manage information unless they also are prepared to buy proper devices to back it up. Computer stores don't help, either. They have no business selling "complete systems" that are missing a tape drive.

Backup Tips and Tricks

The following sections present some ideas to make backing up less painful and more rewarding. The best kind of work is the kind we can get out of. Backing up is enough like work that you just might not do it, unless you can get someone else to do it! If you sucker a batch file into doing the job, you can sit back and smoke a cigar while you back up. This section gives you some tips for avoiding unnecessary work.

Tricks for Improving Backup Frequency

You won't back up if it is difficult, unrewarding, and "not your job." If you have been charged with backing up your own data, or if no one is backing up your data, then you need to come up with a sensible strategy that will improve your own backup frequency. Following are some ideas:

- ✔ Don't back up if you don't need to. If you've just done a backup, gone away for a couple of days, and no one has changed or added any files, you probably don't need to back up the first day you return. TESTBAK.COM, a program that comes with this book, tells you how many bytes you have stored in how many files, how many bytes are in how many files that have not been backed up, and the percent of your stored bytes in the percent of your stored files that have not been backed up. A sample of the TESTBAK.COM output is as follows:

```
F:\PGM\UTILS>testbak f:\

Backup necessity for F:\

1117873075 bytes in 47344 file(s)
    789311 bytes in 123 changed file(s)
         1% of bytes changed in 0% of files
```

- ✔ If your screen looks like this, you have a big hard disk, and you must have just done a backup, because almost nothing has the archive bit set. (The *archive bit* is one of six bits used in a file's attribute byte—the others bits are system, read-only, hidden, directory, and volume label. You could call it the "backed up or not backed up after last edit bit," but archive bit is the way they say it in Silicon Valley.) TEXTBAK does its calculations of changed files by reading directories for file sizes and archive bits. You might put TESTBAK.COM in your AUTOEXEC.BAT and make a decision to do an incremental backup when you have five percent of your bytes or five percent of your files not backed up.

✔ If you are connected to a LAN, see whether you can back up your critical files to a server that is backed up regularly. You can then ask the network manager for assistance in restoring from those backups if something terrible happens to your computer. A laptop computer can be connected to the server via a parallel connection and backed up with a batch file, such as the following:

```
BACKUP1.BAT
REM First, delete any unnecessary files to minimize the
REM amount to be backed up.
REM To back up everything on C: to F:\DAVID, try:
XCOPY C:\*.* F:\DAVID\*.* /S/E/V
REM /S backs up subdirectories from your root directory.
REM /E backs them up even if they are empty.
REM /V verifies that your copies are identical
REM to your originals.
REM If you do this regularly, you might want to use
REM the /M switch, which backs up only those files you have
REM not backed up before. This will speed things up
REM considerably.
REM Use it with a line such as:
REM XCOPY C:\*.* F:\DAVID\*.* /S/E/V/M
```

✔ Buy a tape drive, or set up a low-cost LAN, add a tape drive to it, and share the drive among users of the LAN. Backing up to floppy disks is just too time-consuming.

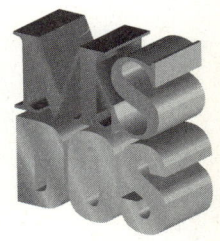

✔ Hire a backup administrator. At minimum wage, your new assistant can professionally do the job for all users in the organization, moving from machine to machine with a portable tape drive (backing up to floppy disk, if you insist.) This person can catalog and store the backups, and can do the job quite well with only minimal training.

The following "Grim Fairy Tale" leads up to the next point: developing an efficient backup strategy.

AUTHOR'S NOTE

Suppose the airport authorities maintained a database of parking tickets. If they could collect on the delinquents in the database, they'd have an extra million dollars in the budget. So they backed up the database daily. Unfortunately, there was some problem with their old tape drive. Perhaps the heads were out of alignment or it was dirty. Perhaps their five-year-old tapes were due for replacement. The clerk who did the backups would see...

```
Abort, Retry, Ignore
```

...whenever he did a backup, but had learned that pressing I (for Ignore) worked just fine. When the database finally disappeared one day, the help desk at the airport learned that none of the 13 backup tapes they owned were readable. The vendor of the non-standard tape drive was no longer in business, and they could find no one who was able to read the tapes.

Moral: ensure that employees know how to back up, that they respond correctly to danger signals, such as `Abort, Retry, Ignore`*, and that all your backups are readable.*

✔ Develop an efficient backup strategy. There is no need to back up everything every day. If you back up everything monthly, back up everything changed or created since the full weekly backup, and back up one or two important files you are working on daily or several times a day, you'll be as safe as necessary.

Suppose that you have an important database on your hard disk, one you can't live without. Consider using a batch file to back it up, as follows:

```
BACKUP2.BAT
CD BACKUP
DEL *.3
REN *.2 *.3
REN *.1 *.2
CD..
PKZIP -EX QF.1 *.* -X@EXCLUDE.DAT
MOVE QF.1 BACKUP
```

This batch file saves three copies of your database. First you change to a backup subdirectory from the database directory. You delete whatever has a file extension of ".3," rename all files that have ".2" extensions with ".3" extensions, and rename all files having ".1" extensions with ".2" extensions. You therefore have no file ending in the extension ".1" because you want this batch file to create a new file ending in the extension ".1". This process is rolling back your backups, and you can retain as many copies of your database as you want.

Then, change back to the database directory (type **CD..**) and use PKZIP (a commonly used compression program) to back up almost everything (using *.*) in this directory. You want maximum compression, so specify **-EX**. And you want the zip file you create to be named QF.1. The switch X@EXCLUDE.DAT tells PKZIP to exclude from the backup any files listed in the file EXCLUDE.DAT. You aren't going to back up these files because you either don't care about them or because you have nice new copies someplace else (such as the program master disks).

Of course, you'll adapt this batch file to your own purposes. You might not, for example, want to exclude anything, and you might value speed over maximizing compression. Your PKZIP line could read...

```
PKZIP QF.1 *.*
```

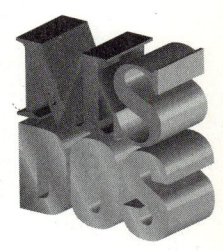

For help with PKZIP, simply type...

```
PKZIP
```

...at the command line. You will see a screen full of help.

When this job is finished, move your backup of everything to the backup directory. MOVE.EXE, which moves copies of files to different directories (in this case MOVE moves QF.1 to the backup directory), is finally provided with DOS! If you don't want to use MOVE, you can replace it with COPY and DEL. You could use COPY alone, rather than MOVE, but then you would have two backup copies and less available storage to use for other purposes. (Incidentally, MOVE also can be used to rename a directory, if you want.)

Of course, having a backup batch file is not quite the same as running it. If you want to back up every time you update the database, one simple way is to incorporate your backup into a batch file that calls the program, as follows:

```
BACKUP3.BAT
REM Code to run the program Bonzo...
BONZO /M /Q
REM Code to back up the mess you've just made with
Bonzo...
REM You can borrow some backup code from BACKUP2.BAT.
```

You may not want to back up every time you run the program. Sometimes you may be in a hurry to get home, and your organization wants machines off at night. To add optional backup to every batch file you have, you can use the CHOICE command that comes with DOS 6. CHOICE allows a batch file to ask for user input, and then branches based on what the user has selected. You can use CHOICE in conjunction with ERRORLEVEL to do your branching. BACKUP4.BAT shows how this might work:

```
BACKUP4.BAT
REM ... program call above here. Now ask user about
backup.
@ECHO OFF
CHOICE Do you want to back up?
```

```
IF ERRORLEVEL 2 THEN GOTO DONE
REM Code to back up here...
:DONE
```

The line...

```
@ECHO OFF
```

...turns off the echo so that you don't see a double prompt from the CHOICE command. The...

```
@
```

...symbol prevents ECHO OFF from displaying. In the CHOICE line, the question need not be enclosed in quotation marks, but you may want to end the line by pressing the space bar because CHOICE will append...

```
[Y,N]?
```

...to the line.

If the user presses **N**, CHOICE issues an error level of 2 (the second choice). The backup code is skipped, and the batch file moves to...

```
:DONE
```

If the user presses **Y**, CHOICE issues an error level of 1, and the backup is performed.

You might wonder why you would bother to back up to the same drive. What if the drive fails? But drive failure is not the only cause of data loss. In fact, it is a minor cause. A second copy of your files in a different directory on the same drive will solve many problems. If the FAT is scrambled or the ROOT is overwritten, your backup file probably is less fragmented than the originals it copied, and is, therefore, more easily recovered.

Dealing with Dupes

If you back up to your hard disk, you have two copies of the file. If you need to edit, which copy of the file do you choose? You probably have done enough work on the wrong file to know this can be a serious problem. Because DOS permits only 11-character file names, many users assume that careful labeling is not possible. Not so.

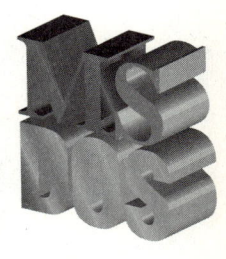

Here are three ways you might solve the problems of not enough (or too many versions) of your favorite thing:

- ✔ If you program, you can create a directory named for the program you are working on. In this directory, the first copy of your program can be named 01.BAS. Name your second version 02, and so on. Save four or five versions a day. When you finish for the day, sort them in order in the directory with a program such as DIRSORT or admire your work in name order with DIR /ON or in date order with DIR /OD. When you begin programming the next day, you can start with the latest version. When you are finished with your program, simply rename the latest version to whatever name you want to use and delete most of the early drafts. (You can delete your first nine drafts with the command DEL 0*.*.)

- ✔ If you are writing the great American novel, you don't want to lose a chapter. You might save your various drafts of Chapter 10 as CHAP10.001, CHAP10.002, and so forth. By using a Save As command, you're assured that you always can go back to the version that existed before the moment when you accidentally deleted the first six pages.

- ✔ Use MOVE rather than COPY whenever you don't want to create extra copies of the file.

Data integrity is severely threatened by the copy process. When two or more copies of a file exist, only one of the copies should be the working copy; all others should be date stamped and clearly identified as backups. MS-DOS, CP/M, and most other microcomputer operating systems, however, do not permit this neat labeling. Thus, you face the possibility that a user will, sooner or later, edit or update the wrong version of a file. This problem can be compounded either by not discovering the problem, or not discovering it until the files have grown so much that it is not possible to determine which portions are the most current.

Backups also can threaten security. If a user backs up a secure mainframe or network file to a local storage medium, then a copy has "escaped" from the system's security controls.

Tracking Backups and Archives

Backups won't do much good if you can't restore efficiently. You can't restore efficiently if you can't even find the disk or tape. Be sure that your disks and tapes are labeled in a useful way. I like to write on a 3.5-inch file card and insert the card in the disk or tape jacket. For backups to tape, I record the drive backed up, then begin a list below it with the date of the backup. With each subsequent backup, I cross out the last date and record a new one.

Keep sets of backup media together. If you back up a drive to a dozen or so floppies, label those floppies with information on where the data came from (machine and drive), when it was backed up, and which disk or tape number each is. A label or file card might read as follows:

```
BACKUP of Bonzo C:, May 5, '93. #3/6
```

> **AUTHOR'S NOTE**
>
> *A client called me one day in panic because her hard drive went belly up. I, of course asked the standard question, "Did you have it backed up?" The reply was a classic. She backed up her data to a tape backup, but she used the same tape each time. So, as Murphy would have it, he chose to break the tape drive in the middle of a backup, and then proceeded to break the hard drive before another backup could be done.*
>
> *Moral: Use alternate tapes or disk sets for regular full backups. That way you always have a full backup in case Murphy drops in.*

Storing Backups and Archives

Hopefully, catastrophic loss of data is not a daily occurrence on your desktop; however, the following "Grim Fairy Tale," based on a true story, could happen to your data.

AUTHOR'S NOTE

Martha had a dust cover for her keyboard, a dust cover for her monitor, and a little house for her mouse. She kept all her neatly labeled disks in a fancy, high-tech plastic box. She put her disk box on the window sill to reduce the clutter on her small, ergonomic desk. During the summer, the air conditioning couldn't keep the room cool, so she just closed the door and left her computer until September. One cool September day, she called to tell me that none of her disks were readable. I explained that a South-facing window sill produces a greenhouse effect, and the temperature on the sill and in her disk box could have reached 120° F. I also explained that a disk will slow cook at much lower temperatures, given long enough. Even hamburger left on the kitchen floor for a week knows this.

Moral: Be cool! Keep your backup media in a cool place.

You need a special place for keeping your backups and archives, and probably some special rules to keep track of things. When labeling and storing backups, remember that the more care you use in filing, the easier retrieval will be. If you don't retrieve often, label carefully and file casually. If you do retrieve often, then you'll save time by filing more carefully. And never file anything you know you'll never need. Here are some specific guidelines:

- ✔ Each user should have her own file box for her working copies. Backup copies of your organization's important files should be kept in a separate, off-limits location, locked and maintained by the person with the key. Each working disk used by a user should belong to that user and should bear the user's name. No one else should be permitted to use such a disk, placing personal librarianship responsibilities on each individual user's shoulders.

- ✔ Make backup copies of every disk you use, especially your masters. Backing up master copies is not considered software piracy, and most software vendors encourage you to do so. Back up your masters before initial use. Back up your data disks after every use.

- ✔ From time to time, test your backups to be certain that they are effective. Remember that heat, humidity, and electromagnetic fields can cause a deterioration in what you've stored. Floppy disks need to be stored under the same temperatures and humidity ranges that people enjoy; extremes can cause damage to both dispositions and data.

- ✔ Store backups in a different location from the location you store originals.

- ✔ Make sure backup disks are labeled "Backup" so that you don't inadvertently edit them, and then later back up over your changes.

Remember that, over time, disks get "weary." Positive charges and negative charges holding your 1's and 0's tend to neutralize each other. You can give renewed life to backed-up and dated disks by periodically copying their contents to newly formatted media. You can then reformat the original backup media to prepare it for use again.

Backing Up a Hard Disk to a Hard Disk

When you back up a big hard disk to tape, it may take about 10 minutes. Do it weekly. But you can back up to another hard disk with a keystroke. With nearly immediate backup, you can afford to back up twice a day.

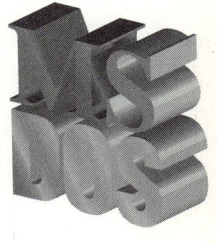

> **AUTHOR'S NOTE**
>
> *My secret weapon...*
>
> *I have a shelf full of hard disks, which I bought for $25 each. Although they were supposed to be broken, nearly all worked after a low-level format. So I've just added one to each of my computers as a second hard disk. To a main menu, I added an option to back up C: to D:. The backup is done by entering the command...*
>
> ```
> XCOPY C:\*.* D:\*.* /S/E/V/M
> ```
>
> *The result is that I have implemented manual disk mirroring.*

There are some advantages to the idea of backing up from one drive to another:

- ✔ If you set up the process correctly and test it, a user can't goof up as when backing up to floppy.

- ✔ Recovery from a hard drive requires few special skills, unlike the task of rescuing data from a damaged tape drive.

- ✔ Backing up to another hard disk with XCOPY is faster than any other approach, and requires nearly no user action, so frequent backup is easy. In fact, you could install the command...

```
XCOPY C:*.* D: /S/E/V/M
```

...in the AUTOEXEC.BAT file so that backup will occur every time the machine is booted, with no user intervention.

There are a couple of drawbacks, unfortunately:

- ✔ Two hard disks will run hotter than one. Do your best to keep your machine cool.

- ✔ You may feel uncomfortable using a hard disk someone else thought was broken, so you may pay more for a hard disk than I do. Your cost is still likely to be less than for a tape drive.

The following "Grim Fairy Tales" could have been prevented with a little forethought.

> **AUTHOR'S NOTE**
>
> *The U.S. Post Office in Washington, DC, responsibly backed up its systems every day and stored their tapes and disks in locked cabinets near the computer. One day a fire swept through the floor of the building that housed the computers. The computers were gone. The tapes were gone. The information was gone.*
>
> *Moral: Off-site storage would have been a good idea.*
>
> *The people at the National Technical Information Service in Alexandria, VA, were smarter—they kept their tapes on a separate floor in the building. One day a small fire broke out in the wiring closet. PVC (polyvinylchloride) on the cable burned and polluted the air. The fire department arrived and sealed off the building. No one will be able to enter it for 100 years. The information in the building must stay there, and won't be much use to anyone 100 years from now.*
>
> *Moral: Off-site storage would have been a very good idea.*

Understanding MSBACKUP

DOS 6.2 comes with MSBACKUP, a modified version of the best-selling Norton Backup for DOS from Symantec (see fig. 18.1). DOS 6 also comes with MWBACKUP, a variation of Norton Backup for Windows (see fig. 18.2). We will talk about them as if they were the same, calling them MSBACKUP/MWBACKUP. You'll see screen shots of each in this chapter, but we won't waste your time telling you which keys to press, or where to click your mouse.

Given the wide variety of other backup products on the market, you may or may not use MSBACKUP/MWBACKUP. Some users no doubt will use it by default, reasoning that because it came in the grab bag of goodies, they might as well use it. But because backing up is such an important part of computing, every organization should take a look at MSBACKUP/MWBACKUP's features before installing and standardizing on it; every organization should consider what features they long for; and every organization should engage in some form of

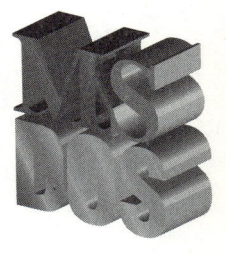

Chapter 18: *Backing Up Your Data*

comparison shopping. Table 18.1 lists some useful features and whether MSBACKUP/MWBACKUP has them.

Figure 18.1
The MSBACKUP Main menu.

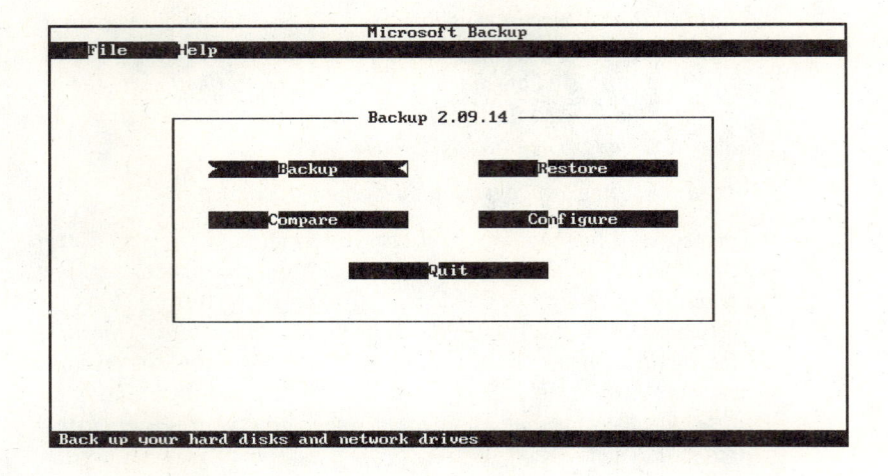

Figure 18.2
The MWBACKUP Main menu.

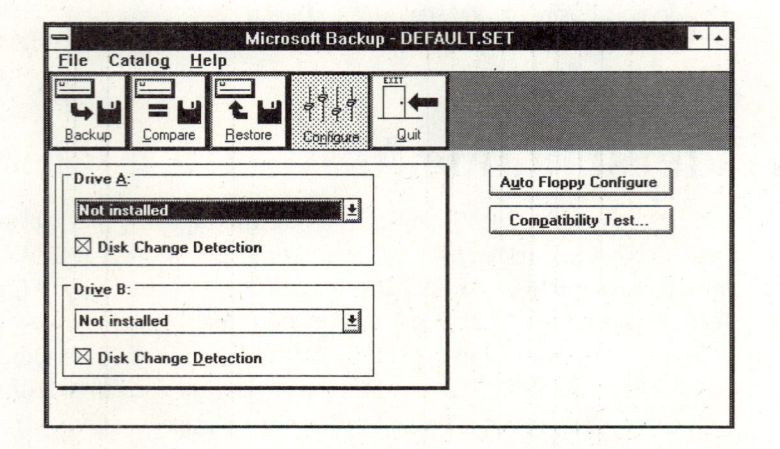

Table 18.1
Backup Options

Feature	Included in MSBACKUP/MWBACKUP
Price	Free!
Scheduling option for unattended backups	No

Understanding MSBACKUP

Feature	Included in MSBACKUP/MWBACKUP
Back up selected files	Yes
Retry busy (open) network files	No
Trustworthy error-correction available as an option during backup	Yes
Different levels (novice, advanced)	No
Ease of use	High
Back up to a variety of tape drives	Only to devices recognized by DOS commands (floppy disks, hard disks, network drives, Bernoulli drives)
Restore from backup media	Yes
Options for using DOS format or a proprietary format for disks	No, only DOS
Control over error correction	Provides error correction, but no control over it
Offers help when you press F1	Yes
Compatibility with your system	High

If you are not backing up your files, or if you are using the old DOS BACKUP and RESTORE programs (from earlier versions of DOS) to do the job, then by all means switch to MSBACKUP/MWBACKUP. (BACKUP is not provided with DOS 6. To restore from backups created with older versions of DOS, you can use RESTORE, which is provided.)

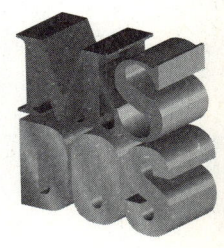

MSBACKUP/MWBACKUP Features

MSBACKUP/MWBACKUP offers three backup types:

- ✔ **Full backup** backs up all selected files and lowers the archive flags to indicate that the file has been backed up. This is a good place to start for your first backup. You might do a full backup once a week.

- ✔ **Incremental backup** backs up whatever you have changed since the last full or incremental backup, using the archive flag as its clue. Anything new will have the archive bit set ("flag raised"), and anything edited since your last full or incremental backup will also. When the incremental backup is completed, it lowers the archive flag so that you won't back it up again until you change it. An incremental backup is a good way to do an interim backup, and you can perform this type of backup daily because it doesn't take long. If, for example, you edit a file every day and you always want to be able to go back to the version of a particular day, incremental backups are well-suited to this purpose.

- ✔ **Differential backup** backs up everything you have changed since the last full backup. It does this by looking to see what files have the archive bit set, and it doesn't change this bit. Thus, if you do a full backup, edit one file, and perform a differential backup, you back up that one file. If you change another file and perform a differential backup, you back up both files. You can perform differential backups between full backups, switching to a full backup whenever the differential backup becomes too time-consuming. The advantage of this approach is that a differential set of backups contains everything new or changed since the last full backup, whereas you may need to go through many incremental sets of backups to get a particular file. Differential backups take more time during backup, but less time during restore. If you rarely need to restore, then incremental backups will save you time overall. If you frequently archive files (remove them from your hard disk temporarily), and then want to restore them (because you are trying to cope with limited hard disk space), then you may find differential backups less time-consuming.

Understanding MSBACKUP 987

Just before backing up, you can choose from a number of options, as shown in figures 18.3 and 18.4.

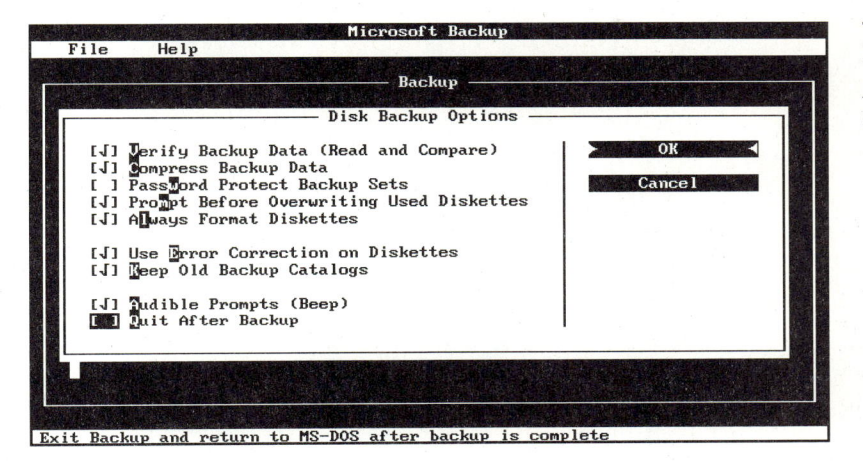

Figure 18.3
MSBACKUP disk backup options.

Figure 18.4
MWBACKUP disk backup options.

The options perform various tasks, as follows:

✔ **Verify Backup Data (Read and Compare)** writes your information to the backup medium, and then reads it from there and compares it with the source information. By default, this option is off. Turning it on will slow you down, but you should have it on. You don't care about doing things fast when you back up. You care about accuracy. Never back up without turning on all the error checking and verification that you can. This option is especially valuable if your computer's memory is none too trustworthy because it deals with accidental changes in your data during the copy process.

- ✔ **Compress Backup Data** is on by default. If you are backing up just a little to floppy disk on a fast machine, leave it on. If you are backing up from a slow machine, be aware that compressing data slows the backup process, but minimizes the number of disks required.

- ✔ **Password Protect Backup Sets** is off by default. Leave it off if you don't think you can remember your password. Turn it on if you have sensitive information and plan to leave your backup disks lying around.

- ✔ **Prompt Before Overwriting Used Diskettes** is on by default. Leave it on unless you are working with a new box of floppy disks, your desktop is immaculate, you are not error-prone, and you have never made a mistake with a computer. The last thing you want to do is make a terrible mistake (overwriting valuable data) when you are trying to be careful.

- ✔ **Always Format Diskettes** is off by default. Turn it on. MSBACKUP will format any disk that has never been formatted or that it finds to be incorrectly formatted. But if you formatted a disk in a different drive, or earlier in the current drive, the alignment of the heads may have changed and the sector addresses may not be very readable. Although formatting floppy disks adds to the backup time, those who truly value their data should turn this option on.

- ✔ **Use Error Correction on Diskettes** devotes about 10 percent of your disk to error correction coding (ECC). Then, if something tragic happens to your backup disks (a jelly donut gets lodged in one, for instance), you have a prayer of getting things back. Although ECC takes more storage space and slows things during backup, it will have a negligible effect on restore times. Verification and ECC are different. With verification, you know that the disk was once readable. With ECC, you have a good chance of recovering something that has been damaged during storage and is no longer readable. This option is on by default.

- ✔ **Keep Old Backup Catalogs** stores the backup disk's directory structure, the names, sizes and attributes of the selected directories and files, the total number of files, the total size of the backup, the name of the setup file used, and the date the backup was made. You can manually delete the oldest catalogs whenever the disks they reference have been reused. Catalogs are named *abymmddn.typ*, in which:

a is the letter of the first drive backed up in this set.

b is the last drive backed up in this set. If you backed up only a single drive, its letter appears twice (CC, for example, for a file describing a backup from drive C).

y is the final year digit (3, for example, indicates 1993).

mm is the two-digit month of the backup.

dd is the two-digit day of the backup.

n is the letter for the ID of this set (A, for example, indicates the first set on this date).

typ is the method. The three types are FUL (full), INC (incremental), and DIF (differential).

> **NOTE** *The term* full, *as used by MSBACKUP, means that the archive bit will be ignored when choosing what to back up. You might choose to back up everything (what you think of as full) or just the files in a certain directory. By choosing full, you choose to back up everything selected, not just those files in your selection that have not been created or changed since your last backup.*
>
> *Therefore, the file name CC31226B.FUL, for example, would indicate the second (shown by the letter B) full backup (shown by the FUL extension) from just drive C (shown by the letter C repeated twice) performed on December 26, 1993 (shown by the numbers 3, 12, and 26).*

✔ **Audible Prompts** is a minor feature. It might be a good idea to select it (the default) so that you don't sit waiting for MSBACKUP/MWBACKUP when MSBACKUP/MWBACKUP is actually waiting for you. A beep whenever it is time to swap disks is a good idea.

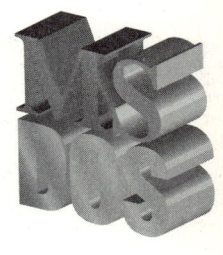

✔ **Quit After Backup** is off by default. Turn this option on if you normally do a full, incremental, or differential backup, and then exit. You'll want to leave it off if you often back up selected directories in various ways.

Configuring MSBACKUP/MWBACKUP

The first time you run MSBACKUP/MWBACKUP, you need to configure it for your machine. You need two identical floppy disks if you are backing up to floppy disk. If you will be backing up to tape, be sure that your tape drive is turned on and you have a spare tape handy. Because MSBACKUP/MWBACKUP will be modifying your CONFIG.SYS and AUTOEXEC.BAT files, you may want to manually back up these files first with the following commands...

```
COPY CONFIG.SYS CONFIG.BAK
COPY AUTOEXEC.BAT AUTOEXEC.BAK
```

MSBACKUP's configuration includes some controls not available to users of MWBACKUP: video colors and lines, and mouse controls. You access these controls by selecting Co**n**figure from the Main menu (see fig. 18.1). The Configure menu is displayed (see fig. 18.5). If you want to try different video or mouse options, choose Video and Mouse. The Video and Mouse menu is displayed, from which you can choose among six additional menus. Figure 18.6 shows you one of these, the Screen Colors menu. Although the defaults in all these menus probably are fine, feel free to experiment with alternatives, all of which are explained briefly on the bottom line of the screen. If you want more explanation, press F1.

> **NOTE** *Changing screen colors is not available in MWBACKUP. It is done in Windows itself.*
>
> *To change the colors of MWBACKUP, go to the Main Group, and then choose Control Panel and Colors. Similarly, mouse controls are found in Control Panel, Mouse.*

Understanding MSBACKUP

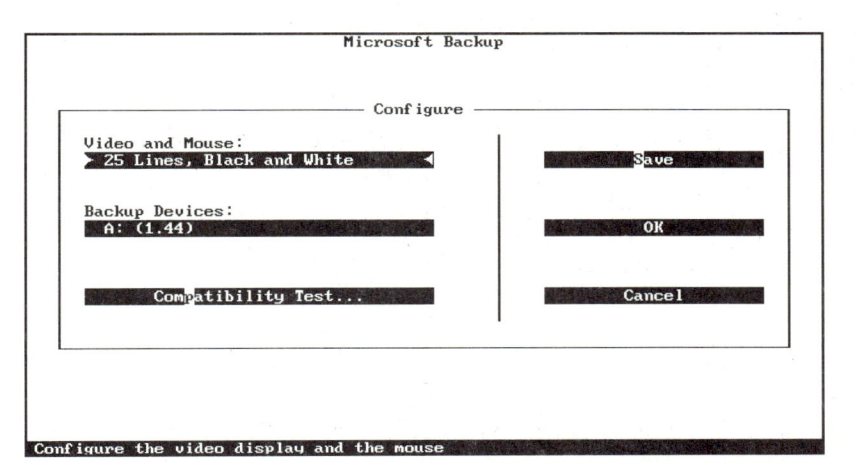

Figure 18.5

The first of the MSBACKUP configuration screens.

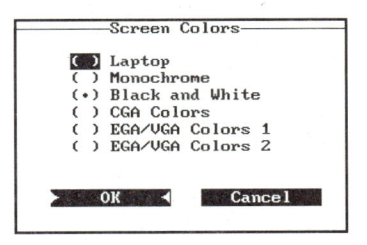

Figure 18.6

The MSBACKUP Screen Colors menu.

For screen colors in MSBACKUP, you can choose from Laptop, Monochrome, Black and White, CGA Colors, EGA/VGA Colors 1, and EGA/VGA Colors 2. The colors don't matter much, but the more colorful you can make this dreaded task, the less irritating it will be. Of greater importance is that you be able to find the cursor on the screen, and determine which options you are choosing when you press Enter. Move to a menu item by pressing the highlighted letter of the option or pressing the Tab key. Select from a multiple choice item (such as the screen colors options) by pressing the space bar, and then pressing Enter. On a laptop, you may find very little difference among the screen colors options. The default proposed by MSBACKUP is probably about the best that you can do.

In MSBACKUP, you also can change the number of lines of information that will be displayed (see fig. 18.7). (In Windows, you can do this to some extent with Setup, Screen in the Main Group.) If you have a large, readable EGA or VGA monitor, you may want 28, 43, or 50 lines. More likely, 25 lines will be fine.

Figure 18.7

The Display Lines menu.

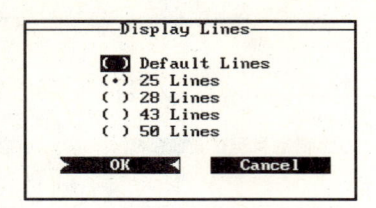

```
┌─Display Lines──────────┐
│  (•) Default Lines     │
│  ( ) 25 Lines          │
│  ( ) 28 Lines          │
│  ( ) 43 Lines          │
│  ( ) 50 Lines          │
│    ◄ OK ►    Cancel    │
└────────────────────────┘
```

Display Lines is not available in MWBACKUP. It is done in Windows itself.

You also can choose whether you want the standard display (text mode, which is the fastest, but also the least visually pleasing); graphical controls; graphical controls and mouse; or graphical controls, mouse, and dialogs. Don't choose a mouse option if you don't have a mouse!

If you have a CGA adapter, you may see snow on it when the screen is rewritten. If so, you can check **R**educe Display Speed. This option slows things down and makes things look better.

If you want to see some slick visuals and are running MSBACKUP on a reasonably perky machine (386+), you may want to select E**x**panding Dialogs to make dialog boxes appear to grow or expand on the screen when you click on them. This is a pleasant effect, and if it will help you back up more frequently, by all means choose this option.

For your mouse, you can control the double-click speed in MSBACKUP. You also can control sensitivity: high sensitivity means that a small movement on your desk equals a large movement on your screen. If you are backing up from your tray table in an airplane, you may find your desktop a bit small and want high sensitivity. You also can control the acceleration of your mouse. If you want your mouse cursor to get to its destination sooner and you are often traveling across the screen, choose rapid acceleration. You also can switch mouse buttons if you are left-handed (and even if you are not). In MWBACKUP, you can change these mouse controls using Control Panel and Mouse.

If you lose this book, just press the F1 key to be reminded of what each option means (we would rather that you buy another book, of course).

When you first use Configuration in MSBACKUP, selecting OK carries you to further hardware tests. MSBACKUP then determines whether the floppy drive change lines are working. Following the on-screen instructions, remove any floppy disks from your drives and start the Floppy Drive Change Line Test.

After that process is finished, your machine will determine how fast your processor and hard disk are, and then try to back up a small amount of information to a floppy disk. For this test of backup reliability, you need two floppy disks of the same capacity (for example, 1.44M 3 1/2-inch floppy disks). They don't need to be formatted. MSBACKUP will execute a backup of several files, running a script called CONFIG$$.SET. MWBACKUP compresses these tests and runs everything automatically when you first run it from Windows. Some small amount of reconfiguration is available with Configure, as you can see in figure 18.2.

Backing Up Everything with MSBACKUP

After you've experimented with MSBACKUP, you'll want to do a full backup. Backing up everything is the easiest selection to perform. Follow these steps:

1. From the Backup screen, choose Bac**k**up From to select a drive. Next, choose Select Fi**l**es. On the letter of the drive you want to back up, press the space bar. Check marks appear on the right side of the screen, which lists files in the root. If you move your cursor down, you will see that there are no check marks next to any of the files in subdirectories.

2. With your cursor on the drive letter (at the top of the screen), press Alt-N to edit the Include list. Your screen will look something like that shown in figure 18.8.

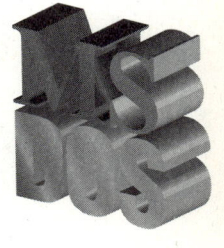

Chapter 18: *Backing Up Your Data*

Figure 18.8

Selecting include files.

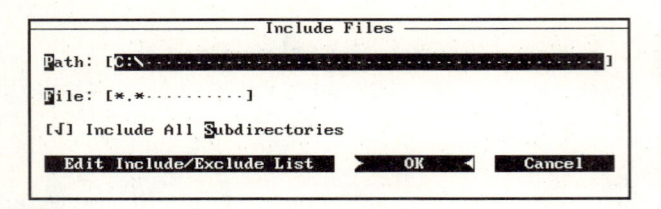

```
┌─────────────── Include Files ───────────────┐
 Path: [C:\............................................]
 File: [*.*..........]
 [√] Include All Subdirectories
 ╞ Edit Include/Exclude List ╡   ► OK ◄    Cancel
└─────────────────────────────────────────────┘
```

3. Press Enter, and MSBACKUP will choose all files in all subdirectories (the default).

4. From the Select Backup Files screen, you can see that all files in all directories are included.

5. Your main Backup screen will show that all files are about to be backed up.

6. Decide to where you want to back up, if you don't want to back up to drive A (which is the default).

7. Decide on the backup type if you don't want Full.

8. Select your backup options.

9. Before beginning the backup, save your hard work with File Save Setup As (press Alt-F and A). I'd name mine DAVIDALL and add some description to Setup File's header (see fig. 18.9). Be aware that MWBACKUP does not do any error checking on your command line, and will save a file name with spaces and other funny non-DOS-like characters. You will want to do your own error checking if you plan to manipulate these files manually in DOS.

Figure 18.9

Saving your set up.

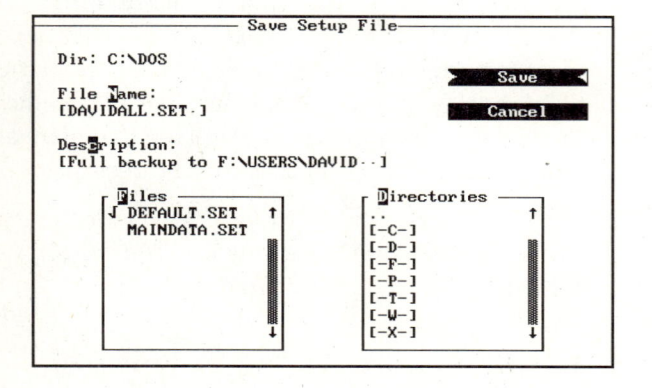

```
┌─────────────── Save Setup File ───────────────┐
 Dir: C:\DOS
                                           ► Save ◄
 File Name:
 [DAVIDALL.SET]                             Cancel
 Description:
 [Full backup to F:\USERS\DAVID..]
  ┌─ Files ────────┐   ┌─ Directories ────┐
  │ √ DEFAULT.SET ↑│   │ ..             ↑ │
  │   MAINDATA.SET │   │ [-C-]            │
  │                │   │ [-D-]            │
  │                │   │ [-F-]            │
  │                │   │ [-P-]            │
  │                │   │ [-T-]            │
  │                │   │ [-W-]            │
  │               ↓│   │ [-X-]          ↓ │
  └────────────────┘   └──────────────────┘
└───────────────────────────────────────────────┘
```

Suppose that you elect to back up to your personal directory, named F:\USERS\DAVID, and your backup set was named CC21227A.FUL. Suppose that your setup file name is DAVIDALL.SET. You will back up to F:\USERS\DAVID\CC21227A.FUL\CC21227A.001. Backing up to a server creates a few additional directories to help with housekeeping.

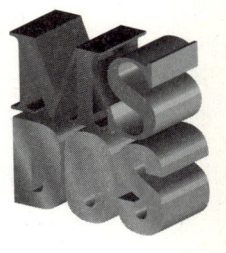

Backing Up Everything with MWBACKUP

MWBACKUP offers the same controls over your selection of files and drives as MSBACKUP, but the method of selecting these controls is much different. Those familiar with Windows won't have much trouble adapting to the scheme. Follow these steps:

1. From the Backup screen, click the drive you want to back up, and then click Select Files. Click the Include button and click Add to add all files to an Include list. To exclude a directory from the list, click on the directory display, and then click on Exclude, and click on Add from the Include/Exclude Files screen. Repeat these tricks until the visual directory shows your intent. Your screen will look something like that shown in figure 18.10.

2. Click OK.

3. Decide to where you want to back up, if you don't want to back up to drive A (the default).

4. Decide on the backup type if you don't want full.

5. Select your backup options.

6. Before beginning the backup, save your hard work with the Setup File option. I'd name mine as DAVIDALL and add some description to Setup File's header (see fig. 18.11).

Suppose that you elect to back up to your personal directory, named F:\USERS\DAVID, on your server and your backup set is named CC21227A.FUL. Suppose that your Setup file name is DAVIDALL.SET. You will back up to F:\USERS\DAVID\CC21227A.FUL\CC21227A.001. Backing up to a server creates a few additional directories to help with housekeeping.

Figure 18.10

Selecting include files with MWBACKUP.

Figure 18.11

Saving your setup with MWBACKUP.

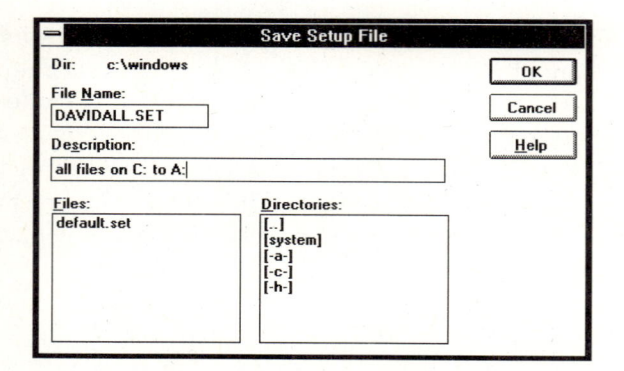

Backing Up Selected Files with MSBACKUP/MWBACKUP

Although making a full backup makes good sense, the time that can be required suggests that you also should have a means of backing up only critical files from time to time. Follow these steps to select just certain files:

1. From the Backup menu, choose Select Files. Press the space bar on the drive letter to turn on or off entries in the root. Press the space bar on a directory letter to turn on or off entries in that directory.

2. In MSBACKUP, press Alt-N to select files or directories to include (in MWBACKUP, press Alt-I). Edit the path and file name (the default is all files, shown with *.*). Decide whether to include all subdirectories by using the Tab key to move to Include All Subdirectories and pressing the space bar to show the checkmark (include) or not show it (don't include). You also can turn this on and off by pressing Alt-S.

3. Edit the Include list to drop any unwanted includes.

4. If you want to exclude certain files, you can do this by choosing Exclude from the Select Backup Files screen (press Alt-X). You can specify certain file types from the backup by setting the path as the root (that is, C:\), the file as *.BAK (to exclude backups from the backup), and checking subdirectories. Your Edit Include/Exclude List would look like that shown in figures 18.12 (MSBACKUP) and 18.13 (MWBACKUP). If you want to individually select files for exclusion, highlight them with your mouse and press Del. To include them, press Ins.

5. After making your selections and checking your work carefully, save it with a Setup file from the main Backup screen.

Restoring from a Backup Set with MSBACKUP/MWBACKUP

Restoring files is something you will want to practice before you actually need to do it.

Your first experiment will be to simulate the loss of one important file. Go to any directory you have just backed up and rename a file. You can, for example, rename MODE.COM to MODE.SAV. Now pretend that you've accidentally lost this file, and need to get it back from your backups. Follow these steps:

1. Choose Restore from the Main menu.

2. Choose Restore From: and select the location to which you originally backed up.

3. Choose Select Files.

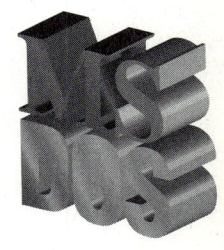

Chapter 18: *Backing Up Your Data*

Figure 18.12
Selecting files to include and exclude in MSBACKUP.

```
                    ┌─ Select Backup Files ─┐
                    │ Edit Include/Exclude List │
    Inc/Exc          Directories              Files      Subdirs

 1. Include C:\                                *.*         Yes
 2. Exclude C:\                                *.BAK       Yes




    [  Edit  ]   [ Del=Delete ]   [ Ins=Copy ]              [ OK ]

Select an include/exclude item to edit, delete, or copy
```

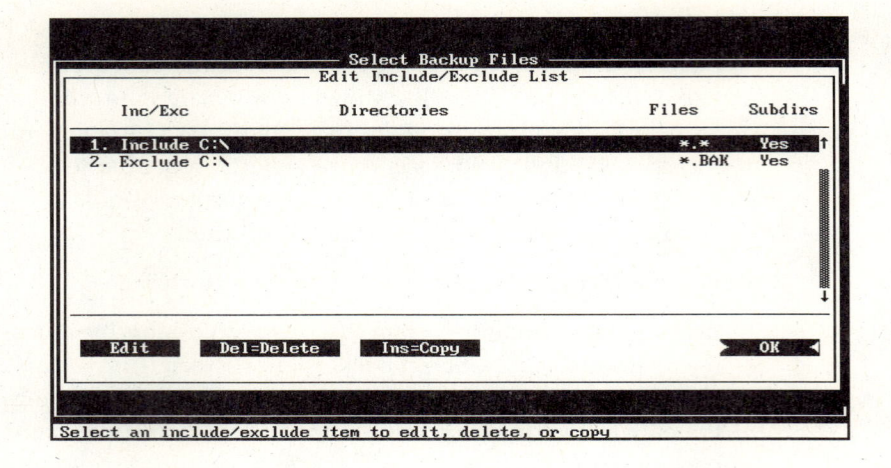

Figure 18.13
Selecting files to include and exclude in MWBACKUP.

```
┌───────────────── Include/Exclude Files ─────────────────┐
 Path:                                            [  OK  ]
 c:\
 File:                                            [ Cancel ]
 *.bak
                                                  [  Add  ]
   ○ Include   ● Exclude
                                                  [ Delete ]
   ☒ Include All Subdirectories
                                                  [  Help  ]
 Include/Exclude List:
 ┌────────────────────────────────┐
 │ Exclude [Sub] c:\*.bak         │
 │                                │
 │                                │
 └────────────────────────────────┘
```

4. Move to the directory on the pop-up list, and use the Tab key to move to the right portion of the screen.

5. Move the highlight down to the file you just renamed, and press the space bar or Ins. A checkmark (MSBACKUP) or box (MWBACKUP) should appear next to it. Your work to this point is shown in figures 18.14 and 18.15.

6. Choose OK. On the Restore screen in MSBACKUP, you should see 1 file selected for restore. In MWBACKUP, you see Selected files: 1 (bytes) in the lower right of the Select Restore Files screen. Press S to begin restore. (In MWBACKUP, you do these things with your mouse.)

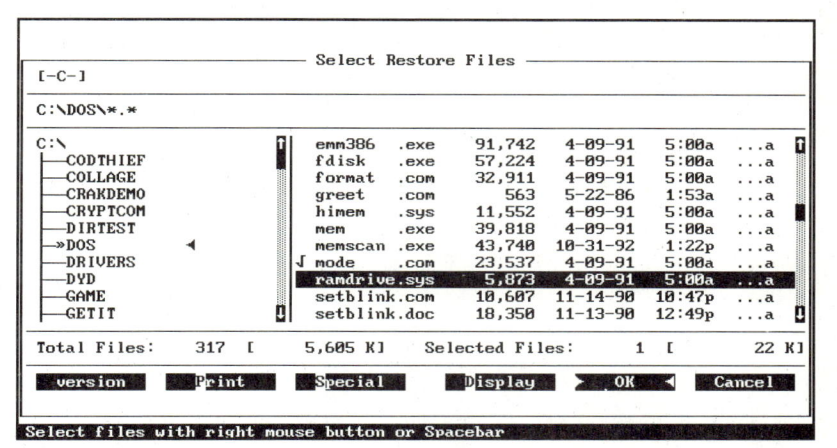

```
                    ┌─── Select Restore Files ────┐
    [-C-]
    C:\DOS\*.*
    C:\                    emm386   .exe    91,742   4-09-91   5:00a  ...a
        ├─CODTHIEF         fdisk    .exe    57,224   4-09-91   5:00a  ...a
        ├─COLLAGE          format   .com    32,911   4-09-91   5:00a  ...a
        ├─CRAKDEMO         greet              563    5-22-86   1:53a  ...a
        ├─CRYPTCOM         himem    .sys    11,552   4-09-91   5:00a  ...a
        ├─DIRTEST          mem      .exe    39,818   4-09-91   5:00a  ...a
        ├─»DOS    ◄        memscan  .exe    43,740  10-31-92   1:22p  ...a
        ├─DRIVERS        √ mode     .com    23,537   4-09-91   5:00a  ...a
        ├─DYD              ramdrive .sys     5,873   4-09-91   5:00a  ...a
        ├─GAME             setblink .com    10,607  11-14-90  10:47p  ...a
        ├─GETIT            setblink .doc    18,350  11-13-90  12:49p  ...a

    Total Files:   317 [  5,605 K]   Selected Files:    1 [    22 K]
    [ Version ]  [ Print ]  [ Special ]  [ Display ]  ► OK ◄  [ Cancel ]
    Select files with right mouse button or Spacebar
```

Figure 18.14
Restoring a file with MSBACKUP.

If things seem to go smoothly and restore seems to have worked, go to the directory where you renamed your test file, and compare the saved copy with the restored copy. You should find that the two files have the same size, date, and time. Run COMP.EXE on the two files (to see whether any bytes differ) by typing...

    COMP MODE.COM MODE.SAV

If you have a general disaster on your drive with many lost files but many good ones remaining, back up your most important files to directories away from their current location before running MSBACKUP/MWBACKUP's restore. To make an emergency backup copy of MYREPORT.DOC, for example, you might type...

    CD\REPORTS
    MD BACKUP
    COPY MYREPORT.DOC BACKUP
    CD BACKUP
    DIR

The last two lines check on the quality of your work, to make sure that MYREPORT.DOC got backed up to a directory named \REPORTS\BACKUP.

If you lose a portion of a directory—or all of a directory or drive, or some files from all over—you need to restore selectively, replacing only what was lost. You don't want to replace your current version of the novel you are writing with last month's version. Be aware that

Chapter 18: *Backing Up Your Data*

MSBACKUP/MWBACKUP will overwrite any existing files in a directory with those from a backup set if the names match!

Figure 18.15
Restoring a file with MWBACKUP.

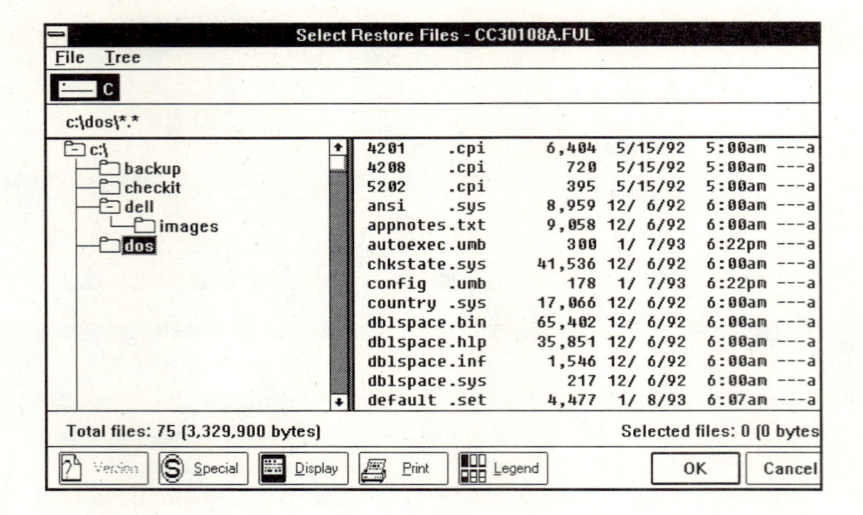

```
            Select Restore Files - CC30108A.FUL
File  Tree
  C
c:\dos\*.*
 c:\              4201    .cpi      6,404  5/15/92  5:00am ---a
   backup         4208    .cpi        720  5/15/92  5:00am ---a
   checkit        5202    .cpi        395  5/15/92  5:00am ---a
   dell           ansi    .sys      8,959 12/ 6/92  6:00am ---a
     images       appnotes.txt      9,058 12/ 6/92  6:00am ---a
   dos            autoexec.umb        300  1/ 7/93  6:22pm ---a
                  chkstate.sys     41,536 12/ 6/92  6:00am ---a
                  config  .umb        178  1/ 7/93  6:22pm ---a
                  country .sys     17,066 12/ 6/92  6:00am ---a
                  dblspace.bin     65,402 12/ 6/92  6:00am ---a
                  dblspace.hlp     35,851 12/ 6/92  6:00am ---a
                  dblspace.inf      1,546 12/ 6/92  6:00am ---a
                  dblspace.sys        217 12/ 6/92  6:00am ---a
                  default .set      4,477  1/ 8/93  6:07am ---a
Total files: 75 (3,329,900 bytes)         Selected files: 0 (0 bytes)
  Version   Special   Display   Print   Legend      OK     Cancel
```

Even if you mark your favorite files as read-only, MSBACKUP/MWBACKUP will replace them.

You can prevent this by selecting Options from the Restore screen. Then, whenever MSBACKUP/MWBACKUP finds that it is asked to restore an existing file, it will report that the file already exists on the hard disk and present choices of overwrite, don't restore, and canceling restore.

If you have an absolute tragedy with your hard disk and the file structure is damaged, I recommend the following steps:

1. Install a tape drive and controller in the victim machine, if you don't have one. (You can rent one for a week, or borrow one from down the hall.)

2. Perform an IMAGE backup to tape using the software that came with your tape drive. Don't bother with a file-by-file backup if the file structure (root or FATs) is damaged.

3. Remove the tape drive and controller, and install them in a "doctor" machine with a hard disk as large as yours (and one with nothing of value on it). Install the backup software for the tape drive and perform an IMAGE RESTORE. Verify that you have re-created the problem exactly. If so, you now can do anything you want to the victim machine (such as reformatting the hard disk).

4. Perform your data recovery miracles on the doctor machine. (See Chapter 19 for miracles.) If you fail on your first try, you can perform another IMAGE RESTORE to the drive and try again. Try until you succeed.

5. When you think you are finished, examine your work carefully to be sure it is perfect. When it is, do an IMAGE BACKUP to a second set of tapes. Pick up the controller, drive, and second set of tapes, install the hardware in the victim machine, and do an IMAGE RESTORE from the second set of (perfect) tapes. Test your work.

Comparing Your Source and Your Backups

If you back up to a server, it is an easy matter to see whether your backup really worked, or to see how much your old files have changed since your last backup.

The MSBACKUP/MWBACKUP Main menu option Compare enables you to choose what to compare, and compare things byte for byte. Compare does not show you the names of any files not backed up in the previous backup. If an old file has been modified, you see an Alert box with the message that the file is a different size. Your only options are to continue or cancel compare. If the file has been changed, but its size has not increased, the message tells you that the file does not match. Make a list of these files, examine them manually (if they are programs, scan them for viruses), and restore from your backups when this seems appropriate.

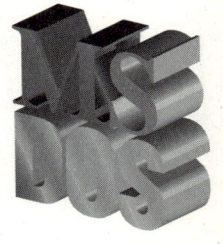

Trouble in River City

If your compatibility test fails, you will be advised to exit from the program, remove any TSRs to free all available memory, then rerun the compatibility test again. If, for example, you see the message...

```
DMA Buffer size too small
```

...you will not be able to perform a backup, compare, or restore until the DMA buffer size is increased. See the Troubleshooting section in your MS-DOS manual.

> *You can correct this problem by increasing the size of the DMA buffer used by EMM386, and then modifying SYSTEM.INI. To increase the DMA buffer size from its default of 32K, you need to do two things:*
>
> 1. *Add the /D:64 switch to the end of your EMM386 line in CONFIG.SYS.*
>
> 2. *Locate the [386Enh] section in the SYSTEM.INI file, and add the DMABuffersize=64 line to it.*

> *This note corrects an error in the Microsoft documentation shipped with DOS 6.2.*

This is not a comforting message because you are likely to have those memory-hungry TSRs running when you run a real backup, and that's where you want to be sure of reliability. You can get the same error message after removing all your TSRs by rebooting with no AUTOEXEC.BAT.

If you exit from your first experience with MSBACKUP/MWBACKUP, and want to start all over (perhaps you have removed some of the silly things from AUTOEXEC.BAT and CONFIG.SYS that, in earlier chapters, we suggested that you add), you can delete all record of your hard work by changing to the directory where

MSBACKUP is stored and typing...

    DIR /OD

This command displays a list of files in date order. You can delete files with the extensions .FUL and .SET that you just created, along with MSBACKUP.INI, DOSBACK.TMP, DOSBACK.RST, and DEFAULT.SET (if they exist). When you run MSBACKUP/MWBACKUP again, you will be asked to configure the program for your computer. Proceed with the configuration. Unfortunately, if MSBACKUP/MWBACKUP doesn't think your DMA chip is up to speed, there is no simple way to configure MSBACKUP/MWBACKUP to not use it. Configuration decisions to use the DMA chip are made automatically, and stored in an uneditable binary file named MSBACKUP.INI (or MWBACKUP.INI).

The Price of Integrity

How fast is MSBACKUP/MWBACKUP? All consultants have learned to answer all questions with the same clever answer: it depends! How fast depends on what options you choose and how fast your machine is.

We didn't want to bring you the results of years of testing MSBACKUP/MWBACKUP on hundreds of different machines. So we chose one, and conducted all our benchmarks on it. Your speed will mirror our results, and be consistently slower or faster, depending on CPU, DMA, cache size, and so forth. All we wanted to do was to see what speed penalty is imposed by various options, as follows:

- ✔ Our fastest time, 2,170K per minute, was turned in using compression with no verify, no format, and no error correction coding (ECC). (MSBACKUP and MWBACKUP seem to operate at about the same speed, despite Windows' reputation for sluggishness.)

- ✔ The second fastest time, 1,934K per minute, was with no ECC, no verify, no format, and no compression. Obviously, compression increases your speed—presumably because in this machine, the CPU (a 33 MHz 80386DX) was faster than the floppy disk drive, and time spent in compression was less than the time saved by writing fewer bytes. On a slower machine, compression might degrade performance.

✔ The option that poses the least risk for your information is ECC, verification, and formatting. This setting was able to back up only 467K per minute with compression. The single largest slowdown in these choices was formatting. When we chose just ECC and verification, we were able to back up 1,144K per minute with compression. This is only two thirds the speed of the fastest option, and it turns a one-hour backup job into an hour and a half. But the quality can be worth it.

> **AUTHOR'S NOTE**
>
> *To explore how good the ECC is, we backed up some files to a 3 1/2-inch 1.44M floppy disk using ECC, and then wrote on the surface of the mylar disk with a ballpoint pen and tried to restore from this disk. We saw the message...*
>
> ```
> Correcting Bad Disk
> ```
>
> *...as the head worked its way past the ink. Only 10 errors were reported, and all 10 were corrected. You should always use ECC. (And don't try any tricks with a ballpoint pen!)*

Using XCOPY for Quick Backup

One drawback of most backup utilities is that they put files in an unreadable (unusable) form until you restore them. A backup alternative to MSBACKUP and MWBACKUP is DOSs XCOPY command. XCOPY stores files in normal format, enabling you to quickly copy them back to your hard disk and use them.

After using either MSBACKUP or MWBACKUP to back up your entire hard disk, run QBACK.BAT every day until your next full backup:

```
@echo off
```

Understanding MSBACKUP **1005**

```
echo *** Quick Backup ***
echo .
:start
echo Insert a FORMATTED floppy disk into drive A,
echo           or hit Ctrl-C if done...
echo .
pause
xcopy c:\*.* /s /m
goto start
```

GOTO, of course, creates an endless loop. Each time a floppy fills up, you see the `Insufficient disk space` message. The loop forces XCOPY to run again, but because of the /M switch, no files will be backed up if they've already been backed up (the /M switch resets the archive bit). When all files have been copied, you get the `0 files copied` message, at which time you can break out of the batch file.

> *If you want to turn off the archive bit of all the files on your disk so that they appear as if they have been backed up, enter* **ATTRIB -A C:*.* /S**.

Getting More Out of MSBACKUP/MWBACKUP

There's more to a good backup than simply knowing what keys to press. You need the good timing of a comedian, the patience of a turtle, and the attention to detail and labeling of a librarian. The following sections present some ideas on how to simulate these multiple personalities.

Backup Cycles and Retention Periods

You probably should devise a backup cycle—a systematic program for what type of backups you will do and when. A backup cycle begins with a full backup and normally contains one or more incremental or differential sets. The length of a cycle is defined, in part, by the likelihood of your needing to recover. If your hard disk is new and working fine, you lock your office at night, and rarely encounter a computer virus, your cycle can be longer than if trouble is your middle name. You might do a full backup monthly, and incremental or differential backups during the month. If you need to restore several times a year, you might want a cycle that is defined by the number of disks required for a differential backup. When you have too many disks, do a full backup and start your cycle over.

The frequency of backups in a cycle is determined in part by the value of the information backed up, and in part by the effort required to perform a backup. Important information should be backed up daily; very important information in constant flux (such as an accounts receivable file) might even be backed up two or three times a day. Unimportant information never needs to be backed up—delete anything you don't need before beginning a backup.

How many backup cycles you store for safe-keeping is called the *retention period*. If your cycle is monthly and you are keeping four sets of full backups, then you have a four-month retention period. The length of the retention period is defined by your need to go back to earlier sets of information. Some government offices require long retention periods. Offices that are experiencing frequent virus infections might want a long retention period for programs, because a new virus that MSAV does not detect may be on one or two backup sets. If your backup media can't always be trusted, then you might want a longer retention period than if you've never experienced a problem with restoration.

How often should you back up? I've heard people suggest that "if you can afford to lose a week's worth of data, then back up every week."

No one can afford to lose anything, but no one can afford to back up every five minutes, either. You need to be a professional gambler, I think, when it comes to backing up. Your long-term costs of backing up should always be lower than your long-terms costs of not backing up. If your hardware is very reliable, the rational gambler's backup frequency will be lower than when the hardware can't be trusted.

Using the Server for Archiving

Your network cannot have a server drive large enough to hold a full copy of each user's hard disk. But you might be able to use it for backup anyway. If the server had a directory named ARCHIVE.ME, for example, some users could back up everything to it on Monday, others on Tuesday, and so forth. David, for example, would back up to F:\ARCHIVE.ME\DAVID, and so forth. The network manager would back up the ARCHIVE.ME directory to a special tape that would be labeled and set aside. After the backup, the entire ARCHIVE.ME directory would be purged to create more room on the server for the next day's backup. If a user ever needed a backup copy of their work, they would go to the network manager, who could find, mount, and restore from the archive tape for them. The user could then restore from F:\ARCHIVE.ME\ to their hard disk.

Backing up MSBACKUP

If you have a catastrophic failure of your hard disk, you will want to have a usable copy of your backup program on floppy disk so that you can use it to restore to another hard disk. Format a high-capacity floppy disk with /S (to make it bootable), and then use the command...

```
COPY MSB*.* A: /V
```

All the DOS 6.2 files that begin with MSB are files you need for MSBACKUP; all those beginning with MWB are needed for MWBACKUP. You can use MWBACKUP to restore a backup set created with MSBACKUP and vice versa. Table 18.2 offers a short explanation of each MSBACKUP file.

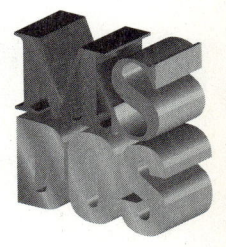

Table 18.2
Important MSBACKUP Files

File	Function
MSBACKUP.EXE	The main program
MSBACKUP.OVL	Additional code called immediately by MSBACKUP.EXE when it loads
MSBACKUP.HLP	Help file for the main program
MSBACKDB.OVL	Code called when you begin a backup to any device other than floppy disk (such as Bernoulli)
MSBACKDR.OVL	Code called when you begin a restore from any device other than floppy disk
MSBACKFB.OVL	Code called when you begin a backup to floppy disk
MSBACKFR.OVL	Help file for backup to floppy disk options
MSBCONFG.OVL	Code called when you choose the Configure option on the Main menu
MSBCONFG.HLP	Help file for configuration options
MSBACKUP.INI	Initialization file for the program—contains a few parameters of interest

None of the files listed in Table 18.3 are critical. As long as your backups are well-labeled, you don't need to back them up to your MSBACKUP rescue disks.

Table 18.3
Less Important MSBACKUP Files

File	Function
DEFAULT.SET	The default setup file—back this up if you edit the defaults and save them as DEFAULT.

Backup Cycles and Retention Periods

File	Function
*.SET	Any other setup files you create.
*.SLT	Something in binary that you're not meant to understand.
*.FUL, *.INC,	Catalogs of your backup sets when you do a full, and *.DIF incremental, or differential backup. Normally stored in the directory housing MSBACKUP, as well as the last file on a set of backup disks.
*.CAT	A master catalog of each of your uses of a given script, stored under the main name you have given. If, for example, you make a script for backing up your DATABASE directory (DATABASE.SET), and then use this script once (making a .FUL, .INC, or .DIF file), then you also create a file named DATABASE.CAT, which lists the backups you've done, the set name, date, and time of backup. Then you load the master catalog for a particular type of backup (for example, your DATABASE.CAT), MSBACKUP/MWBACKUP will merge into it all the backups you've done using that set. You then can automatically restore the latest version of every file you have backed up.

Making Backups More Efficient with Setup Files

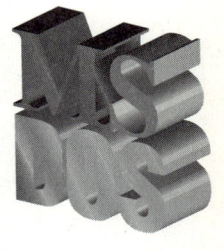

MSBACKUP/MWBACKUP uses setup files to define some of your machine's characteristics (hard-disk size, for example), what you want to back up, and the type of backup to do. You can create a setup file containing all the instructions you want to use in a particular type of backup. When you load the desired setup file, you load the options you previously selected. You are free to edit these options on the screen, but you may want to plunge ahead and use them as is.

Suppose that you work on a large database, and you want to back it up every day. Follow these steps:

1. Follow the instructions earlier in this chapter for "Backing Up Selected Files with MSBACKUP/MWBACKUP."

2. From the menu bar at the top of the screen, select File (press Alt-F) and Choose Save Setup **A**s.

3. Enter a name of eight letters, followed by .SET. We named ours DAVIDALL.SET in figure 18.9 (MSBACKUP) and figure 18.11 (MWBACKUP). Now enter a useful description so that you will know what this backup set does. Save your work.

In the future, when you want to run this backup, you can enter a command at the DOS prompt (or from a batch file) such as...

```
MSBACKUP davidall
```

Substitute the name of your backup set for *davidall*.

We haven't figured out how to get MSBACKUP to run unattended. The only command line options available are /BW, /LCD, and /MDA (which change your screen setup to black and white, LCD (Liquid Crystal Display of your laptop), or IBM monochrome display adapter equivalent, respectively). Obviously, you must attend to it if you are backing up to floppy disk, but a trick to get it to do an unattended backup to your server or Bernoulli drive would be nice.

Repairing Catalogs

If you no longer have access to a drive that holds a copy of your catalog (it has gone to hard disk heaven or you are no longer a network user), if a catalog becomes damaged, or part of your backup set is damaged or missing, you need to rebuild your catalog. You can do this from the Restore menu option Rebuild. When you select Rebuild, you are given a choice of what drive should form the basis for your rebuild, including floppy disks and hard disk directories. The response to the prompt...

    Rebuild Catalog From:

...is wherever your backup files are stored.

Looking at a Model Backup Policy

What should your organization have for a backup policy? It doesn't matter much if users think it's silly or unimportant. Users should discuss catastrophic data loss, come to grips with the issue of who should back up the data, and vote on a policy on their own. Once the users have developed a policy, let them enforce it.

If you can't do this and are looking for a model to use, the following ideas might serve as a starter:

- ✔ Users not connected to a network are expected to back up their own work. The frequency of backup should be proportional to the importance of the information. We recommend one full backup of data files each month, and incremental backups daily. Some information should be backed up more often than other information. Users need only to back up data files. The help desk will be able to restore any supported programs needed.

- ✔ Users connected to a network are expected to back up their critical files to a designated personal directory on the server. The network support staff will ensure that the server is backed up daily.

- ✔ Users who experience data loss and who have not made backups will be excluded from the office Christmas party, be responsible for re-creating the lost information on weekends without pay, or something in-between.

Summary

Backing up is one of the most important things you can ever do. It's especially important in the corporate world because today's organizations depend on computerized information for their survival. Unfortunately, backing up is not glamorous. You probably won't get a commendation for doing it. The immediate rewards, in fact, are less than those for brushing your teeth. Nevertheless, backing up with **MSBACKUP** and **MWBACKUP** can make the chore as pleasant and fast as it will ever get. If you can't bear to back up today, then one day, you will have to utilize the information in Chapter 19—the data-recovery chapter!

MS-DOS

CHAPTER 19

Protecting and Recovering Data

by David Stang

This chapter offers a crash course in data recovery for users of DOS 6.2. Every possible disaster in this chapter is not covered—you won't explore neat ways to trash your system. Instead, this chapter, covers the basics that every reader of this book should know in order to survive and succeed with a computer.

There is little magic in data recovery. Almost every miracle you perform will prove to be nothing more than a combination of motivation, knowledge, skill, and luck. This chapter can provide some of the knowledge (if you'll supply the motivation and the practice to develop the skill). Be aware that luck isn't guaranteed, and not every effort at data recovery succeeds.

Preventing Disasters

You reduce your need for luck by preparing for disaster. If you assume that, sooner or later, you will have to do some data recovery, you can do things to your machine now to make recovery easier later.

General Tips for Disaster Prevention

Following are some tips for avoiding disasters:

- ✔ Take proper care of the machine. Don't move it when it is on. Don't leave laptops in the trunk of your car. Don't leave disks near sources of heat or magnetism. Don't leave computers on unnecessarily, especially if you have severe power fluctuations. Keep your machine cool.

- ✔ Practice good housekeeping. If you won't need a file tomorrow, delete it today. The fewer files you store, the fewer you'll have to back up and the fewer you'll have to sift through during recovery. I name my practice files DELETEME so that I know what I can do with them.

- ✔ Don't place any files in the root directory. FORMAT overwrites the root directory, and recovery of such files is difficult.

- ✔ Make sure that everything you care about is backed up, labeled well, and stored safely.

- ✔ Look before you leap. Use the DIR command on the drive you are planning to format to be sure that this is the one you meant.

- ✔ Watch where you put things, especially with COPY so that you don't overwrite a critical file in the destination directory:

    Before pressing Enter during a copy, study your command line carefully to be certain the file will be going to where you want it to be going.

    After a copy, check the expected destination to ensure that the file landed there.

✔ Another way to ensure that the file is placed where you want it is by changing to the destination directory, and then issuing the COPY command. If, for example, you want to copy a file named from a directory named DIR on drive D to the current (default) directory, type...

   `COPY D:\DIR\X`

✔ In general, avoid use of the same file name for multiple files, except in these cases:

   When you plan to delete the file after this session, you can name it DELETEME or some other name you will always remember.

   When you plan to add the file to other text you are working in, you may want to give your files names such as ADD*xxx*, where *xxx* represents a unique identifier. I then delete such a file after merging it with the document so that I know it no longer needs to be added.

✔ Use UNDELETE /S in your AUTOEXEC.BAT. This is discussed in more detail in a section later in the chapter.

✔ Develop your skills before you need them.

✔ Learn carefully. If you want to conduct some data recovery experiments, practice on a floppy disk you don't care about. If you want to try a new program, be sure to try it carefully. The best experiments are conducted after a backup, on a floppy or at least in a directory set aside for experimentation.

This is not to say that all disasters must be prevented. If you're terrific at data recovery (or become terrific after reading this chapter), you might consider the golden mean: *use a modest level of prevention and expect to need a moderate amount of recovery.* Moderation in all things might cost less than intensive effort in prevention.

> **AUTHOR'S NOTE**
>
> *Taking chances with deletions? If, for example, I have a directory that has 101 files in it and I only want one of them, I might copy the file I want to the root directory, delete all the files in the current directory, and finally move the copied file back to the current directory. Or, I might delete all the files in the current directory, and then undelete the one file I want. Compare the number of keystrokes required by methods 1 and 2, and you will see why I sometimes take a chance with method 2:*
>
> *Method 1:*
>
> ```
> COPY XYZ.COM C:\
> DEL *.*
> MOVE C:\XYZ.COM
> ```
>
> *Method 2:*
>
> ```
> DEL *.*
> UNDELETE XYZ.COM
> ```
>
> *How can you learn such tricks, you ask? Read on, and I'll tell you what I know.*

Preventing Media Damage

You also can make data recovery easier by preventing media damage. Here are some tips:

- ✔ On backup disks, be aware that magnetic recordings fail over time. Don't trust backup disks for too long. From time to time "refresh" them by copying all files from a backup disk to a newly formatted disk. You can reuse the old backup disk by reformatting it (putting fresh sector marks down), and then copying files to it. Disks may last forever, but the information on them won't.

- ✔ If a disk with a bad sector is one that is heavily used (such as a boot floppy disk), you are ready to learn another lesson: disks *don't* last forever. Their lives are shortened by use, especially inside a hot machine, by contact with various surfaces, by rubbing with the heads (especially with dust between head and surface), and so on. Boot floppy disks should be backed up, and replaced with the backup when they fail.

Using MIRROR To Help Prevent Disaster

MIRROR is a DOS 5 utility provided with DOS 6.2 on the supplemental disks. (It is originally from Central Point Software and part of PC Tools, as is UNDELETE and UNFORMAT, which also come with DOS 6.2) MIRROR saves a copy of the system area of your hard disk for later use in recovering files after an erasure or reformatting calamity. (*System area* is defined by the program as the boot record, root, and the first file allocation table, FAT.)

MIRROR comes with a variety of useful options:

DRIVE defines the drive letter you will mirror.

/1 saves only the latest FAT and directory information, rather than saving the current and the previous version.

/PARTN creates a backup copy, on a floppy disk, of your hard disk's master boot record (which contains the partition table) and boot record. UNFORMAT /PARTN restores it.

/TDRIVE-*nnn* turns on "deletion tracking" for drive, specifying that you want to save up to *nnn* deleted files. You can't save more than 999 deleted files, and if your hard disk is nearly overflowing, there may not even be room for this many.

/U unloads MIRROR from memory if you haven't loaded any TSRs after loading MIRROR.

? provides help on-screen.

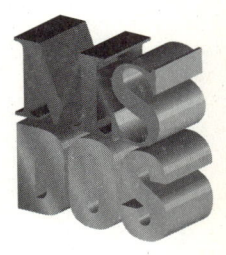

If you run MIRROR by itself, without any switches, you create a file called MIRROR.FIL. This is a read-only file listed in your root directory and physically located near the inside cylinders of the drive you have mirrored. If you run it again, you create MIRROR.BAK by renaming MIRROR.FIL, and then creating a new MIRROR.FIL. If you run it a third time, MIRROR will delete MIRROR.BAK, rename MIRROR.FIL to MIRROR.BAK, and create MIRROR.FIL. These files contain backup copies of the root directory and FAT.

If you run MIRROR /PARTN, you will make a copy on a floppy disk of your master boot record (including partition table) and boot record in a file called PARTNSAV.FIL. You should do this now. Write-protect the floppy disk you saved this file on, label the disk "Hard Disk Rescue Disk," and lock it away. You later will be able to rebuild the master boot record by typing...

    UNFORMAT /PARTN

...which will copy this file back to where it came from.

MIRROR is not a terminate-and-stay-resident (TSR) program unless you run it with the /T switch. If you use this switch, MIRROR loads as a TSR, taking about 6K of memory. As you delete files, MIRROR writes information to a file called PCTRACKR.DEL, which it creates the first time you delete a file after installing MIRROR in memory. PCTRACKR.DEL is marked as a system file in the root directory (system files are hidden, so you won't see it listed), and is stored in the first available clusters that MIRROR can find. PCTRACKR.DEL contains information on the drive, directory, file name, and FAT locations of every file you delete while MIRROR is running as a TSR. PCTRACKR.DEL is of fixed size (defined by your *nnn* on the command line, or by its own judgment of what would be a good size, if you don't specify the *nnn*). MIRROR as a TSR does not protect directories—they are overwritten as you delete files from them and add files to them—but it does protect the critical information needed to recover a file that has not been overwritten.

You run MIRROR with the deletion tracking (/T) switch like this...

    MIRROR /TC

...(you don't specify a colon after the drive letter). If you want to track deletions on several drives, you can list them after the /T by typing...

    MIRROR /TA /TC /TD

The order in which they are listed does not matter, and you can enter them in uppercase or lowercase.

Having said all that, you aren't much better off running MIRROR as a TSR. If you delete a file, and then copy another file to the drive, UNDELETE will be able to report that...

```
Deletion-tracking file contains 1 deleted files. Of
those, 0 files have all clusters available, 0 files have
some clusters available, and 1 files has  no clusters
available. The MS-DOS directory contains 0 deleted files.
Of those, files may be recovered.
```

You will then see a list of the files you have lost, along with the date and time you lost them. Press any key to continue.

Unless you plan to notice accidental deletions the moment they occur, don't bother using MIRROR. Use UNDELETE /S instead. UNDELETE in DOS 6.2 is intended to replace the MIRROR deletion tracking functions.

Although MIRROR is not clever enough to recover files that have been deleted and then overwritten when other files were copied, it does offer two splendid options:

- ✔ You can use MIRROR to back up the master boot record and boot record with /PARTN. This may help you recover from an accidental FORMAT, virus, or other disaster.

- ✔ MIRROR does back up the FAT, root directory, and other files whenever it is run. This is good for protection from all manner of calumny.

Unfortunately, MIRROR makes only two copies of the critical files. If MIRROR is installed in AUTOEXEC.BAT, then it backs things up whenever you reboot. When you experience trouble, you might press Ctrl+Alt+Del as a means of restoring law and order in your machine. You now have backed up the fouled FAT or root directory, and only the older backup is of value. You find things still a shambles, turn the machine off, and call the help desk. They arrive, and do the only thing they shouldn't do: turn the computer on! When AUTOEXEC.BAT runs, the only remaining backup copy of the undamaged system files is replaced with a copy of the damaged system files.

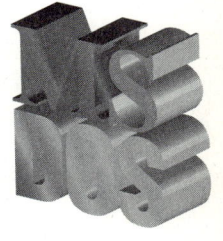

It would be good to ask the help desk gang to boot with a write-protected floppy disk when they make house calls to such a machine. But it would be even better to set up your system to make an unlimited number of spare copies of the key system files using MIRROR.

Here's how to do it. Let's suppose that you want to keep five copies total of your system files named MIRROR.FIL (the most recent copy), MIRROR.BAK (the next most recent), MIRROR.2 (the third most recent), and MIRROR.3 and MIRROR.4. A batch file could copy or rename before MIRROR runs and overwrites, but MIRROR.BAK is set to read-only, and sooner or later we will need to delete the oldest of these files, which we cannot do to a read-only file. So our batch file begins by clearing the read-only attribute from MIRROR.4 (the oldest copy of MIRROR.FIL) using the DOS 6.2 ATTRIB command, as follows...

```
ATTRIB -R MIRROR.4
```

Once MIRROR.4 has lost its read-only attribute, it can be deleted...

```
DEL MIRROR.4
```

Now that we've deleted the old MIRROR.4, we can use the name for MIRROR.3, which is now the oldest file. Let's rename MIRROR.3 to MIRROR.4...

```
REN MIRROR.3 MIRROR.4
```

We also can roll back MIRROR.2 and MIRROR.BAK...

```
REN MIRROR.2 MIRROR.3
REN MIRROR.BAK MIRROR.2
```

Now, we can run MIRROR...

```
MIRROR
```

MIRROR renames MIRROR.FIL to MIRROR.BAK, and creates a new MIRROR.FIL. Now we have an entire set of backups of our FAT and root. Each will have an accurate time and date stamp, so we can recover from any one of them (renaming it to MIRROR.FIL before running UNFORMAT). Following is the complete code for AUTOEXEC.BAT...

```
ATTRIB -R MIRROR.4]
DEL MIRROR.4
REN MIRROR.3 MIRROR.4
REN MIRROR.2 MIRROR.3
REN MIRROR.BAK MIRROR.2
MIRROR
```

On your first few runs, you won't have .4, .3, or .2, so the DEL and REN commands will produce error messages. DEL results in...

```
File not found
```

...and REN results in...

```
Duplicate file name or file not found.
```

Now, with several copies of the root directory, FAT, and other treasures, you can be a bit more casual when you begin data recovery.

Before You Begin

Much of this chapter concerns skills development. If you plan to develop your skills, you can easily practice on floppy disks. You can create a problem on a floppy disk you don't care about, and then practice solving it. Nearly every single data recovery skill can be learned on a 40-cent floppy disk.

When it's time to do real data recovery, unless you have won a Nobel prize for your skill, you should back up the problem, and try to recover the backup copy. If the problem is damage within a file, then you can use commands such as COPY and XCOPY to do your backup. If the problem is with a disk's file structure (damage to boot record, hidden system files, root directory, or FATs), you can use DISKCOPY. If the problem is with a hard disk's file structure, you are in trouble. If the information is very valuable, you can install a tape drive (as suggested in the last chapter) and make an image backup of the drive, restore the image to another machine, and try to recover from the second machine. If this is not feasible, you can experiment with floppy disks on another machine until you are sure that you understand the problem and solution, and then try your tricks on the live problem.

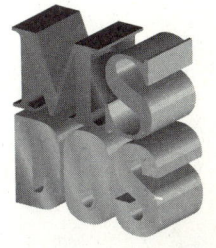

Data-recovery "experts" begin life as klutzes. They find a problem on Jim's machine and install their problem-solving tools, completely obliterating the problem along with any hope of recovery. Then they try to recover and fail. If they are consultants, they also charge $100.

Do not ever attempt to install any recovery tools on a drive on which you are about to perform data recovery. You have a good chance of overwriting (and permanently destroying) the file you are trying to recover. Get those tools installed before you need them, or run recovery tools only from a floppy disk.

This might be a good time to add the utilities from the disk accompanying the book to your hard disk. Put them on your path, perhaps in C:\UTILS.

If you are serious about data recovery, you will need to have some good utilities in your toolbox. Besides the tools that come with DOS and the tools that came on the disk with this book, you should consider buying a program such as Symantec's Norton Utilities, Fifth Generation's Mace Utilities, or Central Point Software's PC Tools. Owning such tools is not enough, of course; you have to know how to use them!

This chapter does not cover these commercial tools at all. Instead, it focuses on the basics of data recovery as you can perform it with the tools provided with DOS and on the disk accompanying this book. As you will see, we cover a lot of ground, and you'll be prepared for the most common problems that arise.

This chapter builds from simple tasks to more complex tasks. The simplest tasks are those involving the tools provided with DOS. You can use these tools to address the most common problems you will face.

Missing Files

You look for a file, and it's not there. Where can it be on your multizigabyte hard disk?

One possibility is that you've merely misplaced it. You can use the DIR command to find it. Move to the root directory. Type...

> **DIR** *filespec* **/S**

...in which *filespec* is the name of the file you are looking for. If you can only remember its first two letters, you can type...

> **DIR AB* /S/P**

...in which AB are the first two letters. The /S switch searches subdirectories, and the /P switch pauses the screen, displaying a page at a time.

If you can't remember the name of the file, but are certain it was a letter to Mr. Smithers, you can use FINDTEXT, provided on the disk accompanying this book. To use this program, type...

> **FINDTEXT**

You will be prompted for the file name to check (you can use wildcards to search for *.DOC, *.*, or M*.*, for example) and the text to search for. If that text is in any of the specified files, it will be found. You'll see the file names as they are searched and the text in context as it is found. Whenever the specified text is found, you have an opportunity to skip to the next file, stop the search, or continue searching within the file. Text search is not case-sensitive. You can practice on known text, if you want, to see how fast and thorough the program is.

Exploring UNDELETE for DOS

Two UNDELETE programs come with DOS 6.2: UNDELETE.EXE (for DOS) and MWUNDEL.EXE (for Windows). If you chose to install DOS 6.2 for both DOS and Windows operation, you will find both in your DOS directory. This section looks at UNDELETE for DOS. The next section discusses MWUNDEL.

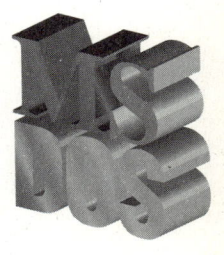

DOS 6.2 offers three levels of protection for accidentally deleted files: Delete Sentry, Delete Tracker, and standard. Standard is the weakest

method of undelete protection and works only if you change your mind about deletion before copying any file to the drive or editing any file. Don't count on it to work at all.

Sentry and Tracker both work through the UNDELETE TSR, which will watch over you and record your deletions. Sentry actually saves a real copy of the file by not marking the FAT as empty and adding a directory entry in a managed hidden subdirectory under the root directory called \SENTRY. Although your free space will not increase when you delete a file and Sentry is running, you will have a near certain chance of recovering the file a day or two later, if you want to recover it.

Tracker is designed for machines that don't have enough space to keep backups of deleted files. Like Sentry, UNDELETE loads into memory and takes just as much memory. When you delete a file, the information stored in the FAT is copied to PCTRACKR.DEL, and then the FAT is zeroed out. Your chance of recovering a deleted file is slightly better with Tracker than with the standard method, but not much.

UNDELETE stores its parameters in UNDELETE.INI. If the file does not exist, UNDELETE creates it with the following parameters:

- ✔ Use the Delete Sentry method on this drive.

- ✔ Save all files except *.TMP, *.VM?, *.WOA, *.SWP, *.SPL, *.RMG, *.IMG, *.THM, and *.DOV files. You may want to drop the *.IMG reference if you do graphics work with *.IMG files, and you may want to add some references to files such as *.BK!, *.BAK, and so on. You can choose to protect a file type by specifying it, and choose to not protect a file type by preceding its specification with a -. Thus, the line...

    ```
    *.*   -*.XYZ  -*.ABC
    ```

    ...would protect all files (*.*) except *.XYZ or *.ABC files.

- ✔ Purge files after seven days. If you are quick on your feet and space is limited, you might want to shrink this number to one or two days with...

    ```
    DAYS=1
    ```

✔ Restrict the amount of disk space to be used for deleted files to 20 percent of total disk space. If your drive is 90 percent full, it will only be a day or two before it is 100 percent full. If your drive is more than 60 percent full, I suggest reducing this number using...

    PERCENTAGE=10

✔ Don't protect any files that have been backed up (ARCHIVE=FALSE). If you want to protect files regardless of whether or not you've backed them up, change this entry in UNDELETE.INI to so that it reads...

    ARCHIVE=TRUE

You can edit the file with EDIT or another text editor.

If you lose a file and have failed with the tricks of the previous section to locate it, or know that you have deleted it, you might be in big trouble. Do not copy any more files to this drive until you have recovered it. Change to the directory where you think the file might have been when it was erased, and type...

    UNDELETE

If you get a `Bad command or file name` message, it is because UNDELETE.EXE is not on your path. Type...

    PATH

...to see what your current path is. If you know where UNDELETE is on your hard disk (for example, in C:\RESCUE), then you can type...

    C:\RESCUE\UNDELETE

If UNDELETE is not on your hard disk, get a copy on a floppy disk from another machine, and then type...

    A:UNDELETE /?

...to see a list of options.

Your options for installing in memory are as follows:

    /S[*drive*] turns on delete-sentry to protect the drive indicated. /SC, for example, turns on delete-sentry for drive C. It also loads UNDELETE into memory, using whatever parameters are defined in UNDELETE.INI. If you don't specify a drive, the default drive is assumed. If, for example, you run UNDELETE from drive C and type...

UNDELETE /S

...drive C will be protected.

/TDRIVE[-*entries*] turns on delete-tracking to protect the drive indicated, loading UNDELETE into memory. If you specify entries, you define the number of deleted files that will be tracked by PCTRACKR.DEL. You can specify any number of entries from 1 to 999 to be tracked. Each 5.5 entries tracked adds about 1K to PCTRACKR.DEL. If you don't specify entries, UNDELETE will choose how many entries to store in PCTRACKR.DEL based on the capacity of the drive—from 25 entries for a 360K floppy disk to 200 entries for a 32M hard disk.

You cannot run both /S and /T switches at the same time. To track 50 entries on drive C, for example, type...

UNDELETE /TC-50

/LOAD loads it in memory, using options stored in UNDELETE.INI (a small file added to the root directory of the protected drive). The file includes information, such as how long deleted files will be retained, what drives will be tracked with UNDELETE's Sentry, and so on. The /LOAD switch makes UNDELETE a TSR, taking about 13K of memory. Network users are not likely to be able to give up such memory, but it is worth a try. You can always unload it (with the /U switch) before running a big application, and then load it back when you exit.

Your options for status checks are as follows:

/LIST lists the deleted files in this directory without bothering to recover any of them.

/STATUS shows what UNDELETE is up to (loaded or not) and what recovery plan (Delete Tracker or Delete Sentry) you are using.

Your options for recovering deleted files are as follows:

/ALL undeletes everything. UNDELETE uses the Delete Sentry method for undeleting, if possible. If Sentry is not in use, /ALL tries Delete Tracker. If this is not possible, UNDELETE will recover files from the DOS directory, supplying a number sign (#) for each first character of recovered files; when two files will have the same name, UNDELETE uses some other character for the first letter of the undeleted file's name.

/DOS recovers only files that are still listed in directories as deleted, prompting for confirmation on each. The switch forces UNDELETE to ignore any Sentry or Tracker files that might exist. (For the life of me, I can't think of why you would want to use this switch!)

/DS uses the deletion sentry files for recovery. If you installed UNDELETE in memory with /S, you don't need to specify this switch on the command line—it is the default.

/DT uses the deletion tracking files produced by UNDELETE /T.

Your one option to remove UNDELETE from memory is as follows:

/U Unloads UNDELETE from memory.

Your one option to remove deleted files permanently is as follows:

/PURGE[*drive***]** purges the contents of the hidden delete-sentry directory (\SENTRY). Don't specify a colon in your drive reference (that is, use /PURGEC, not /PURGEC:). You will lose your ability to recover any erased, overwritten files, but you will protect your erasures from any attackers who might like to take a peek at them. You most often would use this switch when you are trying to install something that requires just a bit more space than you have. Also, if your drive begins to fill, use this option to free some space.

Figure 19.1 shows a sample UNDELETE screen.

Figure 19.1

What you see when using UNDELETE.

```
Using the Delete Sentry method.
      XYZ       COM       307  1-09-93 12:41a  ...A  Deleted:  1-16-93  6:36a

C:\>undelete

UNDELETE - A delete protection facility
Copyright (C) 1987-1993 Central Point Software, Inc.
All rights reserved.

Directory: C:\
File Specifications: *.*

     Delete Sentry control file contains      1 deleted files.

     Deletion-tracking file not found.

     MS-DOS directory contains     1 deleted files.
     Of those,    0 files may be recovered.

Using the Delete Sentry method.
      XYZ       COM       307  1-09-93 12:41a  ...A  Deleted:  1-16-93  6:36a
This file can be 100% undeleted. Undelete (Y/N)?
```

If you get the message...

> Starting cluster is unavailable. This file cannot be recovered with the UNDELETE command. Press any key to continue.

...you won't be able to recover the entire file with any tool. You may be able to recover parts of the file with some tool other than UNDELETE.

> *Your safest approach with UNDELETE, or any other unerasing program, is to carefully select files for unerasing, beginning with the most important. Because many erased directory entries may point to the same clusters, and only one file can truly own a given cluster, start with your most valuable (or most recent) file you want to unerase and work from there. If you recover an older version of a file, you may make one or more clusters unavailable for subsequent recovery of some other file.*
>
> *If you don't know what the most important files are, use UNDELETE to recover erased files until you are told that some of the clusters are in use by another file. Copy the files you have undeleted to a floppy disk, and then delete them again. You will make those clusters available for other files that you can now recover. Of course, some of these recovered files are fouled up, holding clusters that once belonged to another file. In general, the files with the*

most recent dates will be the ones still intact (because they generally will have the most recent deletion dates).

MWUNDEL: Undelete for Windows

When you install DOS 6.2 in a machine on which Windows already is installed, you are given a choice of installing it as a platform for Windows, a standard DOS machine, or both. If you choose installation for Windows, Setup creates a group called Microsoft Tools containing three icons labeled "Anti-Virus," "Backup," and "Undelete." You will get a copy of a file named MWUNDEL.EXE, a program that requires Windows. If you choose DOS, you get UNDELETE.EXE. If you choose both, you will get both.

MWUNDEL can recover accidentally deleted files and directories. It is most effective when your file was protected by Delete Sentry or Delete Tracker, but you may be able to undelete other files, too. On the other hand, if you delete a file in DOS and go into Windows to run MWUNDEL, you have a fair chance of losing the file because Windows writes to the disk. Your best chance of recovering a file that was lost when you were in Windows is to try to recover it while still in Windows; if it was lost when in DOS, try to recover it before going into Windows.

MWUNDEL is not as robust a program as UNDELETE, and its help screens suggest that if a deleted file is missing too much of its data, you will not be able to use Windows Undelete on the file. Instead, you can use the undelete methods available in UNDELETE for MS-DOS to try to get back any of the data that still exists. On the other hand, MWUNDEL can undelete a directory; UNDELETE cannot (you can try UNFORMAT very carefully, if you are using DOS alone, without Windows).

To undelete a file or directory using MWUNDEL, find the file using the Find button. Choose the Undelete option from the Microsoft Tools group. Use Drive/Dir to change to the directory containing the deleted file or directory. If you don't know where it was when it was deleted, but know its name, you can choose Find Deleted File and let MWUNDEL search for the missing file or directory.

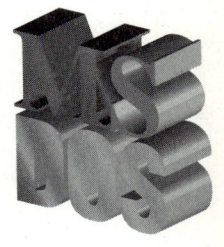

Chapter 19: *Protecting and Recovering Data*

After you have found one or more files, look at their deletion date and current condition in the list of deleted files by clicking on them. Highlight what you want to recover, and then choose the command Undelete or Undelete to.

> *Here is a trick you can do with MWUNDEL but not UNDELETE: if you delete files, and then delete the directory that contained them, you first need to undelete the directory before undeleting the lost files.*

The information you're given on condition is oddly worded. Excellent condition files are those that don't have clusters in use by another file, but may have had one or more clusters overwritten by other files. Good condition files are those with one or more of the clusters in use by other files. Destroyed files are those with no surviving clusters. I would have been less optimistic in my choice of language.

If you want to know the starting cluster of a deleted file or directory, click on the Info button. You will see the information from the list of deleted files displayed in a different format, along with starting cluster information.

After you have highlighted one or more files to undelete, you can click on the Undelete button. For each file, you are asked to enter a new first letter for each of them. Any normal text character will do, so if you don't know, a guess may be fine. Thus, you can delete TEST, select ?EST for recovery, and recover ZEST or PEST. In fact, if you have several copies of a file in your list of deleted files, you can try to recover each of them by providing different first letters.

If you receive a message such as...

```
There is no more deleted directory data on this disk
```

...you must click OK. This is a good time to exit Windows by pressing Alt+F4 and use UNDELETE or other methods for getting this directory back.

About the best part of MWUNDEL is the option Configure Delete Protection in the Options menu along the top menu bar. Configure

Delete Protection allows you to install Sentry, Tracker, or None. None is the default, which is to say no protection at all. The message for this option:

```
Without delete protection, Windows Undelete can often
recover deleted files.
```

Don't plan on it. Do not choose Standard. Choose Sentry, which is explained in the following section.

Choosing Sentry or Tracker causes MWUNDEL to add UNDELETE to your AUTOEXEC.BAT file and writes UNDELETE.INI. MWUNDEL then works with UNDELETE to help you undelete files from Windows.

> **6.2** *An interesting bug in DOS 6 MWUNDEL was that it enabled you to create illegal DOS file names. Fortunately, DOS 6.2 corrects this bug.*

UNDELETE's Sentry

The Sentry option in UNDELETE is extremely powerful. Install the Sentry form of UNDELETE in memory by typing...

UNDELETE /SC

You can place this command in your AUTOEXEC.BAT file so that you can just forget about it. If you are using Windows, you can place this clever line into your AUTOEXEC.BAT by simply clicking Options, Configure Delete Protection or by pressing Alt O, C, and S. Doing this gives you some more questions to answer, as follows:

✔ You can specify that Sentry should save a deleted copy of everything you delete, or only those items that you specify with include and exclude lists. You might choose to exclude *.BK!, for example, if you are a WordPerfect user. If you choose to include *.* and exclude *.BK!, you will keep copies of everything but those WordPerfect backups.

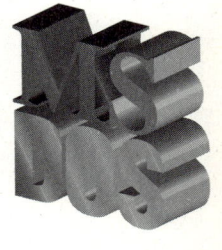

✔ An *archived file* is one that you have backed up, and has the archive bit of the attribute byte set. Presumably these files are less crucial. The default for this option is checked. I would uncheck it so that archived files are saved by Sentry anyway. Anything worth backing up is probably also worth recovering, and backups can't always be trusted.

✔ Windows also asks you to decide when to purge files. There is no reason for the seven-day default proposed. Your computer won't be any heavier on your desktop if you choose 777 days (although the maximum length that Sentry will handle is 255; if you enter **777** days, it will save 255 days in UNDELETE.INI). Power users with little room on their drives might use just one or two days in UNDELETE.INI; dreamier types with lots of space on their drives might leave things at seven.

✔ What should be your limit on disk space for deleted files? It should depend on what you are doing. If your single important task is a 20M database and you have a 60M hard disk, you will want to be able to recover the entire database, so you can set the limit to something like 35 percent to 50 percent. If you run out of disk space, you can always set this number lower.

When you are finished setting these options in Windows, Windows adds the line...

   UNDELETE /LOAD

...as the last line of AUTOEXEC.BAT or AUTOEXEC.SAV (your choice). Your various options are stored in UNDELETE.INI in your DOS directory. UNDELETE is not loaded at all until you run AUTOEXEC.BAT manually or reboot (and run it automatically) or type...

   UNDELETE /LOAD

When you delete a file with UNDELETE /SC in memory, UNDELETE creates a subdirectory under your root directory called SENTRY. Whenever you delete a file, UNDELETE copies the file to a new location; writes the file's size, date, time, and attributes to an entry in the \SENTRY directory; places an ID number instead of the file name in the directory file; and writes the original file name and new ID number in a master file in \SENTRY called CONTROL.FIL. This file is given the attribute "system" which hides and protects it. After the file is fully backed up, UNDELETE then permits the DOS DEL command to delete the file from its original location, and the file appears to be gone.

UNDELETE /S is the most glorious way imaginable to protect your files from accidental deletion. I strongly recommend that every user use this line as one of the last lines in their AUTOEXEC.BAT file. (UNDELETE /LOAD accomplishes the same if Sentry Tracker is specified in UNDELETE.INI.)

Recovering an Erased File Manually

If you have just erased the file you want to recover, recovery is nearly certain. Only one critical item in the directory has been changed during erasure: the first character of the file name in the directory. The entry is otherwise preserved, with a pointer to the FAT. The FAT entries for this file, however, have been zeroed out, and the FAT can't be used to recover the file. But the directory tells you the file's size, so you probably are safe in taking that size in bytes and converting to it clusters, and marking that many consecutive clusters as belonging to the file.

UNDELETE might report...

    Delete Sentry control file not found

or...

    Deletion-tracking file not found

If this is the case, you will be using the DOS file system alone for recovery. The DOS file directory is changed in a very small way when a file listed in it is deleted. The first character of the file is overwritten with an Alt 229. (This is a lowercase Sigma, which looks like a water pistol. Create the character from your keyboard by pressing the Alt key and typing **229** on the numeric keypad.) The FATs also are changed.

Chapter 19: *Protecting and Recovering Data*

> **NOTE**
>
> *The FAT is merely a map, showing where different parts of the file are stored on the hard disk. Each mapped location of the file normally contains information on where to find this piece of the file and where to go next. Each of these entries is erased so that recovery of large, fragmented files is more difficult than recovery of tidy little files.*

You cannot easily view the directory with any of the DOS utilities. Figure 19.2 shows a directory (using DSEDIT on your accompanying disk) in which the file COLLAGE.ZIP has been deleted. Note that the first character of this file is now E5 in hex, which is our Alt 229 water pistol in ASCII.

Figure 19.2

A directory with a deleted file, as displayed by DSEDIT.

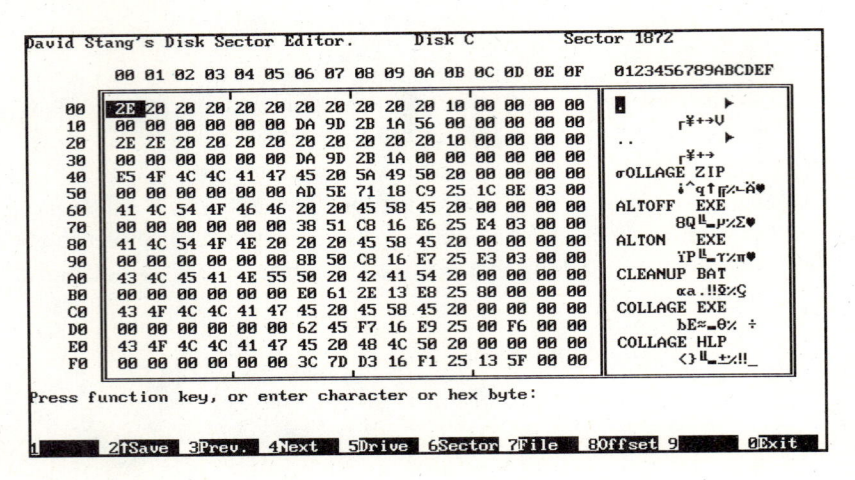

```
David Stang's Disk Sector Editor.      Disk C       Sector 1872
      00 01 02 03 04 05 06 07 08 09 0A 0B 0C 0D 0E 0F   0123456789ABCDEF
  00  2E 20 20 20 20 20 20 20 20 20 10 00 00 00 00 00   .
  10  00 00 00 00 00 00 DA 9D 2B 1A 56 00 00 00 00 00
  20  2E 2E 20 20 20 20 20 20 20 20 10 00 00 00 00 00   ..
  30  00 00 00 00 00 00 DA 9D 2B 1A 00 00 00 00 00 00
  40  E5 4F 4C 4C 41 47 45 20 5A 49 50 20 00 00 00 00   σOLLAGE ZIP
  50  00 00 00 00 00 00 AD 5E 71 18 C9 25 1C 8E 03 00
  60  41 4C 54 4F 46 46 20 20 45 58 45 20 00 00 00 00   ALTOFF  EXE
  70  00 00 00 00 00 00 38 51 C8 16 E6 25 E4 03 00 00
  80  41 4C 54 4F 4E 20 20 20 45 58 45 20 00 00 00 00   ALTON   EXE
  90  00 00 00 00 00 00 8B 50 C8 16 E7 25 E3 03 00 00
  A0  43 4C 45 41 4E 55 50 20 42 41 54 20 00 00 00 00   CLEANUP BAT
  B0  00 00 00 00 00 00 E0 61 2E 13 E8 25 80 00 00 00
  C0  43 4F 4C 4C 41 47 45 20 45 58 45 20 00 00 00 00   COLLAGE EXE
  D0  00 00 00 00 00 00 62 45 F7 16 E9 25 00 F6 00 00
  E0  43 4F 4C 4C 41 47 45 20 48 4C 50 20 00 00 00 00   COLLAGE HLP
  F0  00 00 00 00 00 00 3C 7D D3 16 F1 25 13 5F 00 00
Press function key, or enter character or hex byte:
   1      2↑Save  3Prev.  4Next   5Drive  6Sector 7File   8Offset 9       0Exit
```

An Alternative to SENTRY

Here is a simple batch file alternative to SENTRY. This utility copies the specified file to a directory called C:\GARBAGE (you can specify another drive), and then deletes the file from the original location.

The weakness of this utility, of course, is that it does not purge files from the GARBAGE directory, which continues to grow in size. So, to help you keep track of GARBAGE's size, the following two lines display the directory's current size:

```
echo Current status of C:\GARBAGE
dir c:\garbage ¦ find "file(s)"
```

When the directory starts getting too big, you can purge files manually. You might even want to include these two lines in your AUTOEXEC.BAT file.

SDEL.BAT also includes three error checks. If you don't specify a file name, SDEL reminds you of the syntax. Also, if the specified file does not exist, SDEL notifies that it can't find the specified file. Most importantly, if the specified file already exists in the GARBAGE directory, SDEL displays a warning and the option of continuing or canceling the deletion.

To create SDEL, you need only do three things:

1. Create a directory called GARBAGE on the drive of your choice.

2. Create a keyboard-processing program called ASK.COM by starting DEBUG and entering the following lines:

   E 100 B4 00 CD 16 B4 4C CD 21
   N ASK.COM
   RCX
   8
   W
   Q

   Similar to the CHOICE command, SDEL uses this simple assembly language program to sense what key you press in response to the `Do you want to continue anyway?` prompt. If you press **y** (hex scan code 121) or **Y** (89), SDEL continues and carries out the deletion. If you press **n** (110), **N** (78), or any other key, SDEL aborts the deletion.

3. Create the following batch file.

   ```
   @echo off
   if %1!==! goto oops
   if not exist %1 goto nofile
   if exist c:\garbage\%1 goto already
   :doit
   ```

```
    copy %1 c:\garbage
    del %1
    echo.
    echo %1 safely deleted.
    echo.
    dir c:\garbage ¦ find "file(s)"
    goto end
:already
    echo.
    echo Warning: %1 already exists in C:\GARBAGE
    echo Do you want to continue anyway (Y/N)?
    getkey
    if errorlevel 121 goto doit
    if errorlevel 110 goto end
    if errorlevel 89 goto doit
    if errorlevel 78 goto end
    goto end
:nofile
    echo.
    echo Sorry, %1 does not exist.
    goto end
:oops
    echo.
    echo  Syntax = SDEL filename.ext
    echo.
:end
echo.
```

Understanding Which Is the Most Current Version

One of the most common causes of lost work time is not lost data, but work on the wrong data. If you spend a few hours editing the wrong version of something, you've really fouled things up. Here are some tips for keeping straight on which version is which:

✔ When programming or writing, create a directory just for this program or document. Save the first copy of your file as 01.WK1 (or DBF, WP, and so forth). Save your second as 02.WK1, and so on. When you want to know which version is the latest, there won't be any doubt. And when you need to go back to an older version, you'll be able to. When you are finished with the project, rename your final version, move it to a more meaningful directory, and delete your old copies.

✔ If you find that two directories are very similar, you can use the MOVE command (new with DOS 6.2) to push all the files from one directory into the other. Files that are duplicates won't move. You can compare them manually to see which version you want, and use COPY and DEL to tidy things up.

✔ If you want to view two similar directories side by side, you can use DIRCOMP, available on PCMagNet on CompuServe. The syntax is as follows:

`DIRCOMP DIR1 DIR2`

You will see a list of the two directories, each in alphabetical order. Files of the same name will be listed side by side. If your listing goes by too fast on the screen, type...

`DIRCOMP DIR1 DIR2 ¦ MORE`

Directory Disasters

The directory contains a list of files that are on the disk and information on their starting cluster. This cluster number also happens to be the row in the FAT in which the remaining information on the file begins.

When a file is erased by the user, the first letter of its name in the directory is changed to a special character. Whenever the user accesses the directory (through a DIR or COPY command), DOS treats that file entry as if it weren't there. During a DIR request, DOS doesn't report on the erased file. During a COPY to that medium, DOS finds the first available location in the directory, assuming that the name to be copied does not already occur in the directory, and places the new entry at that location in the directory. An erased file is considered an available location, and the new file name is placed on top of the name of the erased file. Then the file itself is copied to the target disk, covering the old file.

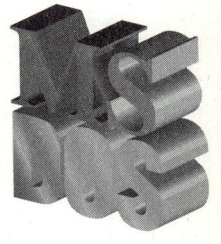

> **NOTE**
>
> DOS doesn't actually erase any of the file contents when you instruct it to. This is because actually erasing the file would take nearly as long as a COPY command. As a result, any file that has been erased can be recovered, providing that no other files have been copied to the disk. Recovering an erased file usually can be done quickly with a program such as UNDELETE, providing that the file has not been overwritten and is not fragmented.

Differences between the Root Directory and Subdirectories

The root directory is the first directory that is read when the machine is booted. Its size is defined by information in the boot sector, as is its starting location. Subdirectories, on the other hand, can be located anywhere on the disk, and can occupy any size, from one cluster on up. A subdirectory is any directory but the root directory. It is a variable-length file that lists other files and directories. Although the boot record defines how to find the root directory, the root directory defines how to find the first layer of subdirectories.

Although DOS maintains two copies of the FAT, it maintains only one copy of the root directory. When FORMAT runs with a /U, it overwrites the root directory, but leaves the subdirectories on a hard disk untouched. Because the root directory has been replaced, there is nothing that references the subdirectories, and they are seemingly lost. The subdirectories, however, all contain some identifying information in their headers that make them unique. Figure 19.3 shows a subdirectory as you normally see it when you type DIR. Notice that it begins with a . entry and a .. entry.

Figure 19.4 shows the first 256 bytes of this directory in hex using DSEDIT (a program on the disk accompanying this book). You can see the . and .. entries at the top right of the screen. In hex, you can see that the first directory entry begins with 2E20202020 (2E hex looks like the dot you see when you type DIR); 32 bytes from the beginning of the first entry, you see the pattern 2E2E202020 (2E2E looks like the double dot). A data recovery utility can use any portion of any such pattern to search for directories on a damaged drive.

Directory Disasters 1041

```
Directory of C:\COLLAGE
.            <DIR>     01-11-93   7:46p
..           <DIR>     01-11-93   7:46p
COLLAGE  ZIP   232988  03-17-92  11:53a
ALTOFF   EXE      996  06-08-91  10:09a
ALTON    EXE      995  06-08-91  10:04a
CLEANUP  BAT      128  09-14-89  12:15p
COLLAGE  EXE    62976  07-23-91   8:43a
COLLAGE  HLP    24339  06-19-91   3:41p
INSTALL  EXE     7462  06-08-91   9:56a
READ     ME      5303  06-20-91   9:07a
S        EXE     6070  06-08-91   8:46p
DS201    PCX     7750  01-16-93   6:38a
SAVE     EXE    27061  06-08-91   9:52a
SHOW     EXE    34317  06-19-91   9:52a
SHOWLITE EXE    26272  06-08-91  10:46a
SNAP     EXE    42421  06-08-91  10:34a
VIEW     EXE    35019  06-08-91   9:51a
20DIR2   PCX    13698  01-16-93   6:50a
20DIR3   PCX    18331  01-16-93   6:51a
      19 file(s)     546126 bytes
                   10690560 bytes free

C:\COLLAGE>
```

Figure 19.3

A subdirectory, after typing DIR.

```
David Stang's Disk Sector Editor.   Disk C       Sector 1872
        00 01 02 03 04 05 06 07 08 09 0A 0B 0C 0D 0E 0F  0123456789ABCDEF
   00   2E 20 20 20 20 20 20 20 20 20 10 00 00 00 00 00  .
   10   00 00 00 00 00 00 DA 9D 2B 1A 56 00 00 00 00 00         ┌¥→V
   20   2E 2E 20 20 20 20 20 20 20 20 10 00 00 00 00 00  ..
   30   00 00 00 00 00 00 DA 9D 2B 1A 00 00 00 00 00 00         ┌¥→
   40   43 4F 4C 4C 41 47 45 20 5A 49 50 20 00 00 00 00  COLLAGE  ZIP
   50   00 00 00 00 00 00 AD 5E 71 18 C9 25 1C 8E 03 00        ¡^q↑╔%∟Ä♥
   60   41 4C 54 4F 46 46 20 20 45 58 45 20 00 00 00 00  ALTOFF   EXE
   70   00 00 00 00 00 00 38 51 C8 16 E6 25 E4 03 00 00        8Q╚▬µ%Σ♥
   80   41 4C 54 4F 4E 20 20 20 45 58 45 20 00 00 00 00  ALTON    EXE
   90   00 00 00 00 00 00 8B 50 C8 16 E7 25 E3 03 00 00        ïP╚▬τ%π♥
   A0   43 4C 45 41 4E 55 50 20 42 41 54 20 00 00 00 00  CLEANUP  BAT
   B0   00 00 00 00 00 00 E0 61 2E 13 E8 25 80 00 00 00        αa.‼Φ%Ç
   C0   43 4F 4C 4C 41 47 45 20 45 58 45 20 00 00 00 00  COLLAGE  EXE
   D0   00 00 00 00 00 00 62 45 F7 16 E9 25 00 F6 00 00        bE≈▬Θ%  ÷
   E0   43 4F 4C 4C 41 47 45 20 48 4C 50 20 00 00 00 00  COLLAGE  HLP
   F0   00 00 00 00 00 00 3C 7D D3 16 F1 25 13 5F 00 00        <}╙▬±%‼_

Press function key, or enter character or hex byte:
 1       2↑Save  3Prev.  4Next   5Drive  6Sector 7File   8Offset 9       0Exit
```

Figure 19.4

The same subdirectory, as displayed by DSEDIT.

Notice that all subdirectories contain a . and a .., reserved names used to point to itself and its parent, respectively. You can search for such characters 32 bytes apart (the width of a directory entry) when you attempt to recover a subdirectory. Once found, you have the list of files it contained. Once you have those, you know the starting cluster of each of these files and its size. From the starting cluster, you can go to the FAT to deduce what other clusters each file occupied. Recovery of files referenced in a directory that is lost when the root directory is overwritten by FORMAT /U (or a virus) is straightforward.

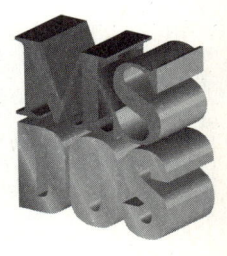

Recovering a Directory Erased with RD

When you delete a directory with RD or RMDIR, you don't delete the directory at all. Because a subdirectory is just a file, you delete it in the same way you delete a file: by replacing the first character of its name with a lowercase sigma—the Greek letter that looks like a water pistol. Figure 19.5 shows a directory listing a valid directory entry, and figure 19.6 shows a directory listing of that same directory after you deleted it. Note that you still know what cluster holds the beginning of the directory.

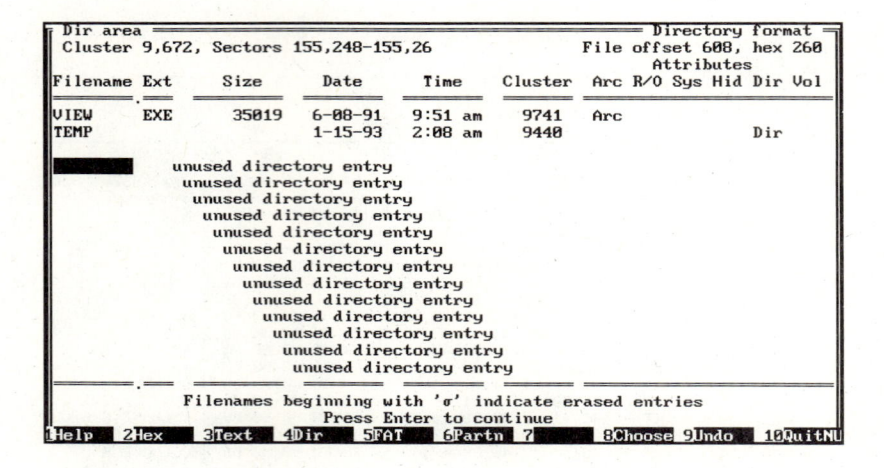

Figure 19.5

A directory with a valid directory, as displayed by Norton Utilities.

```
┌─Dir area ═══════════════════════════════════════════ Directory format─┐
│  Cluster 9,672, Sectors 155,248-155,26              File offset 608, hex 260│
│                                                          Attributes    │
│ Filename Ext     Size      Date      Time    Cluster  Arc R/O Sys Hid Dir Vol│
│                                                                        │
│ VIEW     EXE    35019    6-08-91    9:51 am   9741    Arc              │
│ TEMP                     1-15-93    2:08 am   9440                 Dir │
│ ▓▓▓▓         unused directory entry                                    │
│              unused directory entry                                    │
│              unused directory entry                                    │
│              unused directory entry                                    │
│              unused directory entry                                    │
│              unused directory entry                                    │
│              unused directory entry                                    │
│              unused directory entry                                    │
│              unused directory entry                                    │
│              unused directory entry                                    │
│              unused directory entry                                    │
│              unused directory entry                                    │
│                                                                        │
│         Filenames beginning with 'σ' indicate erased entries           │
│                         Press Enter to continue                        │
│ 1Help  2Hex  3Text  4Dir  5FAT  6Partn  7     8Choose 9Undo  10QuitNU │
└────────────────────────────────────────────────────────────────────────┘
```

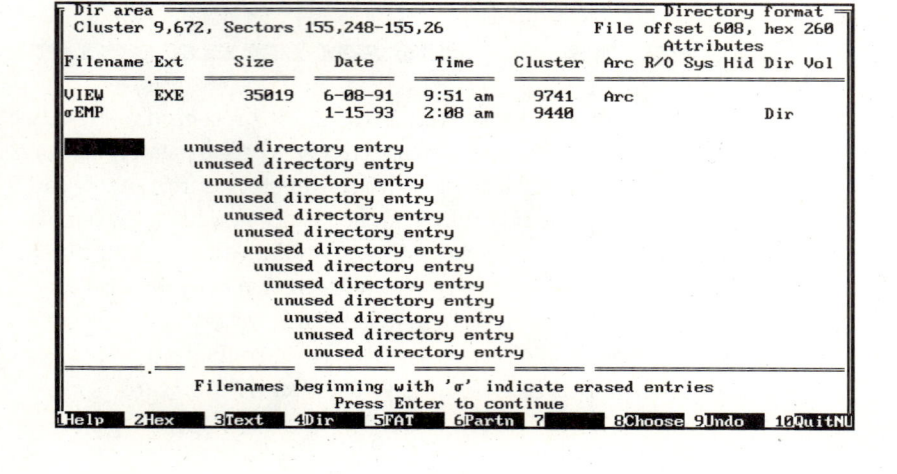

Figure 19.6

A directory with a deleted directory, as displayed by Norton Utilities.

```
┌─Dir area ═══════════════════════════════════════════ Directory format─┐
│  Cluster 9,672, Sectors 155,248-155,26              File offset 608, hex 260│
│                                                          Attributes    │
│ Filename Ext     Size      Date      Time    Cluster  Arc R/O Sys Hid Dir Vol│
│                                                                        │
│ VIEW     EXE    35019    6-08-91    9:51 am   9741    Arc              │
│ σEMP                     1-15-93    2:08 am   9440                 Dir │
│ ▓▓▓▓         unused directory entry                                    │
│              unused directory entry                                    │
│              unused directory entry                                    │
│              unused directory entry                                    │
│              unused directory entry                                    │
│              unused directory entry                                    │
│              unused directory entry                                    │
│              unused directory entry                                    │
│              unused directory entry                                    │
│              unused directory entry                                    │
│              unused directory entry                                    │
│              unused directory entry                                    │
│                                                                        │
│         Filenames beginning with 'σ' indicate erased entries           │
│                         Press Enter to continue                        │
│ 1Help  2Hex  3Text  4Dir  5FAT  6Partn  7     8Choose 9Undo  10QuitNU │
└────────────────────────────────────────────────────────────────────────┘
```

Recovery of a directory could proceed much the same way as recovery of a file, except that you cannot recover files referenced by the directory until it is recognized by DOS. To recover a directory removed by RD, follow these steps:

1. Change to the directory that was the parent of the erased directory.

2. Using a utility, read the directory file.

3. Change the first character of the erased directory name from Alt 229 (which DOS provided) to any valid character.

4. Exit your utility and change to the unerased directory by using the CD command.

5. Assuming that you deleted all files in this directory before removing the directory (a requirement of RD), you need to undelete all of these files. UNDELETE can do this for you, if the files have not been overwritten.

Although UNDELETE will not recover a deleted directory, you can do it if you have not created or deleted on that drive since the time you deleted the directory. Simply go to the directory that listed the directory you just deleted. Create a directory with the exact same name as the one you just deleted. Now change to this directory and run UNDELETE.

The following six steps create the problem:

```
MD MONKEYS
CD MONKEYS
COPY C:\COMMAND.COM
DEL COMMAND.COM
CD..
RD MONKEYS
```

The following three steps solve it:

```
MD MONKEYS
CD MONKEYS
UNDELETE
```

Recovering an Overwritten Root Directory

When a file is overwritten, something writes on top of it. Recovery of an overwritten sector is never possible. If a large file is partially overwritten, recovery of the part not overwritten is possible. The root directory is a moderately large file that is sometimes overwritten by a virus or an anti-virus program. (The Form virus and other viruses derived from Stoned, one of the earliest boot viruses, for example, overwrite the second sector of the root directory on 1.44M floppy disks, placing a copy of the boot record there. If you have more than 16 files in your root directory on such a floppy disk, you lose your easy ability to access them from file 17 on.)

Recovering the files formerly listed in an overwritten sector of the root directory turns out to be unbelievably simple, if all you want back is your files, and don't care what their exact names should be. Suppose that Stoned or Form has just infected your 1.44M floppy disk, and you have lost the second sector of your root directory on that floppy disk. Follow these steps:

1. Edit the root directory with your sector editor, placing valid names where the names go. (You can name all files "A" if you want.)

2. Exit your sector editor and delete all the files whose names you have just created. You won't write to the FAT, because the root directory will say that each of these fake files has a size of 0, and doesn't have a starting cluster. Your deletions will, however, create 16 valid placeholders in the directory.

3. If you had more than 32 files in the root directory when the second sector was overwritten, you will now be able to use the files from 32 on in the list.

4. Run CHKDSK /F on this disk. CHKDSK will notice that you have up to 16 lost chains (files). They are "lost" because, although they have FAT entries (the virus did not overwrite the FAT), they don't have valid root directory entries. Converting lost chains to files actually means writing information in the root directory that corresponds with what is found in the FAT. All your new files will now be a multiple of cluster

size (for example, a 1-byte file will be 512 bytes on this 1.44M floppy disk).

5. CHKDSK /F provides some bizarre names for your recovered files because it cannot guess what the correct names should be. You can type...

   `TYPE FILE0000.CHK`

   ...to see what the name is supposed to be. If it looks like a program, rename it to ABC.COM or ABC.EXE and run it. DOS 6.2 checks inside the file to see whether it is an EXE or COM file before running it, so there is no harm done. (If the file's first two bytes are MZ, it probably is an EXE file.)

Naturally, in all this detective work you also will want to explore the cause of the problem and take steps to prevent its recurrence. Although recovering an overwritten sector makes you look like a miracle worker, you aren't paid well enough to walk on water every day!

Understanding COMMAND.COM

COMMAND.COM is the least of our problems. Nearly nothing can go wrong with it, and nearly everything can be easily corrected. This section, therefore, will be short.

You know that COMMAND.COM loads late in the boot sequence. If you receive the message...

   `Bad or missing Command interpreter`

...it means that IO.SYS (the first of the two hidden system files) has successfully loaded. It probably doesn't mean "bad," but rather "missing." A user can do this by deleting all files in the root directory. Solve your problem by booting with a bootable floppy disk, formatted with the same version of DOS as your hard disk is running. After you've finished booting, look in your root directory for COMMAND.COM. If it is not there, check CONFIG.SYS for a line that begins with SHELL =. If there is such a line, then CONFIG.SYS instructed the loading operating system to look outside the root directory for COMMAND.COM. Look in that directory for

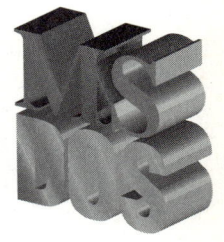

COMMAND.COM. After you've learned that, you can simply copy COMMAND.COM from drive A to wherever it belongs on drive C.

Preventing such problems is easy. First, move COMMAND.COM from your root directory to your DOS directory with the command...

```
MOVE C:\COMMAND.COM C:\DOS\COMMAND.COM
```

Now make it read-only and hidden with the command...

```
ATTRIB +R +H C:\DOS\COMMAND.COM
```

Now add this line to CONFIG.SYS...

```
SHELL=C:\DOS\COMMAND.COM C:\DOS\ /P
```

The SHELL command specifies that you want to do something different with your DOS shell than is specified in your hidden system files (which tell you that COMMAND.COM is the name of the shell and that it is located in the root directory). The first part of the syntax tells the loading operating system that COMMAND.COM is located in C:\DOS. The /P makes this setup permanent so that typing...

```
EXIT
```

...at the DOS prompt will not exit this COMMAND.COM. You can run a second copy of COMMAND.COM by typing...

```
COMMAND
```

... and then exit it by typing...

```
EXIT
```

We just won't lose the main guy. With the /P switch, DOS will run AUTOEXEC.BAT before showing the command prompt.

If you receive the message...

```
Incorrect DOS version
```

...you have attempted to run a version of a program that is incompatible with the COMMAND.COM loaded in memory. This error will be common as you go through the throes of upgrading to DOS 6.2. Most commonly, you will see this from programs, such as COMMAND.COM, FORMAT, and CHKDSK from your old DOS 5. Whenever you see such a message, delete the old version of the program that produced the message (unless you are sharing the system with someone who runs an older version of DOS, and you are booting with your personal disks from drive A).

> **NOTE** *Some viruses infect COMMAND.COM. To detect these viruses, it is a simple matter to memorize the size of COMMAND.COM in bytes and, if you see it has grown by a few thousand bytes, to wonder whether you are infected.*
>
> *To answer the question, boot from a clean floppy disk and run a scanner, such as MSAV (the anti-virus program that comes with DOS 6.2, which is discussed in the next chapter). If you don't think you can memorize the correct size of COMMAND.COM, simply back it up to the same directory and name it COMMAND.BAK. COMMAND.BAK won't get infected with a virus, so if they are the same size, COMMAND.COM probably is not infected. If COMMAND.COM is larger, something is wrong.*

The Hidden System Files

DOS 6.2 loads and executes programs found in two hidden system files prior to loading CONFIG.SYS, COMMAND.COM, or AUTOEXEC.BAT. The first of these programs, IO.SYS, sets up your machine for all the basic input and output it will need to do. The second, MSDOS.SYS, prepares a foundation for DOS, and provides many basic features of the operating system.

These files never seem to get damaged. They are not infected by any common virus. The heads of your hard disk never seem to fly off and dent them. I don't even known why I'm writing this section, except that you would ask for it if I didn't.

Sometimes, however, these files are missing. If they are, you will see the message:

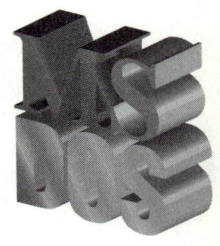

```
Non-System disk or disk error.
Replace and press any key when ready.
```

This message is stored at the bottom of the boot record, and is displayed whenever one of these files (also listed in the boot record) cannot be found.

When you FORMAT without using /S, you create a boot record (with this message), two FATs, and a root directory. When you add a /S to the command line, you add two hidden system files and COMMAND.COM to the drive. In both cases, the boot record is identical.

If you want to make a disk bootable, you won't need to add a boot record, FATs, or a root directory—they already are there. You need to add the two hidden system files and COMMAND.COM. The DOS 6.2 SYS command will do this for you just fine. To make a disk in drive A bootable, type...

SYS A:

This command looks for the two hidden system files and COMMAND.COM on the default drive. If you want to specify where SYS should find them, you can enter a command to copy them from drive B to A, as follows...

SYS B: A:

If SYS can't copy COMMAND.COM, can't find what it is looking for, can't find room on the destination for these three files, or the disk is write-protected, you are notified.

Checking for Changes with UNFORMAT

The DOS 6.2 UNFORMAT includes a switch to compare the system area of a drive with a stored file. If a boot virus has infected a drive, it changes the system area. To determine whether the system area has been changed, follow these steps:

1. Boot with an uninfected, write-protected disk.
2. Type...

   UNFORMAT C: /J

The Hidden System Files

...if you want to search for possible changes on drive C. The J means "just check." Compare with MIRROR.FIL (by answering the next prompt by pressing L) or with MIRROR.BAK (by pressing P). If you want to compare with a known clean version of MIRROR.FIL, you can change the attributes on MIRROR.FIL, rename it, copy a known clean copy of MIRROR.FIL from a floppy disk to the hard disk, and then run this command.

If there is no change, you see the message `The MIRROR image file has been validated. The system area of drive C has been verified to agree with the MIRROR image file.` Because a virus will not modify the file, any mismatch will be of the system area.

Damaged FATs

The FAT contains an entry for each cluster on the disk. A FAT entry has a few values, as follows:

- ✔ An indicator that the cluster is unused.
- ✔ An indicator that the associated cluster has been damaged somehow—is a bad cluster—and should not be used.
- ✔ A pointer to the next cluster for a given file.
- ✔ A marker indicating that this is the last cluster occupied by the file.

The pointer for the next cluster allows for what is called a *linked list*: once you start looking up clusters associated with a given file, each FAT entry tells you what the next cluster is. At the end of the linked list is a special indicator that indicates there are no more clusters associated with the file.

FAT damage comes in several forms:

- ✔ Lost clusters or lost allocation units in which one or more entries in the FAT are not referenced by any directory.

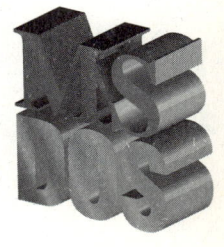

- ✔ Cross-links in which two or more FAT entries point to the same FAT entry.

- ✔ Allocation errors in which the number of FAT entries used by a file does not correspond with the file size as reported in a directory.

- ✔ Mismatched FATs in which the information in one copy of the FAT does not match the information of the other copy.

FATs and the Root Directory during File Copy

What is the order of the process when DOS writes a new file to the disk? Assuming that you issue the command to COPY some huge file to a floppy disk, the DOS writing sequence is as follows:

1. DOS determines where in the directory the file name should be placed. This is the first empty or erased entry.

2. DOS copies the file name to the directory. No size is set yet, and the DIR command will show a file size of 0. No attributes are copied. Initially, the date is set to the current system date and the time is set to the current system time. The archive attribute bit is set, meaning that the destination copy has never been archived.

3. DOS copies the file itself. DOS reads the first FAT on the destination drive and finds a suitable starting location for this file. In DOS 3.3 and later, this will be the first FAT entry that is followed by a sufficient number of contiguous clusters in which the entire file can be accommodated without fragmentation, based on the file size as specified in the origin directory. In DOS 3.3 and later, if there is no such grouping of contiguous clusters, it begins with the first empty FAT entry and fills all available FAT entries, until the file has been stored.

4. DOS uses the directory size information of the origin file to decide how much to copy. If a 1K file has a directory size of 10

bytes, only the first 10 bytes are copied. The destination directory will show a size of 10 bytes.

5. If the origin directory shows a size larger than the FAT says the file is, only the actual file size (as defined in the original FAT) is copied. If, for example, a 1K file has an end-of-file marker at the end of the file and occupies 1K clusters in the FAT but shows 2K in the directory, then only 1K will be copied. The destination directory, however, will show the original directory size of 2K, and sufficient clusters will be allocated to accommodate this new size (on a 360K disk, this will be 4 clusters of 512 bytes each).

6. After the file has been written to the first copy of the FAT, the second FAT is updated to correspond with the first FAT's entries.

7. DOS now reads the directory it has just updated and attempts to record the starting cluster for this file, the size, the date, and the time (from the origin file). That information is now written in the directory entry for the file. If you open the drive door at this moment, you receive the message `Error reading drive`, rather than the message `Error writing drive`. Lost clusters will be created if this operation is interrupted after the FATs are written and before the directory is given a starting cluster pointer.

Using CHKDSK

CHKDSK issued without any switches is a safe command for looking at the condition of your drive. You'll get a report on how large it is, how full it is, and even how much memory is in your computer. CHKDSK, in fact, is a great tool for spotting a virus such as Stoned or FORM. In DOS 6.2, your 640K+ computer should report 655,360 total bytes memory with CHKDSK (a kilobyte is 1,024 bytes, so 655,360/1,024=640K). If you have booted and a member of the Stoned family of viruses is present, CHKDSK will report 2K less. Other boot viruses are likely to change this number too, but by different amounts.

Chapter 19: *Protecting and Recovering Data*

CHKDSK has another option that can be useful. If you want to watch CHKDSK work, you can run it with the /V switch. This slows CHKDSK down to a speed at which your screen can display all your files, but not slow enough to read. Nothing else useful is produced by this switch, unless you want a list of all the files on the drive, in which case you can type...

```
CHKDSK /V > bagem
```

...in which *bagem* is a file in which you want to "bag" the names and directories of all your files. Of course, you also can perform this pipe (with the >) with the DIR command by typing...

```
DIR C:\ /S/ON/B > bagem
```

The /S switch searches the subdirectories of what you have specified, the /ON does things in order of name, and /B uses bare format without any heading or summary information. Experiment with the various options if you need a list of files.

Besides catching boot viruses and telling you how little free space remains on your drive, what good is CHKDSK? The answer is plenty, if you use it wisely. With the /F switch, this command will fix your FAT and directories to correspond to each other. This process usually is a good thing. If a file is listed as longer or shorter in the directory than the FAT claims it is, you will receive the error message...

```
Allocation error. Size adjusted
```

...and the directory entry will be set to match the number of clusters used in the FAT. If you see the error message...

```
Lost clusters in lost chains
```

...the fix is to add a root directory file name for each chain found in the FAT that had no directory entry. (These files may have once been in any directory; they now will be listed in the root directory.)

CHKDSK /F might also report that there are cross-linked files, in which two or more chains in the FAT both reference the same cluster. Because only one of these files can be the valid owner of this cluster, one is surely wrong. A simple fix for one of these two files is to copy both to a floppy disk, and then delete both from your hard disk, and then copy them back. You will have fixed the FAT and ensured that whoever owns that cluster now does not need to share it.

> **NOTE** *If you delete one of the files before copying it, you will make things worse—the cross-linked cluster will not be owned by anyone, and the second file will be recovered as two chains.*

If you frequently find errors when running CHKDSK and you frequently run CHKDSK, then you have some problem worth looking into. Perhaps you reboot the machine while files are being written. Perhaps an ornery program often hangs up the machine when files are opened. Perhaps you remove floppy disks from the drive before the drive light goes out. Whatever the cause, fix the problem.

Understanding the Boot Record

The *boot record* is located in the *boot sector.* This sector is the first on a floppy disk (side 0, cylinder 0, sector 1), and the first sector to be read after the master boot record (MBR) on a hard disk (normally side 1, cylinder 0, sector 1). This is not the Master Boot Record created during partitioning with FDISK. Because the boot record is so important, understanding it is important, and because it occupies just one sector (512 bytes), understanding it is possible.

You can think of the boot record in terms of what information is in it, and where each item of information is located. Location can be defined precisely in terms of how many bytes from the beginning of the sector the item begins, and how many bytes the item uses. The distance from the beginning of the sector is sometimes called the *offset* or *byte offset*. The first byte is located at offset 0.

Table 19.1 lists some offsets and the information contained at those locations.

Table 19.1
Offsets and Their Meanings

Offset	Meaning
4 to 10	Version of MS-DOS with which the disk has been formatted
11 to 12	Number of bytes in each sector
13	Number of sectors in each cluster
14 to 15	Number of reserved sectors
16	Number of copies of the FAT
17 to 18	Number of entries in the root directory
19 to 20	Number of sectors on the disk
21	Disk type
377 to 467	Error messages
470 to 491	Names of the two hidden system files

The first 30 or so bytes of a boot record are very important to DOS. If you damage these bytes on a floppy disk by changing them to your mother's maiden name, for example, and then try to read that floppy disk (with a directory command, for example), DOS will laugh at you and tell you...

```
General failure error reading drive A
```

This is because without the information, DOS is clueless on how big the root directory is, or where it starts. A general failure error usually means that the boot record is wrong. It need not mean anything more. Zigabytes of information are thrown in the trash every day in the U.S. due to just a few missing bytes at the top of a boot record. Lucky our trash is full, and you know all about data recovery.

> **TIP** *One way to repair a boot record is to borrow a boot record from another, identical drive, and then paste it into where it belongs on this disk. (Note that this is something you*

will want to practice from floppy disk to floppy disk because you could wind up with a 360K hard disk if you make a mistake.)

Another way is to FORMAT the drive, and then run UNFORMAT. Practice with this trick on an experimental floppy disk before you need it.

Another way is to display a legitimate boot record on one screen, and manually edit the first 30 bytes (60 hex characters) or so of the culprit drive's boot record, save your work, and try again. Use a sector editor for this trick.

Working with the Master Boot Record

The Master Boot Record is a program located in the master boot sector, which happens to be located on side 0 (the top of your hard disk), cylinder 0 (the outermost band that your heads can read), sector 1. Within this sector is both the main program (which is abbreviated MBR) and a database it reads. That database, called the *partition table*, defines the logical drives you have created with FDISK. It also tells the MBR where to tell the heads to go next, because they will be mighty interested in reading the boot record. The boot record, created with FORMAT, is the next sector that will be read; it is found at the start of every logical drive. When a logical drive is marked active, its boot record is designated as the special one you will read after the MBR. Normally, you will boot from drive C, which normally begins just below the MBR, on side 1, cylinder 0, sector 1.

Having said all that, you should notice that some boot viruses infect the boot sector of disks and MBRs of hard disks.

Repairing the Master Boot Record (Partition Table)

Each disk has a number of concentric tracks. Each track is subdivided into a number of sectors. Each track has the same number of sectors. Tracks are numbered, as are sectors. Any given area on the disk can be accessed if a request is made to read or write data into or out of track X, sector Y. The read or write command is given to the disk controller, which is an interface between the computer itself and the hard disk. The controller figures out what commands to send to the hard disk, the hard disk responds, and the information is read or written as directed.

There are two parts of the Master Boot Record that can be damaged: the program (at the top of the sector) and the data or partition table (near the bottom). Repairing the program is simple. If you are running DOS 5 or DOS 6.2, boot with an uninfected, write-protected floppy disk by typing...

    FDISK /MBR

This command replaces the program. Now try booting with the hard disk. If you can boot, and CHKDSK shows the drive to be the same size as it used to be, you are finished. If you need to edit the partition table, you need to be sure that you enter information exactly as it was before the damage, or you risk losing everything on logical and extended partitions (D, E, and so forth). If you have a machine configured identically to the way this one used to be, try typing the command...

    FDISK /STATUS

...to see how things are partitioned. Only if things are very wrong should you run FDISK without any switches. This is the world's most dangerous command:

    FDISK

Repairing the Master Boot Record (Partition Table)   1057

> **STOP**
>
> *Seek legal counsel before doing this because you may be unemployed this afternoon. You easily can lose everything with just a keystroke or two in the wrong direction. (Are you worried yet? I hope so.) You can exit from FDISK with Esc, as you can see in the bottom line of figure 19.7.*

```
                       MS-DOS Version 6
                    Fixed Disk Setup Program
             (C)Copyright Microsoft Corp. 1983 - 1993

                         FDISK Options

Current fixed disk drive: 1

Choose one of the following:

1. Create DOS partition or Logical DOS Drive
2. Set active partition
3. Delete partition or Logical DOS Drive
4. Display partition information


Enter choice: [1]




Press Esc to exit FDISK
```

Figure 19.7

The opening screen of FDISK.

Another way to peek at your partition table information, to see how your logical drives are organized, is to use the command...

UNFORMAT /L /PARTN /TEST

This command displays the hard disk partition table without modifying it. You'll see the type; size in bytes and sectors; starting cylinder, head, and sector of each partition; and ending cylinder, head, and sector of each partition. This command is more informative than FDISK /STATUS.

> **NOTE**
>
> *Note that viruses rarely modify the partition table information, so your view of the partition table will not be much of a clue as to whether a virus is here or not.*

Recovering from an Accidental Hard Disk Format

A high-level format is performed by the DOS FORMAT command. It rewrites the boot, FAT, and root directory sectors of the disk and reads every cluster looking for unreadable ones so as to flag them in the FAT. There are utilities that keep a copy of these critical tracks in the last clusters of the drive so that they can be located to reconstruct the FAT and root directory in case of accidental FORMAT.

Recovering from a DOS 6.2 FORMAT is easily accomplished with UNFORMAT if you do so moments after finishing formatting and you did not run FORMAT with /U. UNFORMAT is another DOS 6.2 rescue tool (originally from Central Point Software, Inc.). UNFORMAT attempts to recover all the files lost after a format, assuming that you haven't been using the MIRROR command. (If you have been using MIRROR, you can use MIRROR to recover, too.) UNFORMAT runs in two phases: search and repair. The search phase is safe, and you get an opportunity to shut your machine off and take out more insurance before moving on to phase 2. If you don't believe that this trick could possibly work, try this experiment by typing...

```
FORMAT A:
COPY *.* A:
FORMAT A:
UNFORMAT A:
```

You should get all your stuff back.

There is an error in the Microsoft documentation shipped with DOS 6.2. The help displayed by UNFORMAT /? is different than the information displayed by MS-DOS Help. UNFORMAT /? lists several switches, such as /J and /PARTN, which are omitted from HELP UNFORMAT.

> **AUTHOR'S NOTE**
>
> *A low-level format is a prerequisite to a high-level format. A low-level format actually writes the sectors on the disk along with the address marks that identify them. The DOS FORMAT command will only do a low-level format on floppy disks, not on hard disks.*
>
> *The low-level formatting of hard disks is usually done by routines built into the ROM BIOS. On the XT class machines, the format routine is in the disk BIOS, and is invoked by jumping to it with the G command from DEBUG. On AT class machines it is usually an entry in the Setup menu that you invoke by pressing Ctrl+Alt+Esc or some other arcane key combination. Often, third-party software comes with a drive to perform the low-level format. Low-level formatting can be more destructive than high-level formatting. Read the documentation before using such software.*

Recovering Files from Damaged Media

What if during a COPY command, you see the message...

```
Sector not found reading drive  A
Abort, Retry, Ignore, Fail?
```

or perhaps...

```
Data error reading
```

During DISKCOPY, you may see...

```
Unrecoverable read error on A
```

What do these messages mean? The following sections shed some light on these topics.

COPY Clues

The /V option with the COPY command only verifies that it has written what it tried to write. The destination medium is verified, not the source medium. If what is read is damaged, what is written will be damaged.

When you use COPY, you should always respond to the message...

    Abort, Retry, Ignore

...by pressing R (for retry) up to six times or so. Any hard errors—such as a pinhole on the disk—can't be recovered, but any soft errors—weak recording, dust, and so on—are likely to be overcome with enough patience.

COPY detects an error when it either can't read the sector or the CRC at the end of the sector, or when the information read produces a CRC that does not match the CRC recorded at the end of the sector.

COPY doesn't list a file to the screen until the copy is complete, so if you see file X listed and then see an error message, such as

    Sector not found reading drive A

...it means that X is OK, but the next file in the copy process is likely to be damaged.

If you know that a disk has been damaged (you just grabbed it from your dog), you can do a quick check on the extent of the damage by using the COPY command. Simply copy everything to another floppy disk and press I (for ignore) at each prompt. You will be able to see how many files, if any, have been damaged and which ones they are.

DISKCOPY

If a sector mark is damaged and you use DISKCOPY to copy to an unformatted disk, DISKCOPY will create a damaged sector mark. Subsequent attempts to read your copy may produce messages such as Sector not found during read of xxx. Subsequent attempts to copy (with COPY) to this destination floppy disk may produce the error message Sector not found during write of xxx. DISKCOPY will not physically damage a floppy disk, but it will attempt to mimic a physical defect on the source, making a logical or soft error on the target. Such error messages are symptoms of media damage. One sector that the command attempted to access was not readable or writable.

> *You also should know that with DISKCOPY, if files are fragmented on the source, they will be fragmented on the target. COPY, on the other hand, picks up one file at a time, no matter how fragmented, and attempts to place it in contiguous sectors on the destination. When copying to a newly formatted floppy disk, the COPY command eliminates any fragmentation on the source.*

Recovery

There are several recovery procedures, each a bit more cumbersome and powerful than the others, as follows:

- If you can perform a DIR of the media without error, try copying all files (or the files that appear to be sitting on damaged sectors) to another disk. If the problem is on a floppy disk, you'll want to copy to another formatted floppy disk. If the problem is on a hard disk, you can copy the affected file to a new name in the current directory, or a new directory, or a floppy disk.

- If you see the message Abort, Retry, Ignore, DOS is trying to tell you there is a problem. In fact, DOS already is on its third try. Don't select Abort—that gives up, and data recovery acts like you never give up. Don't choose Ignore yet. Ignore copies the file, along with a problem. Unless this is an unimportant word processing file, you don't want such a problem in the destination. COM, EXE, OVL, SYS, BIN, and WKS are all files that are permanently damaged with Ignore. Use Retry at least six times.

- If the problem is on a floppy disk, remove it from the drive, use your index and middle fingers to turn the disk in its jacket, center the disk in its jacket, put it back in your drive, cross those two fingers, and select Retry.

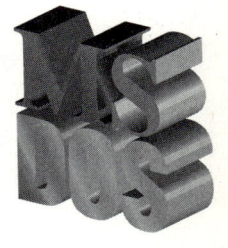

✔ If your media is corrupted beyond recognition, it is time to use your favorite sector editor and try to copy the sectors you can salvage.

Data recovery is serious business. We just hit some highlights in this chapter. If you've lost data, then you must do data recovery. May the force be with you!

Summary

Every day, the value of your computer goes down. And every day, the value of the information in it goes up. With every hard disk sold, there is more stored data and more data to ultimately recover. This will mean that data recovery experts are in shorter supply than ever. If you are good at data recovery, you won't just be a hero in your company. You'll be in a position to go out and get a *real* job. After all, most folks don't seem to be very good at data recovery these days.

What trends will we see in the future? Expect to see sturdier hardware to help reduce data loss. Expect to see Windows and other fancy software used more and more, which will invite more software bugs. So too will you see more viruses and virus removal programs. Users, on average, will get dumber relative to the task. This is because we keep hiring new users (and that pulls the average down) and because the job of recovering network servers, recovering data in OS/2 and NT, and so on, is getting harder.

Thus, having skill in data recovery becomes more and more important. "Murphy" won't visit just *after* a backup, but just *before*. Start now to learn these skills and use your leverage as a data recovery expert for job security and advancement.

MS DOS

CHAPTER 20

Battling Viruses with DOS 6.2

by David Stang

Driving a computer was never quite as easy as driving a car. Now, with computer viruses, it has become more dangerous, too. This is not really a chapter about how to use the new antivirus products bundled with DOS 6.2, although we will cover them. This chapter is about viruses and what you should know to be able to drive your computer safely.

Defining a Virus

Let's begin by defining the term "computer virus." Folks are starting to use the term to refer to all sorts of naughty, unwanted software, but more precision in the definition makes discussion easier.

A *computer virus* is a small program that attaches to other programs and hides in them. Viruses thus require "hosts" and are never stand-alone programs. All viruses replicate, making additional copies of themselves. Most viruses are quite small: the average size of the 987 viruses I have measured is only 1,220 bytes.

A *worm* is software that does not hide in other programs, but is self-sufficient, stand-alone code. Worms, like viruses, make additional copies of themselves.

A *Trojan horse* is a stand-alone program like a worm. Unlike either a virus or a worm, though, it does not make copies of itself.

A *bug* is just a programming error. Bugs were named by Grace Hopper and her gang back in the days of the first computers, when they found a dead moth (which, entomologists note, is not a "bug" at all) lodged in a formerly moving part. Technically, a bug is like a virus in that it hides in a program and requires a host. It is like a Trojan horse in that it does not reproduce. But unlike viruses, bugs occur by accident, rather than by a deliberate act. Bug removal is called *debugging*.

A *joke program* is any code that might simulate the effects of a virus, but does not replicate or cause damage.

A *dropper* is any program that contains a virus and is intended to release the virus when the dropper itself is run. The dropper usually contains the virus in encrypted form so that your scanner does not find any problem with it when it is scanned. I have 155 droppers in my collection of viruses, and the number is growing.

Viruses, worms, Trojans, and bugs can all damage your data, although this is not always the case.

Classifying Viruses

Viruses can be classified in many different ways. Each of these classifications provides another way of understanding the problem.

Viruses can be classified by whether they infect files or the boot areas of disks. Although over half of all infections are from viruses that infect boot areas, only about four percent of virus strains infect the floppy boot record.

If a virus infects files, it may infect only COM files (51 percent of all strains), only EXE files (12 percent of all strains), or both COM and EXE files (31 percent of strains). Some viruses also infect SYS, BIN, OV*, and other file types. A few add their code to both files and boot sectors. Not all viruses that infect COM files infect COMMAND.COM. A few viruses infect COMMAND.COM only (such as Lehigh), many infect all COM files except COMMAND.COM (such as Jerusalem), and some infect all COM files, including COMMAND.COM (such as Frodo). You can get a better sense of what a virus's likely victims are from figure 20.1.

Figure 20.1

What files viruses infect.

A virus doesn't do anything until the program containing it is run, or the boot/master boot sector containing it is loaded and run. When the program is executed, does the virus become memory-resident? All boot viruses and about 60 percent of file viruses become memory-resident. Other viruses sometimes are called *direct action* because they infect immediately whenever an infected program is run.

When a virus attaches to one of your programs, it generally attaches in such a way that its code executes before your program does. If its code is added at the top of your program, the virus is called *prepending*. This is a simple method for attachment to COM files. Often the first bytes of an infected program are a "jump" the virus has placed there, and execution jumps immediately to the virus code, which it has placed at the bottom of the original code. This is called an *appending* virus. There are many other ingenious methods by which viruses can attach to your code.

A few viruses overwrite your programs when they infect them. When a program is overwritten, part or all of its original code is replaced by the virus's code. When your program is overwritten, it will not run; when it won't run, you are sure to detect the virus shortly. As a result, you rarely encounter overwriting viruses "in the wild" (outside of the virus researcher's lab). An overwriting virus cannot be removed from a program in such a way that the program will work again.

Viruses try to be sneaky, and some incorporate ingenious means of escaping your watchful eye. Although 78 percent of all the viruses we have studied use no encryption whatsoever, 14 percent contain an encrypted message, and 8 percent are entirely encrypted.

A *polymorphic virus* is one that can take dozens or hundreds of different forms. Polymorphic viruses are not inherently more dangerous than other viruses, but they are more difficult to detect with anti-virus software, because they can't be caught by matching scan strings. (A *scan string* is a sequence of a few bytes unique to a particular virus, which can be used by a scanner to search your files. If a match is found, the scanner can conclude that the file or boot sector is infected with whatever virus corresponds to the found scan string.) At the time this book was published, there were at least 27 polymorphic viruses, with many more on the way.

In their efforts to avoid detection, virus authors are now building stealth capabilities into their new viruses. A *stealth virus* is one that escapes some method of detection. When Frodo, for example, is in memory, you won't see that it has added any bytes to any of your files. You likely won't find it in any file containing it if all you do is use the TYPE command. And you won't see it listed as a TSR when you run MEM. When this book was published, there were 183 viruses that used one or more stealth techniques.

Understanding Where Viruses Come From

Most virus authors do not sign their work, and it usually requires some detective work to determine where a virus has come from. Table 20.1 shows the place of origin of several viruses. Information for this table was derived from V-Base, the Virus Research Center's Computer Virus Database. (V-Base is included on the disk accompanying this book.) Of the 1,653 viruses described in this database, the place of origin is known for only a handful. Most viruses are first detected at a university or in a city having a university. Most come from industrialized nations.

As a percentage of all computer users, virus authors are more abundant in countries not sharing western concerns for intellectual property. In Asia, Africa, South America, and Eastern Europe there are few copyright laws. Books and software are frequently pirated, and viruses are common.

The frequency of some locations (Bulgaria, for instance) is a result of one or two prolific authors rather than tens of authors. Table 20.1 shows countries producing 10 or more viruses.

Table 20.1
Tallies by Country of Origin

Country	Number of Viruses
Bulgaria	97
Germany	40
Indonesia	14

continues

Table 20.1, Continued
Tallies by Country of Origin

Country	Number of Viruses
Israel	16
Poland	15
Taiwan	18
The Netherlands	13
USA	32
USSR	56

Who Writes Viruses?

Very few virus authors have stepped forward and invited interviews. From what we know, most authors are high school or college students. Nearly all are white males. Most are accomplished programmers in assembly language and perhaps other languages. Motives vary, and we can only speculate. But some authors hint at their motives through quotes in their viruses. Following are some possible motives:

- ✔ Some virus authors are angry. You can infer this from messages in some viruses, such as: `F*** the system (c) 1990`, `Revenge Attacker`, `Death to Pascal`.

- ✔ Some viruses seek attention or recognition for the programming skill of the author. Inside many viruses you can find the names of virus writing groups, such as Armagedon, European Cracking Crew, MAD Virus Factory, Youngsters against McAfee (YAM), HUNGARIAN VIRUS DEVELOPING LABORATORY, Damage inc., and RABID.

- ✔ Some viruses may be written to honor the author's hero: The Eddie viruses, for instance, pay homage to the skeleton mascot of the heavy metal band Iron Maiden, with messages such as `Eddie lives...somewhere in time`. The Ashar virus says, `Dedicated to the dynamic memories of millions of virus who`

Defining a Virus 1071

are no longer with us today. And the Kinnison virus is dedicated to the memory of Sam Kinnison.

- ✔ Some viruses seem to be written by those opposing the blatant software piracy that contributes to the spread of viruses with messages such as `Criminal, be a wiseguy and turn yourself in, if you don't I will`, `Next time be careful with illegal stuff`, `WARNING : USE ONLY ORGINAL PROGRAMS. DON^T COPY IT _ now .. I AM ILL !!`.

- ✔ Some authors do it out of a desire for immortality or the power that is associated with those who create life: `The Big Joke rules forever.`

- ✔ Some see virus writing as a marvelous game, in which they write code to defeat anti-virus products, with messages such as: `I'm sorry John McAfee (NOT!)`, `We have a right to live!!!!!!!!`, `Patricia: Grow some programming knowledge.`

- ✔ Some think viruses are merely funny jokes. Messages from a few such viruses include: `APRIL 1ST HA HA HA YOU HAVE A VIRUS`, `Water detect in Co-processor`, `CRITICAL ERROR 08/15: TOO MANY FINGERS ON KEYBOARD ERROR.`

- ✔ Some spread sociopolitical messages, such as: `Support the power of women`, `Use the power of man`, `LOVE, REMEMBER?`, `HEY SADAM LEAVE QUEIT BEFORE I COME`, `Jews NEVER surrender!"`

- ✔ Some are in love, and write messages to their girlfriends. `Dear Nina, you make me write this virus: Happy new year!`, `Send a FUNNY postcard to: Sylvia`, `Not having found one to do your light justice, mine will still be there: wanting, wishing, waiting.`

Virus authors have as many motives as do other programmers. But virus authors differ from the average programmer in one significant way: they are younger, on average. Most are still in high school or college, and most do their writing evenings, weekends, and on their vacations. Figure 20.2 shows a graph of viruses by month of authorship. This graph shows peaks in the same months that high school and college students have their vacations.

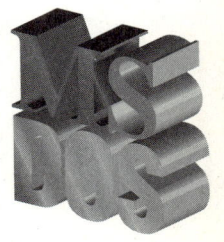

Figure 20.2

Month of virus creation.

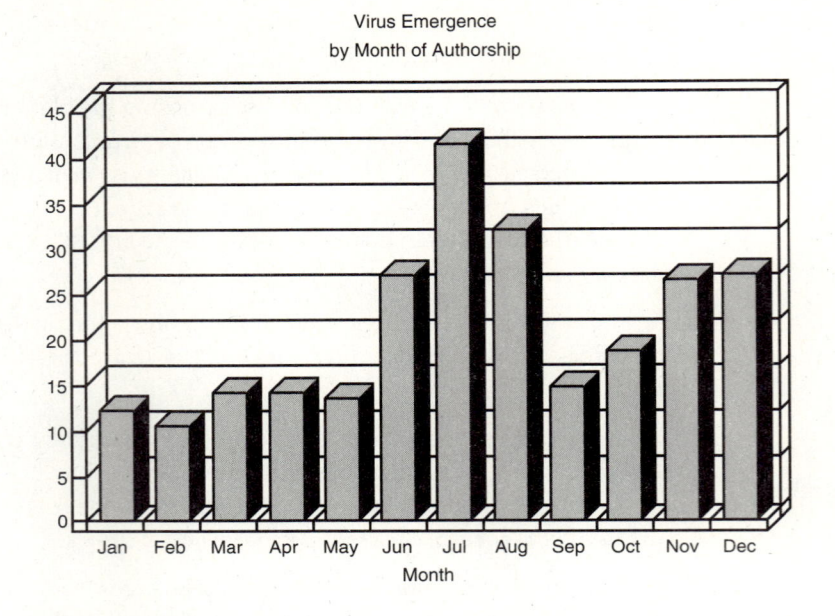

Virus Emergence by Month of Authorship

[Bar chart showing virus counts by month: Jan ~12, Feb ~10, Mar ~13, Apr ~14, May ~13, Jun ~27, Jul ~42, Aug ~32, Sep ~15, Oct ~19, Nov ~27, Dec ~27]

Missile Command (or, Virus Fallout)

Most folks think that the virus problem is something of a battle between themselves, as defenders of their computers, and viruses, as attackers. Sometimes I meet someone who realizes that the warfare is not with viruses, but with virus authors. Once someone asked me why a virus author would want to harm a system he had never even seen, to injure someone he had never met. That is a good question.

The answer may be this: the warfare does not target the user. The warfare is between viruses and anti-virus products, between virus authors and anti-virus product developers. Just as in Missile Command video games, the victims are those who live in the cities below, where the shrapnel lands.

Several reasons tell us that this battle is between vendors and virus authors:

- ✔ For many years, some viruses have targeted specific anti-virus products. In addition to the examples already cited, the virus author known as Dark Avenger has written several viruses that seek anti-virus programs containing the copyright notice of Vesselin Bontchev and destroy or disable them when found. The programs bearing this copyright notice are anti-virus products, which are intended to destroy the work of Dark Avenger. It's a cat-and-mouse game. Similarly, the Peach virus targets the checksum files produced by Central Point Anti-Virus.

✔ Some virus authors seem more interested in getting the attention of anti-virus product developers than in actually spreading their viruses. Some viruses seem to find their way directly to virus researchers, without ever being seen in the field.

✔ Many viruses contain far more code to make them difficult to analyze than they contain code that makes them hard to detect. The Whale virus, for example, is encrypted 64 layers deep. It took anti-virus product developers and researchers several weeks each to take the thing apart, only to find very little of interest inside the virus. Similarly, although Dark Avenger's viruses are typically somewhat difficult to detect, many are resistant to disassembly, producing hundreds of pages of useless source code for a virus that is only a few kilobytes in size. The Dark Avenger's and Trident Polymorphic have self-mutation engines that make viruses based on them much more difficult for anti-virus products to detect, not more lethal or infectious.

✔ Some viruses are designed to spread using your anti-virus product as an agent, hardly a trait that will make you love your anti-virus product more. Viruses like Frodo infect when DOS opens a file. Any scanner or checksum program that opens a file when such viruses are in memory provides the virus with an opportunity to infect it. Your anti-virus product plays right into the hands of such a virus, if it is unable to detect it in memory and act appropriately.

It is not merely the virus author who sees this as an international game of Missile Command, targeting the anti-virus products. The developers of the product also seem to feel this way, targeting the most interesting viruses, and sometimes ignoring the shrapnel that lands on the cities below. Consider the following:

✔ When Whale was first discovered and shared by the virus research community, everyone seemed to stop work in progress to deal with it. The challenge became who could detect it first and who could detect it most efficiently. The same challenge is faced today by products battling the polymorphic viruses. Some products don't detect any polymorphics, others detect almost all of them. Success with the polymorphics, despite their rarity, defines the winners of the Missile Command game.

✔ Anti-virus products seem to focus on scanning, a fun technology to develop if you are a marketing department, because you get to report body counts. No vendor seems to have shown much interest in virus removal—some products can't do it at all, and the rest generally do it poorly. All products detect far more viruses than they remove, a commentary on the vendor's focus on the incoming missiles, rather than the shrapnel landing on the cities.

If the war is now between the virus authors and the anti-virus product developers, and the battleground is in your computer, the results now seem to be clear: the virus authors have won, and continue to win, the battles. The virus authors will win the war, although their viruses will lose some of the battles with anti-virus software. Here's why:

✔ Military historians know that volunteers often fight harder than paid mercenaries. Like a true zealot, a virus author is quite willing to stay up all hours, and to make sacrifices to achieve his or her end; programmers working on anti-virus products, on the other hand, generally go home at 5 p.m.

✔ Military historians know there is strength in union. The virus authors are working together; the anti-virus product developers are working in isolation. The virus authors have several commercially published books available on how to write viruses. They have many BBSs around the world through which they share source code, viruses, and information. The anti-virus product developers get together from time to time, but all their programmers have signed such restrictive nondisclosure agreements that there is little exchange of technology.

✔ Military historians also know that the size of the army affects the outcome. At the moment, there may be 300 to 600 virus authors at work on their projects around the world. The thousands of viruses they have created are battling a few dozen products. In your computer, any one of these viruses may be doing battle with just one product. That one product is the work of just one to six programmers, on average. Very few anti-virus products are the work of more than a half dozen programmers. Because the anti-virus developers are working in isolation, the armies number perhaps 50 to 100 bad guys for every good guy.

✔ One military historian observed that the secret to success is to "get there firstest with the mostest." Surely the two armies are distributed differently. Viruses are free; products must be paid for. Viruses are self-installing; products must be installed. Viruses run automatically; products must be deliberately run by the user. The virus gets there first.

✔ The talent embodied in viruses is certainly beyond that embodied in the average user. Virus authors understand the intricacies of assembly language, the CPU, the operating system, disk and file structure, and the boot process. Few users can claim to have mastered a single application program.

In the warfare between virus authors and anti-virus authors, the only clear loser is the user. To survive, you must get smarter. You must be more determined. And you must not provide needless encouragement to either side. Learning more about viruses, using some good sense, and following some intelligent procedures will defend your data better than any number of anti-virus products you can install.

Understanding the Virus Threat

It is unfortunate that we do not have any trustworthy facts about the frequency or costliness of virus incidents. There is no national center for computer disease control like the National Center for Disease Control.

Emergence of New Viruses

As you can see from figure 20.3, the rate at which new computer viruses are being created continues to increase. About 60 percent of all the viruses that have ever been written through the end of 1992 were written in 1992! We are at the beginning of the problem, not the end.

Figure 20.3

Percent of viruses known at end of 1992, by year of creation.

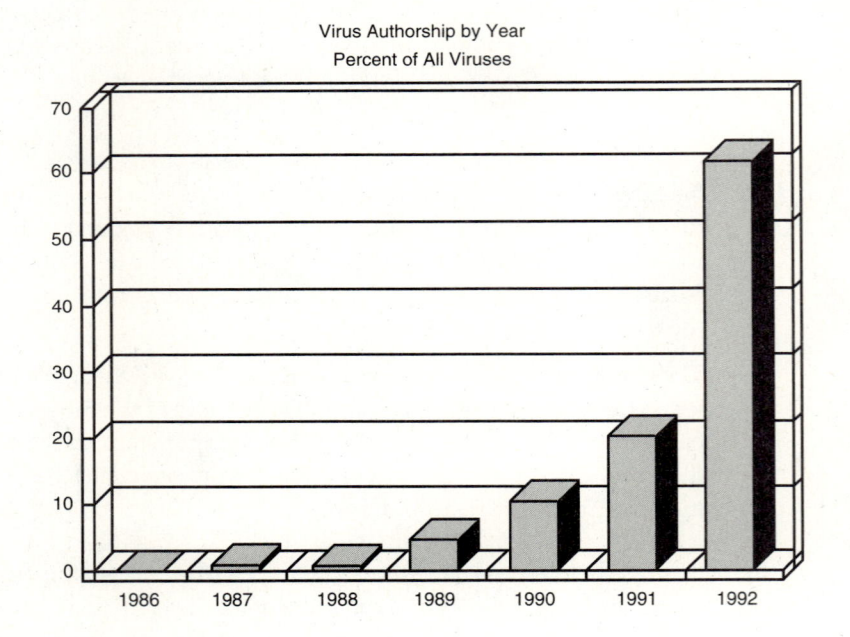

Virus Authorship by Year
Percent of All Viruses

Prevalence

Most viruses are rare. This is partly due to their "newness" and the fact that it takes a long time before a virus can travel from one machine to millions. I've classified 1,633 viruses by their commonness. Here are my conclusions:

- ✔ 48 percent are very rare, perhaps never found "in the wild" (outside the virus researcher's labs).
- ✔ 26 percent are almost never found in the wild.
- ✔ 10 percent are rarely found in the wild.
- ✔ 12 percent sometimes are found in the wild.

✔ 4 percent are among the most common viruses.

What does it mean to be "among the most common viruses?" In the U.S., your chances of infection are slim—despite vendor claims. In a given year, a typical computer is not infected once. In a typical U.S. company in 1992, only 1 in 500 computers was infected once or more. (I made up that statistic, based on informal interviews with students in my virus seminars, but it seems about right.)

Your chance of infection depends on who you are, of course. If, for example, you are a college or high school student, a Macintosh user, or likely to trade software, your chance of infection is much higher. Some high-risk users have averaged an infection once a month!

Your chance of infection also depends on where you live. If you live in Asia or Eastern Europe, you know that viruses spread just as fast as pirated software—rather fast indeed. You may have a dozen infections in your machine this year, many of which can't be detected or removed by the anti-virus products of DOS 6.2.

Infectiousness

How common a virus is depends in part on how old it is. But it also depends on its "infectiousness"—how well it spreads. Infectiousness is affected by things such as compatibility (a virus that hangs up your computer is easily detected), damage immediacy (a virus that causes immediate damage is easily detected), message display (a virus that often displays a message is easily detected), and so forth. I scored many viruses for infectiousness, and found that most are quite infectious (see fig. 20.4).

How Much Damage Do Common Viruses Cause?

I asked my BBS callers to rate the damage experienced by a virus they had gotten. The question was, "How much damage did the virus cause?" Table 20.2 summarizes their responses.

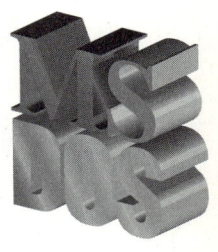

1078 Chapter 20: *Battling Viruses with DOS 6.2*

Figure 20.4
Infectiousness of viruses.

Infectiousness of 1,001 Viruses

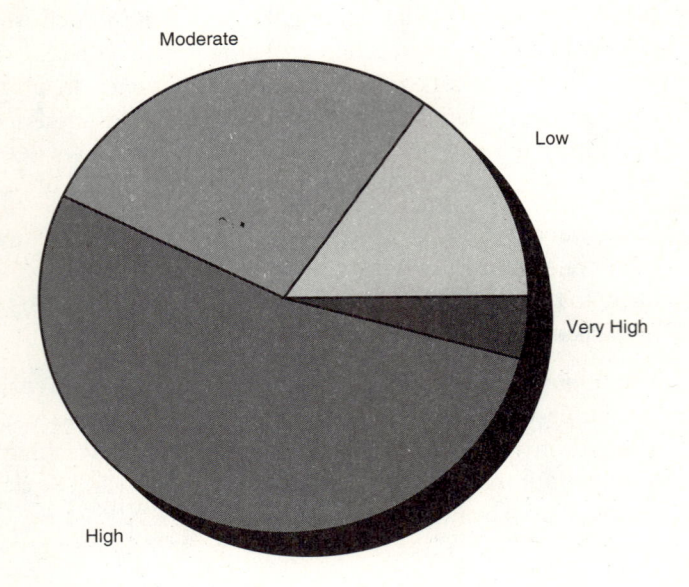

[Pie chart with segments labeled: Moderate, Low, Very High, High]

Table 20.2
BBS Survey of Virus Damage

Answer	Percent of Respondents
A great deal of damage, including lost data	11 percent
A moderate amount of damage, very little or no lost data	15 percent
Very little or no damage, just a nuisance to remove	69 percent
Don't know, or don't want to answer this question	5 percent

The results, seven out of ten incidents are merely a nuisance, are shown in the graph in figure 20.5.

Understanding the Virus Threat 1079

Another way to look at the destructiveness of viruses is to score each virus for damage caused. Such ratings are not influenced by probability of damage (Michelangelo only damages once a year), but by magnitude of damage if it occurs (see fig. 20.6). Table 20.3 summarizes the amount of damage caused by viruses.

Table 20.3
Virus Damage Amount

Damage Amount	Number of Viruses
None	6
Insignificant	191
Minor	423
Substantial	383

The amount of damage to data is shown in the graph in figure 20.6.

Figure 20.5

BBS survey of damage caused by viruses.

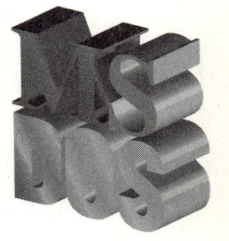

Figure 20.6

Virus damage magnitude based on analysis of over 1,000 viruses.

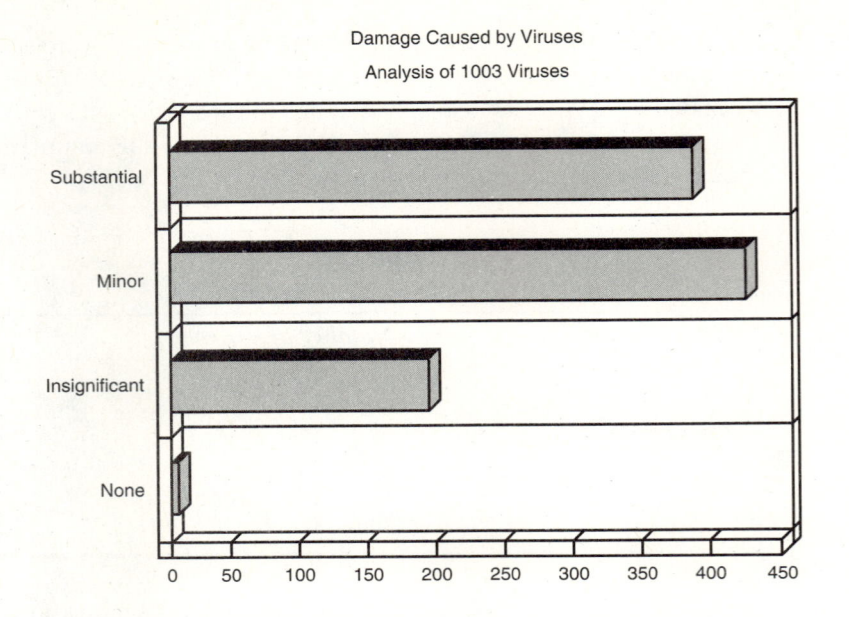

Damage Caused by Viruses
Analysis of 1003 Viruses

- Substantial
- Minor
- Insignificant
- None

0 50 100 150 200 250 300 350 400 450

Although most viruses don't cause much damage, most users attempting to remove a virus can cause a great deal of damage. Doing a low-level format of your hard disk is not the sanest method of removing a file virus, although it is effective! But such efforts will cause more harm than good. We'll talk about recovery later in the chapter.

What Kind of Damage Can Viruses Cause?

What kinds of damage can a virus cause? There is little limit. Some viruses (such as Jerusalem) delete your programs as you try to run them on some special day, such as Friday the 13th. Some (such as Michelangelo) overwrite some or all of your hard disk, given the right circumstances. Others (such as the dBASE virus) may make subtle changes in your databases, changes you are not likely to detect. Other viruses may produce the same symptoms as hardware problems, perhaps leading you to damage your wallet. But, knock on wood, none damage hardware, perhaps because virus authors care too much about computers to let their viruses damage them.

The end of this chapter lists some descriptions of the most common viruses so that you can see what damage these common viruses can cause.

How Serious Is the Virus Threat?

Your exact probability of being infected is a function of two factors: the number of viruses appearing at your door, and the measures you have in place for preventing their entry through that door. The number of viruses "at the door" is determined by the frequency with which new software is brought into your organization (by disk or modem) and the increasing probability that this software is infected. The measures in place are established by policy and procedure.

The magnitude of the threat is difficult to estimate, given the extent of under-reporting, the claims made by those marketing anti-virus products, and the enthusiastic attention that the problem has sometimes received from the press. Victims of crimes, like the rest of us, want to believe in a just world in which good things happen to good people and bad things happen to bad people. Because a virus infection is definitely a bad thing, victims often feel some shame and guilt. No one feels pride when they experience an infection; no one seems to want to talk about it. But it is clear that computer viruses are posing a new threat to safe computing.

Your chance of an infection in the last 12 months may have been only 1 in 500 (that is, if there are 500 computers in your office, perhaps only one of them was infected in the last year). In 1993, this probability may change to 1 in 50. If you get an infection, it is likely that it will be one of the 15 most common viruses, and that means that the probability that the virus is designed to cause serious damage is nearly 0. But unless you or your help staff are careful, the removal might be more damaging than the virus itself.

Today, the real cost of a virus is not merely the damage it causes, but the cost of buying and installing an anti-virus product, of learning how to use it, of the time spent using it, and of coping with false alarms. When you discover that your anti-virus product doesn't remove the virus properly, or doesn't help you recover your data, your costs go even higher. The virus problem is expensive.

You can do something to help make computing safe again. In the next sections, you learn how.

> **AUTHOR'S NOTE**
>
> *A computer virus is amazingly similar to a biological virus. For one thing, it's interesting to observe that not one single virus in history has ever been cured. Yes, medical science has developed vaccines for many viruses, but it has never found a cure. The same is true of the computer virus—although we're not going to stop the users who write this stuff, we can vaccinate our computers from them.*
>
> *This leads to another similarity that is even more important. Viruses, whether biological or logical, are spread by behavior. For example, how many of us would drink out of the same glass as someone who has the flu? No, we alter our behavior so as not to become infected. All the research money in the world will not slow down the spread of a biological virus. Likewise, to prevent our computers from being infected by a logical virus, we must alter our behavior. That's what this chapter is all about.*

Preventing Viruses

Even with inflation, an ounce of prevention is worth a pound of cure.

Preventing viruses seems to be disproportionately difficult when you consider how simple it is to get one. To get a boot virus, simply put an infected disk in drive A and turn your computer on or press Ctrl+Alt+Del. To get a file virus, simply copy an infected file or run it. Anyone who has graduated from boot camp has all the requisite skill.

Given its druthers and a few minutes with an unsuspecting user, one little computer virus may make a dozen perfect copies of itself. One machine might infect no other in your office for a week or two, or it might infect every networked computer in the office in a minute or two.

Infecting every computer in the office can be done quite simply with a scenario like this: Bill goes into work early and runs a golf game for a few minutes that he has borrowed from a friend. The game contains a virus that becomes active in his computer's memory. Other folks start to arrive, and Bill logs in to the network. The menu program, which he runs, is located in a directory where Bill (and therefore his virus) has write permission. The menu is immediately infected. Other staff log in, run the menu, and are infected. By 9:15, the virus is in every computer's memory in the entire organization and is now at work finding homes on each user's hard and floppy disks and backup disks.

Following is a list of some helpful things you can do to reduce the chances that your machine will be infected by a virus; you won't always be able to follow the advice in this section, but do your best, and you will reduce your risk:

- ✔ Don't boot computers from floppy disks that have been in any other computer. Always open the drive A door immediately after using a floppy disk, and always check to see that the drive A door is open before turning on the machine.

- ✔ If the system is to boot from a floppy disk, make sure that the boot floppy disk is labeled to identify the machine it belongs to, and enforce a policy that restricts the use of that floppy disk to that machine.

- ✔ Consider creating a virus scanning machine for employee use. The ideal machine contains a menu-driven product that can scan a floppy disk in drive A or B with the press of a key. All employees could be required to scan all disks they bring from home before taking them to their office, and to scan any disks given them by coworkers or received in the mail before using them.

- ✔ Be wary of the help desk support team as virus propagators. Any software lending library, shared computer, or training room is a potential virus transmission site. At even greater risk is the support team, who may visit a user experiencing difficulties, get a virus on their diagnostic disk, and then move on to another user, infecting that user's machine in the process.

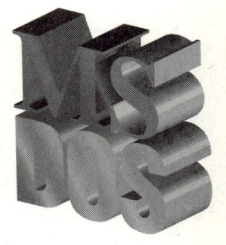

Data Disks and Boot Sector Viruses

If you thought that DOS Boot was the name of a German war movie, you might be surprised to learn that data disks are the most common means by which boot sector viruses are transferred. Over half of office infections are infections of the boot record (on floppy disks) or master boot record (on hard disks). You may think that data disks don't contain a boot record if they are not bootable. But the DOS FORMAT program creates a boot record whenever it is executed. A boot record is all a boot sector virus needs to call a disk home. And every disk has one.

How does a boot sector virus get from a nonbootable floppy disk to a hard disk? It's simple. You put an infected disk in drive A and copy a file or two from it or to it. Perhaps you edit a file on drive A. Five o'clock rolls around and you shut off your machine. Tomorrow you come into work, turn on your machine, and get a cup of coffee. You come in to see the message:

```
Non-System disk or disk error
Replace and press any key when ready.
```

You open the drive door and press Ctrl+Alt+Del. But it is already too late. The virus has already been run as your machine tried to boot from drive A. For many common boot sector viruses, it has infected your hard disk. When you press Ctrl+Alt+Del, you boot from your hard disk, first putting the virus back in memory, and then putting DOS in memory. From now on, every time you access a floppy disk in drive A or B, you'll infect it.

Some older boot sector viruses are not able to infect the hard disk, so they must take another approach. When you boot (or attempt to boot) from an infected floppy disk, the virus goes into memory and looks for another floppy disk in a drive. If it finds one, it may infect the floppy immediately. If the virus can't find one, but your boot was successful, the virus waits in memory until you insert a floppy disk into a disk drive, and then infects the floppy the first time you access it (perhaps with the DIR command).

The morals of this story are as follows:

- ✔ You must learn to remove all disks from your disk drives immediately after using them so that you don't accidentally boot from them.

- ✔ You must never turn on the machine or press Ctrl+Alt+Del without first ensuring that the door to drive A is open.

- ✔ If you normally boot from a floppy disk, it should be your own, personal floppy disk, and it should have a write-protect tab.

- ✔ If you have two drives, you should always try to use drive B for reading and writing floppy disks, and as much as possible try not to use drive A. PCs never try to boot from drive B.

- ✔ With machines that normally boot from the hard disk and that have only one floppy disk drive, you should make that drive B, not drive A, to prevent accidentally booting from it. This can be done by changing the cable connection on the back of the drive, or by moving a jumper on the drive.

Unless you need to write to a floppy disk, the disk should have a write-protect tab on it. This prevents infection of programs on the disk and prevents infection of the boot sector. Although a write-protect tab on a floppy disk won't protect a hard disk from a virus on the floppy disk, it will protect the floppy disk from a virus on the hard disk.

See Chapter 17 to learn to patch the `Non-system disk` *error message of FORMAT.COM with a boot-sector warning.*

Backup

You don't need to be told that backups are important (see Chapter 18). But you may not appreciate your backups today as much as you will the day you need them, the day a virus has destroyed everything in your computer.

Backups can't prevent viruses, but they can prevent the damage and nuisance that a virus can cause. With a good set of backups, a virus is nearly no problem at all. Without a good set of backups, a virus can mean the end of Accounts Receivable—the end of many organizations. Here are the most important things to remember:

- ✔ Back up your hard disks often. The more important the information stored on the hard disk, the more important it is to back it up often.

- ✔ Back up selectively, if this will increase backup speed. Consider backing up everything weekly, and backing up essential, live files daily.

- ✔ Keep multiple sets of backups. If you happen to back up files containing a virus, your previous set of backups may be virus free.

- ✔ If you are backing up to tape, back up by file rather than by image, so that if a virus is later detected and removed, you can omit from your restoration any infected files on the backup tape.

- ✔ Be sure to check for viruses after restoring from your backups. As many as nine out of ten people who eradicate a virus find it back in a month. Infected backup disks can be the culprit.

Access to Bulletin Boards

Many people think that the electronic bulletin board (BBS) is a common source of infection. Some organizations have gone to the trouble of taking modems away from users and not permitting calls to bulletin boards. Although some viruses have been deliberately or accidentally uploaded to bulletin boards, and then downloaded by subsequent callers, the BBS has been unfairly accused of being a threat. We know, for example, that about half of all infections are boot sector infections, and that boot sectors are never downloaded from bulletin boards.

Trojans, on the other hand, are more often distributed through bulletin boards than through any other mechanism, so the BBS is never fully trustworthy. Following are some general precautions concerning bulletin board use:

- ✔ Don't download files from a BBS directory that the SYSOP has labeled "new, untested." Let someone else test your files first!

- ✔ Download shareware from the shareware author's BBS. Most professional shareware authors provide support BBSs for their products. You are guaranteed an uncorrupted version of software when you download it directly from the source. You also are assured of getting the latest program version.

- ✔ Minimize contact with possible carriers of a virus. Bulletin boards full of games, unprotected programs, and discussions of hacking are probably more risky sources of shareware than other boards.

- ✔ Always scan software downloaded from a BBS before running it. Make sure that your scanner is up-to-date.

- ✔ Because scanners normally do not detect Trojans, test downloads on a test computer, or do so just after backing up the system you are about to test a download on.

Virus Response Teams

Even if your organization is not yet ready for a full-time virus expert, you can't afford to delay in assembling an informal support group that will begin now to prepare for disaster. You should create an informal virus response team at each site, and if you have two or more sites, a team at central headquarters or regional headquarters that will back up the local teams.

Your team should be knowledgeable about hardware malfunction, especially how to troubleshoot hard disk problems and how to recover data. After all, most virus alarms turn out to be simple hardware or software problems having nothing to do with viruses. You probably already have a few people on staff who have some knowledge of programs like the Norton Utilities and who can unerase files. Folks like these might volunteer for a virus-busting mission. They can learn more about how viruses work from books on the subject so that when your first virus comes along, they can look it up and decide what to do. They also should be skilled in the use of your organization's anti-virus software so that they can use it to best advantage. The version of the software that they have should be the very latest.

One mission of your virus response team is to ensure that safe, anti-virus preventive measures are being followed. They can do this by helping write policy, training users, working with users one on one, installing anti-virus software on personal computers, and answering questions as they arise. They also might work to ensure that systems are backed up more frequently. All users should be aware that this group exists. Users should know the team's office phone numbers, and users should call them at the first sign of trouble.

Another mission of your virus response team is to get ready for the day that a virus slips through your first line of defense. The team's response should be immediate, thorough, and well-guided, remembering that more damage is normally done by "experts" after an infection than by the virus itself. To prepare, the team should become as well-connected to the world of virus-busting as they can, perhaps through V-Base, a demo version of which is on the disk with this book.

The team would be well-advised to have a removal and recovery plan for the dozen most common viruses. They might want to make copies of the master boot records and boot records of your variously partitioned hard disks, and store them in a safe location. The team may want to make sure that systems are backed up, that files are not fragmented, and that a minimum number of files (CONFIG.SYS, AUTOEXEC.BAT, COMMAND.COM) are in the root directory in case recovery from a FAT-scrambling virus becomes necessary.

In the end, no matter how hard we toil at prevention, virus accidents will happen. We will need to move on to efficient detection.

Detecting Viruses

Most of the procedures outlined in the preceding section for preventing virus infections are good but imperfect. When several procedures are combined, your risk of infection is reduced. But completely eliminating the risk of infection is probably not cost-effective. The "perfect fix" to the virus problem might be putty. Just buy some putty and push it into your disk drive doors, packing a bit onto the connectors on the back of the machine, and you will have prevented the introduction of a virus. Now, if there was no virus in your machine when you applied the putty, you are safe. But software sharing is a necessity of life. We must share software to share information. Putty won't do.

There are two myths about virus detection. The first is that viruses are easy to spot. They drip letters from your screen or put black holes on the screen or turn the letters on the screen upside down or play tunes. The other myth, surprisingly, is just the opposite: viruses are so sneaky that you couldn't catch one with anything but some magic software. For this magic software, nearly everyone thinks "scanner." The fact is that most viruses that spread well show no symptoms, and there are many ways that you can detect and remove a virus with your bare hands!

The next sections discuss several categories of anti-virus software:

- ✔ Checksumming
- ✔ Scanning
- ✔ TSRs and device drivers

Checksumming

The fundamental fact of a virus is that if it is to add its code to another program, it must somehow change that program. You can't eat a cheeseburger without changing your weight. This is a good fact to know, because unlike your weight, we do not expect the "weight" of a program to ever fluctuate naturally.

There is one exception to this, unfortunately. Some programs, such as those written by Borland International, enable you to reconfigure them for different colors and other options. When you make these changes, they can be recorded by the program in itself, thus causing some change. But with this exception, programs are stable creatures, and it is only your documents, spreadsheets, and databases that should ever change. Because viruses do not get into these files, you can use a good method of detecting change in a program as a means of suspecting the introduction of a virus to your system. That is, the only files that should ever change "legally" are files a virus does not infect; the only files that should never change are the files a virus might infect, and must change during the process.

Why Detect Changes?

There are several good reasons why you should detect changes:

- ✔ Viruses have great difficulty infecting your machine without making some change in it. To detect a change is to begin the process of detecting a virus. Although some are concerned that a change-detecting program can't prove there isn't already a virus in your computer, the fact is that you needn't worry about this. If you infect your computer with a dozen viruses, and then measure your computer's state, one of the viruses will change that state in the next hour or so; a remeasurement establishes that something is afoot.

- ✔ Occasionally things go wrong with computer hardware and software. You run CHKDSK and discover many lost clusters in many lost chains. You scrap these clusters, but wonder what files you've lost. A proper change-detection program will give you a list of files deleted since your last run. You can then restore them from your backups.

- ✔ In many organizations, you only want to permit the use of authorized software. Using a proper change-detection program, you can establish what software was added to the machine since your last run. Any extra software will quickly come to your attention.

Each file has a unique fingerprint in the form of a checksum. Changes in any character within the file likely change the checksum. If a file's original checksum is known—perhaps recorded in a file elsewhere— and its current checksum is known, the two values can be compared. Any difference indicates that the file has been changed, and offers reason to investigate further. If a program's size is changed, it must be concluded that some modification has occurred to the file. If the size has not changed, some modification is still possible. A file that

Detecting Viruses

contains the simple message "Hi Mom!" could be modified so that it contained the message "Hi Dad!," and it would not show any change in size. In the same way, an overwriting virus will change the code of a program without changing its size, provided that the program's initial size is larger than the virus.

A much tougher test of whether a file has been modified is to compute the checksum. At the time of this writing, there are no viruses able to modify a file without modifying the file's checksum. Thus any checksum checker will work just fine in catching viruses, providing that you use it to establish checksums before a virus has modified your files.

How is the checksum computed? Simply adding the values of all the characters in the file is not enough, because a file containing just "AE" would produce the same result as a file with just "EA." Rather, the first byte of a file is read, and an algorithm applied to it. This algorithm does something to the value of the byte, such as rotating the bits a certain number of times, and using logical AND or OR to make the bits change to something else. The result of that algorithm is then applied to the next byte of the file. The process is repeated until the final byte is reached, and the remainder is recorded. With most procedures, a small file produces a checksum value of the same size as a large file.

Checksum programs create one or more database files listing programs, their directories, and one or more initial values. When they are run a second time, they can compare their new results against the old list, and report.

DOS 6 comes with MSAV.EXE, which creates checksum database files and can checksum files against these databases. The operation of MSAV is discussed later in this chapter.

Scanning

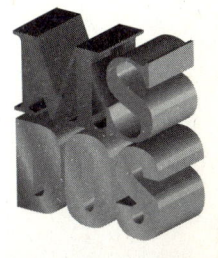

Virus scanners are products designed to help identify viruses within files, boot sectors, master boot sectors, memory, and other hiding places; to name them; and potentially to help remove them. The capability to detect and identify a virus is probably the most important feature of a scanner. Assuming a choice between two scanners that detect every virus ever developed, you should choose the most precise or fastest, providing it makes a clamor or displays a message on-screen when it finds something.

A scanner is critical for providing a precise identification of a virus in your system. Without a precise identification, you can't know the best course of action for removing it, and you can't be sure that you have removed it completely.

Unlike the "change checkers" described previously, or the TSRs described in the next section, the scanner is the only kind of anti-virus program that can spot a virus before it runs. Thus, if you use a scanner to check new software before running it, you can prevent even one of your files from becoming infected.

This praise for scanners must, however, be accompanied by some criticism. Scanners are always out-of-date. Most scanners are usually somewhat incomplete when they are released. No virus researcher has access to every virus on earth. So even if your scanner was absolutely current one month ago, and caught every virus that existed on earth the day it was released, there are now 60 or more viruses that it can't catch. Although your odds of getting a brand new virus are very, very small, you must recognize that scanners will not catch everything.

DOS 6.2 comes with a scanner in the form of MSAV.EXE, the same program that you can use for checksumming.

Using a Scanner

If you plan to use a scanner, you must follow these instructions if you hope to achieve success in detecting viruses:

- ✔ Cold boot the machine to be scanned from an uninfected, write-protected floppy disk. Because a virus can't get past the write-protection mechanism of a floppy disk drive, you are thus assured that no virus has moved into memory, from whence it can defeat your scanner.

- ✔ Run the scanner from the disk you just booted from, and do so before running any other programs—especially programs that are on a drive other than the one you just booted from. Any device driver called by your hard disk's CONFIG.SYS file can contain a virus, as can any program called by your hard disk's AUTOEXEC.BAT file.

✔ Scan the disk you just booted from, to ensure that it is not infected.

✔ Watch your screen carefully during the scanning process, if your scanner does not pause when it detects a virus. In the case of MSAV, you will have to ask for a report and study the report because the identifications fly by too fast on-screen.

✔ Follow the instructions for your scanner carefully. Failure to issue the correct command line may result in a partial scan, and you might inadvertently skip scanning a directory that contains a virus.

TSRs and Device Drivers

Most software, including anti-virus software, is intentionally run by the user, and performs some function when it is run. When it comes to fighting viruses, this approach is beneficial if the user knows when to run a product and is able to run it correctly. Because many users seem unskilled at running anti-virus products, and others don't seem to have a good sense of timing, the anti-virus TSR or device driver will become more popular as a product. TSRs (terminate- and-stay resident software) normally are called by AUTOEXEC.BAT; device drivers always are called by CONFIG.SYS. Both TSRs and device drivers can watch over the user with no further intervention. They can offer the constant vigilance that the user might not provide.

There are advantages and disadvantages of each. TSRs can be installed from the login script for your network. They can be removed from memory without rebooting, if needed, to run a large application. They load after a virus potentially loads (for instance, an infected COMMAND.COM), and thus may be subverted by it.

Device drivers must be loaded when you boot from CONFIG.SYS. They can't be unloaded by either a well-meaning user or a virus. They load before COMMAND.COM, so they are in a better position to monitor COMMAND.COM for infection.

Virus Scanning with MSAV.EXE

MSAV.EXE is the Microsoft anti-virus program, new with DOS 6 and 6.2. MSAV works with all prior versions of DOS. It is loosely based on Central Point Anti-Virus, sharing many of the shortcomings of that product. But MSAV is a limited version of CPAV, and does not offer all of its power. MSAV detects many viruses, and will remove some of them, so it offers some protection. In this section, you learn what MSAV does, how to use it, and its strengths and weaknesses.

Command Line Options

Even if you prefer menus to command line operation, MSAV requires command line operation if you want to scan just one file or just one directory. It can't be made to scan anything but an entire drive from the menu. You can run MSAV with several command-line options:

/S   scans boot sectors and files. (This is the default, so you won't ever need to enter this option.)

/C   scans boot sectors and files, cleaning them if any are found. Don't use this option until you have read the section on "Removal."

/R   generates a report on your activity, which is a great idea. It creates a file named MSAV.RPT in the root of the drive from which you ran MSAV, overwriting any previous copies of this report. If you want to save previous reports, a batch file can rename them or concatenate the current report with your archive of reports, as follows:

```
COPY C:\VARCHIVE.RPT+C:\MSAV.RPT C:\TEMP
DEL C:\VARCHIVE.RPT
REN C:\TEMP C:\VARCHIVE.RPT
MSAV /R
```

In this example, the master archive report is named VARCHIVE.RPT and is stored in the root of drive C. MSAV is run from drive C.

Virus Scanning with MSAV.EXE

/A   scans all drives (including the server, if you are attached) except drives A and B. This speeds things up if you aren't worried about a virus on the disks in drives A and B. Most users have no business scanning the server, in part because others will be charged with this, because it is very time-consuming, and because MSAV can infect every file on the server when it scans the server, if the user has supervisor rights and certain viruses are memory-resident.

/L   scans all local drives except drives A and B. This will be your most common choice for command-line operation. The server is not a local drive, so you will be able to finish the scan in a reasonable time.

/N   indicates no interface. The contents of MSAV.TXT will be displayed instead, if it exists. In this text file, you can put any information you want, such as an explanation of what is happening, and what the user should do if a virus is detected. You probably will choose this option for command-line operation in batch mode. If the text file does not exist, your screen will display...

```
MSAV Copyright (c) 1991-1992 Central
Point     Software, Inc.
Working…
```

...and the path and file names as scanning takes place.

/P   displays the command line interface, rather than the graphic interface. This interface offers more information on what is happening than the /N option, telling you when it is mapping disk directories, scanning memory for viruses, and scanning files for viruses. If used with the /N option, it overrides /N.

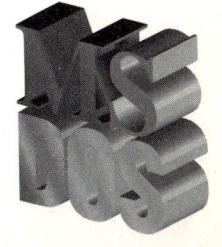

/F prevents display of the names of the files scanned. You can use this option only if you have chosen /N or /P. If, for example, your command line is...

    MSAV /L/N/P

then you will just see:

    MSAV Copyright (c) 1991-1992 Central
    Point Software, Inc.
    Working...

/VIDEO displays help for the video and mouse command line options. Use this switch to find the various switches that can be used to control your screen display and mouse operation when in menu-driven mode. Using...

    MSAV /28/LE

...for example, will run MSAV in menu-driven mode, with a 28-line screen for your VGA, and a left-handed mouse for your left hand.

/H displays a help screen showing the various options other than those controlling video and mouse (/VIDEO).

If you want to exit MSAV after beginning a scan (perhaps because you find it scanning your server), you can press Esc.

Menu-Driven Operation

When you simply type **MSAV** or **MSAV** with any of the mouse/video options, you see a menu like that shown in figure 20.7.

You normally set Options once, and never need to touch them again, because they are saved in a file named MSAV.INI and take effect on each successive run until changed. Display the Options menu by pressing O or F8 (see fig. 20.8). Here is what each of the somewhat confusing options mean:

Virus Scanning with MSAV.EXE

Verify Integrity is used in a session after a session in which you have chosen the second option, Create New Checksums. Verify Integrity compares each file with information you have stored on it in a file called CHKLIST.MS, matching the file's size, attributes, date, time, and checksum. If any of these items is changed, MSAV sounds the alarm (if turned on) and indicates Verify error. If you read the report created by MSAV, you will be able to learn where this `verify error` occurred. It wouldn't hurt to have this option always turned on.

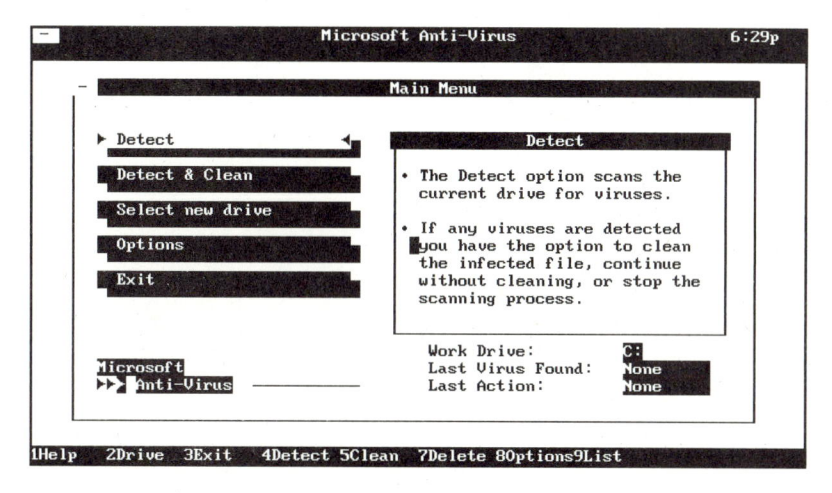

Figure 20.7

The opening screen of MSAV.

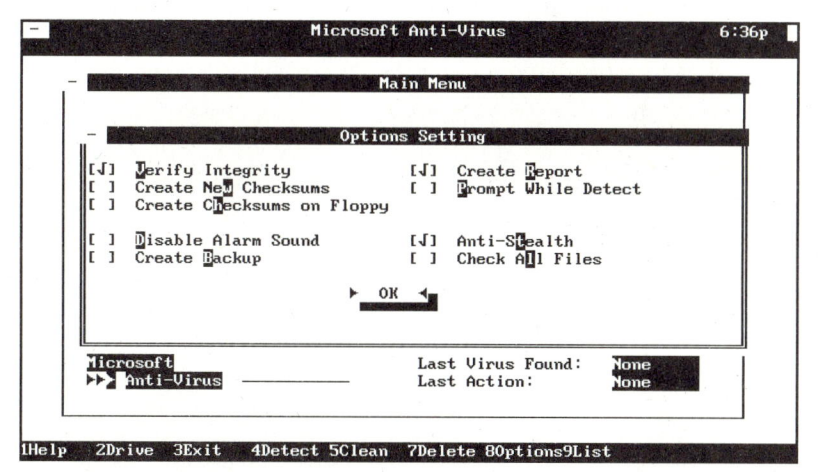

Figure 20.8

The options screen of MSAV.

Create New Checksums generates the file CHKLIST.MS in each directory scanned. If the file already exists, then information on new or changed files is added to it. The first time you choose Create New Checksums, your scanning is slowed slightly as the CHKLIST.MS files are created. On subsequent runs, your speed increases dramatically. You should know that if you add files to a directory, information on these new files will not be added to CHKLIST.MS unless you have this option turned on. The CHKLIST.MS file does not contain information on spreadsheets, databases, and documents, so you need not worry that these will often be changing and foiling your efforts at checksumming. If you ever plan to verify integrity, you should create new checksums just after installing any new software.

> **NOTE**
>
> *If you want to use the Verify Integrity option, then do not use the Create New Checksums option. Integrity verification is always overridden by Create New Checksums, and any changes that have taken place will be recorded as valid, rather than reported. Choosing Create New Checksums can help protect a virus that has infected your system, instead of protecting your system from the virus!*

Create Checksums on Floppy is useful when some merry prankster modifies the Peach virus (which looks for CHKLIST.CPS) to look for CHKLIST.MS. It also is desirable if your drive's storage space is limited, and you don't want extra files in every directory. I'd be inclined to ignore this option, unless you can think of a good reason to use it.

Disable Alarm Sound prevents, when checked, the alarm from sounding when a virus is detected. Virus researchers would be driven insane without this option, but users should never check it. You—and others in your office—should know when MSAV finds a virus.

Create Backup backs up any infected file before attempting to remove the virus from it. After you read my cautions on removal, I hope you agree that this is a terrific option to have checked at all times.

Create Report is an option that should always be chosen, because you might otherwise miss the information that MSAV found in your computer. MSAV fills your screen with pretty boxes and buttons, but only contains a short line showing Last Virus Found. If your machine has more than one virus, you won't know it unless you are a speed-reader and your machine is very slow. To get maximum mileage out of the report created, you can add…

```
MSAV /L/N
MORE ¦TYPE C:\MSAV.RPT
```

…or…

```
MSAV /L
MORE ¦TYPE C:\MSAV.RPT
```

…to a batch file that calls MSAV.

Anti-Stealth is intended to help detect stealth viruses. Because there are now many stealth viruses, it seems wise to always have this option checked.

Check All Files shouldn't be used unless you can think of a good reason. When the option is not checked, you check only executable files: EXE, COM, OVL, OVR, SYS, BIN, APP, CMD, master boot records, and boot records. When the option is checked, you scan everything. Because a virus can't execute from a nonexecutable file, few viruses have any interest in infecting such things, and the infection of text files can hardly be of concern. If a virus adds its code to a spreadsheet or word processing document, you will see this code or otherwise learn about the problem when you try to load the file with your application software. Checking all files may increase your scan time by a factor of three or more, so don't waste your life by scanning everything.

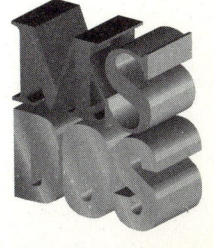

Speed Consequences of Various Options

MSAV performs at two basic speeds: one speed when scanning is done, and another speed when checksumming is done. When checksumming is done, your speed after the first run is about four times as fast as when pure scanning is done. Choosing Verify Integrity from the menu permits checksumming, and checksumming permits MSAV to ignore scanning unless a checksum mismatch is found. I recommend, therefore, that you always have Verify Integrity checked.

In short, I recommend that you normally run MSAV with the following items checked:

- ✔ Verify Integrity
- ✔ Create Report
- ✔ Anti-Stealth

It is recommended that you do not check the following items:

- ✔ Create Checksums on Floppy (too slow)
- ✔ Disable Alarm Sound (You get an alarm sound from your PC only when you have a virus or false alarm, and you will certainly want to know when this happens.)
- ✔ Check All Files (unnecessary and too slow)

When should you create checksums? The best time is just before installing new software, when you trust your system and believe it to be uninfected. When should you verify integrity? The best time is just after installing new software and running it; if a virus is going to come out and modify your existing software, it will likely do it now.

How Good Is MSAV as a Scanner?

Anyone choosing an anti-virus product is hard-pressed to determine which product is the best. If you don't happen to have a thousand viruses or so to test the product, how can you be sure that it detects any of them? Here are the facts about MSAV as a scanner:

Virus Scanning with MSAV.EXE 1101

- ✔ MSAV can detect the 10 most common viruses, which account for 90 percent or so of all infections.

- ✔ MSAV can probably detect most of the 100 or so viruses found from time to time in the wild.

- ✔ MSAV detects many of the polymorphic viruses, but misses some copies of viruses, such as Involuntary and V2P2/Chameleon.

- ✔ MSAV detects Frodo if it is in memory, and removes it from memory. But MSAV does not notice that Frodo has just infected MSAV, and doesn't report this. (Even anti-virus products can get infected.) It doesn't warn you to reboot from an uninfected drive, but rather to simply reboot. If COMMAND.COM is still infected when you reboot, Frodo will be back.

- ✔ MSAV is not particularly fast. We scanned a collection of 10,194 assorted virus samples on a drive with 10,968 programs (68M) and a total of 12,407 files (311.2M). With another anti-virus program, F-PROT (provided on the disk accompanying this book), we were able to scan the samples (and the rest of our hard disk) in 45 minutes. MSAV took 170 minutes for the same job — about four times as long. In another benchmark, MSAV took 5 minutes 36 seconds, and F-Prot took 2 minutes 5 seconds. A minute saved is a minute earned.

- ✔ MSAV misses quite a few viruses. F-Prot (the anti-virus program provided on your disk) detected 1,577 different viruses in my test of 1,590 file viruses; MSAV detected only 1,009 of these files as infected, about 63 percent of the test suite. Thus, while it is fair to claim that MSAV detects over 1,000 viruses, it also is fair to say that MSAV didn't detect over one-third of my virus collection. (There are many viruses I do not own. Whether or not MSAV can detect them is a good question. Because most of the viruses I am missing are brand-new, it is likely that the larger my collection, the lower the percentage of detections.)

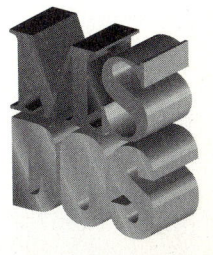

> **NOTE** *Although MSAV may be able to clean a virus, MWAV may not be able to. For example, MSAV can clean the FORMS virus, but MWAV cannot, even though it does detect it.*

✔ MSAV is somewhat casual in its virus identifications. In order to fit virus names into the screen output space, names must be 12 characters. Thus Michelangelo is abbreviated "M.Angelo." MSAV also does not distinguish between related strains of the same virus. For example, MSAV identifies 25 different strains as Friday 13th. MSAV used a total of 677 names for the 1,009 samples it identified as infected, or roughly 1.5 different viruses per name. (In contrast, F-Prot used a different name for each of these samples.) Imprecision in identification is always a concern for those who would like details on what they have been infected with or assurance that the program is able to remove the virus.

A Thorny Boot-Sector Problem

Although MSAV might detect a boot-sector virus (such as STONED or Michelangelo), it may fail to clean it. This problem can be caused either by the virus being on a DoubleSpace-compressed or host drive, or by the fact that all the virus code is not being overwritten.

In the first case, boot-sector viruses alter the DOS startup code located in the boot sector of your hard disk and activate when you start your computer from the infected drive (usually drive C). DoubleSpace-compressed drives do not actually have MS-DOS startup code to corrupt. You can, however, force MSAV to clean all drives, including compressed and host drives, by adding the /C switch.

In the second case, when a boot-sector virus infects a hard disk, it moves the original boot-sector information to another location on the disk and replaces it with virus code. MSAV then finds the original boot-sector information and uses it to overwrite the virus code. The problem arises, however, when the original boot-sector information is incomplete or damaged in some way; the result is that some of the virus code may not be overwritten. So, when MSAV then scans the drive and finds the remnant of the virus code, it reports it as a virus.

To solve this problem, first run CHKDSK. If it reports 655,360 total bytes of memory, you know that the virus is not active. To proceed, back up up all your data, run FDISK /MBR (if the disk was partitioned with FDISK; see Chapter 17 for details and warnings), perform a cold start, and then run MSAV again to verify that the problem has been solved.

If, on the other hand, CHKDSK reports fewer than 655,360 total bytes of memory, the virus may be active and that you need to do the following:

1. Boot from a write-protected system disk that you know is virus free.

2. Insert Disk 3 of the DOS 6 Upgrade set in drive A, log on to A, enter **MSAV C: /C /L**, remove the disk, and then reboot.

3. Scan all hard disks again to ensure that the virus has been removed.

The new location of the original boot-sector information may be different for each boot-sector virus. MSAV can, therefore, clean only the boot-sector viruses on the Microsoft Anti-Virus virus list.

The DOS 6.2 Anti-Virus TSR VSAFE.COM

DOS 6.2 comes with a TSR named VSAFE.COM. It is based on one of two TSRs that Central Point offers with Central Point Anti-Virus. (CPAV also offers two device drivers not included with DOS 6.2.) In testing of anti-virus products done in mid-1992, VSAFE.COM was in the top quarter of the products rated, trailing XTree ViruSafe LAN, XTree ViruSafe, Dr. Solomon's Anti-Virus Toolkit, and Norton AntiVirus.

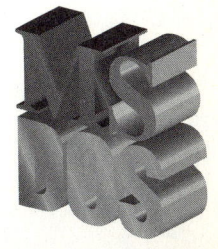

VSAFE.COM has these strengths:

- ✔ Monitors files copied to and from the server.
- ✔ Adds an insignificant amount of time to the boot process and the time required to load applications.
- ✔ Can be loaded high with MS-DOS 6.2, and with QEMM.
- ✔ Takes about 44K of memory, which may or may not be acceptable.

6.2 *The previous item corrects an error in the Microsoft documentation shipped with DOS 6.*

- ✔ Can run while Windows is running. If you will be using Windows, load the VSAFE manager (WNTSRMAN) to ensure that VSAFE messages are displayed in Windows. Do this with this line in WIN.INI:

```
LOAD=WNTSRMAN.EXE
```

Running VSAFE.COM is simple. To get your list of options, type **VSAFE /?**.

Switches for the numbered options are set with a plus or minus. To turn on option 1, for example the syntax is...

```
/1+
```

To turn it off, the syntax is...

```
/1-
```

Switches can be listed in any order, and are not case-sensitive. Precede each switch with a slash (/). Your options include:

/1+	warns of formatting the hard disk. The default is on, so you'll only use this with /1-.
/2+	warns when any program attempts to become memory-resident. The default is off; turn it on.

The DOS 6.2 Anti-Virus TSR VSAFE.COM

/3+	prevents programs from writing to disk. The default is off. Leave it off except perhaps when testing new software.
/4+	checks executables for viruses before permitting DOS 6.2 to load them. The default is on, which is where it should stay.
/5+	checks all disks for boot and master boot viruses. The default is on; leave it on.
/6+	warns of attempts to write to hard disk boot sector or master boot sector. The default is on; leave it on.
/7+	warns of attempt to write to the boot sector of a floppy disk. The default is off. Turn it on unless you do a lot of floppy disk formatting.
/8+	warns of attempt to modify executable files programs. The default is on; leave it on.
/NE	excludes monitoring of expanded memory. Because no viruses load into expanded memory by default, you will want to use this switch to speed things up a bit.
/NX	excludes monitoring of extended memory. Because no viruses load into extended memory, you should use this switch, too.
/N	permits network drivers to load after VSAFE is loaded. This reduces the interference caused by /2+. Use it if you load VSAFE before IPX.
/D	turns off checksumming. This speeds things up a bit, but makes it harder to detect unwanted change. I would not use the /D option.
/U	removes VSAFE from memory. This is a handy switch if you are trying to run a big program that needs all the conventional memory it can get, and you don't have enough upper memory

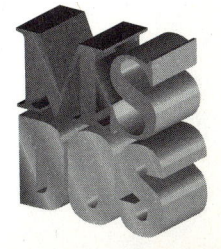

blocks to load VSAFE high. Your batch file can look like this:

```
REM Remove VSAFE from memory:
VSAFE /U
REM Run MightyFat program, that needs
this memory:
MFAT
REM Now that you've exited from MFAT,
you can put VSAFE back in business:
VSAFE /2+ /7+ /NE /NX
```

My recommendations for command line switches when loading after the network drivers are shown as the last line of the previous example (for use in AUTOEXEC.BAT, add /N).

Testing VSAFE.COM

Is VSAFE.COM any good? Should you use it? These questions need to be asked. They need to be asked because, if you want a good anti-virus TSR and VSAFE.COM didn't happen to be terrific, then you would want to use something else. It turns out, however, that VSAFE.COM is quite good, and you can use it in comfort.

We did several tests of VSAFE.COM to see how it performs under a variety of real-world conditions. We loaded it into memory after loading a common memory-resident virus, and loaded it before loading such a virus. We also tried copying an infected file when it was loaded. Table 20.4 summarizes our results.

Table 20.4
VSAFE.COM Test

Method	Result
Loading after a master boot sector infection with Stoned boot sector	If your computer boots with a disk infected with the Stoned virus, your hard disk master is now infected. If you then boot with the hard disk, install- ing the anti-virus TSR or driver,

Method	Result
	VSAFE immediately recognizes the virus infection, identifies the virus as Stoned, and rebuilds the MBR.
Loading after Jerusalem, a memory-resident file infector	If a memory-resident, anti-virus product is loaded after a virus is loaded, the product might fail to detect it or fail to work in a way that you expected. I loaded VSAFE after loading Jerusalem into memory. Jerusalem can go resident from any infected file called by AUTOEXEC.BAT (which is called after COMMAND.COM loads). It is possible for Jerusalem to become resident before the loading of a TSR if an infected file is called by AUTOEXEC before the TSR being called. In my tests, VSAFE reports it has been infected by Jerusalem and recommends using MSAV to remove it. It does not remove the virus from memory.
Loading after Frodo, stealth virus	When the machine boots with a 4096 installed by CONFIG.SYS, you infect every file you open, whether you are running the program, scanning it, or checksumming it. With this virus, it is important for the TSR to be able to detect it in memory and give you a proper warning. VSAFE was able to recognize the virus in memory. It identified the virus as 100 years.

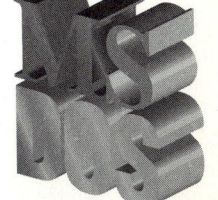

continues

Table 20.4, Continued
VSAFE.COM Test

Method	Result
Loading before Jerusalem	VSAFE identifies the virus as Friday 13th. MSAV can remove it.
Loading before execution of Vienna, a direct-action virus	Vienna is a direct-action virus. As such, any anti-virus TSR or device driver that only monitors memory might not detect it when Vienna infects its first file. I booted the machine with the VSAFE, ran Vienna, and watched what happened. VSAFE detected the virus before it was executed, identifying it as Vienna 62 C.
Copying a file infected with Jerusalem	Any infected user is likely to have many infected files, some of which may be copied by the user from place to place. What happens during such attempts to copy an infected file? VSAFE detects the file as infected with Friday 13th. This is not the preferred name, because perhaps 50 different viruses activate on this date. VSAFE was able to prevent the copy from taking place.
Directory of a disk infected with Stoned	When a floppy disk containing a boot virus is inserted into drive A and the door is closed and you type **DIR A:**, what does VSAFE do? If run with option /5+, VSAFE checks the boot sector for viruses, finds Stoned, and identifies it as Stoned.

The DOS 6.2 Anti-Virus TSR VSAFE.COM

Method	Result
Directory of a disk infected with Cascade	When a floppy disk containing Cascade is inserted into drive A and the door is closed and the user types **DIR A:**, with VSAFE, nothing happens. There was no detection of the virus.
Running a Jerusalem-infected file from the server	About half of all office computers in North America are connected to LANs, which do the bulk of modern storage in these systems. Thus, the server is likely to act as the storage vehicle for a file virus. What happens when a user from a protected workstation attempts to execute a program stored on the server that is infected with a virus? For this test, I used NetWare 3.11, a Compaq SystemPro as a server, and Jerusalem.Standard as the virus. I loaded the anti-virus TSR or driver, logged in, then attempted to run an infected program. With VSAFE.COM I got the message `VSafe Warning. File infected by the Friday 13th virus. For recommended action press any key.` The next screen displayed `Recommended action: Choose continue to repair the file. Do you want to continue?` The options are Stop, Continue, or Boot. If you choose Stop, DOS displays a message telling you it can't execute the drive\path\name of program containing the virus. If

continues

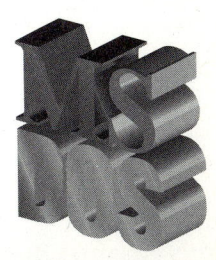

Table 20.4, Continued
VSAFE.COM Test

Method	Result
	you choose Continue, what happens depends on the virus. With the Jerusalem I tested, the message `error while cleaning, file was not cleaned` was displayed. The only option was OK. The infected file was not run, and not cleaned, but five bytes were removed from it. Be sure to run VSAFE /N if you want to load network drivers (IPX,NETX) after VSAFE.

VSAFE is one of the best things to be added to DOS, and probably will satisfy your craving for an anti-virus TSR. It can't do everything and is a bit large for some network users, but it will do fine for most purposes.

Confirming Your Anti-Virus Software's Hunches

Not every suspicious activity turns out to be a virus. You can do much to help ensure a minimal number of false alarms so that you have more energy to respond when there is a real problem.

False Alarms

A false alarm is when an anti-virus product produces a report of a virus, when, in fact, there is no virus in the location the product is examining. False alarms occur in two general locations: memory and the drive surface.

Confirming Your Anti-Virus Software's Hunches

Memory-related false alarms are generally the result of running two anti-virus products consecutively. The first product run uses memory to store its scan strings, which are fragments of real viruses; the second product run matches its scan strings with what it finds in memory, makes a match, and warns the user. The fault here lies in both products: all anti-virus products should remove their scan strings from memory before the program returns control to DOS. And generally, the virus that the second product detects in memory should not be located where the scan string was found in memory, but rather in some other specific location (the bottom of available conventional memory, for instance).

The memory-related false alarm is upsetting, but not debilitating. Turning the machine off and back on clears memory, and a second pass with the scanner that displayed the false alarm now shows memory to be uninfected.

The other kind of false alarm occurs when an anti-virus product concludes that a file is infected. This conclusion is normally based on a match of as few as 10 consecutive bytes between the file being examined and a file of scan strings that the anti-virus product is using. These scan strings, it is widely understood, provide a useful first approximation to answering the question, "Does this file contain this virus?" If part of the virus code is found in the file, then you certainly have reason to look more closely. It is now the task of the anti-virus product to confirm that the file is, indeed, infected with this virus.

Suspicious Behavior

Some alert users spot suspicious activity without the help of an anti-virus product. Not all these suspect behaviors turn out to be viruses. The following list helps familiarize you with some common problems that seem like viruses but aren't:

- ✔ Your machine won't boot. This is quite likely a hardware failure. Viruses rarely do this much damage. If this is Monday morning in the winter, and your hard disk is two years old, its bearings may be worn. Let it warm up by leaving the machine on for a few minutes, and then turn it off and back on. You may be back in business.

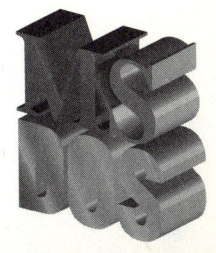

- ✔ You see 1701 on-screen when you turn on your computer. 1701 is the number of the Starship Enterprise and is the error code you see when your hard disk subsystem is not feeling up to par, during the power on self-test. Any number of hardware problems might be the cause, but this is not a virus, because you have not succeeded in reading one byte from the hard disk yet.

- ✔ You tried booting and the computer told you that you were using the wrong version of COMMAND.COM. A virus won't modify COMMAND.COM so that an error message is produced. Most modern viruses are smart enough to not infect COMMAND.COM at all (to help escape your watchful eye). You might have copied some disk to your root directory during your last session and copied over COMMAND.COM. Replace it with the correct version, and your problem will likely go away. To avoid the problem in the future, you can set COMMAND.COM's attributes to read-only, which prevents it from being accidentally overwritten during a copy.

- ✔ You just ran CHKDSK and were told that you had lost clusters and file allocation errors. You also had a cross-link. If you haven't run CHKDSK in some time, or haven't corrected such problems with Norton Disk Doctor or CHKDSK /F, then the problem is normal if unfortunate. Most undoctored machines have some problems like this, which can be caused by dBASE, Windows, or just about any program crash. A few viruses cause progressive cross-linking, but you are not likely to have one of them. Keep your eyes on the machine, run CHKDSK or Norton Disk Doctor more often, and see what you can learn.

- ✔ You just discovered some bad sectors when you ran CHKDSK. Some boot sector viruses will place programs in certain locations and mark those sectors as bad in the FAT (for example, Brain and Italian). Nearly every hard disk, however, will have some bad sectors. It is probably nothing to worry about.

- ✔ You tried copying a file, but got the following message:

    ```
    Error reading drive or Sector not found
    ```

Confirming Your Anti-Virus Software's Hunches   1113

Chances are your drive is due for a low-level format. With most older drives (ST-506, MFM, nontranslating controllers) you can run Norton Disk Doctor, Norton Disk Test, SpinRite, HDTest, Calibrate, or any other nondestructive, low-level format program and correct the situation. With IDE, SCSI, and RLL drives, and drives with translating controllers, you should do a low-level format only if your software supports such drive types.

✔ You just ran your favorite old scanner on your new 200 zigabyte partition, and found a virus in the master boot record! What you might have is older anti-virus software that doesn't recognize the strange look of this large partition. You can determine whether this is a false alarm or a real virus by trying to infect a standard floppy disk. Just put a disk without a write-protect tab in drive A, type **DIR A**, and the disk should be infected. Now run the same scanner against A. Do you have a virus on A? If not, it's time to upgrade your scanner to one of a more recent vintage, one that knows about large partitions. A newer scanner will know about newer viruses. If you have a virus on drive A now, you surely have one where your scanner first reported it.

✔ You were using your favorite program when you noticed that the letters were dripping down the screen. A virus? Maybe. It might be Cascade, but is more likely a joke program called Drippy that your office mate is trying out on you. (Although Cascade only dripped letters in the fall of 1980 and 1988, this virus infects any day of any year. You simply won't see any dripping characters as a side effect.) You need to run a scanner to be sure (or perhaps look in your AUTOEXEC.BAT for something like DRIPPY.COM).

✔ You see the message, `Your PC is now Stoned!` when you turn on your computer. Is that a virus? Yes. That's the Stoned/Marijuana/New Zealand virus. And if you have a ping-pong ball bouncing on your screen, you probably have Ping-Pong/Italian/Bouncing Ball. If you have a black rectangular hole on-screen, you may have Jerusalem. If the letters you type in DOS are displayed in funny colors, it might be Devil's Dance. None of these things seem to be the result of some component no longer working (hardware failure), but of some strange additional controlling force. If it's not you, and not the programs you have grown to love, it may be some new software that's making things happen.

If you were stumped on some of these examples, then *you may want to go back to Chapter 19 and study some more about hardware problems and solutions.*

Real Symptoms

Now that you know about the situations that look like viruses but actually aren't, you should study the following symptoms, which are not likely to be caused by hardware failure but by something else:

- ✔ **Changes in the size of programs**. Any program larger (by a few hundred bytes or more) than another copy of it has possibly been infected by a virus. Viruses never make programs smaller.

- ✔ **Changes in the time stamps**. Most viruses won't affect the date or time stamp, but a few do. If you see a date stamp on a COM or EXE file more recent than when you installed it, you can be suspicious.

- ✔ **Longer loading times**. If a program seems to take a bit longer to load than normal, it may be that a virus has infected it. Check to make sure that nothing has changed in your computer's configuration that might account for this.

- ✔ **Slower operation**. Some viruses slow a program after it has loaded.

- ✔ **Unexplained reduction in available memory**. Running CHKDSK shows you how much memory is available. This value should be the same whenever you boot. If you find less, it may be due to a memory-resident program you have run or possibly a virus.

- ✔ **Bad sectors on your floppy disk**. If CHKDSK tells you that you have bad sectors on a floppy disk today, and you did not have bad sectors yesterday on that floppy disk, a boot sector virus may have written some code to those parts of the disk, and marked them bad. You might have a boot sector virus.

✔ **Programs disappearing**. If you run a program that was in this directory last time you looked, but you see the message…

    Cannot execute filename

…when you run it now, a virus might have deleted it. Run some other program that you can see in that directory, and see whether this error message repeats. If so, and both have been erased, you probably have a virus.

✔ **Unexpected reboots**. If your computer unexpectedly reboots after running your favorite program or when you are doing nothing, a virus might be playing tricks.

✔ **Odd screen action**. If you see characters dripping from the screen, balls bouncing, ambulances driving across the horizon, screen colors changing, a black square on-screen, an unexpected message, or anything else unusual, you may have a virus.

In general, a virus may be responsible for a wide variety of odd computer behavior. One strong symptom (such as a message) or two or more weak symptoms (such as a reduction in memory and an unexpected drive light on) should get you investigating. If you suspect a virus because of the behavior of your computer or software, boot clean and run either MSAV or MWAV. If either product finds a virus, you probably have one. If neither product does, it is possible you have one of the viruses that this version of MSAV or MWAV does not detect. Consider running a newer scanner, such as the latest version of F-PROT, a copy of which is on the disk accompanying this book. Remember, no matter how good your scanner is today, it will not be adequate in a year unless you update it. This won't be as true of checksum or TSR approaches.

Recovering from Viruses

We covered the ounce of prevention in the second part of this chapter. Now you learn about the pound of cure.

If you find a virus in your system and can establish precisely what it is, it is time to remove it from your system. Because the focus of this chapter is MSAV, you first learn about the removal process using MSAV.

> Do not use MSAV, MWAV, or any other product to remove a virus until you read the "Removal Strategies" section later in this chapter.

Finish reading this section, "Recovering from Viruses," now to get an overview of what to do, read the remainder of this chapter, and then outline your own action plan.

Using an Anti-Virus Product

Most anti-virus products offer virus removal capabilities. Usually these functions are built into the scanner, giving you the option to remove a virus from a file the moment it is detected in the file.

Removal of some viruses is fairly straightforward for anti-virus products. Removal of others is more difficult. Many anti-virus products can remove some viruses, but can't remove very many. When choosing a product, ask whether the product can remove all common removable viruses.

Some viruses can't be removed, no matter how clever the author of the anti-virus software. This is because the virus has overwritten some of your original program, effectively erasing it. Without a knowledge of what was supposed to be where the virus "sat down," all an anti-virus product can do is offer to delete the entire program.

Virus Removal with MSAV

If MSAV finds a virus, what should you do next? If you think you should let MSAV clean the infected files, think again. In the case of

some viruses, an anti-virus product makes things worse. Consider the tragic case of MSAV and the Form boot virus. MSAV does a fine job of detecting it on floppy disks and hard disks. It does a fine job of removing it from hard disks. But it makes your 1.44M floppy disks unreadable by writing the wrong sector to the boot sector. You'll see the error message…

```
General failure error reading drive A
```

…after cleaning a floppy disk with MSAV.

This is not to say that there is anything wrong with MSAV—just that it's not perfect. Asking a product to clean up your viruses is not always a good move. Because you may not get a virus more than once a year, you can afford to go slowly and do things right. First, try to decide if you have a virus or a false alarm, as follows:

- ✔ If the virus is detected in memory, but not in any files, and if the virus detected is an extremely rare virus, ask yourself whether another scanner was just run. Any scanner that leaves in memory the scan strings it was using can produce a false alarm when another scanner runs.

- ✔ If the virus is detected in only one program on your hard disk, ask yourself how often you have used this program. If you have used it several times in the past, then any virus in it has had an opportunity to infect other files. If it has not done so yet, it probably won't do so—probably because it isn't a virus! This, too, is probably a false alarm. Don't delete the single program in which the virus was reported. And don't attempt removal. Instead, reboot from an uninfected, write-protected floppy disk, and run another scanner (such as the one provided with this book) to determine if it, too, finds something in this file. If it doesn't, assume that it is a false alarm.

- ✔ If the virus is detected in several programs you use commonly, you almost certainly have an infection. Do not attempt to remove the virus with an anti-virus product yet! You may cause irreparable harm to your files! Instead, read the next section carefully, and follow the steps outlined there.

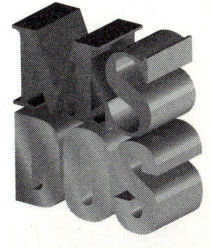

How To Remove a Virus

Removing viruses with MSAV is seemingly as simple as choosing Detect and Clean from the main menu, or running it with the /C switch on the command line.

As simple as it sounds, removing a virus is always a risky business. Viruses were not designed with easy removal in mind. In fact, selection pressures favor viruses that are not easily detected and not easily removed. You should read this section, understand the principles, and follow these steps in sequence:

1. Turn the computer off at the switch. Doing so will remove any virus from memory. Now find a rescue disk you have previously created. This disk should be bootable with DOS 6.2 and should contain MSAV.EXE or your favorite anti-virus program. It must be write-protected.

2. Boot the computer with this disk in drive A. If your machine's setup instructs the machine to boot from drive C first, you need to press a key during the boot process, run Setup, and change this to drive A. You must "boot clean" because, if you boot from the infected drive, you risk putting the virus into memory. A virus that is in memory can interfere with clean up. It can even use the scanner as a means of spreading. (Frodo, for instance, infects every file that is scanned, if it is in memory when you run your scanner.)

3. Don't run any programs from the infected drive. Instead, scan from your clean program, telling the program only to detect, not detect and remove. Identify a few infected programs. Copy these infected files to a floppy disk. Now run the scanner against that disk, telling it to remove.

4. If your scanner reports that it is unable to remove the virus, you will have to go scanner shopping. Before buying the product, ask the vendor if the scanner can remove the virus you have detected. Don't bother buying another scanner if it is unable to remove this virus.

5. If your scanner can remove the virus from the copy of the infected files, then let it do so. Now look at these files carefully. If they are the same size as the original copy or a bit larger, then the virus may have been removed successfully. If they are smaller than the original, they have been damaged by the scanner, and you must not use the scanner to remove this virus from anything. Use another product.

6. If the size of the cleaned files is acceptable, scan them with another scanner to see whether it reports a virus in any of them. If it does, it is because the scanner that cleaned left a bit of virus code in the cleaned file. Although this bit of virus code may be nonfunctional, the false alarms it causes may be costly. Use another scanner to do your removal.

7. If the size of cleaned files is acceptable and your second scanner finds the cleaned files to be virus-free, you should try running each of these samples to see whether they still operate as they should. Some anti-virus products damage files in such a way that they will not operate correctly. You don't want to damage thousands of files on your server. Only if all of these tests are met should you use your product to clean files infected with this virus.

8. You should know that many scanners do a fine job removing a virus from files over a certain size (but not smaller), or from COM files (but not EXE files), and so forth. After removal, study the report carefully to determine whether the scanner claimed to remove all copies of the virus from each file. And run another scanner against the drive to make sure that it has not found any trace of the virus.

Testing Virus Removal with MSAV

The DOS 6.2 manual tells you that MSAV "can detect and remove 1,000 different computer viruses from your system." We have seen that the number 1,000 is a ballpark number for detection. To test MSAV, we simply asked it to remove the viruses from each of our 1,590 infected samples, and then scanned the samples again with F-PROT.

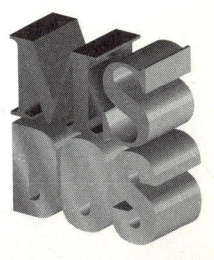

Our effort at removal was frustrating. The machine hung up on 11 different samples, requiring a reboot each time. Each time we rebooted, we lost the report file that MSAV was writing. On one sample, MSAV would not let us continue without deleting the sample, which it did not identify but reported had been destroyed by the virus. Twice, MSAV decided it had completed the removal when it had not checked all directories, and had to be restarted.

The bottom line came when we scanned the collection with F-PROT after trying to remove everything with MSAV. We found that 978 of the 1,590 samples were still infected, so MSAV was able to remove the virus from 612 samples—about 40 percent. At least 21 of the cleaned samples were damaged and would not run correctly. We suggest that you do not use MSAV to remove the following viruses: Sylvia, Vienna, Alabama, Friday the 13th (which MSAV calls Friday COM1), Doteater, Chaos, Dark Avenger, Pathhunt, Yafo, Traceback, Yankee, and Form.

Home-Grown Virus Removal

If you don't use an anti-virus product, can you remove a virus? The answer is yes. There are many programs that will effectively remove certain viruses from your system. Some of these tools are tools you already own, such as SYS, FORMAT, and FDISK. Others are special tools you can purchase. Some virus-removal tools are specialists in master boot record or boot record repair. Others specialize in removing viruses from files. And a few can do some of both.

For a master boot record infection, you can boot clean (from an uninfected, write-protected floppy disk), and then run **FDISK /MBR** with both DOS 5 and DOS 6.2. For a boot record infection, you can run **FORMAT** (writing a new boot record) and then run **UNFORMAT** (to recover everything that FORMAT has lost but the original boot record). For infections of your programs, you can delete all infected files, replacing them with clean backup copies.

If you can learn some key details about your virus, you can safely restore files from infected backups. If, for example, you know that your virus infects only COM files, you can restore all other file types from infected backups and replace any infected COM files with copies from uninfected backups.

If you learn that your virus is a boot sector virus, then you know that none of the files in your backups will be contaminated. Once the boot sector virus is removed from memory, and you have booted from an uninfected disk, you will be able to restore all files from backups infected with a boot sector virus. Just remember to not accidentally boot with one of these floppy disks!

Provided Utilities

Some programs are provided on the accompanying disks to help with the task of virus detection. These programs are discussed in the following sections.

DOSWATCH

DOSWATCH is a TSR that displays information about the current DOS service number at the top of the screen every time an "Interrupt 21" is executed. Interrupt 21 is one of the ways that you can get the attention of the CPU. COMMAND.COM makes it available to the computer and performs all manner of DOS services when this interrupt is used by a program. The services include such things as opening a file, closing a file, deleting a file, and moving the pointer (equivalent to the heads of the drive) to a specific location in the file. DOS services also can find the time and date from the system. Because interrupt 21 does so many things, it is used by most of your programs and by a majority of file viruses. The DOSWATCH program is potentially useful for monitoring what DOS is doing, particularly if a virus is suspected. You type ...

DOSWATCH

...to install it, and you type...

DOSWATCH /U

...to unload it from memory.

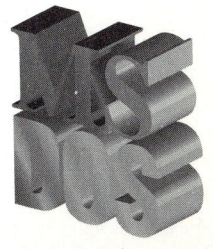

In addition to the DOS service number, messages displayed include:

```
Set disk drive to, Get the DOS time, Get DOS version, Get
disk free space, Change directory to, Create file, Open
file, Close handle, Read from handle, Write to handle,
Delete file, Get current directory, Exec program, Find
first file that matches, and Find next matching file.
```

F-PROT

F-PROT is possibly the world's best anti-virus product. Its scanner detects as many viruses as any in the world, and it does a terrific job at virus removal. You can use it to browse through information on viruses, too. F-PROT is also the cheapest product on the market. It is free for home use, and costs two dollars per machine (or less) for office computers. Complete documentation is included in the zip file.

FINDTEXT

FINDTEXT offers a fast find of text in specified files. If a virus is suspected and any ASCII string for that virus can be identified (such as "PSQRVW"), FINDTEXT may be used to find additional infected files. The text sought need not be normal text. To use it, you type...

FINDTEXT

You can use wild cards when searching files, and can search any file in the current directory. Text search is not case-sensitive. When the selected text is found, it is displayed below the file name in which it was found. You are given the options of continuing in the file (Y), aborting the search (N), or skipping to the next file (Skip).

FULLDIR

When Frodo modifies a file, it also modifies the directory, adding 100 years to the file's date (hence its synonyms, "Century" and "100 Years"). DOS doesn't show the year 2093, just 93, and you conclude the date is unchanged. When Vienna infects a file, it also modifies the directory, changing the file's time to 62 seconds. You can't see the seconds with the DIR command. FULLDIR works about the same way as the internal DIR command does, but it spells out the year as four digits, and shows all the file's time, including seconds. You can run FULLDIR with various wild cards, as you can with the DOS DIR command.

READEXE

If you are trying to figure out whether a virus has modified one of your EXE files, you can use the utility READEXE.EXE. This program reads the header of any EXE and displays the information on your screen. You can test it by asking it to report on itself with the command…

    READEXE READEXE

This information won't make much sense to anyone but programmers, but you can use it to compare a suspect EXE file with an original copy of it that you trust by running READEXE on both files. A virus can't infect an EXE file without changing its header. Any difference you find is important.

REBOOT

REBOOT can be used in a network batch file (such as START.BAT with NOVELL) to reboot any user, based on a conditional test done in that batch file. For example, users found to have a file virus in memory, who have booted from drive A, have an active modem, and so forth, can be rebooted rather than merely logged out. You want them to reboot clean. Perhaps rebooting will be clean, perhaps it will put the virus back in memory. If so, when they log in again, they are rebooted again. After a few of these frustrating cycles, they should be calling the help desk, reporting the symptoms, and getting a proper virus removal treatment.

REBOOT might also be used after AUTOEXEC.BAT has asked a question and branched to code that copied a new CONFIG.SYS and AUTOEXEC.BAT to the root. (The user might want one CONFIG.SYS for Windows, another for Ventura for DOS, and so forth.) You type…

    REBOOT

SHOWINT

SHOWINT displays the interrupt vector table (the first 1K of conventional memory). It is of use to those interested in interrupts hooked by programs and viruses. You type…

```
SHOWINT
```

Once loaded, you can scroll up or down using the arrow keys. Exit SHOWINT by pressing Esc. SHOWINT uses a 256-by-60 virtual screen, permitting scrolling through all 256 possible interrupts.

SNORETIL

SNORETIL can be used in batch files to pause until a specified time. You can use it for evening backup, evening communications, evening virus scanning of a server, and so on. You type…

```
SNORETIL HH:MM[:SS]
```

You must use military (24-hour) time and provide either five or eight characters.

NOTE: If you specify a time that has just passed when SNORETIL is executed, SNORETIL waits nearly a full day to execute.

If you run SNORETIL from a batch file from Windows, do not minimize the application.

V-Base

V-Base is an on-line hypertext database. You can browse through virus information alphabetically, pop up definitions of terms, jump to related viruses, and even search for a word or phrase, such as a synonym or a message the virus has displayed. Full help is provided with F1.

Removal Strategies

Having procedures in place to detect viruses is important. But just as important is a plan for how you will remove whatever you find.

Don't Panic

You must remember that the majority of virus alarms turn out to be false alarms, and are the result of some user, software, or hardware error. Proceed with your detection assuming that, although it may be a virus, it is just as likely to be something else, so note all symptoms carefully, and see what the combination points to.

If the problem turns out to be a virus, it is still important not to panic. You need a cool head to minimize further damage and to remove the virus as cleanly and efficiently as possible. Don't just get out your copy of FORMAT or FDISK and begin your counterattack!

Devise an Action Plan

It might be a good idea for you to have some action plan ready in the event that your organization has an infection. Some of the details to be covered by such a plan are described in the following list. If you are a little late for a plan, and have an infection now, you can try these ideas:

- ✔ If you don't already have one, create a crisis team to take on the assignment. Relieve them of their other duties until you are sure that there is not one copy of this virus still running loose in the organization.

- ✔ Take notes on where the virus has surfaced, and try to draw some intelligent conclusions of how it might have gotten there, and where it might have gone from there. The person to spot the virus first is possibly the one who has been infected the longest. Those they share disks with probably also are infected, if disk sharing has happened in the last few days. Users in your organization with home computers are likely sources of infection.

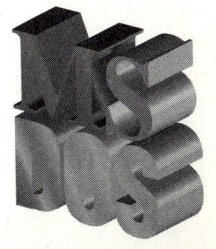

Users who try out the most software are likely to be the most vulnerable. And users with the greatest access to files and machines—the help desk, network manager, and other support staff—are the most common carriers of viruses once the virus has gotten in.

Look at each of these players in your organization and make sure that they are not infected. If you can track down the most likely path, rather than simply sweeping from one end of the building to the other, you will be more efficient in bagging all copies of the virus. After you have recovered, you can spend more time working with these key players to minimize their contribution to your next problem and maximize their contribution to your virus solution.

- ✔ Terminate network connections. Until the virus is removed from the server and prevented from reentering the server (through directory-level access controls, nonstop server scanning, an anti-virus NLM, and so forth), your network provides a terrific means of spreading it. If you clean 99 of 100 workstations and the remaining workstation logs in to the network, you may have 100 more workstations to clean.

- ✔ Brief all users and staff about the situation and give them useful, concrete tasks to perform to help protect themselves, search for additional copies of the virus, and remove any copies found. Don't try to keep this a secret from users. There is nothing embarrassing about a virus. But there should be embarrassment in not asking others for their help.

- ✔ Isolate all systems from each other during the disinfection process, as far as you can. Each office containing an infected system should be closed to distributing disks and files to the outside world until it is virus-free (including every single disk in that office), and each system that is virus-free should temporarily be closed to receiving disks and files from the outside world, until that world can be trusted. Without such isolation, users can spread the virus faster than you can crush it.

- ✔ Arm yourself with the very best anti-virus software. You want to have surefire rapid and accurate detection and an easy-to-use virus removal procedure. If this means running out to the store and doing some hasty shopping for an anti-virus product, do so.

✔ Arm yourself with thorough information about the virus you have discovered. The more you know about your enemy, the better you will be able to deal with it. Call your anti-virus vendor's hotline, call your computer dealer, get a copy of V-Base, call anyone you think may know about this virus. Read what you can about this virus in your virus books.

✔ Remove every single copy of the virus. You want to remove every single copy of the virus from the premises, except perhaps one or two trophies for your wall. This removal includes every single copy on every single hard disk, and every single floppy disk.

✔ Watch for reinfection. If you have just removed a virus from a system and cleaned every single disk on site, you should not yet breathe easily. You are very likely to get another infection in the next few days, from some unnoticed copy of the virus or from the same outside source from which you got the first infection.

But the news on computer viruses is not all bad. Most of the common viruses are not particularly damaging. Some vendors and "experts" have dramatized the virus problem beyond the facts, and your probability of infection is still quite low. And, despite what you can hear from competing anti-virus vendors, and despite some of the shortcomings noted in this chapter, DOS 6.2 comes with a free anti-virus program that is easy to use, will detect nearly every virus you are likely to get in the next year or so, and can remove many of them. Although the virus problem is getting worse, it isn't particularly terrible yet.

> *Your best defense against viruses is not software, as many think. It isn't learning how to use MSAV, MWAV, or VSAFE. Your best defense is good common sense, behavior that minimizes your risk, and intelligence in responding to both false alarms and the occasional real virus. Do what you can to prepare for the big day when a*

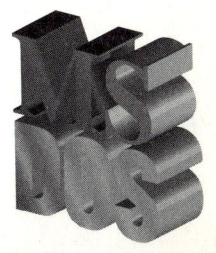

virus is detected. Get streetwise about viruses, and may the force be with you!

Descriptions of Common Viruses

If you get a virus, it is likely one described in this section. Depending on the anti-virus program you use, the virus identified may or may not have the primary name used in this section—you should check the list of synonyms.

Cascade Family

Virus Name:	Cascade Family
Synonyms:	1701, 1704, Falling Letters, Falling Tears, Fall, Autumn Leaves, Second Austrian, Blackjack, Autumn, Waterfall, Russian, Hailstorm
Date of Origin:	October, 1987
Place of Origin:	Switzerland or Germany
Isolated by:	Rudolf Rindler
Host Machine:	PCs and compatibles. The 1704 version contains unsuccessful code intended to prevent infection of machines with a ROM containing an IBM copyright notice.
Use of Memory:	Resident, takes up 2K
Infects:	COM, COMMAND.COM
Encryption:	Self-encryption (see notes that follow)
Symptoms:	In the original version, if the system month is between October 1 and December 31, the system year is

either 1980 or 1988, and the monitor is either CGA or VGA, a cascade display is activated at random intervals. In subsequent modifications, any month and year will do. The cascade display consists of characters falling from the screen, landing and remaining on the bottom line. You also can hear a click from the speaker each time a character "hits" the bottom of the screen. The virus spreads well because these symptoms are not normally displayed.

Bytes Added: 1701 or 1704 bytes (two different versions)

Damage: Affects system run-time operation. Corrupts COM files. Often produces no obvious effects, and thus can be difficult to detect. Can cause problems on Novell networks.

Prevalence: Among the most common viruses

Derived from: A NumLock utility Trojan horse

Scan Code: Uses self-encryption. FA 8B EC E8 00 00 5B 81 EB 31 01 2E F6 87 2A 01 01 74 0F 8D B7 4D 01 BC 82 06 31 34 31 24 46 4C 75 F8.

You also can search at offset 01BH for 31 34 31 24 46 4C 75 F8.

To find the 1704 version, use 0F 8D B7 4D 01 BC 85 06 31 34 31 24 46 4C 75 F8.

To find the Y4 version, use FA 8B CD E8 00 00 5B 81 EB 31 01 2E F6 87 2A 01.

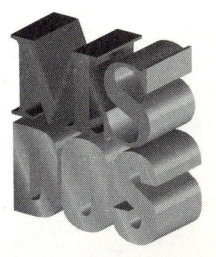

To find the Format version, use 0F 8D B7 4D 01 BC 85 06 31 34 31 24 46 4C 77 F8.

Notes

Cascade was adapted from a Trojan utility which turned off the Num Lock light and mode. The Trojan caused characters on CGA screens to fall to the bottom of the screen. In late 1987, this Trojan was turned into a memory-resident COM virus, and reported by Rudolf Rindler of Switzerland.

Four versions of the virus exist:

- ✔ The 1701 version increases the size of COM files by 1,701 bytes, and infects machines containing an IBM copyright notice in the ROM and clones.

- ✔ The 1704 version increases the size of COM files by 1,704 bytes. The author of this version apparently was editing the 1701 version, and tried to set things so that it would not infect machines with IBM's copyright notice in the ROM. The patch did not work, however, and the 1704 version infects all machines, just as the 1701 version does.

- ✔ The 17Y4 version is nearly identical to the 1704, with just one byte different, resulting in a bug in the virus. The byte change might have occurred during a file copy, and might be the result of a hardware-induced "genetic change," rather than programmer activity.

    You can catch 17Y4 with this scan code for COM files: FA 8B CD E8 00 00 5B 81 EB 31 01 2E F6 87 2A 01 01 74 0F 8D B7 4D 01 BC 85 06 31 34 31 24 46 4C 75 F8.

- ✔ The "YAP" variation has reversed two instructions in an encryption routine, perhaps permitting it to elude some scanner.

Cascade occurs attached to the end of a COM file. The first three bytes of the program are stored in the virus, and replaced by a branch to the beginning of the virus. It becomes memory-resident when the first infected program is run, and it then infects every COM file run (even if the file has an EXE extension).

The Cascade family of viruses is unique in several ways:

- ✔ The virus is encrypted (apart from the first 35 bytes) using an algorithm that includes the length of the host program so that every sample looks different.

- ✔ The mechanics of its activation are complex, being based on randomizations, machine types, monitor type, presence or absence of clock cards, and time of year. In early versions, the virus activates on any machine with a CGA or VGA monitor, in the months of September, October, November or December, in the year 1980 or 1988 (PC and XT systems without clock cards often have the date set to 1980).

- ✔ Occasionally, 1701 triggers a hailstorm. The characters on-screen behave as if they were pinned to the screen, and someone is removing the pins one at a time—it looks a bit like a hailstorm, and has appropriate sound effects. In fact, it is a purely audio-visual effect—nothing is happening to your data. But overreaction—turning the machine off—can result in lost clusters and file damage.

You can catch the virus trying to infect a write-protected floppy disk because DOS displays the message `Abort, Retry, Ignore`.

Dark Avenger 1800

Dark Avenger, the Bulgarian author of the Dark Avenger family of viruses, has distributed the source code widely. He calls this series of viruses "Eddie." The first in this series is Dark Avenger 1800, sometimes called Dark Avenger.1.

Virus Name:	Dark Avenger 1800
Synonyms:	Eddie-1, Black Avenger, Diana, Dark Avenger 1.0, Eddie
Date of Origin:	October 31, 1988

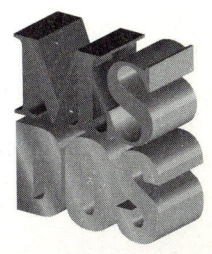

Chapter 20: Battling Viruses with DOS 6.2

Place of Origin:	Bulgaria
Host Machine:	PC compatibles
Use of Memory:	Resident, Stealth
Infects:	COM, EXE
Infectiousness:	Very high
Encryption:	None
Bytes Added:	1,800 bytes
Damage:	Substantial
Prevalence:	Among the most common viruses. Collectively, the family of Dark Avenger viruses are common in the U.S., Europe, and the Soviet Union.
Removable:	Yes
Related:	a, b, c, d, Hi, Rabid, Phoenix Evil, VAN Soft, Dark Avenger 1800.Boroda, Ps!ko

Notes

According to a document prepared by the author of the virus (whose grasp of English was less profound than his mastery of assembly language), "I started writing the virus in early September 1988. In those times there were not any viruses written in Bulgaria, so I decided to write the first Bulgarian virus. VERSION 1.0, 31-OCT-1988 established the most important features of the Eddie virus. Staying resident into high end of memory, it was infecting COM and EXE files, but only when executing them. INT 13 hadn't been handled in any way. This version was damaging infected files only, rather than infected disks. Also, there weren't any messages in it. (I still haven't chosen a name for it.)"

Dark Avenger is the author's pseudonym. Other viruses he may have written include V651, V1800, V2000, V2100, Number of the Beast (512), Anthrax, V800, and derivatives (1226, Proud, Evil, Phoenix). Although

Dark Avenger is sometimes credited with authorship of Nomenklatura and Diamond, they may be the work of others. Murphy was influenced by Dark Avenger, but is the work of another author, as may be Crazy Eddie.

Dark Avenger may be an Iron Maiden fan. Eddie is a 20-foot skeleton that appears on stage with this British heavy metal band, as well as on their album covers. Other band references besides Eddie are honored in these viruses, including "Somewhere in Time," "Only the Good Die Young," and "Number of the Beast."

Dark Avenger also has produced a virus removal program. Running DOCTOR.EXE produces this message on-screen:

```
DOCTOR QUICK! Virus Doctor for the Eddie Virus Version
2.01 10-1-89 Copyright (c) 1988-89 Dark Avenger. All
rights reserved. DOCTOR /? for help.
```

Dark Avenger 1.31

Virus Name:	Dark Avenger 1.31
Synonyms:	Black Avenger, Eddie, Diana
Date of Origin:	January 3, 1989. Released in early March, 1989, after some failed efforts to add self-checksum and other features to Version 1.32.
Place of Origin:	Sofia, Bulgaria. Isolated at U.C. Davis, Davis, California in September, 1989.
Host Machine:	PC compatibles
Use of Memory:	Resident
Infects:	COM, EXE, COMMAND.COM
Bytes Added:	About 1,800 bytes
Damage:	When memory-resident, Dark Avenger infects files through any reads, including viewing the file. It

overwrites a randomly selected sector with the boot sector. Damage occurs after 16 infections, with the counter stored in the boot record.

Intended to be destructive, the author wrote this about its release: "In early March 1989 Version 1.31 was called into existence and started to live its own life to all engineers' and other suckers' terror."

Prevalence: Common worldwide

Derived from: Dark Avenger 1.2. According to the author, "VERSION 1.31, 3-JAN-1989. This became the most common version of Eddie. A code was added to find the INT 13 ROM-vector on many popular XT's and AT's. Also, other messages were added so its length would be exactly 1,800 bytes."

Scan Code: Contains two text strings: "Eddie lives..somewhere in time" at the start of the file and "This program was written in the city of Sofia (C) 1988-89 Dark AvengerDiana P" near the end of the infected file.

You can scan using A4 A5 8B 26 06 00 33 DB 53 FF 64 F5 E8 00 00 5E. You also can use 49 CD 21 BB FF FF B4 48 CD 21 81 EB E7 00 72 7B.

You also can use 9D 73 48 2E 3B 1E 08 07 75 3A 85 DB 74 36 E8 AB 02 9D E8 83 00 72 34.

Related: The author has distributed source code on European bulletin boards, and the virus is in wide circulation. Hymn is a Soviet variant.

Research by: Daniel Kalchev, Matthias Jaenichen, Fridrik Skulason

Notes

Dark Avenger is Bulgaria's first virus author. Dark Avenger 1.31 originated in Sofia, Bulgaria, and was probably imported to the U.S. in September, 1989 by some visiting math professors at U.C. Davis. It was first reported by Randy Dean at the U.C. Davis bookstore.

Dark Avenger not only infects generic COM and EXE files, but also COMMAND.COM. Only files larger than 1,774 bytes are infected. Once in COMMAND.COM, the virus even replicates through the DOS COPY and XCOPY commands, with both the source and destination files being infected in the COPY process. The virus has been named the Dark Avenger because this code appears within the virus.

Dark Avenger 1.31 increases the length of infected COM files by 1,800 bytes. EXE files are rounded up to the next multiple of 16, and the virus is appended.

Dark Avenger 1.31 stays resident in memory (by means of manipulation of memory control blocks) and infects files by means of many DOS functions (such as OPEN, CLOSE, EXEC). For this reason, a file can become infected, not only when it is executed, but even when viewed with PC Tools, when located with some file find program, when copied with COPY or XCOPY, or when read by some anti-virus scanner! During copy commands, both source and target files become infected.

When Dark Avenger 1.31 loads into memory, it begins by destroying the resident portion of COMMAND.COM, which causes reloading of the transient portion. At this time, the virus has already hooked the necessary interrupt and COMMAND.COM is infected first.

Although it stays resident, Dark Avenger 1.31 can't be detected by many programs such as MAPMEM, MI, SMAP, and others. This is because when such a program is executed, the virus finds the program's own memory control block (MCB) and changes it in a way that it looks like the last of the chain of the MCBs (originally the MCB points to the next MCB in which the virus is located). This is especially designed to deceive programs such as MAPMEM.

In addition, in the boot sector, two variables are maintained (at offset 0x08 and 0x0A). The latter is a counter to 15 (initialized to major version of current DOS). It is incremented each time an infected program is executed. When the counter reaches 16, the number from the first variable is used to select a random disk sector, which is then overwritten by the virus. If this sector is used by a file, the file is destroyed. Should the directory sector be selected and overwritten, the results are most unpleasant.

When Dark Avenger 1.31 installs itself, it scans the ROMs of additional controllers to find the address of the INT 0x13 handler (the virus knows how it begins and looks for its own first bytes). After that, it directly calls this address. As a result, the virus can't be detected by a program waiting for INT 0x13. Dark Avenger 1.31 uses INT 0x26 for this, and is detected by many anti-virus programs with this interrupt. The virus affects functions of PC DOS and MS-DOS, such as SetVector and Terminate-and-Stay Resident.

If anti-virus software attempts to set some of the virus's vital interrupts through SetVector, Dark Avenger 1.31 prohibits this. If the anti-virus software directly changes the vector table, when the software terminates (by means of Terminate-and-Stay Resident), the virus restores its vectors.

As an extremely infectious virus, treat Dark Avenger cautiously.

Frodo

Virus Name:	Frodo
Synonyms:	Century, 4096, IDF, 100 Years, 4K, Hidden
Date of Origin:	October, 1989
Place of Origin:	Haifa, Israel
Host Machine:	PC compatibles running DOS 2 or later
Use of Memory:	Resident, Stealth

Infects:	COM, EXE, COMMAND.COM, OV*
Infectiousness:	Very high
Encryption:	None
Symptoms:	Nearly undetectable. COM, EXE, and overlay files grow in size, but the resident virus hides this growth. Cross-links can occur.
Bytes Added:	4,096 bytes for both COM and EXE files. When memory-resident, no change in file size is detected.
Damage:	Substantial. Infects COMMAND.COM, COM, EXE, and overlay files as they are opened (run, copied, or xcopied, attribute changed, or created). From September 22 until December 31, attempts to place a Trojan in boot sectors that is intended to display the message FRODO LIVES but which can hang up the system.
Prevalence:	Among the most common viruses
Removable:	Yes
Related:	Frodo.A, Frodo.B
Scan Code:	E8 08 0B E8 D0 0A E8 9A 0A E8 F6 0A E8 B4 0A 53
	You also can use 87 5E EC FC C3 83 C3 03 81 FB CC 02 72 E9 5B E8 89 0A E4 21.
Research by:	Fridrik Skulason, Alan Solomon

Notes

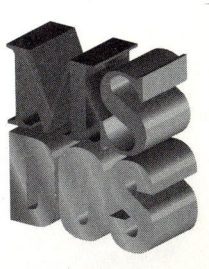

Frodo infects COM, EXE, and overlay files, adding 4,096 bytes to their length. After the virus is resident in memory, the increase in a file's length is not evident from the directory listing. This is done by modifying the first/next function returns so that files with the year greater than 100 are reduced by 4,096 bytes in size. Moreover, once in memory, Frodo infects any executable file that is opened, including those opened with the COPY or XCOPY command.

Some have suggested that through FAT manipulation, the virus destroys files through a slow cross-linking process that would seem to be a hardware problem. The virus not only modifies the FAT, but also changes the number of available sectors. Further destruction of files is likely caused by users who run CHKDSK/F. We have not observed this at our lab.

If the virus is present in memory and you attempt to copy infected files, the new copy of the file will not be infected if the extension is neither COM nor EXE. Thus, one way to disinfect a system is as follows:

1. Copy all the infected files to disks with a nonexecutable file extension. You might, for example, type...

    `COPY *.EXE *.E`

    and

    `COPY *.COM *.C`

2. Shut the system off. Reboot from an uninfected and write-protected disk.

3. Delete any infected files and restore the backed-up files to the original executable file names and extensions. Type...

    `COPY *.C *.COM`

    and

    `COPY *.E *.EXE`

This procedure does not save any cross-linked files, however.

Another procedure is to infect memory by running an infected program, copy all *.COM and *.EXE to nul:, and then to reboot.

- ✔ Infected files will bear a date stamp that is the original date plus 100 years, but you will not notice this because DOS shows you just the last two digits of the year.

✔ On September 22, the virus attempts to modify the boot sector. Systems infected with this virus can hang after September 22 of any year, due to a bug that sends the system into a loop. This is the birthday of Bilbo and Frodo Baggins, in J.R.R. Tolkien's *The Lord of the Rings*.

✔ The virus contains an unused boot sector which, if copied to the boot sector of a disk, displays the message FRODO LIVES. The message appears in large letters on-screen, surrounded by a moving pattern.

Green Caterpillar Family

Virus Name:	Green Caterpillar
Synonyms:	1575, 1591, 1591/1575, Green Caterpillar.1, 1577
Date of Origin:	February, 1990
Place of Origin:	Taiwan
Host Machine:	PC compatibles
Use of Memory:	Resident
Infects:	COM, EXE, COMMAND.COM, OV*
Infectiousness:	Very high
Encryption:	None
Bytes Added:	1,575 to 1,591 bytes
Damage:	Minor
Scan Code:	1F B8 00 01 50 33 C0 CB BE 06 00 AD 3D 92 01 74 DD 3D 79
Propagation:	Infects when a DIR or COPY command is issued, rather than when files are executed. Becomes memory-resident when an infected COM or EXE is run.

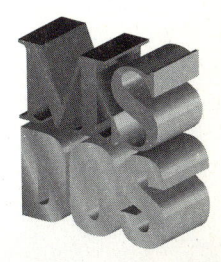

Removable:	Yes
ResQ:	Some researchers suggest that Green Caterpillar only triggers on ATs or PS/2s with a CMOS clock.
Related:	Green Caterpillar.1, Green Caterpillar.2, Green Caterpillar.3
Research by:	Alan Solomon

Notes

Although Green Caterpillar does not reset the date and time stamp, it has become very common. It displays a green caterpillar moving across the screen, munching characters, at some point after a file has been infected for two months.

Jerusalem.Standard

Virus Name:	Jerusalem.Standard
Synonyms:	Jerusalem, Israeli, Friday the 13th, Black Hole, Black Box, PLO, 1808 (EXE), 1813 (COM), sUMsDos, Russian, Hebrew University, Jerusalem B, JV, Black Friday, Morbus Waiblingen, Payday
Date of Origin:	December 24, 1987 (date first detected in Israel)
Place of Origin:	Israel
Author:	Probably written by the author of Suriv.1
Isolated by:	Ysrael Radai. This virus was first discovered at the Hebrew University in Jerusalem.
Host Machine:	PC compatibles running DOS 2 and later

Descriptions of Common Viruses

Use of Memory: Resident. Takes up 2K of memory when resident.

Infects: COM, EXE. Reinfects EXE files until the file becomes too big to fit into memory.

Symptoms: One half hour after activation, a black rectangle appears in the lower left of the screen. Clearing the screen removes the "black hole." The virus redirects Interrupt 8 (among others) and a half hour after an infected program loads, the new timer interrupt introduces a delay that slows down the processor by a factor of 10.

Bytes Added: 1,813 bytes for COM files. 1,808 to 1,823 bytes for EXE files infected for the first time. The reason for the range of bytes is that Jerusalem first adds a padding to EXE files to make them a multiple of 16 and then adds 1,808 bytes. The new EXE file length is, therefore, a multiple of 16 bytes. For EXE files infected for the second or third (or fourth…) time, Jerusalem adds 1,808 bytes.

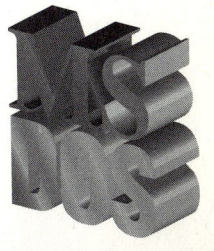

Damage: In addition to the symptoms already mentioned, it slows the system 1/2 hour after activation. It corrupts COM and EXE files. If the file length as recorded in the EXE header is smaller than the actual length of the file, the virus overwrites a portion of the file, rather than appending to it. On every Friday the 13th except in 1987, when an infected program is run, Jerusalem sets the attributes of every program that is to be loaded to read/write, and then deletes them. Users will see `Bad command or filename` or, in DOS 5, `Cannot execute drive:\directory\ filename` repeatedly. This continues despite any changes in the system date until the machine is rebooted. COM files larger than 63,723 bytes are destroyed by overwriting.

Prevalence: Among the most common viruses

Derived from: Suriv 3

Scan Code: 8E D0 BC 00 07 50 B8 C5 00 50 CB FC 06 2E 8C 06 31 00 2E 8C 06 39 00 2E 8C 06 3D 00 2E 8C 06 41 00 8C C0

You also can search at offset 095H for FC B4 E0 CD 21 80 FC E0 73 16.

And you can use 03 F7 2E 8B 8D 11 00 CD 21 8C C8 05 10 00 8E D0.

You will find the text strings "MsDos" and "COMMAND.COM" in the data area of the virus, and "MsDos" as the last five bytes of an infected COM file (this is the signature used there).

Removable: Yes (see notes section)

Related: 1600, Dragon, Jerusalem Sat-13, Messina, Pipi, T1, Timor, Virus #2, Jerusalem 1244, Jerusalem 1361, Jerusalem 1605, Jerusalem 1735, Jerusalem 1767, Jerusalem 2187, Jerusalem A, Jerusalem A-204, Jerusalem Anarkia 1, Jerusalem Anarkia 2, Jerusalem Anarkia 3, Jerusalem AntiCad-2576, Jerusalem AntiCad-2900, Jerusalem AntiCad-

3004, Jerusalem AntiCad-3012, Jerusalem AntiCad-3088, Jerusalem AntiCad-4096-A, Jerusalem AntiCad-4096-Danube, Jerusalem AntiCad-4096-C, Jerusalem AntiCad-4096-Chinese, Jerusalem AntiCad-Tobacco, Jerusalem Antiscan, Jerusalem Apocalypse, Jerusalem Barcelona, Jerusalem Black Friday, Jerusalem Blank, Jerusalem Captain Trips, Jerusalem Carfield, Jerusalem Clipper, Jerusalem Count, Jerusalem Critical, Jerusalem Czech, Jerusalem Discom, Jerusalem Einstein, Jerusalem Feb. 7, Jerusalem Frere A, Jerusalem Frere B, Jerusalem Friday 15, Jerusalem Fu Manchu, Jerusalem G, Jerusalem GP1, Jerusalem GP1 Dropper, Jerusalem Groen Links, Jerusalem IRA, Jerusalem J, Jerusalem January 25th, Jerusalem JVT1, Jerusalem Kylie, Jerusalem Mendoza, Jerusalem Miky, Jerusalem Moctezuma, Jerusalem Mule, Jerusalem Mummy 1.0, Jerusalem Mummy 2.1, Jerusalem Nemesis, Jerusalem Not 13, Jerusalem Nov 30, Jerusalem P, Jerusalem Payday, Jerusalem PcVrsDs, Jerusalem Phenome, Jerusalem PSQR, Jerusalem Puerto, Jerusalem Skism, Jerusalem Skism11, Jerusalem Skism12,Jerusalem Solano-Dyslexia 2.00, Jerusalem Solano-Dyslexia 2.01, Jerusalem Solano-Dyslexia 2.01 Dropper, Jerusalem Solano-Subliminal 1.10, Jerusalem Spanish, Jerusalem Sub zero, Jerusalem sUMFDos,Jerusalem sUMsDos.variants,Jerusalem Sunday,

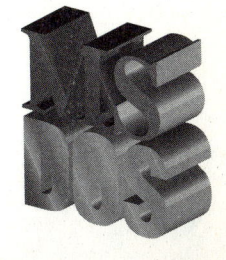

	Jerusalem Sunday.2, Jerusalem Sunday.10, Jerusalem Sunday.A, Jerusalem Sunday.B, Jerusalem Sunday.C, Jerusalem Sunday.D, Jerusalem Sunday.E, Jerusalem Sunday.F, Jerusalem sURIV 3, Jerusalem Swiss, Jerusalem T13, Jerusalem Triple, Jerusalem Turkish, Jerusalem UCNDER, Jerusalem Westwood, Jerusalem Yellow
Propagation:	This virus is a memory-resident infector. Any "clean program" run after an infected program is run becomes infected. Both COM and EXE files are infected. The virus attaches to the beginning of a COM file or to the end of an EXE file. The virus becomes memory-resident when the first infected program is run, and it then infects every program run except COMMAND.COM. COM files are infected once only; EXE files are reinfected each time they are run.
Research by:	Thomas Lippke, Michael Reinschmiedt, Morton Swimmer, Ysrael Radai

Notes

The Jerusalem virus is the most common file-infecting virus in the world, due in part to its intelligent coding, its nondestructiveness, and its age. Over 30 percent of all infections in North America are infections identified as Jerusalem, according to a survey conducted by Dataquest in October, 1991. Its commonness is the cause for its many variants.

Jerusalem attaches to the beginning of a COM file or to the end of an EXE file. A COM file has a five-byte marker attached to the end of the file, after the last byte of the original file. This marker is "MsDos." You see the marker twice in an infected COM file: as the last five bytes and at the top of the virus. At the top of the virus, it is preceded by "sU." (In its predecessor, this was "sURIV*nn*," where *nn* was the version number of Suriv.) "sUMsDos" is not usually found in newer varieties of this virus—the "sU" is nonfunctional, and the "MsDos" can be replaced with anything as a marker. In Jerusalem.Blank, for example, the marker looks like "   " in ASCII and like "20 20 20 20 20" in hex. The virus writes the "MsDos" signature in the infected EXE, but looks for a different signature. This fact suggests that the virus escaped from some programmer's lab prematurely (if it was ever intended to have been released).

Jerusalem is not a stealth virus—it does little to hide itself from the user. But it is well-written. When it tries to infect a file on a write-protected disk, for example, it traps the DOS error message `Write protect error writing drive` so that its presence is less obvious. On the other hand, if the system day and date is Friday the 13th, Jerusalem goes for broke, trying to delete everything you run. On these days, it lets DOS display the `Write protect` error message when it tries to set the file's attributes to read/write. Remove the tab, and it will delete your file for you. Jerusalem does not infect files it deletes on Friday the 13th.

Another sign of Jerusalem's sturdy programming is that it will read the directory entry for a file it is about to infect and remember the date, time, and attributes. It then changes the attributes, if needed, to permit it to write to the file, and then allows DOS to update the date, time, and attributes in the directory with the current date and time. It then goes back into the directory and resets it to the original date, time, and attributes. It is astonishing to consider the amount of work the virus has to do to infect a file, and that it can infect a file without any noticeable delay in the file's loading time (less than a second).

The end of the virus, from offset 0600H, is rubbish and varies from sample to sample.

The names 1808 and 1813 come from the fact that files grow by 1,808 or 1,813 bytes, without changing their date and time or read, write, or hidden attributes.

Although the deletion of files and the slowdown are intended effects, a bug in the program causes the reinfection of EXE files.

The original virus deletes the file you were executing on Friday the 13th, but numerous variants now perform this miracle on a variety of dates.

Recovery on a non-Friday 13th is simple:

1. Reboot the system from an uninfected, write-protected disk.
2. Run your favorite anti-virus product from this disk, and let it remove all copies of the virus from all your files.
3. Install an uninfected anti-virus product on your hard disk and use it to scan and clean every floppy disk in the office.

If you have lost files on Friday the 13th, recovery is nearly as simple:

1. Change the system date to something other than Friday the 13th, and reboot from an uninfected, write-protected floppy disk.
2. Simply record which files were deleted. From a write-protected disk, run an unerase program (such as Norton's QU) and unerase all these files. (If you prefer, restore them from the original disks or from backups.)
3. Follow the procedure outlined earlier for removal.

Stoned.Standard

Virus Name:	Stoned.Standard
Synonyms:	New Zealand, Australian, Hawaii, Marijuana, San Diego, Smithsonian, Hemp
Date of Origin:	Late 1987
Place of Origin:	Wellington, New Zealand. Written by a high school student, spread by another student.

Descriptions of Common Viruses

Host Machine:	PC compatibles running MS-DOS 2 and later
Use of Memory:	Resident. The virus code is 440 bytes, taking one sector of storage. It occupies 2K of memory.
Infects:	F.boot, MBR
Encryption:	None
Unencrypted text:	At offset 18Ah, you can find the unencrypted message "Your PC is now Stoned!..LEGALISE MARIJUANA!"
Symptoms:	The screen sometimes displays Your PC is now Stoned! when booting from an infected floppy disk.
Damage:	Substantial
Prevalence:	Among the most common viruses
Infectiousness:	High
Scan Code:	1E 50 80 FC 02 72 17 80 FC 04 73 12 0A D2 75 0E 33 C0 8E D8 A0 3F 04 A8 01 75 03 E8 07 00
	You also can search at offset 045H for B8 01 02 0E 07 BB 00 02 B9 01.
	Or you can use 04 00 B8 01 02 0E 07 BB 00 02 B9 01 00 33 D2 9C.
	A variant can be detected with 04 00 B8 01 02 0E 07 BB 00 02 33 C9 8B D1 41 9C.
	The virus uses a signature of EA 05 00 C0 as the first four bytes of the boot sector and will not infect a disk containing this signature.
Removable:	Yes

Propagation:

This virus consists of a boot sector only. When attempting to boot from an infected floppy disk (it does not have to be bootable), Stoned immediately becomes memory-resident and infects the first hard disk. It then captures all read and write calls to drive A, checks them for infection, and infects if it does not find its signature in their boot record. When Stoned.Standard has infected the floppy disk's boot sector, the first four bytes of the boot sector are EA 05 00 C0, and down toward the bottom of the boot sector you see the messages "Your PC is now Stoned!" and "LEGALISE." (Sometimes you may see "LEGALISE MARIJUANA!") If the virus displays any messages, it is just the first part, "Your PC is now Stoned!"

During the infection, the original boot sector is copied to head 1, cylinder 0, sector 3 on a floppy disk (usually part of the root). On a hard disk, Stoned.Standard places itself in the master boot record (side 0, cylinder 0, sector 1), and places the original master boot record on side 0, cylinder 0, sector 7, which is usually unused but in some hard disks can be occupied by the FAT. A variant stores the hard disk boot sector at cylinder 0, head 0, sector 2.

The virus is extremely infectious, because infection attempts are triggered by any activity that invokes INT 13h, any read or write, such as DIR or

	TYPE. Hard disks are infected whenever booting from an infected floppy disk.
Related:	Zapper, Sex Revolution 1, Sex Revolution 2, Teraz, b, c, d, e Sonus, Sanded, Nulls, Donald, Flushed, In love, stoned-floppy disk, Mexico, WD1, WD2, WD3, WD4, WD5, WD6, WD7, June 4, Swedish Disaster, Noint, Rostov, Stoned 8, Stoned 16, Damien, Laodung, Stoned 2, Stoned Polish, Stoned B
Research by:	Rainer Anscheit, Alan Solomon

Notes

Stoned.Standard is a polite but imperfect virus. Its author apparently intended no harm, but harm sometimes occurs anyway. If your hard disk has an RLL controller and is infected, it may no longer be bootable. If your hard disk is quite small (10M or less) or is formatted with an old version of DOS, then Stoned will accidentally place the original master boot sector down on top of the FAT, which is stored where the author assumed there would be "slack space." This results in a trashed hard disk. Further accidental damage can be caused to 360K floppy disk disks with more than 96 files in the root and to 1.2M and 1.44M floppy disks with more than 32 entries in the root.

The boot sector contains two character strings: "Your PC is now Stoned!" and "LEGALISE MARIJUANA!" The first of these messages is displayed only when the last three bits of the system clock counter are zero—every eighth time when booting from an infected floppy disk. The second is unreferenced. In some variations, the message is displayed on every 32nd boot. The message does not display when booting from an infected hard disk. When the message is displayed, the system also beeps.

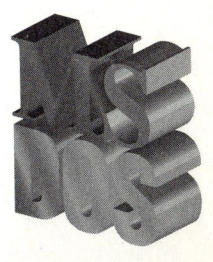

In the original version of this virus, only 360K 5 1/4-inch floppy disks were infected. Although the original version was incapable of infecting a hard disk, other versions (such as Stoned B) are capable of doing so. Neither variant infects floppy disks in drive B or any but the first hard disk.

Some of the harm that any virus does comes at the hands of the recovery "experts." One calamity occurs when the expert decides to kill Stoned on a hard disk by reformatting it with FORMAT. Unfortunately, FORMAT does not touch the master boot record, where Stoned resides. What FORMAT does to a hard disk infected with Stoned is destroy everything but Stoned. Don't use FORMAT against it.

Another calamity comes about with FDISK, a tool that touches the master boot record. With versions of FDISK older than DOS 5, you are certain to destroy your ability to ever see any file that was on the disk. Unless you are using FDISK 5, and enter **FDISK /MBR**, you won't be able to destroy Stoned with FDISK.

Yet another calamity is when you try running FORMAT or FDISK from a floppy disk that is not write-protected. The result is that Stoned immediately transfers itself to that floppy disk with your first DIR command. After running FORMAT or FDISK, the virus is carried on to the next computer. Beware the expert who comes to save you! He can be carrying a virus on his disks.

Learning More about Viruses

There are several books and programs to help you learn more about computer viruses:

- ✔ V-Base, the virus information database. It contains descriptions of about 1,900 different computer viruses, and you can branch through its hypertext to learn more about what a virus was derived from or what has been derived from it. You also can search for any text in the database, such as a message you have seen on-screen. A V-Base sampler is provided on the *Inside MS-DOS 6.2* disk.

- ✔ The International Computer Security Association's *Computer Virus Handbook*, a comprehensive, authoritative book on computer viruses and how to prevent, detect, identify, and recover from them.

These products are available from the Virus Research Center, International Computer Security Association, Suite 33, 5435 Connecticut Ave. NW, Washington DC 20015. The telephone number is (202) 364-8252; the FAX number is (202) 363-1320; the BBS number is (202) 364-0644. You'll find thousands of virus-free files on the board, including the best anti-virus shareware and many pages of information about viruses.

Summary

Life is tough and the job of mastering a computer can make it even tougher. We sure don't need viruses to add to this difficulty. But the viruses *are* coming; each day, we see many new strains, and each month brings the release of yet another totally new virus.

But all is not gloom. The problem is not yet as severe as some have suggested. Most common viruses do little damage. Most products detect all the common viruses and remove them adequately. In addition, many low-cost tools are available—like F-PROT and V-Base—to make your virus fighting easier. We may not live to see the end of viruses, but we won't live to see the end of safe computing, either.

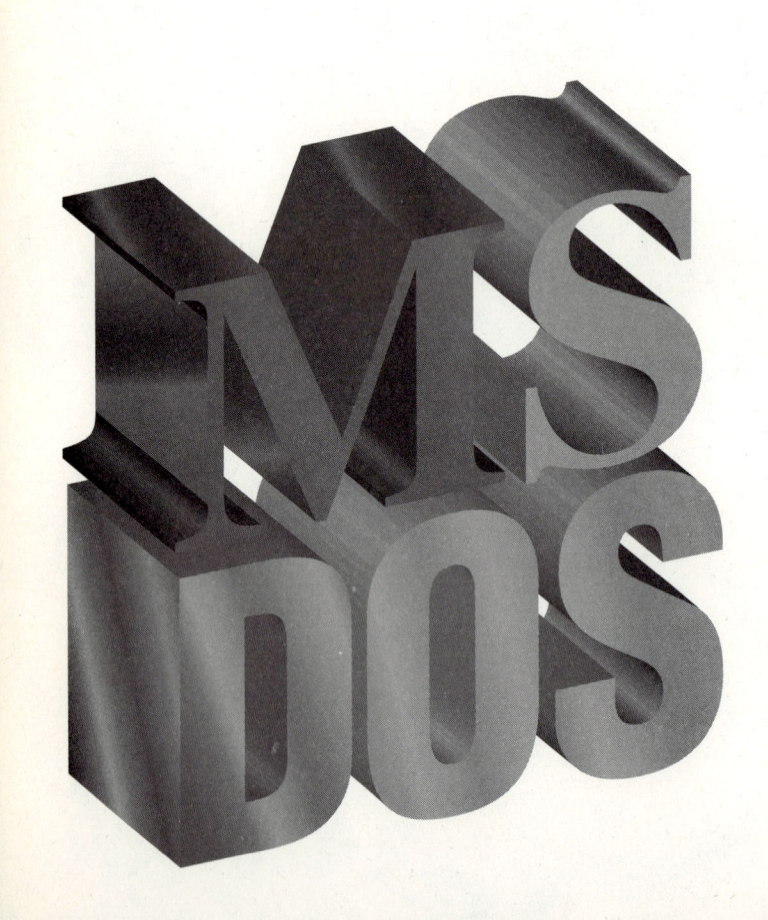

MS DOS

CHAPTER 21

Securing Your PC

by David Stang

This chapter is about some secrets of DOS, some secret things you can do that might make it a bit more secure. Some of the tricks described are dangerous, if not done correctly. We strongly advise you to format a floppy disk, and practice your tricks on it. Only if you are sure that you have things figured out should you attempt any of these feats on your hard disk. If you plan to edit COMMAND.COM, first make a backup copy using the command…

    COPY COMMAND.COM COMMAND.BAK

Now, if you want to go back to where you started, you can simply type…

    COPY COMMAND.BAK COMMAND.COM

…and reboot.

Some of the ideas in this chapter may strike you as terrific. Some may strike you as silly. How they strike you will depend on your need for security and your sense of adventure. Those needing more security and who are short on adventurousness might want to solve their problems with the addition of one of the many security products available for DOS machines. Those with low security needs might want to explore this chapter just to learn a bit more about how the old system works. Those with a high need for security and a thirst for adventure, read on, but consider office politics, support staff training, and other things before plunging in.

> **AUTHOR'S NOTE**
>
> *A vast number of computer users have a great misconception: if I install security measures on my computer, it is secure. Wrong! The best analogy is that your computer is about as secure as the lock on the front door of your house. Thieves prove every day that locks keep out only honest people—if someone wants in bad enough, he'll find a way. Even password programs, such as the one mentioned in the next section and the commercial program FastLock (from Rupp Corporation), are not foolproof.*
>
> *Although some security measures are much more bulletproof than others and keep out even very determined intruders, most keep out only the very casual snooper.*

To do some of the tricks described in this chapter, you will use standard DOS programs. Other tricks require some of the tools provided on the enclosed disk. Still others can be performed from shareware available on CompuServe.

As it comes out of the box, DOS 6.2 is not virus or user-resistant. There are several reasons for this:

- ✔ MS-DOS has ancient roots that go back far before the first virus. There was no consideration for viruses built into the first versions. Based on Q-DOS, a 16-bit operating system developed in the late 1970's with the look and feel of CP/M, modern versions of MS-DOS must remain compatible with their forerunners. This need for "backward compatibility" makes it difficult to add anti-virus components to MS-DOS because any feature that makes an operating system incompatible for a virus is likely to make it incompatible with your favorite software.

✔ Even if MS-DOS had been originally (or recently) designed to be virus-resistant, no operating system this popular could be expected to withstand virus authors for long. Sooner or later, the holes in an operating system become known. It is possible to build an operating system that is resistant to existing viruses. But such an OS can remain virus-resistant only if it does not become popular. Software (and viruses) can always be written to defeat software.

Nevertheless, you can install MS-DOS in such a way that you can defeat most of today's viruses. If everyone were to do this, the viruses of tomorrow would all be able to find workarounds. But we don't expect that most machines will install MS-DOS as described in this chapter. As a consequence, few (or no) virus authors will develop viruses to attack our modifications.

Controlling Access to Your PC

One of the most common security problems in the office occurs when confidential information in your PC is accessed by someone who should not have this access.

There are a few obvious ways you can add security to your machine. The key lock on the front of the AT and later machines, for instance, is something you could use. The original key lock permitted you to leave an application running while the keyboard was disabled. With the lock engaged, you could walk from the machine without fear that someone would interrupt a database sort, a hard disk optimization, or a download from a BBS. But most users don't use those key locks. If you think it might be a good idea to use the lock but you've lost your key, you can buy a replacement lock and keys from a number of suppliers. For extra security, you can lock the case closed with a screw that requires a special tool to remove it. This won't stop everyone, but it will stop all those who are simply curious, or just need to use your machine for a minute or two.

Adding a Password System to Your PC

Passwords offer one of the best and best-known means of providing access control for computers. Mainframe users have used passwords for decades, with good results. And even though some password systems can be beaten by "brute force" (with a program that tries guessing all possible passwords) and with dictionary attacks (with a program that tries all of the words in a stored dictionary) and with user error (taping a written password to the machine or sharing it with other users), passwords are a sound idea.

Oddly, passwords for the PC world have never been available out of the box for users of MS-DOS. You find them in other operating systems for PCs, such as DR DOS, but not in MS-DOS. But that doesn't mean that you can't add passwords to your own DOS 6.2 system.

Password Programs

PASSWRD2.ZIP (from CompuServe) contains the program PASSWORD, an ingenious program you can add to your system. Written by Ray Dittmeier, the program is designed to be placed at the top of your AUTOEXEC.BAT file. It doesn't look like a password program, which may help keep your attackers off balance.

When you run PASSWORD, all you see is the C> prompt on the screen. If someone types anything but the correct password at the prompt, your screen displays…

    Bad command or file name

…and another C> prompt. This continues until the correct password is entered, or the number of incorrect guesses (set by you) has been exceeded. From that point on, no matter what the user does, they see only the C> prompt, along with a bit of disk drive activity for realism. On the other hand, if you enter the correct password at the C> prompt, you see the time and date of the last login, and whether the correct password was entered. With this information, you will know if anyone tried to get into your machine.

The password you start with is *hello*. If you type **PASSWORD**, you see a blank screen with the C> prompt; entering **hello** gives you a report on the last date and time the program was used, and whether the password entered was correct.

After trying the program, install it in your AUTOEXEC.BAT file. You should use @ECHO OFF as the first line of your AUTOEXEC.BAT, the path command as your second line, and the PASSWORD program as your third line. These three lines will run fast enough that an attacker may not have a chance to press Ctrl+Break to prevent PASSWORD from executing. (And you also can run DEVICE=BREAK.SYS in PASSWRD2.ZIP in your CONFIG.SYS to disable the effects of Ctrl+Break.)

Because an attacker might have some chance of looking at your AUTOEXEC.BAT file after you have logged in, you probably will want to rename PASSWORD to something like CHECKMEM.EXE before placing it in AUTOEXEC.BAT, in order to camouflage what is happening.

PASSWORD has several installation options. Each of the following options listed can be placed in any order, separated by spaces:

(*any number*)	defines the number of incorrect password attempts you can make before you are locked out with an endless loop of C prompts and `Bad command or file name` messages. If you don't put a number on the command line, PASSWORD will permit three password attempts. If you place a 0 on the line, an unlimited number of guesses is permitted.
A	sounds an alarm whenever an incorrect password is provided.
O	simulates loading some other operating system, to help confuse intruders. You'll see the message `The Delta Operating System is being loaded` and your drive light will come on. But PASSWORD will work in the normal way, waiting for your password.

W	causes a warm boot after the permitted number of password attempts is permitted.
R	selects some ASCII character at random and displays it for each character that the person logging in types. Your password will still work fine; it just won't display on-screen, which is handy if you often have someone snooping over your shoulder when you log in.
D	displays a dot instead of the letter being typed. If you don't want dots all the time, but today someone is watching you as you turn your computer on, you can enter DOTS as a password. You'll be able to log in with dots echoed for this login, rather than your password.
N	displays nothing at all when the user enters a password.
B	clears the screen and displays nothing—no cursor or other clue about what should happen next.
filename	is the name you give to the file that stores the secret password. In PASSWRD2.ZIP, the file PLS.COM normally contains the secret password. The password is encrypted in the file (along with the time and date and result of the last attempted access to your system), which contains extraneous binary characters that make it look like a real COM file. But you can store the password in any file you want by specifying a filename on the command line. (You also can change the attributes for PLS.COM to make it hidden. Don't

make it read-only, or PASSWORD won't be able to write anything to it!)

After installing PASSWORD and testing it a few times, you should change the password to something other than hello. Do this with the program NEW, also provided in PASSWRD2.ZIP. Type **NEW** at the DOS prompt, and you see the C> prompt. Enter the **hello** password, and you are asked to enter your new password. When you do, it will be written to PLS.COM. From now on, use this new password when you want to log in, until you think the password might have been compromised, then change it again. Your new password can be up to 200 characters long.

Although it is clever, PASSWORD can be defeated. It can be defeated by booting the machine from drive A. (Of course, you may not need a drive named A. If you normally boot from your hard disk, you can physically disable A, or use the cables or jumpers on the drive to make it B.) PASSWORD also can be defeated if the user presses Ctrl+Break before it runs, so be sure to place it early in your AUTOEXEC.BAT.

If you use and like PASSWORD, please register and send a payment to Ray Dittmeier, its author. You'll find more information in PASSWRD2.ZIP.

PASSWRD1.ZIP (on CompuServe) contains a demonstration version of PW, a shareware program that you might want to add to the last line of your AUTOEXEC.BAT. PW asks you for a password. Respond correctly, and the program drops out of memory and lets you proceed. Enter the password wrong once, and you'll get a warning. Enter it wrong twice, and you'll find a disturbing message on-screen, a siren blasting from your PC speaker, and your machine hanging up. Someone who doesn't know the password must reboot to stop the siren. This version of the program works with only one hard-coded password. To change the password, you need to contact the shareware author. Information on how to do this is provided in PASSWRD1.ZIP.

Add a Password to Your Programs

You also can password-protect your programs so that a password is required to run them. The program EPW (in EPW.ZIP on CompuServe) adds a password to any COM or EXE file, preventing the program from running unless the correct password is given. To add a password to DEMO.COM, type…

    EPW -A DEMO.COM

To remove the password, enter…

    EPW -R DEMO.COM

This fine little program will work with everything you have, except for programs that require overlays. Do not password-protect any EXE file in a directory where you find OVL, OVR, or OV* files. If you need to remove the password, do so with the -R option. For safety's sake, make a copy of a program you will password-protect, next password-protect the copy, and then try running the copy. If it works, you can proceed to the real thing. And don't forget your password!

Generating a Non-Guessable Password

Nearly any password you can think of is one that an attacker also can think of. If you choose something like Babylon or Fluffy, for instance, an attacker can use a dictionary attack (running a program that uses a dictionary, and that tries all the words in the dictionary as a password) to guess it in a few minutes.

You can beat that approach by using a non-guessable password that is at least eight characters long. The program PASSWORD (in PASSGEN.ZIP on CompuServe) generates all the random eight-character passwords you might like. All are in uppercase, contain no special characters, and include at least one digit.

If you are afraid you can't remember such gobbledegook, then take a look at PW in PASSGEN2.ZIP (on CompuServe). This program generates passwords that will never be found in any dictionary, but are easier to remember than truly random sequences of numbers and letters. This program gives you six different passwords at a time, and you can run it until it generates a "word" that you think you'll be able to remember.

If you are still afraid you can't remember your password, print it neatly in small letters on a mailing label from your dot-matrix printer, trim the extra white space off the label, and stick the label on the back of a credit card. Because you never want to leave your credit cards loose on your desktop, you won't need to worry about leaving your password lying around either.

Ensuring That Deleted Files Are Deleted

If you read Chapter 19, you know that the DOS commands DEL and ERASE don't actually delete or erase a file, but only its entries in your FATs and the first character of its name in the root. If you want to delete a file so that no one can recover it when you're not looking, you can do so with Mike Johnson's DELETE command (in DELETE.ZIP on CompuServe).

DELETE comes with two dozen command-line parameters, which you can review with the command DELETE /H or DELETE /?. To delete a file by overwriting it eight times, and then removing it from the FAT and root, simply enter…

```
DELETE /G
```

…(perhaps for "grind it up"?). If you are using a slow machine, you are deleting many or large files, or you aren't concerned that the CIA will be visiting with their equipment that can read a file that has only been overwritten once, you can use the /O option to overwrite once and then delete it.

This DELETE command offers a benefit to auditors, too. If you're trying to remove the files GAME.EXE, GOLF.EXE, and BONGO.EXE, and you expect that they might be located just about anywhere on the hard disk, perhaps as hidden files or in a sub-sub-subdirectory, you can enter…

```
DELETE /S /F /O C:\GAME.EXE C:\GOLF.EXE C:\BONGO.EXE
```

The /S looks in all subdirectories (sub-subdirectories, and so forth). The /F forces deletion of these files even if they are system, read-only, or hidden. The /O overwrites the files once, when found.

Replacing Internal Commands

If you want to replace the DOS DEL command with Mike Johnson's DELETE program, the job is simple. First, let's describe the manual method so that you can see what is happening:

✔ First, make a bootable floppy disk in drive A by typing...

   FORMAT A:/S

   You need to edit the COMMAND.COM on this drive to prevent tragedy. Begin by backing up COMMAND.COM to COMMAND.BAK on this drive so that you can get back to where you started if you want.

✔ Use DSEDIT (on the optional, accompanying disk) to edit COMMAND.COM. Look for the command DEL. You'll find many occurrences of these three letters, but the one you are looking for is located near the bottom of the file, in the midst of a list of all the other DOS internal commands. You find it in sector 93 of COMMAND.COM, and can get there as follows:

   1. Press F7 to load a file. Enter the name **COMMAND.COM** at the prompt.

   2. Press F8 to go to a sector offset in this file. Enter **93** to get to the sector having the internal commands in it. Figure 21.1 shows what your screen should look like.

Figure 21.1

A view of COMMAND.COM's internal commands using DSEDIT.

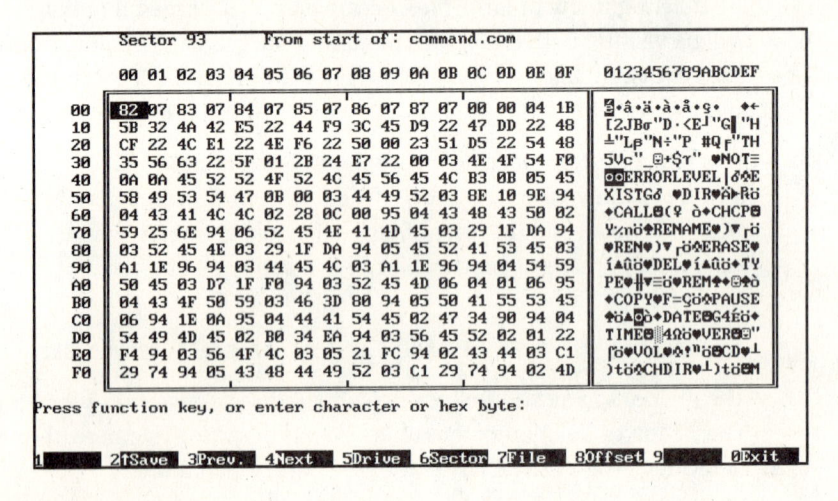

Controlling Access to Your PC 1163

3. Locate DEL (in about the middle of the panel on the right side of the screen) and simply type over one or more of the three letters with other uppercase letters. If you type an X on top of the D in DEL, you disable DEL and enable a new command to delete files, XEL. Because only you know this command, you can delete files when you want, but others can't. If you replace one or more of the letters DEL with a lowercase letter (such as xEL), no one will be able to use it. Why? COMMAND.COM translates your keystrokes to uppercase, and then looks for a match between its uppercase translation and the words in this list. If you type xEL at the keyboard, COMMAND.COM will translate it to XEL, and then determine whether XEL matches xEL. It does not, and you have disabled DEL. Your screen, after making these changes, looks like that in figure 21.2.

4. Write your edits to disk with the command Shift+F2 (Save) and exit DSEDIT by pressing F10 (exit).

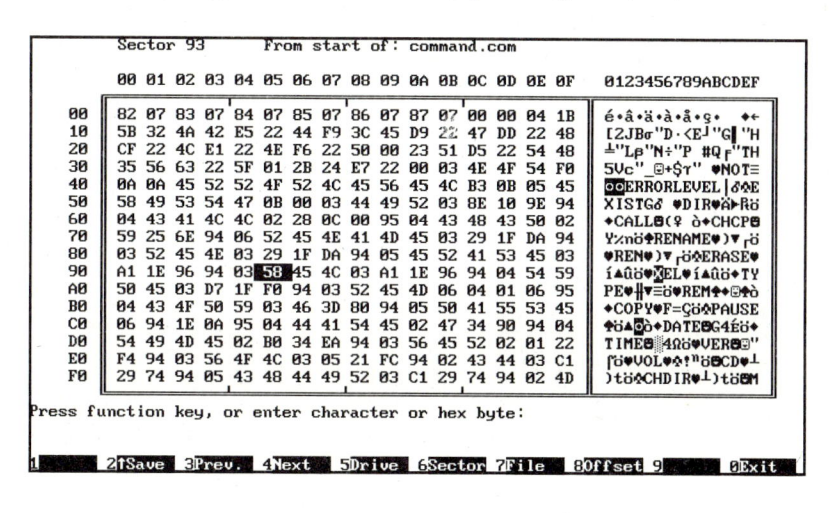

Figure 21.2

After changing DEL to XEL.

5. Run COMMAND.COM by typing...

    COMMAND

    Try out DEL and XEL on a copy of a file you don't need.

Chapter 21: *Securing Your PC*

6. Once you've disabled the DOS DEL command, you can rename DELETE.EXE to DEL.EXE. Place it in one of the first directories on your path so that it will work quickly.

7. The final test of your work is to see whether you can still boot with this COMMAND.COM. With the disk you have been editing in drive A, press Ctrl+Alt+Del and watch your screen.

> *One of the most effective ways to make your computer more secure is to change the internal commands inside COMMAND.COM. Few things frustrate a snooper more than entering* **DIR** *at the prompt only to receive a* `Bad command or file name` *error message. Use DSEDIT, as outlined earlier, to change the names of crucial commands such as: DIR, RENAME, REN, ERASE, DEL, TYPE, COPY, DATE, TIME, VOL, CD, CHDIR, MD, MKDIR, RD, RMDIR, and PATH.*
>
> *You can choose, for example, to reverse the spelling of some commands, such as RID for DIR, NER for REN, or LED for DEL. For other commands, choose a new name, such as FILE for TYPE, or FOOT for PATH. You may even want to change seldom used commands to something bizarre, such as CD%%% for CHDIR.*
>
> *Likewise, rename some of the more important external commands (such as ATTRIB, CHKDSK, LABEL, XCOPY, and so on) to names that are totally unrelated to computers, such as the names of family members, cities, states, or whatever.*
>
> *Keep in mind that if you change the names of commands, you need to edit some of your batch files because they obviously use some of these commands.*

An alternative is to use INT (in INT.ZIP on CompuServe), a neat little COMMAND.COM patcher written by David Masaki. The syntax for INT(ernal) is…

```
INT command-name replacement-name [COMMAND.COM]
```

The *command-name* is the name of the command that you want to turn off, turn on, or rename. This parameter is required.

The *replacement-name* is the name that you want to replace the DOS command name with. Make it exactly the same number of characters as the original name (for instance, DEL can be replaced with XXX, but not with XX or XXXX).

The last parameter is the path and file name of COMMAND.COM. This is optional, and if it is left out, INT will look for the COMSPEC environment setting to find COMMAND.COM. If you have more than one copy of COMMAND.COM that is used, then you should use INT to perform the same action on all copies. This option must contain either a colon (:), backslash(\), or period(.), because INT looks for these characters to distinguish between the options.

> *If you are nervous about all of this, make yourself a bootable floppy disk, copy INT to it, boot with it, and conduct all your experiments there. Remember that the changes you make in the COMMAND.COM file won't take effect until you load the edited file into memory— either by rebooting with it or by running it by typing* **COMMAND**.

Changing the Name of AUTOEXEC.BAT

Some folks think that AUTOEXEC is a vice president of General Motors. Actually, it is the most common name for the default batch file that runs when you boot your machine. The name AUTOEXEC.BAT is defined in COMMAND.COM, and it is there so that you can change the name AUTOEXEC.BAT to another name, if you want. By changing it to something odd, a user who copies files to your drive is less likely to overwrite AUTOEXEC.BAT; an attacker who looks for your AUTOEXEC.BAT in order to defeat some command in it won't find the real, automatically executing batch file you use. You can even place a file named AUTOEXEC.BAT in your root as a decoy, if you want. Others may think this file ran when you booted, but it won't if you make the following change.

Chapter 21: Securing Your PC

To change the name of AUTOEXEC.BAT, using DSEDIT (on the optional disk accompanying this book), look for \AUTOEXEC in COMMAND.COM. Follow these steps:

1. Press F7 to load a file. Enter the name **COMMAND.COM** at the prompt.

2. Press F8 to go to a sector offset from the start of the file. Enter 15 to get to the sector offset within COMMAND.COM that has the internal commands in it.

3. Press the PgDn key to see the second half of this sector. (DSEDIT only displays 256 bytes at a time, and a sector is 512 bytes in size, so you have two screens to view). Figure 21.3 shows what your screen should look like.

Figure 21.3

A view of the reference to \AUTOEXEC.BAT in COMMAND.COM as seen with DSEDIT.

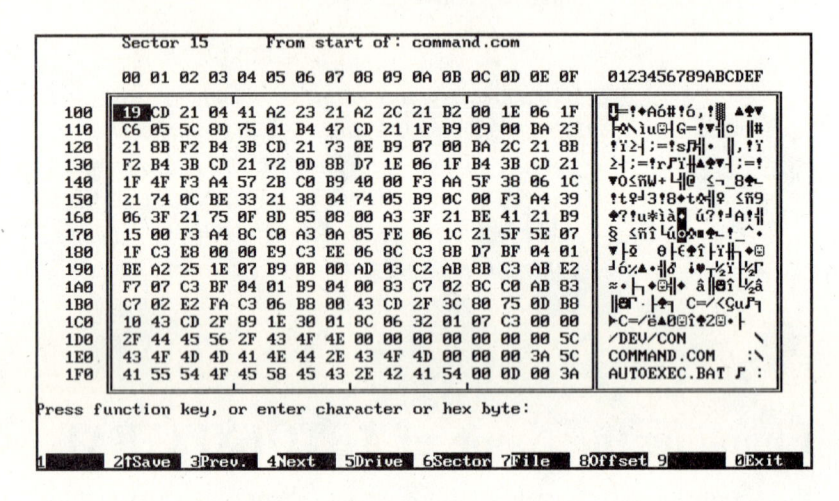

```
Sector 15      From start of: command.com

     00 01 02 03 04 05 06 07 08 09 0A 0B 0C 0D 0E 0F   0123456789ABCDEF

100  19 CD 21 04 41 A2 23 21 A2 2C 21 B2 00 1E 06 1F
110  C6 05 5C 8D 75 01 B4 47 CD 21 1F B9 09 00 BA 23
120  21 8B F2 B4 3B CD 21 73 0E B9 07 00 BA 2C 21 8B
130  F2 B4 3B CD 21 72 0D 8B D7 1E 06 1F B4 3B CD 21
140  1F 4F F3 A4 57 2B C0 B9 40 00 F3 AA 5F 38 06 1C
150  21 74 0C BE 33 21 38 04 74 05 B9 0C 00 F3 A4 39
160  06 3F 21 75 0F 8D 85 08 00 A3 3F 21 BE 41 21 B9
170  15 00 F3 A4 8C C0 A3 0A 05 FE 06 1C 21 5F 5E 07
180  1F C3 E8 00 00 E9 C3 EE 06 8C C3 8B D7 BF 04 01
190  BE A2 25 1E 07 B9 0B 00 AD 03 C2 AB 8B C3 AB E2
1A0  F7 07 C3 BF 04 01 B9 04 00 83 C7 02 8C C0 AB 83
1B0  C7 02 E2 FA C3 06 B8 00 43 CD 2F 3C 80 75 0D B8
1C0  10 43 CD 2F 89 1E 30 01 8C 06 32 01 07 C3 00 00
1D0  2F 44 45 56 2F 43 4F 4E 00 00 00 00 00 00 00 5C   /DEV/CON       \
1E0  43 4F 4D 4D 41 4E 44 2E 43 4F 4D 00 00 00 3A 5C   COMMAND.COM   :\
1F0  41 55 54 4F 45 58 45 43 2E 42 41 54 00 0D 00 3A   AUTOEXEC.BAT ♪ :

Press function key, or enter character or hex byte:

1       2↑Save  3Prev.  4Next   5Drive  6Sector 7File   8Offset 9       0Exit
```

4. Locate \AUTOEXEC.BAT and change it to any other name, such as CARBOSS.BAT. (If you shorten the name, you need to follow the name with 00 in hex. If you lengthen the name, make sure that it occurs before the musical note, 0D hex.) We've done this in figure 21.4.

5. Save your work by pressing Shift+F2 (Save). You see the message `Writing....` Exit by pressing F10.

Controlling Access to Your PC 1167

6. Make a batch file named CARBOSS.BAT in your root. Your batch file might contain something as simple as the line `echo Hello Detroit!`. Test CARBOSS.BAT by typing **CARBOSS** to see that it runs.

Figure 21.4
AUTOEXEC.BAT is now \CARBOSS.BAT in COMMAND.COM.

7. Reboot and see whether the original A:\AUTOEXEC.BAT or A:\CARBOSS.BAT executes. If you've succeeded, A:\CARBOSS.BAT will execute.

Changing AUTOEXEC.BAT to CARBOSS.BAT is hardly a security feature, however. Rather, it simply proves that you don't need to retain the name AUTOEXEC.BAT, which everyone, including hackers, knows. If you want to make your AUTOEXEC.BAT file secure, you can rename it to something else, and then modify COMMAND.COM to look for a file of this new name. If you want to try a super-tricky name, try something like CARBOSS^.BAT, where the ^ character is actually the nonprinting Alt+255 character. The directory view of the file name will look just the same as it does for CARBOSS.BAT, but no one (except you and anyone who knows your secret) will be able to display it with a simple TYPE command (because they won't spell its name correctly). You also can make it a hidden file, and make it read-only, as you will see.

> *To further muddy the water for an unauthorized user, you can create a dummy AUTOEXEC.BAT file, such as this one:*
>
> ```
> @echo off
> cls
> echo            * * *   W A R N I N G !
> W A R N I N G !   W A R N I N G !  * * *
> echo
> U N A U T H O R I Z E D   A C C E S S
> prompt Error 1101
> ```
>
> *If the snoop runs your bogus AUTOEXEC.BAT file, he sees an intimidating (albeit harmless) message and a strange prompt:*
>
> ```
> Error 1101
> ```
>
> *This sounds serious. If he tries to TYPE the file (fat chance if you've patched the internal commands in COMMAND.COM), the result is pretty much the same.*

Changing the Extension of BAT Files

There is nothing in the Ten Commandments that says that your batch files must have a BAT extension. They can all have a TCH extension, a XYZ extension, or a nonprinting extension composed of three repetitions of the Alt+255 key combination. To change the default extensions for batch files using DSEDIT, follow these steps:

1. Go to drive A, back up COMMAND.COM, and load DSEDIT.

2. Press F7 (file) and load COMMAND.COM. Using F8, go to offset sector 93 in this file. Press PgDn to see the bottom half of the sector.

3. Your screen should look like that shown in figure 21.5.

4. Edit the sequence .COM.EXE.BAT to give your batch files whatever extension you want. In figure 21.6, it has been made CAT.

Controlling Access to Your PC **1169**

Figure 21.5

DSEDIT discovers BAT definition in COMMAND.COM.

Figure 21.6

BAT files must now be named with the CAT extension.

5. Save your work with Shift+F2 (Save).

6. Exit DSEDIT and create a CAT file, such as PUSSY.CAT with some simple line such as echo CAT file just ran!. If you don't have one on this disk, create a BAT file, too. You might want to put a line in it such as echo BAT file just ran!. Now run COMMAND.COM (just type **COMMAND**) and try your BAT and CAT files. CAT files should run, BAT files should fail.

This trick also doesn't do much for security. It just proves that you can control your fate. To use the trick to make things more secure, you might do these things:

1. Don't bother with CATs. Instead, you can have all your batch files end in an extension created with three Alt+255 key presses (FF hex). This extension is completely hidden. You'll need to rename batch files and change COMMAND.COM as you just did, replacing .BAT with .^^^. Your screen would look like that shown in figure 21.7.

Figure 21.7

Changing BATs to .^^^s.

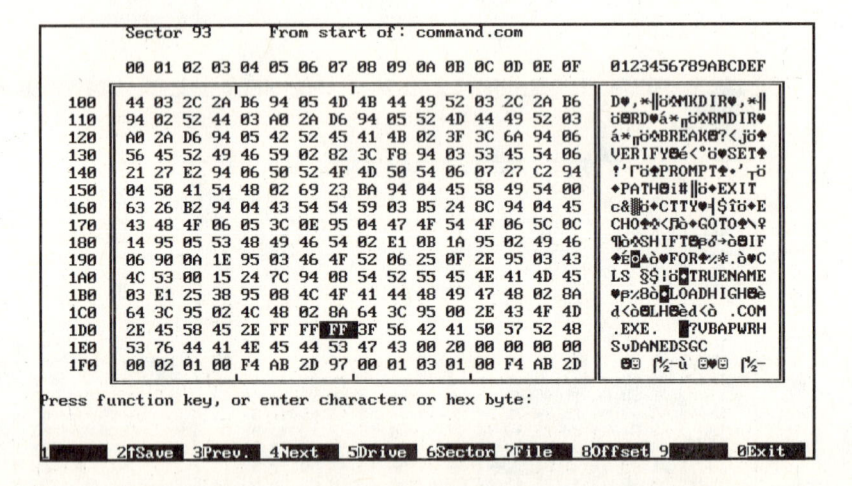

2. If COMMAND.COM is still looking for \CARBOSS.BAT, that's OK. Even if the extension for batch files is XYZ, COMMAND.COM will be happy to process \CARBOSS.BAT for its equivalent of \AUTOEXEC.BAT if you have made this change.

Perform all these experiments on drive A. When you are happy with your results, copy COMMAND.COM to drive C, placing it wherever you specify in your second hidden system file (see the later section "Using Secret Names for COMMAND.COM"). Then be sure to protect it with the read-only attribute with the command...

ATTRIB +R COMMAND.COM

If you want, you also can use +H to hide it.

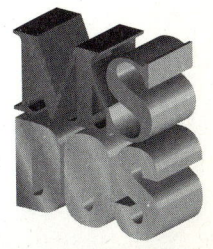

After fully testing your work, if you want to pass on your modified COMMAND.COM to other systems, you can do so either by copying the file to other DOS 6.2 systems (be sure to replace all copies) or with...

```
FORMAT /S
```

...having booted from a modified system.

Logging Bootups

BOOTLOG.BAT keeps track of each time anyone boots the computer by inserting the date and time into BOOT.LOG, an ASCII text file:

```
@echo off
prompt $d $t
type empty.bat > empty.bat
command /c empty.bat >> c:\boot.log
del empty.bat
prompt $P$G
```

TYPE creates a zero-length batch file that is later deleted. The first PROMPT command inserts the date and time that are added to BOOT.LOG because of the >> symbols (without both of the arrows, BOOT.LOG is overwritten, instead of added to).

The last PROMPT command is the one you normally use. It's best to call BOOTLOG.BAT from AUTOEXEC.BAT. For added security, rename it something less obvious.

Blanking the Screen

Here's a neat little screen-blanking trick that uses only the capability of ANSI.SYS. After making sure ANSI is loaded, create BLANK.BAT with the EDIT utility, as follows:

```
@SET P=%PROMPT%
@PROMPT $E[8m

@PROMPT %P%
@SET P=
@CLS
```

This uses ANSI's invisible attribute (8) to blank the screen. Before running BLANK.BAT, however, create UNBLANK.BAT, as follows:

```
@SET P=%PROMPT%
@PROMPT $e[37;40m

@PROMPT %p%
@SET P=
@CLS
```

This returns the screen to normal by setting the colors to white letters on a black background. Rename UNBLANK to any name to provide a password. Be warned, however, that the computer still works normally, even though you can't see what it displays. Also, only DOS is blanked—a user can still execute an application, which displays on the screen because it takes control of the screen directly.

Reprogramming the Keyboard

One of the most diabolical things you can do for security is to reprogram the keyboard. This trick requires a little time to set up, but it's one of the most effective security techniques that you can do with DOS.

Use a text editor that enables you to insert the Esc sequence (EDIT enables you to do so by pressing Ctrl+P, and then Esc). Then use EDIT to create KEYSOFF.BAT, which reprograms the letters a-z (scan codes 97-122) and A-Z (scan codes 65-90) to scan code 254, which is the little block character. No matter which alphanumeric key the user presses, the little block character is all he sees. The contents are as follows:

```
@echo off
echo {ESC}[97;254p
echo {ESC}[98;254p
echo {ESC}[99;254p
echo {ESC}[100;254p
echo {ESC}[101;254p
echo {ESC}[102;254p
echo {ESC}[103;254p
echo {ESC}[104;254p
echo {ESC}[105;254p
echo {ESC}[106;254p
echo {ESC}[107;254p
```

```
echo {ESC}[108;254p
echo {ESC}[109;254p
echo {ESC}[110;254p
echo {ESC}[111;254p
echo {ESC}[112;254p
echo {ESC}[113;254p
echo {ESC}[114;254p
echo {ESC}[115;254p
echo {ESC}[116;254p
echo {ESC}[117;254p
echo {ESC}[118;254p
echo {ESC}[119;254p
echo {ESC}[120;254p
echo {ESC}[121;254p
echo {ESC}[122;254p
echo {ESC}[65;254p
echo {ESC}[66;254p
echo {ESC}[67;254p
echo {ESC}[68;254p
echo {ESC}[69;254p
echo {ESC}[70;254p
echo {ESC}[71;254p
echo {ESC}[72;254p
echo {ESC}[73;254p
echo {ESC}[74;254p
echo {ESC}[75;254p
echo {ESC}[76;254p
echo {ESC}[77;254p
echo {ESC}[78;254p
echo {ESC}[79;254p
echo {ESC}[80;254p
echo {ESC}[81;254p
echo {ESC}[82;254p
echo {ESC}[83;254p
echo {ESC}[84;254p
echo {ESC}[85;254p
echo {ESC}[86;254p
echo {ESC}[87;254p
echo {ESC}[88;254p
echo {ESC}[89;254p
echo {ESC}[90;254p
cls
```

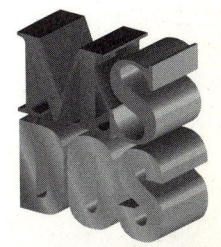

Chapter 21: *Securing Your PC*

> **NOTE** *If you use CTTY NUL to prevent screen echo, make sure that the preceding commands execute before the CTTY NUL command. See Chapter 15 for details on using CTTY NUL.*

Before running KEYSOFF.BAT, create 12345678.BAT, which resets all the keys back to their default values. Obviously, the reason you name this file with numbers is that the alphanumeric keys no longer work. Actually, you can name this file anything you want (such as &^%$#, for example) to provide yourself with a rudimentary password. The contents of 12345678.BAT are as follows:

```
@echo off
echo {ESC}[97;97p
echo {ESC}[98;98p
echo {ESC}[99;99p
echo {ESC}[100;100p
echo {ESC}[101;101p
echo {ESC}[102;102p
echo {ESC}[103;103p
echo {ESC}[104;104p
echo {ESC}[105;105p
echo {ESC}[106;106p
echo {ESC}[107;107p
echo {ESC}[108;108p
echo {ESC}[109;109p
echo {ESC}[110;110p
echo {ESC}[111;111p
echo {ESC}[112;112p
echo {ESC}[113;113p
echo {ESC}[114;114p
echo {ESC}[115;115p
echo {ESC}[116;116p
echo {ESC}[117;117p
echo {ESC}[118;118p
echo {ESC}[119;119p
echo {ESC}[120;120p
echo {ESC}[121;121p
echo {ESC}[122;122p
echo {ESC}[65;65p
```

```
echo {ESC}[66;66p
echo {ESC}[67;67p
echo {ESC}[68;68p
echo {ESC}[69;69p
echo {ESC}[70;70p
echo {ESC}[71;71p
echo {ESC}[72;72p
echo {ESC}[73;73p
echo {ESC}[74;74p
echo {ESC}[75;75p
echo {ESC}[76;76p
echo {ESC}[77;77p
echo {ESC}[78;78p
echo {ESC}[79;79p
echo {ESC}[80;80p
echo {ESC}[81;81p
echo {ESC}[82;82p
echo {ESC}[83;83p
echo {ESC}[84;84p
echo {ESC}[85;85p
echo {ESC}[86;86p
echo {ESC}[87;87p
echo {ESC}[88;88p
echo {ESC}[89;89p
echo {ESC}[90;90p
cls
```

Another trick is to call KEYSOFF.BAT from AUTOEXEC.BAT (make it the last line) in case the snoop tries rebooting. When you boot up, however, you know what to type to restore everything.

Permanently Erasing Files

DOS 6.2's file-recovery features make it a lot harder to lose files by deletion. This is usually a good thing, but there may be times when you want a file to be deleted forever. Of course, you can buy Norton Utilities to get WIPEFILE, which meets government standards, or you can create your own utility that probably stops everybody you need to stop. To create your own utility, write DESTROY.BAT:

```
@echo off
cls
if %1!==! GOTO oops
echo      ==================================
echo             * * * W A R N I N G * * *
echo      ==================================
echo File %1 will be deleted without ANY
echo possibility of recovery!!!
echo .
echo Press Ctrl+C now to abort, or
pause
copy c:\dos\qbasic.exe %1 > NUL
del %1
echo File %1 has been deleted.
goto end
:oops
echo Oops! You forgot to type a filename.
echo          DESTROY filename.ext
:end
```

This simple utility copies the large QBASIC.EXE file over your file, thereby overwriting it, and then erases the file. If someone now undeletes the file, all he or she sees is the binary code of QBASIC.EXE. Of course, you can use any large file by simply including the filespec.

If you need a larger file, use the most mammoth you can find (such as Word for Windows, which is over 1M, or Excel, which is over 2M). Alternately, you can create your own by combining two or more files with the COPY /B command. For example, use this command:

```
COPY C:\DOS\QBASIC /B + C:\WP51\WP.EXE /B +
C:\123\123.EXE /B  %1 > NUL.
```

Controlling Access with Menus and Batch Files

One of the best ways to control access, once your machine has booted, is with a menu system that prevents any user from exiting to DOS

without a password. Creating such a menu system is fairly simple with any of the many menu packages available for DOS 6.2. I am particularly fond of AUTOMENU by Marshall Magee, but you can use whatever you like. Once you have a solid menu system in place, you can add some embellishments, as discussed in the following sections.

Preventing Shelling to DOS from Programs

If your menu system is designed to maintain control of the user and deny him access to the DOS prompt, then you are vulnerable if users can run 1-2-3 or WordPerfect via menu. The problem is that these programs, and many others, have options that permit the user to shell to DOS. Once they've done that, your entire system is vulnerable. But you can disable shelling to DOS with Marc Perkel's COMSPEC (in COMSPEC.ZIP on CompuServe). From your menu, use a command line, such as COMSPEC WP, to call WordPerfect but prevent it from shelling to DOS. If the menu option is to use WordPerfect to edit REPORT.DOC, then the command would be…

```
COMSPEC WP REPORT.DOC
```

Permitting Shelling to DOS with a Password

If you want to permit certain authorized users to shell to DOS from programs, but deny such rights to other users, you can password-protect shelling to DOS with NOSHELL.COM (in NOSHELL.ZIP on CompuServe). Written by Steve Dunn, this program can be configured for any password by running CFG_NOSH. It then runs as a TSR taking only 1.9K of conventional memory unless you load it high. If your DOS shell is COMMAND.COM or 4DOS.COM, it asks users for a password whenever they try shelling to DOS from WordPerfect, 1-2-3, and so on. If the user enters the password correctly, the DOS prompt is displayed. Otherwise, the user never leaves the application.

Passwords are case sensitive with NOSHELL.COM, must be at least 6 characters long, and can be as long as 16 characters.

Preventing Exiting from Batch Files with Ctrl+Break

Ctrl+Break (or Ctrl+C) normally permits a user to break out of a batch file. This is good if the user wrote the batch file and has changed his or her mind about continuing to run it. It is not good if the network manager wrote it, and doesn't want the user dropping to DOS and wandering about the system.

Normally, you prevent the use of Ctrl+Break by placing BREAK ON as the first line of AUTOEXEC.BAT. But this isn't enough if you have a long CONFIG.SYS, and Ctrl+Break is pressed before BREAK ON is issued. And BREAK ON just doesn't seem to work reliably.

Marc Perkel's BREAK.SYS (in BREAK.ZIP on CompuServe) comes to your rescue. Install it in CONFIG.SYS after your memory manager with the line…

```
DEVICE=BREAK.SYS
```

…and put the line BREAK ON in your AUTOEXEC.BAT to turn it on. Now, Ctrl+Break won't stop the execution of a batch file, although it will still terminate the operation of some unruly programs. If you don't want Ctrl+Break to ever work, then your CONFIG.SYS line would be…

```
DEVICE=BREAK.SYS /C
```

A final trick that will absolutely prevent anyone from getting out of a batch file? Try this line at the top of the AUTOEXEC batch file…

```
SHELL=COMMAND.COM /E:400 /C AUTOEXEC.BAT
```

This makes AUTOEXEC.BAT the secondary command processor. You'll lock up the machine with a Ctrl+Break, but you can always reboot with no harm done.

Controlling Access with Encryption

If you encrypt a critical file, then only the user who knows the key and the algorithm to decrypt it will be able to access the contents of that file. LOCKIT (and LOCK386—a faster version for machines with an 80386 or 80486 CPU) by Gary Maddox can encrypt your files.

Running LOCKIT is simple: simply put LOCKIT on your path and type…

```
LOCKIT filename
```

…in which *filename* is the name of the file you want to encrypt or decrypt. You'll be asked for a password. Use the same password to decrypt a file that you used to encrypt it. LOCKIT will encrypt the file (if it is not already) or decrypt it (if it is already encrypted). You'll find this program in LOCKIT.ZIP on CompuServe.

Looking at the Problem of Theft

Theft is one of the big problems confronting users today. The nicest computers seem to contain the most valuable information, and are most often stolen.

Deterring Theft

To deter theft, make your computer difficult to resell. You can spray paint the cover with Day-Glo or other paint color that "ruins" it—without harming its performance. You can stencil your company ID on the frame. You can lock it to the desk.

Recovering from Theft

Even if you try to deter theft, in some organizations it will occur anyway. Schools, libraries, and offices open to the public are especially vulnerable, as are any unguarded laptops in large organizations. Recovering your computer is unlikely; theft is, therefore, the most severe event that can happen to your information. Because the information may be lost even if the computer is recovered, your best defense against this loss is frequent, trustworthy backups.

Rewards

Suppose that someone picks up your laptop, drops it in their bag, and walks away. Suppose that they sell it to someone, who sells it to someone, who turns it on. What will they see? If you happen to be running REWARD.EXE in your AUTOEXEC.BAT, they will see your reward message. Although your reward might not exceed the amount they just paid for your computer, they just might return it anyway.

REWARD.EXE (found in REWARD.ZIP on CompuServe) displays any reward message you like for about 30 seconds or until someone presses a key. Put your name, address, phone, and fax numbers in the message, and you increase the chance that a missing computer may find its way back to you. Thanks to Les Gainous for this clever idea!

Secret ID

Suppose that your computer is recovered by the police. Can you prove it is yours? Most users don't know their machine's serial number or have any identifying information on it but fingerprints and smudges. You can place a secret ID in the slack space of your hard disk (side 0, cylinder 0, sector 2 and beyond). Use DSEDIT to do this as follows:

1. Load DSEDIT from your hard disk, or load it from floppy disk, and then change to drive C by pressing F5.

2. Go to a sector which is completely empty or filled with the same repeating sequence. You should find that sector 2 meets this condition. (The first sector, sector 0, contains the master boot record. If you are using DBLSPACE, the second sector (sector 1) will be used.) Use the PgDn key to look at the entire sector to make sure that it is empty. If it is empty, it is unused and you can write to it. The first sectors are not tracked by the FAT, not used by normal files, and not normally accessible through the DOS file system. But DSEDIT can modify them.

3. Put in your identifying information. A sample is shown in figure 21.8.

Even if a thief reformats the hard disk, these sectors won't be modified.

```
David Stang's Disk Sector Editor.        Disk C          Sector 2

      00 01 02 03 04 05 06 07 08 09 0A 0B 0C 0D 0E 0F    0123456789ABCDEF

00    54 68 69 73 20 63 6F 6D 70 75 74 65 72 00 00 00    This computer
10    68 61 73 00 62 65 65 6E 00 73 74 6F 6C 65 6E 00    has been stolen
20    66 72 6F 6D 00 44 61 76 69 64 00 53 74 61 6E 67    from David Stang
30    00 00 00 00 00 00 00 00 00 00 00 00 00 00 00 00
40    50 6C 65 61 73 65 00 63 61 6C 6C 00 00 00 00 00    Please call
50    00 00 00 00 00 00 00 00 00 00 00 00 00 00 00 00
60    32 30 32 2D 33 36 34 2D 38 32 35 32 00 00 00 00    200-370-8000
70    00 00 00 00 00 00 00 00 00 00 00 00 00 00 00 00
80    63 6F 6C 6C 65 63 74 00 66 6F 72 00 00 00 00 00    collect for
90    52 45 57 41 52 44 21 21 21 00 00 00 00 00 00 00    REWARD!!!
A0    00 00 00 00 00 00 00 00 00 00 00 00 00 00 00 00
B0    00 00 00 00 00 00 00 00 00 00 00 00 00 00 00 00
C0    00 00 00 00 00 00 00 00 00 00 00 00 00 00 00 00
D0    00 00 00 00 00 00 00 00 00 00 00 00 00 00 00 00
E0    00 00 00 00 00 00 00 00 00 00 00 00 00 00 00 00
F0    00 00 00 00 00 00 00 00 00 00 00 00 00 00 00 00

Press function key, or enter character or hex byte:

1         2↑Save  3Prev.  4Next  5Drive  6Sector  7File  8Offset 9         0Exit
```

Figure 21.8

Sector 2 after adding ID info with DSEDIT.

Another good idea is to put some identification inside the computer. If you ever remove the motherboard, put an ID label under it. If you ever remove the hard disk, put some ID on the bottom. And if all you ever do is remove the cover, put your ID wherever you can reach. Thieves won't necessarily open the cover before the computer is sold and before it is recovered by the police.

Redesigning To Prevent Boot Viruses

Boot viruses load before DOS, so you might think that there is not much you can do to defeat them. Au contraire! Here are some ideas:

- ✔ If you have a newer ROM, you may be able to set it up so that the boot sequence does not include drive A. If you can do this, you cannot get a boot virus on your hard disk.

- ✔ If your machine is older, you can eliminate boot viruses and protect the hard disk by eliminating drive A. In most machines, only two floppy disk drives are supported: A and B. For many users, only one floppy disk drive is needed, and this can be drive B. For instructions on setting a machine so that it only has a drive B floppy disk, see *Virus News and Reviews*, January, 1992, p. 46.

✔ All boot viruses are memory resident; when they go into memory, they must allocate some memory for their own use; when they allocate memory, they decrease the memory that is available to users. If you have 640K or more memory in your computer, CHKDSK should report 655,360 total bytes memory. If you get anything less when you run CHKDSK, you may have a boot virus. Similarly, the MEM.EXE program of DOS 5.+ will show 655,360 bytes total conventional memory. You have Stoned, Michelangelo, or a related boot virus if this number is 653,312. Note that some VGA cards may reduce uninfected conventional memory by 1K, so your before and after figures may vary.

✔ You can automate the CHKDSK or MEM test, if you want. After booting, redirect the results of CHKDSK or MEM to a file with one of these commands...

```
CHKDSK > CHECK.MEM
MEM > CHECK.MEM
```

✔ Now, run a simple BASIC program to read the relevant line of this file and pull the appropriate value from it. If the line is correct, the program should exit. Otherwise, the program should hang up the system with a message to call the help desk.

Redesigning To Remove Boot Viruses

There is much you can do to simplify boot-virus removal. One easy step is to back up the master boot record and the boot record from drive C to an emergency floppy disk that you keep with each user or in your storage cabinet. You can do this with MIRROR /PARTN, described in Chapter 19. Many anti-virus programs can do this automatically. Now, if you have reason to believe that you have a virus in the master boot sector or boot sector, all you need to do is boot from an uninfected floppy disk and use UNFORMAT /PARTN to paste the file back to the sector from which it came. This will overwrite the virus and make you virus-free, but it won't guarantee that the virus hasn't caused some damage elsewhere, from which you will still need to recover.

Redesigning To Prevent File Viruses

Preventing file viruses is a bit tougher. You can prevent file viruses by never logging on to the LAN, never downloading a file, and never putting a disk in your drive. Because this is not practical, the following sections give you some other ideas to consider.

MARK and RELEASE

To eliminate a memory-resident virus, try the shareware combination of MARK and RELEASE (found in MARKREL.ZIP on CompuServe). MARK locates where in memory a resident program begins, and RELEASE frees memory back to a previous MARK. Simply place MARK in your AUTOEXEC.BAT file, and then run all programs from a batch file that contains, as its last line…

```
RELEASE
```

This will pull from memory many (not all) of the viruses that might have lodged there.

You don't want to infect RELEASE, of course, so after you do this, you can compare its size with its size before running it, with the DOS 6.2 command COMP…

```
COMP RELEASE.COM RELEASE.PGM
```

This will compare every byte of RELEASE and your backup copy. Because no virus can infect a file without modifying it, you'll find the difference in a jiffy, if there is one. Note that the COMP program must open the file to examine it, so if RELEASE fails to remove a memory-resident virus that infects an open file, you'll likely find no difference when you do this comparison because both will be infected. Thus another approach—perhaps better—would be to assume that

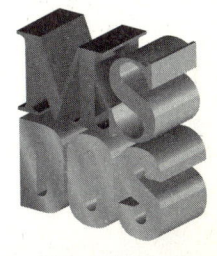

RELEASE gets infected when doing its job, and have your batch program replace RELEASE, after running, with the line…

    COPY RELEASE.BAK RELEASE.COM

This, of course, assumes that you have made a backup copy of RELEASE and have named it RELEASE.BAK.

Using Secret Names for COMMAND.COM

Some of the most common viruses contain code that prevents them from infecting any file named COMMAND.COM. So all you have to do is name all of your files COMMAND.COM. Actually, viruses such as Jerusalem.Standard infect only as you load and execute a file, so you can create a batch file that first copies your program to a file named COMMAND.COM, and then executes COMMAND.COM. Although the largest COM file that will execute is 64K, you can rename any EXE to COM and DOS will have no trouble figuring out that the file is really an EXE. Be aware that this won't work for every virus. Cascade, for instance, infects COMMAND.COM and any other file with the COM extension. To defeat Cascade, you could name all your files COMMAND.EXE—but then you wouldn't defeat certain other viruses. Some variants of Jerusalem, for example, can infect a file named COMMAND.EXE. The renaming trick is one that you might use if your office has had a recurring infection of a particular virus, and you happen to know its taste preferences.

The only place this trick won't work is the directory where a real COMMAND.COM is housed. So why not rename COMMAND.COM to something more sensible (or harder for a virus to remember)?

One way to do this is to use the line…

    SHELL =

…in CONFIG.SYS. You can specify any directory (including a hidden directory or a directory containing Alt+255 (a nonprinting character) as its last character to make it harder for users to damage your shell. This fools a few viruses that look for a file named COMMAND.COM in the root of drive C. And this method makes it possible to temporarily rename any file to COMMAND.COM even in your root

Redesigning To Prevent File Viruses

directory so that you can do the trick described in the previous paragraph. But this method won't fool the virus Frodo and others.

Another way to change the name of COMMAND.COM is more dangerous, and I'd recommend practicing on a bootable floppy disk if you want to try this. In IO.SYS at about offset 32,228 you will see a reference to \COMMAND.COM. You can edit this to show a different name for the file. You then will want to rename COMMAND.COM to match the name you have specified in IO.SYS. Follow these steps:

1. Place DSEDIT on a bootable floppy disk. Load DSEDIT.
2. Load IO.SYS with F7.
3. Go to offset sector 75 by pressing F8.
4. Replace every reference to COMMAND.COM on this screen with something such as 1234567.COM. Figure 21.9 shows how this would look after editing.

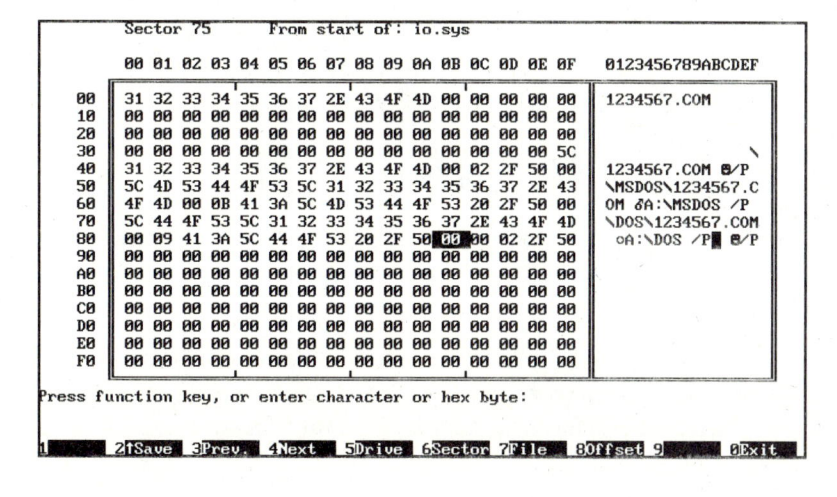

Figure 21.9

Edited IO.SYS showing COMMAND.COM replaced with 1234567.COM.

5. Save your edited IO.SYS by pressing Shift+F2 (Save).
6. Exit and rename all copies of COMMAND.COM on drive A to 1234567.COM (or whatever name you used in IO.SYS).
7. Reboot and see what happens. Everything should be normal.

8. Note that DSEDIT has given IO.SYS today's date and time and discarded its attributes of system, read-only, and hidden. You can set these attributes back (they aren't required, but are good safety features) with the command…

   `ATTRIB +R +S +H IO.SYS`

COMMAND.COM also contains two references to itself. If you change the name in COMMAND.COM to 1234567.COM in IO.SYS, you need to change it inside 1234567.COM, too. With DSEDIT, you will find the reference at the bottom of offset sector 15 and the top of 16. Change it in both places and save your work.

What name should you give to your new COMMAND.COM? You might want to rename it to COMMAND*.COM (where the * is created with the Alt key and 255 from the numeric keypad). Although this might seem like a lot of work, if you boot with this tricked-out system and format from it, you'll automatically transfer these two hidden system files.

Redesigning To Detect Memory-Resident Viruses

Memory-resident viruses must allocate memory or risk being trod upon by your unsuspecting software. Most don't take chances and allocate, thereby decreasing what's available.

DOS 6.2 comes with MEM.EXE, one of the handiest programs around for nailing a memory-resident virus. Now, while your machine doesn't have a file virus, boot it, and immediately run…

   `MEM /C > MEM.OK`

Now add this to the last line of your AUTOEXEC.BAT file…

   `MEM /C > MEM.NOW`

…and add…

   `COMP MEM.OK MEM.NOW`

You will be told `Files are different sizes` or `Compare error at OFFSET` if memory has changed from when you built MEM.OK and when you created MEM.NOW.

If COMP shows that MEM.OK is the same as MEM.NOW, add the following lines to the end of your AUTOEXEC.BAT file:

```
MEM /C > MEM.NOW
COMP MEM.OK MEM.NOW
ECHO
PAUSE
```

If these files don't match, something's fishy. Maybe a virus?

Note that any legitimate change to AUTOEXEC.BAT or CONFIG.SYS causes a somewhat different report from MEM, so you will want to produce a new MEM.OK file after modifying either of these boot files.

Redesigning To Remove (Some) Memory-Resident Viruses

Some programs, such as CLEARMEM.EXE (in CLEARMEM.ZIP, on CompuServe), clear memory. Some viruses will lose their grip and fall to their deaths. CLEARMEM or its equivalents can be called as the last line of whatever batch program you use to call your application software. Naturally, such a virus might like to infect such a program, so you can back it up, using the command…

```
COPY CLEARMEM.EXE CLEARMEM.PGM
```

…and then run it by first copying CLEARMEM.PGM to CLEARMEM.EXE. Then you have at least one good copy (assuming that you don't have a virus that has a taste for .PGM files), and you're always working with a fresh copy.

Redesigning To Detect File Viruses Early

There are two good, inexpensive ways to determine whether a file has been modified: compare its checksum with a stored result, and compare its size. The following sections present a pair of low-cost ideas to do this.

File Size Checks

Only an overwriting virus can infect a file without changing its size, and overwriting viruses are extremely rare. Thus, an almost sure-fire way to determine whether a file is infected is to compare the current sizes of executable files (COMs and EXEs) with former sizes. Do this with the DIR command…

```
DIR C:\*.EXE /S /ON > EXEFILES.OLD
```

This command produces a file named EXEFILES containing all your EXE files listed in alphabetical order (the /ON switch does this), including those files stored in subdirectories.

You can repeat this procedure at intervals, sending your results to EXEFILES.NEW, and then comparing old and new with the command…

```
COMP EXEFILES.OLD EXEFILES.NEW
```

If you try this, you'll discover that EXEFILES.NEW has decreased the available bytes from when you created EXEFILES.OLD. So you can ask COMP to tell you about all but the last few lines with the parameter /N=. Type…

```
COMP /?
```

…for help on how to do this.

This simple approach won't work on an unstable machine — one to which you frequently add or subtract files. For such a machine, I'd recommend that you write a simple program to read the output of DIR C:*.* /S /ON and write a list of files and sizes for all EXE and

COM files. You could run another simple program to match two outputs from this file and report on EXE and COM files that have grown larger by any amount.

Redesigning To Recover Efficiently

You can do a lot to make recovery graceful. Apart from the amazing ideas presented so far, consider some newfangled approaches to backup. For instance:

- ✔ File viruses have a strong preference for your favorite software, often infecting only what you run. So back up your favorite executable files to your hard disk right in the same directory where you keep them. You can copy XYZ.COM to XYZ.COB (B for Backup) and XYZ.EXE to XYZ.EXB. Now, whenever you need to resuscitate something, just boot clean and copy from your backup copy.

- ✔ If you don't want to risk your favorite databases, you can invoke them from a batch file. After leaving your database program, you can automatically back up the database you were using. I use PKZIP (on CompuServe as PKZIP.EXE, a self-extracting archive that does not require PKZIP to do the extraction), and send the backup to a \BACKUP directory. For really important databases, I keep multiple backups by first deleting \BACKUP\DATABASE.8, and then renaming \BACKUP\DATABASE.7 to DATABASE.8 (and so forth), and then using PKZIP to create DATABASE.1.

- ✔ If the boss was too cheap to buy you a tape drive, install a second hard disk in your machine, and use a menu-driven batch file to copy your favorite treasures to it daily. Even a 20M hard disk will hold the important files of most 100M drives. Remember that, if your first hard disk is infected with a file virus, you will be copying it to your backup disk. This approach and the previous one make the machine more resistant to bumbling users and Murphy, but doesn't protect it from viruses.

Redesigning To Slow Hackers

Simple hacks to your modified DOS would include running SYS or FORMAT against your hard disk to replace your hidden system files or your secretly named COMMAND.COM with versions the hacker was more comfortable with. If you already have protected your hard disk by removing the floppy disks, and removed or renamed the SYS and FORMAT programs, this will be difficult for a junior hacker.

If you've removed drive A, the only way a hacker can run SYS or FORMAT is after they've booted with your DOS. But, your DOS can disable their SYS and FORMAT. Find the reference to REN and RENAME in COMMAND.COM, and change these to SYS and FORMAT respectively. By doing this, you make SYS and FORMAT internal commands, and any external programs with these names won't run. There is a drawback: if you do this, you lose your ability to rename files in this system.

Here's how to accomplish this procedure with DSEDIT:

1. On a floppy disk, back up COMMAND.COM to COMMAND.BAK. Load DSEDIT.

2. Load COMMAND.COM (by pressing F7). Go to offset sector 93 by pressing F8.

3. Change REN to SYS and RENAME to FORMAT on this screen, as shown in figure 21.10.

Figure 21.10

Sector 93 of COMMAND.COM after replacing REN with SYS and RENAME with FORMAT with DSEDIT.

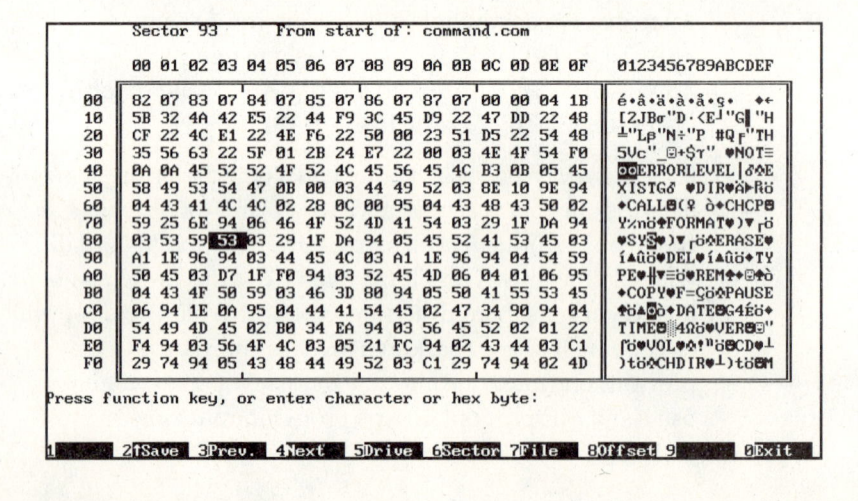

4. Save your work by pressing Shift+F2 (Save).
5. Exit by pressing F10. Load COMMAND.COM by typing…

    COMMAND

    …then try typing…

    SYS

    …or try…

    FORMAT

You should get the following message…

```
Required parameter missing
```

You can edit this message, of course, to something like

```
Invalid command!
```
or
```
Security has been notified!
```
if you want.

Senior hackers could figure this out by running their own disk editor, such as NU (Norton Utilities), so you can make NU an internal command, too. But if they are on to your tricks, they can rename NU to something else, and still run it. In the end, a determined, competent hacker will be able to win. Fortunately, there is a shortage of determined, competent hackers in the world, and all this advice will help you cope with the over-abundance of bumbling users who constitute the greatest part of your menace.

The ideas presented here are the first steps toward a safer DOS. As with any system modifications, they must be done carefully and you must test your work before you can be assured that you have made an improvement. Remember to practice on a floppy disk so that if you really foul things up, you don't need to call the doctor. Good luck and have fun!

Shareware Referenced in This Chapter

On CompuServe, you can join the National Computer Security Association (NCSA) security conference by typing…

    `GO NCSA`

Founded by David Stang, this membership organization works to help users improve their security, reduce the need for data recovery, and battle viruses.

Other chapters of the NCSA exist in Norway, Austria, the UK, Taiwan, and Australia. Call the NCSA US at (800) 488-4595 for more information.

All the following files are on CompuServe:

    BREAK.ZIP

    CLEARMEM.ZIP

    COMSPEC.ZIP

    DELETE.ZIP

    EPW.ZIP

    FPROT116.ZIP

    INT.ZIP

    LOCKIT.ZIP

    MARKREL.ZIP

    NOSHELL.ZIP

    PASSGEN.ZIP

    PASSGEN2.ZIP

    PASSWRD1.ZIP

    PASSWRD2.ZIP

    PKUNZIP.EXE

    REWARD.ZIP

Summary

As you've seen, MS-DOS has never had any significant security features. And yet the privacy and integrity of the information in your computer *must be* protected. How can you protect this information from merry pranksters? The answer is not easily!

Security is an unnatural act. The forces of nature conspire to foil our best efforts. Today, unnatural forces also conspire against us: hackers and viruses are gaining ground, increasingly encroaching on what is ours.

You don't have to be neurotic to want to protect the information in your computer. It is reasonable and responsible to do so. Whether you follow some of the ideas in this chapter or merely lock your office door at night, please remember that security is not a job for someone down the hall. It begins on your desktop. If it doesn't begin there, it will end there!

MS-DOS

Making Connections under DOS 6.2

Interlink and Other Connectivity Solutions 1197
Using DOS 6.2 with Local Area Networks 1239

Part Seven:

MS
DOS

CHAPTER 22

InterLnk and Other Connectivity Solutions

by Bill Camarda

With the growth of laptop computing, more and more people have faced the problem of exchanging information between laptops and their desktop computers.

Until recently, connecting a laptop to your local area network was a cost-prohibitive solution. Some people even resorted to uploading their binary files by modem to a commercial service like CompuServe, and then downloading them by modem into the desktop PC.

And then there was "Sneakernet." But many laptops didn't have a floppy disk drive—or if they did, it wasn't always compatible with the floppy disks on the desktop PCs they needed to connect with. The 3 1/2-inch drives, for example, were built into laptops early on, to save space, but many 286-class machines came with only a 5 1/4-inch 1.2M drive.

Where there's a problem, there's usually an opportunity, and several companies have designed file transfer programs specifically for the purpose of exchanging files between PCs.

These programs can typically work much faster than the normal 19.2K limit of a PC serial port, because they interact directly with the serial port hardware instead of depending on the PC's BIOS to make the connection.

New laptops and desktop PCs nowadays generally use 1.44 3 1/2-inch drives, somewhat abating the problem of connectivity. However, the sheer size of programs and files—often outstripping the capacity of a 1.44M drive—provides a new reason to use file transfer programs.

And there are still all those other PCs and laptops out there (including, quite possibly, yours)...

Three programs, in particular, have become extremely popular, and are representative of the genre:

- ✔ Brooklyn Bridge (Fifth Generation Systems (800) 873-4384)
- ✔ FastLynx (Rupp Brothers (800) 852-7877)
- ✔ LapLink III (Traveling Software (800) 343-8088)

Now someone else has smelled a market: Microsoft. MS-DOS 6 itself comes with a file transfer program, called InterLnk.

What Is InterLnk?

InterLnk is a file transfer program designed to enable you to exchange files between any two PCs that are connected with the appropriate cabling.

InterLnk consists of two separate programs, INTERLNK.EXE and INTERSVR.EXE, but the best way to think about it is as a way to add the disk drives and parallel printers on a remote system to your own. With InterLnk running, you can do nearly anything with those remote disk drives that you could do with drives on your own system.

> **NOTE**
>
> With a few exceptions, these disk management commands won't work with InterLnk:
>
> CHDKSK, DEFRAG, DISKCOMP, DISKCOPY, FDISK, FORMAT, MIRROR, SYS, UNDELETE, UNFORMAT
>
> In addition, if you are running InterLnk on a client system with an older version of DOS, you'll be limited to the capabilities of that version of DOS. For example, if DOS 3.3 is running on your client system, it won't recognize a partition larger than 32M on your server system.

It's also important to note what InterLnk isn't:

- It's not a communications program like Crosstalk (Digital Communications Associates) or Smartcom (Hayes). It won't enable you to connect with a distant computer by modem (though those programs will enable you to establish direct connections between two computers through a null modem cable).

- It's not a remote control program such as PCAnywhere (Symantec) or Carbon Copy (Microcom). Those programs enable you to run a remote computer's programs, using its processor and viewing the results on your computer.

What You Need To Run InterLnk

- Two PCs, each running MS-DOS 3 or higher
- Enough free memory on both systems: 16K on the client, 130K on the server
- A free serial port or bidirectional parallel port on each PC
- A connecting serial or parallel cable

Chapter 22: InterLnk and Other Connectivity Solutions

In most cases, this will be a serial cable. Remember that two kinds of physical RS-232 ports are used by DOS systems: 9-pin (DB9) and 25-pin (DB25), as shown in figure 22.1.

Figure 22.1
9-pin (DB9) and 25-pin (DB25) serial ports.

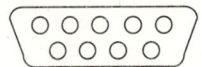

DB-9 (9-PIN SERIAL PORT)

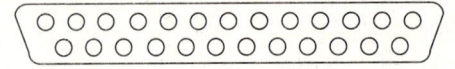

DB-25 (25-PIN SERIAL PORT)

Use table 22.1 to match up correct pinouts on each end. If you have a 9-pin serial connection on your client laptop and a 25-pin connection on your server desktop, for example, use the pinouts listed under Client 9-pin and Server 25-pin.

Table 22.1
InterLnk Serial Cable Pinouts

Client 9-Pin (DB9)	25-Pin (DB25)	Server 25-Pin (DB25)	9-Pin (DB9)	Connection
Pin 5	Pin 7	Pin 7	Pin 5	Ground-Ground
Pin 3	Pin 2	Pin 3	Pin 2	Transmit-Receive
Pin 7	Pin 4	Pin 5	Pin 8	Ready to Send - Clear to Send
Pin 6	Pin 6	Pin 20	Pin 4	Data Set Ready-Data Terminal Ready
Pin 2	Pin 3	Pin 2	Pin 3	Receive-Transmit
Pin 8	Pin 5	Pin 4	Pin 7	Clear to Send-Ready to Send
Pin 4	Pin 20	Pin 6	Pin 6	Data Terminal Ready-Data Set Ready

These cables are widely available. Because they're compatible with those used by LapLink and FastLynx, two popular file transfer programs, you can often get what you want by asking for a LapLink or FastLynx cable.

> **NOTE** *Some other file transfer programs may use incompatible cables.*

Many LapLink-style cables come with both 9-pin and 25-pin connections at each end, as shown in figure 22.2. That's ideal because you'll be able to connect with PCs of any type.

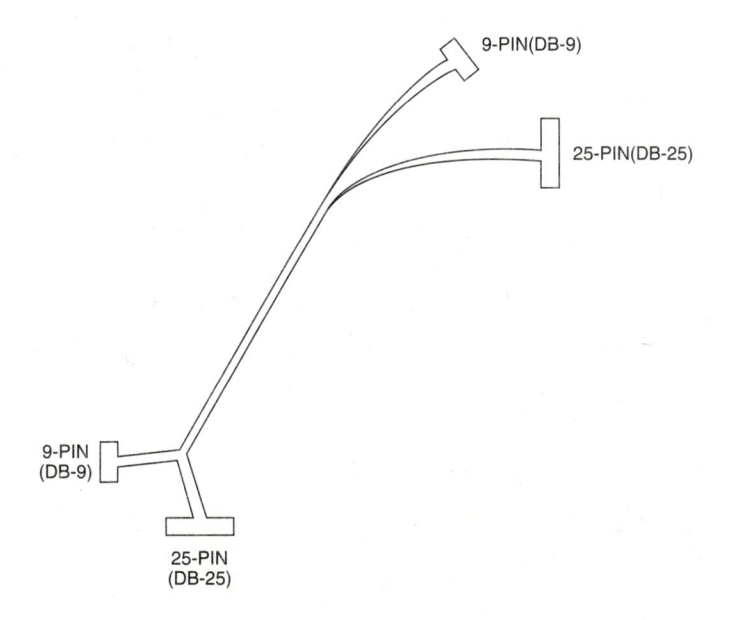

Figure 22.2
LapLink-style cable.

Alternatively, you can adapt a cable with a 25-pin-to-9-pin adapter. If you use one, double-check that it doesn't also change the cable's gender.

The cables described in table 22.1 not only connect systems that are both running InterLnk, but also support uplinking InterLnk to systems that don't already have it. If you don't need to uplink InterLnk, you can use a 3-wire serial cable, with the following connections:

Chapter 22: *InterLnk and Other Connectivity Solutions*

Client 9-Pin (DB9)	25-Pin (DB25)	Server 25-Pin (DB25)	9-Pin (DB9)	*Connection*
Pin 2	Pin 3	Pin 2	Pin 3	Receive-Transmit
Pin 5	Pin 7	Pin 7	Pin 5	Ground-Ground
Pin 3	Pin 2	Pin 3	Pin 2	Transmit-Receive

If the parallel ports on both systems are bidirectional, you can use a parallel cable. (See the discussion on bidirectional ports that follows.) Such a cable should have a DB25 connector on both ends, but is otherwise standard. (Typical parallel cables use a 36-pin connector with "teeth" on the printer end.)

The following pinouts apply to parallel cables:

DB25 25-Pin (Client)	*DB25 25-Pin (Server)*
Pin 2	Pin 15
Pin 3	Pin 13
Pin 4	Pin 12
Pin 5	Pin 10
Pin 6	Pin 11
Pin 15	Pin 2
Pin 13	Pin 3
Pin 12	Pin 4
Pin 10	Pin 5
Pin 11	Pin 6
Pin 25	Pin 25

Note that the first five pins are the reverse of the second set; in other words, it doesn't make any difference which end of the cable is used with which computer.

A parallel cable won't upload InterLnk to a system that doesn't already have it.

Both parallel and serial ports use DB25 connectors. So why don't you ever hear of anyone plugging a parallel cable into a serial connector? Because parallel cables are male on each end, and serial cables are female on each end.

So what would happen if you got a gender-changer and plugged a parallel cable into a serial port? Smell that blue smoke?

Parallel cables actually contain one pin with power running through it; the Centronics standard specifies +5 amperes, which is definitely enough to fry your circuits.

Connecting InterLnk through Parallel Ports

Although serial port InterLnk connections can run at up to 115,200 bps, parallel port connections can work twice that fast—approximately 240,000 bps.

You can often get faster throughput by connecting both systems through their parallel ports. But this works only if the parallel ports on both ends are *bidirectional*: designed specifically to send and receive data.

Traditionally, this wasn't the case: the computer used a parallel port for one purpose—to send data to a printer. And a printer used it for one purpose—to receive data.

To control a printer, however, you need a way for a few tidbits of information to get back to the computer, and so the Centronics parallel standard included four pins to communicate ideas like "paper out," "printer busy," and so on.

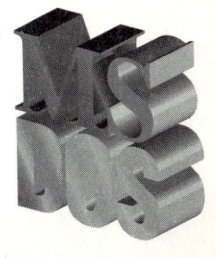

Makers of communications products quickly realized these control lines could be used to transmit data at relatively high speeds across standard parallel ports. Next, hardware manufacturers like IBM added hardware to make their parallel ports bidirectional by design. Many of today's laptops, IBM PS/2s, and some compatibles now contain these true bidirectional parallel ports; InterLnk can take full advantage of them.

Understanding InterLnk Concepts

When two computers are using InterLnk to exchange files, each plays a well-scripted role. The client, running INTERLNK.EXE, is in control, determining which actions to perform on the server's drives. The server, running INTERSVR.EXE, provides support. If you're connecting a laptop to a desktop computer, the laptop will generally be your client.

By the way, this is a more static arrangement than what these days is usually termed *client/server computing*, whereby the server processes complex data requests and forwards them, usually across a LAN, to a user whose system is responsible for the user interface and the ability to make the request. Little of that subtlety is present here: you're simply moving entire files around, from the command line.

From the user's standpoint, the drives on the server system have been remapped as additional drives on the client system. Microsoft calls this *drive redirection*.

For example, if the server contains:

> Drive A
>
> Drive B
>
> Drive C

...and the client contains:

>Drive A
>
>Drive B
>
>Drive C

then the server's drives will appear to the client as:

>Drive D
>
>Drive E
>
>Drive F

The same is true if the server contains only drive A and drive C, as is the case in many laptops. InterLnk starts renumbering after the last drive on the server system—it doesn't "fill in" missing drive name.

> **NOTE** *What if you specified LASTDRIVE=D (or a similarly restrictive LASTDRIVE command) in CONFIG.SYS? It doesn't matter—you get the extra drives anyway.*

InterLnk also redirects one or two parallel printers. These will appear as LPT2 and LPT3 on the client system. (If you already have two parallel ports on each system, only one additional port will be redirected from the server. DOS does not recognize LPT4.)

Uploading InterLnk to Another MS-DOS System

One problem most file transfer programs immediately encounter is that they need to be present on both computers to work. But if you could always copy the file transfer program to the host computer, you'd have no need for it—you'd just copy your files the same way.

You won't have this problem if both computers are running MS-DOS 6.2. InterLnk is already on the system you want to connect with. But most PCs aren't running DOS 6.2 yet. Then what?

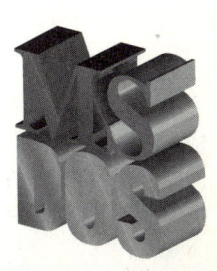

Chapter 22: InterLnk and Other Connectivity Solutions

InterLNK solves the problem the same way many other file transfer programs do. It clones itself onto the remote computer. To perform this magic, both computers need the MODE command *in their current path.*

> **A no-win situation...** Don't run the remote installation program from within Windows.

1. Using a 7-wire serial cable (not a parallel cable or a 3-wire serial cable), connect both computers firmly. Note which serial ports you're using on each computer.

2. On the target computer, switch to the directory where you want to place the files, that is, C:\DOS.

3. Unless you're using the COM1 serial port on your target computer, temporarily disable any SHARE commands from your CONFIG.SYS or AUTOEXEC.BAT files. (Just add the word REM in front of them, and reboot. When you're finished, delete the REMs and reboot again to reactivate SHARE.)

4. On the source computer (where the InterLnk files already exist), type...

    INTERSVR /RCOPY

The following screen appears (see fig. 22.3).

Use the up/down arrow keys to specify the COM (serial) port you will use on the destination computer.

> *InterLnk remote installation supports only COM1 and COM2.*

Uploading InterLnk to Another MS-DOS System **1207**

```
          InterLnk Remote Installation

  InterLnk will copy its program files to another computer that is connected
  to this one by a 7-wire null-modem cable.

  Before continuing, make sure the cable connects the two computers' serial
  ports.

  Specify the serial port of the other computer, and then press ENTER:

                          COM1
                          COM2



Enter=Continue   F3=Exit
```

Figure 22.3

InterLnk Remote Installation opening screen.

5. Type the following command on the target computer...

    MODE COM1(OR 2):2400,N,8,1,P

    This command configures the serial port you've chosen, and sets its parameters: 2400 baud, no parity, 8 bits, 1 stop bit. The P switch tells DOS to keep trying until it works.

    The following messages should appear:

        Resident portion of MODE loaded.

        COM1(or 2): 2400,N,8,1,P

    This is your confirmation that the settings you specified are now active.

6. Still on the target computer, type...

    CTTY COM1(OR 2)

    This command instructs DOS to accept input, not from its keyboard, but from the COM1 port.

7. InterLNK now uploads itself. It first sends a bootstrap program; then the bootstrap program receives INTERSVR.EXE and INTERLNK.EXE. You can follow the progress of the upload on either system. A message displays on the bottom line of the source system, and the following messages appear on the target system:

```
Loading bootstrap
Receiving INTERSVR.EXE (37266) 100%
Receiving INTERLNK.EXE (17133) 100%
```

After both files are copied, each system reverts to its command prompt.

> *Maybe you wonder why you have to use a 7-wire cable for uploading InterLnk, but a 3-wire cable is sufficient for connecting two machines that already contain InterLnk. That's because InterLnk normally handles the handshaking between machines in software—functions like flow control and error control.*
>
> *But if InterLnk isn't present on the server computer, it must rely on the serial port's hardware for this purpose—hence, physical connections to the pins that handle those functions.*

Including InterLnk in Your CONFIG.SYS File

Whether or not you've had to upload the InterLnk programs to your host computer, you still must place INTERLNK.EXE in the CONFIG.SYS file of any computer you plan to use as a client.

This is a disadvantage of InterLnk compared with other file transfer programs. Some of these programs either do not require inclusion in CONFIG.SYS (and the *de rigueur* reboot to make the changes take effect), or if they do require inclusion, they often automate the process—though you might want to check the results.

INTERLNK.EXE (notwithstanding its extension) is a device and needs a DEVICE statement which includes its path and file name:

```
DEVICE=C:\DOS\INTERLNK.EXE
```

Including InterLnk in Your CONFIG.SYS File

By default, InterLnk assumes that three drives are to be redirected from the server. However, you can use the /DRIVES: switch to specify any number of drives—or no drives at all, if you only wish to redirect printers.

To redirect five drives, include the following statement in CONFIG.SYS:

    DEVICE\C:\DOS\INTERLNK.EXE /DRIVES:5

Several other switches are available to adjust the way InterLnk runs from CONFIG.SYS:

> **/NOPRINTER** tells InterLnk not to redirect printers.
>
> **/COM:X** specifies which serial port you want to use on the client machine, that is, /COM:2. If you've added a nonstandard COM port, you can add that port by specifying its hexadecimal address, that is, COM:3F8.

NOTE

> *You're not planning to add a nonstandard COM port? Well, don't be so sure: some add-on serial cards for COM3 and COM4 have indeed used nonstandard addresses. For reference, here's where DOS generally expects to find communications ports in ISA systems:*
>
> > COM1:03F8
> >
> > COM2:02F8
> >
> > COM3:03E8
> >
> > COM4:02E8
>
> *On Micro Channel Architecture systems, which are pretty well standardized, COM1 and COM2 stay the same, but everything else changes:*
>
> > COM3:3220H
> >
> > COM4:3228H
> >
> > COM5:4220H
> >
> > COM6:4228H

COM7:5220H

COM8:5228H

You can generally skip this switch: InterLnk defaults to the first serial port it finds connected to the server.

/LPT:X specifies the parallel port you wish to use on the client machine, if you've made a parallel connection.

Including a /COM: switch and no /LPT: switch tells DOS to search only serial ports. Conversely, including an /LPT: switch and no /COM: switch tells DOS to search only parallel ports.

Limiting InterLnk's search path with one or more of these switches saves a small amount of memory, as shown in table 22.2.

Table 22.2
InterLnk's Varying Memory Requirements

Portion of InterLnk	Amount of Memory
All of InterLnk:	9,536 bytes
InterLnk with /NOPRINTER invoked:	9,344 bytes
InterLnk with /LPT:1 invoked—and not loading support for serial ports:	6,944 bytes
InterLnk with /COM:1 invoked—and not loading support for parallel ports:	7,952 bytes
InterLnk with /COM:1 and /NOPRINTER invoked:	7,760 bytes

The last scenario makes sense if you won't need to print from a printer hooked to the server—merely exchange files through a serial port.

What Happens When INTERLNK.EXE Runs?

When INTERLNK.EXE runs, it first attempts to load into an upper memory block (UMB). If none are available—if they're all full, or if you don't have memory above 640K—INTERLNK.EXE loads into conventional ("low") memory.

However, you can force InterLnk to load "low" by including the /LOW switch:

```
DEVICE\C:\DOS\INTERLNK.EXE /DRIVES:5 /LOW
```

Next, INTERLNK looks for a computer to connect with—a computer that is attached by means of cable and running companion INTERSVR.EXE program. If it finds one, it makes the connection, displaying a screen like the following:

```
            Microsoft Interlnk Version 1.00

Port=COM1
Drive letters redirected: 5 (D: through H:)
Printer ports redirected: 1 (LPT3:)

This Computer              Other Computer
   (Client)                    (Server)
- - - - - - - - - - - - - - - - - - - - - -
    D:    equals         A:
    E:    equals         B:
    F:    equals         C: (80Mb) Mainvolume
    G:    equals         D: (40Mb) Suppvolume
    LPT3: equals         LPT1:
```

The drive size indications reflect the size of the logical drives that exist on the server system. InterLnk also displays any volume labels.

NOTE *If you're running DBLSPACE, INTERLNK reports both the size of the compressed drive and the full size of the host drive that contains it—including bytes that aren't really available because they contain the compressed drive file.*

Chapter 22: *InterLnk and Other Connectivity Solutions*

If there is no available connection when INTERLNK.EXE first loads, you instead get a message like this:

```
Connection NOT established
Drive letters redirected:    5 (D: through H:)
Printer ports redirected:    1 (LPT3:)
```

Whether or not INTERLNK makes a connection, it does redirect your drive assignments. This means that your client system will report phantom drives you never knew you had.

You can see these new drives displayed in DOS Shell or Windows File Manager. They're also visible through your applications. DOS treats them as if they were empty floppy drives—if you double-click on one, it asks you to insert the disk, which of course you can't do. (See figure 22.4.)

Figure 22.4
Phantom drives appearing in DOS Shell.

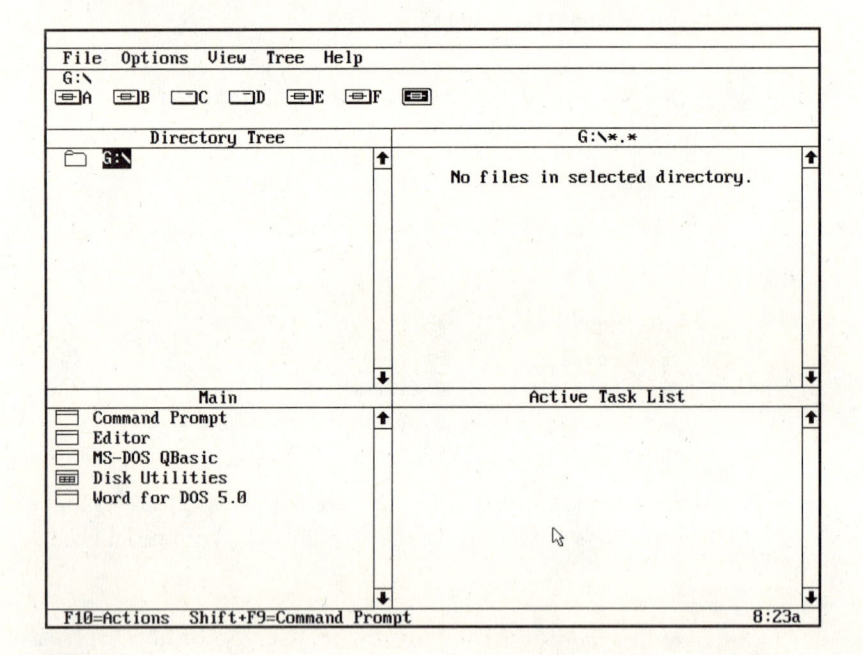

```
File  Options  View  Tree  Help
G:\
 A   B   C   D   E   F

     Directory Tree                    G:\*.*
  G:\                              No files in selected directory.




         Main                       Active Task List
  Command Prompt
  Editor
  MS-DOS QBasic
  Disk Utilities
  Word for DOS 5.0




F10=Actions   Shift+F9=Command Prompt                    8:23a
```

> **NOTE** Remember that the drives won't appear if you run FDISK, CHKDSK, or another command that doesn't work with InterLnk.

If you later run INTERLNK again from the command prompt, and there's still no connection, you'll get this message:

```
Connection NOT established
```

Make sure that a serial or parallel cable connects the server and client computers, and that INTERSVR.EXE is running on the server computer.

Telling InterLnk When To Install

By default, INTERLNK remains in memory whether or not it finds another computer to connect with. This eats up 8-9K of RAM. But you can change that with the /AUTO switch, which places INTERLNK.EXE in memory only if it connects with a system running INTERSVR.EXE. For example:

```
DEVICE\C:\DOS\INTERLNK.EXE /DRIVES:5 /LOW /AUTO
```

Then, if no connection is made, DOS reports…

```
Microsoft Interlnk Version 1.00

Connection NOT established
Driver NOT installed.
```

Unfortunately, you can't then install the driver from the command prompt. Rather, you have to connect your cables, run INTERSVR.EXE on the server system, and then reboot to run CONFIG.SYS again.

Telling InterLnk When To Search

Conversely, you can place InterLnk in memory and tell it not to look for a partner until you're good and ready. Use the /NOSCAN switch:

DEVICE\C:\DOS\INTERLNK.EXE /DRIVES:5 /LOW /NOSCAN

Slowing InterLnk Down

By default, InterLnk attempts to operate at 115,200 baud. This makes it many times as fast as a modem connection, somewhat faster than

a floppy disk, significantly slower than most current hard drives, and much slower than most local area networks.

But there are a few potential problems. First, some computers can't support 115,200 baud. (The IBM PS/2 Model 70 could run at 38,400 baud; the Model 80 at 57,600.)

Second, very fast serial connections can sometimes overwhelm the internal UART chip that manages them. The InterLnk server program tries to cope with this by taking complete control of its system while you are using it.

Nevertheless, in some situations you might have to manually instruct InterLnk to slow down. The /BAUD: switch enables you do this. You can choose any of the following values:

   9600
   19200
   38400
   57600
   115200

For example:

```
DEVICE\C:\DOS\INTERLNK.EXE /DRIVES:5 /BAUD:57600
```

> **NOTE**
>
> *UART to do something about this...* Your computer manages serial communications using a special chip called a universal asynchronous receiver/transmitter, or UART. Among the UART's responsibilities is to accept information and then pass it along to the device at the other end. The faster the data transmission, the more of a challenge this is.
>
> XT-class PCs, and some AT-class PCs, used the 8250 UART, which contained a one-byte buffer that could hold up to eight bits of information until the receiving device was ready for it.

Most AT-class PCs, including most Industry Standard Architecture 386 systems, used the 16450 UART, which contained a two-byte buffer. This was better—but increasingly, it's not good enough. Next came the 16550AN, but it had software problems that limited the usefulness of its 16-byte buffer. What you really want is a 16550AFN.

You can determine what generation UART chip you have by running Microsoft System Diagnostics (MSD). (If you run Windows, exit it first.) If you have a 16550, and you are having problems, pull your serial port if possible. Look for a large 40-pin chip—that's your UART. If it's a 16550AN, it contains the problem code. If the chip is socketed (not soldered), replace it with a 16550AFN.

If you cannot replace your UART, you may want to purchase an add-on multifunction serial port from a supplier like Jameco or JDR Microdevices. It may come with a floppy drive controller which can't be disabled; since your system supports only one floppy controller, use the new floppy controller and disable the one you were previously using.

Then try to make sure that any communications software you purchase takes advantage of this new, larger UART buffer.

Finally, in rare instances an InterLnk serial connection can interfere with a computer's timing. If this happens, the computer may halt during a file transfer.

You can usually solve this problem by adding the /V switch. This ensures that InterLnk will pass every clock timer tick down the interrupt chain, helping both systems maintain their timing. With /V enabled, the status bar speed indicator displays…

```
Speed=Variable.
```

Placing the DEVICE=INTERLNK.EXE Statement

If you're using a RAM drive, the placement of your DEVICE=INTERLNK.EXE statement affects the name assigned to your RAM drive. If, for example, you load INTERLNK before you load your RAM drive, INTERLNK redirects its drives first—and your RAM drive is named G: or H: or I:.

To avoid this, place the DEVICE=INTERLNK.EXE line after the DEVICE=RAMDRIVE.SYS line in CONFIG.SYS.

Connecting the Server with INTERSVR.EXE

Now you've run INTERLNK.EXE from CONFIG.SYS on the client computer, and it's sitting in memory. (In other words, you haven't specified the /AUTO switch.) The next step in making a connection is to run INTERSVR.EXE on the server computer—the computer with which you want to connect with.

We'll assume that INTERSVR.EXE is in your current path. (It should be if the computer is running DOS 6.2—but if you uploaded it using intersvr /RCOPY, it'll be wherever you put it.) To load the server, type...

```
INTERSVR
```

If INTERSVR finds INTERLNK running on another computer, it displays a screen like that shown in figure 22.5.

This tells you the names of the server's drives that are now available for use by the client. The bar at the bottom displays the file currently being transferred, if any, the port used on the server, and the speed of the transmission. If a current drive is active, an asterisk (*) appears next to that drive name. Note that the Alt+F4 combination halts a file transfer and quits InterLnk at the same time.

You can use this screen for reference—all your other InterLnking is done from the client system.

Connecting the Server with INTERSVR.EXE

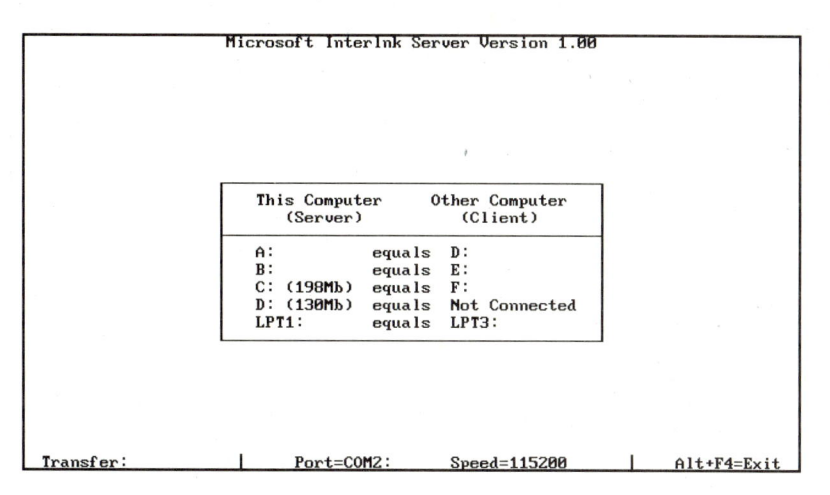

```
         Microsoft InterInk Server Version 1.00



           ┌─────────────────────────────────────┐
           │  This Computer      Other Computer  │
           │     (Server)            (Client)    │
           │                                     │
           │  A:             equals  D:          │
           │  B:             equals  E:          │
           │  C: (198Mb)     equals  F:          │
           │  D: (130Mb)     equals  Not Connected│
           │  LPT1:          equals  LPT3:       │
           │                                     │
           │                                     │
           │                                     │
           └─────────────────────────────────────┘


   Transfer:       |    Port=COM2:     Speed=115200    |   Alt+F4=Exit
```

Figure 22.5
InterLnk Server opening screen.

If INTERSVR does not find INTERLNK running elsewhere, the same screen displays, except for the client drive names and file transfer parameters. Then, when you run INTERLNK on a connected machine, all this information appears.

> **NOTE**
>
> *If you run INTERSVR from inside Windows, or from the DOS Shell with Task Swapping enabled, you'll see a screen that says:*
>
>   You have started the Interlnk server in a
>   task-switching environment. Task-switching,
>   key combinations, and some disk-writing
>   operations are disabled. To restore these
>   functions, exit the server.
>
>   Press ENTER to continue, or F3 to quit.
>
> *You can run INTERSVR.EXE from the Shell or Windows. When you're done, return to the command prompt, and then exit back to the Shell or Windows. (And you can run INTERLNK.EXE on the client without disabling task swapping.)*

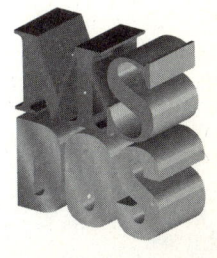

Using InterLnk Switches at the Command Line

You've already learned the switches that are available for use with the DEVICE=INTERLNK statement. Four of these switches also may be used at the command line by either INTERLNK or INTERSVR:

```
/BAUD:# (9600,19200,38400,57600,115200)
/LPT:X  (1,2,3)
/COM:X  (1,2,3,4)
/V
```

However, if your client system has already used a switch to establish a parameter during startup, neither the client nor the server can override it at the command line.

If you have chosen not to place the parallel port code in memory, for example, typing INTERLNK /LPT1 at the command prompt won't put it there. And if you specify /BAUD:57600 in CONFIG.SYS, typing INTERLNK /BAUD:115200 at the command prompt won't change that either.

Three additional switches are available to INTERSVR at the command line. The first is DRIVE, which enables you to choose which drives you want to redirect, and in which order.

In this example, where the client system contains three drives, the server's drives would normally be redirected as follows:

A: -->D:

B: -->E:

C: -->F:

You might prefer to redirect them in a different order, such as:

B: -->D:

C: -->E:

A: -->F:

So you would rearrange the order in which each server drive is assigned the drive name it will use on the client system by typing

INTERSVR B: C: A:

Or you might decide not to redirect one of the drives at all. Perhaps you only want to redirect drives B and C, as follows:

B: -->D:

C: -->E:

Then you would type

INTERSVR B: C:

or, to reverse their order, type

INTERSVR C: B:

Another way to exclude a drive from redirection is to specify it with the /X: parameter. Like the two preceding examples, this statement excludes drive A:

INTERSVR /X:A

When you exclude a drive from redirection, you make it unavailable to the client system.

You also can specify the redirection of a single drive by typing

INTERLNK F=A

and you can cancel a drive's redirection by typing

INTERLNK F=

> *Finally, you can't tell INTERLNK to redirect a server drive that doesn't exist. On a three-drive server, the statement INTERSVR Q: produces the following message:*
>
>   invalid server drive letter - q

Running INTERSVR in Black and White

The InterLnk server expects to run in color: blue, black, and turquoise, to be precise. If you can't see the text on your monochrome system, use the /B switch:

```
INTERSVR /B
```

Using InterLnk To Exchange a File

So let's put it all together. To use InterLnk to exchange a file:

1. Place a `DEVICE=INTERLNK.EXE` statement in your client system's CONFIG.SYS file.

2. Make sure INTERLNK.EXE and INTERSVR.EXE are available on both client and server systems. If they aren't available on the server, upload them using the INTERSVR /RCOPY command and a serial cable.

3. Firmly connect the client and server using the correct serial or parallel cable.

4. At the server's command prompt, type **INTERSVR** with any necessary switches. The server screen will display.

5. At the client's command prompt, type **INTERLNK** with any necessary switches. INTERLNK and INTERSVR both display the connections they have made.

6. When the command prompt returns, copy the file from your drive to the redirected server drive. Let's say your client floppy is on drive A, for example, and your server hard drive C has been redirected to drive F. Then, typing...

    ```
    COPY A:\FILENAME.EXT F:\TRIPFILE
    ```

    ...copies the file from your floppy to the subdirectory \TRIPFILE on your hard drive C.

You can go both ways: copying files from your server to your client...

```
COPY F:\TRIPFILE\REPORT92.WK1 A:
```

7. When you've finished, press Alt+F4 on the server. The server returns to the command prompt, and the client no longer has access to the server's drives.

> **NOTE** *The same wild-card commands that work on a system's own drives also work on drives redirected from the server.*

Running the Client from the DOS Shell

One advantage that many third-party file transfer utilities offer is a graphical, point-and-click user interface that enables you to specify files and directories from lists, and enables you to use a mouse or keyboard shortcuts to move files and directories where you want them to go.

But when you load InterLnk, all you see is the command line (on the client) and a basic screen that offers no interactivity (on the server).

However, DOS itself comes with a Shell that's quite compatible with InterLnk. It's a bit slow, but it gives you access to the Shell's comprehensive, visual file management capabilities.

You can create program groups based on files located on the server drive. And, running the Shell, the client can even perform task swapping.

Whether you like the Shell or not, you will have to admit it makes a pretty competitive DOS-based file transfer GUI.

Troubleshooting InterLnk

If you're having trouble with InterLnk, here's a troubleshooting checklist:

✔ **Problem: Can't upload files using INTERSVR /RCOPY**

Are the cables tightly connected at both ends?

Are they serial cables? Parallel cables won't work here.

Is it a 7-pin serial cable?

Are your MODE settings correct? Did you use the correct port name in your MODE and CTTY commands?

✔ **Problem: No connection**

Again, are the cables tightly connected, and do they match?

Are INTERLNK.EXE or INTERSVR.EXE running at all? If you received the message `Bad command or file name`, they may not be in your current path. Where did you upload them if you used INTERSVR /RCOPY?

Is a proper DEVICE=INTERLNK.EXE statement included in the client system's CONFIG.SYS file? By any chance, does it exclude the COM or LPT port you're using to make the connection?

Are you using DOS 3.0 or later on both machines?

✔ **Problem: File transfer or remote program operation fails**

Did the speed of the file transfer interfere with other system operations? Include the switch /BAUD:57600 (or an even lower rate) in the INTERSVR command and try again.

Could the timing of one system have been disrupted? Try again with the /V switch.

Is the program you are running from the server configured to work with your client? For example, you can't run a Windows program on the server if your client is an XT. Or the program's display might have been customized for the server's computer, not the client's.

✔ **Problem: Can't print from the server's printer**

Are you printing to the correct (redirected) LPT port?

If your DEVICE=INTERLNK.EXE statement included a /NOPRINTER or /COM:X statement, did you delete them and reboot?

More InterLnk Applications

Microsoft positions InterLnk as a solution for laptop connectivity, but it's really more than that, as follows:

✔ It's a workable way of connecting adjacent desktop PCs that aren't networked. You can use InterLnk to exchange large files that can't fit on a floppy disk.

✔ If one of the two systems has extra disk space, you can use that space to back up files from the other system with Microsoft Backup (which supports large backups but not tape drives).

✔ *It's a good emergency solution when a component in* one system fails. For example, you can use InterLnk to view files (and in some cases run programs) on a system with a broken monitor or keyboard. Or, if one system's floppy drive fails, you can use InterLnk to move files back and forth from the floppy drive on the second system.

✔ It's an alternative way to install DOS 6.2 on systems that have only low-density drives. MS-DOS 6.2 is primarily available on 1.44M 3 1/2-inch and 1.2M 5 1/4-inch disks. You may have to special order low-density disks from Microsoft. While you're waiting, you can use InterLnk to run the setup program from a remote high-density floppy drive.

Comparing InterLnk with Third-Party Solutions

When compared with InterLnk, most third-party file transfer programs do have some advantages. These include:

1. Better control over the parameters of a session from within the program.
2. The capability to switch between server and client without leaving the program.

However, InterLnk's capability to run most DOS commands on remote (server) drives, and even to execute programs, is quite impressive. Some third-party products allow only file operations.

Improvements in the DOS commands themselves, such as MOVE and DELTREE, have also made InterLnk more functional than it would have been if it had been introduced with DOS 5.

Linking Your PC to a Macintosh

InterLnk solves the problem of laptop connectivity to PCs, but what about the several million Macintoshes you may run into? Fortunately, there are a variety of solutions for Macintosh connectivity:

- ✔ Interplatform Sneakernet using SuperDrive floppies
- ✔ Running PC software on the Macintosh
- ✔ Direct serial connections between Mac and PC
- ✔ Networking Macs and PCs together
- ✔ File transfer/translation programs

Interplatform Sneakernet Using SuperDrive Floppies

All Macintoshes produced since 1990 come with the SuperDrive, a 3 1/2-inch high-density floppy that can read DOS 720K and 1.44M disks. So if Sneakernet had been a passable option for pure DOS transfer, it can be made to work between platforms as well.

Macintoshes that come with a SuperDrive include

- The Macintosh IIx, IIcx, IIsi, IIci, IIfx
- All Macintosh Quadras
- All Macintosh Powerbook notebook computers except the Powerbook 100, which comes with no disk drive
- All Macintosh Classics
- All Macintosh LC models
- All Macintosh Performa models
- Many SE/30s and SEs (sold after Spring 1990)

This often means the simplest (and cheapest) solution for transferring smaller files is to plunk the disk in a Macintosh drive.

Unfortunately, the normally friendly Macintosh operating system could be more neighborly about how it handles your PC disk. Expect a message like the one shown in figure 22.6.

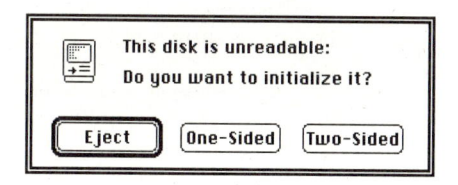

Figure 22.6

Inserting a PC disk in a Macintosh.

Initialize is Mac-speak for Format in the classic, pre-UNFORMAT sense, that is, wipe out your data.

You'll need to run a special utility called Apple File Exchange, which comes with the Macintosh operating system. Look in the Macintosh's System folder, or if it isn't there, use the Find File utility to locate it. In

Chapter 22: InterLnk and Other Connectivity Solutions

System 6, Find File is in the menu under the apple. In System 7, the equivalent Find command is in the menu under File, as shown in figure 22.7.

Figure 22.7

Finding Apple File Exchange with Find File.

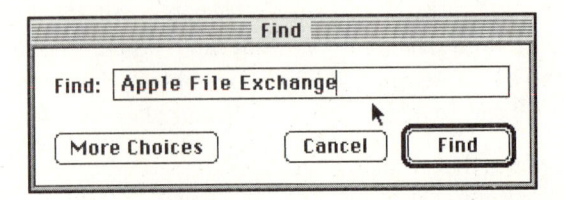

When you've found Apple File Exchange, double-click on it to open it. The contents of your Macintosh's current drive should appear in the left-hand window. The right-hand window should be blank. Now, insert your 3 1/2-inch MS-DOS floppy. Its contents will appear in the box at the right. The menu bar option Mac-to-PC now becomes active.

Click on the file to be moved. Check under Mac-to-PC to see whether or not there is a built-in translator that can help you translate your PC data formats into a Macintosh equivalent. Click on Translate, and the file is moved.

Apple File Exchange comes with every Macintosh that has a SuperDrive, but there are slicker ways of getting the job done. One is DOS Mounter from Dayna Communications (801) 531-0600. Another is AccessPC from Insignia Solutions (415) 694-7600.

Both of these third-party solutions display PC disks on your Macintosh desktop as soon as you insert them—no disconcerting "would you like to initialize this disk" messages. And if you insert a blank disk, you get a choice, as shown in figure 22.8.

Figure 22.8

AccessPC MS-DOS Disk Initialization window.

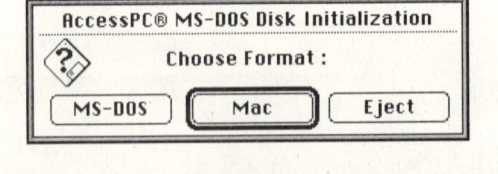

Using these products, you can double-click on a PC PageMaker file and have it open in Macintosh PageMaker (and relatively cleanly, too, since PageMaker's internal translations are quite good).

Up until now, we've talked about only 3 1/2-inch drives—that's all Apple has ever included with its Macintoshes. If you'll regularly need to exchange files from a 5 1/4-inch drive, investigate Kennect Technologies' Drive 1200 and Drive 360, or Dayna's DaynaFile II. (800) 522-1232

A less expensive solution that works with many Macintoshes is a used Apple PC Drive and controller from Sun Remarketing (800) 821-3221. The PC Drive requires Apple File Exchange; it won't work with third-party alternatives. But then, since you'll know that every disk you insert will be a DOS disk—you'll never want to format it.

> *It's not widely known, but two products exist that enable you to follow the reverse path. Central Point Software's (800) 445-2110 Deluxe Option Board replaces your floppy disk controller with one that will also read and write to Macintosh disks. Pacific Microelectronics' (800) 628-3475 Common Link performs a similar software trick.*

Running PC Software on the Macintosh

Remarkably, you can run PC Software on a Macintosh. And there are three ways to do it. The first is pure software—a family of programs called SoftPC and more recently, SoftPC Professional, both published by Insignia Solutions.

With SoftPC, your Macintosh SuperDrive acts as a PC drive, and you set up a Macintosh file that behaves as a DOS partition. Figure 22.9 shows an unexpected sight:

SoftPC mimicked DOS 3.3; SoftPC Professional upgrades to DOS 5. One variant even runs Microsoft Windows—though you need a top-of-the-line Mac Quadra to do it, which points up one of the problems of software emulation: it's slow.

If you already own a PC, you can run it remotely (and faster) from your Macintosh using RunPC (Argosy Software). A TSR sits in memory on the PC, waiting to be called by RunPC through either a serial port connection or a modem. This makes RunPC a solution for controlling your office Macintosh from your home PC, or vice versa.

Figure 22.9

SoftPC running DOS on the Macintosh.

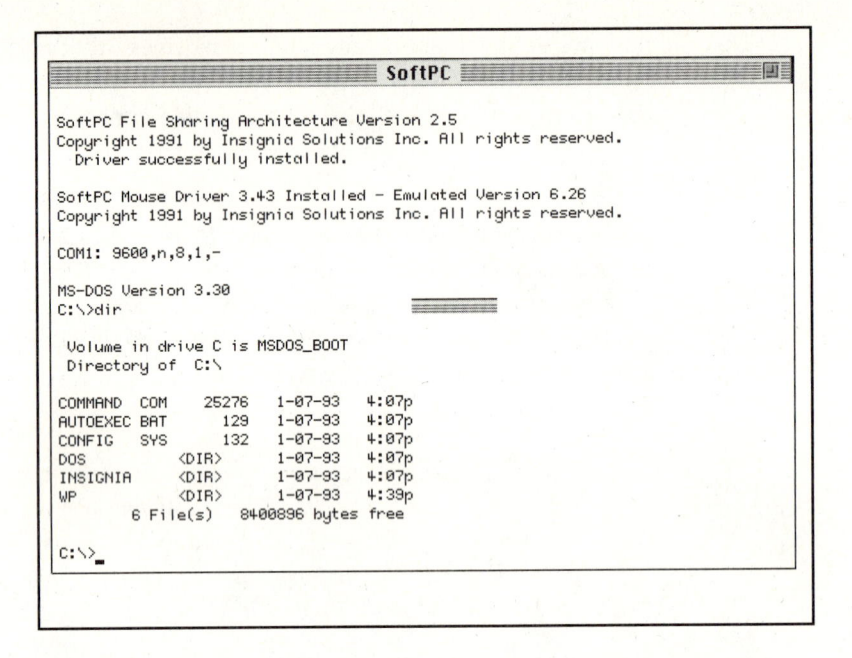

```
                         SoftPC
SoftPC File Sharing Architecture Version 2.5
Copyright 1991 by Insignia Solutions Inc. All rights reserved.
    Driver successfully installed.

SoftPC Mouse Driver 3.43 Installed - Emulated Version 6.26
Copyright 1991 by Insignia Solutions Inc. All rights reserved.

COM1: 9600,n,8,1,-

MS-DOS Version 3.30
C:\>dir

 Volume in drive C is MSDOS_BOOT
 Directory of  C:\

COMMAND  COM      25276  1-07-93   4:07p
AUTOEXEC BAT        129  1-07-93   4:07p
CONFIG   SYS        132  1-07-93   4:07p
DOS          <DIR>        1-07-93   4:07p
INSIGNIA     <DIR>        1-07-93   4:07p
WP           <DIR>        1-07-93   4:39p
        6 File(s)    8400896 bytes free

C:\>_
```

Yet another option is installing a real PC in your Macintosh II's "NuBus" expansion slot. Orange Micro offers the Mac86, Mac286, and Mac386. The Mac386 even enables you to add two standard PC boards to it, if you have the room—some Mac IIs don't. Unfortunately, these boards are often more expensive than purchasing an equivalent MS-DOS computer and RunPC to connect it.

Serial Connections between the Mac and PC

You always can run a null-modem cable between your Macintosh and your PC and upload files through communications software.

A null modem cable is similar to an ordinary serial cable, except that it crosses two pins, fooling both serial ports into thinking they're connected by a modem. Most communications software support null-modem direct connections.

However, you'll need a specialty cable that will connect the Mac's nonstandard round mini-DIN-8 RS-422 serial connection, shown in figure 22.10, with your PC's 9-pin (DB9) or 25-pin (DB25) serial port.

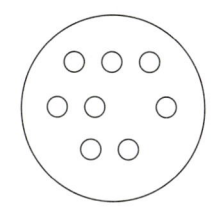

Figure 22.10

Macintosh mini-DIN-8 serial port.

> **NOTE**
>
> *Very old Macintoshes, including the Macintosh 128K, 512K, 512Ke, use a different nonstandard 9-pin serial connector, the DIN-9. Table 22.3 lists the pinouts for Macintosh serial ports and can be used to build compatible cables. One source for such a cable is Cables-to-Go (800) 826-7904.*

Table 22.3
Macintosh Serial Port Pinouts

	Macintosh 128K, 512K, 512Ke (9-Pin)	Macintosh Plus (Most 8-Pin, Some 9-Pin)	Macintosh SE and All Macintoshes Since (8-Pin)
Data carrier detect	None	None	Pin 7
Clock input	None	None	Pin 7
Data terminal ready	None	Pin 1	Pin 1
Clear to send	Pin 7	Pin 2	Pin 2
Receive data RxD+)	Pin 8	Pin 8	Pin 8
Receive data (RxD-)	Pin 9	Pin 5	Pin 5

continues

Table 22.3, Continued
Macintosh Serial Port Pinouts

	Macintosh 128K, 512K, 512Ke (9-Pin)	Macintosh Plus (Most 8-Pin, Some 9-Pin)	Macintosh SE and All Macintoshes Since (8-Pin)
Transmit data (TxD+)	Pin 4	Pin 6	Pin 6
Transmit data (TxD-)	Pin 5	Pin 3	Pin 3
Signal ground	Pin 3	Pin 4	Pin 4
Chassis ground	Pin 1	Shell	Shell
+5V power	Pin 2	None	None
+12V power	Pin 6	None	None

1. Make sure both cables are firmly in place (but don't force them—if you have to, you might have the wrong cable).

2. The printer and phone icons in your software and on the back of your Macintosh are both serial ports—make sure you choose the same port in software that you have physically connected.

3. Set both computers to the same parameters, including baud rate, data bits, stop bits, and parity.

4. Set both computers to direct connect.

5. Set one computer to Originate, and the other to Answer.

6. "Dial" from the originating computer.

7. When connected, make sure both computers are using the same file transfer protocols.

8. Set the sending computer to Upload and the receiving computer to Download.

9. Send the file.

Networking Macs and PCs Together

If you already have a Novell NetWare network, your Macintosh can be added to it using NetWare for Macintosh (800) 453-1267. Alternatively, you can build a small TOPS network—say one Macintosh, one PC, and one LaserWriter.

This requires adding an AppleTalk-compatible card, such as Sitka's FlashCard (415) 769-8700, to your PC, purchasing MacTOPS and DOSTops software, and connecting everything with twisted-pair phone wiring and Farallon PhoneNet (or compatible) connectors (800) 344-7489.

> **NOTE** *We say a small network because TOPS tops out at around 20 workstations. Regrettably, TOPS has fallen somewhat behind the technological curve and at this writing shows few signs of catching up.*

File Translation

Until now, this discussion has glossed over the second half of the problem: file translation. If all you've done is move your raw data onto the Macintosh's hard drive, chances are—unless it's pure ASCII—your data will have formatting that won't be recognizable to the Macintosh application you plan to use it with.

There are two primary solutions, which are good but not perfect:

- ✔ Use applications that come in versions for both the Macintosh and the PC
- ✔ Use file transfer programs that also handle translation

In both cases, advance planning is absolutely essential.

Sibling Applications

If you plan to work extensively across platforms, seriously consider using software that runs on both platforms, for example:

Microsoft Word, WordPerfect (word processing)

Aldus PageMaker, QuarkXpress, FrameMaker (desktop publishing)

Microsoft Excel, Lotus 1-2-3 (spreadsheet)

Claris Filemaker Pro (flat-file database)

Omnis 7 (Relational database)

Adobe Illustrator, Aldus Freehand (illustration)

Adobe Photoshop (photo retouching)

Aldus Persuasion, Microsoft Powerpoint (presentations)

Some of these programs recognize that you are trying to load a DOS file and ask if you want to convert it. In any case, most of these applications include conversion utilities that enable you to convert the files into a form readable by their sister programs.

If possible, standardize on the same generation of program on both platforms. Windows Excel 4.0 files, for example, contain formatting that Macintosh Excel 3.0 hasn't learned about yet.

Even within a generation, conversion utilities aren't always perfect—you may still find you have some cleaning up to do. But they will get you most of the way there. Common translation problems include the following:

- ✔ Changes in colors
- ✔ Inability to read macros and styles
- ✔ Inability to view graphics
- ✔ Shifts in text

Font Substitution

One especially common problem is font substitution. The Windows TrueType font Times New Roman, for example, corresponds to the Macintosh font Times, but they aren't exactly alike.

In particular, the spacing between letters varies. So you may think you've set up a page to fit perfectly, and then you find that it's jumped to the next page when you switch platforms. This is especially annoying in desktop publishing.

The best solution available (and this is not always possible or perfect) is to use the same fonts on both platforms. That means fonts from the same manufacturer, that is, Adobe, Bitstream, or Monotype—not simply fonts with similar names.

Graphics Formats

The Macintosh and PC each support a plethora of graphics standards, but few of them are used on both platforms. Generally, the easiest files to convert are Encapsulated PostScript and TIFF files. If you can't use only TIFF and EPS files, the PC programs Paintshop Pro and Hijaak (Inset Systems (203) 775-5866) specialize in converting among DOS graphics formats. There are DOS and Windows versions.

Because TIFF and EPS files can be large, you may want to compress them: programs that compress and decompress ARC and ZIP formats are available on both platforms.

NOTE *MS-DOS 6.2's DBLSPACE and the popular program Stacker are not compatible with Stuffit (Aladdin Systems), the most widely used Macintosh compression program. Stuffit Deluxe, however, can decompress ARC and ZIP files.*

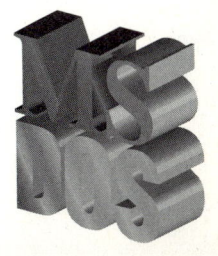

The following list shows some standards, graphics and otherwise, that are reasonably well-supported on both platforms: Macintosh and PC.

Graphics	TIFF, EPS
Text	Rich Text Format (Microsoft)
Database	DBF (dBase)
Spreadsheet	WK1 (Lotus)
Compression	ARC, ZIP

Compatible File Names

If you know a file will need to be translated, use a file name that will be understood on the other end. This is mostly a problem in going from Mac to PC. Mac file names can be up to 31 characters and may include characters that aren't allowed in DOS file names. In translation, your file names may be truncated in ways you won't recognize and may not include an appropriate extension.

Translation and File Transfer Programs

As already mentioned, Apple File Exchange includes limited file translation options. If you need more—and if your sibling programs can't handle the job—seriously consider MacLinkPlus (Dataviz (203) 268-0030), LapLink/Mac III (Traveling Software (800) 682-2652), or Software Bridge (Argosy Software).

MacLinkPlus is available in two versions. MacLinkPlus/PC 7 comes with cables and file transfer software for both PCs and Macs. MacLinkPlus/Translators 7 assumes your data is on disk and includes Dayna's DOS Mounter software to help the Macintosh recognize it.

Both versions contain more than 700 translations, the widest translation library available—even containing selected translations to Sun and NeXT workstations. Some of the translations aren't as robust as those provided by the programs themselves, but if you need the job done, MacLinkPlus is invaluable.

Another option, stronger on file transfer and somewhat lighter on translations, is LapLink Mac III.

MacLinkPlus becomes even more valuable when you use it with XTND-compatible applications. These applications use a new Claris technology, XTND, that automatically connects a file with the appropriate translation resource when you open the file.

LapLink/Mac III contains fewer translators but, quite possibly, the best cross-platform file transfer software available. With LapLink/Mac III, you get Macintosh and PC file transfer software, a cable that supports serial connections at both ends, and a modest set of file translators. Unlike some PC file transfer software, LapLink/Mac (and its sibling, LapLink III) also can work with modems. It also works with AppleTalk networks, which can themselves support PCs.

Software Bridge specializes in text documents. With Software Bridge running, you can double-click on a DOS text document; Software Bridge identifies and translates it, and loads it into the correct Macintosh word processing program, with much of the formatting intact.

Like MacLinkPlus/Translators, Software Bridge comes with a utility for helping the Macintosh automatically recognize DOS disks without fooling around with Apple File Exchange.

Summary

If you need to transfer files between PCs, InterLnk offers a plain but very functional solution. After you get used to thinking of your server's drives as extensions of your client system, you quickly realize the power InterLnk gives you. With the exception of some disk commands—FORMAT, FDISK, CHKDSK, and a few others—if you can do it on your own drives, you can do it on the server system's drives.

InterLnk makes PCs significantly more interoperable. The quest for interoperability has moved forward on the Macintosh platform, also. Many options now are available for connecting these two very dissimilar types of computers.

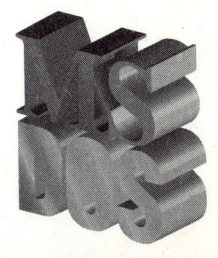

The quest for interoperability has moved forward on the Macintosh platform, also. Someday, who knows? The Apple/IBM operating system, Taligent, and the PowerPC chip they're both developing may make these questions obsolete. But back here in the 20th century, it's a blessing to know that there are now options for connecting Macs and PCs—and for making them work together to get the job done.

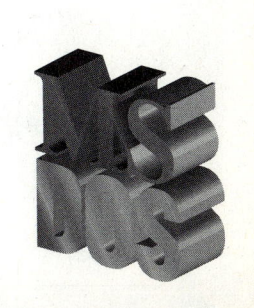

MS-DOS

MS-DOS

CHAPTER 23

Using DOS 6.2 with Local Area Networks

by Bill Camarda

DOS is everywhere. It certainly wasn't originally designed for networking—heck, it wasn't even originally designed for hard disks. But its very ubiquity has ensured the proliferation of local area network solutions which clean up many of its weaknesses and build on the strengths it does have.

This chapter offers a brief overview of how MS-DOS, and especially MS-DOS 6.2, fits into a networked environment. This chapter covers both major networking approaches:

✔ *Dedicated server-based networks*, such as those built around Novell NetWare, in which client systems continue to run MS-DOS, but the server uses an operating system specifically designed for networking.

✓ *Peer-to-peer networks*, in which each DOS-based workstation can act as either a client or server, sharing information from other DOS-based workstations.

This chapter also briefly discusses planning a network, including choosing the hardware and software that underlie today's local area networks.

You'll learn a few DOS commands and some new DOS features, and how they relate (or don't relate) to networking platforms.

Finally, you'll also get some advice on specific upgrades you might need to run MS-DOS 6.2 with various networks. But first, a few definitions....

Understanding Basic Network Terminology

A *local area network* (LAN) is a system of two or more computers, plus specialized hardware and software that enables users to share information across limited distances. LANs themselves may be connected into broader networks, such as *wide area networks* (WANs).

In most cases, each PC on a LAN contains an internal card that enables it to communicate with other computers on the network. These are called network adapter cards or network interface cards. Some very low-speed networks use the PC's built-in serial port; these often are called *zero-slot LANs*.

The PCs themselves, when connected on a LAN, often are called workstations. (Don't confuse this terminology with the high-powered, networked desktop systems from Sun and other manufacturers that are known as workstations.)

> *Laptops sometimes are connected to LANs through external interfaces from companies like Xircom. These interfaces commonly use a laptop's parallel port—still very slow compared with internal cards, but easily two or three times as fast as serial connections.*

In general, computers on a LAN are physically connected by cable, though wireless LANs may now use radio frequencies, replacing some physical connections.

What controls this hardware? A *network operating system* (NOS). NOS components on the client and the server work together to make sure that files, printers, and other resources are available, as appropriate, to each workstation on the network.

On a server-based network, this network operating system works primarily from a file server or dedicated server—a high-powered PC or other computer that does nothing but manage the network and provide files to each workstation on it.

> **NOTE** *Although the term* file server *often is used to mean any kind of LAN server, there are a variety of servers, including FAX and communications servers, which provide FAX and modem services respectively.*

On a peer-to-peer network, each workstation can serve the needs of another workstation as a server and then turn around and request service from another workstation as a client.

> **NOTE** *Technically, you don't need a dedicated computer on a peer-to-peer network. But as a practical matter, once you have several PCs connected together in a peer network, performance can quickly degrade unless you dedicate one PC to network tasks.*

There is growing (but not universal) independence among all these LAN components. For example, a few years ago, if you chose Novell NetWare as your network operating system, that in turn defined the decisions you made about cabling and boards. Now, however, NetWare can operate using a variety of boards and cabling systems.

Chapter 23: *Using DOS 6.2 with Local Area Networks*

> **NOTE**
>
> Ideally, every layer of a network—from the way the physical plugs connect, all the way up to the way applications behave—should be independent. That way, you could choose the best solution at each layer and then could be sure that it would work with the solutions you chose for every other layer.
>
> As it happens, there is a model for this: the Open Systems Interconnection (OSI) model, developed by the International Standards Organization (ISO). (Remember, OSI comes from ISO, not the other way around. You'll be tested in this.) Figure 23.1 shows the seven OSI layers.
>
> Unfortunately, networking customers already have waited several years for truly OSI-compliant products to become widespread. In the meantime, they've chosen instead to purchase products that work right now, which has, in turn, slowed demand for OSI products—and weakened vendor commitment to provide them.
>
> So, with a few exceptions, you should consider the OSI model more as a guide for thinking about LANs than as a hard-and-fast guide to implementing them.

Figure 23.1
OSI layers.

Application (Establishes user interface)
Presentation (Data formats/Security)
Session (Manages the connection)
Transport (Ensures accurate transmission)
Network (Routes data packets)
Data Link (Creates/Double-checks data packets)
Physical (Sends/Receives electrical signals)

How DOS Fits In

If you step away from the significant improvements made by MS-DOS 6.2, MS-DOS 5, and Windows 3.*x*, underneath it all, DOS's architecture hasn't changed much at its core.

- ✔ DOS is still fundamentally a single-tasking operating system, though Windows and other alternatives conspire to disguise or evade that.

> **NOTE**
>
> MS-DOS is single-tasking in large part because its functions are nonreentrant. This means that, with the specific exception of hardware interrupts, DOS must finish every function call it starts. This is in contrast to a reentrant operating system which can suspend a function and run the same function from another task while the first one is waiting.
>
> Windows gets around this handicap through cooperative multitasking: each Windows program must yield control voluntarily at specific times, and wait for Windows to return control to it.
>
> This isn't as efficient or safe as true preemptive multitasking, whereby the operating system itself takes charge of making sure each program gets its share of processor time.
>
> Windows does provide preemptive multitasking for DOS programs running from within it. It does this by creating virtual machines. These make each DOS program think it's working directly under DOS, when in fact it's working with a segment of processor time and memory that masquerades as DOS, and is under Windows' centralized control.
>
> All this requires complex programming and quite a bit of power—which helps to explain why Windows presents special challenges for networking.

✔ The DOS file system still uses very old methods to store, locate, and load files.

> **NOTE**
>
> It was rumored that MS-DOS 6.2 might contain a more advanced file system; perhaps a variant of the High Performance File System available through OS/2. But it doesn't. Rumor now has it that MS-DOS 7 will.

✔ DOS still can only address 640K in conventional memory, notwithstanding the extraordinary, arcane structures that have been built above 640K to evade this limitation.

Each of these limitations presents trouble for a network operating system. Single-tasking limits a network's ability to respond to the needs of many clients quickly. The DOS file system limits the speed and security that can be built into DOS-based networks. The 640K limitation restricts the ability of network operating system programs to run alongside other programs, especially those programs that are on low-end PCs.

This isn't to say that you can't build networks around DOS; most peer-to-peer network operating systems do precisely that. It simply explains why DOS-based network operating systems have tended to be less powerful than NOSs based on UNIX, OS/2, or proprietary multitasking operating systems.

Moreover, DOS has some significant advantages in a networking environment.

✔ It's cheap to buy and work with. DOS requires much less power than preemptive multitasking operating systems like UNIX, OS/2, and Windows NT.

✔ It's widespread and mature. DOS offers a reliable basis for dealing with the functions of a PC that aren't involved in networking.

✔ It offers support for the broadest range of hardware. DOS also has an immense software base.

✔ It contains specific support for file-sharing and file-locking across networks, through the SHARE command.

Planning a LAN

Choosing a LAN actually involves two sets of considerations: managerial and technical. Managerial considerations include:

✔ What problems do you want the LAN to solve now? What problems do you hope it will solve in the future? Which are highest priority? Which problems can you compromise on?

✔ Who will support the LAN when you purchase it? Even in peer-to-peer LANs, generally recognized as easier to live with, a rule of thumb is that someone will spend an hour per workstation per week on network management, including backup. That makes baby-sitting a 40-workstation LAN a full-time job.

✔ What business processes will the LAN affect? Can you streamline these processes before you install the LAN? What opportunities for further streamlining should the LAN offer?

✔ How sophisticated are your users? What training will they need to take maximum advantage of the new LAN?

✔ What are your security requirements?

✔ Who will install and test the network? If you're hiring someone to do it, do they have references? Will you have a single outside source to help solve problems when they arise?

Technical considerations include:

✔ What hardware do you currently have? What do you expect to add in the next few years?

✔ What applications will you implement? For example, heavy use of multimedia across a network can drastically increase the demand on the network and slow it down significantly. Maybe you need a faster network and higher-capacity cabling.

✔ Will you need to connect with remote systems and networks? If so, which ones?

✔ Will you develop client/server applications?

✔ Where will each workstation be? Where will each workgroup be? How extensive are the networking needs of each workgroup?

✔ Will your network have to support mobile computing and remote access, by salespeople and telecommuters for example?

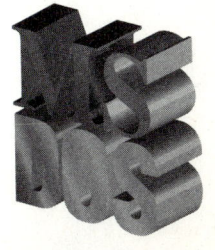

As you can see, technical and business considerations overlap. Some of the technical issues will be discussed next. Keep in mind that your business goals—what you're trying to accomplish—should really drive your technical decision making, not the other way around.

Networking at the Board Level

Early on, you'll need to decide how your networked computers will talk to each other. That means choosing network interface cards.

These cards have two primary responsibilities: to translate signals running inside your computer into signals understood on the network, and to run software that controls how your adapters interface with your wiring.

You have four primary choices:

- ARCnet
- Ethernet (802.3)
- Token Ring (802.5)
- Fiber Distributed Data Interface (FDDI)

ARCnet

ARCnet dates back to a 1977 Datapoint product, the Attached Resource Computer Network. Standard ARCnet runs at 2.5 Mbps—significantly slower than Ethernet or Token Ring, but speed differences often become very fuzzy in real-world applications. The newest version of ARCnet runs at 20 Mbps, leapfrogging conventional Ethernet and Token Ring.

ARCnet originally became popular because it was inexpensive, reliable, relatively easy to install and manage, and could run with either thin coaxial cable (RG62) or cheap twisted-pair telephone wiring.

However, ARCnet's popularity has faded, in part because it's the only major LAN adapter system that isn't based on a public standard.

Many LAN consultants say that's reason enough to disqualify it as a possible solution, because it puts you at the mercy of a relatively small group of suppliers who may or may not keep pace with your networking needs over the long term.

Ethernet-Style Networks

Ethernet was yet another of those incredibly successful inventions that came out of Xerox Corporation's Palo Alto Research Center and made gobs of money for practically everyone but Xerox.

Nowadays, the term *Ethernet* is rarely used to mean the product created by Xerox; it refers to the range of EtherNet-like networks lumped under the public 802.3 standard by the Institute of Electrical and Electronic Engineers (IEEE).

These networks all share a scheme that is euphoniously named *Carrier Sense Multiple Access with Collision Detection (CSMA/CD)*.

CSMA/CD means that your PC first listens to the network to hear if anyone else is transmitting. If not, your PC sends your message—or, more precisely, a frame, which contains up to 1,500 bytes of your message, plus synchronization, address, protocol, and data-checking information.

But some other PC might also have heard a "quiet" network and transmitted at the same time. In that case, the messages collide. Both stations realize it, and each waits before trying again. To make it unlikely that the messages will collide again, each station waits a random amount of time before retransmitting.

Note that five different types of Ethernet networks are recognized by IEEE, each with its own specifications:

- ✔ **10BASE5.** Original Ethernet running at 10 Mbps, using thick coaxial cable.

- ✔ **10BASE2.** Thinnet, running at 10 Mbps, using thin RG58AU coaxial cable.

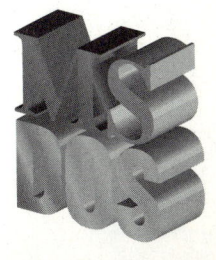

- **1BASE5.** StarLAN, an AT&T variant, running at 1 Mbps over unshielded twisted-pair telephone wire.
- **10BASE-T.** 1BASE5 beefed up to run at 10 Mbps.

Of these, 10BASE2 and 10BASE-T are the most common alternatives.

BASE refers to these standards' use of baseband cable, which can carry only one signal in one direction at one time. For the very largest installations, there is also a broadband Ethernet standard that can carry multiple channels, just as does a cable TV wire:

- **10BROAD36.** Broadband Ethernet running at 10 Mbps for a distance of up to 3,600 meters.

Token Ring Networks (802.5)

Token Ring networks handle communication between PCs in a very different way. Instead of expecting collisions, as Ethernet does, a Token Ring network enables only one user at a time to transmit a message.

The network passes around a unique data frame, called a token, and the sending PC grabs that token when it comes around, inserting its message. The message passes along the network until it arrives at its recipient's workstation; this workstation grabs the message, marks the message as received, and sends the token onward.

When the token arrives at the sender's workstation, the sender realizes that the message has been received in good condition, and spins a new token into the network.

Token Ring networks were popularized by IBM; they theoretically can handle higher traffic levels with more style and grace than the collision-oriented Ethernet. The IEEE has set public Token Ring standards, called the 802.5 standards. Token Ring now comes in 4 Mbps and 16 Mbps versions.

In reality, the performance differences between Token Ring and Ethernet are highly dependent on external factors; it's hard to say which is more efficient.

For example, the time it takes to get information from a server can often depend more on the speed of the server's hard drive than the speed of the network—which is why a fast server hard drive can be a very good investment.

By virtue of IBM's support, Token Ring networks can offer better connectivity with other IBM host computers. Unfortunately, most Token Ring adapter cards are significantly more expensive than Ethernet cards.

IBM Token Ring networks can run on shielded or unshielded twisted pair wiring. If you use unshielded twisted pair, be careful to meet IBM's specifications of 22 AWG or 24 AWG with at least two twists per foot to reduce interference.

Fiber Distributed Data Interface (FDDI)

FDDI extends and adapts the ideas behind IBM Token Ring networking to support the remarkable speed of 100 Mbps over optical fiber. FDDI is a standard set by the American National Standards Institute (ANSI).

Needless to say, this is still prohibitively expensive for small organizations and individuals. An adapter card that might cost $200 under Ethernet and $400 under Token Ring will cost $5,000 under FDDI—not to mention the much higher cost of optical fiber.

Not surprisingly, vendors are attempting to market copper-based variants of FDDI, which maintain the same speed but use less expensive adapters (ballpark, $1,500) and cabling. These so-called CDDI technologies seem promising, but they haven't yet been standardized.

A Few Words about Wiring

As you can see, the adapter technology you choose will somewhat narrow your choice of wiring. Here again, you face the predictable tradeoff of cost versus capacity and reliability. Table 23.1 shows the relative costs, advantages, and limitations of each type of cable.

Table 23.1
Network Cabling Alternatives

Cable Type	Average Cost	Advantages/Disadvantages
Unshielded	9-12 cents/foot	Low cost, wide grade voice twisted pair availability, limited band width and growth potential, requires hub at additional cost.
Unshielded data grade twisted pair (22AWG or 24AWG)	11-15 cents/foot	Low cost, greater growth potential, requires hub at additional cost.
Shielded twisted pair	30-50 cents/foot	Better protection from electrical interference, requires hub.
Baseband coaxial cable (Thinnet)	30-50 cents/foot	Relatively easy to install, relatively high bandwidth, won't carry integrated voice/data signals.
Broadband coaxial (Thicknet) modem-type	$1.00/foot	Expensive; cable requires additional interfaces; bulky; very high bandwidth can also support video and other signals.
Fiber-optic cable	$1.00/foot	Requires specialized expertise, very expensive, will support extensive growth, highly secure.

One common strategy in wiring a building is to create a fiber backbone that carries large amounts of data—say, from floor to floor, or to and from a large computer—and uses twisted pair to individual desktops.

Of course, such a strategy may be largely irrelevant to small users: if you're planning a LAN to connect the PC and laser printer in your home office with the PC in your den, twisted pair should do the job unless you have a very big house.

> *If you're using coax, be aware that some fire codes require fire-resistant plenum cabling.*

Server-Based or Peer-to-Peer?

Your next fundamental decision is whether to go with a server-based network that doesn't use DOS at all on your server, or a peer-to-peer network that builds on DOS for both its client and server tasks.

This decision is highly individual, and based on your specific needs, but table 23.2 can help you make a start. Remember, different peer and server networks have different specific features. These are only generalizations:

Table 23.2
Typical Attributes of Peer-to-Peer and Server-Based Networks

	Peer-to-Peer	*Server-Based*
Cost per workstation	$250-$400	$500-$1000
Need for dedicated server	Not essential but often desirable	Always essential
Connectivity with other networks and hosts	Uneven	Very good

continues

Table 23.2, Continued
Typical Attributes of Peer-to-Peer and Server-Based Networks

	Peer-to-Peer	Server-Based
Support for peripherals (other than printers)	Uneven	Very good
Growth path	Depends on product. You can usually preserve hardware investments if you need to replace NOS.	Very good
Size of networks	Small-Midsized	Midsized-Large
Support for non-DOS clients	Weak	Very good
Training required for users	Limited	Moderate
Ongoing support required	Moderate	Extensive
Network Management tools	Very limited	Extensive
Ease of Moves/Changes	Good	Fair
Security	Moderate	Extensive

Peer-to-Peer Options

The primary peer-to-peer choices are as follows:

- ✔ LANtastic (Artisoft)
- ✔ NetWare Lite (Novell)
- ✔ Windows for Workgroups (Microsoft)

A wide variety of second-level players exists in the peer-to-peer market. Two noteworthy examples are:

POWERLan (Performance Technology), which offers sophisticated interconnectivity with non-DOS based systems and remote LANs; and *WEB* (Webcorp), which is unusually compatible with Novell NetWare, and uses data compression to increase data transmission speeds.

All three of the products in the following discussion can be purchased in the form of starter kits that include the network adapter and cabling required to build a 2-user LAN. NetWare Lite kits, however, are available through third parties, not Novell.

LANtastic

Artisoft's LANtastic is the most popular peer-to-peer LAN, notwithstanding growing competition from two much larger players, Microsoft and Novell. LANtastic's features include:

- ✔ Built-in, sophisticated electronic mail
- ✔ More complete security than most peer networks
- ✔ Relatively low client (24K) and server (58K) memory requirements
- ✔ Support for Windows through the optional LANtastic for Windows
- ✔ Sophisticated print management capabilities that tell users precisely where their jobs stand

LANtastic theoretically can grow to 300 users, though you may want to begin considering full-fledged NetWare or one of its competitors after you reach 75 to 100 users.

Although large LANtastic peer networks share the speed limitations of other large peer networks, these are somewhat mitigated by an excellent built-in read/write disk cache program, LANcache. LANtastic's resource cache also tracks each user's access privileges in memory, cutting the amount of time it takes to open files.

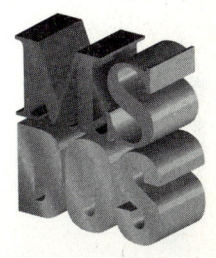

One attractive feature of LANtastic, absent in Windows for Workgroups, is the ability for even stripped-down 8088-based PCs to work as both clients and servers.

If you are only connecting two PCs, LANtastic offers a zero-slot LAN, LANtastic Z, which works through both computers' serial ports. Like all zero-slot LANs, LANtastic Z is very slow compared with "real" networks, but otherwise it works much like "real" LANtastic. You can use it until you expand to a third PC and need more capabilities.

LANtastic may not be ideal if you need to connect with Macintoshes or NetWare networks. In each case, LANtastic offers add-on products that do the job, but they fatten LANtastic's memory requirements. In the case of Macintosh, they are quite limited in capabilities—for example, no electronic mail.

LANtastic also manufactures network boards and offers a number of alternatives. You can purchase an inexpensive, nonstandard board that will only run with LANtastic. Or you can purchase a somewhat more expensive EtherNet-compatible board that will enable you to migrate to another network operating system if you ever decide to do so.

The added flexibility of a standards-based system is almost always worth the extra money. Unfortunately, third-party Ethernet cards may require a special driver at added cost.

NetWare Lite

Recognizing that most local area networks are quite small, Novell introduced NetWare Lite, a stripped-down, easy-to-install version of NetWare for networks comprising no more than 25 computers.

NetWare Lite is very light on memory usage: roughly 27K for client software and 49K for server software. You may have to add a separate 40K disk cache, however.

NetWare Lite uses IPX, the same basic communications protocol as full-scale NetWare. This simplifies migration to NetWare later. In fact, NetWare Lite users can connect to resources on NetWare hosts simply by running the add-on shell program NETX.COM.

However, some elements of NetWare 2.2 and 3.11 are not present on NetWare Lite. These include the higher-level NetWare communications protocol SPX (Sequenced Packet Exchange), and the Bindery, NetWare's mechanism for tracking users and resources. NetWare utilities and programs that require them won't work on NetWare Lite. Rumor has it, however, that the Bindery might not be included in future versions of NetWare, anyway.

> **NOTE**
>
> *This is perhaps a good place to mention networking protocols. Remember the OSI model? Way down at the bottom was the Physical layer, which pretty well corresponds to cables and plugs. One step up was Data Link, which corresponds to things like Ethernet and Token-Ring standards.*
>
> *Now it gets interesting. Real-world networks are full of overlaps between the next three layers: Network, Transport, and Session. That's largely because they predate the OSI standard; some vendor self-interest might occasionally creep into the equation, too.*
>
> *Novell's Internetwork Packet Exchange (IPX) is primarily a network and transport-layer protocol. Another proprietary Novell item, Sequenced Packet Exchange (SPX), sits on top of it and works primarily at the session layer.*
>
> *Fine and dandy, unless you have an MS-DOS-based network application that expects to find NetBIOS there—the long-time standard for MS-DOS network applications.*
>
> *You can purchase NetBIOS from Novell to run these applications, but not everyone's NetBIOS is identical, so don't expect them all to work together.*
>
> *continues*

If this isn't enough, consider TCP/IP, Transport Control Protocol/Internet Protocol, the standard for communications among heterogeneous networks, especially UNIX networks. IP is a network-layer protocol; TCP works at the transport and session layers.

Now do you see why OSI is a better model for thinking about networks than for implementing them?

Legally, you must own a separate copy of any network operating system for each PC. NetWare Lite is copy-protected: you must install from a new copy of NetWare Lite on each PC, and keep track of the copy used by each PC, or else the network will determine that the same copy is running on multiple PCs and display the words License Violation.

One very nice touch: if the server fails, NetWare Lite automatically reconnects your client computer to it when it comes back on-line. Many networks require the client to reboot.

Eagle Technology, Ansel Communications, and Xircom sell kits containing NetWare Lite and all the hardware you need to build a network.

Windows for Workgroups

Windows for Workgroups does not come with DOS 6.2. This program must be purchased separately. Here's a summary of its capabilities:

Windows for Workgroups extends Microsoft Windows 3.1 to provide peer-to-peer networking with other Windows workstations. Computers with Windows for Workgroups also can act as servers to computers running MS-DOS 6.2 with Workgroup Connection. The unfortunate downside to this is that Windows for Workgroups won't permit DOS-only machines to work as servers.

Windows for Workgroups does, however, include basic electronic mail and scheduling, the two fundamental groupware applications. Windows for Workgroups also comes with client software that provides access to NetWare servers.

One very attractive feature of Windows for Workgroups is the way it extends Dynamic Data Exchange (DDE) across the network, permitting you to create documents that automatically update themselves based on new information—whether that information is stored at your workstation or elsewhere on the network.

Not surprisingly, Windows for Workgroups requires significantly more power than other peer-to-peer networks. In fact, you may need 8M to really take full advantage of it—which puts you right up there in OS/2 terrain.

> *Many people choose peer-to-peer LANs in large part to avoid spending money on a dedicated server. That's often a false economy.*
>
> *If your network will have more than a few PCs, by all means consider running a peer-to-peer network because it's cheaper and easier to manage. But dedicate one machine to running the network even though you don't have to.*
>
> *You'll find that networking will slow down a PC more than you might expect—especially if that PC is connected to your workgroup's laser printer or other shared resource.*
>
> *Not only that, but if the individual using that PC reboots, any network activity involving that PC will be disrupted. People on the other end just hate that.*

Server-Based Options

The primary server-based choices are:

- ✔ Novell NetWare
- ✔ Microsoft LAN Manager/IBM LAN Server
- ✔ Banyan VINES

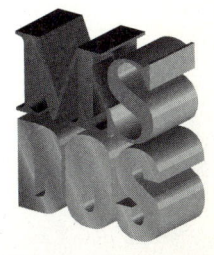

Novell NetWare

Novell NetWare is the mother of all local area network operating systems. By most accounts, NetWare still garners more than 60 percent of all LAN revenue, notwithstanding intense competition from Microsoft.

At this writing, two versions of NetWare exist: NetWare 2.2, designed for 80286-based servers, and NetWare 3.11, designed for 80386 and 80486 servers. Rumor has it than NetWare 4.0 is on the way, with more sophisticated directory services that make it a better solution for enterprise-wide networks in large companies.

NetWare 3.11 is especially powerful. It's able to connect with an extraordinary range of systems. NetWare client software is available for DOS, Macintosh, UNIX, and OS/2.

Connectivity is available to other UNIX systems through TCP/IP and Sun Microsystems' NFS standard, and NetWare's UNIX support is likely to deepen even more now that Novell has bought UNIX Software Laboratories from AT&T, the company that created UNIX.

On the IBM side, NetWare connects to IBM hosts by means of NetWare for SAA and is even resold by IBM. At the hardware level, NetWare runs on Ethernet, Token Ring, and ARCnet.

The NetWare 3.11 server contains a small DOS partition but does its essential work using Novell's own proprietary operating system. NetWare 2.2 uses the older, NetWare 2.*xx* style partitioning in which NetWare either occupies the entire disk or is booted from a startup disk.

On the client side, two elements are required. The first is the NetWare Shell, NETX.COM, which redirects data requests to and from the server. NETX.COM is constantly being updated; the most recent version at this writing is 3.31. The second is the communications protocol program, IPX.COM. You can superimpose a NetBIOS option for compatibility with network applications that need it.

Both versions of NetWare are relatively expensive and very complicated. NetWare client software also eats significantly more memory than many peer-to-peer LANs. By now you've figured out that full-fledged NetWare is probably *not* the solution for hooking up your LAN at home. But if you're connecting large departments throughout a company, well, that's another story.

Microsoft LAN Manager/IBM LAN Server

Both Microsoft LAN Manager and IBM LAN Server are based on OS/2—they date back to the days when Microsoft and IBM were still working together.

Now, Microsoft says LAN Manager, currently in Version 2.2, will migrate to Windows NT when that operating system becomes available. Meanwhile, IBM continues to upgrade the OS/2 platform underlying LAN Server.

LAN Manager and LAN Server continue to trail NetWare badly in sales; however, LAN Manager has picked up the endorsement of a variety of third-party manufacturers, including NCR and Hewlett-Packard.

LAN Manager and LAN Server are sometimes viewed as superior *client/server* environments when compared with NetWare. They're seen as relatively easy to program and are supported by client/server development products like Microsoft's SQL Server, which manages a server database and clients' requests for its data.

Because both LAN Manager and LAN Server are currently OS/2-based, both take advantage of OS/2's High Performance File System to provide faster, more efficient file service than DOS can.

Both support DOS and OS/2 clients; LAN Manager supports Macintoshes as well. Both products require significantly more RAM and disk space on the client workstation than does NetWare.

Clients on a LAN Manager/LAN Server network run a program called the Redirector, comparable to the NetWare Shell in that it determines whether data requests can be handled locally by DOS or must be sent to the Server. The Server runs a separate OS/2 program that manages the network.

Banyan VINES

Banyan VINES offers capabilities similar to Novell NetWare on a UNIX-based platform, along with extensive, standards-based connectivity.

VINES' niche has grown in enterprise-wide networking partly due to its sophisticated StreetTalk directory services, which help it integrate multiple LANs throughout an enterprise. VINES 5.5 makes it easier to use these directory services to build applications that connect multiple sites.

Buying a Server

Assuming that you've decided to centralize much LAN activity in a dedicated PC even if you use a peer-to-peer network, how do you buy a server? Obviously this depends on the size of your network, but in general, you can skimp on:

- ✔ **Monitors.** Buy a cheap VGA, perhaps even a monochrome VGA, unless you're running network management software that depends on color.

- ✔ **Second floppy drives.** Just get a 3 1/2-inch 1.44M; don't bother with the 1.2M if you have a choice.

You should spend on:

- ✔ **Processor speed.** Given the collapse in PC prices, try for at least a 486/33.

- ✔ **Hard drive size and speed.** Try for at least a 300M hard drive, and consider the expandability of SCSI (*see Chapter 4*). (Depending on your users, each workstation will require at least 20M on the server and quite possibly 50M.)

- ✔ **Uninterrupted Power Supply.** Your network will depend heavily (if not totally) on the server. Get a true UPS that always runs your system on its internal power—*not* a switched UPS (or "SPS") that switches over as soon as it realizes the wall power has failed.

Running Your Network with MS-DOS 6.2

In general, MS-DOS 6.2 behaves like MS-DOS 5 when it comes to your network. If your network software worked with DOS 5 but doesn't recognize DOS 6.2, you can sometimes make it work by telling SETVER to tell your network software that it is still running MS-DOS 5. An example appears later in this chapter.

As in DOS 5, run your network software before you enter the DOS Shell.

Some of DOS' new features are less than ideal for networked environments. For example, you might consider avoiding DBLSPACE disk compression on files that will be accessed extensively by network users.

At best, disk compression will slow down access. At worst, you're adding another risk factor to your network—if a compressed volume file crashes, it becomes inaccessible to everyone.

Since Microsoft Backup doesn't support tape drives, it probably won't help you much in backing up large network drives. However, you *can* use it to back up local drives to a large network drive.

These commands can be used on local disks even if they are on a network, but cannot be used on a remote network drive: CHKDSK, DEFRAG, DISKCOMP, FASTOPEN, FDISK, FORMAT, INTERLNK, SYS, UNFORMAT. DEFRAG also may have trouble with some peer-to-peer networks if the server software is running.

On the other hand, a number of new DOS commands make special provisions for networks. Here are some examples of the NET commands that accompany Workgroup Connection:

- ✔ MemMaker sometimes has trouble running if connected to a Token-Ring network. You can tell it to ignore the network by using the command MEMMAKER /T.

- ✔ Microsoft Anti-Virus normally scans network drives. You may wish to disable this feature, using the command MSAV /L.

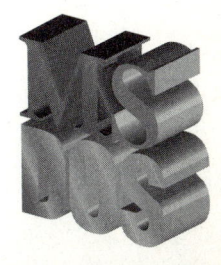

- ✓ Microsoft System Diagnostics (MSD) will display the current network hardware and software you are running.
- ✓ The new environment variable MSDOSDATA enables you to use a local configuration even if you are running a DOS utility located elsewhere on the network.

MS-DOS 6.2, like DOS 5 before it, enables you to load client network drive redirector programs into upper-memory blocks. And DOS 6.2's MemMaker program can help clear space for you to do this.

To save space on client systems, you also might choose to load MS-DOS 6.2 utilities on a server and share them across the network instead of duplicating them on every workstation.

Before installing MS-DOS 6.2 on a networked system, back up your data!

Do You Need a Network Upgrade?

If your network version is incompatible with MS-DOS 6.2, Setup may display a message that begins: "You have specified that your computer is connected to a network...." Setup then will refer you to the README.TXT file that comes with DOS. You may want to review table 23.3 before attempting to set up DOS 6.2 with your network.

Table 23.3
Network Versions Required for MS-DOS 6.2

Network	Version Required	Other Steps Required
LANtastic	3.02 or higher (Versions 2.5 through 3.01 should work if you SETVER to DOS 4.)	Shut down LANtastic server

Network	Version Required	Other Steps Required
AT&T StarGroup (Pre-LAN Manager versions)	N/A	If you have problems with SETVER, set DOS version to 4.0 for the files SETUP.EXE and ATTSTART.EXE. Restart. Deinstall StarGroup. Reinstall StarGroup; tell it you're using DOS 4.0.
Banyan VINES	4.1 and higher	4.0 works if you have (or can copy) REDIRALL.EXE or REDIR4.EXE onto your hard disk.
DEC Pathworks	4.1 and higher	You can make 4.0 compatible with DOS by following the detailed procedures described in README.TXT.
Farallon PhoneNET	Versions after 2.02	N/A
IBM PC LAN	Version 1.34 and higher	Version 1.34 may require an updated REDIR50.EXE file.
IBM DOS LAN Requester	Version 1.30.1 and higher	N/A
Microsoft LAN Manager and MS-NET	N/A	Upgrade client software to Workgroup Connection.

continues

Table 23.3, Continued
Network Versions Required for MS-DOS 6.2

Network	Version Required	Other Steps Required
Net/One PC	N/A	If you have problems, either update LOADNIU.EXE, or place a UBPAUSE command between LOADNIU and XNBIOS in your MSNET.INI or network batch file.
Novell NetWare	NETX Shell 3.31 or higher	After installing DOS 6.2, use SETVER to tell these programs you are running DOS 5: XMSNETX.EXE EMSNETX.EXE XMSNET5.EXE EMSNET5.EXE See README.TXT for more information.
Sitka TOPS	3.0 or higher	Don't use MOVE command; don't load TOPS high.
10Net Plus, DCA 10Net	4.2 and later 3.3 and later	Disable network before installing DOS 6.2; then reenable it.

TIP Updates are often available through the reseller who installed your network, through CompuServe, or through the manufacturer's electronic bulletin board.

Running Networked Applications with MS-DOS 6.2

You can run two kinds of applications across a network: LAN-unaware applications and LAN-aware applications.

A *LAN-unaware* application behaves just as it would if the server's drives were physically attached to your own computer. You can access programs and files on the server, but nobody else can access the same programs or files at the same time.

A *LAN-aware* application sees a network operating system and provides more sophisticated ways for multiple users to share a file and enter data into it concurrently. Many databases, in particular, are LAN-aware.

A step beyond LAN-aware is the *client/server* application, whereby the client application makes a request for specific data from the server; the server processes the request and provides only that data—minimizing network traffic.

Client/server applications, usually databases, tend to require more powerful servers but can make more efficient use of client computers and the network itself. Client/server databases often use *Standard Query Language* (SQL) to make their requests.

Most single-user programs will at least function across the network as LAN-unaware programs (though you should be aware of licensing issues).

However, a few networked applications that ran under MS-DOS 5 may have trouble operating under DOS 6.2. These applications may have been designed to expect DOS 5. You often can use the DOS SETVER command to trick these applications into working with DOS 6.2, or you can upgrade your application to a later version that specifically supports DOS 6.2.

Use the SETVER command to report a DOS version number that your program recognizes, by issuing the following command:

```
SETVER C: PROGRAM.EXE 4.00
```

SETVER should be in your CONFIG.SYS file before you do this. The command might appear in your CONFIG.SYS file like this:

```
DEVICE=C:\DOS\SETVER.EXE
```

You need to reboot your machine in order for these changes to take effect. If these recommendations do not fix your particular problem, contact your software vendor for information regarding that application and its support of DOS 6.2.

Summary

More than half of all business PCs are now networked, and people have even started to talk about *personal LANs*. Real networking is increasingly built into operating systems—even MS-DOS, one of the last holdouts. Maybe the long-delayed "Year of the LAN" has finally arrived.

If so, you're ready with DOS 6.2.

DOS 6.2 will work smoothly as a client in pretty much any standard networked environment, in large part because its guts haven't changed much from DOS 5, and networking providers have had plenty of time to get used to all of DOS's changes. DOS 6.2's (and 5's) ability to load most network drivers into upper memory makes it easier to stay on a network and still get something else done. That's especially true if you're using a DOS-based, peer-to-peer network like LANtastic, NetWare Lite, or Microsoft's Windows for Workgroups. And for the first time, DOS 6.2 not only supports networks, but also has some rudimentary client networking built-in—*if* you run a Microsoft network.

But choosing a network takes you into some new territory, far afield from stand-alone DOS. We've covered:

- ✔ Choosing interface cards: Ethernet, Token Ring, or ARCnet
- ✔ Choosing cabling: coaxial, twisted-pair, and the alternatives within each
- ✔ Choosing between peer-to-peer and server-based networks

Summary

✔ Choosing server hardware

✔ Setting realistic expectations about the business problems you're trying to solve, and the ongoing support you'll need after you have a network

For those who have finally gotten their arms around what's going on in their PCs, the advent of LANs may mean a whole new language to learn and a whole new way to look at computing. But the complexity of networking is manageable. And networks, even small networks, offer opportunities to work much more effectively with your colleagues. That's an offer that is getting harder and harder to pass up.

MS
DOS

Command Reference

Command Reference 1271

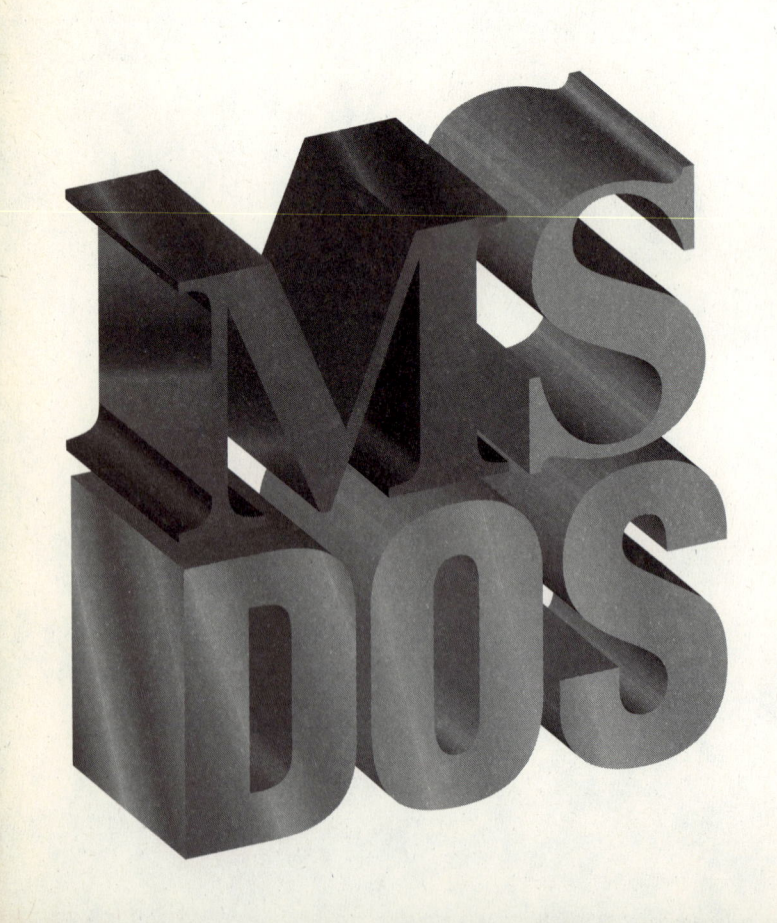

MS-DOS

Command Reference

by Kris Ashton

This chapter is used as a reference to the commands that are available with DOS 6.2.

Each command includes the following information:

- ✔ Purpose
- ✔ Type
- ✔ Syntax
- ✔ Switches
- ✔ Rules and Considerations
- ✔ Examples
- ✔ See Also

The commands covered in this chapter fall into one of several categories:

- ✔ Internal
- ✔ External
- ✔ Device Driver
- ✔ Config
- ✔ Batch
- ✔ Installation

Internal commands are built into the kernel of the operating system. You can execute these commands from any command prompt in any directory. *External* commands are separate programs. To execute external commands, you must be in the directory in which they are located (typically C:\DOS) or the directory must be included in your path statement.

A *device driver* is a program that gives your computer additional capabilities, or enhances its existing capabilities. Device drivers are executed from CONFIG.SYS when your system starts up (boots). CONFIG.SYS may contain other statements that are not device drivers; they may be programs that load device drivers or otherwise enhance your system.

Batch commands are internal commands that are used in DOS batch files. *Installation* commands are external commands used to install, uninstall, or clean up an installation of DOS.

Conventions Used in This Chapter

When entering DOS commands from the command prompt or through batch files, there is no distinction made for uppercase or lowercase letters—with few exceptions, DOS treats them all the same. That means you can enter commands in all uppercase, in all lowercase, or in a mixture of cases if you so desire.

In this command reference, mixed case commands are used to make syntax lines more readable. For those lines, the following conventions are used:

- ✔ The command name is in **BOLD UPPERCASE** letters. Besides any other conventions listed here, the use of **bold** letters indicates something that you need to enter from the keyboard.
- ✔ Parameters and/or switches are in *italic* letters.
- ✔ Anything that is optional is contained within square brackets [ ].
- ✔ Many commands include the parameter:

    ```
    d: or d1: or d:\path
    ```

    used to indicate the drive and directory of the command. Generally, DOS external commands are located in a directory named \DOS, which should be on your system path. If the location is included in the path, then it is not necessary to include it as part of the command.

    Device drivers must have the location specified if they are in a directory other than the root directory, because no path statement is in effect when CONFIG.SYS executes.

    You may also see any combination of

    ```
    [drive][path][filename]
    ```

    used to indicate the location and file name with which the command works. Because these parameters are common to many commands, they are not defined in each command that uses them.

ANSI.SYS

Purpose

Enables you to control your keyboard and display using ANSI control sequences. ANSI controls the location of the cursor on your screen, the colors and attributes of the screen, and enables extended functions on some keyboards.

Type

Device Driver

Syntax

DEVICE=*[d:\path\]***ANSI.SYS** *[/X][/K]*

or

DEVICEHIGH=*[d:\path\]***ANSI.SYS** *[/X][/K]*

Switches

/X   Enables independent remapping of keys on a 101-key keyboard.

/K   Treats a 101-key keyboard as if it were an 84-key keyboard.

Rules and Considerations

ANSI.SYS uses escape sequences to control functions for the display and keyboard. An ANSI escape sequence begins with the escape character and the left bracket character. The characters that follow specify an alphanumeric code that controls a keyboard or display function. ANSI escape sequences are case-sensitive.

When constructing statements in a text editor that use ANSI escape sequences, you cannot type the escape key. Instead, you press a key combination which represents the escape key to the editor. If you use the DOS Editor, press Ctrl+P, then the Esc key, to generate an escape character (which resembles a left arrow). In EDLIN, press Ctrl+V. In both cases, follow the escape character with a left bracket character, then the remainder of the control sequence characters. If you use another editor, refer to its documentation for instructions on inserting escape characters.

To execute an ANSI control sequence, enter it with a text editor as already described, and then save the file. Once the file is saved, it is executed with the TYPE command. If you intend to activate ANSI sequences during execution of a batch file (such as AUTOEXEC.BAT), use $e to represent the escape character.

ANSI sequences may also be activated in conjunction with the PROMPT command, as in the following general format:

PROMPT $e[*sequence*

ANSI control sequences can be used to control the color and attributes of screen text, and the background color of the screen. The general form of the command is:

    $e[attribute;foreground-color;background-colorm

The possible values for this sequence are as follows:

Attribute	Value
Attributes off	0
Bold text	1
Underlined text	4
Blinking text	5
Reverse video	7
Hidden	8

Color	Foreground Value	Background Value
Black	30	40
Red	31	41
Green	32	42
Yellow	33	43
Blue	34	44
Magenta	35	45
Cyan	36	46
White	37	47

ANSI commands can be used to change the display mode. The general form of the command is:

    $e[Typem

Type is one of the following:

Type	Display Mode
0	40x25 Monochrome (text)
1	40x25 Color (text)
2	80x25 Monochrome (text)
3	80x25 Color (text)
4	320x200 (4-color graphics)
5	320x200 Monochrome (graphics)
6	640x200 Monochrome (graphics)
7	Enables line wrapping
13	320x200 color (graphics)
14	640x200 Color (16-color graphics)
15	640x350 Monochrome (2-color graphics)
16	640x350 Color (16-color graphics)
17	640x480 Monochrome (2-color graphics)
18	640x480 Color (16-color graphics)
19	320x200 Color (256-color graphics)

ANSI commands can be used to position the cursor on the screen, using the following commands:

Control Sequence	Effect
$e[row;colH	Moves the cursor to position row, col on the screen.
$e[row,colf	Moves the cursor to position row, col on the screen.
$e[rowA	Moves the cursor up by the number of rows specified.
$e[rowB	Moves the cursor down by the number of rows specified.
$e[colC	Moves the cursor to the right by the number of columns specified.

Control Sequence	Effect
$e[colD	Moves the cursor to the left by the number of columns specified.
$e[s	Saves the current cursor position.
$e[u	Restores the cursor to the last saved position.
$e[=7h	Enables word wrap.
$e[=7l	Disables word wrap.
$e[K	Clears the screen from the cursor to the end of the line.
$e[2J	Erases the screen and moves the cursor to the home position.
$e[0m	Sets the screen for normal (white on black) display.

ANSI sequences can be used to redefine keys on a keyboard. The general form of the command is as follows:

$e[code;string;...p

Code is one or more of the values in the following table. These values represent keys and key combinations that you can reassign or redefine. Be sure to type both the semicolon that is in the code, and any semicolons that are required to separate codes.

String is either an ASCII code representing a character or string of characters, or the character(s) within quotes.

The values shown in parentheses may not be available on all keyboards.

Key	Code	SHIFT+Code	CTRL+Code	ALT+Code
F1	0;59	0;84	0;94	0;104
F2	0;60	0;85	0;95	0;105
F3	0;61	0;86	0;96	0;106

continues

Key	Code	SHIFT+Code	CTRL+Code	ALT+Code
F4	0;62	0;87	0;97	0;107
F5	0;63	0;88	0;98	0;108
F6	0;64	0;89	0;99	0;109
F7	0;65	0;90	0;100	0;110
F8	0;66	0;91	0;101	0;111
F9	0;67	0;92	0;102	0;112
F10	0;68	0;93	0;103	0;113
F11	0;133	0;135	0;137	0;139
F12	0;134	0;136	0;138	0;140
Home	0;71	55	0;119	—
Up Arrow	0;72	56	(0;141)	—
Page Up	0;73	57	0;132	—
Left Arrow	0;75	52	0;115	—
Right Arrow	0;77	54	0;116	—
End	0;79	49	0;117	—
Down Arrow	0;80	50	(0;145)	—
Page Down	0;81	51	0;118	—
Insert	0;82	48	(0;146)	—
Delete	0;83	46	(0;147)	—
Home (gray key)	(224;71)	(224;71)	(224;119)	(224;151)
Up Arrow (gray key)	(224;72)	(224;72)	(224;141)	(224;152)
Page Up (gray key)	(224;73)	(224;73)	(224;132)	(224;153)
Left Arrow (gray key)	(224;75)	(224;75)	(224;115)	(224;155)

ANSI.SYS **1279**

Key	Code	SHIFT+Code	CTRL+Code	ALT+Code
Right Arrow (gray key)	(224;77)	(224;77)	(224;116)	(224;157)
End (gray key)	(224;79)	(224;79)	(224;117)	(224;159)
Down Arrow (gray key)	(224;80)	(224;80)	(224;145)	(224;154)
Page Down (gray key)	(224;81)	(224;81)	(224;118)	(224;161)
Insert (gray key)	(224;82)	(224;82)	(224;146)	(224;162)
Delete (gray key)	(224;83)	(224;83)	(224;147)	(224;163)
Print Screen	—	—	0;114	—
Pause/Break	—	—	0;0	—
Backspace	8	8	127	(0)
Enter	13	—	10	(0)
Tab	9	0;15	(0;148)	(0;165)
Null	0;3	—	—	—
A	97	65	1	0;30
B	98	66	2	0;48
C	99	67	3	0;46
D	100	68	4	0;32
E	101	69	5	0;18
F	102	70	6	0;33
G	103	71	7	0;34

continues

Key	Code	SHIFT+Code	CTRL+Code	ALT+Code
H	104	72	8	0;35
I	105	73	9	0;23
J	106	74	10	0;36
K	107	75	11	0;37
L	108	76	12	0;38
M	109	77	13	0;50
N	110	78	14	0;49
O	111	79	15	0;24
P	112	80	16	0;25
Q	113	81	17	0;16
R	114	82	18	0;19
S	115	83	19	0;31
T	116	84	20	0;20
U	117	85	21	0;22
V	118	86	22	0;47
W	119	87	23	0;17
X	120	88	24	0;45
Y	121	89	25	0;21
Z	122	90	26	0;44
1	49	33	—	0;120
2	50	64	0	0;121
3	51	35	—	0;122
4	52	36	—	0;123
5	53	37	—	0;124
6	54	94	30	0;125
7	55	38	—	0;126
8	56	42	—	0;126

Key	Code	SHIFT+Code	CTRL+Code	ALT+Code
9	57	40	—	0;127
0	48	41	—	0;129
—	45	95	31	0;130
=	61	43	—	0;131
[	91	123	27	0;26
]	93	125	29	0;27
\	92	124	28	0;43
;	59	58	—	0;39
'	39	34	—	0;40
,	44	60	—	0;51
.	46	62	—	0;52
/	47	63	—	0;53
`	96	126	—	(0;41)
ENTER (keypad)	13	—	10	(0;166)
/ (keypad)	47	47	(0;142)	(0;74)
* (keypad)	42	(0;144)	(0;78)	—
- (keypad)	45	45	(0;149)	(0;164)
+ (keypad)	43	43	(0;150)	(0;55)
5 (keypad)	(0;76)	53	(0;143)	—

Examples

To change the screen colors to bold, white text on a blue background, type:

    esc[1;37;44m

To reassign the character string "Dir<Enter>" to the function key F3, enter:

    esc[0;61;"dir";13p

See Also

DEVICE=, PROMPT

APPEND

Purpose

APPEND enables application programs to look for data files in specified directories as if they were the current directory.

Type

External

Syntax

APPEND *[d:\path1\;d:\path2;...][[/X:ON¦:OFF][/PATH:ON¦/PATH:OFF][/E]*

Switches

/X:ON   Directs DOS to search appended directories when executing programs. Can be specified as /X.

/X:OFF   Directs DOS not to search appended directories when executing programs. /X:OFF is the default.

/E   Assigns the list of appended directories to an environment variable. You can only specify this switch once, the first time you use APPEND after starting your system.

Rules and Considerations

APPEND is intended to be used with application programs that use Open File, Open Handle, and Get File Size DOS calls. If a particular program cannot seem to open a data file in an appended directory, try using the /X switch with the command.

Do not use APPEND with Microsoft Windows.

To specify more than one directory, separate the directory names with semicolons. Do not enter each one on a separate line.

If a file in an appended directory has the same name as one in the current directory, the application program will open the file in the current directory. Any new files created by the application are in the current directory.

Examples

To enable application programs to access data files from the D:\DOCS directory, enter the following command:

    APPEND d:\docs

To append the same directory and keep a copy of the appended directory list in the DOS environment, type the following command:

    APPEND /E
    APPEND d:\docs

To delete the appended directories, type the command:

    APPEND;

See Also

PATH, SET

ASSIGN

Purpose

The ASSIGN command redirects for input and output from one disk drive to another. This program is intended for use with floppy drives.

Type

External

Syntax

`ASSIGN [drive1:=drive2:][/STATUS]`

Switches

/STATUS   Lists drive assignments. You may shorten this switch to /STA or /S.

Rules and Considerations

ASSIGN cannot be used on hard drives.

The colon after the drive name is optional.

Do not use ASSIGN with commands that change the disk's logical data areas: programs such as MSBACKUP, JOIN, SUBST, or LABEL.

Examples

To switch drive assignments for floppy drives A: and B:, enter the following command:

`ASSIGN a=b b=a`

To restore the drive assignments, type the following command:

`ASSIGN`

See Also

JOIN, SUBST

ATTRIB

Purpose

The ATTRIB command displays or changes a file's attributes. You can use ATTRIB to control whether the file is a read-only, system, hidden, or archive file.

Type

External

Syntax

ATTRIB *[+attribute/-attribute][[d:\path]filename][/S]*

Switch

/S   Processes files in the current directory and all of its subdirectories.

Rules and Considerations

Use the plus (+) sign to set attributes, and the minus (-) sign to clear attributes. The following attributes can be set or cleared by ATTRIB:

- A   Archive
- H   Hidden
- R   Read-only
- S   System

You can use wild-card characters (? and *) with the file name parameter to display, set, or change attributes.

The System attribute has priority over the others. If a file has the System attribute set, clear that one first and then clear the other attributes.

The ATTRIB command can be used in conjunction with XCOPY to copy a subdirectory or a hard disk to diskettes. First, mark all the files in the directory or hard disk with the Archive attribute. Then, use the XCOPY command as follows:

```
XCOPY *.* a: /M
```

The /M switch causes XCOPY to copy those files whose archive attribute is set, then to clear the archive attribute when the file is copied. When your destination disk is full, simply put in a new one and issue the XCOPY command again.

Examples

To change a file named LETTER.DOC to a read-only file, enter the following command:

```
ATTRIB +r letter.doc
```

To remove the read-only attributes from all the files in the D:\DOCS directory, use this command:

```
ATTRIB -r d:\docs\*.*
```

To make a file a hidden file, type the following:

```
ATTRIB +h d:\path\filename
```

Enter the following command to view the attributes for all the files in a directory:

```
ATTRIB
```

If you want to include all subdirectories, type the following:

```
ATTRIB /S
```

See Also

XCOPY

BREAK

Purpose

The BREAK command is used to control how often DOS checks for the use of Ctrl+C or Ctrl+Break to stop a program.

Type

Internal

Syntax

BREAK *[ON¦OFF]*

Rules and Considerations

DOS normally checks for Ctrl+Break interrupt only when it begins a standard input/output operation, such as reading the keyboard or writing to the screen or printer. This is usually sufficient for most people. If you set BREAK ON, DOS will check for Ctrl+Break sequences during other functions, such as disk I/O operations. The default for BREAK is OFF.

You can activate BREAK ON from CONFIG.SYS or from the command prompt.

Examples

To activate Ctrl+C checking more often, type the command:

BREAK ON

To check the status of Ctrl+C checking, type:

BREAK

BUFFERS

Purpose

The BUFFERS command is used to allocate memory for a specific number of disk buffers; buffers are used by your system for transfers of data between disk and memory.

Type

Config

Syntax

BUFFERS=primary[,secondary]

Rules and Considerations

Buffers require approximately 532 bytes of memory each. While a large number of buffers can sometimes improve disk performance, it can also reduce the amount of memory available to your application programs. Use the MEM command to monitor your system's memory.

If DOS is in the High Memory Area (HMA), and there is enough room, DOS will also place the buffers in the HMA. If you specify more than 48 buffers, however, DOS will not be able to fit the buffers in the HMA and will place them instead in conventional memory.

The primary parameter is the number of primary buffers that are created and used to hold data that has been recently read from disk. The secondary parameter is the number of secondary buffers that are created and used to hold "read-ahead" data; in effect, creating a disk cache. The secondary buffer is best used with 8086 computers. For computers with faster processors, it is best to use a disk cache program such as SMARTDRV.EXE.

> **NOTE**
>
> When using SMARTDRV.EXE, specify a small number of buffers.
>
> SMARTDRV.EXE can handle from 1 to 99 primary buffers, and from 1 to 8 secondary buffers.

The number of buffers that DOS creates by default is based on the configuration of your system, as shown in the following table:

Available Memory	Buffers
<128K RAM, 360K disk	2
<128K RAM, >360K disk	3
128K to 255K RAM	5
256K to 511K RAM	10
512K to 640K RAM	15

Examples

To set the number of buffers at 30, include the following in your CONFIG.SYS file:

```
BUFFERS=30
```

See Also

MEM, SMARTDRV.EXE

CALL

Purpose

The CALL program is used to call one batch program from within another, without causing the original batch program to stop. You can use CALL to nest batch files.

Type

Batch, Internal

Syntax

```
CALL [d:\path]batchname [batch parameters]
```

Rules and Considerations

Batch parameters are used to pass information into one batch file from another. Batch parameters are numbered %1 through %9.

It is possible to create a recursive batch file—one that calls itself. Be sure to include an EXIT command in the batch file, or it will loop endlessly.

Do not use pipes ("¦") or redirection ("<","<<",">", and ">>") with the CALL command.

Examples

To run a program called BATCH.BAT from within a batch file, include the following command in the parent batch file:

```
CALL batch
```

To pass the second parameter to a batch file with the name BATCH.BAT, type the following command:

```
CALL batch %2
```

See Also

CHOICE, ECHO, FOR, GOTO, IF, PAUSE, REM, SHIFT

CHCP

Purpose

The CHCP command enables you to change the active code page that DOS uses for devices that support code page switching.

Type

Internal

Syntax

```
CHCP [nnn]
```

Rules and Considerations

A code page defines the character set that is in use at any given time on your system. There can be two code pages active in memory at one time; use CHCP to switch between them.

Before using the CHCP command, you must first specify the location of the file COUNTRY.SYS by using the COUNTRY command. You must also load the NLSFUNC program into memory.

The code pages that DOS supports are as follows:

437	United States
850	Multilingual (Latin I)
852	Slavic (Latin II)

860	Portuguese
863	Canadian-French
865	Nordic

Examples

Enter the following command to view the active code page setting:

`CHCP`

To change the current code page to Canadian-French, type the following command:

`CHCP 863`

See Also

COUNTRY, MODE <SET DEVICE CODE PAGES>, NLSFUNC

CHDIR (CD)

Purpose

The CHDIR or CD command displays or changes the current directory.

Type

Internal

Syntax

`CHDIR [[d:]\path]`
`CHDIR [..]`

or

`CD [[d:]\path]`
`CD [..]`

Rules and Considerations

CD and CHDIR are equivalent statements.

If no disk drive is indicated, the current drive is used.

CD .. or CHDIR .. is used to move back up the directory tree one level at a time. You can use CD\ to return to the root directory of the current drive.

If you want DOS to start from the root directory, use the backslash (\) as the first character of the path name. Otherwise, DOS assumes that the path starts with the current directory.

Examples

To change to a directory named BUDGET, use the following command:

CD\BUDGET

Perhaps the BUDGET directory included two subdirectories: one called 1992, and the other 1993. To change to the BUDGET\1992 directory, type the following command:

CD\BUDGET\1992

Use the following command to change from any directory or subdirectory back to the root directory:

CD

To display the name of the current directory, type:

CD

See Also

DIR, TREE

CHKDSK

Purpose

The CHKDSK command creates and displays a status report on your system's disk, and fixes any errors it finds.

CHKDSK

Type
External

Syntax
`CHKDSK [[d:\path]filename][/F][/V]`

Switches

/F   Fixes errors found on the disk.

/V   Displays more detailed (verbose) information about the progress of CHKDSK.

Rules and Considerations

CHKDSK reports information similar to the following:

```
Volume MY_DISK   created 06-04-1992 10:45a
Volume Serial Number is 199A-65C2

129652736 bytes total disk space
 39708672 bytes in 33 hidden files
   141312 bytes in 59 directories
 72632320 bytes in 1507 user files
 16736256 bytes available on disk

     2048 bytes in each allocation unit
    63307 total allocation units on disk
     8172 available allocation units on disk

   655360 total bytes memory
   623520 bytes free
```

CHKDSK may report errors, but does not fix them unless the /F option is specified. When you specify the /F option, CHKDSK converts any lost allocation units into files, which you can erase from your disk. The files are named with the format FILE*nnnn*.CHK.

Never run CHKDSK/F when files are open. DOS sometimes interprets open files as errors in the file allocation table; fixing files while they are open can result in lost or damaged files.

Do not use CHKDSK/F when Microsoft Windows or the DOS Task Swapper are running.

CHKDSK does not work on network drives.

Examples

Use the following command to check and display information about your system:

CHKDSK

If you want more detailed information, type the following command:

CHKDSK /V

The following command will check the disk and fix any errors it finds:

CHKDSK /F

CHKSTATE.SYS

Purpose

CHKSTATE.SYS is used by the MEMMAKER memory-optimization program to monitor progress during optimization.

Type

Driver

Syntax

None. Used exclusively by MEMMAKER.

Rules and Considerations

During optimization, MEMMAKER adds CHKSTATE.SYS to your CONFIG.SYS file. When the optimization process is complete, MEMMAKER removes the device driver.

See Also

MEMMAKER, SIZER

CHOICE

Purpose

The CHOICE command is used to get user input during execution of batch files. You can specify a string of text to be displayed as part of the prompt, along with actions to be performed when a selection is made.

Type

External, Batch

Syntax

```
CHOICE [/C[:]keys][text][/N][/S][/T[:]nn,c]
```

Switches

/N
Causes CHOICE to not display a prompt. Any text that appears before the prompt, however, is still displayed.

/S
Causes CHOICE to be case-sensitive. Without this switch, CHOICE will accept input in uppercase or lowercase.

/Tc,nn
Causes CHOICE to pause for an amount of time (in seconds) you specify with nn. After nn seconds have elapsed without user input, CHOICE will default to the character specified by c.

Rules and Considerations

CHOICE enables you to create prompts that are displayed during the execution of a batch file. Each prompt is generally accompanied by a selection of characters that you specify with [keys]; you simply press the appropriate key for the selection you want. When the prompt is displayed, the keys are separated by commas and appear within square brackets, followed by a question mark. When you select a key, the batch file returns an ERRORLEVEL to DOS that corresponds to the key. A batch file may branch as a result of ERRORLEVEL processing.

The first key in the list has the ERRORLEVEL 1 associated with it, the second key ERRORLEVEL 2, and so on. If a key is pressed which is not among those listed, CHOICE sounds a beep. If Ctrl+C or Ctrl+Break are pressed, the batch file returns an ERRORLEVEL of 0.

When you use ERRORLEVELs in a program, you must list them in descending order.

If you do not specify any text to be part of the CHOICE prompt, CHOICE displays a default prompt ([Y,N]?).

Examples

Use the following command if you do not want any text to appear with the prompt,

```
CHOICE /C:ync
```

The following prompt is displayed:

```
[Y,N,C]?
```

To add a text string to the prompt, use the following command:

```
CHOICE /C:ync Enter a Selection
```

With the above statement, the following prompt is displayed:

```
Enter a Selection[Y,N,C]?
```

Use the following command if you want your text to appear without the [Y,N,C]? prompt:

```
CHOICE /C:ync /N Enter a Selection
```

The following prompt is displayed:

```
Enter a Selection
```

To cause the program to wait for input, then proceed with a default if no input is received, type the following:

```
CHOICE /C:ync Enter a Selection /T:5,n
```

The following prompt is displayed:

```
Enter a Selection[Y,N,C]?
```

After waiting for 5 seconds, CHOICE chooses N and returns an ERRORLEVEL of 1. If a key is pressed within the 5 seconds, CHOICE returns the ERRORLEVEL value that corresponds to the selection.

The following batch file demonstrates the use of CHOICE:

```
REM File is named QUESTION.BAT
@ECHO OFF
CHOICE /C:fl /N What is heavier, a pound of feathers or a
pound of lead?
IF ERRORLEVEL 2 GOTO LEAD
IF ERRORLEVEL 1 GOTO FEATHERS
:LEAD
ECHO What LEAD you to that conclusion?
GOTO END
:FEATHERS
ECHO Looks like you WINGed that one!
GOTO END
:END
```

The output from this batch file would look like the following:

```
C:\>question
What is heavier, a pound of feathers or a pound of lead?L
What LEAD you to that conclusion?
C:\>question
What is heavier, a pound of feathers or a pound of lead?F
Looks like you WINGed that one!
```

See Also

ERRORLEVEL, IF

CLEANUP

Purpose

The CLEANUP command is used to remove a previous version of DOS that was saved by the DOS 6.2 installation process.

Type

Installation, External

Syntax

CLEANUP [/B]

Switches

/B   Enables use on a monochrome display.

Rules and Considerations

Use the CLEANUP command when you are sure that all of your applications run properly with DOS 6.2. CLEANUP removes the old version of DOS that the installation program saved.

You cannot use UNINSTALL to replace the earlier version of DOS once CLEANUP has executed.

CLEANUP and DELOLDOS are equivalent commands.

Examples

To remove an earlier version of DOS, type this command:

CLEANUP

See Also

INSTALL, UNINSTALL

CLS

Purpose

The CLS command erases everything on the screen except the command prompt.

Type

Internal

Syntax

CLS

Rules and Considerations

After erasing the screen, the cursor returns to the home position (upper left corner) of the screen.

If you have enabled any screen enhancements with ANSI.SYS, such as text and background colors, they remain active when the screen is cleared.

COMMAND

Purpose

COMMAND loads or reloads a new instance of the DOS command interpreter.

Type

External

Syntax

COMMAND *[d:\path][device][/Cstring][/E:nnnnn][/K:filename] [/P[MSG]]*

COMMAND is most often used in conjunction with the SHELL command. Use the following syntax in your CONFIG.SYS file:

SHELL=*[d:\path\]COMMAND.COM [[d:\path][device][/E:nnnnn][/P[MSG]]*

Switches

/E:*nnn* Specifies the environment size in bytes. The size must be within the range 160 through 32768. The default environment size is 256 bytes.

/C*string* Passes a string to the new copy of the command interpreter, then returns to the prior command interpreter when finished.

/K:file name	Runs the specified command, program, or batch file and then displays the command prompt. The /K switch must be the last switch on the command line. One useful purpose for this switch is to use it to create a start-up batch file for the DOS prompt when working in Windows. Such a batch file acts much like an AUTOEXEC.BAT file does for DOS. Once it runs the commands within it, it then automatically returns you to the DOS prompt. Simply edit the DOSPRMPT.PIF file, typing the /K switch, followed by a batch-file name in the optional parameters box. Because problems with programs that make changes to your AUTOEXEC.BAT can occur, it is not recommended that you use the /K switch on the SHELL command line in CONFIG.SYS.
/P	This option is used when COMMAND is used with the SHELL command in CONFIG.SYS. Causes the new copy of the command interpreter to be permanent.
/MSG	Causes COMMAND to store any error messages in memory, instead of on disk. This switch is useful if you are running COMMAND from a floppy disk. If used, you must include /P.
/F	Undocumented switch that automatically combines the `Not ready reading drive x Abort, Retry, Fail` message with the `Current drive is no longer valid>` message on a failed disk access.
/Y	Instructs COMMAND.COM to interactively execute the batch file specified with the /C switch. To each line of the batch file, the user is prompted to press **Y** or **N** to execute or ignore that line. To step through INTERACT.BAT, for example, enter:

COMMAND Y/ /C/INTERACT

Rules and Considerations

When your computer starts up, DOS loads the command interpreter in two parts. One part is always in memory, while the other part can be overwritten by some application programs. If this happens, DOS must reload that part from disk. The COMSPEC environment variable tells DOS where to find COMMAND on your disk.

You can avoid having to reload the transient part of the command interpreter by using the /P switch, which makes it permanent in memory.

Type the EXIT command to stop a new instance of the command interpreter. Control is returned to the original copy.

You can specify a different device for input and output by using the device parameter. See the CTTY command for more information.

Examples

To start a new command processor that is located in the \SUBDIR directory, type the following:

```
COMMAND c:\subdir
```

To identify the location of the command interpreter and set its environment size, enter the following command:

```
SHELL=c:\dos\command.com /e:1024 /p
```

This command also makes the command interpreter permanent.

See Also

CTTY, COMSPEC, SHELL

COPY

Purpose

The COPY command is used to copy one or more files.

Beginning with version 6.2, COPY asks for confirmation before overwriting an existing file of the same name.

Type

Internal

Syntax

COPY *[d:\path]SOURCE [d:\path][DESTINATION][/V][/A][/B]*

Switches

/V　　　　Verifies that the files were copied correctly.

/A　　　　Indicates that the files are of type ASCII. All characters of the source file are copied except the end-of-file marker. An end-of-file marker is added to the end of the destination file.

/B　　　　Indicates that the files are of type binary. All characters in the file are copied, including end-of-file markers. No end-of-file marker is added to the destination file.

/Y　　　　Beginning with version 6.2, DOS asks for confirmation before overwriting an existing file of the same name. The /Y switch instructs COPY to go ahead and replace any existing files without prompting you for confirmation.

/-Y　　　　Instructs COPY to prompt you for confirmation when replacing an exising file. Used to override the SET COPYCMD=/Y environment variable.

Rules and Considerations

You can copy files from one disk to another or from one directory to another. You also can copy files within the same directory; the destination file in this case must have a new name or you will see the message File cannot be copied onto itself.

Wild-card characters (? and *) can be used to group file names together.

If a destination is not specified, DOS assumes the current directory.

Files can be appended or merged using the + character.

You can indicate a device, such as CON or PRN, as the source or destination.

Files that are zero bytes in size will not be copied. If you want to copy these files, use the XCOPY command. XCOPY also can be used to copy an entire directory, including any subdirectories it may contain.

Examples

To copy MYFILE.TXT from C:\DOCS to A:, type the following:

`COPY C:\DOCS A:`

The copy can be verified by using the following command:

`COPY C:\DOCS A: /V`

To copy MYFILE.TXT from C:\DOCS to D:\BUDGET, type:

`COPY C:\DOCS\MYFILE.TXT D:\BUDGET`

In the previous example it is not necessary to name the destination file, as it will assume the same name it has now. Only the location needs to be specified.

To change the name of a file when it is copied, type:

`COPY d:\path\OLDFILE d:\path\NEWFILE`

To merge two ASCII files, FILE1.TXT and FILE2.TXT to a new file called FILE3.TXT, use the following command:

`COPY FILE1.TXT + FILE2.TXT /A FILE3.TXT`

Copying something from the console to a file is a quick way to create simple batch files. To copy from the screen to a file, use the following command:

`COPY CON filename`

This creates a file in the current directory, which contains any characters that are typed on the screen. To end copying from the screen to the file, press Ctrl+Z.

See Also

DISKCOPY, RENAME, XCOPY

COUNTRY

Purpose

The COUNTRY command customizes DOS for use with a foreign language. COUNTRY sets defaults to use for date and time format, currency, case conversions, and decimal separators.

Type

Config

Syntax

`COUNTRY=code[,page][,[d:\path\]filename]`

Rules and Considerations

By default, DOS uses the United States country code. If you want to change the setting, use COUNTRY in your CONFIG.SYS file. If you do not specify a file name to be used with COUNTRY, DOS uses the file COUNTRY.SYS.

The code parameter specifies which country you want to work with. The page parameter specifies which code page you want to use for that country. Each country has two code pages; DOS uses the first one by default. The following codes and pages are supported:

Country Code	Pages	
Belgium	032	850, 437
Brazil	055	850, 437
Canadian-French	002	863, 850

Country Code		Pages	
Czechoslovakia	042	852, 850
Denmark	045	850, 865
Finland	358	850, 437
France	033	850, 437
Germany	049	850, 437
Hungary	036	852, 850
International English	061	437, 850
Italy	039	850, 437
Latin America	003	850, 437
Netherlands	031	850, 437
Norway	047	850, 865
Poland	048	852, 850
Portugal	351	850, 860
Spain	034	850, 437
Sweden	046	850, 437
Switzerland	041	850, 437
United Kingdom	044	437, 850
United States	001	437, 850
Yugoslavia	038	852, 850

Code pages are available with special versions of DOS for the following countries or languages: Arabic, Israel, Japan, Korea, People's Republic of China, and Taiwan.

Examples

Use the following command to set the country code to Canadian-French:

```
COUNTRY=002 C:\DOS\COUNTRY.SYS
```

Unless the file COUNTRY.SYS is in the boot directory of the start-up disk, you must specify its location, as in the above example.

See Also

DATE, KEYB, TIME

CTTY

Purpose

The CTTY command redirects input or output from your keyboard or screen to another device.

Type

Internal

Syntax

```
CTTY device
```

Rules and Considerations

This command is useful if you have a terminal attached to your serial port and you want to use it instead of your keyboard and screen. You must use the MODE command to set up the communication parameters for the serial port before using this command.

You can specify any of the following devices: PRN, LPT1, LPT2, LPT3, CON, AUX, COM1, COM2, COM3 or COM4.

Many application programs do not depend on DOS for input or output, but rather send input or output directly. These programs are not affected by the CTTY command; it is used only with programs that use DOS to read the keyboard or display output.

Examples

To redirect all screen output and keyboard input to a terminal attached to the COM1 serial port, type the following command:

```
CTTY COM1
```

See Also

COMMAND, MODE

DATE

Purpose

The DATE command is used to display or change the system date.

Type

Internal

Syntax

DATE [mm-dd-yy]

Rules and Considerations

Months (mm) are entered with numbers 1 through 12. Days (dd) are entered with numbers 1 through 31. Years (yy) are entered with numbers 80 through 99, or 1980 through 2099. You can use slashes (/), dashes (-), or periods (.) to separate the parts.

The format used to display the date is determined by the COUNTRY setting that was used in CONFIG.SYS.

Examples

To display the system date and be prompted for a new date, type the following:

DATE

A message similar to the following is displayed:

```
Current date is Sat 01-02-1993
Enter new date (mm-dd-yy):
```

Simply press the Enter key if you do not want to change the date, or enter the new date after the prompt.

Enter any of the following commands to change the system date to January 5, 1993:

```
DATE 1/5/93
DATE 01/05/93
DATE 1-5-93
DATE 1.5.1993
```

See Also

COUNTRY, TIME

DBLSPACE

Purpose

The DBLSPACE command is used to compress a hard disk or a floppy disk, and to configure drives that have been compressed. It is a menu-driven program that enables you to set up and work with a compressed disk. Compressing enables you to store more information on a disk.

Type

External

Syntax

```
DBLSPACE [option]
```

Rules and Considerations

A DoubleSpace-compressed disk is not really a disk. It is a file on a disk, called a compressed volume file. The disk the file is created on is called the uncompressed disk.

When DBLSPACE is used by itself, the DoubleSpace program starts and displays a menu of options for setting up and working with compressed drives. If you specify an option, DBLSPACE carries out the requested command without first going through the menu. There are many options possible, each with its own syntax and other considerations. DBLSPACE includes the following functions:

- ✔ DBLSPACE /AUTOMOUNT, used to turn off or turn on automounting of compressed floppy drives and other compressed removable media.

- ✔ DBLSPACE /CHKDSK, used to check the integrity of the compressed drive's file structure.

- ✔ DBLSPACE /COMPRESS, used to compress a hard or floppy drive.

- ✔ DBLSPACE /CONVSTAC, used to convert a Stacker drive to a DoubleSpace drive.

- ✔ DBLSPACE /CREATE, used to create a new compressed drive.

- ✔ DBLSPACE /DEFRAGMENT, used to remove fragmentation from a compressed drive.

- ✔ DBLSPACE /DELETE, used to remove a compressed drive.

- ✔ DBLSPACE /DOUBLEGUARD, used to turn off or on the DoubleGuard feature, which checks its memory for damage by other programs.

- ✔ DBLSPACE /FORMAT, used to format a compressed drive.

- ✔ DBLSPACE /INFO, used to display information about a compressed drive.

- ✔ DBLSPACE /LIST, used to display a list of drives on your system, including noncompressed drives, floppy drives, and other removable drives. Network drives are not displayed.

- ✔ DBLSPACE /MOUNT, used to mount a compressed volume file. When a compressed volume file is mounted, it is assigned a drive letter name.

- ✔ DBLSPACE /RATIO, used to change the estimated compression ratio that the program uses.

- ✔ DBLSPACE /SIZE, used to change the size of a compressed drive.

- ✔ DBLSPACE /UNCOMPRESS, used to uncompress a drive compressed by Doublespace.

- ✔ DBLSPACE /UNMOUNT, used to unmount a compressed drive.

There are two parts to DoubleSpace: DBLSPACE.BIN and DBLSPACE.SYS. When your system starts up, DBLSPACE.BIN is loaded into the top of conventional memory before any other programs (such as CONFIG.SYS or AUTOEXEC.BAT) are executed; it provides access to your compressed drive(s).

DBLSPACE.SYS determines the final location of DBLSPACE.BIN in memory. If DBLSPACE.SYS is loaded with a DEVICE statement in CONFIG.SYS, DBLSPACE.BIN is moved from the top of conventional memory to the bottom. If DBLSPACE.SYS is loaded with a DEVICEHIGH statement, DBLSPACE.BIN is moved from conventional memory to upper memory, if there is space available.

See Also

DBLSPACE.SYS

DBLSPACE /AUTOMOUNT

Purpose

The DBLSPACE /AUTOMOUNT command is used to turn off or turn on automounting of compressed floppy disks and other compressed removable media.

Type

External

Syntax

```
DBLSPACE /AUTOMOUNT=[0][1]
```

Rules and Considerations

Automounting increases DoubleSpace's resident size by 4K.

Example

To turn off automounting of compressed removable media, enter:

```
DBLSPACE /AUTOMOUNT=0
```

DBLSPACE /CHKDSK

Purpose

The DBLSPACE /CHKDSK command is used to check for file errors on a compressed drive.

Beginning with DOS 6.2, DoubleSpace no longer includes the /CHKDSK switch. Replacing it is the ScanDisk command.

Type

External

Syntax

DBLSPACE /CHKDSK *[d:][/F]*

Switches

/F   Fixes any errors found on the compressed drive.

Rules and Considerations

DoubleSpace Chkdsk only checks the internal structure of the compressed volume file. To check the compressed drive's DOS file allocation table, use the DOS CHKDSK command.

See Also

CHKDSK

DBLSPACE /COMPRESS

Purpose

The DBLSPACE /COMPRESS command compresses files on a hard drive, floppy drive, or other removable drive in order to make more space available.

Type

External

Syntax

`DBLSPACE /COMPRESS d1: [/NEWDRIVE=d2:][/RESERVE=size]`

Switches

/NEWDRIVE=d2:   Specifies the drive letter you want to use for the uncompressed drive. This switch can be abbreviated /NEW.

/RESERVE=size   Specifies the size of the uncompressed drive in megabytes. This switch can be abbreviated /RES.

Rules and Considerations

After DoubleSpace compresses an existing drive, your system includes the existing drive (compressed) and a new uncompressed drive. You can specify the drive letter that is assigned to the uncompressed drive. If you do not, the next available drive letter is used.

DoubleSpace leaves 2M of space, if available, uncompressed on a hard drive. This space is useful if you have files that do not work properly on a compressed drive, such as Windows permanent swap file.

DBLSPACE /COMPRESS cannot be used on a full disk. A hard disk must have 1M of free space; a floppy disk needs 200K.

If you compress a floppy disk, it will have to be MOUNTed each time (after the first time) that you use it.

Examples

Type the following command to compress drive C:

`DBLSPACE /COMPRESS C:`

To compress drive C and leave 10M of free space on the uncompressed drive, type the following command:

`DBLSPACE /COMPRESS C: /RESERVE=10`

DBLSPACE /CONVSTAC

Purpose

The DBLSPACE /CONVSTAC command converts a Stacker volume file to a DoubleSpace compress volume file, and then mounts the newly converted file.

Type

External

Syntax

```
DBLSPACE /CONVSTAC=stacvol d1: [/NEWDRIVE=d2:][/CVF=sss]
```

Switches

/NEWDRIVE=d2: Specifies the drive letter for the newly converted compressed drive. The /NEWDRIVE switch is optional; if you omit it, DoubleSpace assigns the next available drive letter to the newly converted drive. This switch can be abbreviated /NEW.

/CVF=sss Specifies the file name extension for the new compressed volume file. You can specify a number from 000 to 254. By default the next available file extension is used.

Rules and Considerations

You can use drives that have been compressed with Stacker, but they must first be converted to DoubleSpace drives. You specify the Stacker volume to convert with stacvol; the Stacker volume must be on the specified drive.

Examples

To convert an existing Stacker drive, use the following command:

```
DBLSPACE /CONVSTAC=stacvol.000 c:
```

In the above example, stacvol.000 is the name of the Stacker drive which is located on drive C.

DBLSPACE /CREATE

Purpose

The DBLSPACE /CREATE command uses free space on an uncompressed drive to create a new compressed drive.

Type

External

Syntax

```
DBLSPACE /CREATE d1: [/NEWDRIVE=d2:][/SIZE=size¦/RESERVE=size]
```

Switches

/NEWDRIVE=d2: — Specifies the drive letter for the new compressed drive. If you do not specify a drive letter, the next available letter is used. This switch can be abbreviated /NEW.

/RESERVE=size — Specifies how much free space should be left on the uncompressed drive in megabytes. A size of 0 makes the compressed drive as large as possible. This switch can be abbreviated as /RE.

/SIZE=size — Specifies the number of megabytes of uncompressed drive space that you want to use as the new compressed drive. This switch can be abbreviated as /SI.

Rules and Considerations

You can use either the /RESERVE switch or the /SIZE switch, but not both. If neither switch is used, 1M of space is reserved for the uncompressed drive.

Examples

To create a new compressed drive from 10M of uncompressed space on drive D, type the following:

```
DBLSPACE /CREATE D: /SIZE=10
```

DBLSPACE /DEFRAGMENT

Purpose

The DBLSPACE /DEFRAGMENT command is used to unfragment a compressed disk drive, to consolidate the free space on the drive.

Type

External

Syntax

```
DBLSPACE /DEFRAGMENT [d:]
```

Rules and Considerations

If you are going to create a new compressed drive or change the size of an existing drive, you should first unfragment the drive(s). If a drive name is not specified, DoubleSpace will defragment the current drive.

Examples

To defragment the space on drive C, type the following:

```
DBLSPACE /DEFRAGMENT C:
```

DBLSPACE /DELETE

Purpose

Use the DBLSPACE /DELETE command when you want to delete a compressed drive and erase its associated compressed volume file.

Type

External

Syntax

>   DBLSPACE /DELETE d:

Rules and Considerations

DoubleSpace does not allow drive C to be deleted.

If you accidentally delete a drive, you may be able to restore it with the DOS UNDELETE command. Since a compressed drive is simply a file on an uncompressed drive, UNDELETE may be able to recover the file. Nothing must have been written to the disk if this procedure is to have any chance of working.

If you are successful in recovering the deleted compressed volume file, you must remount it using the DBLSPACE /MOUNT command.

Examples

To delete the compressed drive D, enter this command:

>   DBLSPACE /DELETE D:

See Also

DBLSPACE /MOUNT

DBLSPACE /DOUBLEGUARD

Purpose

Turns off or on the DoubleGuard feature, which checks its memory for damage by other programs.

Type

External

Syntax

```
DBLSPACE /DOUBLEGUARD=[0][1]
```

Rules and Considerations

Leaving DoubleGuard enabled (the default) slows down performance by about two percent. If you discover that DoubleSpace is not causing any problems, you may want to disable DoubleGuard.

Example

```
DBLSPACE /DOUBLEGUARD=0
```

DBLSPACE /FORMAT

Purpose

The DBLSPACE /FORMAT command formats a compressed drive.

Type

External

Syntax

```
DBLSPACE /FORMAT d:
```

Rules and Considerations

Using this command causes all data on a compressed drive to be erased. Use caution with this command. It is not possible to unformat a compressed drive.

DoubleSpace does not allow you to format drive C.

Examples

Use the following command to format compressed drive D:

```
DBLSPACE /FORMAT D:
```

DBLSPACE /INFO

Purpose

Use the DBLSPACE /INFO command to display the following information about a compressed drive:

- ✔ Free space
- ✔ Used space
- ✔ The name of its compressed volume file
- ✔ The drive's actual and estimated compression ratios

Type

External

Syntax

```
DBLSPACE [/INFO] d:
```

Rules and Considerations

/INFO can be eliminated from the preceding command, as long as a drive name is specified.

Examples

Type the following command to view information about compressed drive D:

    DBLSPACE D:

DBLSPACE /LIST

Purpose

Use the DBLSPACE /LIST command when you want a description of your system's drives.

Type

External

Syntax

    DBLSPACE /LIST

Rules and Considerations

DoubleSpace does not list network drives.

Examples

To view a list of your system's drives: type the following:

    DBLSPACE /LIST

DoubleSpace displays a list similar to the following:

    <list output here>

DBLSPACE /MOUNT

Purpose

The DBLSPACE /MOUNT command establishes a connection between a compressed volume file and a drive letter name.

Type

External

Syntax

DBLSPACE /**MOUNT**[=nnn] d1: [/NEWDRIVE=d2:]

Switches

=nnn   Specifies the compressed volume file number to be mounted. The file number is the extension of the file DBLSPACE.nnn. If you do not specify a volume to mount, DoubleSpace assumes it is to mount the compressed volume file named DBLSPACE.000. This switch can be abbreviated /MO.

/NEWDRIVE=d2:   Indicates the drive letter that you want to assign to the newly mounted drive.

Rules and Considerations

You do not normally need to mount a compressed drive, unless you have unmounted it. However, you need to mount a compressed volume file (CVF) if it is located on a floppy drive or on a drive that has been unmounted.

You must mount a compressed volume file that you recovered with the DOS UNDELETE command.

Examples

Use this command to mount a previously unmounted compressed drive:

DBLSPACE /**MOUNT**

This command assumes the compressed volume file is on the current drive and is called DBLSPACE.000. To mount a compressed volume file called DBLSPACE.001 on drive D, enter the following:

```
DBLSPACE /MOUNT=001 d:
```

DBLSPACE /UNMOUNT

Purpose

The DBLSPACE /UNMOUNT command is used to unmount a compressed drive.

Type

External

Syntax

```
DBLSPACE /UNMOUNT [d:]
```

Rules and Considerations

If you do not specify a drive to unmount, DoubleSpace unmounts the current drive.

Drive C cannot be unmounted.

Examples

Use the following command to unmount compressed drive D:

```
DBLSPACE /UNMOUNT D:
```

DBLSPACE /RATIO

Purpose

The DBLSPACE /RATIO command changes the compression ratio that DBLSPACE uses to estimate the amount of compression of a drive.

Type

External

Syntax

DBLSPACE /RATIO[=r,r][d:|/ALL]

Switches

    d:|/ALL   Specifies the drive you want to change the ratio for. You can specify an individual drive or you can specify all drives, but not both.

Rules and Considerations

Use this command if you are planning to save files to a drive that has a compression ratio significantly different than those already on the drive.

To change the estimated compression ratio, specify a number using the r,r parameter. Any number from 1.0 to 16.0 may be used. If you don't specify a compression ratio, DoubleSpace uses the average compression ratio for all the files currently on the drive.

Examples

Use the following command to change the compression ratio of drive D to 5 to 1:

    DBLSPACE /RATIO=5 D:

DBLSPACE /SIZE

Purpose

Use the DBLSPACE /SIZE command when you want to change the size of a compressed drive.

Type

External

Syntax

```
DBLSPACE /SIZE[=size1¦/RESERVE=size2] d:
```

Switches

/SIZE=*size1*   Determines the final size of the compressed drive.

/RESERVE=*size2*   Determines the size in megabytes of the uncompressed drive after it is resized.

Rules and Considerations

You can use the /RESERVE= switch or the /SIZE= switch, which specifies the new size of the compressed drive, but not both.

Examples

To change the size of the compress drive D to 100M, type the following command:

```
DBLSPACE /SIZE=100 D:
```

DBLSPACE /UNCOMPRESS

Purpose

Uncompresses a drive that was compressed with DBLSPACE, and removes DBLSPACE.BIN from memory.

Type

External

Syntax

`DBLSPACE /UNCOMPRESS d:`

Rules and Considerations

You must have enough free disk space to successfully uncompress the drive. If there is not enough space, free up enough space by either deleting files or moving them to another drive.

Example

`DBLSPACE /UNCOMPRESS D:`

DBLSPACE.SYS

Purpose

The DBLSPACE.SYS device driver determines the final location of DBLSPACE.BIN in memory.

Type

Device Driver

Syntax

`DEVICE=[d:\path\]DBLSPACE.SYS[/MOVE]`

or

`DEVICEHIGH=[d:\path\]DBLSPACE.SYS[/MOVE]`

Switches

/MOVE — Enables DBLSPACE.BIN to be moved from conventional memory to upper memory, if space exists.

Rules and Considerations

DBLSPACE.SYS does not provide access to your compressed drives; it merely determines the location in memory of the program that *does* allow access, DBLSPACE.BIN.

DBLSPACE.BIN is loaded in conventional memory unless the /MOVE switch is specified; then, it loads into upper memory. If you load the device driver with the DEVICEHIGH statement, DBLSPACE.BIN is moved from conventional memory to upper memory.

Examples

Add the following command to CONFIG.SYS to direct DBLSPACE.SYS to move DBLSPACE.BIN from conventional to upper memory:

```
DEVICEHIGH=DBLSPACE.SYS
```

See Also

DBLSPACE

DEBUG

Purpose

The DEBUG command starts the DOS Debug program that enables you to test and debug executable DOS programs.

Type

External

Syntax

```
DEBUG [[d:\path]filename[testfile-parameters]]
```

Rules and Considerations

When you start the DEBUG program, you see a dash character. The program is waiting for you to enter a command. The following commands are valid for the debug environment:

Command	Function
?	Help. Displays a list of debug commands.
A [address]	Assemble. Assembles 8086/8087/8088 mnemonics.
C [range address]	Compare. Compares two portions of memory.
D [address]	Dump. Displays the contents of memory.
E address [list]	Enter. Enters data into memory starting at a specific address.
F range list	Fill. Fills a range of memory with values you specify.
G [=address][breakpoints]	Go. Runs the program that is in memory. You can specify 1 to 10 temporary breakpoints.
H value1 value2	Hex. Performs hexadecimal arithmetic.
I port	Input. Inputs and displays one byte from a port you specify.
L [address]	Load. Loads contents of a file into memory.
M range address	Move. Moves a block of memory.
N [d:\path]file name	Name. Specifies a file for the Load or Write command.
O port byte-value	Output. Sends one byte to a port you specify.
P [=address][number]	Proceed. Executes a loop, program, subroutine, or interrupt.

Command	Function
Q	Quit. Quits the Debug environment.
R [register-name]	Register. Displays or alters the contents of a memory register.
S range list	Search. Searches a portion of memory for a pattern of byte values that you specify.
T [address][number]	Trace. Single steps to the next instruction and displays registers, flags, and the next instruction.
U [range]	Unassemble. Disassembles bytes and displays their source assembler statements.
W [address]	Write. Writes the file to disk.
XA [count]	Allocates expanded memory.
XD [handle]	Deallocates expanded memory.
XM [lpage][ppage][handle]	Maps expanded memory pages.
XS	Displays expanded memory status.

Examples

Use the following command to start the Debug environment:

    DEBUG

To use Debug to debug a program called PROGRAM.EXE, type:

    DEBUG program.exe

DEFRAG

Purpose

Reorganizes the files on a disk to make them contiguous; this helps to improve the performance of a disk.

Type

External

Syntax

DEFRAG `[d:][/F][/S:order][/V][/B] [/SKIPHIGH] [/LCD\BW\G0][/H]`

or

DEFRAG `[d:][/U][/V][/B][/SKIPHIGH][/LCD\BW\G0][/H]`

Switches

/F	Defragments files and moves them together, leaving no free space between the files.
/U	Defragments files and leaves empty spaces between them.
/B	Restarts your computer after DEFRAG is completed.
/V	Verifies that the data is being written correctly in its new location. Using this option can slow the process significantly.
/H	Moves any hidden files; normally hidden files are not moved.
/S	Specifies a sort order for the files. The following are valid sort orders:

    N   Alphabetic by name

    N-   Reverse alphabetic by name

    E   Alphabetic by extension

    E-   Reverse alphabetic by extension

    D   By date and time, earliest first

DEFRAG 1329

	D-	By date and time, most recent first
	S	By size, smallest first
	S-	By size, largest first
/SKIPHIGH		Loads DEFRAG into conventional memory. By default, DEFRAG loads in upper memory if it is available.
/LCD		Starts the program with an LCD color scheme.
/BW		Starts the program with a black-and-white color scheme.
/GO		Disables a graphic mouse and graphic character set.

Rules and Considerations

DEFRAG does not work on network drives or drives that have been created with INTERLNK.

You should not use this program from within Microsoft Windows—you may lose data.

Examples

Use the following command to defragment drive D, sorting the files alphabetically by name:

```
DEFRAG D: /S:N
```

See Also

CHKDSK, INTERLNK, TREE

DEL (ERASE)

Purpose

The DEL command is used to delete files from a disk. It is equivalent to the ERASE command.

Type

Internal

Syntax

```
DEL [d:\path]filename [/P]
```

or

```
ERASE [d:\path]filename [/P]
```

Switches

/p   Prompts you for confirmation before deleting a file.

Rules and Considerations

You can use wild-card characters (? and *) to delete groups of files. If you type DEL *.* all files are deleted. DOS does not ask you to confirm. Use caution with wild cards; it is probably best to use the DIR command with the group that you intend to delete. This way, you have an opportunity to examine the list of files which are deleted.

You can delete all of the files in a subdirectory by typing the DEL command followed by the subdirectory name. The program asks you to confirm the deletion.

If you accidentally delete a file, you may be able to recover it using the UNDELETE command.

Examples

To delete a file called MYFILE.TXT, type the following command:

```
DEL myfile.txt
```

Use the following command to delete all of the files in the D:\TEMP directory:

```
DEL d:\temp
```

The program prompts you for confirmation before deleting.

DEL (ERASE) **1331**

The following command is used to delete all files in the D:\DOCS directory that have the .TXT extension:

    DEL d:\docs*.txt

Before using a command such as this, you may wish to view the list of files that are deleted. Use the following commands for this procedure:

    DIR d:\docs*.txt

Examine the resulting list of files. If you are sure these are the files you want to delete, continue the procedure:

    DEL d:\docs*.txt

See Also

DELTREE, DIR, TREE, UNDELETE

DELOLDOS

See CLEANUP

DELTREE

Purpose

The DELTREE command deletes a directory and all files that are included in the directory.

Type

External

Syntax

    DELTREE [/Y][d:]path

Switches

v/Y   Enables you to run the DELTREE command without being prompted to confirm each deletion.

Rules and Considerations

The DELTREE command deletes all files and subdirectories included in a directory. It deletes hidden files, system files, and read-only files.

You can use wild-card characters with the DELTREE command. Use caution with wild-card characters. Before using a wild card with this command, you should use DIR to display a list of files that the wild card defines. Be sure these are the files or directories that you want to delete before using DELTREE.

Examples

Use the following command to delete all files and subdirectories in the D:\BUDGET directory:

```
DELTREE d:\budget
```

See Also

DEL, DIR, TREE

DEVICE

Purpose

The DEVICE command is used to install device drivers on your system. Device drivers give your computer additional capabilities, or enhance existing capabilities.

Type

Config

Syntax

```
DEVICE=[d:\path]filename [driver parameters]
```

Switches

None. Individual device drivers may include switches or parameters.

Rules and Considerations

DOS provides a number of device drivers that are loaded with the DEVICE= command in CONFIG.SYS, as follows:

    ANSI.SYS

    DISPLAY.SYS

    DRIVER.SYS

    DBLSPACE.SYS

    EGA.SYS

    EMM386.EXE

    HIMEM.SYS

    INTERLNK.EXE

    POWER.EXE

    RAMDRIVE.SYS

    SETVER.EXE

    SMARTDRV.EXE

Some hardware or software that you purchase may include device drivers. Follow the manufacturer's instructions to install these device drivers.

Some device drivers may be loaded into upper memory using the DEVICEHIGH= command.

COUNTRY.SYS and KEYBOARD.SYS are not device drivers, even though they are named as if they were. They are support files for other programs. Do not use them with DEVICE=.

Examples

To load the device driver ANSI.SYS, use this command:

```
DEVICE=c:\dos\ansi.sys
```

See Also

DEVICEHIGH

DEVICEHIGH

Purpose

The DEVICEHIGH command is used to load device drivers into upper memory, thereby freeing space in conventional memory.

Type

Config

Syntax

```
DEVICEHIGH=[[/L:region1[,minsize1][;region2[,minsize2]...[/S]]
[d:path]filename [driver parameters]
```

Switches

/L:region1[,minsize1]   Specifies the region of upper memory that you want the device driver to load into. By default, DOS loads the largest region of upper memory first. Individual regions of upper memory are called upper memory blocks (UMBs).

/S   Shrinks an upper memory block to its smallest size while a device driver is loading. This switch is normally used by the MEMMAKER command when it is determining the optimal load order of device drivers.

Rules and Considerations

Upper memory blocks must first have been created with a memory manager before you can use this command. Use the command DOS=UMB in your CONFIG.SYS file to create UMBs.

If no UMB space is available, or there is not enough space, the device driver is loaded in conventional memory. DOS does not report this to you when the system starts up.

Refer to Chapter 11 for more information about creating and using Upper Memory Blocks.

Examples

Use the following command to load the device driver ANSI.SYS into upper memory:

```
DEVICEHIGH=c:\dos\ansi.sys
```

See Also

DOS, LOADHIGH

DIR

Purpose

The DIR command is used to display a list of files and subdirectories within a directory.

Type

Internal

Syntax

```
DIR [d:][path][filename][/P][/W][/L][/B][/C][/S]
[/A[:]attributes] [/O[:]sortorder]
```

Switches

/P	Displays one page at a time.
/W	Used for a wide display. Only the file or directory name is used for this display.
/L	Displays unsorted names in lowercase.
/B	Lists only the names of the files or directories.
/C	Displays the compression ratio of files on a DoubleSpace volume.

/S	Lists all occurrences of a file name from the current directory and any subdirectories.
/A:*attributes*	Displays the names of files that have the attributes you specify. Attributes are the following:
H	Hidden files
H-	Files that are not hidden
S	System files
S-	Files other than system files
D	Directories only
D-	Files only
A	Files that have been marked for archive
A-	Files not changed since last backup
R	Read-only files
R-	Files that are not read-only
/O:*sortorder*	Displays the files and directories in a sorted order. Valid sort orders are the following:
N	Alphabetic by name
N-	Reverse alphabetic by name
E	Alphabetic by extension
E-	Reverse alphabetic by extension
D	By date and time, earliest first
D-	By date and time, most recent first
S	By size, smallest first
S-	By size, largest first
G	Directories grouped before files
G-	Directories grouped after files

C	By compression ratio, lowest first
C-	By compression ratio, highest first

Rules and Considerations

By default the DIR command displays the following information:

- ✔ Disk volume label and serial number

- ✔ File name, size in bytes, date and time file was created or last modified

- ✔ Directory name in angle brackets, date and time directory was created

- ✔ Disk summary information, including amount of space used and amount of space remaining on the disk, in bytes

If you find that you use a particular DIR command regularly (that is, with the same switches), you can create an environment variable for that command. For example, if you always specify DIR with the switch /O:D-, add the command SET DIRCMD= /O:D- to your AUTOEXEC.BAT file.

You can redirect the output of the DIR command to a device or to a file, using the redirection character (>). For example, use the DIR>PRN command to print a copy of your directory.

You can use wild-card characters (? and *) with the DIR command, to display groups of files.

Examples

Use this command to display the contents of your disk:

    DIR

The following command displays all files in the directory D:\DOCS:

    DIR d:\docs

To see all files with the TXT extension, use this command:

    DIR *.txt

Add the sortorder switch to sort the preceding listing by file size, as in this command:

```
DIR *.txt /O:S
```

DISKCOMP

Purpose

Use the DISKCOMP command to compare the contents of two floppy disks.

Type

External

Syntax

```
DISKCOMP [d1: [d2:]] [/1][/8]
```

Switches

/1   Compares the first side of the disks, even if they are double-sided.

/8   Compares the first 8 sectors per track, even if the disk contains 9 or 15 sectors.

Rules and Considerations

The DISKCOMP command only works with floppy disks. DISKCOMP cannot compare different types of disks; such as a 3-1/2" disk and a 5-1/4" disk, or a 720K disk and a 1.44M disk. You must use the FC command instead.

The disks that you are comparing can be in the same drive. In this case you use the same drive name for the source drive (d1) and the destination (d2); DOS prompts you to exchange disks during the compare process.

DISKCOMP does not work on network drives, or drives affected by the ASSIGN, JOIN, or SUBST command.

Examples

Use the following command to compare two disks that are of the same type in drive A:

```
DISKCOMP a: a:
```

See Also

DISKCOPY, FC

DISKCOPY

Purpose

DISKCOPY is used to copy the contents of a diskette to another diskette of the same size. If the destination disk (d2) is not formatted, DISKCOPY will format it.

New to DOS 6.2 is the no disk-swap DISKCOPY, which means that multiple disk swaps are no longer needed. DISKCOPY also makes multiple copies of the same disk without having to repeat the original copy step.

Type

External

Syntax

```
DISKCOPY [d1: [d2:]][/V][/1]
```

Switches

/V   Verifies that the files have been copied correctly.

/1   Copies the first side of a disk.

/M   Forces the multi-pass DISKCOPY method.

Rules and Considerations

The DISKCOPY command does not check to see what data may be on a diskette; it simply copies it. Be sure that you do not confuse the original (source) disk with the copy (destination) disk. You should always write-protect a disk to be copied.

DISKCOPY cannot copy different types of disks; such as a 3-1/2" disk and a 5-1/4" disk, or a 720K disk and a 1.44M disk. You must use the COPY command instead.

You can use the /V switch to verify that the files have been copied correctly. Then you do not need to use the DISKCOMP command to compare them.

It is possible to use only one drive with DISKCOPY. In this case both the source drive (d1) and the destination drive (d2) are the same. DISKCOPY prompts you to exchange disks during the copy process.

DISKCOPY does not work on drives affected by the ASSIGN, JOIN, or SUBST command.

Examples

Use the following command to copy the contents of a disk in drive A to another disk in drive A:

```
DISKCOPY a: a:
```

See Also

COPY, DISKCOMP

DISPLAY.SYS

Purpose

The DISPLAY.SYS driver enables support for code page switching for your display. Install this device driver in CONFIG.SYS.

Type

Device Driver

Syntax

    DEVICE=*[d:\path]***DISPLAY.SYS CON***[:]*=**(type**[,*[page]*[,n,m]]**)**

or

    DEVICEHIGH=[d:\path]DISPLAY.SYS
    CON[:]=(type[,[page][,n,m]])

Rules and Considerations

Use the *type* parameter to specify the display adapter you are using. If this parameter is omitted, DISPLAY.SYS checks the hardware and configures itself accordingly. Only EGA and LCD are valid; CGA and MONO are ignored, while EGA supports EGA and VGA.

Use the *page* parameter when you need to specify your display's hardware code page. The following code pages are supported:

    437   United States

    850   Multilingual (Latin I)

    852   Slavic (Latin II)

    860   Portuguese

    863   Canadian-French

    865   Nordic

Use the *n* parameter to specify how many pages (code pages) your display adapter supports. For EGA/VGA adapters, the maximum value is 6; for LCD, the maximum is 1.

Use the *m* parameter to specify the number of subfonts that your display adapter supports for each. The default is 2 for EGA/VGA, and 1 for LCD.

If your video adapter board includes a device driver, it must be installed before you can use this command.

Examples

Use the following command to install DISPLAY.SYS from the \DOS directory, and to specify use of the Canadian-French with two additional code pages:

    DEVICE=c:\dos\display.sys con:=(ega,863,2)

See Also

KEYB, PRINTER.SYS

DOS

Purpose

The DOS command is used to load a portion DOS into the High Memory Area (HMA), and to manage Upper Memory Blocks (UMBs) that were created by a memory manager.

Type

Config

Syntax

    DOS=HIGH¦LOW[,UMB¦,NOUMB]

or

    DOS=[HIGH,¦LOW,]UMB¦NOUMB

Rules and Considerations

The command DOS=HIGH is used to load a large portion of DOS into a memory area called the High Memory Area, leaving more space in conventional memory.

The command DOS=UMB is used to enable DOS to manage upper memory blocks, so you can load device drivers and programs into them.

The command DOS=HIGH or DOS=LOW can be used with or without the UMB parameter. That is, you can have one statement to control where DOS loads, another to control the management of UMBs, or you can combine both functions into one statement.

You must install the device driver HIMEM.SYS or another extended memory manager before using DOS=HIGH. Before using DOS=UMB, you must install an upper memory manager, such as EMM386.EXE.

Refer to Chapter 11 for more information about memory managers.

Examples

To load DOS into the HMA and activate UMB management by DOS, use the following command:

    DOS=HIGH,UMB

See Also

DEVICEHIGH, EMM386.EXE, HIMEM.SYS, LOADHIGH

DOSHELP

Purpose

The DOSHELP command displays a list of DOS commands, and a brief description of each.

Type

External

Syntax

    DOSHELP [command]

or

    command /?

Rules and Considerations

DOSHELP is similar to the HELP command, but the information it contains is not as detailed.

If you type DOSHELP without a command name, you will see a list of DOS commands followed by a brief description. Typing a command name gives you a screen of help for that command.

Examples

Use either of the following commands to see a help screen for the FORMAT command:

```
DOSHELP format
```

or

```
format /?
```

See Also

HELP

DOSKEY

Purpose

The DOSKEY command is used to maintain and display a history of keyboard commands that you can recall and resubmit, and to define keyboard macros. Commands are stored in memory in a command buffer.

Type

External

Syntax

```
DOSKEY [/REINSTALL][/BUFSIZE=size][/MACROS][/HISTORY]
[/INSERT¦OVERSTRIKE][macroname=[text]]
```

Switches

/REINSTALL   Installs a new copy of the program, and clears the command buffer.

DOSKEY   1345

/BUFSIZE=size   Specifies the size of the command
                         buffer, in bytes. The default
                         command buffer size is 512 bytes.
                         The minimum buffer size is 256
                         bytes.

/MACROS   Displays a list of macros currently
                         stored in memory. You can redi-
                         rect the list to a file. This switch
                         can be abbreviated /M.

[macroname=[text]]   Creates a macro that carries out
                         one or more MS-DOS commands
                         (a Doskey macro). Macroname
                         specifies the name you want to
                         assign to the macro.

/HISTORY   Displays a list of the commands
                         currently in the command buffer.
                         You can redirect the list to a file.
                         This switch can be abbreviated /H.

/INSERT | OVERSTRIKE   Specifies whether new text you
                         type overwrites old text when you
                         type commands. The default is
                         /OVERSTRIKE.

Rules and Considerations

You can press the following keys to recall command lines:

Up arrow	Recalls the last command
Down arrow	Recalls the next command
PgUp	Recalls the first command of the session
PgDn	Recalls the most recent command

These commands are used to edit command lines:

Left arrow	Moves cursor back one character
Right arrow	Moves cursor forward one character
Ctrl+left arrow	Moves cursor back one word

Ctrl+right arrow	Moves cursor forward one word
Home	Moves cursor to the beginning of the line
End	Moves cursor to the end of the line
Esc	Clears the command from the screen
F1	Copies a character from a memory buffer to the screen
F2	Searches for the next key you type
F3	Copies the rest of the characters from a memory buffer
F4	Deletes characters, starting with the first one in the memory buffer
F5	Copies current command into memory buffer; clears command line
F6	Puts an end-of-file character at the end of the line
F7	Shows all the commands in the buffer, each numbered
F8	Searches memory for a command that starts with a letter you specify first
F9	Asks for a command number and then displays the command
Alt+F7	Deletes all the commands in the command buffer
Alt+F10	Deletes any macro definitions stored in memory

The following commands are used when creating macros:

$g or $G	Redirects output. Use this character where you would use a redirect symbol (>).

gg or GG	Appends output to the end of a file. Use instead of >>.
$l or $L	Redirects input. Use this instead of <.
$b or $B	Use this character where you would use a pipe (¦).
$$	Uses the dollar sign ($) in a command.
$1-$9	Replaceable parameters used to pass information into a macro.
$*	Represents a batch parameter that is taken from command line input.
T$ or t$	Separates commands. Use either of these special characters to separate commands when you are creating macros or typing commands on the DOSKEY command line. Text specifies the commands you want to record.

To create a macro with DOSKEY, type DOSKEY followed by the name of the macro, an equal sign, and the command that you want the macro to perform. Refer to Chapter 14 for more information about using DOSKEY to work with macros.

Examples

To load the DOSKEY program and use command recall, type the following:

DOSKEY

Use the following command to create a macro that displays a directory with the /P option:

DOSKEY dir=dir/p

The following command creates a macro to type a file, whose name you specify, with the |MORE option:

DOSKEY type=type $1 $bMORE

DOSSHELL

Purpose

The DOSSHELL command starts the DOS Shell, a graphical interface to DOS. You can use a mouse or keyboard to navigate through menus; the menus help you perform common DOS functions without using commands.

Type

External

Syntax

>   **DOSSHELL** `[/T[:res[n]]][/B]` for text mode

or

>   **DOSSHELL** `[/G[:res[n]]][/B]`

Switches

/T   Use this switch to start DOSSHELL in text mode. You can specify low, medium, or high resolution with the *res* parameter, or you can specify the number of lines of resolution with the *n* parameter.

/G   Use this switch to start DOSSHELL in graphics mode. You can specify low, medium, or high resolution with the *res* parameter, or you can specify the number of lines of resolution with the *n* parameter.

/B   Use this switch to start DOSSHELL with a black-and-white color scheme.

Rules and Considerations

Using DOSSHELL enables you to perform *task swapping*, or changing between several active programs. During task swapping, programs that you switch away from are frozen and moved to your hard disk.

DOSSHELL creates a file called DOSSHELL.INI when you use it the first time. This file contains your settings and customization information for DOSSHELL.

Examples

Use this command to start the DOS Shell in graphics mode:

```
DOSSHELL /G
```

DRIVER.SYS

Purpose

The DRIVER.SYS device driver is used to create logical disk drives that are used to refer to physical drives.

Type

Device Driver

Syntax

```
DEVICE=[d:\path]DRIVER.SYS /D:drive /F:type [/C]
[/H:heads] [/S:sectors][/T:tracks]
```

Switches

/D:drive Specifies a number for the physical drive. The first drive on your system, drive A, is drive 0; drive B is drive 1, and a third drive, which would be an external drive, is drive 2.

/F:type Indicates the form factor or type of drive. Valid types are as follows:

0	160K/180K or 320K/360K
1	1.2M
2	720K (3.5")
7	1.44M (3.5")

9	2.88M (3.5")
/C	Indicates whether the drive reports that the door has been opened or closed.
/H:heads	Specifies the number of heads that the drive has.
/S:sectors	Specifies the number of sectors per track.
/T:tracks	Specifies the number of tracks that the drive has.

Rules and Considerations

You may need to use DRIVER.SYS when you install a new external floppy drive in order for DOS to recognize it.

See the DRIVPARM command to reconfigure a drive that is already installed.

Examples

Add the following command to your CONFIG.SYS file if you want to install an external, 1.2M drive:

```
DEVICE=c:\dos\DRIVER.SYS /D:1
```

See Also

DRIVPARM

DRIVPARM

Purpose

Use the DRIVPARM command when you want to modify the format of an existing physical drive. Use this command in CONFIG.SYS.

Type

Config

Syntax

DRIVPARM=/D:drive
[/C][/F:type][/I][/N]
[/S:sectors][/T:tracks]

Switches

/D:*drive*	Indicates the physical drive number. Drive A is number 0, drive B is number 1, and so on.
/C	Specifies whether the drive reports when the door is opened or closed.
/F:*type*	Specifies the form factor or type of drive. Valid types are as follows:
0	160K/180K or 320K/360K
1	1.2M
2	720K (3.5")
5	Hard disk
6	Tape
7	1.44M (3.5")
8	Read/write optical disk
9	2.88M (3.5")
/H:*heads*	Sets the maximum number of heads.
/I	Use this switch to indicate an electronically compatible 3.5" floppy drive if your system ROM does not support this type of drive.
/N	Specifies a non-removable drive.
/S:*sectors*	Indicates the number of sectors per track.
/T:*tracks*	Indicates the number of tracks for a drive.

Rules and Considerations

Use DRIVPARM to change the specifications of a drive that is already installed. This command does not create new logical drives.

Examples

To reconfigure drive B to a 360K format, use the command:

```
DRIVPARM=/d:1 /f:0
```

See Also

DRIVER.SYS

ECHO

Purpose

The ECHO command is used to control the display of command lines during execution of a batch file.

Type

Batch, Internal

Syntax

```
ECHO [ON|OFF]
```

Rules and Considerations

Use the ECHO command when you want to control what displays on the screen during execution of batch files. With ECHO OFF, none of the commands are displayed—only their results. With ECHO ON, commands in a batch file are displayed as it executes.

To echo a blank line, use ECHO with a single period following. There is no space in between.

Insert an at sign (@) in front of the words ECHO OFF and that line does not display on the screen.

Examples

To keep command lines from displaying, use the following command:

```
ECHO off
```

Start the line with the at sign to suppress the ECHO line itself, as in this example:

```
@ECHO off
```

Use the following command to echo a blank line:

```
ECHO.
```

See Also

PAUSE, REM

EDIT

Purpose

Use the EDIT command to start the DOS Editor, a full-screen text-editing program with pull-down menus.

Type

External

Syntax

```
EDIT [[d:][path]filename][/B][/G][/H][/NOHI]
```

Switches

/B	Starts the Editor in black and white.
/G	Enables the fastest screen updating when using a color graphics adapter.
/H	Uses the maximum number of lines for your display.
/NOHI	Disables highlighting, and enables you to use an 8-color display instead of a 16-color display.

Rules and Considerations

EDIT depends on another program, QBASIC.EXE to work properly. QBASIC.EXE must be in the current directory or must be on the system path.

EDIT works with ASCII text files only.

You can use a Microsoft-compatible mouse with EDIT; you must first install the appropriate mouse driver.

Examples

To create a new text file, type the following command:

```
EDIT
```

Use the following command to edit the file MYFILE.TXT:

```
EDIT myfile.txt
```

See Also

QBASIC

EGA.SYS

Purpose

Use EGA.SYS when you want to use the DOS Shell Task Swapper with an EGA monitor. EGA.SYS saves a picture of the display when you switch away from an application, and restores it when you switch back.

Type

Device Driver

Syntax

```
DEVICE=[d:\path]EGA.SYS
```

Rules and Considerations

If you use a mouse on a system with an EGA display, install the driver EGA.SYS before the mouse driver to save memory.

Examples

To install this device driver, add the following line to your CONFIG.SYS file:

```
DEVICE=c:\dos\EGA.SYS
```

See Also

DOSSHELL

EMM386

Purpose

The EMM386 command is used to enable or disable expanded memory support for computers with 80386 or higher processors. EMM386 can also be used to enable or disable support for Weitek coprocessors.

Type

Internal

Syntax

```
EMM386*[ON¦OFF¦AUTO]
```

or

```
EMM386 [W=ON¦W=OFF]
```

Rules and Considerations

The device driver EMM386.EXE must be installed in CONFIG.SYS before this command can be used. EMM386 requires the presence of an 80386 or higher processor. If your computer does not have an 80386 or higher processor, you see the message

```
EMM386 driver not installed.
```

Use EMM386 ON to activate EMM386. This option provides expanded memory emulation, management of Upper Memory Blocks, or both.

Use EMM386 OFF to disable EMM386.

EMM386 AUTO is used to provide expanded memory only when a program requests it.

If your system includes a Weitek coprocessor, use EMM386 W=ON. If this parameter is specified and there is no coprocessor present, you see the message

```
Weitek Coprocessor not installed.
```

Refer to Chapter 11 for more information about memory management.

Examples

Once EMM386.EXE is installed, you can make expanded memory available to a program only when it is requested by typing the following command:

```
EMM386 AUTO
```

See Also

EMM386.EXE

EMM386.EXE

Purpose

The EMM386.EXE device driver is used to simulate expanded memory on a computer with an 80386 or higher processor. EMM386.EXE also is used to provide access to the Upper Memory Area.

Type

Device Driver

EMM386.EXE

Syntax

```
DEVICE=[d:\path]EMM386.EXE
[ON¦OFF¦AUTO][memory][MIN=size]
[W=ON¦W=OFF][Mx¦FRAME=address¦/Paddress][Pn=address]
[X=range][I=range][B=address][L=minXMS][A=altregs]
[H=handles][D=nnn][RAM=range][NOEMS][NOVCPI]
[NOHIGHSCAN][QUIET][WIN=range] [NOHI][ROM=range]
```

Switches

ON | OFF | AUTO	Determines whether EMM386 is actively providing expanded memory and upper memory block support. The default is ON. Use AUTO to disable EMM386, and AUTO to activate memory support only when it is required.
memory	Specifies the amount of memory in kilobytes that is to be allocated as expanded memory.
MIN=size	Specifies the amount of memory that is guaranteed to be available for expanded memory. The default is 256K.
W=ON\W=OFF	Enables or disables Weitek coprocessor support.
Mx	Defines the base address for a page frame, using a number from 1 through 14. Valid addresses are as follows:
1	C000h
2	C400h
3	C800h
4	CC00h
5	D000h
6	D400h
7	D800h
8	DC00h

9	E000h
10	8000h
11	8400h
12	8800h
13	8C00h
14	9000h

FRAME=address	Sets the base address of the page frame segment. Any of the values listed for the M parameter can be used. This parameter cannot be used with M or /P.
/Paddress	Specifies the address of the page frame. Any of the values listed for the M parameter can be used. This parameter cannot be used with M or FRAME=.
Pn=address	Defines a specific page frame address for page *n*. The page must be within the range 0 through 255, and addresses are any listed for the M parameter plus 9400h, 9800h, 9C00h, E400h, E800h, and EC00h.
X=range	Prevents EMM386 from using the specified address range as an upper memory block or a page frame.
I=range	Allows EMM386 to use the specified address range for an upper memory block or a page frame.
B=address	Sets the lowest address that EMM386 can use for memory banking (swapping). The default is 4000h.
A=altregs	Determines the number of fast alternate register sets that are created for multitasking. The default number is 7; each alternate register set increases the size of EMM386.EXE in memory by 200 bytes.

EMM386.EXE

H=*handles*	Determines the number of file handles that are available for EMM386 to use. The default is 64.

NOTE: *The following corrects an error in the Micosoft documentation:*

D=*nnn*	Specifies how much memory in kilobytes is set aside for DMA buffering. The default value is 32.
RAM=*range*	Specifies a range of memory addresses that can be used as upper memory blocks. If no range is specified, EMM386 uses whatever addresses are available.
NOEMS	Provides access to upper memory but does not provide expanded memory.
NOVCPI	Disables support for VCPI applications. If you use this switch to disable VCPI support, you must also use the NOEMS switch.
NOHISCAN	Limits scanning of upper memory area; can be used if you are having problems with EMM386.EXE.
QUIET	Disables the display of EMM386 messages during program loading.
WIN=*range*	Reserves a specified range of memory addresses for use by Microsoft Windows.
NOHI	Prevents any part of EMM386.EXE from loading into the upper memory area, reserving it all for upper memory blocks.
ROM=*range*	Sets aside a range of memory addresses that EMM386 can use for Shadow

RAM—random-access memory that is used to copy programs normally located in ROMs.

Rules and Considerations

The device driver HIMEM.SYS must be installed before you can use this program.

Be cautious when using this program to control memory areas—it is possible to disable your computer. Be sure you have a boot disk nearby before working with memory switches.

If you have a computer with a SCSI or ESDI hard disk controller, double buffering may be required before using EMM386. Install double buffering by adding the following line to your CONFIG.SYS file:

```
DEVICE=c:\dos\SMARTDRV.EXE /double_buffer
```

Refer to Chapter 11 for more information about this program.

Examples

To load the memory manager program with all defaults, type the following lines in your CONFIG.SYS file:

```
DEVICE=c:\dos\HIMEM.SYS
DEVICE=c:\dos\EMM386.EXE
```

Modify the EMM386 statement as follows to allocate 2M of expanded memory:

```
DEVICE=c:\dos\EMM386.EXE 2048
```

Use the following command to exclude the addresses C000h-C7FFh and to place a page frame at address D000h:

```
DEVICE=c:\dos\EMM386.EXE X=C000-C7FF FRAME=D000
```

Type the following command to disable expanded memory, but still provide access to upper memory blocks:

```
DEVICE=c:\dos\EMM386.EXE NOEMS
```

See Also

EMM386, HIMEM.SYS

EXE2BIN

Purpose

The EXE2BIN command is used by programmers to convert .EXE (executable) files to binary format.

Type

External

Syntax

```
EXE2BIN [d1:\path]infile [d2:\path2\][outfile]
```

Rules and Considerations

Infile is the name of the input file that is to be converted. *Outfile* is the name of the converted file.

The input file must be a valid EXE file. It cannot be packed, cannot contain a STACK segment, and the resident code and data portion cannot exceed 64K in size.

If no output file is specified, an output file is created that has the same name as the input file, but with the extension .BIN.

Examples

Use the following command to convert MYPROG.EXE to a binary format file:

```
EXE2BIN myprog.exe
```

EXIT

Purpose

The EXIT command quits the command interpreter and returns to the program that started it.

Type

Internal

Syntax

```
EXIT
```

Rules and Considerations

Use this command to cancel this instance of the command interpreter. An instance is created when you leave an application program temporarily; sometimes known as "exiting to the system." Once you are finished using the command prompt or running your DOS program, type EXIT to return to the calling program.

Examples

If you start a DOS session from within Windows, type the following command to return to Windows when you are finished with DOS:

```
EXIT
```

See Also

COMMAND

EXPAND

Purpose

The EXPAND command is used to expand compressed files from the DOS installation disks. The files are otherwise not usable.

Type

External

Syntax

EXPAND `[d:\path]filename[[d:\path]filename[...]]destination`

Rules and Considerations

Many of the files that come with DOS 6 are in a compressed format, and must be uncompressed to use. While this is done for you by the INSTALL program, you may have a need later to add or reinstall a single file. In this case, the file must be EXPANDed. Compressed files have extensions that end in an underscore.

If you do not enter any file names, EXPAND prompts you for a source file then prompts again for a destination file name. If you enter only a source file name, EXPAND prompts you for a destination file name.

There is a file on DOS 6's Setup Disk 1 called PACKING.LST. This file lists all of the programs included on the disks, and tells you which file is on which disk. Before EXPANDing a file, find out what disk it is on first to save time.

Examples

Use the following command to expand a copy of the FORMAT command from your DOS Setup disks, once you know what disk the program is on:

EXPAND `a:format.co_ d:\dos\format.com`

FASTOPEN

Purpose

The FASTOPEN command is used to cache your directory, which enables DOS to open frequently used files faster.

Type

External

Syntax

`FASTOPEN d1:[=n1] [d2:[=n2]]...[/X]`

Switches

/X Directs FASTOPEN to put the directory cache in expanded memory.

Rules and Considerations

Each time you open a file, FASTOPEN records its name and location in the directory cache. The access time is greatly reduced the next time you want to open the file.

FASTOPEN works on your computer's hard disk; it does not work on network drives.

You can keep track of from 10 to 999 files using the *n* specification. The default value is 48 file names.

FASTOPEN can be executed from the DOS command prompt, from AUTOEXEC.BAT, or from CONFIG.SYS using the INSTALL command.

Do not run programs which compact your hard disk, such as Speed Disk, while this program is loaded.

Do not use this program with the DOS Shell program; your system may lock up.

Examples

Use the following command to install FASTOPEN in CONFIG.SYS, and configure it to track 50 file names:

`INSTALL=c:\dos\FASTOPEN.EXE C:=50`

See Also

INSTALL

FC

Purpose

Use the FC command to compare two files and display their differences.

Type

External

Syntax

FC *[/A][/C][/L][/LBn][/N][/T][/W][/nnn]*
*[d:\path]***file1** *[d:\path]* **file2**

or

FC *[/B][d:\path]***file1** *[d:\path]***file2**

Switches

/A   Abbreviates the output of an ASCII comparison by only displaying the first and last lines of each set of differences.

/C   Ignores the case of letters.

/L   Compares files in ASCII mode, line by line, and attempts to resynchronize the files after finding a mismatch.

/LBn   Sets the number of lines for the internal buffer. The default number of lines is 100; if the number of lines that is different is greater than this, FC cancels the comparison.

/N   Displays the line numbers during comparison.

/T   Does not expand tabs to spaces. Normally tabs are converted to eight spaces.

/W   Compresses tabs and spaces to single spaces in a file.

/nnn   Sets the number of lines that must match before FC considers the files to be synchronized. The default value is 2.

/B   Compares the files in binary mode, byte by byte, and does not attempt to synchronize them after finding mismatches.

Rules and Considerations

You can use wild card characters (? or *) as part of the file names to be compared.

If there are no differences in the files, you see the message

```
FC: no differences encountered.
```

Otherwise the differences are reported by listing the name of the first file, followed by the last line to match in both files, followed by the lines from file1 that are different, followed by the first line to match in both files. Then the name of the second file is displayed, followed by the last line to match, followed by the lines from file2 that are different, followed by the next line to match.

Examples

Use the following command to compare the files BUDGET1.TXT and BUDGET2.TXT:

```
FC /A budget1.txt budget2.txt
```

To compare all of the files in the C:\DOCS directory with the files in the D:\DOCS directory, type the following command:

```
FC c:\docs\*.txt d:\docs\*.txt
```

See Also

DISKCOMP, VERIFY

FCBS

Purpose

The FCBS command sets the number of file control blocks that DOS can have open at one time. Use this command in CONFIG.SYS.

Type

Config

Syntax

FCBS=*nnn*

Rules and Considerations

Some older programs use file control blocks instead of file handles to control files. If you use such programs, you must install this command in your CONFIG.SYS file. File handles are set with the FILES= command.

You can specify from 1 through 255 file control blocks. The default value is 4.

Examples

Add the following command to CONFIG.SYS to set the number of file control blocks at 16:

FCBS=16

See Also

FILES

FDISK

Purpose

The FDISK command is used to configure the partitions on a hard disk.

Type

External

Syntax

FDISK *[/STATUS] [/MBR]*

Switches

/STATUS   Used to display information about a disk's partitions without running the FDISK program.

/MBR   Rebuilds the Master Boot Record of a hard disk without re-creating the partitions, which would cause data loss.

Rules and Considerations

The maximum size of a DOS partition is 2 gigabytes.

FDISK does not work on network drives or InterLnk drives, or drives formed by the SUBST command.

The undocumented switch /MBR can be used to rebuild a disk's Master Boot Record, deleting any virus that may be attached. After using FDISK with this switch, cold boot your system to remove any virus from memory. Refer to Chapter 20 for more information about viruses.

NOTE   *While /MBR can rebuild an existing Master Boot Record, it cannot fix a damaged one.*

Examples

To run the FDISK program to create or modify a disk partition, type the following command:

    FDISK

Follow the prompts that are provided by the program.

Type the following command to cause FDISK to rebuild your hard disk's Master Boot Record, deleting any attached viruses:

    FDISK /MBR

See Also

MSAV, SUBST

FILES

Purpose

The FILES command sets the number of files that DOS can have open at the same time. Use this command in CONFIG.SYS.

Type

Config

Syntax

    FILES=nnn

Rules and Considerations

The default number of files that DOS can access at one time is 8; you may specify up to 255. Most programs need a larger value than 8, or they may produce error messages similar to the following:

    Not enough file handles
    Too many files open

Examples

To set the number of open files at 60, use the following command:

```
FILES=60
```

See Also

BUFFERS, FCBS

FIND

Purpose

The FIND command is used to search for a string of text in one or more files.

Type

External

Syntax

```
FIND [/V][/C][/N][/I]"string"[[d:\path]filename[...]]
```

Switches

/V   Displays all lines that do not contain the string you specified.

/C   Displays a count of the lines that contain the string, but not the lines.

/P   Precedes each line with the line number from the file.

/I   Ignores the case of letters.

Rules and Considerations

The text string that you want to locate must be enclosed in quotation marks. If the text you are searching for contains a quotation mark, simply add a second one to the string.

The FIND command is case-sensitive unless you use the /I switch. That is, there is a difference between the characters "a" and "A".

FIND does not work with wild card characters (? and *). To search for a string in a group of files, you can use the FIND command in a FOR command.

Examples

Use the following command to display all lines from the file LETTER.DOC that contain the string "banana":

```
FIND /I "banana" d:\docs\letter.doc
```

If a string that you want to search for contains quotation marks, use the following example to find it:

```
FIND "The analyst reported that ""this is the best banana"" in her opening remark" d:\docs\letter.doc
```

To search for a string in a group of files, use the following command:

```
FOR %f IN (d:\docs\*.doc) DO FIND "banana" %f
```

See Also

FOR

FOR

Purpose

The FOR command repeats a command for each file in a set of files.

Type

Batch, Internal

Syntax

From the command prompt, type the following:

FOR %variable **IN** (set) **DO** command [command parameters]

To use in a batch file, use the following syntax:

`FOR %%variable IN (set) DO command [command parameters]`

Rules and Considerations

Use %*variable* or %%*variable* to represent variables that are replaced sequentially with each item in the *set*, until the entire set is processed. The set is typically a list of files you want to process.

Processing is done using the command that you specify. You can include any parameters that the command requires.

It is best to avoid using variables %1 through %9, as these variables are more commonly used in batch files. You can use any character for the variable name.

You can use wild-card characters (? and *) in the set if you want to work with groups of files.

Examples

Use the following command to print all text files in the D:\DOCS directory:

`FOR $f IN (d:\docs\*.txt) DO PRINT $f`

FORMAT

Purpose

The FORMAT command is used to format disks. Disks must be formatted before any files can be stored on them.

Type

External

Syntax

`FORMAT d: [/V[:label]][/Q][/U][/F:size][/B¦/S]`
`FORMAT d: [/V[:label]][/Q][/U][/T:tracks/N:sectors][/B¦/S]`

```
FORMAT d: [/V[:label]][/Q][/U][/1][/4][/B¦/S]
FORMAT d: [/Q][/U][/1][/4][/8][/B¦/S]
```

Switches

/V:label	Specifies the volume label, which is used to identify the disk. If you use a volume label, it must not be longer than 11 characters in length. If /V is specified but no label is given, you are prompted for a name. This is useful if you are formatting a number of disks; if a label is specified, all disks will have the same label name. This switch cannot be used with the /8 switch.
/Q	Specifies a quick format, which deletes a previously saved file allocation table and root directory, and does not scan the disk for bad areas.
/U	Specifies an unconditional format, which destroys any existing data. You will not be able to UNFORMAT this disk later.
/F:size	Formats the disk to a specified size. You should use this switch instead of the /T and /F switches whenever possible. The possible size values are as follows:
160	160K single-sided, double-density, 5-1/4" disk
180	180K single-sided, double-density, 5-1/4" disk
320	320K double-sided, double-density, 5-1/4" disk
360	360K double-sided, double-density, 5-1/4" disk
720	720K double-sided, double-density, 3-1/2" disk
1200	1.2M double-sided, high-density, 5-1/4" disk
1440	1.44M double-sided, high-density, 3-1/2" disk
2880	2.88M double-sided, extra-high-density, 3-1/2" disk

/B	Reserves space for the DOS hidden files IO.SYS and MSDOS.SYS. This switch is included for compatibility with earlier versions of DOS; it is not necessary to reserve space for these files with DOS 6.
/S	Formats the disk and copies the system startup files, IO.SYS, MSDOS.SYS, and COMMAND.COM to the disk.
/T	Specifies number of tracks.
/N:sectors	Specifies the number of tracks per sector. If you use this switch you must also use the /T switch. Whenever possible, indicate the format of the drive using the /F switch.
/1	Formats a single side of a disk.
/4	Formats a 5-1/4", double-sided, double-density disk on a 1.2M drive. Use this option only if your drive can read such disks reliably.
/8	Formats a 5-1/4" disk with 8 sectors per track (usually there are 9 sectors per track). This switch enables you to format disks for versions of DOS prior to 2.0.
/AUTOTEST	Undocumented switch that formats the disk without any prompts (such as insert disk prompt, volume label prompt, format another disk prompt) or the usual disk space listing.
/BACKUP	Undocumented switch similar to /AUTOTEST. Formats the disk without any prompts except the volume label prompt. Unlike /AUTOTEST, it displays the usual disk space listing.

Rules and Considerations

By default DOS performs a safe format on a disk. Before the disk is formatted, a copy is made of the disk's file allocation table and root directory, so that the disk can later be unformatted if need be. If you do not want this type of format, you should specify the /U option. On a new disk, an unconditional format is performed by default.

If you do not specify a size, DOS will format the disk according to the capacity of the disk. It is best not to format a disk for a capacity higher than that for which it was designed.

Do not use the FORMAT command on a disk that was prepared using the SUBST command, on a network drive, or on an InterLnk drive.

Examples

To format a new disk in drive A type the following:

```
FORMAT a:
```

Use the following command to format a disk in drive A and give it a volume label name of "budgets."

```
FORMAT a: /V:budgets
```

Type the following command to format a disk in drive A with the name of "boot_disk" and copy the system startup files to the disk:

```
FORMAT a: /S /V:boot_disk
```

See Also

DIR, LABEL, UNFORMAT, VOL

GOTO

Purpose

The GOTO command is used in a batch file to cause a program to jump to another location in the program. The location is identified with a label; the label starts with the colon character.

Type

Batch, Internal

Syntax

```
GOTO label
```

Rules and Considerations

When you use GOTO in a batch file, program control is transferred to the line(s) below the label that you specify.

A label is identified as a line that begins with a colon (:). The first eight characters after the colon are read as the label name, and can include spaces, but not other separators. Labels cannot be executable program statements, as they are ignored by DOS during processing of the batch file.

Refer to Chapter 15 for more information about batch files.

Examples

Use the following command in a batch file to go to a line called SUB1:

```
GOTO sub1
```

Somewhere in the batch program, establish the label:

```
:sub1
```

During batch file execution, program control is transferred to this line, and commands that follow are processed. If no label is found in a program, you see the message

```
Label not found
```

See Also

IF

GRAFTABL

Purpose

The GRAFTABL command enables the use of extended graphics characters in a code page to be displayed in graphics mode.

Type

External

Syntax

    GRAFTABL *[page]*

or

    GRAFTABL */STATUS*

Switch

    /STATUS   Displays the current code page in use.

Rules and Considerations

GRAFTABL is used to enable the display of extended characters only. Use the MODE or CHCP commands to set the code page.

Use one of the following *page* values:

437	United States
850	Multilingual (Latin I)
852	Slavic (Latin II)
860	Portuguese
863	Canadian-French
865	Nordic

Examples

Use the following command to specify the Canadian-French code page:

    GRAFTABL 863

To display the current code page value, type the following:

    GRAFTABL /STATUS

See Also

CHCP, MODE

GRAPHICS

Purpose

The GRAPHICS command is used to set up a printer so that it can print graphics screens when you press PrntScrn.

Type

External

Syntax

```
GRAPHICS [type][[d:\path]filename][/R][/B][/LCD]
[/PRINTBOX:STD¦/PRINTBOX:LCD]
```

Switches

/R   Prints the screen as white characters on a black background, rather than in reverse. Reverse is the default.

/B   Prints the background in color on a color printer.

/LCD   Prints the screen using a liquid crystal display (LCD) aspect ratio. This switch is the same as /PRINTBOX:LCD. The default is to use the CGA aspect ratio, or /PRINTBOX:STD.

Rules and Considerations

You specify the *type* of printer you have by indicating one of the following:

Type	Printer
color1	IBM PC Color Printer with black ribbon

GRAPHICS

Type	Printer
color4	IBM PC Color Printer with RGB ribbon
color8	IBM PC Color Printer with CMY ribbon
hpdefault	Hewlett-Packard PCL printer
deskjet	Hewlett-Packard DeskJet printer
graphics	IBM Personal Graphics Printer, IBM Proprinter, or IBM Quietwriter printer
graphicswide	IBM Personal Graphics Printer with 11-inch wide carriage
laserjet	Hewlett-Packard LaserJet printer
laserjetii	Hewlett-Packard LaserJet II printer
paintjet	Hewlett-Packard PaintJet printer
quietjet	Hewlett-Packard QuietJet printer
quietjetplus	Hewlett-Packard QuietJet Plus printer
ruggedwriter	Hewlett-Packard RuggedWriter printer
ruggedwriterwide	Hewlett-Packard RuggedWriterWide printer
thermal	IBM PC-compatible Thermal printer
thinkjet	Hewlett-Packard ThinkJet printer

The GRAPHICS command uses a printer profile to determine how to set up the printer. By default, it will use the profile GRAPHICS.PRO that is supplied with DOS. If you use another profile, you must specify its name.

Press the Shift+PrntScrn keys to print a graphics screen.

You cannot print a screen on a PostScript printer.

Examples

Type the following command to enable graphics screens to be printed:

```
GRAPHICS
```

HELP

Purpose

The HELP command is used to access the on-line help system for DOS.

Type

External

Syntax

```
HELP [/B][/G][/H][/NOHI][topic]
```

Switches

/B	Enables the use of a monochrome display with a color graphics card.
/G	Provides the fastest update of a CGA display.
/H	Displays the maximum number of lines that are possible for your hardware.
/NOHI	Enables the use of a monitor without high-intensity support; does not use highlighting.

Rules and Considerations

If you enter the command HELP without any parameters, you see a list of all the topics that you can get help with. Simply point to the one you want help with and click your mouse button. If you are using your keyboard, move the cursor down to the command and press Enter.

You can get help for a specific command from the command prompt by typing HELP and the name of the command. This bypasses the list of commands.

Use the /H switch when you want to view as many lines as possible on your screen. On a VGA display this is 50 lines.

Examples

Use the following command to access the help system:

```
HELP
```

For help about the FORMAT command, use this command:

```
HELP format
```

Type the following command to view the help screen with 50 lines for a VGA display:

```
HELP format /h
```

See Also

DOSHELP

HIMEM.SYS

Purpose

The HIMEM.SYS device driver is used to manage extended memory on your system. Install this driver in your CONFIG.SYS file.

Type

Device Driver

Syntax

```
DEVICE=[d:\path]HIMEM.SYS [A20CONTROL:ON¦OFF]
[/CPUCLOCK:ON¦OFF][/EISA] [/HNAMIM=nnn][/INT15=nnn]
[/NUMHANDLES=n] [/MACHINE:nn] [/SHADOWRAM:ON¦OFF][VERBOSE]
```

Switches

A20CONTROL:ON | OFF — Specifies whether HIMEM.SYS takes control of the A20 line even if A20 was on when HIMEM was loaded. The default is ON.

/CPUCLOCK:ON | OFF — Specifies whether HIMEM is to affect the speed of your system's clock. The default is OFF.

/EISA — For use on Enhanced Industry Standard Architecture (EISA) systems with more than 16M of memory; specifies that HIMEM.SYS should allocate all available extended memory. On other systems, all available extended memory is allocated.

/HMAMIN=nnn — Specifies the minimum amount of memory that a program must request to gain access to the High Memory Area. The default is 0; when no amount is specified, the HMA is allocated to the first program that requests it. Only one program can use the HMA.

/INT15=nnn — Allocates an amount of memory in kilobytes that is not controlled by HIMEM.SYS, but is left for those older programs that use the INT15 interface (instead of the XMS standard) to access extended memory. The default amount is 0.

/NUMHANDLES=n — Specifies the number of extended memory block handles that can be used at one time. The default is 32; each additional handle uses 6 bytes of memory.

HIMEM.SYS

/MACHINE:nn — Specifies what type of computer you are using. Usually HIMEM.SYS can detect your machine type and will configure itself accordingly. Some systems may require that you specify the machine type. You can select either a number or a code for the machine types listed in the following table.

Number	Code	Machine Type
1	at	IBM AT or 100% compatible
2	ps2	IBM PS/2
3	ptlcascade	Phoenix Cascade BIOS
4	hpvectra	HP Vectra (A&A+)
5	att6300plus	AT&T 6300 Plus
6	acer1100	Acer 1100
7	toshiba	Toshiba 1600 & 1200XE
8	wyse	Wyse 12.5 Mhz 286
9	tulip	Tulip SX
10	zenith	Zenith ZBIOS
11	at1	IBM PC/AT (alternative delay)
12	at2	IBM PC/AT (alternative delay)
13	at3	IBM PC/AT (alternative delay)
14	fasthp	HP Vectra
15	ibm7552	IBM 7552 Industrial Computer
16	bullmicral	Bull Micral 60
17	dell	Dell XBIOS

/SHADOWRAM:ON | OFF   Specifies whether to disable Shadow RAM—the copying of ROM into RAM.

/VERBOSE   Prevents the display of status and error messages while HIMEM.SYS is starting.

Rules and Considerations

HIMEM.SYS or another extended memory manager must be loaded before programs can access the High Memory Area. Use the command DOS=HIGH if you want to load DOS itself into the HMA.

Refer to Chapter 11 for more information about using a memory manager.

Examples

Add the following command to your CONFIG.SYS file to load HIMEM.SYS with all defaults:

```
DEVICE=c:\dos\HIMEM.SYS
```

For use with an IBM PS/2, the following variation is used:

```
DEVICE=c:\dos\HIMEM.SYS M:2
```

If you have a program that uses Interrupt 15 to access extended memory, reserve 1M for that program with the following command:

```
DEVICE=c:\dos\HIMEM.SYS  /INT15=1024
```

See Also

DOS=, EMM386

IF

Purpose

The IF command is used in a batch file to provide conditional processing. If a specified condition is true, the command that follows is executed. Otherwise the command is ignored.

Type

Batch, Internal

Syntax

    `IF [NOT] condition command`

"Condition" can be any of the following:

    `ERRORLEVEL number`
    `string1==string2`
    `EXIST file name`

Rules and Considerations

The IF command evaluates whether the condition you specify is true. If it is true, then the command you specify is carried out. If it is not true, the command is ignored.

Use the ERRORLEVEL condition when a command returns an exit code. Most commands provide DOS with an exit code. An exit code of 0 generally indicates that a command executed successfully. Other exit codes have various meanings, depending on the specific command. You can instruct the program to do a variety of things based on the value of the exit code.

You can cause your program to branch based upon the comparison of two strings of text. For example, you can set one string to yes, then ask the user for yes/no input. The input can be compared to the known string value, and the program can branch accordingly.

You can cause your program to branch based on whether a file exists or not. Wild-card characters (? and *) are allowed in file names.

Refer to Chapter 15 for more information about batch files.

Examples

Use the following command to look for an exit code. If the exit code is not 0, display the message "No Good":

    `IF ERRORLEVEL 1 ECHO No Good`

To test a user's response to a prompt, use the following command:

```
IF %1==yes GOTO sub1
```

In the preceding example, the batch file must contain a label identified as :sub1. If the comparison is true, the program branches to this location.

The following command tests for the existence of a file called BUDGET.TXT; if the file is found, a message is displayed:

```
IF EXIST d:\docs\budget.txt ECHO Found the File
```

See Also

CHOICE, ECHO, GOTO

INCLUDE

Purpose

The INCLUDE command is used in CONFIG.SYS to include the contents of a configuration block. A configuration block is a block of commands that relate to a specific configuration of hardware and/or memory management, thus enabling multiple configurations for your system.

Type

Config

Syntax

```
INCLUDE=blockname
```

Rules and Considerations

Each configuration block in a CONFIG.SYS file has a name, specified within square brackets. When you INCLUDE one block name inside another block, the commands for the INCLUDEd block are carried out along with the new commands.

Examples

In the following CONFIG.SYS file, three configurations are defined. Notice the use of the INCLUDE command in the example file:

```
[menu]
menuitem basic,Basic configuration
menuitem memmgt,Basic with memory management
menuitem network,Memory management and network

[basic]
files=30
buffers=30

[memmgt]
    INCLUDE basic
device=c:\dos\himem.sys
dos=high,umb
device=c:\dos\emm386.exe
```

See Also

MENU, MENUCOLOR, MENUDEFAULT, MENUITEM, SUBMENU

INSTALL

Purpose

The INSTALL command is used to load a memory-resident utility into memory when your system starts up. It is used in CONFIG.SYS.

Type

Config

Syntax

```
INSTALL=[d:\path]filename [command parameters]
```

Rules and Considerations

INSTALL does not create a program environment when it loads. This means that the program requires slightly less memory than if you load it normally. Programs that require environment variables or shortcut keys may not work when loaded with INSTALL.

Programs that are loaded with INSTALL are loaded after device drivers in CONFIG.SYS, and before any programs in AUTOEXEC.BAT. Programs loaded with INSTALL are loaded into conventional memory.

Programs that respond well to being loaded with INSTALL are FASTOPEN, SHARE, KEYB, and NLSFUNC.

Examples

Use the following command to install FASTOPEN in memory, and to indicate that FASTOPEN is to track 50 file names:

```
INSTALL=c:\dos\fastopen.exe c:=50
```

INTERLNK

Purpose

The INTERLNK command is used to redirect requests for operations on a client computer to a server computer. This is useful if you have a laptop computer that you want to connect to a desktop computer for file or printer sharing. The device driver INTERLNK.EXE must be installed before this can be done.

Type

External

Syntax

```
INTERLNK [client=server]
```

Rules and Considerations

The *client* specifies the letter of the drive that is redirected to a drive on an InterLnk server; it was specified when InterLnk was started.

The *server* specifies the letter of the drive on the InterLnk server that is to be redirected; it must be listed in the This Computer (Server) column of the InterLnk server screen.

When you connect two computers using InterLnk, additional drives are assigned the next available drive letter.

Examples

Type the following command to redirect drive D on an InterLnk server to drive E on a client:

```
INTERLNK e=d
```

See Also

INTERLNK.EXE, INTERSVR

INTERLNK.EXE

Purpose

The INTERLNK.EXE device driver redirects requests for operations on an InterLnk client drive or printer port to a drive or printer port on an InterLnk server. Install this device driver in your CONFIG.SYS file.

Type

Device Driver

Syntax

```
DEVICE=[d:\path]INTERLNK.EXE [/DRIVES:n][/NOPRINTER]
[/COM[:][n¦address]][/AUTO][/NOSCAN][/LOW][/BAUD:rate][/V]
```

Switches

/DRIVES:*n*	Specifies the number of redirected drives. Normally, 3 drives are redirected. If 0 is specified, only printers are redirected.
/NOPRINTER	Specifies that printers are not to be redirected. The default is to redirect all available printer ports.
/COM[:][*n* | *address*]	Designates a serial port to be used for data transfer. You can specify the number of the serial port, such as COM2, or if the port is nonstandard, you can specify its address. If a COM port is specified and an LPT port is omitted, only COM ports are scanned. Normally all available ports are scanned.
/LPT[:][*n* | *address*]	Designates a parallel port to be used for data transfer. Either the number of the port is used, as in LPT1, or the port's address. If you specify an LPT port and omit a COM port, only the parallel ports are scanned.
/AUTO	Installs INTERLNK.EXE in memory only if the client can establish a connection with the server when the client starts up. By default the program is loaded, even if the client is not connected to a server.
/NOSCAN	Installs INTERLNK.EXE in memory, but prevents the program from establishing a connection between a client and a server. By default a client attempts to connect to a server.

/LOW	Loads INTERLNK.EXE into conventional memory. Normally the program loads into upper memory if there is space available.
/BAUD:rate	Sets the maximum rate for serial communications. You can set this rate at 9600, 19200, 38400, 57600, 115200. The default is 115200.
/V	Prevents conflicts with a computer's timer. You should use this switch if you have a serial connection between two computers and one of them stops running when you try to access a drive or printer.

Rules and Considerations

The InterLnk program normally loads all of its code into memory. If you are not using all of the functions of the program you can save memory by not loading those portions of the program that support the functions you do not want. For example, specifying /NOPRINTER causes the program to load without the ability to redirect printers. If you specify the /LPT switch or the /COM switch by themselves, only the program code required to support these functions is loaded.

If you use a serial mouse and you plan to redirect a COM port for data transfer, you should include the /COM switch and specify a COM port other than the one the mouse is using.

When you redirect printer ports and want to print from Microsoft Windows, use the Control Panel to assign the printer to either LPT1.DOS OR LPT2.DOS.

The following commands do not work when InterLnk is active:

CHKDSK	DEFRAG	DISKCOMP
DISKCOPY	FDISK	FORMAT
SYS	UNDELETE	UNFORMAT

Examples

To set up your system for connection on the parallel printer port, add the following line to your CONFIG.SYS file:

    DEVICE=c:\dos\INTERLNK.EXE /LPT1

Use the following line to keep the device driver from loading if the computer is not connected:

    DEVICE=c:\dos\INTERLNK.EXE /LPT1 /AUTO

If you do not want to redirect printers, you can minimize the size of the program in memory by using the following variation of the preceding command:

    DEVICE=c:\dos\INTERLNK.EXE /LPT1 /AUTO /NOPRINTER

See Also

INTERLNK, INTERSVR

INTERSVR

Purpose

The INTERSVR command starts the InterLnk server. An InterLnk server provides serial or parallel file transfer capability through redirected drives, and printing through redirected ports.

Type

External

Syntax

    INTERSVR [d:][/X=drive][/LPT[:][n¦address]]
    [/COM[:][n¦address]] [BAUD:rate][/B][/V]

Use the following syntax to copy files from one computer to another:

    INTERSVR /RCOPY

Switches

/X=*drive*
Specifies a drive that is not to be redirected. By default, all drives are redirected. You can use either /X to specify the drives to not be redirected, or the d: option to specify the drives that you want to be redirected.

/LPT[:][*n | address***]**
Specifies which parallel port to use. You can specify the parallel port either by number, such as LPT1, or you can use its address if it is nonstandard.

/COM[:][*n | address***]**
Specifies which serial port to use. You can specify the serial port either by number, such as COM1, or you can use its address if it is nonstandard.

/BAUD:*rate*
Sets the maximum rate for serial communications. You can set this rate at 9600; 19,200; 38,400; 57,600; 115,200. The default is 115,200.

/B
Displays InterLnk screen output in black-and-white.

/V
Prevents conflicts with a computer's timer. You should use this switch if you have a serial connection between two computers and one of them stops running when you try to access a drive or printer.

/RCOPY
Copies files from one computer to another. The computers must be connected by a 7-wire, null-modem cable on the serial ports, and the MODE command must be available on the computer where InterLnk is installed.

Rules and Considerations

When you connect two computers together, one becomes the *server* and the other the *client*. The server computer must be running the Intersvr program before connections can be made. Both computers must have the device driver INTERLNK.EXE installed.

Drives are redirected in the order that you specify. The first server drive is redirected to the first available client drive, the second server drive to the second client drive, and so on.

> **NOTE** *You cannot redirect network drives or CD-ROM drives.*

Examples

To redirect server drives C and D to the client computer, type the following command:

```
INTERSVR C: D:
```

In the preceding example, if the client computer has drives A, B, and C, the redirected drives appear on that system as drives D and E.

To redirect all server drives except drives A and B, and specify that the connection is on printer port LPT1, use the following command:

```
INTERSVR /X=a /X=b /LPT2
```

See Also

INTERLNK, INTERLNK.EXE

JOIN

Purpose

The JOIN command is used to logically connect a drive to a directory on a different drive.

Type

External

Syntax

    JOIN d1: *d2:path*

or

    JOIN d1: */D*

Switch

    /D   Cancels the JOIN command.

Rules and Considerations

When using JOIN, you specify the drive you want to connect to a directory with the *d1:* parameter. An empty directory must exist at *d2:path*. The empty directory you specify becomes joined to the directory, and the two then appear as the directory name. The drive that you specified to be joined will no longer be recognized by its original name.

The following commands do not work on drives affected by JOIN:

ASSIGN	BACKUP	CHKDSK
DISKCOMP	DISKCOPY	FDISK
FORMAT	LABEL	RECOVER
RESTORE	SYS	

Examples

To join the information on drive A with the D:\DOCS directory, type the following command:

    JOIN a: d:\docs

Use the following command to disconnect the drives:

    JOIN a: /D

KEYB

Purpose

The KEYB command is used to set up an alternate keyboard layout for use with a language other than US English.

Type

External

Syntax

KEYB *[code[,[page][,[d:\path]filename]]]*
[/E][/ID:country]

Switches

/E Specifies the use of an extended keyboard on 8086 computers.

/ID:country Determines the keyboard in use; used with keyboards that have more than one keyboard layout for a particular country. This includes France, Italy, and the United Kingdom, and must be a numeric value from the table below.

Rules and Considerations

The KEYB command works with a keyboard definition file. By default, KEYB uses the file KEYBOARD.SYS that is supplied with DOS. If you want to use a different keyboard definition file, you must specify its name and location.

You must have the code page that you specify installed on your system in order to use it.

Use Ctrl+Alt+F1 to switch between the default and alternate code page.

Values shown in the table may be used for code, page, and country:

Country or Language	Code	Page	Country
Belgium	be	850,437	
Brazil	br	850,437	
Canadian-French	cf	850,863	
Czechoslovakia	cz	852,850 (Czech)	
Czechoslovakia	sl	852,850 (Slovak)	
Denmark	dk	850,865	
Finland	su	850,437	
France	fr	850,437	120,189
Germany	gr	850,437	
Hungary	hu	852,850	
Italy	it	850,437	141,142
Latin America	la	850,437	
Netherlands	nl	850,437	
Norway	no	850,865	
Poland	pl	852,850	
Portugal	po	850,860	
Spain	sp	850,437	
Sweden	sv	850,437	
Switzerland	sf	850,437	
United Kingdom	uk	437,850	166,168
United States	us	437,850	
Yugoslavia	yu	852,850	

Examples

Type the following command to use a Canadian-French keyboard:

```
KEYB cf
```

In this example, KEYB uses the default support file, KEYBOARD.SYS, which is in the \DOS directory. The \DOS directory is on the system path.

See Also

CHCP, INSTALL, KEYBOARD.SYS

LABEL

Purpose

The LABEL command enables you to create, change, or delete a disk's volume label. The volume label is the name of the disk.

Type

External

Syntax

```
LABEL [d:][label name]
```

Rules and Considerations

You can use the LABEL command if you want to give your disk a name, change the name it now has, or delete the name.

You can use up to 11 characters in a label, except for the following:

```
*?\/.,;:+=[]()&^,."
```

If you do not specify a volume name you are prompted for one. If you press Enter when prompted for a name, DOS deletes the current volume name if one exists.

Examples

Use the following command to create a new volume label name for drive D of HARD_DISK_1:

```
LABEL d: hard_disk_1
```

To delete the existing label on drive A, use the following command:

```
LABEL A:
```

When you see the message

```
Delete current volume label?
```

Press **Y** to delete the name.

See Also

DIR, VOL

LASTDRIVE

Purpose

The LASTDRIVE command specifies the maximum number of drives that DOS is able to access.

Type

External

Syntax

```
LASTDRIVE=x
```

Rules and Considerations

NOTE: The following corrects an error in the Microsoft documentation.

The default value for LASTDRIVE is E: or the last drive specification in use on your system.

Memory is allocated for each drive that you specify; indicate only the minimum number of drives for your system.

Examples

Type the following command to enable DOS to recognize drives A through K:

```
LASTDRIVE=k
```

If lastdrive is typed from the command prompt, the last drive setting will be shown. For example, if you set LASTDRIVE=e in your AUTOEXEC.BAT file, then 'LASTDRIVE=E now' will appear on the screen when you type lastdrive at the DOS prompt.

LOADFIX

Purpose

The LOADFIX command is used to force programs to load above the first 64K of conventional memory.

Type

External

Syntax

```
LOADFIX [d:\path]filename [program parameters]
```

Rules and Considerations

Some programs do not function well when loaded in conventional memory below 64K, as they look for DOS, device drivers, or TSRs to be loaded there. If you have moved DOS into the HMA and device drivers and TSRs into upper memory blocks, you may see the message

```
Packed file corrupt
```

when your program loads. Use LOADFIX to load the program into a memory location at which it is more stable.

Indicate any parameters or switches that the program needs.

Refer to Chapter 10 for more information about memory areas.

Examples

To load the program PROGRAM.EXE into a memory location above 64K, add the following line to your AUTOEXEC.BAT file:

```
LOADFIX c:\progs\program.exe
```

LOADHIGH

Purpose

The LOADHIGH program is used to load terminate-stay-resident programs (TSRs) into upper memory blocks, leaving more space in conventional memory. Upper memory blocks must have been created with a memory manager before you can use this command. TSRs are loaded in AUTOEXEC.BAT. This command can be abbreviated LH.

Type

Internal

Syntax

```
LOADHIGH [d:\path]filename [program parameters]
```

or

```
LOADHIGH [/L:region1[,minsize][;region1[,minsize]...]
[/S]] [d:\path]filename [program parameters]
```

Switches

/L:region1,minsize;region1,minsize   Instructs DOS to load the specified program into a particular region in upper memory. By default, DOS loads program into the largest upper memory block first. The *minsize* parameter instructs DOS to set aside a minimum of memory for the program within the upper memory block.

/S Causes the program to shrink to its smallest size while loading. Normally this switch is used by the MEMMAKER program while it is analyzing programs and available memory to determine the best load order. This switch can be used only if you specify a minimum program size with /L.

Rules and Considerations

You can load programs high only on computers with 80386 or higher processors.

Before you can use this command to load programs into upper memory blocks, you must have the statement DOS=UMB in your CONFIG.SYS file. You also must have an upper memory manager, such as EMM386.EXE, installed.

If there is not enough memory available in the upper memory area, DOS will load your program in conventional memory; you are not advised that this is being done. To see where programs have loaded, use the MEM/C command.

Refer to Chapter 11 for more information about memory managers.

Examples

Add the following command to your AUTOEXEC.BAT file to load the program DOSKEY into an upper memory block:

```
LOADHIGH c:\dos\doskey
```

See Also

DEVICEHIGH, DOS, EMM386, HIMEM.SYS, MEM

MEM

Purpose

The MEM command is used to display information about your computer's memory. Use MEM to see how memory is allocated, what memory areas are free, and what programs are currently loaded in memory.

Type

External

Syntax

MEM [/CLASSIFY][/DEBUG][/FREE][/MODULEmodulename][/PAGE]

Switches

/CLASSIFY   Displays the programs that are currently loaded in memory, showing how much conventional and upper memory each program occupies. MEM/CLASSIFY also summarizes overall memory use for the system. Can be abbreviated /C.

/DEBUG   Lists the programs and internal drivers that are currently loaded in memory. This is a much more detailed listing than is provided with the /C switch; it displays a program's location and size in memory. Can be abbreviated /D.

/FREE   Lists the free areas in conventional and upper memory. This option shows the location and size of each free area of conventional memory, and shows the largest free upper memory block in each region of upper memory. Can be abbreviated /F.

/MODULE — Shows how a program module you specify with *modulename* is currently using memory. You can see which area(s) of memory the program is using and the size of each area. Can be abbreviated /M.

/PAGE — Pauses the display after each screen of output, making it easier to read. Can be abbreviated /P.

Rules and Considerations

The MEM command can only display information about expanded memory if it meets the LIM EMS 4.0 standard. MEM can only display information about the upper memory area if a UMB provider such as EMM386.EXE is installed and DOS is managing the upper memory area (as indicated by the command DOS=UMB in CONFIG.SYS).

Examples

Use the following command to display the memory usage of your system, with the memory areas classified:

```
MEM /c
```

The following command displays the memory usage in more detail. Use the /P switch to pause the display:

```
MEM /d /p
```

See Also

CHKDSK, MEMMAKER

MEMMAKER

Purpose

The MEMMAKER command is used to optimize the memory of your system. Optimizing is a process of loading and reloading TSRs and device drivers in order to determine the best fit in upper memory areas.

Type

External

Syntax

    MEMMAKER [/BATCH][/SWAP:drive][/UNDO][/W:n,m][/B]

Switches

/BATCH   Runs the MEMMAKER program in batch mode, and uses all program defaults.

/SWAP:drive   Designates the drive that was your original drive. Use this switch if you are using a disk compression program such as Stac 2.0, and that program has swapped your drive names. You do not need this switch if you used DoubleSpace or Stacker 2.0 disk-compression programs.

/UNDO   Causes MEMMAKER to undo the most recent changes to your CONFIG.SYS and AUTOEXEC.BAT files. Use this switch if you are not satisfied with the way that MEMMAKER ordered your TSRs and device drivers in memory.

/W:n,m   Sets aside an amount of upper memory space for Windows translation buffers. Windows needs two memory areas, designated as *n* and *m*. By default MEMMAKER sets aside 12K for each area. If you do not use Windows, you can specify /W:0,0 and these areas will not be set aside.

/B   Displays MEMMAKER in black and white.

Rules and Considerations

Refer to Chapter 12 for more information about MEMMAKER.

Examples

Type the following command to start the MEMMAKER program and have it determine the best load order for TSRs and device drivers:

    MEMMAKER

Use the following command to revert to the previous settings, if you are unsatisfied with your system's performance after optimization:

    MEMMAKER /undo

See Also

DEVICEHIGH, LOADHIGH, MEM

MENUCOLOR

Purpose

The MENUCOLOR command defines the text and background colors for a startup menu. This command is used in a menu block within your CONFIG.SYS file.

Type

Config

Syntax

    MENUCOLOR=x[,y]

Rules and Considerations

DOS 6 enables you to create a startup menu for your system, in which you list choices of hardware configurations. Each hardware configuration is called a *configuration block*. The MENUCOLOR command is one of several commands that are used when working with the startup menu.

The *x* value specifies the color of the menu text. The *y* value specifies the color of the screen background. You can select the text and background colors from these values:

0	Black
1	Blue
2	Green
3	Cyan
4	Red
5	Magenta
6	Brown
7	White
8	Gray
9	Bright blue
10	Bright green
11	Bright cyan
12	Bright red
13	Bright magenta
14	Yellow
15	Bright white

Refer to Chapter 17 for more information about using configuration menus.

Examples

Use the following command to set your menu colors for cyan text on a gray background:

```
MENUCOLOR 3,8
```

See Also

INCLUDE, MENUDEFAULT, MENUITEM, NUMLOCK, SUBMENU

MENUDEFAULT

Purpose

The MENUDEFAULT command is used in CONFIG.SYS to specify the default configuration block. It also specifies a timeout value, which tells DOS how long to wait before continuing to boot the PC with the default configuration block.

Type

Config

Syntax

```
MENUDEFAULT=blockname[,timeout]
```

Rules and Considerations

You can specify one of the configuration blocks within a startup menu to be the default block. When the system starts and the startup menu is displayed, the default startup option is highlighted. You can specify an amount of time that DOS waits before starting the system using the default configuration (providing no other option was selected).

The timeout value can be from 0 to 90 seconds. If 0 seconds is specified, the system does not wait for a selection to be made and immediately boots with the default configuration.

Examples

Three menu items are contained in the following example. The menu item "basic" is defined as the default, and it loads unless another selection is made within 10 seconds:

```
[menu]
menuitem basic,Basic configuration
menuitem memmgt,Basic with memory management
menuitem network,Memory management and network
menudefault=basic,10
```

See Also

INCLUDE, MENUCOLOR, MENUITEM, NUMLOCK, SUBMENU

MENUITEM

Purpose

The MENUITEM command is used in CONFIG.SYS to identify items on the startup menu.

Type

Config

Syntax

```
MENUITEM=blockname[,text]
```

Rules and Considerations

The startup menu is a list of possible choices that appears when you start your computer. Each item on the list corresponds to a possible hardware and software configuration. The startup menu contains menu configuration blocks, which describe the commands to be carried out if that selection is made.

The *blockname* is used to describe the configuration block, which is described separately in CONFIG.SYS. You can associate *text* with the block name, and if you do, the text is displayed in the startup menu (otherwise the block name is displayed).

Each block in a menu must begin with the block name in square brackets. Also, the menu must start with the word "menu" in square brackets.

Refer to Chapter 17 for more information about configuration menus.

Examples

The following menu defines a startup menu with three options, and specifies menu text for each option:

```
[menu]
menuitem basic,Basic configuration
menuitem memmgt,Basic with memory management
menuitem network,Memory management and network
```

When this system starts up, the following menu is displayed:

```
MS-DOS 6 Startup Menu
=========================
1. Basic configuration
2. Basic with memory management
3. Memory management and network
```

See Also

INCLUDE, MENUCOLOR, MENUDEFAULT, NUMLOCK, SUBMENU

MKDIR

Purpose

The MKDIR command is used to create a directory or subdirectory.

Type

Internal

Syntax

MKDIR *[d:]path*

Rules and Considerations

DOS can support a multilevel directory structure, often referred to as a *tree* structure. The top level of the structure is called the *root*; each drive has a root directory and can contain many levels of subdirectories.

Each subdirectory is a branch of a directory above it, and the branches or levels are separated with backslash (\) characters. The maximum length of any single directory path, from the root to the final subdirectory, cannot exceed 63 characters in length.

To create a directory within the current directory, type **MD** and the directory name. Do not use the backslash character unless you want to create a subdirectory of the root directory and you are not in that directory.

Examples

If you are in the root directory of drive C, you can make a directory called BUDGETS with this command:

    MD BUDGETS

Use the following variation to make two subdirectories of the BUDGETS directory from the root directory of drive C:

    MD BUDGETS\1992
    MD BUDGETS\1993

See Also

CHDR (CD), DIR, RMDR (RD), TREE

MODE

Purpose

The MODE command is used to configure devices that are attached to your system. There are many versions of MODE; each is described separately.

Type

External

Syntax

MODE `[device][/STATUS]`

Switches

device Specifies the name of the device you want information about.

/STATUS Displays information about all devices attached to your system.

Rules and Considerations

You can use the /STATUS option to view the status of a particular device, or all devices attached to your system. This is the same as typing **MODE** without any parameters.

Examples

To display the configuration and status of attached devices, type the following command:

MODE

See Also

MODE (CONFIGURE PRINTER), MODE (CONFIGURE SERIAL PORT),

MODE (REDIRECT PRINTING), MODE (SET DEVICE CODE PAGE),

MODE (SET DISPLAY MODE), MODE (SET TYPEMATIC RATE)

MODE (CONFIGURE PRINTER)

Purpose

This version of the MODE command is used to configure a parallel printer that is attached to your system.

Type

External

Syntax

        `MODE LPTn[:][c][,[l]][,r]`

or

        `MODE LPTn[:][COLS=c][LINES=l][RETRY=R]`

Rules and Considerations

DOS can support up to three parallel printers on a system. They are known as LPT1, LPT2, and LPT3. LPT1, the first parallel port, is often referred to as PRN.

You can specify the number of characters per line your printer is capable of printing with the COLS parameter. The default is 80. The number of lines per inch is specified with the LINES parameter; the default is 6.

The RETRY parameter specifies what action DOS is to take in the event the printer times out. That is, DOS is not able to communicate with the printer for some reason (for example, it may be offline or busy). The following actions may be specified:

B	Return "busy" from a status check of a busy port
E	Return "error" from a status check of a busy port
P	Continue retrying until printer accepts input
R	Return "ready" from a status check of a busy port
N	Take no action. This is the default.

Do not use the RETRY parameter if you are using MODE on a network printer.

Examples

Use the following command to configure a printer attached to LPT1 to use eight lines per inch:

```
MODE LPT1:80,8
```

It is not necessary to specify every parameter in a MODE statement. If, however, you want to specify a number of lines per inch but want to use the default of 80 columns, you can modify the preceding command as follows:

```
MODE LPT1:,8
```

In the preceding example, the comma acts as a placeholder for the COLS parameter.

Type the following command to use defaults for COLS and LINES and cause the printer to retry indefinitely:

```
MODE LPT1:,,p
```

MODE (CONFIGURE SERIAL PRINTER)

Purpose

This version of the MODE command is used to set up communication parameters for a serial printer.

Type

External

Syntax

```
MODE COMn[:][b[,p[,d[,s[,r]]]]]
```

or

```
MODE COMn[:][BAUD=b][PARITY=p][DATA=d][STOP=s][RETRY=r]
```

Rules and Considerations

DOS supports up to four serial ports, known as COM1, COM2, COM3 and COM4.

When you use a serial printer, you must instruct DOS about the printer's communication parameters. You need to refer to your printer's user manual to determine the parameters it uses, and then set the same parameters with the MODE command.

The RETRY parameter specifies what action DOS is to take in the event the printer times out. That is, DOS is not able to communicate with the printer for some reason (for example, it may be offline or busy). The following actions may be specified:

- B   Return "busy" from a status check of a busy port
- E   Return "error" from a status check of a busy port
- P   Continue retrying until printer accepts input
- R   Return "ready" from a status check of a busy port
- N   Take no action. This is the default.

Refer to Chapter 14 for more information about using serial printers.

Examples

If your serial printer is set for 2400 baud, no parity, 8 data bits, and 1 stop bit, type the following command to set the parameters for COM1:

```
MODE COM1:2400,n,8,1
```

MODE (REDIRECT PRINTING)

Purpose

This version of the MODE command is used to redirect output from a parallel port to a serial port on your computer.

Type

External

Syntax

    MODE LPTn[:]=COM1[:]

Rules and Considerations

You can use this command to redirect the output from any one of the three parallel ports that DOS supports, to any one of the four serial ports. Use this command when you have a printer attached to your serial port, but your applications are expecting to print to a parallel port.

> **NOTE** *You must set up the communications parameters for the serial port before output is redirected.*

Examples

Use the following commands to set up the first serial port on your system, and to redirect output from the first parallel port:

    MODE COM1:2400,n,8,1
    MODE LPT1:=COM1

MODE (SET DEVICE CODE PAGE)

Purpose

This version of the MODE command is used to prepare, select, refresh, or display a character set for the device that you specify.

Type

External

MODE (SET DEVICE CODE PAGE)

Syntax

    MODE device CODEPAGE PREPARE=((yyy[...])[d:path]filename)
    MODE device CODEPAGE SELECT=yyy
    MODE device CODEPAGE REFRESH
    MODE device CODEPAGE [/STATUS]

Switch

/STATUS   Displays the numbers of the current character sets that are prepared or selected for the specified device.

Rules and Considerations

In the previous syntax, *device* can be CON, LPT1, LPT2, LPT3, and PRN. CON refers to console—the screen and keyboard.

CODEPAGE PREPARE is used to prepare a character set for use with a device. You must prepare a character set before you can use it. The number of the code page is *yyy*, and the following values are valid code pages:

437	United States
850	Multilingual (Latin I)
852	Slavic (Latin II)
860	Portuguese
863	Canadian-French
865	Nordic

The *[d:path]file name* specifies the name of the code page information file the DOS uses to prepare a code page. DOS includes five code page information files: EGA.CPI, 4201.CPI, 4208.CPI, 5202.CPI, and LCD.CPI.

After a code page is prepared, you select it with the CODEPAGE SELECT command. If a code page is lost as a result of a hardware error, it can be "REFRESHed."

Examples

Use the following command to prepare the Canadian-French character set for use with your keyboard and monitor:

```
MODE con CODEPAGE PREPARE=(863)
```

To use the Canadian-French character set, select it with the following command:

```
MODE con CODEPAGE SELECT=863
```

See Also

CHCP, NLSFUNC

MODE (SET DISPLAY MODE)

Purpose

This version of the MODE command is used to select the active display adapter and its display mode, or to reconfigure the active display adapter. The device driver ANSI.SYS must be installed before you can use this MODE command.

Type

External

Syntax

```
MODE [display adapter][,shift[,T]]
MODE [display adapter][,n]
MODE CON[:][COLS=c][LINES=n]
```

Rules and Considerations

You can use any of the following to describe the display adapter:

40 or 80   Indicates the number of characters per line.

BW40 or BW80	Indicates a color graphics adapter with the color turned off, and specifies the number of characters per line.
CO40 or CO80	Specifies a color monitor with color enabled, and specifies the number of characters per line.
MONO	Specifies a monochrome display adapter with 80 characters per line.
SHIFT	Specifies whether to shift the display to the left or to the right. Use L for left and R for right.

You can use the T option to display a test pattern on your display if you need to align it.

Use the COLS and LINES parameters to specify the number of columns and rows that can be displayed. Columns can be 40 or 80, and lines can be 25, 43, or 50.

Examples

Type the following command to set your display for 50 lines:

```
MODE co80,50
```

MODE (SET TYPEMATIC RATE)

Purpose

This version of the MODE command is used to set the rate at which DOS repeats a character when you hold down a key. Using this command can speed up your keyboard.

Type

External

Syntax

```
MODE CON[:] [RATE=x DELAY=y]
```

Rules and Considerations

This command can be used to speed up your keyboard. You first specify the rate at which DOS repeats a key, using a value from 1 to 32. A value of 1 is equal to 2 characters per second, while a value of 32 is equal to 30 characters per second.

The delay value specifies the amount of time that DOS must wait before repeating a key. You can specify 1, 2, 3, or 4 to represent 0.25, 0.50, 0.75, and 1 second.

> **NOTE** You must use RATE and DELAY together.

Examples

Use the following command to speed up your keyboard's typematic rate:

```
MODE con: delay=1 rate=32
```

MORE

Purpose

The MORE command displays output one screen at a time.

Type

External

Syntax

    MORE<*[d:\path]filename*

or

    command-name ¦ **MORE**

Rules and Considerations

Use the MORE command to view files or directories one screen at a time. After one screen of text displays, you see the following:

```
-- More --
```

Press any key to continue with another screen, or press Ctrl+Break to exit from the display mode.

You can use the redirection symbol (<) to display a file on the screen. When using the pipe (¦), you can use commands such as DIR, SORT, and TYPE.

Examples

Use the following command to display a long text file called LETTER.TXT:

```
MORE<d:\docs\letter.txt
```

The following command has the same function:

```
TYPE d:\docs\letter.txt¦MORE
```

See Also

DIR, SORT, TYPE

MOVE

Purpose

The MOVE command is used to move one or more files from one location to another. MOVE also can be used to rename directories.

6.2 Beginning with version 6.2, MOVE asks for confirmation before overwriting an existing file of the same name.

Type

Internal

Syntax

> **MOVE** *[d:\path]sourcefilename [[d:\path]filename[...]] destination*

Switches

/Y   Instructs MOVE to replace any existing files without prompting you for confirmation.

/-Y   Instructs MOVE to prompt you for confirmation when replacing an existing file. Used to override the SET COPYCMD=/Y environment variable.

Rules and Considerations

You must specify both the source and destination of files to be moved. Files can be moved individually, in groups using wild-card characters (? and *), and in groups by naming several files as the source. If you move groups of files, you cannot rename the files. If a file exists at the destination with the same name as one being moved there, the destination file is overwritten.

The MOVE command can be used to rename a directory. In this case, the original directory name is the source, and the new directory name is the destination. The new directory will occupy the same place in the directory tree as it did before; you cannot move the location of the directory.

Examples

Type the following command to move the file LETTER.TXT from D:\DOCS to D:\BUDGETS:

> **MOVE d:\docs\letter.txt d:\budget**

To move two unrelated files called SMITHLTR.TXT and COMEMO.DOC from D:\DOCS to D:\BUDGETS, type the following command:

```
MOVE d:\docs\smithltr.txt d:\docs\comemo.doc d:\budgets
```

The following command is used to move the file LETTER.TXT, and rename it to JONESLTR.TXT:

```
MOVE d:\docs\letter.txt d:\budgets\jonesltr.txt
```

Use the following command to change the name of the directory D:\BUDGETS\1992 to D:\BUDGETS\1993:

```
MOVE d:\budgets\1992 d:\budgets\1993
```

See Also

COPY, TREE

MSAV

Purpose

The MSAV command is used to scan your system for viruses, and remove them.

Type

External

Syntax

```
MSAV [[d:][/S¦/C][/R][/A¦/L][/N][/P][/F][/VIDEO]
```

Switches

/S   Scans the drive(s) you specified with *d:* and the files on those drives, but does not remove any viruses it finds. This is the default.

/C   Scans the drive(s) you specified and removes any viruses it finds.

/R   Creates a report called MSAV.RPT that lists information about the files checked and viruses found.

Command Reference

/A	Scans all drives except drive A and drive B.
/L	Scans all drives except network drives.
/N	Does not display information on-screen as MSAV scans disks, but displays the report MSAV.TXT when finished. Returns an error code of 86 if viruses are found.
/P	Displays a command-line interface.
/F	Does not display the names of files that have been scanned. Use this switch only with /N or /P.
/VIDEO	Starts MSAV in one of the following modes:
25	Displays 25 lines on the screen. This is the default.
28	Displays 28 lines. Use with VGA adapters only.
43	Displays 43 lines. Use with EGA or VGA adapters only.
50	Displays 50 lines. Use with VGA adapters only.
60	Displays 60 lines. Use with Video 7 adapters only.
IN	Runs MSAV in color, even if a color adapter is not detected.
BW	Runs MSAV in black and white.
MONO	Runs MSAV in monochrome mode.
LCD	Runs MSAV using an LCD color scheme.
FF	Uses the screen's fastest update mode.
BF	Uses the computer's BIOS to display video.
NF	Disables the use of alternate fonts.
BT	Enables the use of a graphics mouse in Windows.
/NGM	Runs MSAV with the default mouse character instead of a graphics character.
/LE	Exchanges left and right mouse buttons.
/IM	Disables the mouse.
/PS2	Resets the mouse if it disappears or locks up.

Rules and Considerations

The Microsoft Anti-Virus program is used to scan your system for viruses. You can instruct the program to remove any virus that it finds, and to create reports about the files it scanned and viruses it found, if any.

You can use the MSAV command with the /N switch in a batch file. When you specify this switch, MSAV does not report the results of the scan on your screen, but instead places the results in a file called MSAV.TXT. If viruses are found, MSAV returns an error code of 86, which you can test for in a batch file. For example, if an error code of 86 is returned from MSAV, you might display a message that viruses were found.

Examples

Use the following command to scan all drives except A and B, and to place the results in a file called MSAV.TXT:

```
MSAV /A /N
```

The following command is used to scan all drives, remove any viruses it finds, and display the results on-screen in using 50 lines:

```
MSAV /C /50
```

MSBACKUP

Purpose

The MSBACKUP command is used to back up one or more files from your hard disk. You can specify that only modified files be backed up, you can schedule backups to occur automatically, and you can restore files with the MSBACKUP command.

Type

External

Syntax

```
MSBACKUP [setup file][/BW][/LCD][/MDA]
```

Switches

/BW	Starts MSBACKUP using a black and white color scheme.
/LCD	Used for computers with LCD displays.
/MDA	Starts MSBACKUP in monochrome mode.

Rules and Considerations

The first time you run the MSBACKUP program you must create a setup file. This file contains your preferences for using the backup program. You can create several preference files, and use any one you want when you run the program. For example, you might create a preference file for a full backup, and another for a weekly backup in which only new or changed files are backed up.

When you run the MSBACKUP program, it creates a backup catalog that contains information about the files you backed up. If you need to restore any files, you can load the backup catalog and select the files you need to restore. The backup catalog contains the following information:

- ✔ Structure of backed-up disk
- ✔ Names, sizes, and attributes of selected files and directories
- ✔ Total number of files
- ✔ Total size of the backup
- ✔ Name of the setup file that was used
- ✔ Date the backup was made

Each backup catalog name is unique, and can be used to identify the backup set that you made. For example, suppose you made a full backup of drives C and D on January 14, 1993. The backup catalog that is created is called CD30114A.FUL. You can decode the backup catalog name as follows:

Character	Meaning
C	The first drive that was backed up
D	The last drive that was backed up

Character	Meaning
3	The last digit of the year the backup was made
01	The month the backup was made
14	The date the backup was made
A	Indicates the first in a possible series of backups made on the same date
.FUL	Indicates a full backup. Other options are INC for incremental, and DIF for differential

Examples

The following command is used to start the MSBACKUP program and create a setup file:

    MSBACKUP

Use the following command with the setup file MONTHLY.SET that defines a monthly backup of new or changed files:

    MSBACKUP monthly

MSD

Purpose

The MSD command is used to run Microsoft System Diagnostics to obtain detailed technical information about your computer.

Type

External

Syntax

    MSD [/B][/I]

or

    MSD [/I][/F[d:\path]filename][/P[d:\path]filename]
    [/S[d:\path]filename]

Switches

/B	Displays in black and white on a color display.
/I	Instructs MSD to not initially detect hardware. You can use this switch if MSD is not working properly.
/F[d:\path]filename	Prompts you for information about yourself, and writes a complete report including that information with a name that you specify. This information may be useful if you need to send this report to a software vendor.
/P[d:\path]filename	Creates a complete MSD report, but does not prompt you for personal information.
/S[d:\path]filename	Creates a summary MSD report, and does not prompt you for personal information.

Rules and Considerations

In the preceding syntax, the first statement is used to work with MSD through an interactive interface. The second statement directs MSD to test your system and create a detailed or summary report. Either method reports information about your system's model and processor, memory, video type, version of DOS, mouse, other adapters, disk drives, LPT ports, COM ports, IRQ status, TSRs in memory, and device drivers in use.

Examples

Use the following command to start the program and work through menus to get information about your computer:

   MSD

To create a detailed report called MYPC.TXT, that included your name, company, and phone number, type the following command:

```
MSD /F d:\msd\mypc.txt
```

NLSFUNC

Purpose

The NLSFUNC command loads country-specific information for national language support. You can use this program from the command prompt, or from within CONFIG.SYS if you are using country-specific information or code-page switching.

Type

External, Config

Syntax

    NLSFUNC *[[d:\path]filename]*

or

    INSTALL=*[d:\path]*NLSFUNC.EXE *[country filename]*

Rules and Considerations

The location and name of the file used in the first syntax above is determined by the COUNTRY setting in your CONFIG.SYS file. If you do not specify a file name, DOS uses the file COUNTRY.SYS.

If you install the NLSFUNC command from CONFIG.SYS, you must include the drive and directory where the program is located, as there is no path established at that time.

Examples

Use the following command to load the program with the default country information found in COUNTRY.SYS:

    NLSFUNC

See Also

    CHCP, COUNTRY, MODE (SET DEVICE CODE PAGE)

NUMLOCK

Purpose

The NUMLOCK command is used to specify whether the NUMLOCK key is initially set to ON or OFF. This command can be used either within a menu block in CONFIG.SYS or as a separate CONFIG.SYS command.

Type

Config

Syntax

NUMLOCK=[ON¦OFF]

Rules and Considerations

This command determines the initial setting for the NUMLOCK key when your computer starts up.

Examples

To set the NUMLOCK key off when your computer starts up, either add the line NUMLOCK=OFF to the menu block in CONFIG.SYS, as follows:

```
[menu]
menuitem basic,Basic configuration
menuitem memmgt,Basic with memory management
menuitem network,Memory management and network
numlock=off
```

or add

```
numlock=off
```

as a separate line anywhere in CONFIG.SYS.

You can also add `numlock=off` as a separate line, anywhere in CONFIG.SYS.

See Also

INCLUDE, MENUDEFAULT, MENUITEM

PATH

Purpose

The PATH command is used to designate a search path for DOS. DOS uses the search path to locate and start executable files in the directories that you specify.

Type

Internal

Syntax

    PATH *[[d:\path][;....]]*

or

    PATH ;

Rules and Considerations

The PATH command is typically included in your AUTOEXEC.BAT file to indicate which directories DOS is to search for executable files. By default, DOS only searches the current directory.

You can use the PATH command with no parameters to view the current search path. To clear the search path, type **PATH ;**.

The search path can be a maximum of 127 characters in length. Separate names of directories with the semicolon (;) character.

Examples

The following command enables DOS to search the directories C:\DOS, C:\UTILS, D:\UTILS, and C:\WINDOWS for executable files:

    PATH c:\dos;c:\utils;d:\utils;c:\windows

See Also

    DIR, TREE

PAUSE

Purpose

The PAUSE command is used to suspend processing in a batch program. A message is displayed instructing the user to continue.

Type

Batch

Syntax

    PAUSE [text]

Rules and Considerations

DOS responds to the PAUSE command by displaying the following message:

```
Press any key to continue ...
```

You can continue processing the batch file by pressing any key, or break out of the batch file by pressing Ctrl+Break.

You can customize the message that is displayed when the batch file suspends by including a string of text after the word PAUSE. The test is displayed on the screen followed by the default message.

Examples

Use the following form of the command to customize the message that is displayed by PAUSE:

    PAUSE Your customized message

When DOS encounters this pause command in a batch file, the following lines are displayed on-screen:

```
Your customized message
Press any key to continue ...
```

See Also

    ECHO

POWER

Purpose

The POWER command is used to reduce power consumption on a computer when applications and devices are not busy. This command is useful for conserving battery power on laptop computers.

Type

External

Syntax

```
POWER [ADV[:MAX¦REG¦MIN]¦STD¦OFF]
```

Rules and Considerations

The device driver POWER.EXE must be installed in your CONFIG.SYS file before you can use this command.

You can control the amount of power conservation by using the following parameters:

MAX	Maximum power conservation.
REG	Balances power conservation with system performance.
MIN	Used if MAX or REG do not conserve power adequately.

If your computer supports the Advanced Power Management specification, you can use the STD parameter to conserve power using the power-management features of your computer's hardware.

Examples

Use the following command to display the current power setting:

```
POWER
```

The command that follows is used to activate maximum power conservation:

```
POWER adv:max
```

See Also

POWER.EXE

POWER.EXE

Purpose

The POWER.EXE device driver is used to reduce power consumption on your computer when applications and devices are not busy. You must install this device driver in CONFIG.SYS.

Type

Device driver

Syntax

```
DEVICE=[d:\path]POWER.EXE [ADV[:MAX|REG|MIN]|STD|OFF][/
LOW]
```

Switch

/LOW Loads the device driver into conventional memory. By default this device driver loads into an upper memory block.

Rules and Considerations

You can control the amount of power conservation by using the following parameters:

MAX Maximum power conservation.

REG Balances power conservation with system performance.

MIN Used if MAX or REG do not conserve power adequately.

If your computer supports the Advanced Power Management specification, you can use the STD parameter to conserve power using the power-management features of your computer's hardware.

Examples

Add the following line to your CONFIG.SYS file to activate power management on your system, using all defaults:

```
DEVICE=c:\dos\power.exe
```

See Also

POWER

PRINT

Purpose

The PRINT command is used to print one or more files to the printer. Files are printed in the background while you continue to use your computer.

Type

External

Syntax

```
PRINT [/D:device][/B:size][/U:ticks][/M:ticks][/S:ticks]
[/Q:qsize][/T][[d:\path]filename[...]][/C][/P]
```

Switches

/D:device   Specifies the name of the print device. The print device can be PRN, LPT1, LPT2, LPT3, COM1, COM2, COM3, or COM4. The default is PRN. PRN and LPT1 are equivalent names.

/B:size   Determines the size of the internal print buffer in bytes. The default print buffer is 512 bytes in size.

/U:*ticks*	Specifies the maximum number of CPU clock ticks that the PRINT command waits for a printer to be available. If a printer is not available within the designated time, the job does not print. The acceptable value of ticks is between 1 and 255.
/M:*ticks*	Specifies the number of CPU clock ticks that PRINT can take to print a character on the printer. The default value is 2. If a character prints too slowly, DOS may display an error. The acceptable value of ticks is between 1 and 255.
/S:*ticks*	Specifies the number of CPU clock ticks that the PRINT scheduler allocates for background printing. The default is 8. Increasing this number gives greater priority to printing in the background, but may slow down applications that are running. The acceptable value of ticks is between 1 and 255.
/Q:*size*	Indicates the number of files that can be in the print queue. You can specify from 4 to 32 files; the default is 10.
/T	Removes all files from the print queue.
/C	Removes the files named from the print queue.
/P	Adds files to the print queue.

Rules and Considerations

The switches /D, /B, /U, /M, /S, and /Q can be used only the first time you use the PRINT command.

Examples

Use the following command to print the file LETTER.TXT:

```
PRINT letter.txt
```

The first time you use the PRINT command and you have not specified a device to print to, you see the following message:

```
Name of list device [PRN]:
```

Press Enter if the printer you want to use is attached to the port LPT1, which is the same as the default PRN.

The following command is used to list the files in the print queue:

```
PRINT
```

If you want to delete the file BUDGET.TXT from the print queue, type the following command:

```
PRINT budget.txt /c
```

PROMPT

Purpose

The PROMPT command is used to change the appearance of the command prompt.

Type

Internal

Syntax

```
PROMPT [text]
```

Rules and Considerations

The default prompt that DOS displays consists of the drive letter name and the greater-than sign. You can customize the appearance of the prompt by using any of the following special characters:

$q	= (equal sign)
$$	$ (dollar sign)
$t	Time

$d	Date
$p	Path, including drive
$v	DOS version number
$n	Drive only
$g	> (greater than sign)
$l	< (less than sign)
$b	¦ (pipe character)
$_	Carriage return/line feed
$e	ASCII escape character
$h	Backspace

If you have the device driver ANSI.SYS installed in your CONFIG.SYS file, you can add color to your prompt or place the cursor anywhere on the screen that you want. Refer to Chapter 14 for more information about customizing the prompt in this way.

Examples

Use the following command to display the drive name, path, and greater than sign:

`PROMPT $p$g`

The following command is used to add the string "Enter a response" to the above prompt:

`PROMPT Enter a response $p$g`

Type the following command to display the date and time as part of the prompt, each on a separate line:

`PROMPT $d$_$t$p$g`

See Also

ANSI.SYS, DATE, TIME, VER

QBASIC

Purpose

The QBASIC command is used to start the DOS Basic program. QBasic is a complete BASIC programming environment.

Type

External

Syntax

`QBASIC [/B][/EDITOR][/G][/H][/MBF] [/NOHI][[/RUN[d:\path]filename]`

Switches

/B	Displays the program in black and white on a color monitor.
/EDITOR	Starts the DOS Editor.
/G	Enables the fastest update of a CGA monitor.
/H	Displays the maximum number of lines for your display.
/MBF	Converts the built-in functions MKS$, MKD$, CVS, and CVD to MKSMBF$, MKDMBF$, CVSMBF, and CVDMBF, respectively.
/NOHI	Enables the use of a monitor that does not support high-intensity video.
/RUN	Runs the program you name.

Rules and Considerations

You must have the file QBASIC.EXE installed on your system before you can use the DOS Editor, EDIT.COM.

> *Do not use the /NOHI switch on Compaq laptop computers.*

Examples

Use the following command to start the Basic environment:

```
QBASIC
```

To use QBasic to run the program GORILLA.BAS, type the following command:

```
QBASIC /run gorilla.bas
```

See Also

EDIT

RAMDRIVE.SYS

Purpose

The RAMDRIVE device driver takes part of your system memory and uses it as if it were a hard disk drive. While a RAM drive appears to you as a normal drive, it is much faster since it is working in your system's RAM memory. This command is used in CONFIG.SYS.

Type

Device driver

Syntax

```
DEVICE=[d:\path]RAMDRIVE.SYS [disksize sectorsize
[NumEntries]] [/E¦/A]
```

Switches

/E   Creates the RAM drive in extended memory. Your system must be configured to use extended memory and you must have an extended memory manager (such as HIMEM.SYS) in place before using this command.

/A   Creates the RAM drive in expanded memory. Your system must be configured to use expanded memory and you must have an expanded memory manager (such as EMM386.EXE) in place before using this command.

Rules and Considerations

If you do not specify a memory area for the RAM drive, it is created in conventional memory. It is strongly recommended that you enable the program to use another memory area for the RAM drive.

You specify the size of the RAM drive in kilobytes using the *disksize* parameter. For example, if you wanted to create a 1024K RAM drive, simply add the number 1024 after the command. The maximum size of the RAM drive is 32,767K or the limit of your available system memory. You also can specify a sector size for the RAM drive; the default sector size is 512 bytes.

The *NumEntries* parameter is used to limit the number of files and directories that can be created in the RAM drive's root directory. If you do not indicate a limit, you can create up to 64 entries in the root directory.

Examples

Add the following line to your CONFIG.SYS file to create a RAM drive in extended memory of 1024K:

```
DEVICE=c:\dos\ramdrive.sys 1024 /e
```

See Also

EMM386.EXE, HIMEM.SYS

REM

Purpose

The REM command is used to include comments in batch files. When a batch file is executed, any line beginning with the word REM is ignored by the command processor.

Type

Internal

Syntax

```
REM [comment]
```

Rules and Considerations

You can include comments in your batch files by beginning each comment line with the word REM. If you include the command ECHO OFF in your batch file, the comments will not be displayed on the screen.

Examples

Add lines similar to the following generic remarks to a batch file:

```
REM This is a line of comment
REM Can be used to temporarily disable batch commands
```

See Also

ECHO

RENAME or REN

Purpose

The RENAME command is used to change the name of a file.

Type

Internal

Syntax

`RENAME [d:\path]file1 file2`

Rules and Considerations

You cannot use the RENAME command across directories. That is, the file that you want to rename cannot be moved to another directory at this time.

You can use wild card characters (? and *) with this command, if the files have the same extension, name, or directory.

If a file already exists called file2, you see the following message:

`Duplicate file name or file not found`

Examples

Type the following command to rename the file LETTER.TXT to LETTER.DOC:

`RENAME letter.txt letter.doc`

The following command is used to rename all files in the directory D:\DOCS that have a .TXT extension to files that have a .DOC extension:

`RENAME d:\docs\*.txt *.doc`

See Also

COPY, MOVE

REPLACE

Purpose

The REPLACE command replaces files on one drive with files of the same name on another drive. REPLACE also can be used to add files to the destination drive or directory.

Type

External

Syntax

    REPLACE *[d1:\path]filename [d2:\path][/A][/P][/R][/W]*

or

    REPLACE *[d1:\path]filename [d2:\path][/P][/R][/S][/W][/U]*

Switches

/A   Adds new files to the destination directory instead of replacing files. This switch cannot be used with /S or /U.

/P   Prompts you for confirmation before replacing files.

/R   Replaces read-only files.

/S   Searches all subdirectories and replaces matching files.

/W   Waits for you to insert a disk before beginning to search for source files.

/U   Replaces only those files on the destination directory that are older than those in the source directory.

Rules and Considerations

The REPLACE command is a good way to keep files current on your disk. For example, you can use REPLACE to move new files onto floppy disks, overwriting any older files whose names match.

Wild-card characters (? and *) can be used with REPLACE.

Examples

To replace an old version of the file LETTER.TXT on drive A with a newer version from drive D, type the following command:

```
REPLACE d:\docs\letter.txt a:
```

Use the following command to replace all files on drive A with matching files from D:\BUDGETS, and have the program prompt you:

```
REPLACE d:\budgets\*.* a: /p
```

See Also

ATTRIB, COPY

RMDIR

Purpose

The RMDIR command is used to remove a directory.

Type

Internal

Syntax

```
RMDIR [d:]path
```

or

```
RD [d:]path
```

Rules and Considerations

Use the RMDIR command to remove any directories that are empty. If a directory contains any subdirectories or hidden files, it cannot be removed until the files or directories are first removed.

RMDIR cannot be used to delete the current directory. You must move to the directory above the current directory in order to remove it.

Examples

Use the following command to remove the directory D:\BUDGETS after all files and subdirectories have been removed:

```
RMDIR d:\budgets
```

See Also
DELTREE

SCANDISK

Purpose
A disk analysis and repair utility that checks and fixes common disk and file errors, such as lost clusters, bad clusters, and cross-linked files.

Type
External

Syntax
```
SCANDISK
```
or
```
SCANDISK [d:][d:...][/ALL][/AUTOFIX][/CHECKONLY]
[/CUSTOM][/FRAGMENT][/MONO][/NOSAVE][/NOSUMMARY]
[/SURFACE]
```

Switches

/ALL	Checks and repairs all local drives.
/AUTOFIX	Fixes damage without prompting. The settings in the SCANDISK.INI file determine how ScanDisk fixes problems.
/CHECKONLY	Checks a drive, but does not repair any damage.
/CUSTOM	Uses the settings in SCANDISK.INI.
/FRAGMENT	Checks the specified file or files for fragmentation in a single directory.
/MONO	Configures ScanDisk for use with a monochrome display.

/NOSAVE	Used with /AUTOFIX, this tells ScanDisk to free lost clusters instead of saving them as files.
/NOSUMMARY	Used with /CHECKONLY or /AUTOFIX, this instructs ScanDisk not to stop at summary screens.
/SURFACE	Immediately performs a surface scan after other checks.

Examples

To check and fix errors on the current drive, enter:

    SCANDISK

To check without fixing errors on the current drive, enter:

    SCANDISK /checkonly

To check and fix errors on multiple drives, enter:

    SCANDISK c: d:

To check and fix errors on all fixed drives, enter:

    SCANDISK /all

To check and fix errors on a CVF named DBLSPACE.000 located in the root directory of drive C, enter:

    SCANDISK c:\dblspace.000

To check a file named PROPOSAL.DOC located in the WINWORD\BUS directory of drive C for fragmentation, enter:

    SCANDISK /FRAGMENT c:\winword\bus\proposal.doc

To check the entire directory above for fragmentation, enter:

    SCANDISK c:\winword\bus*.*

To undo repairs you made previously, enter:

    SCANDISK /undo a:

SET

Purpose

The SET command establishes, changes, or removes environment variables. Environment variables are used to control the behavior of some batch files and programs and to control the way DOS works.

Type

Config

Syntax

   SET [variable=[string]]

Rules and Considerations

The SET command can be used at the command prompt, in AUTOEXEC.BAT, or in CONFIG.SYS to set up the DOS environment.

Use the SET command with no parameters to display the current environment settings. These settings generally include COMSPEC, PATH, PROMPT, and TEMP, among many other possibilities.

Examples

Use the following command to display the current environment variables:

   SET

You can change your path by typing the following command at the command prompt:

   SET path=c:\windows;c:\utils

See Also

COMSPEC, PATH, PROMPT, SHELL

SETVER

Purpose

The SETVER command is used to display the version table and to set the DOS version that is reported to a program or device driver.

Type

External

Syntax

>   **SETVER** *[d:\path][filename n.nn]*

or

>   **SETVER** *[d:\path][filename[/DELETE[/QUIET]]*

Switches

>   /DELETE   Used to delete the version table for the program that you specified. Can be abbreviated /D.
>
>   /QUIET   Used to hide the messages that are normally displayed while entries are being deleted.

Rules and Considerations

Some programs do not work properly with DOS 6.2, as they were designed to run with a previous version. These programs can be made to work properly by changing the DOS version that is reported to them through the version table. This acts to "trick" the program into believing it is working with another version of DOS.

NOTE: You must have the device driver SETVER.EXE installed in your CONFIG.SYS file before you can use this command.

It is only necessary to use this command one time to update the DOS version table. You will need to restart your system in order for the changes to take effect.

Examples

Type the following command to tell the program BANANA.EXE that the version of DOS on this computer is 3.30:

```
SETVER banana.exe 3.30
```

If you install an upgrade to the program BANANA.EXE that operates properly with DOS 6.2, you will need to delete the previous entry from the version table. To delete an entry, use the following command:

```
SETVER banana.exe /D
```

See Also

SETVER.EXE

SETVER.EXE

Purpose

The SETVER.EXE device driver is used to load the DOS version table into memory. It is necessary to use this device driver if you have programs on your system that do not operate properly with DOS 6.2, and must be told that they are running with another version.

Type

Device driver

Syntax

```
DEVICE=[d:\path]SETVER.EXE
```

Rules and Considerations

This device driver must be installed before the DOS version table can be modified. If you are using the SETVER command to modify the version table for a device driver, the command to load it must appear after this command.

Examples

Use the following command to load the DOS version table into memory:

```
DEVICE=c:\dos\SETVER.EXE
```

See Also

SETVER

SHARE

Purpose

The SHARE command installs file sharing and file locking capabilities for your local and network drives. This command is often used in a network or multitasking environment in which applications share data files.

Type

External

Syntax

```
SHARE [/F:space][/L:locks]
```

or

```
INSTALL=[d:\path]SHARE.EXE [/F:space][/L:locks]
```

Switches

/F:space   Allocates an amount of space in memory to hold file sharing information, including the full path and file name of a file being shared. Each file name is typically 20 bytes in length. The default value is 2,048 bytes of storage space.

/L:locks   Designates the number of files that can be locked at one time. The default number is 20.

Rules and Considerations

The SHARE program manages all requests to read to and write from files that may be used in a multitasking environment, so that two people cannot make changes to a file at the same time.

Examples

Add the following line to your CONFIG.SYS file to install the share program with all defaults:

```
INSTALL=c:\dos\SHARE.EXE
```

SHELL

Purpose

The SHELL command is used to indicate the name of the command interpreter that you want to use on your system. Normally, this is COMMAND.COM.

Type

Config

Syntax

```
SHELL=[d:\path]filename [parameters]
```

Rules and Considerations

Normally DOS uses the command interpreter COMMAND.COM and expects to find it in the root directory of your startup drive. If you use another command interpreter, or your command interpreter is in a directory other than the root, you indicate this with a SHELL statement in your CONFIG.SYS file.

The SHELL command does not accept any parameters. If you use an alternate command interpreter that uses parameters, you can include them on the SHELL command line.

Examples

Add the following line to your CONFIG.SYS file if you want to use an alternate command interpreter, ALTSHELL.COM, that is located in the C:\ALT directory:

```
SHELL=c:\alt\altshell.com
```

When using the default command interpreter COMMAND.COM, you can use the SHELL command to set the size of the DOS environment and make the command interpreter permanent. Add the following line to your CONFIG.SYS file:

```
SHELL=c:\dos\command.com /e:1024 /p
```

See Also

COMMAND

SHIFT

Purpose

The SHIFT command changes the position of replaceable parameters in a batch file, which enables you to use more than the default 10 parameters.

Type

External

Syntax

```
SHIFT
```

Rules and Considerations

Batch files can handle 10 replaceable parameters, %0 through %9. The SHIFT command is used to add additional parameters by shifting each parameter down one notch. The new parameter, %9, is added and the original %0 parameter is dropped. The original %0 parameter cannot be retrieved once it has been shifted.

Examples

Batch file parameters before using SHIFT are as follows:

```
%0="first parameter"
%1="second parameter"
%2="third parameter"
```

After adding the SHIFT command to the batch file, the results are as follows:

```
%0="second parameter"
%1="third parameter"
%2=New parameter
```

SIZER.EXE

Purpose

The SIZER.EXE command is used by the MEMMAKER program during memory optimization to determine the size in memory of device drivers and memory resident programs.

Type

External

Rules and Considerations

This command is used exclusively by MEMMAKER, and is added to CONFIG.SYS or AUTOEXEC.BAT during the optimization process. The command is removed at the end of optimization.

Examples

Used by MEMMAKER only.

See Also

MEMMAKER

SMARTDRV.EXE

Purpose

The SMARTDRV.EXE command is used to create a disk cache in your computer's extended memory. A disk cache is used to speed up access to your hard drive.

Type

External, Device Driver

Syntax

> [d:\path]**SMARTDRV.EXE** [[d:[+¦-]]...]
> [/E:ElementSize][InitCache] [WinCache] [/B:<BufferSize>]
> [/C][/R][/L][/Q][/S]

or

> **DEVICE=**[d:\path]**SMARTDRV.EX** /double_buffer

Switches

d:[+¦-]	Enables (+) or disables (-) caching for the drive you specify. If you specify a drive letter without a plus or minus sign, read caching is activated but write caching is not. A plus sign enables both read and write caching; a minus sign disables both.
/E:ElementSize	Specifies the amount of cache in bytes that SMARTDrive moves at one time. Values are 1,024, 2,048, 4,096, and 8,192. The default is 8,192.
InitCache	Specifies the size of the cache in kilobytes when SMARTDrive starts and Windows is not running. If you do not specify a value, SMARTDrive determines how much of your system's extended memory to use for the cache space.

WinCache	Specifies how much SMARTDrive reduces the size of the cache when Windows is running.
/B:*BufferSize*	Specifies the size of the read-ahead buffer. The default read-ahead buffer size is 16K bytes.
/C	Flushes the cache, forcing all information stored to be written back to the hard disk.
/R	Clears the contents of the existing cache and restarts SMARTDrive.
/L	Prevents SMARTDrive from loading into an upper memory block, and instead loads the program in conventional memory.
/Q	Prevents SMARTDrive from displaying messages while it is loading. Compare with the /V switch.
/S	Displays the status of the program and cache(s).
/F	Writes cached data to disk after each command executes. This is the default value. Compare with the /N switch.
/N	Writes cached data to disk when the system is idle, not after each command is executed, as with the /F switch. To ensure all data is written to disk before powering down, you can enter **SMARTDRV /C** at the prompt. Compare with the /F switch.
/V	Instructs SMARTDRV to display status and error messages when it loads. By default, SMARTDRV does not display status messages but does display error messages. Compare with the /Q switch.

Rules and Considerations

By default, all hard disks are read- and write-cached. Floppy drives are only read-cached.

Default values for the cache sizes are shown in the following table.

Extended Memory	*InitCache*	*WinCache*
Up to 1M	All extended memory	none
Up to 2M	1M	256K
Up to 4M	1M	512K
Up to 6M	2M	1M
6M or more	2M	2M

You must have the device driver HIMEM.SYS installed before you can use this command.

SMARTDrive does not cache a compressed drive. A compressed drive is a file on a physical drive. When the physical drive is cached, the compressed drive (file) is also cached.

If your computer has an ESDI or SCSI hard drive installed, you may need to install SMARTDrive as a device driver and activate the double-buffering capability. Refer to Chapter 8 for more information about SMARTDrive with double buffering.

Examples

Add the following command to your AUTOEXEC.BAT file to create a disk cache of 2048 bytes when Windows is not running and 1,024 bytes when Windows is running:

```
c:\dos\SMARTDRV.EXE 2048 1024
```

The following command creates a disk cache of default size for your system, and disables write caching for drive C:

```
c:\dos\SMARTDRV.EXE C
```

Modify the above command as follows to disable all caching for drives A and B:

```
c:\dos\SMARTDRV.EXE C A- B-
```

The following command is added to your CONFIG.SYS file if you have an ESDI or SCSI hard drive:

```
DEVICE=c:\dos\SMARTDRV.EXE /double_buffer
```

SORT

Purpose

The SORT command reads and rearranges data and sends the results to the screen, to a disk file, or to a printer.

Type

External

Syntax

```
SORT [/R][/+n][<][d:\path]file [>output]
```

or

```
[command¦] SORT [/R][/+n][>output]
```

Switches

/R   Sorts in reverse order, from A to Z and then from 9 to 0.

/+n   Sorts the file in order according to the character in column *n*. The default is to start sorting with column 1.

>*output*   Specifies the name of a file if you want the output to go to another file. Or, you can specify the name of a printer, such as LPT1.

Rules and Considerations

SORT works with ASCII text files to sort one line at a time. The "<" symbol pulls the file you want to be sorted from the drive. The ">" symbol directs the output to a file or printer. If you do not specify an output location, the sorted output appears on your screen.

SORT is not case-sensitive. It does not distinguish between uppercase and lowercase letters.

Examples

Use the following command to sort the ASCII file SORTFILE.TXT in the D:\DOCS directory, and store the output in a file called SORTED.TXT in the same directory:

```
SORT <d:\docs\sortfile.txt >d:\docs\sorted.txt
```

You can use the SORT command in combination with DIR to sort your directory listing, as follows:

```
DIR ¦SORT
```

Modify the above command to sort the directory by file size, which is the 9th character, as in the following example:

```
DIR ¦SORT /+9
```

Send the sorted directory listing to the printer with this command:

```
DIR ¦SORT>PRN
```

See Also

DIR, MORE

STACKS

Purpose

The STACKS command controls the dynamic use of data stacks to handle hardware interrupts.

Type

Config

Syntax

   STACKS=*number,size*

Rules and Considerations

DOS allocates one stack each time it receives a hardware interrupt request. You can specify the number and size of the stacks that DOS has to work with. By default, IBM-PCs and PC/XTs are allocated 0 stacks of 0 bytes in size. All other PCs are allocated 9 stacks of 128 bytes in size. You can specify from 8 to 64 stacks, each being from 32 to 512 bytes in size.

Examples

Add the following line to your CONFIG.SYS file to create 9 stacks of 256 bytes each:

   STACKS=9,256

SUBMENU

Purpose

The SUBMENU command is used to define an item in a startup menu that displays another menu when it is selected. This command is used only within a menu block in CONFIG.SYS.

SUBMENU

Type
Config

Syntax
SUBMENU=*blockname[,menutext]*

Rules and Considerations

A startup menu makes it possible for you to start your computer using a number of possible configurations, which you select from a menu when the computer starts up. You can create a "nested" menu system using this command.

A submenu block begins with the name of the block in square brackets. This menu block must be defined somewhere in the CONFIG.SYS file. There can also be text associated with the name of the menu block; if used, the text is what displays when the menu appears during startup.

Examples

The following CONFIG.SYS file defines a startup menu and one submenu:

```
[menu]
menuitem basic,Basic configuration
submenu network,Networks

[network]
menuitem novell,Novell NetWare
menuitem lanman,LAN Manager

[basic]
files=30
buffers=30

[novell]
include=basic
rem Commands for NetWare

[lanman]
include=basic
rem Commands for LAN Manager
```

See Also

MENU, MENUCOLOR, MENUDEFAULT, MENUITEM, INCLUDE

SUBST

Purpose

The SUBST command substitutes a drive letter for any drive and path. You can use this drive letter in commands as if it were a physical drive.

Type

External

Syntax

    SUBST *[d1:[d2:\path]*

or

    SUBST *d1: /D*

Switch

/D   Used to delete a substitution.

Rules and Considerations

The first parameter in the above syntax is a drive letter name. This must be an unused drive letter, and must not be greater than the drive specified in the LASTDRIVE command.

If you are working on a network, do not use any drive letters that are normally associated with your network server.

The second parameter is the drive and path that you want to reassign to the drive letter. When you are finished using the path as a drive, you can delete it using the /D switch.

The following commands should not be used on drives that are affected by SUBST:

ASSIGN	BACKUP	CHKDSK
DEFRAG	DISKCOMP	DISKCOPY
DOSBACK	FDISK	FORMAT
LABEL	SYS	

Examples

Sometimes it is easier to refer to a complicated path as if it were a drive. To use the drive letter G to access the files in the subdirectory D:\BUDGETS\1993\PROJECTA, type the following:

```
SUBST g: d:\budgets\1993\projecta
```

When referring to the above directory, simply call it G:.

To restore the original subdirectory name, use the following command:

```
SUBST g: /D
```

See Also

ASSIGN, JOIN

SWITCHES

Purpose

The SWITCHES command enables special options for MS-DOS. This command is used in your CONFIG.SYS file.

Type

Config

Syntax

```
SWITCHES=/W /K /N /F
```

Switches

/W   Indicates that the file WINA20.386 in another directory other than the root directory. Use this switch with Microsoft Windows 3.0 in enhanced mode if you have moved the WINA20.386 file.

/K   Forces an enhanced keyboard to act like a conventional keyboard.

/N   Prevents the use of the F5 or F8 keys during startup.

/F   Skips the two-second delay after displaying the message "Starting MS-DOS..." during startup.

Rules and Considerations

Use SWITCHES with an enhanced keyboard if a program does not interpret keyboard input correctly. If you use this switch, you must add the /K switch to the ANSI.SYS statement if it was included in your CONFIG.SYS file.

Examples

Add the following line to your CONFIG.SYS file to disable the use of the F5 and F8 keys, and to skip the startup message:

```
SWITCHES /N /F
```

See Also

ANSI.SYS

SYS

Purpose

The SYS command copies the DOS system startup files IO.SYS, MSDOS.SYS, and COMMAND.COM to a drive you specify. The first two files are hidden files, and do not appear on directory listings.

Type

External

Syntax

SYS *[d1\path]d2:*

Rules and Considerations

In the previous syntax, *d1:path* indicates the location of the system files. If this is not specified, DOS looks for them in the current directory. The drive that you want the files copied to is the second parameter.

Earlier versions of DOS required that these files be contiguous on the disk, sometimes requiring a disk to be reformatted to accommodate them. This is no longer the case.

Examples

Type the following command to copy the system startup files to a diskette in drive A:

SYS a:

See Also

COPY, XCOPY

TIME

Purpose

The TIME command is used to display the system time or change the internal clock of your computer.

Type

Internal

Syntax

```
TIME [hours:[minutes[:seconds[.hundredths]]][A|P]]
```

Rules and Considerations

If you use the TIME command without any parameters, the current time is displayed and you are prompted to change it. If you do not want to change the time, simply press Enter.

TIME uses the 24-hour format; when entering times after 12:00 p.m., you must use the 24-hour format or else add the *P* parameter to indicate p.m.

You can change the TIME format by changing the COUNTRY setting in your CONFIG.SYS file. See the COUNTRY command for more information.

Examples

Enter the following command to display the current time:

```
TIME
```

The following command is used to change the time to 2:30 p.m.:

```
TIME 14:30 or TIME 2:30p
```

See Also

COUNTRY, DATE

TREE

Purpose

The TREE command displays a graphical representation of the directory structure for a drive you specify.

Type

External

Syntax

TREE *[d:\path][/F][/A]*

Switches

/F   Displays the names of the files in each directory.

/A   Directs TREE to use text characters when drawing the tree structure, instead of graphics characters. Use this switch on displays that do not support graphics character sets.

Rules and Considerations

If no drive or path is specified, TREE displays the tree structure beginning with the current directory of the current drive.

Examples

Type the following command to display the tree structure for drive C:

TREE

To display the directory structure and show all files, use this command:

TREE /F

Add the MORE pipe to stop the display at each full screen, as in this example:

TREE /F¦more

See Also

DIR

TYPE

Purpose

The TYPE command is used to display the contents of an ASCII text file.

Type

Internal

Syntax

`TYPE [d:\path]filename`

Rules and Considerations

You can redirect output from the TYPE command to a device other than the screen by using the output redirection character (>) and the name of the device, such as PRN. You also can use the MORE pipe to control scrolling of the output on the screen.

It is possible to use the TYPE command with binary files, but the output will not be readable.

Examples

Use the following command to display the file AUTOEXEC.BAT:

`TYPE autoexec.bat`

If a file is too long and scrolls off the screen, you can use the MORE pipe to stop the scrolling at each full screen. Type the following command to display the file LONGFILE.TXT:

`TYPE longfile.txt |MORE`

See Also

MORE, PRINT

UNDELETE

Purpose

The UNDELETE command is used to recover files that have been erased.

Type

External

Syntax

    UNDELETE *[[d:\path]filename][[/DT¦/DS¦/DOS]*

or

    UNDELETE *[/LIST¦/ALL¦/PURGE[d:] ¦/STATUS¦/LOAD¦/U¦ / S[d:]¦/Td:[-entries]]*

Switches

/DT	Recovers only files that are in the deletion-tracking file; prompts for confirmation.
/DS	Recovers only files that are listed in the SENTRY directory; prompts for confirmation.
/DOS	Recovers only files that are internally listed as deleted by DOS; prompts for confirmation.
/LIST	Lists deleted files that can be recovered, but does not recover them. The files that are listed are controlled by the drive, path, and file name that you specify, and the /DT, /DS, and /DOS switches.
/ALL	Recovers deleted files without prompting for confirmation.
/PURGE	Deletes the contents of the SENTRY directory.
/STATUS	Displays the type of delete protection in effect for each drive.
/LOAD	Loads the Undelete TSR into memory using information defined in the UNDELETE.INI file, or default values if this file does not exist.
/U	Unloads the TSR from memory, disabling the capability to undelete files.
/S[d:]	Enables the delete-sentry level of protection and loads the TSR portion of the Undelete program into memory. This program records information needed to recover deleted files on the drive you specify.

/Td[-entries]   Enables the delete tracker lever of protection and loads the TSR portion of the Undelete program into memory. You specify a maximum number of entries, from 1 to 999, for a particular drive.

Rules and Considerations

DOS provides three levels of undelete protection—delete sentry, delete tracker, and MS-DOS.

Delete sentry is the highest level of protection. It uses a hidden directory called SENTRY into which the file you deleted is moved. If you undelete a file, it is moved back to its original location.

Delete tracker provides an intermediate level of protection. It uses a hidden file called PCTRACKER.DEL to record the location of deleted files. You can recover these files provided no other files have written over them on the disk.

The MS-DOS level of protection offers the lowest level of protection, and is automatically enabled when your computer starts up. You may be able to recover files if no other files have been written to the disk.

The first time you use the UNDELETE command, a file called UNDELETE.INI is created that contains your preferences for using the program. You can edit this file with any text editor if you want to make changes. If you do not specify any preferences, the following are set up automatically:

- Use the delete sentry method.
- Save all files.
- Exclude *.tmp, *.vm?, *.woa, *.spl, *.img, *.thm, and *.dov.
- Save archive files.
- Purge files after seven days.
- Restrict the amount of disk space to seven percent of available.

Examples

Use the following command to recover all deleted files on drive C without being prompted:

`UNDELETE c: /ALL`

The following command loads the TSR portion of UNDELETE into memory, creates a hidden directory called SENTRY, and moves all deleted files on drive D to that directory:

`UNDELETE /S d:`

See Also

ERASE

UNFORMAT

Purpose

The UNFORMAT command is used to recover data from a formatted hard or floppy disk, or to rebuild a corrupted disk partition of a hard disk.

Type

External

Syntax

`UNFORMAT d: [/L][/TEST][/P]`

Switches

/L   Lists every file and subdirectory found by UNFORMAT. If this switch is not specified, only subdirectories and fragmented files are listed.

/TEST   Shows how information would be re-created on the unformatted disk, but does not actually unformat the disk.

/P   Sends output messages to a printer connected to LPT1.

Rules and Considerations

UNFORMAT cannot unformat a disk that was formatted with the /U switch.

UNFORMAT cannot unformat files that are fragmented on the disk. If UNFORMAT finds fragmented files, it prompts you for confirmation to truncate the file. You may be able to recover only part of the file. You also may delete the fragmented file.

UNFORMAT can only work on disks whose sectors are 512, 1,024, or 2,048 bytes in size.

Examples

Type the following command to unformat a diskette in drive A:

```
UNFORMAT a:
```

Modify the above command to list all the files on the unformatted disk, as in this example:

```
UNFORMAT a: /L
```

See Also

FORMAT

VER

Purpose

The VER command is used to display the current DOS version.

Type

Internal

Syntax

```
VER
```

Examples

To display the version of DOS that your system is running, enter the following command:

```
VER
```

VERIFY

Purpose

The VERIFY command is used to check that data has been written to your disk accurately.

Type

External

Syntax

```
VERIFY [ON|OFF]
```

Switches

ON|OFF   Specifies whether DOS is to verify that files are copied correctly. The default value is OFF.

Rules and Considerations

If you set VERIFY ON for your system, DOS will check to ensure that data written to disk sectors is correct. If data is not correct, an error code is returned.

The /V option of the DOS COPY or XCOPY command performs the same function as VERIFY.

Examples

To enable disk write verification, enter the following command:

```
VERIFY ON
```

See Also
COPY, XCOPY

VOL

Purpose
The VOL command is used to display the disk volume number and serial number, if they have one.

Type
Internal

Syntax
`VOL [d:]`

Rules and Considerations
If you do not indicate a drive name, DOS will display volume information about the current drive.

The volume label is created with the FORMAT command's /V option, or can be added later with the LABEL command.

Examples
Type the following command to view the current drive's volume label information:

`VOL`

See Also
FORMAT, LABEL

VSAFE

Purpose

The VSAFE command is used to check your system for viruses. If a virus is found, a warning message is displayed. VSAFE is a memory-resident program.

Type

External

Syntax

VSAFE /[option[+¦-]...][/NE][/NX][/Ax][/Cx][/N][/D][/U]

Switches

/option Specifies how VSAFE monitors your system for viruses. Select from one of the following options, using a plus (+) or minus(-) sign to turn the option on or off:

1 Warns of formatting that could erase the hard disk. The default is "on."

2 Warns if a program attempts to stay in memory. The default is "off."

3 Prevents programs from writing to disk. The default is "off."

4 Checks executable files that DOS opens. The default is "on."

5 Checks all disks for boot sector viruses. The default is "on."

6 Warns if attempts are made to write to the boot sector or partition table of a hard disk. The default is "on."

7 Warns if attempts are made to write to the boot sector of a floppy disk. The default is "off."

Command Reference

	8	Warns if attempts are made to modify executable files. The default is "on."
/NE		Does not monitor expanded memory.
/NX		Does not monitor extended memory.
/Ax		Defines the hot key as Alt plus the key specified.
/Cx		Defines the hot key as Ctrl plus the key specified.
/N		Enables network drivers to be loaded after VSAFE starts.
/D		Turns off checksumming.
/U		Removes the VSAFE program from memory.

Rules and Considerations

NOTE: *The following corrects an error in the Microsoft documentation.*

VSAFE occupies approximately 44K of memory.

VSAFE must be disabled before installing Microsoft Windows. If you want to use the VSAFE program with Windows, add the following line to your WIN.INI file:

```
load=wntsrman.exe
```

This command enables VSAFE messages to be displayed in Windows.

Examples

The following command is used to install VSAFE so that it warns if a program attempts to stay in memory and warns if attempts are made to modify the boot sector of a floppy disk:

```
VSAFE /2+ /7+
```

See Also

MSAV

XCOPY

Purpose

The XCOPY command copies files or groups of files, including subdirectories.

> *Beginning with version 6.2, XCOPY asks for confirmation before overwriting an existing file of the same name.* (6.2)

Type

External

Syntax

```
XCOPY source [destination][/A¦/M][/D:date][/P][/E][/V][/W]
```

Switches

/A   Copies only those source files that have had their archive attribute set, but does not modify the archive attribute.

/M   Copies source files that have had their archive attribute set, and turns the archive attribute off.

/D:date   Copies source files that were added or modified after the specified date.

/P   Prompts you for confirmation before creating each destination file.

/S   Copies directories and subdirectories unless they are empty. The default is to copy only a single directory.

/E   Copies directories and subdirectories even if they are empty. You must use the /S switch with this switch.

/V	Verifies each file as it is written to the destination to be sure the two files are identical.
/W	Displays a message and waits for you to respond before copying files.
/Y	Instructs XCOPY to replace any existing files without prompting you for confirmation.
/-Y	Instructs XCOPY to prompt you for confirmation when replacing an exising file. Used to override the SET COPYCMD=/Y environment variable.

Rules and Considerations

This version of XCOPY does not copy system or hidden files. If you want to copy these files, you must first change their file attributes with the ATTRIB command.

XCOPY can be used to copy files from one diskette to another when the diskettes are not the same kind. Normally, you use DISKCOPY to copy a complete diskette, but when the diskettes are not the same, this is not possible.

Examples

Use the following command to copy all of the contents of drive A to a diskette in drive B, including subdirectories:

```
XCOPY a: b: /s
```

Type the following command to copy all files from D:\BUDGETS to a diskette in drive A that have had their archive attributes set, and turn off the archive attribute:

```
XCOPY d:\budgets\*.* /m
```

See Also

ATTRIB, COPY

MS-DOS

Appendix

About the Inside MS-DOS 6.2 Disk 1483

Part Nine:

MS DOS

APPENDIX

About the *Inside MS-DOS 6.2* Disk

by Kris Ashton

During the course of writing this book, the authors have written or discovered several programs and batch files that may be of interest to you. These programs have been placed on a special *Inside MS-DOS 6.2* disk that comes with this book. Many of the programs and batch files on this disk are free of charge. A few programs, however, require a small price to be paid to the program's author. The disk is divided into subdirectories, each representing the chapter in which the program is discussed. Some of the programs may be in a compressed format; others are directly available.

This chapter lists and briefly describes the programs included on the *Inside MS-DOS 6.2* disk.

Batch Files

Purpose

A variety of batch files are included on the disk. These batch files are used as examples throughout the book and are included on the disk so that you don't have to enter them yourself.

Usage

As described in the various chapters (in particular, see Chapter 15) in which the batch files are used.

BAGKEYS.EXE

Purpose

The BAGKEYS program captures keystrokes and sends them to a file called BAGKEYS.DAT. Keystrokes are captured in such a way that they can be played back to re-create the exact strokes the user entered.

Uses for this program include demonstrations and training (by playing back the script stored in BAGKEYS.DAT) and user monitoring (for security purposes).

Usage

To start the program and begin capturing keystrokes, type:

BAGKEYS

To flush the keystroke buffer, close the BAGKEYS.DAT file, and uninstall the program, press Ctrl+Alt+U.

Notes

BAGKEYS does not append a CHR$(10) line feed after each carriage return entered. Therefore, if you use the DOS TYPE command to examine the file BAGKEYS.DAT, the results will not appear correctly. Use the program BAGFIX to add the line feed characters if you want to view the output of BAGKEYS.DAT.

Author

David Stang

BLANK.EXE

Purpose

BLANK is a screen blanker (saver). A screen blanker is useful for protecting personal, private, or sensitive information displayed on-screen. A screen blanker also can prevent burnout of older-style monitors.

Usage

Type the following command to blank the screen after two minutes:

BLANK

Use this command followed by a number that represents the number of seconds the program should wait before blanking the screen, as in the following example:

BLANK 600

In this example, the program waits 600 seconds (10 minutes) before blanking the screen.

To remove the program from memory, enter the following command:

BLANK /U

To restore your screen after it has been blanked, simply press any key.

Notes

BLANK can be run multiple times, each time with a different time interval specified. The last run defines the current wait time before blanking.

The BLANK program works in 25-line character mode only.

Author

David Stang

CDIR.EXE

Purpose

Tired of changing directories with CD? Try CDIR. You'll see all your directories in a pop-up list on-screen. Simply scroll to the directory you want and press Enter. Press the Esc key to remove the pop-up list from the screen.

If your current directory has no subdirectories, the only entry that you see will be that directory.

Usage

Place the CDIR program in a directory called \UTILS and include this directory in your system path. Then, any time you want to change to another directory, use this command:

```
CDIR
```

Notes

This program may not work on huge drives with very complex directory structures.

Author

David Stang

CMOS.EXE

Purpose

Use CMOS to save or restore your CMOS information.

You should save your computer's CMOS information—information about your computer's hardware configuration—to an emergency rescue disk. If your computer's battery fails, or a virus overwrites the CMOS, you will be able to use the CMOS program to restore the configuration that you previously saved.

Usage

To back up your computer's CMOS, enter the following command:

```
CMOS /S
```

This command creates a file called CMOS.DAT on the drive and directory from which you invoked the command. Copy this file to your emergency rescue disk.

If you need to restore your CMOS values, run the program from your rescue disk by typing:

```
CMOS /R
```

Notes

Be sure to copy the file CMOS.EXE to your rescue disk, in case you have to rescue your CMOS. Without CMOS values, your computer will not be able to read your hard disk where the CMOS.EXE program resides. If your computer cannot read the hard disk, it cannot run the program to restore itself!

Author

David Stang

DCOPY.EXE

Purpose

DCOPY is a program for copying disks. It is a replacement for the DOS DISKCOPY command and was written to overcome some of DISKCOPY's shortcomings. DCOPY was designed for systems that have one drive of a particular media size. In these situations, particularly with larger disk capacities such as 1.44M, DISKCOPY involves a series of disk swaps. DCOPY overcomes this limitation, and gives you the option of making multiple copies of a disk after reading the source disk only once.

DCOPY works by creating a "swap pool" to hold the data being copied. The swap pool is created from a combination of memory and hard disk space. All memory in your system can be used to create the swap pool—the hard disk is used only as a last resort.

DCOPY first uses all conventional memory, and then looks for extended memory. DCOPY also can use expanded memory made available by a LIM-compatible driver, Version 3.2 or later. Finally, DCOPY uses hard disk space and creates a temporary swap file.

Usage

Type the following command to copy a disk in drive A:

```
DCOPY A:
```

You see the DCOPY screen, which prompts you through the copying process. You can make multiple copies of the same source disk without needing to read it again.

Notes

DCOPY includes several options that can be executed from the DOS command line, including the following:

> Duplicate or correct bad sectors
>
> Format the floppy disk
>
> Use or exclude normal RAM from the swap pool
>
> Use or exclude extended memory from the swap pool
>
> Use or exclude XMS memory from the swap pool
>
> Use or exclude expanded memory from the swap pool
>
> Use or exclude hard disk space from the swap pool

DCOPY is a shareware program. There is a small charge for the program.

Author

Blue North Software
13112 66th Ave.
Edmonton, AB, Canada T6H 1Y8
(403) 489-9958

DOSWATCH.EXE

Purpose

DOSWATCH is a TSR that displays information about the current DOS service number at the top of the screen every time an INT 21h is executed by a program.

Usage

To install the DOSWATCH program, enter the following command…

```
DOSWATCH
```

Use the following command to uninstall the program from memory:

DOSWATCH /U

Notes

In addition to the DOS service number, the following messages are displayed:

```
Set disk drive to
Get the DOS time
Get the DOS version
Get disk free space
Change directory to
Create a file
Open file
Close handle
Read from handle
Write to handle
Delete file
Get current directory
Execute program
Find first file that matches
Find next matching file
```

Author

David Stang

DSEDIT.EXE

Purpose

DSEDIT is used to edit or view disks or files, sector by sector. The initial display is a dump of the first sector on the drive you choose; you can read another sector, a specific file, or edit the sector you are currently in. The program works with function keys that are defined along the bottom of the screen.

Usage

Use the following command to view or edit the current drive:

DSEDIT

To view or edit another drive, indicate the drive letter, as in the following example:

DSEDIT D:

Notes

Following is a portion of a screen output:

```
00    01 02 03 04 05 06 07 08 09 0A 0B 0C 0D 0E 0F      0123456789
================================================================
00 ¦  EB 3C 90 4D 53 44 4F 53 35 2E 30 00 02 04 01 00 ¦ @#MSDOS6
10 ¦  02 00 02 C3 A2 F8 29 00 11 00 04 00 11 00 00 00 ¦ $#%
20 ¦  00 00 00 00 80 00 29 FC 18 14 1A 4B 4C 55 44 47 ¦      )#
```

You can edit any of the entries by entering the hex or ASCII codes for the changes you want to make.

Author

David Stang

ENVEDIT.EXE

Purpose

The ENVEDIT program allows editing of the DOS master environment. When you start the program, the current DOS environment is listed. Each environment variable appears on a line, and the lines are numbered. You can change any individual line, add lines, or delete lines. Your environment is changed without having to reboot your computer.

Usage

To edit your DOS environment, type the following command:

ENVEDIT

Follow the prompts on-screen to edit, delete, or add lines to the listing of environment variables.

Notes

All environment variables are converted to uppercase. If you experience a problem because an intentionally lowercase environment variable (such as windir) is converted, don't use this program.

Author

David Stang

FIND.EXE

Purpose

You use the FIND program to find a file on your computer. When you invoke the program with a file name, the location of the file on disk is reported.

Usage

To locate a file, such as BANANA.DAT, on disk, enter the following command…

FIND BANANA.DAT

Notes

FIND only works on only the current drive. If you want the program to look on another drive, you must specify the drive before the file name.

Author

David Stang

FINDTEXT.EXE

Purpose

The FINDTEXT program can quickly find a string of text in a file that you specify. If a virus is suspected and any ASCII string for that virus can be identified, you can use FINDTEXT to find additional infected files. The text you seek doesn't need to be normal text.

Usage

To start the FindText program, enter the following command:

```
FINDTEXT
```

You are prompted for the file to search, and the string of text to seek within the specified file.

Notes

You can use wild-card characters when searching files, and you can search any file in the current directory. The text search is not case-sensitive. When the selected text is found, it is displayed below the name of the file in which it was found. You are given the option of continuing in the file, aborting the search, or skipping to the next file.

Appendix: *About the* Inside MS-DOS 6.2 *Disk*

Author

David Stang

F-PROT.EXE

Purpose

F-PROT is an anti-virus program that consists of several modules:

Module	Purpose
VIRSTOP.EXE	A virus-interception program
F-PROT.EXE	Menu-driven main program
SIGN.DEF	Virus signatures
*.TX0	Language files for various languages
VIR-HELP.*	Virus information in various languages
*.DOC	Information about viruses and the package

The main program, F-PROT.EXE, is a menu-driven program that offers options including Scan, Install, Viruses, and Program. Each of the menu selections includes its own separate documentation:

- ✔ Scan searches for viruses, using a large set of virus signatures. You can select where to search and choose from three different search modes.

- ✔ Install is used to configure the program. Installation includes selecting a language to use with the program.

- ✔ Viruses provides information about common viruses and enables you to enter a search pattern for a new virus.

- ✔ Program answers some common questions about the program, such as how to get updates and how to contact the author.

Usage

To start the virus scanning program, use the following command:

   F-PROT

You will see a menu that enables you to install the program, get information about viruses or program updates, or scan for viruses.

To install the memory-resident virus scanner, enter the following command:

   VIRSTOP

This program intercepts known viruses and prevents the execution of any program infected with any of the viruses it recognizes.

Notes

This program includes extensive documentation and information about viruses. There is a small charge for this program.

Author

Frisk Software International
Postholf 7180 IS-127
Reykjavik, Iceland

+354-1-28801 (FAX)

FULLDIR.EXE

Purpose

Use FULLDIR to display full directory information, including full year and time. This program is useful for displaying year and time information that DOS does not normally display, but which some viruses change.

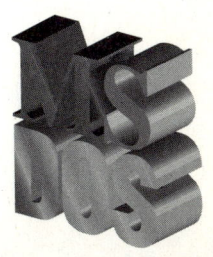

Usage

Use the following command to display all files:

```
FULLDIR
```

You can use wild-card characters with this command. You can, for example, use the following command to display all files ending with BAT:

```
FULLDIR *.BAT
```

Notes

When the Frodo virus modifies a file, it also modifies the directory, adding 100 years to the file's date. DOS does not show the year 2093, for example; it shows just 93, which looks as if the file was unchanged. When the Vienna virus infects a file, it also modifies the directory, changing the file's time to 62 seconds. You can't see the seconds with the DIR command.

FULLDIR works about the same way as the internal DIR command does, but it shows the year as four digits, and shows all the file's time, including seconds. You can run it with the usual DOS wild-card characters.

Author

David Stang

MAKETXT1.EXE

Purpose

MAKETXT1 creates up to 999 files of any desired size up to 1,024 bytes on drives A, B, C, or D. This program is used in data recovery and disk exploration experiments, such as file recovery, cluster examination, and the like.

Usage

Use the following command to create files to be used for data recovery experiments:

```
MAKETXT1
```

Notes

All files created have the name AA and an extension from 001 to 999. There is little error trapping, so the program will overwrite any files of the same name, and will fill the drive if this is possible.

Author

David Stang

NOBOOT.EXE

Purpose

You use NOBOOT to prevent users from rebooting machines with Ctrl+Alt+Del. This program can be helpful if a user often uses this method to exit a program, resulting in cross-links or lost clusters. NOBOOT also can be useful if a user is attempting to bypass security measures on a PC.

Usage

To disable Ctrl+Alt+Del reboots on a computer, add the following command to AUTOEXEC.BAT:

```
NOBOOT
```

Notes

Once NOBOOT is run, the machine must be turned off at the switch.

Author

David Stang

READEXE.EXE

Purpose

You use READEXE to read an EXE file and display its header information. This information is useful in determining what changes, if any, a virus has made to a file.

Usage

To display information about a file, enter the following command:

```
READEXE file name
```

The file name does not include the extension.

To print the output of the program, use the following command:

```
READEXE file name >outputfilename
```

Then, use the DOS PRINT command to print the output file name.

Notes

Following is a sample of the program's output:

```
The header of readexe.EXE contains:
Meaning.............Hex
Signature...........4D5A
Length..............9E00
Size in pages.......1300
```

```
# Reloc. Items......0000
Header Size.........2000
Min Alloc..........4E08
Max Alloc..........FFFF
Stack Seg..........4602
SP reg.............8000
Checksum...........0000
IP reg.............1000
CS reg.............1402
Rel offset.........1E00
Ovl Num............0000
```

Author

David Stang

REBOOT.COM

Purpose

You use the REBOOT program to reboot a computer. This program can be used in a batch file (such as START.BAT with Novell) to reboot any user, based on a conditional test done in that batch file. For example, a user found to have a file virus in memory, who has booted from drive A, and who has an active modem, can be rebooted rather than merely logged out.

This program might also be used after AUTOEXEC.BAT has asked a question and branched to code that copied a new CONFIG.SYS and AUTOEXEC.BAT to the root.

Usage

Use the following command to reboot the computer:

REBOOT

Author

David Stang

SEECODE.BAT

Purpose

You use the SEECODE batch file to test a DOS command for error codes that may be returned. You use SEECODE to test possible outcomes of a command. The codes returned as a result of a particular command can be tested for in a batch file using ERRORLEVEL statements.

Usage

To determine the error code of a DOS command, use the following command…

```
SEECODE command
```

Suppose, for example, that you wanted to test the outcome of the command COPY BANANA.DAT A: and use the result in a batch file. Use the following command:

```
SEECODE COPY BANANA.DAT A:
```

After DOS completes the command you specify, an error code similar to the following is returned:

```
Found error code  0
```

Author

Mark Minasi

SHOWINT.EXE

Purpose

SHOWINT displays the interrupt vector table (the first 1K of conventional memory). This program helps you determine what interrupts are hooked by viruses.

Usage

The following command shows the current interrupts in use:

    SHOWINT

Scroll up or down the list using the arrow keys; exit by pressing Esc.

Notes

SHOWINT uses a 256-by-60 virtual screen, permitting scrolling through all 256 possible interrupts.

Author

David Stang

SNORETIL.EXE

Purpose

You can use SNORETIL in batch files to pause until a specified time. This program can be used for evening backups, evening communications, and the like.

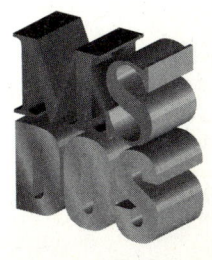

Usage

In the following command, you specify how long you want the program to pause. You must indicate the time using the 24-hour time format:

```
SNORETIL hh:mm[:ss]
```

If, for example, you want a batch file to pause execution until 7:00 p.m., use the following command in the batch file at the point you want it to pause:

```
SNORETIL 15:00
```

Notes

If you specify a time that has just passed when SNORETIL is executed, SNORETIL will wait nearly a full day to execute. If you run it from a batch file from Windows, don't minimize the application.

Author

David Stang

TESTBAK.COM

Purpose

TESTBAK determines the need for backup by examining the archive bit on all files in the current drive and computing total bytes, total files, bytes in changed files, number of changed files, percent of bytes that have changed, and percent of files that have changed. A changed file is one that has the archive bit set, which is normally turned off when a file is backed up and turned on during creation and editing. The archive bit also is set on the destination file when a file is copied or xcopied.

Usage

The following command is used to check the current drive:

```
TESTBAK
```

To test another drive or directory, use the following command:

```
TESTBAK drive:\path
```

Notes

The following is sample output from the program:

```
Backup necessity for C:\
    4714675 bytes in 223 file(s)
    386426 bytes in 33 changed file(s)
    8% of bytes changed in 15% of files
```

Author

David Stang

TURBOBAT.EXE

Purpose

TURBOBAT allows you to compile standard DOS batch files into COM binary programs. This greatly enhances the speed of large batch files by enabling them to run in native code rather than interpreted DOS commands. The resulting .COM files can call nested batch files without losing the parent because the parent calling program is no longer a batch file.

Usage

To run the TURBOBAT compiler, enter the following command:

```
TURBOBAT [options] filename[.ext]
```

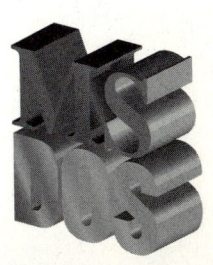

Notes

Options for TURBOBAT are described in the documentation that comes with the program.

TURBOBAT is a multipass batch file compiler. It turns interpreted DOS batch files into binary programs that can execute up to as much as four times faster than normal batch files. TURBOBAT supports all the normal DOS functions that can be called in a batch file and also provides many additional features, including support for many 4DOS/NDOS commands.

There is a small charge for this program.

Author

Foley Hi-Tech Systems
Suite 3002
185 Berry Street
San Francisco, CA 94107
(415) 882-1730

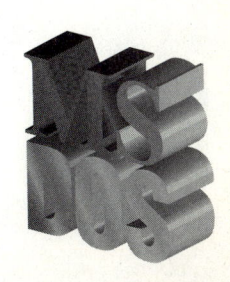

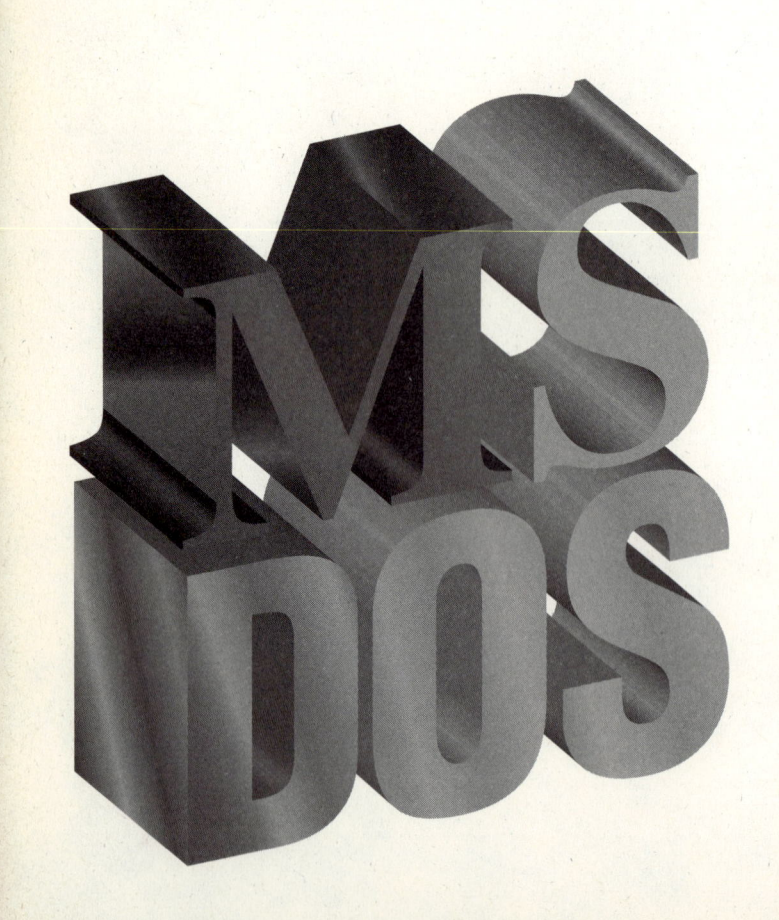

MS DOS

Index

Symbols

$$$ file extension, 328
$_ metast ring character, 287
. (current directory), 86
.. (dot dot) directory reference, 85
@ (ampersand) before commands, 796
[common] block, 887
\ (backslash) root directory, 74
| (verticalbar), piping files, 806
000 file extension, 328
1BASE5 Ethernet network, 1248
3 1/2-inch floppy disks, 901-902
5 1/4-inch floppy disks, 901-902
8-bit computers, memory banks, 569-572
10BASE-T Ethernet network, 1248
10BASE2 Ethernet network, 1247
10BASE5 Ethernet network, 1247
10BROAD36 Ethernet network, 1248
12-bit FAT (file allocation table), 934-936
16-bit computers, memory banks, 572-574
16-bit FAT, 934-936
32-bit computers, memory banks, 574-576
32M limit (hard disks), 23
360K disks, 946
386Max memory manager, 48, 661, 702-713
    general features, 703
    Maximize, 707-713
    obsolete features, 702-703
    special features, 704-705
    syntax, 706-707
640K RAM, 444-445, 451
    addressing limitation, 1244
802.3 (Ethernet) standard, 1247-1248
802.5 (Token-Ring) standard, 1248
8088 memory chips, upgrading, 569
8514/A Graphics, 753

A

A CVF is damaged error message, 142
A20 handlers, 626-632
Abort, Retry, Ignore message, 1060-1061
absolute sectors, 191-192
accelerators (video adapters), 755-760
access
    controlling, 1155-1179
        BAT file extension, changing, 1168-1171
        blanking screen, 1171-1172
        bootups, logging, 1171
        deleted files, 1161

encryption,
  1178-1179
erasing files
  permanently,
  1175-1176
internal commands,
  replacing,
  1162-1165
keyboard,
  reprogramming,
  1172-1175
passwords,
  1156-1161
renaming
  AUTOEXEC.BAT
  file, 1165-1168
with batch files,
  1176-1178
with menus,
  1176-1178
hardware, 106-109
access time, 184,
  565-566, 590-591
activity log, 856-857
actuator arm, 176
adapter cards, 220
adapters, 752-760
  accelerators/
    coprocessors,
    755-756
  color, 754-755
  drivers, 759-760
  local bus, 756-758
  modes, 752
  RAM, 758-759
  resolution, 752-754
add-in boards
  documentation,
  532-533
address lines, 511
addresses (memory),
  442-443
  extended memory,
    472-476
  ROM, 461

addressing
  640K limitation, 1244
  hardware, 104
  sectors, 914
    floppy disks, 915
    hard disks, 915-918
administrators,
  backup, 974
Advanced Power
  Management (APM)
  protocol, 63
alarm utilities, 845-848
algorithms, disk
  compression, 237
Allocation error. Size
  adjusted error
  message, 1052
allocation units,
  192-193, 236
    see also clusters
Always Format
  Diskettes option
  (MSBACKUP/
  MWBACKUP), 988
American National
  Standards Institute
  (ANSI), 1249
American Standard
  Code for Information
  Interchange, *see*
  ASCII
ANSI (American
  National Standards
  Institute), 1249
ANSI.SYS device
  driver, 446, 763-771,
  1273-1282
  cursor movement,
    767-769
  macros, 769-771
  video display
    control, 763-769
anti-virus programs,
  1093
  F-PROT, 1101, 1122,
    1494-1495

  limitations,
    1074-1075
  virus attacks on,
    1072-1075
  VSAFE, 1103-1110
Anti-Virus utility,
  installing, 134, 149
APM (Advanced
  Power Management)
  protocol, 63
APMCHK.ZIP file, 63
APPEND command,
  64, 303-304, 1282-1283
  /X switch, 102-103
  /X:OFF switch, 304
  /X:ON switch, 304
appending viruses,
  1068
Apple File Exchange,
  1234-1235
applications
  programming, 106
ARC file
  extension, 328
archive attribute, 793
archive bit, 973
ARCHIVE.ME
  directory, 1009
archived files, 1034
archiving, 969-971
  with servers, 1009
ARCnet network
  interface cards,
  1246-1247
ASC file extension,
  328
ASCII codes, 26
ASCII files
  comparing, 357-358
  concatenation,
    341-342
  copying, 342-344
ASK.COM
  keyboard-processing
  program, 1037

ASM file extension, 77, 328
ASPI drivers, 226-227
ASQ program (386Max), 705
ASSIGN command, 728-729, 1283-1284
AT-type controllers, 190-191
Attached Resource Computer Network, *see* ARCnet
ATTRIB command, 137, 239, 320-321, 1285-1286
attributes, 320-321
 directories, 321-322
 hidden system files, 957
 setting, 321
Audible Prompts option (MSBACKUP/ MWBACKUP), 989
AUTOEXEC.BAT file, 820-821
 booting without, 38-39
 memory managers, 487-491
 renaming, 1165-1168
automatic sector translation, 229
AUX (virtual device), 799

B

$B metastring character, 287
backfilling (memory management), 552-553
background colors (monitors), 766
background printing, 781-783

backup catalogs, 372-376, 988-989
BACKUP command, 64, 123, 363
 previous DOS versions, 52
backup sets, 375-376
Backup utility, installing, 134, 149
BACKUP2.BAT file, 975
BACKUP3.BAT file, 976
BACKUP4.BAT file, 976-977
backups
 administrators, 974
 archiving, 969-971
 batch file, 975-977
 cycles, 1007
 data, 123
 devices, 971
 disk formats, 55
 DOS disks, 122-123
 fault tolerance, 54
 files, 362-381
  comparing, 380-381
  data compression, 53, 371
  differential backups, 371
  full backups, 368
  incremental backups, 371
  options, 371
  selected files, 996-997
  setup files, 378
  to different directories, 977
  verification, 371
  XCOPY command, 349-351
 floppies, 968
 frequency, improving, 972-983

 hard disks, 981-983
 labeling, 979
 master copies, 981
 MSBACKUP command, 55-56, 993-997, 1010
 MWBACKUP command, 983-985, 995
 need for, determining, 1502-1503
 off-site storage, 983
 policies, 1011
 readability, 974
 refreshing, 1018
 restoring, 997-1001
 storage, 979-981
 to servers, 973
  verifying, 1001-1003
 versus archiving, 970
 virus prevention, 1085-1086
 virus recovery, 969
 XCOPY command, 1006-1011
backward compatibility, 464-466
Bad command or file name error message, 100, 1027
Bad or missing command interpreter error message, 39, 44, 1045
BAGKEYS command, 1484-1485
BAK file extension, 328
band stepper head actuators, 178
banks, installing, 568-572
BAS file extension, 77, 328

baseband coaxial (Thinnet) cabling – bit DIP-type RAM

baseband coaxial
  (Thinnet) cabling,
  1250
Basic Input Output
  System, *see* BIOS
BAT file extension,
  77, 328
batch commands, 1272
Batch Enhancer
  (Norton), 46
batch files, 96,
  791-794, 1484
  activity log, 856-857
  alarm utilities,
    845-848
  AUTOEXEC.BAT,
    820-821
    booting without,
    38-39
    memory managers,
    487-491
    renaming,
    1165-1168
  backups, 975-977
  blank lines, 809-810
  CALL command,
    842-843
  CHOICE command,
    44-46
  command parser,
    831-832
  comments, 838-839
  compiling, 1503-1504
  connecting, 839-844
  controlling access
    with, 1176-1178
  copying different
    disk formats,
    851-852
  CTTY NUL com-
    mand, 843-844
  day of the week
    utility, 849
  default options,
    820-822

delaying, 820-829
designated delays,
  823-825
directories,
  829-830, 853
drives,
  changing, 853
ECHO command,
  794-809
  screen messages,
  796-798
environment
  variables, 835-838
excluding files from
  commands, 850-851
extension, changing,
  1168-1171
File Locator, 849-850
floppy disk
  organizer, 853-854
FO.BAT, 212-214
input/output
  redirection, 801-809
interactive
  execution, 844
macro batch files,
  747
menus, 811-820
  GOTO command,
  816-817
  return codes,
  813-815
  user input, 812-813
nesting, 841-842
notepad, 854-856
on-line help, 834-835
PC Typewriter,
  857-858
preprogrammed
  delays, 822-823
RAM drives, 826-828
recursive delete,
  858-859
replaceable
  parameters, 829-835

SDEL.BAT,
  1037-1039
SEECODE, 1500
sounds, 809-810
testing error levels,
  817-820
toolbox, 845-859
utilizing other batch
  files, 839-840
versus macros,
  742-743
virtual devices,
  798-801
WAITFOR
  command, 828-829
see also commands
baud rates, 774
  InterLnk, 1213-1215
BBSs, virus
  precautions,
  1086-1087
bell character, 809
bezels, 221
bidirectional parallel
  ports (InterLnk),
  1199, 1202-1204
BIN file extension, 77,
  328
binary files, copying,
  342-344
Bindery user-tracking
  program (NetWare),
  1255
BIOS (Basic Input
  Output System), 59,
  104, 921
  bypassing, 111-113
  hard disks
    installation, 228
BIOS parameter
  block, 925
BIOS ROM, 459-461
bit blitting, 756
bit DIP-type
  RAM, 560

BLANK command,
  1485-1486
blank lines (ECHO
  command), 809-810
blanking screen,
  1171-1172
blinking text, 766
blocks
  [common], 887
  data, transferring,
    32-34
Blue North Software,
  1489
BMP file extension,
  77, 328
bold text, 766
Bontchev, Vesselin,
  1073
boot disks
  backing up, 1018
  creating, 487-489,
    1048
boot indicator, 923
boot record, 924-927
  contents, 927-928
  creating, 945-952
  repairing, 1053-1055
  scanning for viruses,
    929-932
  viewing, 929
boot sector, 405, 1053
  viruses, 1084-1085
  *MSAV command,
    1102-1103*
  *transmission of,
    1086*
Boot sector write
  error! error
  message, 141
bootable disks,
  162-165
  creating, 956-958
booting
  "clean" boots,
    38-39, 65

computer
  refusal, 1111
logging bootups,
  1171
prevention,
  1497-1498
sequence, 921-922
  boot record, 924-932
  *FAT (file allocation
    table), 932-962*
  *hidden system files,
    938-940*
  *master boot record,
    creating, 922-924*
  *root directory,
    937-938*
  subdirectories, 938
system, 864-868
viruses, 1055,
  1067-1069, 1181-
  1183
  *checking for,
    1048-1049*
  *CHKDSK command,
    1051-1053*
  contracting, 1082
  removing, 943
  see also rebooting
bootstrap
  program, 925
BREAK command, 94,
  1286-1287
broadband coaxial
  (Thicknet)
  cabling, 1250
Brooklyn Bridge
  (Fifth Generation
  Systems), 1198
buffers, 682-684
  system reserved area
    of memory, 461
BUFFERS command,
  1287-1289
BUFFERS.COM
  (QEMM), 682

bugs, 1066
bulletin boards,
  see BBSs
bus mastering, 388-
  390, 647-659
buses, ISA, 757
BUSETUP.EXE
  file, 158
byte offsets, 1053-1054
bytes, 445
  media
    descriptor, 926
bytes free list, 317

C

C drive, deleting, 259
C file extension, 328
cables, 1249-1251
  hard disks, 221
  InterLnk, 1199-1203
  null modem, linking
    Macintoshes and
    PCs, 1228-1230
cache memory,
  591-592
caches
  size, SMARTDrive,
    394-395
  write-ahead, 188
caching disks, 384-390
CALL command, 94,
  769, 1289-1290
  batch files, 842-843
Canadian-French
  keyboard layout, 740
canceling print
  jobs, 782
capturing video RAM,
  684-685
cards
  network interface,
    1246
    ARCnet, 1246-1247
    Ethernet, 1247-1248
    FDDI, 1249

Token-Ring,
1248-1249
punched, 900
Carrier Sense Multiple Access with Collision Detection, *see* **CSMA/CD**
Cascade Family virus, 1113, 1128-1131
catalogs
  backup, 988-989
  repairing, 1012
CBL file extension, 328
CD command, 84-86, 93, 284-286, 1291-1292
CDDI technologies, 1249
CDIR command, 1486-1487
Central Point Anti-Virus, 1073
CFG file extension, 328
CGA (Color Graphics Adapter), 456, 753
CGM file extension, 328
chains, 202
change-line support, 145, 735
charging times, 590
CHCP command, 94, 1290-1291
CHDIR command, 1291-1292
checkerboard test, 585
CheckIt memory diagnostic program, 587-588
checksum, virus prevention, 1090-1091
child subdirectories, 283
chips
  DRAM, 560

installing, 581
parity, 570
CHKDSK command, 65, 1199, 1261, 1292-1294
  allocation units, size, 192
  defragmenting disks, 423-424
  /F switch, 206, 1052
  hard drive formatted capacity, 912
  lost clusters, 204-208
  options, 1051-1053
  overwritten root directories, recovering, 1044-1045
  /S switch, 1052
  /V switch, 303, 1052
CHKSTATE.SYS command, 1294
CHOICE command, 44-46, 812-813, 977, 1295-1297
  delaying batch files, 820-829
CHP file extension, 328
clean boots, 38-39, 65, 864-865
  disabling, 868
CLEANUP command, 1297-1298
client/server computing, 1204-1205
client/server environments, 1259
client/server programs, 1265-1266
clients,
  INTERLNK.EXE, 868-870, 1204
  connecting to servers, 1216-1217

clock pulses, 919
clock ticks, 589-591, 782
CLOCK$ (virtual device), 799
CLP file extension, 328
CLS command, 94, 763, 1298-1299
clusters, 192-193
  compression programs, 236
  cross-linked, 207
  FAT cluster entries, 201-202
  hard disk size, determining, 955-956
  invalid, 207
  lost, 50, 204-208
  sizes, 954-955
  starting, 203
CMOS command, 1487-1488
CNF file extension, 328
CNV file extension, 328
code, writing, 105-106
code pages, 632, 738-739
codes
  ASCII, 26
  error, testing for commands, 1500
collation sequence, 807
Color Graphics Adapter, *see* **CGA**
color video adapters, 754-755
colors
  menus (MultiConfig), 874-878

COM file extension – commands

screen, changing, 992-993
COM file extension, 77, 97-98, 328
COM1 (virtual device), 799
COM2 (virtual device), 799
COM3 (virtual device), 799
COM4 (virtual device), 799
command buffer, 742
adjusting, 745
COMMAND command, 1299-1301
command histories, 742-750
command lines
creating drives, 251-252
disk compression, 251-252
reading, 90-91
command parser, replaceable parameters, 831-832
COMMAND.COM file, 89-91, 783-784, 792
allocating additional space, 449
conventional memory, 447-450
external commands, 95
finding programs, 92-96
internal commands, 93-95
hidden system files, 939-940
location, 279
moving to C:\DOS directory, 312-313

position-sensitivity, 957-958
reading command line, 90-91
troubleshooting, 1045-1047
wrong version of, 1112
commands
@ (ampersand) preceeding, 796
APPEND, 64, 102-103, 303-304, 1282-1283
ASSIGN, 728-729, 1283-1284
ATTRIB, 137, 239, 320-321, 1285-1286
BACKUP, 64, 123, 363
BAGKEYS, 1484-1485
batch commands, 1272
BLANK, 1485-1486
BREAK, 94, 1286-1287
BUFFERS, 1287-1289
CALL, 94, 769, 842-843, 1289-1290
CD, 84-86, 93, 284-286, 1291-1292
CDIR, 1486-1487
CHCP, 94, 1290-1291
CHDIR, 1291-1292
CHKDSK, 65, 204-208, 912, 1051-1053, 1199, 1261, 1292-1294
CHKSTATE, 1294
CHOICE, 44-46, 812-813, 820-829, 977, 1295-1297
CLEANUP, 1297-1298

CLS, 94, 763, 1298-1299
CMOS, 1487-1488
COMMAND, 1299-1301
command name, 91
COMMAND.COM, 783-784, 792
COMP, 63, 356-359
CONVHEX, 516
COPY, 65, 88, 93, 337-338, 1061, 1301-1304
COPY CON, 800
COUNTRY, 1304-1306
CTTY, 1306-1307
CTTY NUL, 843-844
DATE, 94, 1307-1308
DBLSPACE, 238-242, 251, 1308-1325
DCOPY, 1488-1489
DEBUG, 227, 929, 1325-1327
DECOMP, 64
DEFRAG, 65, 74, 384, 424, 429-430, 1199, 1261, 1327-1329
DEL, 94, 359-360, 1161, 1329-1331
DELTREE, 63, 293-294, 1331-1332
DEVICE, 1332-1333
DEVICE=, 39
DEVICEHIGH, 539-541, 599-601, 1334-1335
DIR, 64-65, 93, 279, 291-292, 316-324, 849, 1016, 1335-1338
DIR FIRST, 320
DIRCMD, 324
DISKCOMP, 1199, 1261, 1338-1339

DISKCOPY, 65,
  122-123, 346-347,
  729-733, 1199,
  1339-1340
DOS, 1342-1343
DOSHELP, 63,
  1343-1344
DOSHELP COPY, 35
DOSKEY, 742-750,
  1344-1347
DOSSHELL,
  1348-1349
DOSWATCH,
  1121-1122,
  1489-1490
DRIVPARM,
  736-737, 1350-1352
DSEDIT, 731-732,
  924, 1040-1041,
  1490-1491
ECHO, 94, 794-798,
  801-810, 1352-1353
ECHO OFF, 795
EDIT, 63, 333-337,
  719-725, 1353-1354
EMM386, 1355-1361
ENVEDIT, 1491-1492
ERASE, 94, 359-360,
  804-805
ERRORLEVEL,
  813-815
EXE2BIN, 1361
EXIT, 1362
EXPAND, 64,
  149-158, 1362-1363
external, 95
F-PROT, 1494-1495
FASTOPEN, 383,
  401-404, 1261,
  1363-1364
FC, 63, 356-359,
  1365-1366
FCBS, 1367
FCBS=, 64

FDISK, 63, 230,
  923-924, 941-945,
  1056-1057, 1199,
  1261, 1368-1369
FDISK /MBR, 943
FILES, 1369-1370
FIND, 808,
  1370-1371,
  1492-1493
FINDTEXT, 1025,
  1122, 1493-1494
FOR, 94, 1371-1372
FORMAT, 65,
  209-216, 231-234,
  945-952, 956-958,
  1058-1059, 1107,
  1120, 1151, 1199,
  1261, 1372-1375
FULLDIR,
  1122-1123,
  1495-1496
GOTO, 94, 816-817,
  1375-1376
GRAFTABL,
  1376-1478
GRAPHICS, 64,
  778-781, 1378-1380
HELP, 63, 1380-1381
HELP COPY, 35-36
HELP DBLSPACE,
  242
HIMEM.SYS,
  1381-1384
IF, 94, 832, 1384-1386
IF ERRORLEVEL, 46
INCLUDE, 885-887,
  1386-1387
INSTALL, 1387-1388
INTERLNK, 1261,
  1388-1992
internal, 93-95, 1272
  replacing, 1162-1165
INTERSVR,
  1392-1394
JOIN, 1394-1395

KEYB, 632, 738-742,
  1396-1398
LABEL, 1398-1399
LASTDRIVE,
  1399-1400
LOADFIX,
  1400-1401
LOADHIGH, 94,
  403, 539-541,
  599-601, 1401-1403
MAKETXT1, 956,
  1496-1497
MD, 81-83, 93, 279
MEM, 30, 59, 64-65,
  491-494, 1403-1404
MEMMAKER,
  1405-1406
MEMMAKER /T,
  1261
MENUCOLOR,
  874-878, 891,
  1406-1408
MENUDEFAULT,
  1408-1409
MENUITEM,
  1409-1410
MIRROR, 1019-1023,
  1199
MKDIR, 282,
  1410-1411
MODE, 771-777,
  1206, 1411-1420
MODE CON,
  750-751
MORE, 808,
  1420-1421
MOVE, 63-65,
  305-306, 354-356,
  1039, 1421-1423
MSAV, 1094-1103,
  1116-1120,
  1423-1425
MSAV /L, 1261
MSBACKUP, *see*
  MSBACKUP
  command

MSD, 1427-1429
MWBACKUP, 362
  backups, 983-990, 995
  configuring, 990-993
  restoring files, 997-1001
  selected files, backing, 996-997
  setup files, 1011-1012
  speed, 1005-1007
NET, 1261-1262
NLSFUNC, 1429
NOBOOT, 1497-1498
NUMLOCK, 891-892, 1430
parameters, 91
PATH, 94, 98-116, 294-300, 1431
PAUSE, 94, 1432
POWER, 1433-1478
PRINT, 781-783, 1435-1437, 1498
PROMPT, 89, 94, 286-291, 764-767, 1437-1438
QBASIC, 63, 1439-1440
RAMDRIVE, 1440-1441
RD, 94, 1042-1043
READEXE, 1123, 1498-1499
REBOOT, 940, 1123, 1499-1500
recalling, 744-745
redirecting disk commands, 728-729
REM, 94, 1442
REN, 94, 360-361
RENAME, 1442-1443
REPLACE, 352-354, 1443-1445
RESTORE, 381
RMDIR, 1445-1446

SCANDISK, 241, 407-409, 1446-1447
SEECODE, 1500
SET, 94, 449, 1448
SETUP, *see* SETUP command
SETVER, 125, 726-727, 1265, 1449-1451
SHARE, 1451-1452
SHELL, 1046, 1452-1453
SHELL=, 39, 146
SHIFT, 94, 1453-1454
SHOWINT, 1124, 1501
SIZER.EXE, 1454
SMARTDRV, 392
SMARTDRV.EXE, 1455-1458
SNORETIL, 1124, 1501-1502
SORT, 808, 1458-1459
STACKS, 1460
SUBMENU, 888-890, 1460-1462
SUBST, 297-298, 1462-1463
Supplemental Disk, 165
SWITCHES, 311, 1463-1464
switches, 91
SYS, 1199, 1261, 1464-1465
SYSEDIT, 167
TEMP, 836
TESTBAK, 1502-1503
testing for error codes, 1500
TIME, 95, 823-825, 1465-1466
TREE, 83-84, 101-102, 301-303, 1466-1467

TRUENAME, 95, 298
TURBOBAT, 1503-1504
TYPE, 95, 331-333, 1467-1468
UNDELETE, 61-62, 1043, 1199, 1468-1471
UNFORMAT, 945-946, 953, 1058-1059, 1120, 1199, 1261, 1471-1472
UNINSTALL, 158-161
VER, 95, 1472-1473
VERIFY, 355-356, 1473-1474
VOL, 95, 1474
.VSAFE, 1475-1476
WAITFOR, 828-829
XCOPY, 65, 347-352, 770, 1006-1011, 1477-1478
XIT, 94
see also batch files
comments
  386Max memory manager, 706
  batch files, 838-839
communications programs
  Crosstalk, 1199
  InterLnk, 32-34
  Smartcom, 1199
communications support, 32-35
COMP command, 63, 356-359
comparators, 571
comparing
  backup files, 380-381
  files, 87, 356-359
    ASCII files, 357-358
  floppy disks, 732-733

compilers, 96-98
compiling batch files, 1503-1504
Compress Backup Data option (MSBACKUP/ MWBACKUP), 988
compressed drives, defragmenting, 421-422
Compressed Volumed Files (CVF), 239, 255-257
compressing ROMs, 705
compression, disk, 23
  DoubleSpace, 23-32, 234-265
  encrypted files, 236
  Huffman encoding, 24-26
  Lempel-Ziv method, 234-235
  run-length encoding, 24-26
compression programs
  allocation units, 236
  backup programs, 53
  clusters, 236
  DoubleSpace, 234-265
  PKZIP, 975
COMPSEC variable, 448
CompuServe, National Computer Security Association, 1192
Computer Virus Database (Virus Research Center), 1069-1070

Computer Virus Handbook, 1150
CON (virtual device), 799
concatenating files, 341-342
CONFIG.SYS device driver, 37
  booting without, 38-39
  device drivers, 446
  HMAs (high memory areas), 498-499
  InterLnk, 1208-1216
  memory managers, 487-491
  MultiConfig
    menus, 872-873
    merging, 870-871
    naming configurations, 871-872
    shared groups of statements, 885-886
    timeouts/defaults, 873-874
  multiple, developing, 40-44
  printing, 799
  UMBs, creating, 537
CONFIG=VAN environment variable, 448
configuration control, 38-66
Configuration Manager, 38-44
configuring
  hard disks, 228-230
  hardware, 87
  MSBACKUP command, 990-993
  MWBACKUP command, 990-993

connecting
  batch files, 839-844
  INTERLNK.EXE program with servers, 1216-1217
Conner CP-2024 20M drive, 903
Conner CP-4044 40M drive, 903
controllers, identifying, 190
conventional memory, 444-451
  COMMAND.COM, 447-450
    allocating additional space, 449
    environment variables, 448-450
  device drivers, 446-447
  environment, 447-450
  environment variables, 448
  interrupt vectors, 445-446
  TSRs, 446-447
  user programs, 450
converting hexadecimal numeric values, 515-517
CONVHEX command, 516
COPY command, 65, 88, 93, 337-338, 1301-1304
  /A switch, 343-344
  /B switch, 343
  COPYCMD environment variable, 340
  error messages, 1060
  fragmented files, 1061

COPY CON command – DBLSPACE command

/V switch, 344-345
/-Y switch, 340
/Y switch, 340
COPY CON command, 800
COPYCMD environment variable, 340
copying
   ASCII files, 342-344
   between devices, 342
   binary files, 342-344
   disks, 346-347
     DCOPY command, 1488-1489
     different disk formats, 851-852
     floppy disks, 729-732
     verfication, 347
   files, 86-88, 337-352
     verification, 344- 345
   subdirectories, 348
Correcting Bad Disk message, 1004
costs
   network cabling, 1249-1251
   peer-to-peer networks, 1251
   server-based networks, 1251
country codes, 739-740
COUNTRY command, 1304-1306
CPI file extension, 328
CPP file extension, 328
CPS file extension, 328
CPUs (central processing units), 920-921
   data paths, 568-569
CRC (cyclic redundancy check), 917

creating
   directories, 81-83
   programs, 96-98
   subdirectories, 279-280
cross-linked clusters, 207
cross-linked files, 50, 404, 1052
cross-platform programs, 1232
Crosstalk (Digital Communications Associates), 1199
CSMA/CD (Carrier Sense Multiple Access with Collision Detection), 1247
Ctrl-F5 (clean boot) keyboard shortcut, 65
CTTY command, 1306-1307
   batch files, 843-844
Current drive must be set to A error message, 144
cursor movement, 767-769
customizing
   directory lists, 324
   keyboard, 737-751
   MicroSoft ScanDisk, 414-415
   SMARTDrive, 395-396
CVF (Compressed Volume Files), 239, 255-257
CVTPACK program, 643-644
cycle times, 589, 591
cycles, backup, 1007
cylinders, 182-183, 909

D

$D metastring character, 287
damaged
   FATs, 1049-1050
   file structures
     data recovery, 1023
     hard disk, 1000-1001
   media
     file recovery, 1059-1062
     preventing, 1018-1019
Dark Avenger viruses, 1072-1073, 1131
DAT file extension, 328
data bits, 775
data blocks, transferring, 32-34
data loss
   causes, 966
   preventing, 1016-1018
data paths, common CPUs, 568-569
data recovery, 1023-1024
data transfer rates, 184-186
DATE command, 94, 1307-1308
day of the week utility, 849
DBF file extension, 329
DBL (DOS batch language) programs, 44-46
DBLSPACE command, 242, 251, 1308-1325
   /? switch, 241
   /AUTOMOUNT=0 switch, 254

1517

DBLSPACE BIN file – DEVICE command

/CHKDSK switch, 255-257
/COM switch, 251
/COMPRESS switch, 251
/CREATE switch, 251
/DEF switch, 258
/DEFRAG switch, 432-433
/DEFRAGMENT switch, 258
/DEL switch, 259
/DOUBLEGUARD =0 switch, 241
/DOUBLEGUARD =1 switch, 241
/FORMAT switch, 262
/H switch, 258
/INFO switch, 262
/LIST switch, 263
/MOUNT switch, 252-253
/NEWDRIVE switch, 251
/NEWDRIVE= switch, 251
/RESERVE switch, 251
/SI switch, 252
/SIZE switch, 252, 259-261
/UNCOMPRESS switch, 238
/UNMOUNT switch, 252
DBLSPACE BIN file, 240
DBLSPACE.INI file, 244, 263-265
DBLSPACE.SYS file, 240
DBR (DOS boot record), 193-194

DCOPY command, 1488-1489
DEBUG command, 227, 929, 1325-1327
decimal addresses (memory maps), 443
DECOMP command, 64
decompressing
  compressed drives, 238
  files, 149-158
dedicated server-based networks, 1239
dedicated servers, 1241
dedicated servos, 916
defaults
  batch files, 820-822
  CONFIG.SYS files (MultiConfig), 873-874
DEFRAG command, 65, 74, 384, 424-430, 1199, 1261, 1327-1329
DEFRAG for DOS (MicroSoft), 421-433
  closing all open programs, 423
  loading, 424-430
defragmentation, 420
  compressed drives, 421-422
  disks, 49-50, 87
  CHKDISK, 423-424
  large disks, 431-432
  DoubleSpaced drives, 258
DEL command, 94, 359-360, 1329-1331
  /P switch, 360
delay time, 750
delaying batch files, 820-829

DELETE command, 1161
Delete Sentry control file not found error, 1035
Delete Sentry level
  MWUNDEL, 1033
  UNDELETE, 1025, 1030, 1033-1035
Delete Tracker level
  MWUNDEL, 1033
  UNDELETE.EXE, 1025, 1030
deleting
  C drive, 259
  directories, 1042-1043
  DoubleSpaced drives, 258-261
  files, 1016-1018
    from subdirectories, 359
  partitions, 232-233
  subdirectories, 293-294
deletion sentry protection level, 62
Deletion-tracking file not found error message, 1035
DELTREE command, 63, 293-294, 1331-1332
designated delays, batch files, 823-825
DESQview, 784
detecting viruses
  anti-virus TSRs, 1093
  checksum changes, 1089-1091
  myths, 1088-1089
  scanning, 1091-1093
DEVICE command, 1332-1333

device drivers – directories **1519**

device drivers, 23, 57, 1272
  ANSI.SYS device driver, 446, 763-771, 1273-1282
    cursor movement, 767-769
    macros, 769-771
    video display control, 763-769
  anti-virus, 1093
  CONFIG.SYS file, 446
    booting without, 38-39
    device drivers, 446
    HMAs (high memory areas), 498-499
    memory managers, 487-491
    MultiConfig, 870-874, 885-886
  conventional memory, 446-447
  DISPLAY.SYS, 1340-1342
  DRIVER.SYS, 733-736, 1349-1350
  EGA.SYS, 1354-1355
  INTERLNK.EXE, 1198, 1204, 1211-1213
    connecting to servers, 1216-1217
    switches, 1213
  memory managers, 533-536
  mouse drivers, 446
  POWER.EXE, 63
  QEMM, 675-676
DEVICE= command, 39
DEVICE=INTERLNK.EXE statement, 1216

DEVICEHIGH command, 539-541, 599-601, 1334-1335
  /L switch, 600
devices
  backup, 971
  copying between, 342
  random access, 900
  sequential access, 900
dialog boxes
  EDIT utility, 724-725
  Problem Found, 409
Dietrich, Lori, 968
DIF file extension, 329, 376
Differential backup option (MSBACKUP/ MWBACKUP), 986
differential backups, 371
DIP (Dual Inline Pin) chips, 560
DIR command, 65, 93, 279, 291-292, 316-324, 1016, 1335-1338
  /A switch, 321-322
  /AHA switch, 322
  /AR switch, 322
  /B switch, 323-324
  /C switch, 64
  /L switch, 323
  /O switch, 322-323
  /P switch, 318
  /S switch, 849
  /W switch, 318
DIR FIRST command, 320
DIRCMD command, 324
DIRCOMP command, 1039
direct action viruses, 1068

direct memory access, 190
DirectAccess DOS, 784
directories, 61, 316-324
  ARCHIVE.ME, 1009
  attributes, 320-322
  bytes free list, 317
  changing, 84, 284-286, 1486-1487
    with batch files, 853
  comparing contents, 1039
  creating, 81-83
    with batch files, 829-830
  differentiating, 1039
  displaying, 318
  erased files, recovering, 1039-1040
  FASTOPEN command, 383, 401-404
  file placement, 353-354
  information, displaying, 1495-1496
  listing, 291-292
  lists, customizing, 324
  moving between, 84-86
  organizing, 306-313
  parent, 80
  path, 76, 98-103, 317-318, 283
    adding directories, 296
    editing, 299-300
    shortening name, 296-297
  purging files, 1036
  recovering, 1031-1033, 1040-1043

relative directory
 addressing, 84-86
renaming, 305-306
root, 74, 276-278,
 925, 937-938
 clearing, 310-313
 overwritten,
 recovery, 1044-1045
 printing, 307
 sizes, 277
 structure, 277-278
 versus
 subdirectories,
 1040-1041
 writing files to disk,
 1050-1051
root directory
 table, 203
searches, 319-320
sorting, 74, 322-323
see also
 subdirectories
directory tree, 276
 saving to disk,
 301-302
 viewing, 83-84,
 301-303
disabling
 clean and
 interactive boots,
 868
 programs for DOS
 installation, 126
 VCPI support, 543
Disaster Recovery
 Planning: Managing
 Risk and Catastrophe
 in Information
 Systems, **966**
disasters, preventing,
 1016-1018
disk caches, 384-390
 bus mastering,
 388-390
 double buffering,
 388-390

MCache, 400
NCache-F, 401
NCache-S, 401
PC Cache, 401
read caching,
 384-385
SMARTDrive,
 390-401
 cache size, 394-395
 customizing,
 395-396
 double buffering, 396
 information, 397-398
 installing, 391-392
 selecting drives to
 cache, 393-394
 storage location, 392
SMARTDrive
 Monitor, 398-400
 third-party, 400-401
 versus processor
 caches, 592
 write caching,
 386-388
disk compression, 23
 algorithms, 237
 alternative to
 DoubleSpace,
 268-269
 DoubleSpace, 23-32,
 234-265
 encrypted files, 236
 from Command
 Line, 251-252
 Huffman encoding,
 24-26
 Lempel-Ziv method,
 234
 LHA program,
 268-269
 PKZIP program,
 268-269
 run-length encoding,
 24-26
disk drives, *see* **drives**

disk formats
 on-the-fly, 55
disk hubs, 902
disk jackets, 902
disk mirroring, 982
disk packs, 900
disk transfers, 644-646
DISKCOMP
 command, 1199, 1261,
 1338-1339
DISKCOPY
 command, 65, 122-
 123, 346-347, 729-733,
 1199, 1339-1340
 sector marks,
 1060-1061
 /V switch, 347
disks
 backups, refreshing,
 1018
 boot disks
 backing up, 1018
 creating, 487-489,
 1048
 boot sectors, 405,
 1084-1085
 bootable, creating,
 956-958
 capacity, 912-914
 components
 information sources,
 960-962
 numbering, 960
 copying, 346-347
 DCOPY command,
 1488-1489
 verfication, 347
 defragmenting, 87
 large disks, 431-432
 DOS disks, backing
 up, 122-123
 editing, 1490-1491
 floppy, *see* floppy
 disks
 formatting, 87

fragmentation,
  49-50, 416-433
  *defragmentation,
    420-422, 432-433*
  *viewing fragmented
    file lists, 419-420*
  hard, *see* hard disks
  information storage,
    918-919
  labeling, 979
  memory, 440-441
  old, 981
  repairing, 50
  ScanDisk, 405-416
  sectors, 910
  sides, 908-909
  storing, 980-981
  tracks, 907-912
    numbering, 909
  troubleshooting,
    404-405
    bad clusters, 405
    cross-linked files, 404
    lost clusters, 404
  viewing, 1490-1491
  writing to, 921
**DISPLAY.SYS device
  driver, 1340-1342**
displaying
  directories, 318
  environment
    variables, 448
  read-only files, 322
**DLL file extension,
  78, 329**
**DLLs (Dynamic Link
  Libraries), 109**
**DMA (direct memory
  access) chips, 920**
  addresses, 646
  disk transfers,
    644-646
**DMA Buffer size too
  small error message,
  1002**

**DOC file extension,
  77, 329**
**documentation,
  on-line, 35-37**
**documenting DOS
  installation, 169-171**
documents
  editing, 335-337
  navigating, 335-336
  see also files, 335-337
DOS
  architectural
    limitations,
    1242-1244
  bypassing, 111-113
  configurations,
    memory
    management,
    489-496
  loading, 200-202
  program support,
    104-115
  user interface, 88-103
DOS 1.1, 22
DOS 2, 22
DOS 3, 22
**DOS 3.3, partitioning
  hard disks, 24**
DOS 5, 21-22
  EMM386.EXE file, 56
  memory manage-
    ment, 46-48
  Memory Manager,
    56-58
  on-line help, 37
  undelete protection,
    61-62
DOS 6.2
  commands, updates,
    63-65
  communications
    support, 32-35
  compared to earlier
    versions, 21-30

configuration
  control, 38-66
installation
  *available space,
    128-129*
  backing up data, 123
  *backing up disks,
    122-123*
  *bootable floppy disk,
    preparing, 162-165*
  *changes to Windows
    INI files, 166-169*
  *current DOS,
    locating, 125*
  *disabling programs,
    126*
  *documenting
    installation,
    169-171*
  *inventory system,
    123-125*
  *manual installation,
    147-149*
  *README.TXT file,
    126-127*
  *SETUP command,
    129-149*
  swapping disks, 137
  *uninstalling,
    158-161*
MemMaker memory
  arranger, 48-49
minor changes in, 65
network software,
  running, 1261-1264
networked
  programs, running,
  1265-1266
on-line
  documentation,
  35-37
required network
  versions, 1262-1264
**DOS batch language
  (DBL) programs,
  44-46**

DOS boot record (DBR), 193-194
DOS command, 1342-1343
DOS environment, 447-450
DOS extenders, 466-472
  DPMI (DOS protected mode interface), 471-472
  GDTs (global descriptor tables), 469
  LDTs (local descriptor tables), 469
  page tables, 469
  VCPI (virtual control program interface), 468-471
DOS master environment, editing, 1491
DOS protected mode interface (DPMI), 471-472
DOSHELP command, 63, 1343-1344
DOSHELP COPY command, 35
DOSKEY command, 742-750, 1344-1347
  command buffer adjustments, 745
  installing, 743-744
  macros
    creating/executing, 745-746
    replaceable parameters, 747-750
    saving, 746-747
  recalling commands, 744-745
DOSKEY Editing Keys, 744-745

DOSSHELL command, 1348-1349
DOSTops software, 1231
DOSWATCH command, 1489-1490
  viruses, removing, 1121-1122
dot pitch, 763
double buffering, 388-390
  SMARTDrive, 396
Double Disk utility (Microsoft), 24
double-sided disks, 909
DoubleGuard, 65, 240-241
DoubleSpace utility, 23-29, 65, 234-265
  ActivateDrive, 264
  creating drives, 247-251
    from Command Line, 251-252
  CVF (Compressed Volume File), 239
  DBLSPACE.INI file, 263-265
  Deframenter, 432-433
  disk compression, 243-246
    alternatives, 268-269
    Custom Setup, 243, 247-251
    Express Setup, 242-243
    from Command Line, 251-252
  DoubleGuard, 66, 240-241
  drives
    changing size, 261
    defragmenting, 258

  deleting, 258-261
  formatting, 262
  information, 262-263
  mounting, 252
  RAM drives, 254
  Stacker drives, 255
  error messages, 266-268
  floppy disks, 253-254
  LastDrive, 264
  MaxFileFragments, 264
  MaxRemovableDrives, 264
  Microsoft Real-Time Compression Interface, 237
  OS/2, 237
  user tips, 238-239
  Windows NT, 237
DPMI (DOS protected mode interface), 471-472
DPMI clients, 471
DPMI servers, 471-472
DPMI support (QEMM), 705
DRAMs (Dynamic Random Access Memories), 560
Drippy program, 1113
drive designator, 76
drive not ready error message, 82
DRIVER.SYS device driver, 733-736, 1349-1350
  /C switch, 735
  /H:HEADS switch, 735
  installing, 734-735
  /S:SECTORS switch, 735
  /T:TRACKS switch, 735

drivers – encryption

drivers, 105
drives
  changing with batch files, 853
  components
    locating, 959
    numbering, 962
  creating
    from Command Line, 251-252
    with DoubleSpace, 247-251
  DoubleSpace
    defragmenting, 258
    deleting, 258-261
    formatting, 262
    information, 262-263
  history, 899-900
  internal operation of, 905-906
  names, 76-78
  reading process, 919-921
  redirection, 1204
  rotation speeds, 905-906
  tape, data transfer, 32
  virtual, data transfer, 33-34
DRIVPARM command, 736-737, 1350-1352
  /C switch, 737
  /D:DRIVE switch, 736
  /F:TYPE switch, 736
  /H:NUMBER switch, 737
  /I switch, 737
  /N switches, 737
  /T:TRACKS switches, 737
drop-down menus, 720
  see also menus

droppers, 1066
DRV file extension, 329
DRW file extension, 77, 329
DSEDIT command, 924, 1040-1041, 1490-1491
  copying files, 731-732
dual-ported RAM, *see* **video RAM**
duplicate files, 977-978
Dynamic Link Libraries, *see* **DLLs**
dynamic linking, 109
dynamic memory, 588-589

E

$E metastring character, 287
ECC (error correction coding), 917, 1003-1004
ECHO command, 94, 1352-1353
  batch files, 794-798, 801-809
  blank lines, 809-810
  output redirection, 804
  sounds, 809-810
ECHO OFF command, 795
EDIT command, 63, 333-337, 719-726, 1353-1354
  changing default file extension, 725-726
  dialog boxes, 724-725
  keyboard operations, 723-725

  loading, 334
  menus, 720-723
Edit menu (EDIT), 722
editing
  DBLSPACE.INI file, 265
  disks, 1490-1491
  documents, 335-337
  DOS environments, 1491
  files, 718-726
  path, 299-300
EGA (Enhanced Graphics Adapter), 753
  memory addresses, 453-454
EGA.SYS device driver, 1354-1355
EISA (Enhanced Industry Standard Architecture), 757
electromagnetic fields, 981
embedded servos, 915-918
EMM386 command, 1355-1356
EMM386.EXE file, 662, 1356-1361
  crashes, 648-649
  DOS 5, 56
  DOS 6.2 changes, 60
  memory managers, 489
    limulating, 544-547
    troubleshooting, 632-640
encoding schemes, 910-922
  Huffman, 24-26
  run-length, 24-26
encrypted files, disk compression, 236
encryption, 1178-1179

end-of-file markers, 325
enhanced graphics adapter, *see* EGA
ENVEDIT command, 1491-1492
environment variables, 448
  batch files, 835-838
  CONFIG=VAN, 448
  COPYCMD, 340
  MSDOSDATA, 1262
  PATH, 449
  PROMPT, 449
environments
  client/server, 1259
  DOS, editing, 1491
ERASE command, 94, 359-360
  input redirection, 804-805
erased files, recovering, 1035-1040
erasing
  files, 87, 359-360
    permanently, 1175-1176
  screen displays, 763
error codes, testing for commands, 1500
error correction coding, *see* ECC
error messages
  A CVF is damaged, 142
  Abort, Retry, Ignore *file recovery*, 1061 *with COPY command*, 1060
  Allocation error. Size adjusted, 1052
  Bad command or file name, 100, 1027
  Bad or missing Command interpreter, 39, 44, 1045

Boot sector write error!, 141
COPY command, 1060
Correcting Bad Disk, 1004
Current drive must be set to A, 144
Delete Sentry control file not found, 1035
Deletion-tracking file not found, 1035
DMA Buffer size too small, 1002
DoubleSpace, 266-268
drive not ready, 82
Error reading drive or Sector not found, 1112
Error updating version table in MSDOS.SYS, 145
File creation, 953
General failure error reading drive A, 82, 922, 1054
Hard disk is not readable or Critical disk error, 142
Incorrect DOS version, 1046
Insufficient disk space, 1007
Invalid drive specification, 730
Lost clusters in lost chains, 1052
Non-System disk or disk error, 929-930, 1048
out of environment space, 450
permanent swap file is corrupt, 266-267

permanent swap files, 266-268
R6003 - Integer Divide by Zero, 265-266
UNRECOVERABLE ERROR - ERROR READING FILE SETUP.INI, 141
unsupported DOS version; upgrade to DOS version 3.1 or higher, 267-268
Windows, 266-268
Error reading drive or Sector not found error mess, 1112
Error updating version table in MSDOS.SYS error message, 145
ERRORLEVEL command, 813-815
errorlevels (MicroSoft ScanDisk), 415-416
errors
  hard, 919
  soft, 920
  walking-bit, 585-586
ESDI (enhanced small device interface), 188-189
Ethernet-style networks, 1247-1248
Examples jump point (Help system), 37
excellent condition files, 1032
exchanging files with InterLnk, 1220-1221
excluding files from commands, 850-851
EXE (executable) files, 77, 97-98, 326, 329
  reading, 1498-1499

EXE2BIN command, 1361
executing macros, 745-746
EXIT command, 1362
EXPAND command, 64, 149-158, 1362-1363
   syntax, 150
expanded memory, 476-482
   FASTOPEN, 403-404
Expanding Dialogs option (MSBACKUP), 992-994
expansion cards, installing memory, 580
expended memory, LIM, 479-481
Express Setup (DoubleSpace), 242-243
Extended DOS Partitions, 232
extended memory, 463-476, 482
   backward compatibility, 464-466
   DOS extenders, 466-472
   memory addresses, 472-476
   privilege rings, 467
   protected mode, 463-466
extended partitions, 196-197
extensions, *see* file extensions
external commands, 95
external floppy drives, 733-736

F

F-Prot anti-virus program, 1101, 1122
F-PROT command, 1494-1495
F5 keyboard shortcut, bypassing startup files, 940
faceplates, 221
false alarms, virus, 1110-1114
Fastback backup utility (Fifth Generation), 54
FastLynx (Rupp Brothers), 1198
FASTOPEN command, 383, 401-404, 1261, 1363-1364
   expanded memory, 403-404
   tracking files, 403-404
   UMBs (Upper Memory Blocks), 403
   /X switch, 403
FATs (file allocation tables), 61, 925, 932-933, 1036
   12-bit versus 16-bit, 934-936
   backing up, 1021-1023
   cluster entries, 201-202
   cross-linked files, 404
   damaged, 1049-1050
   lost clusters, 404
   writing files to disks, 1050-1051
fault tolerance, backup programs, 54

FC command, 63, 356-359, 1365-1366
   comparing ASCII files, 357-358
   /LB# switch, 357
FCBs (File Control Blocks), 682
FCBS command, 1367
FCBS.COM (QEMM), 682
FCBS= command, 64
FDDI (fiber-distributed data interface) networks, 1249
FDISK /MBR command, 943
FDISK command, 230, 923-924, 941-945, 1199, 1261, 1368-1369
   dangers, 1056-1057
   /STATUS switch, 63
fiber-optic cabling, 1250
file allocation tables, *see* FATs
File creation error message, 953
file extensions, 76-78, 327-333
   COM, 97-98
   EXE, 97-98
File Locator, 849-850
File menu (EDIT), 721
file servers, 1241
file specification, 77-79
file structures, damaged
   data recovery, 1023
   hard disk, 1000-1001
file translation, PC to Macintosh, 1231
file viruses, 1067-1069
   contracting, 1082

detecting, 1188-1189
prevention,
  1183-1186
files, 72-86, 325
  APMCHK.ZIP, 63
  archive attribute, 793
  archived, 1034
  backing up, 362-380
    by date, 374
    catalogs, 375-376
    data compression,
      371
    differential backups,
      371
    full backups, 370
    incremental backups,
      371
    options, 371
    to different
      directories, 977
    verifcation, 371
    XCOPY command,
      349-351
  backup sets, 375-376
  batch files, 96,
    791-794, 1484
    activity log, 856-857
    AUTOEXEC.BAT,
      see
      AUTOEXEC.BAT
      file
    BACKUP2.BAT,
      975
    BACKUP3.BAT,
      976
    BACKUP4.BAT,
      976-977
    backups, 975-977
    blank lines, 809-810
    CALL command,
      842-843
    changing drives/
      directories, 853
    CHOICE command,
      44-46

command parser,
  831-832
comments, 838-839
compiling,
  1503-1504
connecting, 839-844
copying different
  disk formats,
  851-852
CTTY NUL
  command, 843-844
day of the week
  utility, 849
default options,
  820-822
delaying, 820-829
designated delays,
  823-825
directories, 829-830
ECHO command,
  794-809
environment
  variables, 835-838
excluding files from
  commands, 850-851
File Locator, 849-850
floppy disk orga-
  nizer, 853-854
FO.BAT, 212-214
input/output
  redirection, 801-809
interactive execution,
  844
menus, 811-820
nesting, 841-842
notepad, 854-856
PC Typewriter,
  857-858
preprogrammed
  delays, 822-823
QBACK.BAT, 1006
RAM drives,
  826-828
recursive delete,
  858-859

replaceable
  parameters, 829-835
sounds, 809-810
TEST.BAT, 45-46
toolbox, 845-859
utilizing other
  batch files, 839-840
versus macros,
  742-743
virtual devices,
  798-801
WAITFOR com-
  mand, 828-829
BUSETUP.EXE, 158
COMMAND.COM,
  89-91
  allocating additional
    space, 449
  conventional
    memory, 447-450
  external commands,
    95
  finding programs,
    92-96
  hidden system files,
    939-940
  internal commands,
    93-95
  location, 279
  moving to C:\DOS
    directory, 312-313
  position-sensitivity,
    957-958
  reading command
    line, 90-91
  troubleshooting,
    1045-1047
  wrong version of,
    1112
comparing, 87
  ASCII files, 357-358
  backup files, 380-381
  contents, 356-359
concatenating,
  341-342

CONFIG.SYS, *see*
  CONFIG.SYS
  device driver
copying, 86-88,
  337-352
  verification, 344-345
creating for data
  recovery
  experiments,
  1496-1497
cross-linked, 50,
  1052
cross-linking, 1112
current version,
  determining,
  1038-1039
DBLSPACE. BIN,
  240
DBLSPACE.INI, 244,
  263-265
DBLSPACE.SYS, 240
decompressing,
  149-158
deleting, 1016-1018
  *from subdirectories,
  359*
duplicates, 977-978
editing, 333-337,
  718-726
end-of-file markers,
  325
erasing, 87, 359-360
  *permanently,
  1175-1176*
excellent condition,
  1032
exchanging with
  InterLnk, 1220-1221
excluding from
  commands in batch
  files, 850-851
floppy disk
  organization, 74-80
good condition, 1032
HELP.HLP, 37

hidden system,
  938-940
  attributes, 957
IO.SYS, 938-940,
  1045-1048
listing, 303
loading, 75
machine-language
  files, 97
maximum number
  on floppy disk,
  953-954
MEMMAKER.STS,
  622-624
MIRROR.FIL, 1019
moving, 87, 354-356
MSDOS.SYS,
  939-940, 1047-1049
MWAV.INI, 168
names, 75
  *drive names,
    including, 76-78*
naming, 325-327,
  1017
  *extensions, 327-333
  renaming, 360-361
  restrictions, 327*
nonexecutable, 326
overwrite
  protection, 338-340
overwriting, 338,
  952-953
  confirmation, 340
piping, 806-809
placement, 353-354,
  958-959
PROGMAN.INI, 167
push and pop, 841
README.TXT,
  126-127, 1262
recovering, 953,
  1031-1033,
  1039-1040
  *from damaged media,
  1059-1062*

*manual recovery,
  1035-1036
MIRROR command,
  1019-1023
misplaced,
  1024-1025
options,
  UNDELETE for
  DOS, 1029-1031*
redirection, 805-806
renaming, 87
restoring, 381,
  997-1001
SCANDISK.INI, 414
searches, 87, 319-320,
  1492-1493
  *nonexecutable files,
  303-304*
selecting for backup,
  373-381
setup files, 378,
  1011-1012
sizes, 954-955
starting cluster, 203
SWAPFILE.EXE, 267
system, hidden,
  1045-1048
SYSTEM.INI,
  167-168
transferring
  *comparison
    InterLnk/third-
    party programs,
    1224
  with InterLnk,
    1198-1199,
    1204-1205*
unerasing, 87
updating, 352-354
viewing, 87
WINFILE.INI, 168
WMBACKUP.INI,
  168
writing to disk,
  1050-1051
see also documents

FILES command,
  1369-1370
FILES.COM (QEMM),
  682
FIND command, 808,
  1370-1371, 1492-1493
Find utility, 37
finding, see searching
  for FINDTEXT
  command, 1025, 1122,
  1493-1494
firmware, 194
fixed frequency
  monitors, 762
FlashCard (Sitka),
  1231
floppy disk organizer,
  853-854
floppy disks, 208-216
  360K, 946
  anatomy, 901-902
  backups, 968
  boot, backing up,
    1018
  boot sector viruses,
    1084-1085
  booting, 487-489
  comparing, 732-733
  components
    information sources,
      960-962
    numbering, 960-962
  controlling, 728-737
  copying, 729-732
  data transfer, 33
  double-sided versus
    single-sided, 909
  DoubleSpace,
    253-254
  external, 733-736
  files
    maximum number
      of, 953-954
    organization, 74-80
  formats, 208
    changes, 736-737
  formatting, 209-216
    format options,
      215-216
    in Windows, 215
    quick formatting,
      211
    safe formats, 211
    unconditional
      formats, 211
  hard-sectoring, 914
  history, 900
  information storage,
    918-919
  logical drives, 733
  magnetic recording,
    904-906
  sectors, 910
    addressing, 915
  sides, 908-909
  size of files,
    determining,
    954-955
  storing, 980-981
  SuperDrive,
    1225-1227
  switches, 948
  tracks, 907-912
    numbering, 909
flux changes, 918
FNT file extension,
  329
FO.BAT batch file,
  212-214
Foley Hi-Tech
  Systems, 1504
FOR command, 94,
  1371-1372
FOR file extension,
  329
foreground color
  (monitors), 766
Form boot virus, 1117,
  1044
FORMAT command,
  65, 209-216, 231-234,
  945-952, 1059, 1199,
  1261, 1372-1375
  limitations, 952
  recovering from,
    1058-1059
  Stoned virus, 1107,
    1151
  switches, 947, 951
    /AUTOTEST,
      211-212
    /BACKUP, 212
    /F, 210
    /U, 211
    /S, 210, 234,
      956-958
  virus removal, 1120
formats
  disks
    on-the-fly, 55
    hard disk, accidental,
      1058-1059
    high-level, 1058-1059
    low-level, 1059
formatted disks,
  capacity, 912-914
formatting
  disks, 87
  DoubleSpaced
    drives, 262
  floppy disks, 209-216
    format options,
      215-216
    in Windows, 215
    quick formatting,
      211
    safe formats, 211
    unconditional
      formats, 211
  hard disks, 233-234
  partitions, 231
FOT file extension,
  329

fragmented files – hard disks

fragmented files
  DISKCOPY,
    1060-1061
  viewing lists,
    419-420
fragmented UMBs,
  537-539
fragmenting disks,
  49-50
frames, system
  reserved area of
  memory, 461
Frisk Software
  International, 1495
Frodo virus, 1067-1069,
  1073, 1101, 1118, 1151,
  1496
FUL file extension,
  376
Full backup option
  (MSBACKUP/
  MWBACKUP), 986
full backups, 370
FULLDIR command,
  1122-1123, 1495-1496
functions,
  nonreentrant, 1243

G

$G metastring
  character, 287
Gap 1 information,
  916
Gap 4 padding, 916
gap bytes, 915
GARBAGE directory,
  purging files, 1036
GDT (global descriptor tables), 469
General failure error
  reading drive A error
  message, 82, 1054
General Failure Error
  Reading Drive C
  error message, 922

Geoworks Desktop,
  783
GIF file extension, 329
gigabytes, 941
global descriptor
  tables (GDT), 469
good condition files,
  1032
GOTO command, 94,
  816-817, 1375-1376
GRAFTABL command, 1376-1478
GRAPHICS command, 64, 1378-1380
  printer support,
    778-779
graphics coprocessors,
  756
graphics mode, 752
  video boards, 456
  Video RAM, 454-455
graphics screens,
  printing, 780-781
Green Caterpillar
  viruses, 1151
GRP file extension,
  78, 329
GRPHICS command
  modifying printer
    profile, 780
  printing graphics
    screens, 780-781
  screen prints,
    778-781

H

$H metastring
  character, 287
hackers, slowing,
  1190-1191
Hard disk is not
  readable or Critical
  disk error error
  message, 142

hard disks
  32M limit, 23
  absolute sectors,
    191-192
  access time, 184
  actuator arm, 176
  adapter cards, 220
  anatomy, 903-904
  ASPI drivers,
    226-227
  backing up to,
    981-983
  bezels, 221
  boot sector viruses,
    1084-1085
  cables, 221
  clusters, 192-193
    cross-linked, 207
    FAT cluster entries,
      201-202
    invalid, 207
    lost, 204-208
    size, determining,
      955-956
  components
    information sources,
      960-962
    locating, 962
    numbering, 960-962
  compressing files,
    27-29
  configuring, 228-230
  controllers,
    identifying, 190
  cylinders, 182-183
  damaged file
    structures,
    1000-1001
  data transfer rates,
    184-186
  DBR (DOS boot
    record), 193-194
  disk caches, 384-390
    bus mastering,
      388-390

double buffering,
388-390
read caching,
384-385
write caching,
386-388
encoding
 techniques, 181-182
faceplates, 221
FORMAT command,
 951-952
formats, accidental,
 1058-1059
formatting, 233-234
hardware, 220-221
head actuators, 178
head crashes, 177
history, 900
IDE, 219
 configuring, 228
 installing, 222-225
information storage,
 918-919
installing, 220-233
interfaces, 186-190
internal operation
 of, 905-906
low-level format-
 ting, 191, 227-228
magnetic recording,
 904-906
master boot record,
 194-195
MemMaker, 612
mounting hardware,
 221
parking, 578
partitioning, 230-234
 DOS 3.3, 24
partitions, 195-199
platters, 176, 908-909
power connector,
 221
read/write heads,
 177
SCSI, 219
 configuring, 228
 installing, 225-227
sectors, 180-182, 910
 addressing, 915-918
storage capacity,
 calculating, 183
storing information,
 179-180
tracks, 180-182,
 907-912
 numbering, 909
hard errors, 919
hard-sectoring, 914
hardcards, 188
hardware
 accessing, 106-109
 addressing, 104
 configuring, 87
 controlling, 104-106
 hard disks, *see* hard
  disks
 InterLnk, 1199-1204
head actuators, 178
head crash, 177
heads, read-write, 903
heat, effect on
 floppys, 980
help, on-line, 35-37
HELP command, 63,
 1380-1381
HELP COPY com-
 mand, 35-36
HELP DBLSPACE
 command, 242
Help menu (EDIT),
 723
HELP.HLP file, 37
Hercules Graphics,
 753
Heumann, Greg, 968
hexadecimal
 addresses (memory
 maps), 443
hexadecimal numeric
 values, 510-521
 converting
  with DOS 6.2,
   516-517
  with Windows
   Calculator, 515-516
 integrated
  motherboards,
  520-521
 memory addressing,
  510-515
 memory maps,
  517-519
 offsets, 519-520
 segments, 519-520
hidden system files,
 938-940, 1045-1048
 attributes, 957
hidden text, 766
high memory areas,
 496-503
 BUFFERS statement,
  499-501
 CONFIG.SYS file,
  498-499
 FILES statement,
  499-501
 filling, 57-58
 HIMEM.SYS file,
  501-503
high-level formats,
 1058-1059
HIMEM.SYS device
 driver, 1381-1384
 adding to
  CONFIG.SYS file,
  40-42
 memory managers,
  489
 XMS Manager,
  501-503
HLP file extension,
 329

HMA (high memory area), 496-503
  CONFIG.SYS file, 498-499
  HIMEM.SYS file, 501-503
horizontal scanning frequency, 760-761
hub rings, 902
Huffman encoding, 24-26

I

IBM 8088, 441
ICO file extension, 329
IDE hard disks, 187-188, 219
  automatic sector translation, 229
  configuring, 228
  installing, 222-225
IDX file extension, 329
IEEE (Institute of Electrical and Electronic Engineers), 1247
IF command, 94, 1384-1386
  checking replaceable pararmeters, 832
IF ERRORLEVEL command, 46
IMG file extension, 329
INC file extension, 376
INCLUDE command, 885-887, 1386-1387
Incorrect DOS version error message, 1046
increasing memory, 650-653
  memory space, 495-496

ROM space, 650-652
video board space, 652-653
Incremental backup option (MSBACKUP/MWBACKUP), 986
incremental backups, 371
INF file extension, 329
INI files, 78, 329
  changes from DOS installation, 166-169
input redirection, 804-805
INSTALL command, 1387-1388
installing
  Anti-Virus utility, 134, 149
  Backup utility, 134, 149
  DOS 6.2
    available space, 128-129
    backing up data, 123
    backing up disks, 122-123
    bootable floppy disk, preparing, 162-165
    changes to Windows INI files, 166-169
    current DOS, locating, 125
    disabling programs, 126
    documenting installation, 169-171
    inventory system, 123-125
    manually, 147-149
    README.TXT file, 126-127
    SETUP command, 129-149
    swapping disks, 137

  uninstalling, 158-161
  DOSKEY, 743-744
  DRIVER.SYS, 734-735
  hard disks, 220-233
    IDE hard disk, 222-225
    SCSI hard disk, 225-227
  InterLnk, 1205-1208
  memory
    chips, 581
    informing the computer, 583
    locations, 579-580
    preparations, 576
    SIMMs, 581-583
    SIPPs, 582
  SMARTDrive, 391-392
  Undelete utility, 134, 149
Institute of Electrical and Electronic Engineers *see* **IEEE**
Insufficient disk space error message, 1007
INT 10 software interrupt, 110
INT 13 software interrupt, 110
INT 15 programs, 502-503
INT 21 software interrupt, 107-109
INT 27 software interrupt, 114-115
integrated motherboards, hexadecimal numeric values, 520-521
interactive batch file execution, 844

interactive boots,
  865-868
interface translation
  buffers, 658
interfaces, hard disk
  interfaces, 186-190
interlacing monitors,
  762
interleave settings,
  184-186
interlinking, 32-34
InterLnk, 32-34,
  1198-1199, 1204-1205
  applications besides
    file exchange, 1223
  baud rate, 1213-1215
  clients or servers,
    868-870
  command line
    switches, 1218-1220
  comparison to
    third-party file
    transfer programs,
    1224
  CONFIG.SYS file,
    1208-1216
  DOS Shell, 1221
  exchanging files,
    1220-1221
  installing on non-
    Version 6 MS-DOS
    systems, 1205-1208
  memory require-
    ments, 1210
  searching for
    connections, 1213
  troubleshooting,
    1222-1223
INTERLNK com-
  mand, 1261, 1388-1392
INTERLNK.EXE
  device driver, 1198,
  1204, 1211-1213
  connecting to
    servers, 1216-1217

switches, 1213
internal commands,
  93-95, 1272
  replacing, 1162-1165
internal print buffer,
  782
International
  Computer Security
  Association, 1150
international
  keyboard options,
  738-742
  code pages, 738-739
  country codes,
    739-740
International
  Standards Organiza-
  tion (ISO), 1242
Interrupt 21, 1121
interrupt pointers, 108
interrupt vector table,
  displaying, 1501
interrupt vectors,
  conventional
  memory, 445-446
interrupts
  software interrupts,
    107-108, 571
    interrupt pointers,
    108
  virus-infected,
    determining, 1501
INTERSVR command,
  1392-1394
  command line
    switches, 1218-1220
INTERSVR.EXE
  program, 1198, 1204
  connecting
    INTERLNK.EXE,
    1216-1217
Invalid drive
  specification error
  messsage, 730
invalid subdirectories,
  207

invalid clusters, 207
inventory programs,
  MSD 2.0a, 51-52
IO.SYS file, 938-940,
  1045-1048
IPX (Internetwork
  packet exchange)
  protocol, 1254-1255
IPX.COM (NetWare
  protocol program),
  1258
ISA (Industry
  Standard
  Architecture) buses,
  757
ISO (International
  Standards
  Organization), 1242

J

Jerusalem virus, 1080,
  1107, 1151
Jillette, Penn, 35
JOIN command,
  1394-1395
joke programs, 1066
jump points, 37

K

Keep Old Backup
  Catalogs option
  (MSBACKUP/
  MWBACKUP),
  988-989
KEYB command, 632,
  738-742, 1396-1398
keyboard
  ASK.COM
    keyboard-
    bypassing program,
    1037
  command history,
    742-750

controlling/
  customizing,
  737-751
 EDIT commands,
  724
 international
  options, 738-742
 menu operations,
  720
 reprogramming,
  1172-1175
 speed enhancement,
  750-751
 TSRs, 632-640
keyboard shortcuts
 Ctrl-F5 (clean boot),
  65
 F5, bypassing
  startup files, 940

L

$L metastring
  character, 288
LABEL command,
  1398-1399
labeling, backups, 979
labels, naming,
  361-362
LAN cards, conflicts,
  38
LAN Manager
  server-based network
  (Microsoft), 1259
LAN Server
  server-based network
  (IBM), 1259
LAN-aware/unaware
  programs, 1265-1266
LANcache disk cache
  program, 1253
LANs (local area
  networks), 32, 1240
 choosing, 1244-1246
 wireless, 1241

zero-slot, 1240
 LANtastic Z, 1254
LANtastic
  peer-to-peer network
  (Artisoft), 1253-1254
LANtastic Z zero-slot
  LAN, 1254
LapLink III (Traveling
  Software), 1198
LapLink/Mac III
  (Traveling Software),
  1234-1235
laptop computers,
  LAN interfaces, 1240
LASTDRIV.COM
  (QEMM), 682
LASTDRIVE command, 1399-1400
launching programs,
  783-785
LCD (liquid crystal
  display) monitors,
  780
LDTs (local descriptor
  tables), 469
Lehigh virus, 29-30,
  1067
Lempel-Ziv method
  (data compression),
  234-235
LET file extension, 329
LGO file extension,
  329
LHA disk
  compression
  program, 268-269
LIB file extension, 329
LIM memory, 479-481
limulating memory
  managers
 EMM386.EXE,
  544-547
 Windows, 657-658

limulation, 543-548
line display options,
  771-773
liners, disk, 902
link editors, 96-98
linked lists, 1049
linking PCs to
  Macintoshes, 1224
 cross-platform
  programs,
  1232-1234
 file translation, 1231
 networks, 1231
 null modem cables,
  1228-1230
 PC software,
  1227-1228
 SuperDrive floppy
  disks, 1225-1227
 transfer programs,
  1234-1235
listing
 directories, 291-292
 files, 303
 macros, 747
lists, linked, 1049
LOADFIX command,
  643-644, 1400-1401
LOADHIGH
  command, 94, 403,
  539-541, 599-601,
  1401-1403
 /L switch, 600, 608
loading
 BUFFERS into
  HMAs, 499-501
 DEFRAG for DOS
  (MicroSoft), 424-430
 DOS FAT (file
  allocation table),
  200-202
 EDIT command, 334
 FILES into HMAs,
  499-501

files, 75
programs
  into UMBs, 539-543
  troubleshooting
    memory managers,
    642-650
local area networks,
  see **LANs**
**local bus memory-
  upgrade cards, 580**
**local bus video,
  756-758**
**local descriptor tables
  (LDTs), 469**
logical drives, 733
**logical memory
  addresses, 507**
**lossless/lossy file
  compression
  algorithms, 237**
**lost clusters, 50,
  204-208**
  FATs, 404
**Lost clusters in lost
  chains error message,
  1052**
Lotus Magellan, 783
**low-level formatting,
  191, 1059**
  hard disks, 227-228
**LPT1/2/3 (virtual
  device), 799**
LST file extension, 329

M

Mace, Paul, 965
**Mace Utilities (Fifth
  Generation), 783, 1024**
**machine-language
  files, 97**
**Macintoshes, linking
  PCs to, 1224**

cross-platform
  programs,
  1232-1234
file translation, 1231,
  1234-1235
networks, 1231
null modem cables,
  1228-1230
PC software,
  1227-1228
SuperDrive floppy
  disks, 1225-1227
**MacLinkPlus
  (Dataviz), 1234-1235**
macro batch files, 747
macros
  ANSI.SYS com-
    mand, 769-771
  creating/executing,
    745-746
  DOSKEY command,
    742-743
  listing, 747
  replaceable
    parameters, 747-750
  saving, 746-747
**MacTOPS software,
  1231**
**magnetic domains,
  918**
magnetic tapes, 904
**MAIL program
  (Windows for
  Workgroups), 35**
**main memory,
  438-441, 439**
**MAKETXT1
  command, 956,
  1496-1497**
**management,
  memory, 56-58,
  661-663**

386Max, 703
  Maximize, 707-713
  *obsolete/special
    features, 702-705*
  syntax, 706-707
DOS 5, 46-48
MemMaker, 668-670
QEMM, 670-701
  *buffers/file handles,
    682-684*
  *device driver,
    675-676*
  *loading TSRs/device
    drivers, 676-678*
  *Manifest utility,
    696-701*
  *Optimize utility,
    686-696*
  shadow RAM, 678
  *Squeeze utility,
    678-682*
  *Stealth utility,
    685-686*
  VIDRAM, 684-685
shadow RAM, 60
test configuration,
  663-668
"yo-yo" programs, 59
**Manifest utility
  (QEMM), 696-701**
**manual disk
  mirroring, 982**
mapping memory
  upper, 522-536
  Windows memory
    managers, 657
**master boot record
  (MBR), 194-195, 921,
  1055**
  creating, 922-924
  displaying, 195
  repairing, 1056-1057

master boot sector, 921
master copies,
 backing up, 981
Max, *see* 386Max
Maximize program
 (386Max), 48
Maxtor XT-1140 hard
 disk, 908
MBR, *see* master boot
 record
MCA (Micro Channel
 Architecture), 757
MCache, 400
MCGA (Multicolor
 Graphics Adapter),
 753
MD command, 81-83,
 93, 279
MDA (Monochrome
 Display Adapter), 753
MDX file extension,
 329
ME file extension, 329
media
 damaged
  file recovery,
   1059-1062
  preventing,
   1018-1019
 random-access, 970
 sequential-access,
  970
media descriptor
 bytes, 926
media descriptors, 933
megabytes, 441-444
megahertz (Mhz), 565
MEM command, 30,
 59, 65, 491-494,
 1403-1404
 /P option, 64
MemMaker, 608-611
 /L switch, 620-621

hard disks, 612
managing memory,
 668-670
options, 613-620
SCSI drives, 612
troubleshooting,
 611-624
**MEMMAKER
command, 46-49,
1405-1406**
 /T switch, 1261
**MEMMAKER.STS
file, 622-624**
memory, 437-441
 cache, 591-592
 command buffer,
  742
 conventional,
  444-451, 482
 disk, 440-441
 dynamic versus
  static, 588-589
 expanded, 479-482
  LIM memory,
   479-481
 extended, 463-476,
  482
 HMA (high memory
  area), 496-503
 increasing, 495-496,
  650-653
  ROM space, 650-652
  video board space,
   652-653
 installing
  chips, 581
  informing the
   computer, 583
  locations, 579-580
  preparations, 576
  SIMMs, 581-583
  SIPPs, 582-593
 InterLnk, 1199

Manifest utility
 (QEMM), 696-701
megabytes, 441-444
optimizing
 386Max, 707-713
 QEMM, 686-696
paging, 457-458
proprietary,
 upgrading, 568
purchasing, 558
 group installation,
  568-576
 RAM package types,
  558-563
 RAM speeds/sizes,
  564-568
RAM, 439
requirements,
 InterLnk, 1210
reserved area, 482
ROM (Read-Only
 Memory), 459
sequential access,
 439
speeds, 565-566,
 589-591
 processor caches,
  591-592
 selecting, 566-568
system reserved
 area, 458-463
testing, 584-587
 programs, 587-588
video, 451
Video RAM, 451,
 454-458, 482
**memory addresses,
442-443**
 EGA, 453-454
 extended memory,
  472-476

memory areas – memory modules

logical, 507
physical, 507
ROM (Read-Only
  Memory), 461
VGA, 453-454
Video RAM, 453-454
memory areas, 443-444
  Video RAM, 455-458
**memory arrangers,
  MemMaker, 48-49**
memory banks, 568
  building
    *8-bit computers,
      569-572*
    *16-bit computers,
      572-574*
    *32-bit computers,
      574-576*
  installing, 569-572
**memory chips (8088),
  upgrading, 569**
**memory management,
  56-58, 551-553, 661-663**
  386Max, 702-713
    Maximize, 707-713
    syntax, 706-707
  backfilling, 552-553
  DOS 5, 46-48
  DOS configurations,
    489-496
  MemMaker, 668-670
  QEMM, 670-701
    *buffers/file handles,
      682-684*
    *device driver,
      675-676*
    *loading TSRs/device
      drivers, 676-678*
    *Manifest utility,
      696-701*
    *Optimize utility,
      686-696*

shadow RAM, 678
*Squeeze utility,
  678-682*
*Stealth utility,
  685-686*
VIDRAM, 684-685
shadow RAM, 60
speed sorting,
  551-552
test configuration,
  663-668
UMBs (upper
  memory blocks),
  596-624
"yo-yo" programs, 59
Memory Manager
  DOS 5, 46-48, 56-58
  DOS 6.2, shadow
    RAM, 60
memory managers
  add-in boards
    documentation,
    532-533
  AUTOEXEC.BAT
    file, 487491
  CONFIG.SYS file,
    487-491
  device drivers,
    533-536
  EMM386.EXE files,
    489
  hexadecimal
    numeric values,
    510-521
  HIMEM.SYS file, 489
  limulation, 543-548
    *EMM386.EXE,
      544-547*
    Windows, 657-658
  mapping upper
    memory, 522-536

memory addressing,
  510-515
MEM utility, 491-494
shadow RAM, 60
troubleshooting,
  523-526, 624-650
  *A20 handlers,
    626-632*
  *bus mastering,
    647-659*
  *EMM386.EXE,
    632-640*
  *keyboard problems,
    625-641*
  *loading programs
    high, 642-650*
  *virtual DMA
    controllers, 646*
  *warm boot problems,
    641-642*
UMBs (upper
  memory blocks),
  506-509, 548
  creating, 537-539
Windows, 655-658
  *interface translation
    buffers, 658*
  *mapping memory,
    657*
  *monochrome region,
    655-656*
  *video drivers,
    655-656*
yo-yo programs,
  605-606
memory maps, 443
  hexadecimal
    numeric values,
    517-519
**memory modules,
  proprietary, 563**

memory protection, 463-464
memory scanners, MSD, 526-532
memory sorting, 551
memory-resident viruses, detecting/ removing, 1186-1187
MENUCOLOR command, 874-878, 891, 1406-1408
MENUDEFAULT command, 1408-1409
MENUITEM command, 1409-1410
menus
  batch files, 811-820
    GOTO command, 816-817
    return codes, 813-815
    user input, 812-813
  CONFIG.SYS files, MultiConfig, 872-873
    coloring, 874-878
  controlling access with, 1176-1178
  selecting items, 720
merging, CONFIG.SYS files, 870-871
metastring characters, 287-288
MFM (modified frequency modulation) encoding, 181, 911-922
Michelangelo virus, 31, 1080

MICRO program (Windows for Workgroups), 35
Microsoft
  DEFRAG for DOS, 421-433
  ScanDisk, 405-416
  Virtual DMA Services, 389
Microsoft Anti-Virus, *see* MSAV
Microsoft Backup for Windows, changes to INI files, 166-168
Microsoft Real-Time Compression Interface (MRCI), 237
Microsoft System Diagnostics, *see* MSD
Microsoft Undelete for Windows, changes to INI files, 166-168
Minasi, Mark, 1500
MIRROR file recovery command, 1199
  options, 1019-1021
  system files, copying, 1022-1023
MIRROR.FIL file, 1019
mirroring, disk, 982
MKDIR command, 282, 1410-1411
MODE command, 1411-1420
  line display, 771-773
  printers
    network, 777
    serial, 774-776

    redirecting ports, 776-777
    timeouts, 777
  uploading InterLnk, 1206
MODE CON command, 750-751
model backup policies, 1012
monitors, 760-763
  dot pitch, 763
  horizontal scanning frequency, 761
  interlacing, 762
  LCD (liquid crystal display), 780
  multisync, 761-762
  vertical refresh rate, 760-761
monochrome adapters/monitors, 456
MORE command, 808, 1420-1421
motherboards, installing memory on, 579
motion sensitivity, disk drives, 905
mountain/valley test, 585
mounting, DoubleSpaced drives, 252
mounting hardware, 221
mouse
  control, MSBACKUP, 994
  menu operations, 720

mouse drivers, 446
  loading TSRs into UMBs, 602-604
MOUSE$ (virtual device), 799
MOUSE.COM driver, loading into UMBs, 59
MOVE command, 63-65, 354-356, 1421-1423
  directories, differentiating, 1039
  renaming directories, 305-306
  restrictions, 355
  verification, 355-356
moving
  between directories, 284-286
  files, 87, 354-356
  verification, 355-356
MRCI (Microsoft Real-Time Compression Interface, 237
MSAV (Microsoft Anti-Virus), 29
  Windows, changes to INI files, 166-168
MSAV command, 1423-1425
  /L switch, 1261
  virus removal, 1116-1119
    testing, 1119-1120
  virus scanning, 1094
    boot sector viruses, 1102-1103
    command line options, 1094-1096
    efficacy, 1100-1102
    menu operation, 1096-1099
    speeds, 1100
MSBACKUP command, 55-56, 64, 362, 1425-1427
  archiving, 970
  backup options, 983-990, 993-997, 1010
  configuring, 990-993
  files, 1010
    restoring, 997-1001
    selected, backing, 996
    setup, 1011-1012
  screen colors, changing, 992-993
  speed, 1005-1007
MSD (Microsoft System Diagnostics), 124, 1215, 1262, 1427-1429
  memory scanners, 526-532
MSD 2.0a inventory program, 51-52
MSDOS.SYS file, 939-940, 1047-1049
MSDOSDATA environment variable, 1262
MSG file extension, 330
MSP file extension, 330
MultiConfig, 862-863, 868-870
  CONFIG.SYS files
    menus, 872-873
    merging, 870-871
  naming configurations, 871-872
  shared groups of statements, 885-886
  timouts/defaults, 873-874
  configurations, AUTOEXEC.BAT file, 878-885
  menus, coloring, 874-878
  NumLock light, 891-892
  submenus, 887-891
multilingual keyboard layout, 740
multiple-configuration control, 38-66
multisync monitors, 761-762
multitasking, 781
  preemptive, 1243
MWAV.INI file, 168
MWBACKUP command, 362
  backup options, 983-990, 995
  configuring, 990-993
  files
    restoring, 997-1001
    selected, backing, 996-997
    setup, 1011-1012
  screen colors, changing, 993
  speed, 1005-1007
MWUNDEL.EXE program (Undelete for Windows), 1031-1033

N

$N metastring character, 288
names
  drive, 76-78
  file, 75-78
  path
    relative, 298-299
    shortening, 296-297
naming
  configurations, 871-872
  files, 325-327, 1017
    extensions, 327-333
    restrictions, 327
  labels, 361-362
  subdirectories, 280-281
  volumes, 361-362
nanoseconds (ns), 589
National Computer Security Association (NCSA), 1192
navigating, documents, 335-336
NCache-F, 401
NCache-S, 401
NCSA (National Computer Security Association), 1192
NDX file extension, 330
nested subdirectories, 282-283
nesting batch files, 841-842
NET commands, 1261-1262
NetWare for Macintosh, 1231
NetWare Lite peer-to-peer network (Novell), 1253-1256
NetWare server-based network (Novell), 1258-1259
  NetWare 2.2, 1258
  NetWare 3.11, 1258
network interface cards, 1246
  ARCnet, 1246-1247
  Ethernet, 1247-1248
  FDDI, 1249
  Token-Ring, 1248-1249
network operating systems (NOSs), 1241
  architectural limitations, DOS, 1242-1244
network software, running
  DOS 6, 1261-1266
  Workgroup Connection, 34-35
networking protocols, 1255-1256
networks
  cabling, 1249-1251
  dedicated server, 1239
  linking Macintoshes and PCs, 1231
  peer-to-peer, 34, 1240-1241
    types, 1252-1257
  printers, MODE command, 777
  server-based
    types, 1257-1260
    versus peer-to-peer, 1251-1252
  version requirements, DOS 6, 1262-1264
NETX.COM (NetWare Shell), 1258
NLSFUNC command, 1429
NMIs (nonmaskable interrupts), 571
NOBOOT command, 1497-1498
Non-System disk or disk error error message, 929-930, 1048
nonexecutable files, 326
noninterlaced monitors, 762
nonmaskable interrupts (NMIs), 571
nonreentrant functions, 1243
nonvolatile disk space, 440-441
Nordic keyboard layout, 741
Norton Backup for DOS (Symantec), 983
Norton Backup for Windows, 983
Norton Commander, 784
Norton Desktop for DOS, 784-785
Norton Utilities (Symantec), 1024
NOS (network operating system), 1241

notepad, 854-856
Notes jump point (Help system), 37
NUL (virtual device), 799
null modem cables, linking Macintoshes and PCs, 1228-1230
numbering
   components, disk, 962
   floppy, 960
   tracks, 909
numeric values, hexadecimal, 510-521
NUMLOCK command, 891-892, 1430
NumLock light, 891-892
nybble DIP-type RAM, 560-561

O

OEM (original equipment manufacturer), 925
off-site storage, 983
offsets (hexadecimal numeric values), 519-520, 1053-1054
on-line documentation, 35-37
on-line help, 35-37
   batch files, 834-835
one-way linked lists, 202
OnTrack Disk Manager (OnTrack Data Systems), 23

Open Systems Interconnection (OSI) model, 1242
operating systems
   network, architectural limitations, DOS, 1242-1244
   reentrant, 1243
   single-tasking on networks, 1242-1244
Optimize program (QEMM), 48
optimizing
   keyboard speed, 750-751
   memory
      386Max, 707-713
      QEMM, 686-696
Options menu (EDIT), 723
Orchid video boards, 51
OS/2 DoubleSpace, 237
OSI (Open Systems Interconnection) model, 1242
   networking protocols, 1255-1256
out of environment space error message, 450
output redirection, 802-804
   ECHO command, 804
overwrite protection, 338-340

overwriting
   files, 338-340, 952-953
      confirmation, 340
   root directories, recovery, 1044-1045
OVL file extension, 77, 330
OVR file extension, 330

P

$P metastring character, 288
page tables (DOS extenders), 469
paging (memory), 457-458
pancake motors, 903
parallel cables, InterLnk, 1202-1203
parallel ports
   InterLnk, 1199, 1202-1204
   redirecting, 776-777
parallel printer ports, 774
parallel-transfer programs, 34
parameters, 91
parent directories, 80
   subdirectories, 283
parity, 775
   chips, 570
parsing, command line, 90-91
partition tables, 405, 921-924, 1055
   repairing, 1056-1057

partitioning, hard
   disks, 230-234
   DOS 3.3, 24
partitions, 195-199
   changing, FDISK,
      941-942
   creating/viewing,
      FDISK, 944-945
   deleting, 232-233
   extended, 196-197,
      232
   formatting, 231
   non-DOS, 197-199
   primary, 196-197,
      233
   size, 231
   status information,
      942
PAS file extension,
   330
PASSWORD
   program, 1156-1159
Password Protect
   Backup Sets option
   (MSBACKUP/
   MWBACKUP), 988
password protection
   programs, 1159-1160
passwords, 1156-1161
patching, 939
path, 76, 98-103, 283,
   317-318
   adding directories,
      296
   common CPUs,
      568-569
   editing, 299-300
   names
      relative, 298-299
      shortening, 296-297

PATH command, 94,
   98-116, 1431
   syntax, 100
PATH environment
   variable, 449
PAUSE command, 94,
   1432
pausing, programs,
   1501-1502
PC Cache, 401
PC support, *see*
   technical support
PC Tools (Central
   Point Software), 783,
   1024
PC Typewriter,
   857-858
PCAnywhere
   (Symantec), 1199
PCMCIA (Personal
   Computer Memory
   Card Industry
   Association), 563
PCs
   files, transferring,
      1198-1199,
      1204-1205
   interlinking, 32-34
   linking to
      Macintoshes, 1224
      *cross-platform
         programs,
         1232-1234*
      file translation, 1231
      networks, 1231
      *null modem cables,
         1228-1230*
      *software, 1227-1228,
         1234-1235*

*SuperDrive floppy
   disks, 1225-1227*
speed, optimizing,
   59-60
PCX file extension, 77,
   330
Peach virus, 1073
peer-to-peer networks,
   34, 1240
   dedicated servers,
      1241
   types, 1252-1253
      *LANtastic (Artisoft),
         1253-1254*
      *NetWare Lite
         (Novell), 1254-1256*
      *Windows for
         Workgroups
         (Microsoft),
         1256-1257*
   versus server-based,
      1251-1252
permanent swap file
   is corrupt error
   message, 266-268
physical memory
   addresses, 507, 646
PIF file extension, 330
piping, 806-809
   collation sequence,
      807
pixels, 752
   bit blitting, 756
PKZIP disk
   compression
   program, 268-269, 975
placement, file,
   958-959
plated media, 176
platters, 176, 908

plug-in expansion cards, 580
polymorphic viruses, 1068, 1101
ports, InterLnk, 1203
   parallel, 1199, 1203-1204
   serial, 1199
Portuguese keyboard layout, 740
position-sensitivity, COMMAND.COM, 957-958
POST (Power On Self Test), 584, 921
PostScript, 781
Power Batch shareware program, 46
POWER command, 63, 1433-1478
power connector (hard disk), 221
POWERLan (Performance Technology) peer-to-peer network, 1253
preemptive multitasking, 1243
prepared code pages, 738
   see also code pages
prepending viruses, 1068
preprogrammed delays, batch files, 822-823
prevention
   booting, 1497-1498
   disaster, general tips, 1016-1018
   virus, 1082-1083
   backups, 1085-1086
   bulletin board precautions, 1086-1087
   virus response teams, 1087-1088
Priam HD 60 hard disk, 908
Primary DOS Partition, 233
primary partitions, 196-197
PRINT command, 1435-1437, 1498
   background printing, 781-783
print queue, 782
printer drivers, 105
printer profile, modifying, 780
printer support, GRAPHICS command, 778-779
printer-sharing devices, 776
printing
   background, 781-783
   canceling print jobs, 782
   CONFIG.SYS file, 799
   controlling, 773-783
   graphics screens, 780-781
   PostScript, 781
   printer profile modifications, 780
   redirecting ports, 776-777
   root directory, 307
   screen prints, 778-781
   serial printers, 774-776
   timeouts, 777
privilege rings, 467
PRN (virtual device), 799
Problem Found dialog box, 409
processor caches, 591-592
profile files (386Max), 704
PROGMAN.INI file, 167
programs
   anti-virus, F-Prot, 1101, 1122, 1494-1495
   Apple File Exchange, 1234-1235
   backup
      features, 53-55
      MSBACKUP, 55-56
   bootstrap, 925
   Brooklyn Bridge (Fifth Generation Systems), 1198
   Carbon Copy (Microcom), 1199
   client/server, 1265-1266
   COMMAND.COM
      hidden system files, 939-940
      troubleshooting, 1045-1047
   communications, InterLnk, 32-34

compression, PKZIP, 975
creating, 96-98
cross-platform, 1232
Crosstalk (Digital Communications Associates), 1199
CVTPACK, 643-644
DBL (DOS batch language), 44-46
defragmentation, 420-421
disabling for DOS installation, 126
disk caching, LANcache, 1253
disk compression
  Double Disk (Microsoft), 24
  Stacker (Stac Electronics), 24
DOS support, 104-115
Drippy, 1113
FastLynx (Rupp Brothers), 1198
file transfer, 1234-1235
file translation, 1234-1235
Find, 37
INT 15, 502-503
InterLnk, 1198-1199, 1204-1216, 1223-1224
  connecting with servers, 1216-1217
inventory, MSD 2.0a, 51-52
joke, 1066

keyboard-processing, ASK.COM, 1037
LAN-aware versus LAN-unaware, 1265-1266
LapLink III (Traveling Software), 1198
LapLink/Mac III (Traveling Software), 1234-1235
launching, 783-785
levels of privilege, 467
load size, 606
LOADFIX, 643-644
loading into UMBs, 542-543
MacLinkPlus (Dataviz), 1234-1235
memory test, 587-588
network,
  Workgroup Connection, 34-35
  on Macintoshes, 1227-1228
parallel-transfer, 34
PASSWORD, 1156-1159
password protection, 1159-1160
pausing, 1501-1502
PCAnywhere (Symantec), 1199
QBASIC, 785-788
serial-transfer, 33-34

shareware
  Power Batch, 46
  TurboBat, 46
Smartcom (Hayes), 1199
sockets, 806
SoftPC/Professional (Insignia Solutions), 1227
Software Bridge (Argosy Software), 1234-1235
SpeedDisk (Norton), 50
TESTBAK.COM, 972-973
unerasing
  MWUNDEL.EXE (Undelete for Windows), 1031-1033
  UNDELETE for DOS, 1025-1031
"yo-yo", 59
Prompt Before Overwriting Used Diskettes option (MSBACKUP/ MWBACKUP), 988
PROMPT command, 89, 94, 286-291, 764-765, 1437-1438
  metastring characters, 287-288
  screen attributes, 765-767
PROMPT environment variable, 449
prompts, 89, 286-287
  customizing, 287-291

proprietary memory, upgrading, 568
proprietary memory modules, 563
proprietary SIMMs, 563
protected mode, extended memory, 463-466
protection, undelete
  DOS 5, 61-62
  DOS 6.2, 62
  UNDELETE for DOS, 1025-1031
protocols
  APM (Advanced Power Management), 63
  IPX, 1254-1255
  networking, 1255-1256
  SPX (Sequenced Packet Exchange), 1255
  TCP/IP (Transport Control Protocol/ Internet Protocol), 1256
PUB file extension, 330
pull-down menus, 720
  see also menus
punched cards/tapes, 900
push and pop, 841

Q

$Q metastring character, 288
QAPlus memory diagnostic program, 587-588
QBACK.BAT file, 1006
QBASIC, 63, 785-788, 1439-1440
  screen messages, 786-787
  screen savers, 785-786
QEMM memory manager (Quarterdeck), 48, 661
  buffers/file handles, 682-684
  device driver, 675-676
  loading TSRs/device drivers, 676-678
  managing memory, 670-701
  Manifest utility, 696-701
  Optimize utility, 686-696
  shadow RAM, 678
  Squeeze feature, 678-682
  Stealth feature, 685-686
  VIDRAM, 684-685
QNX file extension, 330
quick formats, 211
Quit After Backup option (MSBACKUP/ MWBACKUP), 990
quitting write-behind cache, 397

R

R6003 - Integer Divide by Zero error message, 266-268
RAM (random access memory), 439
  640K, 444-445
  interrupt vectors, 445-446
  package types, 558-559
    bit DIP, 560
    nybble DIP, 560-561
    proprietary memory modules, 563
    SIMMs, 561-563
    SIPPs, 562-563
  Shadow RAM, 548-551
  sizes, 564-565
  speeds, 565-566
    selecting, 566-568
  testing, 584-587
  video RAM, 451-458, 684-685, 758-759
  volatility, 439
RAM drives
  batch files, 826-828
  DoubleSpace, 254
RAMDRIVE command, 1440-1441
random access devices, 900
random access memory, *see* RAM
random-access media, 970
RD command, 94
  recovering directories deleted with, 1042-1043
read caching, 384-385
read-only files, displaying, 322
Read-Only Memory, *see* ROM

read-write heads, 177, 903-905
read-write openings, disk, 902
READEXE command, 1123, 1498-1499
reading command lines, 90-91
README.TXT file, 126-127, 1262
REBOOT command, 940, 1123, 1499-1500
rebooting, 1499-1500
Rebuild command (Restore menu, MSBACKUP), 1012
REC file extension, 330
recalling commands, 744-745
records
  boot, 924-927
    contents, 927-928
    creating, 945-952
    repairing, 1053-1055
    scanning for viruses, 929-932
    viewing, 929
  master boot, 921, 1055
    creating, 922-924
    repairing, 1056-1057
recovery
  data, 1023-1024
  directories, 1031-1033, 1040-1041
    erased with RD command, 1042-1043
    overwritten root, 1044-1045

files, 1031-1033
  erased, 1035-1036
  from damaged media, 1062
  misplaced, 1024-1025
  hard disk formats, 1058-1059
recursive delete, 858-859
redirection, 801-809
  disk commands, 728-729
  files, 805-806
  input, 804-805
  output, 802-804
  piping, 806-809
  ports, MODE command, 776-777
reentrant operating systems, 1243
refreshing, backup disks, 1018
relative paths, names, 298-299
relative sector, 923
  numbers, 191-192
REM command, 94, 838, 1442
remote control programs
  Carbon Copy (Microcom), 1199
  PCAnywhere (Symantec), 1199
removing, viruses
  boot, 1182-1183
  memory-resident, 1187
REN command, 94, 360-361

RENAME command, 1442-1443
renaming
  AUTOEXEC.BAT file, 1165-1168
  directories, 305-306
  files, 87, 360-361
repairing disks, ScanDisk (MicroSoft), 405-416
REPLACE command, 352-354, 1443-1445
replaceable parameters
  batch files, 829-835
  macros, 747-750
replacing, internal commands, 1162-1165
RES file extension, 330
reserved area memory, 482
reserved sectors, 925
resolution (video adapters), 752-754
RESTORE command, 381
  previous DOS versions, 52
Restore menu commands (MSBACKUP), Rebuild, 1012
restoring, files, 378-381
  MSBACKUP/ MWBACKUP, 997-1001
retention periods, 1007
retry value, 775

return codes, 813-815
reverse print jobs, 779
reverse video, 766
reverse yo-yo
 programs, 607-608
RFT file extension,
 330
RLE file extension,
 330
RLL (run length
 limited) encoding,
 181-182, 911-922
RMDIR command,
 1445-1446
ROM (Read-Only
 Memory), 59, 110, 459
 addresses, 461
 BIOS ROM, 459-461
 compressing, 705
 increasing memory
  space, 650-652
ROMSearch (386Max),
 704-705
root directories, 74,
 276-278, 925, 937-938
 backing up,
  MIRROR utility,
  1021-1023
 clearing, 310-313
 overwritten,
  recovery, 1044-1045
 printing, 307
 sizes, 277
 structure, 277-278
 versus
  subdirectories, 1040
 writing files to disk,
  1050-1051
root directory table,
 203

run-length encoding,
 24-26

S

safe formats, 211
SAM file extension,
 330
Save As command,
 978
saving
 directory tree to
  disk, 301-302
 macros, 746-747
 setup files, 378
scan strings, 1068
ScanDisk disk repair
 utility (MicroSoft),
 50, 405-416
 closing all open files,
  406-407
 correcting problems,
  409-411
 creating Undo disks,
  411-412
 customizing, 414-415
 deleting lost clusters,
  413
 errorlevels, 415-416
 repairing/scanning
  for errors, 413
 syntax, 412-414
  /Option, 413
  drivename, 412
  path/filename, 413
  volume-name, 412
SCANDISK
 command, 407-409,
 1446-1447
 /ALL switch, 241,
  413

 /AUTOFIX switch,
  413
 /CHECKONLY
  switch, 413
 /CUSTOM switch,
  413
 /MONO switch, 413
 /NOSAVE switch,
  413
 /NOSUMMARY
  switch, 413
 /SURFACE switch,
  413
 /UNDO swtich, 414
SCANDISK.INI file,
 414
scanners, virus, 29, 31,
 1091-1093
 MSAV command,
  1094-1103
screen blanking,
 1171-1172
screen colors,
 changing
 (MSBACKUP),
 992-993
screen messages,
 786-787
 ECHO command,
  796-798
screen prints,
 GRAPHICS
 command, 778-781
screen savers, 785-786,
 1485-1486
screws, organizing,
 578-579
SCSI (small computer
 systems interface),
 189-190

drives, MemMaker, 612
hard disks, 219
configuring, 228
installing, 225-227
SDEL.BAT purge utility, 1037-1039
Seagate ST-225 hard disk, 908
Seagate ST-4038 hard disk, 908
Seagate ST-4096 hard disk, 908
Search menu (EDIT), 722
searches
directory, 319-320
text files, 319
wild cards, 319
file, 87, 319-320, 1492-1493
nonexecutable files, 303-304
text string, 1493-1494
secondary memory, 438-441
sector marks, DISKCOPY, 1060-1061
sector notches, 902
sectors, 180-182, 910, 1056
absolute, 191-192
addressing, 914
floppy disks, 915
hard disks, 915-918
boot, 1053
contents, 927-928
number on drive, 926

overwritten, 1044
reserved, 925
translating, 911-922
security
access, controlling, 1155
BAT file extension, changing, 1168-1171
blanking screen, 1171-1172
bootups, logging, 1171
deleted files, 1161
encryption, 1178-1179
erasing files permanently, 1175-1176
internal commands, replacing, 1162-1165
keyboard, reprogramming, 1172-1175
passwords, 1156-1161
renaming AUTOEXEC.BAT file, 1165-1168
with batch files, 1176-1178
with menus, 1176-1178
backups, 978
redesign
boot virus prevention/removal, 1181-1183

efficient recovery, 1189
file virus prevention/ detection, 1183-1189
memory-resident virus detection/ removal, 1186-1187
slowing hackers, 1190-1191
theft, 1179-1181
SEECODE batch file, 1500
seek time, 184
segments (hexadecimal numeric values), 519-520
selecting
files for backup, 373
menu items, 720
sensitivity, recording, 907
sequential access (memory), 439
sequential access devices, 900
sequential-access media, 970
serial cables, InterLnk, 1199, 1202
serial ports, 774
InterLnk, 1199
linking PCs and Macintoshes, 1228-1230
redirecting, 776-777
serial printers, 774-776
serial-transfer programs, 33-34

server-based networks
types, 1257
  LAN Manager
    (Microsoft), 1259
  LAN Server (IBM),
    1259
  NetWare (Novell),
    1258-1259
  VINES (Banyon),
    1260
versus peer-to-peer,
  1251-1252
servers
archiving with, 1009
backing up to, 973
  verifying, 1001-1003
choosing, 1260
connecting,
  INTERLNK.EXE,
  1216-1217
dedicated, 1241
DPMI, 471-472
file, 1241
InterLnk, 868-870
INTERSVR.EXE,
  1204
**servo-mechanisms,
disk**, 902
servos
dedicated, 916
embedded, 915-918
SET command, 94,
449, 1448
**setting, environment
variables**, 449
**SETUP command,
132-149, 228**
  /B switch, 129
  disabling programs,
    126
  /E switch, 130, 134,
    149

/F switch, 130
/I switch, 130, 139
/M switch, 134
/Q switch, 130, 134
/S switch, 145
troubleshooting,
  139-147
/U switch, 130
setup files, 1011-1012
  saving, 378
**SETVER command,
125, 726-727, 1265,
1449-1451**
**Shadow RAM, 60,
548-551, 678**
**SHARE command,
1451-1452**
**shared statements,
CONFIG.SYS file,
885-886**
shareware programs
  Power Batch, 46
  TurboBat, 46
**SHELL command,
1046, 1452-1453**
**shell programs,
783-785**
  Norton Desktop for
    DOS, 784-785
**SHELL= command,
39, 146**
**shielded twisted
cabling, 1250**
shields, virus, 29-32
**SHIFT command, 94,
1453-1454**
**SHOWINT command,
1124, 1501**
sides, disk, 908-909
signatures, 923

**SIMMs (Single Inline
Memory Modules),
561-562**
  16-bit, 573-574
  installing, 581-583
  proprietary, 563
  speeds/sizes, 564
single-sided disks, 909
**single-tasking
operating systems on
networks, 1242-1244**
**SIPPs (Single Inline
Pin Packages),
562-563**
**SIZER.EXE command,
1454**
sizes
  clusters, 954-956
  files, 954-955
  RAM, 564-565
  SIMMs, 564
  system file, DOS 5
    versus DOS 6, 939
**slack space,
determining, 954-955**
**Slavic keyboard
layout, 740**
**Smartcom (Hayes),
1199**
**SMARTDrive, 65, 383,
390-401**
  alternatives to,
    400-401
  cache size, 394-395
  customizing, 395-396
  double buffering,
    396
  information, 397-398
  installing, 391-392
  quitting, 397

selecting drives to cache, 393-394
storage location, 392
write caching, 386
SMARTDrive Monitor, 398-400
SMARTDRV command, 392, 1455-1458
/? switch, 398
/B:# switch, 395
/C switch, 397
/E:# switch, 396
/L switch, 392
/R switch, 397
/S switch, 397
SNORETIL command, 1124, 1501-1502
sockets, 806
soft errors, 920
SoftPC (Insignia Solutions), 1227
SoftPC Professional (Insignia Solutions), 1227
software
memory management, 661-663
network, running (DOS 6) [.2?], 1261-1264
Software Bridge (Argosy Software), 1234-1235
software interrupts, 107-108, 445, 571
INT 10, 110
INT 13, 110
INT 27, 114-115
interrupt pointers, 108

SORT command, 808, 1458-1459
sorting
directories, 74
DIR command, 322-323
memory, 551
sounds, ECHO command, 809-810
source disks, 729
space, determining disk, 954-955
SPATCH.BAT, 267-268
speed sorting (memory management), 551-552
SpeedDisk utility (Norton), 50
speeds
baud rate, InterLnk, 1213-1215
drive rotation, 905-906
memory, 589-591
processor caches, 591-592
MSBACKUP command, 1005-1007
MSAV program, 1100
MWBACKUP command, 1005-1007
PC, optimizing, 59-60
RAM, 565-566
selecting, 566-568
SIMMs, 564

SpinRite II disk-maintenance program (Gibson Research), 28
SPX (Sequenced Packet Exchange) protocol, 1255
SQL (Standard Query Language), 1265
Squeeze feature (QEMM), 678-682
St-506 interface, 187
Stacker drives, DoubleSpace, 255
Stacker utility (Stac Electronics), 24
STACKS command, 1460
Standard level (MWUNDEL), 1033
Standard level (UNDELETE.EXE), 1025, 1030
Standard Query Language, *see* **SQL**
standards
802.3 (Ethernet), 1247-1248
802.5 (Token-Ring), 1248
Stang, David, 965, 1485, 1488, 1491-1503
startup files, bypassing, 940
statements
CONFIG.SYS files, MultiConfig, 885-886
REM, 838
static electricity, 576-577

static memory versus
    dynamic, 588-589
status checks,
    UNDELETE for DOS,
    1028
Stealth feature
    (QEMM), 685-686
stealth viruses, 1069
stepper motors, 903
Stoned virus, 30-31,
    943, 1044, 1107, 1113,
    1151
stop bits, 775
storage
    backups, 979-981
    capacity, calculating,
        910
    data, disks, 918-919
    off-site, 983
strings
    scan, 1068
    text, searching,
        1493-1494
STY file extension,
    330
subdirectories, 73,
    79-80, 203-204, 278,
    938
    capturing with
        XCOP command,
        349
    copying, 348
    creating, 279-280
    deleting, 293-294,
        1042
    files, deleting, 359
    invalid, 207
    listing, 292
    naming, 280-281
    nested, 282-283
    size, 281-282

versus root directo-
    ries, 1040-1041
viewing, 279
see also directories
SUBMENU command,
    888-890, 1460-1462
submenus,
    MultiConfig, 887-891
SUBST command,
    297-298, 1462-1463
SuperDrive floppy
    disks, 1225-1227
Supplemental Disk,
    commands, 165
SVGA (Super Video
    Graphics Adapter),
    753
SWAPFILE.EXE file,
    267
SWITCHES com-
    mand, 311, 1463-1464
symptoms, virus,
    1111-1115
synchronization bytes,
    915
syntax
    EXPAND command,
        150
    MicroSoft ScanDisk,
        412-414
    PATH command,
        100
SYS command, 1199,
    1261, 1464-1465
SYS file extension, 77,
    330
SYSEDIT command,
    167
system booting
    clean boots, 864-868

    interactive boots,
        865-868
system areas,
    comparing
    (UNFORMAT
    command), 1048-1049
system files
    copying, MIRROR
        utility, 1022-1023
    hidden, 1045-1048
    sizes, DOS 5 versus
        DOS 6, 939
system indicator, 923
system reserved area
    of memory, 458-463
    buffers, 461-463
    frames, 461-463
    ROM (Read-Only
        Memory), 459
system version table,
    updating, 727
SYSTEM.INI file,
    167-168
systems program-
    ming, 106

T

$T metastring
    character, 288
tables, partition,
    921-924, 1055
    repairing, 1056-1057
tabs, write-protect
    (virus prevention),
    1085
tape drives, data
    transfer, 32
tapes
    magnetic, 904
    punched, 900

target disks, 729
TCP/IP (Transport Control Protocol/ Internet Protocol), 1256
technical support, 51-52
TEMP command, 836
terminate-and-stay resident programs, *see* TSRs
TEST.BAT file, 45-46
TESTBAK command, 1502-1503
TESTBAK.COM program, 972-973
testing
　memory, 584-587
　　programs, 587-588
　VSAFE.COM, 1106-1110
testing error levels, batch files, 817-820
tests
　checkerboard, 585
　mountain/valley, 585
　walking-bit, 585-586
text files
　searches, 319
　viewing, 87
text mode, 752
　Video RAM, 454-455
text strings, searching, 1493-1494
text-editing, 718-726
thin film, 176
third-party disk caches, 400-401
TIF file extension, 330

time activation, backup programs, 54
TIME command, 95, 1465-1466
　designated batch file delays, 823-825
timeouts
　CONFIG.SYS files, MultiConfig, 873-874
　printing, 777
times
　access, 565-566, 590-591
　charging, 590
　cycle, 589-591
timing holes, 902
TMP file extension, 330
Toigo, Jon William, 966
Token-Ring networks, 1248-1249
toolbox (batch files), 845-859
tools
　virus removal, 1120-1121
　　DOSWATCH, 1121-1122
　　F-Prot, 1122
　　FINDTEXT, 1122
　　FULLDIR, 1122-1123
　　READEXE, 1123
　　REBOOT, 1123
　　SHOWINT, 1124
　　SNORETIL, 1124
　　V-Base virus database, 1124

TOPS network, 1231
TPI (tracks per inch), 907-908
track density, 907-908
tracks, 180-182, 907, 1056
　numbering, 909
transferring
　data blocks, 32-34
　files
　　comparison InterLnk/third-party programs, 1224
　　with InterLnk, 1198-1199, 1204-1205
translating, sectors, 911-922
TREE command, 83-84, 101-102, 301-303, 1466-1467
　/A switch, 302
　/F switch, 302
Trojan horses, 1066, 1086-1087
troubleshooting
　disks, 404-405
　　bad clusters, 405
　　cross-linked files (FATs), 404
　　lost clusters (FATs), 404
　InterLnk, 1222-1223
　MemMaker, 611-624
　memory managers, 523-526, 624-650
　　A20 handlers, 626-632

bus mastering,
 647-659
EMM386.EXE,
 632-640
keyboard problems,
 625-641
loading programs
 high, 642-650
MSD memory
 scanner, 526-532
virtual DMA
 controllers, 646
warm boot problems,
 641-642
SETUP command,
 139-147
UNINSTALL
 command, 160-161
TRUENAME command, 95, 298
TSRs (terminate-and-stay-resident programs), 57, 113-115
anti-virus, 1093
 VSAFE, 1103-1106
conventional
 memory, 446-447
keyboards, 632-640
loading into UMBs,
 597-601, 601-608
mouse drivers,
 602-604
loading with
 QEMM, 676-678
viruses, 116
yo-yo, loading,
 601-608
TTF file extension, 330
TURBOBAT command, 1503-1504

TurboBat shareware program, 46
turning off/on, DoubleGuard, 241
TXT file extension, 77, 330
TYPE command, 95, 331-333, 1467-1468
typematic rate, 750

U

UARTs (universal asynchronous receiver/transmitters), 1214-1215
DoubleSpace, 239
UI, *see* **user interface**
UMA (upper memory area), 504-505
UMBs (Upper Memory Blocks), 57, 504-518
creating, 509-510,
 537-539
 with CONFIG.SYS,
 537
disabling VCPI
 support, 543
DOS 5 Memory
 Manager, 58
FASTOPEN
 command, 403
fragmented, 537-539
hexadecimal
 numeric values,
 510-521
 integrated
 motherboards,
 520-521

memory addressing,
 510-515
MemMaker, 608-611
memory managers,
 506-509
programs
 arranging for
 maximum space,
 596-624
 loading, 539-543
 load size, 606
 self-loading, 542-543
 yo-yo/reverse,
 607-608
TSRs
 loading, 601-608
 placement, 597-601
unconditional formats, 211
UNDELETE command, 1043, 1199, 1468-1471
/ALL switch, 1029
DOS 5, 61-62
/DS switch, 1029
/DT switch, 1029
/U switch, 1029
UNDELETE for DOS program, 1025-1031
Delete Sentry option,
 1033-1035
installing, 134, 149
options, 1027-1031
undelete protection
DOS 5, 61-62
DOS 6.2, 62
underline text, 766
Undo disks, creating with ScanDisk, 411-412

unerasing files, 87
UNFORMAT command, 945-946, 953, 1058-1059, 1199, 1261, 1471-1472
  boot viruses, checking for, 1048-1049
  virus removal, 1120
unformatted disks, capacity, 912-914
UNINSTALL command, 158-160
  troubleshooting, 160-161
United States code page, 740
universal asynchronous receiver/transmitters, see UARTs
UNIX, virtual devices, 798
UNRECOVERABLE ERROR - ERROR READING FILE SETUP.INI error message, 141
unshielded cabling, 1250
  twisted pair, 1250
unsupported DOS version; upgrade to DOS version 3.1 or higher error message, 267-268
updating
  files, 352-354
    system version table, 727

upper memory, mapping, 522-536
upper memory area, 504-505
Upper Memory Blocks, see UMBs
UPS (Uninterrupted Power Supply), 1260
Use Error Correction on Diskettes option (MSBACKUP/ MWBACKUP), 988
user input in batch files, 812-813
user interface, 88-103
  COMMAND.COM file, 89-91
  prompt, 89
user programs, memory, 450
utilities
  alarm, 845-848
  Anti-Virus, installing, 134, 149
  Backup, installing, 134, 149
  data recovery, 1024
  floppy disks, 728-737
  keyboard control, 737-751
  MEM, 491-494
  print control, 773-783
  QBASIC, 785-788
  Shell programs, 783-785
  Undelete, installing, 134, 149

video control, 751-773
see also commands

V

$V metastring character, 288
V-Base virus database, 1069-1070, 1124
variables
  COMSPEC, 448
  environment, 448
    CONFIG=VAN, 448
    MSDOSDATA, 1262
    PATH, 449
    PROMPT, 449
VCPI (Virtual Control Program Interface), 60, 468-471, 671
  disabling, 543
VER command, 95, 1472-1473
Verify Backup Data option (MSBACKUP/ MWBACKUP), 987
VERIFY command, 355-356, 1473-1474
vertical refresh rate, 760-761
vertical scanning frequency, 760
VESA(Video Electronics Standard Association), 758
VGA (Video Graphics Adapter), 753

VGA (video graphics array), 453-454
  memory addresses, 453-454
VGAswap (386Max), 704
video adapters, 453-456
video boards
  graphics mode, 456
  monochrome adapters, 456
  Orchid, 51
  restricting memory space, 652-653
  Video RAM, 453-454
video drivers, memory managers, 655-656
video graphics array, *see* **VGA**
video memory, 451
Video RAM, 451-458, 482, 758-759
  graphics mode, 454-455
  memory addresses, 453-454
  memory areas, 455-458
  text mode, 454-455
  video boards, 453-454
video system
  adapter, 752-760
  ANSI command, 763-769
  ANSI.SYS command, 769-771
  CLS command, 763
  controlling, 751-773

  dot pitch, 763
  horizontal scanning frequency, 761
  interlacing, 762
  line display options, 771-773
  monitors, 760-763
  multisync monitors, 761-762
  PROMPT command, 764-765
  screen attributes, 765-767
  vertical refresh rate, 760-761
VIDRAM, capturing, 684-685
Vienna virus, 1496
viewing
  boot record, 929
  directory structure, 83-84
  directory tree, 301-303
  disks, 1490-1491
  files, 87
  fragmented file lists, 419-420
  partitions, FDISK, 944-945
  subdirectories, 279
VINES server-based network (Banyon), 1260
virtual control program interface (VCPI), 468-471
virtual devices
  batch files, 798-801
  COPY CON command, 800

  UNIX, 798
virtual DMA controllers, 646
Virtual DMA Services (Microsoft), 389
virtual drives, data transfer, 33-34
Virus Research Center, 1069-1070, 1151
virus response teams, 1087-1088
virus scanners, 29-31
virus shields, 29-32
viruses, 29-32
  appending, 1068
  author motivations, 1070-1071
  attacks on anti-virus products, 1072-1075
  boot, 1055, 1067-1069
    checking for (UNFORMAT command), 1048-1049
    CHKDSK command, 1051-1053
    prevention, 1181-1182
    removing, 943, 1182-1183
  boot record, scanning for, 929-932
  boot sector, 1084-1085
    MSAV command, 1102-1103
    transmission of, 1086

Cascade, 1113, 1151
classifying,
  1067-1069
COMMAND.COM,
  infecting, 1047
damage survey,
  1077-1080
Dark Avenger,
  1072-1073, 1151
detecting
  anti-virus TSRs,
    1093
  checksum changes,
    1089-1091
  myths, 1088-1089
  scanning, 1091-1093
determining, 1057
direct action, 1068
estimated
  magnitude of
  threat, 1081-1083
false alarms,
  1110-1114
file, 1067-1069
  detecting, 1188-1189
  prevention,
    1183-1186
Form, 1044
Form boot, 1117
Frodo, 1067-1069,
  1073, 1101, 1118,
  1151, 1496
infected interrupts,
  determining, 1501
infectiousness, 1077
Jerusalem, 1080,
  1107, 1151
Lehigh, 29-30, 1067
memory-resident
  detecting/removing,
    1186-1187

Michelangelo, 31,
  1080
new, emergence of,
  1076
origins of, 1069-1070
Peach, 1073
polymorphic, 1068,
  1101
potential
  transmission sites,
  1083
prepending, 1068
prevalence,
  1076-1077
preventing,
  1082-1083
  backups, 1085-1086
  bulletin board
    precautions,
    1086-1087
  virus reponse teams,
    1087-1088
  write-protect tabs,
    1085
reference sources,
  1150-1151
removal strategies,
  1125-1128
removal tools,
  1120-1121
  DOSWATCH,
    1121-1122
  F-Prot, 1122
  FINDTEXT, 1122
  FULLDIR,
    1122-1123
  READEXE, 1123
  REBOOT, 1123
  SHOWINT, 1124
  SNORETIL, 1124

V-Base virus
    database, 1124
removing, 1115-1116
  anti-virus products,
    1116
  MSAV command,
    1116-1120
scanning, MSAV
  command,
  1094-1103
stealth, 1069
Stoned, 30-31, 943,
  1044, 1107, 1113,
  1151
symptoms,
  1111-1115
TSRs, 116
types, 1066
Vienna, 1496
Whale, 1073-1074
VL-bus (VESA Local
  bus), 758
voice coil head
  actuators, 178-179, 903
VOL command, 95,
  1474
volatile disk space,
  440
volumes, naming,
  361-362
VSAFE anti-virus
  TSR, 1103-1106
  testing, 1106-1110
VSAFE command,
  1475-1476
VSAFE.COM virus
  shield, 31-32

W

wait states, 590
WAITFOR command, 828-829
walking-bit test, 585-586
WANs (wide area networks), 1240
WAV file extension, 330
WEB (Webcorp) peer-to-peer network, 1253
Whale virus, 1073-1074
wide area networks (WANs), 1240
WINA20.386 file, 311
Winchesters, 900
Windows, 784
  dynamic linking, 109
  error messages, 266-268
  formatting floppy disks, 215
  INI files, changes from DOS installation, 166-169
  memory managers, 655-658
    inteface translation buffers, 658
    limulation, 657-658
    mapping memory, 657
  video drivers, 655-656
Windows API, 109

Windows for Workgroups, 34-35, 1256-1257
Windows NT, 237
WINFILE.INI file, 168
wireless LANs, 1241
wiring, choosing, 1249-1251
  see also cables
WK1 file extension, 330
WK3 file extension, 330
WKQ file extension, 331
WKS file extension, 331
WMBACKUP.INI file, 168
WMF file extension, 77, 331
WordPerfect, memory, 450
Workgroup Connection network program set, 34-35
workstations (LAN), 1240
worms, 1066
WRI file extension, 331
write caching, 386-388
write-ahead caches, 188
write-behind cache, quitting, 397
write-protect tabs, virus prevention, 1085

write-protection, determining, 902
writing
  code, 105-106
  to disks, 921
WRK file extension, 331

X

XCOPY command, 65, 347-352, 1477-1478
  /A switch, 349
  backing up with, 1006-1011
  capturing subdirectories, 349
  /D switch, 351
  /E switch, 349
  /M switch, 349-350
  /S switch, 349
  /V switch, 352
  /W switch, 352, 770
XGA (Extended Graphics Adapter), 753
XIT command, 94
XLC file extension, 331
XLS file extension, 331
XMS Managers
  HIMEM.SYS file, 501-503
  INT 15 programs, 502-503
XT hard disks, 176
XT-type controllers, 190-191
XTree, 783
XTree Gold, 783

Y–Z

YAL file extension, 331
yo-yo programs, 59, 678-682
   loading into UMBs, 601-608
   memory managers, 605-606
   reverse programs, 607-608
zero-slot LANs, 1240
   LANtastic Z, 1254
ZIP file extension, 331

Inside MS-DOS 6.2
Second Edition
REGISTRATION CARD

NRP

Fill out this card to receive information about future DOS books and other New Riders titles!

Name _____ **Title** _____

Company _____

Address _____

City/State/ZIP _____

I bought this book because: _____
_____

I purchased this book from:
- ☐ A bookstore (Name _____)
- ☐ A software or electronics store (Name _____)
- ☐ A mail order (Name of Catalog _____)

I purchase this many computer books each year:
- ☐ 1–4   ☐ 5 or more

I currently use these applications: _____
_____
_____
_____

I found these chapters to be the most informative: _____
_____

I found these chapters to be the least informative: _____
_____

Additional comments: _____
_____

☐ I would like to see my name in print! You may use my name and quote me in future New Riders products and promotions. My daytime phone number is: _____

New Riders Publishing 201 West 103rd Street • Indianapolis, Indiana 46290 USA

Fold Here

PLACE
STAMP
HERE

New Riders Publishing
201 West 103rd Street
Indianapolis, Indiana 46290
USA

WANT MORE INFORMATION?

CHECK OUT THESE RELATED TITLES:

	QTY	PRICE	TOTAL
PCs for Non-Nerds. This lighthearted reference presents information in an easy-to-read, entertaining manner. Provides quick, easy-to-find, no-nonsense answers to questions everyone asks. A great book for the "non-nerd" who wants to learn about personal computers. ISBN: 1-56205-150-4.	____	$18.95	_____
DOS for Non-Nerds. Understanding this popular operating system is easy with fun, step-by-step tutorials. Entertaining and effective instruction gets the reluctant users started immediately with full confidence. ISBN: 1-56205-151-2.	____	$18.95	_____
OS/2 for Non-Nerds. Even nontechnical people can learn how to use OS/2 like a professional with this book. Clear and concise explanations are provided without long-winded, technical discussions. Information is easy to find with the convenient bulleted lists and tables. ISBN: 1-56205-153-9.	____	$18.95	_____
Windows for Non-Nerds. *Windows for Non-Nerds* is written with busy people in mind. With this book, it is extremely easy to find solutions to common Windows problems. Contains only useful information that is of interest to readers and is free of techno-babble and lengthy, technical discussions. Important information is listed in tables or bulleted lists that make it easy to find what you are looking for. ISBN: 1-56205-152-0.	____	$18.95	_____

Name _____

Company _____

Address _____

City _____ State ____ ZIP _____

Phone _____ Fax _____

☐ Check Enclosed   ☐ VISA   ☐ MasterCard

Card # _____ Exp. Date _____

Signature _____

Prices are subject to change. Call for availability and pricing information on latest editions.

Subtotal _____

Shipping _____

$4.00 for the first book and $1.75 for each additional book.

Total _____
Indiana residents add 5% sales tax.

New Riders Publishing 201 West 103rd Street • Indianapolis, Indiana 46290 USA

Orders/Customer Service: 1-800-541-6789
Fax: 1-800-448-3804

OPERATING SYSTEMS

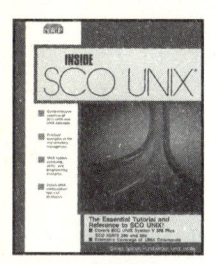

INSIDE SCO UNIX, 2nd EDITION
STEVE GLINES, PETER SPICER,
BEN HUNSBERGER, & KAREN WHITE

Everything users need to know to use the UNIX operating system for everyday tasks.

SCO Xenix 286, SCO Xenix 386, SCO UNIX/System V 386
ISBN: 1-56205-028-1
$29.95 USA

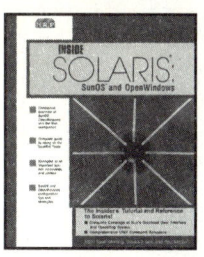

INSIDE SOLARIS SunOS
KARLA SAARI, KITA LONG,
STEVEN R. LEE, & PAUL MARZIN

Comprehensive tutorial and reference to SunOS!

SunOS, Sun's version of UNIX for the SPARC workstation, version 2.0
ISBN: 1-56205-032-X
$29.95 USA

DOS FOR NON-NERDS
MICHAEL GROH

Understanding this popular operating system is easy with this humorous, step-by-step tutorial.

Through DOS 6.0
ISBN: 1-56205-151-2
$18.95 USA

To Order, Call 1-800-428-5331

GRAPHICS TITLES

INSIDE CorelDRAW! 4.0, SPECIAL EDITION
DANIEL GRAY

An updated version of the #1 best-selling tutorial on CorelDRAW!

CorelDRAW! 4.0
ISBN: 1-56205-164-4
$34.95 USA

CorelDRAW! SPECIAL EFFECTS
NEW RIDERS PUBLISHING

An inside look at award-winning techniques from professional CorelDRAW! designers!

CorelDRAW! 4.0
ISBN: 1-56205-123-7
$39.95 USA

CorelDRAW! NOW!
RICHARD FELDMAN

The hands-on tutorial for users who want practical information now!

CorelDRAW! 4.0
ISBN: 1-56205-131-8
$21.95 USA

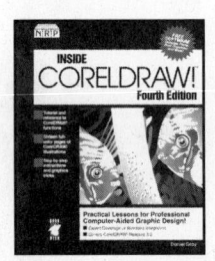

INSIDE CORELDRAW!, FOURTH EDITION
DANIEL GRAY

The popular tutorial approach to learning CorelDRAW!...with complete coverage of version 3.0.

CorelDRAW! 3.0
ISBN: 1-56205-106-7
$24.95 USA

To Order, Call 1-800-428-5331

HOT TOPICS

Get Your Coaching on
HOT TOPICS
from New Riders!

THE FONTS COACH
CHERI ROBINSON

A clear, concise explanation of how fonts work on different platforms!

Beginning-Intermediate

ISBN: 1-56205-130-X
$24.95 USA

THE MODEM COACH
DANA BLANKENHORN, KIMBERLY MAXWELL & KEVIN STOLTZ WITH TOMMY BASS

Everything you need to know to get productive with your modem...fast!

Beginning-Intermediate

ISBN: 1-56205-119-9
$18.95 USA

CRANK IT UP!
KEITH ALESHIRE

Everything you need to know about the hows and whys of computer sound.

Beginning-Intermediate

ISBN: 1-56205-173-3
$16.95 USA

THE GRAPHICS COACH
KATHY MURRAY

The "what you need to know" book about video cards, color monitors, and the many graphic file formats!

Beginning-Intermediate

ISBN: 1-56205-129-6
$24.95 USA

To Order, Call: 1-800-428-5331

WINDOWS TITLES

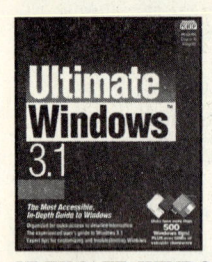

ULTIMATE WINDOWS 3.1

FORREST HOULETTE, JIM BOYCE, RICH WAGNER, & THE BSU RESEARCH STAFF

The most up-to-date reference for Windows available!
Covers 3.1 and related products
ISBN: 1-56205-125-3
$39.95 USA

INSIDE WINDOWS NT

NEW RIDERS PUBLISHING

A complete tutorial and reference to organize and manage multiple tasks and multiple programs in Windows.
Windows NT
ISBN: 1-56205-124-5
$39.95 USA

WINDOWS FOR NON-NERDS

JIM BOYCE & ROB TIDROW

This helpful tutorial for Windows provides novice users with what they need to know to gain computer proficiency...and confidence!
Windows 3.1
ISBN: 1-56205-152-0
$18.95 USA

INTEGRATING WINDOWS APPLICATIONS

ELLEN DANA NAGLER, FORREST HOULETTE, MICHAEL GROH, RICHARD WAGNER, & VALDA HILLEY

This book is a no-nonsense, practical approach for intermediate- and advanced-level Windows users!
Windows 3.1
ISBN: 1-56205-083-4
$34.95 USA

To Order, Call 1-800-428-5331

NETWORKING TITLES

#1 Bestseller!

INSIDE NOVELL NETWARE, SPECIAL EDITION

DEBRA NIEDERMILLER-CHAFFINS & BRIAN L. CHAFFINS

This best-selling tutorial and reference has been updated and made even better!
NetWare 2.2 & 3.11
ISBN: 1-56205-096-6
$34.95 USA

MAXIMIZING NOVELL NETWARE

JOHN JERNEY & ELNA TYMES

Complete coverage of Novell's flagship product...for NetWare system administrators!
NetWare 3.11
ISBN: 1-56205-095-8
$39.95 USA

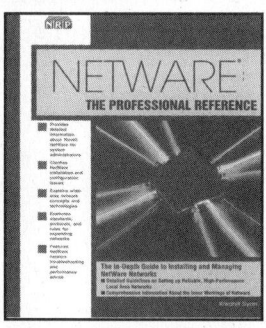

NETWARE: THE PROFESSIONAL REFERENCE, SECOND EDITION

KARANJIT SIYAN

This updated version for professional NetWare administrators and technicians provides the most comprehensive reference available for this phenomenal network system.
NetWare 2.2 & 3.11
ISBN: 1-56205-158-X
$42.95 USA

NETWARE 4: PLANNING AND IMPLEMENTATION

SUNIL PADIYAR

A guide to planning, installing, and managing a NetWare 4.0 network that serves your company's best objectives.
NetWare 4.0
ISBN: 1-56205-159-8
$27.95 USA

To Order, Call 1-800-428-5331

Become a CNE with Help from a Pro!

The NetWare Training Guides are specifically designed and authored to help you prepare for the **Certified NetWare Engineer** exam.

NetWare Training Guide: Managing NetWare Systems

This book clarifies the CNE testing process and provides hints on the best ways to prepare for the CNE examinations. *NetWare Training Guide: Managing NetWare Systems* covers the following sections of the CNE exams:

- NetWare v 2.2 System Manager
- NetWare v 2.2 Advanced System Manager
- NetWare v 3.X System Manager
- NetWare v 3.X Advanced System Manager

ISBN: 1-56205-069-9, **$59.95 USA**

NetWare Training Guide: Networking Technology

This book covers more advanced topics and prepares you for the tough hardware and service/support exams. The following course materials are covered:

- MS-DOS
- Microcomputer Concepts
- Service and Support
- Networking Technologies

ISBN: 1-56205-145-8, **$59.95 USA**

For more information or to place an order, call: 1-800-428-5331